INTERNATIONAL YEARBOOK OF INDUSTRIAL STATISTICS
2013

INTERNATIONAL YEARBOOK
OF
INDUSTRIAL STATISTICS
2013

UNITED NATIONS INDUSTRIAL DEVELOPMENT ORGANIZATION
VIENNA
2013

Published by
Edward Elgar Publishing Limited
The Lypiatts
15 Lansdown Road
Cheltenham
Glos GL50 2JA
UK

Edward Elgar Publishing, Inc.
The William Pratt House
9 Dewey Court
Northampton
Massachusetts 01060-3815
USA

A catalogue record for this book
is available from the British Library

The description and classification of countries, economies and territories in this publication and the arrangement of the material do not imply the expression of any opinion whatsoever on the part of the Secretariat of the United Nations Industrial Development Organization concerning the legal status of any country, territory, city or area, or of its authorities, or concerning the delimitation of its frontiers or boundaries, or regarding its economic system or degree of development. The designation "country, economy or area" covers countries, economies, territories, cities and areas. The designation "region, country, economies or area" extends the preceding one by including groupings of entities designated as "country, economy or area". Designations such as "industrialized" and "developing and emerging industrial" economies are intended for statistical convenience and do not necessarily express a judgement about the stage reached by a particular country, economy or area in the development process.

ISBN 978 1 78195 564 2
ISSN 1025-8493

Printed by MPG Printgroup, UK

Acknowledgements

The 2013 edition of the *International Yearbook of Industrial Statistics* was prepared by a team of statistical staff under the supervision of Shyam Upadhyaya, Chief Statistician of UNIDO. Overall IT support was provided by Valentin Todorov, who managed the integrated statistical databases and produced the final PDF/digital manuscript. Dong Guo contributed to production of selected statistical tables for part I. Kateryna Gumeniuk, P.Y.Rita Liang, Regina McFerren-Zenz, Shohreh Mirzaei, Jürgen Muth and Anja Sedic were involved in the collection of data and the compilation of the regional and country tables. Amadou Boly contributed to the final checking of statistical tables. Liliya Kirchberger and Raphaela Wirth provided administrative support to the team.

Important contributions to the publication were made by consultants Nicolai Christov and Bernhard Karner, who assisted in the development and maintenance of the software infrastructure.

The team members wish to express their sincere thanks to Ludovico Alcorta, Director of the Development Policy, Statistics and Research Branch of UNIDO, for his support of the preparation of this publication.

The co-operation of national statistical offices, the United Nations Statistics Division (UNSD), the Organisation for Economic Co-operation and Development (OECD), the International Monetary Fund, the World Bank and other international and regional agencies in providing the information that has served as the basis of the current publication is gratefully acknowledged.

Acknowledgements

Explanatory notes

Unless otherwise indicated, "manufacturing" includes the industry groups listed under major category D of the *International Standard Industrial Classification of All Economic Activities* (ISIC) [Statistical Papers, Series M, No.4/Rev.3 (United Nations publication, Sales No. E.90.XVII.II)]. It should be noted that many countries have already made a switchover from their national industrial classification schemes that are based on, or related to, Revision 3 of ISIC to those based on, or related to, Revision 4 of ISIC [Statistical Papers, Series M, No.4/Rev.4 (United Nations publication, Sales No. E.08.XVII.25)]. In these instances, "manufacturing" refers to section C in that classification.

However, for few countries data are still presented in accordance with Revision 2 of ISIC [Statistical Papers, Series M, No.4/Rev.2 (United Nations publication, Sales No. E.68.XVII.8)]. In these instances, "manufacturing" refers to major division 3 in that classification.

ISIC code numbers are accompanied by a descriptive title (for example in the case of Revision 3 of ISIC, ISIC 2813: "Manufacture of steam generators, except central heating hot water boilers"). For considerations of space, however, the description is sometimes shortened (that is, ISIC 2813 may be described simply as "Steam generators"). For Revision 2, 3 and 4 of ISIC, all 2-, 3- and 4-digit codes and their corresponding descriptive titles are listed in appendix II to the introduction.

Users are advised to take the note of some changes introduced in this edition. For the first time several statistical tables are presented by economies, which replaces the earlier practice of presenting data by countries and territories. Individual economies are listed alphabetically, whenever appropriate, within two successive categories: "industrialized economies" and "developing and emerging industrial economies". Designation of economies as "industrialized" or "developing and emerging industrial" is based on adjusted manufacturing value added (MVA) per capita, which is a statistical measure derived from the share of MVA in gross domestic product (GDP) at 2005 current prices and GDP per capita in 2005 at the purchasing power parity (PPP) rate. This measure reflects an approximate value of MVA per capita by PPP. An economy is considered to be "industrialized" if its adjusted MVA per capita is higher than 2,500 or its GDP per capita is higher than 20,000 international dollars by PPP. Similarly, an "emerging industrial economy" corresponds to an economy with an adjusted MVA per capita ranging between 1,000 and 2,500 international dollars or an economy whose share of the world MVA is higher than 0.5 per cent. All remaining economies fall in the category of "other developing economies". The list of least developed countries (LDCs) is based on decisions of the United Nations General Assembly. Users are advised to note that MVA per capita presented in the Yearbook are in United States dollars, not in PPP.

Data are also presented by four income groups: high income, upper middle income, lower middle income and low income. These country groups correspond to the World Bank's definition for each income category. The list of economies by all country groups used in the *Yearbook* is given in appendix I to the introduction. Owing to a lack of data, some economies could not be included in their respective groups in some tables.

In the present publication, unless otherwise stated, data for China do not include data for Hong Kong SAR, for Macao SAR or for Taiwan Province of China, which are presented separately under China (Hong Kong SAR), China (Macao SAR) and China (Taiwan Province).

In part I, references to dollars ($) are to United States dollars. National currencies have been converted to dollar equivalents by using period average exchange rates as published in *International Financial Statistics* (International Monetary Fund publication) and other sources.

Data converted to dollars by using current exchange rates are liable to be strongly influenced by fluctuations in exchange rates. Annual variations of data converted in that manner may not reflect movements in the national data.

In part II, for all member countries of the European Monetary Union (EMU), national data are expressed in Euros.

Unless otherwise noted, average annual growth rates are calculated from the data available for each year of a given period (for example, 2005-2010), using a semi-log regression over time. Growth rates are expressed in percentages.

Periods set off by a hyphen (for instance, 2005-2010) include the beginning and end years.

Apparent arithmetical discrepancies, such as percentages that do not add up to precise totals, result from the rounding of basic data or figures known to different degrees of precision.

Three dots (...) indicate that data are not available or are not separately reported.

A dash (-) indicates that an amount is nil or negligible.

The letter "x" designates the item applicable to an economy when several options exist.

To avoid ambiguity, the letters "l", "o" and "O" are not used to designate footnotes.

The following abbreviations and acronyms are used:

ASEAN	Association of Southeast Asian Nations
CACM	Central American Common Market
CARICOM	Caribbean Community
CEMAC	Central African Economic and Monetary Community
CIS	Commonwealth of Independent States
ECOWAS	Economic Community of West African States
EMU	European Monetary Union
EU	European Union
GCC	Cooperation Council for the Arab States of the Gulf
GDP	gross domestic product
ISIC	International Standard Industrial Classification of All Economic Activities
LAIA	Latin American Integration Association
MERCOSUR	Common Market of the South/Mercado Común del Sur
MVA	manufacturing value added
n.e.c.	not elsewhere classified
n.e.s.	not elsewhere specified
OECD	Organisation for Economic Co-operation and Development
PPP	purchasing power parity
SAARC	South Asian Association for Regional Cooperation
SADC	Southern African Development Community
UNIDO	United Nations Industrial Development Organization
UNSD	United Nations Statistics Division
VAT	value added tax
WAEMU/UEMOA	West African Economic and Monetary Union

CONTENTS

PART I. SUMMARY TABLES

SECTION 1.1. THE MANUFACTURING SECTOR

SECTION 1.2. THE MANUFACTURING DIVISIONS / BRANCHES

PART II. COUNTRY TABLES [a/]

[a/] For information on the countries/areas that are not presented, please see page 187.

DATA AVAILABLE ON CD-ROM

UNIDO maintains several databases on industrial statistics, of which new sales versions are made available annually.

INDSTAT2: UNIDO Industrial Statistics Database at the 2-digit level of ISIC code (Revision 3)	☐ Long time series for 166 countries/areas compiled on eight principle indicators (number of establishments, total employment, female employment, wages and salaries paid to employees, output, value added, gross fixed capital formation and index numbers of industrial production) starting from 1963 onwards. The data are arranged at the 2-digit level of ISIC (Revision 3) pertaining to the manufacturing sector, which comprises 23 manufacturing divisions. ☐ All value data are originally stored in national currency values at current prices. The system allows for data conversion from national currency into current U.S. dollars.
INDSTAT4: UNIDO Industrial Statistics Database at the 3- and 4-digit level of ISIC code (Revision 3)	☐ Time series data for 134 countries/areas on seven selected data items including number of establishments, total employment, female employment, wages and salaries paid to employees, output, value added and gross fixed capital formation, starting from 1990 onwards. The data are arranged at the 3- and 4-digit level of ISIC (Revision 3) pertaining to the manufacturing sector, which comprises 151 manufacturing industries. ☐ All value data are originally stored in national currency values at current prices. The system allows for data conversion from national currency into current U.S. dollars.
IDSB: UNIDO Industrial Demand-Supply Balance Database at the 4-digit level of ISIC code (Revision 3)	☐ Time series (starting from 1990) for more than 90 countries on output, imports, exports and apparent consumption (all in current U.S. dollars) at the 4-digit level of ISIC (Revision 3).

Further details on above products may be obtained from:
Statistics Unit, UNIDO
P.O. Box 300
A-1400 Vienna, Austria
Fax: (+43-1) 26026-6802
Email: stat@unido.org
Internet: http://www.unido.org/statistics

INTRODUCTION

This is the nineteenth issue of UNIDO's annual publication, the *International Yearbook of Industrial Statistics*. The *Yearbook* succeeded the *Handbook of Industrial Statistics* which was published biennially by UNIDO up to 1992. At the same time, it replaced the United Nations' *Industrial Statistics Yearbook,* volume I (General Industrial Statistics), which was discontinued after its 1991 edition published in 1993. These changes were in accordance with the recommendations of the United Nations Statistical Commission at its twenty-seventh session, namely that UNIDO, in collaboration with the Organisation for Economic Co-operation and Development (OECD), assumes responsibility for the collection and dissemination of world-wide general industrial statistics, effective 1994. The present *Yearbook* pertains to the manufacturing sector only. UNIDO has also released a separate biennial publication *World Statistics on Mining and Utilities 2012*.

The main purpose of the *Yearbook* is to provide statistical indicators to facilitate international comparisons relating to the manufacturing sector. The data presented were compiled bearing in mind the requirements of international comparability and the standards for this work promulgated by the United Nations. Concepts and definitions are drawn from the *International Recommendations for Industrial Statistics* 2008 (Statistical Papers, Series M, No.90; United Nations publication, Sales No.E.08.XVII.8) and the classification by industry follows the *International Standard Industrial Classification of All Economic Activities*.

The present *Yearbook* consists of two parts. Part I deals with the manufacturing sector as a whole (section 1.1) and with its divisions/ branches (section 1.2). Statistical indicators are presented in terms of percentage distributions, cross-country averages, ratios and real growth rates that facilitate international comparison among selected country groups and/or economies. Graphical presentations followed by a brief description of the overall trend of world industrial growth are also displayed here. In the present publication data for manufacturing divisions/ branches are arranged according to Revision 3 of ISIC at the two- or three-digit level. Part II consists of a series of country/area-specific tables showing detailed data on selected basic statistics that were reported by national statistical offices.

Most countries have made a switchover from their national industrial classifications compatible with Revision 2 to those compatible with Revision 3 of ISIC. Consequently, data for those countries are presented in accordance with Revision 3 of ISIC. In addition, many countries have already made a switchover from their national industrial classifications compatible with Revision 3 to those compatible with Revision 4 of ISIC. These countries are now reporting data in accordance with Revision 4 of ISIC for the first time. However, for few remaining countries, data are still presented in accordance with Revision 2 of ISIC.

Sources and methods

In section 1.1 of part I, manufacturing value added (MVA) was estimated in accordance with the national accounting concept, which represents the net contribution of the manufacturing sector to gross domestic product (GDP). The data on MVA and GDP were obtained from various national and international sources including the World Bank, OECD, the United Nations Statistics Division (UNSD), the International Monetary Fund and regional development banks. These sources were supplemented with estimates generated by UNIDO.

Currently, UNIDO is implementing Revision 4 of ISIC in its database. Data reported in accordance with Revision 4 of ISIC have been converted to Revision 3 of ISIC to facilitate long time series comparison and are displayed in various tables of part I. Therefore, differences may arise from the conversion and users might find discrepancies when comparing converted data of later years with data of earlier years, published in the present edition of the *Yearbook*.

Due to the revision of data received from external sources, there might also be differences between the data presented in the current edition of the *Yearbook* and those shown in previous editions. Figures with respect to population are based on the 2010 revision of data compiled by the Population Division of the United Nations Secretariat.

The information in section 1.2 is drawn from the UNIDO Industrial Statistics Database, as well as data communicated to the United Nations by official national sources. With regard to the member countries of OECD, data were compiled by that organization. Information is solicited through a questionnaire issued jointly by the two organizations.

To facilitate the comparability of the data over time and across economies, see "Explanatory notes", UNIDO has supplemented originally reported data with information obtained from various other sources. The latter include: industrial censuses, statistics supplied by national and international organizations, unpublished data collected in the field by UNIDO as well as estimates made by the UNIDO secretariat.[1]

The indicators presented in tables 1.5 to 1.9 of section 1.2 were derived from estimates of value added at constant 2005 prices. For each economy and industrial division, these value-added estimates were generated by applying production indexes to the 2005 value added base weights, which in turn were generated by UNIDO from various national and international sources.

Except for index numbers of industrial production, the information for the countries and areas other than the OECD member countries, presented in part II, were compiled from (i) the 2010 edition of the UNIDO General Industrial Statistics Questionnaires completed by national statistical offices and (ii) relevant publications issued by national statistical offices. Information referring to OECD member countries is based on data compiled by OECD via questionnaires and incorporated in OECD's Information System on Industrial Statistics as well as in the UNIDO database. With respect to production indexes, data were supplied by UNSD that compiles these data regularly from national sources through the quarterly United Nations Index of Industrial Production Questionnaires.

In section 1.2 of part I and in part II, the measures generally used are census output and census value added. Thus, the costs of non-industrial services are included in value added, whereas the receipts for these services are excluded from output. For a quick reference, appendix III to this introduction provides notes on certain aspects of the data used, and it is recommended that the reader consult them when using the *Yearbook*. A detailed version appears in the individual country notes in part II, which also covers deviations from the standards applied. In general, these notes are also applicable to the estimates that supplement the officially reported data.

---

[1] UNIDO's procedures for estimation are described in *"UNIDO Industrial Statistics Database — Methodological Notes"* (IRD/R.11).

PART I. SUMMARY TABLES

Section 1.1: The manufacturing sector
Section 1.1 comprises tables 1.1 to 1.4. Table 1.1 shows the distribution of world MVA for various regions and groups of economies at constant 2005 prices as well as at current prices.

The reader should be aware that due to variation in official exchange rates the world distribution may change considerably, depending on the choice of the base year.

To maintain comparability over time, composition of each group of economies was kept the same throughout the period. However, due to data limitations, a number of economies listed in appendix I are not included.

China belongs to the group of emerging industrial economies. However, because of the large size of its economy, China is presented separately in tables 1.2 to 1.4.

Table 1.2 presents the shares of selected groups of economies in world MVA and population including industrialized economies. However, in other tables statistics by geographical regions are presented only for developing and emerging industrial economies.

Table 1.3 shows real growth rates and index numbers (2005=100) of total and per-capita MVA as well as values of per-capita MVA for the latest year 2011 for individual economies and for selected country groups. Data referring to country groups were based on cross-country aggregates of MVA in constant 2005 U.S. dollars.

Table 1.4 shows the percentage shares of MVA in GDP estimated at both constant 2005 prices and current prices. The data are presented by individual economies as well as by selected country groups. With respect to the selected country groups, common country samples were taken for both indicators and for all reference years.

Section 1.2: The manufacturing divisions/ branches
Section 1.2 comprises tables 1.5 to 1.11. It focuses on the divisions/branches of the manufacturing sector. The ISIC (Revision 3) definition of manufacturing consists of 23 divisions reported in accordance with a two-digit code and 61 branches reported in accordance with a three-digit code.

In tables 1.5 to 1.9, Recycling (ISIC 37) had to be excluded from the presentation due to data limitations. Data for China and China (Taiwan

Province) are UNIDO estimates. Furthermore, a number of estimates at the country level were also generated to enable regional aggregation or to derive world totals for the latest years.

Table 1.5 shows the world distribution of the respective value added of selected divisions among selected country groups.

Table 1.6 shows the shares of developing regions and the least developed countries in the value added of all developing and emerging economies in selected divisions.

Table 1.7 shows the world's major producers in various industrial divisions as well as the major developing and emerging industrial economies in terms of value added. China, which is the emerging industrial economy in most of the industrial divisions, is presented only among major 'World' economies. However, due to data limitations, it is not presented in all industrial divisions.

Table 1.8 shows the shares of individual divisions in total MVA by country groups.

Table 1.9 shows real growth rates of value added of individual divisions, calculated for selected country groups. The reference periods are 2000-2005 and 2005-2011.

Table 1.10 presents the share of female employees in total employment in individual divisions. For some economies, employment refers to number of persons engaged instead of number of employees (see appendix III of the present introduction). Only a limited number of economies have reported data on female employment at the division level.

Table 1.11 shows, for individual economies, basic indicators that are characteristic of the manufacturing branches. Costs of input materials and utilities are calculated as output minus value added. Costs of labour refer to wages and salaries of employees only. Operating surplus is calculated as value added minus wages and salaries paid to employees.

Information concerning the following branches is excluded from table 1.11: Dressing & dyeing of fur; processing of fur (ISIC 1820); Reproduction of recorded media (ISIC 2230); Coke oven products (ISIC 2310); Refined petroleum products (ISIC 2320); Processing of nuclear fuel (ISIC 2330); Man-made fibres (ISIC 2430); Watches and clocks (ISIC 3330); Railway/ tramway locomotives & rolling stock (ISIC 3520); Aircraft and spacecraft (ISIC 3530); Transport equipment n.e.c. (ISIC 359); Recycling

of metal waste and scrap (ISIC 3710); Recycling of non-metal waste and scrap (ISIC 3720).

PART II. COUNTRY TABLES

Part II comprises country/area-specific tables presenting the following selected industrial statistics: number of establishments, number of employees (or, if not reported, number of persons engaged), wages and salaries paid to employees, output, value added, gross fixed capital formation and index numbers of industrial production. All value data are presented in current national currencies. The data on these items (except gross fixed capital formation and index numbers of industrial production) relate to the last four years for which data were reported. Gross fixed capital formation refers to the last two years for which data were reported. Index numbers of industrial production refer to the period 1999-2010.

Coverage of countries/areas
The countries/areas that are presented in part II are those which reported data during the current round of the UNIDO annual compilation programme of global industrial statistics. Those countries/areas, which reported data only in previous rounds of the UNIDO compilation programme, are not included in the present *Yearbook* but were included in previous editions. At the beginning of part II, those countries/areas are listed together with a reference to the respective editions of the *Yearbook* in which their latest data were presented.

Industrial classification
The classification of industrial activity set out in the tables follows either Revision 2, Revision 3 or Revision 4 of ISIC, at the two-, three- and/or four-digit levels of ISIC depending on the individual country's data reporting scheme. Where information was not provided in this form, the estimates are shown in the most applicable ISIC category. Aggregates for total manufacturing are included. With regard to production indexes, data are arranged either in accordance with the 2-digit level of Revision 3 or Revision 4 of ISIC.

It should be noted that in several cases a figure presented for a 3-digit group does not agree with the sum of data given for the corresponding 4-digit categories. As far as possible, UNIDO resolved these discrepancies with the help of available supplementary information.

Reference unit
For most countries and areas represented, the data shown relate to the activity of "establishments" in the specified industries rather than any other type of industrial unit. In a few cases, however, the concepts of "kind-of-activity unit", "local unit" or

"enterprise" are found. An "establishment" is ideally a unit that engages, under a single ownership or control, in one, or predominantly one, kind of activity at a single location; for example, workshop or factory. A "kind-of-activity unit" differs from the establishment in that there is no restriction with respect to the geographical area in which a given kind of activity is carried out by a single legal entity. A "local unit", on the other hand, comprises all activities carried out under a single ownership or control at a single location and differs from the establishment-type of unit in that there is no restriction on the range of these activities. An "enterprise" is a legal entity possessing the right to conduct business in its own name; for example, to enter into contracts, own property, incur liability for debts, and establish bank accounts. Specific information on the character of the units covered in the tables for each country is set out in the corresponding country note.

Reference period

The statistics in the tables relate, in general, to the calendar year. It should be noted, however, that in many cases where the basic reference period of the industrial inquiry is the calendar year, returns covering proximate fiscal years may be accepted for reporting purposes and the data for these years incorporated in the calendar-year aggregate without adjustment. In a few countries, fiscal years normally used for public accounting purposes have been adopted as the basic reference periods. In the case of fiscal-year coverage, the year indicated in the tables refers to the calendar year in which the major part of the fiscal year falls. In the case of fiscal years from 1 July to 30 June, the year referred to is normally the one in which the fiscal year ends.

Concepts and definitions of the items

The United Nations standards that have been applied in preparing the tables are set out below. All values are in national currency units and are at current prices unless otherwise indicated. Deviations from these concepts and definitions are described in the respective country notes. The country notes referring to OECD member countries are based on information presented in OECD's annual publication "Structural and Demographic Business Statistics".

(1) Number of persons engaged and number of employees

The number of persons engaged is defined as the total number of persons who worked in or for the establishment during the reference year. However, home workers are excluded. The concept covers working proprietors, active business partners and unpaid family workers as well as employees. The figures reported refer normally to the average number of persons

engaged during the reference year, obtained as the sum of the "average number of employees" during the year and the total number of other persons engaged measured for a single period of the year. The category "employees" is intended to include all persons engaged other than working proprietors, active business partners and unpaid family workers. In this publication, preference has been given, whenever possible, to employees over persons engaged.

(2) Wages and salaries

Estimates of wages and salaries include all payments in cash or in kind made to "employees" during the reference year in relation to work done for the establishment. Payments include: (a) direct wages and salaries; (b) remuneration for time not worked; (c) bonuses and gratuities; (d) housing allowances and family allowances paid directly by the employer; and (e) payments in kind.

Compensation of employees is equivalent to wages and salaries plus employers' contributions on behalf of their employees paid to social security, pension and insurance schemes, as well as the benefits received by employees under these schemes and severance and termination pay.

(3) Output

The measure of output normally used in the tables is the census concept that covers only activities of an industrial nature. The value of census output in the case of estimates compiled on a production basis comprises: (a) the value of sale of all products of the establishment; (b) the net change between the beginning and the end of the reference period in the value of work in progress and stocks of goods to be shipped in the same condition as received; (c) the value of industrial work done or industrial services rendered to others; (d) the value of goods shipped in the same condition as received less the amount paid for these goods; and (e) the value of fixed assets produced during the period by the unit for its own use. In the case of estimates compiled on a shipment basis, the net change in the value of stocks of finished goods between the beginning and the end of the reference period is also included.

Gross output is equivalent to census output plus the revenue from activities of a non-industrial nature. Valuation methods differ from country to country. An increasing number of countries are reporting at basic prices, which exclude taxes on commodity and include commodity related subsidies. Other methods of reporting valuation are: (a) at factor costs, which exclude all indirect taxes falling on production and include all current subsidies received in support of production activities; and (b) at producers' prices, which include all indirect taxes except VAT, or any other deductible taxes and exclude all subsidies.

(4) Value added
The measure of value added normally used in the tables is the census concept, which is defined as the value of census output less the value of census input. Items covered in the latter include: (a) value of materials and supplies for production (including cost of all fuels and electricity purchased); and (b) cost of industrial services received (mainly payments for contract and commission work and repair and maintenance work). If input estimates are compiled on a "received" rather than on a "consumed" basis, the result is adjusted for the net change between the beginning and the end of the period in the value of stocks of materials, fuel and other supplies.

Total value added is the national accounting concept. It is ideally represented by the contribution of the establishments in each branch of activity to the gross domestic product. For the measure of total value added, the cost of non-industrial services is deducted and the receipts for non-industrial services are added to census value added. The estimates, whether in terms of census value added or total value added, are gross of depreciation and other provisions for capital consumption, unless otherwise stated. The valuation may be at factor costs, at basic prices or at producers' prices, depending on the treatment of indirect taxes and subsidies as described above.

(5) Gross fixed capital formation
Estimates refer to the value of purchases and own-account construction of fixed assets during the reference year less the value of corresponding sales. The fixed assets covered are those (whether new or used) with a productive life of one year or more. These assets, which are intended for the use of the establishment, include fixed assets made by the establishment's own labour force for its own use. Major additions, alterations and improvements to existing assets that extend their normal economic life or raise their productivity are also included.

New fixed assets include all those that have not been previously used in the country. Thus, newly imported fixed assets are considered new whether or not used before they were imported. Used fixed assets include all those that have been previously used within the country. Transactions in fixed assets include: (a) cost of land purchase and land improvement; (b) buildings and structures; and (c) machinery and equipment.

Countries that have started implementation of recent recommendations for industrial statistics might have extended the coverage of fixed assets to products of research and development, computer software and database and other intellectual property products.

Assets acquired from others are valued at purchasers' prices, which cover all costs directly connected with the acquisition and installation of the items for use. In principle, assets produced on own account are also valued in this manner. However, it may frequently be necessary to value such own-account production at explicit cost, including any imputations that may be required in respect of the employed own-account labour.

Assets produced by one establishment of a multi-establishment enterprise, for the use of another establishment of the same enterprise, should be valued by the receiving establishment as though purchased from outside the enterprise. Sales of assets should be valued at the actual amounts realized rather than at book values.

(6) Index numbers of industrial production
The indexes in the tables are compiled from national indexes that are calculated by use of the Laspeyres formula. The comparison base year is 2005. However, if different base years are used in any economies, the national indexes are converted to the comparison base year.

Appendix I
LIST OF COUNTRIES AND AREAS INCLUDED IN SELECTED GROUPINGS
Industrialized Economies

EU [a/]

Austria
Belgium
Czech Republic
Denmark
Estonia
Finland
France
Germany
Hungary
Ireland
Italy
Lithuania
Luxembourg
Malta
Netherlands
Portugal
Slovakia
Slovenia
Spain
Sweden
United Kingdom

Other Europe

Iceland
Liechtenstein
Norway
Russian Federation
Switzerland

East Asia

China (Hong Kong SAR)
China (Macao SAR)
China (Taiwan Province)
Japan
Malaysia
Republic of Korea
Singapore

West Asia

Bahrain
Kuwait
Qatar
United Arab Emirates

North America

Bermuda
Canada
Greenland
United States of America

Others

Aruba
Australia
British Virgin Islands
Curaçao
French Guiana
French Polynesia
Guam
Israel
New Caledonia
New Zealand
Puerto Rico
United States Virgin Islands

[a/] Excluding non-industrialized EU economies.

Appendix I
LIST OF COUNTRIES AND AREAS INCLUDED IN SELECTED GROUPINGS
Developing and Emerging Industrial Economies by Region

AFRICA

Central Africa

Cameroon
Central African Republic
Chad
Congo
Equatorial Guinea
Gabon
Sao Tome and Principe

Eastern Africa

Burundi
Comoros
Djibouti
Eritrea
Ethiopia
Kenya
Réunion
Rwanda
Somalia
Uganda

North Africa

Algeria
Egypt
Libya
Morocco
South Sudan
Sudan
Tunisia

Southern Africa

Angola
Botswana
Democratic Rep of the Congo
Lesotho
Madagascar
Malawi
Mauritius
Mozambique
Namibia
Seychelles
South Africa
Swaziland
United Republic of Tanzania
Zambia
Zimbabwe

Western Africa

Benin
Burkina Faso
Cape Verde
Côte d'Ivoire
Gambia
Ghana
Guinea
Guinea-Bissau
Liberia
Mali
Mauritania
Niger
Nigeria
Senegal
Sierra Leone
Togo

ASIA AND PACIFIC

China

Central Asia

Kazakhstan
Kyrgyzstan
Mongolia
Tajikistan
Turkmenistan
Uzbekistan

South Asia

Afghanistan
Bangladesh
Bhutan
India
Maldives
Nepal
Pakistan
Sri Lanka

South East Asia

Brunei Darussalam
Cambodia
Indonesia
Lao People's Dem Rep
Myanmar
Philippines
Thailand
Viet Nam

West Asia

Armenia
Azerbaijan
Iran (Islamic Republic of)
Iraq
Jordan
Lebanon
Oman
Palestine
Saudi Arabia
Syrian Arab Republic
Yemen

Other Asia and Pacific

Cook Islands
Democratic People's Rep of Korea
Fiji
Kiribati
Marshall Islands
Micronesia (Federated States of)
Palau
Papua New Guinea
Samoa
Solomon Islands
Timor-Leste
Tonga
Tuvalu
Vanuatu

EUROPE

Albania
Belarus
Bosnia and Herzegovina
Bulgaria
Croatia
Cyprus
Georgia
Greece
Latvia
Montenegro
Poland
Republic of Moldova
Romania
Serbia
The f. Yugoslav Rep of Macedonia
Turkey
Ukraine

LATIN AMERICA

Caribbean

Anguilla
Antigua and Barbuda
Bahamas
Barbados
Cuba
Dominica
Dominican Republic
Grenada
Guadeloupe
Haiti
Jamaica
Martinique
Montserrat
Saint Kitts and Nevis
Saint Lucia
Saint Vincent and the Grenadines
Trinidad and Tobago

Central America

Belize
Costa Rica
El Salvador
Guatemala
Honduras
Mexico
Nicaragua
Panama

South America

Argentina
Bolivia (Plurinational State of)
Brazil
Chile
Colombia
Ecuador
Guyana
Paraguay
Peru
Suriname
Uruguay
Venezuela (Bolivarian Rep of)

Appendix I
LIST OF COUNTRIES AND AREAS INCLUDED IN SELECTED GROUPINGS
Developing and Emerging Industrial Economies by Development

Emerging Industrial Economies (EIEs)

Argentina
Belarus
Brazil
Brunei Darussalam
Bulgaria
Chile
Colombia
Costa Rica
Croatia
Cyprus
Greece
India
Indonesia
Kazakhstan
Latvia
Mauritius
Mexico
Oman
Poland
Romania
Saudi Arabia
Serbia
South Africa
Suriname
Thailand
The f. Yugoslav Rep of Macedonia
Tunisia
Turkey
Ukraine
Uruguay
Venezuela (Bolivarian Rep of)

China

Other Developing Economies

Albania
Algeria
Angola
Anguilla
Antigua and Barbuda
Armenia
Azerbaijan
Bahamas
Barbados
Belize
Bolivia (Plurinational State of)
Bosnia and Herzegovina
Botswana
Cameroon
Cape Verde
Congo
Cook Islands
Côte d'Ivoire
Cuba
Democratic People's Rep of Korea

Dominica
Dominican Republic
Ecuador
Egypt
El Salvador
Equatorial Guinea
Fiji
Gabon
Georgia
Ghana
Grenada
Guadeloupe
Guatemala
Guyana
Honduras
Iran (Islamic Republic of)
Iraq
Jamaica
Jordan
Kenya
Kyrgyzstan
Lebanon
Libya
Maldives
Marshall Islands
Martinique
Micronesia (Federated States of)
Mongolia
Montenegro
Montserrat
Morocco
Namibia
Nicaragua
Nigeria
Pakistan
Palau
Palestine
Panama
Papua New Guinea
Paraguay
Peru
Philippines
Republic of Moldova
Réunion
Saint Kitts and Nevis
Saint Lucia
Saint Vincent and the Grenadines
Seychelles
Sri Lanka
Swaziland
Syrian Arab Republic
Tajikistan
Tonga
Trinidad and Tobago
Turkmenistan
Uzbekistan
Viet Nam
Zimbabwe

Least Developed Countries (LDCs)

Afganistan
Bangladesh
Benin
Bhutan
Burkina Faso
Burundi
Cambodia
Central African Republic
Chad
Comoros
Democratic Rep of the Congo
Djibouti
Eritrea
Ethiopia
Gambia
Guinea
Guinea-Bissau
Haiti
Kiribati
Lao People's Dem Rep
Lesotho
Liberia
Madagascar
Malawi
Mali
Mauritania
Mozambique
Myanmar
Nepal
Niger
Rwanda
Samoa
Sao Tome and Principe
Senegal
Sierra Leone
Solomon Islands
Somalia
South Sudan
Sudan
Timor-Leste
Togo
Tuvalu
Uganda
United Republic of Tanzania
Vanuatu
Yemen
Zambia

Appendix I
LIST OF ALL ECONOMIES INCLUDED IN SELECTED GROUPINGS
Country Groups by Income Categories

(continued)

High income	Upper middle income	Lower middle income	Low income
Andorra	Algeria	Albania	Afghanistan
Anguilla	American Samoa	Armenia	Bangladesh
Aruba	Angola	Belize	Benin
Australia	Antigua and Barbuda	Bhutan	Burkina Faso
Austria	Argentina	Bolivia (Plurinational State of)	Burundi
Bahamas	Azerbaijan	Cameroon	Cambodia
Bahrain	Belarus	Cape Verde	Central African Republic
Barbados	Bosnia and Herzegovina	Congo	Chad
Belgium	Botswana	Côte d'Ivoire	Comoros
Bermuda	Brazil	Djibouti	Democratic People's Rep of Korea
Brunei Darussalam	Bulgaria	Egypt	Democratic Rep of the Congo
Canada	Chile	El Salvador	Eritrea
Cayman Islands	China	Fiji	Ethiopia
China (Hong Kong SAR)	Colombia	Georgia	Gambia
China (Macao SAR)	Costa Rica	Ghana	Guinea
China (Taiwan Province)	Cuba	Guatemala	Guinea-Bissau
Croatia	Dominica	Guyana	Haiti
Curaçao	Dominican Republic	Honduras	Kenya
Cyprus	Ecuador	India	Kyrgyzstan
Czech Republic	Gabon	Indonesia	Liberia
Denmark	Grenada	Iraq	Madagascar
Equatorial Guinea	Iran (Islamic Republic of)	Kiribati	Malawi
Estonia	Jamaica	Lao People's Dem Rep	Mali
Finland	Jordan	Lesotho	Mauritania
France	Kazakhstan	Marshall Islands	Mozambique
French Polynesia	Latvia	Micronesia (Federated States of)	Myanmar
Germany	Lebanon	Mongolia	Nepal
Greece	Libya	Morocco	Niger
Greenland	Lithuania	Nicaragua	Rwanda
Guam	Malaysia	Nigeria	Sierra Leone
Hungary	Maldives	Pakistan	Somalia
Iceland	Mauritius	Palestine	Tajikistan
Ireland	Mexico	Papua New Guinea	Togo
Israel	Montenegro	Paraguay	Uganda
Italy	Namibia	Philippines	United Republic of Tanzania
Japan	Palau	Republic of Moldova	Zimbabwe
Kuwait	Panama	Samoa	
Liechtenstein	Peru	Sao Tome and Principe	
Luxembourg	Romania	Senegal	
Malta	Russian Federation	Solomon Islands	
Netherlands	Saint Lucia	South Sudan	
New Caledonia	Saint Vincent and the Grenadines	Sri Lanka	
New Zealand	Serbia	Sudan	
Norway	Seychelles	Swaziland	
Oman	South Africa	Syrian Arab Republic	
Poland	Suriname	Timor-Leste	
Portugal	Thailand	Tonga	
Puerto Rico	The f. Yugoslav Rep of Macedonia	Tuvalu	
Qatar	Tunisia	Ukraine	
Republic of Korea	Turkey	Uzbekistan	
Saint Kitts and Nevis	Turkmenistan	Vanuatu	
Saudi Arabia	Uruguay	Viet Nam	
Singapore	Venezuela (Bolivarian Rep of)	Yemen	
Slovakia		Zambia	
Slovenia			
Spain			
Sweden			
Switzerland			
Trinidad and Tobago			
United Arab Emirates			
United Kingdom			
United States of America			
United States Virgin Islands			

Appendix I
LIST OF ALL ECONOMIES INCLUDED IN SELECTED GROUPINGS
Other Common Country Groups

(continued)

ASEAN

Brunei Darussalam
Cambodia
Indonesia
Lao People's Dem Rep
Malaysia
Myanmar
Philippines
Singapore
Thailand
Viet Nam

CACM

Costa Rica
El Salvador
Guatemala
Honduras
Nicaragua

CARICOM

Antigua and Barbuda
Bahamas
Barbados
Belize
Dominica
Grenada
Guyana
Haiti
Jamaica
Montserrat
Saint Kitts and Nevis
Saint Lucia
Saint Vincent and the Grenadines
Suriname
Trinidad and Tobago

CEMAC

Cameroon
Central African Republic
Chad
Congo
Equatorial Guinea
Gabon

CIS

Armenia
Azerbaijan
Belarus
Georgia
Kazakhstan
Kyrgyzstan
Republic of Moldova
Russian Federation
Tajikistan
Turkmenistan
Ukraine
Uzbekistan

ECOWAS

Benin
Burkina Faso
Cape Verde
Côte d'Ivoire
Gambia
Ghana
Guinea
Guinea-Bissau
Liberia
Mali
Niger
Nigeria
Senegal
Sierra Leone
Togo

EU

Austria
Belgium
Bulgaria
Cyprus
Czech Republic
Denmark
Estonia
Finland
France
Germany
Greece
Hungary
Ireland
Italy
Latvia
Lithuania
Luxembourg
Malta
Netherlands
Poland
Portugal
Romania
Slovakia
Slovenia
Spain
Sweden
United Kingdom

GCC

Bahrain
Kuwait
Oman
Qatar
Saudi Arabia
United Arab Emirates

LAIA

Argentina
Bolivia (Plurinational State of)
Brazil
Chile
Colombia
Cuba
Ecuador
Mexico
Paraguay
Peru
Uruguay
Venezuela (Bolivarian Rep of)

OECD

Australia
Austria
Belgium
Canada
Chile
Czech Republic
Denmark
Estonia
Finland
France
Germany
Greece
Hungary
Iceland
Ireland
Israel
Italy
Japan
Luxembourg
Mexico
Netherlands
New Zealand
Norway
Poland
Portugal
Republic of Korea
Slovakia
Slovenia
Spain
Sweden
Switzerland
Turkey
United Kingdom
United States of America

MERCOSUR

Argentina
Bolivia (Plurinational State of)
Brazil
Chile
Colombia
Ecuador
Paraguay
Peru
Uruguay
Venezuela (Bolivarian Rep of)

SAARC

Afghanistan
Bangladesh
Bhutan
India
Maldives
Nepal
Pakistan
Sri Lanka

SADC

Angola
Botswana
Democratic Rep of the Congo
Lesotho
Madagascar
Malawi
Mauritius
Mozambique
Namibia
Seychelles
South Africa
Swaziland
United Republic of Tanzania
Zambia
Zimbabwe

WAEMU/UEMOA

Benin
Burkina Faso
Côte d'Ivoire
Guinea-Bissau
Mali
Niger
Senegal
Togo

Appendix II

DETAILED DESCRIPTION OF INTERNATIONAL STANDARD INDUSTRIAL CLASSIFICATION OF ALL ECONOMIC ACTIVITIES (ISIC) - REVISION 2, 3 AND 4

ISIC REVISION 2

ISIC		Description
3		**MANUFACTURING**
311/2		**Food manufacturing**
	3111	Slaughtering, preparing and preserving meat
	3112	Manufacture of dairy products
	3113	Canning and preserving of fruits and vegetables
	3114	Canning, preserving and processing of fish, crustaceans and similar foods
	3115	Manufacture of vegetable and animal oils and fats
	3116	Grain mill products
	3117	Manufacture of bakery products
	3118	Sugar factories and refineries
	3119	Manufacture of cocoa, chocolate and sugar confectionery
	3121	Manufacture of food products not elsewhere classified
	3122	Manufacture of prepared animal feeds
313		**Beverage industries**
	3131	Distilling, rectifying and blending spirits
	3132	Wine industries
	3133	Malt liquors and malt
	3134	Soft drinks and carbonated waters industries
314	**3140**	**Tobacco manufactures**
321		**Manufacture of textiles**
	3211	Spinning, weaving and finishing textiles
	3212	Manufacture of made-up textile goods except wearing apparel
	3213	Knitting mills
	3214	Manufacture of carpets and rugs
	3215	Cordage, rope and twine industries
	3219	Manufacture of textiles not elsewhere classified
322	**3220**	**Manufacture of wearing apparel, except footwear**
323		**Manufacture of leather and products of leather, leather substitutes and fur, except footwear and wearing apparel**
	3231	Tanneries and leather finishing
	3232	Fur dressing and dyeing industries
	3233	Manufacture of products of leather and leather substitutes, except footwear and wearing apparel
324	**3240**	**Manufacture of footwear, except vulcanized or moulded rubber or plastic footwear**

- 20 -

ISIC REVISION 2 (continued)

ISIC		Description
331		**Manufacture of wood and wood and cork products, except furniture**
	3311	Sawmills, planing and other wood mills
	3312	Manufacture of wooden and cane containers and small cane ware
	3319	Manufacture of wood and cork products not elsewhere classified
332	**3320**	**Manufacture of furniture and fixtures, except primarily of metal**
341		**Manufacture of paper and paper products**
	3411	Manufacture of pulp, paper and paperboard
	3412	Manufacture of containers and boxes of paper and paperboard
	3419	Manufacture of pulp, paper and paperboard articles not elsewhere classified
342	**3420**	**Printing, publishing and allied industries**
351		**Manufacture of industrial chemicals**
	3511	Manufacture of basic industrial chemicals except fertilizers
	3512	Manufacture of fertilizers and pesticides
	3513	Manufacture of synthetic resins, plastic materials and man-made fibres except glass
352		**Manufacture of other chemical products**
	3521	Manufacture of paints, varnishes and lacquers
	3522	Manufacture of drugs and medicines
	3523	Manufacture of soap and cleaning preparations, perfumes, cosmetics and other toilet preparations
	3529	Manufacture of chemical products not elsewhere classified
353	**3530**	**Petroleum refineries**
354	**3540**	**Manufacture of miscellaneous products of petroleum and coal**
355		**Manufacture of rubber products**
	3551	Tyre and tube industries
	3559	Manufacture of rubber products not elsewhere classified
356	**3560**	**Manufacture of plastic products not elsewhere classified**
361	**3610**	**Manufacture of pottery, china and earthenware**
362	**3620**	**Manufacture of glass and glass products**
369		**Manufacture of other non-metallic mineral products**
	3691	Manufacture of structural clay products
	3692	Manufacture of cement, lime and plaster
	3699	Manufacture of non-metallic mineral products not elsewhere classified
371	**3710**	**Iron and steel basic industries**
372	**3720**	**Non-ferrous metal basic industries**

ISIC REVISION 2 (continued)

ISIC	Description

381   **Manufacture of fabricated metal products, except machinery and equipment**

3811   Manufacture of cutlery, hand tools and general hardware

3812   Manufacture of furniture and fixtures primarily of metal

3813   Manufacture of structural metal products

3819   Manufacture of fabricated metal products except machinery and equipment not elsewhere classified

382   **Manufacture of machinery except electrical**

3821   Manufacture of engines and turbines

3822   Manufacture of agricultural machinery and equipment

3823   Manufacture of metal and wood working machinery

3824   Manufacture of special industrial machinery and equipment except metal and wood working machinery

3825   Manufacture of office, computing and accounting machinery

3829   Machinery and equipment except electrical not elsewhere classified

383   **Manufacture of electrical machinery, apparatus, appliances and supplies**

3831   Manufacture of electrical industrial machinery and apparatus

3832   Manufacture of radio, television and communication equipment and apparatus

3833   Manufacture of electrical appliances and housewares

3839   Manufacture of electrical apparatus and supplies not elsewhere classified

384   **Manufacture of transport equipment**

3841   Ship building and repairing

3842   Manufacture of railroad equipment

3843   Manufacture of motor vehicles

3844   Manufacture of motorcycles and bicycles

3845   Manufacture of aircraft

3849   Manufacture of transport equipment not elsewhere classified

385   **Manufacture of professional and scientific, and measuring and controlling equipment not elsewhere classified, and of photographic and optical goods**

3851   Manufacture of professional and scientific, and measuring and controlling equipment, not elsewhere classified

3852   Manufacture of photographic and optical goods

3853   Manufacture of watches and clocks

390   **Other manufacturing industries**

3901   Manufacture of jewellery and related articles

3902   Manufacture of musical instruments

3903   Manufacture of sporting and athletic goods

3909   Manufacturing industries not elsewhere classified

* * * * * * * * * *

ISIC REVISION 3

ISIC		Description

D   **MANUFACTURING**

Division 15   **Manufacture of food products and beverages**

151		Production, processing and preservation of meat, fish, fruit, vegetables, oils and fats
	1511	Production, processing and preserving of meat and meat products
	1512	Processing and preserving of fish and fish products
	1513	Processing and preserving of fruit and vegetables
	1514	Manufacture of vegetable and animal oils and fats

152	1520	Manufacture of dairy products

153		Manufacture of grain mill products, starches and starch products, and prepared animal feeds
	1531	Manufacture of grain mill products
	1532	Manufacture of starches and starch products
	1533	Manufacture of prepared animal feeds

154		Manufacture of other food products
	1541	Manufacture of bakery products
	1542	Manufacture of sugar
	1543	Manufacture of cocoa, chocolate and sugar confectionery
	1544	Manufacture of macaroni, noodles, couscous and similar farinaceous products
	1549	Manufacture of other food products n.e.c.

155		Manufacture of beverages
	1551	Distilling, rectifying and blending of spirits; ethyl alcohol production from fermented materials
	1552	Manufacture of wines
	1553	Manufacture of malt liquors and malt
	1554	Manufacture of soft drinks; production of mineral waters

Division 16   **Manufacture of tobacco products**

160	1600	Manufacture of tobacco products

Division 17   **Manufacture of textiles**

171		Spinning, weaving and finishing of textiles
	1711	Preparation and spinning of textile fibres; weaving of textiles
	1712	Finishing of textiles

172		Manufacture of other textiles
	1721	Manufacture of made-up textile articles, except apparel
	1722	Manufacture of carpets and rugs
	1723	Manufacture of cordage, rope, twine and netting
	1729	Manufacture of other textiles n.e.c.

173	1730	Manufacture of knitted and crocheted fabrics and articles

ISIC REVISION 3 (continued)

ISIC		Description

Division 18 **Manufacture of wearing apparel; dressing and dyeing of fur**

| 181 | 1810 | Manufacture of wearing apparel, except fur apparel |
| 182 | 1820 | Dressing and dyeing of fur; manufacture of articles of fur |

Division 19 **Tanning and dressing of leather; manufacture of luggage, handbags, saddlery, harness and footwear**

191		Tanning and dressing of leather; manufacture of luggage, handbags, saddlery and harness
	1911	Tanning and dressing of leather
	1912	Manufacture of luggage, handbags and the like, saddlery and harness
192	1920	Manufacture of footwear

Division 20 **Manufacture of wood and of products of wood and cork, except furniture; manufacture of articles of straw and plaiting materials**

201	2010	Sawmilling and planing of wood
202		Manufacture of products of wood, cork, straw and plaiting materials
	2021	Manufacture of veneer sheets; manufacture of plywood, laminboard, particle board and other panels and boards
	2022	Manufacture of builders' carpentry and joinery
	2023	Manufacture of wooden containers
	2029	Manufacture of other products of wood; manufacture of articles of cork, straw and plaiting materials

Division 21 **Manufacture of paper and paper products**

210		Manufacture of paper and paper products
	2101	Manufacture of pulp, paper and paperboard
	2102	Manufacture of corrugated paper and paperboard and of containers of paper and paperboard
	2109	Manufacture of other articles of paper and paperboard

Division 22 **Publishing, printing and reproduction of recorded media**

221		Publishing
	2211	Publishing of books, brochures, musical books and other publications
	2212	Publishing of newspapers, journals and periodicals
	2213	Publishing of recorded media
	2219	Other publishing
222		Printing and service activities related to printing
	2221	Printing
	2222	Service activities related to printing
223	2230	Reproduction of recorded media

ISIC REVISION 3 (continued)

ISIC		Description

Division 23 — **Manufacture of coke, refined petroleum products and nuclear fuel**

231	2310	Manufacture of coke oven products
232	2320	Manufacture of refined petroleum products
233	2330	Processing of nuclear fuel

Division 24 — **Manufacture of chemicals and chemical products**

241		Manufacture of basic chemicals
	2411	Manufacture of basic chemicals, except fertilizers and nitrogen compounds
	2412	Manufacture of fertilizers and nitrogen compounds
	2413	Manufacture of plastics in primary forms and of synthetic rubber

242		Manufacture of other chemical products
	2421	Manufacture of pesticides and other agro-chemical products
	2422	Manufacture of paints, varnishes and similar coatings, printing ink and mastics
	2423	Manufacture of pharmaceuticals, medicinal chemicals and botanical products
	2424	Manufacture of soap and detergents, cleaning and polishing preparations, perfumes and toilet preparations
	2429	Manufacture of other chemical products n.e.c.

| 243 | 2430 | Manufacture of man-made fibres |

Division 25 — **Manufacture of rubber and plastics products**

251		Manufacture of rubber products
	2511	Manufacture of rubber tyres and tubes; retreading and rebuilding of rubber tyres
	2519	Manufacture of other rubber products

| 252 | 2520 | Manufacture of plastics products |

Division 26 — **Manufacture of other non-metallic mineral products**

| 261 | 2610 | Manufacture of glass and glass products |

269		Manufacture of non-metallic mineral products n.e.c.
	2691	Manufacture of non-structural non-refractory ceramic ware
	2692	Manufacture of refractory ceramic products
	2693	Manufacture of structural non-refractory clay and ceramic products
	2694	Manufacture of cement, lime and plaster
	2695	Manufacture of articles of concrete, cement and plaster
	2696	Cutting, shaping and finishing of stone
	2699	Manufacture of other non-metallic mineral products n.e.c.

Division 27 — **Manufacture of basic metals**

| 271 | 2710 | Manufacture of basic iron and steel |
| 272 | 2720 | Manufacture of basic precious and non-ferrous metals |

ISIC REVISION 3 (continued)

ISIC		Description

273		Casting of metals
	2731	Casting of iron and steel
	2732	Casting of non-ferrous metals

Division 28 — **Manufacture of fabricated metal products, except machinery and equipment**

281		Manufacture of structural metal products, tanks, reservoirs and steam generators
	2811	Manufacture of structural metal products
	2812	Manufacture of tanks, reservoirs and containers of metal
	2813	Manufacture of steam generators, except central heating hot water boilers

289		Manufacture of other fabricated metal products; metal working service activities
	2891	Forging, pressing, stamping and roll-forming of metal; powder metallurgy
	2892	Treatment and coating of metals; general mechanical engineering on a fee or contract basis
	2893	Manufacture of cutlery, hand tools and general hardware
	2899	Manufacture of other fabricated metal products n.e.c.

Division 29 — **Manufacture of machinery and equipment n.e.c.**

291		Manufacture of general purpose machinery
	2911	Manufacture of engines and turbines, except aircraft, vehicle and cycle engines
	2912	Manufacture of pumps, compressors, taps and valves
	2913	Manufacture of bearings, gears, gearing and driving elements
	2914	Manufacture of ovens, furnaces and furnace burners
	2915	Manufacture of lifting and handling equipment
	2919	Manufacture of other general purpose machinery

292		Manufacture of special purpose machinery
	2921	Manufacture of agricultural and forestry machinery
	2922	Manufacture of machine tools
	2923	Manufacture of machinery for metallurgy
	2924	Manufacture of machinery for mining, quarrying and construction
	2925	Manufacture of machinery for food, beverage and tobacco processing
	2926	Manufacture of machinery for textile, apparel and leather production
	2927	Manufacture of weapons and ammunition
	2929	Manufacture of other special purpose machinery

| 293 | 2930 | Manufacture of domestic appliances n.e.c. |

Division 30 — **Manufacture of office, accounting and computing machinery**

| 300 | 3000 | Manufacture of office, accounting and computing machinery |

Division 31 — **Manufacture of electrical machinery and apparatus n.e.c.**

311	3110	Manufacture of electric motors, generators and transformers
312	3120	Manufacture of electricity distribution and control apparatus
313	3130	Manufacture of insulated wire and cable
314	3140	Manufacture of accumulators, primary cells and primary batteries

ISIC REVISION 3 (continued)

ISIC		Description

| 315 | 3150 | Manufacture of electric lamps and lighting equipment |
| 319 | 3190 | Manufacture of other electrical equipment n.e.c. |

Division 32   **Manufacture of radio, television and communication equipment and apparatus**

321	3210	Manufacture of electronic valves and tubes and other electronic components
322	3220	Manufacture of television and radio transmitters and apparatus for line telephony and line telegraphy
323	3230	Manufacture of television and radio receivers, sound or video recording or reproducing apparatus, and associated goods

Division 33   **Manufacture of medical, precision and optical instruments, watches and clocks**

331		Manufacture of medical appliances and instruments and appliances for measuring, checking, testing, navigating and other purposes, except optical instruments
	3311	Manufacture of medical and surgical equipment and orthopaedic appliances
	3312	Manufacture of instruments and appliances for measuring, checking, testing, navigating and other purposes, except industrial process control equipment
	3313	Manufacture of industrial process control equipment
332	3320	Manufacture of optical instruments and photographic equipment
333	3330	Manufacture of watches and clocks

Division 34   **Manufacture of motor vehicles, trailers and semi-trailers**

341	3410	Manufacture of motor vehicles
342	3420	Manufacture of bodies (coachwork) for motor vehicles; manufacture of trailers and semi-trailers
343	3430	Manufacture of parts and accessories for motor vehicles and their engines

Division 35   **Manufacture of other transport equipment**

351		Building and repairing of ships and boats
	3511	Building and repairing of ships
	3512	Building and repairing of pleasure and sporting boats
352	3520	Manufacture of railway and tramway locomotives and rolling stock
353	3530	Manufacture of aircraft and spacecraft
359		Manufacture of transport equipment n.e.c.
	3591	Manufacture of motorcycles
	3592	Manufacture of bicycles and invalid carriages
	3599	Manufacture of other transport equipment n.e.c.

ISIC REVISION 3 (continued)

ISIC		Description

Division 36   **Manufacture of furniture; manufacturing n.e.c..**

361	3610	Manufacture of furniture

369		Manufacturing n.e.c.
	3691	Manufacture of jewellery and related articles
	3692	Manufacture of musical instruments
	3693	Manufacture of sports goods
	3694	Manufacture of games and toys
	3699	Other manufacturing n.e.c.

Division 37   **Recycling**

371	3710	Recycling of metal waste and scrap
372	3720	Recycling of non-metal waste and scrap

* * * * * * * * * *

ISIC REVISION 4

ISIC		Description

C **MANUFACTURING**

Division 10 **Manufacture of food products**

101	1010	Processing and preserving of meat
102	1020	Processing and preserving of fish, crustaceans and molluscs
103	1030	Processing and preserving of fruit and vegetables
104	1040	Manufacture of vegetable and animal oils and fats
105	1050	Manufacture of dairy products
106		Manufacture of grain mill products, starches and starch products
	1061	Manufacture of grain mill products
	1062	Manufacture of starches and starch products
107		Manufacture of other food products
	1071	Manufacture of bakery products
	1072	Manufacture of sugar
	1073	Manufacture of cocoa, chocolate and sugar confectionery
	1074	Manufacture of macaroni, noodles, couscous and similar farinaceous products
	1075	Manufacture of prepared meals and dishes
	1079	Manufacture of other food products n.e.c.
108	1080	Manufacture of prepared animal feeds

Division 11 **Manufacture of beverages**

	1101	Distilling, rectifying and blending of spirits
	1102	Manufacture of wines
	1103	Manufacture of malt liquors and malt
	1104	Manufacture of soft drinks; production of mineral waters and other bottled waters

Division 12 **Manufacture of tobacco products**

| 120 | 1200 | Manufacture of tobacco products |

Division 13 **Manufacture of textiles**

131		Spinning, weaving and finishing of textiles
	1311	Preparation and spinning of textile fibres
	1312	Weaving of textiles
	1313	Finishing of textiles
139		Manufacture of other textiles
	1391	Manufacture of knitted and crocheted fabrics
	1392	Manufacture of made-up textile articles, except apparel
	1393	Manufacture of carpets and rugs
	1394	Manufacture of cordage, rope, twine and netting
	1399	Manufacture of other textiles n.e.c.

ISIC REVISION 4 (continued)

ISIC		Description

Division 14   **Manufacture of wearing apparel**

141	1410	Manufacture of wearing apparel, except fur apparel
142	1420	Manufacture of articles of fur
143	1430	Manufacture of knitted and crocheted apparel

Division 15   **Manufacture of leather and related products**

151		Tanning and dressing of leather; manufacture of luggage, handbags, saddlery and harness; dressing and dyeing of fur
	1511	Tanning and dressing of leather; dressing and dyeing of fur
	1512	Manufacture of luggage, handbags and the like, saddlery and harness

| 152 | 1520 | Manufacture of footwear |

Division 16   **Manufacture of wood and of products of wood and cork, except furniture; manufacture of articles of straw and plaiting materials**

| 161 | 1610 | Sawmilling and planing of wood |

162		Manufacture of products of wood, cork, straw and plaiting materials
	1621	Manufacture of veneer sheets and wood-based panels
	1622	Manufacture of builders' carpentry and joinery
	1623	Manufacture of wooden containers
	1629	Manufacture of other products of wood; manufacture of articles of cork, straw and plaiting materials

Division 17   **Manufacture of paper and paper products**

	1701	Manufacture of pulp, paper and paperboard
	1702	Manufacture of corrugated paper and paperboard and of containers of paper and paperboard
	1709	Manufacture of other articles of paper and paperboard

Division 18   **Printing and reproduction of recorded media**

181		Printing and service activities related to printing
	1811	Printing
	1812	Service activities related to printing

| 182 | 1820 | Reproduction of recorded media |

Division 19   **Manufacture of coke and refined petroleum products**

| 191 | 1910 | Manufacture of coke oven products |
| 192 | 1920 | Manufacture of refined petroleum products |

ISIC REVISION 4 (continued)

ISIC	Description

Division 20 **Manufacture of chemicals and chemical products**

201 Manufacture of basic chemicals, fertilizers and nitrogen compounds, plastics and synthetic rubber in primary forms
2011 Manufacture of basic chemicals
2012 Manufacture of fertilizers and nitrogen compounds
2013 Manufacture of plastics and synthetic rubber in primary forms

202 Manufacture of other chemical products
2021 Manufacture of pesticides and other agrochemical products
2022 Manufacture of paints, varnishes and similar coatings, printing ink and mastics
2023 Manufacture of soap and detergents, cleaning and polishing preparations, perfumes and toilet preparations
2029 Manufacture of other chemical products n.e.c.

203 2030 Manufacture of man-made fibres

Division 21 **Manufacture of pharmaceuticals, medicinal chemical and botanical products**

210 2100 Manufacture of pharmaceuticals, medicinal chemical and botanical products

Division 22 **Manufacture of rubber and plastics products**

221 Manufacture of rubber products
2211 Manufacture of rubber tyres and tubes; retreading and rebuilding of rubber tyres
2219 Manufacture of other rubber products

222 2220 Manufacture of plastics products

Division 23 **Manufacture of other non-metallic mineral products**

231 2310 Manufacture of glass and glass products

239 Manufacture of non-metallic mineral products n.e.c.
2391 Manufacture of refractory products
2392 Manufacture of clay building materials
2393 Manufacture of other porcelain and ceramic products
2394 Manufacture of cement, lime and plaster
2395 Manufacture of articles of concrete, cement and plaster
2396 Cutting, shaping and finishing of stone
2399 Manufacture of other non-metallic mineral products n.e.c.

Division 24 **Manufacture of basic metals**

241 2410 Manufacture of basic iron and steel
242 2420 Manufacture of basic precious and other non-ferrous metals

243 Casting of metals
2431 Casting of iron and steel
2432 Casting of non-ferrous metals

ISIC REVISION 4 (continued)

ISIC		Description

Division 25   **Manufacture of fabricated metal products, except machinery and equipment**

251		Manufacture of structural metal products, tanks, reservoirs and steam generators
	2511	Manufacture of structural metal products
	2512	Manufacture of tanks, reservoirs and containers of metal
	2513	Manufacture of steam generators, except central heating hot water boilers
252	2520	Manufacture of weapons and ammunition
259		Manufacture of other fabricated metal products; metalworking service activities
	2591	Forging, pressing, stamping and roll-forming of metal; powder metallurgy
	2592	Treatment and coating of metals; machining
	2593	Manufacture of cutlery, hand tools and general hardware
	2599	Manufacture of other fabricated metal products n.e.c.

Division 26   **Manufacture of computer, electronic and optical products**

261	2610	Manufacture of electronic components and boards
262	2620	Manufacture of computers and peripheral equipment
263	2630	Manufacture of communication equipment
264	2640	Manufacture of consumer electronics
265		Manufacture of measuring, testing, navigating and control equipment; watches and clocks
	2651	Manufacture of measuring, testing, navigating and control equipment
	2652	Manufacture of watches and clocks
266	2660	Manufacture of irradiation, electromedical and electrotherapeutic equipment
267	2670	Manufacture of optical instruments and photographic equipment
268	2680	Manufacture of magnetic and optical media

Division 27   **Manufacture of electrical equipment**

271	2710	Manufacture of electric motors, generators, transformers and electricity distribution and control apparatus
272	2720	Manufacture of batteries and accumulators
273		Manufacture of wiring and wiring devices
	2731	Manufacture of fibre optic cables
	2732	Manufacture of other electronic and electric wires and cables
	2733	Manufacture of wiring devices
274	2740	Manufacture of electric lighting equipment
275	2750	Manufacture of domestic appliances
279	2790	Manufacture of other electrical equipment

ISIC REVISION 4 (continued)

ISIC		Description

Division 28   **Manufacture of machinery and equipment n.e.c.**

281		Manufacture of general-purpose machinery
	2811	Manufacture of engines and turbines, except aircraft, vehicle and cycle engines
	2812	Manufacture of fluid power equipment
	2813	Manufacture of other pumps, compressors, taps and valves
	2814	Manufacture of bearings, gears, gearing and driving elements
	2815	Manufacture of ovens, furnaces and furnace burners
	2816	Manufacture of lifting and handling equipment
	2817	Manufacture of office machinery and equipment (except computers and peripheral equipment)
	2818	Manufacture of power-driven hand tools
	2819	Manufacture of other general-purpose machinery

282		Manufacture of special-purpose machinery
	2821	Manufacture of agricultural and forestry machinery
	2822	Manufacture of metal-forming machinery and machine tools
	2823	Manufacture of machinery for metallurgy
	2824	Manufacture of machinery for mining, quarrying and construction
	2825	Manufacture of machinery for food, beverage and tobacco processing
	2826	Manufacture of machinery for textile, apparel and leather production
	2829	Manufacture of other special-purpose machinery

Division 29   **Manufacture of motor vehicles, trailers and semi-trailers**

291	2910	Manufacture of motor vehicles
292	2920	Manufacture of bodies (coachwork) for motor vehicles; manufacture of trailers and semi-trailers
293	2930	Manufacture of parts and accessories for motor vehicles

Division 30   **Manufacture of other transport equipment**

301		Building of ships and boats
	3011	Building of ships and floating structures
	3012	Building of pleasure and sporting boats

302	3020	Manufacture of railway locomotives and rolling stock
303	3030	Manufacture of air and spacecraft and related machinery
304	3040	Manufacture of military fighting vehicles

309		Manufacture of transport equipment n.e.c.
	3091	Manufacture of motorcycles
	3092	Manufacture of bicycles and invalid carriages
	3099	Manufacture of other transport equipment n.e.c.

Division 31   **Manufacture of furniture**

310	3100	Manufacture of furniture

ISIC		Description
Division 32		**Other manufacturing**
321		Manufacture of jewellery, bijouterie and related articles
	3211	Manufacture of jewellery and related articles
	3212	Manufacture of imitation jewellery and related articles
322	3220	Manufacture of musical instruments
323	3230	Manufacture of sports goods
324	3240	Manufacture of games and toys
325	3250	Manufacture of medical and dental instruments and supplies
329	3290	Other manufacturing n.e.c.
Division 33		**Repair and installation of machinery and equipment**
331		Repair of fabricated metal products, machinery and equipment
	3311	Repair of fabricated metal products
	3312	Repair of machinery
	3313	Repair of electronic and optical equipment
	3314	Repair of electrical equipment
	3315	Repair of transport equipment, except motor vehicles
	3319	Repair of other equipment
332	3320	Installation of industrial machinery and equipment

* * * * * * * * * *

Country or area	Value added				Output				Employment		
	Factor values	Producers' prices	Unspecified	Mixed	Factor values	Producers' prices	Unspecified	Mixed	Persons engaged	Employees	Mixed
Afghanistan							X			X	
Albania			X					X		X	
Argentina		X				X				X	
Armenia			X			X				X	
Aruba										X	
Australia			X				X		X		
Austria				X			X				X
Azerbaijan	X							X		X	
Bahamas				X				X		X	
Bangladesh	X				X					X	
Belarus		X					X			X	
Belgium	X						X			X	
Bermuda							X		X		
Bolivia (Plurinational State of)		X				X				X	
Botswana		X					X			X	
Brazil	X				X				X		
Bulgaria		X					X			X	
Cambodia		X				X					X
Cameroon							X			X	
Canada			X				X			X	
Cape Verde							X		X		
Chile			X				X			X	
China		X				X				X	
China, Macao SAR		X				X			X		
China, Taiwan Province			X				X		X		
Colombia	X				X					X	
Congo			X				X			X	
Cook Islands			X				X			X	
Croatia										X	
Curaçao		X				X				X	
Cyprus		X				X				X	
Czech Republic				X			X			X	
Denmark				X			X				X
Dominican Republic										X	
Ecuador		X				X				X	
Egypt	X				X						X
Eritrea		X				X				X	
Estonia				X			X			X	
Ethiopia		X				X				X	
Fiji		X				X				X	
Finland				X			X				X
France	X						X			X	
Gambia				X		X				X	
Georgia			X				X				X
Germany	X							X			X
Ghana		X				X				X	
Greece	X							X		X	
Guatemala									X		
Haiti							X			X	
Hungary				X			X			X	
Iceland			X				X			X	
India		X				X					X
Indonesia	X					X				X	
Iran (Islamic Republic of)		X				X				X	
Iraq	X						X			X	
Ireland	X							X		X	
Israel				X				X			X
Italy				X			X			X	
Japan		X					X			X	
Jordan		X				X					X
Kazakhstan							X			X	
Kenya		X					X			X	
Kuwait		X				X				X	
Kyrgyzstan			X			X					X
Lao People's Dem Rep		X				X				X	
Latvia	X				X					X	
Lebanon				X				X		X	

DESCRIPTION OF DATA USED IN SECTION 1.2

Country or area	Value added				Output				Employment		
	Factor values	Producers' prices	Unspecified	Mixed	Factor values	Producers' prices	Unspecified	Mixed	Persons engaged	Employees	Mixed
Lesotho										X	
Lithuania	X							X		X	
Luxembourg	X						X			X	
Madagascar				X				X		X	
Malawi		X				X				X	
Malaysia			X				X			X	
Maldives									X		
Malta	X				X					X	
Mauritius			X				X			X	
Mexico				X				X			X
Mongolia				X				X			X
Morocco	X				X					X	
Myanmar						X				X	
Nepal		X			X					X	
Netherlands	X						X			X	
New Zealand			X				X			X	
Nigeria						X			X		
Norway				X			X			X	
Oman		X				X				X	
Pakistan		X				X				X	
Palestine		X				X					X
Panama		X				X				X	
Papua New Guinea				X				X		X	
Paraguay			X				X			X	
Peru			X				X		X		
Philippines		X			X					X	
Poland				X			X			X	
Portugal	X						X				X
Qatar		X				X					X
Republic of Korea			X				X			X	
Republic of Moldova			X			X				X	
Romania				X				X		X	
Russian Federation			X				X			X	
Rwanda		X			X					X	
Saudi Arabia			X				X				X
Senegal		X						X		X	
Serbia			X				X			X	
Sierra Leone		X				X				X	
Singapore			X					X		X	
Slovakia			X				X				X
Slovenia	X				X					X	
South Africa			X				X			X	
Spain				X			X			X	
Sri Lanka		X			X					X	
Sudan (including South Sudan)		X				X				X	
Suriname			X		X					X	
Sweden	X							X		X	
Switzerland			X				X		X		
Syrian Arab Republic										X	
Tajikistan							X			X	
Thailand				X				X		X	
The f. Yugosl. Rep of Macedonia			X				X			X	
Tonga						X					X
Trinidad and Tobago				X				X		X	
Tunisia			X				X			X	
Turkey				X			X			X	
Turkmenistan							X		X		
Uganda			X							X	
Ukraine			X					X		X	
United Kingdom	X						X			X	
United Republic of Tanzania	X				X					X	
United States of America			X			X				X	
Uruguay		X				X			X		
Viet Nam				X				X		X	
Yemen		X				X				X	
Zimbabwe										X	

Part I
SUMMARY TABLES

Section 1.1

THE MANUFACTURING SECTOR

Major trends of growth and distribution of manufacturing in the world

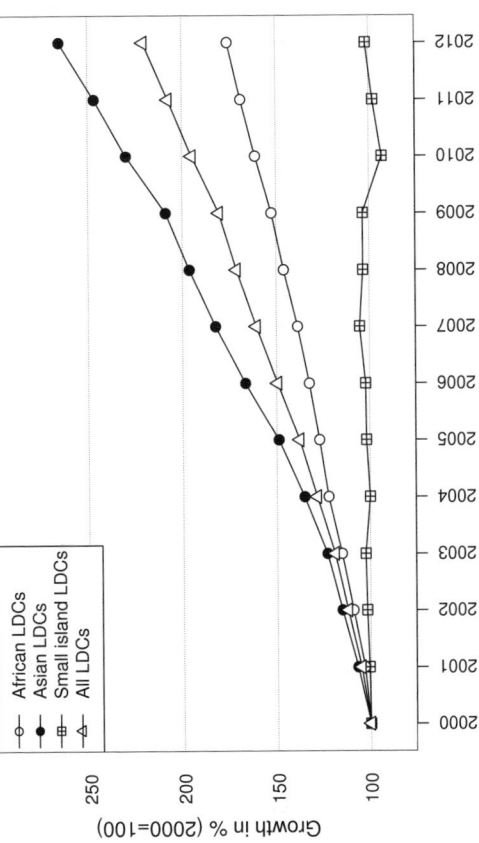

Figure 1: Overall growth trends of world MVA by selected country groups at constant 2005 prices

World industrial production grew smoothly until the onset of the financial crisis in 2009. World MVA, which grew by merely 2.2 percent in 2012, has not yet reached the level of the pre-crisis period. Its effect was particularly strong in industrialized countries. Following a brief period of recovery in 2010, manufacturing in industrialized countries, especially in European countries, has contracted again and is characterized by low growth and there is further risk of another downturn. Developing and emerging industrial economies have maintained a relatively high growth of manufacturing output. However, this growth has faced modest slowdown due to the loss of demand for their manufactured products in external market.

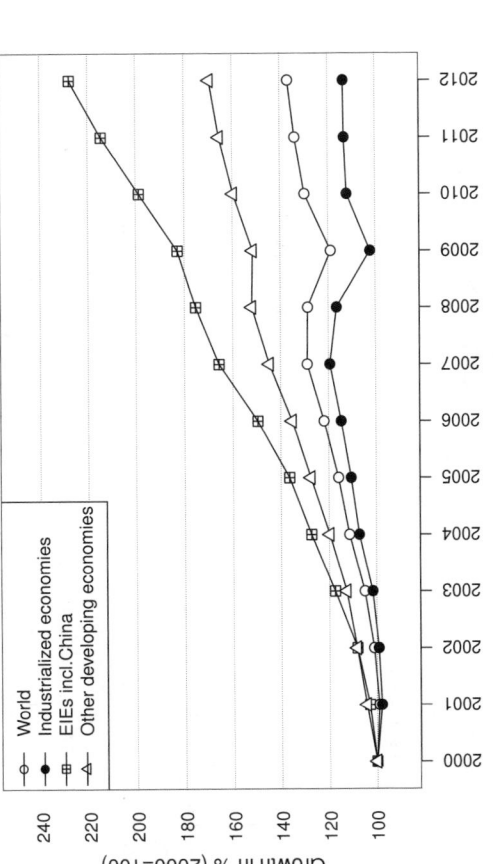

Figure 2: MVA growth trends of least developed countries, 2000-2012

The group of least developed countries (LDCs) includes economies with specific geographic constraints such as lack of territorial access to the sea (landlocked countries) and remoteness and isolation from world markets (small island economies). In both cases, the limitation of external trade hampers the production growth of these countries. In comparison with their African partners, Asian LDCs have the advantage of closer proximity to fast growing economies. Over the last decade, the MVA of Asian LDCs grew by 8.7 percent per annum compared to 5.9 percent of African LDCs. Manufacturing growth has been nominal in small island LDCs which are more oriented towards fishing and service related activities.

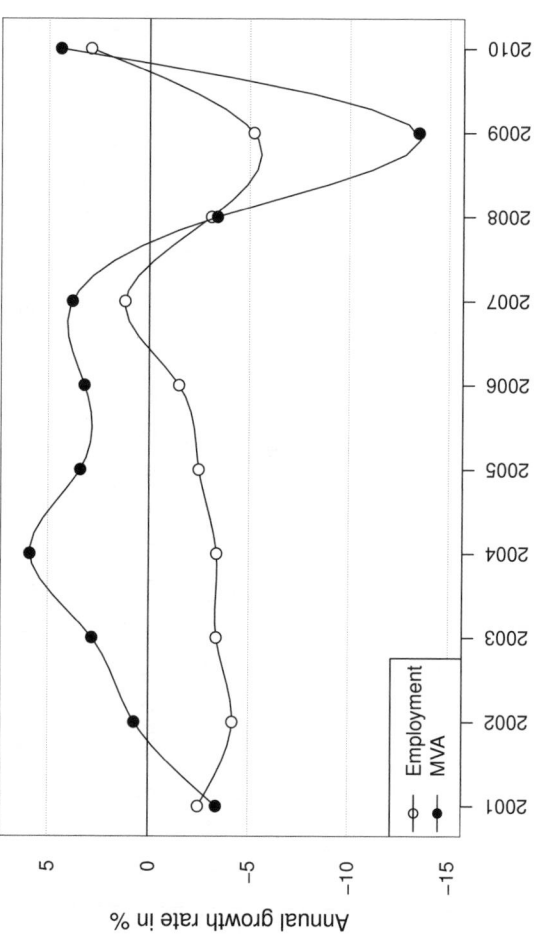

Figure 4: Output and employment in major industrialized countries in the last decade

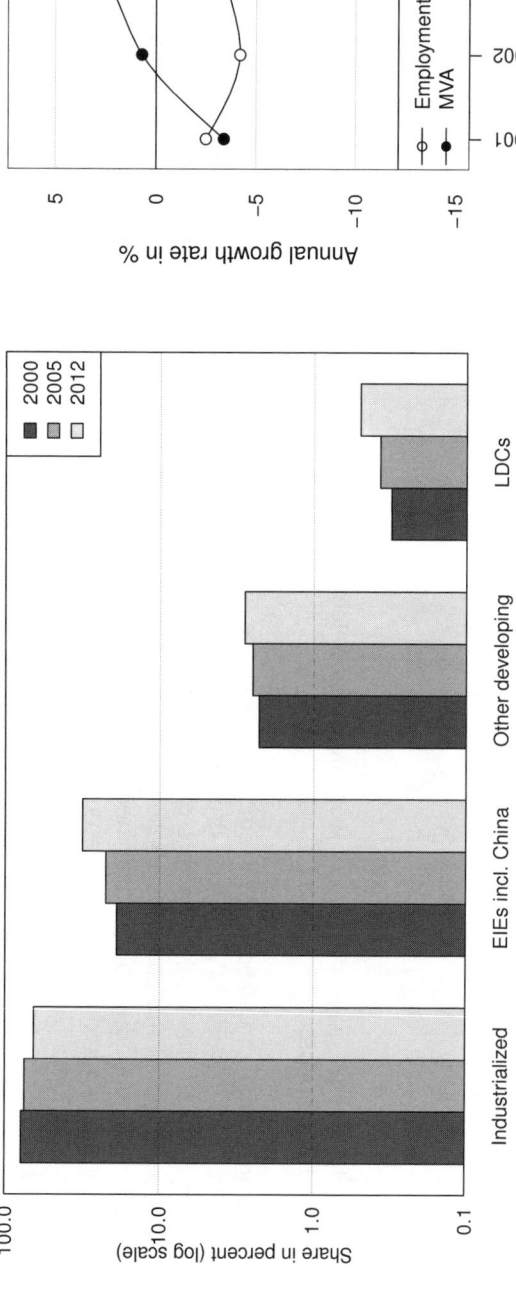

Figure 3: Percentage share (in log scale) of major country groups in world MVA, at constant 2005 prices

The varying pace of industrial growth has changed the share of major country groups in terms of industrial production. Developing and emerging industrial economies have come to occupy an increasing share in world MVA, which rose from 21.8 percent in 2000 to 35.2 percent in 2012. By contrast, the share of industrialized countries over the same period decreased from 78.2 to 64.7 percent. However, from the long-term perspectives the share of industrialized countries in world MVA will remain high as economic advancement pushes more countries into the group of industrialized economies. Since 2000, the number of industrialized economies has increased from 33 to 57. Malaysia, Republic of South Korea, Singapore and the United Arab Emirates were among the new entrants during this period.

The manufacturing sector has not generated much employment in the eight major industrialized countries of the world (Group of Eight or G-8) in the last decade. But job loss declined continuously in the pre-crisis period, and for the first time since 2001, an absolute growth in the number of employees in manufacturing was achieved in 2007. This positive trend was abruptly reversed by the crisis in 2009, when the number of industrial employees again plunged into negative figures. The 2009 crisis also caused decline in labour productivity. At the height of the crisis, as Figure 4 indicates, the net manufacturing output (or MVA) of industrialized countries fell by a much higher rate than the number of employees.

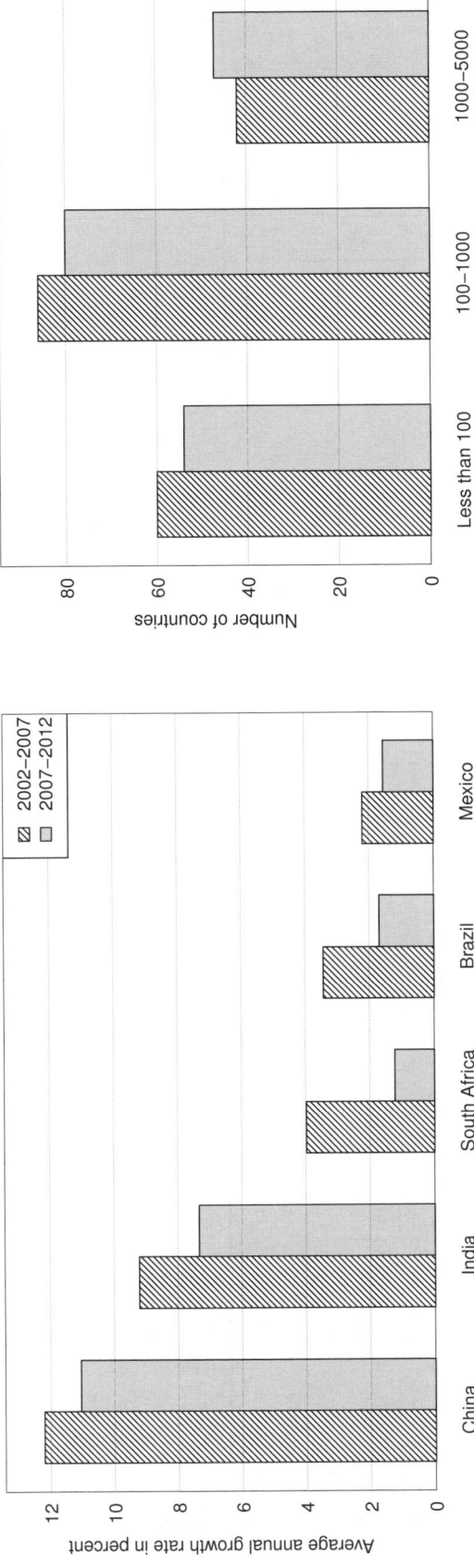

Figure 5: Average annual growth of MVA of selected emerging industrial economies

Although emerging industrial economies as a group maintained a relatively higher growth of MVA, the recent economic recession has decelerated their industrial production. The impact of the recession on individual economies differed mainly due to dependence on export. On account of strong domestic demand, China's average annual growth rate reduced slightly from 12.6 percent in 2002-2007 to 9.9 percent in 2007-2012. However, manufacturing in South Africa, which largely depends on export to Europe, suffered a significant downturn with a reduction in MVA growth from 4.2 percent per annum to a nominal rate of 0.3 percent. In general, the impact of the recession has been more severe in Latin American economies compared to those in Asia.

Figure 6: Change in the number of countries by selected range of MVA per capita, 1992-2012, at constant 2005 prices

MVA per capita is a widely accepted single measure of an economy's industrialization. The number of economies with significant income generated from manufacturing activities has increased in the last 20 years. In 2012, the number of economies with an MVA per capita higher than USD 1000 increased from 53 in 1992 to 66 in 2012. This observation covers 200 economies, for which MVA data exists in UNIDO's database. At the same time, a large number of developing countries have been trapped in low industrial growth for several years. The number of countries with an MVA per capita less than USD 100 decreased from 60 in 1992 to just 55 in 2012.

- 44 -

DISTRIBUTION OF WORLD MVA AMONG SELECTED COUNTRY GROUPS, 2000-2012

Year	Industrialized Economies — Europe EU a/	Industrialized Economies — Europe Other	East Asia	West Asia	North America	Others	Regional groups Africa	Regional groups Asia and Pacific	Regional groups Europe	Regional groups Latin America	Emerging Industrial Economies	Development groups China	Development groups Other Developing Economies	Development groups Least Developed Countries
Percentage share in world total MVA (at constant 2005 prices)														
2000	29.5	2.7	18.3	0.3	25.4	2.2	1.4	11.4	2.6	6.2	12.2	6.9	2.2	0.3
2005	26.7	2.9	18.0	0.5	24.8	1.9	1.4	15.1	2.9	5.8	12.7	9.7	2.5	0.3
2006	26.5	2.9	17.9	0.4	24.2	1.9	1.4	16.0	3.0	5.8	12.9	10.4	2.5	0.4
2007	25.9	2.9	17.7	0.4	23.9	1.8	1.4	17.2	3.1	5.7	12.9	11.5	2.6	0.4
2008	25.2	2.9	17.6	0.4	23.1	1.8	1.4	18.6	3.2	5.8	13.3	12.6	2.7	0.4
2009	23.4	2.8	16.2	0.5	22.6	1.9	1.6	21.9	3.3	5.8	13.9	15.4	2.9	0.4
2010 b/	23.1	2.7	17.2	0.4	22.4	1.8	1.5	21.8	3.3	5.8	13.8	15.3	2.8	0.5
2011 c/	22.8	2.7	16.5	0.4	22.0	1.8	1.4	23.1	3.4	5.9	14.1	16.4	2.8	0.5
2012 c/	21.7	2.7	16.7	0.5	22.0	1.4	1.5	24.3	3.4	5.8	14.3	17.4	2.8	0.5
Percentage share in world total MVA (at current prices)														
2004	28.0	2.6	18.6	0.4	25.1	2.0	1.4	13.9	2.6	5.4	11.8	8.9	2.3	0.3
2005	26.7	2.9	18.0	0.5	24.8	1.9	1.4	15.1	2.9	5.8	12.7	9.7	2.5	0.3
2006	26.2	3.2	16.6	0.4	24.1	1.8	1.5	17.0	3.1	6.1	13.6	11.0	2.7	0.4
2007	26.8	3.5	15.1	0.4	22.2	1.9	1.4	19.1	3.4	6.2	14.3	12.6	2.8	0.4
2008	25.7	3.8	14.5	0.5	20.2	1.8	1.4	21.7	3.7	6.7	15.0	15.0	3.1	0.4
2009	22.5	3.1	14.4	0.5	20.8	1.9	1.6	25.2	3.2	6.8	15.1	17.9	3.3	0.5
2010 b/	21.2	3.4	14.7	0.6	20.2	2.2	1.6	25.4	3.3	7.4	16.3	17.6	3.3	0.5

a/ Excluding non-industrialized EU economies.
b/ Provisional.
c/ Estimate.

Table 1.2

DISTRIBUTION OF WORLD MVA AND POPULATION, SELECTED YEARS
(Percentage)

Country group	MVA at constant 2005 prices					MVA at current prices					Population				
	2000	2005	2010	2011 b/	2012 b/	2006	2007	2008	2009	2010 a/	2000	2005	2010	2011	2012
Industrialized Economies	78.4	74.8	67.6	66.2	65.0	72.3	69.9	66.5	63.2	62.3	18.8	18.2	17.7	17.6	17.5
Emerging Industrial Economies	12.2	12.7	13.8	14.1	14.3	13.6	14.3	15.0	15.1	16.3	33.7	33.9	34.0	34.0	34.0
China	6.9	9.7	15.3	16.4	17.4	11.0	12.6	15.0	17.9	17.6	20.9	20.3	19.7	19.5	19.4
Other Developing Economies	2.3	2.5	2.8	2.8	2.8	2.7	2.8	3.1	3.3	3.3	16.4	16.9	17.4	17.5	17.6
Least Developed Countries	0.3	0.4	0.5	0.5	0.5	0.4	0.4	0.4	0.5	0.5	10.1	10.7	11.3	11.4	11.5
World	100.0	100.0	100.0	100.0	100.0	100.0	100.0	100.0	100.0	100.0	100.0	100.0	100.0	100.0	100.0
Low Income	0.3	0.3	0.4	0.4	0.5	0.3	0.4	0.4	0.5	0.5	10.2	10.8	11.3	11.4	11.6
Lower Middle Income	3.8	4.4	5.2	5.4	5.6	5.0	5.3	5.5	6.0	6.3	34.5	35.2	35.9	36.0	36.1
Upper Middle Income(excl.China)	11.2	11.5	11.7	11.8	11.9	12.3	13.0	14.0	13.1	14.5	17.1	16.9	16.7	16.6	16.6
China	6.9	9.7	15.3	16.4	17.4	11.0	12.6	15.0	17.9	17.6	20.9	20.3	19.7	19.5	19.4
High Income	77.9	74.1	67.3	66.0	64.7	71.4	68.8	65.1	62.6	61.2	17.2	16.8	16.5	16.4	16.3
World	100.0	100.0	100.0	100.0	100.0	100.0	100.0	100.0	100.0	100.0	100.0	100.0	100.0	100.0	100.0
Africa	1.4	1.4	1.5	1.5	1.5	1.4	1.4	1.4	1.6	1.6	12.8	13.5	14.3	14.5	14.7
Asia & Pacific	31.7	35.0	40.9	41.4	42.9	35.4	36.1	38.0	41.6	42.4	60.3	60.3	60.1	60.0	60.0
Europe	34.8	32.5	29.0	28.9	27.9	32.5	33.6	33.2	28.8	27.9	13.1	12.5	12.0	11.9	11.7
Latin America	6.7	6.3	6.2	6.2	5.8	6.6	6.6	7.1	7.3	7.9	8.6	8.6	8.6	8.6	8.6
North America	25.4	24.8	22.4	22.0	22.0	24.1	22.2	20.2	20.8	20.2	5.2	5.1	5.0	5.0	5.0
World	100.0	100.0	100.0	100.0	100.0	100.0	100.0	100.0	100.0	100.0	100.0	100.0	100.0	100.0	100.0

a/ Provisional.
b/ Estimate.

Table 1.3

ANNUAL GROWTH OF MVA, 2000-2011 AND PER-CAPITA MVA, 2011 a/

Country group or economy	Total MVA						Per-capita MVA						
	Growth rate (percentage)		Index (2005 = 100)				Growth rate (percentage)		Index (2005 = 100)				Value (US dollars)
	2000-2005	2005-2011	2008	2009	2010 b/	2011 c/	2000-2005	2005-2011	2008	2009	2010 b/	2011 c/	2011 c/
Industrialized Economies	2.3	-0.5	105	92	101	102	1.7	-1.1	103	90	98	99	4754
EU	0.9	-1.4	105	90	97	98	0.4	-1.8	103	88	94	96	4729
Austria	1.4	1.3	122	105	112	116	0.8	1.0	120	103	109	114	7360
Belgium	0.4	-0.6	103	95	99	100	0.0	-1.2	101	93	96	97	5360
Czech Republic	5.5	4.2	135	119	131	136	5.5	3.7	133	116	128	132	3812
Denmark	-0.9	-0.6	112	98	101	100	-1.2	-1.1	110	96	98	97	5528
Estonia	7.8	-1.9	107	79	96	105	8.2	-1.8	108	80	97	105	1592
Finland	3.9	-0.3	124	100	105	110	3.6	-0.8	123	98	103	107	8097
France	1.2	-1.0	99	89	96	98	0.5	-1.6	98	86	94	94	3918
Germany	1.1	-1.3	107	87	98	102	1.0	-1.2	107	88	98	103	7106
Hungary	5.0	0.7	114	97	108	112	5.2	0.9	114	98	109	113	2357
Ireland	4.1	3.9	107	111	123	128	2.2	2.5	102	105	115	118	...
Italy	-0.9	-3.4	101	84	88	87	-1.5	-3.9	98	82	85	84	4223
Lithuania	10.4	0.8	116	99	107	115	10.9	1.3	118	101	110	118	1694
Luxembourg	1.4	-6.5	93	69	74	72	0.5	-8.4	87	63	67	64	4333
Malta	-4.9	-1.9	110	91	95	92	-5.5	-2.2	109	89	93	90	1817
Netherlands	0.8	0.2	107	98	105	105	0.2	-0.2	106	96	103	102	5094
Portugal	-0.1	-1.8	102	92	95	91	-0.5	-2.0	101	91	94	90	2062
Slovakia	12.6	2.0	148	116	119	125	12.5	1.8	147	115	118	123	2336
Slovenia	4.8	-0.6	117	97	104	103	4.7	-0.8	116	96	103	101	3644
Spain	0.9	-3.1	100	86	89	86	-0.6	-4.2	96	82	83	81	2975
Sweden	5.5	-0.6	105	86	99	108	5.1	-1.3	102	83	96	104	7419
United Kingdom	-0.3	-2.3	99	89	92	90	-0.7	-2.9	97	86	89	87	3882
Other Europe	4.2	0.6	113	100	106	110	4.6	0.6	113	100	107	110	1527
Iceland	1.1	2.0	125	122	109	112	0.0	0.5	119	115	101	102	4884
Liechtenstein	0.2	1.9	122	110	116	119	-0.9	1.3	119	107	113	115	...
Norway	2.5	0.6	109	103	105	105	2.0	-0.5	106	98	99	99	5633
Russian Federation	6.5	0.0	112	96	103	108	6.9	0.1	113	96	104	109	909
Switzerland	1.5	1.6	115	105	112	115	0.8	1.0	113	102	109	111	10110
East Asia	3.2	0.2	109	92	107	106	2.8	-0.3	107	91	105	103	5995
China, Hong Kong SAR	-5.2	0.8	98	90	105	97	-5.2	0.0	96	88	101	93	575
China, Macao SAR	-5.3	-7.1	60	43	82	75	-7.3	-9.3	56	39	72	65	506
China, Taiwan Province	5.9	1.8	100	95	114	117	5.4	1.5	99	93	112	115	4885
Japan	2.2	-1.6	107	86	99	95	2.1	-1.6	107	86	99	95	7374
Malaysia	5.5	1.9	111	101	112	118	3.2	0.2	105	94	103	107	1673

a/ At constant 2005 prices.
b/ Provisional.
c/ Estimate.

Table 1.3
(continued)

ANNUAL GROWTH OF MVA, 2000-2011 AND PER-CAPITA MVA, 2011 [a]

Country group or economy	Total MVA						Per-capita MVA						
	Growth rate (percentage)		Index (2005 = 100)				Growth rate (percentage)		Index (2005 = 100)				Value (US dollars)
	2000-2005	2005-2011	2008	2009	2010 [b]	2011 [c]	2000-2005	2005-2011	2008	2009	2010 [b]	2011 [c]	2011 [c]
Republic of Korea	6.9	5.3	119	117	134	140	6.4	4.8	117	115	131	136	6046
Singapore	5.2	5.6	114	109	141	147	3.5	2.1	102	94	118	121	8966
West Asia	6.7	4.5	116	117	124	133	2.0	-5.3	81	74	73	75	2957
Bahrain	9.2	5.7	132	130	140	145	6.8	-4.7	91	80	80	80	1884
Kuwait	12.7	0.9	89	97	103	112	9.3	-2.8	79	83	86	90	2323
Qatar	8.9	11.7	125	142	164	181	2.3	-3.0	74	73	76	80	4122
United Arab Emirates	4.6	3.6	121	116	119	127	-1.1	-7.5	79	68	65	66	3087
North America	3.1	-0.3	103	93	101	102	2.1	-1.2	100	90	96	97	5530
Bermuda	-6.2	-3.8	98	84	88	...	-6.6	-4.1	96	83	87	...	...
Canada	-0.1	-3.7	91	79	83	84	-1.1	-4.7	88	76	79	79	3867
Greenland	-5.6	1.2	118	114	115	115	-6.0	1.2	118	114	115	115	3133
United States of America	3.4	-0.1	104	95	103	104	2.4	-0.9	101	91	98	99	5714
Others	1.1	0.8	101	100	106	106	-0.2	-0.7	96	94	98	97	4015
Aruba	0.2	-2.5	97	98	91	88	-2.1	-3.6	92	93	86	82	684
Australia	1.2	1.3	100	101	110	109	0.0	-0.4	94	94	100	99	3685
French Polynesia	-1.1	1.6	103	104	107	107	-2.5	0.4	99	99	101	100	1430
Israel	0.4	4.2	124	116	126	132	-1.5	1.8	115	105	113	115	3203
New Caledonia	8.6	0.4	98	81	121	132	6.8	-1.2	93	76	111	119	1851
New Zealand	3.7	-0.7	94	90	97	96	2.3	-1.8	91	86	91	90	3486
Puerto Rico	0.0	-1.6	93	93	92	92	0.1	-1.5	94	94	93	92	8701
Emerging Industrial Economies	4.1	3.6	117	112	122	128	2.7	2.4	112	107	115	119	524
Argentina	3.7	5.7	123	122	134	145	2.8	4.8	119	118	128	137	1396
Belarus	11.1	8.1	137	137	151	163	11.7	8.6	139	139	155	168	1468
Brazil	3.2	1.6	110	100	110	112	1.9	0.7	107	96	105	106	779
Brunei Darussalam	1.8	-1.6	100	91	92	94	-0.3	-3.4	95	84	84	84	2708
Bulgaria	5.4	3.7	127	122	128	126	6.1	4.4	130	125	133	131	675
Chile	3.8	0.1	109	102	101	105	2.6	-0.9	105	98	96	99	1069
Colombia	4.5	2.6	111	105	117	125	2.8	1.1	106	99	109	114	545
Costa Rica	3.9	1.6	114	110	113	117	2.0	0.0	109	103	105	107	972
Croatia	3.7	-2.9	114	92	90	89	4.0	-2.7	115	92	91	90	1347
Cyprus	0.8	-1.4	100	94	93	91	-1.0	-2.6	96	89	87	84	1096
Greece	2.8	-1.5	99	104	91	87	2.4	-1.8	98	102	89	86	1618
India	6.6	8.5	132	144	155	166	5.0	6.9	126	136	144	153	158

[a] At constant 2005 prices.
[b] Provisional.
[c] Estimate.

Table 1.3
(continued)

ANNUAL GROWTH OF MVA, 2000-2011 AND PER-CAPITA MVA, 2011 [a]

Country group or economy	Total MVA						Per-capita MVA							
	Growth rate (percentage)		Index (2005 = 100)				Growth rate (percentage)		Index (2005 = 100)				Value (US dollars)
	2000-2005	2005-2011	2008	2009	2010 [b]	2011 [c]	2000-2005	2005-2011	2008	2009	2010 [b]	2011 [c]	2011 [c]
Indonesia	5.2	4.1	113	116	121	130	3.8	3.0	110	111	115	122	420
Kazakhstan	9.0	3.9	113	109	124	133	8.7	2.8	109	105	118	125	565
Latvia	7.4	-2.3	100	81	93	97	8.1	-1.8	101	82	95	99	771
Mauritius	-0.6	2.6	110	112	114	118	-1.6	2.0	107	109	111	113	982
Mexico	0.3	0.7	107	97	106	110	-0.9	-0.6	103	92	100	102	1482
Oman	10.9	7.0	137	131	143	155	9.3	4.1	126	118	125	132	1362
Poland	6.2	9.0	143	144	161	174	6.3	8.9	142	144	160	173	2251
Romania	6.2	3.1	117	115	121	123	6.6	3.4	118	116	123	125	1206
Saudi Arabia	5.8	4.7	119	121	126	134	1.9	2.0	109	108	110	114	1405
Serbia	-0.8	-1.4	112	95	98	97	-0.3	-1.4	112	95	98	97	359
South Africa	2.7	0.9	115	103	108	111	1.3	0.0	111	98	103	105	897
Suriname	15.7	0.8	109	96	102	106	14.1	-0.2	105	92	97	100	598
Thailand	7.2	3.6	117	110	125	126	6.0	2.9	114	106	121	121	1108
The f. Yugosl. Rep of Macedonia	2.5	-1.8	112	96	94	96	2.2	-2.1	112	96	93	94	410
Tunisia	2.1	4.0	115	111	124	128	1.1	2.9	111	106	117	120	611
Turkey	5.4	3.6	114	106	120	133	4.0	2.2	110	101	113	123	1503
Ukraine	12.0	0.3	117	93	106	116	13.0	1.0	120	95	110	120	380
Uruguay	2.5	3.9	123	118	122	127	2.4	3.5	122	117	121	124	966
Venezuela (Bolivarian Republic of)	0.4	0.0	112	105	103	105	-1.4	-1.6	107	98	94	95	784
China	10.7	11.7	144	162	177	195	10.1	11.2	142	159	172	189	1063
Other Developing Economies	5.0	3.9	117	117	123	127	3.1	2.1	112	109	113	115	196
Albania	15.3	6.9	140	141	151	157	14.7	6.4	138	139	148	153	542
Algeria	2.3	0.1	109	115	99	100	0.8	-1.4	104	108	92	91	159
Angola	8.3	10.0	160	168	172	184	4.7	6.8	146	150	149	155	101
Antigua and Barbuda	2.7	-3.9	109	103	88	84	1.1	-5.0	105	99	83	78	170
Armenia	9.8	1.7	106	104	110	115	9.9	1.5	105	103	109	114	247
Azerbaijan	10.7	1.7	129	112	120	113	9.5	0.4	124	106	112	104	104
Bahamas	4.2	-2.8	90	85	91	92	2.8	-4.1	86	80	85	84	856
Barbados	-4.3	-2.8	96	84	89	87	-4.5	-3.0	96	84	88	86	566
Belize	2.9	6.3	142	159	151	152	0.6	4.2	134	146	136	135	418
Bolivia (Plurinational State of)	3.1	4.7	119	125	128	134	1.1	3.0	113	117	118	121	147
Bosnia and Herzegovina	6.9	2.5	132	123	116	121	6.4	2.6	132	124	117	122	320
Botswana	3.3	4.2	124	118	126	130	2.0	2.8	119	112	117	120	230
Cameroon	2.6	1.7	103	102	107	111	0.3	-0.5	97	94	96	97	158
Cape Verde	-2.6	5.0	117	118	125	129	-4.1	4.0	114	114	119	122	150
Congo	12.8	6.6	126	133	141	147	10.1	3.8	116	119	123	125	86

a/ At constant 2005 prices.
b/ Provisional.
c/ Estimate.

Table 1.3
(continued)

ANNUAL GROWTH OF MVA, 2000-2011 AND PER-CAPITA MVA, 2011 [a]

Country group or economy	Total MVA						Per-capita MVA						
	Growth rate (percentage)		Index (2005 = 100)				Growth rate (percentage)		Index (2005 = 100)				Value (US dollars)
	2000-2005	2005-2011	2008	2009	2010 [b]	2011 [c]	2000-2005	2005-2011	2008	2009	2010 [b]	2011 [c]	2011 [c]
Côte d'Ivoire	-3.3	0.8	95	99	104	97	-4.9	-1.1	90	92	95	87	152
Cuba	-5.0	5.0	129	128	130	132	-5.3	5.0	128	128	130	132	387
Dominica	-0.1	-4.3	89	84	83	83	0.1	-4.0	90	86	84	84	177
Dominican Republic	2.5	2.8	108	107	115	119	1.0	1.4	104	101	107	110	851
Ecuador	4.5	4.9	121	120	128	137	2.7	3.4	116	113	118	125	307
Egypt	3.2	5.9	123	128	135	139	1.3	4.0	117	119	124	125	241
El Salvador	2.3	1.1	107	104	106	108	1.9	0.6	106	102	104	105	633
Equatorial Guinea	...	...	...	...	...	...	...	...	...	...	...	...	48
Fiji	2.0	0.9	99	96	107	110	1.7	-0.1	96	93	102	104	462
Gabon	4.2	2.0	106	102	107	115	2.0	0.1	101	95	97	103	267
Georgia	11.1	5.8	136	127	143	157	12.4	6.4	138	130	148	163	282
Ghana	4.6	2.9	107	105	113	122	2.1	0.4	99	96	101	106	45
Grenada	-2.8	0.4	94	89	103	104	-3.0	0.1	93	88	102	102	199
Guatemala	2.5	2.0	109	108	112	114	0.0	-0.5	101	98	99	99	395
Guyana	-10.8	1.5	103	108	108	112	-11.1	1.3	102	107	107	111	135
Honduras	5.9	1.5	114	104	109	113	3.8	-0.5	107	96	98	100	271
Iran (Islamic Republic of)	10.5	2.4	112	114	117	121	9.1	1.2	108	109	111	112	326
Iraq	-14.3	8.0	122	138	147	161	-16.6	4.9	112	123	127	135	25
Jamaica	-1.0	-1.7	97	92	92	91	-1.8	-2.1	96	90	90	89	284
Jordan	11.1	5.1	128	130	133	139	8.9	2.1	117	115	115	117	449
Kenya	3.3	4.0	117	118	124	128	0.6	1.3	108	107	109	110	61
Kyrgyzstan	0.7	3.8	111	100	111	116	0.4	2.6	107	96	104	108	68
Lebanon	4.3	-1.2	94	90	92	93	2.6	-2.0	91	87	89	89	510
Libya	6.3	-3.8	111	115	118	64	4.3	-5.5	104	106	107	57	238
Maldives	8.6	-2.0	115	97	93	97	7.0	-3.3	110	92	86	89	189
Marshall Islands	0.7	1.3	105	104	109	110	0.7	0.3	103	102	105	104	114
Mongolia	9.7	7.1	147	134	142	167	8.6	5.5	140	126	131	152	86
Montenegro	-0.3	-5.3	87	79	77	77	-0.1	-5.5	87	79	76	76	225
Morocco	3.3	2.5	110	111	114	117	2.2	1.5	107	106	108	110	316
Namibia	6.4	4.0	114	121	121	126	4.4	2.1	108	112	110	113	490
Nicaragua	4.9	3.6	114	113	120	127	3.5	2.2	110	107	113	118	174
Nigeria	8.8	8.5	131	141	152	163	6.2	5.8	121	127	134	140	32
Pakistan	9.5	4.0	123	119	125	131	7.5	2.2	117	111	115	117	142
Palau	...	1.4	87	101	100	107	...	0.9	87	101	100	102	35
Palestine	5.3	3.0	91	91	109	112	3.1	0.4	85	83	96	96	162
Panama	-1.4	3.0	114	114	115	122	-3.1	1.3	108	106	105	111	367
Papua New Guinea	1.8	4.2	115	119	122	129	-0.8	1.8	107	108	109	112	56

a/ At constant 2005 prices.
b/ Provisional.
c/ Estimate.

Table 1.3
(continued)

ANNUAL GROWTH OF MVA, 2000-2011 AND PER-CAPITA MVA, 2011 a/

Country group or economy	Total MVA						Per-capita MVA						
	Growth rate (percentage)		Index (2005 = 100)				Growth rate (percentage)		Index (2005 = 100)				Value (US dollars)
	2000-2005	2005-2011	2008	2009	2010 b/	2011 c/	2000-2005	2005-2011	2008	2009	2010 b/	2011 c/	2011 c/
Paraguay	0.9	1.6	104	102	109	111	-1.1	-0.2	98	95	99	100	175
Peru	5.0	6.2	130	121	137	148	3.7	5.0	126	116	130	139	596
Philippines	3.9	3.2	112	107	119	123	1.9	1.5	107	100	109	111	322
Republic of Moldova	8.3	-3.4	90	75	82	85	10.2	-2.5	94	78	86	90	95
Saint Kitts and Nevis	1.2	-5.2	110	90	76	72	-0.1	-6.4	105	85	72	66	474
Saint Lucia	2.9	5.6	115	139	133	137	1.8	4.5	111	133	126	128	327
Saint Vincent and the Grenadines	0.5	-1.4	98	97	94	93	0.3	-1.4	98	97	94	93	243
Seychelles	-5.2	4.7	106	113	120	128	-6.3	4.0	104	110	116	124	1702
Sri Lanka	2.9	5.8	118	122	131	143	1.7	4.8	114	117	124	135	324
Swaziland	1.4	1.6	106	102	110	110	0.7	0.1	102	97	103	101	727
Syrian Arab Republic	...	8.6	133	145	148	...	...	6.5	125	133	134	...	
Tajikistan	10.6	6.2	121	129	136	144	9.7	4.8	117	122	128	133	100
Tonga	1.9	0.8	97	103	102	102	1.2	0.2	95	100	99	98	200
Trinidad and Tobago	9.2	4.6	136	133	133	135	8.8	4.2	134	131	131	132	883
Uzbekistan	1.8	3.9	109	114	120	125	0.9	2.7	106	109	114	117	52
Viet Nam	11.5	8.8	140	144	156	170	10.3	7.6	135	138	147	159	209
Zimbabwe	-8.9	-2.7	76	82	84	88	-9.0	-2.9	77	83	84	87	60
Least Developed Countries	6.7	6.9	124	131	141	150	4.2	4.6	116	120	127	132	52
Afghanistan	13.7	6.8	115	127	144	152	9.4	4.1	107	115	127	130	49
Bangladesh	6.7	7.8	130	139	148	160	5.0	6.7	126	133	140	149	101
Benin	2.7	2.2	102	105	109	111	-0.5	-0.7	93	93	94	93	39
Bhutan	5.8	10.3	151	162	170	179	2.8	8.3	142	149	155	160	142
Burkina Faso	12.4	4.1	109	115	121	126	9.3	1.1	99	102	104	105	57
Burundi	2.0	0.0	102	103	101	105	-0.6	-2.8	93	91	88	89	16
Cambodia	14.0	6.3	132	111	144	162	12.4	5.1	127	106	136	151	127
Central African Republic	-1.3	-3.2	86	87	88	91	-2.9	-5.0	82	81	80	81	19
Chad	6.7	0.9	100	100	104	105	3.1	-1.8	92	89	91	89	25
Comoros	1.7	2.8	105	110	112	114	-1.0	0.1	97	98	98	97	26
Democratic Rep of the Congo	4.8	5.5	121	117	132	144	1.7	2.6	111	105	115	122	10
Djibouti	3.2	5.1	115	123	127	132	1.2	3.1	108	114	115	118	24
Eritrea	-4.8	-2.3	77	80	80	86	-8.6	-5.3	70	70	69	72	11
Ethiopia	4.3	9.3	128	144	158	169	1.7	6.9	120	132	142	149	11
Gambia	6.1	-1.2	99	96	96	98	3.0	-3.9	91	86	84	83	23
Guinea	1.9	4.1	119	121	122	128	0.3	2.0	113	112	111	113	14
Guinea-Bissau	12.1	1.2	98	100	104	108	9.9	-0.8	93	92	94	95	29
Haiti	0.1	-1.0	104	107	91	97	-1.4	-2.3	99	102	85	89	40
Kiribati	2.6	3.7	129	123	125	127	0.8	2.1	122	115	115	116	59

a/ At constant 2005 prices.
b/ Provisional.
c/ Estimate.

Table 1.3
(continued)

ANNUAL GROWTH OF MVA, 2000-2011 AND PER-CAPITA MVA, 2011 a/

Country group or economy	Total MVA						Per-capita MVA						Value (US dollars)
	Growth rate (percentage)		Index (2005 = 100)				Growth rate (percentage)		Index (2005 = 100)				
	2000-2005	2005-2011	2008	2009	2010 b/	2011 c/	2000-2005	2005-2011	2008	2009	2010 b/	2011 c/	2011 c/
Lao People's Dem Rep	11.0	8.7	141	149	155	169	9.3	7.1	135	140	143	155	69
Lesotho	12.7	2.4	113	105	114	123	11.6	1.4	110	101	108	116	137
Liberia	5.7	7.2	152	151	159	164	3.5	2.5	132	125	126	127	13
Madagascar	2.6	3.9	139	125	122	124	-0.5	0.9	127	111	105	104	37
Malawi	-4.9	9.7	158	165	178	183	-7.4	6.4	145	147	153	152	27
Mali	5.7	-1.4	90	91	93	97	2.5	-4.4	82	81	80	80	10
Mauritania	-1.2	-4.7	68	67	72	73	-3.9	-7.1	63	60	63	63	41
Mozambique	14.3	3.2	107	110	113	124	11.3	0.8	100	100	101	108	48
Myanmar	...	...	...	...	...	...	...	...	...	...	...	...	84
Nepal	0.1	1.1	104	103	106	109	-2.1	-0.8	98	95	96	97	22
Niger	2.9	2.7	107	111	115	116	-0.6	-0.9	96	96	96	94	15
Rwanda	9.6	5.8	121	124	136	146	7.0	2.8	111	111	118	123	24
Samoa	4.3	-5.8	80	64	74	73	3.9	-6.1	80	64	72	71	256
Sao Tome and Principe	5.5	3.9	113	111	123	128	3.8	2.3	108	104	114	116	55
Senegal	3.2	2.3	99	104	110	113	0.4	-0.4	92	94	96	96	102
Sierra Leone	2.4	0.4	116	108	110	108	-2.0	-2.0	107	97	96	93	6
Solomon Islands	-6.4	3.4	109	107	119	125	-9.0	0.7	100	96	104	107	52
Somalia	5.6	2.8	106	109	112	118	3.0	0.5	100	99	100	103	6
Sudan	...	...	116	127	134	135	...	...	...	...	...	...	...
Timor-Leste	3.8	6.1	95	100	108	120	-0.3	3.8	89	92	97	105	12
Togo	1.0	2.8	122	113	117	124	-1.4	0.6	114	104	105	109	36
Tuvalu	0.6	3.5	140	122	122	120	-1.8	3.5	140	122	122	120	22
Uganda	6.0	7.4	122	133	141	154	2.6	4.0	110	117	120	127	29
United Republic of Tanzania	8.2	8.5	130	140	151	163	5.4	5.4	119	125	131	137	40
Vanuatu	-1.7	3.6	118	89	127	127	-4.3	1.0	109	81	111	109	80
Yemen	5.0	4.2	116	118	124	129	1.8	1.1	106	105	106	107	62
Zambia	5.3	5.6	114	124	131	139	2.9	2.8	105	112	115	118	79
Africa	3.0	2.8	115	112	117	119	0.6	0.4	107	102	104	104	127
Central Africa	3.5	2.0	105	104	109	113	0.9	-0.3	98	95	97	98	102
Eastern Africa	3.9	5.3	118	124	131	138	1.1	2.7	109	112	115	118	25
North Africa	3.1	3.6	116	119	122	122	1.5	2.0	110	112	113	111	276
Southern Africa	2.8	1.7	116	106	112	116	0.4	-0.6	108	97	100	101	208
Western Africa	2.9	4.0	109	114	121	124	0.3	1.4	101	103	107	107	42
Asia & Pacific	6.6	5.6	122	125	134	142	4.9	4.1	116	118	125	130	229
China	10.7	11.7	144	162	177	195	10.1	11.2	142	159	172	189	1063
Central Asia	7.6	4.1	113	111	124	133	6.9	2.9	109	106	117	124	201
South Asia	6.8	7.8	130	140	150	160	5.1	6.2	124	132	139	147	149

a/ At constant 2005 prices.
b/ Provisional.
c/ Estimate.

Table 1.3
(continued)

ANNUAL GROWTH OF MVA, 2000-2011 AND PER-CAPITA MVA, 2011 [a]

Country group or economy	Total MVA						Per-capita MVA						
	Growth rate (percentage)		Index (2005 = 100)				Growth rate (percentage)		Index (2005 = 100)				Value (US dollars) [c]
	2000-2005	2005-2011	2008	2009	2010 [b]	2011 [c]	2000-2005	2005-2011	2008	2009	2010 [b]	2011 [c]	2011 [c]
South East Asia	6.1	4.3	117	115	125	131	4.7	3.2	113	110	119	123	417
West Asia	7.5	3.7	117	118	123	127	5.2	1.6	110	109	111	112	367
Other Asia & Pacific	1.7	1.9	104	103	111	115	-0.7	-0.2	98	94	99	101	91
Europe	5.8	4.2	121	115	125	134	5.8	4.0	120	114	124	132	1220
Latin America	2.1	1.8	111	103	112	116	0.7	0.7	107	98	105	108	864
Caribbean	0.2	2.9	114	112	117	120	-0.8	2.1	111	109	112	114	433
Central America	0.6	0.8	108	98	107	111	-0.8	-0.6	103	92	99	102	1196
South America	3.2	2.5	113	106	115	119	1.9	1.4	109	101	109	112	771
World	3.3	1.7	111	102	112	115	2.0	0.5	107	98	106	108	1264
Low Income	6.1	6.9	124	130	141	151	3.7	4.6	117	120	127	133	48
Lower Middle Income	5.9	5.7	122	126	134	142	4.2	4.1	116	118	124	130	190
Upper Middle Income(excl.China)	3.9	2.0	113	104	113	118	2.9	1.0	110	100	108	111	892
China	10.7	11.7	144	162	177	195	10.1	11.2	142	159	172	189	1063
High Income	2.3	-0.4	106	93	102	103	1.5	-1.1	103	90	98	98	5092
African LDCs	5.2	4.9	115	120	127	133	2.3	2.1	106	108	111	113	33
ASEAN	5.9	4.1	115	112	125	131	4.5	2.9	111	107	118	122	551
CACM	3.3	1.7	111	107	111	114	1.5	-0.1	105	100	101	103	444
CARICOM	2.6	0.8	110	107	106	107	1.3	-0.3	107	103	101	101	207
CEMAC	3.4	2.0	105	104	109	113	0.9	-0.3	98	95	97	98	102
CIS	7.3	0.9	114	99	108	114	7.6	0.8	114	99	108	113	642
ECOWAS	3.0	4.2	110	115	122	125	0.4	1.5	102	104	107	107	42
EU	1.1	-1.0	106	92	98	100	0.7	-1.4	104	90	97	98	4233
GCC	6.4	4.7	118	119	125	134	2.5	0.0	101	98	99	103	1884
LAIA	2.0	1.8	111	103	112	116	0.7	0.7	107	98	106	109	920
MERCOSUR	3.2	2.5	113	106	115	119	1.9	1.4	109	101	109	112	772
OECD	2.2	-0.4	106	93	102	103	1.4	-1.1	103	90	98	99	4640
SAARC	6.8	7.8	130	140	150	160	5.1	6.2	124	132	139	147	149
WAEMU	0.4	1.7	99	103	108	106	-2.3	-1.1	91	92	94	90	64

a/ At constant 2005 prices.
b/ Provisional.
c/ Estimate.

Table 1.4

SHARE OF MVA IN GDP, SELECTED YEARS
(Percentage)

Country group or economy	At constant 2005 prices						At current prices					
	2000	2005	2008	2009	2010 a/	2011 b/	2005	2006	2007	2008	2009	2010 a/
Industrialized Economies	15.9	15.8	15.7	14.3	15.2	15.1	15.8	15.5	15.3	14.8	13.8	14.4
EU	16.1	15.5	15.2	13.7	14.4	14.5	15.5	15.4	15.3	14.8	13.3	14.0
Austria	17.5	17.5	19.6	17.5	18.2	18.4	17.5	17.9	18.3	18.5	16.8	17.3
Belgium	16.1	15.3	14.8	14.0	14.3	14.2	15.3	14.8	14.5	13.9	12.8	13.0
Czech Republic	21.0	22.6	26.2	24.2	26.0	26.6	22.6	22.8	23.0	21.3	20.5	21.4
Denmark	13.2	12.0	12.9	12.0	12.1	11.8	12.0	12.0	11.9	12.2	11.3	10.6
Estonia	13.9	14.6	13.8	11.9	14.1	14.3	14.6	14.5	14.0	13.7	12.3	14.3
Finland	19.1	20.3	22.7	19.8	20.2	20.5	20.3	20.9	21.1	19.5	15.6	16.4
France	12.1	11.9	11.3	10.3	11.1	11.0	11.9	11.3	11.2	10.7	9.6	10.5
Germany	20.0	20.6	20.3	17.6	18.9	19.2	20.6	21.2	21.3	20.4	17.2	18.7
Hungary	18.6	19.0	20.6	18.9	20.7	21.1	19.0	19.7	19.3	18.6	18.4	19.6
Ireland	20.9	20.0	19.9	22.2	24.8	25.4	20.0	18.9	18.9	18.8	20.7	23.0
Italy	18.0	16.6	16.3	14.5	14.9	14.7	16.6	16.6	17.0	16.4	14.7	15.0
Lithuania	16.7	18.8	18.0	17.9	19.1	19.3	18.8	18.1	16.7	16.2	14.7	16.4
Luxembourg	9.3	8.2	6.7	5.3	5.5	5.3	8.2	7.4	8.2	7.0	4.9	5.5
Malta	19.5	13.9	13.8	11.6	11.8	11.2	13.9	13.6	13.7	13.8	11.6	11.8
Netherlands	13.0	12.7	12.4	11.8	12.4	12.3	12.7	12.3	12.5	12.2	11.2	11.9
Portugal	13.2	12.6	12.4	11.5	11.7	11.4	12.6	12.3	12.1	11.9	11.3	11.3
Slovakia	15.0	21.4	24.9	20.6	20.2	20.6	21.4	21.8	21.5	21.0	17.8	18.8
Slovenia	19.1	20.2	20.1	18.1	19.2	18.9	20.2	20.0	19.9	18.7	16.5	16.8
Spain	15.8	14.2	13.0	11.7	12.0	11.7	14.2	13.8	13.4	13.3	11.8	12.1
Sweden	15.7	17.4	17.1	14.8	16.2	17.0	17.4	17.3	17.2	15.5	13.5	14.3
United Kingdom	13.9	11.8	11.2	10.4	10.6	10.3	11.8	11.4	11.0	10.5	10.0	10.2
Other Europe	14.6	14.8	14.4	13.4	13.9	13.9	14.8	14.8	14.7	14.6	13.1	14.0
Iceland	10.2	8.7	9.7	10.1	9.4	9.4	8.7	9.5	8.8	11.3	13.3	11.2
Liechtenstein	19.6	19.9	21.4	19.4	20.1	20.1	19.9	20.5	20.8	21.4	19.4	20.1
Norway	8.6	8.7	9.0	8.6	8.8	8.7	8.7	8.9	9.0	8.2	8.8	8.3
Russian Federation	15.7	15.7	14.2	13.2	13.7	13.7	15.7	15.3	15.1	14.9	12.7	14.1
Switzerland	17.7	18.2	19.0	17.7	18.4	18.6	18.2	18.7	18.9	19.0	17.6	18.1
East Asia	21.2	21.9	22.5	20.0	22.1	21.6	21.9	21.7	21.6	20.8	18.9	20.5
China, Hong Kong SAR	3.8	2.4	2.0	1.9	2.0	1.8	2.4	2.3	2.0	1.8	1.7	1.7
China, Macao SAR	7.7	3.2	1.4	1.0	1.5	1.1	3.2	2.9	2.1	1.4	1.0	0.6
China, Taiwan Province	24.6	26.6	24.8	23.6	26.1	25.8	26.6	26.5	26.4	24.8	23.6	……
Japan	21.0	21.5	22.3	19.1	21.2	20.5	21.5	21.2	21.2	20.4	18.0	19.9
Malaysia	29.8	29.6	27.8	25.6	26.6	26.7	29.6	29.4	27.8	26.2	25.5	26.1

a/ Provisional.
b/ Estimate.

Table 1.4
(continued)

SHARE OF MVA IN GDP, SELECTED YEARS
(Percentage)

Country group or economy	At constant 2005 prices						At current prices					
	2000	2005	2008	2009	2010 a/	2011 b/	2005	2006	2007	2008	2009	2010 a/
Republic of Korea	22.4	24.7	26.0	25.5	27.5	27.7	24.7	24.3	24.5	25.0	25.0	27.5
Singapore	26.3	25.6	24.2	23.4	26.4	26.2	25.6	25.5	22.8	20.9	21.7	20.8
West Asia	9.8	9.7	9.1	9.2	9.3	9.3	9.7	8.7	8.5	8.3	9.1	9.3
Bahrain	10.7	12.8	13.7	13.1	13.5	13.7	12.8	14.6	16.1	17.2	15.5	18.0
Kuwait	6.5	7.3	5.6	6.5	6.7	6.7	7.3	5.5	5.5	4.4	5.1	5.3
Qatar	9.4	9.9	7.5	7.6	7.5	7.3	9.9	9.3	9.2	10.7	9.4	10.6
United Arab Emirates	11.1	10.6	10.9	10.7	10.8	11.0	10.6	9.7	9.0	8.6	10.1	9.7
North America	13.6	13.7	13.5	12.7	13.3	13.3	13.7	13.4	13.2	12.6	12.3	12.6
Bermuda	2.6	1.7	1.5	1.3	1.4	...	1.7	1.7	1.5	1.5	1.3	1.5
Canada	16.0	13.9	12.0	10.7	10.9	10.8	13.9	13.2	12.5	11.6	10.4	10.6
Greenland	12.2	9.1	9.7	9.9	9.9	9.7	9.1	10.2	9.9	9.7	9.9	9.9
United States of America	13.4	13.7	13.7	12.9	13.5	13.5	13.7	13.4	13.3	12.8	12.5	12.8
Others	14.8	13.3	12.3	12.0	12.5	12.3	13.3	12.8	12.5	12.0	12.2	12.2
Aruba	3.9	3.7	3.6	4.0	3.8	3.9	3.7	3.8	3.9	3.6	4.0	3.8
Australia	11.1	10.0	9.1	9.0	9.5	9.3	10.0	9.5	9.3	8.7	8.7	9.2
French Polynesia	7.9	6.7	6.6	6.5	6.6	6.5	6.7	6.3	6.7	6.6	6.5	6.6
Israel	15.3	13.7	14.7	13.6	14.2	14.1	13.7	14.0	14.4	13.9	13.3	13.9
New Caledonia	6.8	7.3	6.4	5.2	7.5	7.9	7.3	8.4	10.8	6.4	5.2	7.5
New Zealand	14.6	14.2	12.8	12.2	12.8	12.5	14.2	13.8	14.2	14.2	14.1	14.2
Puerto Rico	47.9	43.0	41.9	42.9	43.3	43.8	43.0	42.6	42.6	43.4	46.2	46.4
Emerging Industrial Economies	16.8	16.7	16.7	16.2	16.5	16.6	16.7	16.6	16.3	16.2	15.9	15.8
Argentina	20.6	21.4	20.9	20.6	20.7	20.6	21.4	20.6	19.5	19.5	19.6	18.8
Belarus	24.4	28.4	29.6	29.5	30.3	31.0	28.4	28.2	27.7	28.5	26.1	27.0
Brazil	15.4	15.5	14.7	13.5	13.8	13.6	15.5	14.1	13.3	14.2	14.4	13.9
Brunei Darussalam	12.8	12.3	12.1	11.1	11.0	10.9	12.3	10.6	10.4	13.7	14.0	12.1
Bulgaria	13.9	13.8	14.6	14.8	15.5	15.0	13.8	13.4	12.8	12.0	13.2	14.0
Chile	15.2	14.9	14.3	13.6	12.8	12.6	14.9	13.5	13.1	12.4	12.5	11.1
Colombia	13.6	14.0	13.2	12.2	13.1	13.2	14.0	14.4	14.5	13.5	13.0	13.9
Costa Rica	20.4	19.6	18.6	18.0	17.8	17.7	19.6	19.5	19.1	18.2	16.1	15.7
Croatia	15.5	14.8	15.0	12.8	12.8	12.6	14.8	14.3	14.5	14.5	13.7	15.5
Cyprus	9.0	7.9	7.0	6.7	6.5	6.4	7.9	7.1	6.5	6.6	6.5	6.3
Greece	9.1	8.8	8.0	8.7	7.9	8.1	8.8	8.6	8.3	9.0	9.4	9.6
India	14.3	14.1	14.9	15.1	14.8	14.9	14.1	14.8	14.7	14.5	14.0	13.6

a/ Provisional.
b/ Estimate.

Table 1.4
(continued)

SHARE OF MVA IN GDP, SELECTED YEARS
(Percentage)

Country group or economy	At constant 2005 prices						At current prices					
	2000	2005	2008	2009	2010 a/	2011 b/	2005	2006	2007	2008	2009	2010 a/
Indonesia	27.1	27.4	26.1	25.5	25.1	25.3	27.4	27.5	27.0	27.8	26.4	24.8
Kazakhstan	12.7	12.0	10.9	10.5	11.1	11.0	12.0	11.6	11.5	11.8	10.9	12.4
Latvia	11.5	11.1	9.4	9.3	10.7	10.6	11.1	10.4	10.1	9.7	9.0	10.9
Mauritius	20.9	17.4	16.4	16.3	15.9	15.7	17.4	17.6	17.0	17.2	16.8	16.0
Mexico	19.7	18.2	17.7	17.1	17.7	17.7	18.2	18.5	18.3	17.9	17.3	17.4
Oman	5.3	8.1	8.7	8.3	8.7	8.9	8.1	10.3	10.4	10.1	9.9	9.5
Poland	14.6	16.3	19.5	19.4	20.8	21.6	16.3	16.5	16.6	16.3	16.4	16.3
Romania	20.8	21.2	20.2	21.2	22.7	22.5	21.2	21.0	20.9	20.0	20.9	22.8
Saudi Arabia	8.5	9.4	10.2	10.3	10.3	10.2	9.4	9.3	9.5	8.3	10.4	9.7
Serbia	19.5	14.4	14.3	12.5	12.8	12.5	14.4	14.5	14.1	14.0	13.6	13.1
South Africa	17.1	16.5	16.4	14.9	15.2	15.2	16.5	15.5	15.1	15.0	13.7	13.2
Suriname	11.1	16.7	16.0	13.7	14.0	13.9	16.7	23.2	23.5	25.3	20.2	21.1
Thailand	32.5	34.7	35.8	34.4	36.4	36.7	34.7	35.0	35.6	34.8	34.2	35.6
The f. Yugosl. Rep of Macedonia	14.4	14.8	14.2	12.3	11.7	11.6	14.8	15.5	17.6	17.2	14.1	13.7
Tunisia	17.2	15.7	15.3	14.3	15.5	16.4	15.7	16.2	16.8	17.2	15.6	16.4
Turkey	17.3	17.3	17.5	17.1	17.8	18.1	17.3	17.2	16.8	16.2	15.0	15.5
Ukraine	14.7	17.3	17.1	15.9	17.4	18.1	17.3	20.1	20.3	17.4	15.5	15.4
Uruguay	13.2	14.9	15.3	14.4	13.7	13.4	14.9	14.5	13.7	14.9	13.1	12.0
Venezuela (Bolivarian Republic of)	16.3	15.1	13.5	13.0	12.9	12.7	15.1	13.9	13.3	13.9	13.4	13.4
China	31.6	32.5	33.3	34.2	33.8	34.2	32.5	32.9	32.9	32.7	32.3	29.6
Other Developing Economies	11.7	12.0	11.8	11.4	11.5	11.8	12.0	11.7	11.4	11.1	11.6	11.4
Albania	8.6	13.3	15.5	15.2	15.7	15.8	13.3	15.1	17.1	16.3	16.5	16.5
Algeria	6.3	5.6	5.7	5.8	4.9	4.8	5.6	5.2	4.9	4.4	5.3	4.6
Angola	3.8	3.5	3.4	3.5	3.5	3.6	3.5	4.8	5.2	4.8	6.1	6.1
Antigua and Barbuda	1.9	1.8	1.9	2.0	1.9	1.9	1.8	1.8	1.7	1.6	1.7	1.6
Armenia	14.7	13.5	10.4	11.9	12.4	12.4	13.5	10.8	9.4	8.8	8.7	9.5
Azerbaijan	7.4	6.5	4.5	3.6	3.6	3.4	6.5	5.8	3.8	4.7	5.5	5.3
Bahamas	4.2	4.2	3.7	3.7	4.0	3.9	4.2	4.4	4.0	3.7	3.6	3.3
Barbados	8.1	5.9	5.5	5.1	5.4	5.2	5.9	5.7	5.4	4.8	4.7	4.3
Belize	9.0	7.8	10.1	11.3	10.5	10.4	7.8	10.3	11.4	12.4	11.5	11.8
Bolivia (Plurinational State of)	11.6	11.6	11.9	12.0	11.9	11.8	11.6	11.3	11.4	11.2	11.6	11.3
Bosnia and Herzegovina	8.4	9.1	10.1	9.7	9.0	9.3	9.1	9.5	11.2	11.4	10.8	11.2
Botswana	3.8	3.5	3.8	3.8	3.8	3.7	3.5	3.2	3.6	3.4	4.0	3.8
Cameroon	18.2	17.3	16.2	15.7	16.0	15.8	17.3	16.4	16.1	16.2	18.8	17.7
Cape Verde	9.1	6.0	5.5	5.4	5.4	5.3	6.0	5.3	4.9	4.8	4.5	4.7
Congo	2.6	4.0	4.6	4.5	4.4	4.4	4.0	3.6	4.0	3.5	4.5	3.8

a/ Provisional.
b/ Estimate.

Table 1.4
(continued)

SHARE OF MVA IN GDP, SELECTED YEARS
(Percentage)

Country group or economy	At constant 2005 prices						At current prices					
	2000	2005	2008	2009	2010 a/	2011 b/	2005	2006	2007	2008	2009	2010 a/
Côte d'Ivoire	21.8	19.3	17.4	17.6	18.0	17.6	19.3	17.8	17.5	18.0	18.2	19.1
Cuba	12.3	7.8	8.0	7.8	7.8	7.7	7.8	7.7	8.3	9.1	8.9	8.7
Dominica	4.5	4.0	3.0	2.9	2.8	2.8	4.0	4.1	3.5	3.0	2.8	2.8
Dominican Republic	22.2	21.1	18.1	17.3	17.2	17.1	21.1	20.4	19.2	21.5	22.6	22.2
Ecuador	9.3	8.9	9.4	9.3	9.6	9.5	8.9	8.9	9.0	9.2	9.2	9.3
Egypt	16.1	15.9	16.0	15.9	16.0	16.2	15.9	15.6	15.0	15.0	15.2	15.1
El Salvador	21.3	21.3	20.9	21.0	21.1	21.2	21.3	20.4	20.0	19.8	19.0	18.8
Equatorial Guinea	0.2	0.2	0.3	0.3	0.3	0.3	0.2	0.2	0.3	0.3	0.4	0.3
Fiji	12.8	12.1	11.7	11.6	12.8	13.0	12.1	12.6	12.0	11.8	11.7	12.9
Gabon	3.5	4.1	4.0	3.9	3.8	3.9	4.1	4.1	4.1	3.5	4.1	3.5
Georgia	10.6	12.1	13.1	12.7	13.5	13.8	12.1	11.1	10.9	10.4	9.9	11.2
Ghana	8.9	8.7	7.5	7.1	7.1	6.7	8.7	9.7	8.6	7.5	6.8	6.4
Grenada	3.4	2.9	2.6	2.6	3.0	3.0	2.9	3.4	3.6	3.3	3.3	3.9
Guatemala	19.2	18.7	17.6	17.4	17.4	17.2	18.7	18.7	18.3	18.5	18.6	18.6
Guyana	11.2	6.9	6.2	6.3	6.1	6.0	6.9	6.9	6.5	7.4	6.7	6.0
Honduras	18.1	19.1	18.4	17.3	17.5	17.6	19.1	19.6	18.0	17.8	16.9	17.1
Iran (Islamic Republic of)	8.4	10.5	10.1	10.1	10.3	10.4	10.5	10.8	10.4	10.5	10.4	10.4
Iraq	2.2	1.6	1.7	1.8	1.9	1.9	1.6	1.3	1.1	0.8	2.2	1.7
Jamaica	9.0	7.6	7.3	7.0	7.1	6.9	7.6	7.4	7.4	7.8	7.8	8.4
Jordan	13.2	16.3	16.6	16.0	16.0	16.3	16.3	17.0	18.9	18.8	17.9	16.8
Kenya	10.8	10.5	10.7	10.5	10.4	10.3	10.5	10.3	10.4	10.8	9.9	10.0
Kyrgyzstan	15.9	12.9	11.7	10.3	11.5	11.4	12.9	11.0	9.9	13.2	14.2	15.4
Lebanon	10.7	10.7	8.5	7.5	7.2	7.1	10.7	9.7	8.8	7.8	7.5	7.3
Libya	5.3	5.3	5.1	5.3	5.2	7.0	5.3	5.0	5.1	4.9	7.4	5.8
Maldives	5.8	6.3	4.9	4.3	3.9	3.9	6.3	5.6	5.2	4.6	3.9	3.5
Marshall Islands	4.4	4.2	4.3	4.2	4.2	4.2	4.2	4.2	4.3	4.2	4.2	4.2
Mongolia	5.1	5.8	6.5	6.0	6.0	6.0	5.8	5.4	6.2	6.6	6.4	6.4
Montenegro	8.5	8.2	5.6	5.4	5.1	5.0	8.2	7.7	5.4	5.4	4.9	4.5
Morocco	15.7	14.6	13.8	13.2	13.1	12.9	14.6	14.1	13.3	12.6	14.2	13.8
Namibia	11.7	12.4	12.0	12.9	12.3	12.3	12.4	14.4	15.7	12.7	13.5	13.8
Nicaragua	14.9	16.4	16.9	16.9	17.3	17.5	16.4	16.4	16.7	16.4	17.1	17.4
Nigeria	2.5	2.8	3.1	3.1	3.1	3.1	2.8	2.6	2.5	2.3	2.4	2.2
Pakistan	13.9	17.5	18.9	17.6	17.8	18.0	17.5	18.0	18.1	19.0	16.3	16.0
Palau	1.8	0.5	0.4	0.5	0.5	0.5	0.5	0.5	0.5	0.5	0.6	0.7
Palestine	11.5	13.0	11.1	10.3	11.5	11.1	13.0	12.2	13.0	10.5	9.9	11.7
Panama	9.1	6.9	5.9	5.7	5.3	5.1	6.9	6.6	6.2	6.2	5.9	5.6
Papua New Guinea	6.0	6.2	6.1	6.0	5.7	5.5	6.2	5.8	5.8	5.6	5.9	5.3

a/ Provisional.
b/ Estimate.

Table 1.4
(continued)

SHARE OF MVA IN GDP, SELECTED YEARS
(Percentage)

Country group or economy	At constant 2005 prices						At current prices					
	2000	2005	2008	2009	2010 a/	2011 b/	2005	2006	2007	2008	2009	2010 a/
Paraguay	15.1	13.9	12.2	12.6	11.6	11.3	13.9	13.7	12.8	12.5	12.9	12.2
Peru	14.4	14.9	15.1	13.9	14.5	14.6	14.9	14.6	14.6	14.8	13.3	15.3
Philippines	24.8	24.1	23.1	21.8	22.5	22.4	24.1	23.6	22.7	22.8	21.3	21.4
Republic of Moldova	12.6	13.3	10.4	9.1	9.3	9.1	13.3	12.5	11.8	11.3	10.6	10.6
Saint Kitts and Nevis	7.4	6.9	7.2	6.2	5.5	5.2	6.9	6.4	6.0	6.0	5.3	4.7
Saint Lucia	4.5	4.8	4.9	7.1	6.5	6.6	4.8	4.6	4.6	4.0	3.6	3.3
Saint Vincent and the Grenadines	5.8	5.1	4.5	4.5	4.5	4.5	5.1	4.3	4.7	4.1	4.4	4.3
Seychelles	15.5	12.6	11.3	12.0	11.9	12.1	12.6	11.6	12.1	11.6	10.7	11.0
Sri Lanka	20.9	19.5	18.9	18.8	18.7	19.0	19.5	19.2	18.5	18.0	18.1	18.0
Swaziland	31.8	30.7	29.7	28.4	29.9	29.9	30.7	30.4	31.1	31.3	34.1	31.1
Syrian Arab Republic	0.6	2.5	2.9	3.0	3.0	...	2.5	5.1	5.0	4.1	4.5	4.5
Tajikistan	20.6	21.0	20.5	20.9	20.8	20.5	21.0	16.7	13.3	10.6	9.6	8.5
Tonga	8.3	7.9	7.5	8.0	7.9	7.9	7.9	7.3	7.6	7.2	6.9	6.5
Trinidad and Tobago	5.1	5.5	6.1	6.2	6.2	6.4	5.5	5.6	5.3	4.2	4.9	5.2
Uzbekistan	9.5	8.1	6.9	6.7	6.5	6.2	8.1	9.8	11.4	11.0	12.4	7.9
Viet Nam	17.1	20.6	23.1	22.6	22.9	23.6	20.6	21.2	21.4	20.3	20.1	19.7
Zimbabwe	15.3	15.1	15.1	15.3	14.4	13.8	15.1	16.0	16.1	16.3	14.2	11.8
Least Developed Countries	9.9	10.3	10.5	10.6	10.7	11.0	10.3	10.3	10.3	9.9	10.3	10.2
Afghanistan	17.5	15.2	13.7	12.6	13.1	13.1	15.2	16.2	17.8	15.3	11.3	11.4
Bangladesh	14.8	15.9	17.1	17.3	17.4	17.6	15.9	16.6	17.2	17.2	17.3	17.3
Benin	7.7	7.5	6.7	6.6	6.7	6.6	7.5	7.1	7.0	6.7	7.0	7.3
Bhutan	7.6	7.1	8.2	8.2	8.1	8.1	7.1	7.6	8.2	8.4	8.2	8.2
Burkina Faso	11.9	14.0	13.0	13.3	13.0	13.0	14.0	13.3	12.8	10.0	9.7	10.5
Burundi	11.9	11.9	10.4	10.2	9.7	9.6	11.9	12.0	11.8	10.4	10.2	9.7
Cambodia	14.6	17.8	18.0	15.2	18.6	19.5	17.8	18.6	17.3	15.3	14.4	14.7
Central African Republic	6.9	7.1	5.6	5.5	5.4	5.4	7.1	7.2	7.4	7.0	6.7	6.2
Chad	7.6	5.2	5.2	5.2	4.8	4.8	5.2	5.1	4.9	4.6	4.9	4.2
Comoros	4.5	4.4	4.4	4.6	4.6	4.6	4.4	4.2	4.2	4.2	4.3	4.3
Democratic Rep of the Congo	6.7	6.4	6.5	6.1	6.4	6.5	6.4	6.0	5.8	5.4	5.3	5.4
Djibouti	2.3	2.3	2.3	2.3	2.3	2.3	2.3	2.2	2.2	2.0	2.0	2.0
Eritrea	10.4	6.4	5.4	5.4	5.4	5.3	6.4	5.7	5.2	5.4	5.4	5.4
Ethiopia	4.7	4.4	4.1	4.3	4.3	4.2	4.4	4.2	4.7	4.4	3.8	4.9
Gambia	5.5	6.5	5.6	5.0	4.8	4.7	6.5	6.7	6.4	5.4	4.6	4.4
Guinea	5.4	3.8	4.1	4.2	4.2	4.2	3.8	3.1	3.8	4.1	4.8	4.4
Guinea-Bissau	4.7	7.2	6.5	6.4	6.4	6.3	7.2	6.9	6.6	6.9	6.8	6.8
Haiti	9.6	10.0	9.7	9.8	8.8	8.8	10.0	10.0	9.8	9.7	9.8	8.8
Kiribati	4.2	4.3	5.5	5.2	5.2	5.2	4.3	4.5	5.2	5.6	5.8	5.7

a/ Provisional.
b/ Estimate.

Table 1.4
(continued)

SHARE OF MVA IN GDP, SELECTED YEARS
(Percentage)

Country group or economy	At constant 2005 prices						At current prices					
	2000	2005	2008	2009	2010 a/	2011 b/	2005	2006	2007	2008	2009	2010 a/
Lao People's Dem Rep	7.5	9.4	10.5	10.3	9.9	10.0	9.4	7.9	8.1	8.4	8.1	7.1
Lesotho	11.9	17.8	17.5	15.9	16.2	16.8	17.8	19.5	17.4	17.4	14.5	11.4
Liberia	3.7	5.7	6.8	6.5	6.5	6.2	5.7	6.8	7.0	6.8	6.5	6.5
Madagascar	12.6	12.7	14.7	13.9	13.4	13.4	12.7	13.1	13.2	12.9	13.1	12.9
Malawi	12.2	8.4	10.7	10.3	10.4	10.2	8.4	9.7	9.6	9.6	9.5	9.5
Mali	3.3	2.9	2.3	2.2	2.2	2.2	2.9	2.8	2.7	2.1	2.0	2.0
Mauritania	11.7	9.2	5.1	5.0	5.1	5.0	9.2	7.0	5.6	3.5	3.7	3.4
Mozambique	10.8	14.0	12.4	11.9	11.5	11.7	14.0	14.6	14.1	12.9	12.3	11.8
Myanmar	9.4	12.8	16.0	17.3	18.8	19.0	12.8	14.0	14.9	16.8	18.2	19.6
Nepal	8.7	7.6	7.0	6.6	6.5	6.4	7.6	7.3	7.2	7.0	6.6	5.9
Niger	6.4	6.1	5.5	5.7	5.5	5.4	6.1	6.0	5.8	5.4	5.7	5.6
Rwanda	6.5	7.0	6.6	6.5	6.7	6.6	7.0	6.8	6.1	6.2	6.4	6.6
Samoa	15.6	15.7	12.1	9.8	11.1	10.7	15.7	13.3	13.7	11.4	8.7	10.0
Sao Tome and Principe	6.5	6.4	5.9	5.5	5.9	5.8	6.4	6.0	5.5	6.8	5.9	6.4
Senegal	14.2	13.2	11.8	12.1	12.2	12.3	13.2	12.6	12.8	11.9	11.8	12.0
Sierra Leone	4.5	2.7	2.6	2.4	2.3	2.1	2.7	2.6	2.4	2.2	2.0	1.9
Solomon Islands	8.3	5.6	4.8	4.7	4.9	4.7	5.6	4.8	4.0	4.0	4.3	3.9
Somalia	2.1	2.2	2.1	2.1	2.1	2.2	2.2	2.2	2.2	2.2	2.2	2.2
Sudan	7.3	6.5	5.8	6.0	6.1	6.4	6.5	6.0	5.8	5.5	6.4	5.3
Timor-Leste	2.0	2.6	2.0	1.9	1.8	1.8	2.6	2.0	1.9	2.3	2.2	2.2
Togo	8.1	8.5	9.6	8.6	8.5	8.7	8.5	9.3	9.2	8.5	7.9	7.9
Tuvalu	0.9	0.8	1.0	0.9	0.8	0.8	0.8	0.9	0.7	1.1	0.9	0.9
Uganda	7.2	7.0	6.5	6.7	6.7	6.9	7.0	7.1	7.1	7.3	7.5	7.7
United Republic of Tanzania	7.6	7.9	8.4	8.5	8.6	8.7	7.9	7.8	7.8	7.8	8.6	8.7
Vanuatu	4.5	3.9	3.8	2.8	3.8	3.8	3.9	3.7	3.4	3.9	3.0	3.8
Yemen	6.8	7.1	7.5	7.4	7.1	8.3	7.1	7.8	8.6	7.1	7.8	6.1
Zambia	10.6	10.7	10.2	10.5	10.3	10.2	10.7	10.4	10.3	9.7	9.3	8.9
Africa	11.6	10.8	10.5	10.0	10.0	10.1	10.8	10.1	9.8	9.1	9.8	9.5
Central Africa	9.8	8.5	7.8	7.5	7.5	7.4	8.5	7.9	7.7	7.0	9.0	7.7
Eastern Africa	7.9	7.5	7.2	7.1	7.0	7.0	7.5	7.4	7.5	7.4	6.7	7.4
North Africa	11.4	10.6	10.6	10.5	10.4	11.0	10.6	10.2	9.9	9.6	11.1	10.4
Southern Africa	15.0	14.2	13.7	12.6	12.8	12.7	14.2	13.4	12.9	12.1	11.8	11.6
Western Africa	6.6	5.9	5.5	5.5	5.4	5.2	5.9	5.4	5.3	4.8	5.1	4.8
Asia & Pacific	15.7	16.4	16.7	16.4	16.5	16.7	16.4	16.9	16.7	16.4	16.3	16.1
China	31.6	32.5	33.3	34.2	33.8	34.2	32.5	32.9	32.9	32.7	32.3	29.6
Central Asia	12.1	11.4	10.3	9.9	10.3	10.2	11.4	11.3	11.3	11.5	11.1	11.3
South Asia	14.4	14.6	15.4	15.4	15.2	15.3	14.6	15.3	15.2	15.2	14.4	14.0

a/ Provisional.
b/ Estimate.

Table 1.4
(continued)

SHARE OF MVA IN GDP, SELECTED YEARS
(Percentage)

Country group or economy	At constant 2005 prices						At current prices					
	2000	2005	2008	2009	2010 a/	2011 b/	2005	2006	2007	2008	2009	2010 a/
South East Asia	26.8	27.6	27.4	26.4	26.9	27.0	27.6	27.8	27.6	27.5	26.3	25.9
West Asia	7.7	9.1	9.2	9.1	9.2	9.5	9.1	9.2	9.0	8.3	9.3	8.9
Other Asia & Pacific	8.1	7.9	7.4	7.1	7.2	7.1	7.9	7.7	7.4	7.0	6.7	6.6
Europe	15.1	15.6	16.4	16.2	17.0	17.5	15.6	15.8	15.8	15.4	14.8	15.4
Latin America	17.0	16.3	15.7	14.8	15.2	15.1	16.3	15.7	15.1	15.2	15.0	14.7
Caribbean	12.9	10.8	10.3	10.1	10.2	10.2	10.8	10.4	10.3	11.0	11.8	11.8
Central America	19.5	18.1	17.6	16.9	17.5	17.5	18.1	18.4	18.1	17.7	17.0	17.1
South America	15.7	15.7	15.0	14.1	14.4	14.3	15.7	14.7	14.0	14.5	14.4	14.1
World	16.4	16.6	16.7	15.8	16.6	16.7	16.6	16.4	16.4	16.1	15.6	15.9
Low Income	10.9	11.2	11.6	11.5	11.7	11.8	11.2	11.2	11.3	11.1	11.1	11.5
Lower Middle Income	15.7	16.0	16.1	15.8	15.8	16.0	16.0	16.4	16.1	15.9	15.6	15.1
Upper Middle Income(excl.China)	17.0	16.7	16.0	15.2	15.7	15.8	16.7	16.2	15.8	15.6	15.0	15.2
China	31.6	32.5	33.3	34.2	33.8	34.2	32.5	32.9	32.9	32.7	32.3	29.6
High Income	15.7	15.6	15.5	14.2	15.1	15.0	15.6	15.3	15.1	14.6	13.7	14.3
African LDCs	8.1	7.9	7.4	7.4	7.4	7.5	7.9	7.6	7.4	7.0	7.1	6.9
ASEAN	27.2	27.7	27.0	25.8	26.8	26.8	27.7	27.7	27.0	26.6	25.7	25.4
CACM	19.6	19.4	18.6	18.2	18.3	18.2	19.4	19.3	18.7	18.4	17.7	17.5
CARICOM	6.9	6.5	6.5	6.5	6.5	6.5	6.5	7.0	6.9	6.6	6.8	7.0
CEMAC	9.8	8.5	7.8	7.5	7.5	7.4	8.5	7.9	7.7	7.0	9.0	7.7
CIS	15.5	15.7	14.4	13.4	14.0	14.1	15.7	15.5	15.3	15.0	12.9	14.0
ECOWAS	6.5	5.9	5.5	5.5	5.4	5.2	5.9	5.4	5.3	4.9	5.1	4.8
EU	16.0	15.4	15.2	13.8	14.5	14.6	15.4	15.3	15.3	14.8	13.3	14.0
GCC	8.9	9.5	9.6	9.7	9.7	9.6	9.5	9.1	9.0	8.4	9.7	9.5
LAIA	17.1	16.4	15.8	14.9	15.3	15.2	16.4	15.8	15.2	15.3	15.0	14.8
MERCOSUR	15.7	15.8	15.0	14.1	14.4	14.3	15.8	14.7	14.0	14.5	14.4	14.1
OECD	15.8	15.7	15.7	14.3	15.2	15.1	15.7	15.4	15.3	14.8	13.7	14.5
SAARC	14.4	14.6	15.4	15.4	15.2	15.3	14.6	15.3	15.2	15.2	14.4	14.0
WAEMU	14.5	12.9	11.5	11.7	11.7	11.4	12.9	12.1	11.9	11.3	11.2	11.6

a/ Provisional.
b/ Estimate.

Section 1.2

THE MANUFACTURING DIVISIONS / BRANCHES

Table 1.5

DISTRIBUTION OF WORLD VALUE ADDED, SELECTED DIVISIONS AND YEARS a/
(Percentage)

| ISIC Division | Year | Industrialized Economies | | | | | | | Developing & Emerging Industrial Economies | | | | World |
| | | All Economies | Europe | | East Asia | West Asia | North America | Others | All Economies | Emerging Industrial c/ Economies | Other Developing Economies | Least Developing Countries | |
			EU b/	Other									
15 Food and beverages	2000	74.5	26.0	2.8	15.5	0.3	27.5	2.4	25.5	20.8	4.4	0.3	100.0
	2005	70.0	24.7	2.9	13.6	0.3	26.2	2.3	30.0	25.6	4.1	0.3	100.0
	2011	59.6	20.9	2.9	11.0	0.3	22.7	1.8	40.4	36.0	4.1	0.3	100.0
16 Tobacco products	2000	57.6	13.8	1.9	6.3	0.0	34.6	1.0	42.4	34.0	7.9	0.5	100.0
	2005	48.5	9.8	2.2	6.4	0.0	29.1	1.0	51.5	44.8	5.8	0.9	100.0
	2011	29.7	6.2	1.8	5.4	0.0	15.5	0.8	70.3	64.6	4.6	1.1	100.0
17 Textiles	2000	63.8	26.7	1.0	17.2	0.0	17.7	1.2	36.2	30.5	4.9	0.8	100.0
	2005	50.9	21.7	0.9	11.9	0.1	15.3	1.0	49.1	41.7	6.1	1.3	100.0
	2011	29.7	14.1	0.7	7.1	0.0	7.1	0.7	70.3	63.0	5.6	1.7	100.0
18 Wearing apparel, fur	2000	65.4	32.8	1.1	12.1	0.1	18.1	1.2	34.6	28.1	5.9	0.6	100.0
	2005	47.3	24.3	1.2	9.2	0.1	11.3	1.2	52.7	44.5	7.4	0.8	100.0
	2011	29.0	15.8	1.0	5.8	0.2	5.5	0.7	71.0	62.7	6.9	1.4	100.0
19 Leather, leather products and footwear	2000	59.0	40.0	0.6	10.0	0.1	7.3	1.0	41.0	29.8	10.8	0.4	100.0
	2005	47.2	31.8	0.9	8.3	0.2	5.1	0.9	52.8	46.8	5.3	0.7	100.0
	2011	25.8	17.2	1.0	4.2	0.1	2.7	0.6	74.2	68.6	4.9	0.7	100.0
20 Wood products (excl. furniture)	2000	83.9	32.4	4.3	12.6	0.3	31.2	3.1	16.1	13.4	2.5	0.2	100.0
	2005	81.1	31.3	4.6	9.7	0.4	32.0	3.1	18.9	16.8	2.0	0.1	100.0
	2011	68.9	32.4	5.1	7.7	0.5	20.3	2.9	31.1	29.2	1.6	0.3	100.0
21 Paper and paper products	2000	81.3	25.4	2.0	15.0	0.3	37.1	1.5	18.7	17.1	1.2	0.4	100.0
	2005	74.5	24.8	1.9	14.0	0.3	32.1	1.4	25.5	24.0	1.3	0.2	100.0
	2011	59.7	22.6	1.6	12.2	0.4	21.9	1.0	40.3	38.8	1.3	0.2	100.0
22 Printing and publishing	2000	90.3	44.6	3.6	16.0	0.3	22.5	3.3	9.7	8.9	0.7	0.1	100.0
	2005	87.7	44.6	3.5	15.4	0.3	20.1	3.8	12.3	11.3	0.9	0.1	100.0
	2011	82.6	43.5	3.5	16.9	0.4	15.2	3.1	17.4	16.1	1.2	0.1	100.0
23 Coke, refined petroleum products, nuclear fuel	2000	68.4	14.8	9.2	9.9	2.0	31.2	1.3	31.6	27.2	4.4	0.0	100.0
	2005	66.7	13.5	9.1	9.9	2.0	31.0	1.2	33.3	29.4	3.9	0.0	100.0
	2011	56.9	12.3	9.7	9.0	1.9	23.1	0.9	43.1	39.2	3.8	0.1	100.0
24 Chemicals and chemical products	2000	80.8	26.5	2.8	17.9	0.1	32.4	1.1	19.2	17.3	1.7	0.2	100.0
	2005	76.2	25.1	2.9	16.1	0.1	30.9	1.1	23.8	21.8	1.8	0.2	100.0
	2011	64.3	22.5	3.0	13.6	0.0	24.1	1.1	35.7	33.7	1.9	0.1	100.0

a/ At constant 2005 prices.
b/ Excluding non-industrialized EU economies.
c/ Including China.

Table 1.5
(continued)

DISTRIBUTION OF WORLD VALUE ADDED, SELECTED DIVISIONS AND YEARS a/
(Percentage)

ISIC Division	Year	Industrialized Economies — All Economies	Europe — EU b/	Europe — Other	East Asia	West Asia	North America	Others	Dev & Emerging — All Economies	Emerging Industrial c/ Economies	Other Developing Economies	Least Developing Countries	World
25 Rubber and plastics products	2000	85.6	31.4	1.4	23.5	0.0	28.0	1.3	14.4	13.3	1.1	0.0	100.0
	2005	80.1	29.6	1.5	22.0	0.0	25.7	1.3	19.9	18.6	1.3	0.0	100.0
	2011	69.7	27.5	2.1	19.9	0.0	19.1	1.1	30.3	28.7	1.5	0.1	100.0
26 Non-metallic mineral products	2000	75.7	32.4	2.3	18.1	0.9	20.4	1.6	24.3	20.9	3.3	0.1	100.0
	2005	68.4	28.9	2.7	14.5	1.1	19.4	1.8	31.6	27.4	4.0	0.2	100.0
	2011	54.2	23.8	2.4	12.0	1.3	12.8	1.9	45.8	40.3	5.2	0.3	100.0
27 Basic metals	2000	73.4	22.1	5.9	23.0	0.5	19.8	2.1	26.6	24.2	2.3	0.1	100.0
	2005	59.7	17.4	5.4	19.3	0.4	15.4	1.8	40.3	38.0	2.3	0.0	100.0
	2011	32.0	10.2	3.2	11.5	0.4	5.5	1.2	68.0	66.6	1.4	0.0	100.0
28 Fabricated metal products	2000	89.8	37.5	1.9	21.1	0.2	27.1	2.0	10.2	9.2	0.9	0.1	100.0
	2005	85.1	38.2	2.1	17.7	0.3	24.7	2.1	14.9	13.8	1.0	0.1	100.0
	2011	74.8	36.7	2.2	14.7	0.3	18.7	2.2	25.2	23.9	1.3	0.0	100.0
29 Machinery and equipment n.e.c.	2000	89.5	36.9	3.0	23.2	0.1	25.5	0.8	10.5	9.6	0.8	0.1	100.0
	2005	83.2	35.0	2.8	22.9	0.1	21.6	0.8	16.8	16.3	0.5	0.0	100.0
	2011	68.4	33.4	2.6	19.2	0.1	12.5	0.6	31.6	30.9	0.6	0.1	100.0
30 Office, accounting and computing machinery	2000	84.7	25.5	0.9	31.1	0.7	26.3	0.2	15.3	14.0	1.3	0.0	100.0
	2005	73.6	15.1	0.5	28.6	0.7	28.5	0.2	26.4	24.9	1.5	0.0	100.0
	2011	56.1	12.7	0.3	17.7	0.5	24.8	0.1	43.9	42.6	1.3	0.0	100.0
31 Electrical machinery and apparatus	2000	86.0	38.1	2.1	18.2	0.3	26.7	0.6	14.0	12.6	1.3	0.1	100.0
	2005	77.1	34.9	2.1	18.8	0.3	20.3	0.7	22.9	21.3	1.5	0.1	100.0
	2011	59.9	27.8	2.2	17.1	0.2	12.1	0.5	40.1	39.0	1.1	0.0	100.0
32 Radio,television and communication equipment	2000	85.8	20.6	2.2	43.8	0.2	17.9	1.1	14.2	13.2	1.0	0.0	100.0
	2005	80.1	14.8	1.7	41.6	0.1	21.0	0.9	19.9	18.9	1.0	0.0	100.0
	2011	71.8	11.6	1.0	41.3	0.1	17.3	0.5	28.2	27.5	0.7	0.0	100.0
33 Medical, precision and optical instruments	2000	95.5	32.3	5.5	14.8	0.3	40.9	1.7	4.5	4.1	0.4	0.0	100.0
	2005	92.6	29.7	5.4	12.8	0.3	42.9	1.5	7.4	6.9	0.5	0.0	100.0
	2011	85.5	26.7	4.8	13.5	0.3	38.9	1.3	14.5	14.1	0.4	0.0	100.0
34 Motor vehicles, trailers, semi-trailers	2000	84.2	30.1	1.0	25.6	0.1	26.7	0.7	15.8	14.9	0.9	0.0	100.0
	2005	79.4	28.3	0.9	26.1	0.1	23.3	0.7	20.6	19.5	1.1	0.0	100.0
	2011	67.1	25.9	1.1	28.2	0.1	11.2	0.6	32.9	31.4	1.4	0.1	100.0

a/ At constant 2005 prices.
b/ Excluding non-industrialized EU economies.
c/ Including China.

Table 1.5
(continued)

DISTRIBUTION OF WORLD VALUE ADDED, SELECTED DIVISIONS AND YEARS [a]
(Percentage)

| ISIC Division | Year | Industrialized Economies | | | | | | | Developing & Emerging Industrial Economies | | | | World |
		All Economies	Europe EU [b]	Europe Other	East Asia	West Asia	North America	Others	All Economies	Emerging Industrial [c] Economies	Other Developing Economies	Least Developing Countries	
35 Other transport equipment	2000	89.8	32.8	3.1	9.5	0.4	42.4	1.6	10.2	9.3	0.8	0.1	100.0
	2005	84.4	29.7	2.6	11.8	0.4	38.3	1.6	15.6	14.5	1.0	0.1	100.0
	2011	73.5	27.0	2.7	11.2	0.3	31.0	1.3	26.5	25.0	1.4	0.1	100.0
36 Furniture; manufacturing n.e.c.	2000	86.4	34.1	2.0	16.6	0.3	31.6	1.8	13.6	11.4	2.2	0.0	100.0
	2005	80.2	30.3	2.2	12.2	0.4	33.2	1.9	19.8	17.2	2.5	0.1	100.0
	2011	68.1	25.6	2.1	12.2	0.5	26.1	1.6	31.9	28.3	3.6	0.0	100.0

a/ At constant 2005 prices.
b/ Excluding non-industrialized EU economies.
c/ Including China.

Table 1.6

DISTRIBUTION OF VALUE ADDED OF SELECTED DIVISIONS AMONG DEVELOPING REGIONS, 2005 AND 2011 [a/]
(Percentage)

| ISIC Division | All Developing & Emerging Industrial Economies | | | | | | | | | | Least Developed Countries | |
| | Africa | | Asia and Pacific b/ | | Europe | | Latin America | | All Economies | | | |
	2005	2011	2005	2011	2005	2011	2005	2011	2005	2011	2005	2011
15 Food and beverages	6.2	4.2	43.1	58.5	12.2	9.3	38.5	28.0	100.0	100.0	0.9	0.7
16 Tobacco products	4.0	2.9	73.5	84.2	9.1	4.7	13.4	8.2	100.0	100.0	1.6	1.6
17 Textiles	4.6	2.5	70.0	84.8	13.0	6.1	12.4	6.6	100.0	100.0	2.5	2.5
18 Wearing apparel, fur	8.4	4.5	61.0	80.0	18.3	7.9	12.3	7.6	100.0	100.0	1.5	2.0
19 Leather, leather products and footwear	4.7	2.5	62.9	78.4	10.6	5.9	21.8	13.2	100.0	100.0	1.4	1.0
20 Wood products (excl. furniture)	12.9	6.2	51.3	67.7	19.9	17.6	15.9	8.5	100.0	100.0	0.5	0.7
21 Paper and paper products	3.8	2.4	61.9	74.3	7.1	4.9	27.2	18.4	100.0	100.0	0.6	0.3
22 Printing and publishing	6.5	4.6	34.8	45.4	24.0	21.8	34.7	28.2	100.0	100.0	0.5	0.4
23 Coke,refined petroleum products,nuclear fuel	3.1	2.5	51.4	65.3	13.6	9.4	31.9	22.8	100.0	100.0	0.1	0.1
24 Chemicals and chemical products	3.2	2.0	62.3	76.2	6.4	4.5	28.1	17.3	100.0	100.0	0.9	0.5
25 Rubber and plastics products	4.5	3.1	58.4	70.0	13.3	10.8	23.8	16.1	100.0	100.0	0.3	0.2
26 Non-metallic mineral products	6.9	4.7	56.5	70.5	14.6	10.1	22.0	14.7	100.0	100.0	0.6	0.5
27 Basic metals	3.3	0.9	68.6	89.6	8.0	2.9	20.1	6.6	100.0	100.0	0.1	0.1
28 Fabricated metal products	7.1	3.9	57.6	73.0	17.6	11.9	17.7	11.2	100.0	100.0	0.3	0.2
29 Machinery and equipment n.e.c.	4.0	1.6	67.3	82.5	12.3	7.7	16.4	8.2	100.0	100.0	0.0	0.0
30 Office, accounting and computing machinery	1.4	0.4	86.3	93.9	1.3	0.6	11.0	5.1	100.0	100.0	0.0	0.0
31 Electrical machinery and apparatus	3.9	1.9	72.8	86.6	9.9	5.2	13.4	6.3	100.0	100.0	0.3	0.1
32 Radio,television and communication equipment	0.8	0.5	90.5	95.6	3.4	2.1	5.3	1.8	100.0	100.0	0.1	0.1
33 Medical, precision and optical instruments	2.5	1.1	72.6	84.6	10.7	6.8	14.2	7.5	100.0	100.0	0.0	0.0
34 Motor vehicles, trailers, semi-trailers	3.7	2.2	52.4	65.1	10.1	8.2	33.8	24.5	100.0	100.0	0.1	0.1
35 Other transport equipment	2.8	1.3	70.2	80.7	16.4	10.2	10.6	7.8	100.0	100.0	0.6	0.4
36 Furniture; manufacturing n.e.c.	9.0	6.2	55.7	68.6	16.7	12.1	18.6	13.1	100.0	100.0	0.4	0.2

a/ At constant 2005 prices.
b/ Including China.

Table 1.7

MAJOR PRODUCERS IN SELECTED DIVISIONS, 2005 AND 2011 [a/]

	World				Developing & emerging industrial economies			
	2005		2011		2005		2011	
Economy	Economy	Share [b/] (percentage)	Economy	Share [b/] (percentage)	Economy	Share [c/] (percentage)	Economy	Share [c/] (percentage)
Food and beverages (ISIC 15)								
	United States of America	24.0	United States of America	20.9	Mexico	19.6	Mexico	17.2
	Japan	11.3	China	17.1	Brazil	12.1	Brazil	11.0
	China	7.1	Japan	8.9	Argentina	5.7	Argentina	7.6
	Germany	4.8	Germany	4.2	Indonesia	5.3	Indonesia	6.5
	Mexico	4.5	Mexico	4.0	Turkey	4.9	India	5.1
	United Kingdom	4.4	United Kingdom	3.5	India	4.4	Turkey	4.6
	France	3.9	France	3.3	Poland	4.1	Poland	4.4
	Italy	3.0	Brazil	2.6	Thailand	4.1	Thailand	3.8
	Brazil	2.8	Italy	2.5	South Africa	3.0	Saudi Arabia	2.9
	Spain	2.6	Spain	2.2	Saudi Arabia	2.8	South Africa	2.8
	Canada	2.2	Russian Federation	1.9	Colombia	2.6	Viet Nam	2.7
	Russian Federation	1.9	Canada	1.8	Philippines	2.4	Colombia	2.6
	Australia	1.6	Argentina	1.8	Greece	2.1	Romania	2.1
	Republic of Korea	1.4	Indonesia	1.5	Venezuela (Bolivarian Republic of)	1.9	Philippines	1.9
	Argentina	1.3	Australia	1.2	Chile	1.8	Greece	1.9
	Sum of above	**76.8**	**Sum of above**	**77.4**	**Sum of above**	**76.8**	**Sum of above**	**77.1**
Tobacco products (ISIC 16)								
	United States of America	27.3	China	41.6	Indonesia	28.2	Indonesia	41.9
	China	23.5	United States of America	14.8	Mexico	11.9	Mexico	10.4
	Indonesia	7.9	Indonesia	12.1	Poland	9.8	India	5.3
	Japan	4.4	Japan	3.4	India	6.2	Poland	5.2
	Mexico	3.3	Mexico	3.0	Dominican Republic	4.3	Bangladesh	3.6
	India	2.7	India	1.5	Thailand	3.6	Turkey	3.3
	Poland	2.1	Poland	1.5	Turkey	3.4	Morocco	3.2
	United Kingdom	2.0	United Kingdom	1.4	Brazil	3.3	Thailand	2.8
	Netherlands	1.9	Netherlands	1.2	Pakistan	3.0	Pakistan	2.4
	Republic of Korea	1.8	Republic of Korea	1.1	Bangladesh	2.8	Brazil	2.3
	Bangladesh	1.7	Bangladesh	1.0	Morocco	2.7	Dominican Republic	2.3
	Turkey	1.2	Turkey	0.9	Philippines	2.5	Viet Nam	1.8
	Morocco	1.1	Morocco	0.9	Viet Nam	1.9	Venezuela (Bolivarian Republic of)	1.7
	Switzerland	1.0	Switzerland	0.9	Venezuela (Bolivarian Republic of)	1.7	Sri Lanka	1.5
	Russian Federation	1.0	Russian Federation	0.8	Egypt	1.5	Argentina	1.5
	Sum of above	**82.9**	**Sum of above**	**86.1**	**Sum of above**	**86.8**	**Sum of above**	**89.2**

a/ China is presented only among 'World', depending on data availability.
b/ In world total value added at constant 2005 prices.
c/ In total value added of developing and emerging industrial economies at constant 2005 prices.

Table 1.7

MAJOR PRODUCERS IN SELECTED DIVISIONS, 2005 AND 2011 [a/]

Textiles (ISIC 17)

World 2005 Economy	Share b/ (%)	World 2011 Economy	Share b/ (%)	Developing & emerging 2005 Economy	Share c/ (%)	Developing & emerging 2011 Economy	Share c/ (%)
China	21.2	China	46.1	Turkey	17.5	India	17.4
United States of America	13.9	United States of America	6.4	India	14.4	Turkey	13.3
Italy	7.8	Italy	4.7	Indonesia	10.6	Indonesia	12.8
Japan	7.2	Japan	4.4	Pakistan	8.6	Pakistan	10.1
Turkey	4.9	India	4.2	Mexico	6.4	Bangladesh	7.1
India	4.0	Turkey	3.2	Brazil	5.6	Mexico	5.6
Germany	3.0	Indonesia	3.1	Bangladesh	4.4	Brazil	4.7
Indonesia	3.0	Pakistan	2.4	Thailand	4.3	Egypt	3.0
Republic of Korea	2.9	Germany	2.2	Peru	3.8	Peru	2.9
Pakistan	2.4	Republic of Korea	1.8	South Africa	3.3	Thailand	2.7
France	2.4	Bangladesh	1.7	Egypt	2.1	South Africa	2.1
United Kingdom	2.2	United Kingdom	1.5	Argentina	1.7	Argentina	2.1
Mexico	1.8	Mexico	1.3	Poland	1.5	Poland	1.7
Spain	1.7	France	1.3	Colombia	1.4	Colombia	1.5
Brazil	1.6	Brazil	1.1	Romania	1.3	Iran (Islamic Republic of)	1.4
Sum of above	**80.0**	**Sum of above**	**85.4**	**Sum of above**	**86.9**	**Sum of above**	**88.4**

Wearing apparel, fur (ISIC 18)

World 2005 Economy	Share b/ (%)	World 2011 Economy	Share b/ (%)	Developing & emerging 2005 Economy	Share c/ (%)	Developing & emerging 2011 Economy	Share c/ (%)
China	21.5	China	47.4	Turkey	15.2	Turkey	11.6
Italy	9.7	Italy	8.9	South Africa	7.2	Peru	6.9
United States of America	9.2	United States of America	4.6	Indonesia	7.2	Indonesia	6.4
Republic of Korea	4.7	Republic of Korea	3.3	Thailand	5.7	India	6.1
Turkey	3.9	Turkey	2.8	Romania	5.6	South Africa	6.0
Japan	3.6	Japan	1.7	Brazil	5.6	Bangladesh	5.8
Peru	3.2	Peru	1.6	Peru	5.4	Viet Nam	5.6
Germany	2.7	Germany	1.5	India	5.3	Brazil	5.4
Indonesia	2.4	Indonesia	1.4	Sri Lanka	3.1	Thailand	4.6
United Kingdom	2.4	United Kingdom	1.4	Morocco	2.7	Sri Lanka	3.8
India	2.2	India	1.4	Viet Nam	2.6	Romania	3.5
South Africa	2.2	South Africa	1.4	Mexico	2.5	Bulgaria	3.2
Bangladesh	2.1	Bangladesh	1.3	Philippines	2.5	Morocco	2.9
Viet Nam	1.8	Viet Nam	1.3	Bulgaria	2.5	Saudi Arabia	2.7
Brazil	1.8	Brazil	1.2	Greece	2.4	Colombia	2.5
Sum of above	**73.2**	**Sum of above**	**81.2**	**Sum of above**	**75.5**	**Sum of above**	**77.0**

a/ China is presented only among 'World', depending on data availability.
b/ In world total value added at constant 2005 prices.
c/ In total value added of developing and emerging industrial economies at constant 2005 prices.

Table 1.7

MAJOR PRODUCERS IN SELECTED DIVISIONS, 2005 AND 2011 a/

Leather, leather products and footwear (ISIC 19)

World				Developing & emerging industrial economies			
2005		2011		2005		2011	
Economy	Share b/ (percentage)	Economy	Share b/ (percentage)	Economy	Share c/ (percentage)	Economy	Share c/ (percentage)
China	22.6	China	48.9	Brazil	16.4	Indonesia	12.4
Italy	17.5	Italy	9.0	Indonesia	10.2	Argentina	11.8
Brazil	5.0	Indonesia	3.1	Turkey	7.3	Brazil	11.5
Japan	4.8	Argentina	3.0	Argentina	6.6	Viet Nam	8.0
United States of America	4.5	Brazil	2.9	Thailand	6.5	Turkey	6.1
France	3.5	Japan	2.4	Mexico	5.8	India	6.0
Spain	3.2	United States of America	2.3	Viet Nam	5.7	Mexico	5.8
Indonesia	3.1	Viet Nam	2.0	India	5.1	Romania	4.7
Germany	2.3	France	1.9	Romania	5.0	Peru	4.4
Republic of Korea	2.2	Spain	1.6	South Africa	4.4	South Africa	4.0
Turkey	2.2	Turkey	1.5	Peru	3.8	Bangladesh	2.8
Argentina	2.0	India	1.5	Bangladesh	2.3	Thailand	2.5
Thailand	2.0	Mexico	1.5	Poland	1.7	Croatia	2.1
Portugal	1.8	Germany	1.4	Saudi Arabia	1.5	Saudi Arabia	1.8
Mexico	1.7	Republic of Korea	1.3	Colombia	1.4	Colombia	1.7
Sum of above	**78.4**	**Sum of above**	**84.3**	**Sum of above**	**83.7**	**Sum of above**	**85.6**

Wood products (excl. furniture) (ISIC 20)

World				Developing & emerging industrial economies			
2005		2011		2005		2011	
Economy	Share b/ (percentage)	Economy	Share b/ (percentage)	Economy	Share c/ (percentage)	Economy	Share c/ (percentage)
United States of America	25.7	China	17.9	Indonesia	20.5	Turkey	13.3
Japan	7.7	United States of America	15.3	Brazil	10.8	Poland	11.1
Canada	6.3	Germany	6.5	South Africa	9.4	Indonesia	9.3
Germany	6.0	Japan	5.8	Poland	7.5	South Africa	9.2
China	5.3	Italy	5.1	Turkey	6.4	Brazil	9.1
Italy	5.2	Canada	5.1	Romania	4.1	Romania	7.4
United Kingdom	3.9	United Kingdom	3.3	Thailand	3.9	India	2.6
France	3.1	France	3.2	Peru	2.7	Saudi Arabia	2.4
Spain	2.8	Spain	2.5	Côte d'Ivoire	2.7	Croatia	2.4
Austria	2.8	Austria	2.3	Serbia	2.4	Thailand	2.3
Russian Federation	2.1	Russian Federation	2.2	Latvia	1.9	Peru	2.0
Australia	2.0	Switzerland	2.1	Cameroon	1.9	Argentina	1.9
Switzerland	1.8	Sweden	2.1	Chile	1.9	Latvia	1.9
Sweden	1.8	Australia	1.9	Croatia	1.7	Viet Nam	1.8
Turkey	1.7	Turkey	1.8	Greece	1.7	Chile	1.6
Sum of above	**78.2**	**Sum of above**	**77.1**	**Sum of above**	**79.5**	**Sum of above**	**78.3**

a/ China is presented only among 'World', depending on data availability.
b/ In world total value added at constant 2005 prices.
c/ In total value added of developing and emerging industrial economies at constant 2005 prices.

Table 1.7

MAJOR PRODUCERS IN SELECTED DIVISIONS, 2005 AND 2011 [a/]

Paper and paper products (ISIC 21)

World				Developing & emerging industrial economies			
2005		2011		2005		2011	
Economy	Share [b/] (percentage)	Economy	Share [b/] (percentage)	Economy	Share [c/] (percentage)	Economy	Share [c/] (percentage)
United States of America	27.7	China	24.8	Mexico	17.5	Mexico	16.9
Japan	11.4	United States of America	19.3	Indonesia	16.5	Brazil	14.7
China	10.5	Japan	9.8	Brazil	15.6	Indonesia	14.6
Germany	5.9	Germany	6.0	Argentina	5.6	Argentina	6.8
Canada	4.4	Italy	2.8	India	5.6	India	6.1
Italy	3.2	Canada	2.7	Turkey	4.9	Turkey	5.1
France	2.8	Mexico	2.6	Thailand	4.0	Poland	4.0
Mexico	2.6	France	2.3	South Africa	3.3	Saudi Arabia	3.6
Indonesia	2.5	Brazil	2.3	Poland	3.3	Thailand	3.2
United Kingdom	2.4	Indonesia	2.2	Saudi Arabia	3.3	South Africa	3.1
Brazil	2.3	Finland	2.1	Colombia	2.5	Colombia	2.3
Finland	2.3	United Kingdom	2.0	Chile	1.6	Venezuela (Bolivarian Republic of)	2.1
Sweden	2.0	Spain	1.8	Pakistan	1.6	Chile	2.0
Spain	2.0	Sweden	1.8	Venezuela (Bolivarian Republic of)	1.5	Pakistan	1.3
Republic of Korea	1.7	Republic of Korea	1.5	Greece	1.2	Uruguay	1.2
Sum of above	**83.7**	**Sum of above**	**84.0**	**Sum of above**	**88.0**	**Sum of above**	**87.0**

Printing and publishing (ISIC 22)

World				Developing & emerging industrial economies			
2005		2011		2005		2011	
Economy	Share [b/] (percentage)	Economy	Share [b/] (percentage)	Economy	Share [c/] (percentage)	Economy	Share [c/] (percentage)
United States of America	18.0	United States of America	13.4	Brazil	15.8	Brazil	13.6
Japan	12.1	Japan	13.3	Mexico	13.0	Mexico	12.4
United Kingdom	10.8	United Kingdom	9.4	Turkey	8.0	India	8.6
Germany	9.5	Germany	9.0	Greece	7.3	Turkey	8.0
France	5.0	China	4.9	Poland	7.0	Poland	7.2
Italy	4.7	France	4.4	India	6.3	Greece	6.6
Netherlands	3.5	Italy	4.1	South Africa	5.8	South Africa	4.2
Australia	3.0	Ireland	4.0	Argentina	4.1	Romania	4.1
Spain	2.8	Spain	3.5	Saudi Arabia	3.5	Indonesia	3.8
Canada	2.1	Netherlands	3.0	Thailand	3.4	Saudi Arabia	3.7
China	2.1	Australia	2.4	Romania	3.1	Argentina	3.5
Ireland	1.9	Republic of Korea	1.9	Colombia	2.9	Thailand	3.2
Republic of Korea	1.8	Canada	1.8	Venezuela (Bolivarian Republic of)	2.7	Colombia	2.6
Brazil	1.6	Brazil	1.7	Peru	1.6	Croatia	2.0
Switzerland	1.4	Mexico	1.6		1.5	Peru	2.0
Sum of above	**80.3**	**Sum of above**	**78.4**	**Sum of above**	**86.0**	**Sum of above**	**85.5**

a/ China is presented only among 'World', depending on data availability.
b/ In world total value added at constant 2005 prices.
c/ In total value added of developing and emerging industrial economies at constant 2005 prices.

Table 1.7

MAJOR PRODUCERS IN SELECTED DIVISIONS, 2005 AND 2011 a/

World				Developing & emerging industrial economies			
2005		2011		2005		2011	
Economy	Share b/ (percentage)	Economy	Share b/ (percentage)	Economy	Share c/ (percentage)	Economy	Share c/ (percentage)
Coke, refined petroleum products, nuclear fuel (ISIC 23)							
United States of America	30.1	United States of America	22.3	Brazil	23.4	India	25.1
Russian Federation	8.9	China	18.8	India	22.1	Brazil	22.5
China	8.3	Russian Federation	9.5	Poland	7.4	Poland	8.5
Brazil	5.8	India	6.1	Venezuela (Bolivarian Republic of)	6.0	Venezuela (Bolivarian Republic of)	5.5
India	5.5	Brazil	5.5	Turkey	4.8	Colombia	4.6
Spain	3.2	Spain	3.0	Philippines	4.7	Philippines	3.8
Republic of Korea	2.7	Republic of Korea	2.4	Colombia	4.1	Iran (Islamic Republic of)	3.6
Japan	2.6	Japan	2.3	Argentina	3.4	Turkey	3.4
Poland	2.3	Poland	2.1	Iran (Islamic Republic of)	2.7	Argentina	3.0
China, Taiwan Province	2.3	China, Taiwan Province	2.1	Ukraine	2.6	Greece	2.1
Malaysia	1.9	Malaysia	2.0	Greece	2.2	Pakistan	1.8
Germany	1.9	Germany	2.0	Ecuador	1.8	Ukraine	1.6
Venezuela (Bolivarian Republic of)	1.5	Venezuela (Bolivarian Republic of)	1.3	Thailand	1.6	Ecuador	1.4
France	1.4	France	1.3	Pakistan	1.5	Thailand	1.4
United Kingdom	1.3	Netherlands	1.2	Mexico	1.3	Kazakhstan	1.4
Sum of above	**79.7**	**Sum of above**	**81.9**	**Sum of above**	**89.6**	**Sum of above**	**89.7**
Chemicals and chemical products (ISIC 24)							
United States of America	29.3	United States of America	22.9	Mexico	20.6	Mexico	16.4
Japan	12.0	China	21.0	India	14.9	India	14.5
China	9.2	Japan	9.3	Brazil	12.1	Brazil	10.8
Germany	6.7	Germany	6.1	Saudi Arabia	6.3	Indonesia	8.9
France	3.6	France	3.3	Indonesia	5.8	Argentina	6.7
United Kingdom	3.5	United Kingdom	2.8	Argentina	4.9	Saudi Arabia	6.7
Mexico	3.0	Mexico	2.4	Turkey	4.4	Turkey	4.8
India	2.6	India	2.1	Thailand	3.0	Iran (Islamic Republic of)	3.1
Republic of Korea	2.2	Republic of Korea	2.1	Poland	2.8	Poland	2.9
Italy	2.1	Italy	2.1	Venezuela (Bolivarian Republic of)	2.1	Thailand	2.7
Brazil	1.8	Ireland	1.7	Colombia	2.1	Colombia	2.3
Ireland	1.7	Brazil	1.6	Pakistan	2.1	Venezuela (Bolivarian Republic of)	1.8
Canada	1.6	Switzerland	1.6	Iran (Islamic Republic of)	2.1	Egypt	1.7
Spain	1.6	Spain	1.3	Egypt	1.8	South Africa	1.7
Switzerland	1.4	Indonesia	1.3	South Africa	1.7	Pakistan	1.6
Sum of above	**82.3**	**Sum of above**	**81.6**	**Sum of above**	**86.7**	**Sum of above**	**86.6**

a/ China is presented only among 'World', depending on data availability.
b/ In world total value added at constant 2005 prices.
c/ In total value added of developing and emerging industrial economies at constant 2005 prices.

Table 1.7

MAJOR PRODUCERS IN SELECTED DIVISIONS, 2005 AND 2011 [a/]

	World				Developing & emerging industrial economies			
	2005		**2011**		**2005**		**2011**	
	Economy	Share [b/] (percentage)	Economy	Share [b/] (percentage)	Economy	Share [c/] (percentage)	Economy	Share [c/] (percentage)
Rubber and plastics products (ISIC 25)								
	United States of America	23.4	United States of America	17.5	Brazil	12.3	Brazil	11.3
	China	16.7	China	16.0	Indonesia	11.3	India	9.3
	Japan	8.5	Japan	14.6	Mexico	10.8	Poland	9.0
	Germany	6.7	Germany	8.5	Thailand	10.0	Mexico	8.8
	United Kingdom	4.5	Italy	3.9	Turkey	8.7	Thailand	8.3
	Italy	4.4	France	3.6	India	6.9	Turkey	8.1
	France	4.3	Republic of Korea	3.3	Poland	5.7	Indonesia	7.9
	Republic of Korea	3.1	United Kingdom	3.2	South Africa	4.3	Argentina	5.2
	Canada	2.3	Spain	2.0	Argentina	4.0	South Africa	4.7
	Spain	2.3	Brazil	1.6	Saudi Arabia	3.5	Saudi Arabia	3.8
	Brazil	1.6	Canada	1.6	Colombia	2.3	Colombia	2.6
	Indonesia	1.5	Russian Federation	1.4	Romania	1.9	Romania	2.3
	Mexico	1.4	India	1.3	Venezuela (Bolivarian Republic of)	1.8	Venezuela (Bolivarian Republic of)	1.7
	Thailand	1.3	Poland	1.3	Greece	1.6	Philippines	1.6
	Turkey	1.2	Mexico	1.2	Philippines	1.5	Iran (Islamic Republic of)	1.5
	Sum of above	**83.2**	**Sum of above**	**81.1**	**Sum of above**	**86.6**	**Sum of above**	**86.1**
Non-metallic mineral products (ISIC 26)								
	United States of America	17.8	China	23.9	Mexico	17.3	Mexico	14.3
	China	11.1	United States of America	11.6	Turkey	10.8	India	9.7
	Japan	10.9	Japan	8.5	India	8.2	Turkey	9.0
	Italy	5.7	Germany	4.8	Brazil	6.9	Brazil	6.9
	Germany	5.4	Italy	4.3	Indonesia	5.7	Poland	5.8
	Spain	4.6	Spain	3.3	Poland	4.3	Indonesia	5.0
	Mexico	3.5	Mexico	3.1	Saudi Arabia	4.2	Iran (Islamic Republic of)	4.8
	France	3.1	France	2.6	Thailand	3.6	Saudi Arabia	4.5
	United Kingdom	3.1	Republic of Korea	2.3	South Africa	3.3	Viet Nam	3.6
	Republic of Korea	2.3	United Kingdom	2.3	Iran (Islamic Republic of)	3.1	Pakistan	3.4
	India	2.2	India	2.1	Greece	2.6	Egypt	3.0
	Turkey	1.8	Turkey	2.0	Egypt	2.5	Romania	2.9
	Russian Federation	1.7	Russian Federation	1.7	Pakistan	2.4	Thailand	2.8
	Canada	1.6	Australia	1.7	Romania	2.2	South Africa	2.6
	Australia	1.5	Brazil	1.5	Venezuela (Bolivarian Republic of)	2.1	Argentina	1.9
	Sum of above	**76.3**	**Sum of above**	**75.7**	**Sum of above**	**79.2**	**Sum of above**	**80.2**

a/ China is presented only among 'World', depending on data availability.
b/ In world total value added at constant 2005 prices.
c/ In total value added of developing and emerging industrial economies at constant 2005 prices.

Table 1.7

MAJOR PRODUCERS IN SELECTED DIVISIONS, 2005 AND 2011 [a]

Basic metals (ISIC 27)

World — Economy (2005)	Share b/ (%)	World — Economy (2011)	Share b/ (%)	Developing & emerging — Economy (2005)	Share c/ (%)	Developing & emerging — Economy (2011)	Share c/ (%)
China	20.9	China	55.3	India	18.7	India	26.6
Japan	14.1	Japan	8.3	Brazil	13.1	Brazil	12.3
United States of America	13.3	United States of America	4.6	Chile	9.4	Mexico	7.7
Germany	5.8	Germany	3.9	Mexico	9.1	Chile	6.3
Russian Federation	4.6	India	3.4	Turkey	6.3	Turkey	6.2
India	3.7	Russian Federation	2.7	Argentina	4.4	Argentina	5.5
Republic of Korea	3.6	Republic of Korea	2.4	Iran (Islamic Republic of)	4.3	Indonesia	4.4
Brazil	2.6	Brazil	1.6	Venezuela (Bolivarian Republic of)	3.8	Iran (Islamic Republic of)	3.9
Italy	2.2	Italy	1.3	Kazakhstan	3.3	Ukraine	3.8
Canada	2.0	Australia	1.2	Indonesia	3.3	Kazakhstan	3.4
Chile	1.8	Mexico	1.0	Egypt	3.1	Egypt	2.2
Mexico	1.8	Canada	0.9	South Africa	3.0	Poland	1.9
Australia	1.7	Spain	0.9	Thailand	2.2	South Africa	1.7
France	1.6	France	0.8	Poland	2.1	Thailand	1.6
Spain	1.5	Chile	0.8		1.9	Romania	1.4
Sum of above	**81.2**	**Sum of above**	**89.1**	**Sum of above**	**88.0**	**Sum of above**	**88.9**

Fabricated metal products (ISIC 28)

World — Economy (2005)	Share b/ (%)	World — Economy (2011)	Share b/ (%)	Developing & emerging — Economy (2005)	Share c/ (%)	Developing & emerging — Economy (2011)	Share c/ (%)
United States of America	22.5	United States of America	17.0	Brazil	12.9	Poland	13.0
Japan	13.5	China	15.5	Turkey	8.7	Brazil	11.8
Germany	10.5	Germany	11.3	Poland	7.8	India	11.1
Italy	7.5	Japan	10.7	India	7.7	Mexico	7.4
China	6.0	Italy	6.4	Thailand	7.5	Turkey	6.5
France	4.7	France	4.3	Mexico	7.4	South Africa	6.2
United Kingdom	4.5	United Kingdom	3.3	South Africa	7.3	Thailand	5.3
Spain	3.5	Spain	3.1	Greece	6.1	Greece	4.1
Canada	2.2	Republic of Korea	2.4	Indonesia	4.5	Saudi Arabia	4.1
Republic of Korea	2.1	Canada	1.7	Saudi Arabia	3.8	Peru	3.3
Australia	1.5	Netherlands	1.6	Romania	2.9	Romania	2.7
Netherlands	1.4	Australia	1.3	Argentina	2.4	Argentina	2.5
China, Taiwan Province	1.4	Austria	1.3	Peru	2.0	Indonesia	2.5
Sweden	1.3	Poland	1.3	Venezuela (Bolivarian Republic of)	1.7	Viet Nam	1.9
Switzerland	1.3	Switzerland	1.2	Iran (Islamic Republic of)	1.6	Iran (Islamic Republic of)	1.7
Sum of above	**83.9**	**Sum of above**	**82.4**	**Sum of above**	**84.3**	**Sum of above**	**84.1**

a/ China is presented only among 'World', depending on data availability.
b/ In world total value added at constant 2005 prices.
c/ In total value added of developing and emerging industrial economies at constant 2005 prices.

Table 1.7

MAJOR PRODUCERS IN SELECTED DIVISIONS, 2005 AND 2011 [a/]

Machinery and equipment n.e.c. (ISIC 29)

World				Developing & emerging industrial economies			
2005		2011		2005		2011	
Economy	Share [b/] (percentage)	Economy	Share [b/] (percentage)	Economy	Share [c/] (percentage)	Economy	Share [c/] (percentage)
United States of America	20.0	China	23.3	Brazil	15.8	India	17.7
Japan	18.6	Japan	14.8	India	13.0	Brazil	14.8
Germany	13.4	Germany	14.0	Turkey	12.4	Poland	12.4
China	9.1	United States of America	11.3	Mexico	10.4	Turkey	10.1
Italy	6.4	Italy	5.1	Thailand	6.6	Mexico	9.4
United Kingdom	3.5	Republic of Korea	3.0	Poland	6.5	Thailand	6.3
France	3.1	France	2.7	South Africa	6.3	South Africa	4.0
Republic of Korea	2.8	United Kingdom	2.4	Venezuela (Bolivarian Republic of)	3.8	Iran (Islamic Republic of)	2.8
Spain	1.7	Spain	1.6	Romania	2.7	Saudi Arabia	2.4
India	1.5	India	1.5	Saudi Arabia	2.5	Argentina	2.2
Canada	1.4	Sweden	1.5	Indonesia	2.3	Indonesia	2.1
Switzerland	1.4	Austria	1.4	Argentina	2.2	Romania	2.1
Sweden	1.2	Switzerland	1.3	Iran (Islamic Republic of)	1.8	Egypt	2.0
Brazil	1.2	Brazil	1.2	Egypt	1.8	Venezuela (Bolivarian Republic of)	1.8
Netherlands	1.2	Canada	1.2	Ukraine	1.7	Greece	1.2
Austria	1.1						
Sum of above	**86.4**	**Sum of above**	**86.3**	**Sum of above**	**89.8**	**Sum of above**	**91.3**

Office, accounting and computing machinery (ISIC 30)

World				Developing & emerging industrial economies			
2005		2011		2005		2011	
Economy	Share [b/] (percentage)	Economy	Share [b/] (percentage)	Economy	Share [c/] (percentage)	Economy	Share [c/] (percentage)
United States of America	27.0	China	38.8	Mexico	31.9	Mexico	29.2
China	19.9	United States of America	23.7	Philippines	19.5	Philippines	17.3
Japan	14.5	Japan	7.9	India	13.5	Brazil	13.1
China, Taiwan Province	6.1	Germany	7.0	Brazil	11.4	Thailand	12.6
Germany	4.6	China, Taiwan Province	3.6	Thailand	8.7	India	10.0
Singapore	3.3	Singapore	2.8	South Africa	4.9	Viet Nam	6.6
Republic of Korea	3.0	Republic of Korea	2.5	Poland	1.4	South Africa	3.1
Malaysia	2.7	Ireland	1.8	Viet Nam	1.3	Poland	1.8
United Kingdom	2.2	Mexico	1.5	Romania	1.1	Romania	1.0
France	2.2	France	1.3	Costa Rica	0.9	Iran (Islamic Republic of)	0.8
Canada	2.1	Canada	1.1	Turkey	0.8	Turkey	0.8
Philippines	1.8	Philippines	0.9	Croatia	0.8	Costa Rica	0.7
Mexico	1.5	Malaysia	0.8	Algeria	0.6	Algeria	0.5
Brazil	1.3	Brazil	0.7	Iran (Islamic Republic of)	0.5	Croatia	0.5
India	0.9	Thailand	0.6	Ukraine	0.5	Kazakhstan	0.4
Sum of above	**93.1**	**Sum of above**	**95.0**	**Sum of above**	**97.8**	**Sum of above**	**98.4**

a/ China is presented only among 'World', depending on data availability.
b/ In world total value added at constant 2005 prices.
c/ In total value added of developing and emerging industrial economies at constant 2005 prices.

Table 1.7

MAJOR PRODUCERS IN SELECTED DIVISIONS, 2005 AND 2011 a/

Electrical machinery and apparatus (ISIC 31)

	World				Developing & emerging industrial economies			
	2005		**2011**		**2005**		**2011**	
	Economy	Share b/ (percentage)	Economy	Share b/ (percentage)	Economy	Share c/ (percentage)	Economy	Share c/ (percentage)
	United States of America	18.8	China	28.6	India	14.8	India	31.2
	Germany	14.5	Japan	13.9	Mexico	12.4	Mexico	10.5
	Japan	14.4	Germany	12.6	Brazil	10.2	Brazil	7.4
	China	11.6	United States of America	11.1	Turkey	7.8	Saudi Arabia	6.8
	Italy	4.6	India	3.6	Saudi Arabia	7.6	Turkey	6.8
	France	3.7	France	2.7	Thailand	6.2	Poland	6.1
	United Kingdom	3.4	Italy	2.7	Indonesia	5.9	Thailand	4.3
	Republic of Korea	2.6	Republic of Korea	2.2	Poland	5.5	South Africa	4.0
	Spain	2.0	Spain	1.8	South Africa	4.6	Indonesia	3.3
	India	1.7	United Kingdom	1.8	Philippines	3.9	Iran (Islamic Republic of)	2.4
	Canada	1.5	Switzerland	1.2	Romania	2.7	Philippines	1.9
	Mexico	1.4	Mexico	1.2	Iran (Islamic Republic of)	2.3	Romania	1.8
	China, Taiwan Province	1.2	Czech Republic	1.2	Argentina	1.4	Argentina	1.3
	Brazil	1.1	Canada	1.0	Greece	1.2	Ukraine	1.3
	Russian Federation	1.0	Austria	1.0	Egypt	1.2	Viet Nam	1.2
	Sum of above	**83.5**	**Sum of above**	**86.3**	**Sum of above**	**87.7**	**Sum of above**	**90.3**

Radio, television and communication equipment (ISIC 32)

	World				Developing & emerging industrial economies			
	2005		**2011**		**2005**		**2011**	
	Economy	Share b/ (percentage)	Economy	Share b/ (percentage)	Economy	Share c/ (percentage)	Economy	Share c/ (percentage)
	Japan	20.5	China	21.8	Thailand	33.4	India	30.0
	United States of America	20.2	United States of America	16.8	Indonesia	14.6	Indonesia	26.4
	China	13.6	Japan	15.5	Philippines	11.7	Thailand	14.9
	Republic of Korea	9.9	Republic of Korea	12.8	Brazil	11.6	Philippines	7.5
	China, Taiwan Province	8.0	China, Taiwan Province	11.3	India	7.5	Brazil	4.5
	Germany	3.2	Germany	4.3	Turkey	5.7	Poland	3.8
	India	2.1	India	1.9	Mexico	3.0	Turkey	3.7
	Indonesia	2.1	Indonesia	1.7	Poland	2.3	Mexico	2.0
	Finland	2.0	Finland	1.6	Costa Rica	1.0	Viet Nam	0.8
	Thailand	1.6	Thailand	1.0	Viet Nam	1.0	Egypt	0.8
	Malaysia	1.5	Malaysia	0.9	Romania	1.0	Romania	0.7
	Italy	1.5	France	0.9	Egypt	0.9	Argentina	0.6
	Singapore	1.1	Singapore	0.9	Greece	0.9	Costa Rica	0.5
	United Kingdom	1.1	United Kingdom	0.8	South Africa	0.8	South Africa	0.5
	Sweden	1.1	Russian Federation	0.8	Argentina	0.6	Iran (Islamic Republic of)	0.4
	Netherlands	1.0	Sweden	0.7				
	Sum of above	**89.4**	**Sum of above**	**92.9**	**Sum of above**	**96.0**	**Sum of above**	**97.1**

a/ China is presented only among 'World', depending on data availability.
b/ In world total value added at constant 2005 prices.
c/ In total value added of developing and emerging industrial economies at constant 2005 prices.

Table 1.7

MAJOR PRODUCERS IN SELECTED DIVISIONS, 2005 AND 2011 [a/]

Medical, precision and optical instruments (ISIC 33)

World 2005 Economy	Share [b/] (percentage)	World 2011 Economy	Share [b/] (percentage)	Developing & emerging 2005 Economy	Share [c/] (percentage)	Developing & emerging 2011 Economy	Share [c/] (percentage)
United States of America	41.6	United States of America	38.0	Brazil	14.4	Brazil	15.9
Japan	10.6	Japan	11.5	India	12.9	Poland	14.8
Germany	10.5	China	11.0	Thailand	10.7	India	11.6
United Kingdom	4.8	Germany	10.0	Mexico	9.3	Thailand	9.7
Switzerland	4.1	Switzerland	3.8	Poland	8.9	Mexico	8.4
China	4.0	United Kingdom	3.8	Philippines	8.8	Philippines	7.8
France	4.0	France	3.5	Turkey	5.1	Turkey	5.5
Italy	3.5	Italy	2.2	South Africa	4.4	South Africa	3.4
Ireland	1.4	Ireland	1.5	Romania	4.1	Romania	3.3
Canada	1.3	Sweden	1.0	Saudi Arabia	2.5	Saudi Arabia	2.4
Sweden	1.1	Israel	1.0	Greece	2.1	Greece	2.4
Republic of Korea	1.1	Republic of Korea	1.0	Costa Rica	2.0	Argentina	2.1
Israel	1.0	Canada	0.9	Argentina	1.5	Costa Rica	1.8
Netherlands	0.9	Netherlands	0.8	Ukraine	1.5	Venezuela (Bolivarian Republic of)	1.3
Russian Federation	0.9	Denmark	0.7	Indonesia	1.5	Indonesia	1.3
Sum of above	90.8	Sum of above	90.7	Sum of above	90.3	Sum of above	91.7

Motor vehicles, trailers, semi-trailers (ISIC 34)

World 2005 Economy	Share [b/] (percentage)	World 2011 Economy	Share [b/] (percentage)	Developing & emerging 2005 Economy	Share [c/] (percentage)	Developing & emerging 2011 Economy	Share [c/] (percentage)
Japan	21.7	Japan	23.3	Mexico	30.3	Mexico	26.6
United States of America	19.6	China	14.8	Brazil	13.6	India	17.0
Germany	13.9	Germany	13.8	India	10.4	Brazil	13.2
China	5.9	United States of America	9.1	Turkey	8.9	Turkey	7.6
Mexico	4.5	Mexico	4.8	Thailand	8.8	Thailand	6.9
Republic of Korea	3.8	Republic of Korea	4.3	Indonesia	7.3	Indonesia	5.7
India	3.7	India	3.1	South Africa	4.4	Poland	5.4
France	3.6	France	2.6	Iran (Islamic Republic of)	3.8	Iran (Islamic Republic of)	4.5
Brazil	2.6	Brazil	2.4	Poland	3.7	Argentina	3.6
Canada	2.0	Canada	2.1	Argentina	2.2	South Africa	3.1
United Kingdom	1.9	United Kingdom	1.5	Pakistan	1.1	Romania	1.1
Spain	1.5	Spain	1.5	Philippines	0.9	Pakistan	1.0
Italy	1.5	Turkey	1.4	Romania	0.7	Philippines	0.6
Turkey	1.3	Thailand	1.3	Colombia	0.6	Colombia	0.6
Thailand	1.3	Sweden	1.2	Ukraine	0.5	Ukraine	0.5
Sum of above	88.8	Sum of above	87.2	Sum of above	97.2	Sum of above	97.4

a/ China is presented only among 'World', depending on data availability.
b/ In world total value added at constant 2005 prices.
c/ In total value added of developing and emerging industrial economies at constant 2005 prices.

Table 1.7

MAJOR PRODUCERS IN SELECTED DIVISIONS, 2005 AND 2011 [a/]

Other transport equipment (ISIC 35)

World				Developing & emerging industrial economies			
2005		2011		2005		2011	
Economy	Share [b/] (percentage)	Economy	Share [b/] (percentage)	Economy	Share [c/] (percentage)	Economy	Share [c/] (percentage)
United States of America	34.9	United States of America	28.2	India	18.5	India	24.6
United Kingdom	8.0	China	16.1	Indonesia	16.4	Brazil	15.4
Germany	7.1	United Kingdom	7.0	Brazil	13.0	Indonesia	10.2
China	6.2	Germany	6.9	Thailand	6.3	Turkey	7.1
Japan	5.9	France	5.9	Turkey	6.0	Romania	5.4
France	5.6	Republic of Korea	5.0	Poland	5.4	Viet Nam	5.1
Republic of Korea	3.7	Japan	4.2	Romania	4.9	Poland	4.9
Canada	3.4	Canada	2.7	Greece	3.7	Thailand	3.5
Italy	3.4	India	2.6	Ukraine	3.2	Ukraine	3.1
Spain	1.8	Italy	2.5	Croatia	2.8	Iran (Islamic Republic of)	2.5
India	1.8	Norway	1.8	South Africa	2.7	Greece	2.5
Indonesia	1.6	Brazil	1.6	Iran (Islamic Republic of)	2.2	South Africa	2.0
Norway	1.4	Spain	1.5	Viet Nam	2.2	Croatia	1.9
Brazil	1.2	Singapore	1.3	Philippines	1.9	Mexico	1.5
Singapore	1.1	Indonesia	1.1	Mexico	1.9	Philippines	1.5
Sum of above	**87.1**	**Sum of above**	**88.4**	**Sum of above**	**91.1**	**Sum of above**	**91.2**

Furniture; manufacturing n.e.c. (ISIC 36)

World				Developing & emerging industrial economies			
2005		2011		2005		2011	
Economy	Share [b/] (percentage)	Economy	Share [b/] (percentage)	Economy	Share [c/] (percentage)	Economy	Share [c/] (percentage)
United States of America	29.5	United States of America	23.8	South Africa	10.8	Turkey	10.1
Japan	9.1	China	18.2	Turkey	9.5	Poland	8.9
China	7.3	Japan	9.9	Brazil	8.7	Brazil	8.6
Italy	6.5	Germany	5.5	Thailand	8.3	South Africa	8.0
Germany	6.2	Italy	5.3	Poland	7.4	Peru	7.9
United Kingdom	4.8	United Kingdom	3.7	Indonesia	6.1	Indonesia	5.6
Spain	3.7	Spain	2.6	Peru	5.9	India	5.6
Canada	3.4	Canada	2.3	India	5.8	Mexico	5.4
France	2.9	France	2.3	Mexico	5.5	Thailand	4.8
Republic of Korea	1.4	Turkey	1.4	Romania	3.9	Kenya	4.3
Poland	1.4	Poland	1.2	Saudi Arabia	2.8	Romania	4.2
Brazil	1.3	Brazil	1.2	Dominican Republic	2.7	Saudi Arabia	2.9
Australia	1.2	Australia	1.2	Greece	1.9	Dominican Republic	2.6
Austria	1.2	Austria	1.1	Colombia	1.7	Philippines	2.4
South Africa	1.1	South Africa	1.1	Philippines	1.6	Cuba	1.6
Sum of above	**81.0**	**Sum of above**	**80.8**	**Sum of above**	**82.6**	**Sum of above**	**82.9**

a/ China is presented only among 'World', depending on data availability.
b/ In world total value added at constant 2005 prices.
c/ In total value added of developing and emerging industrial economies at constant 2005 prices.

Table 1.8

STRUCTURE OF MVA IN SELECTED COUNTRY GROUPS, SELECTED YEARS [a]
(Percentage)

ISIC Division	Year	Industrialized Economies — Europe — EU [b]	Industrialized Economies — Europe — Other	Industrialized Economies — East Asia	Industrialized Economies — West Asia	Industrialized Economies — North America	Industrialized Economies — Others	Industrialized Economies — All Economies	Developing & Emerging Industrial Economies — Emerging Industrial Economies [c]	Developing & Emerging Industrial Economies — Other Developing Economies	Developing & Emerging Industrial Economies — Least Developed Countries	Developing & Emerging Industrial Economies — All Economies
15 Food and beverages	2000	10.5	11.9	9.6	11.8	12.2	18.6	11.1	17.5	23.8	21.9	16.4
	2005	11.1	12.6	9.1	11.6	12.6	18.7	11.4	17.9	22.8	21.7	14.7
	2011	10.6	12.7	7.6	11.8	14.8	17.1	11.2	17.9	22.6	19.7	12.1
16 Tobacco products	2000	0.8	1.0	0.5	0.0	2.0	1.0	1.1	2.8	5.6	6.0	3.6
	2005	0.6	1.1	0.5	0.0	1.7	1.0	0.9	2.4	3.8	7.5	3.0
	2011	0.4	0.9	0.4	0.0	1.2	1.0	0.6	2.6	3.0	8.5	2.5
17 Textiles	2000	2.7	1.1	2.6	0.3	2.0	2.4	2.3	5.2	6.7	16.5	5.8
	2005	2.1	0.8	1.7	0.2	1.6	1.8	1.7	4.2	7.4	20.5	5.2
	2011	1.5	0.6	1.0	0.3	0.9	1.3	1.2	3.3	6.3	23.4	4.4
18 Wearing apparel, fur	2000	2.3	0.8	1.3	0.7	1.4	1.6	1.7	3.6	5.5	8.1	3.8
	2005	1.4	0.7	0.8	0.7	0.7	1.3	1.0	2.9	5.4	7.7	3.4
	2011	1.1	0.7	0.6	0.9	0.5	1.0	0.8	2.0	5.3	13.0	3.0
19 Leather, leather products and footwear	2000	1.2	0.2	0.4	0.3	0.3	0.5	0.6	1.7	4.4	2.5	2.0
	2005	0.8	0.2	0.3	0.3	0.2	0.4	0.4	1.3	1.6	3.1	1.4
	2011	0.6	0.3	0.2	0.3	0.1	0.3	0.2	1.1	1.5	2.8	1.3
20 Wood products (excl. furniture)	2000	2.1	3.0	1.3	1.7	2.2	4.0	2.0	1.9	2.2	1.4	1.7
	2005	2.1	3.0	1.0	1.7	2.3	3.9	2.0	1.7	1.7	1.1	1.4
	2011	1.9	2.6	0.6	1.9	1.5	3.2	1.5	1.2	1.0	1.6	1.1
21 Paper and paper products	2000	2.5	2.0	2.3	3.0	4.1	2.9	3.0	3.0	1.6	7.1	3.0
	2005	2.6	1.9	2.2	2.9	3.7	2.7	2.8	3.0	1.7	2.9	2.9
	2011	2.5	1.6	1.9	3.0	3.2	2.2	2.5	2.9	1.6	1.8	2.7
22 Printing and publishing	2000	6.2	5.2	3.4	3.3	3.4	9.0	4.6	2.7	1.3	1.6	2.1
	2005	6.0	4.4	3.0	3.3	2.9	9.1	4.2	2.6	1.6	1.4	1.8
	2011	5.2	3.6	2.8	3.4	2.3	7.2	3.7	2.5	1.5	1.1	1.2

a/ Percentage shares of individual divisions in total MVA at constant 2005 prices.
b/ Excluding non-industrialized EU economies.
c/ Including China.

Table 1.8
(continued)

STRUCTURE OF MVA IN SELECTED COUNTRY GROUPS, SELECTED YEARS a/
(Percentage)

ISIC Division	Year	Industrialized Economies — Europe EU b/	Industrialized Economies — Europe Other	East Asia	West Asia	North America	Others	All Economies	Developing & Emerging Industrial Economies — Emerging Industrial Economies c/	Other Developing Economies	Least Developed Countries	All Economies
23 Coke, refined petroleum products, nuclear fuel	2000	1.8	11.8	1.8	24.2	4.2	3.2	3.1	6.9	7.3	1.1	6.2
	2005	1.9	12.3	2.1	23.5	4.7	3.1	3.4	6.4	6.9	0.8	5.2
	2011	1.8	12.5	1.8	20.0	4.4	2.6	3.1	5.6	6.0	0.5	3.7
24 Chemicals and chemical products	2000	9.8	10.9	10.1	2.7	13.1	8.1	11.0	11.7	8.4	14.3	11.3
	2005	10.9	12.1	10.4	3.6	14.4	8.8	12.0	11.7	9.6	15.0	11.3
	2011	11.1	12.8	9.1	3.1	15.2	10.0	11.8	11.7	10.1	11.5	10.4
25 Rubber and plastics products	2000	4.7	2.2	5.4	0.2	4.6	3.8	4.7	3.8	2.2	1.9	3.5
	2005	4.7	2.2	5.2	0.2	4.4	3.8	4.6	4.1	2.6	1.7	3.5
	2011	4.5	3.0	4.5	0.2	4.0	3.6	4.3	3.9	2.7	1.1	3.0
26 Non-metallic mineral products	2000	4.6	3.5	3.9	13.2	3.2	4.6	4.0	5.4	6.2	4.1	5.5
	2005	4.5	4.0	3.3	13.4	3.2	5.1	3.8	5.4	7.7	5.0	5.3
	2011	4.0	3.5	2.7	14.4	2.7	6.1	3.3	5.1	9.3	5.1	4.5
27 Basic metals	2000	4.1	11.5	6.5	8.5	4.0	7.7	5.0	7.8	5.8	2.1	7.9
	2005	4.0	11.8	6.6	8.8	3.8	7.5	5.0	8.4	6.6	2.2	10.1
	2011	3.8	10.5	5.9	10.1	2.7	8.9	4.5	7.9	5.6	1.8	15.1
28 Fabricated metal products	2000	9.1	5.0	7.8	4.1	7.2	9.7	8.0	4.0	2.8	2.0	3.9
	2005	9.4	4.9	6.4	4.2	6.5	9.6	7.5	4.1	3.2	2.0	4.0
	2011	9.5	5.0	5.2	4.6	6.2	10.9	7.2	4.0	3.6	2.0	3.8
29 Machinery and equipment n.e.c.	2000	10.9	9.4	10.4	3.2	8.3	4.5	9.7	4.3	3.3	0.3	4.9
	2005	11.3	8.6	11.0	3.2	7.5	4.5	9.7	4.9	2.3	0.5	5.9
	2011	13.0	8.9	10.2	3.2	6.2	4.6	9.9	5.6	2.6	0.6	7.2
30 Office, accounting and computing machinery	2000	1.2	0.4	2.3	3.1	1.4	0.2	1.5	0.7	0.9	0.0	1.2
	2005	0.8	0.3	2.3	3.1	1.7	0.2	1.4	0.6	1.0	0.0	1.6
	2011	1.1	0.2	2.1	3.1	2.7	0.3	1.8	0.7	1.2	0.0	2.2

a/ Percentage shares of individual divisions in total MVA at constant 2005 prices.
b/ Excluding non-industrialized EU economies.
c/ Including China.

Table 1.8
(continued)

STRUCTURE OF MVA IN SELECTED COUNTRY GROUPS, SELECTED YEARS a/
(Percentage)

ISIC Division	Year	Industrialized Economies							Developing & Emerging Industrial Economies			
		Europe		East Asia	West Asia	North America	Others	All Economies	Emerging Industrial Economies c/	Other Developing Economies	Least Developed Countries	All Economies
		EU b/	Other									
31 Electrical machinery and apparatus	2000	4.8	2.8	3.5	3.2	3.7	1.5	4.0	2.6	2.2	2.5	2.8
	2005	4.7	2.7	3.8	3.2	2.9	1.7	3.8	2.8	2.4	1.8	3.4
	2011	5.0	3.4	4.2	3.2	2.8	1.7	4.0	3.5	2.1	0.6	4.3
32 Radio,television and communication equipment	2000	3.4	3.9	11.0	3.1	3.2	3.5	5.2	2.4	2.3	1.0	3.7
	2005	3.2	3.5	13.2	3.1	4.8	3.3	6.2	2.4	2.6	1.0	4.6
	2011	4.2	3.1	20.7	3.1	8.1	3.9	9.8	3.9	2.6	1.0	6.1
33 Medical, precision and optical instruments	2000	3.3	5.8	2.3	3.2	4.5	3.4	3.5	0.7	0.6	0.1	0.7
	2005	3.5	5.9	2.2	3.1	5.4	3.2	3.9	0.8	0.7	0.0	0.9
	2011	3.9	6.1	2.7	3.2	7.3	3.8	4.6	0.9	0.6	0.0	1.3
34 Motor vehicles, trailers, semi-trailers	2000	7.5	2.6	9.7	3.2	7.3	3.4	7.7	7.4	2.9	1.6	6.3
	2005	8.2	2.4	11.2	3.1	7.2	3.7	8.3	8.4	3.9	1.2	6.5
	2011	8.0	3.0	12.0	3.1	4.4	3.8	7.7	9.6	4.7	1.3	6.0
35 Other transport equipment	2000	2.9	2.8	1.3	3.2	4.1	2.8	2.9	1.5	1.0	2.0	1.4
	2005	3.0	2.4	1.8	3.1	4.1	2.9	3.0	1.8	1.3	1.5	1.7
	2011	3.5	3.0	2.0	3.2	5.1	3.1	3.5	2.1	1.9	1.5	2.0
36 Furniture; manufacturing n.e.c.	2000	3.6	2.2	2.6	3.8	3.6	3.6	3.3	2.4	3.0	1.9	2.3
	2005	3.2	2.2	1.9	3.7	3.7	3.7	3.0	2.2	3.2	1.4	2.2
	2011	2.8	2.0	1.8	3.9	3.7	3.4	2.8	2.0	4.2	1.1	2.1
D Total manufacturing	2000	100.0	100.0	100.0	100.0	100.0	100.0	100.0	100.0	100.0	100.0	100.0
	2005	100.0	100.0	100.0	100.0	100.0	100.0	100.0	100.0	100.0	100.0	100.0
	2011	100.0	100.0	100.0	100.0	100.0	100.0	100.0	100.0	100.0	100.0	100.0

a/ Percentage shares of individual divisions in total MVA at constant 2005 prices.
b/ Excluding non-industrialized EU economies.
c/ Including China.

Table 1.9

ANNUAL GROWTH OF VALUE ADDED OF DIVISIONS, SELECTED COUNTRY GROUPS, 2000-2005 AND 2005-2011 [a/]
(Percentage)

ISIC Division	Industrialized Economies		Developing & Emerging Industrial Economies						World	
			Emerging Industrial Economies [b/]		Other Developing Economies		Least Developed Countries			
	2000-2005	2005-2011	2000-2005	2005-2011	2000-2005	2005-2011	2000-2005	2005-2011	2000-2005	2005-2011
15 Food and beverages	1.3	0.7	3.8	3.5	0.9	3.8	5.0	3.5	2.6	3.3
16 Tobacco products	-3.2	-5.0	-0.3	5.4	-6.1	-0.6	10.3	7.1	0.3	3.2
17 Textiles	-4.6	-6.4	0.4	-1.0	4.6	0.5	9.2	8.5	0.0	2.1
18 Wearing apparel, fur	-9.1	-3.7	-0.1	-3.0	1.2	3.0	4.0	13.8	-2.9	3.9
19 Leather, leather products and footwear	-8.0	-5.6	-0.7	0.5	-18.8	4.1	7.5	3.9	-3.7	3.9
20 Wood products (excl. furniture)	0.7	-4.9	2.2	-1.8	-2.1	-4.9	-2.0	12.9	1.4	-2.1
21 Paper and paper products	0.1	-1.6	3.6	3.1	3.2	2.9	-13.3	-2.9	1.8	2.0
22 Printing and publishing	-0.8	-1.6	3.0	2.8	5.2	4.0	2.6	1.4	-0.3	-0.7
23 Coke,refined petroleum products,nuclear fuel	3.1	-0.7	2.1	1.2	-0.4	1.2	0.1	-1.4	3.7	1.6
24 Chemicals and chemical products	2.7	0.2	4.1	3.2	4.8	5.0	6.5	2.1	4.0	3.0
25 Rubber and plastics products	0.7	-0.9	5.3	2.9	5.8	4.3	2.7	0.5	2.0	1.5
26 Non-metallic mineral products	0.2	-2.1	4.1	1.8	6.5	7.5	9.1	6.4	2.3	2.0
27 Basic metals	1.2	-1.6	5.5	1.6	5.9	0.6	5.5	1.1	5.7	8.1
28 Fabricated metal products	-0.5	-0.5	3.9	2.4	4.0	6.3	5.6	6.0	0.6	1.6
29 Machinery and equipment n.e.c.	0.9	0.5	7.1	5.1	-3.9	7.0	15.3	10.6	2.6	3.7
30 Office, accounting and computing machinery	-0.2	3.7	6.9	3.5	4.8	7.6	-3.4	-2.2	2.9	8.0
31 Electrical machinery and apparatus	-0.3	1.4	5.6	8.1	4.5	2.6	-2.6	-13.2	2.0	5.7
32 Radio,television and communication equipment	5.6	8.2	4.6	11.6	4.5	3.9	6.5	5.3	7.1	9.9
33 Medical, precision and optical instruments	2.6	3.7	5.3	5.0	4.3	3.1	4.5	6.8	3.3	4.9
34 Motor vehicles, trailers, semi-trailers	2.7	-1.0	6.7	5.0	7.7	6.7	-1.0	10.6	4.0	1.8
35 Other transport equipment	1.0	2.9	7.7	7.0	6.4	11.0	-1.2	9.8	2.4	5.3
36 Furniture; manufacturing n.e.c.	-1.0	-1.0	2.5	2.0	3.3	8.4	-2.4	1.4	0.6	1.6

a/ At constant 2005 prices.
b/ Including China.

Table 1.9
(continued)

ANNUAL GROWTH OF VALUE ADDED OF DIVISIONS, SELECTED COUNTRY GROUPS, 2000-2005 AND 2005-2011 [a/]
(Percentage)

ISIC Division	All Economies		Developing & Emerging Industrial Economies							
			Africa		Asia and Pacific [b/]		Europe		Latin America	
	2000-2005	2005-2011	2000-2005	2005-2011	2000-2005	2005-2011	2000-2005	2005-2011	2000-2005	2005-2011
15 Food and beverages	5.9	8.3	-2.7	2.4	12.9	13.6	4.4	3.7	2.2	3.0
16 Tobacco products	4.4	8.8	-3.4	2.8	6.9	11.4	0.0	-3.1	-1.3	0.0
17 Textiles	6.7	8.2	-3.5	-2.6	10.8	11.7	0.4	-4.7	0.6	-1.9
18 Wearing apparel, fur	5.9	8.9	-0.5	-0.7	12.9	13.7	-1.7	-4.7	-1.0	0.9
19 Leather, leather products and footwear	1.3	9.9	-2.1	-0.3	4.8	13.7	-2.5	-0.5	-3.7	2.2
20 Wood products (excl. furniture)	4.9	7.0	-1.1	-6.2	8.9	12.8	1.8	4.1	3.7	-4.2
21 Paper and paper products	8.0	10.1	2.9	2.1	11.9	13.4	6.5	3.5	2.4	3.5
22 Printing and publishing	4.7	5.3	2.8	-1.3	8.6	9.9	5.6	3.8	1.3	1.9
23 Coke,refined petroleum products,nuclear fuel	4.7	5.6	0.6	2.4	9.3	9.4	0.5	-0.4	1.1	0.6
24 Chemicals and chemical products	8.9	10.2	4.6	2.8	14.2	13.8	7.1	3.7	1.5	2.0
25 Rubber and plastics products	8.9	8.9	3.4	2.8	12.9	12.4	10.7	4.9	1.7	1.9
26 Non-metallic mineral products	8.2	8.8	4.6	2.6	13.1	13.1	4.7	1.7	2.0	1.2
27 Basic metals	15.3	17.4	2.1	-3.1	23.1	22.6	6.1	-0.3	4.7	-1.4
28 Fabricated metal products	8.6	10.5	1.5	0.4	14.2	15.0	6.0	3.7	1.1	2.5
29 Machinery and equipment n.e.c.	13.7	15.1	2.2	0.4	20.9	19.2	10.2	6.5	0.9	2.1
30 Office, accounting and computing machinery	17.0	17.1	3.3	-2.8	21.2	18.8	2.8	2.6	1.6	2.7
31 Electrical machinery and apparatus	13.0	16.1	0.6	3.7	19.2	19.6	4.7	4.1	0.9	1.6
32 Radio,television and communication equipment	14.6	15.9	-1.2	5.1	16.1	16.9	10.2	9.5	1.5	-3.2
33 Medical, precision and optical instruments	14.8	15.4	4.7	1.4	21.7	18.1	5.3	8.7	1.6	4.7
34 Motor vehicles, trailers, semi-trailers	10.1	10.3	2.9	-0.9	18.0	15.3	18.1	5.3	1.1	3.5
35 Other transport equipment	12.6	15.2	0.0	1.2	18.0	18.0	0.8	5.5	10.6	10.5
36 Furniture; manufacturing n.e.c.	9.0	9.9	0.3	3.4	17.6	13.7	2.7	4.1	1.5	4.2

a/ At constant 2005 prices.
b/ Including China.

Table 1.10

SHARE OF FEMALES IN TOTAL EMPLOYMENT BY DIVISION, SELECTED YEARS
(Percentage)

ISIC Division	Azerbaijan 2006	Azerbaijan 2010	Bulgaria 2006	Bulgaria 2010	Croatia 2006	Croatia 2010	Cyprus 2006	Cyprus 2010	Ethiopia 2006	Ethiopia 2009
15 Food and beverages	32.1	26.1	50.4	50.1	42.6	43.9	46.3	48.4	18.8	25.2
16 Tobacco products	15.8	16.4	48.4	56.1	42.9	37.9	...	53.8	43.7	39.6
17 Textiles	50.2	27.0	69.8	71.4	74.0	75.6	58.8	62.7	47.2	49.8
18 Wearing apparel, fur	61.4	37.6	88.6	89.4	87.1	86.8	86.5	94.1	62.4	66.7
19 Leather, leather products and footwear	51.1	36.0	...	81.3	80.0	79.9	56.7	57.5	27.6	33.4
20 Wood products (excl. furniture)	14.0	16.9	27.2	25.7	29.0	29.6	9.2	10.2	12.5	16.1
21 Paper and paper products	34.6	32.0	45.7	47.1	31.1	29.2	42.6	42.7	29.5	34.2
22 Printing and publishing	29.5	29.9	54.0	46.1	48.8	42.3	47.1	38.4	43.8	42.4
23 Coke,refined petroleum products,nuclear fuel	36.4	31.9	...	23.9	31.2	32.0	16.9	...	...	...
24 Chemicals and chemical products	37.2	38.5	47.2	48.1	39.5	40.5	52.8	50.3	33.9	35.7
25 Rubber and plastics products	15.6	13.7	37.9	40.4	29.0	29.8	29.1	28.1	36.8	35.5
26 Non-metallic mineral products	18.1	10.5	25.3	26.8	20.4	21.0	13.4	13.8	16.4	16.3
27 Basic metals	19.9	6.1	23.1	22.9	17.2	16.8	15.4	19.9	12.3	15.4
28 Fabricated metal products	17.4	11.6	24.2	21.7	13.7	11.4	14.2	13.1	34.0	18.4
29 Machinery and equipment n.e.c.	25.7	12.4	27.4	32.0	15.5	15.5	17.2	22.9	9.4	15.9
30 Office, accounting and computing machinery	31.8	24.8	51.3	47.6	27.0	21.5	...	...	...	...
31 Electrical machinery and apparatus	26.4	19.3	47.8	49.1	32.1	33.8	26.9	...	30.4	25.0
32 Radio,television and communication equipment	33.5	30.8	54.1	59.6	45.6	43.9	43.5	...	...	...
33 Medical, precision and optical instruments	22.8	37.1	48.1	52.6	42.6	49.8	56.5	...	...	...
34 Motor vehicles, trailers, semi-trailers	11.9	4.3	22.7	69.3	35.4	24.7	34.1	10.2	11.4	16.8
35 Other transport equipment	12.8	15.9	17.7	22.0	9.9	10.4	16.3	26.3	...	26.7
36 Furniture; manufacturing n.e.c.	15.2	11.3	33.3	36.7	32.3	34.6	33.3	32.9	12.4	14.4
37 Recycling	15.4	...	22.9	...	23.9	...	13.3	...	...	...
D Total manufacturing	29.2	21.0	51.5	51.0	37.6	35.8	35.9	35.1	29.5	30.9

Table 1.10

SHARE OF FEMALES IN TOTAL EMPLOYMENT BY DIVISION, SELECTED YEARS
(Percentage)

ISIC Division	Georgia		India		Indonesia		Iran (Islamic Republic of)		Japan	
	2006	2010	2006	2008	2006	2009	2006	2009	2006	2007
15 Food and beverages	37.9	38.5	17.2	17.7	41.8	38.5	13.3	15.6	56.5	56.6
16 Tobacco products	27.4	24.1	18.6	14.3	81.2	81.4	7.5	6.3	20.1	19.8
17 Textiles	48.5	40.5	15.5	17.2	56.0	55.4	13.7	13.9	56.7	56.8
18 Wearing apparel, fur	85.4	84.6	44.7	41.2	79.3	78.8	43.9	52.8	82.5	82.1
19 Leather, leather products and footwear	26.1	37.0	22.6	24.3	68.7	67.1	8.4	9.1	48.9	49.1
20 Wood products (excl. furniture)	11.2	16.5	5.5	6.1	37.4	35.2	2.4	3.6	25.6	25.0
21 Paper and paper products	32.3	38.3	6.8	6.2	21.6	21.3	13.4	16.3	30.5	30.7
22 Printing and publishing	55.4	58.3	4.4	5.0	30.0	28.5	9.5	14.0	30.4	30.4
23 Coke,refined petroleum products,nuclear fuel	...	...	1.2	1.5	9.6	9.8	4.0	4.2	10.4	10.6
24 Chemicals and chemical products	44.2	43.9	9.8	9.2	33.6	34.2	13.1	11.6	26.1	26.1
25 Rubber and plastics products	22.9	23.7	4.9	5.1	38.8	38.5	9.7	12.7	35.4	35.1
26 Non-metallic mineral products	15.8	13.6	3.5	3.5	24.2	23.7	6.9	6.2	21.8	21.5
27 Basic metals	14.7	14.2	0.8	0.9	8.1	8.4	2.9	3.9	11.2	11.2
28 Fabricated metal products	14.9	10.8	1.3	1.4	22.6	22.3	5.5	5.7	24.4	24.1
29 Machinery and equipment n.e.c.	14.9	14.5	1.2	1.1	30.8	23.3	6.3	7.0	19.6	19.4
30 Office, accounting and computing machinery	0.0	...	8.2	9.4	29.9	71.5	29.7	24.2	...	...
31 Electrical machinery and apparatus	26.9	10.2	5.6	5.0	46.6	46.2	13.4	20.1	34.1	33.5
32 Radio,television and communication equipment	...	...	12.4	11.6	67.0	70.7	17.4	22.7	32.5	31.6
33 Medical, precision and optical instruments	43.3	37.1	13.7	12.8	48.3	58.2	22.7	21.9	33.1	32.9
34 Motor vehicles, trailers, semi-trailers	24.0	...	2.1	2.5	13.1	12.4	5.2	5.5	16.0	16.0
35 Other transport equipment	22.0	20.5	0.6	0.7	13.5	12.6	5.3	4.2	11.8	11.6
36 Furniture; manufacturing n.e.c.	21.5	24.0	12.3	11.2	42.6	45.5	8.2	9.3	33.6	33.7
37 Recycling	...	...	18.7	...	45.3	40.3	18.9	27.3	16.5	16.3
D Total manufacturing	32.6	32.6	11.5	10.9	48.6	47.4	9.4	10.2	31.9	31.6

Table 1.10

SHARE OF FEMALES IN TOTAL EMPLOYMENT BY DIVISION, SELECTED YEARS
(Percentage)

ISIC Division	Jordan		Kuwait		Kyrgyzstan		Lithuania		Malaysia	
	2006	2010	2006	2010	2006	2010	2006	2010	2006	2010
15 Food and beverages	7.4	7.9	6.1	6.0	38.1	39.7	58.6	56.9	32.3	32.6
16 Tobacco products	12.2	17.8	...	...	41.3	38.2	27.5	19.1	50.3	32.4
17 Textiles	23.2	20.9	1.3	0.6	39.7	67.6	72.3	69.3	42.8	35.7
18 Wearing apparel, fur	47.2	32.6	8.9	9.0	40.5	66.8	89.4	81.1	70.1	60.6
19 Leather, leather products and footwear	7.0	1.4	2.2	1.8	46.3	32.5	65.3	62.1	54.5	40.1
20 Wood products (excl. furniture)	0.3	1.1	0.3	0.4	3.5	5.1	24.2	27.0	31.2	26.6
21 Paper and paper products	11.1	11.9	1.8	2.3	30.9	24.4	44.6	45.5	29.3	28.3
22 Printing and publishing	12.9	11.6	5.2	6.0	28.4	21.6	58.2	44.7	36.3	32.8
23 Coke,refined petroleum products,nuclear fuel	2.2	2.1	2.5	2.6	38.9	25.1	27.3	24.4	13.1	16.5
24 Chemicals and chemical products	17.3	21.5	4.8	4.0	27.2	31.3	40.1	36.6	27.2	27.2
25 Rubber and plastics products	5.8	7.6	1.0	1.9	36.3	22.5	30.6	34.9	40.8	33.3
26 Non-metallic mineral products	1.6	1.5	1.1	2.8	26.0	18.5	25.9	26.6	19.1	18.5
27 Basic metals	1.3	2.1	1.8	2.1	9.5	9.8	22.8	22.8	15.1	18.0
28 Fabricated metal products	1.1	2.4	0.8	0.9	28.1	30.5	18.9	20.0	25.9	22.5
29 Machinery and equipment n.e.c.	3.6	3.5	0.5	0.7	31.8	35.2	27.5	37.3	26.5	28.1
30 Office, accounting and computing machinery	...	...	...	...	...	...	26.6	42.5	58.5	50.2
31 Electrical machinery and apparatus	8.7	6.0	1.6	1.7	47.3	44.3	66.7	52.7	56.7	41.4
32 Radio,television and communication equipment	0.0	0.0	...	...	40.6	45.6	53.6	49.0	67.1	58.9
33 Medical, precision and optical instruments	15.0	18.8	1.2	0.5	27.0	21.2	51.4	55.1	70.2	66.1
34 Motor vehicles, trailers, semi-trailers	6.0	5.3	1.4	1.6	37.6	36.8	13.5	45.2	17.5	23.0
35 Other transport equipment	3.3	5.2	1.8	1.4	0.0	18.8	19.6	31.6	18.5	16.2
36 Furniture; manufacturing n.e.c.	4.5	3.6	0.4	0.3	33.3	43.3	39.3	46.1	25.7	24.5
37 Recycling	...	...	...	...	0.0	0.0	19.7	...	17.7	...
D Total manufacturing	12.3	12.4	3.4	3.7	35.9	34.3	48.0	46.6	41.3	34.9

Table 1.10

SHARE OF FEMALES IN TOTAL EMPLOYMENT BY DIVISION, SELECTED YEARS
(Percentage)

ISIC Division	Morocco		Philippines		Sri Lanka		Turkey		Viet Nam	
	2007	2010	2006	2008	2006	2010	2006	2008	2006	2010
15 Food and beverages	33.6	40.7	36.2	37.9	42.0	40.7	21.9	22.7	56.0	52.2
16 Tobacco products	7.0	7.1	35.1	37.9	64.4	67.2	32.0	24.9	48.3	42.0
17 Textiles	47.8	46.6	55.5	50.5	58.6	47.9	30.9	28.9	69.3	61.4
18 Wearing apparel, fur	83.1	80.2	73.3	73.3	77.2	75.1	49.0	46.8	83.1	81.6
19 Leather, leather products and footwear	45.7	44.7	54.2	50.3	60.0	47.4	18.8	18.3	83.1	78.4
20 Wood products (excl. furniture)	6.5	6.5	21.7	20.3	32.0	26.2	4.5	7.2	50.7	42.6
21 Paper and paper products	18.0	17.8	24.9	27.1	9.1	26.9	17.9	17.1	37.3	39.4
22 Printing and publishing	19.6	23.0	37.3	35.7	30.0	19.8	26.9	22.1	42.4	43.4
23 Coke,refined petroleum products,nuclear fuel	5.7	7.6	25.7	22.9	14.9	…	38.5	11.7	…	20.4
24 Chemicals and chemical products	23.6	24.9	33.9	33.6	28.6	32.7	14.9	15.1	39.5	39.3
25 Rubber and plastics products	26.9	24.7	37.9	37.5	37.2	32.6	14.5	14.3	45.7	48.0
26 Non-metallic mineral products	9.1	8.1	22.5	16.0	30.2	19.3	11.2	9.9	31.6	32.1
27 Basic metals	7.2	6.5	16.8	14.9	5.1	10.1	6.7	6.0	20.5	20.4
28 Fabricated metal products	9.6	8.0	30.9	31.5	48.1	19.5	11.1	9.7	25.8	27.8
29 Machinery and equipment n.e.c.	19.7	16.7	44.7	51.2	5.5	10.1	11.9	15.1	22.5	27.4
30 Office, accounting and computing machinery	31.2	40.3	80.3	72.4	88.7	65.8	30.0	18.7	78.3	0.0
31 Electrical machinery and apparatus	53.1	57.9	58.6	50.8	25.7	29.0	26.1	25.0	67.0	52.7
32 Radio,television and communication equipment	65.1	62.1	73.3	72.1	74.4	62.7	29.7	28.8	60.6	78.8
33 Medical, precision and optical instruments	29.2	30.3	69.0	72.5	20.0	…	…	32.5	64.5	70.4
34 Motor vehicles, trailers, semi-trailers	13.1	9.0	37.2	56.9	16.0	6.9	8.9	9.2	36.2	42.5
35 Other transport equipment	23.1	36.1	11.2	13.8	37.8	37.4	6.9	5.3	21.0	25.1
36 Furniture; manufacturing n.e.c.	29.1	18.8	38.8	38.0	43.6	41.1	16.2	12.0	50.7	51.2
37 Recycling	44.0	4.0	17.3	…	30.0	21.6	17.2	16.5	37.2	43.8
D Total manufacturing	47.7	44.2	51.6	49.4	52.2	55.0	23.1	21.2	59.2	57.7

Table 1.11

SELECTED CHARACTERISTICS OF BRANCHES, SELECTED YEARS AND ECONOMIES

Processed meat,fish,fruit,vegetables,fats (ISIC 151)

Economy	Latest year (LY)	Value added per employee (current 1000 dollars) 2000	Value added per employee (current 1000 dollars) LY	Wages and salaries per employee (current 1000 dollars) 2000	Wages and salaries per employee (current 1000 dollars) LY	Percentage in output a/ — Costs of input materials and utilities 2000	2006	LY	Costs of labour 2000	2006	LY	Operating surplus 2000	2006	LY
Industrialized Economies														
EU														
Austria	2009	43.4	71.3	20.6	37.3	72.8	...	76.9	12.9	...	12.1	14.3	...	11.0
Belgium	2009	49.7	99.3	22.5	44.7	83.1	83.9	85.5	7.7	7.4	6.5	9.3	8.7	7.9
Denmark	2009	...	106.1	...	68.7	...	79.7	78.2	...	12.9	14.1	...	7.4	7.7
Estonia	2010	5.6	20.6	2.8	9.8	76.5	...	77.9	11.7	...	10.5	11.8	...	11.6
Finland	2009	39.3	76.3	22.6	38.2	75.0	76.0	74.5	14.3	13.5	12.8	10.6	10.5	12.8
Germany	2009	27.6	59.6	16.3	30.7	79.1	82.3	83.2	12.3	9.3	8.6	8.6	8.4	8.1
Hungary	2009	8.9	21.2	3.6	10.0	81.2	...	80.2	7.6	...	9.4	11.1	...	10.4
Ireland	2009	35.0	66.7	17.7	38.7	82.4	...	84.4	8.9	...	9.1	8.7	...	6.5
Italy	2009	42.3	67.5	17.1	33.4	84.5	...	87.4	6.3	...	6.2	9.2	...	6.4
Lithuania	2010	3.4	11.8	1.8	6.0	83.7	85.2	85.0	8.5	8.1	7.6	7.8	6.7	7.4
Malta	2008	35.9	61.5	10.4	19.3	65.0	68.0	64.2	10.1	11.0	11.2	24.9	21.0	24.6
Portugal	2009	...	33.6	7.8	15.7	...	82.5	82.1	7.8	8.2	8.4	...	9.3	9.5
Slovenia	2010	15.5	31.7	11.5	21.1	80.0	81.3	79.2	14.9	14.3	13.8	5.1	4.4	6.9
Spain	2009	28.7	62.7	13.7	29.3	82.5	82.1	82.1	8.3	8.1	8.3	9.1	9.8	9.6
Sweden	2009	46.4	71.5	24.4	37.5	75.6	79.6	79.5	12.8	11.3	10.7	11.6	9.1	9.7
United Kingdom	2009	...	79.1	...	39.6	...	75.9	76.4	...	14.3	11.8	...	9.9	11.8
Other Europe														
Norway	2008	48.1	110.6	28.2	61.1	78.7	81.6	80.3	12.5	11.8	10.9	8.8	6.5	8.8
Russian Federation	2009	...	25.1	0.8	5.7	...	68.8	71.9	8.4	5.6	6.4	...	25.7	21.7
East Asia														
Japan	2010	67.6	73.8	16.4	19.1	68.2	68.5	68.7	7.7	7.4	8.1	24.1	24.1	23.2
Malaysia	2010	18.3	41.6	4.1	6.2	87.5	91.3	90.2	2.8	1.8	1.5	9.7	6.9	8.3
Republic of Korea	2008	40.9	63.2	10.5	16.6	65.3	69.4	70.8	8.9	8.7	7.7	25.7	21.9	21.5
Singapore	2010	27.3	41.2	15.3	22.4	80.8	80.0	80.3	10.7	9.6	10.7	8.4	10.4	9.0
West Asia														
Kuwait	2010	...	22.8	...	10.8	...	74.8	70.3	...	13.9	14.0	...	11.4	15.7

a/ At current prices.

Table 1.11
(continued)

SELECTED CHARACTERISTICS OF BRANCHES, SELECTED YEARS AND ECONOMIES

Processed meat,fish,fruit,vegetables,fats (ISIC 151)

Economy	Latest year (LY)	Value added per employee (current 1000 dollars)		Wages and salaries per employee (current 1000 dollars)		Percentage in output [a]								
						Costs of input materials and utilities			Costs of labour			Operating surplus		
		2000	LY	2000	LY	2000	2006	LY	2000	2006	LY	2000	2006	LY
North America														
Canada	2009	46.9	91.1	17.4	33.2	72.8	...	66.4	10.1	...	12.3	17.1	...	21.4
United States of America	2008	92.4	128.3	25.2	32.0	66.4	64.0	69.4	9.2	8.3	7.6	24.4	27.7	23.0
Others														
Israel	2009	35.3	50.0	23.9	29.6	78.3	81.9	81.4	14.7	12.8	11.0	7.1	5.3	7.6
Developing & EIE														
Albania	2010	2.6	8.4	0.7	2.4	76.6	78.7	76.7	6.1	6.8	6.8	17.3	14.5	16.5
Azerbaijan	2010	...	31.1	0.2	4.7	...	87.5	84.3	3.2	0.9	2.4	...	11.6	13.3
Brazil	2010	18.0	43.0	4.1	9.0	74.2	69.3	70.7	5.9	6.0	6.2	19.9	24.7	23.2
Bulgaria	2010	1.9	10.6	0.9	3.7	87.8	86.2	83.5	5.8	4.1	5.7	6.4	9.7	10.8
Chile	2008	31.2	41.1	6.8	9.4	54.1	58.5	65.3	9.9	8.2	7.9	36.0	33.2	26.8
China	2007	...	20.7	...	2.3	...	73.4	73.6	...	2.8	2.9	...	23.8	23.5
Cyprus	2010	24.5	50.1	12.0	25.2	81.8	81.5	81.2	9.0	8.5	9.5	9.3	10.0	9.3
Egypt	2010	...	10.0	...	2.9	...	67.8	79.2	...	5.5	6.0	...	26.7	14.8
Eritrea	2010	2.4	4.1	0.6	1.0	70.3	...	48.6	7.0	...	12.5	22.8	...	38.8
Ethiopia	2009	3.5	3.5	0.7	0.8	58.1	66.7	65.5	7.8	11.1	8.3	34.1	22.2	26.1
Georgia	2010	3.4	6.7	0.2	2.4	71.0	88.6	80.5	1.7	5.6	7.1	27.3	5.9	12.4
Greece	2007	...	58.8	...	25.3	...	71.9	72.7	...	12.3	11.8	...	15.7	15.5
India	2009	4.1	8.3	0.8	1.5	92.7	92.3	93.1	1.4	1.1	1.3	5.9	6.6	5.6
Indonesia	2009	7.1	27.1	0.8	1.8	74.1	71.9	72.2	3.0	2.8	1.9	22.9	25.2	25.9
Iran (Islamic Republic of)	2009	38.6	23.4	9.1	5.9	72.0	73.5	78.3	6.6	6.7	5.5	21.4	19.7	16.2
Jordan	2010	9.7	37.2	3.5	6.1	79.1	75.1	74.2	7.6	3.9	4.2	13.3	21.0	21.5
Kyrgyzstan	2010	...	15.5	0.2	1.3	...	75.8	43.9	3.1	4.9	4.8	...	19.3	51.4
Latvia	2009	5.5	12.6	2.2	5.2	70.5	77.2	76.9	11.8	9.1	9.6	17.8	13.7	13.5
Malawi	2008	1.5	9.6	0.8	2.1	...	77.6	76.4	21.7	4.4	5.1	...	18.0	18.5
Mongolia	2010	8.5	3.2	0.5	1.3	81.6	86.4	79.6	6.9	6.1	7.9	11.5	7.5	12.5
Morocco	2010	...	12.1	3.4	5.0	73.1	80.8	78.8	10.9	...	8.8	16.0	...	12.4
Oman	2008	20.6	35.2	6.0	10.6	67.1	75.3	72.8	9.6	8.4	8.2	23.3	16.3	18.9
Philippines	2009	...	13.8	...	3.4	...	82.4	79.8	...	5.8	5.0	...	11.8	15.1
Poland	2010	...	18.9	...	9.1	...	83.1	83.6	...	7.8	7.9	...	9.1	8.5
Romania	2010	...	14.7	...	5.9	64.2	86.2	83.2	...	7.0	6.7	...	6.9	10.1
The f. Yugosl. Rep of Macedonia	2009	30.8	14.1	5.7	6.9	69.0	76.6	76.1	5.8	16.0	11.7	25.2	7.4	12.2
Turkey	2010	...	14.4	...	5.4	...	89.5	92.8	...	4.7	2.7	...	5.8	4.5
United Republic of Tanzania	2010	...	19.5	...	1.4	...	77.1	76.4	...	4.6	1.7	...	18.3	21.9
Uruguay	2007	15.1	17.6	8.1	6.6	82.4	...	82.4	9.4	...	6.6	8.2	...	11.0

a/ At current prices.

Table 1.11

SELECTED CHARACTERISTICS OF BRANCHES, SELECTED YEARS AND ECONOMIES

Dairy products (ISIC 1520)

Economy	Latest year (LY)	Value added per employee (current 1000 dollars)		Wages and salaries per employee (current 1000 dollars)		Percentage in output [a]								
						Costs of input materials and utilities			Costs of labour			Operating surplus		
		2000	LY	2000	LY	2000	2006	LY	2000	2006	LY	2000	2006	LY
Industrialized Economies														
EU														
Austria	2009	51.7	108.5	28.2	51.5	84.7	81.6	81.5	8.4	8.3	8.8	6.9	10.1	9.7
Belgium	2009	46.9	119.9	26.9	51.4	88.2	86.2	82.5	6.8	6.6	7.5	5.0	7.2	10.0
Czech Republic	2007	9.1	29.0	3.6	11.3	87.2	89.2	87.4	5.0	5.1	4.9	7.8	5.6	7.7
Estonia	2010	6.9	28.5	3.6	12.3	84.5	83.6	84.0	8.1	7.1	6.9	7.4	9.2	9.1
Finland	2008	40.6	85.6	24.4	50.3	85.8	84.0	84.7	8.5	8.8	9.0	5.7	7.1	6.3
France	2009	42.9	80.7	21.5	40.9	86.1	86.0	85.5	7.0	7.1	7.3	6.9	6.9	7.1
Germany	2009	60.0	96.9	29.2	50.9	85.8	86.9	87.7	6.9	6.4	6.5	7.3	6.8	5.8
Hungary	2009	12.0	30.1	4.1	12.7	83.5	82.4	80.1	5.6	8.1	8.4	10.9	9.4	11.5
Ireland	2009	75.8	89.0	26.1	59.0	78.8	79.8	88.6	7.3	7.8	7.6	13.9	12.4	3.9
Italy	2009	49.6	102.7	20.1	37.8	81.3	82.4	81.6	7.6	7.3	6.8	11.1	10.2	11.6
Lithuania	2010	5.0	22.6	2.9	9.0	81.1	77.5	83.7	11.1	7.7	6.4	7.9	14.8	9.8
Malta	2008	20.2	25.4	10.5	17.7	81.3	79.0	87.8	9.7	10.4	8.6	9.0	10.6	3.7
Netherlands	2008	66.2	120.4	31.7	62.2	86.5	87.1	89.5	6.5	6.3	5.4	7.1	6.6	5.1
Portugal	2009	26.4	57.7	9.7	21.2	83.5	81.5	80.6	6.0	6.6	7.1	10.5	12.0	12.3
Slovakia	2009	4.1	27.7	2.3	12.6	90.4	91.1	84.2	5.3	5.3	7.2	4.3	3.6	8.6
Slovenia	2010	17.1	50.1	14.1	25.6	88.5	...	82.7	9.5	...	8.8	2.0	...	8.5
Spain	2009	47.2	101.1	19.3	40.2	80.3	80.3	78.8	8.1	7.6	8.4	11.6	12.1	12.8
Sweden	2009	33.1	85.3	27.2	41.9	87.1	78.4	79.9	10.6	9.6	9.9	2.3	12.1	10.2
United Kingdom	2009	53.5	73.7	26.6	35.1	78.3	79.5	79.5	10.8	10.4	9.8	10.9	10.1	10.7
Other Europe														
Norway	2008	56.3	105.0	32.8	67.4	77.8	79.6	77.4	13.0	14.6	14.5	9.3	5.8	8.1
Russian Federation	2010	...	19.0	0.8	6.3	...	79.2	80.4	5.6	7.3	6.5	...	13.6	13.0
East Asia														
Japan	2010	158.5	213.7	35.9	40.3	68.7	70.6	69.6	7.1	6.1	5.7	24.2	23.3	24.7
Malaysia	2010	33.4	23.4	7.5	9.8	73.2	80.8	84.0	6.1	6.0	6.7	20.8	13.2	9.3
Republic of Korea	2008	137.6	234.0	16.6	29.3	60.0	56.9	58.8	4.8	5.4	5.2	35.2	37.7	36.1
West Asia														
Kuwait	2010	...	36.9	...	17.1	...	66.1	66.0	...	12.9	15.8	...	21.0	18.2

a/ At current prices.

Table 1.11
(continued)

SELECTED CHARACTERISTICS OF BRANCHES, SELECTED YEARS AND ECONOMIES

Dairy products (ISIC 1520)

| Economy | Latest year (LY) | Value added per employee (current 1000 dollars) | | Wages and salaries per employee (current 1000 dollars) | | Percentage in output [a] | | | | | | | | |
| | | | | | | Costs of input materials and utilities | | | Costs of labour | | | Operating surplus | | |
		2000	LY	2000	LY	2000	2006	LY	2000	2006	LY	2000	2006	LY
North America														
Canada	2009	92.8	139.7	24.3	39.9	73.6	80.0	72.5	6.9	7.7	7.9	19.4	12.3	19.7
United States of America	2008	152.0	204.6	34.7	44.6	67.0	67.8	72.4	7.5	7.0	6.0	25.5	25.2	21.6
Others														
Israel	2009	55.1	82.4	31.3	38.2	69.9	70.9	71.7	17.1	15.9	13.1	13.0	13.2	15.2
Developing & EIE														
Albania	2010	8.1	10.3	0.9	2.5	65.3	75.6	73.1	4.1	3.5	6.5	30.6	20.8	20.4
Azerbaijan	2010	...	111.8	0.1	2.3	...	87.5	63.0	0.0	0.2	0.8	...	12.3	36.2
Brazil	2010	29.5	72.6	5.3	9.7	63.2	66.1	62.5	6.6	7.6	5.0	30.2	26.3	32.5
Bulgaria	2010	2.4	10.8	1.0	4.6	84.1	81.5	81.2	6.4	5.8	7.9	9.5	12.7	10.8
Chile	2008	49.4	54.6	8.9	12.1	60.0	62.8	71.5	7.2	7.0	6.3	32.8	30.2	22.2
China	2007	...	23.1	...	2.8	...	70.3	70.8	...	3.6	3.6	...	26.1	25.7
Cyprus	2010	27.2	49.0	13.4	29.0	71.8	68.6	72.8	13.9	17.7	16.1	14.4	13.7	11.1
Ecuador	2008	14.7	29.1	2.6	7.0	74.3	80.7	76.8	4.5	5.4	5.6	21.2	13.9	17.6
Egypt	2010	...	21.8	...	3.7	...	78.2	70.0	...	3.0	5.0	...	18.8	25.0
Eritrea	2010	1.3	5.0	0.8	1.6	68.9	80.8	78.7	17.8	5.2	6.9	13.3	14.0	14.4
Ethiopia	2009	3.2	7.8	0.4	1.3	53.1	56.0	66.7	6.4	5.2	5.6	40.6	38.8	27.7
Georgia	2010	...	7.8	...	4.0	...	74.0	75.7	...	12.0	12.4	...	14.0	11.9
Greece	2007	...	63.6	...	29.0	...	73.4	75.4	...	10.8	11.2	...	15.8	13.4
India	2009	6.6	9.4	1.8	3.1	87.1	92.2	90.4	3.6	3.2	3.2	9.3	4.6	6.4
Indonesia	2009	...	23.4	...	3.0	...	70.4	88.0	...	2.4	1.5	...	27.2	10.5
Iran (Islamic Republic of)	2009	37.7	19.5	10.8	7.2	81.6	77.2	81.1	5.3	6.0	7.0	13.2	16.9	11.9
Jordan	2010	8.1	20.4	3.0	4.6	75.5	79.2	66.8	9.0	7.2	7.4	15.6	13.6	25.8
Kyrgyzstan	2010	...	10.1	0.4	2.2	...	64.8	70.8	7.2	7.4	6.3	...	27.7	22.9
Latvia	2010	8.4	22.7	3.2	9.6	70.6	81.1	81.9	11.0	7.6	7.6	18.4	11.3	10.4
Mongolia	2008	...	3.0	0.4	0.9	...	73.1	82.3	13.1	11.9	5.5	...	15.0	12.2
Morocco	2010	17.3	34.8	6.6	13.6	75.6	74.8	74.5	9.3	4.1	9.9	15.0	15.2	15.5
Oman	2010	27.9	40.3	6.4	6.9	71.4	80.7	79.0	6.6	3.7	3.6	22.0	23.6	17.4
Philippines	2008	...	112.6	...	13.3	...	72.6	72.2	...	6.9	3.3	...	9.5	24.5
Poland	2009	8.0	29.6	...	11.4	84.3	83.6	80.9	...	8.9	7.3	...	8.9	11.7
Romania	2010	...	15.8	...	6.0	68.8	82.2	79.9	...	15.6	7.6	...	10.5	12.5
The f. Yugosl. Rep of Macedonia	2010	...	22.8	...	9.2	...	73.9	73.7	...	4.4	10.6	...	36.8	15.7
United Republic of Tanzania	2007	...	8.7	...	0.9	...	58.8	58.8	...	...	4.3	...	...	36.9
Uruguay	2007	26.4	24.9	16.7	11.1	74.7	...	80.3	16.1	...	8.7	9.3	...	10.9

a/ At current prices.

Table 1.11

SELECTED CHARACTERISTICS OF BRANCHES, SELECTED YEARS AND ECONOMIES

Grain mill products; starches; animal feeds (ISIC 153)

Economy	Latest year (LY)	Value added per employee (current 1000 dollars)		Wages and salaries per employee (current 1000 dollars)		Percentage in output a/								
						Costs of input materials and utilities			Costs of labour			Operating surplus		
		2000	LY	2000	LY	2000	2006	LY	2000	2006	LY	2000	2006	LY
Industrialized Economies														
EU														
Austria	2009	49.2	118.0	24.6	49.3	74.2	72.1	77.3	12.9	10.5	9.5	12.9	17.4	13.2
Belgium	2009	75.5	155.6	31.8	58.1	85.9	87.8	89.7	5.9	5.5	3.9	8.1	6.7	6.5
Czech Republic	2007	11.3	33.3	4.1	12.8	81.6	80.5	81.8	6.7	7.5	7.0	11.7	12.0	11.2
Denmark	2009	53.2	110.3	32.5	72.6	86.3	81.7	83.4	8.3	11.3	10.9	5.3	7.0	5.7
Estonia	2010	6.5	33.7	2.6	11.2	70.3	...	83.0	12.1	...	5.7	17.6	...	11.4
Finland	2009	57.2	107.7	26.1	52.2	83.7	...	82.6	7.5	...	8.4	8.9	...	9.0
France	2009	55.4	109.4	24.2	49.1	82.1	81.7	83.2	7.8	8.5	7.5	10.1	9.8	9.3
Germany	2009	66.9	112.1	28.7	52.3	77.0	78.6	80.5	9.9	9.4	9.1	13.1	12.0	10.4
Hungary	2009	14.7	50.6	4.0	14.1	77.5	76.6	78.4	6.2	7.6	6.0	16.3	15.8	15.6
Ireland	2009	54.2	104.3	23.5	44.9	81.1	89.3	84.5	8.2	8.4	6.7	10.7	2.2	8.8
Italy	2009	59.3	126.8	20.3	44.2	87.9	85.1	85.8	4.1	5.3	4.9	7.9	9.7	9.2
Lithuania	2010	7.8	34.1	3.0	12.4	81.0	82.9	83.8	7.4	5.8	5.9	11.6	11.3	10.3
Malta	2008	35.1	71.1	12.9	22.4	82.0	83.4	83.6	6.6	7.3	5.2	11.3	9.3	11.3
Netherlands	2008	59.4	135.2	29.7	59.7	86.8	85.5	86.8	6.6	7.1	5.8	6.6	7.4	7.4
Portugal	2009	27.2	58.5	10.4	21.2	86.7	85.7	85.9	5.1	6.1	5.1	8.2	8.2	9.0
Slovakia	2008	4.4	31.8	2.3	14.1	86.3	79.6	86.8	7.1	7.0	5.8	6.6	13.3	7.4
Slovenia	2010	18.0	35.1	12.6	18.6	80.8	73.6	77.6	13.5	16.5	11.8	5.8	9.9	10.5
Spain	2009	47.9	88.7	18.1	37.5	86.6	87.1	87.8	5.1	5.1	5.2	8.3	7.8	7.0
United Kingdom	2009	76.3	139.0	34.3	45.0	75.0	71.6	74.6	11.3	10.8	8.2	13.8	17.6	17.2
Other Europe														
Russian Federation	2010	...	25.3	0.8	6.1	...	76.7	76.0	5.9	6.6	5.8	...	16.7	18.2
East Asia														
Japan	2010	142.8	175.0	24.2	24.5	79.1	80.4	80.1	3.5	2.9	2.8	17.3	16.8	17.1
Malaysia	2010	20.1	22.7	4.8	8.3	83.0	85.4	85.5	4.1	3.9	5.3	12.9	10.7	9.2
Republic of Korea	2008	125.6	191.5	16.2	28.0	73.5	73.5	75.4	3.4	4.3	3.6	23.0	22.2	21.0
Singapore	2008	33.4	71.8	24.3	32.8	78.1	84.1	80.6	15.9	12.9	8.9	6.0	2.9	10.6

a/ At current prices.

Table 1.11
(continued)

SELECTED CHARACTERISTICS OF BRANCHES, SELECTED YEARS AND ECONOMIES

Grain mill products; starches; animal feeds (ISIC 153)

Economy	Latest year (LY)	Value added per employee (current 1000 dollars) 2000	Value added per employee LY	Wages and salaries per employee (current 1000 dollars) 2000	Wages and salaries per employee LY	Percentage in output [a] — Costs of input materials and utilities 2000	2006	LY	Costs of labour 2000	2006	LY	Operating surplus 2000	2006	LY
North America														
Canada	2009	94.5	109.5	23.6	43.7	65.1	...	80.5	8.7	...	7.8	26.2	...	11.7
United States of America	2008	222.9	420.6	36.9	48.5	57.1	56.1	61.7	7.1	5.9	4.4	35.8	37.9	33.9
Others														
Israel	2009	67.5	137.5	28.2	39.4	81.0	87.0	84.5	7.9	5.4	4.5	11.1	7.6	11.1
Developing & EIE														
Azerbaijan	2010	...	62.1	0.3	2.3	70.8	87.5	71.4	2.5	0.5	1.1	23.6	12.0	27.5
Brazil	2010	27.2	71.9	5.2	11.8	...	65.1	64.2	5.6	5.5	5.9	...	29.4	30.0
Bulgaria	2010	3.6	20.1	1.2	4.9	84.1	82.2	83.1	5.2	4.7	4.1	10.7	13.1	12.7
Chile	2008	59.5	82.1	8.5	14.1	62.1	75.3	77.3	5.4	4.3	3.9	32.5	20.3	18.8
China	2007	...	29.1	...	2.2	...	73.0	73.4	...	2.0	2.0	...	25.1	24.6
Cyprus	2010	26.6	70.3	12.6	30.3	81.8	81.6	78.6	8.6	9.0	9.2	9.5	9.4	12.2
Ecuador	2008	11.0	24.1	1.7	6.8	85.8	85.3	81.8	2.2	4.6	5.1	12.0	10.1	13.0
Egypt	2010	...	16.8	...	3.1	...	83.7	76.7	...	4.9	4.3	...	11.4	19.0
Ethiopia	2009	3.5	3.8	0.7	0.7	80.7	79.8	84.2	3.9	4.5	3.0	15.4	15.6	12.9
Greece	2007	...	71.6	...	29.6	...	75.2	76.2	...	11.1	9.9	...	13.7	14.0
India	2009	2.0	5.6	0.5	1.1	92.1	90.1	91.4	2.1	2.0	1.7	5.8	7.9	6.8
Indonesia	2009	6.3	17.0	0.6	1.9	76.5	65.1	81.1	2.1	2.7	2.1	21.3	32.2	16.8
Iran (Islamic Republic of)	2009	36.3	20.1	7.9	6.2	56.2	67.2	79.8	9.5	8.9	6.2	34.2	23.9	14.0
Jordan	2010	15.7	18.7	4.4	4.6	89.1	87.0	85.1	3.0	4.9	3.7	7.8	8.0	11.2
Kyrgyzstan	2010	...	11.8	0.3	0.9	71.9	95.6	73.8	1.2	2.7	2.1	...	1.8	24.1
Latvia	2010	11.2	14.3	4.1	4.3	72.0	72.2	79.0	10.2	7.8	6.2	17.8	19.9	14.7
Malawi	2009	5.0	8.8	1.9	2.2	82.9	95.5	91.1	6.6	1.9	2.2	10.5	2.6	6.7
Mongolia	2008	1.2	19.4	0.3	3.0	82.9	57.9	72.6	4.6	2.0	4.2	12.5	40.1	23.1
Morocco	2010	13.4	23.9	4.3	7.0	90.7	91.1	90.3	3.0	...	2.8	6.3	...	6.8
Oman	2010	58.9	82.3	13.7	18.4	76.0	80.8	73.9	5.6	5.7	5.9	18.4	13.5	20.2
Philippines	2008	...	45.6	...	3.8	...	86.4	73.8	...	2.9	2.2	...	10.7	24.0
Poland	2009	...	36.6	...	12.0	72.7	80.2	79.5	...	6.1	6.7	...	13.7	13.8
Romania	2010	...	13.9	...	5.1	...	85.7	81.5	...	9.5	6.7	...	4.7	11.7
Turkey	2009	33.7	28.2	5.0	8.2	75.1	89.7	83.3	3.7	3.2	4.9	21.2	7.1	11.9
United Republic of Tanzania	2007	...	28.2	...	4.5	...	55.9	55.9	...	7.1	7.1	...	37.0	37.1
Uruguay	2007	25.6	25.9	12.3	8.7	78.0	...	81.8	10.5	...	6.1	11.4	...	12.1

a/ At current prices.

Table 1.11

SELECTED CHARACTERISTICS OF BRANCHES, SELECTED YEARS AND ECONOMIES

Other food products (ISIC 154)

Economy	Latest year (LY)	Value added per employee (current 1000 dollars)		Wages and salaries per employee (current 1000 dollars)		Percentage in output a/								
						Costs of input materials and utilities			Costs of labour			Operating surplus		
		2000	LY	2000	LY	2000	2006	LY	2000	2006	LY	2000	2006	LY
Industrialized Economies														
EU														
Austria	2009	33.9	59.8	18.8	32.8	55.9	59.6	58.8	24.4	22.4	22.6	19.7	17.9	18.6
Belgium	2009	43.1	85.3	18.9	37.7	71.6	76.1	75.5	12.5	10.7	10.8	15.9	13.2	13.7
Czech Republic	2007	7.6	20.9	3.4	9.3	72.7	70.8	70.7	12.0	12.7	13.0	15.3	16.5	16.3
Denmark	2009	39.5	70.0	22.8	46.5	62.1	64.9	65.8	21.9	22.0	22.7	16.0	13.1	11.5
Estonia	2010	5.7	18.7	2.8	10.1	66.3	67.6	68.5	16.6	18.8	17.0	17.0	13.6	14.5
Finland	2009	34.0	74.2	20.6	39.6	68.7	66.1	65.8	19.0	18.7	18.2	12.3	15.2	16.0
France	2009	37.8	66.1	16.6	32.5	67.2	68.7	68.0	14.4	15.5	15.7	18.4	15.8	16.3
Germany	2009	27.1	48.3	15.9	28.0	67.6	65.9	68.2	19.0	18.6	18.4	13.3	15.5	13.4
Hungary	2009	7.5	18.4	3.1	8.3	72.9	69.3	71.0	11.1	12.6	13.2	16.0	18.1	15.9
Italy	2009	46.7	73.4	16.4	31.3	70.3	71.8	72.9	10.4	12.0	11.5	19.2	16.2	15.5
Lithuania	2010	4.2	12.6	2.3	6.9	72.1	69.9	71.6	15.4	15.5	15.5	12.5	14.7	12.9
Luxembourg	2008	31.2	56.3	17.9	37.9	49.7	48.7	48.6	28.8	34.8	34.6	21.5	16.6	16.8
Malta	2008	18.7	23.2	7.9	14.0	55.4	63.3	63.0	18.8	22.0	22.3	25.8	14.7	14.7
Netherlands	2008	45.1	99.1	20.8	42.1	67.9	67.4	72.0	14.7	13.2	11.9	17.3	19.4	16.1
Portugal	2009	13.8	26.1	6.6	13.7	65.8	64.6	65.4	16.3	18.0	18.1	17.9	17.4	16.5
Slovakia	2009	3.5	22.5	2.0	10.6	78.8	68.8	69.9	12.3	11.4	14.2	8.9	19.9	15.9
Slovenia	2010	17.7	33.9	12.4	21.1	66.3	61.6	63.7	23.5	22.2	22.6	10.2	16.2	13.7
Spain	2009	28.3	59.7	13.8	30.0	64.6	66.0	67.0	17.3	16.3	16.6	18.1	17.7	16.4
Sweden	2009	45.5	66.4	22.7	34.7	63.7	65.8	68.1	18.1	17.3	16.7	18.2	16.9	15.2
United Kingdom	2009	52.5	77.6	23.6	36.0	59.6	56.2	62.6	18.1	18.3	17.4	22.3	25.5	20.0
Other Europe														
Norway	2008	40.8	89.2	24.3	55.3	59.3	61.4	63.1	24.2	23.6	22.8	16.5	14.9	14.0
Russian Federation	2010	...	15.7	1.0	6.2	...	67.9	72.1	9.8	11.3	11.0	...	20.8	16.9
East Asia														
Japan	2010	74.0	87.3	19.6	23.6	55.0	55.9	56.3	11.9	11.3	11.8	33.1	32.8	31.9
Malaysia	2010	12.2	19.0	3.7	6.0	71.0	78.6	77.6	8.7	7.7	7.0	20.2	13.7	15.3
Republic of Korea	2008	71.3	99.9	12.8	20.8	50.4	56.2	57.2	8.9	10.0	8.9	40.7	33.8	33.8
West Asia														
Kuwait	2010	...	13.0	...	8.2	...	63.7	72.5	...	19.7	17.4	...	16.6	10.1

a/ At current prices.

Table 1.11
(continued)

SELECTED CHARACTERISTICS OF BRANCHES, SELECTED YEARS AND ECONOMIES

Other food products (ISIC 154)

Economy	Latest year (LY)	Value added per employee (current 1000 dollars)		Wages and salaries per employee (current 1000 dollars)		Percentage in output [a]								
						Costs of input materials and utilities			Costs of labour			Operating surplus		
	(LY)	2000	LY	2000	LY	2000	2006	LY	2000	2006	LY	2000	2006	LY
North America														
United States of America	2008	140.8	175.5	30.8	36.8	41.0	42.8	46.5	12.9	12.0	11.2	46.1	45.2	42.3
Others														
Israel	2009	29.8	33.0	19.5	21.6	59.7	64.3	64.5	26.3	24.2	23.3	14.0	11.5	12.3
Developing & EIE														
Azerbaijan	2010	...	28.3	0.1	2.3	...	87.5	69.1	0.4	1.6	2.5	...	11.0	28.4
Brazil	2010	14.7	36.0	3.8	9.4	58.2	55.9	52.1	10.7	10.3	12.5	31.1	33.8	35.4
Bulgaria	2010	2.1	8.7	1.0	4.0	80.9	78.3	74.7	8.8	9.1	11.8	10.3	12.6	13.5
Chile	2008	51.1	40.0	6.7	9.8	31.2	46.4	50.5	9.0	11.5	12.1	59.8	42.1	37.3
China	2007	...	17.8	...	2.5	...	68.0	68.7	...	4.3	4.4	...	27.7	26.9
Cyprus	2010	17.9	31.2	9.5	18.9	54.3	63.3	53.0	24.2	8.7	28.5	21.5	28.0	18.5
Ecuador	2008	10.9	24.5	2.5	5.0	75.5	71.0	61.6	5.5	7.9	7.8	19.0	21.1	30.5
Egypt	2010	...	8.7	...	2.7	...	74.9	69.0	...	6.2	9.6	...	18.9	21.3
Eritrea	2010	2.7	2.7	0.8	0.9	67.2	57.8	76.8	9.6	6.7	7.9	23.2	35.5	15.3
Ethiopia	2009	10.1	5.4	0.9	1.2	35.6	82.7	62.5	5.5	5.5	8.6	58.8	11.8	28.9
Georgia	2010	0.7	4.1	0.4	1.5	83.3	67.4	81.3	8.2	13.9	6.9	8.5	18.7	11.8
Greece	2007	...	53.3	...	25.8	...	80.3	66.2	...	4.8	16.3	...	15.0	17.5
India	2009	2.8	5.3	0.9	1.5	81.3	66.4	83.7	5.9	7.1	4.7	12.8	26.5	11.6
Indonesia	2009	3.4	11.5	0.8	1.4	64.8	62.7	58.9	8.7	13.1	4.9	26.5	24.1	36.2
Iran (Islamic Republic of)	2009	22.4	15.7	9.4	6.3	67.7	71.2	65.0	13.5	10.4	14.0	18.8	18.4	21.0
Jordan	2010	5.8	10.6	2.4	3.8	72.0	70.2	72.9	11.5	5.4	9.8	16.4	24.4	17.3
Kyrgyzstan	2010	...	9.3	0.6	1.4	...	62.4	72.7	5.0	13.6	4.0	...	23.9	23.3
Latvia	2010	5.2	13.4	2.6	7.0	70.5	77.8	72.8	14.8	8.8	14.1	14.6	13.4	13.1
Malawi	2008	1.0	5.4	0.3	1.3	54.0	79.0	77.7	11.9	11.7	5.3	34.1	9.3	17.0
Mongolia	2008	1.6	4.1	0.6	2.0	73.1	67.8	74.0	10.0	...	12.6	16.9	...	13.4
Morocco	2010	11.0	23.4	5.1	8.1	71.8	...	73.1	13.0	...	9.3	15.1	...	17.5
Oman	2010	13.8	27.5	5.0	7.7	54.8	...	58.1	16.4	...	11.8	28.8	...	30.1
Philippines	2008	...	15.1	...	4.1	69.7	68.6	72.6	...	7.6	7.4	...	23.8	20.1
Poland	2009	10.8	27.8	...	9.1	62.5	68.2	65.7	...	10.0	11.3	...	21.8	23.0
Romania	2010	...	9.6	...	4.0	...	79.6	75.4	...	11.0	10.3	...	9.5	14.3
The f. Yugosl. Rep of Macedonia	2010	...	9.1	...	5.6	...	60.3	70.3	...	26.1	18.4	...	13.5	11.4
Turkey	2009	23.4	20.2	9.8	10.2	66.6	76.9	76.8	14.0	11.6	11.8	19.3	11.5	11.4
United Republic of Tanzania	2007	...	1.8	...	0.8	...	66.8	66.8	...	14.8	14.7	...	18.5	18.6
Uruguay	2007	31.0	33.3	10.6	5.3	55.3	...	63.5	15.3	...	5.9	29.4	...	30.7

a/ At current prices.

Table 1.11

SELECTED CHARACTERISTICS OF BRANCHES, SELECTED YEARS AND ECONOMIES

Beverages (ISIC 155)

Economy	Latest year (LY)	Value added per employee (current 1000 dollars)		Wages and salaries per employee (current 1000 dollars)		Percentage in output [a]								
						Costs of input materials and utilities			Costs of labour			Operating surplus		
		2000	LY	2000	LY	2000	2006	LY	2000	2006	LY	2000	2006	LY
Industrialized Economies														
EU														
Austria	2009	61.7	171.4	30.3	55.3	64.5	63.9	73.5	17.4	14.6	8.6	18.1	21.5	18.0
Belgium	2009	75.0	194.2	30.5	63.5	71.0	70.0	74.2	11.8	10.3	8.4	17.2	19.8	17.4
Denmark	2009	68.9	139.7	32.4	71.4	67.0	72.8	66.8	15.5	14.5	17.0	17.5	12.7	16.2
Estonia	2010	13.9	50.6	4.9	17.3	73.8	68.4	64.0	9.2	9.6	12.3	16.9	22.0	23.7
Finland	2009	...	137.7	...	54.7	...	66.2	67.0	...	13.9	13.1	...	20.0	19.9
France	2009	93.9	154.6	28.8	53.9	72.6	75.4	76.0	8.4	8.0	8.4	19.0	16.5	15.6
Germany	2009	62.1	92.8	30.8	51.9	72.2	72.6	75.2	13.7	14.0	13.9	14.0	13.4	10.9
Hungary	2009	14.1	40.7	5.3	14.2	76.3	77.4	76.1	9.0	8.0	8.4	14.8	14.6	15.6
Ireland	2009	182.3	157.6	34.1	75.4	55.9	64.5	81.1	8.2	8.9	9.1	35.9	26.5	9.9
Italy	2009	68.8	115.6	21.2	44.3	79.1	83.1	81.3	6.4	6.9	7.2	14.4	10.0	11.5
Lithuania	2010	11.8	33.7	4.1	11.9	63.3	68.9	75.9	12.9	8.4	8.5	23.9	22.7	15.6
Luxembourg	2009	74.4	149.8	27.4	57.2	59.4	62.1	64.1	15.0	13.1	13.7	25.6	24.8	22.2
Malta	2008	33.7	54.2	12.8	27.1	48.4	48.4	55.2	19.6	21.0	22.4	31.9	30.5	22.4
Netherlands	2008	116.4	201.8	34.0	59.1	66.3	72.3	73.9	9.8	9.1	7.7	23.8	18.6	18.5
Portugal	2009	38.4	70.7	11.8	23.4	73.1	75.7	74.3	8.3	9.0	8.5	18.6	15.2	17.2
Slovakia	2009	5.2	36.3	2.4	14.0	81.8	78.1	75.5	8.4	9.2	9.5	9.9	12.7	15.1
Slovenia	2010	26.9	63.3	16.8	29.0	75.7	62.6	67.8	15.1	15.0	14.7	9.2	22.4	17.4
Spain	2009	72.2	139.3	23.6	46.3	71.7	71.0	69.0	9.2	9.4	10.3	19.1	19.5	20.7
Sweden	2009	81.8	125.0	28.6	49.4	66.9	68.5	71.3	11.6	10.6	11.3	21.5	20.9	17.4
United Kingdom	2007	112.0	170.8	34.4	66.8	67.5	69.7	71.6	10.0	11.6	11.1	22.5	18.7	17.3
Other Europe														
Russian Federation	2010	...	41.4	1.5	9.2	...	60.9	67.3	7.9	6.2	7.3	...	32.9	25.4
East Asia														
Japan	2010	300.2	390.0	31.2	34.3	63.8	64.8	61.8	3.8	3.6	3.4	32.4	31.6	34.8
Malaysia	2010	29.6	40.9	6.1	9.2	67.4	59.2	75.8	6.7	4.3	5.4	25.9	36.6	18.8
Republic of Korea	2008	193.2	332.3	16.1	31.1	39.0	42.0	42.5	5.1	5.9	5.4	55.9	52.1	52.1
Singapore	2010	51.9	160.4	24.4	43.4	68.8	...	59.3	14.7	...	11.0	16.5	...	29.7
West Asia														
Kuwait	2010	...	30.7	...	13.9	...	68.8	74.8	...	12.2	11.4	...	19.0	13.8

a/ At current prices.

Table 1.11
(continued)

SELECTED CHARACTERISTICS OF BRANCHES, SELECTED YEARS AND ECONOMIES

Beverages (ISIC 155)

Economy	Latest year (LY)	Value added per employee (current 1000 dollars)		Wages and salaries per employee (current 1000 dollars)		Percentage in output a/								
						Costs of input materials and utilities			Costs of labour			Operating surplus		
		2000	LY	2000	LY	2000	2006	LY	2000	2006	LY	2000	2006	LY
North America														
Canada	2008	134.6	247.3	28.8	44.1	41.5	37.0	37.9	12.5	11.6	11.1	46.0	51.4	51.1
United States of America	2008	219.6	332.9	39.7	46.2	53.4	47.9	49.1	8.4	7.2	7.1	38.2	45.0	43.8
Developing & EIE														
Albania	2010	3.9	12.9	1.3	3.8	65.9	73.6	73.3	11.7	6.4	7.8	22.5	20.0	18.8
Azerbaijan	2010	...	17.9	0.8	4.5	...	87.5	56.0	10.4	8.0	11.1	...	4.5	32.9
Botswana	2010	36.0	57.0	0.4	0.9	75.5	72.6	72.6	0.2	0.2	0.4	24.3	27.2	26.9
Brazil	2010	40.6	105.8	6.1	12.6	48.1	48.6	44.5	7.8	7.8	6.6	44.0	43.6	48.9
Bulgaria	2010	4.8	19.2	1.5	5.9	79.0	77.1	72.5	6.5	7.4	8.4	14.5	15.5	19.1
Chile	2008	82.4	135.0	9.4	15.6	40.7	48.4	45.7	6.8	6.5	6.3	52.5	45.1	48.1
China	2007	...	25.5	...	2.7	...	62.4	62.3	...	4.0	4.0	...	33.6	33.7
Cyprus	2010	48.2	71.0	15.6	36.9	57.7	55.6	55.2	13.7	21.9	23.3	28.6	22.5	21.5
Ecuador	2008	23.8	39.5	2.1	5.9	61.6	59.3	59.3	3.3	6.3	6.0	35.1	34.4	34.6
Egypt	2010	...	14.1	...	6.2	...	50.0	66.8	...	6.9	14.5	...	43.1	18.7
Eritrea	2010	18.5	42.5	1.4	1.5	36.8	37.9	24.8	4.7	4.3	2.6	58.5	57.8	72.6
Ethiopia	2009	10.5	20.0	1.0	2.2	28.6	44.8	45.9	6.9	8.2	6.1	64.5	47.0	48.0
Georgia	2010	2.6	14.9	0.7	4.3	71.3	75.1	65.8	7.8	8.8	9.9	20.9	16.1	24.3
Greece	2007	...	115.1	...	40.9	...	60.7	61.5	...	15.3	13.7	...	24.1	24.8
India	2009	6.0	13.5	1.4	2.4	77.5	63.7	74.3	5.2	3.7	4.6	17.4	32.6	21.1
Indonesia	2009	7.4	16.5	0.9	1.7	51.6	58.4	51.8	5.6	10.0	4.9	42.8	31.6	43.3
Iran (Islamic Republic of)	2009	44.5	28.5	12.3	8.4	49.6	55.4	63.7	14.0	13.9	10.6	36.4	30.7	25.7
Jordan	2010	24.8	51.1	4.2	7.6	46.2	51.3	51.8	9.2	8.4	7.1	44.6	40.3	41.0
Kyrgyzstan	2010	...	7.3	0.4	1.6	...	64.9	61.6	6.7	9.7	8.4	...	25.4	30.0
Latvia	2010	18.4	31.4	4.8	13.1	52.5	77.7	79.2	12.4	8.1	8.7	35.1	14.2	12.2
Malawi	2009	7.6	16.5	1.5	5.0	65.7	53.1	82.7	6.9	6.8	5.2	27.5	40.1	12.1
Mexico	2010	49.3	67.0	7.5	7.8	54.4	59.6	56.1	6.9	...	5.1	38.6	...	38.8
Mongolia	2008	4.7	15.2	0.5	3.0	42.5	61.9	65.7	5.9	5.4	6.8	51.6	32.7	27.5
Morocco	2010	45.3	62.4	7.8	14.1	48.2	44.9	52.4	9.0	...	10.7	42.8	...	36.9
Oman	2010	12.2	27.3	6.4	10.2	78.2	61.2	57.3	11.4	12.9	16.0	10.3	26.0	26.7
Philippines	2008	...	56.2	...	7.6	...	59.4	64.4	...	5.1	4.8	...	35.6	30.7
Poland	2009	57.3	94.5	...	17.1	42.8	74.7	71.6	...	5.5	5.1	...	19.8	23.3
Romania	2010	...	41.9	...	9.1	66.4	75.6	68.1	...	8.1	6.9	...	16.3	25.0
The f. Yugosl. Rep of Macedonia	2010	...	36.7	...	14.6	...	67.1	57.3	...	11.4	17.0	...	21.5	25.7
Turkey	2009	82.8	71.7	10.6	16.3	50.5	74.9	73.4	6.4	6.9	6.0	43.2	18.2	20.5
United Republic of Tanzania	2007	...	36.1	...	5.8	...	61.6	61.6	...	6.2	6.1	...	32.2	32.3
Uruguay	2007	71.1	69.1	23.1	13.8	46.0	...	53.7	17.5	...	9.3	36.5	...	37.1

a/ At current prices.

Table 1.11

SELECTED CHARACTERISTICS OF BRANCHES, SELECTED YEARS AND ECONOMIES

Tobacco products (ISIC 1600)

Economy	Latest year (LY)	Value added per employee (current 1000 dollars)		Wages and salaries per employee (current 1000 dollars)		Percentage in output a/								
						Costs of input materials and utilities			Costs of labour			Operating surplus		
		2000	LY	2000	LY	2000	2006	LY	2000	2006	LY	2000	2006	LY
Industrialized Economies														
EU														
Austria	2009	127.3	221.5	44.5	111.0	59.6	...	93.1	14.1	...	3.4	26.3	...	3.4
Belgium	2008	75.4	164.1	24.6	46.2	86.7	81.7	85.2	4.3	4.5	4.2	8.9	13.8	10.6
Germany	2009	133.4	170.1	41.7	77.7	87.2	90.1	90.4	4.0	4.0	4.4	8.8	5.9	5.2
Hungary	2009	39.0	73.7	8.7	25.5	66.6	...	90.6	7.5	...	3.3	25.9	...	6.2
Italy	2009	44.2	352.1	20.4	60.4	63.8	...	46.2	16.7	...	9.2	19.5	...	44.6
Lithuania	2010	32.8	77.4	9.4	26.6	79.3	77.9	30.3	5.9	5.8	23.9	14.8	16.3	45.7
Portugal	2008	...	129.6	16.9	41.0	...	54.6	53.8	8.0	7.0	14.6	...	38.3	31.5
Spain	2009	72.5	192.2	25.5	60.1	59.9	58.0	47.6	14.1	19.9	16.4	26.0	22.1	36.0
Other Europe														
Russian Federation	2010	...	203.8	3.3	19.2	...	64.2	58.7	4.3	4.4	3.9	...	31.4	37.4
East Asia														
Japan	2010	950.3	1582.7	66.2	83.3	76.3	75.4	80.1	1.7	0.8	1.0	22.1	23.8	18.9
Malaysia	2010	8.9	124.8	2.7	14.4	78.8	72.5	54.3	6.4	3.1	5.3	14.7	24.4	40.4
Republic of Korea	2008	675.7	627.5	32.8	44.2	35.8	44.3	45.4	3.1	3.3	3.8	61.1	52.4	50.7

a/ At current prices.

Table 1.11
(continued)

SELECTED CHARACTERISTICS OF BRANCHES, SELECTED YEARS AND ECONOMIES

Tobacco products (ISIC 1600)

Economy	Latest year (LY)	Value added per employee (current 1000 dollars) 2000	LY	Wages and salaries per employee (current 1000 dollars) 2000	LY	Percentage in output [a/] — Costs of input materials and utilities 2000	2006	LY	Costs of labour 2000	2006	LY	Operating surplus 2000	2006	LY
North America														
United States of America	2008	1414.6	1734.3	52.9	60.6	14.6	12.8	16.0	3.2	3.0	2.9	82.2	84.2	81.1
Developing & EIE														
Albania	2010	3.2	6.5	1.2	2.5	66.5	84.2	72.3	12.3	9.3	10.6	21.2	6.5	17.1
Azerbaijan	2010	...	13.0	0.8	4.7	...	87.5	73.7	5.7	8.5	9.5	...	4.0	16.8
Brazil	2010	76.0	161.5	10.2	27.1	42.5	53.1	54.0	7.7	6.9	7.7	49.7	40.0	38.3
Bulgaria	2010	8.4	27.4	2.6	10.2	66.2	68.0	87.2	10.5	13.6	4.8	23.3	18.5	8.0
China	2007	...	206.2	...	8.6	...	26.0	22.7	...	3.3	3.2	...	70.8	74.1
Ecuador	2008	20.5	26.4	3.9	9.4	64.9	...	68.9	6.7	...	11.1	28.4	...	20.0
Eritrea	2010	67.8	128.8	2.6	21.5	49.2	39.2	28.3	1.9	4.1	12.0	48.9	56.7	59.7
Ethiopia	2009	25.8	35.8	1.4	2.1	30.9	37.1	24.9	3.8	5.5	4.4	65.4	57.4	70.7
Fiji	2007	...	15.7	...	7.6	...	79.5	78.0	...	10.6	10.5	...	9.9	11.4
Georgia	2010	...	22.7	...	6.6	...	82.6	79.0	...	5.2	6.1	...	12.3	14.9
Greece	2007	...	129.9	...	56.4	...	61.1	57.8	...	17.0	18.3	...	21.9	23.9
India	2009	1.9	3.7	0.4	0.6	64.7	57.3	66.2	7.4	6.9	5.9	27.9	35.8	27.9
Indonesia	2009	7.5	11.2	0.6	1.1	56.2	29.9	66.4	3.6	4.9	3.4	40.2	65.3	30.2
Iran (Islamic Republic of)	2009	41.3	27.7	15.1	16.4	37.1	45.0	39.3	23.0	15.0	35.9	39.9	40.0	24.8
Jordan	2010	197.7	386.6	6.3	7.8	29.3	36.0	28.8	2.3	2.0	1.4	68.4	62.0	69.8
Kenya	2010	...	19.1	...	5.9	64.0	64.0	64.0	...	4.2	5.5	...	31.8	30.5
Kyrgyzstan	2010	...	...	0.7	11.9	...	60.2	67.1	5.1	8.2	10.2	...	31.6	22.6
Mexico	2010	254.6	928.0	13.7	1.2	30.2	17.7	18.1	3.7	...	1.0	66.0	...	80.9
Mongolia	2008	...	29.7	...	5.3	...	83.2	74.2	...	2.2	1.0	...	14.6	24.8
Philippines	2008	...	84.0	...	20.7	...	65.5	51.9	...	3.6	3.0	...	30.8	45.1
Poland	2009	175.1	74.9	...	4.9	26.0	93.2	87.7	10.0	2.7	3.4	...	4.0	8.9
Republic of Moldova	2010	...	10.2	1.6	18.2	...	78.7	77.8	...	14.4	10.7	...	6.8	11.5
Romania	2007	14.0	39.1	2.5	14.4	70.5	93.5	94.9	5.2	3.5	2.4	24.2	2.9	2.7
The f. Yugosl. Rep of Macedonia	2010	...	29.0	...	19.1	...	64.3	52.9	...	22.0	23.4	...	13.7	23.8
Turkey	2009	111.3	45.3	12.4	...	39.0	64.3	72.1	6.8	15.7	11.8	54.2	20.1	16.2
United Republic of Tanzania	2010	...	22.1	...	1.5	...	70.5	52.6	...	9.6	3.3	...	19.9	44.1
Uruguay	2008	311.4	283.8	34.7	36.3	30.6	...	22.6	7.7	...	9.9	61.6	...	67.5

a/ At current prices.

Table 1.11

SELECTED CHARACTERISTICS OF BRANCHES, SELECTED YEARS AND ECONOMIES

Spinning, weaving and finishing of textiles (ISIC 171)

Economy	Latest year (LY)	Value added per employee (current 1000 dollars)		Wages and salaries per employee (current 1000 dollars)		Percentage in output a/								
						Costs of input materials and utilities			Costs of labour			Operating surplus		
		2000	LY	2000	LY	2000	2006	LY	2000	2006	LY	2000	2006	LY
Industrialized Economies														
EU														
Austria	2009	41.1	63.5	24.6	42.4	63.5	67.7	66.9	21.8	21.0	22.1	14.7	11.3	11.0
Belgium	2009	44.8	57.0	20.7	34.9	68.8	73.7	73.9	14.4	14.5	15.9	16.8	11.7	10.1
Czech Republic	2007	7.1	18.9	3.2	9.2	71.4	71.8	71.5	12.9	14.2	13.9	15.7	13.9	14.6
Denmark	2009	...	97.7	...	70.8	...	64.9	68.3	...	22.7	23.0	12.5	12.5	8.7
Finland	2009	34.4	57.7	19.7	35.1	65.3	63.3	54.0	19.8	23.3	28.0	14.9	13.3	18.0
France	2009	33.7	50.2	19.1	41.0	74.8	76.2	74.0	14.3	16.0	21.2	10.9	7.8	4.8
Germany	2009	36.9	49.7	24.6	36.4	66.2	70.0	69.0	22.5	19.2	22.7	11.3	10.8	8.3
Hungary	2009	5.9	17.1	2.9	9.6	69.5	67.0	69.4	14.9	17.3	17.2	15.6	15.7	13.4
Italy	2009	41.2	47.2	17.5	30.6	68.6	72.1	73.7	13.3	14.0	17.0	18.1	13.9	9.2
Lithuania	2010	3.6	13.0	2.7	7.9	69.8	66.1	69.7	22.9	21.3	18.4	7.2	12.6	12.0
Malta	2008	45.6	87.1	14.0	20.6	49.5	57.6	51.5	15.5	16.9	11.5	34.9	25.4	37.0
Netherlands	2008	46.1	88.0	25.7	47.3	64.8	...	65.9	19.6	...	18.3	15.6	...	15.8
Portugal	2009	14.2	20.4	7.2	14.1	68.5	...	68.4	15.9	...	21.8	15.6	...	9.8
Slovenia	2010	11.0	28.5	8.7	19.4	73.4	72.4	75.8	21.2	17.2	16.5	5.4	10.4	7.7
Spain	2009	27.5	47.5	14.2	32.2	69.0	69.8	69.7	16.0	18.0	20.5	15.0	12.2	9.8
Sweden	2009	36.4	55.8	19.6	32.5	66.2	65.7	64.5	18.2	19.2	20.7	15.6	15.1	14.8
United Kingdom	2009	38.8	43.0	24.8	29.9	63.1	64.1	67.2	23.6	22.7	22.9	13.3	13.2	10.0
Other Europe														
Norway	2008	34.3	68.8	24.8	50.1	60.6	58.7	63.0	28.5	26.7	27.0	10.9	14.6	10.0
East Asia														
Japan	2010	64.8	68.5	20.1	20.6	55.4	55.3	56.1	13.8	13.0	13.2	30.8	31.7	30.7
Malaysia	2010	17.3	20.2	4.3	5.7	69.2	83.6	77.1	7.7	6.5	6.5	23.1	9.9	16.4
Republic of Korea	2008	44.6	58.4	13.1	19.7	56.9	60.7	62.1	12.6	14.0	12.8	30.5	25.3	25.1
Singapore	2007	38.8	29.7	17.9	18.4	74.7	81.9	86.4	11.7	11.0	8.4	13.6	7.1	5.2

a/ At current prices.

Table 1.11
(continued)

SELECTED CHARACTERISTICS OF BRANCHES, SELECTED YEARS AND ECONOMIES

Spinning, weaving and finishing of textiles (ISIC 171)

Economy	Latest year (LY)	Value added per employee (current 1000 dollars) 2000	LY	Wages and salaries per employee (current 1000 dollars) 2000	LY	Costs of input materials and utilities 2000	2006	LY	Costs of labour 2000	2006	LY	Operating surplus 2000	2006	LY
North America														
Canada	2009	48.4	68.3	21.1	36.8	56.3	55.4	51.8	19.0	21.6	26.0	24.7	23.0	22.2
United States of America	2008	61.2	74.1	26.4	30.5	59.8	59.3	65.1	17.3	14.9	14.4	22.9	25.8	20.6
Developing & EIE														
Brazil	2010	15.0	26.5	4.1	9.2	58.1	60.4	57.5	11.4	12.9	14.8	30.5	26.7	27.7
Bulgaria	2010	1.8	10.3	1.0	4.4	75.7	78.6	78.5	13.4	6.3	9.2	10.9	15.2	12.2
Chile	2008	16.9	21.5	7.6	10.4	56.1	63.0	68.8	19.9	17.5	15.1	24.0	19.6	16.1
China	2007	...	10.8	...	2.0	...	74.6	74.2	...	4.9	4.8	...	20.5	21.1
Cyprus	2010	19.8	21.6	10.0	15.5	54.5	56.8	58.0	23.1	21.2	30.1	22.4	22.0	11.9
Ecuador	2008	9.4	15.2	1.3	4.6	70.5	66.3	66.6	4.0	10.5	10.1	25.5	23.2	23.4
Egypt	2010	...	4.3	...	3.0	...	57.2	63.5	...	20.8	25.3	...	22.0	11.1
Eritrea	2010	1.2	4.0	0.3	1.5	59.7	55.7	52.0	10.2	18.1	18.3	30.1	26.3	29.6
Ethiopia	2009	1.2	2.7	0.6	0.8	61.9	75.1	62.9	18.2	14.0	11.1	19.9	10.9	26.0
Greece	2007	...	39.2	...	27.4	...	65.5	69.6	...	21.0	21.2	...	13.5	9.2
India	2009	2.9	5.4	1.1	1.6	81.4	81.2	82.2	7.1	5.5	5.3	11.5	13.3	12.5
Indonesia	2009	4.6	9.8	0.7	1.4	66.5	65.2	63.0	4.9	5.6	5.3	28.5	29.2	31.7
Iran (Islamic Republic of)	2009	16.1	11.7	8.5	5.7	62.7	67.7	67.3	19.7	16.1	16.0	17.6	16.3	16.7
Jordan	2010	19.9	37.3	4.3	8.0	57.5	57.1	47.6	9.3	11.8	11.2	33.2	31.1	41.2
Kyrgyzstan	2010	...	2.0	0.2	0.8	...	62.5	73.6	3.9	11.0	10.7	...	26.6	15.7
Latvia	2010	5.1	16.5	3.0	5.3	59.6	76.0	69.5	23.8	14.9	9.8	16.6	9.1	20.6
Mexico	2010	15.0	19.2	5.3	6.3	61.5	69.9	67.4	13.6	...	10.7	24.9	...	21.9
Mongolia	2008	3.7	4.5	1.1	1.7	76.9	87.9	90.5	6.6	7.0	3.6	16.5	5.0	6.0
Morocco	2010	8.5	9.9	3.8	5.3	64.0	69.8	72.0	16.0	...	15.0	20.0	...	13.0
Oman	2010	25.1	89.7	9.8	11.3	53.1	57.0	36.0	18.3	22.6	8.0	28.6	20.5	56.0
Philippines	2008	...	5.9	...	2.9	...	81.6	80.5	...	11.4	9.7	...	7.0	9.7
Poland	2009	7.1	16.3	...	8.5	65.4	67.0	68.1	...	16.2	16.7	...	16.7	15.2
Romania	2010	...	14.6	...	5.3	...	75.5	73.9	...	16.2	9.5	...	8.3	16.6
Sri Lanka	2010	...	10.5	...	1.7	...	38.6	59.4	...	6.9	6.6	...	54.5	34.0
Turkey	2009	18.7	17.0	5.7	7.3	62.7	78.3	77.5	11.3	8.8	9.7	26.0	12.9	12.8
United Republic of Tanzania	2007	...	8.1	...	1.0	...	43.6	43.6	...	7.0	7.0	...	49.3	49.4
Uruguay	2007	21.5	17.1	11.3	8.0	71.5	...	78.6	15.0	...	10.1	13.5	...	11.4

a/ At current prices.

Table 1.11

SELECTED CHARACTERISTICS OF BRANCHES, SELECTED YEARS AND ECONOMIES

Other textiles (ISIC 172)

Economy	Latest year (LY)	Value added per employee (current 1000 dollars)		Wages and salaries per employee (current 1000 dollars)		Percentage in output [a]								
						Costs of input materials and utilities			Costs of labour			Operating surplus		
		2000	LY	2000	LY	2000	2006	LY	2000	2006	LY	2000	2006	LY
Industrialized Economies														
EU														
Austria	2009	44.6	68.3	20.7	40.0	55.4	60.6	62.5	20.6	19.9	21.9	23.9	19.5	15.6
Belgium	2009	44.9	68.5	20.6	37.8	74.9	75.8	71.0	11.5	12.6	16.0	13.6	11.6	13.0
Czech Republic	2007	6.7	21.6	3.1	8.9	69.7	67.9	69.7	13.9	11.8	12.4	16.4	20.3	17.9
Denmark	2009	41.1	91.0	26.5	65.5	65.1	68.1	67.3	22.6	20.6	23.6	12.4	11.3	9.2
Estonia	2010	5.2	20.3	2.9	10.0	76.1	72.3	71.4	13.3	13.0	14.1	10.6	14.7	14.5
Finland	2009	51.4	66.0	23.1	39.8	57.1	60.1	62.9	19.3	20.3	22.3	23.7	19.6	14.8
France	2009	34.2	59.7	18.7	38.5	69.9	69.8	67.1	16.5	18.1	21.3	13.6	12.1	11.6
Germany	2009	36.7	59.3	21.7	38.8	65.9	65.0	67.9	20.1	20.4	21.0	13.9	14.6	11.1
Hungary	2009	5.1	11.7	2.6	6.7	73.0	57.3	64.3	13.7	19.9	20.5	13.3	22.8	15.2
Italy	2009	41.5	64.3	14.8	29.8	73.7	73.2	75.7	9.4	11.2	11.3	16.9	15.6	13.0
Lithuania	2010	6.8	16.0	2.6	6.8	79.8	71.3	68.8	7.8	13.8	13.2	12.4	14.9	18.0
Malta	2008	11.3	28.0	6.6	18.8	56.9	62.5	64.3	25.2	20.1	24.0	17.9	17.4	11.7
Netherlands	2008	50.7	89.8	26.8	45.7	69.0	70.9	71.0	16.4	14.3	14.8	14.6	14.8	14.3
Portugal	2009	12.6	22.3	6.5	13.5	66.5	69.9	71.2	17.3	17.4	17.5	16.2	12.7	11.3
Slovakia	2009	2.2	16.8	1.7	9.0	68.4	68.5	69.6	23.7	16.1	16.2	7.9	15.3	14.2
Slovenia	2010	13.8	31.3	9.6	21.3	71.3	68.9	64.1	19.9	17.1	24.4	8.8	14.0	11.5
Spain	2009	24.8	44.9	12.5	29.4	68.4	69.4	69.8	15.8	16.9	19.8	15.7	13.6	10.4
Sweden	2009	45.5	60.1	22.7	35.4	61.6	61.7	62.8	19.1	20.2	22.0	19.2	18.1	15.3
United Kingdom	2009	35.3	54.6	21.4	27.7	60.0	61.9	57.4	24.2	22.0	21.6	15.8	16.1	21.0
Other Europe														
Norway	2008	40.0	95.2	25.8	57.0	61.9	63.6	61.6	24.6	23.3	23.0	13.5	13.2	15.4
East Asia														
Japan	2010	64.1	70.7	13.9	18.2	58.2	60.2	62.0	9.1	9.0	9.8	32.7	30.8	28.2
Malaysia	2010	8.6	11.7	3.5	5.6	63.9	70.5	73.9	14.6	15.4	12.6	21.5	14.0	13.5
Republic of Korea	2008	41.7	71.4	12.0	21.1	57.8	64.4	66.6	12.2	10.8	9.9	30.0	24.8	23.5
Singapore	2010	21.6	26.8	15.9	18.3	63.2	...	66.4	27.0	...	22.9	9.8	...	10.6
West Asia														
Kuwait	2010	...	15.1	...	7.2	...	62.6	62.0	...	19.3	18.1	...	18.1	19.9

a/ At current prices.

Table 1.11
(continued)

SELECTED CHARACTERISTICS OF BRANCHES, SELECTED YEARS AND ECONOMIES

Other textiles (ISIC 172)

Economy	Latest year (LY)	Value added per employee (current 1000 dollars) 2000	LY	Wages and salaries per employee (current 1000 dollars) 2000	LY	Percentage in output [a] Costs of input materials and utilities 2000	2006	LY	Costs of labour 2000	2006	LY	Operating surplus 2000	2006	LY
North America														
Canada	2008	48.0	74.3	20.2	37.4	53.1	51.9	53.9	19.7	22.9	23.2	27.2	25.2	22.9
United States of America	2008	67.0	96.4	26.6	33.4	58.2	52.6	55.7	16.6	13.5	15.3	25.2	34.0	28.9
Others														
Israel	2009	26.6	49.7	19.5	26.3	63.8	73.7	67.6	26.5	18.0	17.1	9.7	8.4	15.2
Developing & EIE														
Azerbaijan	2010	...	4.4	0.1	3.3	...	82.6	70.0	25.9	14.1	22.4	...	3.3	7.7
Brazil	2010	13.9	27.2	4.2	8.6	56.2	56.8	58.5	13.4	13.9	13.1	30.5	29.3	28.4
Bulgaria	2010	1.7	7.1	1.0	3.3	72.6	75.5	70.2	15.6	10.4	14.1	11.8	14.1	15.6
Chile	2008	14.7	25.7	6.8	10.9	57.0	58.5	59.8	20.0	15.7	17.0	23.0	25.8	23.2
China	2007	...	10.9	...	2.1	...	73.2	73.2	...	5.4	5.2	...	21.4	21.6
Cyprus	2010	14.9	28.9	7.9	19.3	60.7	52.4	59.5	20.8	25.1	27.1	18.5	22.5	13.5
Ecuador	2008	8.8	13.4	0.9	4.3	60.8	69.7	64.4	3.9	9.2	11.6	35.3	21.1	24.0
Egypt	2010	...	7.4	...	2.8	...	49.8	75.2	...	8.3	9.3	...	41.9	15.5
Ethiopia	2009	1.3	1.5	0.5	0.6	49.2	57.4	61.4	21.3	3.6	16.3	29.5	39.0	22.2
Georgia	2010	0.4	4.8	0.2	2.3	90.1	63.2	61.5	5.7	17.8	18.5	4.2	19.0	20.1
Greece	2007	...	48.0	...	22.8	...	82.1	61.2	...	5.2	18.4	...	12.8	20.4
India	2009	3.5	4.8	0.9	1.6	78.2	61.6	82.4	5.5	8.7	6.0	16.4	29.7	11.6
Indonesia	2009	2.8	3.8	0.6	1.3	64.5	64.2	62.9	7.8	10.1	12.9	27.7	25.7	24.2
Iran (Islamic Republic of)	2009	15.1	14.2	6.2	5.5	69.1	59.3	66.5	12.6	10.4	13.1	18.3	30.3	20.4
Jordan	2010	10.0	12.7	2.9	4.0	58.1	39.7	65.2	12.3	3.8	10.8	29.6	56.5	24.0
Kyrgyzstan	2010	4.2	4.4	0.3	1.2	66.9	65.3	58.9	7.3	14.7	10.9	13.6	20.0	30.3
Latvia	2010	1.3	14.2	2.5	6.8	40.1	76.8	64.8	19.5	15.6	16.8	46.1	7.6	18.4
Malawi	2009	14.3	3.3	0.3	2.1	66.5	72.0	65.8	13.8	...	21.0	21.3	...	13.2
Mexico	2010	5.3	15.0	5.2	5.3	67.2	71.1	66.6	12.2	...	11.9	14.1	...	21.6
Morocco	2010	...	7.7	3.0	4.8	...	56.2	73.3	18.7	13.8	16.6	...	30.0	10.1
Oman	2010	...	16.1	...	8.1	...	64.8	59.1	...	14.2	20.6	...	20.9	20.3
Philippines	2008	9.9	5.6	...	2.9	63.3	69.0	74.0	...	12.9	13.5	...	18.1	12.5
Poland	2009	...	17.4	...	7.9	...	65.9	66.3	...	21.4	15.2	...	12.6	18.5
Romania	2010	...	8.5	...	4.4	...	44.7	72.1	...	26.6	14.5	...	28.7	13.5
Sri Lanka	2010	...	4.7	...	1.7	...	65.4	53.7	...	30.8	17.1	...	3.8	29.2
The f. Yugosl. Rep of Macedonia	2010	...	6.9	...	3.6	...	76.2	68.9	...	9.8	16.1	...	14.0	15.0
Turkey	2009	21.7	18.2	4.6	7.4	54.4	...	77.8	9.7	...	9.0	35.9	...	13.2
Uruguay	2007	12.3	15.9	8.4	10.5	61.6	...	61.3	26.4	...	25.5	12.1	...	13.2

a/ At current prices.

Table 1.11

SELECTED CHARACTERISTICS OF BRANCHES, SELECTED YEARS AND ECONOMIES

Knitted and crocheted fabrics and articles (ISIC 1730)

| Economy | Latest year (LY) | Value added per employee (current 1000 dollars) | | Wages and salaries per employee (current 1000 dollars) | | Percentage in output [a] | | | | | | | | |
| | | | | | | Costs of input materials and utilities | | | Costs of labour | | | Operating surplus | | |
		2000	LY	2000	LY	2000	2006	LY	2000	2006	LY	2000	2006	LY
Industrialized Economies														
EU														
Austria	2009	36.6	51.8	22.2	40.2	72.4	56.3	47.7	16.8	27.3	40.5	10.8	16.5	11.7
Belgium	2009	30.8	39.9	14.7	26.6	61.3	73.0	71.4	18.5	14.1	19.0	20.2	13.0	9.5
Czech Republic	2007	4.9	13.8	2.8	7.7	67.0	60.7	62.2	18.7	21.6	20.9	14.3	17.7	16.9
Denmark	2009	...	77.9	...	63.4	...	74.4	70.3	...	16.2	24.2	...	9.4	5.5
Estonia	2010	2.9	13.1	1.8	7.6	53.6	...	48.0	29.0	...	30.1	17.4	...	21.9
Finland	2009	28.8	46.1	17.9	34.6	59.2	59.6	63.6	25.4	27.7	27.3	15.4	12.8	9.1
France	2009	31.0	62.5	18.3	38.7	66.0	68.4	58.8	20.1	18.2	25.5	13.9	13.4	15.7
Germany	2008	33.8	70.5	20.2	40.2	64.3	67.0	69.0	21.4	21.1	17.7	14.4	11.9	13.3
Hungary	2009	3.8	12.3	2.0	5.9	64.2	52.8	28.7	18.8	32.3	34.3	17.0	14.9	37.0
Ireland	2008	14.2	25.7	9.5	17.2	54.3	63.0	66.7	30.4	19.6	22.2	15.2	17.4	11.1
Italy	2009	33.6	49.0	12.9	25.3	73.7	74.2	75.2	10.1	11.2	12.8	16.2	14.6	12.0
Lithuania	2010	4.0	9.0	2.4	5.6	62.2	62.0	62.9	22.6	22.2	23.1	15.2	15.8	14.0
Netherlands	2008	33.9	88.6	17.7	46.9	65.0	...	50.0	18.2	...	26.5	16.8	...	23.5
Portugal	2009	11.4	17.8	6.3	11.9	72.7	...	63.8	14.9	...	24.3	12.4	...	12.0
Slovakia	2009	1.5	9.1	1.5	7.0	68.3	...	69.4	31.7	...	23.6	0.0	...	6.9
Slovenia	2010	10.1	20.6	8.6	17.5	64.5	68.8	51.2	30.3	26.6	41.5	5.3	4.7	7.3
Spain	2009	21.9	45.2	12.0	26.2	68.4	69.2	69.7	17.3	17.8	17.6	14.3	12.9	12.7
Sweden	2009	37.2	54.8	19.6	31.7	65.4	69.8	62.9	18.2	16.6	21.5	16.4	13.6	15.6
United Kingdom	2007	31.9	48.7	22.9	36.0	59.2	58.7	61.6	29.4	27.7	28.4	11.4	13.6	10.0
Other Europe														
Norway	2008	30.9	71.7	22.6	55.3	55.3	67.2	71.5	32.6	24.8	22.0	12.1	8.1	6.5
East Asia														
Japan	2010	43.1	53.9	12.5	16.4	57.8	55.4	61.5	12.2	11.5	11.8	30.0	33.1	26.8
Malaysia	2010	10.5	10.0	3.7	5.7	67.5	74.4	82.0	11.6	11.6	10.3	20.9	14.0	7.7
Republic of Korea	2008	41.8	64.6	11.9	19.5	61.4	63.8	66.0	11.0	10.4	10.3	27.6	25.8	23.7
Singapore	2007	26.4	11.5	13.8	7.4	80.3	81.3	78.0	10.3	14.3	14.1	9.4	4.4	7.9

a/ At current prices.

Table 1.11
(continued)

SELECTED CHARACTERISTICS OF BRANCHES, SELECTED YEARS AND ECONOMIES

Knitted and crocheted fabrics and articles (ISIC 1730)

Economy	Latest year (LY)	Value added per employee (current 1000 dollars)		Wages and salaries per employee (current 1000 dollars)		Percentage in output a/								
						Costs of input materials and utilities			Costs of labour			Operating surplus		
		2000	LY	2000	LY	2000	2006	LY	2000	2006	LY	2000	2006	LY
North America														
Canada	2009	30.4	58.8	16.2	31.4	49.1	49.6	46.8	27.2	27.3	28.4	23.7	23.2	24.8
United States of America	2008	47.3	67.8	21.4	28.9	54.5	53.3	56.9	20.6	15.8	18.4	24.9	30.9	24.7
Others														
Israel	2009	21.4	53.6	16.6	27.2	64.9	67.4	59.8	27.3	23.0	20.4	7.8	9.6	19.8
Developing & EIE														
Azerbaijan	2010	…	6.9	0.3	5.0	…	82.6	79.6	26.2	7.0	14.8	…	10.4	5.5
Brazil	2010	14.8	21.8	3.7	7.2	60.5	65.4	45.5	9.7	10.5	17.8	29.7	24.1	36.6
Bulgaria	2010	2.0	6.8	1.0	3.7	60.8	64.6	62.4	20.5	16.5	20.2	18.7	18.8	17.3
Chile	2008	16.7	9.3	6.8	5.1	50.1	57.4	56.8	20.4	21.1	24.0	29.5	21.5	19.2
China	2007	…	8.2	…	2.3	…	72.5	72.1	…	7.7	8.0	…	19.8	20.0
Cyprus	2010	11.9	26.6	8.4	18.0	59.0	53.8	46.4	28.9	26.0	36.2	12.1	20.2	17.4
Ecuador	2008	7.0	13.3	1.0	4.4	64.5	69.3	72.6	5.3	11.4	9.1	30.2	19.2	18.3
Egypt	2010	…	3.1	…	1.4	…	58.5	68.1	…	15.1	14.4	…	26.4	17.5
Eritrea	2010	2.1	4.6	0.7	1.0	51.1	39.5	28.7	15.2	17.8	15.9	33.7	42.7	55.4
Ethiopia	2009	0.7	0.2	0.3	0.2	47.1	51.4	80.1	20.3	11.3	19.2	32.6	37.3	0.8
Greece	2007	…	40.8	…	23.7	…	70.0	70.5	…	15.4	17.1	…	14.7	12.4
India	2009	3.5	3.6	0.8	1.4	81.8	85.4	81.4	4.1	4.5	7.5	14.1	10.1	11.1
Indonesia	2009	2.0	5.7	0.7	1.3	66.8	52.0	72.2	10.9	14.0	6.3	22.4	34.0	21.5
Iran (Islamic Republic of)	2009	17.6	9.0	8.2	4.8	55.4	57.7	58.9	20.7	16.3	21.8	23.9	26.0	19.3
Jordan	2010	2.4	7.8	1.8	3.4	76.7	56.5	50.0	18.1	24.1	22.2	5.2	19.4	27.8
Kyrgyzstan	2010	…	7.1	0.2	1.3	…	69.1	70.3	22.7	19.6	5.6	…	11.3	24.1
Latvia	2010	7.6	6.9	3.1	4.1	52.4	67.8	61.0	19.7	17.1	23.4	28.0	15.1	15.6
Malawi	2009	0.9	1.2	0.4	0.5	79.0	…	88.9	9.8	…	5.1	11.2	…	6.1
Mongolia	2008	1.2	1.9	0.8	1.4	72.9	93.2	76.8	17.8	4.3	18.0	9.4	2.5	5.2
Morocco	2010	4.1	6.1	2.5	4.4	69.7	68.7	67.1	18.3	…	23.8	12.0	…	9.1
Philippines	2008	…	5.2	…	2.9	…	76.0	63.8	…	15.0	20.1	…	9.0	16.1
Poland	2008	7.5	19.3	…	8.7	59.9	67.5	63.0	…	14.0	16.7	…	18.5	20.3
Romania	2010	…	8.4	…	4.5	…	57.8	50.1	…	33.2	26.5	…	9.1	23.4
Sri Lanka	2010	…	6.9	…	1.7	…	31.1	53.9	…	8.8	11.5	…	60.1	34.7
The f. Yugosl. Rep of Macedonia	2010	…	6.1	…	3.6	…	66.7	55.8	…	20.8	26.1	…	12.4	18.2
Turkey	2009	17.6	13.8	4.0	6.3	61.2	74.8	80.2	8.8	10.8	9.0	30.0	14.4	10.8
Uruguay	2007	10.4	7.7	5.9	4.6	49.7	…	55.8	28.4	…	26.1	21.9	…	18.0

a/ At current prices.

Table 1.11

SELECTED CHARACTERISTICS OF BRANCHES, SELECTED YEARS AND ECONOMIES

Wearing apparel, except fur apparel (ISIC 1810)

Economy	Latest year (LY)	Value added per employee (current 1000 dollars)		Wages and salaries per employee (current 1000 dollars)		Percentage in output [a]								
						Costs of input materials and utilities			Costs of labour			Operating surplus		
		2000	LY	2000	LY	2000	2006	LY	2000	2006	LY	2000	2006	LY
Industrialized Economies														
EU														
Austria	2009	...	56.4	...	30.3	...	63.4	64.9	...	21.2	18.9	...	15.4	16.3
Czech Republic	2007	4.6	12.6	2.3	6.7	57.8	59.6	58.8	21.4	23.0	22.0	20.8	17.3	19.2
Denmark	2009	41.6	107.9	27.4	67.7	71.7	...	71.9	18.6	...	17.6	9.7	...	10.5
Estonia	2010	4.1	11.2	2.4	6.8	53.8	...	50.7	27.1	...	29.9	19.1	...	19.4
Finland	2008	28.0	63.3	17.6	37.5	64.5	62.3	65.7	22.3	21.5	20.3	13.3	16.2	14.0
France	2009	28.6	64.5	17.1	37.9	72.6	69.7	63.2	16.4	16.1	21.7	11.0	14.3	15.2
Germany	2009	33.8	65.6	20.8	39.8	73.2	73.7	73.3	16.5	14.7	16.1	10.3	11.5	10.5
Hungary	2009	3.8	9.8	2.2	6.2	56.2	63.9	49.6	24.9	21.2	31.8	18.9	14.9	18.6
Italy	2009	31.4	45.8	12.7	25.5	70.7	74.4	77.2	11.9	11.2	12.7	17.4	14.4	10.1
Lithuania	2010	3.0	8.2	1.8	5.0	42.1	56.4	56.4	34.6	26.7	26.6	23.3	16.9	17.0
Malta	2008	...	23.5	...	12.6	...	64.4	77.0	...	23.9	12.3	...	11.7	10.7
Portugal	2009	8.7	14.0	5.4	10.4	64.3	...	62.3	22.2	...	28.1	13.5	...	9.7
Slovakia	2009	1.8	9.8	1.4	7.3	62.1	...	50.8	31.3	...	36.7	6.6	...	12.6
Slovenia	2010	9.6	19.7	8.0	16.1	50.3	49.8	48.7	41.4	41.6	42.0	8.3	8.6	9.2
Spain	2009	18.0	44.5	9.8	27.0	67.5	70.4	68.6	17.7	17.3	19.0	14.8	12.2	12.3
Sweden	2009	40.7	63.5	18.9	37.1	66.0	71.5	72.7	15.8	12.7	15.9	18.2	15.8	11.3
Other Europe														
Norway	2008	34.2	115.2	22.2	53.1	60.2	63.9	63.4	25.9	17.8	16.9	14.0	18.2	19.7
East Asia														
Japan	2010	36.8	45.2	10.8	12.2	47.6	46.9	47.9	15.4	15.0	14.1	37.0	38.1	38.0
Malaysia	2010	5.9	8.2	3.2	4.6	67.7	72.1	69.7	17.3	16.0	17.0	15.0	11.9	13.3
Republic of Korea	2008	27.6	87.0	10.4	18.2	52.5	49.7	49.4	17.9	13.5	10.6	29.6	36.8	40.0
Singapore	2008	16.8	21.8	11.0	14.6	76.7	67.2	70.9	15.3	23.6	19.6	8.0	9.3	9.6
West Asia														
Kuwait	2010	...	11.8	...	6.2	...	34.7	39.2	...	34.3	32.2	...	31.0	28.6

a/ At current prices.

Table 1.11
(continued)

SELECTED CHARACTERISTICS OF BRANCHES, SELECTED YEARS AND ECONOMIES

Wearing apparel, except fur apparel (ISIC 1810)

Economy	Latest year (LY)	Value added per employee (current 1000 dollars) 2000	Value added per employee (current 1000 dollars) LY	Wages and salaries per employee (current 1000 dollars) 2000	Wages and salaries per employee (current 1000 dollars) LY	Percentage in output a/ — Costs of input materials and utilities 2000	Costs of input materials and utilities 2006	Costs of input materials and utilities LY	Costs of labour 2000	Costs of labour 2006	Costs of labour LY	Operating surplus 2000	Operating surplus 2006	Operating surplus LY
North America														
Canada	2008	30.9	43.9	15.1	28.4	50.2	52.5	51.2	24.3	29.4	31.6	25.5	18.2	17.2
United States of America	2008	56.5	61.2	20.1	26.0	54.0	47.2	52.6	16.3	17.0	20.1	29.7	35.7	27.3
Others														
Israel	2009	20.8	25.0	15.0	19.4	63.3	70.7	70.0	26.5	21.8	23.3	10.2	7.6	6.7
Developing & EIE														
Brazil	2010	...	14.3	...	5.7	...	...	46.2	...	...	21.4	...	...	32.4
Bulgaria	2010	1.4	4.8	0.8	2.7	53.7	61.7	61.1	26.1	19.8	21.8	20.3	18.5	17.0
Chile	2008	12.0	18.4	6.4	8.3	62.3	59.1	55.8	20.0	18.0	19.9	17.7	23.0	24.3
China	2007	...	7.6	...	2.4	...	70.9	70.8	...	8.5	9.2	...	20.6	20.0
Cyprus	2010	15.7	26.3	7.8	19.8	60.5	60.2	51.6	19.7	25.9	36.4	19.8	14.0	12.0
Ecuador	2008	3.2	11.6	0.8	3.9	67.1	57.2	55.8	7.8	15.2	14.7	25.1	27.6	29.5
Egypt	2010	...	4.6	...	2.2	35.9	56.2	54.6	26.8	16.6	22.1	37.3	27.2	23.3
Eritrea	2010	1.8	4.1	0.7	1.0	55.8	66.7	57.2	24.3	12.8	10.0	19.9	20.5	32.8
Ethiopia	2009	0.9	0.8	0.5	0.7	60.5	61.9	81.5	24.8	31.6	15.0	14.7	6.5	3.5
Georgia	2010	0.3	4.0	0.2	2.1	...	56.5	50.6	...	27.0	26.3	...	16.5	23.1
Greece	2007	2.5	38.5	...	19.9	77.9	67.3	66.9	6.9	17.0	17.1	15.1	15.7	16.0
India	2009	2.2	3.2	0.8	1.6	63.2	75.3	78.1	12.7	10.4	10.6	24.2	14.3	11.3
Indonesia	2009	12.1	5.7	0.8	1.3	61.7	57.3	42.5	20.2	15.5	13.5	18.1	27.2	44.0
Iran (Islamic Republic of)	2010	4.0	11.7	6.4	5.3	36.3	53.5	50.9	27.5	22.4	22.2	36.2	24.1	26.9
Jordan	2010	...	14.9	1.7	3.2	...	46.2	37.5	...	10.5	13.5	...	43.3	49.1
Kyrgyzstan	2010	3.4	27.4	0.2	1.0	50.2	74.0	77.8	28.7	0.6	0.8	21.1	25.4	21.3
Latvia	2009	2.2	8.1	2.0	4.6	36.0	53.9	57.8	14.8	23.7	24.2	49.2	22.4	18.0
Malawi	2010	10.3	2.5	0.5	0.7	65.2	73.2	64.8	12.8	14.4	9.5	22.0	12.3	25.7
Mexico	2008	0.7	11.8	3.8	4.8	60.1	67.7	56.6	33.6	...	17.6	6.3	...	25.8
Mongolia	2010	3.5	0.8	0.6	0.6	58.1	...	69.5	28.4	...	24.3	13.5	...	6.1
Morocco	2010	6.0	5.1	2.3	3.7	63.1	59.6	60.2	17.3	...	28.7	19.7	...	11.1
Oman	2008	...	7.9	2.8	2.9	...	54.7	48.7	...	30.0	19.2	...	15.4	32.2
Philippines	2009	5.4	3.4	...	2.2	49.5	63.7	65.9	...	24.3	22.4	...	12.0	11.7
Poland	2010	...	9.6	...	5.8	54.2	55.2	53.4	...	24.7	27.9	...	20.1	18.7
Romania	2010	...	6.9	...	3.9	...	57.4	57.3	...	34.0	24.3	...	8.6	18.5
Sri Lanka	2010	...	5.0	...	1.2	...	42.9	53.0	...	11.7	11.7	...	45.4	35.3
The f. Yugosl. Rep of Macedonia	2009	12.7	5.0	3.9	3.8	67.1	51.5	41.9	10.1	39.7	44.4	22.9	8.7	13.7
Turkey	2010	...	11.0	...	6.3	...	80.4	80.7	...	10.6	11.1	...	9.0	8.2
United Republic of Tanzania	2010	...	3.7	...	0.5	...	20.7	36.5	...	4.1	8.4	...	75.3	55.1
Uruguay	2007	9.7	7.8	5.8	4.9	62.3	...	72.2	22.7	...	17.5	15.0	...	10.2

a/ At current prices.

Table 1.11

SELECTED CHARACTERISTICS OF BRANCHES, SELECTED YEARS AND ECONOMIES

Tanning, dressing and processing of leather (ISIC 191)

Economy	Latest year	Value added per employee (current 1000 dollars)		Wages and salaries per employee (current 1000 dollars)		Percentage in output [a]								
						Costs of input materials and utilities			Costs of labour			Operating surplus		
	(LY)	2000	LY	2000	LY	2000	2006	LY	2000	2006	LY	2000	2006	LY
Industrialized Economies														
EU														
Austria	2009	32.5	48.2	15.9	31.2	78.2	...	67.3	10.6	...	21.1	11.1	...	11.6
Estonia	2010	3.1	12.2	2.1	8.5	67.2	61.4	56.3	21.5	24.4	30.6	11.3	14.1	13.1
Finland	2008	38.3	68.2	18.7	36.4	65.8	50.0	51.6	16.8	28.6	25.8	17.5	21.4	22.6
France	2009	37.1	83.0	17.8	36.7	59.4	57.7	45.7	19.4	19.9	24.0	21.2	22.4	30.2
Germany	2009	31.0	58.5	20.9	34.7	70.1	69.8	67.0	20.2	16.5	19.5	9.7	13.6	13.5
Hungary	2009	...	15.9	...	8.5	...	61.3	74.2	...	12.8	13.8	...	25.9	12.0
Ireland	2009	27.9	68.3	16.8	22.8	77.9	...	57.1	13.2	...	14.3	8.8	...	28.6
Italy	2009	40.8	57.8	15.1	31.5	80.3	80.8	80.1	7.3	8.3	10.8	12.4	10.9	9.0
Lithuania	2010	5.4	7.9	2.3	5.2	83.3	59.6	77.8	7.2	13.7	14.8	9.5	26.7	7.4
Malta	2008	10.0	21.2	8.1	18.7	61.8	61.2	58.3	31.1	35.1	36.7	7.1	3.7	4.9
Netherlands	2008	46.0	62.4	24.4	36.3	74.7	...	70.5	13.4	...	17.1	11.9	...	12.3
Portugal	2009	12.3	24.6	7.1	14.6	75.6	...	72.3	14.1	...	16.4	10.3	...	11.3
Slovenia	2010	13.4	21.4	10.2	18.4	78.6	85.6	79.4	16.3	12.8	17.6	5.1	1.7	2.9
Spain	2009	24.3	53.7	12.9	30.2	74.6	71.8	68.2	13.5	17.0	17.9	11.9	11.2	13.9
Sweden	2009	42.2	72.6	21.3	34.4	68.8	...	61.9	15.7	...	18.0	15.4	...	20.0
United Kingdom	2007	43.0	65.5	19.5	36.4	61.6	62.5	61.5	17.4	21.4	21.4	21.0	16.1	17.1
Other Europe														
Norway	2008	...	69.4	...	55.5	...	70.4	73.8	...	24.7	20.9	...	4.9	5.2
East Asia														
Japan	2010	67.6	66.9	13.8	12.7	58.8	61.3	60.9	8.4	8.6	7.4	32.8	30.2	31.7
Malaysia	2010	6.1	10.2	3.4	5.0	71.9	76.2	70.6	15.7	11.7	14.4	12.5	12.2	15.0
Republic of Korea	2008	50.4	93.9	13.4	29.4	67.0	65.5	68.0	8.8	10.2	10.0	24.2	24.3	22.0
Singapore	2010	30.3	50.5	13.8	25.6	78.0	76.9	68.1	10.0	14.0	16.2	12.0	9.2	15.7

a/ At current prices.

Table 1.11
(continued)

SELECTED CHARACTERISTICS OF BRANCHES, SELECTED YEARS AND ECONOMIES

Tanning, dressing and processing of leather (ISIC 191)

Economy	Latest year (LY)	Value added per employee (current 1000 dollars)		Wages and salaries per employee (current 1000 dollars)		Percentage in output a/								
						Costs of input materials and utilities			Costs of labour			Operating surplus		
		2000	LY	2000	LY	2000	2006	LY	2000	2006	LY	2000	2006	LY
North America														
Canada	2008	30.4	42.6	14.9	27.2	61.5	51.8	51.0	18.9	29.4	31.4	19.6	18.8	17.6
United States of America	2008	73.9	82.8	25.2	32.5	52.2	50.2	55.0	16.3	16.8	17.6	31.5	33.0	27.4
Developing & EIE														
Azerbaijan	2010	...	31.7	...	7.0	...	70.9	62.3	...	5.0	8.3	...	24.1	29.3
Brazil	2010	8.8	19.4	3.2	7.2	73.4	70.6	64.9	9.6	10.0	13.0	17.0	19.4	22.1
Bulgaria	2010	2.2	5.3	1.0	3.0	78.4	...	66.7	10.3	...	18.6	11.2	...	14.8
Chile	2008	11.7	16.4	6.2	8.6	76.8	67.1	68.2	12.3	12.6	16.8	11.0	20.3	15.1
China	2007	...	9.6	...	2.4	...	72.7	73.0	...	6.5	6.6	...	20.8	20.4
Cyprus	2010	18.0	16.3	10.3	15.6	51.2	47.2	61.5	27.9	22.0	37.0	20.8	30.8	1.5
Ecuador	2008	5.4	8.4	0.9	3.6	74.1	70.9	75.0	4.2	10.1	10.6	21.7	19.0	14.4
Egypt	2010	...	4.6	...	1.8	...	62.0	76.6	...	2.0	9.1	...	36.0	14.3
Eritrea	2010	2.8	3.9	0.9	1.3	69.4	80.2	66.9	10.4	10.3	10.7	20.3	9.5	22.4
Ethiopia	2009	3.6	3.6	1.1	1.3	72.3	80.7	81.2	8.4	6.4	6.9	19.4	12.9	11.9
Georgia	2010	...	7.6	...	3.4	...	62.3	63.4	...	12.4	16.5	...	25.3	20.1
Greece	2007	...	40.4	...	21.9	...	64.6	67.1	...	16.5	17.8	...	19.0	15.1
India	2009	1.9	4.4	0.8	1.5	90.1	87.5	83.6	4.1	3.8	5.6	5.8	8.7	10.8
Indonesia	2009	3.0	4.2	0.6	1.3	66.8	59.4	72.1	6.9	15.2	8.4	26.3	25.4	19.6
Iran (Islamic Republic of)	2009	28.2	17.4	6.4	4.8	70.8	70.3	70.9	6.6	6.0	8.0	22.6	23.8	21.1
Jordan	2010	10.1	6.3	4.5	1.6	66.9	74.7	50.7	14.6	21.9	12.3	18.5	3.4	37.0
Latvia	2010	4.1	5.1	1.3	3.4	52.2	73.6	78.8	15.3	13.2	14.2	32.5	13.2	7.0
Mongolia	2008	1.1	2.4	0.5	1.0	64.7	81.0	67.7	16.1	11.5	13.2	19.2	7.5	19.1
Morocco	2010	5.8	8.4	3.0	5.2	75.7	68.1	67.6	12.5	...	20.2	11.9	...	12.2
Philippines	2008	...	15.1	...	3.0	...	77.1	62.2	...	8.6	7.4	...	14.3	30.4
Romania	2010	...	8.8	...	4.8	...	65.0	60.4	...	25.9	21.3	...	9.1	18.3
The f. Yugosl. Rep of Macedonia	2010	...	7.6	...	2.8	...	60.9	48.6	...	32.3	18.9	...	6.8	32.6
Turkey	2009	16.6	14.1	4.4	6.5	69.4	82.7	79.7	8.1	7.9	9.3	22.5	9.4	11.0
United Republic of Tanzania	2007	...	2.4	...	0.2	...	69.1	68.9	...	2.7	2.6	...	28.2	28.4
Uruguay	2007	40.8	17.9	12.9	8.4	80.3	...	80.6	6.2	...	9.1	13.5	...	10.3

a/ At current prices.

Table 1.11

SELECTED CHARACTERISTICS OF BRANCHES, SELECTED YEARS AND ECONOMIES

Footwear (ISIC 1920)

Economy	Latest year (LY)	Value added per employee (current 1000 dollars) 2000	Value added LY	Wages and salaries per employee (current 1000 dollars) 2000	Wages LY	Percentage in output a/ — Costs of input materials and utilities 2000	2006	LY	Costs of labour 2000	2006	LY	Operating surplus 2000	2006	LY
Industrialized Economies														
EU														
Austria	2009	31.3	95.7	17.5	41.5	66.8	65.3	69.0	18.6	16.6	13.5	14.6	18.1	17.5
Czech Republic	2007	3.8	12.2	2.6	7.7	65.6	59.6	59.5	23.1	27.6	25.5	11.3	12.7	15.1
Estonia	2010	5.4	13.5	2.9	8.3	68.3	53.7	51.7	16.9	29.6	29.7	14.9	16.7	18.5
Finland	2009	31.3	51.2	17.2	29.0	58.1	57.0	59.5	23.1	24.2	22.9	18.8	18.8	17.6
France	2009	26.2	57.9	16.6	35.6	65.8	67.4	56.7	21.6	20.9	26.6	12.6	11.7	16.7
Germany	2009	34.9	58.4	21.0	35.6	71.7	73.4	69.8	17.0	14.4	18.4	11.3	12.2	11.8
Hungary	2009	3.9	10.3	2.3	6.4	56.6	63.7	65.1	25.6	23.2	21.6	17.7	13.1	13.3
Ireland	2009	24.6	86.8	14.1	34.7	53.3	...	70.6	26.7	...	11.8	20.0	...	17.6
Italy	2009	29.6	46.7	12.6	25.1	73.9	73.2	77.3	11.1	12.1	12.2	15.0	14.7	10.5
Lithuania	2010	...	10.4	...	6.4	...	58.3	60.0	...	23.1	24.8	...	18.6	15.2
Netherlands	2008	29.6	76.1	18.3	38.1	65.6	65.2	62.5	21.2	19.1	18.8	13.1	15.6	18.8
Portugal	2009	9.3	18.3	5.8	11.4	70.7	69.2	67.7	18.2	19.0	20.2	11.1	11.8	12.2
Slovakia	2009	1.9	13.9	1.5	8.4	73.9	74.3	73.4	20.9	14.9	16.2	5.2	10.8	10.4
Slovenia	2010	11.4	21.9	9.3	17.8	64.2	63.1	72.7	29.1	26.1	22.2	6.7	10.8	5.1
Spain	2009	17.0	40.9	9.5	21.5	74.9	75.3	73.2	14.1	13.9	14.1	11.0	10.8	12.7
Sweden	2009	31.9	50.3	19.9	34.2	69.9	...	74.7	18.7	...	17.2	11.4	10.8	8.1
United Kingdom	2009	46.7	51.3	23.6	30.3	49.2	53.1	56.8	25.7	28.2	25.5	25.1	18.7	17.7
Other Europe														
Norway	2008	...	73.7	...	43.9	...	77.7	77.8	...	18.3	13.2	...	4.0	9.0
East Asia														
Japan	2010	51.9	61.7	15.0	16.8	60.9	60.7	60.6	11.3	11.0	10.7	27.8	28.3	28.7
Malaysia	2010	4.6	11.7	2.9	5.7	67.3	65.8	69.1	20.6	15.1	15.1	12.1	19.1	15.8
Republic of Korea	2008	28.7	68.5	11.0	16.5	55.5	56.8	51.4	17.0	14.9	11.7	27.5	28.3	36.9
Singapore	2010	28.6	13.6	19.2	10.0	62.0	82.9	63.9	25.5	11.2	26.6	12.5	5.9	9.5
West Asia														
Kuwait	2010	...	23.0	...	10.2	...	58.1	55.6	...	17.9	19.8	...	24.0	24.6

a/ At current prices.

Table 1.11
(continued)

SELECTED CHARACTERISTICS OF BRANCHES, SELECTED YEARS AND ECONOMIES

Footwear (ISIC 1920)

Economy	Latest year (LY)	Value added per employee (current 1000 dollars)		Wages and salaries per employee (current 1000 dollars)		Percentage in output [a]								
						Costs of input materials and utilities			Costs of labour			Operating surplus		
		2000	LY	2000	LY	2000	2006	LY	2000	2006	LY	2000	2006	LY
North America														
Canada	2009	31.4	41.9	15.7	25.5	49.0	47.2	53.1	25.5	29.2	28.5	25.4	23.6	18.3
United States of America	2008	56.0	82.3	22.9	29.7	54.7	47.1	45.5	18.5	20.5	19.7	26.8	32.4	34.8
Others														
Israel	2009	24.8	38.3	18.0	20.1	66.9	69.1	54.4	24.1	25.0	24.0	9.0	5.9	21.6
Developing & EIE														
Azerbaijan	2010	...	6.1	0.2	3.3	55.9	70.9	62.9	14.1	11.0	20.1	29.6	18.0	16.9
Brazil	2010	8.0	17.3	2.6	6.2	...	51.4	45.1	14.6	18.8	19.6	...	29.8	35.3
Bulgaria	2010	1.2	5.0	0.8	2.6	61.3	...	55.4	24.4	...	23.3	14.4	...	21.3
Chile	2008	14.7	28.1	6.5	9.9	49.0	54.5	53.3	22.7	15.3	16.5	28.3	30.1	30.3
China	2007	...	6.1	...	2.4	55.8	71.1	70.1	25.4	11.3	11.6	18.8	17.6	18.3
Cyprus	2010	17.4	21.6	10.0	15.4	75.3	48.4	56.9	5.6	29.1	30.8	19.1	22.5	12.3
Ecuador	2008	4.4	10.9	1.0	4.6	...	69.3	71.0	...	11.4	12.2	...	19.3	16.8
Egypt	2010	...	6.7	...	1.6	57.0	57.6	41.4	13.1	16.0	14.4	29.9	26.3	44.2
Eritrea	2010	2.0	2.8	0.6	0.9	64.0	55.1	61.6	10.1	9.9	13.0	25.9	34.9	25.5
Ethiopia	2009	2.6	2.7	0.7	0.7	...	65.4	68.8	...	9.2	8.1	...	25.5	23.1
Georgia	2010	...	2.4	...	1.3	...	87.3	66.8	...	7.3	17.7	...	5.4	15.5
Greece	2007	...	41.8	...	21.9	83.0	61.0	61.6	5.7	20.6	20.1	11.3	18.4	18.3
India	2009	2.4	4.3	0.8	1.6	58.7	81.9	82.1	12.7	6.3	6.8	28.6	11.9	11.1
Indonesia	2009	2.6	6.1	0.8	1.5	61.7	55.3	53.5	27.8	14.5	11.6	10.5	30.2	34.9
Iran (Islamic Republic of)	2010	9.9	9.7	7.2	4.8	73.2	62.5	64.5	12.4	14.2	17.7	14.3	23.3	17.8
Jordan	2009	5.9	19.0	2.7	6.4	80.4	62.8	44.1	14.7	5.6	19.0	4.8	31.7	36.9
Malawi	2010	1.1	10.1	0.8	1.6	64.4	62.1	57.0	17.6	7.9	6.7	18.0	30.0	36.3
Mexico	2010	8.7	11.4	4.3	5.5	60.3	68.5	69.5	27.0	...	14.8	12.6	...	15.7
Morocco	2010	4.0	8.2	2.8	4.8	49.8	58.3	56.1	20.4	...	25.8	29.8	...	18.1
Oman	2008	12.3	6.6	5.0	5.6	...	56.6	82.8	...	11.2	14.5	...	32.1	2.7
Philippines	2009	...	4.1	...	1.8	66.0	72.4	66.5	...	13.5	14.3	...	14.0	19.2
Poland	2010	5.6	13.5	...	6.7	...	78.8	61.5	...	18.4	19.0	...	2.8	19.6
Romania	2010	...	7.3	...	4.1	...	62.3	64.1	...	29.8	20.0	...	7.9	15.9
Sri Lanka	2010	...	4.3	...	1.4	...	57.2	54.7	...	14.4	14.5	...	28.4	30.8
The f. Yugosl. Rep of Macedonia	2009	...	4.5	4.8	3.9	60.5	45.8	47.2	14.3	42.3	46.3	25.3	11.9	6.5
Turkey	2010	13.2	12.2	...	5.7	...	80.2	79.6	...	8.5	9.6	...	11.3	10.8
United Republic of Tanzania	2010	...	1.5	...	0.3	...	88.8	69.3	...	6.7	5.3	...	4.5	25.4
Uruguay	2007	14.1	9.2	5.5	3.8	66.1	...	62.8	13.2	...	15.2	20.7	...	22.0

a/ At current prices.

Table 1.11

SELECTED CHARACTERISTICS OF BRANCHES, SELECTED YEARS AND ECONOMIES

Sawmilling and planing of wood (ISIC 2010)

Economy	Latest year (LY)	Value added per employee (current 1000 dollars)		Wages and salaries per employee (current 1000 dollars)		Percentage in output a/								
						Costs of input materials and utilities			Costs of labour			Operating surplus		
		2000	LY	2000	LY	2000	2006	LY	2000	2006	LY	2000	2006	LY
Industrialized Economies														
EU														
Austria	2009	55.6	76.7	21.2	39.1	72.3	73.2	77.4	10.6	10.1	11.5	17.1	16.8	11.1
Belgium	2009	40.2	87.1	18.4	33.6	78.1	81.0	73.2	10.1	7.5	10.3	11.9	11.5	16.4
Czech Republic	2007	5.5	24.9	3.1	8.8	82.3	85.5	79.2	10.0	7.5	7.4	7.7	7.0	13.4
Denmark	2009	41.8	76.2	26.2	62.5	67.1	67.1	73.0	20.6	20.6	22.1	12.3	12.4	4.9
Estonia	2010	6.9	40.6	2.6	11.4	78.5	79.0	74.8	8.0	7.6	7.1	13.5	13.4	18.1
Finland	2009	51.8	52.5	22.5	38.2	80.2	82.5	86.7	8.6	7.6	9.7	11.2	10.0	3.6
France	2009	34.6	63.8	17.7	38.5	67.8	68.6	70.3	16.5	17.4	17.9	15.7	13.9	11.8
Germany	2009	38.5	53.9	18.8	34.8	72.7	75.2	80.3	13.3	10.5	12.7	13.9	14.3	7.0
Hungary	2009	4.6	11.6	2.0	6.1	71.1	72.2	74.6	12.9	12.8	13.4	16.1	15.0	12.0
Italy	2009	37.5	59.4	13.5	26.2	73.2	72.6	77.0	9.7	8.7	10.2	17.1	18.7	12.9
Lithuania	2010	3.1	12.0	1.7	5.3	76.3	76.1	75.9	12.9	12.2	10.6	10.8	11.7	13.5
Netherlands	2008	56.2	79.1	26.6	38.2	70.6	68.9	68.9	13.9	14.5	15.0	15.5	16.6	16.1
Portugal	2009	12.4	22.4	6.2	12.9	73.8	71.4	70.0	13.2	14.5	17.3	13.0	14.1	12.7
Slovakia	2009	2.6	14.4	1.6	8.5	75.0	76.1	71.6	15.6	12.2	16.7	9.4	11.7	11.6
Slovenia	2010	13.7	32.7	9.3	18.8	71.6	66.9	73.0	19.3	16.9	15.6	9.2	16.2	11.5
Spain	2009	23.9	43.6	11.5	25.2	73.7	72.4	69.8	12.7	13.9	17.4	13.6	13.7	12.7
Sweden	2009	51.7	73.4	23.9	39.7	79.6	78.8	82.7	9.5	8.4	9.4	11.0	12.8	7.9
United Kingdom	2009	38.0	51.5	19.3	29.3	59.7	58.8	65.3	20.5	18.0	19.8	19.9	23.2	15.0
Other Europe														
Norway	2008	51.6	88.2	27.6	59.2	69.9	76.0	75.8	16.1	14.0	16.2	14.0	9.9	7.9
Russian Federation	2010	...	15.2	0.8	4.5	...	60.8	61.6	16.5	10.1	11.5	...	29.1	26.9
East Asia														
Japan	2010	63.4	80.6	6.9	10.7	63.8	65.6	62.0	3.9	4.5	5.1	32.3	29.9	33.0
Malaysia	2010	7.6	10.3	3.1	5.0	72.4	81.3	79.6	11.2	10.9	10.0	16.4	7.8	10.4
Republic of Korea	2008	44.3	69.4	12.2	20.4	60.1	68.1	69.7	11.0	9.6	8.9	28.9	22.3	21.4
Singapore	2007	35.6	32.1	22.5	15.0	58.6	...	47.4	26.2	...	24.6	15.3	...	28.0

a/ At current prices.

Table 1.11
(continued)

SELECTED CHARACTERISTICS OF BRANCHES, SELECTED YEARS AND ECONOMIES

Economy	Latest year (LY)	Sawmilling and planing of wood (ISIC 2010)												
		Value added per employee (current 1000 dollars)		Wages and salaries per employee (current 1000 dollars)		Percentage in output [a/]								
						Costs of input materials and utilities			Costs of labour			Operating surplus		
		2000	LY	2000	LY	2000	2006	LY	2000	2006	LY	2000	2006	LY
North America														
Canada	2009	64.7	73.3	26.7	40.0	64.2	67.1	64.7	14.8	16.0	19.3	21.0	16.9	16.1
United States of America	2008	60.5	79.2	27.0	37.0	69.7	69.4	70.0	13.5	12.0	14.0	16.8	18.6	16.0
Developing & EIE														
Brazil	2010	6.4	18.8	2.3	6.5	47.2	50.6	47.3	18.5	14.4	18.2	34.3	35.0	34.6
Bulgaria	2010	1.1	5.6	0.7	2.3	86.2	79.6	76.5	8.9	6.9	9.6	4.9	13.5	14.0
Chile	2008	38.2	40.0	7.4	9.0	45.1	61.1	59.7	10.6	8.7	9.0	44.3	30.3	31.3
China	2007	...	12.6	...	1.9	...	69.7	68.9	...	5.3	4.7	...	25.0	26.4
Cyprus	2010	15.3	49.3	9.3	19.1	59.8	53.9	41.8	24.3	20.1	22.5	15.9	25.9	35.6
Ecuador	2008	6.5	11.1	1.4	3.1	62.9	71.2	73.5	8.0	8.3	7.3	29.1	20.5	19.2
Georgia	2010	0.5	3.6	0.2	2.1	71.1	63.7	60.2	13.2	10.8	23.2	15.7	25.5	16.6
Greece	2007	...	45.7	...	22.0	...	69.7	68.4	...	16.7	15.2	...	13.6	16.5
India	2009	1.0	2.1	0.4	0.9	87.3	92.7	92.2	4.9	3.0	3.3	7.8	4.3	4.5
Indonesia	2009	2.2	9.2	0.6	0.9	61.9	69.8	50.7	9.6	14.4	5.1	28.4	15.8	44.2
Iran (Islamic Republic of)	2009	12.8	17.4	8.0	8.4	50.7	32.9	32.9	30.6	63.2	32.2	18.7	4.0	34.9
Jordan	2010	10.7	22.0	2.2	2.5	74.2	81.9	38.7	5.2	10.4	6.9	20.6	7.7	54.5
Kyrgyzstan	2010	5.1	1.4	0.1	0.6	68.0	16.0	49.7	10.6	15.1	22.3	21.4	68.8	28.0
Latvia	2010	7.7	21.8	1.7	5.7	84.7	73.6	74.1	7.0	7.8	6.8	8.3	18.6	19.1
Morocco	2008	...	8.6	3.5	3.6	...	79.7	73.9	13.3	...	10.8	...	...	15.3
Philippines	2009	6.7	5.3	...	1.9	72.5	69.1	68.6	...	10.7	11.2	...	20.2	20.3
Poland	2010	...	13.8	...	6.6	...	71.8	72.3	...	11.4	13.3	...	16.8	14.4
Romania	2010	...	9.6	...	3.0	...	80.9	76.1	...	9.7	7.6	...	9.3	16.3
Sri Lanka	2010	...	8.1	...	1.8	...	24.4	57.7	...	18.1	9.4	...	57.5	32.9
The f. Yugosl. Rep of Macedonia	2010	9.4	4.9	3.1	3.4	72.3	50.2	65.9	9.0	36.5	24.1	18.7	13.3	10.1
Turkey	2009	...	15.9	...	5.3	...	82.1	80.4	...	5.4	6.5	...	12.5	13.1
United Republic of Tanzania	2010	...	10.6	...	1.0	...	...	56.1	...	...	4.0	...	...	39.9
Uruguay	2007	22.7	22.3	8.6	6.2	66.5	...	72.6	12.7	...	7.6	20.7	...	19.8

a/ At current prices.

Table 1.11

SELECTED CHARACTERISTICS OF BRANCHES, SELECTED YEARS AND ECONOMIES

Products of wood, cork, straw, etc. (ISIC 202)

Economy	Latest year (LY)	Value added per employee (current 1000 dollars)		Percentage in output a/											
				Wages and salaries per employee (current 1000 dollars)		Costs of input materials and utilities			Costs of labour			Operating surplus		
		2000	LY	2000	LY	2000	2006	LY	2000	2006	LY	2000	2006	LY
Industrialized Economies														
EU														
Austria	2009	36.7	78.2	21.6	41.6	64.9	66.5	67.9	20.7	17.5	17.1	14.4	16.0	15.0
Belgium	2009	55.5	100.1	20.7	41.8	72.8	72.3	69.5	10.2	9.8	12.7	17.0	17.9	17.8
Czech Republic	2007	7.0	28.6	3.0	9.0	73.7	68.9	70.5	11.5	10.0	9.2	14.9	21.1	20.3
Denmark	2009	40.5	76.2	28.1	59.9	60.9	62.9	65.9	27.1	25.0	26.8	12.0	12.1	7.3
Estonia	2010	6.2	24.7	2.8	11.1	70.5	69.3	70.7	13.6	14.3	13.2	16.0	16.4	16.1
Finland	2009	39.8	45.4	21.3	36.2	65.8	71.8	78.0	18.3	16.0	17.6	16.0	12.2	4.5
France	2009	35.3	60.4	17.9	36.6	71.0	70.4	69.1	14.7	15.5	18.7	14.3	14.1	12.2
Germany	2009	35.1	63.9	23.6	38.1	64.5	69.0	71.3	23.8	17.1	17.1	11.7	13.9	11.6
Hungary	2009	5.6	15.7	2.4	7.7	72.1	72.8	73.2	12.0	13.5	13.2	15.9	13.6	13.6
Ireland	2008	34.1	71.0	18.5	45.9	71.1	69.5	66.3	15.7	18.4	21.8	13.2	12.0	11.9
Italy	2009	39.6	58.7	13.6	27.8	68.7	69.6	71.1	10.7	11.7	13.7	20.6	18.7	15.2
Lithuania	2010	3.6	13.6	2.1	6.2	69.8	69.5	74.0	17.3	14.8	11.9	12.9	15.7	14.1
Malta	2008	17.5	23.4	5.8	14.5	49.0	65.5	65.8	16.9	21.9	21.2	34.2	12.6	13.0
Netherlands	2008	44.3	85.9	23.7	48.2	65.4	...	67.8	18.5	...	18.1	16.1	...	14.1
Portugal	2009	16.0	25.4	7.2	14.8	77.8	75.3	74.9	10.1	11.6	14.6	12.1	13.1	10.5
Slovakia	2009	3.3	13.8	1.8	9.8	77.2	78.0	80.6	12.3	8.7	13.9	10.5	13.3	5.5
Slovenia	2010	12.6	26.6	10.0	19.2	72.3	69.2	71.0	22.0	20.2	21.0	5.7	10.6	8.1
Spain	2009	23.9	47.5	11.8	28.9	71.4	69.7	68.1	14.1	15.6	19.4	14.4	14.7	12.5
Sweden	2009	43.2	68.0	22.3	37.2	68.1	68.7	70.3	16.5	15.8	16.3	15.4	15.6	13.4
United Kingdom	2009	43.5	52.9	22.6	32.5	61.3	63.5	66.1	20.1	20.6	20.8	18.7	16.0	13.1
Other Europe														
Norway	2008	40.1	88.3	27.3	58.9	66.3	65.2	66.5	22.9	22.4	22.4	10.7	12.4	11.2
Russian Federation	2010	...	20.8	0.6	5.4	...	59.4	56.9	24.2	12.4	11.2	...	28.2	32.0
East Asia														
Japan	2010	69.1	79.1	13.3	17.2	60.1	61.6	64.4	7.7	7.4	7.8	32.2	31.0	27.9
Malaysia	2010	8.9	13.9	2.6	4.7	67.8	74.3	73.8	9.5	8.0	8.8	22.6	17.7	17.5
Republic of Korea	2008	46.6	78.1	13.3	23.1	59.2	64.9	65.7	11.7	12.0	10.1	29.2	23.1	24.2
Singapore	2010	25.6	29.9	15.9	18.3	76.5	79.4	66.6	14.6	15.0	20.5	8.9	5.6	12.9
West Asia														
Kuwait	2010	...	16.5	...	6.9	...	65.4	64.8	...	14.9	14.7	...	19.7	20.4

a/ At current prices.

Table 1.11
(continued)

SELECTED CHARACTERISTICS OF BRANCHES, SELECTED YEARS AND ECONOMIES

Products of wood, cork, straw, etc. (ISIC 202)

Economy	Latest year (LY)	Value added per employee (current 1000 dollars)		Wages and salaries per employee (current 1000 dollars)		Percentage in output [a]								
						Costs of input materials and utilities			Costs of labour			Operating surplus		
		2000	LY	2000	LY	2000	2006	LY	2000	2006	LY	2000	2006	LY
North America														
Canada	2009	63.9	71.1	24.4	37.1	56.0	59.0	59.6	16.8	18.6	21.1	27.2	22.5	19.3
United States of America	2008	61.5	73.8	27.1	33.0	56.3	56.9	57.2	19.3	17.8	19.2	24.4	25.3	23.7
Others														
Israel	2009	30.1	35.2	23.0	24.6	64.8	66.2	61.7	27.0	28.5	26.8	8.2	5.3	11.5
Developing & EIE														
Azerbaijan	2010	...	4.5	0.1	4.0	...	82.0	53.8	7.2	10.5	40.9	...	7.5	5.3
Brazil	2010	9.7	25.9	3.0	8.1	49.6	55.9	52.8	15.5	13.0	14.8	34.8	31.1	32.3
Bulgaria	2010	2.0	9.1	1.0	3.6	80.7	74.1	74.2	9.2	8.5	10.2	10.1	17.4	15.6
Chile	2008	34.5	57.3	6.8	10.8	44.5	54.4	50.6	11.0	10.1	9.3	44.5	35.5	40.1
China	2007	...	12.0	...	2.1	...	71.6	70.6	...	5.4	5.2	...	23.0	24.3
Cyprus	2010	20.9	35.3	10.8	24.5	56.3	58.8	59.6	22.7	24.0	28.0	21.0	17.3	12.4
Ecuador	2008	9.4	64.2	1.6	5.2	67.0	52.4	37.5	5.6	8.0	5.0	27.4	39.6	57.5
Egypt	2010	...	7.3	...	3.0	...	70.5	64.9	...	12.6	14.2	...	17.0	20.9
Georgia	2010	0.6	4.5	0.2	2.7	65.6	66.2	61.2	11.3	12.5	23.6	23.1	21.4	15.2
Greece	2007	...	44.6	...	21.6	...	65.2	64.9	...	17.5	17.0	...	17.3	18.1
India	2009	1.9	4.6	0.7	1.5	82.2	87.5	84.8	6.5	5.0	4.9	11.4	7.5	10.4
Indonesia	2009	4.2	7.4	0.8	1.5	63.7	60.6	55.5	6.9	...	9.3	29.3	27.6	35.2
Iran (Islamic Republic of)	2009	22.8	21.8	9.7	7.2	54.2	62.3	61.3	19.6	10.1	12.8	26.2	32.6	25.9
Jordan	2010	5.3	5.0	2.3	1.8	66.8	58.4	66.7	14.3	9.0	11.9	18.9	17.8	21.3
Kyrgyzstan	2010	...	5.6	0.2	0.6	60.0	65.2	71.5	10.0	17.0	2.8	22.1	12.1	25.6
Latvia	2010	7.9	28.5	3.5	7.8	69.9	76.6	67.6	17.9	11.2	8.9	20.4	...	23.6
Mexico	2008	12.3	13.4	4.0	5.6	47.8	74.3	73.8	9.7	...	11.0	34.4	...	15.3
Mongolia	2010	1.1	9.2	0.4	4.5	66.3	...	80.2	17.8	...	9.8	19.5	...	10.0
Morocco	2010	7.6	9.1	3.2	5.4	49.0	75.5	77.6	14.2	9.7	13.3	29.8	...	9.1
Oman	2008	10.5	39.9	4.4	5.9	67.6	37.6	26.6	21.2	8.8	10.9	...	52.6	62.5
Philippines	2009	...	6.5	...	2.6	...	89.8	80.8	...	9.4	7.7	...	1.4	11.5
Poland	2010	11.6	21.4	...	8.0	...	70.8	70.7	...	11.2	11.0	...	19.8	18.3
Romania	2010	...	16.7	...	4.9	...	79.9	75.6	...	...	7.1	...	8.9	17.3
The f. Yugosl. Rep of Macedonia	2010	...	5.2	...	3.5	...	51.3	63.5	...	31.3	24.5	...	17.4	12.0
Turkey	2009	31.3	24.1	5.1	7.4	57.4	...	79.6	7.0	...	6.3	35.6	...	14.1
Uruguay	2007	8.5	13.4	5.5	5.6	53.2	...	64.1	30.6	...	15.0	16.2	...	20.9

a/ At current prices.

Table 1.11

SELECTED CHARACTERISTICS OF BRANCHES, SELECTED YEARS AND ECONOMIES

Paper and paper products (ISIC 210)

| Economy | Latest year (LY) | Value added per employee (current 1000 dollars) | | Wages and salaries per employee (current 1000 dollars) | | Percentage in output a/ | | | | | | | | |
| | | | | | | Costs of input materials and utilities | | | Costs of labour | | | Operating surplus | | |
		2000	LY	2000	LY	2000	2006	LY	2000	2006	LY	2000	2006	LY
Industrialized Economies														
EU														
Austria	2009	87.6	125.3	32.3	58.8	67.2	69.0	68.4	12.1	13.7	14.8	20.7	17.2	16.8
Belgium	2009	70.2	186.3	28.9	54.4	71.2	77.4	58.6	11.9	10.9	12.1	17.0	11.7	29.3
Czech Republic	2007	17.5	38.1	4.3	12.5	72.9	75.2	74.6	6.6	8.4	8.3	20.5	16.4	17.1
Denmark	2009	55.9	100.7	34.1	74.8	64.0	64.9	65.5	22.0	24.5	25.6	14.0	10.6	8.9
Estonia	2010	12.0	50.6	4.1	13.6	72.0	75.6	72.5	9.7	10.1	7.4	18.4	14.3	20.2
Finland	2009	123.7	97.0	32.0	57.9	64.4	75.4	82.5	9.2	9.9	10.5	26.4	14.7	7.1
France	2009	50.1	80.4	24.3	46.3	75.2	76.6	73.8	12.0	13.6	15.0	12.8	9.7	11.1
Germany	2009	57.3	92.0	30.5	52.3	68.8	70.8	71.9	16.6	15.5	16.0	14.6	13.8	12.1
Hungary	2009	14.2	35.7	4.9	14.7	78.3	74.3	71.6	7.5	12.3	11.7	14.1	13.5	16.7
Ireland	2009	56.2	71.5	26.1	52.9	61.9	75.0	65.6	17.7	22.2	25.4	20.4	2.8	9.0
Italy	2009	54.1	71.6	20.0	37.8	75.2	78.0	80.1	9.1	9.7	10.5	15.6	12.3	9.4
Lithuania	2010	6.0	26.1	3.2	10.1	72.8	76.3	72.7	14.5	10.1	10.6	12.6	13.6	16.8
Malta	2008	20.1	30.1	11.2	22.4	62.0	63.5	64.7	21.1	22.3	26.2	16.9	14.2	9.0
Netherlands	2008	58.1	110.2	29.4	58.7	70.4	72.0	73.6	15.0	14.5	14.1	14.6	13.5	12.3
Portugal	2009	62.1	76.9	13.2	26.0	59.7	68.6	76.1	8.6	8.5	8.1	31.8	22.9	15.8
Slovakia	2009	11.4	48.9	2.6	15.8	73.1	78.5	76.9	6.1	5.6	7.5	20.8	15.8	15.6
Slovenia	2010	22.8	42.8	12.8	25.6	79.5	78.2	78.9	11.5	12.9	12.6	9.0	8.8	8.5
Spain	2009	51.3	87.3	19.6	41.6	70.3	72.1	71.4	11.4	12.3	13.6	18.4	15.6	15.0
Sweden	2009	105.3	123.3	28.6	49.7	62.7	72.2	73.8	10.2	10.1	10.6	27.2	17.7	15.7
United Kingdom	2007	62.5	88.5	32.5	49.5	64.9	76.2	70.7	18.3	16.5	16.4	16.9	7.3	12.9
Other Europe														
Norway	2008	102.6	105.4	38.7	72.0	58.4	73.7	81.3	15.7	15.9	12.8	25.9	10.4	5.9
Russian Federation	2010	...	33.7	1.6	8.1	...	68.9	69.8	7.8	8.5	7.3	...	22.6	23.0
Switzerland	2007	72.7	...	42.0	...	65.3	67.2	67.4	20.0	20.3	19.0	14.7	12.5	13.6
East Asia														
Japan	2010	114.8	143.3	29.1	34.5	62.5	65.5	66.3	9.5	8.4	8.1	28.0	26.1	25.6
Malaysia	2010	16.9	16.0	4.4	6.6	68.2	77.9	75.3	8.3	8.5	10.1	23.6	13.5	14.6
Republic of Korea	2008	79.7	105.4	16.0	26.4	63.5	64.2	68.4	7.3	9.5	7.9	29.2	26.3	23.7
Singapore	2010	43.3	49.2	19.0	28.7	60.5	74.2	75.8	17.4	15.4	14.1	22.1	10.4	10.1
West Asia														
Kuwait	2010	...	32.1	...	11.4	...	74.8	71.9	...	12.1	10.0	...	13.1	18.1
North America														
Canada	2009	127.0	108.9	36.3	47.6	53.6	61.1	58.7	13.2	15.0	18.1	33.1	23.9	23.2

a/ At current prices.

Table 1.11
(continued)

SELECTED CHARACTERISTICS OF BRANCHES, SELECTED YEARS AND ECONOMIES

Paper and paper products (ISIC 210)

Economy	Latest year (LY)	Value added per employee (current 1000 dollars) 2000	LY	Wages and salaries per employee (current 1000 dollars) 2000	LY	Percentage in output [a] — Costs of input materials and utilities 2000	2006	LY	Costs of labour 2000	2006	LY	Operating surplus 2000	2006	LY
United States of America	2008	141.8	196.3	41.0	51.0	52.6	52.7	55.7	13.7	12.1	11.5	33.7	35.2	32.8
Others														
Israel	2009	44.2	53.2	27.6	30.9	64.4	72.0	68.7	22.3	18.4	18.2	13.4	9.7	13.1
New Zealand	2009	49.2	81.8	...	45.3	66.8	72.3	76.7	...	14.2	12.9	...	13.5	10.4
Developing & EIE														
Azerbaijan	2010	...	9.2	0.1	3.7	...	69.6	62.3	5.2	5.2	15.2	...	25.2	22.5
Brazil	2010	45.8	75.9	7.8	16.1	46.8	51.3	52.9	9.0	9.2	10.0	44.2	39.5	37.1
Bulgaria	2010	1.7	13.5	1.2	4.2	83.9	78.6	74.6	11.3	7.5	7.9	4.8	13.9	17.5
China	2007	...	17.4	...	2.4	...	72.5	72.5	...	3.9	3.7	...	23.6	23.8
Cyprus	2010	22.8	43.1	11.8	25.4	63.3	63.0	62.0	18.9	20.9	22.4	17.7	16.2	15.6
Ecuador	2008	15.1	38.0	2.4	6.3	82.8	80.4	69.4	2.7	5.8	5.1	14.5	13.8	25.5
Egypt	2010	...	13.7	...	3.6	...	67.5	75.0	...	5.2	6.6	29.0	27.3	18.4
Eritrea	2010	2.4	2.9	0.7	0.6	58.4	44.7	44.6	12.6	14.8	11.3	32.8	40.5	44.1
Ethiopia	2009	3.5	7.3	0.8	1.3	57.8	58.4	58.7	9.5	9.1	7.3	...	32.5	34.0
Fiji	2009	...	13.6	...	1.7	...	76.2	67.9	...	8.1	3.9	23.1	15.7	28.2
Georgia	2010	1.1	8.7	0.5	3.6	60.2	76.6	67.7	16.7	10.5	13.4	...	12.9	18.9
Greece	2007	...	56.8	...	29.8	...	69.5	72.0	...	14.9	14.7	18.9	15.6	13.3
India	2009	5.7	6.9	1.3	2.2	75.5	78.2	82.9	5.7	5.4	5.5	20.6	16.4	11.7
Indonesia	2009	9.4	37.3	1.0	2.9	77.0	57.3	56.6	2.4	4.9	3.4	25.9	37.8	40.0
Iran (Islamic Republic of)	2009	41.0	16.6	12.0	7.4	63.5	67.1	65.1	10.7	12.9	15.7	22.1	20.0	19.2
Jordan	2010	14.4	24.6	3.9	7.2	69.8	67.1	71.1	8.1	7.2	8.5	21.8	25.7	20.4
Latvia	2009	8.9	23.5	2.9	9.5	67.8	70.9	72.9	10.4	10.9	11.0	44.8	18.2	16.1
Malawi	2010	19.4	9.5	2.7	4.1	47.8	84.1	85.3	7.4	7.4	6.3	34.5	8.6	8.4
Mauritius	2010	16.4	17.8	3.4	13.0	56.6	68.2	65.7	8.9	8.8	25.0	27.9	23.0	9.3
Mexico	2010	43.2	42.6	7.4	10.3	66.3	70.7	71.5	5.8	...	6.9	13.2	...	21.6
Mongolia	2008	0.8	9.4	0.5	2.9	65.1	...	81.1	21.6	...	5.8	25.2	...	13.1
Morocco	2010	22.4	33.2	6.0	10.5	65.6	69.6	73.3	9.2	9.7	8.4	23.4	21.0	18.3
Oman	2010	18.1	76.7	6.6	8.1	63.1	69.3	42.3	13.5	...	6.1	...	...	51.6
Philippines	2008	...	13.6	...	3.9	...	83.2	79.3	...	6.1	5.9	...	10.7	14.9
Poland	2009	16.4	39.9	...	12.1	74.7	71.4	69.1	10.6	8.0	9.3	...	20.5	21.5
Republic of Moldova	2010	...	5.6	0.5	2.4	...	85.2	81.1	...	7.3	8.1	...	7.5	10.8
Romania	2010	8.0	15.8	1.2	5.8	64.4	81.3	78.6	5.2	11.4	7.8	30.4	7.3	13.6
Sri Lanka	2010	...	7.8	...	1.7	...	70.7	69.3	...	7.1	6.5	...	22.2	24.2
The f. Yugosl. Rep of Macedonia	2010	...	12.9	...	8.1	65.7	65.6	60.7	...	23.1	24.7	22.6	11.3	14.7
Turkey	2009	31.3	30.0	10.7	11.8	65.7	78.8	79.6	11.7	7.6	8.0	22.6	13.7	12.4
United Republic of Tanzania	2007	...	14.0	...	3.6	...	36.4	36.4	...	16.3	16.3	...	47.3	47.3

a/ At current prices.

Table 1.11

SELECTED CHARACTERISTICS OF BRANCHES, SELECTED YEARS AND ECONOMIES

Publishing (ISIC 221)

Economy	Latest year (LY)	Value added per employee (current 1000 dollars)		Wages and salaries per employee (current 1000 dollars)		Percentage in output a/								
						Costs of input materials and utilities			Costs of labour			Operating surplus		
	(LY)	2000	LY	2000	LY	2000	2006	LY	2000	2006	LY	2000	2006	LY
Industrialized Economies														
EU														
Austria	2008	74.5	120.3	35.9	64.2	62.0	65.2	58.8	18.3	17.4	22.0	19.7	17.4	19.2
Belgium	2008	69.4	149.6	31.7	66.7	69.1	68.2	64.6	14.1	15.3	15.8	16.8	16.6	19.6
Czech Republic	2007	12.5	39.5	5.2	18.4	75.8	72.8	69.0	10.1	13.1	14.4	14.1	14.1	16.6
Denmark	2008	31.8	92.1	22.7	59.7	57.9	59.7	55.1	30.1	29.1	29.1	12.0	11.2	15.8
Estonia	2007	7.9	25.9	5.1	14.9	64.7	58.8	57.5	22.6	23.8	24.5	12.6	17.4	18.0
Finland	2008	49.3	90.4	26.7	53.3	59.6	60.8	62.3	21.9	21.8	22.3	18.5	17.3	15.5
France	2008	61.9	97.3	33.0	63.7	68.5	67.9	67.7	16.8	17.9	21.1	14.7	14.2	11.2
Germany	2007	52.6	75.0	28.0	41.1	62.4	63.4	63.3	20.1	20.7	20.1	17.6	15.9	16.6
Hungary	2008	16.9	40.7	4.7	20.9	71.5	64.6	62.5	7.9	16.9	19.2	20.6	18.5	18.3
Ireland	2008	71.6	121.4	30.0	76.9	41.8	45.5	42.0	24.3	24.5	36.7	33.9	30.0	21.2
Italy	2008	88.4	155.1	33.1	69.3	68.9	70.2	71.4	11.6	11.2	12.8	19.4	18.7	15.8
Lithuania	2008	6.7	15.6	4.0	9.6	62.1	70.5	74.9	22.4	16.4	15.5	15.4	13.1	9.6
Luxembourg	2008	...	108.5	...	76.6	35.0	45.1	40.6	26.5	39.5	41.9	38.6	15.4	17.5
Malta	2008	27.1	31.2	11.0	19.0	...	53.0	41.3	...	31.6	35.8	...	15.5	22.9
Netherlands	2008	73.0	125.4	32.7	61.5	57.3	62.4	58.9	19.1	17.6	20.2	23.6	20.0	20.9
Portugal	2008	31.5	50.7	15.9	30.0	67.4	...	66.1	16.5	...	20.1	16.1	...	13.8
Slovakia	2008	4.7	35.6	2.7	15.2	69.7	67.4	60.5	17.2	14.5	16.8	13.1	18.1	22.7
Slovenia	2007	32.9	49.2	25.9	33.4	59.2	64.4	65.7	32.2	23.8	23.3	8.6	11.8	11.1
Spain	2008	56.5	94.0	24.4	48.3	59.6	61.5	50.8	17.5	17.8	25.3	22.9	20.8	23.9
Sweden	2008	49.8	82.4	27.8	48.8	67.7	68.9	68.9	18.0	16.7	18.4	14.3	14.4	12.7
United Kingdom	2007	74.2	112.0	35.6	56.8	56.7	53.6	53.8	20.8	22.6	23.4	22.6	23.8	22.8
Other Europe														
Norway	2008	47.1	131.6	30.2	80.9	55.8	58.9	59.7	28.3	25.9	24.8	15.9	15.2	15.5
Russian Federation	2010	...	17.3	1.4	8.2	...	46.6	45.1	...	17.1	26.1	...	36.3	28.8
East Asia														
Malaysia	2008	22.3	25.5	6.7	10.3	50.7	55.3	63.7	14.7	13.8	14.7	34.5	31.0	21.7
West Asia														
Kuwait	2010	...	29.5	...	29.4	...	48.5	62.2	...	25.0	37.7	...	26.5	0.2

a/ At current prices.

Table 1.11
(continued)

SELECTED CHARACTERISTICS OF BRANCHES, SELECTED YEARS AND ECONOMIES

Publishing (ISIC 221)

Economy	Latest year (LY)	Value added per employee (current 1000 dollars)		Wages and salaries per employee (current 1000 dollars)		Percentage in output [a]								
						Costs of input materials and utilities			Costs of labour			Operating surplus		
		2000	LY	2000	LY	2000	2006	LY	2000	2006	LY	2000	2006	LY
Others														
Israel	2009	37.4	30.4	25.9	27.2	59.7	58.6	65.2	27.9	32.8	31.2	12.4	8.6	3.6
Developing & EIE														
Azerbaijan	2009	...	6.9	0.5	2.1	...	69.6	60.5	22.9	6.2	12.3	...	24.3	27.2
Brazil	2007	31.7	52.0	8.8	12.9	36.0	33.8	32.1	17.8	17.1	16.8	46.2	49.1	51.1
Bulgaria	2007	5.6	14.2	1.3	3.9	72.3	72.8	69.6	6.6	8.2	8.5	21.1	19.0	21.9
Chile	2008	38.6	30.6	11.6	15.2	32.0	57.8	55.9	20.5	18.0	21.9	47.5	24.2	22.2
Cyprus	2007	30.5	55.4	17.0	31.3	55.7	54.1	51.4	24.6	27.2	27.5	19.6	18.7	21.1
Ecuador	2008	5.5	18.5	2.1	8.2	71.1	59.2	60.5	11.4	14.8	17.5	17.6	26.0	22.0
Georgia	2010	0.8	5.6	0.4	2.6	63.2	57.8	59.6	21.2	11.9	18.6	15.5	30.3	21.8
Greece	2007	...	98.8	...	34.1	...	59.1	55.7	...	17.1	15.3	...	23.8	29.0
India	2007	7.6	17.4	2.5	5.1	70.5	68.0	66.0	9.7	9.6	9.9	19.8	22.3	24.1
Indonesia	2009	14.6	11.4	0.9	2.4	46.6	49.5	56.0	3.2	10.0	9.2	50.3	40.4	34.8
Iran (Islamic Republic of)	2009	30.6	14.5	9.2	9.5	44.5	44.4	51.9	16.7	31.7	31.6	38.8	23.9	16.6
Jordan	2010	17.1	27.0	6.4	9.8	44.3	43.0	47.0	20.6	16.9	19.3	35.0	40.1	33.7
Kyrgyzstan	2007	...	2.9	0.7	1.6	31.3	...	58.4	28.2	24.2	22.1	40.5	...	19.5
Latvia	2009	9.7	17.6	4.0	9.4	62.3	53.1	56.9	10.7	20.9	23.0	27.0	25.9	20.1
Malawi	2008	3.5	11.6	1.0	6.5	54.3	68.0	55.5	23.3	30.5	24.9	22.4	1.5	19.6
Mongolia	2008	6.7	4.2	3.4	2.2	52.1	80.5	77.6	27.4	9.9	11.7	20.6	9.6	10.7
Morocco	2010	10.8	13.3	6.2	7.8	55.1	49.3	63.4	...	...	21.5	...	...	15.1
Poland	2008	27.4	58.2	...	25.3	...	58.2	57.4	...	19.0	18.5	...	22.9	24.1
Romania	2008	...	13.0	...	8.4	...	71.6	78.7	...	14.2	13.8	...	14.2	7.4
Sri Lanka	2010	...	4.4	...	1.1	...	73.6	41.3	...	12.0	14.5	...	14.4	44.1
The f. Yugosl. Rep of Macedonia	2010	...	15.1	...	9.4	...	59.0	53.4	...	30.8	29.1	...	10.2	17.5
Uruguay	2007	31.8	16.4	15.6	9.4	50.9	...	58.7	24.1	...	23.7	25.1	...	17.6

[a] At current prices.

Table 1.11

SELECTED CHARACTERISTICS OF BRANCHES, SELECTED YEARS AND ECONOMIES

Printing and related service activities (ISIC 222)

Economy	Latest year (LY)	Value added per employee (current 1000 dollars)		Wages and salaries per employee (current 1000 dollars)		Percentage in output [a]								
						Costs of input materials and utilities			Costs of labour			Operating surplus		
		2000	LY	2000	LY	2000	2006	LY	2000	2006	LY	2000	2006	LY
Industrialized Economies														
EU														
Austria	2009	53.9	92.8	30.0	52.2	51.2	54.8	57.3	27.2	24.7	24.0	21.6	20.5	18.7
Belgium	2008	53.7	107.8	24.9	50.9	63.1	65.4	65.4	17.1	16.1	16.3	19.8	18.5	18.3
Czech Republic	2007	...	27.0	...	11.6	...	67.7	70.8	...	12.2	12.6	...	20.1	16.7
Denmark	2008	47.8	99.0	32.7	70.7	55.5	58.3	59.9	30.5	27.3	28.7	14.0	14.4	11.5
Estonia	2010	9.8	30.3	4.5	12.4	63.6	63.0	66.8	16.7	15.4	13.6	19.7	21.7	19.6
Finland	2009	46.5	68.8	24.3	42.8	57.1	60.1	61.6	22.4	21.7	23.9	20.5	18.1	14.5
France	2009	38.6	68.9	22.7	44.3	62.9	64.5	64.0	21.8	21.8	23.1	15.3	13.7	12.9
Germany	2009	45.7	65.5	26.4	43.0	54.2	60.2	64.0	26.5	22.9	23.6	19.4	16.9	12.3
Hungary	2009	8.1	19.2	3.3	9.7	69.7	66.5	67.9	12.5	16.2	16.1	17.8	17.3	15.9
Ireland	2009	43.2	77.9	22.7	50.1	52.1	65.7	53.3	25.2	28.9	30.1	22.7	5.4	16.6
Italy	2009	43.2	65.6	18.2	34.7	64.5	64.0	66.3	15.0	14.3	17.9	20.5	21.7	15.9
Lithuania	2010	6.3	15.7	2.8	7.1	65.3	66.8	69.5	15.3	13.3	13.9	19.4	19.9	16.7
Luxembourg	2006	60.3	75.3	30.4	47.3	44.3	49.3	49.3	28.1	31.9	31.9	27.5	18.8	18.8
Malta	2008	29.5	49.8	12.0	27.7	54.1	66.2	69.2	18.7	17.8	17.1	27.1	16.1	13.7
Netherlands	2009	49.2	83.0	25.6	48.2	57.9	61.5	63.6	22.0	22.5	21.2	20.1	16.0	15.3
Portugal	2009	21.4	36.5	9.9	18.3	55.8	55.5	56.7	20.5	22.1	21.8	23.7	22.5	21.6
Slovakia	2008	5.3	25.6	2.7	12.1	73.8	73.8	70.4	13.4	12.2	14.0	12.8	14.0	15.6
Slovenia	2010	17.3	38.4	12.4	22.0	68.6	62.7	67.1	22.5	20.6	18.9	8.9	16.8	14.0
Spain	2009	32.4	62.0	16.8	34.2	60.6	59.4	60.1	20.4	21.2	21.9	19.0	19.4	17.9
Sweden	2009	46.4	67.1	25.0	41.0	61.9	64.4	65.6	20.5	19.6	21.1	17.6	16.0	13.4
United Kingdom	2009	56.7	69.9	31.4	43.4	51.0	50.5	53.6	27.2	26.8	28.8	21.8	22.7	17.6
Other Europe														
Norway	2008	52.8	111.4	35.2	69.9	59.0	58.8	61.2	27.3	25.7	24.4	13.7	15.5	14.5
Russian Federation	2010	...	16.5	1.1	7.4	...	62.5	62.3	17.7	13.6	16.8	...	23.9	20.9
East Asia														
Japan	2010	87.6	100.0	23.4	28.2	53.8	53.6	56.3	12.3	11.7	12.3	33.8	34.7	31.4
Malaysia	2010	11.3	14.8	4.6	6.9	59.8	68.5	64.4	16.4	15.2	16.6	23.8	16.3	19.0
Republic of Korea	2008	38.3	60.7	13.2	23.2	50.9	48.6	51.2	17.0	18.8	18.6	32.2	32.6	30.2
Singapore	2010	48.4	58.5	22.7	33.7	50.5	54.1	49.4	23.3	24.5	29.1	26.3	21.4	21.4
West Asia														
Kuwait	2010	...	21.5	...	11.7	...	56.9	58.7	...	25.0	22.5	...	18.1	18.8

a/ At current prices.

Table 1.11
(continued)

SELECTED CHARACTERISTICS OF BRANCHES, SELECTED YEARS AND ECONOMIES

Printing and related service activities (ISIC 222)

Economy	Latest year (LY)	Value added per employee (current 1000 dollars) 2000	LY	Wages and salaries per employee (current 1000 dollars) 2000	LY	Percentage in output a/ — Costs of input materials and utilities 2000	2006	LY	Costs of labour 2000	2006	LY	Operating surplus 2000	2006	LY
North America														
Canada	2009	55.1	91.5	25.9	39.9	45.2	43.0	32.9	25.8	28.2	29.3	29.0	28.8	37.8
United States of America	2008	77.7	99.0	34.6	41.5	39.5	39.4	39.5	26.9	25.2	25.4	33.6	35.3	35.1
Developing & EIE														
Azerbaijan	2010	...	9.1	0.5	3.0	...	69.6	69.6	12.2	9.7	10.1	41.4	20.8	20.4
Brazil	2010	15.3	35.5	4.9	10.4	39.1	44.9	45.5	19.5	17.5	16.0	18.2	37.6	38.5
Bulgaria	2010	4.0	12.8	1.6	4.5	69.7	70.0	68.6	12.2	8.7	11.2	31.6	21.2	20.2
Chile	2008	30.9	29.0	11.1	13.2	50.6	59.2	54.3	17.9	17.8	20.8	25.5	22.9	24.9
China	2007	...	12.4	...	2.8	...	67.2	67.4	25.0	7.3	7.5	22.9	25.5	25.2
Cyprus	2008	25.5	53.2	12.6	27.3	49.5	56.6	56.2	7.5	23.8	22.4	29.5	19.6	21.3
Ecuador	2008	7.2	14.4	1.8	5.3	69.6	64.1	71.9	15.0	11.3	10.3	39.7	24.7	17.8
Egypt	2010	...	9.9	...	3.7	...	62.9	48.7	13.7	10.3	19.2	18.1	26.8	32.1
Eritrea	2010	3.2	6.2	1.1	1.1	55.6	55.8	53.0	12.2	11.1	8.1	20.7	33.1	38.9
Ethiopia	2009	3.6	5.1	0.9	1.4	46.6	61.7	50.7	12.5	11.5	13.4	54.0	26.7	35.9
Georgia	2010	0.9	9.4	0.3	3.6	69.7	62.0	61.9	19.9	8.0	14.8	26.1	30.0	23.3
Greece	2007	...	157.0	...	29.0	70.7	53.9	51.3	13.0	10.3	9.0	22.2	35.8	39.7
India	2009	3.8	9.2	1.1	2.8	33.6	74.5	71.7	21.3	7.4	8.6	37.6	18.1	19.8
Indonesia	2009	2.9	16.3	0.6	1.8	54.1	50.7	68.4	18.7	9.5	3.4	12.2	39.8	28.2
Iran (Islamic Republic of)	2009	17.1	16.7	7.4	5.8	64.8	49.9	67.0	16.7	19.3	11.5	26.5	30.8	21.4
Jordan	2010	9.2	15.7	3.4	4.8	43.7	63.6	57.0	13.5	13.8	13.1	24.9	22.6	30.0
Kyrgyzstan	2010	...	5.1	0.5	1.6	71.1	...	53.0	11.0	19.6	15.1	16.8	...	31.8
Latvia	2010	10.2	19.7	3.4	7.2	60.1	73.4	72.3	18.5	10.2	10.2	28.7	16.4	17.6
Malawi	2009	1.8	7.8	1.0	2.9	64.1	79.6	67.0	20.1	7.4	12.4	27.1	13.0	20.6
Mexico	2010	22.9	18.2	7.7	7.6	64.7	60.6	65.5	...	...	14.4	...	...	20.1
Mongolia	2008	1.7	5.4	0.5	1.7	51.2	69.3	64.3	...	12.6	11.0	...	18.2	24.7
Morocco	2010	7.6	13.3	4.0	7.9	...	68.1	69.2	...	...	18.3	...	12.5	12.5
Oman	2010	12.8	19.3	5.3	6.5	64.2	50.4	45.1	20.1	16.5	18.3	28.7	33.1	36.5
Philippines	2008	...	6.3	...	3.0	...	67.9	73.0	...	12.5	13.1	...	19.6	13.9
Poland	2009	16.2	27.7	...	11.2	...	64.5	67.7	...	12.0	13.0	...	23.4	19.3
Romania	2010	...	16.2	...	5.8	...	64.9	69.0	...	14.9	11.1	...	20.2	19.9
Sri Lanka	2010	...	7.3	...	2.5	...	66.9	56.4	...	5.3	15.1	...	27.8	28.5
The f. Yugosl. Rep of Macedonia	2010	...	12.5	...	7.7	...	59.1	61.7	...	26.2	23.5	...	14.8	14.7
Turkey	2009	25.8	18.3	9.2	8.0	57.8	77.7	74.5	15.0	9.4	11.1	27.1	12.9	14.4
United Republic of Tanzania	2007	...	16.6	...	6.9	...	55.7	55.7	...	18.5	18.5	...	25.8	25.9

a/ At current prices.

Table 1.11

SELECTED CHARACTERISTICS OF BRANCHES, SELECTED YEARS AND ECONOMIES

Basic chemicals (ISIC 241)

Economy	Latest year (LY)	Value added per employee (current 1000 dollars)		Wages and salaries per employee (current 1000 dollars)		Percentage in output [a]								
						Costs of input materials and utilities			Costs of labour			Operating surplus		
		2000	LY	2000	LY	2000	2006	LY	2000	2006	LY	2000	2006	LY
Industrialized Economies														
EU														
Austria	2008	112.9	189.3	40.1	75.7	69.2	74.3	80.8	11.0	8.6	7.7	19.9	17.1	11.5
Belgium	2008	129.1	230.6	42.2	89.7	74.2	79.3	83.4	8.4	7.3	6.5	17.3	13.4	10.1
Denmark	2006	90.7	162.5	45.5	73.5	64.0	57.2	57.2	18.0	19.3	19.3	17.9	23.4	23.4
Estonia	2007	4.9	52.6	3.5	12.4	89.4	78.5	73.7	7.6	6.7	6.2	3.0	14.8	20.1
Finland	2008	103.1	201.4	32.1	66.4	70.5	76.6	76.2	9.2	8.6	7.8	20.3	14.8	16.0
France	2008	84.5	166.6	31.6	67.6	78.7	83.5	81.9	8.0	7.4	7.3	13.3	9.0	10.7
Germany	2008	83.8	181.4	43.4	79.7	68.4	71.9	73.1	16.4	13.3	11.8	15.2	14.8	15.1
Hungary	2008	24.4	89.0	5.8	23.5	77.1	79.1	82.8	5.5	4.8	4.5	17.4	16.0	12.7
Italy	2008	71.9	91.8	25.9	52.7	80.6	86.9	88.7	7.0	6.5	6.5	12.4	6.6	4.8
Lithuania	2008	6.6	87.3	5.6	21.0	91.9	83.6	86.3	6.8	5.3	3.3	1.3	11.0	10.4
Netherlands	2008	137.0	289.7	42.5	87.1	80.4	85.9	86.6	6.1	4.4	4.0	13.6	9.8	9.4
Portugal	2008	57.4	134.9	18.2	38.4	79.0	...	82.4	6.7	...	5.0	14.3	...	12.6
Slovakia	2008	8.3	35.9	2.7	15.7	78.9	83.0	88.8	6.9	5.0	4.9	14.2	11.9	6.3
Slovenia	2007	23.2	54.7	15.2	26.3	77.9	74.6	75.3	14.4	12.2	11.9	7.6	13.2	12.8
Spain	2008	87.7	165.4	27.3	60.1	74.1	79.7	81.4	8.1	7.6	6.7	17.9	12.6	11.8
Sweden	2008	84.6	187.9	30.6	63.4	71.9	72.5	73.7	10.2	9.2	8.9	18.0	18.3	17.4
United Kingdom	2007	82.5	185.9	44.5	66.8	74.9	79.6	82.7	13.5	6.3	6.2	11.6	14.0	11.1
Other Europe														
Norway	2007	158.7	247.4	88.5	89.2	63.5	70.3	72.5	20.4	10.6	9.9	16.1	19.0	17.6
Russian Federation	2010	...	56.2	1.3	9.2	...	68.2	69.1	10.7	5.5	5.0	...	26.2	25.9
East Asia														
Japan	2007	293.8	284.1	54.1	49.4	57.3	69.8	72.3	7.9	4.9	4.8	34.8	25.3	22.9
Malaysia	2008	79.7	122.1	9.1	14.7	68.2	70.0	73.8	3.6	2.6	3.2	28.2	27.4	23.1
West Asia														
Kuwait	2010	...	165.6	...	63.6	...	50.4	82.6	...	10.3	6.7	...	39.3	10.7

a/ At current prices.

Table 1.11
(continued)

SELECTED CHARACTERISTICS OF BRANCHES, SELECTED YEARS AND ECONOMIES

Basic chemicals (ISIC 241)

Economy	Latest year (LY)	Value added per employee (current 1000 dollars)		Wages and salaries per employee (current 1000 dollars)		Percentage in output a/								
						Costs of input materials and utilities			Costs of labour			Operating surplus		
		2000	LY	2000	LY	2000	2006	LY	2000	2006	LY	2000	2006	LY
North America														
Canada	2008	209.3	339.4	40.3	69.3	65.9	75.7	76.4	6.6	4.9	4.8	27.5	19.4	18.8
United States of America	2008	231.8	455.9	52.8	66.9	61.5	58.4	67.1	8.8	5.5	4.8	29.7	36.1	28.1
Developing & EIE														
Azerbaijan	2009	...	9.9	0.7	3.7	...	76.7	57.3	10.9	8.8	16.2	...	14.5	26.4
Brazil	2007	82.0	128.5	13.4	20.7	68.6	72.5	71.5	5.1	4.7	4.6	26.3	22.8	23.9
Bulgaria	2007	6.7	31.8	2.3	6.2	80.7	81.5	75.2	6.7	5.0	4.8	12.7	13.5	19.9
Chile	2008	207.6	714.6	15.5	31.4	66.8	65.2	59.2	2.5	2.1	1.8	30.8	32.7	39.0
China	2007	...	26.3	...	3.0	...	76.3	75.0	...	3.0	2.8	...	20.8	22.2
Ecuador	2008	32.1	41.3	3.0	7.3	74.4	71.4	76.3	2.4	6.9	4.2	23.2	21.7	19.5
Eritrea	2010	2.4	8.9	1.4	2.2	63.4	26.3	54.6	21.9	13.9	11.1	14.6	59.8	34.3
Ethiopia	2009	1.9	3.1	0.7	1.1	39.5	...	62.0	20.4	21.6	13.7	40.0	...	24.3
Georgia	2010	1.5	11.8	0.9	5.3	54.8	61.9	69.2	27.3	9.3	13.8	17.9	28.8	17.0
Greece	2007	...	117.1	...	42.2	...	77.8	77.3	...	11.3	8.2	...	10.9	14.5
India	2007	17.0	35.1	2.5	4.7	78.2	80.8	79.3	3.2	2.7	2.8	18.6	16.5	18.0
Indonesia	2009	22.8	58.2	2.5	5.5	62.9	65.5	65.3	4.1	2.8	3.3	33.0	31.7	31.4
Iran (Islamic Republic of)	2009	272.5	134.4	18.7	14.2	26.0	57.3	55.9	5.1	3.4	4.6	68.9	39.3	39.5
Jordan	2010	30.4	91.5	7.9	12.0	80.8	69.8	57.6	5.0	6.0	5.6	14.2	24.2	36.8
Latvia	2007	5.6	17.8	2.5	4.6	60.7	76.1	61.7	17.5	8.6	9.9	21.7	15.3	28.4
Malawi	2009	7.3	14.8	1.2	4.8	73.6	87.8	92.1	4.2	4.6	2.5	22.2	7.6	5.3
Mexico	2010	61.3	111.5	13.4	25.5	70.9	75.4	83.1	6.4	...	3.9	22.8	...	13.0
Mongolia	2008	0.9	7.1	0.4	0.5	69.9	17.6	66.0	15.3	...	2.2	14.8	...	31.9
Morocco	2010	31.7	104.1	11.5	35.2	68.6	72.3	72.9	11.4	4.4	9.2	20.0	68.8	17.9
Oman	2010	44.3	441.0	7.4	19.5	46.7	26.8	32.3	8.9	5.6	3.0	44.4	15.1	64.7
Poland	2008	21.5	74.8	...	19.8	71.1	79.3	76.0	...	9.8	6.4	...	5.6	17.6
Romania	2008	...	23.0	...	13.1	82.4	84.5	82.6	...	5.9	9.9	...	45.0	7.5
Sri Lanka	2010	...	80.5	...	1.7	...	49.1	56.0	...	31.6	0.9	...	28.4	43.0
The f. Yugosl. Rep of Macedonia	2010	...	28.3	0.7	10.7	...	40.0	59.0	7.8	...	15.6	...	...	25.5
Ukraine	2010	...	2.2	0.7	3.8	...	...	81.2	7.8	8.0	6.6	...	1.4	...
United Republic of Tanzania	2007	...	...	...	2.0	...	81.3	...	...	17.3	17.2	...	...	1.5
Uruguay	2007	47.5	64.5	22.3	18.1	69.3	...	76.9	14.4	...	6.5	16.3	...	16.6

a/ At current prices.

Table 1.11

SELECTED CHARACTERISTICS OF BRANCHES, SELECTED YEARS AND ECONOMIES

Other chemicals (ISIC 242)

Economy	Latest year (LY)	Value added per employee (current 1000 dollars)		Wages and salaries per employee (current 1000 dollars)		Percentage in output a/								
						Costs of input materials and utilities			Costs of labour			Operating surplus		
		2000	LY	2000	LY	2000	2006	LY	2000	2006	LY	2000	2006	LY
Industrialized Economies														
EU														
Austria	2009	74.5	153.7	34.0	61.0	60.7	54.5	60.7	18.0	16.6	15.6	21.4	28.9	23.7
Belgium	2009	115.1	207.6	38.9	78.3	60.9	60.2	62.7	13.2	11.6	14.1	25.9	28.1	23.2
Estonia	2010	13.8	71.2	4.1	19.4	67.5	75.6	72.6	9.6	7.2	7.5	23.0	17.2	19.9
France	2009	78.8	132.0	33.1	57.5	72.8	69.0	70.2	11.4	11.8	13.0	15.8	19.3	16.8
Germany	2009	66.3	139.8	37.5	66.4	65.8	63.8	64.4	19.4	17.3	16.9	14.9	18.9	18.7
Hungary	2009	...	74.2	...	24.7	...	54.8	59.6	...	12.6	13.5	...	32.5	26.9
Italy	2009	77.1	133.4	29.1	53.8	70.0	74.1	71.1	11.3	10.8	11.7	18.7	15.0	17.3
Lithuania	2010	4.5	38.7	3.4	11.2	70.3	71.4	78.7	22.2	12.3	6.2	7.5	16.2	15.2
Malta	2008	23.1	207.2	10.7	36.1	67.7	45.5	40.3	15.0	18.2	10.4	17.3	36.3	49.3
Netherlands	2008	78.1	152.0	33.2	65.9	73.8	72.1	71.8	11.1	13.8	12.2	15.1	14.2	16.0
Portugal	2009	35.0	58.9	14.7	25.3	67.3	...	75.8	13.8	...	10.4	19.0	...	13.8
Slovakia	2009	6.1	26.3	2.7	13.2	81.4	...	82.5	8.3	...	8.7	10.3	...	8.7
Slovenia	2007	37.3	50.1	21.9	26.3	67.7	56.5	76.6	19.0	16.5	12.3	13.3	27.1	11.1
Spain	2009	57.6	112.8	26.0	53.7	68.5	70.6	71.0	14.2	13.4	13.8	17.3	16.0	15.2
United Kingdom	2007	...	180.8	...	70.0	...	55.9	57.0	...	16.5	16.7	...	27.5	26.3
Other Europe														
Norway	2007	88.8	221.1	41.4	81.0	63.7	52.3	53.6	16.9	17.4	17.0	19.4	30.3	29.4
Russian Federation	2010	...	29.9	1.0	8.4	...	67.2	69.9	6.0	11.0	8.4	...	21.8	21.7
East Asia														
Japan	2010	302.3	367.4	46.8	52.4	47.0	46.9	49.3	8.2	7.5	7.2	44.8	45.6	43.5
Malaysia	2010	22.5	28.3	6.2	8.8	70.6	75.3	78.3	8.1	6.7	6.7	21.3	18.1	15.0
Republic of Korea	2008	109.2	201.4	17.2	27.5	50.6	48.8	50.7	7.8	7.9	6.7	41.6	43.4	42.5
Singapore	2010	209.8	...	38.6	58.0	62.6	...	...	6.9	...	4.6	30.5	...	...
West Asia														
Kuwait	2010	...	39.2	...	15.3	...	62.5	67.1	...	13.5	12.8	...	24.0	20.0

a/ At current prices.

Table 1.11
(continued)

SELECTED CHARACTERISTICS OF BRANCHES, SELECTED YEARS AND ECONOMIES

Other chemicals (ISIC 242)

Economy	Latest year (LY)	Value added per employee (current 1000 dollars) 2000	Value added per employee LY	Wages and salaries per employee (current 1000 dollars) 2000	Wages and salaries per employee LY	Percentage in output a/ — Costs of input materials and utilities 2000	2006	LY	Costs of labour 2000	2006	LY	Operating surplus 2000	2006	LY
North America														
Canada	2009	114.9	116.5	31.8	47.1	54.0	48.7	46.7	12.7	16.8	21.6	33.3	34.5	31.8
United States of America	2008	284.8	459.1	47.7	64.5	37.9	36.5	38.4	10.4	8.3	8.6	51.7	55.2	52.9
Others														
Israel	2009	61.7	143.5	34.7	49.5	63.9	58.5	60.2	20.3	11.6	13.7	15.8	29.9	26.0
Developing & EIE														
Azerbaijan	2010	...	6.0	0.3	4.0	...	76.7	44.5	2.1	13.4	37.0	...	9.9	18.6
Brazil	2010	44.0	91.8	10.7	22.4	51.5	53.9	52.4	11.8	11.5	11.6	36.7	34.6	36.0
Bulgaria	2007	5.6	15.3	1.6	4.3	69.6	71.4	72.0	8.9	7.8	7.8	21.5	20.8	20.1
Chile	2008	56.9	68.8	13.7	20.1	42.1	46.9	49.1	13.9	14.4	14.9	44.0	38.6	36.0
China	2007	...	23.5	...	3.4	...	67.7	67.7	...	4.7	4.6	...	27.6	27.6
Cyprus	2010	34.9	61.5	13.6	28.4	60.9	59.4	60.2	15.3	18.4	18.3	23.8	22.2	21.5
Ecuador	2008	37.0	41.8	2.6	8.1	50.2	73.1	66.7	3.4	7.6	6.4	46.3	19.3	26.8
Egypt	2010	...	22.3	...	5.4	49.7	61.0	61.6	6.4	8.1	9.4	43.8	30.9	29.1
Eritrea	2010	5.2	6.9	0.7	1.2	62.3	61.5	55.9	5.1	6.0	7.8	32.5	32.5	36.4
Ethiopia	2009	6.1	10.9	0.8	0.2	64.0	71.4	65.0	9.8	5.2	0.8	26.2	23.4	34.2
Georgia	2010	1.4	11.3	0.4	4.0	...	58.8	52.9	...	11.6	16.7	...	29.6	30.4
Greece	2007	6.7	78.7	1.5	35.2	75.2	64.3	61.3	5.4	16.6	17.3	19.4	19.1	21.4
India	2009	8.6	17.9	1.6	3.2	60.2	71.3	69.5	7.3	5.3	5.5	32.5	23.4	25.0
Indonesia	2009	45.0	60.1	10.6	2.7	62.4	53.9	54.3	8.9	5.8	2.1	28.7	40.3	43.7
Iran (Islamic Republic of)	2009	18.6	37.2	4.9	9.1	61.1	64.7	61.1	10.3	9.1	9.5	28.6	26.2	29.4
Jordan	2010	...	49.4	0.3	11.8	...	63.7	57.6	12.7	10.5	10.2	...	25.8	32.3
Kyrgyzstan	2010	9.6	6.3	3.5	1.2	53.5	74.5	65.4	17.0	5.3	6.5	29.6	20.2	28.1
Latvia	2009	8.1	17.5	2.1	4.5	78.9	53.8	65.0	5.5	16.7	9.1	15.7	29.4	26.0
Malawi	2008	1.7	22.0	0.8	4.3	84.7	69.6	66.3	7.0	6.7	6.6	8.4	23.7	27.1
Mongolia	2010	22.6	9.6	10.1	3.3	67.2	63.9	62.8	14.7	12.7	12.9	18.1	23.4	24.4
Morocco	2010	38.9	54.0	7.8	21.1	63.7	62.5	59.9	7.3	...	15.7	29.0	24.4	24.4
Oman	2008	...	52.7	...	10.4	...	62.4	56.6	...	9.1	8.6	...	28.5	34.9
Philippines	2009	...	25.2	...	8.0	...	74.6	77.5	...	8.7	7.2	...	16.7	15.4
Poland	2010	...	50.8	...	16.5	60.1	67.1	65.6	...	10.4	11.2	...	22.5	23.2
Romania	2010	...	32.8	...	9.5	...	70.5	66.0	...	12.6	9.9	...	16.9	24.2
Sri Lanka	2010	...	17.2	...	1.9	...	68.2	50.0	...	3.0	5.5	...	28.8	44.5
The f. Yugosl. Rep of Macedonia	2009	...	37.7	...	14.3	48.2	53.3	44.4	...	24.2	21.2	...	22.5	34.4
Turkey	2009	79.1	25.9	14.9	14.3	48.2	...	67.4	9.7	...	18.0	42.0	...	14.6
Uruguay	2007	37.0	30.1	21.4	15.0	60.4	...	65.8	22.9	...	17.0	16.7	...	17.2

a/ At current prices.

Table 1.11

SELECTED CHARACTERISTICS OF BRANCHES, SELECTED YEARS AND ECONOMIES

Rubber products (ISIC 251)

Economy	Latest year (LY)	Value added per employee (current 1000 dollars)		Wages and salaries per employee (current 1000 dollars)		Percentage in output [a]								
						Costs of input materials and utilities			Costs of labour			Operating surplus		
		2000	LY	2000	LY	2000	2006	LY	2000	2006	LY	2000	2006	LY
Industrialized Economies														
EU														
Austria	2009	53.3	85.2	29.2	55.3	56.9	63.0	69.9	23.6	18.4	19.5	19.5	18.7	10.5
Belgium	2009	57.8	95.4	26.6	50.4	66.5	69.9	72.2	15.4	11.2	14.7	18.1	18.9	13.1
Czech Republic	2007	14.6	48.8	4.8	12.9	69.9	77.8	76.1	9.9	6.1	6.3	20.2	16.1	17.5
Denmark	2009	43.6	90.5	32.6	65.3	60.2	...	60.8	29.8	...	28.3	10.0	...	10.9
Estonia	2010	8.9	25.1	3.8	12.3	64.8	63.2	65.3	15.0	17.9	17.0	20.2	19.0	17.7
Finland	2009	58.9	64.0	27.3	39.6	53.9	60.0	73.2	21.3	16.8	16.6	24.7	23.3	10.2
France	2009	43.0	70.9	23.8	48.3	63.6	69.0	58.5	20.1	17.5	28.3	16.3	13.5	13.2
Germany	2009	49.5	73.6	31.3	52.2	59.1	64.2	63.9	25.8	20.7	25.6	15.1	15.1	10.5
Hungary	2009	11.1	40.6	4.9	15.9	72.5	71.4	66.3	12.1	14.1	13.2	15.4	14.5	20.5
Ireland	2009	28.9	51.8	20.2	44.6	64.2	60.9	79.6	25.0	24.6	17.6	10.8	14.5	2.8
Italy	2009	45.6	64.9	20.6	37.3	66.5	75.0	70.9	15.1	12.4	16.7	18.4	12.6	12.4
Lithuania	2010	2.0	16.2	1.9	6.8	80.7	68.9	70.0	18.4	14.9	12.5	1.0	16.2	17.5
Luxembourg	2007	65.8	110.0	47.9	68.8	54.7	65.9	64.3	32.9	21.5	22.3	12.3	12.6	13.4
Malta	2008	35.6	37.2	16.1	20.6	35.2	46.8	47.1	29.2	30.1	29.4	35.5	23.1	23.5
Netherlands	2008	52.8	104.9	28.2	56.4	59.4	64.6	62.8	21.7	20.8	20.0	18.9	14.6	17.2
Slovakia	2009	7.6	36.6	3.2	14.4	74.7	77.7	73.2	10.7	8.0	10.5	14.6	14.3	16.3
Slovenia	2010	25.5	59.5	16.0	30.0	73.0	70.3	71.5	17.0	14.3	14.3	10.0	15.4	14.1
Spain	2009	46.0	76.1	21.5	41.3	58.8	63.6	63.3	19.3	18.3	19.9	21.9	18.1	16.8
Sweden	2009	46.9	67.4	22.6	42.2	61.8	65.0	69.6	18.4	18.5	19.1	19.8	16.4	11.4
United Kingdom	2009	49.0	63.3	31.5	37.2	55.8	61.6	65.6	28.3	19.8	20.2	15.8	18.6	14.2
Other Europe														
Norway	2008	42.4	116.0	27.7	72.3	57.2	50.3	62.7	27.9	30.1	23.3	14.9	19.5	14.1
East Asia														
Japan	2010	109.3	120.7	34.0	40.8	53.4	57.6	60.0	14.5	12.4	13.5	32.1	30.0	26.5
Malaysia	2010	12.5	20.6	3.6	6.6	67.9	84.7	82.3	9.2	5.8	5.7	22.9	9.5	12.0
Republic of Korea	2008	61.6	103.0	16.0	29.3	53.4	55.4	58.8	12.1	12.0	11.7	34.4	32.7	29.4
Singapore	2010	36.8	57.3	19.1	30.2	69.9	59.9	56.9	15.6	19.0	22.7	14.5	21.0	20.4
West Asia														
Kuwait	2010	...	17.6	...	8.3	...	66.6	77.7	...	15.5	10.5	...	17.8	11.8

a/ At current prices.

Table 1.11
(continued)

SELECTED CHARACTERISTICS OF BRANCHES, SELECTED YEARS AND ECONOMIES

Rubber products (ISIC 251)

Economy	Latest year (LY)	Value added per employee (current 1000 dollars)		Wages and salaries per employee (current 1000 dollars)		Percentage in output [a]								
						Costs of input materials and utilities			Costs of labour			Operating surplus		
		2000	LY	2000	LY	2000	2006	LY	2000	2006	LY	2000	2006	LY
North America														
Canada	2009	62.7	80.1	29.5	39.6	57.4	59.5	59.4	20.0	20.8	20.1	22.6	19.7	20.6
United States of America	2008	89.1	103.2	35.4	43.4	47.8	55.1	59.9	20.7	17.8	16.9	31.5	27.1	23.2
Others														
Israel	2009	35.9	45.2	30.7	32.2	61.7	70.9	67.2	32.7	21.4	23.4	5.6	7.6	9.5
Developing & EIE														
Brazil	2010	23.6	47.9	6.9	14.5	54.2	56.8	58.3	13.4	11.3	12.6	32.4	31.9	29.1
Bulgaria	2010	2.5	12.5	1.2	4.6	74.7	81.6	74.4	12.6	8.5	9.5	12.7	9.9	16.2
Chile	2008	40.5	39.8	10.6	17.2	49.7	62.8	66.2	13.2	14.4	14.6	37.0	22.8	19.2
China	2007	...	16.6	...	2.6	...	73.7	72.1	...	4.3	4.3	...	22.0	23.6
Cyprus	2010	17.3	41.2	9.7	20.4	56.9	57.0	56.5	24.1	20.4	21.5	19.0	22.6	22.0
Ecuador	2008	17.3	10.0	3.5	3.4	74.7	77.3	62.6	5.2	10.0	12.7	20.2	12.7	24.7
Egypt	2010	...	17.8	...	4.5	...	76.0	71.2	...	7.0	7.3	...	17.0	21.5
Ethiopia	2009	11.9	10.1	1.5	1.7	51.2	43.0	66.4	5.9	7.5	5.6	42.8	49.5	28.0
Georgia	2010	1.1	9.4	0.5	1.6	69.4	...	71.8	13.5	...	4.8	17.0	...	23.4
Greece	2007	...	80.0	...	31.3	...	64.7	62.9	...	13.5	14.5	...	21.8	22.6
India	2009	6.1	12.4	1.4	3.2	74.6	85.4	77.4	5.9	4.7	5.8	19.5	9.9	16.8
Indonesia	2009	4.2	15.7	1.0	1.7	74.4	75.0	71.1	5.9	3.2	3.1	19.7	21.8	25.7
Iran (Islamic Republic of)	2009	41.0	25.0	11.4	8.7	60.0	60.4	62.6	11.1	11.9	13.0	28.9	27.7	24.4
Jordan	2010	7.6	36.2	3.2	5.9	58.9	72.2	52.9	17.5	11.3	7.6	23.6	16.4	39.4
Latvia	2010	4.9	18.9	2.2	8.5	53.8	69.4	76.5	21.0	11.0	10.5	25.2	19.6	12.9
Mexico	2010	30.4	31.8	10.6	9.0	57.0	72.3	64.2	15.0	...	10.1	27.9	...	25.7
Oman	2008	8.0	14.1	5.9	8.3	66.1	31.8	55.7	25.2	8.0	26.1	8.7	60.2	18.2
Philippines	2009	...	12.2	...	3.8	...	74.4	78.3	...	8.5	6.8	...	17.1	14.9
Poland	2010	14.3	33.6	...	12.1	65.2	71.3	68.3	...	10.9	11.4	...	17.8	20.3
Romania	2010	...	34.9	...	8.1	69.3	79.2	75.5	...	10.8	5.7	...	10.0	18.8
Sri Lanka	2010	...	12.0	...	1.8	...	49.3	52.8	...	8.8	6.9	...	41.9	40.3
The f. Yugosl. Rep of Macedonia	2010	...	9.0	...	4.2	...	62.1	50.5	...	24.6	22.9	...	13.3	26.6
Turkey	2009	43.7	36.1	12.8	16.7	49.6	74.1	69.6	14.8	11.9	14.1	35.7	14.0	16.3
United Republic of Tanzania	2007	...	5.5	...	1.0	...	54.0	54.0	...	8.6	8.6	...	37.4	37.4
Uruguay	2007	15.0	6.8	13.7	4.9	67.9	...	77.9	29.2	...	15.7	2.9	...	6.4

a/ At current prices.

Table 1.11

SELECTED CHARACTERISTICS OF BRANCHES, SELECTED YEARS AND ECONOMIES

Plastic products (ISIC 2520)

Economy	Latest year (LY)	Value added per employee (current 1000 dollars)		Wages and salaries per employee (current 1000 dollars)		Percentage in output a/								
						Costs of input materials and utilities			Costs of labour			Operating surplus		
		2000	LY	2000	LY	2000	2006	LY	2000	2006	LY	2000	2006	LY
Industrialized Economies														
EU														
Austria	2009	47.0	88.0	25.6	47.5	62.6	63.2	63.9	20.4	18.9	19.5	17.0	17.8	16.6
Belgium	2009	62.2	107.5	28.4	53.2	70.7	74.5	70.3	13.4	11.6	14.7	15.9	13.9	15.0
Czech Republic	2007	9.6	28.8	3.9	11.6	74.1	75.2	74.3	10.4	10.2	10.3	15.5	14.6	15.4
Denmark	2009	47.1	124.9	29.8	74.1	57.3	60.0	53.0	27.0	22.9	27.9	15.6	17.1	19.1
Estonia	2010	7.6	25.4	3.2	13.1	72.9	74.9	75.0	11.6	11.4	12.9	15.6	13.8	12.1
Finland	2009	49.8	83.2	23.1	45.6	59.9	65.6	65.1	18.6	17.4	19.1	21.4	17.0	15.8
France	2009	40.2	73.1	20.9	42.1	69.5	71.5	68.3	15.8	15.7	18.3	14.7	12.8	13.4
Germany	2009	44.4	71.3	26.4	44.5	62.7	66.1	65.7	22.2	19.1	21.4	15.1	14.8	12.9
Hungary	2009	10.7	24.8	3.6	10.6	73.3	74.0	72.2	9.1	10.9	11.8	17.7	15.2	15.9
Ireland	2009	43.2	66.3	19.9	45.7	62.9	65.0	67.5	17.1	19.2	22.5	20.0	15.8	10.1
Italy	2009	45.4	72.6	17.7	34.9	70.8	75.6	72.8	11.4	10.6	13.0	17.8	13.8	14.1
Lithuania	2010	6.0	22.7	2.4	8.3	76.8	74.2	78.8	9.5	7.6	7.8	13.8	18.2	13.4
Luxembourg	2008	81.1	115.4	39.0	61.6	64.8	73.8	72.0	16.9	15.9	14.9	18.3	10.3	13.0
Malta	2008	18.3	35.8	10.5	20.1	48.5	54.8	59.9	29.5	24.2	22.5	22.1	21.0	17.5
Netherlands	2008	49.6	97.0	25.7	51.5	68.0	69.8	70.5	16.5	16.1	15.7	15.5	14.2	13.8
Portugal	2009	21.4	42.0	9.7	19.6	71.2	...	71.3	13.1	...	13.4	15.7	...	15.3
Slovakia	2009	4.4	22.6	2.4	12.2	81.5	81.7	77.4	10.2	8.8	12.2	8.3	9.4	10.5
Slovenia	2010	16.7	40.6	11.2	22.9	74.9	70.6	68.8	16.8	14.4	17.6	8.3	14.9	13.6
Spain	2009	34.4	66.7	16.5	36.2	68.7	71.9	69.2	15.0	14.3	16.7	16.3	13.9	14.1
Sweden	2009	48.8	73.7	24.1	40.7	63.4	65.0	67.4	18.0	16.8	18.0	18.5	18.2	14.6
United Kingdom	2009	46.4	68.7	25.4	38.5	60.2	63.2	63.8	21.8	21.1	20.3	18.0	15.7	15.9
Other Europe														
Norway	2008	45.3	111.0	31.2	67.4	64.0	66.9	69.1	24.8	21.0	18.8	11.2	12.1	12.1
East Asia														
Japan	2010	92.0	117.2	24.1	31.4	59.4	61.4	61.3	10.6	9.7	10.4	29.9	28.9	28.4
Malaysia	2010	11.1	15.8	3.7	6.9	66.0	76.1	74.6	11.4	10.4	11.0	22.6	13.5	14.4
Republic of Korea	2008	47.9	80.6	13.4	22.3	60.5	63.5	65.2	11.1	10.7	9.6	28.5	25.8	25.2
Singapore	2010	28.8	38.1	15.6	24.6	67.3	69.3	68.2	17.7	18.9	20.6	15.0	11.8	11.3
West Asia														
Kuwait	2010	...	27.9	...	10.8	...	67.0	71.6	...	10.9	10.9	...	22.1	17.5

a/ At current prices.

Table 1.11
(continued)

SELECTED CHARACTERISTICS OF BRANCHES, SELECTED YEARS AND ECONOMIES

Plastic products (ISIC 2520)

Economy	Latest year (LY)	Value added per employee (current 1000 dollars) 2000	Value added per employee LY	Wages and salaries per employee (current 1000 dollars) 2000	Wages and salaries per employee LY	Percentage in output [a] — Costs of input materials and utilities 2000	2006	LY	Costs of labour 2000	2006	LY	Operating surplus 2000	2006	LY
North America														
Canada	2009	59.5	83.8	23.3	38.7	54.1	56.1	56.4	17.9	18.5	20.1	28.0	25.3	23.5
United States of America	2008	85.7	117.3	31.4	38.8	48.7	52.4	54.3	18.8	15.3	15.1	32.5	32.2	30.6
Others														
Israel	2009	39.8	54.2	24.3	31.7	63.9	68.8	66.8	22.1	16.6	19.4	14.0	14.7	13.8
Developing & EIE														
Azerbaijan	2010	...	4.7	...	3.4	...	80.2	71.1	...	5.1	21.1	...	14.8	7.8
Brazil	2010	16.5	35.0	5.2	10.8	63.6	62.2	58.3	11.5	11.6	12.9	24.9	26.2	28.8
Bulgaria	2010	2.4	10.4	1.1	3.6	77.5	79.9	78.5	10.0	5.3	7.3	12.5	14.9	14.2
Chile	2008	24.4	40.1	7.5	13.7	58.5	61.6	65.0	12.8	12.0	11.9	28.7	26.4	23.0
China	2007	...	12.7	...	2.6	...	73.9	73.7	...	5.1	5.4	...	21.0	20.8
Cyprus	2010	22.1	42.8	12.4	25.3	58.5	59.4	61.9	23.2	23.0	22.6	18.2	17.6	15.6
Ecuador	2008	13.8	51.6	1.8	5.5	69.9	70.9	54.8	3.9	6.3	4.8	26.2	22.8	40.4
Egypt	2010	...	7.5	...	2.2	...	74.1	79.7	...	6.2	6.0	...	19.7	14.3
Eritrea	2010	6.5	3.2	0.9	0.8	31.7	60.8	37.8	9.3	10.4	15.0	59.0	28.8	47.2
Ethiopia	2009	4.3	4.6	0.7	0.2	58.9	61.4	62.7	7.0	4.9	1.6	34.2	33.7	35.7
Georgia	2010	0.9	5.5	0.5	2.7	84.8	71.6	76.9	9.1	14.0	11.3	6.1	14.4	11.8
Greece	2007	...	61.1	...	26.5	...	66.5	66.3	...	14.6	14.6	...	18.9	19.1
India	2009	4.5	9.9	1.0	2.2	82.2	84.9	81.9	4.0	3.6	4.0	13.8	11.5	14.1
Indonesia	2009	3.9	7.5	0.7	1.6	65.2	61.5	72.7	6.5	8.7	5.9	28.4	29.8	21.5
Iran (Islamic Republic of)	2009	24.4	18.3	8.2	6.1	66.7	67.4	63.9	11.2	9.6	12.1	22.1	23.0	24.0
Jordan	2010	9.3	22.4	3.0	5.6	69.6	68.4	70.4	9.9	7.0	7.4	20.5	24.7	22.2
Kyrgyzstan	2010	...	7.9	0.4	1.4	...	89.2	70.2	4.6	3.2	5.4	...	7.6	24.5
Latvia	2010	8.4	14.9	1.9	6.9	68.4	78.0	79.1	7.1	9.1	9.6	24.5	12.9	11.3
Malawi	2009	2.2	4.6	0.8	2.7	72.0	83.6	77.2	9.8	15.6	13.2	18.2	0.8	9.6
Mexico	2010	21.4	23.2	6.2	6.6	67.0	72.2	71.4	9.5	...	8.1	23.5	...	20.5
Morocco	2010	8.9	15.2	4.2	7.4	69.9	75.0	76.4	14.2	8.4	11.4	15.9	16.7	12.2
Oman	2010	18.1	33.5	5.2	6.8	62.0	75.0	58.1	11.0	9.4	8.4	27.0	18.0	33.5
Poland	2009	12.2	27.9	...	10.0	71.3	72.5	69.4	...	8.8	11.0	...	10.5	19.6
Romania	2010	...	14.2	...	5.4	63.2	80.7	79.2	...	...	7.9	...	18.4	13.0
The f. Yugosl. Rep of Macedonia	2010	...	10.2	...	4.6	...	64.3	68.3	...	17.3	14.3	30.5	12.3	17.4
Turkey	2009	29.8	23.3	6.4	8.1	61.2	81.6	78.0	8.3	6.2	7.6	...	13.1	14.3
United Republic of Tanzania	2010	...	10.6	...	1.0	...	82.4	44.0	...	4.5	5.4	...	...	50.6
Uruguay	2007	20.8	19.8	10.3	8.7	68.7	...	79.6	15.4	...	9.0	15.8	...	11.4

a/ At current prices.

Table 1.11

SELECTED CHARACTERISTICS OF BRANCHES, SELECTED YEARS AND ECONOMIES

Glass and glass products (ISIC 2610)

Economy	Latest year (LY)	Value added per employee (current 1000 dollars)		Wages and salaries per employee (current 1000 dollars)		Percentage in output a/								
						Costs of input materials and utilities			Costs of labour			Operating surplus		
	(LY)	2000	LY	2000	LY	2000	2006	LY	2000	2006	LY	2000	2006	LY
Industrialized Economies														
EU														
Austria	2009	60.1	89.2	26.1	52.4	41.6	42.0	51.6	25.3	25.5	28.4	33.1	32.5	20.0
Belgium	2009	61.4	100.2	30.6	59.7	65.7	...	73.5	17.1	...	15.8	17.2	...	10.7
Czech Republic	2007	12.6	31.6	4.1	11.7	59.7	62.2	62.7	13.2	13.4	13.8	27.0	24.4	23.5
Denmark	2009	42.8	84.6	28.0	62.3	58.9	59.3	63.3	26.9	25.2	27.0	14.2	15.5	9.7
Estonia	2010	15.8	50.9	5.2	15.5	67.7	69.1	61.8	10.7	11.2	11.6	21.6	19.6	26.6
Finland	2008	47.9	99.8	24.5	47.5	56.2	56.2	57.0	22.5	21.3	20.5	21.4	22.5	22.6
France	2009	47.7	70.1	24.5	43.4	62.9	64.7	63.0	19.0	19.1	22.9	18.1	16.2	14.1
Germany	2009	48.9	77.6	27.4	46.9	59.4	62.9	64.6	22.8	20.0	21.4	17.8	17.1	14.0
Hungary	2009	10.9	28.6	3.6	12.4	58.4	67.7	72.0	13.6	11.2	12.1	28.0	21.2	15.9
Ireland	2007	61.5	81.5	26.4	50.1	42.3	63.5	59.5	24.7	25.1	24.9	32.9	11.5	15.6
Italy	2009	50.1	67.3	19.1	36.0	65.7	67.8	68.9	13.1	13.3	16.6	21.2	18.8	14.5
Lithuania	2010	6.3	16.0	3.8	7.7	67.7	74.8	74.7	19.5	12.0	12.1	12.8	13.2	13.2
Malta	2008	17.5	25.7	7.5	16.8	51.7	59.7	68.9	20.7	20.1	20.3	27.6	20.2	10.8
Netherlands	2008	64.4	122.2	30.2	59.0	63.0	61.7	60.1	17.3	20.2	19.3	19.7	18.1	20.7
Portugal	2009	26.6	68.3	11.3	22.8	59.7	...	59.7	17.2	...	13.4	23.1	...	26.9
Slovakia	2009	5.4	25.2	2.5	13.3	67.8	69.8	71.1	14.8	13.4	15.3	17.5	16.9	13.6
Slovenia	2010	15.0	30.0	11.2	22.4	66.9	59.5	64.1	24.6	25.0	26.7	8.5	15.5	9.2
Spain	2009	45.2	67.7	19.0	39.5	59.8	64.2	66.7	16.9	16.9	19.4	23.3	19.0	13.9
Sweden	2008	42.0	98.7	23.1	49.5	62.6	65.2	65.2	20.6	16.6	17.4	16.9	18.1	17.3
United Kingdom	2009	54.1	63.5	28.5	40.1	56.1	58.7	68.6	23.1	23.0	19.8	20.8	18.3	11.6
Other Europe														
Norway	2008	53.0	114.6	32.4	68.9	56.9	63.1	60.7	26.3	23.9	23.6	16.8	13.1	15.7
Russian Federation	2010	...	18.4	0.9	7.2	...	60.6	68.9	16.2	10.2	12.2	...	29.2	18.8
East Asia														
Japan	2010	148.4	261.0	39.4	48.4	49.4	45.8	48.6	13.4	10.3	9.5	37.1	43.9	41.9
Malaysia	2010	41.9	34.7	5.9	12.4	50.8	77.4	68.4	7.0	10.4	11.3	42.2	12.2	20.3
Republic of Korea	2008	113.8	180.0	18.9	27.4	41.5	52.2	51.0	9.7	9.1	7.5	48.8	38.7	41.5
Singapore	2010	73.2	73.0	18.1	23.1	57.8	59.1	54.5	10.5	13.9	14.4	31.8	27.0	31.1
West Asia														
Kuwait	2010	...	33.2	...	10.7	...	59.2	53.2	...	15.7	15.0	...	25.1	31.7

a/ At current prices.

Table 1.11
(continued)

SELECTED CHARACTERISTICS OF BRANCHES, SELECTED YEARS AND ECONOMIES

Economy	Latest year (LY)	Value added per employee (current 1000 dollars)		Wages and salaries per employee (current 1000 dollars)		Percentage in output [a]								
						Costs of input materials and utilities			Costs of labour			Operating surplus		
		2000	LY	2000	LY	2000	2006	LY	2000	2006	LY	2000	2006	LY
North America														
Canada	2009	69.0	93.8	27.3	42.0	47.8	47.7	47.5	20.7	20.8	23.5	31.5	31.5	29.0
United States of America	2008	112.5	133.9	36.3	45.0	39.0	44.8	45.8	19.7	18.0	18.2	41.3	37.1	35.9
Others														
New Zealand	2008	...	87.1	...	40.2	...	54.0	52.2	...	18.0	22.1	...	28.0	25.7
Developing & EIE														
Brazil	2010	31.2	69.9	8.5	15.2	50.2	48.4	45.3	13.6	11.5	11.9	36.2	40.1	42.8
Bulgaria	2010	2.1	26.5	1.4	5.7	80.0	66.0	71.4	13.2	5.5	6.2	6.8	28.5	22.4
Chile	2008	60.9	55.0	10.7	13.7	37.5	38.8	53.4	10.9	13.8	11.6	51.5	47.5	35.0
China	2007	...	13.0	...	2.3	...	68.1	69.1	...	5.5	5.4	...	26.4	25.6
Cyprus	2010	19.0	42.3	8.7	19.6	60.5	56.5	56.5	18.0	22.2	20.2	21.5	21.3	23.3
Ecuador	2008	11.8	38.4	3.7	6.6	80.0	57.9	51.5	6.3	6.8	8.4	13.7	35.3	40.1
Egypt	2010	...	7.8	...	2.4	...	42.9	49.0	...	12.3	15.7	...	44.8	35.3
Eritrea	2010	...	6.6	...	1.1	...	77.7	62.3	...	8.5	6.5	...	13.7	31.2
Ethiopia	2009	3.6	4.6	0.8	0.8	31.0	48.3	50.5	15.0	8.6	8.1	54.0	43.0	41.3
Georgia	2010	1.6	7.5	0.6	3.1	69.8	66.6	64.8	10.7	7.6	14.4	19.4	25.8	20.8
Greece	2007	...	71.3	...	31.9	...	58.5	58.6	...	21.8	18.6	...	19.7	22.9
India	2009	4.2	9.1	1.3	2.3	73.4	73.0	72.5	7.9	7.2	6.8	18.7	19.8	20.7
Indonesia	2009	...	6.4	...	3.1	...	52.5	62.3	...	10.1	18.3	...	37.4	19.4
Iran (Islamic Republic of)	2009	34.0	23.4	9.3	7.7	49.1	55.0	51.4	13.9	15.1	16.0	37.0	29.8	32.6
Jordan	2010	7.8	9.2	3.2	3.8	63.7	58.1	59.6	14.8	12.6	16.5	21.5	29.2	23.9
Kyrgyzstan	2010	...	2.8	...	2.1	...	71.2	67.4	...	8.6	24.4	...	20.2	8.2
Latvia	2010	5.1	28.4	2.5	10.8	60.0	72.7	66.9	19.5	14.0	12.5	20.6	13.3	20.6
Mexico	2010	34.3	35.3	8.4	8.9	49.3	63.5	65.6	12.5	...	8.7	38.3	...	25.7
Morocco	2010	15.2	20.2	4.7	7.3	46.0	61.5	61.4	16.8	...	14.0	37.2	...	24.7
Oman	2010	18.3	57.3	6.8	10.5	53.7	69.0	35.9	17.2	10.4	11.7	29.2	20.6	52.3
Philippines	2008	...	18.0	...	6.0	...	66.8	72.8	...	11.6	9.2	...	21.6	18.1
Poland	2008	11.1	35.9	...	14.6	58.6	61.9	64.4	...	13.5	14.5	...	24.6	21.1
Romania	2010	...	14.6	...	5.1	51.3	78.7	72.8	...	17.9	9.6	...	3.4	17.6
The f. Yugosl. Rep of Macedonia	2010	...	6.1	...	5.7	...	64.0	68.4	...	32.3	29.8	...	3.7	1.8
United Republic of Tanzania	2008	...	6.3	...	0.3	...	77.4	48.7	...	5.5	2.1	...	17.2	49.2
Uruguay	2007	19.0	11.7	10.0	6.3	70.3	...	63.6	15.7	...	19.7	14.0	...	16.8

a/ At current prices.

Table 1.11

SELECTED CHARACTERISTICS OF BRANCHES, SELECTED YEARS AND ECONOMIES

Non-metallic mineral products n.e.c. (ISIC 269)

Economy	Latest year (LY)	Value added per employee (current 1000 dollars)		Wages and salaries per employee (current 1000 dollars)		Percentage in output a/								
						Costs of input materials and utilities			Costs of labour			Operating surplus		
		2000	LY	2000	LY	2000	2006	LY	2000	2006	LY	2000	2006	LY
Industrialized Economies														
EU														
Austria	2009	57.3	93.2	30.3	53.9	58.8	61.3	66.0	21.8	18.8	19.6	19.4	19.9	14.4
Belgium	2009	61.9	114.7	26.0	49.5	67.2	...	68.4	13.8	...	13.6	19.0	...	18.0
Czech Republic	2007	14.0	47.7	4.5	13.4	64.2	67.0	63.8	11.4	10.2	10.1	24.4	22.8	26.1
Denmark	2009	54.8	111.8	31.2	76.0	56.3	58.8	60.2	24.9	24.1	27.0	18.8	17.1	12.8
Estonia	2010	11.2	26.7	4.0	14.5	57.8	52.7	66.3	15.1	14.5	18.4	27.1	32.8	15.4
Finland	2009	59.0	81.4	23.8	42.8	61.2	63.8	65.7	15.7	15.9	18.0	23.1	20.4	16.2
France	2009	48.9	101.3	22.9	45.8	67.9	68.6	68.4	15.0	12.8	14.3	17.1	18.6	17.3
Germany	2009	48.7	81.7	27.6	47.5	60.7	64.4	66.5	22.3	19.7	19.5	17.1	15.9	14.0
Hungary	2009	13.8	34.2	4.4	13.4	62.0	65.3	66.9	12.1	11.1	13.0	25.9	23.6	20.2
Ireland	2009	66.0	95.9	23.5	52.4	57.4	58.9	69.2	15.1	14.3	16.8	27.5	26.8	14.0
Italy	2009	50.1	70.8	18.4	35.6	66.6	69.5	72.8	12.3	11.6	13.7	21.1	18.9	13.6
Lithuania	2010	3.5	14.3	2.6	7.8	73.4	62.1	75.1	20.1	12.4	13.6	6.5	25.5	11.3
Malta	2008	18.4	33.5	8.2	16.2	58.6	61.4	69.2	18.4	16.3	14.9	23.1	22.4	15.9
Netherlands	2008	67.0	125.0	28.6	56.3	61.2	65.0	68.7	16.6	16.1	14.1	22.3	18.9	17.2
Portugal	2009	24.5	39.1	8.8	18.1	58.9	...	65.1	14.7	...	16.1	26.4	...	18.8
Slovakia	2009	5.5	35.8	2.5	15.2	72.8	66.8	69.6	12.0	10.2	12.8	15.1	22.9	17.5
Slovenia	2010	19.2	45.5	12.8	24.0	71.7	64.5	68.8	18.9	15.2	16.5	9.4	20.3	14.8
Spain	2009	42.5	73.5	16.9	40.0	62.4	66.7	66.4	15.0	12.8	18.3	22.6	20.5	15.3
Sweden	2009	53.1	88.7	25.4	43.6	63.7	66.0	67.9	17.3	15.3	15.8	19.0	18.7	16.3
United Kingdom	2009	52.2	52.5	25.4	37.8	56.4	57.3	71.9	21.2	19.3	20.2	22.3	23.4	7.9
Other Europe														
Norway	2008	65.2	141.1	33.8	77.0	59.7	66.1	67.6	20.9	19.3	17.7	19.4	14.6	14.7
Russian Federation	2010	...	15.1	0.9	7.1	...	63.2	69.4	13.0	13.0	14.5	...	23.8	16.1
East Asia														
Japan	2010	103.8	121.4	20.2	24.5	52.0	52.1	56.5	9.3	8.3	8.8	38.7	39.6	34.7
Malaysia	2010	17.9	26.7	4.5	8.0	62.0	71.3	73.4	9.7	9.1	8.0	28.4	19.6	18.7
Republic of Korea	2008	83.2	128.2	14.9	25.4	53.3	56.9	58.1	8.4	8.8	8.3	38.4	34.3	33.6
Singapore	2010	28.4	52.6	17.9	24.0	81.3	79.9	77.5	11.7	10.7	10.2	6.9	9.4	12.2
West Asia														
Kuwait	2010	...	38.1	...	12.7	...	65.0	69.1	...	10.0	10.3	...	24.9	20.6

a/ At current prices.

Table 1.11
(continued)

SELECTED CHARACTERISTICS OF BRANCHES, SELECTED YEARS AND ECONOMIES

Non-metallic mineral products n.e.c. (ISIC 269)

Economy	Latest year (LY)	Value added per employee (current 1000 dollars) 2000	Value added per employee (current 1000 dollars) LY	Wages and salaries per employee (current 1000 dollars) 2000	Wages and salaries per employee (current 1000 dollars) LY	Costs of input materials and utilities 2000	Costs of input materials and utilities 2006	Costs of input materials and utilities LY	Costs of labour 2000	Costs of labour 2006	Costs of labour LY	Operating surplus 2000	Operating surplus 2006	Operating surplus LY
North America														
Canada	2008	86.2	140.6	28.0	46.9	49.1	52.8	54.4	16.5	16.0	15.2	34.4	31.2	30.4
United States of America	2008	107.3	150.5	35.0	43.8	46.9	45.4	50.8	17.3	14.1	14.3	35.7	40.5	34.8
Others														
New Zealand	2008	...	89.3	...	36.0	...	63.1	59.1	...	15.8	16.5	...	21.1	24.4
Developing & EIE														
Azerbaijan	2010	...	17.0	0.7	5.9	46.7	67.1	75.4	25.6	6.3	8.5	...	26.7	16.1
Brazil	2010	16.2	35.4	3.9	9.3	...	51.6	51.4	12.7	12.8	12.8	40.6	35.6	35.8
Bulgaria	2010	3.3	17.5	1.4	5.5	75.8	71.2	68.0	10.2	5.3	10.1	14.0	23.5	21.9
Chile	2008	52.0	83.6	10.4	15.3	46.4	58.8	58.9	10.8	8.5	7.5	42.8	32.7	33.6
China	2007	...	14.3	...	2.3	...	68.8	68.8	...	5.1	4.9	...	26.0	26.3
Cyprus	2010	37.6	68.7	15.2	33.8	59.4	63.9	69.2	16.4	13.5	15.1	24.1	22.5	15.7
Ecuador	2008	25.7	44.7	3.1	6.3	61.5	60.5	60.9	4.7	5.1	5.5	33.8	34.5	33.6
Egypt	2010	...	31.8	...	3.8	...	55.7	54.5	...	7.2	5.5	...	37.1	40.0
Eritrea	2010	1.8	4.1	0.7	1.1	62.4	67.5	59.8	14.6	12.6	10.8	23.0	19.9	29.4
Ethiopia	2009	5.2	7.3	0.8	0.5	50.5	53.4	51.5	7.7	5.7	3.2	41.8	40.8	45.3
Georgia	2010	1.4	6.9	0.6	3.2	69.9	75.0	78.2	13.8	9.0	10.0	16.3	16.0	11.8
Greece	2007	...	85.2	...	34.5	...	62.6	63.6	...	13.8	14.7	...	23.5	21.6
India	2009	5.1	12.3	1.1	1.8	69.3	65.4	63.2	6.4	5.0	5.3	24.4	29.6	31.5
Indonesia	2009	...	18.0	...	2.4	...	52.3	44.2	...	7.8	7.6	...	39.9	48.2
Iran (Islamic Republic of)	2009	30.9	29.2	9.1	7.4	44.4	43.0	39.9	16.4	16.1	15.3	39.2	41.0	44.8
Jordan	2010	14.8	30.3	3.9	5.4	52.8	51.6	52.2	12.5	7.0	8.5	34.7	41.5	39.3
Latvia	2010	7.4	18.1	3.0	9.2	63.8	67.5	78.5	14.5	8.2	10.9	21.7	24.3	10.6
Malawi	2009	6.4	22.5	3.3	4.4	78.2	74.6	69.4	11.1	8.7	5.9	10.7	16.7	24.7
Mongolia	2008	...	5.8	...	2.2	...	78.4	67.9	...	13.5	12.0	...	8.1	20.1
Morocco	2010	14.0	43.6	4.0	10.0	50.8	68.7	54.0	14.1	9.8	10.6	35.1	...	35.5
Oman	2010	21.8	56.3	5.5	9.3	43.5	33.2	32.2	14.2	6.5	11.2	42.3	57.0	56.5
Philippines	2008	...	34.0	...	5.4	...	70.3	64.5	...	10.1	5.6	...	23.3	29.9
Poland	2009	...	39.1	...	11.6	...	61.7	62.8	...	10.9	11.1	...	28.1	26.1
Romania	2010	...	31.5	...	7.5	61.5	67.0	63.1	...	9.0	8.7	...	22.1	28.2
Sri Lanka	2010	...	19.0	...	2.4	...	71.3	62.3	...	16.0	4.7	...	19.7	33.0
The f. Yugosl. Rep of Macedonia	2010	33.2	29.2	6.7	9.5	48.1	56.8	57.0	10.4	7.9	14.0	41.5	27.2	29.0
Turkey	2009	...	27.3	...	9.5	...	70.4	74.5	...	4.7	8.9	...	21.7	16.6
United Republic of Tanzania	2007	...	40.1	...	4.6	...	59.8	59.8	...	...	4.6	...	35.5	35.5
Uruguay	2007	23.1	25.0	15.2	9.8	60.2	...	63.9	26.3	...	14.2	13.5	...	21.9

a/ At current prices.

Table 1.11

SELECTED CHARACTERISTICS OF BRANCHES, SELECTED YEARS AND ECONOMIES

Basic iron and steel (ISIC 2710)

Economy	Latest year (LY)	Value added per employee (current 1000 dollars)		Wages and salaries per employee (current 1000 dollars)		Percentage in output a/								
						Costs of input materials and utilities			Costs of labour			Operating surplus		
		2000	LY	2000	LY	2000	2006	LY	2000	2006	LY	2000	2006	LY
Industrialized Economies														
EU														
Austria	2008	67.7	187.2	34.5	59.8	62.5	68.7	69.6	19.1	12.2	9.7	18.4	19.1	20.7
Belgium	2008	73.9	145.3	33.4	69.7	74.1	79.9	82.5	11.7	7.8	8.4	14.2	12.3	9.1
Denmark	2009	44.0	67.6	31.8	65.5	68.4	73.1	77.6	22.8	12.0	21.7	8.8	14.9	0.7
France	2009	66.0	98.0	28.0	62.6	74.7	78.9	82.7	10.8	7.8	11.1	14.6	13.3	6.3
Germany	2009	60.0	93.6	33.3	57.2	71.3	75.5	78.5	15.9	11.0	13.2	12.8	13.4	8.4
Ireland	2008	43.7	104.3	24.9	55.8	68.1	59.3	66.8	18.1	19.9	17.8	13.7	20.8	15.5
Italy	2009	56.6	58.0	22.2	37.9	79.3	81.7	87.2	8.1	5.5	8.4	12.6	12.7	4.4
Lithuania	2010	7.1	13.6	3.9	10.2	77.5	76.7	87.7	12.4	13.3	9.2	10.1	10.0	3.0
Netherlands	2008	84.7	131.2	34.0	69.5	62.8	68.9	77.5	15.0	13.7	11.9	22.3	17.4	10.6
Portugal	2008	40.5	113.8	13.1	28.8	82.3	...	87.8	5.7	...	3.1	12.0	...	9.1
Slovakia	2008	7.7	58.5	3.2	19.0	79.6	67.3	77.3	8.6	7.6	7.4	11.9	25.1	15.4
Slovenia	2010	19.1	49.7	13.1	26.4	80.1	81.5	80.5	13.6	8.7	10.4	6.3	9.7	9.1
Spain	2009	70.3	58.4	24.4	49.1	74.2	77.7	87.6	8.9	6.6	10.4	16.8	15.7	2.0
Sweden	2009	69.9	54.9	29.2	46.0	68.1	77.1	86.0	13.3	8.0	11.7	18.6	14.9	2.3
United Kingdom	2007	51.6	152.3	36.1	63.6	75.6	79.7	73.2	17.1	11.4	11.2	7.3	8.8	15.6
Other Europe														
Norway	2008	73.2	415.5	38.1	73.6	73.6	77.6	63.4	13.7	10.3	6.5	12.7	12.2	30.1
Russian Federation	2010	...	40.1	1.5	9.6	...	69.3	78.3	8.5	5.4	5.2	...	25.3	16.5
East Asia														
Japan	2010	193.8	222.3	48.6	55.3	65.6	68.7	81.1	8.6	5.0	4.7	25.8	26.3	14.2
Malaysia	2010	14.7	38.5	5.5	14.8	86.3	86.8	84.1	5.1	3.3	6.1	8.6	9.9	9.8
Republic of Korea	2008	146.8	315.9	20.2	39.5	67.7	68.7	72.7	4.4	4.4	3.4	27.9	26.9	23.9
West Asia														
Kuwait	2010	...	42.7	...	20.6	...	82.9	87.0	...	3.1	6.3		14.0	6.7

a/ At current prices.

Table 1.11
(continued)

SELECTED CHARACTERISTICS OF BRANCHES, SELECTED YEARS AND ECONOMIES

Basic iron and steel (ISIC 2710)

Economy	Latest year (LY)	Value added per employee (current 1000 dollars) 2000	LY	Wages and salaries per employee (current 1000 dollars) 2000	LY	Percentage in output [a] — Costs of input materials and utilities 2000	2006	LY	Costs of labour 2000	2006	LY	Operating surplus 2000	2006	LY
North America														
Canada	2009	97.3	115.6	38.2	59.7	61.2	67.0	70.5	15.2	11.7	15.2	23.5	21.3	14.3
United States of America	2008	125.8	295.9	46.1	59.8	61.2	62.4	65.2	14.2	8.5	7.0	24.6	29.1	27.7
Others														
Israel	2009	71.6	51.6	33.4	35.6	71.4	84.2	86.7	13.4	8.8	9.2	15.3	7.0	4.1
Developing & EIE														
Azerbaijan	2010	...	13.3	0.2	4.2	...	80.3	58.9	30.7	8.9	13.1	...	10.8	28.0
Brazil	2010	61.6	137.8	10.7	25.0	55.1	58.1	62.2	7.8	5.5	6.9	37.1	36.4	30.9
Chile	2008	55.0	74.8	16.8	19.4	59.2	63.9	75.4	12.5	8.5	6.4	28.3	27.5	18.2
China	2007	...	38.9	...	4.0	...	72.4	73.3	...	3.0	2.7	...	24.6	24.0
Ethiopia	2009	8.3	20.7	1.2	1.3	66.1	77.7	65.3	5.0	2.2	2.1	28.9	20.0	32.6
Georgia	2010	0.3	12.0	0.2	4.0	86.5	85.3	66.1	8.7	5.2	11.3	4.8	9.5	22.7
Greece	2007	...	112.3	...	41.6	...	73.6	83.6	...	6.1	6.1	...	20.3	10.3
India	2009	7.9	24.9	2.5	3.5	80.7	80.1	81.8	6.2	2.7	2.5	13.2	17.2	15.6
Indonesia	2009	16.7	40.4	2.5	8.5	77.0	78.5	77.5	3.4	3.3	4.7	19.6	18.2	17.8
Iran (Islamic Republic of)	2009	94.7	58.7	17.9	13.1	58.4	62.5	70.9	7.9	4.9	6.5	33.8	32.6	22.6
Jordan	2010	35.4	85.7	4.2	10.4	60.7	67.3	63.0	4.7	3.3	4.5	34.7	29.5	32.5
Mexico	2010	83.7	166.0	10.9	18.0	70.3	72.7	66.1	3.9	...	3.7	25.8	...	30.2
Morocco	2010	25.7	28.6	5.8	10.6	77.8	84.2	89.4	5.0	2.0	4.0	17.1	13.8	6.7
Oman	2009	14.1	65.2	3.5	11.7	88.2	71.3	83.9	2.9	5.7	2.9	8.8	23.1	13.2
Poland	2010	15.6	29.1	...	14.8	76.7	82.3	83.9	...	8.8	8.1	...	8.9	7.9
Romania	2010	...	16.0	...	9.8	79.0	81.8	89.2	...	6.6	6.6	...	...	4.2
The f. Yugosl. Rep of Macedonia	2010	...	14.4	...	8.8	...	92.1	90.5	...	5.2	5.8	...	2.7	3.7
United Republic of Tanzania	2010	...	7.4	...	1.0	...	89.3	72.4	...	3.8	3.9	...	6.9	23.8

a/ At current prices.

Table 1.11

SELECTED CHARACTERISTICS OF BRANCHES, SELECTED YEARS AND ECONOMIES

Basic precious and non-ferrous metals (ISIC 2720)

Economy	Latest year (LY)	Value added per employee (current 1000 dollars)		Wages and salaries per employee (current 1000 dollars)		Percentage in output a/								
						Costs of input materials and utilities			Costs of labour			Operating surplus		
		2000	LY	2000	LY	2000	2006	LY	2000	2006	LY	2000	2006	LY
Industrialized Economies														
EU														
Austria	2009	61.3	127.0	30.5	55.0	79.4	78.6	80.4	10.3	7.7	8.5	10.4	13.7	11.1
Belgium	2008	84.9	162.8	32.9	66.7	82.4	90.2	87.4	6.8	4.7	5.2	10.8	5.1	7.4
Czech Republic	2006	13.2	31.2	4.9	11.1	83.3	84.7	84.7	6.2	5.4	5.4	10.6	9.9	9.9
France	2008	70.3	92.2	27.8	56.8	81.4	82.9	88.3	7.4	5.7	7.2	11.3	11.4	4.5
Germany	2009	66.4	96.5	35.1	59.9	77.0	84.4	80.9	12.2	8.5	11.9	10.8	7.1	7.3
Hungary	2008	23.0	45.6	6.8	20.0	81.3	82.6	80.1	5.6	6.1	8.7	13.1	11.3	11.2
Italy	2009	64.2	68.3	22.7	39.4	83.5	89.7	88.5	5.8	4.0	6.6	10.7	6.3	4.9
Lithuania	2010	3.4	35.6	1.6	4.9	76.1	76.8	90.5	11.1	3.9	1.3	12.8	19.3	8.2
Malta	2008	...	29.4	...	7.6	...	64.5	62.9	...	8.6	9.5	...	26.9	27.6
Netherlands	2008	67.4	104.8	31.4	64.3	75.4	81.0	85.1	11.4	8.7	9.1	13.1	10.4	5.8
Portugal	2009	28.8	34.8	11.0	20.6	73.6	...	80.0	10.1	...	11.9	16.3	...	8.1
Slovakia	2008	14.3	87.8	2.9	16.6	75.6	80.3	79.1	5.0	3.0	4.0	19.4	16.7	17.0
Slovenia	2010	26.0	48.7	15.2	25.7	87.3	82.0	85.2	7.4	6.5	7.8	5.2	11.6	7.0
Spain	2008	77.8	135.2	23.8	49.1	78.7	83.3	85.5	6.5	4.0	5.3	14.8	12.7	9.3
Sweden	2008	67.8	104.3	28.5	51.6	77.4	84.6	89.1	9.5	5.1	5.4	13.1	10.2	5.5
United Kingdom	2007	69.0	148.5	33.6	59.0	75.7	79.2	79.0	11.8	8.6	8.3	12.4	12.2	12.6
Other Europe														
Norway	2008	152.0	176.9	41.7	89.8	73.1	77.3	83.6	7.4	6.7	8.3	19.5	16.0	8.1
Russian Federation	2010	...	109.9	2.9	11.0	...	58.4	65.3	10.0	3.5	3.5	...	38.1	31.3
East Asia														
Japan	2010	150.7	211.5	44.5	50.5	73.3	73.5	79.8	7.9	4.8	4.8	18.8	21.7	15.4
Malaysia	2010	27.4	29.6	5.8	7.7	77.0	89.2	85.8	4.8	3.1	3.7	18.1	7.7	10.5
Republic of Korea	2008	92.0	183.7	17.0	29.4	75.3	80.8	81.9	4.6	3.0	2.9	20.1	16.2	15.2
West Asia														
Kuwait	2010	...	26.3	...	7.8	...	75.8	74.7	...	9.3	7.5	...	14.9	17.8

a/ At current prices.

Table 1.11
(continued)

SELECTED CHARACTERISTICS OF BRANCHES, SELECTED YEARS AND ECONOMIES

Economy	Latest year (LY)	Value added per employee (current 1000 dollars)		Wages and salaries per employee (current 1000 dollars)		Percentage in output [a]								
						Costs of input materials and utilities			Costs of labour			Operating surplus		
		2000	LY	2000	LY	2000	2006	LY	2000	2006	LY	2000	2006	LY
North America														
Canada	2009	132.6	235.5	36.5	62.5	64.7	59.8	68.2	9.7	7.4	8.4	25.6	32.8	23.4
United States of America	2008	114.9	219.3	39.0	53.0	67.1	71.9	73.2	11.2	6.8	6.5	21.7	21.3	20.3
Others														
Israel	2009	31.2	51.0	25.0	33.2	80.4	80.1	77.8	15.7	9.2	14.4	3.9	10.7	7.7
Developing & EIE														
Brazil	2010	61.4	101.8	9.3	21.4	55.3	63.0	71.4	6.8	4.9	6.0	37.9	32.1	22.6
Bulgaria	2010	8.5	39.8	2.6	9.8	83.7	89.1	94.3	5.1	1.1	1.4	11.2	9.7	4.3
Chile	2008	320.4	1625.6	23.3	40.3	55.6	39.0	43.6	3.2	1.8	1.4	41.2	59.2	55.0
China	2007	..	38.3	..	3.5	..	75.2	75.2	..	2.2	2.2	..	22.6	22.6
Ecuador	2008	..	43.1	..	7.7	..	79.4	84.5	..	3.3	2.8	..	17.3	12.7
Greece	2007	..	95.7	..	32.2	..	84.2	84.4	..	5.2	5.3	..	10.6	10.4
India	2009	11.9	23.6	2.0	4.8	76.8	74.5	85.0	3.9	2.2	3.0	19.2	23.3	11.9
Indonesia	2009	18.8	45.8	1.8	5.3	63.9	71.7	67.4	3.4	3.3	3.8	32.7	25.1	28.8
Iran (Islamic Republic of)	2009	106.9	54.2	19.6	11.6	54.0	60.8	74.7	8.4	5.6	5.4	37.5	33.6	19.9
Jordan	2010	16.0	27.9	3.7	4.8	64.8	57.7	64.7	8.0	4.4	6.0	27.1	37.9	29.3
Kyrgyzstan	2010	..	125.0	0.4	16.9	..	75.9	58.6	1.0	12.1	5.6	..	12.0	35.8
Mexico	2010	55.7	99.2	7.7	11.1	73.4	74.4	81.3	3.7	..	2.1	22.9	..	16.6
Morocco	2010	13.6	29.2	4.1	7.4	81.1	73.9	76.5	5.7	11.6	5.9	13.2	14.5	17.5
Oman	2008	38.6	310.7	11.4	19.2	50.3	83.1	39.4	14.6	0.9	3.7	35.0	16.0	56.8
Philippines	2008	..	82.1	..	7.5	..	81.0	86.4	..	5.4	1.2	..	13.6	12.3
Poland	2010	15.3	44.8	..	17.7	79.8	75.2	79.5	..	7.6	8.1	..	17.2	12.4
Romania	2010	..	42.9	..	11.0	83.8	67.0	74.3	..	4.6	6.6	..	28.5	19.1
Sri Lanka	2009	..	37.3	..	0.9	..	46.1	70.2	..	4.8	0.7	..	49.1	29.1
The f. Yugosl. Rep of Macedonia	2010	..	31.5	..	9.9	..	78.4	90.9	..	..	2.9	..	..	6.3
Turkey	2008	29.8	52.8	10.5	13.7	76.1	86.8	86.1	8.4	2.9	3.6	15.5	10.2	10.3
United Republic of Tanzania	2010	..	3.6	..	1.0	..	88.8	84.9	..	10.7	4.3	..	0.4	10.7

Basic precious and non-ferrous metals (ISIC 2720)

a/ At current prices.

Table 1.11

SELECTED CHARACTERISTICS OF BRANCHES, SELECTED YEARS AND ECONOMIES

Casting of metals (ISIC 273)

Economy	Latest year (LY)	Value added per employee (current 1000 dollars)		Wages and salaries per employee (current 1000 dollars)		Percentage in output [a]								
						Costs of input materials and utilities			Costs of labour			Operating surplus		
		2000	LY	2000	LY	2000	2006	LY	2000	2006	LY	2000	2006	LY
Industrialized Economies														
EU														
Austria	2009	47.5	77.3	26.5	52.6	56.7	65.1	61.9	24.1	22.0	25.9	19.1	12.9	12.1
Belgium	2009	47.3	67.9	27.1	45.1	64.2	69.7	71.1	20.5	17.2	19.2	15.3	13.1	9.7
Czech Republic	2007	7.6	23.6	3.9	11.8	69.0	73.4	73.7	15.9	13.6	13.2	15.1	13.0	13.2
Denmark	2009	39.0	80.9	28.1	69.1	51.1	57.7	65.6	35.2	28.8	29.3	13.7	13.6	5.0
Finland	2009	...	50.5	...	35.8	...	61.7	62.4	...	23.9	26.7	...	14.4	10.9
France	2009	34.2	61.2	20.2	41.1	65.5	69.3	65.6	20.4	19.4	23.1	14.1	11.3	11.3
Germany	2009	44.2	64.6	29.2	48.2	57.3	63.4	64.3	28.2	22.4	26.6	14.5	14.2	9.0
Hungary	2009	8.5	21.8	3.8	11.2	66.4	69.6	73.5	15.1	14.1	13.6	18.5	16.3	12.9
Ireland	2009	62.7	54.7	19.3	43.8	60.6	33.3	64.3	12.1	33.3	28.6	27.3	33.3	7.1
Italy	2009	45.1	57.7	19.6	33.2	70.4	76.1	73.5	12.8	10.8	15.3	16.7	13.1	11.2
Lithuania	2010	3.3	10.2	3.1	8.9	65.2	59.4	63.6	32.6	24.7	31.9	2.2	15.9	4.5
Netherlands	2008	43.1	76.0	25.5	47.2	64.3	70.0	71.4	21.1	18.8	17.8	14.6	11.3	10.8
Portugal	2009	19.7	34.2	9.5	19.4	59.4	...	67.9	19.5	...	18.2	21.1	...	13.9
Slovakia	2009	3.6	20.7	2.7	12.9	75.0	75.8	74.5	18.8	12.6	15.9	6.3	11.5	9.6
Slovenia	2010	16.2	38.8	11.6	22.9	69.9	67.3	66.8	21.5	18.0	19.7	8.6	14.7	13.6
Spain	2009	37.4	59.7	19.4	38.5	65.6	70.6	69.4	17.9	14.1	19.7	16.6	15.3	10.8
Sweden	2009	50.0	48.6	24.0	37.0	55.6	63.2	66.3	21.3	20.4	25.6	23.1	16.3	8.1
United Kingdom	2007	45.0	67.6	26.7	41.9	52.9	56.8	62.2	27.9	26.9	23.4	19.2	16.3	14.4
Other Europe														
Norway	2008	44.5	99.2	32.3	69.9	52.9	61.3	65.3	34.2	25.5	24.5	12.9	13.2	10.2
East Asia														
Japan	2010	90.0	115.9	31.3	35.3	54.1	59.6	56.6	15.9	12.9	13.2	29.9	27.5	30.2
Malaysia	2010	15.3	15.1	4.9	7.2	74.4	82.7	70.6	8.2	6.9	14.1	17.4	10.4	15.4
Republic of Korea	2008	46.8	101.3	15.4	26.8	53.1	65.4	68.1	15.5	10.2	8.5	31.5	24.4	23.5
West Asia														
Kuwait	2010	...	13.5	...	7.5	...	46.7	50.9	...	31.7	27.3	...	21.7	21.8

a/ At current prices.

Table 1.11
(continued)

SELECTED CHARACTERISTICS OF BRANCHES, SELECTED YEARS AND ECONOMIES

Casting of metals (ISIC 273)

Economy	Latest year (LY)	Value added per employee (current 1000 dollars)		Wages and salaries per employee (current 1000 dollars)		Percentage in output [a]								
						Costs of input materials and utilities			Costs of labour			Operating surplus		
		2000	LY	2000	LY	2000	2006	LY	2000	2006	LY	2000	2006	LY
North America														
Canada	2009	60.5	105.7	31.5	48.7	47.1	52.9	67.4	27.6	25.2	15.0	25.4	21.8	17.6
United States of America	2008	78.3	107.6	35.3	44.7	41.2	47.3	51.3	26.5	21.2	20.2	32.3	31.6	28.4
Others														
Israel	2009	...	39.3	...	30.8	...	...	56.8	...	24.9	33.8	...	...	9.4
Developing & EIE														
Azerbaijan	2010	...	5.9	0.3	2.3	...	80.3	59.6	40.5	8.2	15.9	...	11.4	24.5
Brazil	2010	9.3	31.4	4.2	11.7	52.3	56.1	56.4	21.3	16.0	16.2	26.4	27.9	27.4
Bulgaria	2010	1.9	8.7	1.1	4.2	73.1	75.0	74.1	15.4	11.3	12.5	11.5	13.7	13.4
China	2007	...	15.5	...	2.5	...	72.7	72.6	...	4.6	4.5	...	22.7	22.9
Ecuador	2008	3.4	13.6	0.6	4.2	41.1	64.1	63.1	10.2	12.2	11.5	48.7	23.8	25.4
Egypt	2010	...	6.5	...	2.7	...	84.9	76.9	...	10.1	9.5	...	5.0	13.5
Greece	2007	...	48.8	...	24.4	...	64.7	66.7	...	13.7	16.7	...	21.6	16.7
India	2009	2.5	8.4	1.2	2.3	81.2	83.0	81.2	9.3	5.5	5.1	9.6	11.5	13.7
Indonesia	2009	12.5	52.8	1.3	3.3	71.2	54.1	50.3	3.0	3.5	3.1	25.8	42.5	46.6
Iran (Islamic Republic of)	2009	21.8	18.5	10.4	8.2	55.4	55.3	60.1	21.2	16.7	17.7	23.4	28.0	22.1
Jordan	2010	3.3	14.5	3.1	2.5	73.5	51.7	71.7	25.6	5.3	4.8	0.9	43.0	23.5
Kyrgyzstan	2010	...	6.2	0.1	0.8	...	...	79.6	34.5	...	2.5	...	...	17.9
Mexico	2010	14.1	30.7	6.1	7.2	61.0	...	63.7	16.9	17.3	8.6	22.1	...	27.8
Mongolia	2008	1.4	1.3	1.0	0.9	77.2	...	95.4	15.6	...	3.2	7.2	...	1.4
Morocco	2010	5.4	15.3	4.1	8.1	31.2	38.6	75.5	52.5	...	13.0	16.3	...	11.5
Oman	2010	...	43.0	...	8.6	...	56.6	13.4	...	17.8	17.4	...	25.7	69.3
Philippines	2008	7.5	13.0	...	4.4	66.7	69.0	81.8	...	7.6	6.1	...	23.4	12.1
Poland	2009	...	23.1	...	10.8	65.2	69.3	70.5	...	14.8	13.7	...	15.9	15.8
Romania	2010	...	13.3	...	5.7	...	82.3	79.7	...	12.8	8.6	...	4.8	11.6
Sri Lanka	2010	...	14.1	...	2.5	...	47.2	70.5	...	13.5	5.2	...	39.3	24.3
The f. Yugosl. Rep of Macedonia	2010	...	8.7	...	7.7	...	80.2	90.2	...	12.0	8.7	...	7.8	1.1
Turkey	2009	22.0	23.5	9.0	10.9	53.4	72.4	68.6	19.0	11.1	14.6	27.5	16.5	16.8
United Republic of Tanzania	2007	...	9.8	...	3.0	...	86.7	86.7	...	4.2	4.1	...	9.2	9.2

a/ At current prices.

- 137 -

Table 1.11

SELECTED CHARACTERISTICS OF BRANCHES, SELECTED YEARS AND ECONOMIES

Struct.metal products;tanks;steam generators (ISIC 281)

Economy	Latest year (LY)	Value added per employee (current 1000 dollars)		Wages and salaries per employee (current 1000 dollars)		Percentage in output [a]								
						Costs of input materials and utilities			Costs of labour			Operating surplus		
	(LY)	2000	LY	2000	LY	2000	2006	LY	2000	2006	LY	2000	2006	LY
Industrialized Economies														
EU														
Austria	2009	44.5	89.4	25.1	47.1	58.2	61.9	61.1	23.6	19.8	20.5	18.2	18.3	18.4
Belgium	2009	45.6	88.6	23.8	45.4	65.8	69.6	69.9	17.8	16.8	15.4	16.4	13.7	14.7
Czech Republic	2006	8.4	21.7	4.2	10.1	72.8	75.6	75.6	13.5	11.4	11.4	13.7	13.0	13.0
Estonia	2010	5.8	24.9	3.4	14.1	72.8	...	70.4	15.8	...	16.7	11.4	...	12.9
Finland	2009	42.6	70.9	23.7	41.6	67.8	64.1	67.3	18.0	21.3	19.2	14.3	14.6	13.5
France	2009	39.7	73.8	21.4	40.5	63.8	66.0	66.2	19.6	19.3	18.6	16.7	14.7	15.3
Germany	2009	38.7	68.3	25.9	43.4	63.3	62.0	66.5	24.5	20.3	21.3	12.2	17.7	12.2
Hungary	2009	8.2	18.4	3.4	10.4	65.4	69.8	67.4	14.4	14.3	18.3	20.3	15.9	14.2
Ireland	2006	39.9	58.1	20.1	38.9	63.2	68.6	68.6	18.6	21.0	21.0	18.3	10.3	10.3
Italy	2009	38.3	68.4	16.0	31.0	69.5	70.8	68.5	12.7	13.2	14.3	17.7	16.0	17.2
Lithuania	2010	4.5	15.4	2.2	7.2	69.5	69.4	69.1	14.7	14.2	14.5	15.8	16.4	16.5
Malta	2008	14.6	33.9	7.4	15.7	62.9	60.9	59.4	18.9	18.5	18.8	18.2	20.5	21.9
Netherlands	2007	43.1	88.7	25.9	48.5	68.2	70.1	70.4	19.1	17.5	16.2	12.7	12.4	13.4
Portugal	2009	15.2	31.3	8.2	17.2	70.1	...	68.3	16.2	...	17.4	13.7	...	14.3
Slovakia	2008	3.4	23.5	2.3	12.6	78.5	73.6	80.8	14.6	11.1	10.3	6.9	15.3	8.9
Slovenia	2010	15.1	34.3	11.4	23.0	76.0	69.1	68.7	18.1	17.2	21.0	5.9	13.7	10.3
Spain	2009	26.3	53.8	14.2	32.4	66.9	67.8	63.6	17.8	17.6	21.9	15.3	14.7	14.5
Sweden	2009	45.8	71.6	24.8	41.3	65.6	69.3	65.9	18.6	16.7	19.6	15.8	14.0	14.4
United Kingdom	2007	48.0	94.6	32.5	50.1	62.6	57.9	59.3	25.3	21.6	21.6	12.0	20.6	19.2
Other Europe														
Norway	2008	40.3	106.3	31.2	70.1	59.9	62.8	63.8	31.0	26.0	23.8	9.0	11.2	12.3
Russian Federation	2010	...	14.3	1.0	7.4	...	68.9	69.0	9.9	13.4	15.9	...	17.7	15.0
East Asia														
Japan	2010	100.2	121.9	23.4	30.2	58.9	60.4	62.9	9.6	8.1	9.2	31.5	31.5	27.9
Malaysia	2010	11.0	15.7	4.4	6.6	68.7	74.6	72.9	12.4	12.3	11.3	18.8	13.2	15.8
Republic of Korea	2008	50.9	106.8	16.9	25.2	61.5	67.8	67.4	12.8	10.4	7.7	25.7	21.8	24.9
Singapore	2010	20.4	41.5	14.0	22.2	72.6	69.6	62.5	18.8	20.7	20.1	8.6	9.7	17.4
West Asia														
Kuwait	2010	...	15.6	...	9.2	...	68.3	69.5	...	15.3	18.0	...	16.4	12.4

a/ At current prices.

Table 1.11
(continued)

SELECTED CHARACTERISTICS OF BRANCHES, SELECTED YEARS AND ECONOMIES

Struct.metal products;tanks;steam generators (ISIC 281)

Economy	Latest year (LY)	Value added per employee (current 1000 dollars) 2000	Value added per employee LY	Wages and salaries per employee (current 1000 dollars) 2000	Wages and salaries per employee LY	Percentage in output a/ — Costs of input materials and utilities 2000	2006	LY	Costs of labour 2000	2006	LY	Operating surplus 2000	2006	LY
North America														
Canada	2009	56.9	85.1	26.0	43.0	51.4	56.1	53.2	22.2	23.4	23.7	26.4	20.5	23.1
United States of America	2008	79.9	113.7	33.9	43.4	49.1	50.7	51.9	21.6	18.3	18.4	29.3	30.9	29.7
Others														
Israel	2009	28.6	39.7	22.7	28.7	67.1	70.5	67.5	26.0	21.6	23.6	6.9	7.9	9.0
Developing & EIE														
Azerbaijan	2010	...	14.0	0.7	6.0	...	80.3	62.2	17.3	17.4	16.2	...	2.2	21.6
Brazil	2010	10.6	30.8	4.2	11.3	53.8	52.2	47.5	18.4	16.2	19.3	27.8	31.6	33.3
Bulgaria	2010	1.7	8.6	1.1	3.9	75.3	79.7	75.1	16.6	7.0	11.3	8.1	13.4	13.6
Chile	2008	...	28.6	...	11.0	...	59.2	58.5	...	18.9	16.0	...	21.9	25.5
China	2007	...	18.4	...	3.0	...	73.7	72.9	...	4.1	4.4	...	22.2	22.7
Cyprus	2010	20.9	40.1	10.5	23.1	65.3	64.2	66.5	17.4	18.4	19.3	17.4	17.4	14.2
Ecuador	2008	7.2	35.0	1.1	5.8	64.8	74.9	61.6	5.5	9.2	6.3	29.7	15.9	32.1
Egypt	2010	...	9.0	...	3.3	...	70.2	70.0	...	14.5	10.9	...	15.2	19.1
Eritrea	2010	5.7	6.2	1.0	1.5	52.2	49.3	52.4	8.8	10.4	11.7	39.0	40.3	35.9
Ethiopia	2009	1.9	7.9	0.5	0.1	58.0	68.7	63.9	11.4	6.9	0.6	30.6	24.4	35.5
Georgia	2010	0.6	6.7	0.4	4.4	77.0	71.5	62.2	15.7	15.4	24.4	7.3	13.2	13.4
Greece	2007	...	97.3	...	23.7	...	66.3	63.5	...	9.3	8.9	...	24.4	27.6
India	2009	3.3	12.8	1.8	2.9	79.0	79.1	75.6	11.8	4.9	5.6	9.3	16.0	18.8
Indonesia	2009	15.2	26.9	1.6	3.3	60.1	50.0	63.9	4.1	8.2	4.4	35.9	41.8	31.7
Iran (Islamic Republic of)	2009	33.2	19.6	14.2	7.5	52.9	61.5	64.1	20.2	14.5	13.7	26.9	24.0	22.1
Jordan	2010	6.4	8.9	2.3	3.5	59.9	67.7	64.2	14.7	9.1	13.9	25.4	23.2	21.9
Kyrgyzstan	2010	...	6.1	0.3	1.6	...	...	66.8	9.3	19.7	8.6	...	24.6	24.6
Latvia	2010	5.5	16.2	2.1	7.5	60.6	70.4	76.1	15.2	11.1	11.0	24.3	18.5	12.9
Malawi	2009	1.1	8.9	0.6	3.7	69.4	65.7	82.4	16.0	10.9	7.2	14.6	23.4	10.4
Mongolia	2008	1.4	6.6	0.6	4.2	70.7	85.4	86.5	12.2	7.5	8.5	17.1	7.1	5.0
Morocco	2010	7.2	13.6	4.2	7.7	56.5	73.2	72.2	25.5	...	15.7	18.0	12.1	12.1
Oman	2010	9.3	64.6	6.0	6.6	51.5	54.9	21.6	31.4	16.0	8.0	17.2	29.1	70.4
Poland	2009	10.7	26.8	...	11.6	67.6	65.5	63.6	...	14.9	15.8	...	19.5	20.7
Romania	2010	...	11.4	...	5.4	...	73.6	74.1	...	16.4	12.3	...	10.0	13.7
Sri Lanka	2010	...	8.9	...	1.3	...	59.4	52.6	...	17.6	7.0	...	23.0	40.4
The f. Yugosl. Rep of Macedonia	2008	...	8.2	...	6.5	...	81.0	66.6	...	17.2	26.6	...	1.8	6.9
Turkey	2008	27.9	18.0	6.5	7.8	55.5	81.9	80.5	10.3	7.6	8.4	34.1	10.5	11.1
United Republic of Tanzania	2007	...	0.3	...	0.1	...	67.9	67.8	...	7.7	7.6	...	24.4	24.6
Uruguay	2007	16.0	18.4	10.7	7.7	59.7	...	77.4	26.9	...	9.4	13.4	...	13.2

a/ At current prices.

Table 1.11

SELECTED CHARACTERISTICS OF BRANCHES, SELECTED YEARS AND ECONOMIES

Other metal products; metal working services (ISIC 289)

Economy	Latest year (LY)	Value added per employee (current 1000 dollars)		Wages and salaries per employee (current 1000 dollars)		Percentage in output a/								
						Costs of input materials and utilities			Costs of labour			Operating surplus		
		2000	LY	2000	LY	2000	2006	LY	2000	2006	LY	2000	2006	LY
Industrialized Economies														
EU														
Austria	2009	47.7	86.8	25.1	49.5	54.7	58.5	60.9	23.8	19.9	22.3	21.5	21.5	16.8
Belgium	2009	49.4	83.9	24.2	45.7	63.4	67.0	64.6	17.9	15.1	19.3	18.7	17.9	16.1
Czech Republic	2007	8.7	29.7	3.8	11.3	68.8	66.9	67.8	13.5	11.9	12.2	17.6	21.2	20.0
Estonia	2010	7.1	26.2	3.3	12.4	70.0	...	69.5	13.9	...	14.5	16.1	...	16.0
Finland	2009	45.9	67.8	22.5	40.9	51.7	57.8	58.4	23.7	21.7	25.1	24.6	20.5	16.5
France	2009	39.6	71.2	21.3	44.4	61.2	64.0	60.0	20.9	20.1	24.9	17.9	15.8	15.1
Germany	2009	45.1	66.8	27.2	44.3	55.4	58.9	62.2	26.9	22.7	25.0	17.7	18.4	12.7
Hungary	2009	8.3	21.8	3.4	11.9	64.3	66.4	63.2	14.6	14.7	20.1	21.1	18.8	16.7
Ireland	2009	40.4	82.2	20.6	55.4	54.2	54.4	50.0	23.3	25.1	33.7	22.5	20.5	16.3
Italy	2009	44.7	62.7	16.7	31.9	63.0	67.8	67.0	13.8	13.3	16.8	23.2	18.9	16.2
Lithuania	2010	3.1	15.7	2.2	8.9	64.2	75.6	66.6	25.2	13.8	19.0	10.6	10.6	14.4
Malta	2008	26.3	29.5	10.5	17.7	53.5	73.7	77.3	18.5	18.3	13.6	28.0	8.1	9.1
Netherlands	2007	46.5	89.5	24.6	44.3	60.6	64.3	65.1	20.8	18.6	17.3	18.6	17.1	17.6
Portugal	2008	16.6	32.3	8.0	16.6	64.4	...	63.5	17.2	...	18.8	18.4	...	17.7
Slovakia	2009	4.2	19.1	2.2	12.9	71.6	70.8	76.8	14.9	13.5	15.6	13.5	15.7	7.6
Slovenia	2010	15.7	38.1	10.4	22.4	71.0	66.6	67.9	19.2	16.9	18.9	9.8	16.5	13.2
Spain	2009	34.1	63.6	17.2	37.1	61.7	64.5	60.6	19.2	18.4	23.0	19.0	17.1	16.4
Sweden	2009	42.6	68.0	22.6	40.2	56.9	61.1	64.3	22.9	18.5	21.1	20.3	20.4	14.6
United Kingdom	2009	48.8	63.0	27.4	34.1	48.9	52.6	54.7	28.7	25.5	24.5	22.4	21.8	20.8
Other Europe														
Norway	2008	46.9	112.6	30.6	68.7	56.6	57.7	60.5	28.3	25.9	24.1	15.1	16.4	15.4
Russian Federation	2010	...	9.2	0.8	6.5	...	74.1	72.3	5.9	17.9	19.5	...	8.0	8.2
East Asia														
Japan	2010	85.9	98.4	23.4	26.5	53.1	55.6	56.0	12.8	11.7	11.9	34.1	32.7	32.2
Malaysia	2010	14.6	17.9	4.5	7.4	72.2	79.7	76.4	8.7	8.1	9.8	19.1	12.2	13.8
Republic of Korea	2008	42.4	74.1	13.6	23.1	52.0	57.0	59.8	15.4	14.5	12.5	32.6	28.5	27.7
Singapore	2010	35.4	49.6	18.0	28.2	71.9	75.1	75.1	14.3	13.5	14.2	13.8	11.4	10.8
West Asia														
Kuwait	2010	...	34.7	...	12.8	...	66.8	76.4	...	14.9	8.7	...	18.3	14.9

a/ At current prices.

Table 1.11
(continued)

SELECTED CHARACTERISTICS OF BRANCHES, SELECTED YEARS AND ECONOMIES

Other metal products; metal working services (ISIC 289)

Economy	Latest year (LY)	Value added per employee (current 1000 dollars)		Wages and salaries per employee (current 1000 dollars)		Percentage in output [a] Costs of input materials and utilities			Costs of labour			Operating surplus		
	(LY)	2000	LY	2000	LY	2000	2006	LY	2000	2006	LY	2000	2006	LY
North America														
Canada	2009	59.8	81.5	26.9	44.3	49.1	52.7	55.4	22.9	25.1	24.2	28.1	22.2	20.4
United States of America	2008	80.9	112.5	35.1	44.0	42.2	45.0	45.3	25.0	22.0	21.4	32.7	32.9	33.3
Others														
Israel	2009	47.5	42.9	27.2	30.1	50.4	59.2	56.0	28.5	25.8	30.9	21.2	15.0	13.1
Developing & EIE														
Azerbaijan	2010	...	9.7	0.3	5.5	...	80.3	59.5	30.1	17.3	23.2	...	2.4	17.3
Brazil	2010	16.2	35.6	5.3	12.0	54.2	57.1	48.7	14.9	13.4	17.2	30.9	29.5	34.0
Bulgaria	2010	2.4	11.3	1.0	4.8	75.8	72.9	62.4	10.3	9.2	16.0	13.8	17.9	21.6
Chile	2008	25.3	43.5	9.1	14.1	55.4	63.6	67.8	16.0	13.2	10.4	28.6	23.2	21.7
China	2007	...	13.9	...	2.7	...	73.3	73.1	...	5.2	5.2	...	21.6	21.7
Cyprus	2010	23.7	48.7	11.1	27.5	54.0	53.0	49.6	21.7	25.1	28.5	24.3	21.9	21.9
Ecuador	2008	24.3	37.1	2.6	6.8	59.6	69.8	71.2	4.4	7.7	5.3	36.0	22.5	23.6
Egypt	2010	...	9.8	...	2.9	...	78.8	74.8	...	7.6	7.5	13.7	13.7	17.7
Eritrea	2010	1.6	3.1	0.7	0.9	53.9	...	50.6	21.0	...	14.6	25.0	...	34.8
Ethiopia	2009	2.8	8.2	0.8	0.8	53.7	65.0	69.2	13.0	8.7	2.8	33.3	26.3	28.0
Georgia	2010	0.8	6.0	0.4	2.7	56.7	77.4	60.3	22.9	11.1	17.8	20.4	11.4	21.9
Greece	2007	...	85.9	...	25.7	...	63.9	61.9	...	11.7	11.4	...	24.3	26.7
India	2009	3.8	7.4	1.1	2.4	77.8	78.0	78.0	6.6	5.7	7.1	15.6	15.5	14.9
Indonesia	2009	6.0	17.7	1.0	2.4	62.2	65.0	54.2	6.4	5.7	6.2	31.3	29.3	39.6
Iran (Islamic Republic of)	2009	27.0	18.7	8.9	7.2	57.1	66.3	69.6	14.2	10.8	11.8	28.7	22.9	18.6
Jordan	2010	10.0	22.7	3.0	4.3	66.9	60.4	68.7	10.0	5.3	5.9	23.1	34.2	25.4
Latvia	2010	6.3	12.1	2.2	5.5	53.3	67.4	58.7	16.3	13.5	18.6	30.3	19.1	22.7
Malawi	2007	5.0	1.7	2.2	0.8	79.4	87.9	84.2	9.3	11.7	7.2	11.3	0.3	8.6
Mongolia	2008	0.5	4.3	0.2	2.8	82.3	77.0	80.2	7.9	14.9	13.0	9.7	8.1	6.8
Morocco	2010	9.1	16.7	4.9	8.3	65.9	74.2	75.3	18.5	...	12.2	15.7	...	12.5
Oman	2010	14.5	48.9	4.7	10.8	48.9	55.4	34.6	16.4	12.7	14.4	34.7	31.9	51.0
Philippines	2008	...	10.4	...	3.4	...	80.1	76.6	...	7.3	7.7	...	12.7	15.7
Poland	2009	12.5	26.8	...	11.1	61.0	68.0	61.1	...	11.3	16.1	...	20.7	22.8
Romania	2010	...	13.3	...	6.5	...	72.7	68.0	...	18.0	15.5	...	9.3	16.5
Sri Lanka	2010	...	6.1	...	1.5	...	45.3	56.9	...	25.5	10.6	...	29.3	32.5
The f. Yugosl. Rep of Macedonia	2010	...	7.3	...	5.0	54.8	67.4	63.7	13.2	22.4	25.0	32.0	10.2	11.3
Turkey	2009	21.9	19.2	6.4	9.1	...	79.2	74.3	...	8.5	12.1	...	12.2	13.6
United Republic of Tanzania	2007	...	4.4	...	2.6	...	86.0	86.0	...	8.1	8.1	...	5.8	5.9
Uruguay	2007	19.3	19.3	12.2	8.2	70.0	...	67.3	19.0	...	14.0	10.9	...	18.7

a/ At current prices.

Table 1.11

SELECTED CHARACTERISTICS OF BRANCHES, SELECTED YEARS AND ECONOMIES

General purpose machinery (ISIC 291)

Economy	Latest year (LY)	Value added per employee (current 1000 dollars)		Wages and salaries per employee (current 1000 dollars)		Percentage in output a/								
						Costs of input materials and utilities			Costs of labour			Operating surplus		
		2000	LY	2000	LY	2000	2006	LY	2000	2006	LY	2000	2006	LY
Industrialized Economies														
EU														
Austria	2009	53.4	103.4	29.8	55.7	60.8	63.3	64.8	21.9	18.4	19.0	17.3	18.3	16.2
Belgium	2009	63.4	121.3	28.9	56.5	65.9	71.0	72.0	15.5	12.7	13.0	18.5	16.4	14.9
Czech Republic	2007	8.7	31.0	4.5	13.1	67.3	74.9	74.8	16.9	10.9	10.6	15.8	14.2	14.5
Denmark	2009	46.1	115.2	33.2	78.7	58.6	61.8	74.4	29.8	25.7	17.5	11.6	12.5	8.1
Estonia	2010	4.6	22.0	3.4	13.1	71.7	66.0	64.3	21.0	18.4	21.2	7.2	15.6	14.5
Finland	2009	50.5	97.8	27.3	51.2	70.8	73.5	73.5	15.8	13.9	13.9	13.4	12.6	12.6
France	2009	44.2	89.3	24.4	49.2	67.4	66.7	66.5	18.0	17.0	18.5	14.6	16.3	15.0
Germany	2009	50.5	85.1	34.0	60.5	60.1	63.6	64.8	26.9	22.2	25.0	13.1	14.2	10.2
Hungary	2009	8.6	69.6	4.1	14.8	62.7	68.6	52.1	17.9	14.5	10.2	19.4	16.8	37.7
Ireland	2009	52.5	109.5	23.9	52.5	60.1	56.1	63.2	18.2	15.3	17.7	21.8	28.6	19.2
Italy	2009	49.2	84.4	20.0	41.0	68.1	71.6	70.6	12.9	12.5	14.3	18.9	15.9	15.1
Lithuania	2010	3.1	22.8	2.9	9.5	63.6	63.1	64.0	34.0	17.8	14.9	2.4	19.1	21.1
Malta	2008	17.9	28.4	8.2	19.5	67.5	63.3	71.2	14.9	16.8	19.7	17.6	19.9	9.1
Netherlands	2008	46.8	107.6	27.4	57.5	64.9	68.2	68.1	20.6	17.8	17.0	14.5	14.0	14.8
Portugal	2009	20.3	38.9	10.2	20.2	67.9	71.1	68.3	16.2	14.2	16.5	15.9	14.8	15.3
Slovakia	2009	3.7	24.3	2.3	13.5	75.7	75.5	71.8	15.1	10.4	15.7	9.2	14.1	12.6
Slovenia	2010	16.9	41.6	12.4	24.9	69.2	68.0	69.1	22.6	19.1	18.5	8.2	12.9	12.4
Spain	2009	37.1	77.7	19.4	42.5	64.5	67.2	64.1	18.6	16.9	19.6	16.9	15.9	16.3
Sweden	2009	56.1	88.9	28.3	45.8	63.5	68.1	66.2	18.4	15.4	17.4	18.1	16.5	16.4
United Kingdom	2007	50.1	95.6	31.6	51.6	61.1	60.8	61.8	24.6	22.9	20.7	14.4	16.3	17.6
Other Europe														
Norway	2008	49.3	162.3	34.6	87.1	68.5	70.3	69.8	22.1	17.9	16.2	9.4	11.8	14.0
Russian Federation	2010	...	15.6	0.7	8.8	...	62.1	62.5	43.4	23.2	21.2	...	14.7	16.3
East Asia														
Japan	2010	103.7	134.7	35.6	45.9	63.3	60.6	60.6	12.6	11.2	13.4	24.1	28.2	26.0
Malaysia	2010	21.7	23.4	5.5	9.6	69.2	78.6	77.8	7.8	6.8	9.1	23.0	14.5	13.1
Republic of Korea	2008	57.5	110.4	16.1	26.8	59.9	63.3	64.0	11.2	10.2	8.7	28.9	26.5	27.3
Singapore	2010	37.2	56.8	19.6	33.8	67.7	66.7	74.1	17.0	15.1	15.4	15.3	18.1	10.5
West Asia														
Kuwait	2010	...	20.8	...	8.8	...	61.9	69.7	...	21.3	12.8	...	16.8	17.5

a/ At current prices.

Table 1.11
(continued)

SELECTED CHARACTERISTICS OF BRANCHES, SELECTED YEARS AND ECONOMIES

General purpose machinery (ISIC 291)

Economy	Latest year	Value added per employee (current 1000 dollars)		Wages and salaries per employee (current 1000 dollars)		Percentage in output a/								
						Costs of input materials and utilities			Costs of labour			Operating surplus		
	(LY)	2000	LY	2000	LY	2000	2006	LY	2000	2006	LY	2000	2006	LY
North America														
United States of America	2008	103.8	150.1	39.6	48.8	50.7	51.9	51.9	18.8	15.6	15.6	30.5	32.5	32.4
Others														
Israel	2009	42.0	66.3	37.3	48.1	61.6	61.2	62.7	34.0	27.9	27.1	4.3	10.9	10.3
Developing & EIE														
Azerbaijan	2010	...	10.3	0.6	2.4	...	54.4	54.3	28.8	18.8	10.5	...	26.9	35.2
Brazil	2010	23.5	55.2	7.8	17.6	50.8	58.4	55.6	16.4	13.3	14.1	32.8	28.3	30.3
Bulgaria	2010	2.8	14.7	1.4	5.9	69.3	75.6	68.8	15.9	11.0	12.5	14.8	13.3	18.7
Chile	2008	17.7	32.0	8.1	15.5	47.9	57.5	56.5	23.9	20.2	21.1	28.2	22.3	22.5
China	2007	...	17.6	...	3.1	...	72.8	73.0	...	4.7	4.8	...	22.4	22.2
Cyprus	2007	22.4	46.4	11.8	24.3	59.5	56.5	57.8	21.3	24.7	22.1	19.1	18.8	20.1
Ecuador	2008	5.7	11.6	0.9	4.2	69.2	69.6	72.3	5.0	11.9	10.0	25.8	18.5	17.7
Egypt	2010	...	8.1	...	3.2	...	65.5	73.8	...	11.5	10.2	...	23.0	16.0
Eritrea	2010	...	1.0	...	1.0	...	26.5	82.4	...	3.5	16.5	...	70.1	1.1
Ethiopia	2008	1.2	3.8	0.3	0.9	53.0	79.4	63.4	13.5	1.5	8.6	33.4	19.1	28.0
Georgia	2010	2.9	8.3	1.0	4.6	40.6	38.3	39.0	20.6	28.9	34.2	38.9	32.8	26.8
Greece	2007	...	61.6	...	27.8	...	56.5	57.2	...	18.7	19.3	...	24.8	23.4
India	2009	6.0	17.6	2.2	4.4	73.8	75.9	72.3	9.5	6.0	7.0	16.7	18.1	20.7
Indonesia	2009	5.3	15.3	1.4	3.0	57.3	69.8	49.7	11.2	7.8	9.8	31.5	22.4	40.5
Iran (Islamic Republic of)	2009	28.6	25.2	9.9	7.8	59.6	62.7	66.0	14.0	12.4	10.6	26.3	24.9	23.4
Jordan	2010	8.7	25.0	3.8	7.5	68.3	68.7	59.0	13.7	10.2	12.3	18.0	21.1	28.7
Kyrgyzstan	2010	...	2.0	0.2	1.2	...	...	87.1	21.7	5.9	7.3	...	...	5.6
Latvia	2009	5.3	19.7	2.5	8.7	61.0	66.3	57.4	18.7	15.2	18.7	20.4	18.6	23.9
Mexico	2010	25.0	53.9	7.6	11.6	57.5	66.2	52.2	13.0	...	10.2	29.5	...	37.5
Mongolia	2008	0.7	1.1	0.6	0.5	80.4	...	57.6	16.0	...	16.7	3.7	...	25.7
Morocco	2010	8.4	14.3	5.4	8.1	63.3	61.0	61.8	23.6	...	21.5	13.1	...	16.7
Oman	2010	21.0	49.3	7.1	10.7	59.8	47.7	52.9	13.5	5.9	10.2	26.7	46.4	36.8
Poland	2009	11.2	33.9	...	13.2	60.3	63.7	65.5	...	15.4	13.4	...	20.9	21.1
Romania	2010	...	21.4	...	7.8	60.6	69.3	62.3	...	25.3	13.8	...	5.4	24.0
Sri Lanka	2010	...	13.3	...	1.8	...	52.4	50.6	...	9.9	6.9	...	37.7	42.5
The f. Yugosl. Rep of Macedonia	2010	...	17.7	...	6.8	...	62.8	48.7	...	31.2	19.6	...	6.1	31.7
Turkey	2009	22.7	23.8	8.1	10.0	51.0	76.9	71.7	17.5	9.9	11.9	31.5	13.2	16.4
Uruguay	2007	13.3	17.0	13.1	10.2	58.7	...	47.7	40.9	...	31.5	0.5	...	20.8

a/ At current prices.

Table 1.11

SELECTED CHARACTERISTICS OF BRANCHES, SELECTED YEARS AND ECONOMIES

Special purpose machinery (ISIC 292)

Economy	Latest year (LY)	Value added per employee (current 1000 dollars)		Wages and salaries per employee (current 1000 dollars)		Percentage in output [a]								
						Costs of input materials and utilities			Costs of labour			Operating surplus		
		2000	LY	2000	LY	2000	2006	LY	2000	2006	LY	2000	2006	LY
Industrialized Economies														
EU														
Austria	2009	51.2	95.7	29.5	58.0	61.5	63.1	67.6	22.2	19.1	19.7	16.3	17.8	12.8
Belgium	2009	55.9	91.0	28.5	52.1	70.6	64.5	65.1	15.0	18.6	20.0	14.4	16.9	14.9
Czech Republic	2007	8.1	26.4	4.1	12.9	64.0	69.2	70.9	18.3	14.8	14.3	17.7	16.0	14.8
Denmark	2009	...	95.0	...	76.4	...	...	63.8	...	...	29.1	...	...	7.1
Estonia	2010	6.2	30.0	3.4	14.9	61.8	...	67.3	21.0	...	16.2	17.3	...	16.4
Finland	2009	51.3	72.6	27.7	49.2	67.3	71.8	70.7	17.6	15.5	19.9	15.1	12.7	9.4
France	2009	45.9	79.7	25.2	49.9	68.4	71.1	66.3	17.3	17.5	21.1	14.3	11.4	12.6
Germany	2009	50.3	77.8	33.5	57.9	62.0	65.5	66.3	25.3	21.5	25.1	12.7	13.1	8.6
Hungary	2009	8.4	25.6	4.1	12.2	64.0	66.9	64.8	17.6	15.5	16.7	18.4	17.5	18.5
Ireland	2009	34.9	111.6	20.9	51.2	60.3	62.5	61.1	23.8	21.0	17.8	15.9	16.5	21.0
Italy	2009	49.4	67.8	21.4	38.7	70.3	72.5	73.2	12.9	12.9	15.3	16.8	14.7	11.5
Lithuania	2010	4.2	16.5	2.9	8.0	56.4	51.7	63.1	30.2	24.1	18.0	13.4	24.2	18.9
Malta	2008	27.6	43.8	11.7	22.6	31.9	61.4	67.0	28.9	17.5	17.0	39.1	21.1	16.0
Netherlands	2008	...	111.8	...	61.1	65.0	...	71.6	15.7	...	15.5	19.3	...	12.9
Portugal	2009	20.8	43.9	10.8	23.6	58.7	...	70.9	21.4	...	15.6	19.9	...	13.5
Slovakia	2009	2.5	22.0	2.2	15.3	75.6	72.4	72.4	21.6	16.1	19.2	2.9	11.6	8.4
Slovenia	2010	16.5	40.8	11.8	26.0	68.6	63.6	64.9	22.4	22.4	22.4	9.1	14.1	12.8
Spain	2009	35.6	68.3	19.0	41.5	63.2	65.7	62.0	19.6	19.2	23.1	17.2	15.1	14.9
Sweden	2009	54.4	55.4	27.5	47.3	67.0	69.5	78.9	16.7	14.4	18.0	16.3	16.0	3.1
United Kingdom	2007	53.7	102.8	32.6	52.3	61.8	61.8	63.0	23.2	20.0	18.8	15.1	18.1	18.2
Other Europe														
Norway	2008	50.1	209.9	36.4	97.6	60.1	69.8	70.1	29.0	17.4	13.9	10.9	12.8	16.0
Russian Federation	2010	...	10.4	0.9	6.9	...	65.6	66.0	19.5	21.3	22.4	...	13.2	11.6
East Asia														
Japan	2010	105.1	122.6	31.0	36.4	57.3	61.8	62.3	12.6	9.5	11.2	30.1	28.7	26.5
Malaysia	2010	14.0	19.0	5.3	7.4	62.2	72.3	71.3	14.4	11.2	11.1	23.4	16.6	17.5
Republic of Korea	2008	53.2	95.5	16.3	27.1	56.3	62.2	62.6	13.4	11.0	10.6	30.3	26.8	26.8
Singapore	2010	42.4	74.3	20.5	32.3	63.0	73.3	71.6	17.8	14.2	12.3	19.2	12.5	16.0
West Asia														
Kuwait	2010	...	10.3	...	8.5	...	21.9	42.5	...	68.8	47.4	...	9.3	10.1

a/ At current prices.

Table 1.11
(continued)

SELECTED CHARACTERISTICS OF BRANCHES, SELECTED YEARS AND ECONOMIES

Special purpose machinery (ISIC 292)

Economy	Latest year (LY)	Value added per employee (current 1000 dollars) 2000	LY	Wages and salaries per employee (current 1000 dollars) 2000	LY	Percentage in output [a] — Costs of input materials and utilities 2000	2006	LY	Costs of labour 2000	2006	LY	Operating surplus 2000	2006	LY
North America														
United States of America	2008	110.9	165.4	42.4	52.6	50.1	52.1	52.9	19.1	15.9	15.0	30.8	32.0	32.1
Others														
Israel	2009	63.8	48.9	39.7	42.5	63.5	...	65.2	22.7	...	30.2	13.8	...	4.6
Developing & EIE														
Azerbaijan	2010	...	21.3	0.7	3.8	...	54.4	67.9	16.2	14.2	5.7	...	31.4	26.4
Brazil	2010	20.4	53.6	7.1	16.2	53.2	54.9	56.8	16.3	15.0	13.1	30.5	30.1	30.2
Bulgaria	2010	2.1	9.6	1.3	4.8	62.9	67.0	63.2	22.2	14.9	18.4	14.9	18.1	18.4
Chile	2008	23.5	34.2	11.1	21.9	45.3	53.4	61.3	25.8	20.6	24.8	28.9	25.9	13.9
China	2007	...	16.2	...	3.1	...	71.3	71.1	...	5.6	5.5	...	23.2	23.4
Cyprus	2007	23.1	54.7	10.6	27.6	51.5	57.7	63.4	22.3	23.1	18.4	26.2	19.3	18.2
Ecuador	2008	...	56.6	1.2	5.2	...	74.1	46.9	8.3	7.3	4.9	...	18.6	48.3
Egypt	2010	...	9.4	...	4.0	...	60.0	50.8	...	25.7	20.9	...	14.3	28.2
Georgia	2010	...	6.7	...	2.4	...	80.5	30.2	...	9.3	25.2	...	10.2	44.6
Greece	2007	...	51.2	...	29.8	...	62.6	65.0	...	20.8	20.4	...	16.6	14.6
India	2009	5.4	14.5	1.9	4.2	75.1	79.1	76.1	8.6	6.2	6.9	16.3	14.7	17.0
Indonesia	2009	6.2	24.7	1.2	2.6	60.2	55.0	30.1	7.7	11.7	7.4	32.1	33.4	62.5
Iran (Islamic Republic of)	2009	24.1	16.2	11.1	7.5	55.3	64.3	67.0	20.5	12.4	15.2	24.1	23.3	17.7
Jordan	2010	5.7	23.8	2.4	4.1	65.9	66.8	60.0	14.4	8.1	6.9	19.7	25.1	33.2
Kyrgyzstan	2010	...	3.1	0.3	2.6	41.3	59.0	54.3	28.8	...	37.8	32.0	...	7.9
Latvia	2010	5.3	16.7	2.4	9.7	62.0	21.4	63.0	26.7	22.0	21.5	19.2	19.0	15.6
Morocco	2010	7.1	12.1	3.5	7.7	27.1	21.8	66.4	18.8	22.1	21.5	55.4	56.2	12.0
Oman	2010	37.9	43.7	9.1	13.3	57.3	76.3	20.1	17.5	4.9	24.3	...	18.8	55.6
Philippines	2008	...	14.6	...	3.6	56.9	63.2	67.6	...	15.5	7.9	...	21.3	24.4
Poland	2009	9.4	26.7	...	12.0	...	69.0	61.6	...	29.2	17.3	...	1.8	21.1
Romania	2010	...	9.6	...	4.9	...	61.4	80.1	...	22.3	10.1	...	16.3	9.9
Sri Lanka	2010	...	3.0	...	1.6	...	61.6	56.1	...	17.2	22.5	...	21.2	21.4
The f. Yugosl. Rep of Macedonia	2010	...	10.5	...	5.8	56.5	72.9	56.3	17.8	11.2	24.4	25.8	15.9	19.3
Turkey	2009	22.0	18.9	9.0	8.3	76.2	...	75.2	9.1	...	11.0	14.7	...	13.9
Uruguay	2007	51.3	15.3	19.7	7.8	...	...	60.9	...	...	20.0	...	...	19.1

a/ At current prices.

Table 1.11

SELECTED CHARACTERISTICS OF BRANCHES, SELECTED YEARS AND ECONOMIES

Domestic appliances n.e.c. (ISIC 2930)

Economy	Latest year (LY)	Value added per employee (current 1000 dollars)		Wages and salaries per employee (current 1000 dollars)		Percentage in output a/								
						Costs of input materials and utilities			Costs of labour			Operating surplus		
		2000	LY	2000	LY	2000	2006	LY	2000	2006	LY	2000	2006	LY
Industrialized Economies														
EU														
Austria	2009	48.6	104.1	26.2	49.0	58.6	64.2	61.9	22.4	16.1	17.9	19.0	19.7	20.2
Belgium	2008	44.1	108.1	22.3	46.2	62.9	63.2	66.7	18.7	17.6	14.2	18.4	19.2	19.1
Czech Republic	2007	7.6	25.0	3.8	10.5	70.4	76.0	75.7	14.8	9.8	10.2	14.8	14.2	14.1
Denmark	2009	...	103.5	...	71.3	...	...	62.1	...	...	26.1	...	...	11.8
Finland	2009	41.8	76.2	23.8	43.9	67.8	62.9	60.5	18.3	18.6	22.8	13.8	18.6	16.8
France	2009	43.7	90.8	24.5	46.8	72.3	71.4	64.9	15.5	14.5	18.1	12.2	14.2	17.0
Germany	2009	51.7	89.3	33.6	61.2	63.4	64.8	65.3	23.9	23.2	23.8	12.8	12.0	10.9
Hungary	2009	9.5	25.6	3.7	10.2	76.2	75.5	75.9	9.3	8.6	9.6	14.5	15.8	14.5
Ireland	2008	36.8	90.8	18.6	52.7	58.8	60.8	50.0	20.8	20.9	29.0	20.4	18.3	21.0
Italy	2009	45.3	68.2	19.5	37.0	72.9	78.6	73.9	11.7	11.3	14.1	15.4	10.1	11.9
Lithuania	2010	4.1	16.6	2.7	7.5	74.6	79.7	71.9	16.9	11.8	12.6	8.5	8.4	15.4
Netherlands	2008	...	212.4	...	130.4	61.0	...	67.4	19.1	...	20.0	19.9	...	12.6
Portugal	2009	23.8	49.5	9.4	19.0	72.4	...	70.0	10.9	...	11.5	16.7	...	18.5
Slovenia	2010	17.0	43.8	11.5	23.6	79.0	72.4	71.8	14.2	14.4	15.2	6.7	13.1	13.0
Spain	2009	35.4	70.8	18.6	40.8	71.8	69.8	72.3	14.8	14.4	16.0	13.4	15.7	11.7
Sweden	2009	38.6	51.0	24.7	43.8	67.6	73.1	70.7	20.8	17.0	25.2	11.7	9.8	4.2
United Kingdom	2009	45.0	72.6	25.3	43.3	63.1	69.0	67.2	20.8	18.4	19.6	16.1	12.6	13.2
Other Europe														
Norway	2008	105.8	84.5	68.7	64.7	56.7	63.6	68.1	28.1	24.3	24.4	15.1	12.1	7.4
Russian Federation	2010	...	13.6	0.9	6.8	...	74.4	82.7	12.4	13.2	8.7	...	12.4	8.6
East Asia														
Japan	2010	131.3	214.7	36.0	43.3	60.2	61.8	54.7	10.9	9.0	9.1	28.9	29.2	36.1
Malaysia	2010	15.7	19.9	6.2	9.5	77.2	84.7	84.4	8.9	4.9	7.5	13.9	10.4	8.1
Republic of Korea	2008	71.3	110.8	14.9	25.6	62.0	67.0	70.3	8.0	7.5	6.9	30.0	25.5	22.8
Singapore	2010	40.4	50.1	25.6	29.6	76.0	60.7	69.8	15.2	13.8	17.9	8.8	25.5	12.4
West Asia														
Kuwait	2010	...	18.2	...	8.7	...	54.7	64.8	...	17.5	16.8	...	27.8	18.4

a/ At current prices.

Table 1.11 (continued)

SELECTED CHARACTERISTICS OF BRANCHES, SELECTED YEARS AND ECONOMIES

Domestic appliances n.e.c. (ISIC 2930)

Economy	Latest year (LY)	Value added per employee (current 1000 dollars)		Wages and salaries per employee (current 1000 dollars)		Percentage in output [a]								
						Costs of input materials and utilities			Costs of labour			Operating surplus		
		2000	LY	2000	LY	2000	2006	LY	2000	2006	LY	2000	2006	LY
North America														
Canada	2008	58.8	81.3	24.2	43.1	58.6	58.1	58.0	17.0	21.1	22.3	24.4	20.8	19.7
United States of America	2008	101.8	158.8	32.6	39.9	56.2	57.5	58.4	14.0	10.9	10.5	29.8	31.5	31.2
Developing & EIE														
Azerbaijan	2010	...	1.9	0.1	1.2	...	54.4	51.9	34.4	22.2	29.8	...	23.4	18.4
Brazil	2010	28.1	65.4	7.6	24.2	57.9	61.9	59.1	11.4	9.5	15.2	30.7	28.7	25.8
Bulgaria	2010	...	18.4	...	6.6	...	78.3	77.5	...	7.5	8.0	...	14.2	14.4
Chile	2008	31.8	40.4	7.5	12.1	62.4	64.7	62.1	8.9	11.3	11.4	28.7	24.0	26.5
China	2007	...	15.7	...	3.0	...	77.7	76.5	...	4.3	4.6	...	18.0	18.9
Cyprus	2010	18.0	37.4	10.2	21.4	58.6	64.1	62.9	23.4	16.6	21.2	17.9	19.3	15.9
Ecuador	2008	4.7	13.4	1.4	4.6	80.4	78.2	75.2	6.0	8.5	8.5	13.6	13.3	16.2
Egypt	2010	...	13.4	...	3.5	...	78.9	73.0	...	5.9	7.1	...	15.3	19.9
Greece	2007	...	64.6	...	29.9	...	61.0	65.5	...	17.1	16.0	...	21.9	18.5
India	2009	6.3	17.8	1.6	2.8	76.8	81.9	80.6	6.0	3.7	3.1	17.2	14.4	16.3
Indonesia	2009	7.0	24.3	1.0	1.7	67.8	62.5	62.5	4.8	9.5	2.6	27.5	28.0	34.9
Iran (Islamic Republic of)	2009	39.1	18.8	10.2	6.3	60.5	59.3	65.8	10.3	12.0	11.4	29.2	28.8	22.8
Jordan	2010	10.6	30.0	3.6	5.8	64.8	61.9	55.1	12.0	8.4	8.7	23.2	29.7	36.2
Latvia	2009	1.1	6.6	...	4.6	...	51.0	78.6	...	33.7	14.8	...	15.2	6.6
Morocco	2010	10.4	20.1	4.8	8.7	77.1	73.3	65.2	10.6	5.1	15.0	12.3	16.2	19.8
Oman	2010	18.7	30.9	6.7	9.7	49.4	78.8	52.8	18.1	8.2	14.8	32.5	33.4	32.4
Philippines	2008	...	23.3	...	7.7	...	58.4	79.9	...	6.8	6.7	...	16.3	13.5
Poland	2009	9.7	38.3	...	11.7	70.4	76.8	81.8	...	10.2	5.6	...	10.6	12.7
Romania	2008	...	18.7	...	8.6	56.9	79.3	78.3	...	6.0	9.9	...	53.7	11.8
Sri Lanka	2010	...	10.8	...	3.3	...	40.2	70.0	...	12.2	9.1	...	26.3	20.9
The f. Yugosl. Rep of Macedonia	2010	...	10.9	...	5.1	...	61.5	72.4	...	7.2	12.9	36.0	15.9	14.7
Turkey	2009	42.8	44.8	8.8	16.8	54.7	76.9	76.7	9.3	10.0	8.8	...	53.5	14.5
United Republic of Tanzania	2007	...	24.9	...	3.9	...	36.4	36.4	...	...	10.0	...	...	53.6
Uruguay	2007	21.4	36.0	12.2	9.0	59.7	...	49.8	23.1	...	12.5	17.2	...	37.7

a/ At current prices.

Table 1.11

SELECTED CHARACTERISTICS OF BRANCHES, SELECTED YEARS AND ECONOMIES

Office, accounting and computing machinery (ISIC 3000)

Economy	Latest year	Value added per employee (current 1000 dollars)		Wages and salaries per employee (current 1000 dollars)		Percentage in output a/								
						Costs of input materials and utilities			Costs of labour			Operating surplus		
	(LY)	2000	LY	2000	LY	2000	2006	LY	2000	2006	LY	2000	2006	LY
Industrialized Economies														
EU														
Austria	2009	61.0	85.7	23.8	59.5	82.5	63.0	56.6	6.8	20.0	30.1	10.6	17.0	13.3
Belgium	2009	56.7	97.7	29.9	69.4	65.7	76.4	73.9	18.1	10.0	18.6	16.2	13.5	7.6
Denmark	2009	56.6	116.1	36.5	94.3	61.6	63.4	64.3	24.8	20.8	29.0	13.6	15.8	6.7
Estonia	2010	11.0	22.5	4.2	13.3	84.6	86.4	78.9	5.8	6.3	12.5	9.5	7.3	8.6
Finland	2009	...	61.2	25.8	45.9	...	73.3	74.2	14.2	15.0	19.4	...	11.7	6.5
France	2009	70.7	96.2	42.7	53.1	77.0	75.6	77.4	13.9	16.2	12.5	9.1	8.2	10.1
Germany	2009	81.8	89.7	44.5	63.6	74.7	71.9	72.5	13.7	16.6	19.5	11.5	11.5	8.0
Hungary	2009	19.2	33.4	4.1	15.1	91.2	88.9	86.5	1.9	3.3	6.1	6.9	7.8	7.4
Ireland	2009	116.2	182.6	23.2	64.2	86.7	89.3	92.1	2.7	2.5	2.8	10.6	8.2	5.1
Italy	2009	46.2	74.4	22.4	39.9	82.4	86.6	84.1	8.5	10.7	8.5	9.1	2.7	7.4
Lithuania	2010	2.4	22.2	1.9	10.5	87.0	76.4	75.1	10.6	10.0	11.8	2.5	13.6	13.1
Malta	2007	...	21.3	...	16.1	...	82.2	82.2	...	13.4	13.4	...	4.3	4.3
Netherlands	2008	69.7	83.2	36.6	65.6	79.4	74.1	77.2	10.8	16.0	18.0	9.8	10.0	4.8
Portugal	2009	32.5	70.7	14.1	25.7	80.6	...	79.6	8.4	...	7.4	11.0	...	13.0
Slovakia	2009	3.9	25.7	2.6	12.8	71.9	67.7	78.3	18.8	14.5	10.8	9.4	17.7	10.8
Slovenia	2010	21.3	47.3	14.9	35.5	77.3	69.9	70.4	15.9	20.5	22.2	6.8	9.6	7.4
Spain	2008	68.8	57.1	32.5	37.1	79.3	78.6	79.2	9.8	13.6	13.5	10.9	7.8	7.3
Sweden	2009	46.8	75.8	29.2	47.7	69.0	70.4	64.5	19.3	14.3	22.3	11.6	15.3	13.2
United Kingdom	2007	61.0	108.1	38.4	51.1	83.4	65.3	54.1	10.4	20.9	21.7	6.1	13.9	24.2
Other Europe														
Norway	2008	...	280.6	...	84.3	...	81.9	70.6	...	17.4	8.8	...	0.7	20.6
Russian Federation	2010	...	34.5	0.7	10.8	...	71.6	67.3	4.5	6.9	10.2	...	21.5	22.5
East Asia														
Japan	2010	110.0	177.9	43.5	53.0	78.9	...	67.9	8.4	...	9.6	12.8	...	22.6
Malaysia	2010	20.6	26.7	4.8	6.4	85.8	88.3	81.5	3.3	3.1	4.4	10.9	8.6	14.1
Republic of Korea	2008	128.1	145.9	18.9	24.1	72.7	61.5	58.9	4.0	7.9	6.8	23.3	30.7	34.3
Singapore	2010	100.8	257.2	18.6	33.7	85.4	83.2	81.8	2.7	4.1	2.4	11.9	12.7	15.8

a/ At current prices.

Table 1.11
(continued)

SELECTED CHARACTERISTICS OF BRANCHES, SELECTED YEARS AND ECONOMIES

Office, accounting and computing machinery (ISIC 3000)

Economy	Latest year (LY)	Value added per employee (current 1000 dollars) 2000	Value added per employee (current 1000 dollars) LY	Wages and salaries per employee (current 1000 dollars) 2000	Wages and salaries per employee (current 1000 dollars) LY	Percentage in output [a/] — Costs of input materials and utilities 2000	Costs of input materials and utilities 2006	Costs of input materials and utilities LY	Costs of labour 2000	Costs of labour 2006	Costs of labour LY	Operating surplus 2000	Operating surplus 2006	Operating surplus LY
North America														
Canada	2009	79.9	127.0	34.0	50.9	64.7	55.6	59.1	15.0	19.7	16.4	20.3	24.7	24.5
United States of America	2008	214.1	381.8	52.5	63.2	60.3	48.0	44.5	9.8	8.8	9.2	30.0	43.2	46.3
Developing & EIE														
Brazil	2010	74.6	57.7	13.6	18.6	64.5	67.4	73.3	6.4	8.9	8.6	29.0	23.7	18.1
Bulgaria	2010	2.6	27.0	1.3	7.2	82.7	77.8	66.7	8.6	6.7	8.9	8.7	15.5	24.4
China	2007	...	20.4	...	4.1	...	83.3	85.0	...	2.5	3.0	...	14.2	11.9
Egypt	2010	...	7.2	...	3.1	...	74.0	87.5	...	7.7	5.4	...	18.3	7.1
Greece	2007	...	...	...	...	80.2	...	52.4	4.6	...	4.8	15.2	...	42.9
India	2009	10.8	23.2	2.5	5.0	54.8	79.3	81.0	8.3	3.4	4.1	37.0	17.3	14.9
Iran (Islamic Republic of)	2009	47.7	37.6	8.7	8.5	...	46.8	54.2	6.4	17.1	10.4	...	36.2	35.4
Kyrgyzstan	2010	...	2.1	0.3	0.8	79.1	50.8	73.2	3.4	29.8	10.4	17.5	19.4	16.4
Latvia	2010	13.8	7.9	2.2	3.6	82.9	73.0	77.5	2.4	4.6	10.1	14.7	22.5	12.4
Mexico	2010	58.1	14.2	8.0	7.3	53.9	91.5	70.3	27.8	...	15.4	18.2	...	14.3
Morocco	2010	12.4	15.9	7.5	7.2	...	78.9	64.3	...	3.6	16.1	...	...	19.5
Philippines	2008	...	16.2	...	3.9	61.8	84.3	79.0	19.7	10.9	5.1	...	12.1	15.9
Poland	2009	22.1	33.2	...	12.9	...	72.8	64.1	...	23.1	14.0	...	16.3	21.9
Republic of Moldova	2010	...	6.4	0.3	4.4	...	55.4	40.0	...	7.0	40.8	...	21.4	19.2
Sri Lanka	2010	...	5.0	...	1.3	...	58.1	32.8	...	16.5	17.4	...	34.8	49.9
The f. Yugosl. Rep of Macedonia	2010	...	22.3	...	10.0	...	65.3	68.0	...	2.4	14.4	...	18.2	17.6
Turkey	2009	53.1	51.0	7.3	20.1	76.1	93.2	89.6	3.3	...	4.1	20.6	4.4	6.3
Uruguay	2007	13.7	17.9	3.8	10.4	81.7	...	54.0	5.0	...	26.8	13.3	...	19.2

a/ At current prices.

Table 1.11

SELECTED CHARACTERISTICS OF BRANCHES, SELECTED YEARS AND ECONOMIES

Electric motors, generators and transformers (ISIC 3110)

Economy	Latest year (LY)	Value added per employee (current 1000 dollars)		Wages and salaries per employee (current 1000 dollars)		Percentage in output a/								
						Costs of input materials and utilities			Costs of labour			Operating surplus		
		2000	LY	2000	LY	2000	2006	LY	2000	2006	LY	2000	2006	LY
Industrialized Economies														
EU														
Austria	2009	63.4	112.1	31.8	74.2	65.7	69.9	68.6	17.2	17.1	20.8	17.1	12.9	10.6
Belgium	2009	62.2	115.0	29.6	59.7	62.2	69.0	71.9	18.0	15.2	14.6	19.8	15.8	13.5
Czech Republic	2007	9.8	28.5	3.7	11.3	71.4	71.8	74.7	10.8	9.9	10.0	17.9	18.3	15.3
Denmark	2009	47.3	111.5	31.4	75.8	76.1	79.4	62.2	15.9	13.9	25.7	8.0	6.7	12.1
Estonia	2010	8.7	33.4	4.0	15.4	66.8	72.3	72.2	15.3	12.4	12.8	17.9	15.3	15.0
Finland	2009	60.8	105.1	28.3	51.8	68.5	66.4	63.0	14.7	15.3	18.2	16.9	18.3	18.8
France	2009	43.0	86.8	23.0	51.8	66.4	68.3	66.1	17.9	16.0	20.2	15.7	15.7	13.7
Germany	2009	47.2	99.1	29.3	67.2	66.4	68.0	62.6	20.8	19.3	25.4	12.7	12.7	12.1
Hungary	2009	7.6	24.8	4.5	11.9	65.2	78.3	72.1	20.4	12.2	13.4	14.3	9.5	14.5
Italy	2009	40.2	84.4	17.0	40.0	65.1	74.3	70.1	14.8	10.8	14.2	20.1	15.0	15.7
Lithuania	2010	...	17.1	...	9.4	...	68.7	70.6	...	20.4	16.2	...	10.9	13.2
Malta	2008	12.8	32.2	8.8	22.4	42.7	44.4	48.1	39.2	28.7	36.1	18.1	26.9	15.8
Netherlands	2008	49.7	119.9	25.9	61.8	67.2	64.2	69.6	17.1	17.8	15.7	15.7	18.0	14.7
Portugal	2009	21.7	76.3	11.6	28.1	75.8	72.9	82.3	12.9	15.0	6.5	11.3	12.1	11.2
Slovakia	2009	5.0	25.4	2.2	14.2	81.9	83.1	78.2	8.0	8.1	12.1	10.2	8.8	9.6
Slovenia	2010	20.7	46.8	14.1	24.8	72.4	69.0	66.6	18.8	16.3	17.7	8.9	14.7	15.7
Spain	2009	46.2	98.7	23.1	47.7	77.7	77.4	74.3	11.1	9.7	12.4	11.2	12.9	13.3
Sweden	2009	47.6	108.1	28.0	51.0	68.0	72.6	68.1	18.8	13.5	15.0	13.1	13.9	16.9
United Kingdom	2009	66.6	71.6	29.3	41.9	60.5	66.7	62.2	17.4	15.9	22.1	22.1	17.4	15.7
Other Europe														
Norway	2008	59.7	104.9	39.0	86.7	61.8	68.1	78.7	24.9	19.9	17.6	13.3	12.0	3.7
East Asia														
Japan	2010	79.1	109.9	32.8	43.0	63.4	63.3	63.7	15.2	13.2	14.2	21.4	23.6	22.1
Malaysia	2010	8.6	13.7	3.2	7.5	73.3	68.7	79.1	10.0	15.4	11.4	16.7	15.9	9.5
Republic of Korea	2008	44.8	81.8	13.8	25.5	64.0	66.7	66.6	11.1	11.4	10.4	24.9	22.0	23.0
Singapore	2010	44.6	55.3	21.0	31.7	76.3	83.0	76.0	11.2	7.9	13.8	12.5	9.2	10.2

a/ At current prices.

Table 1.11
(continued)

SELECTED CHARACTERISTICS OF BRANCHES, SELECTED YEARS AND ECONOMIES

Electric motors, generators and transformers (ISIC 3110)

Economy	Latest year (LY)	Value added per employee (current 1000 dollars)		Wages and salaries per employee (current 1000 dollars)		Percentage in output [a] — Costs of input materials and utilities			Costs of labour			Operating surplus		
		2000	LY	2000	LY	2000	2006	LY	2000	2006	LY	2000	2006	LY
North America														
Canada	2009	62.2	89.1	27.9	43.6	54.3	57.4	52.6	20.5	22.4	23.2	25.2	20.2	24.2
United States of America	2008	80.2	139.8	30.1	42.1	47.1	53.0	53.1	19.9	16.2	14.1	33.1	30.8	32.8
Others														
Israel	2009	37.9	57.2	28.1	37.5	58.4	62.6	62.4	30.8	23.9	24.7	10.8	13.5	12.9
Developing & EIE														
Azerbaijan	2010	...	11.1	0.4	3.8	...	57.4	76.2	9.8	6.3	8.0	...	36.3	15.8
Brazil	2010	22.0	53.3	7.8	16.3	53.8	59.9	62.0	16.3	12.9	11.6	29.9	27.2	26.4
Bulgaria	2010	2.0	14.2	1.2	5.9	72.3	75.5	70.0	16.1	10.1	12.4	11.6	14.5	17.6
Chile	2008	25.1	61.7	11.6	18.3	62.5	51.8	63.4	17.3	12.7	10.9	20.3	35.5	25.7
China	2007	...	15.5	...	3.1	...	74.0	73.2	...	5.5	5.4	...	20.5	21.4
Cyprus	2010	15.6	54.0	9.3	25.7	43.9	47.3	59.0	33.5	28.7	19.5	22.5	24.0	21.5
Ecuador	2008	8.0	29.2	1.3	6.0	71.4	75.8	72.5	4.7	6.4	5.7	23.8	17.8	21.8
Egypt	2010	...	12.8	...	4.0	...	75.7	70.1	...	14.6	9.3	...	9.7	20.5
Greece	2007	...	58.1	...	38.0	...	65.4	69.3	...	17.9	20.1	...	16.7	10.6
India	2009	5.6	16.2	3.1	4.0	75.6	78.7	78.3	13.3	3.3	5.4	11.1	17.9	16.3
Indonesia	2009	12.8	21.9	1.0	4.1	31.3	60.9	33.5	5.5	4.7	12.4	63.2	34.4	54.0
Iran (Islamic Republic of)	2009	33.1	53.3	12.1	10.1	66.5	70.5	55.9	12.2	9.6	8.4	21.3	19.9	35.7
Jordan	2010	22.3	21.7	5.1	4.6	78.1	86.9	86.6	5.0	4.5	2.9	16.9	8.5	10.6
Kyrgyzstan	2010	...	4.8	0.3	2.0	...	...	49.2	36.3	24.4	21.4	...	...	29.4
Latvia	2010	4.2	15.9	2.0	10.6	77.0	66.5	69.4	11.0	14.6	20.4	12.0	18.9	10.2
Mexico	2010	21.4	31.3	8.5	9.7	63.8	63.2	59.1	14.4	...	12.6	21.8	...	28.3
Morocco	2010	9.8	12.2	5.9	6.7	58.2	68.0	63.8	25.0	21.1	19.9	16.8	...	16.3
Philippines	2008	...	45.8	...	5.9	...	49.9	76.5	...	14.2	3.1	...	29.0	20.5
Poland	2009	10.3	31.2	...	13.0	64.6	67.0	61.3	...	19.2	16.2	...	18.8	22.5
Romania	2009	...	13.9	...	6.8	...	77.6	76.3	...	10.6	11.6	...	3.2	12.1
Sri Lanka	2010	...	21.5	...	2.6	...	61.9	50.8	...	24.8	5.9	...	27.5	43.3
The f. Yugosl. Rep of Macedonia	2010	...	9.5	...	6.3	...	60.7	50.5	...	...	32.9	...	14.5	16.6
Turkey	2009	28.8	52.0	11.1	17.5	59.6	74.7	67.9	15.6	10.3	10.7	24.7	15.0	21.3
United Republic of Tanzania	2007	...	2.5	...	1.5	...	83.9	83.9	...	9.4	9.3	...	6.7	6.8

a/ At current prices.

Table 1.11

SELECTED CHARACTERISTICS OF BRANCHES, SELECTED YEARS AND ECONOMIES

Electricity distribution & control apparatus (ISIC 3120)

Economy	Latest year (LY)	Value added per employee (current 1000 dollars)		Wages and salaries per employee (current 1000 dollars)		Percentage in output a/								
						Costs of input materials and utilities			Costs of labour			Operating surplus		
		2000	LY	2000	LY	2000	2006	LY	2000	2006	LY	2000	2006	LY
Industrialized Economies														
EU														
Austria	2008	50.0	104.3	26.5	56.1	55.4	61.2	61.8	23.7	20.3	20.5	21.0	18.5	17.7
Belgium	2008	61.9	103.9	33.4	58.1	63.3	68.2	64.4	19.8	18.9	19.9	16.9	12.8	15.7
Czech Republic	2007	9.9	30.4	4.5	12.7	71.5	65.8	70.6	12.9	12.2	12.3	15.6	22.0	17.2
Denmark	2008	47.5	112.1	31.0	69.3	53.4	61.4	60.1	30.4	23.7	24.7	16.2	14.9	15.2
Estonia	2007	8.3	33.3	4.5	14.2	61.2	75.7	74.2	21.1	10.4	11.0	17.7	13.9	14.8
Finland	2008	45.2	73.6	24.3	46.7	62.5	68.1	69.2	20.2	19.4	19.6	17.3	12.5	11.3
France	2008	50.1	101.2	25.8	56.7	65.2	73.6	73.2	18.0	14.3	15.0	16.8	12.1	11.8
Germany	2008	62.0	103.6	40.4	75.3	58.9	64.2	63.4	26.8	26.3	26.6	14.3	9.5	10.0
Hungary	2008	9.9	30.1	4.2	14.5	68.7	69.2	70.6	13.3	13.3	14.2	18.0	17.5	15.2
Ireland	2008	71.2	94.7	19.8	52.7	53.8	63.8	65.5	12.9	20.4	19.2	33.4	15.8	15.3
Italy	2008	49.4	109.7	21.1	45.9	65.0	67.2	67.9	15.0	13.9	13.5	20.1	18.9	18.7
Lithuania	2010	8.8	10.8	3.4	6.2	64.4	68.7	47.0	13.6	16.7	30.4	21.9	14.5	22.6
Malta	2008	15.0	57.0	11.8	24.7	76.4	63.4	61.0	18.6	15.7	16.9	5.0	20.9	22.1
Netherlands	2008	54.4	117.6	31.7	56.1	63.4	63.4	62.3	21.3	18.6	18.0	15.2	18.0	19.7
Slovakia	2008	3.8	27.2	2.2	13.6	77.0	73.1	75.7	13.5	14.5	12.2	9.5	12.4	12.2
Slovenia	2010	14.1	22.6	11.1	19.4	63.1	62.1	54.3	29.1	24.2	39.1	7.8	13.7	6.5
Spain	2008	44.5	88.9	19.9	46.3	60.4	60.7	64.4	17.7	16.8	18.5	21.9	22.5	17.0
Sweden	2008	51.4	111.8	26.3	52.2	66.7	60.8	64.2	17.1	17.5	16.7	16.2	21.7	19.1
United Kingdom	2007	47.5	76.1	29.9	52.9	57.4	60.8	61.3	26.9	24.7	26.9	15.7	14.5	11.8
Other Europe														
Norway	2008	43.6	125.4	27.3	72.3	56.6	58.4	60.0	27.2	24.9	23.1	16.2	16.7	16.9
East Asia														
Japan	2010	93.0	99.0	35.1	38.0	59.7	65.2	62.4	15.2	12.6	14.4	25.1	22.2	23.1
Malaysia	2010	12.7	13.3	4.4	6.3	70.2	78.0	73.4	10.3	9.8	12.7	19.5	12.3	14.0
Republic of Korea	2006	53.0	82.8	14.7	24.8	58.1	63.8	63.8	11.7	10.8	10.8	30.3	25.3	25.3
Singapore	2008	33.0	47.4	18.9	26.3	66.3	80.8	77.4	19.3	10.9	12.5	14.5	8.3	10.1
West Asia														
Kuwait	2010	...	31.9	...	13.4	...	51.2	70.7	...	17.1	12.3	...	31.7	17.0

a/ At current prices.

Table 1.11
(continued)

SELECTED CHARACTERISTICS OF BRANCHES, SELECTED YEARS AND ECONOMIES

Electricity distribution & control apparatus (ISIC 3120)

Economy	Latest year (LY)	Value added per employee (current 1000 dollars)		Wages and salaries per employee (current 1000 dollars)		Percentage in output a/								
						Costs of input materials and utilities			Costs of labour			Operating surplus		
		2000	LY	2000	LY	2000	2006	LY	2000	2006	LY	2000	2006	LY
North America														
Canada	2009	69.1	102.1	27.6	47.7	55.0	49.2	48.2	18.0	24.1	24.2	27.0	26.8	27.6
United States of America	2008	108.2	154.5	36.9	48.8	43.2	44.4	44.6	19.4	18.0	17.5	37.5	37.6	37.9
Developing & EIE														
Brazil	2007	26.0	39.9	9.4	11.4	44.5	53.7	53.3	20.1	14.0	13.3	35.4	32.3	33.4
Bulgaria	2010	2.5	5.9	1.2	3.6	68.7	71.4	43.6	15.0	11.5	34.7	16.3	17.0	21.6
Chile	2008	25.4	27.7	9.6	13.9	46.0	55.7	57.2	20.4	20.2	21.4	33.6	24.1	21.4
China	2007	...	20.1	...	3.4	...	70.5	71.6	...	4.9	4.9	...	24.5	23.6
Ecuador	2008	5.9	8.0	1.8	4.7	66.2	75.6	68.1	10.1	6.7	18.8	23.7	17.7	13.1
Egypt	2010	...	7.3	...	1.6	...	71.6	58.8	...	6.0	8.8	...	22.3	32.3
Georgia	2010	0.4	4.2	0.3	2.4	85.9	...	54.4	10.9	...	26.1	3.2	...	19.5
Greece	2007	...	55.6	...	28.7	...	59.8	60.3	...	18.1	20.5	...	22.0	19.2
India	2009	5.6	17.0	2.2	2.8	75.0	73.0	69.8	10.0	5.2	4.9	15.0	21.8	25.3
Indonesia	2009	5.3	14.1	1.2	1.9	62.6	60.2	75.6	8.7	7.8	3.2	28.7	29.7	21.2
Iran (Islamic Republic of)	2009	30.3	22.6	10.4	6.7	50.7	55.3	63.7	17.0	15.0	10.7	32.4	25.6	25.6
Jordan	2010	7.6	49.2	2.9	7.1	48.3	63.1	38.8	19.8	11.3	8.8	32.0	20.7	52.3
Latvia	2007	9.7	26.0	3.5	11.5	42.4	64.3	63.9	21.1	15.0	16.0	36.5	20.7	20.1
Mexico	2010	...	24.8	...	7.4	...	65.9	68.7	...	...	9.3	...	...	22.0
Morocco	2010	10.0	17.2	5.6	9.2	50.7	46.3	63.9	27.9	7.2	19.3	21.4	22.4	16.8
Oman	2008	21.8	42.1	8.8	10.6	62.1	70.4	61.3	15.4	...	9.8	22.5	...	28.9
Poland	2010	11.9	35.4	...	16.2	61.0	63.8	61.9	...	15.8	17.4	...	20.4	20.6
The f. Yugosl. Rep of Macedonia	2009	...	6.5	...	5.7	...	60.9	62.1	...	18.8	33.6	...	20.3	4.3
Turkey	2009	32.0	24.1	10.3	10.0	41.3	74.2	75.8	18.8	11.7	10.0	39.9	14.0	14.2

a/ At current prices.

Table 1.11

SELECTED CHARACTERISTICS OF BRANCHES, SELECTED YEARS AND ECONOMIES

Insulated wire and cable (ISIC 3130)

| Economy | Latest year (LY) | Value added per employee (current 1000 dollars) | | Wages and salaries per employee (current 1000 dollars) | | Percentage in output [a] | | | | | | | | |
| | | | | | | Costs of input materials and utilities | | | Costs of labour | | | Operating surplus | | |
		2000	LY	2000	LY	2000	2006	LY	2000	2006	LY	2000	2006	LY
Industrialized Economies														
EU														
Austria	2009	50.3	74.8	29.4	45.0	61.0	78.3	77.8	22.8	12.8	13.4	16.2	8.9	8.8
Belgium	2009	52.0	98.2	28.5	58.0	74.4	82.1	75.7	14.1	10.5	14.4	11.6	7.4	9.9
Czech Republic	2007	10.5	23.4	3.9	10.5	74.4	83.5	82.8	9.6	6.9	7.7	16.0	9.6	9.5
Denmark	2009	...	108.0	...	69.1	...	72.1	68.4	...	16.0	20.2	...	11.9	11.4
Estonia	2010	...	38.1	...	15.6	...	80.0	77.1	...	10.2	9.4	...	9.8	13.6
Finland	2008	45.2	98.1	25.1	48.6	76.0	83.0	78.9	13.3	10.2	10.5	10.7	6.8	10.6
France	2008	55.0	102.2	26.1	50.0	72.7	79.8	77.8	13.0	10.4	10.9	14.4	9.8	11.4
Germany	2008	47.0	84.0	29.0	52.4	70.5	79.5	78.9	18.2	12.5	13.1	11.3	7.9	7.9
Hungary	2008	8.9	21.4	3.8	11.0	67.3	85.3	85.3	14.0	6.3	7.6	18.7	8.4	7.2
Ireland	2008	32.0	149.4	20.5	71.8	73.8	...	79.2	16.8	...	10.0	9.4	...	10.8
Italy	2008	43.3	88.2	21.6	42.7	81.2	87.6	87.1	9.4	5.0	6.2	9.5	7.4	6.6
Lithuania	2010	5.4	12.7	2.7	6.5	76.0	79.8	76.0	11.7	5.7	12.3	12.2	14.4	11.8
Malta	2008	...	185.1	...	15.4	...	50.4	63.4	...	3.2	3.0	...	46.4	33.5
Netherlands	2008	66.1	126.1	29.6	59.5	64.6	77.8	75.2	15.8	12.6	11.7	19.6	9.7	13.1
Portugal	2008	27.1	67.0	12.4	27.9	79.5	85.2	83.6	9.4	5.9	6.8	11.1	8.9	9.6
Slovakia	2008	3.1	11.9	2.0	8.9	82.7	71.8	71.3	11.0	16.3	21.3	6.3	11.9	7.4
Slovenia	2009	13.4	27.7	13.4	23.1	71.4	33.3	73.9	28.6	33.3	21.7	0.0	33.3	4.3
Spain	2008	39.0	100.6	18.7	48.2	76.4	81.0	83.2	11.4	7.4	8.1	12.3	11.6	8.8
Sweden	2008	67.7	136.8	28.8	52.6	69.6	78.8	75.0	12.9	9.6	9.6	17.5	11.6	15.4
United Kingdom	2007	53.9	96.3	24.1	49.1	61.4	79.4	67.8	17.2	14.8	16.4	21.3	5.8	15.8
Other Europe														
Norway	2008	56.4	213.7	44.1	92.9	73.3	71.7	69.4	20.8	15.4	13.3	5.8	12.9	17.3
Russian Federation	2010	...	17.4	1.3	8.4	...	81.4	86.1	7.0	5.3	6.7	...	13.2	7.2
East Asia														
Japan	2010	120.5	148.8	44.8	54.3	68.9	75.6	78.3	11.6	6.6	7.9	19.5	17.8	13.8
Malaysia	2010	14.6	21.6	4.8	7.3	78.8	86.6	87.4	6.9	4.9	4.3	14.3	8.5	8.3
Republic of Korea	2006	88.4	151.9	16.4	26.6	65.5	68.9	68.9	6.4	5.5	5.5	28.1	25.6	25.6
Singapore	2008	44.7	71.0	21.7	29.1	71.2	70.0	74.4	14.0	10.5	10.5	14.9	19.5	15.1
West Asia														
Kuwait	2010	...	86.7	...	40.1	...	68.4	84.8	...	3.8	7.0	...	27.8	8.2

a/ At current prices.

Table 1.11
(continued)

SELECTED CHARACTERISTICS OF BRANCHES, SELECTED YEARS AND ECONOMIES

Insulated wire and cable (ISIC 3130)

| Economy | Latest year | Value added per employee (current 1000 dollars) | | Wages and salaries per employee (current 1000 dollars) | | Percentage in output a/ | | | | | | | | |
| | | | | | | Costs of input materials and utilities | | | Costs of labour | | | Operating surplus | | |
	(LY)	2000	LY	2000	LY	2000	2006	LY	2000	2006	LY	2000	2006	LY
North America														
Canada	2009	100.0	120.6	26.8	45.0	58.7	65.9	67.6	11.1	12.7	12.1	30.2	21.3	20.3
United States of America	2008	136.0	153.0	37.1	47.2	58.5	64.9	67.3	11.4	9.4	10.1	30.2	25.7	22.6
Developing & EIE														
Brazil	2007	25.5	45.5	7.4	10.7	71.3	74.3	74.9	8.3	6.0	5.9	20.4	19.7	19.2
Bulgaria	2010	5.8	17.1	1.8	6.1	82.1	84.2	87.9	5.7	3.2	4.4	12.3	12.5	7.8
Chile	2008	14.4	21.8	6.3	9.9	65.9	71.6	77.7	14.9	11.4	10.2	19.2	17.0	12.1
China	2007	...	30.5	...	3.1	...	75.7	76.3	...	2.3	2.4	...	22.0	21.3
Ecuador	2008	9.3	37.8	1.8	6.2	83.1	81.4	83.0	3.3	2.6	2.8	13.6	16.0	14.2
Egypt	2010	...	38.5	...	4.2	...	80.2	57.2	...	2.3	4.7	...	17.5	38.1
Greece	2007	...	92.0	...	32.3	...	83.9	84.8	...	5.2	5.3	...	10.8	9.9
India	2009	8.1	12.3	1.7	2.7	83.0	87.9	87.4	3.5	1.8	2.7	13.6	10.3	9.9
Indonesia	2009	6.1	18.1	1.2	1.7	69.2	76.1	63.9	6.2	3.1	3.4	24.6	20.8	32.6
Iran (Islamic Republic of)	2009	40.3	34.9	10.8	7.5	71.4	72.6	71.1	7.7	4.9	6.2	20.9	22.5	22.7
Jordan	2010	23.9	20.1	4.3	4.2	76.6	78.4	80.0	4.2	2.6	4.2	19.2	19.0	15.8
Morocco	2010	22.4	39.2	6.9	14.5	71.8	81.8	84.6	8.7	...	5.7	19.5	...	9.7
Oman	2010	53.7	107.2	7.9	21.3	70.6	94.8	85.7	4.3	1.6	2.8	25.1	3.6	11.4
Philippines	2006	...	12.5	...	2.6	...	87.4	87.4	...	2.6	2.6	...	10.0	10.0
Poland	2008	18.4	32.5	...	11.7	74.1	83.4	80.4	...	4.7	7.0	...	12.0	12.5
Romania	2010	...	25.7	...	8.5	...	80.6	88.4	...	6.1	3.9	...	13.3	7.8
Turkey	2009	33.9	32.8	8.3	12.0	70.4	89.1	88.1	7.3	3.5	4.3	22.3	7.4	7.6

a/ At current prices.

Table 1.11

SELECTED CHARACTERISTICS OF BRANCHES, SELECTED YEARS AND ECONOMIES

Accumulators, primary cells and batteries (ISIC 3140)

Economy	Latest year (LY)	Value added per employee (current 1000 dollars)		Wages and salaries per employee (current 1000 dollars)		Percentage in output a/								
						Costs of input materials and utilities			Costs of labour			Operating surplus		
		2000	LY	2000	LY	2000	2006	LY	2000	2006	LY	2000	2006	LY
Industrialized Economies														
EU														
Austria	2009	64.4	113.1	31.3	60.9	64.7	68.3	74.7	17.1	16.3	13.6	18.1	15.4	11.7
Belgium	2008	69.8	164.8	29.9	73.2	69.5	47.5	36.3	13.1	22.0	28.3	17.4	30.5	35.4
Czech Republic	2007	8.4	43.4	3.4	15.5	75.7	...	84.3	9.9	...	5.6	14.5	...	10.1
Denmark	2008	...	90.0	...	45.0	...	72.0	50.0	...	8.0	25.0	...	20.0	25.0
France	2009	33.3	71.2	21.8	50.4	74.2	72.1	65.0	16.8	18.5	24.8	9.0	9.4	10.2
Germany	2009	41.0	81.4	33.0	60.2	71.8	75.4	79.9	22.7	16.3	14.8	5.5	8.3	5.2
Hungary	2009	13.1	26.4	3.8	14.4	81.7	91.2	93.1	5.3	3.2	3.8	13.0	5.6	3.1
Ireland	2009	34.1	53.4	20.5	35.6	70.6	61.1	66.7	17.6	22.2	22.2	11.8	16.7	11.1
Italy	2009	42.3	77.8	21.5	36.8	73.6	83.8	79.8	13.4	11.4	9.6	13.0	4.7	10.6
Lithuania	2010	...	11.6	...	3.3	...	60.9	77.8	...	17.4	6.3	...	21.6	16.0
Netherlands	2008	50.4	236.6	23.6	67.6	72.0	67.2	65.6	13.1	12.1	9.8	14.9	20.7	24.6
Slovenia	2010	17.2	55.4	12.9	25.7	75.0	69.3	80.0	18.8	13.6	9.3	6.3	17.0	10.7
Spain	2009	49.0	70.0	22.9	47.0	68.0	73.3	78.5	15.0	13.7	14.4	17.1	13.0	7.1
Sweden	2008	...	93.7	...	38.4	...	...	65.9	...	...	14.0	...	...	20.1
United Kingdom	2007	54.7	94.0	28.5	47.0	62.6	66.7	64.0	19.5	21.1	18.0	17.9	12.3	18.0
East Asia														
Japan	2010	143.1	149.7	46.2	60.3	66.6	70.1	72.8	10.8	10.1	11.0	22.6	19.7	16.3
Malaysia	2010	15.2	23.1	4.7	7.2	63.9	71.2	73.3	11.3	10.2	8.3	24.9	18.7	18.4
Republic of Korea	2008	62.2	223.2	16.4	35.9	65.2	64.8	62.3	9.2	10.8	6.1	25.6	24.4	31.6
Singapore	2010	80.2	90.5	23.5	47.9	52.5	63.2	66.9	13.9	13.5	17.5	33.6	23.3	15.5

a/ At current prices.

Table 1.11
(continued)

SELECTED CHARACTERISTICS OF BRANCHES, SELECTED YEARS AND ECONOMIES

Accumulators, primary cells and batteries (ISIC 3140)

Economy	Latest year (LY)	Value added per employee (current 1000 dollars) 2000	Value added per employee (current 1000 dollars) LY	Wages and salaries per employee (current 1000 dollars) 2000	Wages and salaries per employee (current 1000 dollars) LY	Costs of input materials and utilities 2000	Costs of input materials and utilities 2006	Costs of input materials and utilities LY	Costs of labour 2000	Costs of labour 2006	Costs of labour LY	Operating surplus 2000	Operating surplus 2006	Operating surplus LY
North America														
Canada	2009	55.3	72.0	22.0	45.2	60.4	65.7	58.5	15.7	20.6	26.0	23.9	13.7	15.4
United States of America	2008	128.8	153.2	37.7	46.6	48.3	53.8	59.6	15.1	15.3	12.3	36.6	31.0	28.1
Developing & EIE														
Azerbaijan	2008	..	5.3	0.3	4.0	68.2	57.3	59.1	33.2	17.9	30.5	..	24.7	10.4
Brazil	2010	19.7	35.3	7.3	13.9	..	56.3	64.6	11.8	12.7	13.9	20.0	31.0	21.5
Bulgaria	2010	4.4	26.0	1.7	7.6	71.7	73.9	83.6	10.6	8.5	4.8	17.7	17.6	11.6
China	2007	..	14.1	..	3.1	..	74.2	75.5	..	5.2	5.4	..	20.6	19.2
Ecuador	2008	10.1	14.1	3.2	4.2	79.5	77.3	77.0	6.5	7.7	6.8	13.9	15.0	16.2
Ethiopia	2008	1.1	13.8	0.4	1.1	47.7	84.3	72.6	17.2	..	2.2	35.1	..	25.2
Greece	2007	..	79.6	..	26.5	..	65.9	70.3	..	7.3	9.9	..	26.8	19.8
India	2009	7.8	18.7	1.6	3.2	68.7	79.2	71.6	6.3	4.3	4.9	25.0	16.5	23.5
Indonesia	2009	52.4	25.6	1.9	2.5	59.7	67.6	60.9	1.4	4.1	3.8	38.9	28.4	35.3
Iran (Islamic Republic of)	2009	62.8	17.8	9.1	11.8	52.6	74.6	73.2	6.9	11.3	17.8	40.5	14.1	9.0
Morocco	2010	13.0	24.7	7.7	8.8	60.2	68.3	54.1	23.5	..	16.3	16.3	..	29.7
Oman	2010	21.4	37.1	6.0	7.8	62.8	71.4	65.1	10.4	7.0	7.4	26.8	21.7	27.6
Philippines	2008	..	14.7	..	5.3	..	66.8	64.7	..	8.7	12.6	..	24.6	22.7
Poland	2009	15.5	41.9	..	16.0	74.7	77.1	75.1	..	8.0	9.5	..	14.9	15.4
Turkey	2009	41.4	39.8	7.9	16.3	50.8	75.5	78.3	9.4	10.2	8.8	39.7	14.3	12.8
United Republic of Tanzania	2010	..	35.0	..	2.1	..	73.8	29.7	..	5.0	4.2	..	21.2	66.1

a/ At current prices.

Table 1.11

SELECTED CHARACTERISTICS OF BRANCHES, SELECTED YEARS AND ECONOMIES

Lighting equipment and electric lamps (ISIC 3150)

Economy	Latest year	Value added per employee (current 1000 dollars)		Wages and salaries per employee (current 1000 dollars)		Percentage in output a/								
						Costs of input materials and utilities			Costs of labour			Operating surplus		
	(LY)	2000	LY	2000	LY	2000	2006	LY	2000	2006	LY	2000	2006	LY
Industrialized Economies														
EU														
Austria	2009	60.7	100.3	28.5	52.7	50.5	54.7	58.1	23.2	25.8	22.0	26.3	19.5	19.9
Belgium	2009	61.9	89.6	25.4	45.9	53.6	58.7	58.6	19.0	18.4	21.2	27.4	22.9	20.2
Czech Republic	2007	6.8	21.1	3.4	10.9	71.5	...	78.6	14.1	...	11.1	14.4	...	10.3
Denmark	2009	43.4	76.8	27.8	70.7	60.8	60.8	62.2	25.1	26.3	34.9	14.1	12.9	3.0
Finland	2009	48.6	81.5	23.6	40.3	62.2	58.6	53.3	18.4	18.3	23.1	19.5	23.1	23.6
France	2009	36.6	82.6	19.7	51.6	64.1	63.0	59.8	19.3	19.8	25.1	16.6	17.2	15.1
Germany	2009	45.3	77.5	27.3	54.5	53.9	57.1	61.2	27.9	24.8	27.3	18.3	18.1	11.5
Hungary	2009	11.3	25.9	4.3	9.7	68.4	50.6	58.3	12.0	9.4	15.7	19.6	40.0	26.1
Ireland	2008	35.8	72.9	16.8	53.0	56.4	53.3	62.1	20.5	26.7	27.6	23.1	20.0	10.3
Italy	2009	40.7	69.4	16.8	34.5	69.2	72.0	72.7	12.7	11.0	13.6	18.0	17.0	13.7
Lithuania	2010	3.5	22.3	2.4	7.2	59.8	79.4	80.0	27.8	6.4	6.5	12.4	14.2	13.6
Malta	2008	23.0	37.9	11.2	15.7	40.3	58.8	58.2	29.0	18.2	17.3	30.7	23.0	24.5
Netherlands	2008	37.6	102.4	21.3	72.1	70.3	68.9	64.3	16.8	17.6	25.1	12.9	13.5	10.6
Slovakia	2009	2.9	23.6	2.0	11.4	80.4	...	75.6	13.7	...	11.8	5.9	...	12.6
Slovenia	2010	17.0	56.4	10.2	27.7	74.4	73.9	77.7	15.4	21.7	10.9	10.3	4.3	11.3
Spain	2009	28.3	56.8	15.5	36.3	67.8	68.9	68.9	17.6	17.1	19.9	14.5	14.0	11.2
Sweden	2008	45.1	78.4	23.1	42.6	64.5	...	63.5	18.2	...	19.9	17.3	...	16.7
United Kingdom	2007	41.5	73.0	25.8	42.0	61.0	52.4	56.5	24.3	23.4	25.0	14.7	24.2	18.5
Other Europe														
Norway	2008	41.0	109.8	32.5	66.6	63.6	58.1	58.0	28.9	27.0	25.5	7.6	14.9	16.5
East Asia														
Japan	2010	108.2	132.3	36.3	44.4	59.6	60.0	65.1	13.6	11.2	11.7	26.8	28.8	23.2
Malaysia	2010	20.4	17.1	5.0	6.8	63.4	83.9	70.1	8.9	7.5	12.0	27.7	8.6	18.0
Republic of Korea	2008	37.5	75.6	12.4	23.9	56.1	58.5	64.1	14.5	12.7	11.4	29.4	28.8	24.5
Singapore	2010	18.5	54.6	16.0	27.8	73.9	74.5	46.0	22.7	20.4	27.4	3.5	5.1	26.5

a/ At current prices.

Table 1.11
(continued)

SELECTED CHARACTERISTICS OF BRANCHES, SELECTED YEARS AND ECONOMIES

Lighting equipment and electric lamps (ISIC 3150)

Economy	Latest year (LY)	Value added per employee (current 1000 dollars)		Wages and salaries per employee (current 1000 dollars)		Percentage in output [a]								
						Costs of input materials and utilities			Costs of labour			Operating surplus		
		2000	LY	2000	LY	2000	2006	LY	2000	2006	LY	2000	2006	LY
North America														
Canada	2009	49.6	71.8	22.1	37.1	52.4	50.4	58.7	21.2	29.6	21.4	26.4	20.1	20.0
United States of America	2008	99.9	106.5	31.6	42.5	43.5	43.7	44.1	17.9	22.5	22.3	38.6	33.8	33.6
Developing & EIE														
Brazil	2010	16.1	29.7	6.6	12.2	49.5	56.7	53.4	20.5	26.6	19.2	30.0	16.7	27.4
Bulgaria	2010	1.7	11.0	0.9	3.7	80.6	77.9	72.3	9.8	5.5	9.1	9.5	16.6	18.5
Chile	2008	40.1	30.7	7.9	10.1	28.4	68.7	67.5	14.0	13.0	10.7	57.6	18.3	21.8
China	2007	...	8.2	...	2.6	...	74.2	75.0	...	7.6	7.8	...	18.2	17.2
Ecuador	2008	219.4	9.1	35.8	3.6	46.0	76.3	71.4	8.8	10.9	11.4	45.2	12.9	17.2
Egypt	2010	...	7.4	...	3.4	...	67.6	67.5	...	12.1	15.0	...	20.3	17.5
Georgia	2006	...	14.9	...	4.6	...	55.8	55.8	...	13.6	13.6	...	30.6	30.6
Greece	2007	...	67.9	...	25.9	...	58.6	59.4	...	11.8	15.5	...	29.6	25.1
India	2009	4.4	8.2	1.3	2.4	72.7	76.4	77.1	7.8	6.9	6.8	19.5	16.7	16.1
Indonesia	2009	7.5	10.0	1.2	1.8	51.5	54.9	60.6	7.9	9.7	7.0	40.6	35.4	32.4
Iran (Islamic Republic of)	2009	26.4	16.1	9.6	5.9	56.2	54.9	62.8	15.9	19.7	13.8	27.9	25.4	23.4
Jordan	2010	21.0	29.0	4.3	6.5	46.6	51.9	53.1	10.9	9.5	10.6	42.5	38.6	36.4
Kyrgyzstan	2010	...	3.1	0.5	2.0	65.1	...	56.4	12.7	23.6	28.3	...	...	15.3
Latvia	2010	4.2	7.8	2.5	5.4	66.6	...	83.6	20.9	...	11.3	14.0	...	5.1
Mexico	2010	15.5	18.8	7.3	9.4	66.6	72.0	56.5	15.6	...	21.7	17.8	...	21.8
Morocco	2010	7.6	11.2	5.0	6.0	56.9	68.3	65.1	28.2	...	18.8	14.9	...	16.2
Oman	2010	16.1	102.3	4.2	8.3	62.8	60.7	68.1	9.7	20.8	2.6	27.5	18.5	29.3
Philippines	2008	...	6.6	...	3.9	70.4	67.6	74.7	...	12.1	14.8	...	20.3	10.6
Poland	2009	10.5	35.7	...	11.2	...	66.0	62.3	...	11.2	11.9	...	22.9	25.8
Romania	2010	...	17.0	...	7.1	...	68.9	77.9	...	17.6	9.2	...	13.5	12.9
The f. Yugosl. Rep of Macedonia	2010	...	10.9	...	4.8	...	60.6	67.2	...	10.6	14.5	...	28.9	18.3
Turkey	2009	19.2	14.4	5.7	7.0	55.4	79.1	79.3	13.2	9.4	10.1	31.4	11.5	10.7

a/ At current prices.

Table 1.11

SELECTED CHARACTERISTICS OF BRANCHES, SELECTED YEARS AND ECONOMIES

Other electrical equipment n.e.c. (ISIC 3190)

Economy	Latest year (LY)	Value added per employee (current 1000 dollars)		Wages and salaries per employee (current 1000 dollars)		Percentage in output a/								
						Costs of input materials and utilities			Costs of labour			Operating surplus		
		2000	LY	2000	LY	2000	2006	LY	2000	2006	LY	2000	2006	LY
Industrialized Economies														
EU														
Austria	2009	56.2	101.6	22.6	56.4	55.9	66.3	59.0	17.7	16.6	22.8	26.4	17.0	18.2
Belgium	2009	56.4	100.6	28.8	61.4	62.2	64.7	59.3	19.3	19.3	24.9	18.5	16.1	15.9
Czech Republic	2007	8.3	27.6	3.7	11.3	69.3	71.7	72.3	13.8	13.2	11.3	16.9	15.1	16.4
Denmark	2008	42.6	101.4	28.8	67.5	58.4	66.3	61.8	28.1	23.7	25.4	13.5	10.0	12.8
Estonia	2010	6.5	14.7	3.7	7.0	59.2	46.1	57.9	23.0	31.7	20.0	17.9	22.2	22.1
Finland	2009	40.2	55.2	21.4	38.2	68.0	65.9	66.9	17.0	17.2	22.9	15.0	16.9	10.2
France	2009	42.6	78.2	24.3	47.9	71.1	68.4	61.5	16.5	17.9	23.6	12.4	13.6	14.9
Germany	2009	51.6	88.2	30.5	55.6	61.9	65.4	59.3	22.5	21.4	25.6	15.6	13.2	15.0
Hungary	2009	14.2	27.4	4.3	12.1	86.6	74.6	70.1	4.1	12.0	13.2	9.3	13.4	16.7
Ireland	2009	39.9	86.6	19.0	47.1	69.2	72.4	53.5	14.6	15.4	25.3	16.2	12.1	21.2
Italy	2009	40.7	74.9	18.5	34.9	70.3	66.2	69.1	13.5	13.8	14.4	16.2	20.0	16.5
Malta	2008	31.5	115.3	14.1	31.1	50.0	37.0	36.4	22.3	18.8	17.1	27.6	44.2	46.4
Netherlands	2008	55.8	108.6	27.4	64.5	65.0	69.4	69.7	17.2	18.1	18.0	17.8	12.5	12.3
Portugal	2009	14.0	30.8	8.8	18.4	68.8	...	69.8	19.7	...	18.0	11.5	...	12.2
Slovakia	2009	2.9	13.9	2.1	12.9	67.9	71.7	83.9	22.9	12.9	15.0	9.2	15.4	1.2
Slovenia	2010	16.7	47.0	11.8	26.3	70.2	63.8	60.9	21.0	17.2	21.9	8.8	19.0	17.2
Spain	2009	35.7	84.3	18.4	42.0	65.4	68.4	67.7	17.8	15.7	16.1	16.7	15.9	16.2
Sweden	2009	45.3	94.4	24.3	50.2	69.1	62.0	68.3	16.6	20.1	16.8	14.3	17.9	14.8
United Kingdom	2009	52.0	83.5	30.8	43.4	56.3	62.2	51.0	25.9	20.8	25.5	17.8	17.0	23.5
Other Europe														
Norway	2007	45.3	120.4	33.8	76.0	67.1	65.4	62.9	24.6	25.0	23.4	8.3	9.6	13.7
East Asia														
Japan	2010	86.8	125.4	33.5	38.3	70.9	69.5	61.7	11.2	9.8	11.7	17.9	20.8	26.6
Malaysia	2010	11.3	13.1	3.7	6.2	62.2	75.0	69.7	12.4	9.4	14.5	25.4	15.7	15.9
Republic of Korea	2008	46.6	71.0	13.2	22.1	59.6	68.3	58.2	11.5	10.1	13.0	28.9	21.5	28.8
Singapore	2010	26.5	63.5	22.3	35.7	82.4	65.2	70.4	14.7	17.0	16.7	2.8	17.8	12.9

a/ At current prices.

Table 1.11
(continued)

SELECTED CHARACTERISTICS OF BRANCHES, SELECTED YEARS AND ECONOMIES

Other electrical equipment n.e.c. (ISIC 3190)

Economy	Latest year (LY)	Value added per employee (current 1000 dollars)		Wages and salaries per employee (current 1000 dollars)		Percentage in output [a]								
						Costs of input materials and utilities			Costs of labour			Operating surplus		
		2000	LY	2000	LY	2000	2006	LY	2000	2006	LY	2000	2006	LY
North America														
Canada	2009	57.1	88.6	24.3	46.7	53.4	55.9	50.8	19.8	25.7	25.9	26.8	18.4	23.3
United States of America	2008	108.4	124.9	39.3	50.5	50.6	51.0	52.6	17.9	17.0	19.2	31.5	32.0	28.2
Developing & EIE														
Azerbaijan	2010	...	54.3	0.2	3.9	...	57.3	44.5	29.8	25.9	4.0	...	16.8	51.5
Brazil	2010	21.0	46.4	6.4	15.9	54.8	60.2	54.5	13.8	13.0	15.6	31.4	26.8	29.9
Bulgaria	2010	2.4	12.1	1.0	5.2	68.4	79.7	77.2	14.0	5.3	9.8	17.6	15.0	13.0
Chile	2008	13.6	30.3	6.4	11.3	40.9	49.6	52.4	27.7	19.6	17.8	31.4	30.8	29.8
China	2007	...	17.5	...	3.0	...	70.0	70.6	...	4.8	5.1	...	25.2	24.3
Ecuador	2008	2.8	66.3	0.8	6.5	58.0	83.8	69.8	11.4	4.3	2.9	30.7	11.9	27.2
Egypt	2010	...	54.6	...	5.1	...	49.6	95.2	...	9.5	0.5	...	40.9	4.4
Georgia	2010	0.9	7.2	0.4	3.1	73.5	51.5	54.8	10.1	14.6	19.4	16.4	33.8	25.8
Greece	2007	...	79.6	...	30.6	78.4	56.5	56.7	6.7	10.1	16.7	14.9	33.3	26.7
India	2009	4.5	7.5	1.4	2.7	78.4	81.5	83.7	6.7	4.7	5.8	14.9	13.8	10.5
Indonesia	2009	1.5	51.9	0.7	3.3	62.6	38.0	55.7	16.7	14.2	2.8	20.7	47.8	41.4
Iran (Islamic Republic of)	2009	18.2	27.4	6.5	8.8	67.0	73.7	69.4	11.9	8.0	9.8	21.1	18.4	20.8
Latvia	2010	4.9	25.5	2.7	7.5	64.1	...	53.3	20.2	...	13.8	15.7	...	32.9
Morocco	2008	7.2	10.1	3.9	6.1	75.1	80.5	76.4	13.4	...	14.3	11.5	...	9.3
Philippines	2009	12.5	6.3	...	4.9	61.7	75.9	83.6	...	7.9	12.6	...	16.2	3.8
Poland	2010	...	39.8	...	12.6	...	71.7	50.8	...	12.5	15.6	...	15.9	33.7
Romania	2010	...	19.0	...	6.6	...	74.8	73.6	...	19.5	9.2	...	5.7	17.2
The f. Yugosl. Rep of Macedonia	2010	...	11.1	...	8.0	...	58.8	87.5	...	20.0	9.1	...	21.2	3.4
Turkey	2009	20.4	20.8	10.7	9.0	56.2	73.2	77.2	23.1	13.3	9.9	20.7	13.5	12.9

a/ At current prices.

Table 1.11

SELECTED CHARACTERISTICS OF BRANCHES, SELECTED YEARS AND ECONOMIES

Electronic valves, tubes, etc. (ISIC 3210)

Economy	Latest year (LY)	Value added per employee (current 1000 dollars)		Wages and salaries per employee (current 1000 dollars)		Percentage in output [a]								
						Costs of input materials and utilities			Costs of labour			Operating surplus		
	(LY)	2000	LY	2000	LY	2000	2006	LY	2000	2006	LY	2000	2006	LY
Industrialized Economies														
EU														
Austria	2009	67.1	94.9	26.3	60.2	56.6	61.8	59.5	17.0	19.2	25.7	26.4	19.0	14.8
Belgium	2009	77.6	106.5	32.2	60.5	69.3	63.4	66.6	12.7	17.2	19.0	18.0	19.4	14.4
Czech Republic	2007	8.5	23.1	3.5	10.5	59.3	71.9	80.6	16.7	11.1	8.8	24.0	17.0	10.5
Denmark	2009	39.7	96.5	26.5	68.9	56.7	62.0	65.0	28.9	26.9	25.0	14.4	11.0	10.0
Estonia	2010	7.0	15.6	3.1	10.9	56.9	75.6	85.2	19.4	11.1	10.4	23.8	13.4	4.4
Finland	2009	45.5	56.8	22.1	42.2	58.0	72.4	67.5	20.4	20.2	24.1	21.6	7.5	8.4
France	2009	56.6	79.2	26.3	51.8	73.1	66.7	65.7	12.5	18.2	22.4	14.4	15.0	11.9
Germany	2009	76.2	80.1	34.2	56.6	62.7	70.6	74.4	16.7	15.3	18.1	20.6	14.1	7.5
Hungary	2009	9.0	24.5	4.1	11.6	76.2	74.1	78.7	10.9	6.7	10.1	12.9	19.2	11.2
Italy	2009	68.6	68.6	22.0	37.4	59.8	63.0	60.8	12.9	18.3	21.4	27.3	18.7	17.8
Lithuania	2010	10.7	17.4	4.5	9.4	61.4	...	77.4	16.3	...	12.3	22.2	...	10.3
Malta	2008	92.7	49.5	15.0	28.7	83.4	89.0	89.6	2.7	5.1	6.0	13.9	5.9	4.4
Portugal	2009	34.9	19.3	10.9	18.8	73.9	...	90.4	8.2	...	9.4	17.9	...	0.2
Slovakia	2009	2.2	27.0	2.1	10.8	86.8	80.8	84.4	12.4	5.2	6.2	0.8	14.0	9.4
Slovenia	2010	14.1	45.1	10.0	22.0	64.4	66.5	67.4	25.2	19.8	15.9	10.4	13.7	16.7
Spain	2009	42.5	60.1	19.7	37.6	59.5	67.8	66.1	18.8	18.9	21.2	21.7	13.3	12.7
United Kingdom	2009	73.3	66.9	33.7	39.4	58.4	64.3	63.5	19.1	18.6	21.5	22.5	17.2	15.0
Other Europe														
Norway	2008	47.6	146.8	34.4	74.2	70.0	64.4	67.7	21.6	20.2	16.3	8.4	15.4	15.9
East Asia														
Japan	2010	139.7	156.8	43.7	51.0	62.6	61.8	63.9	11.7	10.7	11.7	25.7	27.5	24.4
Malaysia	2010	25.7	30.6	5.3	9.8	74.8	83.2	80.2	5.2	5.3	6.3	20.0	11.5	13.5
Republic of Korea	2008	142.4	182.7	19.9	32.3	41.7	50.8	55.6	8.1	8.4	7.8	50.1	40.8	36.5
Singapore	2008	102.4	109.8	23.3	34.2	72.2	73.8	79.4	6.3	6.2	6.4	21.5	20.0	14.2

a/ At current prices.

Table 1.11
(continued)

SELECTED CHARACTERISTICS OF BRANCHES, SELECTED YEARS AND ECONOMIES

Electronic valves, tubes, etc. (ISIC 3210)

| Economy | Latest year | Value added per employee (current 1000 dollars) | | Wages and salaries per employee (current 1000 dollars) | | Percentage in output [a] | | | | | | | | |
| | | | | | | Costs of input materials and utilities | | | Costs of labour | | | Operating surplus | | |
	(LY)	2000	LY	2000	LY	2000	2006	LY	2000	2006	LY	2000	2006	LY
North America														
Canada	2009	109.7	72.9	28.9	42.1	56.4	52.3	52.7	11.5	26.7	27.3	32.1	21.0	20.0
United States of America	2008	193.5	195.3	47.6	56.0	36.8	35.2	39.4	15.5	15.6	17.4	47.7	49.2	43.2
Others														
Israel	2009	129.5	143.9	32.5	40.3	33.7	49.1	37.1	16.7	28.7	17.6	49.7	22.2	45.3
Developing & EIE														
Azerbaijan	2010	..	5.8	0.2	2.7	..	57.4	49.2	26.6	13.0	23.6	..	29.7	27.2
Brazil	2010	23.8	36.2	7.3	13.1	61.0	57.0	56.9	12.0	13.7	15.6	27.0	29.3	27.5
Bulgaria	2010	2.3	16.3	1.2	6.3	77.1	73.6	70.9	12.4	9.4	11.3	10.5	17.0	17.8
Chile	2008	17.9	35.3	7.2	15.2	63.1	35.0	38.3	14.9	45.2	26.5	22.0	19.8	35.2
China	2007	..	14.2	..	3.6	..	73.4	74.8	..	5.7	6.3	..	20.9	18.9
Egypt	2010	..	9.4	..	3.4	..	71.8	75.5	..	3.9	8.8	..	24.3	15.7
Greece	2007	7.2	42.3	1.9	31.7	71.1	63.3	60.0	7.8	30.0	30.0	21.1	6.7	10.0
India	2009	15.6	12.4	1.5	3.6	61.5	70.0	75.1	3.8	9.1	7.2	34.7	20.9	17.7
Indonesia	2009	28.3	12.9	6.7	1.9	55.9	65.1	48.1	10.5	7.3	7.5	33.6	27.6	44.4
Iran (Islamic Republic of)	2009	..	13.9	0.3	7.2	..	53.7	67.4	27.6	19.8	17.0	..	26.4	15.7
Kyrgyzstan	2010	6.9	5.3	2.3	2.3	43.2	..	52.1	19.0	23.4	20.5	37.8	..	27.4
Latvia	2010	24.0	23.4	5.5	8.5	59.8	44.3	52.3	9.3	24.5	17.2	31.0	31.2	30.5
Mexico	2010	8.7	16.3	5.6	8.6	64.1	71.5	38.2	23.3	..	32.6	12.6	..	29.2
Morocco	2008	..	24.8	..	11.2	..	49.3	16.2	..	..	38.0	..	..	45.9
Philippines	2009	9.4	14.7	..	4.5	58.8	77.0	80.7	..	5.7	5.9	..	17.3	13.4
Poland	2010	..	22.7	..	10.0	..	64.9	82.3	..	18.7	7.8	..	16.4	9.9
Romania	2010	..	15.3	..	7.8	..	53.6	60.2	..	34.4	20.3	..	12.0	19.5
The f. Yugosl. Rep of Macedonia	2010	..	9.3	..	4.6	..	57.2	65.9	..	32.1	16.7	..	10.6	17.4
Turkey	2009	17.9	20.2	7.3	9.5	52.7	..	68.6	19.3	10.5	14.8	28.0	..	16.6

a/ At current prices.

Table 1.11

SELECTED CHARACTERISTICS OF BRANCHES, SELECTED YEARS AND ECONOMIES

TV/radio transmitters; line comm. apparatus (ISIC 3220)

Economy	Latest year (LY)	Value added per employee (current 1000 dollars)		Wages and salaries per employee (current 1000 dollars)		Percentage in output a/								
						Costs of input materials and utilities			Costs of labour			Operating surplus		
	(LY)	2000	LY	2000	LY	2000	2006	LY	2000	2006	LY	2000	2006	LY
Industrialized Economies														
EU														
Austria	2009	77.6	111.5	46.9	85.2	56.7	54.1	66.9	26.2	23.0	25.3	17.1	22.9	7.8
Belgium	2009	97.4	130.8	43.4	93.7	65.7	57.6	72.9	15.3	20.6	19.4	19.0	21.8	7.7
Denmark	2009	39.7	118.2	28.1	85.3	76.7	53.4	56.8	16.5	27.8	31.2	6.8	18.8	12.0
Finland	2009	164.9	102.9	31.2	87.8	67.7	69.7	85.2	6.1	8.8	12.6	26.2	21.5	2.2
Germany	2009	51.9	90.2	41.8	62.2	72.9	76.1	65.3	21.9	16.9	23.9	5.3	7.1	10.8
Hungary	2009	21.3	46.6	6.0	14.8	65.6	61.9	89.6	9.7	15.8	3.3	24.8	22.3	7.1
Italy	2009	57.2	75.8	26.3	47.4	79.3	71.9	74.5	9.5	15.0	15.9	11.2	13.1	9.5
Lithuania	2010	11.2	25.4	5.6	13.6	59.3	64.2	68.7	20.4	12.4	16.7	20.3	23.4	14.6
Netherlands	2008	...	71.1	...	51.5	71.1	63.0	69.6	23.8	17.9	22.0	5.1	19.1	8.4
Portugal	2009	41.7	53.0	22.1	25.9	74.0	...	71.3	13.8	...	14.0	12.2	...	14.7
Slovakia	2009	4.1	15.3	2.4	11.1	70.9	73.8	83.0	17.3	19.7	12.3	11.8	6.6	4.7
Spain	2009	53.9	84.9	33.8	43.9	70.5	70.6	61.1	18.5	16.6	20.1	11.0	12.7	18.8
Sweden	2008	62.6	195.8	36.3	74.5	87.5	...	74.1	7.2	...	9.8	5.2	...	16.0
United Kingdom	2007	97.2	149.7	42.3	78.5	66.2	64.0	64.0	14.7	16.2	18.8	19.1	19.7	17.1
Other Europe														
Norway	2008	93.4	142.6	53.2	88.3	65.1	71.7	73.6	19.9	19.7	16.4	15.0	8.6	10.1
East Asia														
Japan	2010	213.5	186.1	48.0	60.0	66.1	67.5	66.1	7.6	8.1	10.9	26.3	24.3	23.0
Malaysia	2010	33.0	22.5	4.8	8.0	76.4	87.6	82.7	3.4	2.8	6.1	20.2	9.6	11.2
Republic of Korea	2008	105.5	318.9	15.1	30.9	70.1	59.7	56.0	4.3	5.1	4.3	25.6	35.2	39.7
Singapore	2010	94.8	66.6	32.2	45.3	79.6	71.5	70.0	6.9	4.3	20.5	13.4	24.1	9.6

a/ At current prices.

Table 1.11
(continued)

SELECTED CHARACTERISTICS OF BRANCHES, SELECTED YEARS AND ECONOMIES

TV/radio transmitters; line comm. apparatus (ISIC 3220)

| Economy | Latest year (LY) | Value added per employee (current 1000 dollars) | | Wages and salaries per employee (current 1000 dollars) | | Percentage in output a/ | | | | | | | | |
| | | | | | | Costs of input materials and utilities | | | Costs of labour | | | Operating surplus | | |
		2000	LY	2000	LY	2000	2006	LY	2000	2006	LY	2000	2006	LY
North America														
Canada	2009	172.8	132.5	34.2	45.2	61.4	57.5	39.8	7.6	21.7	20.5	30.9	20.8	39.7
United States of America	2008	258.4	241.4	67.8	69.4	47.5	47.7	43.3	13.8	11.4	16.3	38.8	40.9	40.4
Developing & EIE														
Brazil	2010	87.3	91.6	13.0	23.8	61.3	72.5	65.0	5.8	5.4	9.1	32.9	22.1	25.9
Bulgaria	2010	2.9	21.8	1.6	6.1	63.6	58.0	57.6	20.5	8.9	11.8	15.9	33.1	30.6
China	2007	...	27.9	...	5.6	...	76.9	78.9	...	3.5	4.3	...	19.6	16.8
Ecuador	2008	5.6	15.9	1.5	8.2	59.7	59.4	72.5	10.6	15.3	14.2	29.8	25.3	13.3
Egypt	2010	...	12.9	...	3.2	...	61.8	72.3	...	6.9	6.8	...	31.3	20.8
Greece	2007	...	84.1	...	38.7	...	65.8	53.3	...	19.0	21.5	...	15.2	25.2
India	2009	5.0	11.0	2.3	4.8	80.8	77.0	82.0	8.8	4.4	7.8	10.3	18.6	10.1
Indonesia	2009	9.1	21.8	1.1	1.7	51.8	40.6	17.2	5.9	1.8	6.6	42.3	57.6	76.2
Iran (Islamic Republic of)	2008	51.7	23.6	10.9	8.7	51.0	60.9	69.8	10.3	15.2	11.2	38.7	23.8	19.0
Latvia	2008	4.8	23.1	2.1	15.2	57.5	53.1	69.7	18.8	12.9	19.9	23.7	34.0	10.4
Mongolia	2008	0.5	0.4	0.2	0.3	75.1	39.7	53.8	10.3	...	35.0	14.6	...	11.2
Poland	2009	18.6	25.6	...	13.4	76.5	76.5	80.1	...	11.4	10.4	...	12.1	9.5
Romania	2007	...	39.8	...	18.5	...	76.4	72.8	...	12.5	12.7	...	11.1	14.6
The f. Yugosl. Rep of Macedonia	2010	...	9.3	...	5.1	...	53.7	66.9	...	36.2	18.1	...	10.1	15.0
Turkey	2008	79.8	64.7	22.5	37.5	38.5	...	55.7	17.3	25.8	25.7	44.1	...	18.6

a/ At current prices.

Table 1.11

SELECTED CHARACTERISTICS OF BRANCHES, SELECTED YEARS AND ECONOMIES

TV and radio receivers and associated goods (ISIC 3230)

Economy	Latest year (LY)	Value added per employee (current 1000 dollars)		Wages and salaries per employee (current 1000 dollars)		Percentage in output a/								
						Costs of input materials and utilities			Costs of labour			Operating surplus		
		2000	LY	2000	LY	2000	2006	LY	2000	2006	LY	2000	2006	LY
Industrialized Economies														
EU														
Austria	2009	60.3	149.1	33.8	77.3	74.5	61.3	49.6	14.3	18.6	26.1	11.2	20.1	24.3
Belgium	2008	81.8	178.1	30.7	74.1	76.9	65.1	55.1	8.7	11.9	18.7	14.4	23.0	26.2
Denmark	2008	35.3	101.1	25.3	59.5	67.2	74.2	73.1	23.5	16.8	15.8	9.2	9.1	11.1
Finland	2009	54.1	66.2	26.6	47.3	64.8	69.8	61.1	17.3	27.9	27.8	17.9	2.3	11.1
France	2009	38.1	64.0	22.8	47.1	82.4	73.4	66.8	10.5	16.8	24.4	7.1	9.8	8.8
Germany	2009	53.7	83.1	33.8	64.2	69.0	67.8	69.9	19.6	18.2	23.2	11.5	14.0	6.8
Hungary	2008	12.6	48.0	4.2	16.2	90.5	91.0	92.0	3.2	2.6	2.7	6.3	6.4	5.3
Ireland	2009	56.3	156.3	17.8	47.2	71.8	...	67.9	8.9	...	9.7	19.2	...	22.4
Italy	2009	39.7	58.9	17.8	33.6	74.8	73.0	79.3	11.3	13.9	11.8	13.9	13.1	8.9
Lithuania	2010	4.5	17.6	2.8	7.9	76.9	88.8	89.1	14.4	7.1	4.9	8.7	4.1	6.0
Malta	2008	59.5	143.2	12.4	32.1	57.2	62.5	65.0	8.9	5.1	7.8	33.9	32.4	27.2
Netherlands	2008	...	125.1	...	60.1	72.1	...	71.5	13.8	...	13.7	14.1	...	14.8
Portugal	2009	25.8	47.9	11.7	23.8	83.6	82.7	82.9	7.4	7.4	8.5	9.0	10.0	8.6
Slovakia	2009	3.3	13.6	2.0	13.0	81.5	89.8	98.3	11.1	1.3	1.7	7.4	8.8	0.1
Slovenia	2010	13.6	44.0	9.5	24.0	87.3	67.6	68.6	8.9	17.6	17.1	3.8	14.7	14.3
Spain	2009	30.9	88.9	19.5	47.8	86.4	85.9	78.5	8.6	6.5	11.6	5.0	7.7	9.9
Sweden	2009	52.0	76.1	27.2	41.9	78.2	...	61.9	11.4	...	21.0	10.4	...	17.1
United Kingdom	2007	47.8	149.8	27.3	58.5	73.4	63.8	59.2	15.1	17.9	15.9	11.4	18.3	24.8
Other Europe														
Norway	2008	63.7	149.6	36.0	70.9	78.5	60.1	59.5	12.1	21.5	19.2	9.3	18.4	21.3
East Asia														
Japan	2010	105.5	193.7	35.6	61.4	67.6	71.3	73.9	10.9	8.4	8.3	21.5	20.3	17.8
Malaysia	2010	12.8	40.9	4.3	9.1	87.2	90.9	86.9	4.3	4.6	2.9	8.4	4.5	10.2
Republic of Korea	2008	50.2	71.2	13.5	33.0	68.3	59.8	66.1	8.5	12.9	15.7	23.2	27.3	18.2
Singapore	2010	33.0	46.4	20.6	36.7	86.5	84.1	93.3	8.4	13.3	5.3	5.1	2.6	1.4

a/ At current prices.

Table 1.11
(continued)

SELECTED CHARACTERISTICS OF BRANCHES, SELECTED YEARS AND ECONOMIES

TV and radio receivers and associated goods (ISIC 3230)

Economy	Latest year (LY)	Value added per employee (current 1000 dollars)		Wages and salaries per employee (current 1000 dollars)		Percentage in output [a]								
						Costs of input materials and utilities			Costs of labour			Operating surplus		
		2000	LY	2000	LY	2000	2006	LY	2000	2006	LY	2000	2006	LY
North America														
Canada	2009	63.8	77.4	24.5	40.5	49.8	46.5	45.4	19.2	28.0	28.6	30.9	25.5	26.0
United States of America	2008	66.5	143.2	20.1	45.8	64.9	65.8	64.2	10.6	8.7	11.4	24.5	25.5	24.3
Developing & EIE														
Brazil	2010	44.1	102.7	7.9	14.7	68.2	66.6	67.9	5.7	5.3	4.6	26.1	28.1	27.5
Bulgaria	2009	2.7	8.2	1.2	6.0	58.3	80.0	57.1	19.4	16.1	31.3	22.3	3.9	11.5
China	2007	...	20.0	...	3.9	...	80.6	82.2	...	2.7	3.5	...	16.7	14.3
Egypt	2010	...	10.2	...	3.6	...	80.6	70.2	...	5.9	10.5	...	13.5	19.4
India	2009	10.7	28.5	1.7	4.1	86.1	92.1	85.1	2.2	2.5	2.2	11.7	5.5	12.8
Indonesia	2009	6.5	17.2	1.2	2.0	76.4	52.3	82.5	4.3	4.3	2.1	19.3	43.4	15.4
Iran (Islamic Republic of)	2009	63.0	26.1	13.7	8.2	67.3	69.6	69.2	7.1	9.8	9.6	25.6	20.6	21.2
Latvia	2009	2.8	13.3	2.5	7.1	53.7	50.5	53.9	40.2	21.6	24.5	6.1	28.0	21.5
Mexico	2010	41.8	17.2	4.9	9.4	71.5	68.9	45.3	3.3	...	30.0	25.1	...	24.7
Morocco	2010	4.5	10.0	3.2	8.6	76.2	62.5	37.9	16.9	...	53.3	6.9	...	8.8
Philippines	2008	...	7.3	...	3.6	...	72.5	86.9	...	3.7	6.5	...	23.8	6.6
Poland	2009	8.5	37.8	...	10.3	90.3	91.5	89.9	...	3.7	2.8	...	4.8	7.4
Romania	2009	...	10.7	...	4.4	...	83.6	81.2	...	8.7	7.7	...	7.7	11.1
Sri Lanka	2010	...	1.4	...	1.3	...	70.5	91.7	...	10.0	8.1	...	19.5	0.2
The f. Yugosl. Rep of Macedonia	2010	...	8.6	...	7.3	...	64.2	54.4	...	24.1	39.0	...	11.7	6.7
Turkey	2008	51.9	37.8	12.7	16.3	74.1	85.8	88.1	6.3	4.8	5.2	19.6	9.4	6.8

a/ At current prices.

Table 1.11

SELECTED CHARACTERISTICS OF BRANCHES, SELECTED YEARS AND ECONOMIES

Medical, measuring, testing appliances, etc. (ISIC 331)

Economy	Latest year (LY)	Value added per employee (current 1000 dollars)		Wages and salaries per employee (current 1000 dollars)		Percentage in output [a]								
						Costs of input materials and utilities			Costs of labour			Operating surplus		
		2000	LY	2000	LY	2000	2006	LY	2000	2006	LY	2000	2006	LY
Industrialized Economies														
EU														
Austria	2009	41.7	84.5	23.2	46.4	47.9	49.0	53.0	28.9	25.0	25.8	23.1	26.0	21.2
Belgium	2009	58.9	77.6	25.5	50.4	63.4	70.3	78.9	15.8	14.1	13.7	20.7	15.6	7.4
Czech Republic	2007	10.0	30.0	4.2	12.8	68.1	71.3	60.2	13.5	14.6	16.9	18.5	14.0	22.9
Denmark	2009	56.4	130.7	34.0	83.3	53.6	51.6	55.5	28.0	26.0	28.4	18.4	22.4	16.2
Estonia	2010	7.6	29.9	3.6	13.5	68.7	71.4	67.9	14.6	15.7	14.5	16.7	12.9	17.6
Finland	2009	56.2	103.9	26.9	52.0	56.6	60.7	59.4	20.8	19.9	20.3	22.6	19.3	20.3
France	2009	51.2	100.4	28.2	56.2	63.4	61.1	55.5	20.1	21.5	24.9	16.5	17.4	19.6
Germany	2009	47.9	80.1	29.7	52.4	53.6	54.5	56.5	28.7	25.6	28.5	17.7	19.9	15.0
Hungary	2009	7.4	26.1	4.1	11.8	67.5	63.9	59.7	17.9	15.9	18.3	14.6	20.2	22.1
Ireland	2009	92.9	177.0	22.3	53.2	49.5	...	54.4	12.1	...	13.7	38.4	...	31.9
Italy	2009	52.1	80.1	21.7	38.1	60.5	64.4	66.9	16.4	15.3	15.8	23.0	20.2	17.4
Lithuania	2010	5.5	19.2	3.0	8.2	62.6	59.8	54.3	20.1	17.6	19.6	17.2	22.6	26.1
Malta	2008	34.7	35.2	13.2	22.1	52.2	52.4	53.6	18.2	31.8	29.1	29.6	15.8	17.3
Netherlands	2008	54.4	113.5	29.2	60.2	57.5	...	67.1	22.8	...	17.5	19.7	...	15.5
Portugal	2009	21.1	38.0	10.8	17.8	61.6	...	59.1	19.7	...	19.2	18.7	...	21.6
Slovakia	2009	6.0	26.2	2.7	11.9	72.1	62.9	64.6	12.5	15.0	16.0	15.4	22.1	19.4
Slovenia	2010	17.3	36.2	13.0	22.4	63.9	64.5	56.9	27.0	23.4	26.6	9.1	12.1	16.4
Spain	2009	42.7	74.6	21.1	37.4	60.6	61.7	54.6	19.5	20.1	22.7	19.9	18.2	22.6
Sweden	2009	56.1	113.3	30.0	51.0	64.4	58.0	60.2	19.1	17.9	17.9	16.5	24.0	21.9
United Kingdom	2009	58.3	90.3	31.5	45.3	54.0	52.4	54.1	24.9	23.4	23.0	21.1	24.2	22.9
Other Europe														
Norway	2008	58.8	162.2	44.4	96.1	65.2	64.5	63.6	26.3	23.8	21.6	8.5	11.7	14.9
Russian Federation	2010	...	14.9	0.7	8.5	...	54.7	55.4	16.6	21.6	25.6	...	23.7	19.0
East Asia														
Japan	2010	112.8	134.3	36.6	43.1	47.6	54.5	55.8	17.0	12.4	14.2	35.4	33.1	30.0
Malaysia	2010	11.8	18.0	4.8	7.9	72.0	72.2	70.2	11.3	8.4	13.0	16.7	19.3	16.8
Republic of Korea	2008	52.6	79.1	13.9	23.7	52.9	55.4	56.7	12.4	14.7	13.0	34.6	29.8	30.3
Singapore	2008	99.4	103.0	21.4	31.1	53.8	61.4	65.3	9.9	11.6	10.5	36.2	27.0	24.2
West Asia														
Kuwait	2010	...	21.3	...	16.4	...	53.8	50.8	...	36.6	37.8	...	9.6	11.4

a/ At current prices.

Table 1.11
(continued)

SELECTED CHARACTERISTICS OF BRANCHES, SELECTED YEARS AND ECONOMIES

Medical, measuring, testing appliances, etc. (ISIC 331)

Economy	Latest year (LY)	Value added per employee (current 1000 dollars) 2000	LY	Wages and salaries per employee (current 1000 dollars) 2000	LY	Percentage in output a/ Costs of input materials and utilities 2000	2006	LY	Costs of labour 2000	2006	LY	Operating surplus 2000	2006	LY
North America														
United States of America	2008	125.1	210.8	45.5	64.4	34.7	33.4	33.6	23.7	21.5	20.3	41.5	45.0	46.1
Developing & EIE														
Azerbaijan	2009	24.1	4.2	0.3	2.8	...	57.3	65.1	31.0	37.7	23.2		5.0	11.7
Brazil	2010	1.8	46.5	7.0	14.9	41.6	43.2	42.0	17.0	18.8	18.6	41.4	38.0	39.4
Bulgaria	2010	37.1	15.0	1.0	4.4	66.7	69.5	55.7	19.0	10.7	12.9	14.3	19.8	31.4
Chile	2008	...	23.5	11.3	12.6	55.5	73.8	47.0	13.5	15.6	28.4	31.0	10.6	24.6
China	2007	20.9	16.7	...	3.4	...	67.2	68.5	...	6.6	6.5		26.2	25.1
Cyprus	2010	2.3	44.1	10.5	30.4	38.6	36.2	37.8	30.8	36.4	42.9	30.6	27.5	19.3
Ecuador	2008	0.2	15.7	0.9	3.7	66.9	63.8	52.7	12.6	10.7	11.1	20.5	25.5	36.3
Georgia	2010	...	4.4	0.1	2.4	65.1	53.1	59.6	21.4	17.4	22.2	13.4	29.5	18.2
Greece	2007	5.8	88.8	...	21.9	...	49.7	57.4	...	11.2	10.5		39.0	32.1
India	2008	5.3	13.4	1.8	3.8	73.6	74.8	66.3	8.2	7.0	9.6	18.2	18.2	24.1
Indonesia	2009	20.9	13.6	1.3	2.1	47.9	61.8	42.8	12.8	5.6	8.9	39.3	32.6	48.3
Iran (Islamic Republic of)	2009	6.0	19.3	8.3	6.6	60.1	50.9	64.3	15.9	17.7	12.3	24.0	31.3	23.4
Jordan	2010	6.6	18.4	3.1	5.0	62.8	60.3	44.6	19.1	14.4	14.9	18.1	25.3	40.5
Latvia	2010	25.0	14.7	2.6	6.8	58.6	55.8	59.9	16.6	15.6	18.6	24.9	28.6	21.5
Mexico	2010	...	21.6	5.5	10.1	51.6	59.9	46.7	10.6	...	24.9	37.8	...	28.4
Mongolia	2008	10.2	2.6	0.6	2.3	...	53.1	65.1	9.5	13.4	31.0		33.5	3.9
Morocco	2010	...	19.1	5.0	9.1	74.7	77.9	76.5	12.3	...	11.2	13.0	...	12.3
Philippines	2008	17.1	9.5	...	4.2	...	82.3	63.5	...	5.7	16.2		12.0	20.2
Poland	2009	...	25.1	...	11.1	46.4	60.4	58.4	...	16.2	18.3		23.4	23.3
Romania	2010	...	20.0	...	7.4	...	68.1	65.2	...	17.4	12.9		14.5	21.8
The f. Yugosl. Rep of Macedonia	2010	...	19.8	...	12.0	...	37.4	41.6	...	31.4	35.4		31.2	23.0
Turkey	2009	38.7	22.3	7.9	8.9	36.0	...	67.7	13.1	...	12.9	50.9	...	19.4

a/ At current prices.

Table 1.11

SELECTED CHARACTERISTICS OF BRANCHES, SELECTED YEARS AND ECONOMIES

Optical instruments & photographic equipment (ISIC 3320)

Economy	Latest year (LY)	Value added per employee (current 1000 dollars)		Wages and salaries per employee (current 1000 dollars)		Percentage in output a/ Costs of input materials and utilities			Costs of labour			Operating surplus		
		2000	LY	2000	LY	2000	2006	LY	2000	2006	LY	2000	2006	LY
Industrialized Economies														
EU														
Austria	2009	46.3	96.3	24.4	52.1	46.9	46.7	51.2	28.0	24.5	26.4	25.1	28.8	22.4
Belgium	2008	46.8	144.3	28.5	58.3	72.1	65.9	65.1	17.0	17.1	14.1	10.9	17.1	20.8
Denmark	2009	122.9	99.2	32.6	88.2	45.7	55.5	69.5	14.4	22.0	27.1	39.9	22.5	3.4
Finland	2009	42.8	90.6	20.4	60.4	56.3	...	40.0	20.8	...	40.0	22.9	...	20.0
France	2009	42.1	92.7	22.6	58.1	58.9	62.1	55.6	22.1	20.9	27.8	19.1	17.0	16.6
Germany	2009	51.1	86.0	31.2	61.6	54.9	55.2	59.6	27.5	24.0	28.9	17.5	20.8	11.5
Hungary	2009	7.1	20.3	3.4	12.2	63.6	54.3	57.5	17.7	21.9	25.5	18.7	23.9	17.1
Ireland	2009	...	63.3	...	49.2	...	40.6	69.1	...	13.0	24.0	...	46.4	6.9
Italy	2008	51.7	73.1	16.7	34.3	62.5	60.4	65.5	12.1	14.6	16.2	25.4	25.1	18.3
Lithuania	2010	12.9	62.2	5.5	23.6	63.1	59.0	49.7	15.7	18.9	19.1	21.2	22.0	31.2
Malta	2008	20.4	16.2	10.9	9.2	39.3	...	55.8	32.4	...	25.2	28.3	...	19.0
Netherlands	2008	74.3	126.1	27.1	56.3	49.9	...	56.0	18.2	...	19.7	31.8	...	24.4
Portugal	2009	23.3	28.9	10.3	21.0	59.4	63.0	57.7	18.0	15.6	30.8	22.6	21.5	11.5
Slovenia	2009	18.5	25.9	9.9	25.9	59.4	48.0	66.7	21.9	30.7	33.3	18.8	21.3	0.0
Spain	2008	34.8	74.2	19.9	43.7	60.9	59.7	49.8	22.4	18.0	29.6	16.7	22.3	20.6
Sweden	2009	55.9	89.7	33.0	45.5	64.7	57.9	63.7	20.9	17.1	18.4	14.4	24.9	17.9
United Kingdom	2007	40.1	104.1	28.3	46.6	52.4	55.0	49.9	33.6	28.0	22.4	14.0	17.0	27.7
Other Europe														
Norway	2008	37.5	122.7	30.1	69.9	59.0	47.5	50.7	32.9	32.0	28.1	8.1	20.5	21.2
East Asia														
Japan	2010	75.1	105.6	29.4	39.8	61.0	59.0	79.1	15.3	13.0	7.9	23.8	28.0	13.0
Malaysia	2010	10.2	10.5	4.6	5.4	82.5	87.1	84.8	8.0	6.2	7.9	9.5	6.8	7.3
Republic of Korea	2008	36.5	77.9	11.4	21.7	50.6	66.1	66.7	15.4	10.7	9.3	34.0	23.2	24.0
Singapore	2010	33.0	80.0	16.7	31.6	56.3	...	60.1	22.1	...	15.7	21.6	...	24.1

a/ At current prices.

Table 1.11
(continued)

SELECTED CHARACTERISTICS OF BRANCHES, SELECTED YEARS AND ECONOMIES

Optical instruments & photographic equipment (ISIC 3320)

Economy	Latest year (LY)	Value added per employee (current 1000 dollars) 2000	Value added per employee LY	Wages and salaries per employee (current 1000 dollars) 2000	Wages and salaries per employee LY	Percentage in output [a/] — Costs of input materials and utilities 2000	Costs of input materials and utilities 2006	Costs of input materials and utilities LY	Costs of labour 2000	Costs of labour 2006	Costs of labour LY	Operating surplus 2000	Operating surplus 2006	Operating surplus LY
North America														
United States of America	2008	126.0	174.4	34.8	50.4	33.7	35.2	36.4	18.3	19.5	18.4	48.0	45.3	45.2
Others														
Israel	2009	80.6	100.0	52.5	68.3	48.8	62.4	55.6	33.3	28.0	30.3	17.8	9.6	14.1
Developing & EIE														
Azerbaijan	2010	...	17.7	0.1	5.2	...	56.7	65.1	33.3	10.0	10.2	...	33.3	24.6
Brazil	2010	17.2	42.5	5.0	15.6	44.6	39.6	61.4	15.9	14.8	14.2	39.5	45.7	24.4
Bulgaria	2010	2.3	11.0	1.4	6.1	58.8	69.2	62.5	25.0	13.1	20.7	16.2	17.6	16.8
Chile	2008	18.6	28.1	9.3	17.1	41.7	56.6	57.1	28.9	40.2	26.2	29.4	3.2	16.7
China	2007	...	10.8	...	3.8	...	77.0	76.7	...	6.6	8.1	...	16.4	15.2
Ecuador	2008	4.0	14.1	1.2	5.0	57.0	71.6	70.2	12.9	8.6	10.6	30.0	19.7	19.2
Egypt	2010	...	4.7	...	2.8	...	65.4	66.5	...	11.2	19.7	...	23.4	13.9
India	2009	7.2	11.2	1.9	3.3	61.0	59.4	60.2	10.1	8.3	11.7	28.9	32.3	28.2
Indonesia	2009	10.3	3.4	1.0	1.9	40.6	45.4	46.1	5.5	14.5	31.0	53.9	40.1	23.0
Iran (Islamic Republic of)	2007	13.8	68.6	8.0	12.6	62.9	64.0	62.4	21.5	13.7	6.9	15.7	22.3	30.7
Latvia	2010	10.5	55.3	2.7	13.4	39.1	58.1	47.0	15.7	23.8	12.8	45.2	18.1	40.2
Mexico	2010	46.5	49.7	6.9	14.7	58.7	73.8	43.2	6.1	...	16.8	35.2	...	40.1
Morocco	2010	7.9	2.2	4.9	1.8	48.3	57.1	86.1	31.9	...	11.4	19.8	...	2.5
Oman	2010	58.3	210.1	17.6	21.8	54.5	55.9	15.5	13.7	12.0	8.7	31.8	32.1	75.7
Poland	2009	14.3	30.2	...	11.2	59.0	62.6	67.2	...	13.1	12.1	...	24.3	20.7
Turkey	2008	33.1	22.4	6.0	10.1	23.6	68.6	76.7	13.9	7.1	10.4	62.6	24.3	12.8

a/ At current prices.

Table 1.11

SELECTED CHARACTERISTICS OF BRANCHES, SELECTED YEARS AND ECONOMIES

Motor vehicles (ISIC 3410)

Economy	Latest year (LY)	Value added per employee (current 1000 dollars)		Wages and salaries per employee (current 1000 dollars)		Percentage in output [a]								
						Costs of input materials and utilities			Costs of labour			Operating surplus		
		2000	LY	2000	LY	2000	2006	LY	2000	2006	LY	2000	2006	LY
Industrialized Economies														
EU														
Austria	2009	65.8	149.4	31.6	62.0	76.0	83.0	75.5	11.5	6.9	10.2	12.5	10.0	14.3
Belgium	2009	58.2	95.0	31.2	52.7	81.3	80.2	83.8	10.0	8.5	9.0	8.7	11.3	7.2
Estonia	2007	...	31.3	...	17.8	...	62.3	62.4	...	18.9	21.5	...	18.7	16.2
Finland	2009	44.5	64.5	25.4	44.8	59.1	71.2	72.2	23.4	16.3	19.3	17.6	12.5	8.5
France	2009	71.9	63.6	28.6	55.8	86.9	87.1	81.9	5.2	7.6	15.8	7.9	5.3	2.2
Germany	2009	53.1	86.1	41.6	73.6	80.6	78.2	83.1	15.2	14.3	14.5	4.2	7.5	2.4
Hungary	2009	79.1	124.0	6.7	21.4	82.5	82.9	81.1	1.5	2.3	3.3	16.0	14.8	15.7
Italy	2009	41.2	71.3	21.3	32.7	86.0	85.9	84.2	7.2	6.2	7.2	6.8	7.8	8.5
Lithuania	2010	1.0	12.7	1.8	6.1	...	87.7	84.4	...	7.5	7.5	...	4.9	8.0
Malta	2007	...	12.2	...	6.4	...	80.9	80.9	...	10.0	10.0	...	9.1	9.1
Netherlands	2007	79.6	310.5	31.1	57.6	79.5	70.8	72.4	8.0	7.6	5.1	12.5	21.6	22.4
Portugal	2009	58.0	73.4	14.0	27.6	79.6	87.1	84.6	4.9	4.8	5.8	15.5	8.0	9.6
Slovenia	2010	20.8	65.1	14.2	26.9	94.8	90.0	89.3	3.6	4.5	4.4	1.6	5.5	6.3
Spain	2009	52.6	77.0	24.3	45.0	85.1	85.6	86.8	6.9	6.4	7.7	8.0	8.1	5.5
United Kingdom	2007	51.2	147.4	39.3	68.9	84.9	81.8	82.1	11.6	10.1	8.4	3.5	8.0	9.5
East Asia														
Japan	2010	242.0	280.1	66.4	75.0	77.7	72.9	78.9	6.1	4.4	5.6	16.2	22.7	15.5
Malaysia	2010	32.4	39.6	6.0	9.9	83.8	81.5	84.4	3.0	3.8	3.9	13.2	14.7	11.7
Republic of Korea	2008	142.4	227.3	27.0	53.5	61.8	66.9	67.5	7.2	7.2	7.6	30.9	25.8	24.8

a/ At current prices.

Table 1.11
(continued)

SELECTED CHARACTERISTICS OF BRANCHES, SELECTED YEARS AND ECONOMIES

Motor vehicles (ISIC 3410)

Economy	Latest year (LY)	Value added per employee (current 1000 dollars)		Wages and salaries per employee (current 1000 dollars)		Percentage in output a/								
						Costs of input materials and utilities			Costs of labour			Operating surplus		
		2000	LY	2000	LY	2000	2006	LY	2000	2006	LY	2000	2006	LY
North America														
Canada	2009	280.9	158.7	42.9	61.1	72.5	82.1	80.2	4.2	6.6	7.6	23.3	11.3	12.2
United States of America	2008	190.0	234.0	51.3	59.1	72.8	72.2	73.4	7.3	6.7	6.7	19.8	21.1	19.9
Developing & EIE														
Azerbaijan	2010	...	3.1	0.2	0.9	...	45.1	50.6	5.2	0.7	13.7	...	54.2	35.7
Brazil	2010	53.6	201.3	16.0	35.9	67.2	69.5	62.5	9.8	6.8	6.7	23.0	23.7	30.8
Chile	2008	30.3	85.2	15.3	26.8	91.8	77.9	87.5	4.1	3.7	3.9	4.1	18.4	8.6
China	2007	...	47.5	...	4.9	...	77.4	75.8	...	2.5	2.5	...	20.1	21.7
Ecuador	2008	18.1	63.8	3.0	7.6	91.0	87.6	89.0	1.5	1.5	1.3	7.5	10.9	9.7
Egypt	2010	...	17.9	...	3.8	...	75.7	76.7	...	5.9	5.0	...	18.4	18.4
Greece	2007	...	58.9	...	34.1	...	64.6	64.8	...	26.0	20.3	...	9.4	14.8
India	2009	9.7	34.0	3.5	6.8	86.0	81.8	85.1	5.0	2.8	3.0	9.0	15.4	11.9
Indonesia	2009	67.4	156.5	2.4	2.9	54.4	17.5	38.6	1.6	1.7	1.1	44.0	80.8	60.3
Iran (Islamic Republic of)	2009	127.9	82.4	23.0	16.8	65.8	71.4	74.8	6.1	4.2	5.1	28.0	24.4	20.1
Mexico	2010	102.0	150.4	11.7	20.0	74.1	76.2	81.1	3.0	...	2.5	22.9	...	16.3
Morocco	2010	23.7	28.7	8.8	10.2	69.9	68.9	80.6	11.2	...	6.9	19.0	...	12.5
Oman	2010	...	6.9	...	3.0	...	12.5	16.3	...	25.4	36.6	...	62.2	47.1
Philippines	2008	...	85.0	...	10.3	...	85.3	68.3	...	3.2	3.8	...	11.4	27.9
Poland	2009	19.1	65.5	...	17.2	86.4	86.2	85.1	...	3.1	3.9	...	10.7	10.9
Turkey	2009	77.6	62.3	13.5	23.3	64.2	84.5	82.7	6.2	5.3	6.5	29.6	10.2	10.8

a/ At current prices.

Table 1.11

SELECTED CHARACTERISTICS OF BRANCHES, SELECTED YEARS AND ECONOMIES

Automobile bodies, trailers & semi-trailers (ISIC 3420)

Economy	Latest year (LY)	Value added per employee (current 1000 dollars) 2000	LY	Wages and salaries per employee (current 1000 dollars) 2000	LY	Percentage in output a/ — Costs of input materials and utilities 2000	2006	LY	Costs of labour 2000	2006	LY	Operating surplus 2000	2006	LY
Industrialized Economies														
EU														
Austria	2009	41.1	68.3	21.3	43.4	65.0	64.8	67.4	18.1	18.8	20.7	16.9	16.4	11.9
Belgium	2009	43.7	71.4	23.4	36.3	73.9	78.2	74.0	14.0	11.0	13.2	12.1	10.8	12.8
Czech Republic	2007	...	24.3	...	12.1	...	78.3	81.2	...	10.3	9.4	...	11.5	9.4
Denmark	2009	44.6	79.4	30.9	67.7	72.4	70.4	68.8	19.1	20.6	26.6	8.5	9.1	4.6
Estonia	2007	...	23.9	...	12.0	...	71.6	72.3	...	15.2	13.9	...	13.2	13.8
Finland	2009	41.3	56.1	23.5	39.0	65.3	67.7	68.4	19.7	20.3	22.0	15.0	12.0	9.6
France	2009	34.9	59.1	19.9	39.0	71.1	71.8	70.1	16.5	16.2	19.7	12.4	12.0	10.2
Germany	2009	40.4	57.7	26.6	44.5	71.0	75.9	75.0	19.1	13.6	19.3	9.9	10.6	5.7
Hungary	2009	12.0	20.0	4.6	12.5	78.8	83.3	77.9	8.1	9.4	13.8	13.1	7.3	8.3
Italy	2009	36.8	49.1	19.1	32.6	75.5	76.6	76.6	12.7	13.1	15.6	11.8	10.3	7.9
Lithuania	2010	4.1	59.4	2.4	11.0	86.2	82.4	74.9	7.9	5.4	4.7	5.9	12.2	20.5
Luxembourg	2009	...	71.3	...	40.8	...	66.7	73.1	...	17.4	15.4	15.9	...	11.5
Malta	2008	20.7	35.9	7.7	22.6	49.6	50.4	51.9	18.7	35.4	30.3	31.7	14.2	17.8
Netherlands	2008	35.4	81.4	23.0	50.2	72.5	74.3	76.0	17.8	16.2	14.8	9.6	9.5	9.2
Portugal	2009	13.8	26.9	8.0	17.8	68.9	...	67.4	18.0	...	21.6	13.1	...	11.1
Slovenia	2010	15.6	45.7	10.9	25.2	82.6	80.5	83.8	12.2	8.4	8.9	5.2	11.1	7.3
Spain	2009	31.6	46.8	15.5	33.7	73.9	76.6	71.0	12.8	13.4	20.9	13.3	10.1	8.1
Sweden	2009	45.5	74.2	24.2	39.5	68.3	73.9	65.1	16.9	15.0	18.6	14.8	11.1	16.3
United Kingdom	2009	40.9	51.3	27.2	32.4	70.2	67.9	71.4	19.8	17.3	18.0	10.0	14.8	10.6
Other Europe														
Norway	2008	43.6	87.1	30.3	63.7	67.5	73.8	74.8	22.6	18.6	18.4	9.9	7.6	6.8
East Asia														
Japan	2010	111.8	107.9	55.4	46.7	78.3	86.8	67.2	10.8	8.2	14.2	11.0	4.9	18.6
Malaysia	2010	13.7	17.7	4.3	7.9	64.3	75.6	74.1	11.2	8.9	11.6	24.5	15.5	14.3
Republic of Korea	2008	41.5	75.5	15.8	25.1	79.7	64.2	70.7	7.7	11.0	9.7	12.5	24.8	19.5
West Asia														
Kuwait	2010	...	20.4	...	11.5	...	71.9	71.9	...	11.3	15.9	...	16.8	12.2

a/ At current prices.

Table 1.11
(continued)

SELECTED CHARACTERISTICS OF BRANCHES, SELECTED YEARS AND ECONOMIES

Automobile bodies, trailers & semi-trailers (ISIC 3420)

Economy	Latest year (LY)	Value added per employee (current 1000 dollars)		Wages and salaries per employee (current 1000 dollars)		Percentage in output [a]								
						Costs of input materials and utilities			Costs of labour			Operating surplus		
		2000	LY	2000	LY	2000	2006	LY	2000	2006	LY	2000	2006	LY
North America														
Canada	2009	65.8	59.7	25.5	39.8	56.1	64.6	62.1	17.0	20.7	25.3	26.8	14.7	12.6
United States of America	2008	57.3	80.2	27.4	37.9	61.3	63.8	64.3	18.5	15.5	16.9	20.2	20.6	18.8
Developing & EIE														
Brazil	2010	16.9	38.5	6.0	13.5	60.2	62.9	62.6	14.1	12.5	13.1	25.7	24.6	24.3
Bulgaria	2010	1.4	10.7	1.0	4.4	71.4	77.8	60.0	20.0	10.3	16.5	8.6	12.0	23.5
Chile	2008	17.5	53.4	8.0	14.9	57.4	64.7	54.0	19.6	12.9	12.8	23.0	22.4	33.2
China	2007	..	25.2	..	4.5	..	77.9	78.7	..	3.6	3.8	..	18.5	17.5
Cyprus	2010	..	53.7	..	31.3	..	59.8	64.1	..	24.2	20.9	..	16.1	15.0
Ecuador	2008	1.6	7.5	0.8	3.7	81.5	81.3	81.8	8.8	9.4	9.0	9.7	9.3	9.3
Egypt	2010	..	7.9	..	4.1	..	90.3	82.4	..	5.0	9.2	..	4.6	8.4
Eritrea	2010	6.3	3.4	0.7	1.1	50.9	..	37.5	5.1	..	19.9	44.0	..	42.5
Ethiopia	2009	19.0	8.1	1.1	0.6	72.6	73.8	69.6	1.5	5.7	2.1	25.8	20.5	28.4
Greece	2007	..	58.1	..	26.2	..	62.5	63.1	..	18.1	16.7	..	19.4	20.2
India	2009	1.8	4.8	1.2	2.0	80.9	84.1	79.5	12.8	7.1	8.3	6.3	8.8	12.1
Indonesia	2009	2.6	17.2	0.6	1.9	45.6	47.0	35.4	12.7	14.1	6.9	41.7	39.0	57.6
Iran (Islamic Republic of)	2010	13.8	16.9	5.7	5.8	61.7	73.9	74.3	15.8	9.7	8.8	22.5	16.4	16.9
Jordan	2010	14.6	7.3	4.0	3.1	67.8	66.3	67.3	8.8	10.2	13.7	23.4	23.5	19.0
Kyrgyzstan	2007	..	1.1	0.4	0.0	..	..	53.7	25.0	..	0.6	..	..	45.7
Latvia	2009	5.0	22.3	1.7	7.0	57.6	82.9	79.1	14.5	7.0	6.5	27.9	10.1	14.4
Malawi	2010	..	6.9	..	4.2	..	79.2	82.5	..	11.3	10.5	..	9.5	7.0
Mexico	2010	18.8	27.5	5.6	8.7	64.5	71.7	62.2	10.6	..	12.0	24.8	..	25.9
Morocco	2010	6.1	19.6	5.1	6.2	81.3	83.7	77.0	15.6	..	7.3	3.1	..	15.7
Oman	2008	6.6	8.9	3.9	6.1	40.9	..	59.6	34.4	..	27.8	24.7	..	12.6
Philippines	2009	..	4.8	..	2.3	..	64.3	84.2	..	8.0	7.8	..	27.7	8.0
Poland	2009	8.2	19.0	..	9.8	74.6	78.7	75.0	..	9.4	13.0	..	11.9	12.1
Turkey	2009	18.0	12.7	5.9	6.7	63.7	84.4	81.4	11.9	6.9	9.9	24.4	8.7	8.7

a/ At current prices.

Table 1.11

SELECTED CHARACTERISTICS OF BRANCHES, SELECTED YEARS AND ECONOMIES

Parts/accessories for automobiles (ISIC 3430)

Economy	Latest year (LY)	Value added per employee (current 1000 dollars)		Wages and salaries per employee (current 1000 dollars)		Percentage in output a/								
						Costs of input materials and utilities			Costs of labour			Operating surplus		
		2000	LY	2000	LY	2000	2006	LY	2000	2006	LY	2000	2006	LY
Industrialized Economies														
EU														
Austria	2009	71.9	82.0	26.9	51.7	65.3	72.1	69.7	13.0	12.3	19.1	21.7	15.6	11.2
Belgium	2009	54.1	77.7	26.3	46.9	72.9	78.3	75.4	13.2	11.4	14.8	13.9	10.3	9.8
Denmark	2008	42.7	93.2	31.5	61.8	55.6	...	56.4	32.8	...	28.9	11.6	...	14.7
Estonia	2010	...	36.9	...	13.1	...	68.8	68.0	...	12.2	11.3	...	...	20.7
Finland	2009	41.8	48.1	23.3	36.5	61.3	63.9	73.1	21.5	18.0	20.4	17.1	19.0	6.5
France	2009	45.6	69.5	24.4	49.3	76.2	75.6	76.7	12.8	13.5	16.5	11.0	18.0	6.8
Germany	2009	52.7	73.0	34.5	57.0	65.4	68.4	74.3	22.7	20.3	20.1	11.9	10.9	5.6
Hungary	2009	17.0	30.2	4.6	13.1	69.1	77.6	79.1	8.4	7.4	9.1	22.5	11.4	11.9
Ireland	2008	43.5	84.3	21.4	49.9	67.1	68.0	72.6	16.1	17.3	16.2	16.7	15.0	11.2
Italy	2009	42.3	55.4	20.0	34.2	72.6	75.2	75.8	12.9	12.5	14.9	14.4	14.7	9.2
Lithuania	2010	...	14.3	...	8.9	...	72.8	37.1	...	18.4	39.1	...	12.3	23.8
Netherlands	2007	40.8	102.7	25.9	51.6	69.4	68.8	72.1	19.4	15.7	14.0	11.2	8.9	13.9
Portugal	2009	21.0	36.2	9.5	20.0	74.3	...	78.3	11.7	...	12.0	14.1	15.5	9.7
Slovakia	2009	6.3	20.8	2.4	12.1	68.3	87.8	85.0	12.0	6.2	8.8	19.7	6.0	6.2
Slovenia	2010	17.7	43.7	12.1	24.1	76.7	68.8	71.8	15.8	16.1	15.6	7.4	15.2	12.6
Spain	2009	41.6	62.2	20.3	44.1	70.9	75.4	76.9	14.2	13.3	16.4	14.9	11.3	6.7
Sweden	2009	48.4	58.7	25.3	38.4	68.7	73.2	73.3	16.3	14.0	17.5	15.0	12.8	9.3
United Kingdom	2007	45.5	82.2	31.0	51.6	64.9	70.5	73.0	23.9	18.6	16.9	11.2	10.9	10.1
Other Europe														
Norway	2008	52.0	94.8	35.2	75.4	60.8	67.4	70.9	26.6	23.6	23.2	12.6	9.0	6.0
East Asia														
Japan	2010	97.6	140.1	42.0	51.8	69.6	70.8	67.6	13.1	11.0	12.0	17.3	18.2	20.4
Malaysia	2010	14.0	20.6	4.0	7.0	65.2	75.3	74.5	9.8	10.2	8.6	24.9	14.5	16.8
Republic of Korea	2008	55.8	93.8	15.7	27.4	61.2	66.5	68.8	10.9	9.3	9.1	27.9	24.2	22.0
West Asia														
Kuwait	2010	...	18.8	...	10.3	...	53.3	65.9	...	29.1	18.6	...	17.7	15.4

a/ At current prices.

Table 1.11
(continued)

SELECTED CHARACTERISTICS OF BRANCHES, SELECTED YEARS AND ECONOMIES

Parts/accessories for automobiles (ISIC 3430)

Economy	Latest year (LY)	Value added per employee (current 1000 dollars)		Wages and salaries per employee (current 1000 dollars)		Percentage in output [a/]								
						Costs of input materials and utilities			Costs of labour			Operating surplus		
		2000	LY	2000	LY	2000	2006	LY	2000	2006	LY	2000	2006	LY
North America														
Canada	2008	75.9	100.4	30.0	47.7	58.2	61.1	61.5	16.5	17.9	18.3	25.3	21.0	20.2
United States of America	2008	103.9	118.8	44.1	47.2	56.8	59.0	63.3	18.3	15.1	14.6	24.9	25.9	22.1
Developing & EIE														
Azerbaijan	2010	..	3.7	0.3	1.1	..	45.2	41.6	67.8	24.5	17.4	..	30.3	41.0
Brazil	2010	25.6	52.1	8.2	16.5	55.7	60.5	60.5	14.2	11.8	12.5	30.1	27.7	27.0
Bulgaria	2010	2.6	10.6	1.3	5.2	62.1	75.8	80.1	18.7	8.6	9.8	19.2	15.5	10.1
Chile	2008	18.1	16.4	8.4	10.7	49.1	52.8	81.9	23.7	29.4	11.8	27.2	17.7	6.3
China	2007	..	16.6	..	3.0	..	74.6	73.3	..	4.8	4.8	..	20.5	21.9
Cyprus	2010	17.5	52.8	10.1	32.2	55.2	56.8	50.4	26.0	24.7	30.2	18.8	18.5	19.4
Ecuador	2008	5.5	24.1	1.2	5.1	67.9	76.2	67.7	7.0	8.3	6.8	25.1	15.5	25.6
Egypt	2010	..	10.9	..	3.1	..	43.3	76.6	..	8.3	6.6	..	48.4	16.8
Eritrea	2010	2.3	4.0	1.2	1.1	55.3	57.9	63.9	23.1	16.1	10.1	21.7	26.0	26.0
Ethiopia	2008	7.2	10.7	0.6	1.2	17.3	53.5	63.2	6.7	9.1	4.2	76.0	37.5	32.6
Georgia	2009	0.2	6.0	0.1	1.8	67.4	71.7	62.0	11.6	11.6	11.4	20.9	16.7	26.6
Greece	2007	..	50.3	..	22.1	..	52.1	49.0	..	20.8	22.4	..	27.1	28.6
India	2009	5.7	10.5	1.8	2.9	74.3	79.6	77.7	8.0	5.6	6.1	17.7	14.8	16.2
Indonesia	2009	20.7	43.9	1.9	2.7	46.2	64.5	43.1	4.8	4.8	3.5	48.9	30.6	53.4
Iran (Islamic Republic of)	2009	35.9	26.0	10.3	7.9	66.2	63.9	68.5	9.7	9.7	9.6	24.1	26.4	21.9
Jordan	2010	5.0	11.0	3.0	4.2	77.6	65.4	58.9	13.7	14.4	15.8	8.8	20.2	25.3
Kyrgyzstan	2010	1.8	5.5	0.2	2.4	64.3	..	64.1	10.6	14.7	15.8	18.5	..	20.1
Latvia	2010	28.5	38.7	0.9	14.2	68.9	78.0	65.4	17.2	12.4	12.7	22.1	9.6	21.9
Mexico	2010	9.0	27.8	8.3	8.0	66.6	70.2	65.7	9.0	..	9.9	16.2	..	24.5
Morocco	2010	7.9	10.1	4.6	6.3	24.9	66.7	69.4	17.2	24.0	19.2	40.5	28.1	11.4
Oman	2008	..	10.9	3.6	9.1	..	47.9	63.9	34.6	5.0	30.3	..	11.6	5.8
Philippines	2009	10.8	9.4	..	4.2	73.6	83.3	79.9	..	8.0	9.0	..	16.9	11.1
Poland	2010	..	28.8	..	11.2	..	75.2	75.7	..	15.1	9.4	..	7.8	14.9
Romania	2009	..	15.4	..	7.3	..	77.1	76.7	..	17.4	11.0	..	27.1	12.3
Sri Lanka	2010	..	1.6	..	1.3	..	55.5	46.2	..	19.4	42.2	..	12.8	11.6
The f. Yugosl. Rep of Macedonia	2010	..	136.1	..	8.1	..	67.8	59.6	..	..	2.4	28.0	..	38.0
Turkey	2009	23.6	22.5	8.2	11.9	56.9	72.2	75.1	15.1	10.8	13.1	..	17.0	11.8

a/ At current prices.

Table 1.11

SELECTED CHARACTERISTICS OF BRANCHES, SELECTED YEARS AND ECONOMIES

Building and repairing of ships and boats (ISIC 351)

Economy	Latest year (LY)	Value added per employee (current 1000 dollars)		Wages and salaries per employee (current 1000 dollars)		Percentage in output a/								
						Costs of input materials and utilities			Costs of labour			Operating surplus		
		2000	LY	2000	LY	2000	2006	LY	2000	2006	LY	2000	2006	LY
Industrialized Economies														
EU														
Austria	2009	47.1	49.6	26.0	42.5	55.6	61.4	73.1	24.5	17.5	23.1	19.9	21.1	3.8
Belgium	2008	42.6	94.0	24.9	50.6	60.7	65.3	65.2	23.0	19.5	18.7	16.3	15.1	16.1
Czech Republic	2006	...	37.6	...	8.4	...	61.8	61.8	...	8.6	8.6	...	29.7	29.7
Estonia	2010	8.8	33.8	3.3	13.1	59.9	...	68.0	15.0	...	12.4	25.0	...	19.6
Finland	2008	29.9	70.3	23.8	49.3	79.1	76.2	77.6	16.7	14.7	15.7	4.3	9.1	6.7
France	2009	44.8	61.3	21.2	50.2	76.3	68.2	82.3	11.2	17.0	14.5	12.5	14.8	3.2
Germany	2009	41.3	76.3	30.5	61.5	75.2	76.5	79.6	18.3	13.9	16.5	6.5	9.6	4.0
Hungary	2009	6.8	12.9	2.5	7.5	51.1	64.7	68.4	17.8	20.7	18.4	31.1	14.6	13.2
Ireland	2008	28.9	75.2	21.0	48.7	56.0	...	55.3	32.0	27.6	28.9	12.0	...	15.8
Italy	2009	43.1	62.9	18.2	38.8	70.3	76.1	81.9	12.6	10.6	11.2	17.2	13.4	6.9
Lithuania	2010	5.9	80.0	4.1	39.5	54.7	61.1	42.5	31.6	21.9	28.4	13.7	16.9	29.1
Netherlands	2008	46.5	127.0	27.7	64.5	75.7	77.5	80.1	14.5	12.1	10.1	9.8	10.3	9.8
Portugal	2009	18.4	31.8	12.7	25.4	63.3	68.5	63.8	25.4	18.5	28.8	11.3	13.0	7.4
Slovenia	2010	21.4	31.7	12.9	27.2	66.7	68.8	84.1	20.0	15.6	13.6	13.3	15.6	2.3
Spain	2009	23.6	68.1	18.7	49.4	72.8	76.2	84.1	21.5	17.1	11.5	5.7	6.7	4.3
Sweden	2009	47.3	52.5	24.6	42.8	65.0	63.4	72.8	18.2	19.7	22.2	16.8	16.9	5.0
United Kingdom	2009	51.0	51.2	30.1	37.4	54.1	60.7	66.1	27.1	28.3	24.7	18.8	11.0	9.1
Other Europe														
Norway	2008	50.9	127.1	37.9	87.6	66.6	73.6	74.1	24.9	18.8	17.9	8.5	7.6	8.0
East Asia														
Japan	2010	135.5	205.3	38.4	48.2	64.8	70.3	69.2	10.0	7.8	7.2	25.2	21.9	23.6
Malaysia	2010	14.1	22.7	7.4	8.9	62.5	78.1	84.3	19.7	7.3	6.2	17.8	14.6	9.5
Republic of Korea	2008	79.7	154.2	24.3	41.7	56.5	67.2	67.3	13.3	11.3	8.9	30.2	21.6	23.9
Singapore	2010	21.6	33.1	14.4	17.5	66.8	73.5	60.4	22.1	15.0	21.0	11.1	11.5	18.7
West Asia														
Kuwait	2010	...	18.8	...	13.2	...	63.1	45.4	...	25.4	38.5	...	11.5	16.1

a/ At current prices.

Table 1.11
(continued)

SELECTED CHARACTERISTICS OF BRANCHES, SELECTED YEARS AND ECONOMIES

Building and repairing of ships and boats (ISIC 351)

Economy	Latest year (LY)	Value added per employee (current 1000 dollars)		Wages and salaries per employee (current 1000 dollars)		Percentage in output [a]								
						Costs of input materials and utilities			Costs of labour			Operating surplus		
		2000	LY	2000	LY	2000	2006	LY	2000	2006	LY	2000	2006	LY
North America														
Canada	2009	58.2	58.0	27.7	38.7	38.9	52.9	53.9	29.1	27.5	30.8	32.0	19.6	15.3
United States of America	2008	68.1	111.8	34.1	46.0	49.1	46.9	45.2	25.5	22.2	22.5	25.4	30.9	32.2
Developing & EIE														
Brazil	2010	15.2	45.7	4.7	16.1	53.5	54.3	50.9	14.5	15.5	17.3	32.0	30.2	31.8
Bulgaria	2009	4.3	8.1	1.8	6.1	73.5	66.5	84.2	11.1	14.7	12.0	15.3	18.9	3.9
Chile	2008	23.5	27.9	9.6	12.2	42.3	56.6	62.0	23.7	19.4	16.6	34.0	24.0	21.3
China	2007	...	29.2	...	4.6	...	74.3	71.3	...	4.9	4.5	...	20.8	24.2
Cyprus	2010	22.5	37.2	12.4	17.1	51.0	52.0	61.4	27.1	24.2	17.7	22.0	23.8	20.9
Ecuador	2008	4.8	8.4	1.6	4.1	76.6	37.8	59.2	7.7	14.0	20.1	15.7	48.2	20.7
Georgia	2010	2.5	5.5	0.9	3.2	57.7	...	51.6	15.0	...	27.6	27.3	...	20.8
Greece	2007	...	83.1	...	33.2	...	50.6	47.2	...	25.2	21.1	...	24.1	31.7
India	2009	2.6	25.2	1.9	5.4	88.9	79.3	60.1	8.0	7.9	8.6	3.0	12.8	31.3
Indonesia	2009	7.0	22.6	1.1	2.8	76.6	53.3	45.4	3.7	5.6	6.8	19.7	41.1	47.8
Iran (Islamic Republic of)	2009	25.2	34.4	12.3	8.8	46.4	59.0	78.4	26.2	10.7	5.5	27.4	30.3	16.0
Jordan	2010	16.5	42.6	6.1	13.2	50.0	56.5	31.1	18.6	32.1	21.3	31.4	11.4	47.6
Latvia	2008	8.2	31.9	3.3	13.6	57.9	71.6	69.2	17.1	12.4	13.2	25.0	16.0	17.6
Mexico	2010	13.7	23.7	7.4	9.3	65.6	35.7	47.5	18.5	...	20.6	15.9	...	31.9
Morocco	2009	9.4	19.4	6.7	12.0	53.6	52.0	50.0	33.0	...	30.9	13.4	...	19.2
Oman	2010	10.0	11.2	2.9	4.6	63.0	...	44.6	10.7	...	22.8	26.3	...	32.6
Poland	2009	10.4	39.6	...	15.7	76.8	72.0	58.6	...	17.5	16.4	...	10.5	25.0
Turkey	2009	24.2	23.4	11.2	10.2	53.3	78.2	78.5	21.6	10.8	9.3	25.1	11.1	12.1
Uruguay	2007	18.8	15.3	11.3	11.8	47.0	...	43.6	32.0	...	43.3	21.0	...	13.1

a/ At current prices.

Table 1.11

SELECTED CHARACTERISTICS OF BRANCHES, SELECTED YEARS AND ECONOMIES

Furniture (ISIC 3610)

Economy	Latest year (LY)	Value added per employee (current 1000 dollars)		Wages and salaries per employee (current 1000 dollars)		Percentage in output [a]								
						Costs of input materials and utilities			Costs of labour			Operating surplus		
		2000	LY	2000	LY	2000	2006	LY	2000	2006	LY	2000	2006	LY
Industrialized Economies														
EU														
Austria	2009	34.3	57.9	18.9	36.1	49.0	57.6	58.8	28.1	24.3	25.7	22.9	18.1	15.5
Belgium	2009	39.2	74.5	19.2	35.5	70.7	72.5	67.6	14.4	13.6	15.4	14.9	14.0	17.0
Czech Republic	2007	6.9	22.8	3.5	10.1	76.7	74.8	75.3	11.6	11.1	10.9	11.7	14.1	13.8
Denmark	2009	40.5	92.6	26.7	65.3	63.9	63.8	63.7	23.8	22.5	25.6	12.3	13.7	10.7
Estonia	2010	5.4	17.1	2.8	9.7	68.3	70.3	71.3	16.7	16.5	16.3	15.0	13.2	12.4
Finland	2009	37.0	52.6	20.1	35.4	60.3	65.4	66.1	21.6	20.0	22.8	18.1	14.6	11.1
France	2009	33.2	64.0	18.6	38.4	68.0	71.0	64.7	18.0	17.8	21.2	14.0	11.3	14.1
Germany	2009	38.9	64.1	25.3	41.6	65.8	67.3	66.0	22.2	19.5	22.1	11.9	13.2	11.9
Hungary	2009	4.6	13.7	2.3	7.5	70.0	69.4	68.4	15.1	16.0	17.2	14.9	14.6	14.4
Italy	2009	38.9	56.2	14.7	29.7	72.8	73.7	72.8	10.3	11.9	14.4	16.9	14.4	12.8
Lithuania	2010	3.8	14.3	2.2	7.3	69.2	72.0	72.8	17.7	16.9	13.8	13.1	11.1	13.4
Luxembourg	2009	31.7	71.4	20.1	39.7	48.6	60.0	52.6	32.6	30.0	26.3	18.8	10.0	21.1
Malta	2008	15.0	25.9	7.4	14.5	49.3	56.0	54.1	25.2	24.1	25.6	25.6	19.9	20.2
Netherlands	2008	40.2	81.1	22.0	45.7	64.5	66.7	66.4	19.4	19.9	18.9	16.1	13.5	14.7
Portugal	2009	11.3	19.2	6.1	12.1	66.4	68.4	63.6	18.0	18.4	22.9	15.6	13.2	13.5
Slovakia	2009	2.6	17.8	1.9	10.5	85.7	76.6	73.2	10.3	9.6	15.9	4.0	13.7	11.0
Slovenia	2010	13.1	22.8	9.8	18.5	68.6	65.0	65.2	23.5	23.8	28.2	7.8	11.2	6.6
Spain	2009	23.2	42.7	12.7	28.7	67.5	66.7	64.0	17.8	18.9	24.2	14.7	14.4	11.8
Sweden	2009	33.5	64.1	20.9	37.8	65.1	70.3	68.0	21.8	16.1	18.9	14.7	13.6	13.1
United Kingdom	2009	36.4	42.0	21.1	24.6	59.2	61.5	61.8	23.7	22.5	22.4	17.1	16.0	15.8
Other Europe														
Norway	2008	40.7	92.2	27.2	58.7	63.1	61.2	64.9	24.7	23.8	22.4	12.2	15.0	12.7
Russian Federation	2010	...	9.5	0.7	4.8	...	64.1	69.4	8.9	11.8	15.4	...	24.1	15.3
East Asia														
Japan	2010	72.3	75.0	19.5	23.8	56.0	57.6	59.2	11.8	10.9	13.0	32.2	31.5	27.8
Malaysia	2010	8.2	11.4	3.2	5.3	68.2	76.5	72.0	12.2	11.7	13.0	19.6	11.8	15.0
Republic of Korea	2008	43.6	75.4	12.5	21.7	57.4	64.9	65.9	12.2	10.8	9.8	30.4	24.3	24.3
Singapore	2010	21.2	31.5	15.2	19.7	72.2	70.1	66.9	19.8	22.4	20.7	7.9	7.5	12.4
West Asia														
Kuwait	2010	...	15.4	...	8.1	...	58.2	62.3	...	22.6	19.9	...	19.2	17.9

a/ At current prices.

Table 1.11
(continued)

SELECTED CHARACTERISTICS OF BRANCHES, SELECTED YEARS AND ECONOMIES

Furniture (ISIC 3610)

Economy	Latest year (LY)	Value added per employee (current 1000 dollars) 2000	Value added per employee (current 1000 dollars) LY	Wages and salaries per employee (current 1000 dollars) 2000	Wages and salaries per employee (current 1000 dollars) LY	Percentage in output [a] — Costs of input materials and utilities 2000	2006	LY	Costs of labour 2000	2006	LY	Operating surplus 2000	2006	LY
North America														
Canada	2009	52.5	57.9	22.2	31.4	55.1	56.6	49.2	19.0	22.0	27.6	25.9	21.4	23.2
United States of America	2008	67.9	97.0	28.4	36.2	48.2	51.0	50.1	21.7	18.6	18.6	30.2	30.4	31.3
Others														
Israel	2009	28.3	30.1	22.2	20.6	63.4	69.6	63.2	28.7	20.6	25.2	7.9	9.8	11.6
Developing & EIE														
Azerbaijan	2010	...	5.2	0.1	2.9	...	74.7	76.5	4.0	5.9	13.2	...	19.4	10.3
Brazil	2010	8.7	22.0	3.2	7.6	62.5	63.0	56.6	14.1	13.6	15.0	23.5	23.4	28.5
Bulgaria	2010	1.6	6.7	0.8	2.8	73.7	73.6	72.6	13.3	10.4	11.5	13.0	16.0	15.9
Chile	2008	18.0	23.2	5.7	9.6	51.2	56.1	55.1	15.6	18.6	18.5	33.3	25.4	26.4
China	2007	...	9.3	...	2.6	...	73.4	73.3	...	7.3	7.5	...	19.3	19.1
Cyprus	2010	20.8	38.5	10.6	23.3	51.9	53.2	52.5	24.4	26.8	28.7	23.7	20.0	18.8
Ecuador	2008	7.0	15.5	1.1	4.2	68.4	69.7	67.9	5.1	10.1	8.8	26.6	20.2	23.4
Egypt	2010	...	4.2	...	2.0	...	67.1	70.3	...	12.9	14.3	...	20.0	15.4
Eritrea	2010	3.5	5.8	1.3	0.9	54.1	52.8	44.2	16.7	13.7	8.9	29.2	33.5	47.0
Ethiopia	2009	1.9	2.7	0.7	0.6	51.9	58.8	61.5	17.1	12.2	8.5	31.1	29.0	30.0
Georgia	2010	0.4	7.1	0.2	2.9	67.5	73.3	68.0	12.8	10.8	13.2	19.7	15.9	18.8
Greece	2007	...	36.5	...	20.8	...	57.3	56.1	...	18.6	25.0	...	24.0	18.9
India	2009	4.0	7.4	1.6	3.4	81.8	79.8	80.5	7.2	9.9	8.8	11.0	10.3	10.7
Indonesia	2009	1.8	4.1	0.6	1.3	61.1	55.7	57.9	13.7	13.6	13.3	25.2	30.7	28.8
Iran (Islamic Republic of)	2010	17.1	12.6	7.4	6.7	50.9	60.1	62.7	21.2	15.5	19.8	27.9	24.4	17.5
Jordan	2010	5.6	8.3	2.2	3.0	62.0	58.0	61.5	15.2	15.5	13.9	22.8	26.5	24.6
Kyrgyzstan	2010	...	5.4	0.3	0.9	...	68.7	59.4	5.5	7.7	6.9	...	23.5	33.7
Latvia	2009	5.2	9.6	2.0	5.2	58.7	65.3	72.2	15.9	15.6	14.9	25.4	19.0	12.9
Malawi	2010	...	2.3	...	1.1	...	61.7	64.1	...	21.3	17.7	...	17.0	18.2
Mexico	2008	12.6	14.6	4.6	7.2	63.9	69.3	62.1	13.1	...	18.8	22.9	...	19.1
Mongolia	2010	1.1	5.6	0.5	2.3	58.7	69.6	78.3	17.9	12.8	9.0	23.3	17.6	12.7
Morocco	2010	10.8	16.6	5.8	9.5	48.5	71.6	68.3	27.7	...	18.1	23.9	...	13.6
Oman	2008	14.4	22.0	4.8	7.6	44.8	44.8	52.2	18.3	11.3	16.4	36.9	43.9	31.4
Philippines	2009	...	5.1	...	2.5	...	67.5	72.4	...	14.6	13.4	...	17.9	14.1
Poland	2010	7.8	18.2	...	8.3	71.6	72.0	70.4	...	12.4	13.4	...	15.5	16.1
Romania	2009	...	8.6	4.3	4.3	52.7	74.8	73.7	...	17.3	13.0	...	7.9	13.3
Turkey	2010	18.6	12.6	...	6.3	59.4	79.2	77.5	9.4	10.7	11.2	31.2	10.1	11.3
United Republic of Tanzania	2009	...	5.2	...	0.8	...	73.3	58.0	...	4.4	6.4	...	22.3	35.6
Uruguay	2007	17.8	10.0	9.2	5.8	70.1	...	73.1	15.4	...	15.7	14.4	...	11.3

a/ At current prices.

Table 1.11

SELECTED CHARACTERISTICS OF BRANCHES, SELECTED YEARS AND ECONOMIES

Manufacturing n.e.c. (ISIC 369)

Economy	Latest year (LY)	Value added per employee (current 1000 dollars)		Wages and salaries per employee (current 1000 dollars)		Percentage in output a/								
						Costs of input materials and utilities			Costs of labour			Operating surplus		
		2000	LY	2000	LY	2000	2006	LY	2000	2006	LY	2000	2006	LY
Industrialized Economies														
EU														
Austria	2009	48.0	83.6	23.3	46.2	59.3	63.0	83.3	19.8	16.7	9.3	21.0	20.4	7.5
Belgium	2009	42.0	85.8	19.0	36.0	77.6	81.8	81.3	10.1	8.0	7.9	12.3	10.2	10.9
Czech Republic	2007	6.6	23.3	3.0	8.9	64.5	63.1	64.2	16.2	13.7	13.7	19.3	23.2	22.1
Denmark	2009	...	99.4	...	62.3	...	66.8	62.7	...	21.1	23.4	...	12.0	13.9
Estonia	2010	5.4	25.7	2.8	10.7	67.2	58.6	69.4	16.9	16.8	12.8	15.9	24.6	17.8
Finland	2009	43.8	68.2	20.5	40.0	56.4	65.9	63.9	20.4	18.2	21.2	23.2	15.9	14.9
France	2009	37.1	76.3	20.1	44.6	68.4	66.9	62.1	17.1	18.6	22.2	14.5	14.5	15.7
Germany	2009	35.3	69.9	21.8	36.6	57.0	57.5	58.5	26.6	22.5	21.8	16.4	20.1	19.8
Hungary	2009	4.4	18.8	2.3	8.6	65.4	64.0	64.8	17.7	15.4	16.2	16.9	20.6	19.1
Italy	2009	37.9	58.7	14.4	28.5	74.6	72.6	73.0	9.7	10.4	13.1	15.8	17.0	13.9
Lithuania	2010	2.8	14.9	1.9	6.8	62.8	59.9	60.8	24.9	19.2	17.8	12.3	20.9	21.4
Luxembourg	2008	38.0	78.5	24.2	52.3	77.1	57.1	50.0	14.6	28.6	33.3	8.3	14.3	16.7
Malta	2008	39.9	65.3	12.4	27.5	56.9	49.0	57.8	13.4	19.5	17.8	29.7	31.5	24.4
Netherlands	2008	46.9	96.6	21.4	50.2	62.9	66.5	66.7	16.9	16.9	17.3	20.2	16.6	16.0
Portugal	2009	14.3	22.0	7.5	12.5	70.3	70.7	67.3	15.6	16.6	18.6	14.2	12.6	14.2
Slovakia	2009	2.9	19.7	1.8	10.4	69.8	67.1	73.2	18.9	16.5	14.1	11.3	16.5	12.7
Slovenia	2010	12.5	39.0	8.8	22.4	65.2	66.7	65.5	24.7	17.4	19.8	10.1	16.0	14.7
Spain	2009	28.4	53.8	14.1	32.6	64.5	65.6	65.5	17.7	17.7	20.9	17.8	16.7	13.6
Sweden	2009	43.0	75.3	21.5	36.4	60.0	...	62.3	20.0	...	18.2	20.0	16.7	19.5
United Kingdom	2009	46.4	77.2	19.7	38.9	56.9	56.0	57.1	18.3	22.7	21.6	24.8	21.3	21.3
Other Europe														
Norway	2008	44.6	99.6	29.1	60.1	51.5	60.3	59.6	31.6	27.0	24.4	16.9	12.7	16.1
Russian Federation	2010	...	29.5	0.8	6.2	...	65.7	62.4	12.7	8.2	8.0	...	26.2	29.6
East Asia														
Japan	2010	86.4	108.1	19.4	26.7	60.3	62.3	58.4	8.9	9.0	10.3	30.8	28.7	31.4
Malaysia	2010	9.3	15.3	3.7	5.9	67.9	80.5	78.6	12.6	10.3	8.3	19.5	9.3	13.1
Republic of Korea	2008	37.0	56.1	12.4	19.7	55.4	57.4	60.1	14.9	15.9	14.0	29.6	26.8	25.8
Singapore	2010	38.1	33.6	17.7	23.0	71.0	82.4	81.6	13.4	12.5	12.7	15.6	5.1	5.8
West Asia														
Kuwait	2010	...	17.0	...	7.1	...	72.2	78.5	...	12.1	9.0	...	15.7	12.6

a/ At current prices.

Table 1.11
(continued)

SELECTED CHARACTERISTICS OF BRANCHES, SELECTED YEARS AND ECONOMIES

Manufacturing n.e.c. (ISIC 369)

Economy	Latest year (LY)	Value added per employee (current 1000 dollars) 2000	Value added per employee LY	Wages and salaries per employee (current 1000 dollars) 2000	Wages and salaries per employee LY	Costs of input materials and utilities 2000	Costs of input materials and utilities 2006	Costs of input materials and utilities LY	Costs of labour 2000	Costs of labour 2006	Costs of labour LY	Operating surplus 2000	Operating surplus 2006	Operating surplus LY
North America														
Canada	2008	44.6	68.9	19.3	36.3	50.7	56.1	60.6	21.4	25.0	20.8	27.9	18.8	18.7
United States of America	2008	77.0	129.2	29.7	40.5	46.2	44.4	44.6	20.8	17.9	17.4	33.0	37.8	38.0
Others														
Israel	2009	26.9	26.8	19.1	20.5	70.0	69.9	69.6	21.4	19.4	23.2	8.7	10.7	7.2
Developing & EIE														
Azerbaijan	2010	...	8.0	0.2	0.7	...	74.7	32.1	6.6	7.1	6.2	...	18.3	61.7
Brazil	2010	13.6	28.1	4.0	8.9	42.4	43.3	43.9	16.8	18.8	17.6	40.8	37.8	38.5
Bulgaria	2010	2.0	11.2	1.0	4.0	68.4	...	66.8	16.0	...	11.7	15.5	...	21.5
Chile	2008	27.8	31.3	7.7	11.8	46.2	50.4	56.1	14.8	14.1	16.5	38.9	35.5	27.4
China	2007	...	7.7	...	2.5	...	72.6	73.3	...	8.5	8.5	...	18.8	18.2
Cyprus	2010	20.5	40.9	8.9	23.3	63.3	55.0	56.9	15.8	25.4	24.6	20.9	19.6	18.5
Ecuador	2008	5.4	22.9	1.2	5.9	63.8	60.5	57.5	7.9	12.1	10.8	28.4	27.4	31.6
Georgia	2010	...	5.9	...	3.0	...	60.2	61.2	...	24.5	20.1	...	15.3	18.7
Greece	2007	...	31.8	...	20.2	...	58.1	56.4	...	18.8	27.7	...	23.1	15.9
India	2009	4.4	8.0	1.1	2.2	81.5	89.2	95.7	4.8	3.1	1.2	13.7	7.7	3.1
Indonesia	2009	2.6	5.1	0.7	1.3	57.9	50.4	48.6	10.7	10.2	13.1	31.4	39.4	38.2
Iran (Islamic Republic of)	2009	19.0	13.9	7.4	4.9	62.7	56.9	73.5	14.5	15.3	9.4	22.8	27.8	17.2
Jordan	2010	4.8	20.3	2.9	3.6	49.5	66.6	80.6	30.7	7.2	3.4	19.8	26.2	16.0
Latvia	2010	5.0	12.2	2.3	5.5	40.3	57.4	60.4	27.8	17.5	18.1	31.9	25.1	21.5
Malawi	2009	3.4	11.2	1.6	4.4	68.4	63.9	50.2	15.2	22.4	19.6	16.4	13.8	30.2
Mexico	2010	19.1	15.9	5.6	8.8	53.6	66.2	48.0	13.6	...	28.7	32.8	...	23.3
Mongolia	2008	0.8	1.7	0.4	1.0	67.6	67.5	74.2	17.0	16.5	15.5	15.4	16.0	10.3
Morocco	2010	11.3	15.3	6.4	8.0	61.9	70.6	71.4	21.6	...	15.0	16.5	...	13.6
Oman	2010	12.6	16.1	4.9	7.3	83.3	51.9	66.6	6.5	13.7	15.1	10.2	34.4	18.3
Philippines	2008	...	6.0	...	2.8	...	69.7	69.5	...	16.1	14.3	...	14.2	16.2
Poland	2009	8.9	21.6	...	7.9	66.3	70.4	66.7	...	12.8	12.2	...	16.8	21.2
Romania	2010	...	9.8	...	4.6	57.7	70.1	62.7	...	18.7	17.5	...	11.2	19.8
The f. Yugosl. Rep of Macedonia	2010	...	8.6	...	3.7	...	45.9	35.1	...	23.6	27.6	...	30.5	37.3
Turkey	2009	31.2	20.6	4.3	6.9	59.1	87.3	88.6	5.7	5.2	3.8	35.3	7.5	7.6
Uruguay	2007	14.1	12.3	8.6	6.6	52.9	...	58.2	28.7	...	22.2	18.4	...	19.6

a/ Percentage in output

a/ At current prices.

Part II
COUNTRY TABLES

- 187 -

Countries/areas for which data were presented in previous editions of the *Yearbook* but not in part II of the current edition

Country/area	Latest edition in which data were presented	Country/area	Latest edition in which data were presented	Country/area	Latest edition in which data were presented
Algeria	2001	Gabon	1998	Panama	2009
Angola	1997	Gambia	2012	Papua New Guinea	2006
Argentina	2007	Ghana	2007	Paraguay	2008
Aruba	2004	Greece	2011	Puerto Rico	2009
Bahrain	1996	Grenada	1999	Republic of Korea	2012
Bangladesh	2004	Guatemala	2009	Rwanda	2002
Barbados	2001	Haiti	2001	Saint Lucia	2001
Belize	1995	Honduras	1999	Saint Vincent and the Grenadines	2004
Benin	2003	Iceland	2011	Saudi Arabia	2009
Bolivia (Plurinational State of)	2006	Indonesia	2012	Serbia and Montenegro	2005
Bosnia and Herzegovina	1999	Iraq	2001	Sierra Leone	2011
Burkina Faso	2001	Jamaica	2009	Solomon Islands	1999
Burundi	1995	Kazakhstan	2010	Sudan	2006
Cambodia	2004	Lao People's Democratic Republic	2002	Suriname	2007
Cameroon	2012	Lebanon	2012	Swaziland	1999
Cape Verde	2000	Lesotho	2012	Switzerland	2011
Central African Republic	1998	Madagascar	2009	Tajikistan	2011
Chad	1998	Malawi	2012	Thailand	2010
Chile	2012	Maldives	2004	Tonga	2007
Congo	2012	Malta	2011	Trinidad and Tobago	2010
Cook Islands	2010	Mongolia	2011	Tunisia	2011
Côte d'Ivoire	2000	Mozambique	2003	Turkmenistan	2003
Curaçao	2012	Namibia	1998	Uganda	2009
Czech Republic	2011	Nepal	2012	Uruguay	2012
Dominican Republic	2000	Netherlands Antilles	2011	Venezuela (Bolivarian Republic of)	2002
Ecuador	2012	Niger	2006	Yemen	2009
El Salvador	2001	Nigeria	2007	Zambia	1997
Ethiopia	2012	Pakistan	2010	Zimbabwe	2003

Afghanistan

Supplier of information:
Central Statistics Office, Kabul.

Basic source of data:
Survey on registered establishments; administrative source.

Major deviations from ISIC (Revision 3):
None reported.

Reference period:
Calendar year.

Scope:
All registered establishments.

Method of data collection:
Direct interview in the field.

Type of enumeration:
Complete enumeration.

Adjusted for non-response:
Yes.

Concepts and definitions of variables:
No deviations from the standard UN concepts and definitions are reported.

Related national publications:
None reported.

Afghanistan

		Number of establishments (number)					Number of employees (number)					Wages and salaries paid to employees (thousands of Afghan Afghani)				
ISIC	Industry	Note	2007	2008	2009	2010	Note	2007	2008	2009	2010	Note	2007	2008	2009	2010
151	Processed meat,fish,fruit,vegetables,fats															
1511	Processing/preserving of meat															
1512	Processing/preserving of fish															
1513	Processing/preserving of fruit & vegetables															
1514	Vegetable and animal oils and fats															
1520	Dairy products															
153	Grain mill products; starches; animal feeds															
1531	Grain mill products															
1532	Starches and starch products															
1533	Prepared animal feeds															
154	Other food products															
1541	Bakery products		206	212	199	195		5300	5431	5400	4893		305280	322376	343440	322938
1542	Sugar															
1543	Cocoa, chocolate and sugar confectionery															
1544	Macaroni, noodles & similar products															
1549	Other food products n.e.c.															
155	Beverages															
1551	Distilling, rectifying & blending of spirits															
1552	Wines															
1553	Malt liquors and malt															
1554	Soft drinks; mineral waters															
1600	Tobacco products															
171	Spinning, weaving and finishing of textiles															
1711	Textile fibre preparation; textile weaving															
1712	Finishing of textiles															
172	Other textiles															
1721	Made-up textile articles, except apparel															
1722	Carpets and rugs		57	64	66	66		6700	6917	6902	6820		385920	423324	438969	450120
1723	Cordage, rope, twine and netting															
1729	Other textiles n.e.c.															
1730	Knitted and crocheted fabrics and articles															
1810	Wearing apparel, except fur apparel															
1820	Dressing & dyeing of fur; processing of fur															
191	Tanning, dressing and processing of leather															
1911	Tanning and dressing of leather															
1912	Luggage, handbags, etc.; saddlery & harness															
1920	Footwear															
2010	Sawmilling and planing of wood															
202	Products of wood, cork, straw, etc.															
2021	Veneer sheets, plywood, particle board, etc.															
2022	Builders' carpentry and joinery															
2023	Wooden containers															
2029	Other wood products; articles of cork/straw		50	45	37	32		1600	1520	1497	1405		92160	96672	95202	92730
210	Paper and paper products															
2101	Pulp, paper and paperboard															
2102	Corrugated paper and paperboard															
2109	Other articles of paper and paperboard															
221	Publishing															
2211	Publishing of books and other publications		60	63	63	70		2290	2290	2290	2307		131904	140148	145644	152262
2212	Publishing of newspapers, journals, etc.															
2213	Publishing of recorded media															
2219	Other publishing															

222	Printing and related service activities	...	...	...	...	...	...	...	...	...	...	...	...
2221	Printing	...	...	...	...	...	...	...	...	...	...	...	...
2222	Service activities related to printing	...	...	...	...	...	...	...	...	...	...	...	...
2230	Reproduction of recorded media	...	...	...	...	...	...	...	...	...	...	...	...
2310	Coke oven products	...	...	...	...	...	...	...	...	...	...	...	...
2320	Refined petroleum products	...	...	...	...	...	...	...	...	...	...	...	...
2330	Processing of nuclear fuel	...	...	...	...	...	...	...	...	...	...	...	...
241	Basic chemicals	...	...	...	...	...	...	...	...	...	...	...	...
2411	Basic chemicals, except fertilizers	...	...	...	...	...	...	...	...	...	...	...	...
2412	Fertilizers and nitrogen compounds	...	...	...	...	...	...	...	...	...	...	...	...
2413	Plastics in primary forms; synthetic rubber	...	...	...	...	...	...	...	...	...	...	...	...
242	Other chemicals	12	14	11	13	1920	2133	2133	2131	110592	130536	135028	140646
2421	Pesticides and other agro-chemical products	...	...	...	...	...	...	...	...	...	...	...	...
2422	Paints, varnishes, printing ink and mastics	...	...	...	...	...	...	...	...	...	...	...	...
2423	Pharmaceuticals, medicinal chemicals, etc.	...	...	...	...	...	...	...	...	...	...	...	...
2424	Soap, cleaning & cosmetic preparations	...	...	...	...	...	...	...	...	...	...	...	...
2429	Other chemical products n.e.c.	...	...	...	...	...	...	...	...	...	...	...	...
2430	Man-made fibres	...	...	...	...	...	...	...	...	...	...	...	...
251	Rubber products	...	...	...	...	...	...	...	...	...	...	...	...
2511	Rubber tyres and tubes	...	...	...	...	...	...	...	...	...	...	...	...
2519	Other rubber products	...	...	...	...	...	...	...	...	...	...	...	...
2520	Plastic products	61	58	58	55	2500	2030	2030	2001	132480	124236	129168	132066
2610	Glass and glass products	...	...	...	...	...	...	...	...	...	...	...	...
269	Non-metallic mineral products n.e.c.	...	...	...	...	...	...	...	...	...	...	...	...
2691	Pottery, china and earthenware	...	...	...	...	...	...	...	...	...	...	...	...
2692	Refractory ceramic products	...	...	...	...	...	...	...	...	...	...	...	...
2693	Struct.non-refractory clay; ceramic products	...	...	...	...	...	...	...	...	...	...	...	...
2694	Cement, lime and plaster	...	...	...	...	...	...	...	...	...	...	...	...
2695	Articles of concrete, cement and plaster	93	101	105	105	2400	5503	5510	5497	270720	326780	385190	425670
2696	Cutting, shaping & finishing of stone	...	...	...	...	...	...	...	...	...	...	...	...
2699	Other non-metallic mineral products n.e.c.	...	...	...	...	...	...	...	...	...	...	...	...
2710	Basic iron and steel	...	...	...	...	...	...	...	...	...	...	...	...
2720	Basic precious and non-ferrous metals	...	...	...	...	...	...	...	...	...	...	...	...
273	Casting of metals	...	...	...	...	...	...	...	...	...	...	...	...
2731	Casting of iron and steel	...	...	...	...	...	...	...	...	...	...	...	...
2732	Casting of non-ferrous metals	...	...	...	...	...	...	...	...	...	...	...	...
281	Struct.metal products;tanks;steam generators	...	...	...	...	...	...	...	...	...	...	...	...
2811	Structural metal products	...	...	...	...	...	...	...	...	...	...	...	...
2812	Tanks, reservoirs and containers of metal	...	...	...	...	...	...	...	...	...	...	...	...
2813	Steam generators	...	...	...	...	...	...	...	...	...	...	...	...
289	Other metal products; metal working services	86	78	80	75	2570	2440	2432	2392	148042	149328	154675	157872
2891	Metal forging/pressing/stamping/roll-forming	...	...	...	...	...	...	...	...	...	...	...	...
2892	Treatment & coating of metals	...	...	...	...	...	...	...	...	...	...	...	...
2893	Cutlery, hand tools and general hardware	...	...	...	...	...	...	...	...	...	...	...	...
2899	Other fabricated metal products n.e.c.	...	...	...	...	...	...	...	...	...	...	...	...
291	General purpose machinery	...	...	...	...	...	...	...	...	...	...	...	...
2911	Engines & turbines (not for transport equipment)	...	...	...	...	...	...	...	...	...	...	...	...
2912	Pumps, compressors, taps and valves	...	...	...	...	...	...	...	...	...	...	...	...
2913	Bearings, gears, gearing & driving elements	...	...	...	...	...	...	...	...	...	...	...	...
2914	Ovens, furnaces and furnace burners	...	...	...	...	...	...	...	...	...	...	...	...
2915	Lifting and handling equipment	...	...	...	...	...	...	...	...	...	...	...	...
2919	Other general purpose machinery	...	...	...	...	...	...	...	...	...	...	...	...
292	Special purpose machinery	...	...	...	...	...	...	...	...	...	...	...	...
2921	Agricultural and forestry machinery	...	...	...	...	...	...	...	...	...	...	...	...
2922	Machine tools	...	...	...	...	...	...	...	...	...	...	...	...
2923	Machinery for metallurgy	...	...	...	...	...	...	...	...	...	...	...	...
2924	Machinery for mining & construction	...	...	...	...	...	...	...	...	...	...	...	...
2925	Food/beverage/tobacco processing machinery	...	...	...	...	...	...	...	...	...	...	...	...
2926	Machinery for textile, apparel and leather	...	...	...	...	...	...	...	...	...	...	...	...
2927	Weapons and ammunition	...	...	...	...	...	...	...	...	...	...	...	...
2929	Other special purpose machinery	...	...	...	...	...	...	...	...	...	...	...	...

continued

Afghanistan

ISIC Revision 3

ISIC	Industry	Number of establishments (number)					Number of employees (number)					Wages and salaries paid to employees (thousands of Afghan Afghani)				
		Note	2007	2008	2009	2010	Note	2007	2008	2009	2010	Note	2007	2008	2009	2010
2930	Domestic appliances n.e.c.		...	...	...	...		...	...	...	...		...	...	...	...
3000	Office, accounting and computing machinery		...	...	...	...		...	...	...	...		...	...	...	...
3110	Electric motors, generators and transformers		...	...	...	...		...	...	...	...		...	...	...	...
3120	Electricity distribution & control apparatus		...	...	...	...		...	...	...	...		...	...	...	...
3130	Insulated wire and cable		...	...	...	...		...	...	...	...		...	...	...	...
3140	Accumulators, primary cells and batteries		...	...	...	...		...	...	...	...		...	...	...	...
3150	Lighting equipment and electric lamps		...	...	...	...		...	...	...	...		...	...	...	...
3190	Other electrical equipment n.e.c.		...	...	...	...		...	...	...	...		...	...	...	...
3210	Electronic valves, tubes, etc.		...	...	...	...		...	...	...	...		...	...	...	...
3220	TV/radio transmitters; line comm. apparatus		...	...	...	...		...	...	...	...		...	...	...	...
3230	TV and radio receivers and associated goods		...	...	...	...		...	...	...	...		...	...	...	...
331	Medical, measuring, testing appliances, etc.		...	...	...	...		...	...	...	...		...	...	...	...
3311	Medical, surgical and orthopaedic equipment		...	...	...	...		...	...	...	...		...	...	...	...
3312	Measuring/testing/navigating appliances,etc.		...	...	...	...		...	...	...	...		...	...	...	...
3313	Industrial process control equipment		...	...	...	...		...	...	...	...		...	...	...	...
3320	Optical instruments & photographic equipment		...	...	...	...		...	...	...	...		...	...	...	...
3330	Watches and clocks		...	...	...	...		...	...	...	...		...	...	...	...
3410	Motor vehicles		...	...	...	...		...	...	...	...		...	...	...	...
3420	Automobile bodies, trailers & semi-trailers		...	...	...	...		...	...	...	...		...	...	...	...
3430	Parts/accessories for automobiles		...	...	...	...		...	...	...	...		...	...	...	...
351	Building and repairing of ships and boats		...	...	...	...		...	...	...	...		...	...	...	...
3511	Building and repairing of ships		...	...	...	...		...	...	...	...		...	...	...	...
3512	Building/repairing of pleasure/sport. boats		...	...	...	...		...	...	...	...		...	...	...	...
3520	Railway/tramway locomotives & rolling stock		...	...	...	...		...	...	...	...		...	...	...	...
3530	Aircraft and spacecraft		...	...	...	...		...	...	...	...		...	...	...	...
359	Transport equipment n.e.c.		...	...	...	...		...	...	...	...		...	...	...	...
3591	Motorcycles		...	...	...	...		...	...	...	...		...	...	...	...
3592	Bicycles and invalid carriages		...	...	...	...		...	...	...	...		...	...	...	...
3599	Other transport equipment n.e.c.		...	...	...	...		...	...	...	...		...	...	...	...
3610	Furniture		...	...	...	...		...	...	...	...		...	...	...	...
369	Manufacturing n.e.c.		...	...	...	...		...	...	...	...		...	...	...	...
3691	Jewellery and related articles		...	...	...	...		...	...	...	...		...	...	...	...
3692	Musical instruments		...	...	...	...		...	...	...	...		...	...	...	...
3693	Sports goods		...	...	...	...		...	...	...	...		...	...	...	...
3694	Games and toys		...	...	...	...		...	...	...	...		...	...	...	...
3699	Other manufacturing n.e.c.		183	196	192	195		6327	7056	7042	8254		364428	431832	447871	544764
3710	Recycling of metal waste and scrap		...	...	...	...		...	...	...	...		...	...	...	...
3720	Recycling of non-metal waste and scrap		...	...	...	...		...	...	...	...		...	...	...	...
D	Total manufacturing	a/	808	831	811	806	a/	31607	35320	35236	35700	a/	1941526	2145232	2275187	2419068

a/ Sum of available data.

Afghanistan

Afghanistan

ISIC	Industry	Output (millions of Afghan Afghani)					Value added (millions of Afghan Afghani)					Gross fixed capital formation (millions of Afghan Afghani)		
		Note	2007	2008	2009	2010	Note	2007	2008	2009	2010	Note	2009	2010
151	Processed meat,fish,fruit,vegetables,fats		...	...	...	...		...	...	...	...		...	...
1511	Processing/preserving of meat		...	...	...	...		...	...	...	...		...	...
1512	Processing/preserving of fish		...	...	...	...		...	...	...	...		...	...
1513	Processing/preserving of fruit & vegetables		...	...	...	...		...	...	...	...		...	...
1514	Vegetable and animal oils and fats		...	...	...	...		...	...	...	...		...	...
1520	Dairy products		...	...	...	...		...	...	...	...		...	...
153	Grain mill products; starches; animal feeds		...	...	...	...		...	...	...	...		...	...
1531	Grain mill products		...	...	...	...		...	...	...	...		...	...
1532	Starches and starch products		...	...	...	...		...	...	...	...		...	...
1533	Prepared animal feeds		1804	1791	2269	1870		...	...	...	...		...	...
154	Other food products		...	...	...	...		...	...	...	...		...	...
1541	Bakery products		...	...	...	...		...	...	...	...		...	...
1542	Sugar		...	...	...	...		...	...	...	...		...	...
1543	Cocoa, chocolate and sugar confectionery		...	...	...	...		...	...	...	...		...	...
1544	Macaroni, noodles & similar products		...	...	...	...		...	...	...	...		...	...
1549	Other food products n.e.c.		...	...	...	...		...	...	...	...		...	...
155	Beverages		...	...	...	...		...	...	...	...		...	...
1551	Distilling, rectifying & blending of spirits		...	...	...	...		...	...	...	...		...	...
1552	Wines		...	...	...	...		...	...	...	...		...	...
1553	Malt liquors and malt		...	...	...	...		...	...	...	...		...	...
1554	Soft drinks; mineral waters		...	...	...	...		...	...	...	...		...	...
1600	Tobacco products		...	...	...	...		...	...	...	...		...	...
171	Spinning, weaving and finishing of textiles		...	...	...	...		...	...	...	...		...	...
1711	Textile fibre preparation; textile weaving		...	...	...	...		...	...	...	...		...	...
1712	Finishing of textiles		...	...	...	...		...	...	...	...		...	...
172	Other textiles		...	...	...	...		...	...	...	...		...	...
1721	Made-up textile articles, except apparel		...	...	...	...		...	...	...	...		...	...
1722	Carpets and rugs		997	915	445	965		...	...	...	...		...	...
1723	Cordage, rope, twine and netting		...	...	...	...		...	...	...	...		...	...
1729	Other textiles n.e.c.		...	...	...	...		...	...	...	...		...	...
1730	Knitted and crocheted fabrics and articles		...	...	...	...		...	...	...	...		...	...
1810	Wearing apparel, except fur apparel		...	...	...	...		...	...	...	...		...	...
1820	Dressing & dyeing of fur; processing of fur		...	...	...	...		...	...	...	...		...	...
191	Tanning, dressing and processing of leather		...	...	...	...		...	...	...	...		...	...
1911	Tanning and dressing of leather		...	...	...	...		...	...	...	...		...	...
1912	Luggage, handbags, etc.; saddlery & harness		...	...	...	...		...	...	...	...		...	...
1920	Footwear		...	...	...	...		...	...	...	...		...	...
2010	Sawmilling and planing of wood		...	...	...	...		...	...	...	...		...	...
202	Products of wood, cork, straw, etc.		...	...	...	...		...	...	...	...		...	...
2021	Veneer sheets, plywood, particle board, etc.		...	...	...	...		...	...	...	...		...	...
2022	Builders' carpentry and joinery		...	...	...	...		...	...	...	...		...	...
2023	Wooden containers		...	...	...	...		...	...	...	...		...	...
2029	Other wood products; articles of cork/straw		392	366	371	435		...	...	...	...		...	...
210	Paper and paper products		...	...	...	...		...	...	...	...		...	...
2101	Pulp, paper and paperboard		...	...	...	...		...	...	...	...		...	...
2102	Corrugated paper and paperboard		...	...	...	...		...	...	...	...		...	...
2109	Other articles of paper and paperboard		...	...	...	...		...	...	...	...		...	...
221	Publishing		180	180	193	240		...	...	...	...		...	...
2211	Publishing of books and other publications		...	...	...	...		...	...	...	...		...	...
2212	Publishing of newspapers, journals, etc.		...	...	...	...		...	...	...	...		...	...
2213	Publishing of recorded media		...	...	...	...		...	...	...	...		...	...
2219	Other publishing		...	...	...	...		...	...	...	...		...	...

continued

Afghanistan

ISIC	Industry	Output Note	2007	2008	2009	2010	Value added Note	2007	2008	2009	2010	GFCF Note	2009	2010
222	Printing and related service activities		...	...	...	...		...	...	...	...		...	...
2221	Printing		...	...	...	...		...	...	...	...		...	...
2222	Service activities related to printing		...	...	...	...		...	...	...	...		...	...
2230	Reproduction of recorded media		...	...	...	...		...	...	...	...		...	...
2310	Coke oven products		...	...	...	...		...	...	...	...		...	...
2320	Refined petroleum products		...	...	...	...		...	...	...	...		...	...
2330	Processing of nuclear fuel		...	...	...	...		...	...	...	...		...	...
241	Basic chemicals		...	...	...	...		...	...	...	...		...	...
2411	Basic chemicals, except fertilizers		...	...	...	...		...	...	...	...		...	...
2412	Fertilizers and nitrogen compounds		...	...	...	...		...	...	...	...		...	...
2413	Plastics in primary forms; synthetic rubber		...	...	...	...		...	...	...	...		...	...
242	Other chemicals		240	817	878	889		...	...	...	...		...	...
2421	Pesticides and other agro-chemical products		...	...	...	...		...	...	...	...		...	...
2422	Paints, varnishes, printing ink and mastics		...	...	...	...		...	...	...	...		...	...
2423	Pharmaceuticals, medicinal chemicals, etc.		...	...	...	...		...	...	...	...		...	...
2424	Soap, cleaning & cosmetic preparations		...	...	...	...		...	...	...	...		...	...
2429	Other chemical products n.e.c.		...	...	...	...		...	...	...	...		...	...
2430	Man-made fibres		...	...	...	...		...	...	...	...		...	...
251	Rubber products		...	...	...	...		...	...	...	...		...	...
2511	Rubber tyres and tubes		...	...	...	...		...	...	...	...		...	...
2519	Other rubber products		...	...	...	...		...	...	...	...		...	...
2520	Plastic products		817	878	921	1057		...	...	...	...		...	...
2610	Glass and glass products		...	...	...	...		...	...	...	...		...	...
269	Non-metallic mineral products n.e.c.		...	...	...	...		...	...	...	...		...	...
2691	Pottery, china and earthenware		...	...	...	...		...	...	...	...		...	...
2692	Refractory ceramic products		...	...	...	...		...	...	...	...		...	...
2693	Struct.non-refractory clay; ceramic products		...	...	...	...		...	...	...	...		...	...
2694	Cement, lime and plaster		1743	1762	1845	1973		...	...	...	...		...	...
2695	Articles of concrete, cement and plaster		...	...	...	...		...	...	...	...		...	...
2696	Cutting, shaping & finishing of stone		...	...	...	...		...	...	...	...		...	...
2699	Other non-metallic mineral products n.e.c.		...	...	...	...		...	...	...	...		...	...
2710	Basic iron and steel		...	...	...	...		...	...	...	...		...	...
2720	Basic precious and non-ferrous metals		...	...	...	...		...	...	...	...		...	...
273	Casting of metals		...	...	...	...		...	...	...	...		...	...
2731	Casting of iron and steel		...	...	...	...		...	...	...	...		...	...
2732	Casting of non-ferrous metals		...	...	...	...		...	...	...	...		...	...
281	Struct.metal products;tanks;steam generators		...	...	...	...		...	...	...	...		...	...
2811	Structural metal products		...	...	...	...		...	...	...	...		...	...
2812	Tanks, reservoirs and containers of metal		...	...	...	...		...	...	...	...		...	...
2813	Steam generators		...	...	...	...		...	...	...	...		...	...
289	Other metal products; metal working services		392	391	382	422		...	...	...	...		...	...
2891	Metal forging/pressing/stamping/roll-forming		...	...	...	...		...	...	...	...		...	...
2892	Treatment & coating of metals		...	...	...	...		...	...	...	...		...	...
2893	Cutlery, hand tools and general hardware		...	...	...	...		...	...	...	...		...	...
2899	Other fabricated metal products n.e.c.		...	...	...	...		...	...	...	...		...	...
291	General purpose machinery		...	...	...	...		...	...	...	...		...	...
2911	Engines & turbines (not for transport equipment)		...	...	...	...		...	...	...	...		...	...
2912	Pumps, compressors, taps and valves		...	...	...	...		...	...	...	...		...	...
2913	Bearings, gears, gearing & driving elements		...	...	...	...		...	...	...	...		...	...
2914	Ovens, furnaces and furnace burners		...	...	...	...		...	...	...	...		...	...
2915	Lifting and handling equipment		...	...	...	...		...	...	...	...		...	...
2919	Other general purpose machinery		...	...	...	...		...	...	...	...		...	...

Output — (millions of Afghan Afghani)
Value added — (millions of Afghan Afghani)
Gross fixed capital formation — (millions of Afghan Afghani)

292	Special purpose machinery				
2921	Agricultural and forestry machinery				
2922	Machine tools				
2923	Machinery for metallurgy				
2924	Machinery for mining & construction				
2925	Food/beverage/tobacco processing machinery				
2926	Machinery for textile, apparel and leather				
2927	Weapons and ammunition				
2929	Other special purpose machinery				
2930	Domestic appliances n.e.c.				
3000	Office, accounting and computing machinery				
3110	Electric motors, generators and transformers				
3120	Electricity distribution & control apparatus				
3130	Insulated wire and cable				
3140	Accumulators, primary cells and batteries				
3150	Lighting equipment and electric lamps				
3190	Other electrical equipment n.e.c.				
3210	Electronic valves, tubes, etc.				
3220	TV/radio transmitters; line comm. apparatus				
3230	TV and radio receivers and associated goods				
331	Medical, measuring, testing appliances, etc.				
3311	Medical, surgical and orthopaedic equipment				
3312	Measuring/testing/navigating appliances,etc.				
3313	Industrial process control equipment				
3320	Optical instruments & photographic equipment				
3330	Watches and clocks				
3410	Motor vehicles				
3420	Automobile bodies, trailers & semi-trailers				
3430	Parts/accessories for automobiles				
3510	Building and repairing of ships and boats				
3511	Building and repairing of ships				
3512	Building/repairing of pleasure/sport. boats				
3520	Railway/tramway locomotives & rolling stock				
3530	Aircraft and spacecraft				
359	Transport equipment n.e.c.				
3591	Motorcycles				
3592	Bicycles and invalid carriages				
3599	Other transport equipment n.e.c.				
3610	Furniture				
369	Manufacturing n.e.c.				
3691	Jewellery and related articles				
3692	Musical instruments				
3693	Sports goods				
3694	Games and toys				
3699	Other manufacturing n.e.c.	1268	1448	1468	1519
3710	Recycling of metal waste and scrap				
3720	Recycling of non-metal waste and scrap				
D	Total manufacturing a/	7833	8548	8772	9370

a/ Sum of available data.

Albania

Supplier of information:
Institute of Statistics, Tirana.

Basic source of data:
Structural business statistics; annual survey.

Major deviations from ISIC (Revision 3):
The data presented in ISIC (Revision 3) were originally classified according to NACE (Revision 1).

Reference period:
Calendar year.

Scope:
All registered enterprises.

Method of data collection:
Direct interview in the field.

Type of enumeration:
Enterprises with five or more employees are completely enumerated; enterprises with less than five employees are sampled.

Adjusted for non-response:
Yes.

Concepts and definitions of variables:
Output includes deductible subsidies and indirect taxes and is valued at basic prices.
Value added is valued at basic prices.

Related national publications:
Structural Survey Economic Enterprises - 2010, published by the Institute of Statistics, Tirana.

Albania

ISIC	Industry	Ent. Note	Ent. 2007	Ent. 2008	Ent. 2009	Ent. 2010	Emp. Note	Emp. 2007	Emp. 2008	Emp. 2009	Emp. 2010	Wage Note	Wage 2007	Wage 2008	Wage 2009	Wage 2010
	ISIC Revision 3		**Number of enterprises (number)**					**Number of employees (number)**					**Wages and salaries paid to employees (millions of Albanian Leks)**			
151	Processed meat,fish,fruit,vegetables,fats	a/	144	168	134	237	a/	1794	1849	2029	2253	a/	427.1	554.1	524.8	572.7
1511	Processing/preserving of meat	a/	78	100	62	116	a/	1392	1517	1659	1756	a/	321.7	438.7	416.7	434.9
1512	Processing/preserving of fish		…	…	…	…		…	…	…	…		…	…	…	…
1513	Processing/preserving of fruit & vegetables		28	33	33	50		141	159	172	267		29.9	50.2	45.8	63.8
1514	Vegetable and animal oils and fats		37	35	39	70		261	173	197	230		75.5	65.2	62.3	74.0
1520	Dairy products		333	294	280	450		399	505	304	426		83.0	163.1	79.7	110.2
153	Grain mill products; starches; animal feeds	b/	1726	2085	1979	2106	b/	2894	2462	3082	2725	b/	695.9	816.8	902.0	775.5
1531	Grain mill products		…	…	…	…		…	…	…	…		…	…	…	…
1532	Starches and starch products		…	…	…	…		…	…	…	…		…	…	…	…
1533	Prepared animal feeds		…	…	…	…		…	…	…	…		…	…	…	…
154	Other food products	b/	…	…	…	…	b/	…	…	…	…	b/	…	…	…	…
1541	Bakery products		…	…	…	…		…	…	…	…		…	…	…	…
1542	Sugar		…	…	…	…		…	…	…	…		…	…	…	…
1543	Cocoa, chocolate and sugar confectionery		…	…	…	…		…	…	…	…		…	…	…	…
1544	Macaroni, noodles & similar products		…	…	…	…		…	…	…	…		…	…	…	…
1549	Other food products n.e.c.		…	…	…	…		…	…	…	…		…	…	…	…
155	Beverages		175	261	154	191		1445	1427	1417	1804		507.5	576.6	528.2	708.4
1551	Distilling, rectifying & blending of spirits		…	…	…	…		…	…	…	…		…	…	…	…
1552	Wines		…	…	…	…		…	…	…	…		…	…	…	…
1553	Malt liquors and malt		…	…	…	…		…	…	…	…		…	…	…	…
1554	Soft drinks; mineral waters		…	…	…	…		…	…	…	…		…	…	…	…
1600	Tobacco products	c/	4	3	5	11	c/	174	147	123	185	c/	43.3	41.2	30.4	48.2
171	Spinning, weaving and finishing of textiles		870	834	708	871		12639	13162	11845	14105		2637.8	3658.5	2875.5	3537.5
1711	Textile fibre preparation; textile weaving	c/	…	…	…	…	c/	…	…	…	…	c/	…	…	…	…
1712	Finishing of textiles		…	…	…	…		…	…	…	…		…	…	…	…
172	Other textiles	c/	…	…	…	…	c/	…	…	…	…	c/	…	…	…	…
1721	Made-up textile articles, except apparel		…	…	…	…		…	…	…	…		…	…	…	…
1722	Carpets and rugs		…	…	…	…		…	…	…	…		…	…	…	…
1723	Cordage, rope, twine and netting		…	…	…	…		…	…	…	…		…	…	…	…
1729	Other textiles n.e.c.		…	…	…	…		…	…	…	…		…	…	…	…
1730	Knitted and crocheted fabrics and articles	c/	…	…	…	…	c/	…	…	…	…	c/	…	…	…	…
1810	Wearing apparel, except fur apparel	c/	…	…	…	…	c/	…	…	…	…	c/	…	…	…	…
1820	Dressing & dyeing of fur; processing of fur	c/	…	…	…	…	c/	…	…	…	…	c/	…	…	…	…
191	Tanning, dressing and processing of leather	d/	124	128	145	120	d/	9850	9041	8832	10254	d/	2281.7	2797.2	2181.0	2585.9
1911	Tanning and dressing of leather		…	…	…	…		…	…	…	…		…	…	…	…
1912	Luggage, handbags, etc.; saddlery & harness		…	…	…	…		…	…	…	…		…	…	…	…
1920	Footwear	d/	…	…	…	…	d/	…	…	…	…	d/	…	…	…	…
2010	Sawmilling and planing of wood	e/	534	664	548	395	e/	975	900	865	948	e/	220.6	312.1	223.5	270.3
202	Products of wood, cork, straw, etc.	e/	…	…	…	…	e/	…	…	…	…	e/	…	…	…	…
2021	Veneer sheets, plywood, particle board, etc.		…	…	…	…		…	…	…	…		…	…	…	…
2022	Builders' carpentry and joinery		…	…	…	…		…	…	…	…		…	…	…	…
2023	Wooden containers		…	…	…	…		…	…	…	…		…	…	…	…
2029	Other wood products; articles of cork/straw		…	…	…	…		…	…	…	…		…	…	…	…
210	Paper and paper products	f/	259	283	272	365	f/	2126	2301	2982	3765	f/	591.9	840.2	1155.5	1344.1
2101	Pulp, paper and paperboard		…	…	…	…		…	…	…	…		…	…	…	…
2102	Corrugated paper and paperboard		…	…	…	…		…	…	…	…		…	…	…	…
2109	Other articles of paper and paperboard		…	…	…	…		…	…	…	…		…	…	…	…
221	Publishing	f/	…	…	…	…	f/	…	…	…	…	f/	…	…	…	…
2211	Publishing of books and other publications		…	…	…	…		…	…	…	…		…	…	…	…
2212	Publishing of newspapers, journals, etc.		…	…	…	…		…	…	…	…		…	…	…	…
2213	Publishing of recorded media		…	…	…	…		…	…	…	…		…	…	…	…
2219	Other publishing		…	…	…	…		…	…	…	…		…	…	…	…

222	Printing and related service activities	f/					f/					f/				
2221	Printing															
2222	Service activities related to printing	f/					f/					f/				
2230	Reproduction of recorded media															
2310	Coke oven products	g/					g/					g/				
2320	Refined petroleum products	g/					g/					g/				
2330	Processing of nuclear fuel	g/					g/					g/				
241	Basic chemicals	g/	146	189	178	162	g/	3921	3742	3492	3530	g/	2163.3	2864.1	1861.9	2170.3
2411	Basic chemicals, except fertilizers															
2412	Fertilizers and nitrogen compounds															
2413	Plastics in primary forms; synthetic rubber															
242	Other chemicals															
2421	Pesticides and other agro-chemical products	g/					g/					g/				
2422	Paints, varnishes, printing ink and mastics															
2423	Pharmaceuticals, medicinal chemicals, etc.															
2424	Soap, cleaning & cosmetic preparations															
2429	Other chemical products n.e.c.															
2430	Man-made fibres	g/					g/					g/				
251	Rubber products	g/					g/					g/				
2511	Rubber tyres and tubes															
2519	Other rubber products															
2520	Plastic products	g/					g/					g/				
2610	Glass and glass products	h/	668	602	854	826	h/	3568	4178	4113	4746	h/	1352.7	2355.7	2039.0	235.4
269	Non-metallic mineral products n.e.c.	h/					h/					h/				
2691	Pottery, china and earthenware															
2692	Refractory ceramic products															
2693	Struct.non-refractory clay; ceramic products															
2694	Cement, lime and plaster															
2695	Articles of concrete, cement and plaster															
2696	Cutting, shaping & finishing of stone															
2699	Other non-metallic mineral products n.e.c.															
2710	Basic iron and steel	i/	1245	1299	1330	1229	i/	5228	5393	5015	5948	i/	1902.6	2760.7	2302.0	2795.1
2720	Basic precious and non-ferrous metals	i/					i/					i/				
273	Casting of metals	i/					i/					i/				
2731	Casting of iron and steel	i/					i/					i/				
2732	Casting of non-ferrous metals	i/					i/					i/				
281	Struct.metal products;tanks;steam generators	i/					i/					i/				
2811	Structural metal products															
2812	Tanks, reservoirs and containers of metal															
2813	Steam generators															
289	Other metal products; metal working services	i/					i/					i/				
2891	Metal forging/pressing/stamping/roll-forming															
2892	Treatment & coating of metals															
2893	Cutlery, hand tools and general hardware															
2899	Other fabricated metal products n.e.c.															
291	General purpose machinery	i/					i/					i/				
2911	Engines & turbines (not for transport equipment)															
2912	Pumps, compressors, taps and valves	i/					i/					i/				
2913	Bearings, gears, gearing & driving elements															
2914	Ovens, furnaces and furnace burners															
2915	Lifting and handling equipment															
2919	Other general purpose machinery															
292	Special purpose machinery															
2921	Agricultural and forestry machinery	i/					i/					i/				
2922	Machine tools															
2923	Machinery for metallurgy															
2924	Machinery for mining & construction															
2925	Food/beverage/tobacco processing machinery															
2926	Machinery for textile, apparel and leather															
2927	Weapons and ammunition															
2929	Other special purpose machinery															

continued

Albania

ISIC	Industry	Number of enterprises (number)					Number of employees (number)					Wages and salaries paid to employees (millions of Albanian Leks)				
		Note	2007	2008	2009	2010	Note	2007	2008	2009	2010	Note	2007	2008	2009	2010
2930	Domestic appliances n.e.c.	i/	...	...	...	...	i/	...	...	...	...	i/	...	...	...	...
3000	Office, accounting and computing machinery	j/	65	58	160	160	j/	870	893	794	730	j/	277.5	453.0	439.5	354.3
3110	Electric motors, generators and transformers	j/	...	...	...	...	j/	...	...	...	...	j/	...	...	...	...
3120	Electricity distribution & control apparatus	j/	...	...	...	...	j/	...	...	...	...	j/	...	...	...	...
3130	Insulated wire and cable	j/	...	...	...	...	j/	...	...	...	...	j/	...	...	...	...
3140	Accumulators, primary cells and batteries	j/	...	...	...	...	j/	...	...	...	...	j/	...	...	...	...
3150	Lighting equipment and electric lamps	j/	...	...	...	...	j/	...	...	...	...	j/	...	...	...	...
3190	Other electrical equipment n.e.c.	j/	...	...	...	...	j/	...	...	...	...	j/	...	...	...	...
3210	Electronic valves, tubes, etc.	j/	...	...	...	...	j/	...	...	...	...	j/	...	...	...	...
3220	TV/radio transmitters; line comm. apparatus	j/	...	...	...	...	j/	...	...	...	...	j/	...	...	...	...
3230	TV and radio receivers and associated goods	j/	...	...	...	...	j/	...	...	...	...	j/	...	...	...	...
331	Medical, measuring, testing appliances, etc.	i/	...	...	...	...	i/	...	...	...	...	i/	...	...	...	...
3311	Medical, surgical and orthopaedic equipment		...	...	...	...		...	...	...	...		...	...	...	...
3312	Measuring/testing/navigating appliances,etc.		...	...	...	...		...	...	...	...		...	...	...	...
3313	Industrial process control equipment		...	...	...	...		...	...	...	...		...	...	...	...
3320	Optical instruments & photographic equipment	j/	...	...	...	...	j/	...	...	...	...	j/	...	...	...	...
3330	Watches and clocks	j/	...	...	...	...	j/	...	...	...	...	j/	...	...	...	...
3410	Motor vehicles	j/	...	...	...	...	j/	...	...	...	...	j/	...	...	...	...
3420	Automobile bodies, trailers & semi-trailers	j/	...	...	...	...	j/	...	...	...	...	j/	...	...	...	...
3430	Parts/accessories for automobiles	j/	...	...	...	...	j/	...	...	...	...	j/	...	...	...	...
351	Building and repairing of ships and boats	i/	...	...	...	...	i/	...	...	...	...	i/	...	...	...	...
3511	Building and repairing of ships		...	...	...	...		...	...	...	...		...	...	...	...
3512	Building/repairing of pleasure/sport. boats		...	...	...	...		...	...	...	...		...	...	...	...
3520	Railway/tramway locomotives & rolling stock	j/	...	...	...	...	j/	...	...	...	...	j/	...	...	...	...
3530	Aircraft and spacecraft	j/	...	...	...	...	j/	...	...	...	...	j/	...	...	...	...
359	Transport equipment n.e.c.	j/	...	...	...	...	j/	...	...	...	...	j/	...	...	...	...
3591	Motorcycles		...	...	...	...		...	...	...	...		...	...	...	...
3592	Bicycles and invalid carriages		...	...	...	...		...	...	...	...		...	...	...	...
3599	Other transport equipment n.e.c.		...	...	...	...		...	...	...	...		...	...	...	...
3610	Furniture	k/	623	678	797	1051	k/	1906	1949	2368	2425	k/	466.5	678.0	683.0	760.7
369	Manufacturing n.e.c.	k/	...	...	...	...	k/	...	...	...	...	k/	...	...	...	...
3691	Jewellery and related articles		...	...	...	...		...	...	...	...		...	...	...	...
3692	Musical instruments		...	...	...	...		...	...	...	...		...	...	...	...
3693	Sports goods		...	...	...	...		...	...	...	...		...	...	...	...
3694	Games and toys		...	...	...	...		...	...	...	...		...	...	...	...
3699	Other manufacturing n.e.c.		...	...	...	...		...	...	...	...		...	...	...	...
3710	Recycling of metal waste and scrap	m/	20	79	48	55	m/	60	127	159	188	m/	26.0	62.6	67.0	80.4
3720	Recycling of non-metal waste and scrap	m/	...	...	...	...	m/	...	...	...	...	m/	...	...	...	...
D	Total manufacturing	n/	6936	7625	7592	8229	n/	47849	48076	47420	54032	n/	13677.2	18933.9	15892.8	16348.9

a/ 1511 includes 1512.
b/ 153 includes 154.
c/ 171 includes 172, 1730, 1810 and 1820.
d/ 191 includes 1920.
e/ 2010 includes 202.
f/ 210 includes 221, 222 and 2230.
g/ 241 includes 2310, 2320, 2330, 242, 2430, 251 and 2520.
h/ 2610 includes 269.
i/ 2710 includes 2720, 273, 281, 289, 291, 292 and 2930.
j/ 3000 includes 31, 32, 33, 34 and 35.

k/ 3610 includes 369.
m/ 3710 includes 3720.
n/ Sum of available data.

Albania

ISIC	Industry	Note	Output (millions of Albanian Leks)				Note	Value added (millions of Albanian Leks)				Note	Gross fixed capital formation (millions of Albanian Leks)	
			2007	2008	2009	2010		2007	2008	2009	2010		2009	2010
151	Processed meat,fish,fruit,vegetables,fats	a/	5214.7	4436.8	7023.7	8438.4	a/	1008.2	1571.8	1653.4	1968.0	a/	195.9	535.3
1511	Processing/preserving of meat	a/	2791.2	2805.7	4181.8	4610.5	a/	761.1	1031.8	1145.1	1210.9	a/	88.2	372.6
1512	Processing/preserving of fish													
1513	Processing/preserving of fruit & vegetables		376.1	277.9	377.1	574.3		58.3	92.7	119.3	195.7		54.0	29.0
1514	Vegetable and animal oils and fats		2047.4	1353.2	2464.8	3253.6		188.8	447.3	389.0	561.4		53.7	133.7
1520	Dairy products		2246.5	1687.8	1266.2	1703.1		420.3	419.4	181.4	457.4		97.0	556.6
153	Grain mill products; starches; animal feeds	b/	12656.1	15577.3	12225.8	14697.3	b/	2576.2	2650.5	3081.6	3145.4	b/	695.8	671.0
1531	Grain mill products		...	...	...	...		...	...	...	...		...	...
1532	Starches and starch products		...	...	...	...		...	...	...	...		...	...
1533	Prepared animal feeds	b/	...	...	...	...	b/	...	...	...	...	b/	...	...
154	Other food products		...	...	...	...		...	...	...	...		...	...
1541	Bakery products		...	...	...	...		...	...	...	...		...	...
1542	Sugar		...	...	...	...		...	...	...	...		...	...
1543	Cocoa, chocolate and sugar confectionery		...	...	...	...		...	...	...	...		...	...
1544	Macaroni, noodles & similar products		...	...	...	...		...	...	...	...		...	...
1549	Other food products n.e.c.		7314.9	7010.7	8728.7	9031.8		1941.9	1725.0	1702.0	2410.6		564.0	2500.5
155	Beverages		...	...	...	...		...	...	...	...		...	...
1551	Distilling, rectifying & blending of spirits		...	...	...	...		...	...	...	...		...	...
1552	Wines		...	...	...	...		...	...	...	...		...	...
1553	Malt liquors and malt		...	...	...	...		...	...	...	...		...	...
1554	Soft drinks; mineral waters		442.2	214.9	252.0	453.4		89.0	43.7	58.9	125.6		6.0	-
1600	Tobacco products	c/	11175.1	10272.3	9375.5	11415.2	c/	5129.7	5899.0	5776.9	6868.8	c/	690.3	318.5
171	Spinning, weaving and finishing of textiles	c/	...	...	...	...	c/	...	...	...	...	c/	...	...
1711	Textile fibre preparation; textile weaving		...	...	...	...		...	...	...	...		...	...
1712	Finishing of textiles		...	...	...	...		...	...	...	...		...	...
172	Other textiles	c/	...	...	...	...	c/	...	...	...	...	c/	...	...
1721	Made-up textile articles, except apparel		...	...	...	...		...	...	...	...		...	...
1722	Carpets and rugs		...	...	...	...		...	...	...	...		...	...
1723	Cordage, rope, twine and netting	c/	...	...	...	...	c/	...	...	...	...	c/	...	...
1729	Other textiles n.e.c.	c/	...	...	...	...	c/	...	...	...	...	c/	...	...
1730	Knitted and crocheted fabrics and articles	c/	...	...	...	...	c/	...	...	...	...	c/	...	...
1810	Wearing apparel, except fur apparel	d/	9156.2	9069.6	11691.8	14502.6	d/	3847.1	3778.7	4642.1	6311.0	d/	978.3	601.0
1820	Dressing & dyeing of fur; processing of fur		...	...	...	...		...	...	...	...		...	...
191	Tanning, dressing and processing of leather	d/	...	...	...	...	d/	...	...	...	...	d/	...	...
1911	Tanning and dressing of leather		...	...	...	...		...	...	...	...		...	...
1912	Luggage, handbags, etc.; saddlery & harness		...	...	...	...		...	...	...	...		...	...
1920	Footwear	e/	2864.0	2523.8	2730.6	2596.8	e/	858.2	854.6	902.5	741.5	e/	223.6	345.9
2010	Sawmilling and planing of wood	e/	...	...	...	...	e/	...	...	...	...	e/	...	...
202	Products of wood, cork, straw, etc.		...	...	...	...		...	...	...	...		...	...
2021	Veneer sheets, plywood, particle board, etc.		...	...	...	...		...	...	...	...		...	...
2022	Builders' carpentry and joinery		...	...	...	...		...	...	...	...		...	...
2023	Wooden containers		...	...	...	...		...	...	...	...		...	...
2029	Other wood products; articles of cork/straw	f/	4922.2	5328.6	9277.5	13767.9	f/	1420.8	1754.3	3333.3	5397.1	f/	2891.2	1300.0
210	Paper and paper products		...	...	...	...		...	...	...	...		...	...
2101	Pulp, paper and paperboard		...	...	...	...		...	...	...	...		...	...
2102	Corrugated paper and paperboard		...	...	...	...		...	...	...	...		...	...
2109	Other articles of paper and paperboard		...	...	...	...		...	...	...	...		...	...
221	Publishing	f/	...	...	...	...	f/	...	...	...	...	f/	...	...
2211	Publishing of books and other publications		...	...	...	...		...	...	...	...		...	...
2212	Publishing of newspapers, journals, etc.		...	...	...	...		...	...	...	...		...	...
2213	Publishing of recorded media		...	...	...	...		...	...	...	...		...	...
2219	Other publishing		...	...	...	...		...	...	...	...		...	...

continued

Albania

ISIC Revision 3		Output (Note)	Output (millions of Albanian Leks)				Value added (Note)	Value added (millions of Albanian Leks)				Gross fixed capital formation (Note)	Gross fixed capital formation (millions of Albanian Leks)	
ISIC	Industry	Note	2007	2008	2009	2010	Note	2007	2008	2009	2010	Note	2009	2010
222	Printing and related service activities	f/	...	...	...	...	f/	...	...	...	...	f/	...	...
2221	Printing		...	...	...	...		...	...	...	...		...	...
2222	Service activities related to printing		...	...	...	...		...	...	...	...		...	...
2230	Reproduction of recorded media	f/	...	...	...	...	f/	...	...	...	...	f/	...	...
2310	Coke oven products	g/	...	...	...	...	g/	...	...	...	...	g/	...	...
2320	Refined petroleum products	g/	...	...	...	...	g/	...	...	...	...	g/	...	...
2330	Processing of nuclear fuel	g/	...	...	...	...	g/	...	...	...	...	g/	...	...
241	Basic chemicals	g/	22316.3	22140.2	18421.7	16724.5	g/	6084.4	4908.6	4314.3	2362.1	g/	962.0	1458.8
2411	Basic chemicals, except fertilizers		...	...	...	...		...	...	...	...		...	...
2412	Fertilizers and nitrogen compounds		...	...	...	...		...	...	...	...		...	...
2413	Plastics in primary forms; synthetic rubber		...	...	...	...		...	...	...	...		...	...
242	Other chemicals	g/	...	...	...	...	g/	...	...	...	...	g/	...	...
2421	Pesticides and other agro-chemical products		...	...	...	...		...	...	...	...		...	...
2422	Paints, varnishes, printing ink and mastics		...	...	...	...		...	...	...	...		...	...
2423	Pharmaceuticals, medicinal chemicals, etc.		...	...	...	...		...	...	...	...		...	...
2424	Soap, cleaning & cosmetic preparations		...	...	...	...		...	...	...	...		...	...
2429	Other chemical products n.e.c.		...	...	...	...		...	...	...	...		...	...
2430	Man-made fibres		...	...	...	...		...	...	...	...		...	...
251	Rubber products	g/	...	...	...	...	g/	...	...	...	...	g/	...	...
2511	Rubber tyres and tubes	g/	...	...	...	...	g/	...	...	...	...	g/	...	...
2519	Other rubber products		...	...	...	...		...	...	...	...		...	...
2520	Plastic products	g/	...	...	...	...	g/	...	...	...	...	g/	...	...
2610	Glass and glass products	h/	21510.9	22111.4	28263.3	34064.9	h/	5109.1	8218.2	7455.7	8708.8	h/	2181.6	1617.7
269	Non-metallic mineral products n.e.c.	h/	...	...	...	...	h/	...	...	...	...	h/	...	...
2691	Pottery, china and earthenware		...	...	...	...		...	...	...	...		...	...
2692	Refractory ceramic products		...	...	...	...		...	...	...	...		...	...
2693	Struct.non-refractory clay; ceramic products		...	...	...	...		...	...	...	...		...	...
2694	Cement, lime and plaster		...	...	...	...		...	...	...	...		...	...
2695	Articles of concrete, cement and plaster		...	...	...	...		...	...	...	...		...	...
2696	Cutting, shaping & finishing of stone		...	...	...	...		...	...	...	...		...	...
2699	Other non-metallic mineral products n.e.c.		...	...	...	...		...	...	...	...		...	...
2710	Basic iron and steel	i/	23859.8	32745.7	27571.7	35680.6	i/	5317.2	8218.2	3879.6	9883.2	i/	2884.6	2539.3
2720	Basic precious and non-ferrous metals	i/	...	...	...	...	i/	...	...	...	...	i/	...	...
273	Casting of metals	i/	...	...	...	...	i/	...	...	...	...	i/	...	...
2731	Casting of iron and steel		...	...	...	...		...	...	...	...		...	...
2732	Casting of non-ferrous metals		...	...	...	...		...	...	...	...		...	...
281	Struct.metal products;tanks;steam generators	i/	...	...	...	...	i/	...	...	...	...	i/	...	...
2811	Structural metal products		...	...	...	...		...	...	...	...		...	...
2812	Tanks, reservoirs and containers of metal		...	...	...	...		...	...	...	...		...	...
2813	Steam generators		...	...	...	...		...	...	...	...		...	...
289	Other metal products; metal working services	i/	...	...	...	...	i/	...	...	...	...	i/	...	...
2891	Metal forging/pressing/stamping/roll-forming		...	...	...	...		...	...	...	...		...	...
2892	Treatment & coating of metals		...	...	...	...		...	...	...	...		...	...
2893	Cutlery, hand tools and general hardware		...	...	...	...		...	...	...	...		...	...
2899	Other fabricated metal products n.e.c.		...	...	...	...		...	...	...	...		...	...
291	General purpose machinery	i/	...	...	...	...	i/	...	...	...	...	i/	...	...
2911	Engines & turbines (not for transport equipment)		...	...	...	...		...	...	...	...		...	...
2912	Pumps, compressors, taps and valves		...	...	...	...		...	...	...	...		...	...
2913	Bearings, gears, gearing & driving elements		...	...	...	...		...	...	...	...		...	...
2914	Ovens, furnaces and furnace burners		...	...	...	...		...	...	...	...		...	...
2915	Lifting and handling equipment		...	...	...	...		...	...	...	...		...	...
2919	Other general purpose machinery		...	...	...	...		...	...	...	...		...	...

292	Special purpose machinery	...	...	...	...	i/	...	...	...	...	i/	...	...	i/
2921	Agricultural and forestry machinery	...	...	...	...		...	...	...	...		...	...	
2922	Machine tools	...	...	...	...		...	...	...	...		...	...	
2923	Machinery for metallurgy	...	...	...	...		...	...	...	...		...	...	
2924	Machinery for mining & construction	...	...	...	...		...	...	...	...		...	...	
2925	Food/beverage/tobacco processing machinery	...	...	...	...		...	...	...	...		...	...	
2926	Machinery for textile, apparel and leather	...	...	...	...		...	...	...	...		...	...	
2927	Weapons and ammunition	...	...	...	...		...	...	...	...		...	...	
2929	Other special purpose machinery	...	...	...	...		...	...	...	...		...	...	
2930	Domestic appliances n.e.c.	...	...	...	...	i/	...	...	...	...	i/	58.1	50.7	i/
3000	Office, accounting and computing machinery	1686.8	2312.7	2928.4	2011.9	i/	756.2	1134.1	1486.9	1013.9	i/	...	...	i/
3110	Electric motors, generators and transformers	...	...	...	...	i/	...	...	...	...	i/	...	...	i/
3120	Electricity distribution & control apparatus	...	...	...	...	i/	...	...	...	...	i/	...	...	i/
3130	Insulated wire and cable	...	...	...	...	i/	...	...	...	...	i/	...	...	i/
3140	Accumulators, primary cells and batteries	...	...	...	...	i/	...	...	...	...	i/	...	...	i/
3150	Lighting equipment and electric lamps	...	...	...	...	i/	...	...	...	...	i/	...	...	i/
3190	Other electrical equipment n.e.c.	...	...	...	...	i/	...	...	...	...	i/	...	...	i/
3210	Electronic valves, tubes, etc.	...	...	...	...	i/	...	...	...	...	i/	...	...	i/
3220	TV/radio transmitters; line comm. apparatus	...	...	...	...	i/	...	...	...	...	i/	...	...	i/
3230	TV and radio receivers and associated goods	...	...	...	...	i/	...	...	...	...	i/	...	...	i/
331	Medical, measuring, testing appliances, etc.	...	...	...	...	i/	...	...	...	...	i/	...	...	i/
3311	Medical, surgical and orthopaedic equipment	...	...	...	...		...	...	...	...		...	...	
3312	Measuring/testing/navigating appliances,etc.	...	...	...	...		...	...	...	...		...	...	
3313	Industrial process control equipment	...	...	...	...		...	...	...	...		...	...	
3320	Optical instruments & photographic equipment	...	...	...	...	i/	...	...	...	...	i/	...	...	i/
3330	Watches and clocks	...	...	...	...	i/	...	...	...	...	i/	...	...	i/
3410	Motor vehicles	...	...	...	...	i/	...	...	...	...	i/	...	...	i/
3420	Automobile bodies, trailers & semi-trailers	...	...	...	...	i/	...	...	...	...	i/	...	...	i/
3430	Parts/accessories for automobiles	...	...	...	...	i/	...	...	...	...	i/	...	...	i/
351	Building and repairing of ships and boats	...	...	...	...	i/	...	...	...	...	i/	...	...	i/
3511	Building and repairing of ships	...	...	...	...		...	...	...	...		...	...	
3512	Building/repairing of pleasure/sport. boats	...	...	...	...		...	...	...	...		...	...	
3520	Railway/tramway locomotives & rolling stock	...	...	...	...	i/	...	...	...	...	i/	...	...	i/
3530	Aircraft and spacecraft	...	...	...	...	i/	...	...	...	...	i/	...	...	i/
359	Transport equipment n.e.c.	...	...	...	...	i/	...	...	...	...	i/	...	...	i/
3591	Motorcycles	...	...	...	...		...	...	...	...		...	...	
3592	Bicycles and invalid carriages	...	...	...	...		...	...	...	...		...	...	
3599	Other transport equipment n.e.c.	...	...	...	...		...	...	...	...		...	...	
3610	Furniture	5175.6	5254.6	5885.3	6557.0	k/	1478.0	1594.7	1846.9	1921.1	k/	384.3	818.1	k/
369	Manufacturing n.e.c.	...	...	...	...	k/	...	...	...	...	k/	...	...	k/
3691	Jewellery and related articles	...	...	...	...		...	...	...	...		...	...	
3692	Musical instruments	...	...	...	...		...	...	...	...		...	...	
3693	Sports goods	...	...	...	...		...	...	...	...		...	...	
3694	Games and toys	...	...	...	...		...	...	...	...		...	...	
3699	Other manufacturing n.e.c.	...	...	...	...		...	...	...	...		...	...	
3710	Recycling of metal waste and scrap	1693.9	1553.3	619.4	2926.0	m/	60.1	121.9	75.6	187.7	m/	14.4	46.4	m/
3720	Recycling of non-metal waste and scrap	...	...	...	...	m/	...	...	...	...	m/	...	...	m/
D	Total manufacturing	132235.0	142239.7	146261.5	174571.3	n/	36096.3	42892.7	40391.3	51502.1	n/	12827.1	13359.9	n/

a/ 1511 includes 1512.
b/ 153 includes 154.
c/ 171 includes 172, 1730, 1810 and 1820.
d/ 191 includes 1920.
e/ 2010 includes 202.
f/ 210 includes 221, 222 and 2230.
g/ 241 includes 2310, 2320, 2330, 242, 2430, 251 and 2520.
h/ 2610 includes 269.
i/ 2710 includes 2720, 273, 281, 289, 291, 292 and 2930.
j/ 3000 includes 31, 32, 33, 34 and 35.

k/ 3610 includes 369.
m/ 3710 includes 3720.
n/ Sum of available data.

Albania

Index numbers of industrial production

ISIC Revision 3		Note	1999	2000	2001	2002	2003	2004	2005	2006	2007	2008	2009	2010
								(2005=100)						
ISIC	Industry													
15	Food and beverages	a/	...	...	...	...	91	103	100	122	125	150	149	159
16	Tobacco products	a/	...	...	...	...	...	...	...	...	...	...	...	...
17	Textiles	b/	...	...	...	...	90	99	100	107	103	115	116	134
18	Wearing apparel, fur	b/	...	...	...	...	...	...	...	...	...	...	...	...
19	Leather, leather products and footwear		...	...	...	...	110	102	100	122	111	143	209	236
20	Wood products (excl. furniture)		...	...	...	...	105	95	100	105	125	143	183	191
21	Paper and paper products	c/	...	...	...	...	88	79	100	87	89	120	115	256
22	Printing and publishing	c/	...	...	...	...	...	...	...	...	...	...	...	...
23	Coke,refined petroleum products,nuclear fuel	d/	...	...	...	...	66	73	100	78	70	73	123	77
24	Chemicals and chemical products	d/	...	...	...	...	...	...	...	...	...	...	...	...
25	Rubber and plastics products	d/	...	...	...	...	...	...	...	...	...	...	...	...
26	Non-metallic mineral products	e/	...	...	...	...	78	87	100	128	149	178	221	252
27	Basic metals	e/	...	...	...	...	101	81	100	82	114	127	109	146
28	Fabricated metal products	e/	...	...	...	...	...	...	...	...	...	...	...	...
29	Machinery and equipment n.e.c.	e/	...	...	...	...	...	...	...	...	...	...	...	...
30	Office, accounting and computing machinery	e/	...	...	...	...	...	...	...	...	...	...	...	...
31	Electrical machinery and apparatus	e/	...	...	...	...	...	...	...	...	...	...	...	...
32	Radio,television and communication equipment	e/	...	...	...	...	...	...	...	...	...	...	...	...
33	Medical, precision and optical instruments	e/	...	...	...	...	...	...	...	...	...	...	...	...
34	Motor vehicles, trailers, semi-trailers	e/	...	...	...	...	...	...	...	...	...	...	...	...
35	Other transport equipment	e/	...	...	...	...	...	...	...	...	...	...	...	...
36	Furniture; manufacturing n.e.c.	f/	...	...	...	...	89	115	100	100	125	141	125	132
37	Recycling	f/	...	...	...	...	...	...	...	...	...	...	...	...
D	Total manufacturing		...	...	...	...	87	90	100	106	113	132	152	172

a/ 15 includes 16.
b/ 17 includes 18.
c/ 21 includes 22.
d/ 23 includes 24 and 25.
e/ 27 includes 28, 29, 30, 31, 32, 33, 34 and 35.
f/ 36 includes 37.

Armenia

Supplier of information:
National Statistical Service of the Republic of Armenia, Yerevan.

Basic source of data:
Annual survey; administrative source.

Major deviations from ISIC (Revision 4):
None reported.

Reference period:
Calendar year.

Scope:
All registered establishments.

Method of data collection:
Direct interview in the field and statistical reports from large and medium establishments.

Type of enumeration:
Complete enumeration for medium and large establishments; sample survey for small establishments.

Adjusted for non-response:
No.

Concepts and definitions of variables:
No deviations from the standard UN concepts and definitions are reported.

Related national publications:
The Statistical Yearbook of Armenia, published by the National Statistical Service of the Republic of Armenia, Yerevan.

Armenia

ISIC	Industry	Number of establishments (number)					Number of employees (number)					Wages and salaries paid to employees (millions of Armenian Drams)				
		Note	2007	2008	2009	2010	Note	2007	2008	2009	2010	Note	2007	2008	2009	2010
1010	Processing/preserving of meat		...	...	83	81		...	...	...	...		...	...	...	...
1020	Processing/preserving of fish, etc.		...	...	4	3		...	...	...	...		...	...	...	...
1030	Processing/preserving of fruit,vegetables		...	...	20	22		...	...	...	...		...	...	...	...
1040	Vegetable and animal oils and fats		...	...	5	6		...	...	...	...		...	...	...	...
1050	Dairy products		...	...	69	72		...	...	...	...		...	...	...	...
106	Grain mill products,starches and starch products		...	...	24	28		...	...	...	...		...	...	...	...
1061	Grain mill products		...	...	24	28		...	...	...	...		...	...	...	...
1062	Starches and starch products		...	...	-	-		...	...	...	...		...	...	...	...
107	Other food products		...	...	446	493		...	...	...	...		...	...	...	...
1071	Bakery products		...	...	423	468		...	...	...	...		...	...	...	...
1072	Sugar		...	...	10	14		...	...	...	...		...	...	...	...
1073	Cocoa, chocolate and sugar confectionery		...	...	13	11		...	...	...	...		...	...	...	...
1074	Macaroni, noodles, couscous, etc.		...	...	-	-		...	...	...	...		...	...	...	...
1075	Prepared meals and dishes		...	...	-	-		...	...	...	...		...	...	...	...
1079	Other food products n.e.c.		...	...	-	-		...	...	...	...		...	...	...	...
1080	Prepared animal feeds		...	...	64	83		...	...	...	...		...	...	...	...
1101	Distilling, rectifying and blending of spirits		...	...	41	41		...	...	...	...		...	...	...	...
1102	Wines		...	...	19	21		...	...	...	...		...	...	...	...
1103	Malt liquors and malt		...	...	-	-		...	...	...	...		...	...	...	...
1104	Soft drinks,mineral waters,other bottled waters		...	...	-	-		...	...	...	...		...	...	...	...
1200	Tobacco products		...	...	4	4		...	...	...	...		...	...	...	...
131	Spinning, weaving and finishing of textiles		...	...	1	1		...	...	...	...		...	...	...	...
1311	Preparation and spinning of textile fibres		...	...	-	-		...	...	...	...		...	...	...	...
1312	Weaving of textiles		...	...	-	-		...	...	...	...		...	...	...	...
1313	Finishing of textiles		...	...	-	-		...	...	...	...		...	...	...	...
139	Other textiles		...	...	11	14		...	...	...	...		...	...	...	...
1391	Knitted and crocheted fabrics		...	...	1	3		...	...	...	...		...	...	...	...
1392	Made-up textile articles, except apparel		...	...	-	1		...	...	...	...		...	...	...	...
1393	Carpets and rugs		...	...	7	6		...	...	...	...		...	...	...	...
1394	Cordage, rope, twine and netting		...	...	-	-		...	...	...	...		...	...	...	...
1399	Other textiles n.e.c.		...	...	1	2		...	...	...	...		...	...	...	...
1410	Wearing apparel, except fur apparel		...	...	55	50		...	...	...	...		...	...	...	...
1420	Articles of fur		...	...	-	-		...	...	...	...		...	...	...	...
1430	Knitted and crocheted apparel		...	...	23	19		...	...	...	...		...	...	...	...
151	Leather;luggage,handbags,saddlery,harness;fur		...	...	13	17		...	...	...	...		...	...	...	...
1511	Tanning/dressing of leather; dressing of fur		...	...	4	4		...	...	...	...		...	...	...	...
1512	Luggage,handbags,etc.;saddlery/harness		...	...	9	13		...	...	...	...		...	...	...	...
1520	Footwear		...	...	27	28		...	...	...	...		...	...	...	...
1610	Sawmilling and planing of wood		...	...	21	19		...	...	...	...		...	...	...	...
162	Wood products, cork, straw, plaiting materials		...	...	51	51		...	...	...	...		...	...	...	...

Code	Description					Value
1621	Veneer sheets and wood-based panels	...	...	...	...	1
1622	Builders' carpentry and joinery	...	...	...	...	1
1623	Wooden containers	...	...	...	...	34
1629	Other wood products;articles of cork,straw	...	...	...	...	10
1701	Pulp, paper and paperboard	...	...	...	...	-
1702	Corrugated paper and paperboard	...	...	...	...	-
1709	Other articles of paper and paperboard	...	...	...	...	-
181	Printing and service activities related to printing	...	...	...	...	130
1811	Printing	...	...	...	...	26
1812	Service activities related to printing	...	...	...	...	82
1820	Reproduction of recorded media	...	...	...	...	3
1910	Coke oven products	...	...	...	...	-
1920	Refined petroleum products	...	...	...	...	-
201	Basic chemicals,fertilizers, etc.	...	...	...	...	10
2011	Basic chemicals	...	...	...	...	2
2012	Fertilizers and nitrogen compounds	...	...	...	...	-
2013	Plastics and synthetic rubber in primary forms	...	...	...	...	5
202	Other chemical products	...	...	...	...	-
2021	Pesticides and other agrochemical products	...	...	...	...	-
2022	Paints,varnishes;printing ink and mastics	...	...	...	...	-
2023	Soap,cleaning and cosmetic preparations	...	...	...	...	-
2029	Other chemical products n.e.c.	...	...	...	...	-
2030	Man-made fibres	...	...	...	...	14
2100	Pharmaceuticals,medicinal chemicals, etc.	...	...	...	...	-
221	Rubber products	...	...	...	...	9
2211	Rubber tyres and tubes	...	...	...	...	-
2219	Other rubber products	...	...	...	...	9
2220	Plastics products	...	...	...	...	93
2310	Glass and glass products	...	...	...	...	12
239	Non-metallic mineral products n.e.c.	...	...	...	...	6
2391	Refractory products	...	...	...	...	-
2392	Clay building materials	...	...	...	...	-
2393	Other porcelain and ceramic products	...	...	...	...	-
2394	Cement, lime and plaster	...	...	...	...	-
2395	Articles of concrete, cement and plaster	...	...	...	...	-
2396	Cutting, shaping and finishing of stone	...	...	...	...	-
2399	Other non-metallic mineral products n.e.c.	...	...	...	...	6
2410	Basic iron and steel	...	...	...	...	6
2420	Basic precious and other non-ferrous metals	...	...	...	...	1
243	Casting of metals	...	...	...	...	1
2431	Casting of iron and steel	...	...	...	...	-
2432	Casting of non-ferrous metals	...	...	...	...	-
251	Struct.metal products, tanks, reservoirs	...	...	...	...	134
2511	Structural metal products	...	...	...	...	114
2512	Tanks, reservoirs and containers of metal	...	...	...	...	20

The second numeric column reads: 1, 2, 33, 11, -, -, -, 112, 16, 75, 3, -, -, 12, 5, -, 3, -, -, -, -, -, 13, -, 10, -, 10, 195, 13, 6, -, -, -, -, -, -, -, 6, 5, 1, 4, -, -, 45, 29, 16

continued

Armenia

ISIC Revision 4		Number of establishments (number)					Number of employees (number)					Wages and salaries paid to employees (millions of Armenian Drams)				
ISIC	Industry	Note	2007	2008	2009	2010	Note	2007	2008	2009	2010	Note	2007	2008	2009	2010
2513	Steam generators, excl. hot water boilers		…	…	-	-		…	…	…	…		…	…	…	…
2520	Weapons and ammunition		…	…	-	-		…	…	…	…		…	…	…	…
259	Other metal products;metal working services		…	…	37	38		…	…	…	…		…	…	…	…
2591	Forging,pressing,stamping,roll-forming of metal		…	…	2	2		…	…	…	…		…	…	…	…
2592	Treatment and coating of metals; machining		…	…	3	3		…	…	…	…		…	…	…	…
2593	Cutlery, hand tools and general hardware		…	…	2	3		…	…	…	…		…	…	…	…
2599	Other fabricated metal products n.e.c.		…	…	29	30		…	…	…	…		…	…	…	…
2610	Electronic components and boards		…	…	10	6		…	…	…	…		…	…	…	…
2620	Computers and peripheral equipment		…	…	6	6		…	…	…	…		…	…	…	…
2630	Communication equipment		…	…	7	8		…	…	…	…		…	…	…	…
2640	Consumer electronics		…	…	2	2		…	…	…	…		…	…	…	…
265	Measuring,testing equipment; watches, etc.		…	…	15	13		…	…	…	…		…	…	…	…
2651	Measuring/testing/navigating equipment,etc.		…	…	10	9		…	…	…	…		…	…	…	…
2652	Watches and clocks		…	…	5	4		…	…	…	…		…	…	…	…
2660	Irradiation/electromedical equipment,etc.		…	…	-	-		…	…	…	…		…	…	…	…
2670	Optical instruments and photographic equipment		…	…	4	3		…	…	…	…		…	…	…	…
2680	Magnetic and optical media		…	…	-	-		…	…	…	…		…	…	…	…
2710	Electric motors,generators,transformers,etc.		…	…	8	10		…	…	…	…		…	…	…	…
2720	Batteries and accumulators		…	…	-	1		…	…	…	…		…	…	…	…
273	Wiring and wiring devices		…	…	8	10		…	…	…	…		…	…	…	…
2731	Fibre optic cables		…	…	-	-		…	…	…	…		…	…	…	…
2732	Other electronic and electric wires and cables		…	…	8	9		…	…	…	…		…	…	…	…
2733	Wiring devices		…	…	-	1		…	…	…	…		…	…	…	…
2740	Electric lighting equipment		…	…	6	4		…	…	…	…		…	…	…	…
2750	Domestic appliances		…	…	15	12		…	…	…	…		…	…	…	…
2790	Other electrical equipment		…	…	9	8		…	…	…	…		…	…	…	…
281	General-purpose machinery		…	…	9	10		…	…	…	…		…	…	…	…
2811	Engines/turbines,excl.aircraft,vehicle engines		…	…	1	1		…	…	…	…		…	…	…	…
2812	Fluid power equipment		…	…	3	2		…	…	…	…		…	…	…	…
2813	Other pumps, compressors, taps and valves		…	…	1	1		…	…	…	…		…	…	…	…
2814	Bearings, gears, gearing and driving elements		…	…	-	1		…	…	…	…		…	…	…	…
2815	Ovens, furnaces and furnace burners		…	…	4	5		…	…	…	…		…	…	…	…
2816	Lifting and handling equipment		…	…	-	-		…	…	…	…		…	…	…	…
2817	Office machinery, excl.computers,etc.		…	…	-	-		…	…	…	…		…	…	…	…
2818	Power-driven hand tools		…	…	-	-		…	…	…	…		…	…	…	…
2819	Other general-purpose machinery		…	…	-	-		…	…	…	…		…	…	…	…
282	Special-purpose machinery		…	…	16	16		…	…	…	…		…	…	…	…
2821	Agricultural and forestry machinery		…	…	4	2		…	…	…	…		…	…	…	…
2822	Metal-forming machinery and machine tools		…	…	1	1		…	…	…	…		…	…	…	…
2823	Machinery for metallurgy		…	…	6	8		…	…	…	…		…	…	…	…
2824	Mining, quarrying and construction machinery		…	…	1	1		…	…	…	…		…	…	…	…

2825	Food/beverage/tobacco processing machinery	...	...	...	1	1	...
2826	Textile/apparel/leather production machinery	...	...	...	-	-	...
2829	Other special-purpose machinery	...	...	...	3	3	...
2910	Motor vehicles	...	...	...	-	-	...
2920	Automobile bodies, trailers and semi-trailers	...	...	...	1	-	...
2930	Parts and accessories for motor vehicles	...	...	...	-	-	...
301	Building of ships and boats	...	...	...	-	-	...
3011	Building of ships and floating structures	...	...	...	-	-	...
3012	Building of pleasure and sporting boats	...	...	...	-	-	...
3020	Railway locomotives and rolling stock	...	...	...	-	-	...
3030	Air and spacecraft and related machinery	...	...	...	-	-	...
3040	Military fighting vehicles	...	...	...	-	-	...
309	Transport equipment n.e.c.	...	...	...	1	1	...
3091	Motorcycles	...	...	...	-	-	...
3092	Bicycles and invalid carriages	...	...	...	1	1	...
3099	Other transport equipment n.e.c.	...	...	...	-	-	...
3100	Furniture	...	...	...	100	105	...
321	Jewellery, bijouterie and related articles	...	...	...	45	41	...
3211	Jewellery and related articles	...	...	...	-	-	...
3212	Imitation jewellery and related articles	...	...	...	41	36	...
3220	Musical instruments	...	...	...	-	-	...
3230	Sports goods	...	...	...	1	1	...
3240	Games and toys	...	...	...	6	7	...
3250	Medical and dental instruments and supplies	...	...	...	-	-	...
3290	Other manufacturing n.e.c.	...	...	...	20	23	...
331	Repair of fabricated metal products/machinery	...	...	...	-	5	...
3311	Repair of fabricated metal products	...	...	...	10	8	...
3312	Repair of machinery	...	...	...	3	2	...
3313	Repair of electronic and optical equipment	...	...	...	6	7	...
3314	Repair of electrical equipment	...	...	...	-	-	...
3315	Repair of transport equip., excl. motor vehicles	...	...	...	-	-	...
3319	Repair of other equipment	...	...	...	-	-	...
3320	Installation of industrial machinery/equipment	...	...	...	-	-	...
C	Total manufacturing	...	76900	71500	2147	2241	92528 / 100502

Armenia

ISIC	Industry	Output at producers' prices (millions of Armenian Drams)					Value added (millions of Armenian Drams)					Gross fixed capital formation (millions of Armenian Drams)		
		Note	2007	2008	2009	2010	Note	2007	2008	2009	2010	Note	2009	2010
1010	Processing/preserving of meat		...	...	12017	12232		...	...	...	...		...	...
1020	Processing/preserving of fish, etc.		...	...	8	5		...	...	...	...		...	...
1030	Processing/preserving of fruit,vegetables		...	...	6116	8563		...	...	...	...		...	...
1040	Vegetable and animal oils and fats		...	...	492	578		...	...	...	...		...	...
1050	Dairy products		...	...	30671	31733		...	...	...	...		...	...
106	Grain mill products,starches and starch products		...	...	23235	25649		...	...	...	...		...	...
1061	Grain mill products		...	...	23235	25649		...	...	...	...		...	...
1062	Starches and starch products		...	...	-	-		...	...	...	...		...	...
107	Other food products		...	...	73833	74027		...	...	...	...		...	...
1071	Bakery products		...	...	71753	71893		...	...	...	...		...	...
1072	Sugar		...	...	1561	1560		...	...	...	...		...	...
1073	Cocoa, chocolate and sugar confectionery		...	...	519	574		...	...	...	...		...	...
1074	Macaroni, noodles, couscous, etc.		...	...	-	-		...	...	...	...		...	...
1075	Prepared meals and dishes		...	...	-	-		...	...	...	...		...	...
1079	Other food products n.e.c.		...	...	-	-		...	...	...	...		...	...
1080	Prepared animal feeds		...	...	23382	35365		...	...	...	...		...	...
1101	Distilling, rectifying and blending of spirits		...	...	31756	45676		...	...	...	...		...	...
1102	Wines		...	...	2069	4175		...	...	...	...		...	...
1103	Malt liquors and malt		...	...	-	-		...	...	...	...		...	...
1104	Soft drinks,mineral waters,other bottled waters		...	...	-	...		...	...	...	...		...	...
1200	Tobacco products		...	...	14239	19889		...	...	...	...		...	...
131	Spinning, weaving and finishing of textiles		...	...	6	-		...	...	...	...		...	...
1311	Preparation and spinning of textile fibres		...	...	-	-		...	...	...	...		...	...
1312	Weaving of textiles		...	...	-	-		...	...	...	...		...	...
1313	Finishing of textiles		...	...	-	-		...	...	...	...		...	...
139	Other textiles		...	...	178	99		...	...	...	...		...	...
1391	Knitted and crocheted fabrics		...	...	12	21		...	...	...	...		...	...
1392	Made-up textile articles, except apparel		...	...	-	9		...	...	...	...		...	...
1393	Carpets and rugs		...	...	154	63		...	...	...	...		...	...
1394	Cordage, rope, twine and netting		...	...	-	-		...	...	...	...		...	...
1399	Other textiles n.e.c.		...	...	6	4		...	...	...	...		...	...
1410	Wearing apparel, except fur apparel		...	...	2785	2637		...	...	...	...		...	...
1420	Articles of fur		...	...	-	-		...	...	...	...		...	...
1430	Knitted and crocheted apparel		...	...	942	886		...	...	...	...		...	...
151	Leather;luggage,handbags,saddlery,harness;fur		...	...	403	604		...	...	...	...		...	...
1511	Tanning/dressing of leather; dressing of fur		...	...	51	48		...	...	...	...		...	...
1512	Luggage,handbags,etc.:saddlery/harness		...	...	353	555		...	...	...	...		...	...
1520	Footwear		...	...	411	474		...	...	...	...		...	...
1610	Sawmilling and planing of wood		...	...	84	144		...	...	...	...		...	...
162	Wood products, cork, straw, plaiting materials		...	...	709	1275		...	...	...	...		...	...

1621	Veneer sheets and wood-based panels	6	9
1622	Builders' carpentry and joinery	17	98
1623	Wooden containers	540	857
1629	Other wood products;articles of cork,straw	62	200
1701	Pulp, paper and paperboard	-	-
1702	Corrugated paper and paperboard	-	-
1709	Other articles of paper and paperboard	-	-
181	Printing and service activities related to printing	8695	9292
1811	Printing	2645	2661
1812	Service activities related to printing	5403	5925
1820	Reproduction of recorded media	51	29
1910	Coke oven products	-	-
1920	Refined petroleum products	3962	2817
201	Basic chemicals,fertilizers, etc.	292	205
2011	Basic chemicals	-	-
2012	Fertilizers and nitrogen compounds	303	650
2013	Plastics and synthetic rubber in primary forms	-	-
202	Other chemical products	-	-
2021	Pesticides and other agrochemical products	-	-
2022	Paints,varnishes;printing ink and mastics	-	-
2023	Soap,cleaning and cosmetic preparations	-	-
2029	Other chemical products n.e.c.	-	-
2030	Man-made fibres	3859	4250
2100	Pharmaceuticals,medicinal chemicals, etc.	-	-
221	Rubber products	293	803
2211	Rubber tyres and tubes	-	-
2219	Other rubber products	293	803
2220	Plastics products	13504	14360
2310	Glass and glass products	6196	9016
239	Non-metallic mineral products n.e.c.	155	236
2391	Refractory products	-	-
2392	Clay building materials	-	-
2393	Other porcelain and ceramic products	-	-
2394	Cement, lime and plaster	-	-
2395	Articles of concrete, cement and plaster	-	-
2396	Cutting, shaping and finishing of stone	-	-
2399	Other non-metallic mineral products n.e.c.	155	236
2410	Basic iron and steel	34232	49435
2420	Basic precious and other non-ferrous metals	2119	2196
243	Casting of metals	4208	5878
2431	Casting of iron and steel	-	-
2432	Casting of non-ferrous metals	-	-
251	Struct.metal products, tanks, reservoirs	1831	2956
2511	Structural metal products	1530	2579
2512	Tanks, reservoirs and containers of metal	301	376

continued

Armenia

ISIC	Industry	Note	Output at producers' prices (millions of Armenian Drams) 2007	2008	2009	2010	Note	Value added (millions of Armenian Drams) 2007	2008	2009	2010	Note	Gross fixed capital formation (millions of Armenian Drams) 2009	2010
2513	Steam generators, excl. hot water boilers		...	...	-	-		...	...	...	...		...	...
2520	Weapons and ammunition		...	...	-	-		...	...	...	...		...	...
259	Other metal products;metal working services		...	...	2106	2469		...	...	...	...		...	...
2591	Forging,pressing,stamping,roll-forming of metal		...	...	145	264		...	...	...	...		...	...
2592	Treatment and coating of metals; machining		...	...	481	539		...	...	...	...		...	...
2593	Cutlery, hand tools and general hardware		...	...	86	232		...	...	...	...		...	...
2599	Other fabricated metal products n.e.c.		...	...	1393	1433		...	...	...	...		...	...
2610	Electronic components and boards		...	...	212	351		...	...	...	...		...	...
2620	Computers and peripheral equipment		...	...	408	400		...	...	...	...		...	...
2630	Communication equipment		...	...	958	943		...	...	...	...		...	...
2640	Consumer electronics		...	...	31	187		...	...	...	...		...	...
265	Measuring,testing equipment; watches, etc.		...	...	1852	2663		...	...	...	...		...	...
2651	Measuring/testing/navigating equipment,etc.		...	...	1329	2063		...	...	...	...		...	...
2652	Watches and clocks		...	...	524	600		...	...	...	...		...	...
2660	Irradiation/electromedical equipment,etc.		...	...	-	-		...	...	...	...		...	...
2670	Optical instruments and photographic equipment		...	...	320	142		...	...	...	...		...	...
2680	Magnetic and optical media		...	...	-	-		...	...	...	...		...	...
2710	Electric motors,generators,transformers,etc.		...	...	628	922		...	...	...	...		...	...
2720	Batteries and accumulators		...	...	-	299		...	...	...	...		...	...
273	Wiring and wiring devices		...	...	673	609		...	...	...	...		...	...
2731	Fibre optic cables		...	...	-	-		...	...	...	...		...	...
2732	Other electronic and electric wires and cables		...	...	663	605		...	...	...	...		...	...
2733	Wiring devices		...	...	9	4		...	...	...	...		...	...
2740	Electric lighting equipment		...	...	43	50		...	...	...	...		...	...
2750	Domestic appliances		...	...	738	894		...	...	...	...		...	...
2790	Other electrical equipment		...	...	1062	1430		...	...	...	...		...	...
281	General-purpose machinery		...	...	328	236		...	...	...	...		...	...
2811	Engines/turbines,excl.aircraft,vehicle engines		...	...	93	78		...	...	...	...		...	...
2812	Fluid power equipment		...	...	68	93		...	...	...	...		...	...
2813	Other pumps, compressors, taps and valves		...	...	34	25		...	...	...	...		...	...
2814	Bearings, gears, gearing and driving elements		...	...	7	8		...	...	...	...		...	...
2815	Ovens, furnaces and furnace burners		...	...	126	32		...	...	...	...		...	...
2816	Lifting and handling equipment		...	...	-	-		...	...	...	...		...	...
2817	Office machinery, excl.computers,etc.		...	...	-	-		...	...	...	...		...	...
2818	Power-driven hand tools		...	...	-	-		...	...	...	...		...	...
2819	Other general-purpose machinery		...	...	-	-		...	...	...	...		...	...
282	Special-purpose machinery		...	...	522	461		...	...	...	...		...	...
2821	Agricultural and forestry machinery		...	...	32	12		...	...	...	...		...	...
2822	Metal-forming machinery and machine tools		...	...	2	1		...	...	...	...		...	...
2823	Machinery for metallurgy		...	...	216	177		...	...	...	...		...	...
2824	Mining, quarrying and construction machinery		...	...	4	15		...	...	...	...		...	...

2825	Food/beverage/tobacco processing machinery	249	230
2826	Textile/apparel/leather production machinery	19	26
2829	Other special-purpose machinery	-	-
2910	Motor vehicles	-	-
2920	Automobile bodies, trailers and semi-trailers	-	-
2930	Parts and accessories for motor vehicles	-	-
301	Building of ships and boats	-	-
3011	Building of ships and floating structures	-	-
3012	Building of pleasure and sporting boats	-	-
3020	Railway locomotives and rolling stock	-	-
3030	Air and spacecraft and related machinery	-	-
3040	Military fighting vehicles	-	-
309	Transport equipment n.e.c.	6	4
3091	Motorcycles	-	-
3092	Bicycles and invalid carriages	6	4
3099	Other transport equipment n.e.c.	-	-
3100	Furniture	2080	1951
321	Jewellery, bijouterie and related articles	6527	9682
3211	Jewellery and related articles	-	-
3212	Imitation jewellery and related articles	6474	9639
3220	Musical instruments	-	-
3230	Sports goods	57	58
3240	Games and toys	798	893
3250	Medical and dental instruments and supplies	-	-
3290	Other manufacturing n.e.c.	-	-
331	Repair of fabricated metal products/machinery	4158	3798
3311	Repair of fabricated metal products	-	44
3312	Repair of machinery	2832	1984
3313	Repair of electronic and optical equipment	14	55
3314	Repair of electrical equipment	1149	1583
3315	Repair of transport equip., excl. motor vehicles	-	-
3319	Repair of other equipment	-	-
3320	Installation of industrial machinery/equipment	-	-
C	Total manufacturing	443572	544803

Armenia

Index numbers of industrial production

ISIC Revision 3

(2005=100)

ISIC	Industry	Note	1999	2000	2001	2002	2003	2004	2005	2006	2007	2008	2009	2010
15	Food and beverages		66	69	75	81	93	95	100	104	111	119	112	128
16	Tobacco products		47	48	37	59	74	88	100	95	93	98	115	129
17	Textiles		41	51	52	56	81	134	100	98	88	69	34	31
18	Wearing apparel, fur		126	93	131	119	146	140	100	97	95	102	91	105
19	Leather, leather products and footwear		118	156	124	148	105	103	100	162	215	268	248	330
20	Wood products (excl. furniture)		44	90	89	111	123	119	100	123	129	98	96	166
21	Paper and paper products		20	29	33	37	84	102	100	118	111	103	93	162
22	Printing and publishing		71	81	78	68	78	86	100	127	171	190	173	179
23	Coke,refined petroleum products,nuclear fuel		...	...	...	...	...	...	...	...	...	...	...	...
24	Chemicals and chemical products		64	76	64	51	41	64	100	88	105	88	59	56
25	Rubber and plastics products		31	25	24	30	54	73	100	118	170	190	222	227
26	Non-metallic mineral products		46	35	38	50	63	79	100	109	132	140	106	120
27	Basic metals		19	40	58	71	77	75	100	105	119	108	130	138
28	Fabricated metal products		38	30	33	47	60	75	100	127	183	238	224	286
29	Machinery and equipment n.e.c.		51	65	96	73	85	112	100	114	119	99	97	86
30	Office, accounting and computing machinery		10	9	8	74	107	146	100	91	97	100	60	59
31	Electrical machinery and apparatus		46	73	71	79	93	95	100	108	145	151	103	136
32	Radio,television and communication equipment		50	57	88	67	137	79	100	115	206	293	199	179
33	Medical, precision and optical instruments		48	52	81	73	102	106	100	108	122	130	62	71
34	Motor vehicles, trailers, semi-trailers		13	103	33	16	19	39	100	106	101	341	-	-
35	Other transport equipment		119	39	33	53	70	280	100	98	261	158	71	57
36	Furniture; manufacturing n.e.c.		54	50	52	93	121	102	100	77	42	36	21	23
37	Recycling		231	300	265	174	150	114	100	69	250	285	213	269
D	Total manufacturing		52	56	61	77	92	91	100	98	99	100	91	102

Australia

Supplier of information:
Australian Bureau of Statistics, Canberra.

Basic source of data:
Economic activity survey; business activity statement data derived from Australian Taxation Office.

Major deviations from ISIC (Revision 3):
Data have been compiled on the basis of the Australian and New Zealand Standard Industrial Classification (ANZSIC). This classification is not fully compatible with ISIC (Revision 3), especially at a high level of disaggregation.

Reference period:
Fiscal year ending 30 June of the year indicated.

Scope:
All enterprises.

Method of data collection:
Not reported.

Type of enumeration:
Not reported.

Adjusted for non-response:
Yes.

Concepts and definitions of variables:
No deviations from the standard UN concepts and definitions are reported.

Related national publications:
Australian System of National Accounts, published by the Australian Bureau of Statistics, Canberra.

Australia

ISIC	Industry	Establishments (number) Note	2007	2008	2009	2010	Persons engaged (thousands) Note	2007	2008	2009	2010	Wages and salaries (millions of Australian Dollars) Note	2007	2008	2009	2010
151	Processed meat,fish,fruit,vegetables,fats		...	...	...	...		...	...	...	...		...	...	...	...
1511	Processing/preserving of meat		...	...	...	...		...	...	60.6	59.1		2492	2711	2820	2612
1512	Processing/preserving of fish		...	...	...	...		...	...	3.6	3.3		116	112	127	109
1513	Processing/preserving of fruit & vegetables		...	...	...	...		...	...	12.5	12.6		653	676	639	663
1514	Vegetable and animal oils and fats		...	...	...	...		...	...	1.8	1.6		120	124	116	114
1520	Dairy products		...	...	...	...		...	...	21.2	20.0		1075	1211	1178	1287
153	Grain mill products; starches; animal feeds		...	...	...	...		...	...	...	...		...	...	...	...
1531	Grain mill products		...	...	...	...		...	...	23.3	23.3		1034	1074	1138	1009
1532	Starches and starch products		...	...	...	...		...	...	9.1	9.6		438	520	486	630
1533	Prepared animal feeds		...	...	...	...		...	...	...	...		...	164	...	...
154	Other food products		...	...	...	...		...	...	...	...		...	...	...	...
1541	Bakery products		...	...	...	...		...	...	61.1	61.7		1693	1939	2071	1726
1542	Sugar		...	...	...	...		...	...	5.1	4.9		275	303	312	318
1543	Cocoa, chocolate and sugar confectionery		...	...	...	...		...	...	15.3	13.6		740	748	776	715
1544	Macaroni, noodles & similar products		...	...	...	...		...	...	...	...		...	...	...	...
1549	Other food products n.e.c.		...	...	...	...		...	...	15.1	15.2		648	634	659	626
155	Beverages		...	...	...	...		...	...	...	...		...	...	...	...
1551	Distilling, rectifying & blending of spirits		...	...	...	...		...	...	...	...		...	...	...	...
1552	Wines		...	...	...	...		...	...	15.5	16.7		797	737	849	830
1553	Malt liquors and malt		...	...	...	...		...	...	4.1	3.6		260	280	316	303
1554	Soft drinks; mineral waters		...	...	...	...		...	...	7.8	8.0		470	492	513	511
1600	Tobacco products		...	...	...	...		...	...	...	...		...	...	...	...
171	Spinning, weaving and finishing of textiles		...	...	...	...		...	...	...	...		...	...	...	...
1711	Textile fibre preparation; textile weaving		...	...	...	...		...	...	1.1	0.5		57	60	49	23
1712	Finishing of textiles		...	...	...	...		...	...	...	...		...	...	...	...
172	Other textiles		...	...	...	...		...	...	...	...		...	...	...	...
1721	Made-up textile articles, except apparel		...	...	...	...		...	...	...	...		...	...	...	...
1722	Carpets and rugs		...	...	...	...		...	...	2.2	2.2		143	132	141	121
1723	Cordage, rope, twine and netting		...	...	...	...		...	...	0.6	0.5		21	19	23	20
1729	Other textiles n.e.c.		...	...	...	...		...	...	...	...		...	...	...	...
1730	Knitted and crocheted fabrics and articles		...	...	...	...		...	...	1.5	1.3		72	65	74	66
1810	Wearing apparel, except fur apparel		...	...	...	...		...	...	20.9	19.7		626	630	682	618
1820	Dressing & dyeing of fur; processing of fur		...	...	...	...	a/	...	...	...a/	...a/		...	...	...	...
191	Tanning, dressing and processing of leather		...	...	...	...		...	...	...	...		...	...	...	...
1911	Tanning and dressing of leather		...	...	...	...	a/	...	...	2.9a/	2.8a/		90	101	99	96
1912	Luggage, handbags, etc.; saddlery & harness		...	...	...	...		...	...	...	...		...	...	...	...
1920	Footwear		...	...	...	...	a/	...	...	...a/	...a/		...	...	...	...
2010	Sawmilling and planing of wood		...	...	...	...		...	...	14.1	13.9		703	751	659	701
202	Products of wood, cork, straw, etc.		...	...	...	...		...	...	34.6	34.6		1379	1496	1478	1523
2021	Veneer sheets, plywood, particle board, etc.		...	...	...	...		...	...	1.1	1.3		59	61	63	68
2022	Builders' carpentry and joinery		...	...	...	...		...	...	...	...		...	...	...	...
2023	Wooden containers		...	...	...	...		...	...	...	...		...	...	...	...
2029	Other wood products; articles of cork/straw		...	...	...	...		...	...	4.9	4.5		163	184	182	177
210	Paper and paper products		...	...	...	...		...	...	...	...		...	...	...	...
2101	Pulp, paper and paperboard		...	...	...	...		...	...	20.8	20.5		1470	1530	1446	1459
2102	Corrugated paper and paperboard		...	...	...	...		...	...	4.8	4.1		354	369	317	335
2109	Other articles of paper and paperboard		...	...	...	...		...	...	5.9	6.7		472	492	510	504
221	Publishing		...	...	...	...		...	...	...	...		...	...	...	...
2211	Publishing of books and other publications		...	...	...	...		...	...	...	...		...	...	...	...
2212	Publishing of newspapers, journals, etc.		...	...	...	...		...	...	...	...		...	...	...	...
2213	Publishing of recorded media		...	...	...	...		...	...	...	...		...	...	...	...
2219	Other publishing		...	...	...	...		...	...	...	...		...	...	...	...

Code						%	%
222	Printing and related service activities	2128	2424	2327	2223	47.4	47.9
2221	Printing	2035	2319	2231	2116	44.8	45.3
2222	Service activities related to printing	93	105	96	107	2.6	2.6
2230	Reproduction of recorded media	118	130	120	98	2.4	2.4
2310	Coke oven products	165	147	130	125	2.1	2.5
2320	Refined petroleum products	462	635	618	578	5.3	3.7
2330	Processing of nuclear fuel						
241	Basic chemicals	778	710	633	570	9.1	10.0
2411	Basic chemicals, except fertilizers	298	264	331	257	3.7	3.4
2412	Fertilizers and nitrogen compounds						
2413	Plastics in primary forms; synthetic rubber						
242	Other chemicals						
2421	Pesticides and other agro-chemical products	111	106	94	97	1.7	1.7
2422	Paints, varnishes, printing ink and mastics	1309	1158	1074	1009	15.0	15.1
2423	Pharmaceuticals, medicinal chemicals, etc.	452	436	431	466	7.8	7.0
2424	Soap, cleaning & cosmetic preparations	328	277	221	215	2.7	3.4
2429	Other chemical products n.e.c.						
2430	Man-made fibres	158	144	171	156	2.4	2.7
251	Rubber products						
2511	Rubber tyres and tubes						
2519	Other rubber products	2606	2605	2701	2681	48.7	45.3
2520	Plastic products	691	695	340	405	8.3	9.1
2610	Glass and glass products						
269	Non-metallic mineral products n.e.c.						
2691	Pottery, china and earthenware						
2692	Refractory ceramic products	286	358	333	338	5.4	4.9
2693	Struct.non-refractory clay; ceramic products	1372	1355	1561	1537	21.8 b/	22.1 b/
2694	Cement, lime and plaster					.. b/	.. b/
2695	Articles of concrete, cement and plaster						
2696	Cutting, shaping & finishing of stone	340	357	323	336	6.9	6.7
2699	Other non-metallic mineral products n.e.c.	1607	1762	1744	1632	23.8	22.7
2710	Basic iron and steel	2145	2124	1995	1762	21.1	22.1
2720	Basic precious and non-ferrous metals						
273	Casting of metals	559	610	784	717	10.0	9.3
2731	Casting of iron and steel	273	227	349	319	4.7	4.5
2732	Casting of non-ferrous metals						
281	Struct.metal products;tanks;steam generators	3118	3136	2946	2622	66.7	59.2
2811	Structural metal products	391	415	436	437	11.5	9.3
2812	Tanks, reservoirs and containers of metal						
2813	Steam generators	1760	1688	1773	1593	43.3	37.4
289	Other metal products; metal working services						
2891	Metal forging/pressing/stamping/roll-forming						
2892	Treatment & coating of metals						
2893	Cutlery, hand tools and general hardware						
2899	Other fabricated metal products n.e.c.						
291	General purpose machinery						
2911	Engines & turbines (not for transport equipment)	262	232	217	213	4.3	4.1
2912	Pumps, compressors, taps and valves						
2913	Bearings, gears, gearing & driving elements						
2914	Ovens, furnaces and furnace burners	393	446	495	441	7.3	7.4
2915	Lifting and handling equipment	307	297	247	221	5.5	5.4
2919	Other general purpose machinery	1571	1546	1360	1387	29.1	27.6
292	Special purpose machinery						
2921	Agricultural and forestry machinery	325	347	293	300	7.2	6.6
2922	Machine tools	249	258	224	244	5.8	5.5
2923	Machinery for metallurgy	741	669	570	554	10.5	10.3
2924	Machinery for mining & construction						
2925	Food/beverage/tobacco processing machinery						
2926	Machinery for textile, apparel and leather						
2927	Weapons and ammunition	256	273	273	289	5.7	5.2
2929	Other special purpose machinery						

continued

Australia

ISIC	Industry	Establishments (number) Note	2007	2008	2009	2010	Persons engaged (thousands) Note	2007	2008	2009	2010	Wages and salaries (millions of Australian Dollars) Note	2007	2008	2009	2010
2930	Domestic appliances n.e.c.		...	...	...	...		...	...	6.6	6.0		330	340	370	330
3000	Office, accounting and computing machinery		...	...	...	...		...	...	16.9	15.3		991	1078	966	919
3110	Electric motors, generators and transformers		...	...	...	...		...	...	...	...		...	...	...	...
3120	Electricity distribution & control apparatus		...	...	...	...		...	...	...	...		...	...	...	...
3130	Insulated wire and cable		...	...	...	...		...	...	3.0	2.8		179	159	174	176
3140	Accumulators, primary cells and batteries		...	...	...	...		...	...	...	...		...	...	...	...
3150	Lighting equipment and electric lamps		...	...	...	...		...	...	4.6	4.7		234	219	233	239
3190	Other electrical equipment n.e.c.		...	...	...	...		...	...	12.1	11.4		621	658	667	644
3210	Electronic valves, tubes, etc.		...	...	...	...		...	...	...	...		...	...	...	...
3220	TV/radio transmitters; line comm. apparatus		...	...	...	...		...	...	...	...		...	...	...	...
3230	TV and radio receivers and associated goods		...	...	...	...		...	...	...	...		...	...	...	...
331	Medical, measuring, testing appliances, etc.		...	...	...	...		...	...	...	...		...	...	...	...
3311	Medical, surgical and orthopaedic equipment		...	...	...	...		...	...	11.0	11.2		527	504	534	587
3312	Measuring/testing/navigating appliances,etc.		...	...	...	...		...	...	...	...		...	...	...	...
3313	Industrial process control equipment		...	...	...	...		...	...	...	...		...	...	...	...
3320	Optical instruments & photographic equipment		...	...	...	...		...	...	1.5	1.3		82	90	73	69
3330	Watches and clocks		...	...	...	...		...	...	...	...		...	...	...	...
3410	Motor vehicles		...	...	...	...		...	...	20.2	17.1		1792	1694	1523	1281
3420	Automobile bodies, trailers & semi-trailers		...	...	...	...		...	...	15.5	11.5		625	757	629	614
3430	Parts/accessories for automobiles		...	...	...	...		...	...	18.3	14.5		1198	1139	962	858
351	Building and repairing of ships and boats		...	...	...	...		...	...	...	...		...	...	...	...
3511	Building and repairing of ships		...	...	...	...		...	...	8.2	7.9		472	527	514	646
3512	Building/repairing of pleasure/sport. boats		...	...	...	...		...	...	9.3	6.1		336	376	310	235
3520	Railway/tramway locomotives & rolling stock		...	...	...	...		...	...	6.4	5.1		415	488	500	487
3530	Aircraft and spacecraft		...	...	...	...		...	...	14.5	13.4		765	849	966	972
359	Transport equipment n.e.c.		...	...	...	...		...	...	0.7	1.1		15	15	12	60
3591	Motorcycles		...	...	...	...		...	...	...	...		...	...	...	...
3592	Bicycles and invalid carriages		...	...	...	...		...	...	...	...		...	...	...	...
3599	Other transport equipment n.e.c.		...	...	...	...		...	...	...	...		...	...	...	...
3610	Furniture		...	...	...	...		...	...	26.1	25.3		...	...	...	951
369	Manufacturing n.e.c.		...	...	...	...		...	...	15.7	15.2		...	...	...	495
3691	Jewellery and related articles		...	...	...	...		...	...	2.9c/	4.5		...	...	...	109
3692	Musical instruments		...	...	...	...		...	...	...	...		...	...	...	...
3693	Sports goods		...	...	...	...		...	...	..c/	...		...	...	...	...
3694	Games and toys		...	...	...	...		...	...	..c/	...		...	...	...	...
3699	Other manufacturing n.e.c.		...	...	...	...		...	...	...	...		...	...	...	...
3710	Recycling of metal waste and scrap		...	...	...	...		...	...	...	...		...	...	...	...
3720	Recycling of non-metal waste and scrap		...	...	...	...		...	...	...	...		...	...	...	...
D	Total manufacturing		...	...	...	...		...	...	1007.8	955.0		50190	52745	53158	51853

a/ 191 includes 1820 and 1920.
b/ 2694 includes 2695.
c/ 3692 includes 3693 and 3694.

Australia

ISIC	Industry	Note	Output (millions of Australian Dollars) 2007	2008	2009	2010	Note	Value added (millions of Australian Dollars) 2007	2008	2009	2010	Note	Gross fixed capital formation (millions of Australian Dollars) 2009	2010
151	Processed meat,fish,fruit,vegetables,fats		18408	18574	20111	19922		3749	4144	4359	4240		...	...
1511	Processing/preserving of meat		1330	1212	1386	1407		152	155	234	305		...	...
1512	Processing/preserving of fish		4738	4867	5168	5485		1169	1336	1301	1239		...	...
1513	Processing/preserving of fruit & vegetables		1783	2091	3314	2716		258	254	333	174		...	...
1514	Vegetable and animal oils and fats		11338	13571	12522	13011		1976	2367	2039	2328		...	...
1520	Dairy products		8507	...	9417	9519		1814	1758	1769	2183		...	...
153	Grain mill products; starches; animal feeds		4150	4904	5301	6451		917	949	954	1170		...	...
1531	Grain mill products		...	...	...	...		...	...	...	...		...	...
1532	Starches and starch products		...	769	...	...		...	258	...	...		...	...
1533	Prepared animal feeds		...	3162	...	...		...	452	...	...		...	...
154	Other food products												...	...
1541	Bakery products		7068	7231	7684	8126		2795	3140	3323	3319		...	...
1542	Sugar		2783	2093	1882	2267		510	491	586	624		...	...
1543	Cocoa, chocolate and sugar confectionery		4614	4898	5339	5222		1569	1475	1652	1249		...	...
1544	Macaroni, noodles & similar products												...	...
1549	Other food products n.e.c.		4575	4345	4450	4596		1106	1047	956	1078		...	...
155	Beverages												...	...
1551	Distilling, rectifying & blending of spirits		6248	5219	5725	5779		1455	1347	1136	1395		...	...
1552	Wines		...	3871	4199	...		...	1436	1863	...		...	...
1553	Malt liquors and malt		4389	4365	4423	4966		1586	1524	1617	1791		...	...
1554	Soft drinks; mineral waters												...	...
1600	Tobacco products												...	...
171	Spinning, weaving and finishing of textiles		221	239	225	136		70	92	70	38		...	...
1711	Textile fibre preparation; textile weaving		...	...	...	...		...	...	...	...		...	...
1712	Finishing of textiles		...	...	...	...		...	...	...	...		...	...
172	Other textiles		...	...	...	...		...	...	...	...		...	...
1721	Made-up textile articles, except apparel		...	...	...	...		...	...	...	...		...	...
1722	Carpets and rugs		1076	1004	924	946		235	228	241	200		...	...
1723	Cordage, rope, twine and netting		157	165	194	142		40	41	33	37		...	...
1729	Other textiles n.e.c.		...	...	...	...		...	...	...	...		...	...
1730	Knitted and crocheted fabrics and articles		267	265	263	251		115	112	88	108		...	...
1810	Wearing apparel, except fur apparel	a/	3535	3751	3626	3477		1088	1148	1120	1144		...	...
1820	Dressing & dyeing of fur; processing of fur	a/	734	777	608	650		173	194	173	189		...	...
191	Tanning, dressing and processing of leather		...	...	...	...		...	...	...	...		...	...
1911	Tanning and dressing of leather		...	...	...	...		...	...	...	...		...	...
1912	Luggage, handbags, etc.; saddlery & harness		...	...	...	...		...	...	...	...		...	...
1920	Footwear	a/	...	...	...	...		...	...	...	...		...	...
2010	Sawmilling and planing of wood		4523	5145	4794	4693		1572	1740	1472	1310		...	...
202	Products of wood, cork, straw, etc.		7065	7954	7704	7999		2448	2680	2740	2902		...	...
2021	Veneer sheets, plywood, particle board, etc.		414	477	442	468		104	124	118	96		...	...
2022	Builders' carpentry and joinery												...	...
2023	Wooden containers												...	...
2029	Other wood products; articles of cork/straw		767	952	888	885		285	330	355	348		...	...
210	Paper and paper products		9589	9904	9542	9657		2755	2953	2842	2633		...	...
2101	Pulp, paper and paperboard		2582	2763	2584	2429		648	671	538	433		...	...
2102	Corrugated paper and paperboard		2980	3185	3033	3306		898	1072	924	975		...	...
2109	Other articles of paper and paperboard		...	...	...	...		...	...	...	...		...	...
221	Publishing		...	...	...	...		...	...	...	...		...	...
2211	Publishing of books and other publications		...	...	...	...		...	...	...	...		...	...
2212	Publishing of newspapers, journals, etc.		...	...	...	...		...	...	...	...		...	...
2213	Publishing of recorded media		...	...	...	...		...	...	...	...		...	...
2219	Other publishing		...	...	...	...		...	...	...	...		...	...

continued

Australia

		Output (millions of Australian Dollars)					Value added (millions of Australian Dollars)					Gross fixed capital formation (millions of Australian Dollars)		
ISIC	Industry	Note	2007	2008	2009	2010	Note	2007	2008	2009	2010	Note	2009	2010
222	Printing and related service activities		8903	8871	9334	8696		3777	3851	4173	3817			
2221	Printing		8616	8590	9008	8395		3603	3687	3992	3649			
2222	Service activities related to printing		287	281	327	300		174	165	181	168			
2230	Reproduction of recorded media		458	559	542	487		202	220	234	217			
2310	Coke oven products		1183	1349	1782	1745		290	334	322	437			
2320	Refined petroleum products		35478	36471	46625	23845		2285	2954	829	1146			
2330	Processing of nuclear fuel													
241	Basic chemicals		6087	6651	7778	7501		1648	1877	1956	1726			
2411	Basic chemicals, except fertilizers													
2412	Fertilizers and nitrogen compounds		3121	4327	3676	3545		817	1024	963	1022			
2413	Plastics in primary forms; synthetic rubber													
242	Other chemicals													
2421	Pesticides and other agro-chemical products		846	843	1001	1037		174	180	135	121			
2422	Paints, varnishes, printing ink and mastics													
2423	Pharmaceuticals, medicinal chemicals, etc.		7179	7953	8668	10021		1925	2032	2528	2844			
2424	Soap, cleaning & cosmetic preparations		2861	2945	3087	3337		962	960	1006	1176			
2429	Other chemical products n.e.c.		1459	1617	1721	2145		656	638		953			
2430	Man-made fibres													
251	Rubber products		770	838	701	832		265	325	269	327			
2511	Rubber tyres and tubes													
2519	Other rubber products													
2520	Plastic products		15263	16480	15160	15245		4913	5584	4946	5063			
2610	Glass and glass products		2142	1917	3634	3394		890	817	1574	1327			
269	Non-metallic mineral products n.e.c.													
2691	Pottery, china and earthenware													
2692	Refractory ceramic products													
2693	Struct.non-refractory clay; ceramic products	b/	1587	1593	1576	1448	b/	704	681	673	568			
2694	Cement, lime and plaster	b/	10392	11579	10438	10417	b/	2995	3280	2823	2862			
2695	Articles of concrete, cement and plaster													
2696	Cutting, shaping & finishing of stone		1687	1751	1845	1939		595	640	736	655			
2699	Other non-metallic mineral products n.e.c.													
2710	Basic iron and steel		14387	17006	18565	14649		3753	4452	5209	2722			
2720	Basic precious and non-ferrous metals		39654	40796	44903	38619		9892	9267	6413	2724			
273	Casting of metals													
2731	Casting of iron and steel		3690	4144	4221	3243		1441	1357	1795	1087			
2732	Casting of non-ferrous metals		3586	3797	3600	2678		530	483	628	311			
281	Struct.metal products;tanks;steam generators													
2811	Structural metal products		14601	15502	17053	15582		4648	4937	5369	5452			
2812	Tanks, reservoirs and containers of metal		2429	2381	2387	2337		855	896	944	870			
2813	Steam generators													
289	Other metal products; metal working services		7649	8055	8212	7870		2878	3038	3139	3184			
2891	Metal forging/pressing/stamping/roll-forming													
2892	Treatment & coating of metals													
2893	Cutlery, hand tools and general hardware													
2899	Other fabricated metal products n.e.c.													
291	General purpose machinery													
2911	Engines & turbines (not for transport equipment)		1134	1124	1261	1223		380	406	462	358			
2912	Pumps, compressors, taps and valves													
2913	Bearings, gears, gearing & driving elements													
2914	Ovens, furnaces and furnace burners													
2915	Lifting and handling equipment		2161	2243	2231	2090		731	745	771	638			
2919	Other general purpose machinery		1056	1104	1743	1560		339	410	525	502			

Code									
292	Special purpose machinery	2538	2878	2366	2460	8248	9206	7752	7320
2921	Agricultural and forestry machinery	553	626	500	492	1908	2527	1908	1722
2922	Machine tools	378	516	...	...	928	1103	873	934
2923	Machinery for metallurgy	...	...	...	...	...	...	...	...
2924	Machinery for mining & construction	1215	1243	...	...	4059	4147	3623	3255
2925	Food/beverage/tobacco processing machinery	...	...	...	...	...	...	...	...
2926	Machinery for textile, apparel and leather	...	...	...	...	...	...	...	...
2927	Weapons and ammunition	392	492	466	476	1353	1429	1348	1409
2929	Other special purpose machinery	720	772	707	604	2391	2582	2378	2103
2930	Domestic appliances n.e.c.	1472	1641	1748	1756	4132	4899	4766	4967
3000	Office, accounting and computing machinery	...	...	...	...	...	...	...	...
3110	Electric motors, generators and transformers	...	...	...	...	...	...	...	...
3120	Electricity distribution & control apparatus	...	...	...	...	...	...	...	...
3130	Insulated wire and cable	306	335	322	384	1642	1689	1817	1811
3140	Accumulators, primary cells and batteries	403	400	330	379	1288	1279	1089	1132
3150	Lighting equipment and electric lamps	946	982	1090	1044	3892	4142	3566	3550
3190	Other electrical equipment n.e.c.	...	...	...	...	...	...	...	...
3210	Electronic valves, tubes, etc.	...	...	...	...	...	...	...	...
3220	TV/radio transmitters; line comm. apparatus	...	...	...	...	...	...	...	...
3230	TV and radio receivers and associated goods	...	...	...	...	...	...	...	...
331	Medical, measuring, testing appliances, etc.	1296	1357	1122	1084	2891	3102	2348	2482
3311	Medical, surgical and orthopaedic equipment	...	...	...	...	...	...	...	...
3312	Measuring/testing/navigating appliances,etc.	...	...	...	...	...	...	...	...
3313	Industrial process control equipment	...	...	...	...	...	...	...	...
3320	Optical instruments & photographic equipment	118	126	127	121	345	381	393	296
3330	Watches and clocks	...	...	...	...	...	...	...	...
3410	Motor vehicles	1593	2171	2415	2510	10109	12441	14656	13824
3420	Automobile bodies, trailers & semi-trailers	1078	1116	1285	1024	3351	3575	3691	3184
3430	Parts/accessories for automobiles	1451	1537	2022	2036	4681	5128	5625	5842
351	Building and repairing of ships and boats	...	...	...	...	...	...	...	...
3511	Building and repairing of ships	979	510	677	578	2637	1839	1954	1777
3512	Building/repairing of pleasure/sport. boats	447	961	940	631	1221	1640	1829	1688
3520	Railway/tramway locomotives & rolling stock	881	...	...	1332	2815	3157	2694	2412
3530	Aircraft and spacecraft	1516	1557	1577	...	3920	3853	2843	3394
359	Transport equipment n.e.c.	113	...	...	...	420	70	79	74
3591	Motorcycles	...	...	...	...	...	...	...	...
3592	Bicycles and invalid carriages	...	...	...	...	...	...	...	...
3599	Other transport equipment n.e.c.	...	...	...	...	...	...	...	...
3610	Furniture	1600	1731	1777	1611	4604	4756	5263	5043
369	Manufacturing n.e.c.	895	939	899	825	2692	2841	2806	2778
3691	Jewellery and related articles	202	...	256	224	725	...	847	810
3692	Musical instruments	...	151c/	163c/	158c/	...	437c/	453c/	511c/
3693	Sports goods	...	..c/	..c/	..c/	...	..c/	..c/	..c/
3694	Games and toys	...	..c/	..c/	..c/	...	..c/	..c/	..c/
3699	Other manufacturing n.e.c.	...	...	480	442	...	...	1506	1456
3710	Recycling of metal waste and scrap	...	...	...	...	...	...	...	...
3720	Recycling of non-metal waste and scrap	...	...	...	...	...	...	...	...
D	Total manufacturing	96809	105154	107331	101815	381165	420921	395667	377246

a/ 191 includes 1820 and 1920.
b/ 2694 includes 2695.
c/ 3692 includes 3693 and 3694.

Australia

Index numbers of industrial production

ISIC Revision 3			(2005=100)											
ISIC	Industry	Note	1999	2000	2001	2002	2003	2004	2005	2006	2007	2008	2009	2010
15	Food and beverages	a/	93	94	98	98	99	99	100	99	100	100	97	...
16	Tobacco products	a/	...	...	...	...	...	...	...	...	...	...	...	...
17	Textiles	b/	126	124	121	117	115	115	100	92	91	95	85	...
18	Wearing apparel, fur	b/	...	...	...	...	...	...	...	...	...	...	...	...
19	Leather, leather products and footwear	b/	...	...	...	...	...	...	...	...	...	...	...	...
20	Wood products (excl. furniture)	c/	89	96	94	97	99	99	100	96	94	90	84	...
21	Paper and paper products	c/	...	...	...	...	...	...	...	...	...	...	...	...
22	Printing and publishing		79	88	94	95	101	107	100	96	97	99	82	...
23	Coke,refined petroleum products,nuclear fuel	d/	91	95	97	98	104	100	100	97	95	97	88	...
24	Chemicals and chemical products	d/	...	...	...	...	...	...	...	...	...	...	...	...
25	Rubber and plastics products	d/	...	...	...	...	...	...	...	...	...	...	...	...
26	Non-metallic mineral products	e/	74	78	80	85	93	96	100	112	114	119	119	...
27	Basic metals	e/	96	92	92	98	102	103	100	100	110	123	119	...
28	Fabricated metal products	e/	...	...	...	...	...	...	...	...	...	...	...	...
29	Machinery and equipment n.e.c.	f/	84	83	87	88	94	100	100	104	104	107	101	...
30	Office, accounting and computing machinery	f/	...	...	...	...	...	...	...	...	...	...	...	...
31	Electrical machinery and apparatus	f/	...	...	...	...	...	...	...	...	...	...	...	...
32	Radio,television and communication equipment	f/	...	...	...	...	...	...	...	...	...	...	...	...
33	Medical, precision and optical instruments	f/	...	...	...	...	...	...	...	...	...	...	...	...
34	Motor vehicles, trailers, semi-trailers	f/	...	...	...	...	...	...	...	...	...	...	...	...
35	Other transport equipment	f/	...	...	...	...	...	...	...	...	...	...	...	...
36	Furniture; manufacturing n.e.c.	g/	83	85	88	97	102	109	100	90	90	101	97	...
37	Recycling	g/	...	...	...	...	...	...	...	...	...	...	...	...
D	Total manufacturing		91	92	94	96	100	101	100	100	102	106	99	...

a/ 15 includes 16.
b/ 17 includes 18 and 19.
c/ 20 includes 21.
d/ 23 includes 24 and 25.
e/ 27 includes 28.
f/ 29 includes 30, 31, 32, 33, 34 and 35.
g/ 36 includes 37.

Austria

Supplier of information:
Statistics Austria, Vienna.
Industrial statistics for the OECD countries are compiled by the OECD secretariat, which
supplies them to UNIDO.

Basic source of data:
Annual survey; administrative data.

Major deviations from ISIC (Revision 4):
Data have been converted from the national NACE-related classification system (ÖNACE)
to ISIC (Revision 4) by the OECD.

Reference period:
Calendar year.

Scope:
All enterprises.

Method of data collection:
Not reported.

Type of enumeration:
Not reported.

Adjusted for non-response:
Not reported.

Concepts and definitions of variables:
No deviations from the standard UN concepts and definitions are reported.

Related national publications:
Statistical Yearbook of Austria, published by Statistics Austria, Vienna.

Austria

		Number of enterprises (number)					Number of employees (number)					Wages and salaries paid to employees (millions of Euros)				
ISIC	Industry	Note	2006	2007	2008	2009	Note	2006	2007	2008	2009	Note	2006	2007	2008	2009
1010	Processing/preserving of meat		..	..	1092	1058		..	..	15728	16112		..	..	378	393
1020	Processing/preserving of fish, etc.		..	..	6	5		..	..	139	128		..	..	4	4
1030	Processing/preserving of fruit,vegetables		..	..	112	112		..	..	3659	3592		..	..	135	135
1040	Vegetable and animal oils and fats		..	..	61	63		..	..	...	...		..	..	...	...
1050	Dairy products		..	..	158	165		..	..	4786	4584		..	..	167	170
106	Grain mill products,starches and starch products		..	..	132	135		..	..	1771	1832		..	..	57	61
1061	Grain mill products		..	..	128	132		..	..	1273	1310		..	..	38	41
1062	Starches and starch products		..	..	4	3		..	..	498	522		..	..	18	20
107	Other food products		..	..	2061	2035		..	..	36783	36795		..	..	872	868
1071	Bakery products		..	..	1864	1825		..	..	28754	29079		..	..	588	607
1072	Sugar		..	..	1	1		..	..	...	...		..	..	...	...
1073	Cocoa, chocolate and sugar confectionery		..	..	30	33		..	..	2209	1842		..	..	83	58
1074	Macaroni, noodles, couscous, etc.		..	..	39	46		..	..	459	466		..	..	11	12
1075	Prepared meals and dishes		..	..	14	15		..	..	827	812		..	..	24	23
1079	Other food products n.e.c.		..	..	113	115		..	..	...	...		..	..	...	...
1080	Prepared animal feeds		..	..	56	51		..	..	1984	1887		..	..	70	71
1101	Distilling, rectifying and blending of spirits		..	..	335a/	332a/		..	..	8943a/	8898a/		..	..	345a/	354a/
1102	Wines		..	..	...a/	...a/		..	..	...a/	...a/		..	..	...a/	...a/
1103	Malt liquors and malt		..	..	...a/	...a/		..	..	...a/	...a/		..	..	...a/	...a/
1104	Soft drinks,mineral waters,other bottled waters		..	..	...a/	...a/		..	..	...a/	...a/		..	..	...a/	...a/
1200	Tobacco products		..	..	1	1		..	..	2549	2477		..	..	192	198
131	Spinning, weaving and finishing of textiles		..	..	160	159		..	..	4482	3961		..	..	140	121
1311	Preparation and spinning of textile fibres		..	..	18	15		..	..	1232	956		..	..	39	31
1312	Weaving of textiles		..	..	45	41		..	..	2351	2132		..	..	75	65
1313	Finishing of textiles		..	..	97	103		..	..	899	873		..	..	27	25
139	Other textiles		..	..	495	464		..	..	5323	4797		..	..	151	138
1391	Knitted and crocheted fabrics		..	..	31	25		..	..	309	267		..	..	10	9
1392	Made-up textile articles, except apparel		..	..	115	115		..	..	1699	1640		..	..	42	40
1393	Carpets and rugs		..	..	19	19		..	..	313	284		..	..	9	8
1394	Cordage, rope, twine and netting		..	..	17	15		..	..	...	...		..	..	...	...
1399	Other textiles n.e.c.		..	..	313	290		..	..	...	...		..	..	...	...
1410	Wearing apparel, except fur apparel		..	..	672	651		..	..	6586	6231		..	..	142	136
1420	Articles of fur		..	..	53	45		..	..	81	71		..	..	1	1
1430	Knitted and crocheted apparel		..	..	27	29		..	..	1648	1554		..	..	52	45
151	Leather;luggage,handbags,saddlery,harness;fur		..	..	98	96		..	..	2604	2363		..	..	57	53
1511	Tanning/dressing of leather; dressing of fur		..	..	36	36		..	..	2289	2043		..	..	50	46
1512	Luggage,handbags,etc.;saddlery/harness		..	..	62	60		..	..	315	320		..	..	7	7
1520	Footwear		..	..	88	83		..	..	1652	1539		..	..	49	46
1610	Sawmilling and planing of wood		..	..	1094	1077		..	..	11474	9944		..	..	335	280
162	Wood products, cork, straw, plaiting materials		..	..	1865	1800		..	..	22315	21275		..	..	668	637

- 225 -

Code	Industry	(1)	(2)	(3)	(4)	(5)	(6)
1621	Veneer sheets and wood-based panels	32	30	4509	3982	182	158
1622	Builders' carpentry and joinery	1396	1325	15867	15542	442	438
1623	Wooden containers	110	108	1073	992	26	24
1629	Other wood products;articles of cork,straw	327	337	866	759	19	17
1701	Pulp, paper and paperboard	37	36	8166	7582	381	365
1702	Corrugated paper and paperboard	65	63	5873	5668	221	210
1709	Other articles of paper and paperboard	52	51	4411	3962	184	153
181	Printing and service activities related to printing	985	935	14264	13176	548	495
1811	Printing	727	698	12638	11779	496	450
1812	Service activities related to printing	258	237	1626	1397	51	45
1820	Reproduction of recorded media	28	23	1358	1420	58	50
1910	Coke oven products	-	-	-	-	-	-
1920	Refined petroleum products	5	5	2549	2477	192	198
201	Basic chemicals,fertilizers, etc.	80	72	6367	6347	329	323
2011	Basic chemicals	44	40	979	975	51	49
2012	Fertilizers and nitrogen compounds	13	13	...	...	...	...
2013	Plastics and synthetic rubber in primary forms	23	19	...	...	...	...
202	Other chemical products	251	245	8456	8105	343	336
2021	Pesticides and other agrochemical products	8	7	266	285	13	13
2022	Paints,varnishes;printing ink and mastics	46	42	3233	2998	129	119
2023	Soap,cleaning and cosmetic preparations	124	126	2605	2492	101	103
2029	Other chemical products n.e.c.	73	70	2352	2330	101	100
2030	Man-made fibres	5	5	2525	2204	130	111
2100	Pharmaceuticals,medicinal chemicals, etc.	82	82	10532	10683	471	489
221	Rubber products	48	48	3201	2837	124	113
2211	Rubber tyres and tubes	6	6	99	97	2	2
2219	Other rubber products	42	42	3102	2740	121	111
2220	Plastics products	551	557	25541	25010	869	855
2310	Glass and glass products	167	173	10617	9466	400	357
239	Non-metallic mineral products n.e.c.	1237	1199	24104	23032	921	893
2391	Refractory products	12	12	1622	1418	70	58
2392	Clay building materials	24	26	1007	1007	42	42
2393	Other porcelain and ceramic products	180	170	1476	1473	...	51
2394	Cement, lime and plaster	12	12	1508	1476	70	70
2395	Articles of concrete, cement and plaster	360	352	12057	11797	467	474
2396	Cutting, shaping and finishing of stone	571	549	3113	2968	81	79
2399	Other non-metallic mineral products n.e.c.	78	78	3247	2893	139	121
2410	Basic iron and steel	50	49	...	...	...	...
2420	Basic precious and other non-ferrous metals	50	51	6846	6587	293	261
243	Casting of metals	64	62	7253	6545	291	248
2431	Casting of iron and steel	19	18	2519	2387	107	95
2432	Casting of non-ferrous metals	45	44	4734	4158	184	152
251	Struct.metal products, tanks, reservoirs	1287	1292	26866	22479	909	883
2511	Structural metal products	1231	1233	23332		765	738
2512	Tanks, reservoirs and containers of metal	51	51	3212	3249	130	131

continued

Austria

ISIC	Industry	Number of enterprises (number)					Number of employees (number)					Wages and salaries paid to employees (millions of Euros)				
		Note	2006	2007	2008	2009	Note	2006	2007	2008	2009	Note	2006	2007	2008	2009
2513	Steam generators, excl. hot water boilers		...	...	5	8		...	...	322	321		...	...	14	13
2520	Weapons and ammunition		...	...	43	46		...	...	860	886		...	...	33	35
259	Other metal products;metal working services		...	...	2715	2522		...	...	44098	42247		...	...	1548	1482
2591	Forging,pressing,stamping,roll-forming of metal		...	...	500	455		...	...	5960	5717		...	...	184	195
2592	Treatment and coating of metals; machining		...	...	735	730		...	...	12356	11651		...	...	402	382
2593	Cutlery, hand tools and general hardware		...	...	1078	955		...	...	17866	17384		...	...	697	642
2599	Other fabricated metal products n.e.c.		...	...	402	382		...	...	7916	7495		...	...	265	264
2610	Electronic components and boards		...	...	111	106		...	...	8821	8463		...	...	400	367
2620	Computers and peripheral equipment		...	...	54	38		...	...	892	888		...	...	38	41
2630	Communication equipment		...	...	76	73		...	...	4551	4498		...	...	246	276
2640	Consumer electronics		...	...	31	28		...	...	1354	1258		...	...	72	70
265	Measuring,testing equipment; watches, etc.		...	...	249	248		...	...	4800	4802		...	...	188	187
2651	Measuring/testing/navigating equipment,etc.		...	...	218	217		...	...	4655	4665		...	...	183	183
2652	Watches and clocks		...	...	31	31		...	...	145	137		...	...	5	5
2660	Irradiation/electromedical equipment,etc.		...	...	50	50		...	...	1782	1886		...	...	74	75
2670	Optical instruments and photographic equipment		...	...	19	20		...	...	873	880		...	...	34	33
2680	Magnetic and optical media		...	...	-	-		...	...	-	-		...	...	-	-
2710	Electric motors,generators,transformers,etc.		...	...	198	197		...	...	24739	24248		...	...	1316	1296
2720	Batteries and accumulators		...	...	5	4		...	...	460	479		...	...	20	21
273	Wiring and wiring devices		...	...	50	46		...	...	3295	3170		...	...	114	105
2731	Fibre optic cables		...	...	2	1		...	...	...	...		...	...	...	...
2732	Other electronic and electric wires and cables		...	...	29	27		...	...	1682	1635		...	...	58	53
2733	Wiring devices		...	...	19	18		...	...	...	...		...	...	...	...
2740	Electric lighting equipment		...	...	87	84		...	...	3849	3823		...	...	142	145
2750	Domestic appliances		...	...	50	51		...	...	4882	4738		...	...	175	167
2790	Other electrical equipment		...	...	74	84		...	...	7536	7041		...	...	306	286
281	General-purpose machinery		...	...	707	669		...	...	36632	36701		...	...	1526	1471
2811	Engines/turbines,excl.aircraft,vehicle engines		...	...	31	28		...	...	3703	1788		...	...	136	83
2812	Fluid power equipment		...	...	42	44		...	...	1649	1799		...	...	65	65
2813	Other pumps, compressors, taps and valves		...	...	50	46		...	...	5647	5649		...	...	247	240
2814	Bearings, gears, gearing and driving elements		...	...	38	40		...	...	4120	4428		...	...	186	186
2815	Ovens, furnaces and furnace burners		...	...	66	69		...	...	2637	2716		...	...	107	101
2816	Lifting and handling equipment		...	...	144	141		...	...	9290	9241		...	...	421	402
2817	Office machinery, excl.computers,etc.		...	...	14	10		...	...	271	279		...	...	8	9
2818	Power-driven hand tools		...	...	17	16		...	...	112	109		...	...	4	4
2819	Other general-purpose machinery		...	...	305	275		...	...	9203	10692		...	...	353	383
282	Special-purpose machinery		...	...	697	672		...	...	37682	35569		...	...	1610	1478
2821	Agricultural and forestry machinery		...	...	131	120		...	...	5854	5809		...	...	223	214
2822	Metal-forming machinery and machine tools		...	...	148	138		...	...	6062	5642		...	...	250	222
2823	Machinery for metallurgy		...	...	15	18		...	...	608	628		...	...	27	28
2824	Mining, quarrying and construction machinery		...	...	50	43		...	...	4930	4662		...	...	216	191

2825	Food/beverage/tobacco processing machinery	59	55	...	1853	1743	...	...	76	72
2826	Textile/apparel/leather production machinery	24	22	...	747	620	...	...	33	25
2829	Other special-purpose machinery	270	276	...	17628	16465	...	...	786	725
2910	Motor vehicles	27	24	...	15502	14579	...	...	743	651
2920	Automobile bodies, trailers and semi-trailers	191	183	...	3835	3459	...	...	121	108
2930	Parts and accessories for motor vehicles	83	82	...	13874	12039	...	...	529	448
301	Building of ships and boats	30	30	...	221	196	...	...	6	6
3011	Building of ships and floating structures	-	-	...	-	-	...	...	-	-
3012	Building of pleasure and sporting boats	30	30	...	221	196	...	...	6	6
3020	Railway locomotives and rolling stock	14	9	...	4675	...	...	...	280	40
3030	Air and spacecraft and related machinery	18	17	...	928	887	...	...	40	40
3040	Military fighting vehicles	1	1	...	...	1870	...	...	...	...
309	Transport equipment n.e.c.	13	15	...	1528	...	...	...	52	59
3091	Motorcycles	3	4	...	...	...	...	...	...	...
3092	Bicycles and invalid carriages	9	10	...	339	344	...	...	10	11
3099	Other transport equipment n.e.c.	1	1	...	...	...	...	...	...	...
3100	Furniture	3373	3201	...	28816	27910	...	...	739	725
321	Jewellery, bijouterie and related articles	441	434	...	1413	1338	...	...	42	42
3211	Jewellery and related articles	411	397	...	...	...	...	...	...	...
3212	Imitation jewellery and related articles	30	37	...	616	723	...	...	16	22
3220	Musical instruments	201	197	...	3747	3397	...	...	128	119
3230	Sports goods	80	80	...	2127	2017	...	...	80	74
3240	Games and toys	80	74	...	7978	7942	...	...	222	227
3250	Medical and dental instruments and supplies	918	880	...	1575	1514	...	...	43	42
3290	Other manufacturing n.e.c.	163	168	...	...	...	...	...	...	...
331	Repair of fabricated metal products/machinery	1276	1320	...	11417	11259	...	...	416	426
3311	Repair of fabricated metal products	55	56	...	1098	1046	...	...	49	47
3312	Repair of machinery	972	994	...	3827	3798	...	...	119	120
3313	Repair of electronic and optical equipment	59	64	...	1854	1956	...	...	86	95
3314	Repair of electrical equipment	96	100	...	385	488	...	...	10	18
3315	Repair of transport equip., excl. motor vehicles	66	78	...	4164	3902	...	...	151	146
3319	Repair of other equipment	28	28	...	89	69	...	...	2	1
3320	Installation of industrial machinery/equipment	346	357	...	6919	6743	...	...	297	292
C	Total manufacturing	26081	25319	...	616255	591109	...	...	22989	22025

a/ 1101 includes 1102, 1103 and 1104.

Austria

ISIC	Industry	Note	Output (millions of Euros)				Note	Value added at factor values (millions of Euros)				Note	Gross fixed capital formation (millions of Euros)	
			2006	2007	2008	2009		2006	2007	2008	2009		2008	2009
1010	Processing/preserving of meat		...	...	3070	3188		...	...	706	711		107	95
1020	Processing/preserving of fish, etc.		...	...	23	27		...	...	9	10		5	3
1030	Processing/preserving of fruit,vegetables		...	...	1421	1199		...	...	308	297		41	52
1040	Vegetable and animal oils and fats		...	...	...	...		...	...	...	...		...	...
1050	Dairy products		...	...	2149	1931		...	...	335	358		99	89
106	Grain mill products,starches and starch products		...	...	651	634		...	...	151	149		30	35
1061	Grain mill products		...	...	430	394		...	...	93	92		21	24
1062	Starches and starch products		...	...	221	241		...	...	59	57		8	10
107	Other food products		...	...	4075	3846		...	...	1608	1583		180	155
1071	Bakery products		...	...	2051	2073		...	...	1043	1076		118	98
1072	Sugar		...	...	...	...		...	...	...	...		...	...
1073	Cocoa, chocolate and sugar confectionery		...	...	570	271		...	...	180	105		14	11
1074	Macaroni, noodles, couscous, etc.		...	...	71	70		...	...	24	22		4	7
1075	Prepared meals and dishes		...	...	124	134		...	...	38	42		6	4
1079	Other food products n.e.c.		...	...	...	...		...	...	...	...		...	...
1080	Prepared animal feeds		...	...	789	758		...	...	181	167		25	21
1101	Distilling, rectifying and blending of spirits		...	...	4176a/	4139a/		...	...	945a/	1098a/		152a/	151a/
1102	Wines		...	...	...a/	...a/		...	...	...a/	...a/		...a/	...a/
1103	Malt liquors and malt		...	...	...a/	...a/		...	...	...a/	...a/		...a/	...a/
1104	Soft drinks,mineral waters,other bottled waters		...	...	...a/	...a/		...	...	...a/	...a/		...a/	...a/
1200	Tobacco products		...	...	7996	5753		...	...	628	395		319	143
131	Spinning, weaving and finishing of textiles		...	...	690	547		...	...	212	181		28	18
1311	Preparation and spinning of textile fibres		...	...	251	180		...	...	58	44		11	4
1312	Weaving of textiles		...	...	340	279		...	...	115	102		15	9
1313	Finishing of textiles		...	...	99	88		...	...	39	34		2	5
139	Other textiles		...	...	740	629		...	...	266	236		23	16
1391	Knitted and crocheted fabrics		...	...	90	66		...	...	17	17		-	-
1392	Made-up textile articles, except apparel		...	...	195	187		...	...	67	70		9	4
1393	Carpets and rugs		...	...	45	42		...	...	13	13		1	2
1394	Cordage, rope, twine and netting		...	...	...	...		...	...	...	...		...	...
1399	Other textiles n.e.c.		...	...	...	...		...	...	...	...		...	...
1410	Wearing apparel, except fur apparel		...	...	774	720		...	...	263	253		13	10
1420	Articles of fur		...	...	6	6		...	...	3	3		-	-
1430	Knitted and crocheted apparel		...	...	129	111		...	...	77	58		4	3
151	Leather;luggage,handbags,saddlery,harness;fur		...	...	379	251		...	...	110	82		7	5
1511	Tanning/dressing of leather; dressing of fur		...	...	353	228		...	...	97	73		7	5
1512	Luggage,handbags,etc.;saddlery/harness		...	...	26	23		...	...	14	9		-	-
1520	Footwear		...	...	374	342		...	...	107	106		8	6
1610	Sawmilling and planing of wood		...	...	3146	2430		...	...	692	549		173	95
162	Wood products, cork, straw, plaiting materials		...	...	4122	3734		...	...	1339	1197		194	149

Code	Description	(1)	(2)	(3)	(4)	(5)	(6)	(7)	(8)	(9)	(10)
1621	Veneer sheets and wood-based panels	73	79	319	449	:	1167	1673	:	:	:
1622	Builders' carpentry and joinery	68	106	803	802	:	2379	2227	:	:	:
1623	Wooden containers	6	6	45	56	:	120	146	:	:	:
1629	Other wood products;articles of cork,straw	3	2	30	32	:	68	76	:	:	:
1701	Pulp, paper and paperboard	100	122	739	798	:	2940	3587	:	:	:
1702	Corrugated paper and paperboard	63	45	456	440	:	1149	1296	:	:	:
1709	Other articles of paper and paperboard	48	42	358	364	:	824	898	:	:	:
181	Printing and service activities related to printing	94	103	880	998	:	2061	2284	:	:	:
1811	Printing	88	95	804	913	:	1911	2116	:	:	:
1812	Service activities related to printing	6	7	76	84	:	149	168	:	:	:
1820	Reproduction of recorded media	78	37	213	215	:	493	493	:	:	:
1910	Coke oven products	-	-	-	-	:	-	-	:	:	:
1920	Refined petroleum products	143	319	395	628	:	5753	7996	:	:	:
201	Basic chemicals,fertilizers, etc.	191	342	649	824	:	3397	4286	:	:	:
2011	Basic chemicals	:	:	:	:	:	:	:	:	:	:
2012	Fertilizers and nitrogen compounds	11	10	58	226	:	369	649	:	:	:
2013	Plastics and synthetic rubber in primary forms	:	:	:	:	:	:	:	:	:	:
202	Other chemical products	94	153	745	760	:	2246	2209	:	:	:
2021	Pesticides and other agrochemical products	5	8	50	32	:	170	140	:	:	:
2022	Paints,varnishes;printing ink and mastics	17	20	207	228	:	545	615	:	:	:
2023	Soap,cleaning and cosmetic preparations	38	22	284	280	:	638	626	:	:	:
2029	Other chemical products n.e.c.	35	103	203	220	:	893	828	:	:	:
2030	Man-made fibres	56	97	333	328	:	748	805	:	:	:
2100	Pharmaceuticals,medicinal chemicals, etc.	237	264	1334	1180	:	3047	2748	:	:	:
221	Rubber products	23	24	174	257	:	579	734	:	:	:
2211	Rubber tyres and tubes	-	-	6	8	:	10	13	:	:	:
2219	Other rubber products	23	24	168	249	:	569	721	:	:	:
2220	Plastics products	190	280	1585	1697	:	4385	4884	:	:	:
2310	Glass and glass products	109	152	608	652	:	1257	1396	:	:	:
239	Non-metallic mineral products n.e.c.	237	300	1546	1750	:	4548	5141	:	:	:
2391	Refractory products	9	21	81	141	:	298	378	:	:	:
2392	Clay building materials	11	11	61	:	:	165	:	:	:	:
2393	Other porcelain and ceramic products	18	18	86	:	:	194	:	:	:	:
2394	Cement, lime and plaster	35	55	176	187	:	468	519	:	:	:
2395	Articles of concrete, cement and plaster	133	154	808	839	:	2464	2709	:	:	:
2396	Cutting, shaping and finishing of stone	11	9	151	142	:	304	301	:	:	:
2399	Other non-metallic mineral products n.e.c.	19	32	183	251	:	655	835	:	:	:
2410	Basic iron and steel	:	:	:	:	:	:	:	:	:	:
2420	Basic precious and other non-ferrous metals	63	98	602	691	:	3075	4083	:	:	:
243	Casting of metals	65	95	364	451	:	956	1291	:	:	:
2431	Casting of iron and steel	28	32	152	191	:	411	510	:	:	:
2432	Casting of non-ferrous metals	37	62	213	259	:	545	781	:	:	:
251	Struct.metal products, tanks, reservoirs	153	175	1677	1669	:	4311	4730	:	:	:
2511	Structural metal products	118	151	1373	1367	:	3569	3971	:	:	:
2512	Tanks, reservoirs and containers of metal	33	23	283	287	:	668	690	:	:	:

continued

Austria

ISIC	Industry	Output Note	Output 2006	Output 2007	Output 2008	Output 2009	VA Note	VA 2006	VA 2007	VA 2008	VA 2009	GFCF Note	GFCF 2008	GFCF 2009
			(millions of Euros)					(millions of Euros)					(millions of Euros)	
2513	Steam generators, excl. hot water boilers		...	...	69	74		...	...	15	22		1	2
2520	Weapons and ammunition		...	...	196	266		...	...	85	107		12	12
259	Other metal products;metal working services		...	...	8191	7077		...	...	3031	2640		477	447
2591	Forging,pressing,stamping,roll-forming of metal		...	...	1122	997		...	...	364	299		71	57
2592	Treatment and coating of metals; machining		...	...	2461	2153		...	...	794	674		119	126
2593	Cutlery, hand tools and general hardware		...	...	3085	2622		...	...	1375	1204		211	208
2599	Other fabricated metal products n.e.c.		...	...	1523	1305		...	...	499	463		75	57
2610	Electronic components and boards		...	...	1788	1426		...	...	706	578		93	51
2620	Computers and peripheral equipment		...	...	144	113		...	...	56	55		3	2
2630	Communication equipment		...	...	1289	1091		...	...	339	361		14	15
2640	Consumer electronics		...	...	279	268		...	...	142	135		16	6
265	Measuring,testing equipment; watches, etc.		...	...	746	716		...	...	366	338		30	16
2651	Measuring/testing/navigating equipment,etc.		...	...	717	695		...	...	354	329		30	16
2652	Watches and clocks		...	...	28	21		...	...	12	9		1	-
2660	Irradiation/electromedical equipment,etc.		...	...	458	437		...	...	201	161		15	11
2670	Optical instruments and photographic equipment		...	...	118	125		...	...	62	61		15	9
2680	Magnetic and optical media		...	...	-	-		...	...	-	-		-	-
2710	Electric motors,generators,transformers,etc.		...	...	6640	6239		...	...	2430	1957		212	249
2720	Batteries and accumulators		...	...	184	154		...	...	51	39		8	4
273	Wiring and wiring devices		...	...	780	647		...	...	210	190		24	18
2731	Fibre optic cables		...	...	...	...		...	...	...	...		...	...
2732	Other electronic and electric wires and cables		...	...	513	396		...	...	107	88		9	7
2733	Wiring devices		...	...	...	...		...	...	...	...		...	...
2740	Electric lighting equipment		...	...	681	659		...	...	283	276		40	31
2750	Domestic appliances		...	...	1115	932		...	...	423	355		65	35
2790	Other electrical equipment		...	...	1583	1256		...	...	671	515		88	43
281	General-purpose machinery		...	...	8961	7762		...	...	3051	2731		318	275
2811	Engines/turbines,excl.aircraft,vehicle engines		...	...	871	319		...	...	273	83		55	17
2812	Fluid power equipment		...	...	336	254		...	...	139	94		9	7
2813	Other pumps, compressors, taps and valves		...	...	1360	1165		...	...	514	416		73	49
2814	Bearings, gears, gearing and driving elements		...	...	881	750		...	...	392	342		50	55
2815	Ovens, furnaces and furnace burners		...	...	530	595		...	...	177	218		12	8
2816	Lifting and handling equipment		...	...	3108	2584		...	...	920	867		81	74
2817	Office machinery, excl.computers,etc.		...	...	56	53		...	...	17	17		-	2
2818	Power-driven hand tools		...	...	26	23		...	...	10	9		-	-
2819	Other general-purpose machinery		...	...	1793	2018		...	...	609	686		37	63
282	Special-purpose machinery		...	...	9502	7468		...	...	3121	2399		301	187
2821	Agricultural and forestry machinery		...	...	1698	1415		...	...	494	385		62	47
2822	Metal-forming machinery and machine tools		...	...	1419	1161		...	...	477	365		58	26
2823	Machinery for metallurgy		...	...	148	200		...	...	64	81		16	6
2824	Mining, quarrying and construction machinery		...	...	1555	994		...	...	484	278		55	26

2825	Food/beverage/tobacco processing machinery	330	290	...	...	128	128	8	11
2826	Textile/apparel/leather production machinery	98	67	...	...	38	27	4	3
2829	Other special-purpose machinery	4254	3342	...	...	1436	1136	97	68
2910	Motor vehicles	8931	6397	...	...	1967	1568	199	208
2920	Automobile bodies, trailers and semi-trailers	729	521	...	...	224	170	26	24
2930	Parts and accessories for motor vehicles	3643	2349	...	...	962	711	243	138
301	Building of ships and boats	25	26	...	...	7	7	4	1
3011	Building of ships and floating structures	-	-	...	...	-	-	-	-
3012	Building of pleasure and sporting boats	25	26	...	...	7	7	4	1
3020	Railway locomotives and rolling stock	2186	...	...	...	619	...	23	...
3030	Air and spacecraft and related machinery	158	109	...	...	77	20	25	9
3040	Military fighting vehicles	...	537	...	...	...	97	...	10
309	Transport equipment n.e.c.	601	...	...	...	86	...	24	...
3091	Motorcycles	95	97	...	...	28	26	1	1
3092	Bicycles and invalid carriages	...	...	...	...	...	...	...	...
3099	Other transport equipment n.e.c.	...	...	...	...	...	...	...	...
3100	Furniture	3155	2826	...	...	1224	1164	93	100
321	Jewellery, bijouterie and related articles	1323	1931	...	...	149	119	3	6
3211	Jewellery and related articles	...	...	...	...	...	...	...	...
3212	Imitation jewellery and related articles	...	...	...	...	...	...	...	...
3220	Musical instruments	52	61	...	...	34	35	3	2
3230	Sports goods	595	601	...	...	181	157	24	15
3240	Games and toys	721	464	...	...	285	157	21	16
3250	Medical and dental instruments and supplies	787	743	...	...	442	392	47	18
3290	Other manufacturing n.e.c.	188	174	...	...	87	73	8	7
331	Repair of fabricated metal products/machinery	1478	1478	...	...	779	703	78	108
3311	Repair of fabricated metal products	154	144	...	...	82	72	2	2
3312	Repair of machinery	533	499	...	...	268	251	12	12
3313	Repair of electronic and optical equipment	289	306	...	...	130	137	3	4
3314	Repair of electrical equipment	30	58	...	...	15	24	1	2
3315	Repair of transport equip., excl. motor vehicles	463	464	...	...	280	216	60	87
3319	Repair of other equipment	9	7	...	...	4	3	-	-
3320	Installation of industrial machinery/equipment	1597	1442	...	...	533	471	20	15
C	Total manufacturing	161935	139487	...	...	47331	41614	7212	5785

a/ 1101 includes 1102, 1103 and 1104.

Austria

Index numbers of industrial production

ISIC Revision 4

(2005=100)

ISIC	Industry	Note	1999	2000	2001	2002	2003	2004	2005	2006	2007	2008	2009	2010
10	Food products		91	94	95	97	96	98	100	106	107	106	104	105
11	Beverages		86	90	91	94	97	97	100	102	110	108	105	103
12	Tobacco products		66	69	75	98	106	106	100	102	92	93	...	...
13	Textiles		124	126	122	127	126	110	100	99	103	96	80	89
14	Wearing apparel		140	127	114	108	108	106	100	105	102	94	87	84
15	Leather and related products		107	107	119	104	94	96	100	73	64	63	51	44
16	Wood/wood products/cork,excl. furniture		74	80	80	81	89	96	100	109	112	105	94	103
17	Paper and paper products		85	90	88	92	94	100	100	104	107	109	97	106
18	Printing and reproduction of recorded media		84	89	94	94	98	97	100	105	113	113	104	108
19	Coke and refined petroleum products		97	107	112	71	74	96	100	117	117	162	146	142
20	Chemicals and chemical products		72	77	79	81	82	90	100	107	119	124	109	115
21	Pharmaceuticals,medicinal chemicals, etc.		71	75	81	91	97	90	100	105	124	119	133	148
22	Rubber and plastics products		86	94	97	95	97	100	100	110	117	117	105	110
23	Other non-metallic mineral products		90	91	95	93	96	100	100	105	109	105	87	93
24	Basic metals		74	82	87	88	88	96	100	110	117	118	87	108
25	Fabricated metal products, except machinery		72	75	78	78	85	94	100	105	110	113	94	102
26	Computer, electronic and optical products		94	110	102	97	84	91	100	105	134	134	117	140
27	Electrical equipment		76	94	88	86	86	94	100	108	115	126	118	120
28	Machinery and equipment n.e.c.		68	74	78	83	84	94	100	114	125	134	105	113
29	Motor vehicles, trailers and semi-trailers		63	73	76	75	78	98	100	105	104	97	73	85
30	Other transport equipment		65	62	64	84	104	96	100	108	115	129	128	96
31	Furniture		102	99	98	94	93	99	100	105	109	105	99	98
32	Other manufacturing		71	101	108	98	96	104	100	107	112	116	113	113
33	Repair and installation of machinery/equipment		72	75	74	79	82	97	100	101	116	128	118	129
C	Total manufacturing		78	85	87	87	89	96	100	107	114	116	101	108

Azerbaijan

Supplier of information:
State Statistical Committee of the Republic of Azerbaijan, Baku.

Basic source of data:
Annual survey.

Major deviations from ISIC (Revision 4):
None reported.

Reference period:
Calendar year.

Scope:
All enterprises.

Method of data collection:
Mail questionnaires.

Type of enumeration:
Complete enumeration.

Adjusted for non-response:
No.

Concepts and definitions of variables:
Wages and salaries excludes housing and family allowances paid directly by the employer and payments in kind.

Related national publications:
Statistical Yearbook "Industry of Azerbaijan", published by State Statistical Committee of the Republic of Azerbaijan, Baku.

Azerbaijan

ISIC	Industry	Number of enterprises (number)					Number of employees (number)					Wages and salaries paid to employees (thousands of Azerbaijani Manat)			
		Note	2007	2008	2009	2010	Note	2007	2008	2009	2010	Note	2007	2008	2009	2010
1010	Processing/preserving of meat		36	31	30	20		600	628	577	2224		844	1300	1287	11533
1020	Processing/preserving of fish, etc.		14	10	10	10		620	578	535	366		1088	1221	1076	1453
1030	Processing/preserving of fruit,vegetables		77	77	56	56		1839	2230	2238	2431		2926	4508	4513	6599
1040	Vegetable and animal oils and fats		6	5	4	4		706	691	505	563		1233	1464	1102	1416
1050	Dairy products		36	35	32	31		879	1141	1134	1001		1262	2037	2095	1845
106	Grain mill products,starches and starch products		76	69	55	55		2187	1979	1874	1619		1712	2298	2446	2997
1061	Grain mill products		76	69	55	55		2187	1979	1874	1619		1712	2298	2446	2997
1062	Starches and starch products		-	-	-	-		-	-	-	-		-	-	-	-
107	Other food products		252	247	229	230		8953	9733	10537	6836		7901	14132	15210	12502
1071	Bakery products		200	193	182	182		5024	5216	5690	4189		4519	7986	8186	7132
1072	Sugar		9	10	6	6		1035	1452	1521	1058		1391	2938	3219	2599
1073	Cocoa, chocolate and sugar confectionery		17	16	15	15		1251	1105	953	780		840	1237	1253	1559
1074	Macaroni, noodles, couscous, etc.		9	10	6	6		378	521	406	203		242	486	369	205
1075	Prepared meals and dishes		-	-	-	1		-	-	-	5		-	-	-	4
1079	Other food products n.e.c.		17	18	20	20		1265	1439	1967	601		909	1485	2183	1003
1080	Prepared animal feeds		2	3	3	3		6	34	39	49		25	...	...	107
1101	Distilling, rectifying and blending of spirits		11	11	27	24		1039	932	666	981		1383	1197	837	1372
1102	Wines		24	27	17	18		1586	1628	1463	958		2378	2818	2917	2700
1103	Malt liquors and malt		15	15	23	23		505	532	482	497		3386	4383	3856	4121
1104	Soft drinks,mineral waters,other bottled waters		63	63	69	69		1886	2165	2334	2767		4810	8127	8895	10709
1200	Tobacco products		12	10	9	8		884	944	879	561		2574	2583	2651	2115
131	Spinning, weaving and finishing of textiles		41	45	46	45		6905	6488	4193	4857		6009	8833	8369	8217
1311	Preparation and spinning of textile fibres		35	38	39	38		3825	3593	2803	2518		3293	4836	4605	4329
1312	Weaving of textiles		6	7	7	7		3080	2895	1390	2339		2716	3997	3764	3888
1313	Finishing of textiles		-	-	-	-		-	-	-	-		-	-	-	-
139	Other textiles		56	56	68	40		2634	1830	499	391		727	848	836	1025
1391	Knitted and crocheted fabrics		8	8	14	8		23	22	16	4		...	...	...	-
1392	Made-up textile articles, except apparel		12	12	15	10		127	80	76	146		93	100	91	140
1393	Carpets and rugs		27	27	28	16		2313	1571	261	149		338	423	361	372
1394	Cordage, rope, twine and netting		1	1	2	2		28	56	73	78		128	152	251	355
1399	Other textiles n.e.c.		8	8	9	4		143	101	73	14		168	173	133	131
1410	Wearing apparel, except fur apparel		72	77	81	79		2052	1579	1969	2768		2070	3245	3821	6792
1420	Articles of fur		1	-	-	1		2	-	-	2		-	-	-	1
1430	Knitted and crocheted apparel		20	22	14	10		517	478	395	148		533	726	641	616
151	Leather;luggage,handbags,saddlery,harness;fur		9	9	9	9		499	426	272	214		683	818	565	1200
1511	Tanning/dressing of leather; dressing of fur		6	6	6	6		449	372	222	177		618	721	464	1042
1512	Luggage,handbags,etc.;saddlery/harness		3	3	3	3		50	54	50	37		65	97	101	158
1520	Footwear		17	16	16	12		380	323	365	488		474	688	925	1294
1610	Sawmilling and planing of wood		10	10	8	10		194	160	211	149		281	392	418	402
162	Wood products, cork, straw, plaiting materials		69	69	79	63		1433	1309	1645	1482		2021	2723	2724	4772

1621	Veneer sheets and wood-based panels	2	2	3	3	7	5	4	42	6	6	6	62
1622	Builders' carpentry and joinery	56	55	66	53	1024	1073	1200	1156	1670	2330	2406	4424
1623	Wooden containers	2	2	1	1	84	48	71	59	144	97	76	67
1629	Other wood products;articles of cork,straw	9	10	9	6	318	183	370	225	201	289	236	219
1701	Pulp, paper and paperboard	1	7	7	8	7	46	48	137	12	86	109	404
1702	Corrugated paper and paperboard	9	8	6	4	261	364	366	284	483	651	841	941
1709	Other articles of paper and paperboard	8	8	6	8	152	142	132	167	138	199	180	409
181	Printing and service activities related to printing	191	193	195	153	1546	1541	2630	1592	3273	4061	4788	3833
1811	Printing	167	167	169	137	1340	1340	2394	1408	3068	3788	4477	3528
1812	Service activities related to printing	24	26	26	16	206	201	236	184	205	273	311	305
1820	Reproduction of recorded media	9	7	5	3	168	95	115	61	147	326	384	59
1910	Coke oven products	-	-	-	-	-	-	-	-	-	-	-	-
1920	Refined petroleum products	6	5	7	9	6351	6330	5622	5303	25223	36273	33899	32338
201	Basic chemicals,fertilizers, etc.	44	47	43	37	7699	7206	6829	7130	17733	19856	19593	30502
2011	Basic chemicals	31	34	32	29	2742	2546	2263	6916	8107	9483	9402	...
2012	Fertilizers and nitrogen compounds	1	1	1	1	328	336	312	188	401	650	484	461
2013	Plastics and synthetic rubber in primary forms	12	12	10	7	4629	4324	4254	...	9225	9723	9707	...
202	Other chemical products	51	52	47	40	2664	2598	2371	1313	3659	4509	5151	4237
2021	Pesticides and other agrochemical products	1	1	-	...	34	34	30	27	42	69	70	70
2022	Paints,varnishes;printing ink and mastics	26	26	23	17	345	480	333	367	649	1056	968	1771
2023	Soap,cleaning and cosmetic preparations	19	19	19	15	774	731	707	439	515	772	1146	1429
2029	Other chemical products n.e.c.	5	6	5	8	1511	1353	1301	480	2453	2612	2967	967
2030	Man-made fibres	-	-	-	-	-	-	-	-	-	-	-	-
2100	Pharmaceuticals,medicinal chemicals, etc.	9	8	5	8	178	141	130	140	161	189	198	319
221	Rubber products	12	12	10	10	782	708	152	634	164	129	127	144
2211	Rubber tyres and tubes	6	6	5	4	622	580	41	532	82	71	62	52
2219	Other rubber products	6	6	5	6	160	128	111	102	82	58	65	92
2220	Plastics products	81	83	75	77	2697	2924	3265	3338	3787	6573	7153	9126
2310	Glass and glass products	25	29	27	22	1571	1893	1322	1193	4021	6544	3912	4579
239	Non-metallic mineral products n.e.c.	245	269	280	258	7722	7773	7138	8029	17506	24879	26455	37749
2391	Refractory products	7	7	7	2	522	108	96	15	96	...	...	...
2392	Clay building materials	2	2	3	3	94	101	51	1127	150	202	155	5488
2393	Other porcelain and ceramic products	51	53	51	49	2079	1987	1670	35	3109	3999	3645	58
2394	Cement, lime and plaster	30	34	36	31	1369	1363	1244	931	7749	9088	10743	11297
2395	Articles of concrete, cement and plaster	99	106	104	96	2983	2804	2504	3773	5446	6822	6738	12363
2396	Cutting, shaping and finishing of stone	54	59	59	53	648	646	739	616	901	1417	1545	1891
2399	Other non-metallic mineral products n.e.c.	2	8	20	24	27	764	834	1532	55	3229	3504	6342
2410	Basic iron and steel	15	17	17	14	4506	4365	4028	4851	12125	14414	12323	16465
2420	Basic precious and other non-ferrous metals	11	14	15	14	3720	4158	3734	3454	11273	15770	5564	2327
243	Casting of metals	11	11	10	2	1428	1417	698	39	1763	2518	1688	73
2431	Casting of iron and steel	7	7	6	1	1386	1364	643	12	1730	2468	1618	30
2432	Casting of non-ferrous metals	4	4	4	1	42	53	55	27	33	50	70	43
251	Struct.metal products, tanks, reservoirs	58	55	49	54	2957	3123	2980	3611	10013	17515	15694	17474
2511	Structural metal products	52	51	49	49	2927	3111	2974	3564	9994	17500	15685	17409
2512	Tanks, reservoirs and containers of metal	6	4	...	4	30	12	6	16	19	15	9	30

continued

Azerbaijan

ISIC Revision 4

		Number of enterprises (number)				Number of employees (number)				Wages and salaries paid to employees (thousands of Azerbaijani Manat)			
ISIC	Industry	2007	2008	2009	2010	2007	2008	2009	2010	2007	2008	2009	2010
2513	Steam generators, excl. hot water boilers	-	-	-	1	-	-	-	31	-	-	-	35
2520	Weapons and ammunition	-	-	-	-	-	-	-	-	-	-	-	-
259	Other metal products;metal working services	29	29	25	25	2041	1850	1773	1021	5287	4512	4430	3732
2591	Forging,pressing,stamping,roll-forming of metal	9	9	7	3	1040	1028	1001	131	1143	1503	1935	459
2592	Treatment and coating of metals; machining	6	4	3	2	284	115	79	63	3065	1296	867	780
2593	Cutlery, hand tools and general hardware	3	3	2	1	198	259	213	65	247	447	427	66
2599	Other fabricated metal products n.e.c.	11	13	13	19	519	448	480	762	832	1266	1201	2427
2610	Electronic components and boards	4	6	6	5	321	418	366	468	256	601	671	1009
2620	Computers and peripheral equipment	9	9	9	1	308	328	366	334	632	846	618	655
2630	Communication equipment	7	9	11	9	380	355	461	421	820	941	1211	1391
2640	Consumer electronics	-	-	-	-	-	-	-	-	-	-	-	-
265	Measuring,testing equipment; watches, etc.	8	8	15	15	840	864	1048	829	1091	1628	1435	2815
2651	Measuring/testing/navigating equipment,etc.	8	8	15	15	840	864	1048	829	1091	1628	1435	2815
2652	Watches and clocks												
2660	Irradiation/electromedical equipment,etc.	-	-	-	-	-	-	-	-	-	-	-	-
2670	Optical instruments and photographic equipment	-	-	-	2	-	-	-	178	-	-	-	741
2680	Magnetic and optical media	-	-	-	1	19	11	15	10	-	-	-	116
2710	Electric motors,generators,transformers,etc.	17	19	20	21	1057	1027	689	799	1042	1416	1570	2405
2720	Batteries and accumulators	7	6	5	4	190	148	123	9	407	484	...	9
273	Wiring and wiring devices	17	15	17	7	372	303	474	221	669	806	1025	240
2731	Fibre optic cables	6	6	7	6	201	164	260	205	513	597	867	196
2732	Other electronic and electric wires and cables	11	9	10	1	171	139	214	16	156	209	158	44
2733	Wiring devices												
2740	Electric lighting equipment	13	13	11	8	1721	1414	226	637	768	936	754	603
2750	Domestic appliances	3	3	3	5	233	244	88	175	531	664	591	548
2790	Other electrical equipment												
281	General-purpose machinery	36	38	55	51	5065	4282	3390	3226	9926	11905	9040	6097
2811	Engines/turbines,excl.aircraft,vehicle engines	6	4	3	1	639	579	181	3	301	362	292	6
2812	Fluid power equipment	-	-	-	1	-	-	-	2	-	-	-	6
2813	Other pumps, compressors, taps and valves	7	8	18	17	2366	1724	1278	945	4812	5481	4804	2464
2814	Bearings, gears, gearing and driving elements	2	3	7	8	91	83	38	258	112	130	55	838
2815	Ovens, furnaces and furnace burners	2	1	1	1	106	74	81	16	554	404	420	74
2816	Lifting and handling equipment	6	7	7	7	636	547	738	795	1017	1400	882	1004
2817	Office machinery, excl.computers,etc.	-	-	-	1	-	-	-	5	-	-	-	6
2818	Power-driven hand tools	-	-	-	1	-	-	-	38	-	-	-	130
2819	Other general-purpose machinery	13	15	19	14	1227	1275	1074	1164	3130	4129	2587	1569
282	Special-purpose machinery	40	35	34	21	1911	2404	1959	1602	4484	5081	4470	4643
2821	Agricultural and forestry machinery	18	14	14	11	387	307	183	455	428	469	350	1305
2822	Metal-forming machinery and machine tools	7	4	4	-	80	82	64	-	107	187	92	-
2823	Machinery for metallurgy	1	2	2	1	99	198	229	91	173	426	567	276
2824	Mining, quarrying and construction machinery	9	9	7	2	745	1001	719	270	1160	1630	1049	529

2825	Food/beverage/tobacco processing machinery	2	2	3	2	17	19	14	11	19	34	25	35
2826	Textile/apparel/leather production machinery	-	-	-	5	583	797	750	775	2597	2336	2387	2498
2829	Other special-purpose machinery	3	4	4	3	612	591	111	568	117	190	202	395
2910	Motor vehicles	2	2	2	1	9	6	5	-	9	6	5	-
2920	Automobile bodies, trailers and semi-trailers	1	1	1	3	298	296	297	32	468	677	762	28
2930	Parts and accessories for motor vehicles	3	3	2	3	-	-	-	-	-	-	-	3193
301	Building of ships and boats	-	-	-	-	-	-	-	-	-	-	-	-
3011	Building of ships and floating structures	-	-	-	-	-	-	-	-	-	-	-	-
3012	Building of pleasure and sporting boats	-	-	-	-	-	-	-	-	-	-	-	-
3020	Railway locomotives and rolling stock	9	12	8	8	4551	4423	4259	3689	8281	10065	9746	8986
3030	Air and spacecraft and related machinery	-	-	-	1	-	-	-	12	-	-	-	43
3040	Military fighting vehicles	-	-	-	-	-	-	-	-	-	-	-	-
309	Transport equipment n.e.c.	-	-	1	-	-	-	219	-	-	-	2075	-
3091	Motorcycles	-	-	-	-	-	-	-	-	-	-	-	-
3092	Bicycles and invalid carriages	-	-	1	-	-	-	219	-	-	-	2075	-
3099	Other transport equipment n.e.c.	-	-	-	-	-	-	-	-	-	-	-	-
3100	Furniture	95	97	94	85	2336	3227	3215	2923	2645	5586	5782	6817
321	Jewellery, bijouterie and related articles	17	17	16	12	590	565	465	387	421	533	466	310
3211	Jewellery and related articles	17	17	16	12	590	565	465	385	421	533	466	309
3212	Imitation jewellery and related articles	-	-	-	-	..	..	2	2	-	-	-	-
3220	Musical instruments	2	2	1	1	19	3	2	3	9	5	3	3
3230	Sports goods	-	-	-	-	-	-	-	-	-	-	-	-
3240	Games and toys	1	-	-	-	3	2	2	3	3	4	4	3
3250	Medical and dental instruments and supplies	49	56	46	6	352	351	..	..	..	..	..	898
3290	Other manufacturing n.e.c.	45	39	32	36	691	582	681	625	518	1033	829	283
331	Repair of fabricated metal products/machinery	45	39	32	37	6158	5965	4370	3734	23802	38039	34383	17432
3311	Repair of fabricated metal products	17	13	6	9	..	..	..	2	-	-	-	1
3312	Repair of machinery	-	-	-	1	..	..	..	554	-	-	-	2197
3313	Repair of electronic and optical equipment	-	-	-	1	..	..	..	2	-	-	-	3
3314	Repair of electrical equipment	-	-	-	1	..	..	..	39	-	-	-	29
3315	Repair of transport equip., excl. motor vehicles	28	26	26	20	6158	5965	4370	3131	23802	38039	34383	15199
3319	Repair of other equipment	-	-	-	1	..	..	..	6	-	-	-	3
3320	Installation of industrial machinery/equipment	3	3	3	5	95	96	91	189	278	289	242	825
C	Total manufacturing	2122	2149	2106	1914	110887	110387	99067	94723	218265	305148	284156	308987

Azerbaijan

ISIC Revision 4			Output at factor values (thousands of Azerbaijani Manat)					Value added at factor values (thousands of Azerbaijani Manat)					Gross fixed capital formation (thousands of Azerbaijani Manat)		
ISIC	Industry	Note	2007	2008	2009	2010	Note	2007	2008	2009	2010	Note	2009	2010
1010	Processing/preserving of meat		242585	473158	502150	772518		...	...	153981	103405		631	1302
1020	Processing/preserving of fish, etc.		6729	4457	2707	1741		...	...	830	399		-	135
1030	Processing/preserving of fruit,vegetables		77851	76175	76030	63149		...	...	23314	22553		-	31431
1040	Vegetable and animal oils and fats		31218	36870	40716	50324		...	...	12485	13000		9647	510
1050	Dairy products		293835	115021	146565	242857		...	...	44943	89807		8246	2211
106	Grain mill products,starches and starch products		264990	317435	290542	290663		...	...	89093	83039		-	6153
1061	Grain mill products		264990	317435	290542	290663		...	...	89093	83039		-	6153
1062	Starches and starch products													
107	Other food products		337638	357777	461494	503236		...	...	141513	155326		14103	11096
1071	Bakery products		242998	256845	323670	375805		...	...	99251	115501		2371	4962
1072	Sugar		68608	77274	104079	99802		...	...	31915	29449		10564	3230
1073	Cocoa, chocolate and sugar confectionery		5363	6988	7319	8521		...	...	2244	3806		22	700
1074	Macaroni, noodles, couscous, etc.		2513	4333	2095	5885		...	...	642	883		1146	-
1075	Prepared meals and dishes		...	...	...	13		...	...	-	7		...	-
1079	Other food products n.e.c.		18156	12337	24331	13210		...	...	7461	5680		-	2204
1080	Prepared animal feeds		10	115	86	73		...	...	20	35		-	-
1101	Distilling, rectifying and blending of spirits		15445	9715	20420	17079		...	...	6262	6177		422	-
1102	Wines		22465	25315	17531	18638		...	...	5376	8037		2016	755
1103	Malt liquors and malt		24626	36901	42719	38425		...	...	23216	25721		12139	1837
1104	Soft drinks,mineral waters,other bottled waters		69498	75316	72489	96063		...	...	22228	34965		6636	-
1200	Tobacco products		22399	21748	21669	22273		...	...	6645	5854		-	111
131	Spinning, weaving and finishing of textiles		30908	46008	29974	24849		...	...	12994	8108		33823	6658
1311	Preparation and spinning of textile fibres		28274	30122	20454	12512		...	...	6527	3217		32726	4984
1312	Weaving of textiles		2634	15886	9520	12337		...	...	6467	4891		1097	1674
1313	Finishing of textiles													
139	Other textiles		5142	4427	3957	4583		...	...	1004	1377		260	138
1391	Knitted and crocheted fabrics		65	43	3	5		...	...	-	1		-	1
1392	Made-up textile articles, except apparel		348	467	1095	642		...	...	279	158		-	-
1393	Carpets and rugs		779	1523	1423	2531		...	...	361	934		260	-
1394	Cordage, rope, twine and netting		653	1217	1400	1329		...	...	355	261		-	137
1399	Other textiles n.e.c.		3297	1177	...	...		...	...	9	23		-	23
1410	Wearing apparel, except fur apparel		17536	19213	21856	30540		...	...	6688	6248		148	315
1420	Articles of fur		4	-	-	16		...	...	-	12		-	-
1430	Knitted and crocheted apparel		5796	6837	4493	4151		...	...	1140	845		-	-
151	Leather;luggage,handbags,saddlery,harness;fur		11956	11152	9392	14440		...	...	3446	5438		4306	-
1511	Tanning/dressing of leather; dressing of fur		11555	10602	8869	13770		...	...	3254	5193		4304	-
1512	Luggage,handbags,etc.;saddlery/harness		401	550	523	670		...	...	192	245		2	-
1520	Footwear		4222	5880	7667	6426		...	...	2813	2383		120	-
1610	Sawmilling and planing of wood		709	695	...	483		...	...	131	223		74	263
162	Wood products, cork, straw, plaiting materials		17683	14936	10349	11664		...	...	4707	5389		485	-

1621	Veneer sheets and wood-based panels	53	66	62	199	28	111	-	-
1622	Builders' carpentry and joinery	12311	12848	7427	8734	3378	3873	485	-
1623	Wooden containers	733	496	459	1058	209	838	-	-
1629	Other wood products;articles of cork,straw	4586	1526	2401	1673	1092	567	99	450
1701	Pulp, paper and paperboard	13	1610	954	1579	577	1066	642	-
1702	Corrugated paper and paperboard	5714	8228	6835	6388	2702	2138	-	-
1709	Other articles of paper and paperboard	844	789	3116	3575	1032	1152	27	356
181	Printing and service activities related to printing	29281	44944	41972	38108	16594	11592	5194	88
1811	Printing	27468	43106	37325	31768	14756	9355	5193	63
1812	Service activities related to printing	1813	1838	4647	6340	1838	2237	1	25
1820	Reproduction of recorded media	1298	1383	1205	276	439	92	-	-
1910	Coke oven products	-	-	-	-	-	-	-	-
1920	Refined petroleum products	2118233	2399971	1844844	2160566	999300	985646	26697	56289
201	Basic chemicals,fertilizers, etc.	188917	188390	120683	108810	51501	37443	21637	113
2011	Basic chemicals	86693	58725	52774	15628	22521	8076	15449	113
2012	Fertilizers and nitrogen compounds	1788	4034	1458	1402	623	621	-	-
2013	Plastics and synthetic rubber in primary forms	100436	125631	66451	91780	28357	28746	6188	1460
202	Other chemical products	23357	30703	11447	11490	4884	6566	762	-
2021	Pesticides and other agrochemical products	64	91	...	...	-	-	-	29
2022	Paints,varnishes;printing ink and mastics	4227	11725	4814	1970	2054	674	-	-
2023	Soap,cleaning and cosmetic preparations	1915	1547	4190	2854	1787	987	762	1431
2029	Other chemical products n.e.c.	17151	17340	2443	6666	1043	4905	-	-
2030	Man-made fibres	-	-	-	-	-	-	-	-
2100	Pharmaceuticals,medicinal chemicals, etc.	742	655	737	1013	315	404	4	17
221	Rubber products	235	119	347	124	103	68	4	17
2211	Rubber tyres and tubes	14	1	184	33	55	27	-	-
2219	Other rubber products	221	118	163	91	48	41	17504	4155
2220	Plastics products	36895	69836	59449	43197	17597	12495	35762	7177
2310	Glass and glass products	7296	10701	5367	7850	2452	3722	28713	22927
239	Non-metallic mineral products n.e.c.	245682	341801	364197	444339	87611	109238	-	-
2391	Refractory products	322	386	26	39	16	18	-	12294
2392	Clay building materials	359	400	319	8036	142	2680	-	-
2393	Other porcelain and ceramic products	14507	13945	13179	25	2566	16	-	-
2394	Cement, lime and plaster	136267	170284	126374	112610	34195	40440	22249	8585
2395	Articles of concrete, cement and plaster	88279	122060	71734	80822	9410	11330	4405	1652
2396	Cutting, shaping and finishing of stone	5696	7620	8633	11038	2336	2492	2059	396
2399	Other non-metallic mineral products n.e.c.	252	27106	143932	231769	38946	52262	-	-
2410	Basic iron and steel	108966	159387	45121	125902	16955	51689	4513	1823
2420	Basic precious and other non-ferrous metals	139518	156723	29952	8807	11255	1629	262	737
243	Casting of metals	30171	32835	13712	458	5153	185	151	562
2431	Casting of iron and steel	30055	32612	13338	89	5012	46	111	175
2432	Casting of non-ferrous metals	116	223	374	369	141	139	-	-
251	Struct.metal products, tanks, reservoirs	65856	82039	76779	107790	29134	40710	-	-
2511	Structural metal products	65812	81970	76779	106057	29134	39636	-	-
2512	Tanks, reservoirs and containers of metal	44	69	-	64	-	31	-	-

continued

Azerbaijan

ISIC	Industry	Note	Output at factor values (thousands of Azerbaijani Manat)				Note	Value added at factor values (thousands of Azerbaijani Manat)				Note	Gross fixed capital formation (thousands of Azerbaijani Manat)	
			2007	2008	2009	2010		2007	2008	2009	2010		2009	2010
2513	Steam generators, excl. hot water boilers		-	-	-	1669		...	...	-	1043		-	-
2520	Weapons and ammunition		-	-	-	-		...	...	-	-		-	-
259	Other metal products;metal working services		59112	84662	24442	27285		...	...	9185	10514		11001	118
2591	Forging,pressing,stamping,roll-forming of metal		16800	37198	5336	3216		...	...	2005	2094		11001	1
2592	Treatment and coating of metals; machining		28141	30374	1147	1312		...	...	431	1061		-	-
2593	Cutlery, hand tools and general hardware		1121	1743	2141	2787		...	...	805	932		-	117
2599	Other fabricated metal products n.e.c.		13050	15347	15818	19970		...	...	5944	6427		-	-
2610	Electronic components and boards		1358	4934	2859	4272		...	...	997	2171		15267	8264
2620	Computers and peripheral equipment		8997	4001	5001	...		...	...	894	2		9064	-
2630	Communication equipment		3496	5142	10808	22763		...	...	3770	8560		544	1747
2640	Consumer electronics		-	-	-	-		...	...	-	-		-	-
265	Measuring,testing equipment; watches, etc.		4137	7511	17544	20201		...	...	6119	8460		25683	80110
2651	Measuring/testing/navigating equipment,etc.		4137	7511	17544	20201		...	...	6119	8460		25683	80110
2652	Watches and clocks		-	-	-	-		...	...	-	-		-	-
2660	Irradiation/electromedical equipment,etc.		-	-	-	-		...	...	-	-		-	-
2670	Optical instruments and photographic equipment		-	-	-	7231		...	...	-	2522		-	4291
2680	Magnetic and optical media		-	-	-	140		...	...	-	50		-	-
2710	Electric motors,generators,transformers,etc.		19372	20134	23973	29964		...	...	6490	7126		3804	3656
2720	Batteries and accumulators		1244	1586	13	4		...	...	5	4		-	-
273	Wiring and wiring devices		5434	6264	6069	29293		...	...	2870	6293		832	803
2731	Fibre optic cables		3098	3131	5440	28887		...	...	2553	6185		97	803
2732	Other electronic and electric wires and cables		2336	3133	629	406		...	...	317	108		735	-
2733	Wiring devices		-	-	-	-		...	...	-	-		-	-
2740	Electric lighting equipment		-	-	-	-		...	...	-	-		-	-
2750	Domestic appliances		7460	15511	2746	2025		...	...	821	975		11	-
2790	Other electrical equipment		1458	2158	7471	13743		...	...	2606	7627		445	-
281	General-purpose machinery		40584	54294	63516	58192		...	...	18987	26605		893	10829
2811	Engines/turbines,excl.aircraft,vehicle engines		1835	3337	299	204		...	...	89	80		893	-
2812	Fluid power equipment		-	-	-	40		...	...	-	25		-	-
2813	Other pumps, compressors, taps and valves		14955	18016	33919	14004		...	...	10140	9914		-	-
2814	Bearings, gears, gearing and driving elements		854	915	646	4648		...	...	193	3073		-	106
2815	Ovens, furnaces and furnace burners		679	587	986	2523		...	...	295	1483		-	-
2816	Lifting and handling equipment		7024	10696	12416	15771		...	...	3712	5596		-	10644
2817	Office machinery, excl.computers,etc.		-	-	-	22		...	...	-	8		-	-
2818	Power-driven hand tools		-	-	-	1047		...	...	-	264		-	79
2819	Other general-purpose machinery		15237	20743	15250	19933		...	...	4558	6162		-	-
282	Special-purpose machinery		41021	36668	29814	93031		...	...	8092	29797		45544	56713
2821	Agricultural and forestry machinery		2989	2296	19874	72204		...	...	5941	20526		579	11
2822	Metal-forming machinery and machine tools		905	1453	701	-		...	...	210	-		186	-
2823	Machinery for metallurgy		695	1641	1445	1132		...	...	432	589		578	422
2824	Mining, quarrying and construction machinery		15795	21020	4352	1274		...	...	480	753		-	9

2825	Food/beverage/tobacco processing machinery	64	38	2488	...	744	...	-	-
2826	Textile/apparel/leather production machinery	-	-	-	-	-	-	44201	56271
2829	Other special-purpose machinery	20573	10220	...	18421	285	7929	-	-
2910	Motor vehicles	6924	922	422	2882	196	1424	-	-
2920	Automobile bodies, trailers and semi-trailers	351	1816	30	-	14	-	2256	24
2930	Parts and accessories for motor vehicles	9793	14528	...	161	41	94	-	-
301	Building of ships and boats	-	-	-	-	-	-	-	-
3011	Building of ships and floating structures	-	-	-	-	-	-	-	-
3012	Building of pleasure and sporting boats	-	-	-	-	-	7959	2292	278
3020	Railway locomotives and rolling stock	16121	16523	14041	10111	-	-	-	-
3030	Air and spacecraft and related machinery	...	...	...	107	-	87	-	1
3040	Military fighting vehicles	...	...	7083	-	6531	-	-	-
309	Transport equipment n.e.c.	-	7083	-	-	-	-	-	-
3091	Motorcycles	-	-	-	-	-	-	-	-
3092	Bicycles and invalid carriages	-	-	7083	-	-	-	-	-
3099	Other transport equipment n.e.c.	-	7083	-	-	6531	-	3145	7318
3100	Furniture	25887	32784	35713	51462	9213	12104	-	-
321	Jewellery, bijouterie and related articles	1019	903	878	704	227	388	-	-
3211	Jewellery and related articles	1019	903	878	701	227	387	-	-
3212	Imitation jewellery and related articles	-	-	-	3	-	1	15	-
3220	Musical instruments	128	89	5	5	1	3	-	-
3230	Sports goods	-	-	-	-	-	-	-	-
3240	Games and toys	...	-	-	-	-	1553	-	33
3250	Medical and dental instruments and supplies	-	-	-	2399	3910	6159	-	-
3290	Other manufacturing n.e.c.	12246	12213	7403	8942	75184	26420	8023	7575
331	Repair of fabricated metal products/machinery	145689	186534	165790	63835	75184	26420	122	-
3311	Repair of fabricated metal products	...	...	...	6	-	3	-	-
3312	Repair of machinery	25447	28448	7072	13731	1104	5162	-	-
3313	Repair of electronic and optical equipment	...	...	...	4	-	2	...	-
3314	Repair of electrical equipment	...	...	...	184	-	47	-	-
3315	Repair of transport equip., excl. motor vehicles	120242	158086	158718	49870	74080	21186	7901	7575
3319	Repair of other equipment	...	...	...	40	-	20	...	-
3320	Installation of industrial machinery/equipment	1103	1577	550	2445	175	840	-	23
C	Total manufacturing	4919197	5700012	4836072	5735674	1966761	2011913	363991	340290

Azerbaijan

ISIC Revision 4 — Index numbers of industrial production (2005=100)

ISIC	Industry	Note	1999	2000	2001	2002	2003	2004	2005	2006	2007	2008	2009	2010
10	Food products		⋮	⋮	⋮	⋮	⋮	⋮	100	102	106	108	111	114
11	Beverages		⋮	⋮	⋮	⋮	⋮	⋮	100	125	155	147	129	143
12	Tobacco products		⋮	⋮	⋮	⋮	⋮	⋮	100	92	70	54	48	45
13	Textiles		⋮	⋮	⋮	⋮	⋮	⋮	100	77	54	41	29	28
14	Wearing apparel		⋮	⋮	⋮	⋮	⋮	⋮	100	92	98	79	94	104
15	Leather and related products		⋮	⋮	⋮	⋮	⋮	⋮	100	80	125	94	99	118
16	Wood/wood products/cork,excl. furniture		⋮	⋮	⋮	⋮	⋮	⋮	100	99	154	266	90	107
17	Paper and paper products		⋮	⋮	⋮	⋮	⋮	⋮	100	149	157	179	365	406
18	Printing and reproduction of recorded media		⋮	⋮	⋮	⋮	⋮	⋮	100	96	129	129	130	132
19	Coke and refined petroleum products		⋮	⋮	⋮	⋮	⋮	⋮	100	102	110	120	107	116
20	Chemicals and chemical products		⋮	⋮	⋮	⋮	⋮	⋮	100	114	77	97	61	82
21	Pharmaceuticals,medicinal chemicals, etc.		⋮	⋮	⋮	⋮	⋮	⋮	⋮	⋮	⋮	⋮	⋮	⋮
22	Rubber and plastics products		⋮	⋮	⋮	⋮	⋮	⋮	100	80	106	117	99	87
23	Other non-metallic mineral products		⋮	⋮	⋮	⋮	⋮	⋮	100	102	130	117	98	89
24	Basic metals		⋮	⋮	⋮	⋮	⋮	⋮	100	115	76	88	30	43
25	Fabricated metal products, except machinery		⋮	⋮	⋮	⋮	⋮	⋮	100	86	164	235	123	115
26	Computer, electronic and optical products		⋮	⋮	⋮	⋮	⋮	⋮	100	65	60	27	23	28
27	Electrical equipment		⋮	⋮	⋮	⋮	⋮	⋮	100	175	196	116	90	165
28	Machinery and equipment n.e.c.		⋮	⋮	⋮	⋮	⋮	⋮	100	158	248	264	224	421
29	Motor vehicles, trailers and semi-trailers		⋮	⋮	⋮	⋮	⋮	⋮	100	2231	3266	3749	862	⋮
30	Other transport equipment		⋮	⋮	⋮	⋮	⋮	⋮	⋮	⋮	⋮	⋮	⋮	⋮
31	Furniture		⋮	⋮	⋮	⋮	⋮	⋮	100	121	127	134	134	32
32	Other manufacturing		⋮	⋮	⋮	⋮	⋮	⋮	⋮	⋮	⋮	⋮	⋮	⋮
33	Repair and installation of machinery/equipment		⋮	⋮	⋮	⋮	⋮	⋮	⋮	⋮	⋮	⋮	⋮	⋮
C	Total manufacturing		⋮	⋮	⋮	⋮	⋮	⋮	100	107	115	122	113	124

Bahamas

Supplier of information:
Department of Statistics, Nassau.

Basic source of data:
Annual sample survey.

Major deviations from ISIC (Revision 4):
None reported.

Reference period:
Calendar year.

Scope:
Data refer to establishments with 10 or more reported establishments.

Method of data collection:
Mail questionnaires and direct interviews in the field.

Type of enumeration:
Sample survey.

Adjusted for non-response:
No.

Concepts and definitions of variables:
No deviation from the standard UN concepts and definitions are reported.

Related national publications:
None reported.

Bahamas

ISIC Revision 4			Number of establishments (number)					Number of employees (number)					Wages and salaries (Bahamian Dollars)				
ISIC	Industry	Note	2006	2007	2008	2009	Note	2006	2007	2008	2009	Note	2006	2007	2008	2009
10	Food products		...	...	32	32		...	...	425	453		...	...	...	...
11	Beverages		...	...	17	18		...	...	604	608		...	...	...	...
12	Tobacco products		...	...	...	...		...	...	...	...		...	...	...	...
13	Textiles		...	...	16	16		...	...	101	76		...	...	...	...
14	Wearing apparel		...	...	68	66		...	...	138	142		...	...	...	...
15	Leather and related products		...	...	1	1		...	...	18	18		...	...	...	...
16	Wood/wood products/cork,excl. furniture		...	...	17	17		...	...	93	77		...	...	...	...
17	Paper and paper products		...	...	3	3		...	...	37	37		...	...	...	...
18	Printing and reproduction of recorded media		...	...	63	64		...	...	430	473		...	...	...	...
19	Coke and refined petroleum products		...	...	...	...		...	...	...	...		...	...	...	...
20	Chemicals and chemical products		...	...	6	6		...	...	120	120		...	...	...	...
21	Pharmaceuticals,medicinal chemicals, etc.		...	...	1	1		...	...	74	74		...	...	...	...
22	Rubber and plastics products		...	...	4	5		...	...	78	80		...	...	...	...
23	Other non-metallic mineral products		...	...	19	20		...	...	332	329		...	...	...	...
24	Basic metals		...	...	7	8		...	...	89	100		...	...	...	...
25	Fabricated metal products, except machinery		...	...	49	52		...	...	500	521		...	...	...	...
26	Computer, electronic and optical products		...	...	...	...		...	...	...	...		...	...	...	...
27	Electrical equipment		...	...	4	4		...	...	28	28		...	...	...	...
28	Machinery and equipment n.e.c.		...	...	1	1		...	...	2	2		...	...	...	...
29	Motor vehicles, trailers and semi-trailers		...	...	...	...		...	...	...	...		...	...	...	...
30	Other transport equipment		...	...	...	...		...	...	...	...		...	...	...	...
31	Furniture		...	...	36	36		...	...	208	208		...	...	...	...
32	Other manufacturing		...	...	13	15		...	...	42	42		...	...	...	...
33	Repair and installation of machinery/equipment		...	...	20	20		...	...	758	758		...	...	...	...
C	Total manufacturing		...	...	377a/	385a/		...	...	4077a/	4146a/		...	...	...	...

a/ Sum of available data.

Belarus

Supplier of information:
National Statistical Committee of the Republic of Belarus, Minsk.

Basic source of data:
Annual survey of registered establishments.

Major deviations from ISIC (Revision 3):
The data presented in ISIC (Revision 3) were originally classified according to NACE (Revision 1.1).

Reference period:
Calendar year.

Scope:
All establishments.

Method of data collection:
Mail questionnaires.

Type of enumeration:
Complete enumeration.

Adjusted for non-response:
Not reported.

Concepts and definitions of variables:
Number of employees includes home workers.
Wages and salaries was computed by UNIDO from reported monthly average of wages and salaries per employee.

Related national publications:
Small and Medium-Sized Business in the Republic of Belarus; Labour and Employment in the Republic of Belarus, both published by National Statistical Committee of the Republic of Belarus, Minsk.

Belarus

ISIC Revision 3		Number of establishments (number)					Number of employees (number)					Wages and salaries paid to employees (millions of Belarusian Roubles)				
ISIC	Industry	Note	2007	2008	2009	2010	Note	2007	2008	2009	2010	Note	2007	2008	2009	2010
15	Food and beverages	a/	828	897	805	815	a/	148819	148901	149436	151762	a/	1232007	1547065	1788898	2294070
16	Tobacco products	a/	...	...	...	...	a/	...	...	...	...	a/	...	...	...	...
17	Textiles	b/	1243	1619	1481	1577	b/	110691	114379	107129	104160	b/	624520	810921	841923	1036862
18	Wearing apparel, fur	b/	...	...	...	...	b/	...	...	...	...	b/	...	...	...	...
19	Leather, leather products and footwear		103	129	115	115		17688	17226	16737	17138		122620	145866	160106	208245
20	Wood products (excl. furniture)		1084	1323	1175	1267		55383	56497	50264	48615		354948	463969	442253	533808
21	Paper and paper products	c/	875	1013	937	997	c/	31523	32896	32128	32444	c/	271790	350342	373721	469486
22	Printing and publishing	c/	20	20	12	18	c/	9009	9618	9965	9954	c/	162317	216973	265720	296513
23	Coke,refined petroleum products,nuclear fuel		...	...	...	...		...	...	...	...		...	...	...	...
24	Chemicals and chemical products		364	390	359	361		56968	56069	56695	63243		619506	818452	976091	1627658
25	Rubber and plastics products		679	935	965	1018		38717	41885	41237	41375		374719	490642	519488	640233
26	Non-metallic mineral products		485	865	826	918		69338	73570	71883	72051		654522	884743	956288	1172114
27	Basic metals	d/	869	1218	1261	1395	d/	69740	81869	72024	72099	d/	741113	1134221	1034438	1255117
28	Fabricated metal products	d/	...	...	...	...	d/	...	...	...	...	d/	...	...	...	...
29	Machinery and equipment n.e.c.	e/	778	885	930	980	e/	156283	160177	150808	145531	e/	1527452	2077407	2033233	2391597
30	Office, accounting and computing machinery	e/	...	...	...	...	e/	...	...	...	...	e/	...	...	...	...
31	Electrical machinery and apparatus	f/	864	980	814	881	f/	77544	78530	74165	72670	f/	615787	806965	832714	1051768
32	Radio,television and communication equipment	f/	...	...	...	...	f/	...	...	...	...	f/	...	...	...	...
33	Medical, precision and optical instruments	f/	...	...	...	...	f/	...	...	...	...	f/	...	...	...	...
34	Motor vehicles, trailers, semi-trailers	g/	112	120	123	118	g/	76879	66493	70670	65000	g/	818683	904346	907823	1106816
35	Other transport equipment	g/	...	...	...	...	g/	...	...	...	...	g/	...	...	...	...
36	Furniture; manufacturing n.e.c.	h/	695	1126	1153	1235	h/	45149	46858	46527	46559	h/	330829	423523	470358	594813
37	Recycling	h/	...	...	...	...	h/	...	...	...	...	h/	...	...	...	...
D	Total manufacturing		8999	11520	10956	11695		963731	984968	949668	942601		8450818	11075435	11603059	14679103

a/ 15 includes 16.
b/ 17 includes 18.
c/ 21 includes 22.
d/ 27 includes 28.
e/ 29 includes 30.
f/ 31 includes 32 and 33.
g/ 34 includes 35.
h/ 36 includes 37.

Belarus

ISIC Revision 3			Output (billions of Belarusian Roubles)					Value added (billions of Belarusian Roubles)					Gross fixed capital formation (billions of Belarusian Roubles)	
ISIC	Industry	Note	2007	2008	2009	2010	Note	2007	2008	2009	2010	Note	2009	2010
15	Food and beverages		...	22244.6a/	26335.3a/	...		...	6443.0a/	7821.7a/	...		...	...
16	Tobacco products		...	...a/	...a/	...		...	...a/	...a/	...		...	...
17	Textiles		...	4492.8b/	4516.6b/	...		...	1548.9b/	1732.9b/	...		...	...
18	Wearing apparel, fur		...	...b/	...b/	...		...	...b/	...b/	...		...	...
19	Leather, leather products and footwear		...	932.9	996.6	...		...	331.6	400.5	...		...	...
20	Wood products (excl. furniture)		...	2209.2	2067.3	...		...	813.6	787.9	...		...	...
21	Paper and paper products		...	2312.3c/	2384.4c/	...		...	719.0c/	736.5c/	...		...	...
22	Printing and publishing		...	...c/	...c/	...		...	...c/	...c/	...		...	...
23	Coke,refined petroleum products,nuclear fuel		...	26696.6	23811.4	...		...	2047.2	1796.1	...		...	...
24	Chemicals and chemical products		...	13194.3	10965.5	...		...	6132.2	4672.4	...		...	...
25	Rubber and plastics products		...	4175.9	4166.3	...		...	1457.9	1422.2	...		...	...
26	Non-metallic mineral products		...	6541.3	6767.3	...		...	2454.0	2517.1	...		...	...
27	Basic metals		...	9658.9d/	8071.8d/	...		...	2659.5d/	2310.5d/	...		...	...
28	Fabricated metal products		...	...d/	...d/	...		...	...d/	...d/	...		...	...
29	Machinery and equipment n.e.c.		...	12395.4e/	12067.4e/	...		...	3970.1e/	4156.5e/	...		...	...
30	Office, accounting and computing machinery		...	...e/	...e/	...		...	...e/	...e/	...		...	...
31	Electrical machinery and apparatus		...	4858.7f/	4661.5f/	...		...	1586.6f/	1683.7f/	...		...	...
32	Radio,television and communication equipment		...	...f/	...f/	...		...	...f/	...f/	...		...	...
33	Medical, precision and optical instruments		...	...f/	...f/	...		...	...f/	...f/	...		...	...
34	Motor vehicles, trailers, semi-trailers		...	8166.7g/	5376.5g/	...		...	2584.0g/	1573.0g/	...		...	...
35	Other transport equipment		...	...g/	...g/	...		...	...g/	...g/	...		...	...
36	Furniture; manufacturing n.e.c.		...	3219.9h/	2990.6h/	...		...	1237.3h/	1195.8h/	...		...	...
37	Recycling		...	...h/	...h/	...		...	...h/	...h/	...		49345.5	...
D	Total manufacturing		87917.0	121099.4	115178.5	150882.2		24200.9	33984.9	32807.0	39513.1			

a/ 15 includes 16.
b/ 17 includes 18.
c/ 21 includes 22.
d/ 27 includes 28.
e/ 29 includes 30.
f/ 31 includes 32 and 33.
g/ 34 includes 35.
h/ 36 includes 37.

Belarus

Index numbers of industrial production

(2005=100)

ISIC Revision 3		Note	1999	2000	2001	2002	2003	2004	2005	2006	2007	2008	2009	2010
ISIC	Industry													
15	Food and beverages		...	...	...	...	...	...	...	...	...	...	...	...
16	Tobacco products		...	...	...	...	...	...	...	...	...	...	...	...
17	Textiles		...	...	...	...	...	...	...	...	...	...	...	...
18	Wearing apparel, fur		...	...	...	...	...	...	...	...	...	...	...	...
19	Leather, leather products and footwear		...	...	...	...	...	...	...	...	...	...	...	...
20	Wood products (excl. furniture)		...	...	...	...	...	...	...	...	...	...	...	...
21	Paper and paper products		...	...	...	...	...	...	...	...	...	...	...	...
22	Printing and publishing		...	...	...	...	...	...	...	...	...	...	...	...
23	Coke,refined petroleum products,nuclear fuel		...	...	...	...	...	...	...	...	...	...	...	...
24	Chemicals and chemical products		...	...	...	...	...	...	...	...	...	...	...	...
25	Rubber and plastics products		...	...	...	...	...	...	...	...	...	...	...	...
26	Non-metallic mineral products		...	...	...	...	...	...	...	...	...	...	...	...
27	Basic metals		...	...	...	...	...	...	...	...	...	...	...	...
28	Fabricated metal products		...	...	...	...	...	...	...	...	...	...	...	...
29	Machinery and equipment n.e.c.		...	...	...	...	...	...	...	...	...	...	...	...
30	Office, accounting and computing machinery		...	...	...	...	...	...	...	...	...	...	...	...
31	Electrical machinery and apparatus		...	...	...	...	...	...	...	...	...	...	...	...
32	Radio,television and communication equipment		...	...	...	...	...	...	...	...	...	...	...	...
33	Medical, precision and optical instruments		...	...	...	...	...	...	...	...	...	...	...	...
34	Motor vehicles, trailers, semi-trailers		...	...	...	...	...	...	...	...	...	...	...	...
35	Other transport equipment		...	...	...	...	...	...	...	...	...	...	...	...
36	Furniture; manufacturing n.e.c.		...	...	...	...	...	...	...	...	...	...	...	...
37	Recycling		...	...	...	...	...	...	...	...	...	...	...	...
D	Total manufacturing		61	66	70	73	78	90	100	113	124	139	135	151

Belgium

Supplier of information:
National Institute of Statistics (Institut National de Statistique), Brussels. Industrial statistics for the OECD countries are compiled by the OECD secretariat, which supplies them to UNIDO.

Basic source of data:
Annual survey; administrative data.

Major deviations from ISIC (Revision 4):
Data have been converted from the NACE-BEL classification system to ISIC (Revision 4) by the OECD.

Reference period:
Calendar year.

Scope:
All registered enterprises.

Method of data collection:
Not reported.

Type of enumeration:
Not reported.

Adjusted for non-response:
Not reported.

Concepts and definitions of variables:
No deviations from the standard UN concepts and definitions are reported.

Related national publications:
None reported.

Belgium

ISIC	Industry	Number of enterprises (number)					Number of employees (number)					Wages and salaries paid to employees (millions of Euros)				
		Note	2006	2007	2008	2009	Note	2006	2007	2008	2009	Note	2006	2007	2008	2009
1010	Processing/preserving of meat		...	...	823	764		...	...	13434	13300		...	...	351	384
1020	Processing/preserving of fish, etc.		...	...	56	37		...	...	1063	1026		...	...	30	32
1030	Processing/preserving of fruit, vegetables		...	...	202	187		...	...	7891	7909		...	...	247	263
1040	Vegetable and animal oils and fats		...	...	...	34		...	...	...	2240		...	...	...	109
1050	Dairy products		...	...	442	474		...	...	7237	7105		...	...	249	263
106	Grain mill products,starches and starch products		...	...	109	89		...	...	2436	1909		...	...	106	88
1061	Grain mill products		...	...	...	...		...	...	...	...		...	...	...	...
1062	Starches and starch products		...	...	...	...		...	...	...	...		...	...	...	...
107	Other food products		...	...	5818	5535		...	...	43084	43066		...	...	1118	1169
1071	Bakery products		...	...	...	4681		...	...	...	26057		...	...	...	527
1072	Sugar		...	...	11	9		...	...	1261	1063		...	...	60	51
1073	Cocoa, chocolate and sugar confectionery		...	...	...	528		...	...	...	7140		...	...	...	241
1074	Macaroni, noodles, couscous, etc.		...	...	...	21		...	...	...	731		...	...	...	24
1075	Prepared meals and dishes		...	...	26	31		...	...	1566	1777		...	...	50	58
1079	Other food products n.e.c.		...	...	...	265		...	...	...	6299		...	...	...	268
1080	Prepared animal feeds		...	...	149	175		...	...	3174	3163		...	...	113	124
1101	Distilling, rectifying and blending of spirits		...	...	337a/	336a/		...	...	10230a/	9672a/		...	...	420a/	442a/
1102	Wines		...	...	...a/	...a/		...	...	...a/	...a/		...	...	...a/	...a/
1103	Malt liquors and malt		...	...	...a/	...a/		...	...	...a/	...a/		...	...	...a/	...a/
1104	Soft drinks,mineral waters,other bottled waters		...	...	...a/	...a/		...	...	...a/	...a/		...	...	...a/	...a/
1200	Tobacco products		...	...	...	...		...	...	...	...		...	...	...	...
131	Spinning, weaving and finishing of textiles		...	...	694	745		...	...	9633	8407		...	...	249	211
1311	Preparation and spinning of textile fibres		...	...	219	213		...	...	1850	1668		...	...	43	34
1312	Weaving of textiles		...	...	173	247		...	...	6256	5393		...	...	167	140
1313	Finishing of textiles		...	...	302	285		...	...	1527	1346		...	...	38	38
139	Other textiles		...	...	895	720		...	...	15332	14736		...	...	430	401
1391	Knitted and crocheted fabrics		...	...	...	31		...	...	...	356		...	...	...	10
1392	Made-up textile articles, except apparel		...	...	526	345		...	...	3152	3247		...	...	79	79
1393	Carpets and rugs		...	...	168	196		...	...	9854	9005		...	...	282	250
1394	Cordage, rope, twine and netting		...	...	...	18		...	...	...	247		...	...	...	7
1399	Other textiles n.e.c.		...	...	...	130		...	...	...	1881		...	...	...	55
1410	Wearing apparel, except fur apparel		...	...	...	1082		...	...	...	4998		...	...	...	119
1420	Articles of fur		...	...	31	41		...	...	46	52		...	...	1	1
1430	Knitted and crocheted apparel		...	...	52	43		...	...	463	418		...	...	9	8
151	Leather;luggage,handbags,saddlery,harness;fur		...	...	...	...		...	...	...	...		...	...	...	...
1511	Tanning/dressing of leather; dressing of fur		...	...	...	...		...	...	...	...		...	...	...	...
1512	Luggage,handbags,etc.;saddlery/harness		...	...	...	...		...	...	...	...		...	...	...	...
1520	Footwear		...	...	53	92		...	...	268	292		...	...	6	7
1610	Sawmilling and planing of wood		...	...	368	317		...	...	2311	1818		...	...	58	44
162	Wood products, cork, straw, plaiting materials		...	...	1346	1573		...	...	10039	9148		...	...	298	275

1621	Veneer sheets and wood-based panels	...	61	...	2894	...	104
1622	Builders' carpentry and joinery	...	1045	...	4383	...	124
1623	Wooden containers	89	151	1125	1265	29	32
1629	Other wood products;articles of cork,straw	317	316	753	605	17	15
1701	Pulp, paper and paperboard	137	135	5165	5506	169	190
1702	Corrugated paper and paperboard	...	...	...	...	...	...
1709	Other articles of paper and paperboard	...	...	...	...	...	...
181	Printing and service activities related to printing	4426	4612b/	16526	16945b/	568	595b/
1811	Printing	1904	2007	13194	14029	465	501
1812	Service activities related to printing	2521	...b/	3333	...b/	104	...b/
1820	Reproduction of recorded media	197	45c/	198	4410c/	6	465c/
1910	Coke oven products	...	...c/	...	...c/	...	...c/
1920	Refined petroleum products	...	...	...	...	...	...
201	Basic chemicals,fertilizers, etc.	249	246	24931	24906	1526	1540
2011	Basic chemicals	34	136	720	17004	35	1065
2012	Fertilizers and nitrogen compounds	...	21	...	590	...	29
2013	Plastics and synthetic rubber in primary forms	...	89	...	7312	...	446
202	Other chemical products	...	390	...	17133	...	889
2021	Pesticides and other agrochemical products	116	12	4022	1305	197	93
2022	Paints,varnishes;printing ink and mastics	...	114	...	3969	...	199
2023	Soap,cleaning and cosmetic preparations	...	155	...	5755	...	236
2029	Other chemical products n.e.c.	...	109	...	6103	...	361
2030	Man-made fibres	...	19	...	1081	...	39
2100	Pharmaceuticals,medicinal chemicals, etc.	...	142	3893	18614	137	1126
221	Rubber products	97	94	...	2868	...	104
2211	Rubber tyres and tubes	...	39	...	946	...	26
2219	Other rubber products	...	55	846	1922	...	78
2220	Plastics products	836	781	21956	20373	846	780
2310	Glass and glass products	...	284	...	8814	802	379
239	Non-metallic mineral products n.e.c.	1378	1491	22886	21187	...	755
2391	Refractory products	81	80	...	1094	39	38
2392	Clay building materials	...	...	1165	2409	...	135
2393	Other porcelain and ceramic products	...	12	...	12710	...	429
2394	Cement, lime and plaster	...	540	...	2625	...	66
2395	Articles of concrete, cement and plaster	...	680	...	1389	...	56
2396	Cutting, shaping and finishing of stone	...	54	...	...	...	...
2399	Other non-metallic mineral products n.e.c.	...	...	...	...	...	...
2410	Basic iron and steel	...	...	...	...	...	...
2420	Basic precious and other non-ferrous metals	100	84	2949	2740	113	89
243	Casting of metals	53	43	2251	2179	91	74
2431	Casting of iron and steel	47	41	698	562	22	16
2432	Casting of non-ferrous metals	...	...	...	...	...	...
251	Struct.metal products, tanks, reservoirs	...	2571	...	25756	...	841
2511	Structural metal products	2096	2294	16996	17511	530	561
2512	Tanks, reservoirs and containers of metal	179	162	5123	4435	172	139

continued

Belgium

ISIC	Industry	Number of enterprises (number)					Number of employees (number)					Wages and salaries paid to employees (millions of Euros)				
		Note	2006	2007	2008	2009	Note	2006	2007	2008	2009	Note	2006	2007	2008	2009
2513	Steam generators, excl. hot water boilers		...	...	...	115		...	...	...	3810		...	...	...	141
2520	Weapons and ammunition		...	...	...	39		...	...	...	1710		...	...	...	77
259	Other metal products;metal working services		...	...	3896	4339		...	...	27794	27056		...	...	891	838
2591	Forging,pressing,stamping,roll-forming of metal		...	...	561	700		...	...	2279	2369		...	...	72	70
2592	Treatment and coating of metals; machining		...	...	2446	2805		...	...	15825	15787		...	...	486	473
2593	Cutlery, hand tools and general hardware		...	...	421	386		...	...	3300	2951		...	...	114	102
2599	Other fabricated metal products n.e.c.		...	...	468	446		...	...	6390	5948		...	...	220	193
2610	Electronic components and boards		...	...	...	153		...	...	...	5399		...	...	...	235
2620	Computers and peripheral equipment		...	...	112	181		...	...	806	1081		...	...	35	54
2630	Communication equipment		...	...	...	48		...	...	...	5542		...	...	...	374
2640	Consumer electronics		...	...	...	...		...	...	...	...		...	...	...	...
265	Measuring,testing equipment; watches, etc.		...	...	127	...		...	...	2710	...		...	...	132	...
2651	Measuring/testing/navigating equipment,etc.		...	...	101	120		...	...	2591	2417		...	...	127	107
2652	Watches and clocks		...	...	26	...		...	...	118	...		...	...	5	...
2660	Irradiation/electromedical equipment,etc.		...	...	...	33		...	...	...	358		...	...	...	13
2670	Optical instruments and photographic equipment		...	...	...	...		...	...	...	...		...	...	...	...
2680	Magnetic and optical media		...	...	...	...		...	...	...	...		...	...	...	...
2710	Electric motors,generators,transformers,etc.		...	...	...	253		...	...	...	4517		...	...	...	194
2720	Batteries and accumulators		...	...	...	...		...	...	...	...		...	...	...	...
273	Wiring and wiring devices		...	...	34	37		...	...	2765	2841		...	...	110	126
2731	Fibre optic cables		...	...	...	...		...	...	...	...		...	...	...	...
2732	Other electronic and electric wires and cables		...	...	...	19		...	...	...	2250		...	...	...	94
2733	Wiring devices		...	...	...	...		...	...	...	...		...	...	...	...
2740	Electric lighting equipment		...	...	...	235		...	...	...	2451		...	...	...	81
2750	Domestic appliances		...	...	86	...		...	...	1345	...		...	...	44	...
2790	Other electrical equipment		...	...	...	75		...	...	...	2873		...	...	...	127
281	General-purpose machinery		...	...	1129	1047		...	...	23776	21694		...	...	965	883
2811	Engines/turbines,excl.aircraft,vehicle engines		...	...	51	24		...	...	4092	1913		...	...	185	98
2812	Fluid power equipment		...	...	8	48		...	...	440	757		...	...	16	24
2813	Other pumps, compressors, taps and valves		...	...	...	34		...	...	...	3841		...	...	...	161
2814	Bearings, gears, gearing and driving elements		...	...	...	46		...	...	...	3123		...	...	...	123
2815	Ovens, furnaces and furnace burners		...	...	40	52		...	...	442	430		...	...	15	16
2816	Lifting and handling equipment		...	...	219	272		...	...	2499	3278		...	...	80	118
2817	Office machinery, excl.computers,etc.		...	...	34	...		...	...	110	...		...	...	3	...
2818	Power-driven hand tools		...	...	14	...		...	...	63	...		...	...	2	...
2819	Other general-purpose machinery		...	...	623	537		...	...	8783	8260		...	...	332	340
282	Special-purpose machinery		...	...	707	661		...	...	17203	15729		...	...	665	565
2821	Agricultural and forestry machinery		...	...	...	140		...	...	...	3980		...	...	...	145
2822	Metal-forming machinery and machine tools		...	...	...	121		...	...	...	938		...	...	...	34
2823	Machinery for metallurgy		...	...	...	7		...	...	...	248		...	...	...	9
2824	Mining, quarrying and construction machinery		...	...	69	73		...	...	1223	4496		...	...	58	147

2825	Food/beverage/tobacco processing machinery	...	74	78	...	955	867	...	...	29	31
2826	Textile/apparel/leather production machinery	...	...	45	...	...	2573	...	...	...	91
2829	Other special-purpose machinery	...	...	196	...	...	2626	...	...	...	109
2910	Motor vehicles	...	40	32	...	24069	21532	...	...	961	817
2920	Automobile bodies, trailers and semi-trailers	...	214	245	...	7258	5619	...	...	215	147
2930	Parts and accessories for motor vehicles	...	...	180	...	...	11258	...	...	...	380
301	Building of ships and boats	...	26	...	...	347	...	...	...	10	...
3011	Building of ships and floating structures	...	...	...	...	...	...	...	...	...	...
3012	Building of pleasure and sporting boats	...	...	16	...	...	12	...	...	...	...
3020	Railway locomotives and rolling stock	...	...	9	...	5211	1153	...	...	...	56
3030	Air and spacecraft and related machinery	...	66	44	...	...	5144	...	...	212	221
3040	Military fighting vehicles	...	-	-	...	-	-	...	...	-	-
309	Transport equipment n.e.c.	...	...	...	...	...	...	...	...	...	...
3091	Motorcycles	...	...	...	...	...	...	...	...	...	...
3092	Bicycles and invalid carriages	...	...	73	...	...	472	...	...	...	17
3099	Other transport equipment n.e.c.	...	...	7	...	...	17	...	...	...	1
3100	Furniture	...	1782	2269	...	13024	13103	...	...	326	335
321	Jewellery, bijouterie and related articles	...	818	784	...	1102	1033	...	...	22	24
3211	Jewellery and related articles	...	...	737	...	...	1009	...	...	...	23
3212	Imitation jewellery and related articles	...	...	47	...	...	23	...	...	...	1
3220	Musical instruments	...	137	98	...	95	74	...	...	2	1
3230	Sports goods	...	...	43	...	...	56	...	...	...	1
3240	Games and toys	...	69	63	...	652	567	...	...	20	18
3250	Medical and dental instruments and supplies	...	...	...	...	...	...	...	...	...	...
3290	Other manufacturing n.e.c.	...	319	452	...	1187	1007	...	...	32	27
331	Repair of fabricated metal products/machinery	...	968	1110	...	8574	9638	...	...	322	369
3311	Repair of fabricated metal products	...	122	102	...	997	2342	...	...	30	83
3312	Repair of machinery	...	620	753	...	4045	3757	...	...	160	145
3313	Repair of electronic and optical equipment	...	...	...	...	...	...	...	...	...	...
3314	Repair of electrical equipment	...	...	65	...	...	239	...	...	...	9
3315	Repair of transport equip., excl. motor vehicles	...	...	168	...	...	2825	...	...	...	109
3319	Repair of other equipment	...	5	...	...	679	...	...	...	25	...
3320	Installation of industrial machinery/equipment	...	90	147	...	1497	6672	...	...	62	262
C	Total manufacturing	...	37209	37981	...	546743	524751	...	...	21189	20553

a/ 1101 includes 1102, 1103 and 1104.
b/ 181 includes 1820.
c/ 1910 includes 1920.

Belgium

ISIC Revision 4		Output (millions of Euros)					Value added at factor values (millions of Euros)					Gross fixed capital formation (millions of Euros)		
ISIC	Industry	Note	2006	2007	2008	2009	Note	2006	2007	2008	2009	Note	2008	2009
1010	Processing/preserving of meat		...	...	5149	4934		...	...	778	787		147	135
1020	Processing/preserving of fish, etc.		...	...	408	381		...	...	70	76		12	17
1030	Processing/preserving of fruit,vegetables		...	...	2689	3056		...	...	583	657		158	170
1040	Vegetable and animal oils and fats		...	...	...	3726		...	...	...	229		...	27
1050	Dairy products		...	...	3977	3499		...	...	695	613		76	97
106	Grain mill products,starches and starch products		...	...	1949	2013		...	...	256	318		45	21
1061	Grain mill products		...	...	...	...		...	...	...	...		...	...
1062	Starches and starch products		...	...	...	...		...	...	...	...		...	...
107	Other food products		...	...	10157	10783		...	...	2511	2645		501	621
1071	Bakery products		...	...	...	3110		...	...		1157		...	297
1072	Sugar		...	...	876	939		...	...	197	226		31	30
1073	Cocoa, chocolate and sugar confectionery		...	...	...	3655		...	...	...	507		...	68
1074	Macaroni, noodles, couscous, etc.		...	...	...	207		...	...	...	58		...	8
1075	Prepared meals and dishes		...	...	440	558		...	...	95	132		10	22
1079	Other food products n.e.c.		...	...		2314		...	...		564			196
1080	Prepared animal feeds		...	...	3062	3477		...	...	278	250		55	54
1101	Distilling, rectifying and blending of spirits		...	...	4420a/	5240a/		...	...	1210a/	1352a/		270a/	228a/
1102	Wines		...	...	...a/	...a/		...	...	...a/	...a/		...a/	...a/
1103	Malt liquors and malt		...	...	...a/	...a/		...	...	...a/	...a/		...a/	...a/
1104	Soft drinks,mineral waters,other bottled waters		...	...	...a/	...a/		...	...	...a/	...a/		...a/	...a/
1200	Tobacco products		...	...	...	...		...	...	...	...		...	...
131	Spinning, weaving and finishing of textiles		...	...	1628	1323		...	...	425	345		62	54
1311	Preparation and spinning of textile fibres		...	...	357	242		...	...	63	56		9	12
1312	Weaving of textiles		...	...	1016	804		...	...	295	223		43	22
1313	Finishing of textiles		...	...	255	277		...	...	68	65		10	21
139	Other textiles		...	...	3077	2507		...	...	741	727		111	73
1391	Knitted and crocheted fabrics		...	...	...	55		...	...	...	16		...	1
1392	Made-up textile articles, except apparel		...	...	502	473		...	...	124	136		24	19
1393	Carpets and rugs		...	...	2031	1634		...	...	462	462		63	46
1394	Cordage, rope, twine and netting		...	...	...	55		...	...	...	16		...	2
1399	Other textiles n.e.c.		...	...	...	291		...	...	...	98		...	5
1410	Wearing apparel, except fur apparel		...	...	...	1104		...	...	...	268		...	35
1420	Articles of fur		...	...	7	10		...	...	2	1		-	1
1430	Knitted and crocheted apparel		...	...	52	42		...	...	15	12		2	1
151	Leather;luggage,handbags,saddlery,harness;fur		...	...	...	...		...	...	...	...		...	...
1511	Tanning/dressing of leather; dressing of fur		...	...	...	...		...	...	...	...		...	...
1512	Luggage,handbags,etc.;saddlery/harness		...	...	...	...		...	...	...	...		...	...
1520	Footwear		...	...	46	58		...	...	14	14		3	3
1610	Sawmilling and planing of wood		...	...	870	426		...	...	162	114		81	64
162	Wood products, cork, straw, plaiting materials		...	...	2755	2159		...	...	772	659		533	96

Code							
1621	Veneer sheets and wood-based panels	..	929	..	297	..	28
1622	Builders' carpentry and joinery	..	841	..	254	..	42
1623	Wooden containers	375	291	71	69	11	8
1629	Other wood products;articles of cork,straw	101	98	31	39	6	18
1701	Pulp, paper and paperboard	..	..	..	..	..	..
1702	Corrugated paper and paperboard	1202	1144	352	370	58	49
1709	Other articles of paper and paperboard	..	..	..	..	..	..
181	Printing and service activities related to printing	3501	3392b/	1250	1258b/	306	542b/
1811	Printing	2915	2783	1015	1046	223	436
1812	Service activities related to printing	586	586	235	..	83	..
1820	Reproduction of recorded media	42	...b/	10	...b/	7	...b/
1910	Coke oven products	..	32019c/	..	754c/	..	283c/
1920	Refined petroleum products	..	...c/	..	...c/	..	...c/
201	Basic chemicals,fertilizers, etc.	23636	17534	3923	3780	749	740
2011	Basic chemicals	..	12278	..	2806	..	487
2012	Fertilizers and nitrogen compounds	641	358	98	64	8	41
2013	Plastics and synthetic rubber in primary forms	..	4898	..	910	..	213
202	Other chemical products	..	6372	..	1694	..	166
2021	Pesticides and other agrochemical products	..	326	..	170	..	17
2022	Paints,varnishes;printing ink and mastics	2059	1508	406	370	47	26
2023	Soap,cleaning and cosmetic preparations	..	2200	..	459	..	58
2029	Other chemical products n.e.c.	..	2338	..	694	..	66
2030	Man-made fibres	..	578	..	85	..	5
2100	Pharmaceuticals,medicinal chemicals, etc.	1502	7947	348	3648	..	843
221	Rubber products	..	709	..	197	82	26
2211	Rubber tyres and tubes	..	205	..	60	..	5
2219	Other rubber products	..	504	..	138	..	21
2220	Plastics products	6894	5317	1782	1577	264	240
2310	Glass and glass products	..	2399	..	636	..	179
239	Non-metallic mineral products n.e.c.	6081	5542	1726	1750	461	358
2391	Refractory products	..	..	..	..	..	..
2392	Clay building materials	281	255	-68	97	22	19
2393	Other porcelain and ceramic products	..	..	..	..	..	..
2394	Cement, lime and plaster	..	1172	..	418	..	62
2395	Articles of concrete, cement and plaster	..	2967	..	927	..	174
2396	Cutting, shaping and finishing of stone	..	477	..	144	..	87
2399	Other non-metallic mineral products n.e.c.	..	534	..	115	..	9
2410	Basic iron and steel	..	..	..	..	..	..
2420	Basic precious and other non-ferrous metals	..	..	..	..	..	..
243	Casting of metals	581	464	173	134	82	24
2431	Casting of iron and steel	463	381	148	111	29	22
2432	Casting of non-ferrous metals	117	83	25	23	53	3
251	Struct.metal products, tanks, reservoirs	4093	5451	..	1642	199	190
2511	Structural metal products	1214	3743	1255	1125	30	150
2512	Tanks, reservoirs and containers of metal	..	850	366	276	..	26

continued

Belgium

ISIC	Industry	Output (millions of Euros) Note	2006	2007	2008	2009	Value added at factor values (millions of Euros) Note	2006	2007	2008	2009	Gross fixed capital formation (millions of Euros) Note	2008	2009
2513	Steam generators, excl. hot water boilers		...	...	...	858		...	...	...	241		...	14
2520	Weapons and ammunition		...	...	...	359		...	...	...	146		...	13
259	Other metal products;metal working services		...	...	6311	4753		...	...	1909	1610		331	322
2591	Forging,pressing,stamping,roll-forming of metal		...	...	767	471		...	...	166	126		37	27
2592	Treatment and coating of metals; machining		...	...	3083	2384		...	...	1030	917		201	219
2593	Cutlery, hand tools and general hardware		...	...	622	399		...	...	210	162		30	17
2599	Other fabricated metal products n.e.c.		...	...	1839	1498		...	...	503	405		64	59
2610	Electronic components and boards		...	...	...	1240		...	...	...	414		...	78
2620	Computers and peripheral equipment		...	...	223	291		...	...	69	76		17	10
2630	Communication equipment		...	...	...	1926		...	...	...	522		...	21
2640	Consumer electronics		...	...				...	...					
265	Measuring,testing equipment, watches, etc.		...	...	927	...		...	...	257	...		11	...
2651	Measuring/testing/navigating equipment,etc.		...	...	911	711		...	...	253	178		11	15
2652	Watches and clocks		...	...	16	...		...	...	4	...		-	...
2660	Irradiation/electromedical equipment,etc.		...	...	...	95		...	...	...	20		...	3
2670	Optical instruments and photographic equipment		...	...	...	...		...	...	...	...		...	...
2680	Magnetic and optical media		...	...	...	...		...	...	...	...		...	...
2710	Electric motors,generators,transformers,etc.		...	...	...	1333		...	...	...	374		...	29
2720	Batteries and accumulators		...	...	...	...		...	...	...	...		...	...
273	Wiring and wiring devices		...	...	725	819		...	...	179	211		17	14
2731	Fibre optic cables		...	...	...	...		...	...	...	...		...	...
2732	Other electronic and electric wires and cables		...	...	...	654		...	...	...	159		...	13
2733	Wiring devices		...	...	...	...		...	...	...	...		...	...
2740	Electric lighting equipment		...	...	...	382		...	...	...	158		...	11
2750	Domestic appliances		...	...	313	511		...	...	103	...		8	...
2790	Other electrical equipment		...	...	...	...		...	...	...	208		...	13
281	General-purpose machinery		...	...	8437	6770		...	...	2288	1895		197	152
2811	Engines/turbines,excl.aircraft,vehicle engines		...	...	1942	1135		...	...	362	207		51	17
2812	Fluid power equipment		...	...	67	90		...	...	25	41		1	4
2813	Other pumps, compressors, taps and valves		...	...	...	1311		...	...	...	515		...	17
2814	Bearings, gears, gearing and driving elements		...	...	...	716		...	...	...	212		...	33
2815	Ovens, furnaces and furnace burners		...	...	81	91		...	...	32	32		2	3
2816	Lifting and handling equipment		...	...	678	723		...	...	167	251		11	17
2817	Office machinery, excl.computers,etc.		...	...	19	...		...	...	4	...		1	...
2818	Power-driven hand tools		...	...	8	...		...	...	3	...		-	...
2819	Other general-purpose machinery		...	...	2576	2696		...	...	729	631		58	61
282	Special-purpose machinery		...	...	3910	3050		...	...	1322	1034		162	88
2821	Agricultural and forestry machinery		...	...	...	992		...	...	...	282		...	41
2822	Metal-forming machinery and machine tools		...	...	...	219		...	...	...	69		...	7
2823	Machinery for metallurgy		...	...	...	30		...	...	...	16		...	1
2824	Mining, quarrying and construction machinery		...	...	496	581		...	...	98	271		8	9

2825	Food/beverage/tobacco processing machinery	3	6	57	55	167	169
2826	Textile/apparel/leather production machinery	11	...	137	...	518	...
2829	Other special-purpose machinery	16	...	204	...	543	...
2910	Motor vehicles	258	312	1472	1780	9073	12509
2920	Automobile bodies, trailers and semi-trailers	18	56	289	428	1112	2002
2930	Parts and accessories for motor vehicles	63	...	630	...	2563	...
301	Building of ships and boats	...	12	...	17	...	83
3011	Building of ships and floating structures	...	...	...	...	...	...
3012	Building of pleasure and sporting boats	...	...	1	...	3	...
3020	Railway locomotives and rolling stock	7	...	184	...	271	...
3030	Air and spacecraft and related machinery	36	48	383	377	1022	1171
3040	Military fighting vehicles	-	-	-	-	-	-
309	Transport equipment n.e.c.	...	...	...	...	...	...
3091	Motorcycles	...	...	...	...	...	...
3092	Bicycles and invalid carriages	4	...	37	...	152	...
3099	Other transport equipment n.e.c.	-	...	...	...	2	...
3100	Furniture	119	103	703	698	2169	2313
321	Jewellery, bijouterie and related articles	25	8	64	103	573	610
3211	Jewellery and related articles	12	...	61	...	566	...
3212	Imitation jewellery and related articles	13	...	3	...	7	...
3220	Musical instruments	1	1	3	6	8	15
3230	Sports goods	-	-	3	...	12	...
3240	Games and toys	1	4	39	44	89	113
3250	Medical and dental instruments and supplies	15	...	...	78	...	277
3290	Other manufacturing n.e.c.	15	15	60	...	221	...
331	Repair of fabricated metal products/machinery	61	73	605	563	1506	1581
3311	Repair of fabricated metal products	8	15	134	61	280	184
3312	Repair of machinery	29	34	259	301	662	842
3313	Repair of electronic and optical equipment	...	...	...	...	...	...
3314	Repair of electrical equipment	4	...	15	...	60	...
3315	Repair of transport equip., excl. motor vehicles	17	...	162	...	398	146
3319	Repair of other equipment	...	4	...	42	...	...
3320	Installation of industrial machinery/equipment	23	7	400	96	1117	373
C	Total manufacturing	7423	8400	44747	49160	198556	251239

a/ 1101 includes 1102, 1103 and 1104.
b/ 181 includes 1820.
c/ 1910 includes 1920.

Belgium

- 258 -

ISIC	Industry	Note	1999	2000	2001	2002	2003	2004	2005	2006	2007	2008	2009	2010
10	Food products		..	84	92	93	95	97	100	105	108	115	113	116
11	Beverages		..	88	92	93	101	102	100	99	102	100	102	99
12	Tobacco products		..	87	90	96	98	111	100	93	95	115	114	123
13	Textiles		..	108	111	109	103	104	100	104	107	97	79	83
14	Wearing apparel		..	116	123	118	112	103	100	98	88	72	60	56
15	Leather and related products		..	157	148	134	112	107	100	99	94	97	82	81
16	Wood/wood products/cork,excl. furniture		..	81	85	92	93	98	100	108	111	102	101	108
17	Paper and paper products		..	96	98	98	99	101	100	104	111	111	106	108
18	Printing and reproduction of recorded media		..	88	92	88	94	97	100	106	106	120	106	101
19	Coke and refined petroleum products		..	102	109	120	119	114	100	98	101	99	92	96
20	Chemicals and chemical products		..	93	91	93	95	98	100	103	103	104	80	92
21	Pharmaceuticals,medicinal chemicals, etc.		..	53	65	70	84	100	100	107	102	112	113	140
22	Rubber and plastics products		..	94	92	94	97	100	100	103	108	107	95	100
23	Other non-metallic mineral products		..	101	101	98	98	101	100	107	110	111	94	92
24	Basic metals		..	80	81	84	97	98	100	110	106	112	83	99
25	Fabricated metal products, except machinery		..	95	99	98	101	103	100	104	112	112	94	98
26	Computer, electronic and optical products		..	128	107	84	90	103	100	74	120	125	98	106
27	Electrical equipment		..	110	107	104	95	99	100	101	105	107	90	95
28	Machinery and equipment n.e.c.		..	90	96	89	88	92	100	114	134	144	107	117
29	Motor vehicles, trailers and semi-trailers		..	74	91	87	80	93	100	103	102	95	67	81
30	Other transport equipment		..	70	80	86	77	93	100	100	118	116	109	110
31	Furniture		..	103	104	99	93	97	100	103	108	107	101	103
32	Other manufacturing		..	93	98	101	98	98	100	101	100	93	89	95
33	Repair and installation of machinery/equipment		..	89	96	89	87	93	100	98	106	122	105	95
C	Total manufacturing		..	86	91	91	94	99	100	103	109	111	96	104

ISIC Revision 4

Index numbers of industrial production

(2005=100)

Bermuda

Supplier of information:
Department of Statistics, Government of Bermuda, Hamilton.

Basic source of data:
Annual employment survey; annual economic activities survey.

Major deviations from ISIC (Revision 3):
None reported.

Reference period:
Calendar year.

Scope:
All economically active establishments.

Method of data collection:
Mail questionnaires; online survey.

Type of enumeration:
Complete enumeration for number of establishments, number of persons engaged and number of female employees; sample survey for output and gross fixed capital formation.

Adjusted for non-response:
Yes.

Concepts and definitions of variables:
Number of persons engaged is the average of a reference week around the middle of the year.

Related national publications:
Annual Employment Briefs; Annual Gross Domestic Report, both published by the Department of Statistics, Government of Bermuda, Hamilton.

Bermuda

ISIC Revision 3		Number of establishments (number)					Number of persons engaged (number)					Wages and salaries (Bermuda Dollars)				
ISIC	Industry	Note	2007	2008	2009	2010	Note	2007	2008	2009	2010	Note	2007	2008	2009	2010
151	Processed meat,fish,fruit,vegetables,fats		…	…	…	…		…	…	…	…		…	…	…	…
1511	Processing/preserving of meat		…	…	…	…		…	…	…	…		…	…	…	…
1512	Processing/preserving of fish		…	…	…	…		…	…	…	…		…	…	…	…
1513	Processing/preserving of fruit & vegetables		…	…	…	…		…	…	…	…		…	…	…	…
1514	Vegetable and animal oils and fats		…	…	…	…		…	…	…	…		…	…	…	…
1520	Dairy products		2	2	2	2		20	9	12	9		…	…	…	…
153	Grain mill products; starches; animal feeds		…	…	…	…		…	…	…	…		…	…	…	…
1531	Grain mill products		…	…	…	…		…	…	…	…		…	…	…	…
1532	Starches and starch products		…	…	…	…		…	…	…	…		…	…	…	…
1533	Prepared animal feeds		…	…	…	…		…	…	…	…		…	…	…	…
154	Other food products		…	…	…	…		…	…	…	…		…	…	…	…
1541	Bakery products		8	9	9	9		72	74	76	77		…	…	…	…
1542	Sugar		…	…	…	…		…	…	…	…		…	…	…	…
1543	Cocoa, chocolate and sugar confectionery		…	…	…	…		…	…	…	…		…	…	…	…
1544	Macaroni, noodles & similar products		…	…	…	…		…	…	…	…		…	…	…	…
1549	Other food products n.e.c.		…	…	…	…		…	…	…	…		…	…	…	…
155	Beverages		…	…	…	…		…	…	…	…		…	…	…	…
1551	Distilling, rectifying & blending of spirits		…	…	…	…		…	…	…	…		…	…	…	…
1552	Wines		…	…	…	…		…	…	…	…		…	…	…	…
1553	Malt liquors and malt		…	…	…	…		…	…	…	…		…	…	…	…
1554	Soft drinks; mineral waters		1	1	1	1		110	108	104	100		…	…	…	…
1600	Tobacco products		…	…	…	…		…	…	…	…		…	…	…	…
171	Spinning, weaving and finishing of textiles		…	…	…	…		…	…	…	…		…	…	…	…
1711	Textile fibre preparation; textile weaving		…	…	…	…		…	…	…	…		…	…	…	…
1712	Finishing of textiles		…	…	…	…		…	…	…	…		…	…	…	…
172	Other textiles		…	…	…	…		…	…	…	…		…	…	…	…
1721	Made-up textile articles, except apparel		4	3	3	3		9	9	10	9		…	…	…	…
1722	Carpets and rugs		…	…	…	…		…	…	…	…		…	…	…	…
1723	Cordage, rope, twine and netting		…	…	…	…		…	…	…	…		…	…	…	…
1729	Other textiles n.e.c.		1	1	1	1		5	4	4	3		…	…	…	…
1730	Knitted and crocheted fabrics and articles		…	…	…	…		…	…	…	…		…	…	…	…
1810	Wearing apparel, except fur apparel		6	6	6	6		11	11	9	9		…	…	…	…
1820	Dressing & dyeing of fur; processing of fur		…	…	…	…		…	…	…	…		…	…	…	…
191	Tanning, dressing and processing of leather		…	…	…	…		…	…	…	…		…	…	…	…
1911	Tanning and dressing of leather		…	…	…	…		…	…	…	…		…	…	…	…
1912	Luggage, handbags, etc.; saddlery & harness		…	…	…	…		…	…	…	…		…	…	…	…
1920	Footwear		…	…	…	…		…	…	…	…		…	…	…	…
2010	Sawmilling and planing of wood		1	1	1	1		4	3	4	3		…	…	…	…
202	Products of wood, cork, straw, etc.		…	…	…	…		…	…	…	…		…	…	…	…
2021	Veneer sheets, plywood, particle board, etc.		…	…	…	…		…	…	…	…		…	…	…	…
2022	Builders' carpentry and joinery		1	1	1	1		6	5	5	5		…	…	…	…
2023	Wooden containers		…	…	…	…		…	…	…	…		…	…	…	…
2029	Other wood products; articles of cork/straw		9	7	7	7		16	14	13	13		…	…	…	…
210	Paper and paper products		…	…	…	…		…	…	…	…		…	…	…	…
2101	Pulp, paper and paperboard		…	…	…	…		…	…	…	…		…	…	…	…
2102	Corrugated paper and paperboard		…	…	…	…		…	…	…	…		…	…	…	…
2109	Other articles of paper and paperboard		…	…	…	…		…	…	…	…		…	…	…	…
221	Publishing		…	…	…	…		…	…	…	…		…	…	…	…
2211	Publishing of books and other publications		7	6	4	3		16	19	13	13		…	…	…	…
2212	Publishing of newspapers, journals, etc.		3	3	3	3		202	190	183	163		…	…	…	…
2213	Publishing of recorded media		…	…	…	…		…	…	…	…		…	…	…	…
2219	Other publishing		6	7	6	7		13	13	12	15		…	…	…	…

Code	Description	9	10	10	10	93	94	81	70
222	Printing and related service activities								
2221	Printing								
2222	Service activities related to printing								
2230	Reproduction of recorded media								
2310	Coke oven products								
2320	Refined petroleum products								
2330	Processing of nuclear fuel								
241	Basic chemicals								
2411	Basic chemicals, except fertilizers								
2412	Fertilizers and nitrogen compounds								
2413	Plastics in primary forms; synthetic rubber								
242	Other chemicals								
2421	Pesticides and other agro-chemical products	2	2	2	2	16	13	14	14
2422	Paints, varnishes, printing ink and mastics								
2423	Pharmaceuticals, medicinal chemicals, etc.	1	1	1		4	6	6	8
2424	Soap, cleaning & cosmetic preparations								
2429	Other chemical products n.e.c.								
2430	Man-made fibres								
251	Rubber products								
2511	Rubber tyres and tubes								
2519	Other rubber products	2	3	3	3	8	11	9	7
2520	Plastic products	2	1	1	1	10	9	11	8
2610	Glass and glass products								
269	Non-metallic mineral products n.e.c.								
2691	Pottery, china and earthenware								
2692	Refractory ceramic products		1		1				1
2693	Struct.non-refractory clay; ceramic products								
2694	Cement, lime and plaster	3	3	3	3	103	99	119	103
2695	Articles of concrete, cement and plaster								
2696	Cutting, shaping & finishing of stone								
2699	Other non-metallic mineral products n.e.c.								
2710	Basic iron and steel								
2720	Basic precious and non-ferrous metals								
273	Casting of metals								
2731	Casting of iron and steel					7	8	6	6
2732	Casting of non-ferrous metals	2	2	2	2	7	8	6	6
281	Struct.metal products;tanks;steam generators								
2811	Structural metal products								
2812	Tanks, reservoirs and containers of metal								
2813	Steam generators								
289	Other metal products; metal working services	24	23	23	22	43	42	44	44
2891	Metal forging/pressing/stamping/roll-forming								
2892	Treatment & coating of metals								
2893	Cutlery, hand tools and general hardware	2			2				
2899	Other fabricated metal products n.e.c.								
291	General purpose machinery								
2911	Engines & turbines (not for transport equipment)								
2912	Pumps, compressors, taps and valves								
2913	Bearings, gears, gearing & driving elements								
2914	Ovens, furnaces and furnace burners								
2915	Lifting and handling equipment								
2919	Other general purpose machinery								
292	Special purpose machinery								
2921	Agricultural and forestry machinery								
2922	Machine tools								
2923	Machinery for metallurgy								
2924	Machinery for mining & construction								
2925	Food/beverage/tobacco processing machinery								
2926	Machinery for textile, apparel and leather								
2927	Weapons and ammunition								
2929	Other special purpose machinery								

continued

Bermuda

ISIC Revision 3		Number of establishments					Number of persons engaged					Wages and salaries (Bermuda Dollars)				
		Note	(number)				Note	(number)				Note				
ISIC	Industry		2007	2008	2009	2010		2007	2008	2009	2010		2007	2008	2009	2010
2930	Domestic appliances n.e.c.		…	…	…	…		…	…	…	…		…	…	…	…
3000	Office, accounting and computing machinery		…	…	…	…		…	…	…	…		…	…	…	…
3110	Electric motors, generators and transformers		…	…	…	…		…	…	…	…		…	…	…	…
3120	Electricity distribution & control apparatus		…	…	…	…		…	…	…	…		…	…	…	…
3130	Insulated wire and cable		…	…	…	…		…	…	…	…		…	…	…	…
3140	Accumulators, primary cells and batteries		…	…	…	…		…	…	…	…		…	…	…	…
3150	Lighting equipment and electric lamps		…	…	…	…		…	…	…	…		…	…	…	…
3190	Other electrical equipment n.e.c.		…	2	2	2		…	9	10	9		…	…	…	…
3210	Electronic valves, tubes, etc.		…	…	…	…		…	…	…	…		…	…	…	…
3220	TV/radio transmitters; line comm. apparatus		…	…	…	…		…	…	…	…		…	…	…	…
3230	TV and radio receivers and associated goods		…	…	…	…		…	…	…	…		…	…	…	…
331	Medical, measuring, testing appliances, etc.		…	…	…	…		…	…	…	…		…	…	…	…
3311	Medical, surgical and orthopaedic equipment		…	…	…	…		…	…	…	…		…	…	…	…
3312	Measuring/testing/navigating appliances,etc.		…	…	…	…		…	…	…	…		…	…	…	…
3313	Industrial process control equipment		…	…	…	…		…	…	…	…		…	…	…	…
3320	Optical instruments & photographic equipment		…	…	…	…		…	…	…	…		…	…	…	…
3330	Watches and clocks		…	…	…	…		…	…	…	…		…	…	…	…
3410	Motor vehicles		…	…	…	…		…	…	…	…		…	…	…	…
3420	Automobile bodies, trailers & semi-trailers		…	…	…	…		…	…	…	…		…	…	…	…
3430	Parts/accessories for automobiles		…	…	…	…		…	…	…	…		…	…	…	…
351	Building and repairing of ships and boats		30	28	26	25		61	65	64	67		…	…	…	…
3511	Building and repairing of ships		…	…	…	…		…	…	…	…		…	…	…	…
3512	Building/repairing of pleasure/sport. boats		…	…	…	…		…	…	…	…		…	…	…	…
3520	Railway/tramway locomotives & rolling stock		…	…	…	…		…	…	…	…		…	…	…	…
3530	Aircraft and spacecraft		…	…	…	…		…	…	…	…		…	…	…	…
359	Transport equipment n.e.c.		…	…	…	…		…	…	…	…		…	…	…	…
3591	Motorcycles		…	…	…	…		…	…	…	…		…	…	…	…
3592	Bicycles and invalid carriages		…	…	…	…		…	…	…	…		…	…	…	…
3599	Other transport equipment n.e.c.		…	…	…	…		…	…	…	…		…	…	…	…
3610	Furniture		32	32	32	28		91	95	91	78		…	…	…	…
369	Manufacturing n.e.c.		4	4	4	4		5	5	6	7		…	…	…	…
3691	Jewellery and related articles		…	…	…	…		…	…	…	…		…	…	…	…
3692	Musical instruments		…	…	…	…		…	…	…	…		…	…	…	…
3693	Sports goods		…	…	…	…		…	…	…	…		…	…	…	…
3694	Games and toys		…	…	…	…		…	…	…	…		…	…	…	…
3699	Other manufacturing n.e.c.		…	…	…	…		…	…	…	…		…	…	…	…
3710	Recycling of metal waste and scrap		…	…	…	…		…	…	…	…		…	…	…	…
3720	Recycling of non-metal waste and scrap		…	…	…	…		…	…	…	…		…	…	…	…
D	Total manufacturing		162	158	154	148		935	915	906	841		…	…	…	…

Bermuda

ISIC Revision 3		Output (thousands of Bermuda Dollars)					Value added (thousands of Bermuda Dollars)					Gross fixed capital formation (thousands of Bermuda Dollars)	
ISIC	Industry	Note	2007	2008	2009	2010	Note	2007	2008	2009	2010	Note	2009	2010
151	Processed meat,fish,fruit,vegetables,fats		..	..	..	..		..	..	..	..		..	..
1511	Processing/preserving of meat		..	..	..	..		..	..	..	..		..	..
1512	Processing/preserving of fish		..	..	..	..		..	..	..	..		..	..
1513	Processing/preserving of fruit & vegetables		..	..	..	..		..	..	..	..		..	..
1514	Vegetable and animal oils and fats		..	..	..	..		..	..	..	..		..	..
1520	Dairy products		3627	186	399	140		..	..	..	..		7	-
153	Grain mill products; starches; animal feeds		..	..	..	..		..	..	..	..		..	..
1531	Grain mill products		..	..	..	..		..	..	..	..		..	..
1532	Starches and starch products		..	..	..	..		..	..	..	..		..	..
1533	Prepared animal feeds		..	..	..	..		..	..	..	..		..	..
154	Other food products		8956	9679	9912	9883		..	..	..	..		32	129
1541	Bakery products			9679	9912	9883		..	..	..	..		32	129
1542	Sugar		..	..	..	..		..	..	..	..		..	..
1543	Cocoa, chocolate and sugar confectionery		..	..	..	..		..	..	..	..		..	..
1544	Macaroni, noodles & similar products		..	..	..	..		..	..	..	..		..	..
1549	Other food products n.e.c.		..	..	..	..		..	..	..	..		..	..
155	Beverages		14696	14696	11105	10782		..	..	..	..		745	254
1551	Distilling, rectifying & blending of spirits		..	..	..	..		..	..	..	..		..	..
1552	Wines		..	..	..	..		..	..	..	..		..	..
1553	Malt liquors and malt		..	..	..	..		..	..	..	..		..	..
1554	Soft drinks; mineral waters		14062	14696	11105	10782		..	..	..	..		745	254
1600	Tobacco products		..	..	..	..		..	..	..	..		..	..
171	Spinning, weaving and finishing of textiles		..	..	..	..		..	..	..	..		..	..
1711	Textile fibre preparation; textile weaving		..	..	..	..		..	..	..	..		..	..
1712	Finishing of textiles		..	..	..	..		..	..	..	..		..	..
172	Other textiles			1628	1626	1478		..	..	..	..		-16	-14
1721	Made-up textile articles, except apparel		829	835	876	814		..	..	..	..		-	-
1722	Carpets and rugs		..	..	..	..		..	..	..	..		..	..
1723	Cordage, rope, twine and netting		985	794	751	663		..	..	..	..		-16	-14
1729	Other textiles n.e.c.		..	..	..	..		..	..	..	..		..	..
1730	Knitted and crocheted fabrics and articles		4111	..	..	2829		..	..	..	..		-	107
1810	Wearing apparel, except fur apparel		..	..	..	..		..	..	..	..		..	..
1820	Dressing & dyeing of fur; processing of fur		..	..	..	..		..	..	..	..		..	..
191	Tanning, dressing and processing of leather		..	..	..	..		..	..	..	..		..	..
1911	Tanning and dressing of leather		..	..	..	..		..	..	..	..		..	..
1912	Luggage, handbags, etc.; saddlery & harness		..	..	..	..		..	..	..	..		..	..
1920	Footwear		..	..	..	..		..	..	..	..		..	..
2010	Sawmilling and planing of wood		2272	1933	1451	1088		..	..	..	..		-25	-19
202	Products of wood, cork, straw, etc.			2530	2933	2193		..	..	..	..		40	-18
2021	Veneer sheets, plywood, particle board, etc.		..	..	..	..		..	..	..	..		..	..
2022	Builders' carpentry and joinery		849	896	956	861		..	..	..	..		34	9
2023	Wooden containers		..	..	..	..		..	..	..	..		..	..
2029	Other wood products; articles of cork/straw		1242	1634	1977	1331		..	..	..	..		6	-27
210	Paper and paper products		..	..	..	..		..	..	..	..		..	..
2101	Pulp, paper and paperboard		..	..	..	..		..	..	..	..		..	..
2102	Corrugated paper and paperboard		..	..	..	..		..	..	..	..		..	..
2109	Other articles of paper and paperboard		..	..	..	..		..	..	..	..		..	..
221	Publishing			47197	37556	36361		..	..	..	..		729	1398
2211	Publishing of books and other publications		4130	4145	4383	2789		..	..	..	..		6	555
2212	Publishing of newspapers, journals, etc.		28187	33468	30538	29610		..	..	..	..		634	809
2213	Publishing of recorded media		3031	9584	2636	3962		..	..	..	..		24	34
2219	Other publishing		..	..	..	..		..	..	..	..		..	..

continued

Bermuda

ISIC	Industry	Output (thousands of Bermuda Dollars)					Value added (thousands of Bermuda Dollars)					Gross fixed capital formation (thousands of Bermuda Dollars)		
		Note	2007	2008	2009	2010	Note	2007	2008	2009	2010	Note	2009	2010
222	Printing and related service activities		18562	18044	17946	16501		…	…	…	…		66	-710
2221	Printing		…	…	…	…		…	…	…	…		…	…
2222	Service activities related to printing		…	…	…	…		…	…	…	…		…	…
2230	Reproduction of recorded media		…	…	…	…		…	…	…	…		…	…
2310	Coke oven products		…	…	…	…							…	…
2320	Refined petroleum products													
2330	Processing of nuclear fuel		…	…	…	…							…	…
241	Basic chemicals		…	…	…	…							…	…
2411	Basic chemicals, except fertilizers		…	…	…	…							…	…
2412	Fertilizers and nitrogen compounds		…	…	…	…							…	…
2413	Plastics in primary forms; synthetic rubber		…	…	…	…							…	…
242	Other chemicals			5393	5835	5184							20	163
2421	Pesticides and other agro-chemical products		…	…	…	…							…	…
2422	Paints, varnishes, printing ink and mastics		4786	4299	4735	3789							154	128
2423	Pharmaceuticals, medicinal chemicals, etc.		…	…	…	…							…	…
2424	Soap, cleaning & cosmetic preparations		875	1094	1100	1395							-135	35
2429	Other chemical products n.e.c.		…	…	…	…							…	…
2430	Man-made fibres		…	…	…	…							…	…
251	Rubber products		…	…	…	…							…	…
2511	Rubber tyres and tubes		…	…	…	…							…	…
2519	Other rubber products		…	…	…	…							…	…
2520	Plastic products		1466	308	272	248							…	-
2610	Glass and glass products		940	959	1125	2189							30	-123
269	Non-metallic mineral products n.e.c.			44068	39574	31758							372	-1476
2691	Pottery, china and earthenware		…	…	…	…							…	…
2692	Refractory ceramic products													
2693	Struct.non-refractory clay; ceramic products			300	1621	108							…	-3
2694	Cement, lime and plaster		…	…	…	…							…	…
2695	Articles of concrete, cement and plaster		40056	42802	37503	31270							499	-1413
2696	Cutting, shaping & finishing of stone		141	966	450	379							-128	-59
2699	Other non-metallic mineral products n.e.c.		…	…	…	…							…	…
2710	Basic iron and steel		…	…	…	…							…	…
2720	Basic precious and non-ferrous metals		…	…	…	…							…	…
273	Casting of metals		…	…	…	…							…	…
2731	Casting of iron and steel		…	…	…	…							…	…
2732	Casting of non-ferrous metals													
281	Struct.metal products;tanks;steam generators		1049	890	838	873							-	11
2811	Structural metal products		…	…	…	…							…	…
2812	Tanks, reservoirs and containers of metal		…	…	…	…							…	…
2813	Steam generators		…	…	…	…							…	…
289	Other metal products; metal working services		4721	4442	5739	5032							20	68
2891	Metal forging/pressing/stamping/roll-forming		…	…	…	…							…	…
2892	Treatment & coating of metals		…	…	…	…							…	…
2893	Cutlery, hand tools and general hardware		…	…	…	…							…	…
2899	Other fabricated metal products n.e.c.		…	…	…	…							…	…
291	General purpose machinery				179	179							4	4
2911	Engines & turbines (not for transport equipment)		…	…	…	…							…	…
2912	Pumps, compressors, taps and valves		…	…	…	…							…	…
2913	Bearings, gears, gearing & driving elements		…	…	…	…							…	…
2914	Ovens, furnaces and furnace burners		…	…	…	…							…	…
2915	Lifting and handling equipment		…	…	…	…							…	…
2919	Other general purpose machinery		…	…	…	…							…	…

ISIC Revision 3

Code	Description							
292	Special purpose machinery	...	...		...	...	...	...
2921	Agricultural and forestry machinery	...	...		...	...	...	...
2922	Machine tools	...	...		...	...	...	...
2923	Machinery for metallurgy	...	...		...	...	...	...
2924	Machinery for mining & construction	...	...		...	...	...	...
2925	Food/beverage/tobacco processing machinery	...	...		...	...	...	...
2926	Machinery for textile, apparel and leather	...	...		...	...	...	...
2927	Weapons and ammunition	...	...		...	...	...	...
2929	Other special purpose machinery	...	...		...	...	...	...
2930	Domestic appliances n.e.c.	...	...		...	...	...	...
3000	Office, accounting and computing machinery	38	-		...	...	...	...
3110	Electric motors, generators and transformers			a/	...	...	...	...
3120	Electricity distribution & control apparatus			a/	...	...	...	...
3130	Insulated wire and cable			a/	...	...	...	...
3140	Accumulators, primary cells and batteries			a/	...	...	...	...
3150	Lighting equipment and electric lamps			a/	...	...	...	...
3190	Other electrical equipment n.e.c.	...	...		...	...	...	...
3210	Electronic valves, tubes, etc.	...	...		...	...	...	...
3220	TV/radio transmitters; line comm. apparatus	...	...		...	...	...	...
3230	TV and radio receivers and associated goods	...	...		...	...	...	...
331	Medical, measuring, testing appliances, etc.	...	...		...	...	...	...
3311	Medical, surgical and orthopaedic equipment	...	...		...	...	...	...
3312	Measuring/testing/navigating appliances,etc.	...	...		...	...	...	...
3313	Industrial process control equipment	...	...		...	...	...	...
3320	Optical instruments & photographic equipment	...	...		...	...	...	...
3330	Watches and clocks	...	...		...	...	...	...
3410	Motor vehicles	...	...		...	...	...	...
3420	Automobile bodies, trailers & semi-trailers	...	...		...	...	...	...
3430	Parts/accessories for automobiles	469	210		10544	12933	12145	
351	Building and repairing of ships and boats	...	...					9322
3511	Building and repairing of ships	...	...		...	...	...	...
3512	Building/repairing of pleasure/sport. boats	...	...		...	...	...	...
3520	Railway/tramway locomotives & rolling stock	...	...		...	...	...	...
3530	Aircraft and spacecraft	...	...		470	...	...	...
359	Transport equipment n.e.c.	...	...		...	...	...	...
3591	Motorcycles	...	...		...	...	...	...
3592	Bicycles and invalid carriages	...	...		...	...	...	...
3599	Other transport equipment n.e.c.	...	...		...	...	...	...
3610	Furniture	-49	-112		7175	7880	9703	6818
369	Manufacturing n.e.c.	17	...		543	496	756	637
3691	Jewellery and related articles	...	...		...	...	...	...
3692	Musical instruments	...	...		...	...	...	...
3693	Sports goods	...	...		...	...	...	...
3694	Games and toys	-659	...		...	...	...	...
3699	Other manufacturing n.e.c.	...	...		...	...	...	...
3710	Recycling of metal waste and scrap	...	...		...	...	...	...
3720	Recycling of non-metal waste and scrap	250	2121		...	...	...	...
D	Total manufacturing				147943	161379	178672	164111

a/ 3110 includes 3120, 3130, 3140, 3150 and 3190.

Botswana

Supplier of information:
Central Statistics Office, Gaborone.

Basic source of data:
Survey of employment and employees (biannual); census of production and distribution (annual).

Major deviations from ISIC (Revision 3):
None reported.

Reference period:
Fiscal year ending 30 June of the year indicated.

Scope:
Licensed establishments with one or more paid employees.

Method of data collection:
Mail questionnaires.

Type of enumeration:
Not reported.

Adjusted for non-response:
Yes.

Concepts and definitions of variables:
Wages and salaries refers only to direct wages and salaries.

Related national publications:
Statistical Bulletin (quarterly); Employment Survey Report (annual); National Accounts of Botswana (annual), all published by the Central Statistics Office, Gaborone.

Botswana

ISIC	Industry		Establishments (number)					Number of employees (number)					Wages and salaries paid to employees (thousands of Botswana Pula)			
		Note	2007	2008	2009	2010	Note	2007	2008	2009	2010	Note	2007	2008	2009	2010
151	Processed meat,fish,fruit,vegetables,fats		...	...	...	...		...	...	...	...		...	...	...	...
1511	Processing/preserving of meat		...	...	...	...		1243	2130	2672	1645		6577	9730	11820	8170
1512	Processing/preserving of fish		...	...	...	...		...	...	...	...		...	...	...	...
1513	Processing/preserving of fruit & vegetables		...	...	...	...		...	...	...	...		...	...	...	...
1514	Vegetable and animal oils and fats		...	...	...	...		...	...	...	...		...	...	...	...
1520	Dairy products		...	...	...	...		419	440	341	350		863	1361	1387	1187
153	Grain mill products; starches; animal feeds		...	...	...	...		2635	2293	2153	2287		4415	6352	4225	5917
1531	Grain mill products		...	...	...	...		...	...	...	...		...	...	...	...
1532	Starches and starch products		...	...	...	...		...	...	...	...		...	...	...	...
1533	Prepared animal feeds		...	...	...	...		...	...	...	...		...	...	...	...
154	Other food products		...	...	...	...		...	...	...	...		...	...	...	...
1541	Bakery products		...	...	...	...		1938	2387	1667	1749		2849	2811	2104	2183
1542	Sugar		...	...	...	...		...	...	...	...		...	...	...	...
1543	Cocoa, chocolate and sugar confectionery		...	...	...	...	a/	...	...	...	...	a/	...	...	...	...
1544	Macaroni, noodles & similar products		...	...	...	...	a/	...	...	...	...	a/	...	...	...	...
1549	Other food products n.e.c.		...	...	...	...	a/	284	795	777	826	a/	728	1920	2264	2505
155	Beverages		...	...	...	...		1237	717	1035	1476		2688	2415	5267	9142
1551	Distilling, rectifying & blending of spirits		...	...	...	...		...	...	...	...		...	...	...	...
1552	Wines		...	...	...	...		...	...	...	...		...	...	...	...
1553	Malt liquors and malt		...	...	...	...		...	...	...	...		...	...	...	...
1554	Soft drinks; mineral waters		...	...	...	...		...	...	...	...		...	...	...	...
1600	Tobacco products		...	...	...	...		...	...	...	...		...	...	...	...
171	Spinning, weaving and finishing of textiles		...	...	...	...	b/	2987b/	2982b/	...	2461b/	b/	3499	4117	3154	3713
1711	Textile fibre preparation; textile weaving		...	...	...	...		...	...	...	...		...	...	...	...
1712	Finishing of textiles		...	...	...	...		...	...	...	...		...	...	...	...
172	Other textiles		...	...	...	...	b/	..b/	..b/	...	..b/	b/	..b/	...	...	...
1721	Made-up textile articles, except apparel		...	...	...	...		...	...	...	...		...	...	...	...
1722	Carpets and rugs		...	...	...	...		...	...	...	...		...	...	...	...
1723	Cordage, rope, twine and netting		...	...	...	...		...	...	...	...		...	...	...	...
1729	Other textiles n.e.c.		...	...	...	...		...	...	...	...		...	...	...	...
1730	Knitted and crocheted fabrics and articles		...	...	...	...	b/	..b/	..b/	...	..b/	b/	...	...	...	...
1810	Wearing apparel, except fur apparel		...	...	...	...	c/	4853	3651	5239	4765	c/	4853	3779	4225	4501
1820	Dressing & dyeing of fur; processing of fur		...	...	...	...	c/	...	216	177	496	c/	...	168	351	865
191	Tanning, dressing and processing of leather		...	...	...	...		...	...	...	...		...	...	...	...
1911	Tanning and dressing of leather		...	...	...	...		335	453	235	262		...	...	...	...
1912	Luggage, handbags, etc.; saddlery & harness		...	...	...	...		...	...	...	...		...	...	...	...
1920	Footwear		...	...	...	...	d/	553	560	517	550	d/	423	391	349	395
2010	Sawmilling and planing of wood		...	...	...	...	d/	416	503	612	1287	d/	497	821	692	2493
202	Products of wood, cork, straw, etc.		...	...	...	...		...	...	...	...		...	...	...	...
2021	Veneer sheets, plywood, particle board, etc.		...	...	...	...		...	...	...	...		...	...	...	...
2022	Builders' carpentry and joinery		...	...	...	...		...	...	...	...		...	...	...	...
2023	Wooden containers		...	...	...	...		...	...	...	...		...	...	...	...
2029	Other wood products; articles of cork/straw		...	...	...	...		...	...	...	...		...	...	...	...
210	Paper and paper products		...	...	...	...		...	...	...	...		682	668	470	422
2101	Pulp, paper and paperboard		...	...	...	...		...	...	...	...		...	...	...	...
2102	Corrugated paper and paperboard		...	...	...	...		...	...	...	...		...	...	...	...
2109	Other articles of paper and paperboard		...	...	...	...		...	...	...	...		...	...	...	...
221	Publishing		...	...	...	...	e/	1311	1723	1548	1764	e/	3249	4596	7789	14781
2211	Publishing of books and other publications		...	...	...	...		...	...	...	...		...	...	...	...
2212	Publishing of newspapers, journals, etc.		...	...	...	...		...	...	...	...		...	...	...	...
2213	Publishing of recorded media		...	...	...	...		...	...	...	...		...	...	...	...
2219	Other publishing		...	...	...	...		...	...	...	...		...	...	...	...

Code	Description	1	2	3	4		5	6	7	8	
222	Printing and related service activities										
2221	Printing										
2222	Service activities related to printing										
2230	Reproduction of recorded media										
2310	Coke oven products										
2320	Refined petroleum products										
2330	Processing of nuclear fuel					e/					e/
241	Basic chemicals	6806	4225	6004	3014	f/	1231	894	1577	1025	f/
2411	Basic chemicals, except fertilizers										
2412	Fertilizers and nitrogen compounds										
2413	Plastics in primary forms; synthetic rubber										
242	Other chemicals										
2421	Pesticides and other agro-chemical products					f/					f/
2422	Paints, varnishes, printing ink and mastics										
2423	Pharmaceuticals, medicinal chemicals, etc.										
2424	Soap, cleaning & cosmetic preparations										
2429	Other chemical products n.e.c.										
2430	Man-made fibres					f/					f/
251	Rubber products	1568	1273	2411	1217	g/	648	578	839	478	g/
2511	Rubber tyres and tubes										
2519	Other rubber products										
2520	Plastic products	7757	6811	4201	2924	g/	2774	2707	2604	1966	g/
2610	Glass and glass products										
269	Non-metallic mineral products n.e.c.					h/					h/
2691	Pottery, china and earthenware					h/					h/
2692	Refractory ceramic products										
2693	Struct.non-refractory clay; ceramic products										
2694	Cement, lime and plaster	690	549	403	403	f/	56	54	53	53	f/
2695	Articles of concrete, cement and plaster										
2696	Cutting, shaping & finishing of stone										
2699	Other non-metallic mineral products n.e.c.										
2710	Basic iron and steel			1648i/	77i/				173i/	83i/	
2720	Basic precious and non-ferrous metals										
273	Casting of metals										
2731	Casting of iron and steel			..i/	..i/				..i/	..i/	
2732	Casting of non-ferrous metals			..i/	..i/				..i/	..i/	
281	Struct.metal products;tanks;steam generators	7097	7954	7314	6729	j/	3555	4277	4311	4296	j/
2811	Structural metal products										
2812	Tanks, reservoirs and containers of metal										
2813	Steam generators										
289	Other metal products; metal working services					j/					j/
2891	Metal forging/pressing/stamping/roll-forming										
2892	Treatment & coating of metals										
2893	Cutlery, hand tools and general hardware										
2899	Other fabricated metal products n.e.c.										
291	General purpose machinery	2914	3790	1422	2248	k/	783	777	648	1119	k/
2911	Engines & turbines (not for transport equipment)										
2912	Pumps, compressors, taps and valves										
2913	Bearings, gears, gearing & driving elements										
2914	Ovens, furnaces and furnace burners										
2915	Lifting and handling equipment										
2919	Other general purpose machinery										
292	Special purpose machinery					k/					k/
2921	Agricultural and forestry machinery										
2922	Machine tools										
2923	Machinery for metallurgy										
2924	Machinery for mining & construction										
2925	Food/beverage/tobacco processing machinery										
2926	Machinery for textile, apparel and leather										
2927	Weapons and ammunition										
2929	Other special purpose machinery										

continued

Botswana

ISIC	Industry	Establishments Note	Est 2007	Est 2008	Est 2009	Est 2010	No. of employees Note	Emp 2007	Emp 2008	Emp 2009	Emp 2010	Wages Note	Wage 2007	Wage 2008	Wage 2009	Wage 2010
			(number)					(number)					(thousands of Botswana Pula)			
2930	Domestic appliances n.e.c.	k/	…	…	…	…	k/	…	…	…	…	k/	…	…	…	…
3000	Office, accounting and computing machinery		…	…	…	…		462	…	679	…		1126	…	1644	…
3110	Electric motors, generators and transformers		…	…	…	…		…	…	…	…		…	…	…	…
3120	Electricity distribution & control apparatus		…	…	…	…		…	…	…	…		…	…	…	…
3130	Insulated wire and cable		…	…	…	…		…	…	…	…		…	…	…	…
3140	Accumulators, primary cells and batteries		…	…	…	…		…	…	…	…		…	…	…	…
3150	Lighting equipment and electric lamps		…	…	…	…		…	…	…	…		…	…	…	…
3190	Other electrical equipment n.e.c.		…	…	…	…		…	…	…	…		…	…	…	…
3210	Electronic valves, tubes, etc.		…	…	…	…		…	…	…	…		…	…	…	…
3220	TV/radio transmitters; line comm. apparatus		…	…	…	…		16	17	104	252		74	119	589	803
3230	TV and radio receivers and associated goods		…	…	…	…		…	…	…	…		…	…	…	…
331	Medical, measuring, testing appliances, etc.		…	…	…	…		269m/	185m/	…	…		761m/	633m/	…	…
3311	Medical, surgical and orthopaedic equipment		…	…	…	…		…	…	…	…		…	…	…	…
3312	Measuring/testing/navigating appliances,etc.		…	…	…	…		…	…	…	…		…	…	…	…
3313	Industrial process control equipment		…	…	…	…		…	…	…	…		…	…	…	…
3320	Optical instruments & photographic equipment		…	…	…	…		…m/	…m/				…m/	…m/		
3330	Watches and clocks		…	…	…	…		…m/	…m/				…m/	…m/		
3410	Motor vehicles	n/	…	…	…	…	n/	196	306	133	214	n/	524	481	388	941
3420	Automobile bodies, trailers & semi-trailers	n/	…	…	…	…	n/	…	…	…	…	n/	…	…	…	…
3430	Parts/accessories for automobiles	n/	…	…	…	…	n/	…	…	…	…	n/	…	…	…	…
351	Building and repairing of ships and boats		…	…	…	…		…	…	…	…		…	…	…	…
3511	Building and repairing of ships		…	…	…	…		…	…	…	…		…	…	…	…
3512	Building/repairing of pleasure/sport. boats		…	…	…	…		…	…	…	…		…	…	…	…
3520	Railway/tramway locomotives & rolling stock		…	…	…	…		…	…	…	…		…	…	…	…
3530	Aircraft and spacecraft		…	…	…	…		…	…	…	…		…	…	…	…
359	Transport equipment n.e.c.		…	…	…	…		…	…	…	…		…	…	…	…
3591	Motorcycles		…	…	…	…		…	…	…	…		…	…	…	…
3592	Bicycles and invalid carriages		…	…	…	…		…	…	…	…		…	…	…	…
3599	Other transport equipment n.e.c.		…	…	…	…		…	…	…	…		…	…	…	…
3610	Furniture		…	…	…	…		5235	4218	4178	4233		5423	3983	5261	5320
369	Manufacturing n.e.c.		…	…	…	…		1413	1740	819	952		2501	…	1089	1269
3691	Jewellery and related articles		…	…	…	…		376	371	1052	1329		250	247	2152	3328
3692	Musical instruments		…	…	…	…		…	…	…	…		…	…	…	…
3693	Sports goods		…	…	…	…		…	…	…	…		…	…	…	…
3694	Games and toys		…	…	…	…		…	…	…	…		…	…	…	…
3699	Other manufacturing n.e.c.		…	…	…	…		…	…	…	…		…	…	…	…
3710	Recycling of metal waste and scrap		…	…	…	…		6	…	88	421		…	…	…	…
3720	Recycling of non-metal waste and scrap		…	…	…	…		…	…	…	…		…	…	168	972
D	Total manufacturing		…	…	…	…		35204	35888	35796	36366		57941	67592	79990	95289

a/ 1549 includes 1543 and 1544.
b/ 171 includes 172 and 1730.
c/ 1810 includes 1820.
d/ 2010 includes 202.
e/ 221 includes 222.
f/ 241 includes 242 and 2430.
g/ 251 includes 2520.
h/ 2610 includes 269.
i/ 2710 includes 2720 and 273.
j/ 2811 includes 289.

k/ 291 includes 292 and 2930.
m/ 331 includes 3320 and 3330.
n/ 3410 includes 3420 and 3430.

Botswana

ISIC	Industry	Note	Output (millions of Botswana Pula) 2007	2008	2009	2010	Note	Value added (millions of Botswana Pula) 2007	2008	2009	2010	Note	Gross fixed capital formation (millions of Botswana Pula) 2009	2010
15	Food and beverages	a/	2308.9	2803.7	3415.4	4021.4	a/	599.9	727.7	877.4	1029.8		...	...
16	Tobacco products		...	...	...	...		...	...	...	...		...	...
17	Textiles		396.0	508.1	594.5	550.9		109.5	140.0	164.1	152.1		...	...
18	Wearing apparel, fur		...	...	...	...		...	...	...	...		...	...
19	Leather, leather products and footwear	a/	40.8	29.3	30.1	39.1	a/	12.1	8.7	13.0	15.6		...	...
20	Wood products (excl. furniture)		...	...	...	...		...	...	...	...		...	...
21	Paper and paper products		...	...	...	...		...	...	...	...		...	...
22	Printing and publishing		...	...	...	...		...	...	...	...		...	...
23	Coke,refined petroleum products,nuclear fuel		...	...	...	...		...	...	...	...		...	...
24	Chemicals and chemical products		...	...	...	...		...	...	...	...		...	...
25	Rubber and plastics products		...	...	...	...		...	...	...	...		...	...
26	Non-metallic mineral products		...	...	...	...		...	...	...	...		...	...
27	Basic metals		...	...	...	...		...	...	...	...		...	...
28	Fabricated metal products		...	...	...	...		...	...	...	...		...	...
29	Machinery and equipment n.e.c.		...	...	...	...		...	...	...	...		...	...
30	Office, accounting and computing machinery		...	...	...	...		...	...	...	...		...	...
31	Electrical machinery and apparatus		...	...	...	...		...	...	...	...		...	...
32	Radio,television and communication equipment		...	...	...	...		...	...	...	...		...	...
33	Medical, precision and optical instruments		...	...	...	...		...	...	...	...		...	...
34	Motor vehicles, trailers, semi-trailers		...	...	...	...		...	...	...	...		...	...
35	Other transport equipment	a/	8914.5	8736.1	9609.7	11971.5	a/	1980.5	2234.4	2288.8	2659.2		...	...
36	Furniture; manufacturing n.e.c.		...	...	...	...		...	...	...	...		...	...
37	Recycling		...	...	...	...		...	...	...	...		...	...
D	Total manufacturing		11711.5	12077.2	13649.6	16582.9		2716.0	3111.2	3343.2	3856.7		...	...

a/ Data are aggregated from incomplete 3- and/or 4-digit level of ISICs.

Brazil

Concepts and definitions of variables:
Output excludes value of goods shipped in the same condition as received less the amount paid for these goods.
Value added excludes net change between the beginning and end of the year in the stocks of fuels and materials and supplies (deductible).

Related national publications:
Annual Industrial Survey - Enterprise Issue, published by Fundação Instituto Brasileiro de Geografía e Estatística (IBGE), Rio de Janeiro.

Supplier of information:
Fundação Instituto Brasileiro de Geografía e Estatística (IBGE), Rio de Janeiro.

Basic source of data:
Annual industrial survey.

Major deviations from ISIC (Revision 4):
None reported.

Reference period:
Calendar year.

Scope:
Local units with five or more persons engaged.

Method of data collection:
Not reported.

Type of enumeration:
Sample survey.

Adjusted for non-response:
Yes.

Brazil

		Number of establishments					Number of employees					Wages and salaries paid to employees				
			(number)					(number)					(millions of Brazilian Reais)			
ISIC	Industry	Note	2007	2008	2009	2010	Note	2007	2008	2009	2010	Note	2007	2008	2009	2010
1010	Processing/preserving of meat		2476	2589	2625	2621		390129	405674	405987	421408		4329.8	4996.2	5517.6	6093.9
1020	Processing/preserving of fish, etc.		247	314	253	277		14468	15370	15694	17475		149.3	172.8	182.1	217.1
1030	Processing/preserving of fruit,vegetables		1505	1492	1412	1422		82691	83457	84740	78555		1007.0	1013.6	1190.9	1284.1
1040	Vegetable and animal oils and fats		849	874	835	756		36106	32384	32280	35599		855.9	976.8	1010.5	1183.7
1050	Dairy products		3910	3593	3464	3327		103062	104543	105173	108257		1689.5	1821.5	1753.5	1851.1
106	Grain mill products,starches and starch products		2814	3068	3368	2709		98471	105876	113474	111340		1625.8	1896.7	2130.2	2302.8
1061	Grain mill products		...	...	...	...		...	...	...	...		...	...	...	...
1062	Starches and starch products		...	...	...	...		...	...	...	...		...	...	...	...
107	Other food products		10402	14542	15106	16292		512772	564184	649756	695723		6316.2	7256.3	9946.3	11456.7
1071	Bakery products		...	...	...	...		...	...	...	...		...	...	...	...
1072	Sugar		...	...	...	...		...	...	...	...		...	...	...	...
1073	Cocoa, chocolate and sugar confectionery		...	...	...	...		...	...	...	...		...	...	...	...
1074	Macaroni, noodles, couscous, etc.		...	...	...	...		...	...	...	...		...	...	...	...
1075	Prepared meals and dishes		...	...	...	...		...	...	...	...		...	...	...	...
1079	Other food products n.e.c.		...	...	...	...		...	...	...	...		...	...	...	...
1080	Prepared animal feeds		...	...	...	...		...	...	...	...		...	...	...	...
1101	Distilling, rectifying and blending of spirits		...	...	...	...		...	...	...	...		...	...	...	...
1102	Wines		...	...	...	...		...	...	...	...		...	...	...	...
1103	Malt liquors and malt		...	...	...	...		...	...	...	...		...	...	...	...
1104	Soft drinks,mineral waters,other bottled waters		...	...	...	...		...	...	...	...		...	...	...	...
1200	Tobacco products		225	314	210	201		17819	18164	17424	17523		623.2	726.9	788.3	834.8
131	Spinning, weaving and finishing of textiles		2604	2577	2631	2810		202514	189068	184291	190769		2509.7	2630.9	2697.7	3090.9
1311	Preparation and spinning of textile fibres		...	...	...	...		...	...	...	...		...	...	...	...
1312	Weaving of textiles		...	...	...	...		...	...	...	...		...	...	...	...
1313	Finishing of textiles		...	...	...	...		...	...	...	...		...	...	...	...
139	Other textiles		2936	3204	3381	3482		97295	110553	112358	117386		1168.0	1413.9	1569.8	1777.9
1391	Knitted and crocheted fabrics		...	...	...	...		...	...	...	...		...	...	...	...
1392	Made-up textile articles, except apparel		...	...	...	...		...	...	...	...		...	...	...	...
1393	Carpets and rugs		...	...	...	...		...	...	...	...		...	...	...	...
1394	Cordage, rope, twine and netting		...	...	...	...		...	...	...	...		...	...	...	...
1399	Other textiles n.e.c.		...	...	...	...		...	...	...	...		...	...	...	...
1410	Wearing apparel, except fur apparel		24966	26242	27451	26977		537756	590207	621608	652907		4295.2	5068.1	6068.7	6559.2
1420	Articles of fur		750	636	683	649		15196	15459	17250	18449		146.5	171.4	202.3	232.1
1430	Knitted and crocheted apparel		...	...	...	...		...	...	...	...		...	...	...	...
151	Leather;luggage,handbags,saddlery,harness;fur		1988	2207	1978	1955		73866	70741	65897	65120		751.5	825.4	790.6	825.1
1511	Tanning/dressing of leather; dressing of fur		...	...	...	...		...	...	...	...		...	...	...	...
1512	Luggage,handbags,etc.;saddlery/harness		...	...	...	...		...	...	...	...		...	...	...	...
1520	Footwear		5649	6013	5707	6080		328161	322754	328481	355514		2867.9	3062.6	3204.1	3862.0
1610	Sawmilling and planing of wood		4359	4129	4068	4043		97238	87717	82521	89567		921.7	889.3	900.5	1021.0
162	Wood products, cork, straw, plaiting materials		4501	4778	4683	4662		127009	123246	118172	113135		1296.9	1511.7	1521.5	1621.5

1621	Veneer sheets and wood-based panels	…	…	…	…	…	…	…	…	…	…	…	…
1622	Builders' carpentry and joinery	…	…	…	…	…	…	…	…	…	…	…	…
1623	Wooden containers	…	…	…	…	…	…	…	…	…	…	…	…
1629	Other wood products;articles of cork,straw	…	…	…	…	…	…	…	…	…	…	…	…
1701	Pulp, paper and paperboard	…	…	…	…	…	…	…	…	…	…	…	…
1702	Corrugated paper and paperboard	…	…	…	…	…	…	…	…	…	…	…	…
1709	Other articles of paper and paperboard	5508	6071	6789	6742	96657	103618	109051	115428	1458.6	1690.9	1856.9	2117.9
181	Printing and service activities related to printing	…	…	…	…	…	…	…	…	…	…	…	…
1811	Printing	…	…	…	…	…	…	…	…	…	…	…	…
1812	Service activities related to printing	54	40	81	51	4175	3675	3687	3629	98.3	91.1	88.9	91.8
1820	Reproduction of recorded media	2	3	6	6	144	166	230	272	3.1	2.3	4.1	5.1
1910	Coke oven products	175	195	192	202	34584	39593	39931	39867	3591.3	4455.4	4935.2	5508.7
1920	Refined petroleum products	1912	1951	1970	1987	222293	264744	220438	213238	6162.9	7371.7	6645.7	7077.1
201	Basic chemicals,fertilizers, etc.	…	…	…	…	…	…	…	…	…	…	…	…
2011	Basic chemicals	…	…	…	…	…	…	…	…	…	…	…	…
2012	Fertilizers and nitrogen compounds	…	…	…	…	…	…	…	…	…	…	…	…
2013	Plastics and synthetic rubber in primary forms	4352	4369	4478	4467	160497	172452	175569	190437	4625.0	5239.7	5820.1	6617.7
202	Other chemical products	…	…	…	…	…	…	…	…	…	…	…	…
2021	Pesticides and other agrochemical products	…	…	…	…	…	…	…	…	…	…	…	…
2022	Paints,varnishes;printing ink and mastics	…	…	…	…	…	…	…	…	…	…	…	…
2023	Soap,cleaning and cosmetic preparations	…	…	…	…	…	…	…	…	…	…	…	…
2029	Other chemical products n.e.c.	49	57	53	50	7411	7385	6849	6474	187.0	213.5	186.2	196.7
2030	Man-made fibres	878	858	776	798	89866	94096	93352	97677	3585.4	4049.3	4415.8	4735.0
2100	Pharmaceuticals,medicinal chemicals, etc.	2142	2099	2110	2026	95658	93436	93045	95465	1996.0	2154.1	2117.3	2437.1
221	Rubber products	…	…	…	…	…	…	…	…	…	…	…	…
2211	Rubber tyres and tubes	…	…	…	…	…	…	…	…	…	…	…	…
2219	Other rubber products	7490	7561	7071	7981	283420	283705	294787	329438	4336.8	4855.5	5188.4	6280.0
2220	Plastics products	13310	13952	14101	15158	318096	343194	344298	384233	4094.5	4957.8	5216.2	6293.9
2310	Glass and glass products	496	486	478	524	34200	32894	34265	38250	717.3	789.5	846.6	1022.5
239	Non-metallic mineral products n.e.c.	…	…	…	…	…	…	…	…	…	…	…	…
2391	Refractory products	…	…	…	…	…	…	…	…	…	…	…	…
2392	Clay building materials	…	…	…	…	…	…	…	…	…	…	…	…
2393	Other porcelain and ceramic products	…	…	…	…	…	…	…	…	…	…	…	…
2394	Cement, lime and plaster	…	…	…	…	…	…	…	…	…	…	…	…
2395	Articles of concrete, cement and plaster	…	…	…	…	…	…	…	…	…	…	…	…
2396	Cutting, shaping and finishing of stone	…	…	…	…	…	…	…	…	…	…	…	…
2399	Other non-metallic mineral products n.e.c.	…	…	…	…	…	…	…	…	…	…	…	…
2410	Basic iron and steel	889	909	929	937	127527	133197	122298	135106	4462.8	5208.1	5007.6	5942.1
2420	Basic precious and other non-ferrous metals	635	695	641	693	48522	49634	46898	49581	1583.8	1790.5	1736.4	1863.5
243	Casting of metals	…	…	…	…	…	…	…	…	…	…	…	…
2431	Casting of iron and steel	…	…	…	…	…	…	…	…	…	…	…	…
2432	Casting of non-ferrous metals	1124	1145	1245	1318	46270	48754	46363	52543	776.5	903.6	874.1	1082.0
251	Struct.metal products, tanks, reservoirs	5200	5423	5994	5678	127007	138326	141647	151644	1901.4	2253.0	2397.7	3011.5
2511	Structural metal products	…	…	…	…	…	…	…	…	…	…	…	…
2512	Tanks, reservoirs and containers of metal	…	…	…	…	…	…	…	…	…	…	…	…

continued

Brazil

ISIC	Industry	Number of establishments (number)					Number of employees (number)					Wages and salaries paid to employees (millions of Brazilian Reais)				
		Note	2007	2008	2009	2010	Note	2007	2008	2009	2010	Note	2007	2008	2009	2010
2513	Steam generators, excl. hot water boilers		...	...	...	...		...	...	...	...		...	...	...	...
2520	Weapons and ammunition		18	20	17	40		6027	6324	6908	7063		145.3	164.5	195.1	257.0
259	Other metal products;metal working services		12200	12743	12776	13176		324834	346015	324622	356414		5314.5	6346.4	6223.9	7338.5
2591	Forging,pressing,stamping,roll-forming of metal		...	...	...	...		...	...	...	...		...	...	...	...
2592	Treatment and coating of metals; machining		...	...	...	...		...	...	...	...		...	...	...	...
2593	Cutlery, hand tools and general hardware		...	...	...	...		...	...	...	...		...	...	...	...
2599	Other fabricated metal products n.e.c.		...	...	...	...		...	...	...	...		...	...	...	...
2610	Electronic components and boards		471	541	501	537		25517	25537	21693	22320		496.9	528.7	383.2	515.4
2620	Computers and peripheral equipment		478	505	514	506		40019	45323	46472	47537		967.5	1274.2	1340.5	1553.9
2630	Communication equipment		222	222	220	228		26699	21527	24204	22370		942.8	897.3	1196.1	937.3
2640	Consumer electronics		289	278	266	265		28798	28446	27261	35090		489.3	624.2	752.1	909.6
265	Measuring,testing equipment; watches, etc.		711	893	753	720		33632	38667	33603	33859		874.2	1010.8	1049.2	1159.4
2651	Measuring/testing/navigating equipment,etc.		...	...	...	...		...	...	...	...		...	...	...	...
2652	Watches and clocks		...	...	...	...		...	...	...	...		...	...	...	...
2660	Irradiation/electromedical equipment,etc.		228	222	207	213		5777	6778	5771	5826		101.2	129.3	127.9	135.8
2670	Optical instruments and photographic equipment		77	61	71	82		1954	1834	2771	2531		29.6	35.6	63.0	69.7
2680	Magnetic and optical media		7	7	5	6		366	770	242	157		5.7	11.9	5.3	3.4
2710	Electric motors,generators,transformers,etc.		1403	1386	1461	1495		108512	117524	113815	120775		2537.7	3224.2	3370.7	3459.6
2720	Batteries and accumulators		125	126	128	123		10946	11580	11154	11987		239.2	259.9	260.7	292.9
273	Wiring and wiring devices		...	...	...	...		...	...	...	...		...	...	...	...
2731	Fibre optic cables		...	...	...	...		...	...	...	...		...	...	...	...
2732	Other electronic and electric wires and cables		...	...	...	...		...	...	...	...		...	...	...	...
2733	Wiring devices		...	...	...	...		...	...	...	...		...	...	...	...
2740	Electric lighting equipment		522	454	472	483		15060	14080	14288	15521		336.0	251.3	247.9	334.1
2750	Domestic appliances		378	316	356	361		48252	46593	51644	56135		1120.6	1221.3	1389.9	2392.3
2790	Other electrical equipment		592	642	732	714		19137	20223	21930	25934		343.6	407.6	487.4	726.2
281	General-purpose machinery		4156	3961	4050	4459		187737	191108	193621	208184		4542.3	5178.5	5309.5	6433.0
2811	Engines/turbines,excl.aircraft,vehicle engines		...	...	...	...		...	...	...	...		...	...	...	...
2812	Fluid power equipment		...	...	...	...		...	...	...	...		...	...	...	...
2813	Other pumps, compressors, taps and valves		...	...	...	...		...	...	...	...		...	...	...	...
2814	Bearings, gears, gearing and driving elements		...	...	...	...		...	...	...	...		...	...	...	...
2815	Ovens, furnaces and furnace burners		...	...	...	...		...	...	...	...		...	...	...	...
2816	Lifting and handling equipment		...	...	...	...		...	...	...	...		...	...	...	...
2817	Office machinery, excl.computers,etc.		...	...	...	...		...	...	...	...		...	...	...	...
2818	Power-driven hand tools		...	...	...	...		...	...	...	...		...	...	...	...
2819	Other general-purpose machinery		...	...	...	...		...	...	...	...		...	...	...	...
282	Special-purpose machinery		...	...	...	...		178013	186820	175630	200501		4014.1	4808.2	4655.6	5822.3
2821	Agricultural and forestry machinery		4255	4329	4616	4669		...	...	...	...		...	...	...	...
2822	Metal-forming machinery and machine tools		...	...	...	...		...	...	...	...		...	...	...	...
2823	Machinery for metallurgy		...	...	...	...		...	...	...	...		...	...	...	...
2824	Mining, quarrying and construction machinery		...	...	...	...		...	...	...	...		...	...	...	...

2825	Food/beverage/tobacco processing machinery	:	:	:	:	:	:	:	:	:	:	:	:
2826	Textile/apparel/leather production machinery	:	:	:	:	:	:	:	:	:	:	:	:
2829	Other special-purpose machinery	1088	1011	1070	1098	120754	127978	124917	137437	6019.1	7060.0	7350.6	8677.3
2910	Motor vehicles	891	936	975	930	52290	56658	57322	64731	944.8	1168.8	1202.7	1535.4
2920	Automobile bodies, trailers and semi-trailers	1995	2169	2279	2376	282874	294458	289556	327446	6974.3	7956.0	8097.5	9479.3
2930	Parts and accessories for motor vehicles	224	251	243	256	17933	20605	27153	32777	424.3	472.1	718.3	927.1
301	Building of ships and boats	:	:	:	:	:	:	:	:	:	:	:	:
3011	Building of ships and floating structures	:	:	:	:	:	:	:	:	:	:	:	:
3012	Building of pleasure and sporting boats	48	43	47	45	9457	8623	5351	9260	261.0	352.4	234.2	575.7
3020	Railway locomotives and rolling stock	38	47	51	57	23782	24062	19500	20657	1364.1	1351.2	1036.1	1409.6
3030	Air and spacecraft and related machinery	1	2	3	2	9	99	384	31	0.6	4.3	17.1	16.1
3040	Military fighting vehicles	384	382	377	371	34292	39217	35281	37099	740.9	897.8	863.3	963.5
309	Transport equipment n.e.c.	:	:	:	:	:	:	:	:	:	:	:	:
3091	Motorcycles	:	:	:	:	:	:	:	:	:	:	:	:
3092	Bicycles and invalid carriages	:	:	:	:	:	:	:	:	:	:	:	:
3099	Other transport equipment n.e.c.	9254	9365	9416	9580	226118	225182	233458	256269	2285.4	2558.4	2808.8	3420.3
3100	Furniture	1055	1157	1164	1123	20482	22669	21950	22999	224.8	251.7	304.7	308.9
321	Jewellery, bijouterie and related articles	:	:	:	:	:	:	:	:	:	:	:	:
3211	Jewellery and related articles	:	:	:	:	:	:	:	:	:	:	:	:
3212	Imitation jewellery and related articles	74	80	80	78	1978	1915	1652	1971	24.5	25.4	21.0	34.2
3220	Musical instruments	181	213	176	244	5164	5644	4954	5348	58.7	73.0	67.3	78.1
3230	Sports goods	467	352	353	405	15017	15146	14389	15586	156.5	193.5	198.5	233.9
3240	Games and toys	945	990	1126	1121	36574	34879	40625	41259	581.2	598.4	741.2	826.6
3250	Medical and dental instruments and supplies	1795	1951	1995	2011	48980	55231	53323	55780	663.1	769.2	833.1	928.4
3290	Other manufacturing n.e.c.	3431	3779	4024	4597	116241	127833	133846	156448	2166.6	2556.8	2878.4	3467.8
331	Repair of fabricated metal products/machinery	:	:	:	:	:	:	:	:	:	:	:	:
3311	Repair of fabricated metal products	:	:	:	:	:	:	:	:	:	:	:	:
3312	Repair of machinery	:	:	:	:	:	:	:	:	:	:	:	:
3313	Repair of electronic and optical equipment	:	:	:	:	:	:	:	:	:	:	:	:
3314	Repair of electrical equipment	:	:	:	:	:	:	:	:	:	:	:	:
3315	Repair of transport equip., excl. motor vehicles	:	:	:	:	:	:	:	:	:	:	:	:
3319	Repair of other equipment	635	694	993	874	11371	15711	21133	18382	154.1	245.5	344.5	350.1
3320	Installation of industrial machinery/equipment	:	:	:	:	:	:	:	:	:	:	:	:
C	Total manufacturing	168389	178054	181403	185032	6823147	7148094	7203410	7698138	122438.8	140851.5	149426.5	172637.7

Brazil

- 278 -

ISIC	Industry	Output at factor values (millions of Brazilian Reais)					Value added at factor values (millions of Brazilian Reais)					Gross fixed capital formation (Brazilian Reais)		
		Note	2007	2008	2009	2010	Note	2007	2008	2009	2010	Note	2009	2010
1010	Processing/preserving of meat		56681	70517	68282	77949		17666	21757	19133	22954		...	...
1020	Processing/preserving of fish, etc.		1684	1917	1957	2555		604	669	713	1049		...	...
1030	Processing/preserving of fruit,vegetables		12009	10723	12002	13604		5186	4560	4787	5746		...	...
1040	Vegetable and animal oils and fats		37605	47254	45199	48401		7108	10693	10458	12066		...	...
1050	Dairy products		25455	28938	32546	36883		8538	10242	11800	13820		...	...
106	Grain mill products,starches and starch products		31664	38914	38285	39286		10568	12618	13245	14083		...	...
1061	Grain mill products		...	...	...	...		...	...	...	...		...	...
1062	Starches and starch products													
107	Other food products		52392	58403	73658	91927		22601	26879	35656	44016		...	...
1071	Bakery products													
1072	Sugar		...	...	...	...		...	...	...	...		...	...
1073	Cocoa, chocolate and sugar confectionery		...	...	...	...		...	...	...	...			
1074	Macaroni, noodles, couscous, etc.		...	...	...	...		...	...	...	...			
1075	Prepared meals and dishes		...	...	...	...		...	...	...	...			
1079	Other food products n.e.c.		...	...	...	...		...	...	...	...			
1080	Prepared animal feeds		...	...	...	...		...	...	...	...			
1101	Distilling, rectifying and blending of spirits		...	...	...	...		...	...	...	...			
1102	Wines		...	...	...	...		...	...	...	...			
1103	Malt liquors and malt		...	...	...	...		...	...	...	...			
1104	Soft drinks,mineral waters,other bottled waters		...	...	...	...		...	...	...	...		...	...
1200	Tobacco products		8538	9997	10805	10820		4259	5065	5641	4980			
131	Spinning, weaving and finishing of textiles		17420	17836	17044	20925		6997	7355	7188	8894			
1311	Preparation and spinning of textile fibres		...	...	...	...		...	...	...	...			
1312	Weaving of textiles		...	...	...	...		...	...	...	...			
1313	Finishing of textiles		...	...	...	...		...	...	...	...			
139	Other textiles		10033	11416	12100	13560		3756	4615	4934	5625			
1391	Knitted and crocheted fabrics		...	...	...	...		...	...	...	...			
1392	Made-up textile articles, except apparel		...	...	...	...		...	...	...	...			
1393	Carpets and rugs		...	...	...	...		...	...	...	...		...	...
1394	Cordage, rope, twine and netting		...	...	...	...		...	...	...	...		...	...
1399	Other textiles n.e.c.		...	...	...	...		...	...	...	...		...	...
1410	Wearing apparel, except fur apparel		22887	24908	27975	30654		10730	11425	14003	16478		...	...
1420	Articles of fur		836	954	1050	1301		436	478	598	709		...	...
1430	Knitted and crocheted apparel		8133	8140	6002	6353		2171	2639	2154	2228		...	...
151	Leather;luggage,handbags,saddlery,harness;fur		...	...	...	...		...	...	...	...		...	...
1511	Tanning/dressing of leather; dressing of fur		...	...	...	...		...	...	...	...		...	...
1512	Luggage,handbags,etc.;saddlery/harness		...	...	...	...		...	...	...	...		...	...
1520	Footwear		15141	16542	16068	19673		7218	8404	8687	10808		...	...
1610	Sawmilling and planing of wood		5975	5588	5023	5622		2987	2819	2554	2965		...	...
162	Wood products, cork, straw, plaiting materials		10124	11702	9097	10930		4473	5199	4200	5156		...	...

1621	Veneer sheets and wood-based panels	:	:	:	:	:	:	:	:
1622	Builders' carpentry and joinery	:	:	:	:	:	:	:	:
1623	Wooden containers	:	:	:	:	:	:	:	:
1629	Other wood products;articles of cork,straw	:	:	:	:	:	:	:	:
1701	Pulp, paper and paperboard	:	:	:	:	:	:	:	:
1702	Corrugated paper and paperboard	:	:	:	:	:	:	:	:
1709	Other articles of paper and paperboard	:	:	:	:	:	:	:	:
181	Printing and service activities related to printing	8417	9775	10760	13249	4771	5637	5808	7219
1811	Printing	:	:	:	:	:	:	:	:
1812	Service activities related to printing	:	:	:	:	:	:	:	:
1820	Reproduction of recorded media	1330	1246	1267	1193	897	772	806	753
1910	Coke oven products	44	92	85	114	10	28	29	32
1920	Refined petroleum products	99675	117911	96349	109761	64346	75636	63559	75952
201	Basic chemicals,fertilizers, etc.	100810	122479	92366	104497	30386	37616	28747	33779
2011	Basic chemicals	:	:	:	:	:	:	:	:
2012	Fertilizers and nitrogen compounds	:	:	:	:	:	:	:	:
2013	Plastics and synthetic rubber in primary forms	52434	61151	62419	68130	20319	23268	23711	27572
202	Other chemical products	:	:	:	:	:	:	:	:
2021	Pesticides and other agrochemical products	:	:	:	:	:	:	:	:
2022	Paints,varnishes;printing ink and mastics	:	:	:	:	:	:	:	:
2023	Soap,cleaning and cosmetic preparations	:	:	:	:	:	:	:	:
2029	Other chemical products n.e.c.	:	:	:	:	:	:	:	:
2030	Man-made fibres	2294	2349	1934	2141	899	876	744	841
2100	Pharmaceuticals,medicinal chemicals, etc.	24044	27003	28504	29512	15621	17055	17530	18947
221	Rubber products	16271	17770	16109	19299	6918	7320	6783	8044
2211	Rubber tyres and tubes	:	:	:	:	:	:	:	:
2219	Other rubber products	:	:	:	:	:	:	:	:
2220	Plastics products	36985	41024	41643	48740	13817	15524	17064	20311
2310	Glass and glass products	6216	6743	7168	8591	3194	3464	3722	4702
239	Non-metallic mineral products n.e.c.	32129	40113	41230	49347	15431	19044	19736	23961
2391	Refractory products	:	:	:	:	:	:	:	:
2392	Clay building materials	:	:	:	:	:	:	:	:
2393	Other porcelain and ceramic products	:	:	:	:	:	:	:	:
2394	Cement, lime and plaster	:	:	:	:	:	:	:	:
2395	Articles of concrete, cement and plaster	:	:	:	:	:	:	:	:
2396	Cutting, shaping and finishing of stone	:	:	:	:	:	:	:	:
2399	Other non-metallic mineral products n.e.c.	:	:	:	:	:	:	:	:
2410	Basic iron and steel	83304	105406	68660	86745	34239	44759	24910	32763
2420	Basic precious and other non-ferrous metals	30984	29755	23801	31024	10716	9968	7447	8879
243	Casting of metals	4776	6129	5125	6665	2260	2602	2422	2907
2431	Casting of iron and steel	:	:	:	:	:	:	:	:
2432	Casting of non-ferrous metals	:	:	:	:	:	:	:	:
251	Struct.metal products, tanks, reservoirs	11658	14792	14349	15640	5286	6759	7658	8218
2511	Structural metal products	:	:	:	:	:	:	:	:
2512	Tanks, reservoirs and containers of metal	:	:	:	:	:	:	:	:

continued

Brazil

ISIC	Industry	Output at factor values (millions of Brazilian Reais) Note	2007	2008	2009	2010	Value added at factor values (millions of Brazilian Reais) Note	2007	2008	2009	2010	Gross fixed capital formation (Brazilian Reais) Note	2009	2010
2513	Steam generators, excl. hot water boilers		...	...	...	...		...	...	...	...		...	...
2520	Weapons and ammunition		699	792	1000	1179		412	505	621	835		...	...
259	Other metal products;metal working services		39072	47992	40794	49307		17493	21197	19371	23293		...	...
2591	Forging,pressing,stamping,roll-forming of metal		...	...	...	...		...	...	...	...		...	...
2592	Treatment and coating of metals; machining		...	...	...	...		...	...	...	...		...	...
2593	Cutlery, hand tools and general hardware		...	...	...	...		...	...	...	...		...	...
2599	Other fabricated metal products n.e.c.		...	...	...	...		...	...	...	...		...	...
2610	Electronic components and boards		4088	4385	2501	3294		1450	1719	1017	1421		...	...
2620	Computers and peripheral equipment		12681	18014	14501	18106		3623	5277	4144	4829		...	...
2630	Communication equipment		18407	14893	10870	10290		5652	5653	3785	3605		...	...
2640	Consumer electronics		8707	13078	13513	19769		2739	3382	3860	6340		...	...
265	Measuring,testing equipment; watches, etc.		4925	5333	4735	5609		2571	2832	2686	3112		...	...
2651	Measuring/testing/navigating equipment,etc.		...	...	...	...		...	...	...	...		...	...
2652	Watches and clocks		...	...	...	...		...	...	...	...		...	...
2660	Irradiation/electromedical equipment,etc.		688	880	847	1006		371	487	480	506		...	...
2670	Optical instruments and photographic equipment		212	208	411	490		117	120	160	189		...	...
2680	Magnetic and optical media		94	135	74	27		33	70	38	12		...	...
2710	Electric motors,generators,transformers,etc.		23435	29040	26027	29792		8419	10946	9825	11326		...	...
2720	Batteries and accumulators		1792	2252	1988	2102		565	755	836	744		...	...
273	Wiring and wiring devices		...	...	...	...		...	...	...	...		...	...
2731	Fibre optic cables		...	...	...	...		...	...	...	...		...	...
2732	Other electronic and electric wires and cables		...	...	...	...		...	...	...	...		...	...
2733	Wiring devices		...	...	...	...		...	...	...	...		...	...
2740	Electric lighting equipment		1305	1440	1202	1738		561	614	496	810		...	...
2750	Domestic appliances		11083	11209	13971	15776		4185	4456	5398	6458		...	...
2790	Other electrical equipment		2249	3039	3001	4647		1165	1477	1374	2115		...	...
281	General-purpose machinery		35509	39687	35170	45497		14439	16353	15332	20205		...	...
2811	Engines/turbines,excl.aircraft,vehicle engines		...	...	...	...		...	...	...	...		...	...
2812	Fluid power equipment		...	...	...	...		...	...	...	...		...	...
2813	Other pumps, compressors, taps and valves		...	...	...	...		...	...	...	...		...	...
2814	Bearings, gears, gearing and driving elements		...	...	...	...		...	...	...	...		...	...
2815	Ovens, furnaces and furnace burners		...	...	...	...		...	...	...	...		...	...
2816	Lifting and handling equipment		...	...	...	...		...	...	...	...		...	...
2817	Office machinery, excl.computers,etc.		...	...	...	...		...	...	...	...		...	...
2818	Power-driven hand tools		...	...	...	...		...	...	...	...		...	...
2819	Other general-purpose machinery		...	...	...	...		...	...	...	...		...	...
282	Special-purpose machinery		35105	43649	33518	46656		14206	17504	14300	19488		...	...
2821	Agricultural and forestry machinery		...	...	...	...		...	...	...	...		...	...
2822	Metal-forming machinery and machine tools		...	...	...	...		...	...	...	...		...	...
2823	Machinery for metallurgy		...	...	...	...		...	...	...	...		...	...
2824	Mining, quarrying and construction machinery		...	...	...	...		...	...	...	...		...	...

2825	Food/beverage/tobacco processing machinery	…	…	…	…	…	…	…	…
2826	Textile/apparel/leather production machinery	…	…	…	…	…	…	…	…
2829	Other special-purpose machinery	…	…	…	…	…	…	…	…
2910	Motor vehicles	92080	113968	106629	129722	29422	40624	38274	48677
2920	Automobile bodies, trailers and semi-trailers	7387	9780	8232	11712	2686	3471	3669	4384
2930	Parts and accessories for motor vehicles	58885	66882	61447	76063	23136	26184	25334	30034
301	Building of ships and boats	3604	3666	4922	5370	1516	1674	2309	2635
3011	Building of ships and floating structures	…	…	…	…	…	…	…	…
3012	Building of pleasure and sporting boats	…	…	…	…	…	…	…	…
3020	Railway locomotives and rolling stock	1656	2187	1563	2641	1026	966	714	1206
3030	Air and spacecraft and related machinery	9569	11800	9335	8900	3319	3922	2601	3364
3040	Military fighting vehicles	3	26	92	120	1	15	57	85
309	Transport equipment n.e.c.	12655	14732	12332	14306	4689	5391	4617	5164
3091	Motorcycles	…	…	…	…	…	…	…	…
3092	Bicycles and invalid carriages	…	…	…	…	…	…	…	…
3099	Other transport equipment n.e.c.	…	…	…	…	…	…	…	…
3100	Furniture	15950	17676	18321	22846	6307	7048	7628	9923
321	Jewellery, bijouterie and related articles	804	919	968	1107	487	571	638	764
3211	Jewellery and related articles	…	…	…	…	…	…	…	…
3212	Imitation jewellery and related articles	…	…	…	…	…	…	…	…
3220	Musical instruments	112	130	107	175	65	73	61	98
3230	Sports goods	340	396	455	544	170	202	269	310
3240	Games and toys	1010	1126	1121	1298	520	586	632	694
3250	Medical and dental instruments and supplies	3360	3764	4275	4806	2037	2175	2612	3007
3290	Other manufacturing n.e.c.	4515	5129	4796	5849	2286	2663	2640	3168
331	Repair of fabricated metal products/machinery	9298	11431	12430	13420	5655	6848	7324	8855
3311	Repair of fabricated metal products	…	…	…	…	…	…	…	…
3312	Repair of machinery	…	…	…	…	…	…	…	…
3313	Repair of electronic and optical equipment	…	…	…	…	…	…	…	…
3314	Repair of electrical equipment	…	…	…	…	…	…	…	…
3315	Repair of transport equip., excl. motor vehicles	…	…	…	…	…	…	…	…
3319	Repair of other equipment	…	…	…	…	…	…	…	…
3320	Installation of industrial machinery/equipment	561	1080	1305	1352	341	640	880	909
C	Total manufacturing	1334291	1559586	1434065	1686309	548358	647795	606938	727843

Brazil

Index numbers of industrial production

ISIC Revision 3

(2005=100)

ISIC	Industry	Note	1999	2000	2001	2002	2003	2004	2005	2006	2007	2008	2009	2010
15	Food and beverages		93	91	95	96	94	98	100	103	107	107	108	115
16	Tobacco products		172	159	151	91	85	101	100	104	95	89	87	80
17	Textiles		97	102	97	97	93	102	100	101	105	103	97	101
18	Wearing apparel, fur		114	124	112	118	104	105	100	95	100	103	95	102
19	Leather, leather products and footwear		118	118	113	112	101	103	100	97	95	89	81	86
20	Wood products (excl. furniture)		84	87	86	90	95	102	100	91	88	79	65	76
21	Paper and paper products		79	82	82	85	90	97	100	102	103	108	107	111
22	Printing and publishing		89	98	87	91	92	90	100	102	102	103	100	104
23	Coke,refined petroleum products,nuclear fuel		99	97	101	98	96	99	100	102	105	105	104	105
24	Chemicals and chemical products		91	98	92	91	92	98	100	101	105	106	106	113
25	Rubber and plastics products		98	102	97	97	94	101	100	102	108	111	100	113
26	Non-metallic mineral products		98	99	97	96	93	97	100	103	108	117	111	122
27	Basic metals		82	90	90	93	99	102	100	103	110	113	93	110
28	Fabricated metal products		90	92	94	96	91	100	100	99	104	107	91	113
29	Machinery and equipment n.e.c.		65	77	81	83	87	101	100	104	122	130	106	131
30	Office, accounting and computing machinery		...	...	...	59	64	85	100	152	173	158	147	167
31	Electrical machinery and apparatus		65	71	86	85	87	93	100	109	124	128	103	112
32	Radio,television and communication equipment		65	86	83	74	74	88	100	100	99	96	72	74
33	Medical, precision and optical instruments		...	...	...	93	90	97	100	109	114	132	116	140
34	Motor vehicles, trailers, semi-trailers		60	71	71	69	72	94	100	101	117	126	110	137
35	Other transport equipment		43	52	65	79	86	95	100	102	116	165	169	169
36	Furniture; manufacturing n.e.c.		...	...	...	...	...	...	...	...	...	...	...	...
37	Recycling		...	...	...	...	...	...	...	...	...	...	...	...
D	Total manufacturing		83	88	89	90	90	97	100	103	109	112	104	115

Bulgaria

Supplier of information:
National Statistical Institute of the Republic of Bulgaria, Sofia.

Basic source of data:
Census/exhaustive survey.

Major deviations from ISIC (Revision 4):
None reported.

Reference period:
Calendar year.

Scope:
All enterprises.

Method of data collection:
Mail questionnaires and online survey.

Type of enumeration:
Complete enumeration.

Adjusted for non-response:
No.

Concepts and definitions of variables:
Output is at basic prices.

Related national publications:
Statistical Yearbook of the Republic of Bulgaria, published by the National Statistical Institute of the Republic of Bulgaria, Sofia.

Bulgaria

ISIC	Industry	Number of enterprises (number)					Number of employees (number)					Wages and salaries paid to employees (thousands of Bulgarian Leva)				
		Note	2007	2008	2009	2010	Note	2007	2008	2009	2010	Note	2007	2008	2009	2010
1010	Processing/preserving of meat		…	475	510	491		…	17830	17844	17606		…	71554	89132	95091
1020	Processing/preserving of fish, etc.		…	31	33	34		…	1311	1309	1327		…	4735	5384	5572
1030	Processing/preserving of fruit, vegetables		…	318	336	329		…	7928	7544	7427		…	36553	41745	42430
1040	Vegetable and animal oils and fats		…	85	79	78		…	2532	2350	2543		…	13512	14386	14969
1050	Dairy products		…	273	301	296		…	8355	9218	9339		…	48085	57348	62946
106	Grain mill products, starches and starch products		…	163	148	155		…	3478	2846	2637		…	21693	20624	20738
1061	Grain mill products		…	…	143	150		…	…	…	…		…	15790	…	…
1062	Starches and starch products		…	…	5	5		…	…	…	…		…	…	…	…
107	Other food products		…	2970	3173	3235		…	41016	40944	38334		…	189904	221701	229244
1071	Bakery products		…	2400	2575	2622		…	28480	28942	27241		…	106713	128911	136711
1072	Sugar		…	7	10	9		…	1312	980	681		…	9188	10013	7216
1073	Cocoa, chocolate and sugar confectionery		…	131	135	134		…	4878	4815	4565		…	42045	47054	50947
1074	Macaroni, noodles, couscous, etc.		…	26	27	30		…	283	268	362		…	952	1052	1466
1075	Prepared meals and dishes		…	43	48	52		…	1901	1631	1796		…	7416	8152	10977
1079	Other food products n.e.c.		…	363	378	388		…	4162	4308	3689		…	23590	26519	21927
1080	Prepared animal feeds		…	106	104	96		…	1768	1732	1613		…	9217	10146	10221
1101	Distilling, rectifying and blending of spirits		…	209	273	309		…	2656	2481	2411		…	11695	11652	11610
1102	Wines		…	161	200	218		…	4975	4368	3935		…	23583	24138	23188
1103	Malt liquors and malt		…	15	16	13		…	2689	2533	2426		…	33916	35879	36152
1104	Soft drinks,mineral waters,other bottled waters		…	265	246	241		…	6063	5953	5587		…	56035	56608	53735
1200	Tobacco products		…	30	26	27		…	4215	4309	4452		…	61479	62727	67163
131	Spinning, weaving and finishing of textiles		…	151	144	132		…	9569	7372	6549		…	56432	45023	42999
1311	Preparation and spinning of textile fibres		…	53	46	47		…	5086	4048	4085		…	34055	29122	30572
1312	Weaving of textiles		…	64	56	48		…	3973	2752	2009		…	20458	13528	9747
1313	Finishing of textiles		…	34	42	37		…	510	572	455		…	1919	2374	2680
139	Other textiles		…	498	529	472		…	7160	5068	5082		…	29939	23197	25149
1391	Knitted and crocheted fabrics		…	6	7	10		…	215	144	137		…	642	532	509
1392	Made-up textile articles, except apparel		…	193	181	158		…	3939	2356	2676		…	15745	10843	13318
1393	Carpets and rugs		…	15	18	16		…	692	533	469		…	3213	2757	2674
1394	Cordage, rope, twine and netting		…	31	35	27		…	192	154	105		…	667	614	386
1399	Other textiles n.e.c.		…	253	288	261		…	2122	1881	1695		…	9672	8451	8262
1410	Wearing apparel, except fur apparel		…	4509	4594	4200		…	118300	100388	91217		…	401327	373704	363860
1420	Articles of fur		…	22	30	31		…	94	130	91		…	287	434	277
1430	Knitted and crocheted apparel		…	260	264	249		…	12036	10482	8690		…	60829	54598	47428
151	Leather;luggage,handbags,saddlery,harness;fur		…	111	116	104		…	2394	2015	1779		…	8985	7416	7803
1511	Tanning/dressing of leather; dressing of fur		…	32	33	26		…	431	252	173		…	1148	804	605
1512	Luggage,handbags,etc.;saddlery/harness		…	79	83	78		…	1963	1763	1606		…	7837	6612	7198
1520	Footwear		…	416	418	396		…	15624	13925	14018		…	49912	51411	53815
1610	Sawmilling and planing of wood		…	823	842	756		…	5910	4702	4844		…	17449	15334	16264
162	Wood products, cork, straw, plaiting materials		…	1153	1214	1183		…	11530	9785	8733		…	57413	49181	46631

Code	Description	(1)	(2)	(3)		(4)	(5)	(6)		(7)	(8)	(9)
1621	Veneer sheets and wood-based panels	23318	21944	29170	⋮	2669	2772	3591	⋮	35	34	39	⋮
1622	Builders' carpentry and joinery	7650	11746	11489	⋮	2046	2754	3003	⋮	316	340	322	⋮
1623	Wooden containers	4804	3931	4805	⋮	1336	1139	1525	⋮	158	152	171	⋮
1629	Other wood products;articles of cork,straw	10859	11560	11949	⋮	2682	3120	3411	⋮	674	688	621	⋮
1701	Pulp, paper and paperboard	11160	8791	14529	⋮	1241	1166	1803	⋮	18	20	19	⋮
1702	Corrugated paper and paperboard	25934	25331	26075	⋮	4116	4294	4737	⋮	195	193	190	⋮
1709	Other articles of paper and paperboard	16351	18562	16854	⋮	3240	3899	4092	⋮	305	333	311	⋮
181	Printing and service activities related to printing	59331	62539	57596	⋮	8830	9376	9161	⋮	1123	1135	957	⋮
1811	Printing	55351	58557	54320	⋮	8025	8519	8351	⋮	767	754	641	⋮
1812	Service activities related to printing	3980	3982	3276	⋮	805	857	810	⋮	356	381	316	⋮
1820	Reproduction of recorded media	843	1185	1141	⋮	126	125	137	⋮	16	15	15	⋮
1910	Coke oven products	...	-	...	⋮	...	-	-	⋮	-	-	...	⋮
1920	Refined petroleum products	70514	...	...	⋮	2961	...	...	⋮	17	19	21	⋮
201	Basic chemicals,fertilizers, etc.	43412	40156	53397	⋮	3767	3879	4735	⋮	134	120	130	⋮
2011	Basic chemicals	25172	22523	27171	⋮	1846	1865	2335	⋮	106	98	107	⋮
2012	Fertilizers and nitrogen compounds	18064	17531	26026	⋮	1887	1997	2352	⋮	18	16	16	⋮
2013	Plastics and synthetic rubber in primary forms	176	102	200	⋮	34	17	48	⋮	10	6	7	⋮
202	Other chemical products	67220	...	62621	⋮	8579	...	...	⋮	436	...	...	⋮
2021	Pesticides and other agrochemical products	2487	...	1780	⋮	251	...	...	⋮	15	...	...	⋮
2022	Paints,varnishes;printing ink and mastics	12129	13548	16440	⋮	1440	1750	2323	⋮	75	70	75	⋮
2023	Soap,cleaning and cosmetic preparations	31742	28862	24649	⋮	4349	4454	4555	⋮	179	172	172	⋮
2029	Other chemical products n.e.c.	20862	21270	19752	⋮	2539	2867	2563	⋮	167	160	157	⋮
2030	Man-made fibres	3049	...	...	⋮	534	...	...	⋮	4	...	...	⋮
2100	Pharmaceuticals,medicinal chemicals, etc.	71008	...	65598	⋮	7200	...	...	⋮	60	62	62	⋮
221	Rubber products	18499	16385	16184	⋮	2701	2549	2731	⋮	214	216	211	⋮
2211	Rubber tyres and tubes	289	363	465	⋮	72	78	101	⋮	41	45	48	⋮
2219	Other rubber products	18210	16022	15719	⋮	2629	2471	2630	⋮	173	171	163	⋮
2220	Plastics products	99669	106992	99967	⋮	18977	21702	23837	⋮	1704	1840	1695	⋮
2310	Glass and glass products	31832	32169	32544	⋮	3759	3985	4248	⋮	142	153	141	⋮
239	Non-metallic mineral products n.e.c.	152986	170562	180685	⋮	18722	22946	26351	⋮	1314	1405	1330	⋮
2391	Refractory products	3213	3192	3590	⋮	448	482	547	⋮	14	12	12	⋮
2392	Clay building materials	16117	18146	23683	⋮	2382	3129	4372	⋮	54	64	57	⋮
2393	Other porcelain and ceramic products	28577	25582	28264	⋮	2915	2825	3275	⋮	168	175	164	⋮
2394	Cement, lime and plaster	25270	25202	25140	⋮	2142	2164	2078	⋮	69	68	61	⋮
2395	Articles of concrete, cement and plaster	49181	65640	78861	⋮	6612	9402	11906	⋮	554	609	596	⋮
2396	Cutting, shaping and finishing of stone	7542	9185	9667	⋮	1522	1924	2180	⋮	266	286	264	⋮
2399	Other non-metallic mineral products n.e.c.	23086	23615	11480	⋮	2701	3020	1993	⋮	189	191	176	⋮
2410	Basic iron and steel	54017	87166	118167	⋮	4639	7116	8953	⋮	41	41	46	⋮
2420	Basic precious and other non-ferrous metals	72243	58963	65465	⋮	4967	4491	4916	⋮	40	38	41	⋮
243	Casting of metals	24548	22801	35830	⋮	3977	4041	5206	⋮	134	137	129	⋮
2431	Casting of iron and steel	20429	19381	31936	⋮	3268	3407	4455	⋮	71	73	81	⋮
2432	Casting of non-ferrous metals	4119	3420	3894	⋮	709	634	751	⋮	63	64	48	⋮
251	Struct.metal products, tanks, reservoirs	75693	94661	98872	⋮	13203	16760	19706	⋮	1437	1611	1558	⋮
2511	Structural metal products	66610	80599	84540	⋮	11734	14478	16981	⋮	1369	1529	1485	⋮
2512	Tanks, reservoirs and containers of metal	8196	12752	11168	⋮	1350	2020	2149	⋮	57	72	62	⋮

continued

Bulgaria

ISIC	Industry	Number of enterprises (number)					Number of employees (number)					Wages and salaries paid to employees (thousands of Bulgarian Leva)				
		Note	2007	2008	2009	2010	Note	2007	2008	2009	2010	Note	2007	2008	2009	2010
2513	Steam generators, excl. hot water boilers		...	11	10	11		...	576	262	119		...	3164	1310	887
2520	Weapons and ammunition		...	19	21	23		...	12467	13178	13427		...	77908	83749	87442
259	Other metal products;metal working services		...	2508	2700	2562		...	28007	25514	22518		...	150441	142705	138797
2591	Forging,pressing,stamping,roll-forming of metal		...	48	47	40		...	1666	1024	446		...	8750	4922	2838
2592	Treatment and coating of metals; machining		...	1316	1374	1273		...	10802	9982	9045		...	60926	59108	57007
2593	Cutlery, hand tools and general hardware		...	147	124	125		...	3614	3048	2679		...	23578	18720	18959
2599	Other fabricated metal products n.e.c.		...	997	1155	1124		...	11925	11460	10348		...	57187	59956	59993
2610	Electronic components and boards		...	99	101	97		...	3357	2546	2696		...	27926	22219	25210
2620	Computers and peripheral equipment		...	33	33	35		...	436	282	360		...	2581	1672	2710
2630	Communication equipment		...	85	83	65		...	1660	1201	1118		...	11317	8009	10013
2640	Consumer electronics		...	10	16	21		...	311	259	300		...	2204	2192	2741
265	Measuring,testing equipment; watches, etc.		...	101	107	104		...	2457	2508	2204		...	15290	17648	16344
2651	Measuring/testing/navigating equipment,etc.		...	97	103	98		...	...	2468	2156		...	15036	17366	16011
2652	Watches and clocks		...	4	4	6		...	...	40	48		...	...	282	333
2660	Irradiation/electromedical equipment,etc.		...	23	12	6		...	234	...	...		...	1546	...	...
2670	Optical instruments and photographic equipment		...	26	25	31		...	1305	1119	1108		...	10454	9218	9954
2680	Magnetic and optical media		...	9	9	5		...	78	...	...		...	691	...	...
2710	Electric motors,generators,transformers,etc.		...	183	162	164		...	7201	5813	6186		...	48331	40691	53773
2720	Batteries and accumulators		...	13	11	7		...	1873	1378	1380		...	17472	13797	15441
273	Wiring and wiring devices		...	51	52	56		...	3856	4590	4768		...	23962	25092	29905
2731	Fibre optic cables		...	...	...	-		...	...	...	...		...	...	...	-
2732	Other electronic and electric wires and cables		...	16	17	18		...	1229	1166	1190		...	11377	8747	10807
2733	Wiring devices		...	...	...	38		...	...	...	3578		...	12572	...	19098
2740	Electric lighting equipment		...	71	82	80		...	1130	1004	797		...	5079	4868	4298
2750	Domestic appliances		...	58	63	57		...	3937	3584	3159		...	35591	34125	30821
2790	Other electrical equipment		...	120	160	145		...	2245	1850	1454		...	11954	12369	11213
281	General-purpose machinery		...	476	449	447		...	24340	19638	19011		...	176469	139913	166057
2811	Engines/turbines,excl.aircraft,vehicle engines		...	18	13	13		...	922	428	376		...	7028	2576	2240
2812	Fluid power equipment		...	26	26	29		...	4135	2757	3170		...	33291	20369	32078
2813	Other pumps, compressors, taps and valves		...	42	42	41		...	3832	2875	2769		...	36686	29609	33235
2814	Bearings, gears, gearing and driving elements		...	19	15	16		...	1728	2505	2500		...	10417	15814	18535
2815	Ovens, furnaces and furnace burners		...	12	14	12		...	94	71	175		...	514	406	1637
2816	Lifting and handling equipment		...	139	117	119		...	7368	5734	4539		...	48571	34681	33724
2817	Office machinery, excl.computers,etc.		...	13	10	13		...	667	642	917		...	6041	7690	10919
2818	Power-driven hand tools		...	5	7	7		...	1696	1165	888		...	10420	5259	5558
2819	Other general-purpose machinery		...	202	205	197		...	3898	3461	3677		...	23501	23509	28131
282	Special-purpose machinery		...	517	469	458		...	11987	9447	9029		...	79036	62050	63990
2821	Agricultural and forestry machinery		...	63	60	62		...	1286	1069	970		...	6766	6276	5911
2822	Metal-forming machinery and machine tools		...	102	84	77		...	3571	2518	2194		...	22924	15617	15365
2823	Machinery for metallurgy		...	9	8	14		...	747	627	714		...	6873	5625	3836
2824	Mining, quarrying and construction machinery		...	36	28	22		...	1125	718	884		...	9104	6948	7250

2825	Food/beverage/tobacco processing machinery	94	99	104	2759	2342	2393	17948	13929	18261
2826	Textile/apparel/leather production machinery	11	10	8	228	125	95	1411	455	445
2829	Other special-purpose machinery	202	180	171	2271	2048	1779	14010	13200	12922
2910	Motor vehicles	3	…	-	…	…	-	…	…	-
2920	Automobile bodies, trailers and semi-trailers	19	…	25	…	…	381	2715	…	2468
2930	Parts and accessories for motor vehicles	77	81	85	9852	9878	9668	56241	64809	74865
301	Building of ships and boats	45	42	33	3333	2537	1882	32364	21922	16268
3011	Building of ships and floating structures	33	30	25	3202	2490	1862	31735	21675	16179
3012	Building of pleasure and sporting boats	12	12	8	131	47	20	629	246	89
3020	Railway locomotives and rolling stock	13	14	13	2564	…	…	24587	…	…
3030	Air and spacecraft and related machinery	3	3	3	-	…	…	-	…	…
3040	Military fighting vehicles	-	-	-	-	-	-	-	-	-
309	Transport equipment n.e.c.	24	27	27	…	898	1014	3819	4056	5310
3091	Motorcycles	-	-	-	-	-	-	-	-	-
3092	Bicycles and invalid carriages	20	22	20	1121	898	996	3729	4056	5250
3099	Other transport equipment n.e.c.	4	5	7	90	…	18	90	…	60
3100	Furniture	2192	2407	2253	27412	23031	19630	100124	90811	81680
321	Jewellery, bijouterie and related articles	246	263	246	910	846	705	4046	4040	3880
3211	Jewellery and related articles	225	242	228	819	776	659	3826	3836	3719
3212	Imitation jewellery and related articles	21	21	18	91	70	46	220	204	161
3220	Musical instruments	15	18	19	130	144	158	772	971	1136
3230	Sports goods	29	33	33	728	969	1309	5217	7570	10796
3240	Games and toys	30	26	19	1856	1433	1409	6339	5477	7540
3250	Medical and dental instruments and supplies	532	620	613	1958	1899	1630	9233	10278	8354
3290	Other manufacturing n.e.c.	431	470	451	2124	2097	1614	9326	10053	7040
331	Repair of fabricated metal products/machinery	1733	2004	1954	17215	14192	13799	138372	116970	118790
3311	Repair of fabricated metal products	135	168	152	2236	1475	1188	16527	9213	7565
3312	Repair of machinery	900	985	982	9272	6698	6562	66655	50555	51428
3313	Repair of electronic and optical equipment	194	222	211	222	227	215	1002	1319	1335
3314	Repair of electrical equipment	190	232	229	711	837	805	4423	6161	5681
3315	Repair of transport equip., excl. motor vehicles	252	299	283	4629	4884	4938	47968	49391	52430
3319	Repair of other equipment	62	98	97	145	71	91	1797	332	351
3320	Installation of industrial machinery/equipment	179	233	212	2432	1416	1062	31810	26458	15471
C	Total manufacturing	30288	32177	30728	608206	540756	498327	3408376	3243525	3220107

Bulgaria

		Output (millions of Bulgarian Leva)					Value added at factor values (millions of Bulgarian Leva)					Gross fixed capital formation (millions of Bulgarian Leva)		
ISIC	Industry	Note	2007	2008	2009	2010	Note	2007	2008	2009	2010	Note	2009	2010
1010	Processing/preserving of meat		…	1683.2	1735.0	1708.0		…	203.7	203.0	237.0		…	…
1020	Processing/preserving of fish, etc.		…	59.2	58.0	62.0		…	13.9	14.0	13.0		…	…
1030	Processing/preserving of fruit,vegetables		…	499.4	507.0	506.0		…	89.3	106.0	111.0		…	…
1040	Vegetable and animal oils and fats		…	338.6	318.0	476.0		…	65.7	41.0	93.0		…	…
1050	Dairy products		…	695.1	727.0	794.0		…	103.6	141.0	149.0		…	…
106	Grain mill products,starches and starch products		…	533.9	404.0	490.0		…	88.6	72.0	91.0		…	…
1061	Grain mill products		…	…				…	…				…	…
1062	Starches and starch products		…					…					…	…
107	Other food products		…	2033.2	1862.0	1943.0		…	520.5	474.0	491.0		…	…
1071	Bakery products		…	906.1	857.0	894.0		…	245.2	260.0	262.0		…	…
1072	Sugar		…	242.2	175.0	136.0		…	39.0	13.0	-8.0		…	…
1073	Cocoa, chocolate and sugar confectionery		…	503.7	483.0	562.0		…	123.9	120.0	142.0		…	…
1074	Macaroni, noodles, couscous, etc.		…	9.9	9.0	13.0		…	2.5	3.0	4.0		…	…
1075	Prepared meals and dishes		…	74.5	59.0	76.0		…	15.8	13.0	20.0		…	…
1079	Other food products n.e.c.		…	296.8	279.0	262.0		…	94.1	65.0	71.0		…	…
1080	Prepared animal feeds		…	243.2	255.0	257.0		…	29.8	34.0	35.0		…	…
1101	Distilling, rectifying and blending of spirits		…	241.3	109.0	209.0		…	28.1	23.0	34.0		…	…
1102	Wines		…	362.4	286.0	256.0		…	57.8	60.0	43.0		…	…
1103	Malt liquors and malt		…	516.6	483.0	476.0		…	121.5	129.0	140.0		…	…
1104	Soft drinks,mineral waters,other bottled waters		…	635.8	592.0	538.0		…	207.4	190.0	190.0		…	…
1200	Tobacco products		…	1586.6	1597.0	1410.0		…	156.6	124.0	180.0		…	…
131	Spinning, weaving and finishing of textiles		…	650.0	420.0	466.0		…	115.4	81.0	100.0		…	…
1311	Preparation and spinning of textile fibres		…	444.5	308.0	380.0		…	60.1	50.0	77.0		…	…
1312	Weaving of textiles		…	192.2	95.0	70.0		…	50.0	25.0	16.0		…	…
1313	Finishing of textiles		…	13.3	17.0	16.0		…	5.3	6.0	7.0		…	…
139	Other textiles		…	222.4	160.0	178.0		…	71.0	52.0	53.0		…	…
1391	Knitted and crocheted fabrics		…	9.8	7.0	9.0		…	2.4	2.0	2.0		…	…
1392	Made-up textile articles, except apparel		…	120.1	85.0	102.0		…	34.1	25.0	28.0		…	…
1393	Carpets and rugs		…	…	18.0	17.0		…	…	6.0	…		…	…
1394	Cordage, rope, twine and netting		…		3.0	3.0		…		1.0	…		…	…
1399	Other textiles n.e.c.		…	65.5	47.0	47.0		…	26.4	18.0	17.0		…	…
1410	Wearing apparel, except fur apparel		…	1786.0	1556.0	1667.0		…	740.6	661.0	648.0		…	…
1420	Articles of fur		…	1.0	1.0	1.0		…	0.4	…	…		…	…
1430	Knitted and crocheted apparel		…	279.9	249.0	228.0		…	103.5	94.0	87.0		…	…
151	Leather;luggage,handbags,saddlery,harness;fur		…	66.0	39.0	42.0		…	18.0	12.0	14.0		…	…
1511	Tanning/dressing of leather; dressing of fur		…	15.0	9.0	10.0		…	2.7	…	1.0		…	…
1512	Luggage,handbags,etc.;saddlery/harness		…	50.9	30.0	32.0		…	15.3	12.0	13.0		…	…
1520	Footwear		…	231.2	207.0	231.0		…	92.8	92.0	103.0		…	…
1610	Sawmilling and planing of wood		…	230.1	147.0	170.0		…	48.9	36.0	40.0		…	…
162	Wood products, cork, straw, plaiting materials		…	562.8	426.0	458.0		…	131.9	109.0	118.0		…	…

Code	Product									
1621	Veneer sheets and wood-based panels	…	321.4	233.0	275.0	…	66.4	50.0	65.0	…
1622	Builders' carpentry and joinery	…	85.3	67.0	49.0	…	23.5	20.0	14.0	…
1623	Wooden containers	…	65.0	46.0	58.0	…	10.2	11.0	15.0	…
1629	Other wood products;articles of cork,straw	…	91.2	80.0	76.0	…	31.8	28.0	24.0	…
1701	Pulp, paper and paperboard	…	199.8	72.0	…	…	8.9	13.0	…	…
1702	Corrugated paper and paperboard	…	325.6	292.0	309.0	…	81.0	89.0	83.0	…
1709	Other articles of paper and paperboard	…	207.8	194.0	…	…	47.8	45.0	…	…
181	Printing and service activities related to printing	…	544.9	528.0	532.0	…	176.3	168.0	167.0	…
1811	Printing	…	507.8	495.0	497.0	…	163.1	155.0	155.0	…
1812	Service activities related to printing	…	37.1	33.0	35.0	…	13.2	13.0	12.0	…
1820	Reproduction of recorded media	…	33.6	25.0	26.0	…	15.0	10.0	8.0	…
1910	Coke oven products	…	-	-	-	…	-	-	-	…
1920	Refined petroleum products	…	…	…	…	…	…	72.0	119.0	…
201	Basic chemicals,fertilizers, etc.	…	1274.9	624.0	912.0	…	191.4	47.0	76.0	…
2011	Basic chemicals	…	524.5	336.0	…	…	119.5	78.0	…	…
2012	Fertilizers and nitrogen compounds	…	745.4	287.0	453.0	…	71.3	-31.0	…	…
2013	Plastics and synthetic rubber in primary forms	…	5.0	1.0	…	…	0.7	…	…	…
202	Other chemical products	…	…	…	…	…	…	…	…	…
2021	Pesticides and other agrochemical products	…	245.9	186.0	172.0	…	42.4	44.0	33.0	…
2022	Paints,varnishes;printing ink and mastics	…	342.6	356.0	397.0	…	68.3	95.0	90.0	…
2023	Soap,cleaning and cosmetic preparations	…	351.1	280.0	324.0	…	75.0	76.0	94.0	…
2029	Other chemical products n.e.c.	…	…	…	…	…	…	…	…	…
2030	Man-made fibres	…	…	…	…	…	…	217.0	…	…
2100	Pharmaceuticals,medicinal chemicals, etc.	…	…	…	…	…	…	…	…	…
221	Rubber products	…	144.7	142.0	195.0	…	36.9	39.0	50.0	…
2211	Rubber tyres and tubes	…	4.8	3.0	3.0	…	1.7	1.0	1.0	…
2219	Other rubber products	…	139.8	139.0	192.0	…	35.3	38.0	49.0	…
2220	Plastics products	…	1624.9	1250.0	1358.0	…	331.7	322.0	292.0	…
2310	Glass and glass products	…	606.8	493.0	514.0	…	207.3	138.0	147.0	…
239	Non-metallic mineral products n.e.c.	…	2846.3	1837.0	1515.0	…	876.0	565.0	485.0	…
2391	Refractory products	…	19.0	22.0	14.0	…	7.0	6.0	5.0	…
2392	Clay building materials	…	222.3	148.0	167.0	…	89.8	54.0	68.0	…
2393	Other porcelain and ceramic products	…	158.2	127.0	152.0	…	50.3	46.0	55.0	…
2394	Cement, lime and plaster	…	871.1	477.0	399.0	…	362.1	180.0	157.0	…
2395	Articles of concrete, cement and plaster	…	1305.9	747.0	483.0	…	279.6	175.0	107.0	…
2396	Cutting, shaping and finishing of stone	…	81.2	64.0	54.0	…	29.8	23.0	21.0	…
2399	Other non-metallic mineral products n.e.c.	…	188.5	252.0	246.0	…	57.4	81.0	72.0	…
2410	Basic iron and steel	…	2027.4	937.0	1053.0	…	22.3	…	…	…
2420	Basic precious and other non-ferrous metals	…	3907.1	3696.0	5081.0	…	22.1	…	292.0	…
243	Casting of metals	…	278.2	153.0	197.0	…	65.0	41.0	51.0	…
2431	Casting of iron and steel	…	237.9	120.0	138.0	…	58.2	33.0	39.0	…
2432	Casting of non-ferrous metals	…	40.4	33.0	59.0	…	6.8	8.0	12.0	…
251	Struct.metal products, tanks, reservoirs	…	1390.4	914.0	670.0	…	289.8	226.0	167.0	…
2511	Structural metal products	…	1240.3	813.0	598.0	…	252.9	196.0	146.0	…
2512	Tanks, reservoirs and containers of metal	…	125.6	95.0	68.0	…	30.4	29.0	19.0	…

continued

Bulgaria

ISIC Revision 4		Output (millions of Bulgarian Leva)					Value added at factor values (millions of Bulgarian Leva)					Gross fixed capital formation (millions of Bulgarian Leva)		
ISIC	Industry	Note	2007	2008	2009	2010	Note	2007	2008	2009	2010	Note	2009	2010
2513	Steam generators, excl. hot water boilers		…	24.5	6.0	4.0		…	6.4	1.0	2.0		…	
2520	Weapons and ammunition		…	300.8	293.0	402.0		…	117.4	129.0	158.0		…	
259	Other metal products;metal working services		…	1415.9	1043.0	1045.0		…	444.5	331.0	344.0		…	
2591	Forging,pressing,stamping,roll-forming of metal		…	121.5	43.0	26.0		…	40.7	2.0	6.0		…	
2592	Treatment and coating of metals; machining		…	487.9	412.0	384.0		…	164.9	136.0	142.0		…	
2593	Cutlery, hand tools and general hardware		…	124.1	86.0	99.0		…	51.5	39.0	44.0		…	
2599	Other fabricated metal products n.e.c.		…	682.4	502.0	536.0		…	187.4	154.0	152.0		…	…
2610	Electronic components and boards		…	236.2	143.0	223.0		…	72.3	39.0	65.0		…	
2620	Computers and peripheral equipment		…	28.5	17.0	24.0		…	7.0	6.0	8.0		…	
2630	Communication equipment		…	97.4	78.0	85.0		…	29.0	28.0	36.0		…	
2640	Consumer electronics		…	22.6	7.0	…		…	3.5	3.0	…		…	
265	Measuring,testing equipment; watches, etc.		…	122.1	138.0	139.0		…	36.4	42.0	49.0		…	
2651	Measuring/testing/navigating equipment,etc.		…	117.7	135.0	136.0		…	34.9	41.0	48.0		…	
2652	Watches and clocks		…	4.4	3.0	3.0		…	1.4	1.0	1.0		…	
2660	Irradiation/electromedical equipment,etc.		…	32.1	…	…		…	15.0	…	18.0		…	
2670	Optical instruments and photographic equipment		…	41.5	37.0	48.0		…	19.6	17.0	18.0		…	…
2680	Magnetic and optical media		…	10.1	…	…		…	5.0	…	…		…	
2710	Electric motors,generators,transformers,etc.		…	460.4	345.0	433.0		…	118.3	110.0	130.0		…	
2720	Batteries and accumulators		…	278.1	207.0	323.0		…	66.7	46.0	53.0		…	
273	Wiring and wiring devices		…	280.2	206.0	302.0		…	53.6	49.0	61.0		…	
2731	Fibre optic cables		…	…	…	-		…	…	…	-		…	
2732	Other electronic and electric wires and cables		…	236.0	158.0	247.0		…	32.8	25.0	30.0		…	
2733	Wiring devices		…	79.0	63.0	55.0		…	…	…	31.0		…	
2740	Electric lighting equipment		…		…	47.0		…	20.2	17.0	13.0		…	
2750	Domestic appliances		…	431.4	417.0	383.0		…	86.8	102.0	86.0		…	…
2790	Other electrical equipment		…	153.8	114.0	114.0		…	41.4	28.0	26.0		…	
281	General-purpose machinery		…	1596.6	978.0	1327.0		…	470.2	289.0	414.0		…	
2811	Engines/turbines,excl.aircraft,vehicle engines		…	48.7	25.0	28.0		…	17.4	6.0	8.0		…	
2812	Fluid power equipment		…	211.9	99.0	193.0		…	74.3	39.0	70.0		…	
2813	Other pumps, compressors, taps and valves		…	359.7	225.0	…		…	115.4	71.0	…		…	
2814	Bearings, gears, gearing and driving elements		…	81.2	91.0	153.0		…	14.0	24.0	54.0		…	
2815	Ovens, furnaces and furnace burners		…		4.0	…		…		1.0	…		…	
2816	Lifting and handling equipment		…	460.9	232.0	264.0		…	117.7	55.0	76.0		…	
2817	Office machinery, excl.computers,etc.		…	94.6	75.0	129.0		…	29.5	27.0	43.0		…	…
2818	Power-driven hand tools		…		15.0	…		…		1.0	…		…	
2819	Other general-purpose machinery		…	255.2	212.0	269.0		…	68.7	65.0	80.0		…	
282	Special-purpose machinery		…	638.4	353.0	404.0		…	201.8	127.0	136.0		…	
2821	Agricultural and forestry machinery		…	48.0	33.0	35.0		…	…	…	14.0		…	
2822	Metal-forming machinery and machine tools		…	159.3	86.0	90.0		…	44.9	28.0	28.0		…	
2823	Machinery for metallurgy		…	43.3	22.0	31.0		…	…	…	10.0		…	
2824	Mining, quarrying and construction machinery		…	77.8	31.0	35.0		…	21.1	10.0	10.0		…	

2825	Food/beverage/tobacco processing machinery	...	165.4	101.0	132.0	50.4	35.0	43.0	...
2826	Textile/apparel/leather production machinery	...	7.7	2.0	2.0	2.4	1.0	1.0	...
2829	Other special-purpose machinery	...	137.0	78.0	79.0	47.1	31.0	30.0	...
2910	Motor vehicles	...	...	...	-	...	...	-	...
2920	Automobile bodies, trailers and semi-trailers	...	...	...	15.0	...	...	6.0	...
2930	Parts and accessories for motor vehicles	...	605.3	569.0	763.0	93.6	108.0	152.0	...
301	Building of ships and boats	...	251.7	183.0	...	49.5	29.0	...	...
3011	Building of ships and floating structures	...	249.5	182.0	121.0	49.5	29.0	...	...
3012	Building of pleasure and sporting boats	...	2.2	1.0	...	-	...	...	...
3020	Railway locomotives and rolling stock	...	259.2	...	148.0	57.8	...	40.0	...
3030	Air and spacecraft and related machinery	...	1.4	...	...	...	...	...	...
3040	Military fighting vehicles	...	-	-	-	-	-	-	...
309	Transport equipment n.e.c.	...	96.3	94.0	116.0	...	20.0	20.0	...
3091	Motorcycles	...	-	-	-	-	-	-	...
3092	Bicycles and invalid carriages	...	95.6	94.0	116.0	20.5	20.0	20.0	...
3099	Other transport equipment n.e.c.	...	0.7	...	...	...	...	...	...
3100	Furniture	...	920.2	710.0	708.0	261.0	215.0	194.0	...
321	Jewellery, bijouterie and related articles	...	29.1	27.0	28.0	10.6	9.0	10.0	...
3211	Jewellery and related articles	...	27.3	25.0	25.0	10.0	9.0	9.0	...
3212	Imitation jewellery and related articles	...	1.7	2.0	3.0	0.6	...	1.0	...
3220	Musical instruments	...	2.6	3.0	4.0	1.3	1.0	2.0	...
3230	Sports goods	...	34.8	62.0	102.0	11.5	16.0	28.0	...
3240	Games and toys	...	76.4	56.0	75.0	28.5	20.0	28.0	...
3250	Medical and dental instruments and supplies	...	65.6	65.0	53.0	24.1	29.0	18.0	...
3290	Other manufacturing n.e.c.	...	83.0	80.0	50.0	21.4	27.0	18.0	...
331	Repair of fabricated metal products/machinery	...	757.9	615.0	567.0	325.2	269.0	262.0	...
3311	Repair of fabricated metal products	...	73.5	48.0	32.0	27.5	15.0	15.0	...
3312	Repair of machinery	...	402.8	291.0	280.0	152.7	118.0	116.0	...
3313	Repair of electronic and optical equipment	...	9.6	10.0	8.0	5.2	5.0	4.0	...
3314	Repair of electrical equipment	...	30.1	28.0	23.0	9.9	13.0	10.0	...
3315	Repair of transport equip., excl. motor vehicles	...	235.2	233.0	...	127.6	116.0	116.0	...
3319	Repair of other equipment	...	6.7	5.0	...	2.2	2.0	...	...
3320	Installation of industrial machinery/equipment	...	197.0	212.0	101.0	79.0	82.0	40.0	...
C	Total manufacturing	...	47938.9	37209.0	41484.0	8367.0	7596.0	8065.0	...

Bulgaria

ISIC Revision 4		Index numbers of industrial production (2005=100)												
ISIC	Industry	Note	1999	2000	2001	2002	2003	2004	2005	2006	2007	2008	2009	2010
10	Food products		…	64	64	69	81	92	100	107	117	123	112	117
11	Beverages		…	79	75	69	82	101	100	105	121	126	98	88
12	Tobacco products		…	98	89	83	94	100	100	75	86	101	106	97
13	Textiles		…	62	61	81	97	102	100	113	125	104	70	66
14	Wearing apparel		…	49	56	69	89	103	100	110	113	100	74	69
15	Leather and related products		…	66	67	76	90	95	100	110	120	112	79	78
16	Wood/wood products/cork,excl. furniture		…	48	48	59	77	91	100	114	119	111	70	82
17	Paper and paper products		…	50	44	52	77	95	100	97	108	108	76	124
18	Printing and reproduction of recorded media		…	92	85	78	78	75	100	103	113	118	116	111
19	Coke and refined petroleum products		…	…	…	…	…	…	100	…	…	…	…	…
20	Chemicals and chemical products		…	74	76	70	79	85	100	100	105	116	78	95
21	Pharmaceuticals,medicinal chemicals, etc.		…	97	94	92	101	97	100	101	109	102	77	87
22	Rubber and plastics products		…	53	55	55	81	96	100	100	114	133	107	111
23	Other non-metallic mineral products		…	52	50	57	67	87	100	123	144	149	88	80
24	Basic metals		…	52	45	47	60	96	100	111	111	112	96	97
25	Fabricated metal products, except machinery		…	49	55	66	63	79	100	113	127	135	86	97
26	Computer, electronic and optical products		…	61	73	113	122	83	100	86	99	98	99	105
27	Electrical equipment		…	48	47	55	71	85	100	122	147	161	130	143
28	Machinery and equipment n.e.c.		…	54	53	61	72	96	100	114	132	139	101	107
29	Motor vehicles, trailers and semi-trailers		…	58	56	66	56	65	100	124	151	128	106	154
30	Other transport equipment		…	57	59	60	76	81	100	130	134	163	104	82
31	Furniture		…	36	39	48	71	100	100	122	152	146	92	98
32	Other manufacturing		…	71	71	72	87	110	100	121	149	142	147	136
33	Repair and installation of machinery/equipment		…	63	64	72	85	98	100	115	120	133	92	113
C	Total manufacturing		…	61	63	68	80	93	100	109	119	120	93	97

Canada

Supplier of information:
Statistics Canada, Ottawa.
Industrial statistics for the OECD countries are compiled by the OECD secretariat, which supplies them to UNIDO.

Basic source of data:
Annual survey of manufacturing; business register.

Major deviations from ISIC (Revision 4):
None reported.

Reference period:
Calendar year.

Scope:
All establishments.

Method of data collection:
Mail questionnaires.

Type of enumeration:
Not reported.

Adjusted for non-response:
Yes.

Concepts and definitions of variables:
No deviations from the standard UN concepts and definitions are reported.

Related national publications:
None reported.

Canada

- 294 -

ISIC	Industry		Establishments (number)					Number of employees (thousands)					Wages and salaries (millions of Canadian Dollars)			
		Note	2006	2007	2008	2009	Note	2006	2007	2008	2009	Note	2006	2007	2008	2009
1010	Processing/preserving of meat		...	...	...	...		...	...	79	79		...	...	2910	2900
1020	Processing/preserving of fish, etc.		...	...	...	...		...	...	...	...		...	...	...	...
1030	Processing/preserving of fruit,vegetables		...	...	...	...		...	...	26	27		...	...	1084	1108
1040	Vegetable and animal oils and fats		...	...	...	...		...	...	...	...		...	...	...	...
1050	Dairy products		...	...	...	...		...	...	22	22		...	...	990	997
106	Grain mill products,starches and starch products		...	...	...	...		...	...	...	...		...	...	...	...
1061	Grain mill products		...	...	...	...		...	...	...	...		...	...	...	...
1062	Starches and starch products		...	...	...	...		...	...	...	...		...	...	...	...
107	Other food products		...	...	...	...		...	...	...	...		...	...	...	...
1071	Bakery products		...	...	...	...		...	...	...	...		...	...	...	...
1072	Sugar		...	...	...	...		...	...	...	...		...	...	...	...
1073	Cocoa, chocolate and sugar confectionery		...	...	...	...		...	...	...	...		...	...	...	...
1074	Macaroni, noodles, couscous, etc.		...	...	...	...		...	...	2	2		...	...	78	84
1075	Prepared meals and dishes		...	...	...	...		...	...	...	...		...	...	...	...
1079	Other food products n.e.c.		...	...	...	...		...	...	2	2		...	...	102	113
1080	Prepared animal feeds		...	...	...	...		...	...	9	9		...	...	433	433
1101	Distilling, rectifying and blending of spirits		...	...	...	...		...	...	5	5		...	...	210	218
1102	Wines		...	...	...	...		...	...	...	...		...	...	...	...
1103	Malt liquors and malt		...	...	...	...		...	...	8	8		...	...	467	489
1104	Soft drinks,mineral waters,other bottled waters		...	...	...	...		...	...	11	11		...	...	441	452
1200	Tobacco products		...	...	...	...		...	...	...	...		...	...	...	...
131	Spinning, weaving and finishing of textiles		...	...	...	...		...	...	14	13		...	...	611	545
1311	Preparation and spinning of textile fibres		...	...	...	...		...	...	6	6		...	...	238	215
1312	Weaving of textiles		...	...	...	...		...	...	3	3		...	...	170	142
1313	Finishing of textiles		...	...	...	...		...	...	4	4		...	...	202	187
139	Other textiles		...	...	...	...		...	...	...	...		...	...	...	...
1391	Knitted and crocheted fabrics		...	...	...	...		...	...	-	-		...	...	20	17
1392	Made-up textile articles, except apparel		...	...	...	...		...	...	18	15		...	...	784	650
1393	Carpets and rugs		...	...	...	...		...	...	2	2		...	...	88	71
1394	Cordage, rope, twine and netting		...	...	...	...		...	...	...	...		...	...	...	...
1399	Other textiles n.e.c.		...	...	...	...		...	...	36	34		...	...	1550	1450
1410	Wearing apparel, except fur apparel		...	...	...	...		...	...	...	...		...	...	...	...
1420	Articles of fur		...	...	...	...		...	...	...	...		...	...	...	...
1430	Knitted and crocheted apparel		...	...	...	...		...	...	3	3		...	...	120	96
151	Leather;luggage,handbags,saddlery,harness;fur		...	...	...	...		...	...	...	...		...	...	...	...
1511	Tanning/dressing of leather; dressing of fur		...	...	...	...		...	...	-	-		...	...	11	9
1512	Luggage,handbags,etc.;saddlery/harness		...	...	...	...		...	...	...	...		...	...	...	...
1520	Footwear		...	...	...	...		...	...	3	2		...	...	73	65
1610	Sawmilling and planing of wood		...	...	...	...		...	...	54	46		...	...	2477	2099
162	Wood products, cork, straw, plaiting materials		...	...	...	...		...	...	67	58		...	...	2881	2471

1621	Veneer sheets and wood-based panels	886	749	20	17
1622	Builders' carpentry and joinery	1286	1075	33	28
1623	Wooden containers	172	154	5	4
1629	Other wood products;articles of cork,straw	538	493	10	10
1701	Pulp, paper and paperboard	2561	2216	37	32
1702	Corrugated paper and paperboard	834	820	16	16
1709	Other articles of paper and paperboard	3160	2873	67	61
181	Printing and service activities related to printing	680	626	15	14
1811	Printing	416	382	9	9
1812	Service activities related to printing	264	243	6	5
1820	Reproduction of recorded media	130	95	3	2
1910	Coke oven products	149	154	2	2
1920	Refined petroleum products	...	...	...	...
201	Basic chemicals,fertilizers, etc.	1997	1823	31	28
2011	Basic chemicals	1387	1324	21	21
2012	Fertilizers and nitrogen compounds	64	63	2	2
2013	Plastics and synthetic rubber in primary forms	547	436	7	6
202	Other chemical products	2617	2660	45	46
2021	Pesticides and other agrochemical products	49	54	1	1
2022	Paints,varnishes;printing ink and mastics	535	498	10	10
2023	Soap,cleaning and cosmetic preparations	225	224	5	5
2029	Other chemical products n.e.c.	1808	1884	30	31
2030	Man-made fibres	88	67	2	1
2100	Pharmaceuticals,medicinal chemicals, etc.	848	868	19	20
221	Rubber products	1253	1122	27	25
2211	Rubber tyres and tubes	366	338	7	6
2219	Other rubber products	887	784	21	19
2220	Plastics products	3790	3324	87	75
2310	Glass and glass products	810	731	16	15
239	Non-metallic mineral products n.e.c.	113	96	...	...
2391	Refractory products	9	7	2	2
2392	Clay building materials	...	...	-	-
2393	Other porcelain and ceramic products	359	321	6	5
2394	Cement, lime and plaster	1164	1087	24	23
2395	Articles of concrete, cement and plaster	...	...	...	...
2396	Cutting, shaping and finishing of stone	1027	795	20	16
2399	Other non-metallic mineral products n.e.c.	2057	1553	29	23
2410	Basic iron and steel	2350	1841	33	26
2420	Basic precious and other non-ferrous metals	879	722	15	13
243	Casting of metals	604	506	10	9
2431	Casting of iron and steel	275	216	5	4
2432	Casting of non-ferrous metals	4304	3950	88	80
251	Struct.metal products, tanks, reservoirs	3000	2720	62	56
2511	Structural metal products	1025	971	21	20
2512	Tanks, reservoirs and containers of metal	...	...	...	...

continued

Canada

ISIC	Industry	Establishments (number) Note	2006	2007	2008	2009	Number of employees (thousands) Note	2006	2007	2008	2009	Wages and salaries paid to employees (millions of Canadian Dollars) Note	2006	2007	2008	2009
2513	Steam generators, excl. hot water boilers		...	...	...	...		...	...	4	4		...	...	279	260
2520	Weapons and ammunition		...	...	...	...		...	...	...	...		...	...	...	...
259	Other metal products;metal working services		...	...	...	...		...	...	145	124		...	...	7383	6299
2591	Forging,pressing,stamping,roll-forming of metal		...	...	...	...		...	...	19	15		...	...	973	742
2592	Treatment and coating of metals; machining		...	...	...	...		...	...	48	43		...	...	2312	2066
2593	Cutlery, hand tools and general hardware		...	...	...	...		...	...	54	46		...	...	2881	2503
2599	Other fabricated metal products n.e.c.		...	...	...	...		...	...	24	20		...	...	1218	989
2610	Electronic components and boards		...	...	...	...		...	...	17	15		...	...	852	742
2620	Computers and peripheral equipment		...	...	...	...		...	...	8	6		...	...	450	351
2630	Communication equipment		...	...	...	...		...	...	23	22		...	...	1154	1149
2640	Consumer electronics		...	...	...	...		...	...	2	3		...	...	118	125
265	Measuring,testing equipment; watches, etc.		...	...	...	...		...	...	...	...		...	...	...	...
2651	Measuring/testing/navigating equipment,etc.		...	...	...	...		...	...	28	26		...	...	1635	1569
2652	Watches and clocks		...	...	...	...		...	...	...	...		...	...	...	...
2660	Irradiation/electromedical equipment,etc.		...	...	...	...		...	...	...	...		...	...	...	...
2670	Optical instruments and photographic equipment		...	...	...	...		...	...	15	13		...	...	832	720
2680	Magnetic and optical media		...	...	...	...		...	...	...	...		...	...	...	...
2710	Electric motors,generators,transformers,etc.		...	...	...	...		...	...	20	20		...	...	971	982
2720	Batteries and accumulators		...	...	...	...		...	...	1	1		...	...	48	36
273	Wiring and wiring devices		...	...	...	...		...	...	...	...		...	...	...	...
2731	Fibre optic cables		...	...	...	...		...	...	4	4		...	...	216	203
2732	Other electronic and electric wires and cables		...	...	...	...		...	...	...	...		...	...	...	...
2733	Wiring devices		...	...	...	...		...	...	4	3		...	...	188	157
2740	Electric lighting equipment		...	...	...	...		...	...	5	4		...	...	227	173
2750	Domestic appliances		...	...	...	...		...	...	...	...		...	...	...	...
2790	Other electrical equipment		...	...	...	...		...	...	4	3		...	...	189	156
281	General-purpose machinery		...	...	...	...		...	...	...	...		...	...	...	...
2811	Engines/turbines,excl.aircraft,vehicle engines		...	...	...	...		...	...	12	10		...	...	758	621
2812	Fluid power equipment		...	...	...	...		...	...	...	...		...	...	...	...
2813	Other pumps, compressors, taps and valves		...	...	...	...		...	...	85	76		...	...	4950	4535
2814	Bearings, gears, gearing and driving elements		...	...	...	...		...	...	2	2		...	...	110	85
2815	Ovens, furnaces and furnace burners		...	...	...	...		...	...	8	7		...	...	396	343
2816	Lifting and handling equipment		...	...	...	...		...	...	21	16		...	...	1034	796
2817	Office machinery, excl.computers,etc.		...	...	...	...		...	...	...	...		...	...	...	...
2818	Power-driven hand tools		...	...	...	...		...	...	...	...		...	...	...	...
2819	Other general-purpose machinery		...	...	...	...		...	...	4	4		...	...	158	176
282	Special-purpose machinery		...	...	...	...		...	...	...	...		...	...	...	...
2821	Agricultural and forestry machinery		...	...	...	...		...	...	2	1		...	...	95	78
2822	Metal-forming machinery and machine tools		...	...	...	...		...	...	7	6		...	...	401	320
2823	Machinery for metallurgy		...	...	...	...		...	...	...	...		...	...	...	...
2824	Mining, quarrying and construction machinery		...	...	...	...		...	...	...	...		...	...	...	...

2825	Food/beverage/tobacco processing machinery	…	…	…	…
2826	Textile/apparel/leather production machinery	…	…	…	…
2829	Other special-purpose machinery	…	…	…	…
2910	Motor vehicles	53	44	3688	3038
2920	Automobile bodies, trailers and semi-trailers	7	5	304	210
2930	Parts and accessories for motor vehicles	…	…	…	…
301	Building of ships and boats	9	8	390	362
3011	Building of ships and floating structures	6	6	261	267
3012	Building of pleasure and sporting boats	3	3	129	95
3020	Railway locomotives and rolling stock	…	…	…	…
3030	Air and spacecraft and related machinery	…	…	…	…
3040	Military fighting vehicles	…	…	…	…
309	Transport equipment n.e.c.	…	…	…	…
3091	Motorcycles	…	…	…	…
3092	Bicycles and invalid carriages	…	…	…	…
3099	Other transport equipment n.e.c.	…	…	…	…
3100	Furniture	71	61	2534	2210
321	Jewellery, bijouterie and related articles	…	…	…	…
3211	Jewellery and related articles	…	…	…	…
3212	Imitation jewellery and related articles	…	…	…	…
3220	Musical instruments	…	…	…	…
3230	Sports goods	…	…	…	…
3240	Games and toys	…	…	…	…
3250	Medical and dental instruments and supplies	…	…	…	…
3290	Other manufacturing n.e.c.	…	…	…	…
331	Repair of fabricated metal products/machinery	…	…	…	…
3311	Repair of fabricated metal products	…	…	…	…
3312	Repair of machinery	…	…	…	…
3313	Repair of electronic and optical equipment	…	…	…	…
3314	Repair of electrical equipment	…	…	…	…
3315	Repair of transport equip., excl. motor vehicles	…	…	…	…
3319	Repair of other equipment	…	…	…	…
3320	Installation of industrial machinery/equipment	…	…	…	…
C	Total manufacturing	…	…	…	…

Canada

ISIC	Industry	Output Note	Output 2006	Output 2007	Output 2008	Output 2009	Value added Note	VA 2006	VA 2007	VA 2008	VA 2009	GFCF Note	GFCF 2008	GFCF 2009
			(millions of Canadian Dollars)					(millions of Canadian Dollars)					(millions of Canadian Dollars)	
1010	Processing/preserving of meat		...	...	24200	24000		...	...	7347	7333		...	...
1020	Processing/preserving of fish, etc.		...	...	...	...		...	...	...	...		...	...
1030	Processing/preserving of fruit,vegetables		...	...	8527	8700		...	...	3627	3663			
1040	Vegetable and animal oils and fats		...	...	...	...		...	...	...	...			
1050	Dairy products		...	...	12600	12700		...	...	3318	3493			
106	Grain mill products,starches and starch products		...	...	...	...		...	...	...	...			
1061	Grain mill products		...	...	...	...		...	...	...	...			
1062	Starches and starch products		...	...	...	...		...	...	...	...			
107	Other food products		...	...	...	...		...	...	...	...			
1071	Bakery products		...	...	...	...		...	...	...	...			
1072	Sugar		...	...	...	...		...	...	...	...			
1073	Cocoa, chocolate and sugar confectionery		...	...	606	672		...	...	241	263			
1074	Macaroni, noodles, couscous, etc.		...	...	...	...		...	...	...	...			
1075	Prepared meals and dishes		...	...	917	1036		...	...	323	350			
1079	Other food products n.e.c.		...	...	5693	5570		...	...	1084	1086			
1080	Prepared animal feeds		...	...	1676	1693		...	...	962	935			
1101	Distilling, rectifying and blending of spirits		...	...	...	...		...	...	...	...			
1102	Wines		...	...	...	...		...	...	...	...			
1103	Malt liquors and malt		...	...	4411	4671		...	...	3486	3712			
1104	Soft drinks,mineral waters,other bottled waters		...	...	4069	4033		...	...	1859	1887			
1200	Tobacco products		...	...	...	...		...	...	...	...			
131	Spinning, weaving and finishing of textiles		...	...	2365	2098		...	...	1108	1012			
1311	Preparation and spinning of textile fibres		...	...	976	871		...	...	435	400			
1312	Weaving of textiles		...	...	762	617		...	...	340	280			
1313	Finishing of textiles		...	...	627	610		...	...	333	332			
139	Other textiles		...	...	...	...		...	...	...	...			
1391	Knitted and crocheted fabrics		...	...	134	91		...	...	43	32			
1392	Made-up textile articles, except apparel		...	...	4948	3501		...	...	1764	1329			
1393	Carpets and rugs		...	...	546	448		...	...	269	210			
1394	Cordage, rope, twine and netting		...	...	...	...		...	...	...	...			
1399	Other textiles n.e.c.		...	...	6301	5878		...	...	2996	2865			
1410	Wearing apparel, except fur apparel		...	...	...	...		...	...	...	...			
1420	Articles of fur		...	...	...	...		...	...	...	...			
1430	Knitted and crocheted apparel		...	...	385	306		...	...	214	180			
151	Leather;luggage,handbags,saddlery,harness;fur		...	...	...	...		...	...	...	...			
1511	Tanning/dressing of leather; dressing of fur		...	...	42	34		...	...	17	16			
1512	Luggage,handbags,etc.;saddlery/harness		...	...	...	...		...	...	...	...			
1520	Footwear		...	...	259	226		...	...	118	106			
1610	Sawmilling and planing of wood		...	...	13800	10900		...	...	4720	3849			
162	Wood products, cork, straw, plaiting materials		...	...	13700	11700		...	...	5293	4731			

1621	Veneer sheets and wood-based panels	3834	4522	1565	1402
1622	Builders' carpentry and joinery	4306	5167	2457	2028
1623	Wooden containers	593	656	279	268
1629	Other wood products;articles of cork,straw	2925	3339	992	1034
1701	Pulp, paper and paperboard	17300	20600	7309	5911
1702	Corrugated paper and paperboard	4268	4353	1797	1743
1709	Other articles of paper and paperboard	11200	12300	6420	5828
181	Printing and service activities related to printing	2135	2372	1586	1434
1811	Printing	1487	1645	1075	986
1812	Service activities related to printing	648	727	511	448
1820	Reproduction of recorded media	302	430	251	178
1910	Coke oven products	2989	3516	892	824
1920	Refined petroleum products	...	...	...	...
201	Basic chemicals,fertilizers, etc.	18500	23700	7393	6801
2011	Basic chemicals	11200	12800	5263	4829
2012	Fertilizers and nitrogen compounds	613	581	126	143
2013	Plastics and synthetic rubber in primary forms	6671	10300	2004	1828
202	Other chemical products	13400	13200	6716	6946
2021	Pesticides and other agrochemical products	970	869	451	525
2022	Paints,varnishes;printing ink and mastics	2947	3071	1254	1141
2023	Soap,cleaning and cosmetic preparations	1270	1270	510	536
2029	Other chemical products n.e.c.	8198	8000	4501	4744
2030	Man-made fibres	488	637	201	147
2100	Pharmaceuticals,medicinal chemicals, etc.	2968	2934	1695	1785
221	Rubber products	5589	6117	2377	2271
2211	Rubber tyres and tubes	1831	1844	439	563
2219	Other rubber products	3758	4272	1938	1708
2220	Plastics products	16500	19100	8050	7201
2310	Glass and glass products	3106	3649	1863	1632
239	Non-metallic mineral products n.e.c.	...	...	...	...
2391	Refractory products	389	450	247	202
2392	Clay building materials	32	34	21	21
2393	Other porcelain and ceramic products	...	...	...	...
2394	Cement, lime and plaster	2545	2734	1524	1411
2395	Articles of concrete, cement and plaster	6025	6794	2929	2716
2396	Cutting, shaping and finishing of stone	...	...	...	...
2399	Other non-metallic mineral products n.e.c.	6289	8010	2982	2346
2410	Basic iron and steel	10200	17100	5044	3008
2420	Basic precious and other non-ferrous metals	21800	30300	10200	6939
243	Casting of metals	4810	7244	2594	1568
2431	Casting of iron and steel	4018	6061	1988	1206
2432	Casting of non-ferrous metals	792	1183	606	362
251	Struct.metal products, tanks, reservoirs	16700	18700	8451	7809
2511	Structural metal products	12000	13600	5855	5341
2512	Tanks, reservoirs and containers of metal	3701	3951	1949	1912

continued

Canada

		Output					Value added					Gross fixed capital formation		
		(millions of Canadian Dollars)					(millions of Canadian Dollars)					(millions of Canadian Dollars)		
ISIC	Industry	Note	2006	2007	2008	2009	Note	2006	2007	2008	2009	Note	2008	2009
2513	Steam generators, excl. hot water boilers		...	...	1114	1033		...	...	646	556		...	...
2520	Weapons and ammunition		...	...	...	...		...	...	...	...		...	...
259	Other metal products;metal working services		...	...	31300	26000		...	...	14200	11600		...	...
2591	Forging,pressing,stamping,roll-forming of metal		...	...	5214	3856		...	...	2048	1445		...	...
2592	Treatment and coating of metals; machining		...	...	9383	8398		...	...	4411	3817		...	...
2593	Cutlery, hand tools and general hardware		...	...	11700	9903		...	...	5710	4644		...	...
2599	Other fabricated metal products h.e.c.		...	...	4909	3800		...	...	2049	1715		...	...
2610	Electronic components and boards		...	...	3324	2719		...	...	1751	1286		...	...
2620	Computers and peripheral equipment		...	...	2784	2142		...	...	1049	876		...	...
2630	Communication equipment		...	...	5579	5598		...	...	3124	3369		...	...
2640	Consumer electronics		...	...	390	437		...	...	212	239		...	...
265	Measuring,testing equipment; watches, etc.		...	...	...	...		...	...	...	...		...	...
2651	Measuring/testing/navigating equipment,etc.		...	...	5102	5355		...	...	3034	3156		...	...
2652	Watches and clocks		...	...	...	...		...	...	...	...		...	...
2660	Irradiation/electromedical equipment,etc.		...	...	...	...		...	...	...	...		...	...
2670	Optical instruments and photographic equipment		...	...	...	...		...	...	...	...		...	...
2680	Magnetic and optical media		...	...	3609	3307		...	...	1875	1656		...	...
2710	Electric motors,generators,transformers,etc.		...	...	4194	4229		...	...	1912	2005		...	...
2720	Batteries and accumulators		...	...	181	137		...	...	66	57		...	...
273	Wiring and wiring devices		...	...	...	...		...	...	...	...		...	...
2731	Fibre optic cables		...	...	2070	1677		...	...	676	543		...	...
2732	Other electronic and electric wires and cables		...	...	768	648		...	...	403	335		...	...
2733	Wiring devices		...	...	991	811		...	...	399	335		...	...
2740	Electric lighting equipment		...	...	...	...		...	...	...	...		...	...
2750	Domestic appliances		...	...	842	600		...	...	386	295		...	...
2790	Other electrical equipment		...	...	...	...		...	...	...	...		...	...
281	General-purpose machinery		...	...	5999	5748		...	...	2152	2133		...	...
2811	Engines/turbines,excl.aircraft,vehicle engines		...	...	...	...		...	...	...	...		...	...
2812	Fluid power equipment		...	...	27700	24900		...	...	12300	10800		...	...
2813	Other pumps, compressors, taps and valves		...	...	459	356		...	...	208	163		...	...
2814	Bearings, gears, gearing and driving elements		...	...	1476	1140		...	...	690	549		...	...
2815	Ovens, furnaces and furnace burners		...	...	4714	3500		...	...	1939	1518		...	...
2816	Lifting and handling equipment		...	...	...	...		...	...	...	...		...	...
2817	Office machinery, excl.computers,etc.		...	...	593	672		...	...	326	347		...	...
2818	Power-driven hand tools		...	...	...	...		...	...	...	...		...	...
2819	Other general-purpose machinery		...	...	297	230		...	...	172	139		...	...
282	Special-purpose machinery		...	...	1429	1115		...	...	713	514		...	...
2821	Agricultural and forestry machinery		...	...	...	...		...	...	...	...		...	...
2822	Metal-forming machinery and machine tools		...	...	...	...		...	...	...	...		...	...
2823	Machinery for metallurgy		...	...	...	...		...	...	...	...		...	...
2824	Mining, quarrying and construction machinery		...	...	...	...		...	...	...	...		...	...

2825	Food/beverage/tobacco processing machinery	:	:	:	:
2826	Textile/apparel/leather production machinery	:	:	:	:
2829	Other special-purpose machinery	:	:	:	:
2910	Motor vehicles	48900	39900	8498	7894
2920	Automobile bodies, trailers and semi-trailers	1259	830	466	315
2930	Parts and accessories for motor vehicles	:	:	:	:
301	Building of ships and boats	1259	1175	584	542
3011	Building of ships and floating structures	762	830	353	394
3012	Building of pleasure and sporting boats	497	345	232	148
3020	Railway locomotives and rolling stock	:	:	:	:
3030	Air and spacecraft and related machinery	:	:	:	:
3040	Military fighting vehicles	:	:	:	:
309	Transport equipment n.e.c.	:	:	:	:
3091	Motorcycles	:	:	:	:
3092	Bicycles and invalid carriages	:	:	:	:
3099	Other transport equipment n.e.c.	:	:	:	:
3100	Furniture	9201	8016	4668	4072
321	Jewellery, bijouterie and related articles	:	:	:	:
3211	Jewellery and related articles	:	:	:	:
3212	Imitation jewellery and related articles	:	:	:	:
3220	Musical instruments	:	:	:	:
3230	Sports goods	:	:	:	:
3240	Games and toys	:	:	:	:
3250	Medical and dental instruments and supplies	:	:	:	:
3290	Other manufacturing n.e.c.	:	:	:	:
331	Repair of fabricated metal products/machinery	:	:	:	:
3311	Repair of fabricated metal products	:	:	:	:
3312	Repair of machinery	:	:	:	:
3313	Repair of electronic and optical equipment	:	:	:	:
3314	Repair of electrical equipment	:	:	:	:
3315	Repair of transport equip., excl. motor vehicles	:	:	:	:
3319	Repair of other equipment	:	:	:	:
3320	Installation of industrial machinery/equipment	:	:	:	:
C	Total manufacturing	:	:	:	:

Canada

Index numbers of industrial production

ISIC Revision 3

(2005=100)

ISIC	Industry	Note	1999	2000	2001	2002	2003	2004	2005	2006	2007	2008	2009	2010
15	Food and beverages		86	90	96	95	94	96	100	103	102	102	103	105
16	Tobacco products		190	187	159	155	135	110	100	85	53	55	61	60
17	Textiles		119	133	128	130	117	113	100	90	76	67	55	56
18	Wearing apparel, fur		129	154	148	136	133	113	100	90	77	60	50	56
19	Leather, leather products and footwear		206	241	206	199	158	122	100	90	96	89	81	83
20	Wood products (excl. furniture)		77	85	81	90	90	94	100	99	89	74	64	71
21	Paper and paper products		95	99	93	98	98	99	100	89	90	82	71	72
22	Printing and publishing		91	98	104	102	98	100	100	98	98	97	90	86
23	Coke,refined petroleum products,nuclear fuel		97	93	106	103	105	104	100	94	96	92	88	91
24	Chemicals and chemical products		83	93	95	99	102	102	100	101	97	93	83	87
25	Rubber and plastics products		84	94	93	100	99	102	100	93	91	83	69	73
26	Non-metallic mineral products		75	81	86	88	92	96	100	101	103	98	84	90
27	Basic metals		84	91	89	93	92	97	100	100	97	97	72	82
28	Fabricated metal products		83	103	100	102	99	98	100	102	102	94	80	84
29	Machinery and equipment n.e.c.		85	95	95	94	91	98	100	101	100	96	81	86
30	Office, accounting and computing machinery		71	106	92	95	94	100	100	103	106	102	89	117
31	Electrical machinery and apparatus		103	130	127	108	94	100	100	96	96	93	82	87
32	Radio,television and communication equipment		169	213	104	83	82	94	100	100	98	103	96	101
33	Medical, precision and optical instruments		72	82	80	86	91	96	100	106	103	99	100	91
34	Motor vehicles, trailers, semi-trailers		99	100	92	95	95	96	100	96	93	73	53	68
35	Other transport equipment		96	103	99	85	90	92	100	105	113	117	109	100
36	Furniture; manufacturing n.e.c.		90	102	100	107	101	104	100	95	89	80	72	74
37	Recycling		...	...	...	...	...	...	...	...	...	...	...	...
D	Total manufacturing		91	101	97	97	96	98	100	99	97	90	79	83

China

Concepts and definitions of variables:
No deviations from the standard UN concepts and definitions are reported.

Related national publications:
Statistical Yearbook of China (annual), published by the National Bureau of Statistics, Beijing.

Supplier of information:
National Bureau of Statistics, Beijing.

Basic source of data:
Annual census/exhaustive survey.

Major deviations from ISIC (Revision 3):
'Other manufacturing n.e.c. (ISIC 3699)' includes 'Maintenance and repair of motor vehicles (ISIC 5020)'; 'TV and radio receivers and associated goods (ISIC 3230) includes 'Mobile communication & terminal equipment manufacturing'.

Reference period:
Calendar year.

Scope:
Prior to 2010: all industrial enterprises with annual revenue from principal business above 5 million Chinese Yuan; from 2010 onwards: all industrial enterprises with annual revenue from principal business above 20 million Chinese Yuan.

Method of data collection:
Mail questionnaires; online survey.

Type of enumeration:
Complete enumeration.

Adjusted for non-response:
No.

China

ISIC Revision 3		Number of enterprises (number)					Number of employees (thousands)					Wages and salaries paid to employees (billions of Chinese Yuan)				
ISIC	Industry	Note	2007	2008	2009	2010	Note	2007	2008	2009	2010	Note	2007	2008	2009	2010
151	Processed meat,fish,fruit,vegetables,fats		10860	13346	13187	13644		1934	2240	2208	2416		33.5	47.5	77.2	87.2
1511	Processing/preserving of meat		3215	3932	4206	4375		685	807	886	1003		11.5	16.2	28.7	36.2
1512	Processing/preserving of fish		2014	2380	2474	2471		449	478	495	511		8.3	10.6	21.5	19.8
1513	Processing/preserving of fruit & vegetables		3363	4244	4149	4381		524	608	559	605		8.4	12.4	16.6	19.8
1514	Vegetable and animal oils and fats		2268	2790	2358	2417		276	347	268	298		5.3	8.2	10.4	11.4
1520	Dairy products		988	1078	1076	1065		248	254	266	278		5.4	7.0	10.3	10.8
153	Grain mill products; starches; animal feeds		7740	9895	10601	11175		752	951	1037	1145		12.8	20.9	37.5	40.6
1531	Grain mill products		4272	5633	6105	6494		319	438	467	523		4.7	8.6	14.0	16.6
1532	Starches and starch products		782	969	988	985		156	173	186	193		2.2	3.4	9.5	7.9
1533	Prepared animal feeds		2686	3293	3508	3696		278	340	384	429		5.9	8.9	14.0	16.1
154	Other food products		7044	8985	10029	10724		1316	1534	1642	1792		25.2	35.9	52.6	60.4
1541	Bakery products		993	1320	1493	1547		188	234	262	287		3.5	5.3	7.4	8.4
1542	Sugar		292	318	309	307		150	155	145	148		2.7	3.0	4.1	4.4
1543	Cocoa, chocolate and sugar confectionery		554	736	816	901		103	132	144	165		2.7	4.0	4.7	6.0
1544	Macaroni, noodles & similar products		950	1201	1290	1354		258	293	308	325		4.3	6.8	9.8	11.6
1549	Other food products n.e.c.		4255	5410	6121	6615		617	720	783	867		12.0	16.8	26.6	29.9
155	Beverages		3660	4334	4456	4692		916	1018	1046	1129		19.0	26.3	37.1	44.2
1551	Distilling, rectifying & blending of spirits		1586	1904	1996	2122		400	449	452	496		6.5	10.0	15.1	18.7
1552	Wines		280	349	228	246		34	41	26	27		0.8	1.0	1.2	1.3
1553	Malt liquors and malt		585	584	584	558		245	251	251	246		5.3	6.4	8.8	9.1
1554	Soft drinks; mineral waters		1209	1497	1648	1766		236	278	316	359		6.5	8.8	11.9	15.0
1600	Tobacco products		150	156	158	151		186	198	200	211		12.2	15.1	16.0	21.4
171	Spinning, weaving and finishing of textiles		16600	19472	18800	19035		4150	4217	3913	3989		62.9	82.4	101.2	120.6
1711	Textile fibre preparation; textile weaving		14096	16478	15956	16183		3557	3556	3285	3336		51.6	67.3	83.8	100.3
1712	Finishing of textiles		2504	2994	2844	2852		593	661	628	653		11.3	15.2	17.4	20.3
172	Other textiles		6026	7513	7129	7236		1060	1207	1074	1081		17.1	26.1	27.8	32.5
1721	Made-up textile articles, except apparel		3123	3859	3433	3405		604	701	567	566		9.7	15.0	14.7	17.3
1722	Carpets and rugs		327	385	371	360		87	84	73	70		1.1	1.6	1.6	2.0
1723	Cordage, rope, twine and netting		255	323	331	316		32	39	35	33		0.5	0.9	0.8	0.9
1729	Other textiles n.e.c.		2321	2946	2994	3155		338	383	399	412		5.7	8.7	10.7	12.3
1730	Knitted and crocheted fabrics and articles		6824	7942	7854	8463		1394	1436	1422	1631		24.8	30.2	34.2	46.5
1810	Wearing apparel, except fur apparel		21495	25770	18348	18629		5477	5892	4464	4427		99.2	126.7	111.6	130.0
1820	Dressing & dyeing of fur; processing of fur		391	503	537	583		55	62	68	74		0.8	1.0	1.6	2.2
191	Tanning, dressing and processing of leather		2611	3180	3158	3251		643	753	707	688		11.5	14.9	17.4	20.3
1911	Tanning and dressing of leather		783	821	844	881		160	193	180	152		3.2	3.7	5.0	5.1
1912	Luggage, handbags, etc.; saddlery & harness		1828	2359	2314	2370		483	560	526	536		8.3	11.2	12.4	15.2
1920	Footwear		4868	5656	5624	5897		2108	2274	2137	2322		38.1	47.7	53.3	65.1
2010	Sawmilling and planing of wood		954	1389	1491	1648		105	144	152	167		1.5	2.7	3.4	4.3
202	Products of wood, cork, straw, etc.		7987	10193	9903	10258		1147	1371	1242	1329		18.4	27.2	30.7	39.1
2021	Veneer sheets, plywood, particle board, etc.		4357	5590	5782	5996		619	774	750	799		9.7	15.6	19.0	24.0
2022	Builders' carpentry and joinery		725	1007	1106	1233		108	130	138	159		2.2	2.8	3.5	4.8
2023	Wooden containers		313	414	444	450		33	29	30	35		0.5	0.6	0.9	1.1
2029	Other wood products; articles of cork/straw		2592	3182	2571	2579		388	438	324	337		6.0	8.2	7.3	9.2
210	Paper and paper products		11373	13181	10022	10357		2086	2237	1551	1603		37.6	49.8	42.6	54.1
2101	Pulp, paper and paperboard		3560	3963	871	836		794	832	140	128		13.9	18.2	3.8	4.0
2102	Corrugated paper and paperboard		6248	7193	7087	7323		1101	1172	1176	1214		19.9	26.0	32.3	41.9
2109	Other articles of paper and paperboard		1565	2025	2064	2198		192	234	235	262		3.8	5.6	6.4	8.2
221	Publishing		...	...	...			...	...	...			...	...	...	
2211	Publishing of books and other publications		...	...	...			...	...	...			...	...	...	
2212	Publishing of newspapers, journals, etc.		...	...	...			...	...	...			...	...	...	
2213	Publishing of recorded media		...	...	...			...	...	...			...	...	...	
2219	Other publishing		...	...	...			...	...	...			...	...	...	

Code	ISIC category												
222	Printing and related service activities	5001	6372	6532	6770	712	805	809	839	15.4	20.4	22.8	26.3
2221	Printing	4785	6084	6260	6485	680	766	776	807	14.6	19.4	21.8	25.1
2222	Service activities related to printing	216	288	272	285	32	39	33	32	0.8	1.0	1.0	1.2
2230	Reproduction of recorded media	82	109	86	80	12	16	12	12	0.3	0.5	0.4	0.5
2310	Coke oven products	901	957	843	794	378	412	399	428	6.8	9.1	16.3	18.5
2320	Refined petroleum products	1244	1454	1489	1525	423	438	440	483	17.5	20.6	25.4	32.7
2330	Processing of nuclear fuel	...	...	...	...	...	...	...	...	...	...	...	...
241	Basic chemicals	11042	12723	12862	13109	2212	2423	2385	2514	49.8	67.2	84.9	100.3
2411	Basic chemicals, except fertilizers	6848	7887	7978	8033	1159	1292	1290	1354	26.7	36.9	45.8	53.9
2412	Fertilizers and nitrogen compounds	2184	2483	2631	2650	707	733	744	747	13.4	17.5	24.7	28.0
2413	Plastics in primary forms; synthetic rubber	2010	2353	2253	2426	346	398	350	413	9.7	12.8	14.3	18.5
242	Other chemicals	17954	22317	22846	23544	3037	3471	3648	3978	77.9	109.0	134.6	158.4
2421	Pesticides and other agro-chemical products	809	965	974	959	161	181	179	192	3.1	4.5	6.3	6.8
2422	Paints, varnishes, printing ink and mastics	3065	3818	3804	3948	289	331	334	371	7.7	10.5	13.4	15.4
2423	Pharmaceuticals, medicinal chemicals, etc.	5748	6524	6807	7039	1374	1508	1605	1732	31.5	44.0	62.4	72.4
2424	Soap, cleaning & cosmetic preparations	1086	1360	988	990	227	253	230	245	13.3	19.6	11.0	13.6
2429	Other chemical products n.e.c.	7246	9650	10273	10608	987	1199	1299	1438	22.2	30.5	41.5	50.2
2430	Man-made fibres	1494	1942	1859	1852	436	427	390	415	8.8	10.6	12.0	14.4
251	Rubber products	3086	3929	4009	4148	659	745	765	812	12.9	18.1	23.5	28.7
2511	Rubber tyres and tubes	500	605	626	629	263	305	323	333	5.5	8.1	11.7	13.9
2519	Other rubber products	2586	3324	3383	3519	397	440	443	480	7.4	10.0	11.8	14.9
2520	Plastic products	15214	19297	19206	20265	2205	2456	2423	2688	44.0	59.9	66.6	83.9
2610	Glass and glass products	3648	4438	4564	4839	817	911	908	1005	14.0	20.1	24.1	30.7
269	Non-metallic mineral products n.e.c.	21258	26839	27498	29417	3774	4196	4141	4395	65.1	92.0	110.4	134.4
2691	Pottery, china and earthenware	1896	2173	2337	2424	568	569	567	614	9.5	12.2	13.6	17.7
2692	Refractory ceramic products	1630	2120	2142	2320	258	285	304	317	4.2	6.8	8.3	9.2
2693	Struct.non-refractory clay; ceramic products	3304	4735	5233	5720	634	764	798	866	10.7	15.8	20.2	25.7
2694	Cement, lime and plaster	5383	5694	5625	5451	1225	1207	1174	1142	19.4	24.5	30.6	35.1
2695	Articles of concrete, cement and plaster	4019	5407	5492	6262	527	650	599	694	10.4	15.0	16.5	21.8
2696	Cutting, shaping & finishing of stone	1779	2255	2439	2648	194	262	267	288	4.1	7.1	8.7	10.1
2699	Other non-metallic mineral products n.e.c.	3247	4455	4230	4592	369	459	432	474	6.8	10.6	12.4	14.9
2710	Basic iron and steel	7161	8012	7773	7881	3044	3135	3230	3456	91.5	115.3	166.1	192.8
2720	Basic precious and non-ferrous metals	6117	7434	7283	7409	1487	1756	1681	1811	39.1	52.4	71.5	87.3
273	Casting of metals	5065	6788	6869	7193	619	733	724	813	12.0	17.2	22.6	27.5
2731	Casting of iron and steel	4481	6022	6111	6402	543	637	628	708	9.9	14.6	18.4	23.4
2732	Casting of non-ferrous metals	584	766	758	791	76	96	96	105	2.1	2.6	4.2	4.2
281	Struct.metal products;tanks;steam generators	6826	10126	9419	9808	1030	1327	1189	1287	23.4	35.3	37.8	46.3
2811	Structural metal products	5028	7718	7923	8272	693	940	956	1038	14.8	24.0	29.1	36.2
2812	Tanks, reservoirs and containers of metal	1095	1494	568	588	201	234	81	92	5.0	6.7	2.8	3.4
2813	Steam generators	703	914	928	948	136	153	153	157	3.6	4.5	5.9	6.7
289	Other metal products; metal working services	18183	23339	21180	21916	2896	3272	2656	2842	59.0	80.6	74.0	91.3
2891	Metal forging/pressing/stamping/roll-forming	1414	2043	2089	2135	187	236	238	253	3.6	5.8	8.4	8.8
2892	Treatment & coating of metals	1466	2139	2109	2157	196	252	253	269	4.0	6.4	6.8	8.2
2893	Cutlery, hand tools and general hardware	4419	5242	5160	5314	772	806	746	783	14.9	19.2	19.2	23.8
2899	Other fabricated metal products n.e.c.	10884	13915	11822	12310	1742	1979	1419	1538	36.5	49.2	39.6	50.5
291	General purpose machinery	15835	22202	22052	23608	2812	3323	3242	3623	67.0	94.2	116.8	141.6
2911	Engines & turbines (not for transport equipment)	716	889	848	873	237	235	222	245	6.7	7.6	10.8	11.3
2912	Pumps, compressors, taps and valves	4495	6150	6380	6915	697	828	823	920	15.6	22.7	27.7	32.8
2913	Bearings, gears, gearing & driving elements	2549	3446	3392	3584	472	555	518	561	9.0	13.2	15.6	20.3
2914	Ovens, furnaces and furnace burners	581	798	298	330	78	84	30	35	1.6	2.2	1.1	1.3
2915	Lifting and handling equipment	1463	2114	2150	2302	313	388	406	432	9.0	13.2	17.6	20.6
2919	Other general purpose machinery	6031	8805	8984	9604	1014	1233	1242	1429	25.1	35.3	44.0	55.3
292	Special purpose machinery	16379	22996	22765	24056	2894	3646	3406	3740	67.7	102.9	119.1	147.7
2921	Agricultural and forestry machinery	1107	1392	1493	1556	250	268	263	262	3.9	5.4	8.4	9.3
2922	Machine tools	3362	4488	3842	4133	593	655	567	636	13.4	18.1	18.6	23.4
2923	Machinery for metallurgy	814	1160	1188	1278	158	197	198	219	4.2	6.5	7.7	9.6
2924	Machinery for mining and construction	2477	3689	3921	4205	529	695	740	830	13.6	21.6	28.8	38.0
2925	Food/beverage/tobacco processing machinery	690	844	911	967	113	110	117	126	2.2	3.0	4.5	4.8
2926	Machinery for textile, apparel and leather	1487	1674	1594	1666	251	248	226	245	5.2	6.1	6.7	8.2
2927	Weapons and ammunition	...	...	...	...	...	...	...	...	...	...	...	...
2929	Other special purpose machinery	6442	9683	9816	10251	1001	1305	1296	1423	25.1	37.7	44.4	54.2

continued

China

ISIC	Industry	Note	Number of enterprises (number)				Note	Number of employees (thousands)				Note	Wages and salaries paid to employees (billions of Chinese Yuan)			
			2007	2008	2009	2010		2007	2008	2009	2010		2007	2008	2009	2010
2930	Domestic appliances n.e.c.		2672	3463	3714	3856		836	994	1008	1174		19.4	29.6	35.1	46.4
3000	Office, accounting and computing machinery		1386	1621	1592	1569		1414	1612	1593	1770		44.6	71.6	66.5	81.8
3110	Electric motors, generators and transformers		3987	5434	5544	5846		956	1141	1123	1271		22.8	31.5	36.6	47.9
3120	Electricity distribution & control apparatus		3083	4143	4304	4449		502	575	626	684		13.1	17.6	22.8	28.1
3130	Insulated wire and cable		3645	4643	4653	4765		578	689	717	816		13.7	19.1	22.6	28.4
3140	Accumulators, primary cells and batteries		1061	1439	1522	1637		402	486	507	613		9.5	15.7	16.3	23.7
3150	Lighting equipment and electric lamps		2595	3240	3270	3442		632	667	647	701		12.3	15.6	17.1	22.3
3190	Other electrical equipment n.e.c.		2696	3682	2689	2751		503	658	510	528		11.5	18.1	17.4	18.8
3210	Electronic valves, tubes, etc.		7350	10036	10105	10786		3103	3653	3539	4289		84.2	113.8	117.1	159.0
3220	TV/radio transmitters; line comm. apparatus		1511	1789	1454	1371		806	929	587	641		34.6	49.2	52.3	59.8
3230	TV and radio receivers and associated goods		1611	1944	1886	1887		1035	1055	1008	1113		30.9	37.2	45.8	46.5
331	Medical, measuring, testing appliances, etc.		4130	5432	5265	5422		738	892	814	903		19.1	28.1	30.1	37.4
3311	Medical, surgical and orthopaedic equipment		881	1200	1262	1310		173	223	233	253		4.4	7.0	8.6	10.0
3312	Measuring/testing/navigating appliances,etc.		2355	3028	2740	2803		439	502	405	445		10.8	15.4	13.9	17.1
3313	Industrial process control equipment		894	1204	1263	1309		126	167	176	205		3.9	5.8	7.6	10.3
3320	Optical instruments & photographic equipment		890	1009	980	989		356	380	346	382		10.2	10.9	11.2	14.5
3330	Watches and clocks		401	426	402	400		130	122	112	123		2.4	2.6	2.5	3.1
3410	Motor vehicles		766	914	934	941		790	827	958	1104		29.5	34.8	67.6	82.4
3420	Automobile bodies, trailers & semi-trailers		330	429	448	464		104	114	100	131		3.5	5.1	4.0	6.1
3430	Parts/accessories for automobiles		7579	10331	10904	11953		1615	1928	2003	2380		37.0	52.7	68.1	93.8
351	Building and repairing of ships and boats		780	1177	1296	1384		304	463	519	646		10.7	18.8	32.2	35.9
3511	Building and repairing of ships		740	1110	1229	1317		298	455	511	638		10.6	18.5	32.0	35.7
3512	Building/repairing of pleasure/sport. boats		40	67	67	67		6	8	8	8		0.1	0.2	0.2	0.3
3520	Railway/tramway locomotives & rolling stock		622	810	836	847		271	304	328	344		7.6	9.6	14.6	18.4
3530	Aircraft and spacecraft		181	217	220	237		301	314	325	337		10.2	13.2	15.5	18.7
359	Transport equipment n.e.c.		2852	3508	3374	3429		623	672	614	664		12.2	16.5	19.8	22.1
3591	Motorcycles		2055	2585	2464	2533		465	498	457	498		8.8	12.2	14.9	16.9
3592	Bicycles and invalid carriages		693	780	760	723		140	155	137	146		3.2	3.9	3.7	4.5
3599	Other transport equipment n.e.c.		104	143	150	173		18	20	20	20		0.3	0.4	...	0.7
3610	Furniture		4110	5386	5576	5934		913	1044	986	1117		18.3	24.5	26.1	35.0
369	Manufacturing n.e.c.		9212	11013	11542	11849		2304	2515	2516	2620		43.2	54.4	63.5	76.0
3691	Jewellery and related articles		398	510	531	553		135	164	157	182		3.2	4.5	4.3	5.7
3692	Musical instruments		276	320	317	313		71	76	71	71		1.4	1.6	1.6	2.1
3693	Sports goods		1043	1297	1306	1331		296	318	311	327		5.5	6.7	7.3	9.1
3694	Games and toys		1712	1990	1943	1964		651	747	674	702		12.5	15.0	15.4	17.7
3699	Other manufacturing n.e.c.		5783	6896	7445	7688		1151	1209	1303	1338		20.7	26.6	34.9	41.4
3710	Recycling of metal waste and scrap		451	713	741	818		53	116	110	107		1.3	3.0	3.1	3.5
3720	Recycling of non-metal waste and scrap		201	374	424	484		13	26	27	32		0.3	0.6	0.8	1.1
D	Total manufacturing	a/	330163	417045	405183	422532	a/	72304	81464	77195	83915	a/	1594.4	2181.0	2592.1	3153.6

a/ Sum of available data.

China

ISIC	Industry	Note	Output at producers' prices (billions of Chinese Yuan) 2007	2008	2009	2010	Note	Value added at producers' prices (billions of Chinese Yuan) 2007	2008	2009	2010	Note	Gross fixed capital formation (billions of Chinese Yuan) 2009	2010
151	Processed meat,fish,fruit,vegetables,fats		1155.4	1548.6	1653.6	2024.0		304.5	...	...	...		...	...
1511	Processing/preserving of meat		383.1	513.7	608.3	765.4		102.4	...	...	...		...	...
1512	Processing/preserving of fish		202.6	242.6	278.9	315.8		53.2	...	...	...		...	...
1513	Processing/preserving of fruit & vegetables		204.8	274.0	267.5	345.3		61.3	...	...	...		...	...
1514	Vegetable and animal oils and fats		364.8	518.4	498.9	597.5		87.6	...	...	...		...	...
1520	Dairy products		149.4	165.7	187.6	220.1		43.7	...	...	...		...	...
153	Grain mill products; starches; animal feeds		626.8	886.5	1076.2	1385.2		166.7	...	...	...		...	...
1531	Grain mill products		263.2	369.9	468.5	622.7		71.4	...	...	...		...	...
1532	Starches and starch products		105.4	140.5	159.4	197.6		31.7	...	...	...		...	...
1533	Prepared animal feeds		258.3	376.1	448.4	564.9		63.7	...	...	...		...	...
154	Other food products		569.8	733.1	887.8	1120.0		178.6	...	...	...		...	...
1541	Bakery products		59.7	81.3	101.2	127.6		19.0	...	...	...		...	...
1542	Sugar		56.2	62.8	61.4	80.5		19.2	...	...	...		...	...
1543	Cocoa, chocolate and sugar confectionery		42.4	55.4	67.6	89.8		13.5	...	...	...		...	...
1544	Macaroni, noodles & similar products		97.3	131.1	159.0	191.1		30.9	...	...	...		...	...
1549	Other food products n.e.c.		314.2	402.7	498.6	631.0		95.9	...	...	...		...	...
155	Beverages		471.7	577.2	672.6	810.9		177.8	...	...	...		...	...
1551	Distilling, rectifying & blending of spirits		181.6	228.9	274.3	347.8		74.6	...	...	...		...	...
1552	Wines		22.3	28.5	24.2	30.4		8.8	...	...	...		...	...
1553	Malt liquors and malt		101.8	113.1	122.0	132.0		40.0	...	...	...		...	...
1554	Soft drinks; mineral waters		166.0	206.6	252.0	300.6		54.5	...	...	...		...	...
1600	Tobacco products		377.6	448.9	492.5	584.3		291.9	...	...	...		...	...
171	Spinning, weaving and finishing of textiles		1320.3	1464.1	1556.3	1915.2		340.9	...	...	...		...	...
1711	Textile fibre preparation; textile weaving		1082.8	1197.6	1275.1	1586.2		284.4	...	...	...		...	...
1712	Finishing of textiles		237.5	266.5	281.2	329.0		56.5	...	...	...		...	...
172	Other textiles		327.7	423.4	434.8	515.2		87.8	...	...	...		...	...
1721	Made-up textile articles, except apparel		186.5	243.2	233.6	275.0		50.1	...	...	...		...	...
1722	Carpets and rugs		18.7	23.0	25.1	28.8		5.9	...	...	...		...	...
1723	Cordage, rope, twine and netting		9.2	12.8	14.2	14.6		2.6	...	...	...		...	...
1729	Other textiles n.e.c.		113.2	144.5	161.9	196.8		29.1	...	...	...		...	...
1730	Knitted and crocheted fabrics and articles		311.7	356.6	393.3	518.1		87.0	...	...	...		...	...
1810	Wearing apparel, except fur apparel		1080.9	1297.0	1057.7	1253.0		315.6	...	...	...		...	...
1820	Dressing & dyeing of fur; processing of fur		22.6	30.6	38.5	46.5		6.7	...	...	...		...	...
191	Tanning, dressing and processing of leather		173.5	197.1	216.7	257.1		46.9	...	...	...		...	...
1911	Tanning and dressing of leather		90.9	96.9	107.9	120.0		24.0	...	...	...		...	...
1912	Luggage, handbags, etc.; saddlery & harness		82.7	100.2	108.8	137.1		22.8	...	...	...		...	...
1920	Footwear		327.9	377.3	409.7	501.3		98.0	...	...	...		...	...
2010	Sawmilling and planing of wood		32.2	52.5	65.5	85.7		10.0	...	...	...		...	...
202	Products of wood, cork, straw, etc.		356.4	475.3	538.5	682.7		104.9	...	...	...		...	...
2021	Veneer sheets, plywood, particle board, etc.		224.7	304.2	355.9	445.9		65.1	...	...	...		...	...
2022	Builders' carpentry and joinery		43.2	55.1	69.5	96.9		12.4	...	...	...		...	...
2023	Wooden containers		8.8	10.5	12.5	18.0		2.5	...	...	...		...	...
2029	Other wood products; articles of cork/straw		79.7	105.6	100.6	121.8		24.8	...	...	...		...	...
210	Paper and paper products		1003.7	1224.1	841.2	1062.5		276.0	...	...	...		...	...
2101	Pulp, paper and paperboard		411.5	498.5	78.8	85.1		113.4	...	...	...		...	...
2102	Corrugated paper and paperboard		516.6	626.7	647.9	826.3		141.2	...	...	...		...	...
2109	Other articles of paper and paperboard		75.6	99.0	114.5	151.1		21.4	...	...	...		...	...
221	Publishing		...	...	...	...		...	...	...	...		...	...
2211	Publishing of books and other publications		...	...	...	...		...	...	...	...		...	...
2212	Publishing of newspapers, journals, etc.		...	...	...	...		...	...	...	...		...	...
2213	Publishing of recorded media		...	...	...	...		...	...	...	...		...	...
2219	Other publishing		...	...	...	...		...	...	...	...		...	...

continued

China

ISIC Revision 3		Note	Output at producers' prices (billions of Chinese Yuan)				Note	Value added at producers' prices (billions of Chinese Yuan)				Note	Gross fixed capital formation (billions of Chinese Yuan)	
ISIC	Industry		2007	2008	2009	2010		2007	2008	2009	2010		2009	2010
222	Printing and related service activities		206.5	260.2	291.1	349.2		67.4	...	...	...		...	...
2221	Printing		197.8	249.5	280.3	336.0		64.3	...	...	...		...	...
2222	Service activities related to printing		8.7	10.7	10.8	13.1		3.1	...	...	...		...	...
2230	Reproduction of recorded media		5.3	8.3	6.2	7.1		1.8	...	...	...		...	...
2310	Coke oven products		248.7	421.3	377.5	485.5		78.8	...	...	...		...	...
2320	Refined petroleum products		1534.1	1836.8	1765.6	2431.0		230.2	...	...	...		...	...
2330	Processing of nuclear fuel		...	...	...	...		...	...	...	...		...	...
241	Basic chemicals		1769.4	2173.2	2107.5	2766.9		442.7	...	...	...		...	...
2411	Basic chemicals, except fertilizers		953.7	1158.6	1184.1	1582.4		245.6	...	...	...		...	...
2412	Fertilizers and nitrogen compounds		351.3	443.4	457.8	548.1		98.1	...	...	...		...	...
2413	Plastics in primary forms; synthetic rubber		464.3	571.2	465.6	636.3		99.0	...	...	...		...	...
242	Other chemicals		1684.7	2163.0	2534.5	3207.6		543.3	...	...	...		...	...
2421	Pesticides and other agro-chemical products		94.6	128.6	133.2	162.6		26.0	...	...	...		...	...
2422	Paints, varnishes, printing ink and mastics		200.5	233.4	263.1	324.6		56.8	...	...	...		...	...
2423	Pharmaceuticals, medicinal chemicals, etc.		636.2	787.5	944.3	1174.1		228.7	...	...	...		...	...
2424	Soap, cleaning & cosmetic preparations		157.3	182.7	172.9	198.3		56.8	...	...	...		...	...
2429	Other chemical products n.e.c.		596.2	830.8	1020.9	1348.0		175.1	...	...	...		...	...
2430	Man-made fibres		400.8	384.1	368.0	476.4		77.5	...	...	...		...	...
251	Rubber products		298.2	377.4	429.7	540.0		83.1	...	...	...		...	...
2511	Rubber tyres and tubes		173.2	215.1	243.7	306.6		45.2	...	...	...		...	...
2519	Other rubber products		125.0	162.4	185.9	233.4		38.0	...	...	...		...	...
2520	Plastic products		809.3	981.4	1064.4	1349.6		212.5	...	...	...		...	...
2610	Glass and glass products		261.8	349.4	388.6	502.7		80.9	...	...	...		...	...
269	Non-metallic mineral products n.e.c.		1314.5	1771.7	2059.6	2652.3		410.7	...	...	...		...	...
2691	Pottery, china and earthenware		97.7	122.0	144.2	191.0		33.9	...	...	...		...	...
2692	Refractory ceramic products		116.3	159.6	195.0	253.9		39.6	...	...	...		...	...
2693	Struct.non-refractory clay; ceramic products		203.2	262.8	325.8	421.2		62.3	...	...	...		...	...
2694	Cement, lime and plaster		410.8	519.4	620.4	757.7		130.0	...	...	...		...	...
2695	Articles of concrete, cement and plaster		224.3	321.5	368.4	498.5		65.1	...	...	...		...	...
2696	Cutting, shaping & finishing of stone		84.1	120.8	137.1	155.7		26.3	...	...	...		...	...
2699	Other non-metallic mineral products n.e.c.		178.0	265.7	268.5	374.4		53.4	...	...	...		...	...
2710	Basic iron and steel		3370.3	4472.8	4263.6	5183.4		900.7	...	...	...		...	...
2720	Basic precious and non-ferrous metals		1743.2	2018.1	1970.0	2698.1		432.6	...	...	...		...	...
273	Casting of metals		266.4	380.0	442.6	586.9		73.1	...	...	...		...	...
2731	Casting of iron and steel		206.4	303.3	355.9	473.1		57.9	...	...	...		...	...
2732	Casting of non-ferrous metals		60.0	76.7	86.7	113.8		15.2	...	...	...		...	...
281	Struct.metal products;tanks;steam generators		530.9	730.0	713.9	866.6		143.9	...	...	...		...	...
2811	Structural metal products		338.7	483.3	550.5	680.6		93.5	...	...	...		...	...
2812	Tanks, reservoirs and containers of metal		108.8	143.6	46.1	55.8		28.6	...	...	...		...	...
2813	Steam generators		83.4	103.2	117.3	130.1		21.8	...	...	...		...	...
289	Other metal products; metal working services		1140.5	1421.9	1283.1	1590.6		306.4	...	...	...		...	...
2891	Metal forging/pressing/stamping/roll-forming		97.9	146.5	174.0	212.9		28.2	...	...	...		...	...
2892	Treatment & coating of metals		86.5	113.8	127.1	162.4		21.4	...	...	...		...	...
2893	Cutlery, hand tools and general hardware		214.4	252.6	262.1	326.5		57.3	...	...	...		...	...
2899	Other fabricated metal products n.e.c.		741.7	908.9	719.9	888.7		199.5	...	...	...		...	...
291	General purpose machinery		1389.2	1809.7	1947.5	2495.3		375.5	...	...	...		...	...
2911	Engines & turbines (not for transport equipment)		136.4	152.2	160.8	202.3		38.6	...	...	...		...	...
2912	Pumps, compressors, taps and valves		287.2	386.9	421.2	548.2		80.3	...	...	...		...	...
2913	Bearings, gears, gearing & driving elements		135.2	199.7	217.6	273.9		40.6	...	...	...		...	...
2914	Ovens, furnaces and furnace burners		34.1	41.8	15.6	20.8		9.6	...	...	...		...	...
2915	Lifting and handling equipment		216.9	292.1	320.8	390.4		53.7	...	...	...		...	...
2919	Other general purpose machinery		579.5	737.1	811.5	1059.7		152.6	...	...	...		...	...

Code						
292	Special purpose machinery	1235.4	1722.9	1881.3	2457.8	356.6
2921	Agricultural and forestry machinery	108.9	135.3	161.6	177.2	27.3
2922	Machine tools	244.1	292.4	272.1	371.9	71.0
2923	Machinery for metallurgy	81.3	114.6	125.7	150.1	23.5
2924	Machinery for mining & construction	301.7	475.6	563.6	793.4	85.2
2925	Food/beverage/tobacco processing machinery	40.9	47.9	57.4	70.3	12.5
2926	Machinery for textile, apparel and leather	91.0	87.5	95.2	136.4	23.3
2927	Weapons and ammunition	...	...	...	...	...
2929	Other special purpose machinery	367.4	521.4	605.6	758.5	113.9
2930	Domestic appliances n.e.c.	425.4	517.6	570.9	729.3	99.8
3000	Office, accounting and computing machinery	1464.8	1612.2	1593.2	1942.5	219.4
3110	Electric motors, generators and transformers	422.0	573.1	677.9	880.4	112.9
3120	Electricity distribution & control apparatus	269.9	334.6	400.0	496.9	76.8
3130	Insulated wire and cable	566.7	706.2	752.4	946.0	134.2
3140	Accumulators, primary cells and batteries	175.8	278.8	302.6	446.7	43.1
3150	Lighting equipment and electric lamps	157.2	186.5	201.6	250.0	39.3
3190	Other electrical equipment n.e.c.	228.3	310.9	250.8	283.3	67.1
3210	Electronic valves, tubes, etc.	1331.6	1553.7	1574.5	2095.1	336.0
3220	TV/radio transmitters; line comm. apparatus	813.9	883.1	470.9	546.7	171.3
3230	TV and radio receivers and associated goods	883.0	861.4	858.4	962.5	157.2
331	Medical, measuring, testing appliances, etc.	296.6	382.6	403.7	520.1	93.5
3311	Medical, surgical and orthopaedic equipment	61.0	83.2	97.3	117.8	19.9
3312	Measuring/testing/navigating appliances,etc.	161.1	193.4	185.4	236.5	48.4
3313	Industrial process control equipment	74.5	106.0	120.9	165.7	25.2
3320	Optical instruments & photographic equipment	124.9	139.1	117.4	143.8	29.1
3330	Watches and clocks	18.5	20.0	20.6	23.0	5.3
3410	Motor vehicles	1181.2	1299.5	1709.4	2323.9	285.6
3420	Automobile bodies, trailers & semi-trailers	93.9	90.5	55.6	112.8	20.0
3430	Parts/accessories for automobiles	763.7	987.0	1207.7	1686.6	204.2
351	Building and repairing of ships and boats	235.7	385.5	494.0	593.1	67.7
3511	Building and repairing of ships	234.5	383.6	491.0	590.1	67.4
3512	Building/repairing of pleasure/sport. boats	1.2	1.9	3.0	2.9	0.3
3520	Railway/tramway locomotives & rolling stock	96.6	135.4	185.3	256.3	27.5
3530	Aircraft and spacecraft	102.4	119.9	135.3	159.8	29.2
359	Transport equipment n.e.c.	262.8	310.5	309.4	362.0	62.7
3591	Motorcycles	209.8	246.1	248.0	287.9	51.4
3592	Bicycles and invalid carriages	43.1	50.6	45.0	55.0	9.4
3599	Other transport equipment n.e.c.	9.9	13.7	16.4	19.1	1.9
3610	Furniture	242.5	307.3	343.1	441.5	64.7
369	Manufacturing n.e.c.	508.7	615.3	723.7	894.5	135.7
3691	Jewellery and related articles	76.1	93.7	99.9	149.1	14.9
3692	Musical instruments	14.2	17.3	17.6	21.6	3.8
3693	Sports goods	57.5	71.5	74.9	90.1	14.5
3694	Games and toys	95.1	112.1	120.8	143.4	26.1
3699	Other manufacturing n.e.c.	265.8	320.7	410.6	490.2	76.4
3710	Recycling of metal waste and scrap	59.4	101.2	127.5	206.3	13.7
3720	Recycling of non-metal waste and scrap	8.7	12.6	16.9	24.3	2.5
D	Total manufacturing a/	37250.7	46269.8	47920.0	60955.8	9853.3a/

a/ Sum of available data.

China, Hong Kong SAR

Supplier of information:
Census and Statistics Department, Hong Kong SAR.

Basic source of data:
Annual survey.

Major deviations from ISIC (Revision 4):
Data presented in accordance with ISIC (Revision 4) were originally classified according to Hong Kong Standard Industrial Classification (HSIC) system.

Reference period:
Calendar year.

Scope:
All privately owned establishments.

Method of data collection:
Mail questionnaires; direct interview in the field.

Type of enumeration:
Sample survey.

Adjusted for non-response:
Yes.

Concepts and definitions of variables:
Wages and salaries is compensation of employees.
Output refers to gross output.
Value added refers to total value added.

Related national publications:
Key Statistics on Business Performance and Operating Characteristics of the Industrial Sector, published by the Census and Statistics Department, Hong Kong SAR.

China, Hong Kong SAR

ISIC Revision 4		Number of establishments (number)					Number of employees (number)					Wages and salaries paid to employees (millions of Hong Kong Dollars)				
ISIC — Industry	Note	Note	2007	2008	2009	2010	Note	2007	2008	2009	2010	Note	2007	2008	2009	2010
10 Food products			745	768	762	763		22900	23800	22900	23200		3080	3678	3171	3415
11 Beverages	a/	a/	21	20	20	19	a/	3400	3400	3900	3700	a/	772	757	835	819
12 Tobacco products	a/	a/	...	...	...	...	a/	...	...	...	...	a/	...	...	...	...
13 Textiles			740	701	613	574		6600	6900	5700	5000		1228	1284	1298	996
14 Wearing apparel			1458	1334	1157	1015		23300	19400	15400	11600		2992	3000	2176	1788
15 Leather and related products	b/	b/	1703	2047	1920	1825	b/	6400	6400	6100	6500	b/	1330	1177	1135	1203
16 Wood/wood products/cork,excl. furniture	b/	b/	...	...	...	...	b/	...	...	...	...	b/	...	...	...	...
17 Paper and paper products	c/	c/	3246	3232	3032	2980	c/	16800	18200	18500	16700	c/	3120	3227	3463	3200
18 Printing and reproduction of recorded media	c/	c/	...	...	...	...	c/	...	...	...	...	c/	...	...	...	...
19 Coke and refined petroleum products	d/	d/	550	556	503	493	d/	3500	3400	3500	3600	d/	918	791	695	751
20 Chemicals and chemical products	e/	e/	272	260	268	297	e/	5200	4700	4900	5300	e/	861	977	1021	967
21 Pharmaceuticals,medicinal chemicals, etc.	e/	e/	...	...	...	...	e/	...	...	...	...	e/	...	...	...	...
22 Rubber and plastics products	d/	d/	...	...	...	...	d/	...	...	...	...	d/	...	...	...	...
23 Other non-metallic mineral products	d/	d/	...	...	...	...	d/	...	...	...	...	d/	...	...	...	...
24 Basic metals	f/	f/	877	864	837	717	f/	4100	5000	5000	3600	f/	701	873	877	700
25 Fabricated metal products, except machinery	f/	f/	...	...	...	...	f/	...	...	...	...	f/	...	...	...	...
26 Computer, electronic and optical products	g/	g/	321	299	299	295	g/	9600	9300	9600	8900	g/	1529	1642	1679	1565
27 Electrical equipment	g/	g/	...	...	...	...	g/	...	...	...	...	g/	...	...	...	...
28 Machinery and equipment n.e.c.	h/	h/	635	472	451	417	h/	3400	3500	3900	3600	h/	699	816	743	847
29 Motor vehicles, trailers and semi-trailers	h/	h/	...	...	...	...	h/	...	...	...	...	h/	...	...	...	...
30 Other transport equipment	h/	h/	...	...	...	...	h/	...	...	...	...	h/	...	...	...	...
31 Furniture	b/	b/	...	...	...	...	b/	...	...	...	...	b/	...	...	...	...
32 Other manufacturing	b/	b/	...	...	...	...	b/	...	...	...	...	b/	...	...	...	...
33 Repair and installation of machinery/equipment	b/	b/	834	866	890	924	b/	9000	8500	10000	10000	b/	2379	2193	2628	2758
C Total manufacturing			11402	11419	10752	10320		114300	112500	109400	101700		19610	20415	19721	19009

a/ 11 includes 12.
b/ 15 includes 16, 31 and 32.
c/ 17 includes 18.
d/ 19 includes 22 and 23.
e/ 20 includes 21.
f/ 24 includes 25.
g/ 26 includes 27.
h/ 28 includes 29 and 30.

China, Hong Kong SAR

ISIC Revision 4		Output at producers' prices (millions of Hong Kong Dollars)					Value added at producers' prices (millions of Hong Kong Dollars)					Gross fixed capital formation (millions of Hong Kong Dollars)		
ISIC	Industry	Note	2007	2008	2009	2010	Note	2007	2008	2009	2010	Note	2009	2010
10	Food products		17500	18514	19701	23424		6346	6086	5712	5867		589	717
11	Beverages	a/	5122	5236	5180	5588	a/	1788	1618	1760	2180	a/	188	274
12	Tobacco products	a/	...	...	...	...	a/	...	...	...	...	a/	12	39
13	Textiles		7718	6474	4402	3875		1512	1314	1252	1071		25	47
14	Wearing apparel		19122	13861	10986	11907		3914	3474	3187	2420		31	60
15	Leather and related products	b/	10884	7792	7289	8344	b/	2434	2072	2121	2006	b/	...	...
16	Wood/wood products/cork,excl. furniture	b/	...	...	...	...	b/	...	...	...	...	b/	406	342
17	Paper and paper products	c/	15242	16243	14635	16557	c/	5979	5573	5071	5222	c/	...	...
18	Printing and reproduction of recorded media	c/	...	...	...	...	c/	...	...	...	...	c/	...	...
19	Coke and refined petroleum products	d/	6380	5700	4975	5389	d/	1882	1507	1407	1449	d/	77	125
20	Chemicals and chemical products	e/	10752	8778	7603	10515	e/	2023	2077	2177	2295	e/	823	225
21	Pharmaceuticals,medicinal chemicals, etc.	e/	...	...	...	...	e/	...	...	...	...	e/	...	...
22	Rubber and plastics products	d/	...	...	...	...	d/	...	...	...	...	d/	...	...
23	Other non-metallic mineral products	d/	...	...	...	...	d/	...	...	...	...	d/	23	72
24	Basic metals	f/	27609	48721	43258	69242	f/	936	1097	1151	1435	f/	...	...
25	Fabricated metal products, except machinery	f/	...	...	...	...	f/	...	...	...	...	f/	137	99
26	Computer, electronic and optical products	g/	8809	10554	11597	9908	g/	2887	2829	2514	2611	g/	...	...
27	Electrical equipment	g/	...	...	...	...	g/	...	...	...	...	g/	13	27
28	Machinery and equipment n.e.c.	h/	4736	3582	4210	6574	h/	1579	1480	1544	2799	h/	...	...
29	Motor vehicles, trailers and semi-trailers	h/	...	...	...	...	h/	...	...	...	...	h/	...	...
30	Other transport equipment	h/	...	...	...	...	h/	...	...	...	...	h/	...	...
31	Furniture	b/	...	...	...	...	b/	...	...	...	...	b/	...	...
32	Other manufacturing	b/	11131	13594	12884	17368	b/	4057	4654	4232	5606	b/	999	350
33	Repair and installation of machinery/equipment		...	...	...	...		...	...	...	...		...	...
C	Total manufacturing		145006	159048	146720	188690		35338	33780	32129	34961		3323	2378

a/ 11 includes 12.
b/ 15 includes 16, 31 and 32.
c/ 17 includes 18.
d/ 19 includes 22 and 23.
e/ 20 includes 21.
f/ 24 includes 25.
g/ 26 includes 27.
h/ 28 includes 29 and 30.

China, Hong Kong SAR

- 314 -

Index numbers of industrial production

ISIC Revision 4 — (2005=100)

ISIC	Industry	Note	1999	2000	2001	2002	2003	2004	2005	2006	2007	2008	2009	2010
10	Food products	a/	...	...	...	...	...	...	100	110	125	128	127	135
11	Beverages	a/	...	...	...	...	...	...	...	...	...	...	...	...
12	Tobacco products	a/	...	...	...	...	...	...	...	...	...	...	...	...
13	Textiles		...	...	...	...	...	...	100	98	90	80	62	57
14	Wearing apparel		...	...	...	...	...	...	100	99	83	65	46	40
15	Leather and related products	b/	...	...	...	...	...	...	100	106	114	114	109	116
16	Wood/wood products/cork,excl. furniture	b/	...	...	...	...	...	...	...	...	...	...	...	...
17	Paper and paper products	c/	...	...	...	...	...	...	100	103	105	105	97	98
18	Printing and reproduction of recorded media	c/	...	...	...	...	...	...	...	...	...	...	...	...
19	Coke and refined petroleum products	b/	...	...	...	...	...	...	...	...	...	...	...	...
20	Chemicals and chemical products	b/	...	...	...	...	...	...	...	...	...	...	...	...
21	Pharmaceuticals,medicinal chemicals, etc.	b/	...	...	...	...	...	...	...	...	...	...	...	...
22	Rubber and plastics products	b/	...	...	...	...	...	...	...	...	...	...	...	...
23	Other non-metallic mineral products	b/	...	...	...	...	...	...	...	...	...	...	...	...
24	Basic metals	d/	...	...	...	...	...	...	100	97	86	77	69	76
25	Fabricated metal products, except machinery	d/	...	...	...	...	...	...	...	...	...	...	...	...
26	Computer, electronic and optical products	d/	...	...	...	...	...	...	...	...	...	...	...	...
27	Electrical equipment	d/	...	...	...	...	...	...	...	...	...	...	...	...
28	Machinery and equipment n.e.c.	d/	...	...	...	...	...	...	...	...	...	...	...	...
29	Motor vehicles, trailers and semi-trailers	d/	...	...	...	...	...	...	...	...	...	...	...	...
30	Other transport equipment	d/	...	...	...	...	...	...	...	...	...	...	...	...
31	Furniture	b/	...	...	...	...	...	...	...	...	...	...	...	...
32	Other manufacturing	b/	...	...	...	...	...	...	...	...	...	...	...	...
33	Repair and installation of machinery/equipment	b/	...	...	...	...	...	...	...	...	...	...	...	...
C	Total manufacturing		...	...	...	...	...	...	100	102	101	94	86	89

a/ 10 includes 11 and 12.
b/ 15 includes 16, 19, 20, 21, 22, 23, 31, 32 and 33.
c/ 17 includes 18.
d/ 24 includes 25, 26, 27, 28, 29 and 30.

China, Macao SAR

Supplier of information:
Statistics and Census Service, Macao SAR.

Basic source of data:
Annual sample survey.

Major deviations from ISIC (Revision 3):
None reported.

Reference period:
Calendar year.

Scope:
All establishments.

Method of data collection:
Mail questionnaires; direct interview in the field.

Type of enumeration:
Systematic stratified sampling estimation method.

Adjusted for non-response:
Yes.

Concepts and definitions of variables:
No deviations from the standard UN concepts and definitions are reported.

Related national publications:
Brief report on Industrial Survey, published by the Statistics and Census Service, Macao SAR.

China, Macao SAR

ISIC	Industry	Note	Number of establishments (number) 2007	2008	2009	2010	Note	Number of persons engaged (number) 2007	2008	2009	2010	Note	Wages and salaries paid to employees (millions of Macao Patacas) 2007	2008	2009	2010
15	Food and beverages		199	219	234	247		2495	2778	3151	3559		181.6	214.9	248.9	269.2
16	Tobacco products		...	...	...	...		...	...	...	...		...	...	...	...
17	Textiles		55	40	32	26		2789	2097	1250	1029		193.8	153.5	98.0	81.8
18	Wearing apparel, fur		372	308	272	212		18168	14517	9264	4970		1009.3	857.5	577.2	315.9
19	Leather, leather products and footwear		11	4	3	3		394	104	48	51		19.8	4.3	2.5	2.6
20	Wood products (excl. furniture)		...	...	...	...		...	...	...	...		...	...	...	...
21	Paper and paper products		...	...	...	...		...	...	...	...		...	...	...	...
22	Printing and publishing		147	153	126	143		1319	1276	1377	1470		137.6	120.1	159.1	147.3
23	Coke,refined petroleum products,nuclear fuel		-	-	-	...		-	-	-	...		-	-	-	...
24	Chemicals and chemical products		...	...	...	...		...	...	...	...		...	...	...	...
25	Rubber and plastics products		...	...	...	...		...	...	...	...		...	...	...	...
26	Non-metallic mineral products		16	16	15	14		516	425	431	396		95.2	74.2	58.1	53.9
27	Basic metals		-	-	-	...		-	-	-	...		-	-	-	...
28	Fabricated metal products		...	...	...	...		...	...	...	...		...	...	...	...
29	Machinery and equipment n.e.c.		...	...	...	...		...	...	...	...		...	...	...	...
30	Office, accounting and computing machinery		1	1	1	1		...	...	...	...		...	...	...	...
31	Electrical machinery and apparatus		7	7	6	6		...	...	...	...		...	...	...	...
32	Radio,television and communication equipment		...	...	...	...		...	...	...	...		...	...	...	...
33	Medical, precision and optical instruments		...	...	...	...		...	...	...	...		...	...	...	...
34	Motor vehicles, trailers, semi-trailers		...	...	...	...		...	...	...	...		...	...	...	...
35	Other transport equipment															
36	Furniture; manufacturing n.e.c.		307a/	298a/	313b/	253b/		2507a/	2467a/	2382b/	1833b/		238.3a/	215.9a/	238.9b/	197.5b/
37	Recycling		...	...	...	...		...	...	...	...		...	...	...	...
D	Total manufacturing		1115	1046	1002	905		28523	24004	18208	13599		1912.9	1679.9	1419.3	1104.4

a/ 36 includes 16,20,21,24,25,28,29,32,33,34 and 35.
b/ 36 includes 16,20,21,24,25,28,29,32,33,34,35 and 37.

China, Macao SAR

| | | | Output at producers' prices | | | | | Value added at producers' prices | | | | | Gross fixed capital formation | |
| | | | (millions of Macao Patacas) | | | | | (millions of Macao Patacas) | | | | | (millions of Macao Patacas) | |
ISIC	Industry	Note	2007	2008	2009	2010	Note	2007	2008	2009	2010	Note	2009	2010
15	Food and beverages		646.8	634.9	672.2	900.2		356.2	350.3	363.4	454.9		36.4	47.5
16	Tobacco products		1877.5	1631.5	1026.9	919.1		352.2	291.1	189.6	152.4		133.9	5.4
17	Textiles		7650.3	6125.9	3529.6	1715.6		1557.0	1106.5	671.4	430.5		-7.0	3.4
18	Wearing apparel, fur		149.2	9.4	7.7	7.9		27.9	0.6	3.0	2.6		-	-
19	Leather, leather products and footwear		...	...	...	...		...	...	...	...		...	...
20	Wood products (excl. furniture)													
21	Paper and paper products		631.6	547.6	562.0	459.5		248.1	219.3	202.1	216.2		22.9	245.4
22	Printing and publishing		-	-	-	...		-	-	-	...		-	...
23	Coke,refined petroleum products,nuclear fuel		...	...	...	...		...	...	...	...		...	...
24	Chemicals and chemical products		...	...	...	...		...	...	...	...		...	...
25	Rubber and plastics products		1194.7	820.2	351.3	316.9		301.0	149.0	68.4	44.8		18.4	17.3
26	Non-metallic mineral products		...	...	...	...		...	...	...	...		-	...
27	Basic metals		-	-	-	...		-	-	-	...		-	...
28	Fabricated metal products		...	...	...	...		...	...	...	...		...	...
29	Machinery and equipment n.e.c.		...	...	...	...		...	...	...	...		...	...
30	Office, accounting and computing machinery		...	...	...	...		...	...	...	...		...	...
31	Electrical machinery and apparatus		...	...	...	...		...	...	...	...		...	...
32	Radio,television and communication equipment		...	...	...	...		...	...	...	...		...	...
33	Medical, precision and optical instruments		...	...	...	...		...	...	...	...		...	...
34	Motor vehicles, trailers, semi-trailers		...	...	...	...		...	...	...	...		...	...
35	Other transport equipment		1019.5a/	1054.2a/	1152.4b/	996.6b/		350.5a/	429.7a/	491.0b/	425.2b/		33.2b/	32.6b/
36	Furniture; manufacturing n.e.c.		...	...	...	...		...	...	...	...		...	...
37	Recycling		...	...	...	...		...	...	...	...		...	...
D	Total manufacturing		13769.5	11379.3	7620.2	5743.4		3321.8	2635.3	2062.6	1818.1		241.8	353.7

a/ 36 includes 16,20,21,24,25,28,29,32,33,34 and 35.
b/ 36 includes 16,20,21,24,25,28,29,32,33,34,35 and 37.

China, Macao SAR

	ISIC Revision 3		Index numbers of industrial production (2005=100)											
ISIC	Industry	Note	1999	2000	2001	2002	2003	2004	2005	2006	2007	2008	2009	2010
15	Food and beverages		...	...	...	...	...	...	...	...	...	...	...	...
16	Tobacco products		38	56	59	60	75	93	100	99	99	102	102	110
17	Textiles		125	78	87	107	122	113	100	111	115	68	18	10
18	Wearing apparel, fur		144	101	106	123	144	139	100	92	86	60	15	9
19	Leather, leather products and footwear		...	...	...	...	...	...	...	...	...	...	...	...
20	Wood products (excl. furniture)		...	...	...	...	...	...	...	...	...	...	...	...
21	Paper and paper products		...	...	...	...	...	...	...	...	...	...	...	...
22	Printing and publishing		...	...	...	...	...	...	...	...	...	...	...	...
23	Coke,refined petroleum products,nuclear fuel		...	...	...	...	...	...	...	...	...	...	...	...
24	Chemicals and chemical products		...	...	...	...	...	...	...	...	...	...	...	...
25	Rubber and plastics products		...	...	...	...	...	...	...	...	...	...	...	...
26	Non-metallic mineral products		42	26	26	18	40	43	100	140	136	101	33	33
27	Basic metals		...	...	...	...	...	...	...	...	...	...	...	...
28	Fabricated metal products		...	...	...	...	...	...	...	...	...	...	...	...
29	Machinery and equipment n.e.c.		...	...	...	...	...	...	...	...	...	...	...	...
30	Office, accounting and computing machinery		...	...	...	...	...	...	...	...	...	...	...	...
31	Electrical machinery and apparatus		...	...	...	...	...	...	...	...	...	...	...	...
32	Radio,television and communication equipment		...	...	...	...	...	...	...	...	...	...	...	...
33	Medical, precision and optical instruments		...	...	...	...	...	...	...	...	...	...	...	...
34	Motor vehicles, trailers, semi-trailers		...	...	...	...	...	...	...	...	...	...	...	...
35	Other transport equipment		...	...	...	...	...	...	...	...	...	...	...	...
36	Furniture; manufacturing n.e.c.		...	...	...	...	...	...	...	...	...	...	...	...
37	Recycling		...	...	...	...	...	...	...	...	...	...	...	...
D	Total manufacturing		132	94	100	116	136	128	100	99	94	63	29	31

Colombia

Supplier of information:
Departamento Administrativo Nacional de Estadística, Bogotá.

Basic source of data:
Not reported.

Major deviations from ISIC (Revision 3):
Data presented in accordance with ISIC (Revision 3) were originally classified according to the national classification system.

Reference period:
Fiscal year.

Scope:
Not reported.

Method of data collection:
Mail questionnaires.

Type of enumeration:
Sample survey.

Adjusted for non-response:
Not reported.

Concepts and definitions of variables:
Wages and salaries refers to permanent and temporary staff hired directly by the establishment.

Related national publications:
None reported.

Colombia

ISIC	Industry	Note	Number of establishments (number)				Note	Number of employees (number)				Note	Wages and salaries paid to employees (billions of Colombian Pesos)			
			2007	2008	2009	2010		2007	2008	2009	2010		2007	2008	2009	2010
151	Processed meat,fish,fruit,vegetables,fats		272	296	320	357		24304	26713	26737	28399		277.8	332.9	366.1	392.1
1511	Processing/preserving of meat		:	:	:	:		:	:	:	:		:	:	:	:
1512	Processing/preserving of fish		:	:	:	:		:	:	:	:		:	:	:	:
1513	Processing/preserving of fruit & vegetables		:	:	:	:		:	:	:	:		:	:	:	:
1514	Vegetable and animal oils and fats		:	:	:	:		:	:	:	:		:	:	:	:
1520	Dairy products		139	144	167	180		11740	13045	12756	13465		161.0	193.1	199.4	222.3
153	Grain mill products; starches; animal feeds		205	224	232	239		12271	12729	12905	13618		168.5	185.5	201.5	220.8
1531	Grain mill products		:	:	:	:		:	:	:	:		:	:	:	:
1532	Starches and starch products		:	:	:	:		:	:	:	:		:	:	:	:
1533	Prepared animal feeds		:	:	:	:		:	:	:	:		:	:	:	:
154	Other food products		739	772	870	932		40891	42648	44976	46506		551.7	596.3	688.1	707.5
1541	Bakery products		:	:	:	:		:	:	:	:		:	:	:	:
1542	Sugar		:	:	:	:		:	:	:	:		:	:	:	:
1543	Cocoa, chocolate and sugar confectionery		:	:	:	:		:	:	:	:		:	:	:	:
1544	Macaroni, noodles & similar products		:	:	:	:		:	:	:	:		:	:	:	:
1549	Other food products n.e.c.		:	:	:	:		:	:	:	:		:	:	:	:
155	Beverages		130	147	149	138		9842	10588	10344	10036		207.7	223.5	241.5	246.4
1551	Distilling, rectifying & blending of spirits		:	:	:	:		:	:	:	:		:	:	:	:
1552	Wines		:	:	:	:		:	:	:	:		:	:	:	:
1553	Malt liquors and malt		:	:	:	:		:	:	:	:		:	:	:	:
1554	Soft drinks; mineral waters		:	:	:	:		:	:	:	:		:	:	:	:
1600	Tobacco products		6	6	6	6		1734	1064	1176	1081		45.3	27.0	37.2	32.2
171	Spinning, weaving and finishing of textiles		125	130	151	165		17315	16089	14745	14654		209.1	209.1	197.1	197.9
1711	Textile fibre preparation; textile weaving		:	:	:	:		:	:	:	:		:	:	:	:
1712	Finishing of textiles		:	:	:	:		:	:	:	:		:	:	:	:
172	Other textiles		134	141	169	191		7081	7491	6795	7299		81.1	91.4	89.8	94.4
1721	Made-up textile articles, except apparel		:	:	:	:		:	:	:	:		:	:	:	:
1722	Carpets and rugs		:	:	:	:		:	:	:	:		:	:	:	:
1723	Cordage, rope, twine and netting		:	:	:	:		:	:	:	:		:	:	:	:
1729	Other textiles n.e.c		78	77	83	85		10270	9638	9511	9475		146.6	146.4	148.9	137.0
1730	Knitted and crocheted fabrics and articles		729	763	950	1068		55774	53555	48421	49625		424.6	452.7	430.4	463.4
1810	Wearing apparel, except fur apparel		110	119	127	134		4939	4668	4604	5007		47.2	44.0	43.6	52.6
1820	Dressing & dyeing of fur; processing of fur		:	:	:	:		:	:	:	:		:	:	:	:
191	Tanning, dressing and processing of leather		:	:	:	:		:	:	:	:		:	:	:	:
1911	Tanning and dressing of leather		:	:	:	:		:	:	:	:		:	:	:	:
1912	Luggage, handbags, etc.; saddlery & harness		:	:	:	:		:	:	:	:		:	:	:	:
1920	Footwear		219	232	284	296		8570	8623	9354	9926		69.7	75.1	92.2	96.5
2010	Sawmilling and planing of wood		51	57	71	77		950	1115	1305	1511		10.0	11.8	13.3	15.7
202	Products of wood, cork, straw, etc.		77	78	116	137		2767	2968	3623	3962		28.9	30.7	38.4	43.3
2021	Veneer sheets, plywood, particle board, etc.		:	:	:	:		:	:	:	:		:	:	:	:
2022	Builders' carpentry and joinery		:	:	:	:		:	:	:	:		:	:	:	:
2023	Wooden containers		:	:	:	:		:	:	:	:		:	:	:	:
2029	Other wood products; articles of cork/straw		:	:	:	:		:	:	:	:		:	:	:	:
210	Paper and paper products		242	256	174	190		18138	18333	14799	14628		310.8	336.7	299.9	293.3
2101	Pulp, paper and paperboard		:	:	:	:		:	:	:	:		:	:	:	:
2102	Corrugated paper and paperboard		:	:	:	:		:	:	:	:		:	:	:	:
2109	Other articles of paper and paperboard		:	:	:	:		:	:	:	:		:	:	:	:
221	Publishing		121	230	272	266		9778	13463	12709	13648		179.8	247.7	266.6	252.9
2211	Publishing of books and other publications		:	:	:	:		:	:	:	:		:	:	:	:
2212	Publishing of newspapers, journals, etc.		:	:	:	:		:	:	:	:		:	:	:	:
2213	Publishing of recorded media		:	:	:	:		:	:	:	:		:	:	:	:
2219	Other publishing		:	:	:	:		:	:	:	:		:	:	:	:

ISIC Revision 3

222	Printing and related service activities	214.6	204.0	183.9	172.7	15329	12458	11507	12385	445	417	285	302
2221	Printing	…	…	…	…	…	…	…	…	…	…	…	…
2222	Service activities related to printing	…	…	…	…	…	…	…	…	…	…	…	…
2230	Reproduction of recorded media	13.7	…	0.8	…	1092	…	…	…	8	…	5	…
2310	Coke oven products	…	…	…	…	…	…	…	…	…	…	…	…
2320	Refined petroleum products	110.2	119.9	126.0	82.2	4051	3503	2534	3531	53	40	36	37
2330	Processing of nuclear fuel	…	…	…	…	…	…	…	…	…	…	…	…
241	Basic chemicals	207.1	196.5	188.1	177.2	8165	7819	7213	7687	179	165	156	144
2411	Basic chemicals, except fertilizers	…	…	…	…	…	…	…	…	…	…	…	…
2412	Fertilizers and nitrogen compounds	…	…	…	…	…	…	…	…	…	…	…	…
2413	Plastics in primary forms; synthetic rubber	1016.2	975.5	883.1	769.1	44850	42298	38677	37884	653	614	548	475
242	Other chemicals	…	…	…	…	…	…	…	…	…	…	…	…
2421	Pesticides and other agro-chemical products	…	…	…	…	…	…	…	…	…	…	…	…
2422	Paints, varnishes, printing ink and mastics	…	…	…	…	…	…	…	…	…	…	…	…
2423	Pharmaceuticals, medicinal chemicals, etc.	…	…	…	…	…	…	…	…	…	…	…	…
2424	Soap, cleaning & cosmetic preparations	…	…	…	…	…	…	…	…	…	…	…	…
2429	Other chemical products n.e.c.	21.3	18.6	18.5	…	1136	814	783	…	8	8	6	…
2430	Man-made fibres	70.0	63.2	66.7	63.1	4032	3803	3247	3883	112	102	87	78
251	Rubber products	63.2	…	…	…	…	…	…	…	…	…	…	…
2511	Rubber tyres and tubes	483.5	456.6	421.8	380.0	33390	30805	26465	29523	686	635	552	493
2519	Other rubber products	100.9	91.8	86.1	76.3	5303	4773	4187	4645	91	87	66	63
2520	Plastic products	399.9	373.8	364.0	311.2	24249	24553	20871	22692	404	373	339	322
2610	Glass and glass products	…	…	…	…	…	…	…	…	…	…	…	…
269	Non-metallic mineral products n.e.c.	…	…	…	…	…	…	…	…	…	…	…	…
2691	Pottery, china and earthenware	…	…	…	…	…	…	…	…	…	…	…	…
2692	Refractory ceramic products	…	…	…	…	…	…	…	…	…	…	…	…
2693	Struct.non-refractory clay; ceramic products	…	…	…	…	…	…	…	…	…	…	…	…
2694	Cement, lime and plaster	…	…	…	…	…	…	…	…	…	…	…	…
2695	Articles of concrete, cement and plaster	…	…	…	…	…	…	…	…	…	…	…	…
2696	Cutting, shaping & finishing of stone	…	…	…	…	…	…	…	…	…	…	…	…
2699	Other non-metallic mineral products n.e.c.	216.7	222.2	198.2	173.0	9633	10277	9104	9726	142	129	120	106
2710	Basic iron and steel	44.0	39.5	36.7	33.8	2490	2152	2031	2155	51	49	40	41
2720	Basic precious and non-ferrous metals	…	…	…	…	…	…	…	…	…	…	…	…
273	Casting of metals	…	…	…	…	…	…	…	…	…	…	…	…
2731	Casting of iron and steel	…	…	…	…	…	…	…	…	…	…	…	…
2732	Casting of non-ferrous metals	134.8	112.0	90.1	64.6	11338	7237	6685	5895	308	263	196	165
281	Struct.metal products;tanks;steam generators	…	…	…	…	…	…	…	…	…	…	…	…
2811	Structural metal products	…	…	…	…	…	…	…	…	…	…	…	…
2812	Tanks, reservoirs and containers of metal	…	…	…	…	…	…	…	…	…	…	…	…
2813	Steam generators	…	…	…	…	…	…	…	…	…	…	…	…
289	Other metal products; metal working services	204.2	186.0	172.8	163.0	15673	14173	11509	13740	440	384	330	300
2891	Metal forging/pressing/stamping/roll-forming	…	…	…	…	…	…	…	…	…	…	…	…
2892	Treatment & coating of metals	…	…	…	…	…	…	…	…	…	…	…	…
2893	Cutlery, hand tools and general hardware	…	…	…	…	…	…	…	…	…	…	…	…
2899	Other fabricated metal products n.e.c.	139.3	121.4	106.3	94.4	10183	8694	7759	8485	273	244	212	202
291	General purpose machinery	…	…	…	…	…	…	…	…	…	…	…	…
2911	Engines & turbines (not for transport equipment)	…	…	…	…	…	…	…	…	…	…	…	…
2912	Pumps, compressors, taps and valves	…	…	…	…	…	…	…	…	…	…	…	…
2913	Bearings, gears, gearing & driving elements	…	…	…	…	…	…	…	…	…	…	…	…
2914	Ovens, furnaces and furnace burners	…	…	…	…	…	…	…	…	…	…	…	…
2915	Lifting and handling equipment	…	…	…	…	…	…	…	…	…	…	…	…
2919	Other general purpose machinery	116.7	100.3	83.6	67.5	9413	7052	6066	6176	307	269	227	184
292	Special purpose machinery	…	…	…	…	…	…	…	…	…	…	…	…
2921	Agricultural and forestry machinery	…	…	…	…	…	…	…	…	…	…	…	…
2922	Machine tools	…	…	…	…	…	…	…	…	…	…	…	…
2923	Machinery for metallurgy	…	…	…	…	…	…	…	…	…	…	…	…
2924	Machinery for mining & construction	…	…	…	…	…	…	…	…	…	…	…	…
2925	Food/beverage/tobacco processing machinery	…	…	…	…	…	…	…	…	…	…	…	…
2926	Machinery for textile, apparel and leather	…	…	…	…	…	…	…	…	…	…	…	…
2927	Weapons and ammunition	…	…	…	…	…	…	…	…	…	…	…	…
2929	Other special purpose machinery	…	…	…	…	…	…	…	…	…	…	…	…

continued

Colombia

ISIC	Industry	Number of establishments (number)				Note	Number of employees (number)				Note	Wages and salaries paid to employees (billions of Colombian Pesos)				Note
		2007	2008	2009	2010		2007	2008	2009	2010		2007	2008	2009	2010	
2930	Domestic appliances n.e.c.	25	22	27	27		5156	5610	3398	5108		65.5	73.0	70.3	71.6	
3000	Office, accounting and computing machinery	...	3	8	10		...	84	211	316		...	0.8	2.8	3.9	
3110	Electric motors, generators and transformers	36	41	42	40		3418	3572	3964	4115		67.6	79.8	87.0	87.8	
3120	Electricity distribution & control apparatus	34	34	41	48		1783	1886	1549	2519		22.9	26.7	29.1	42.7	
3130	Insulated wire and cable	7	8	9	9		965	1102	1083	1171		19.1	22.2	24.2	24.9	
3140	Accumulators, primary cells and batteries	11	10	11	10		1203	1198	1030	1176		19.1	19.5	20.2	20.8	
3150	Lighting equipment and electric lamps	34	36	34	34		1558	1851	1234	1620		19.8	25.0	26.5	24.7	
3190	Other electrical equipment n.e.c.	35	34	41	45		3435	3431	1109	2587		32.7	33.5	31.3	26.7	
3210	Electronic valves, tubes, etc.	10	12	16	15		624	518	451	573		5.1	5.2	5.5	6.0	
3220	TV/radio transmitters; line comm. apparatus	4	4	3	3		396	...	107	111		6.1	...	2.0	2.3	
3230	TV and radio receivers and associated goods	4	4	4	3		85	98	109	70		0.8	1.0	1.0	1.0	
331	Medical, measuring, testing appliances, etc.	46	53	67	79		2184	2261	2496	2967		24.5	25.5	33.4	36.1	
3311	Medical, surgical and orthopaedic equipment	...	...	...	...		...	...	...	...		...	...	...	...	
3312	Measuring/testing/navigating appliances,etc.	...	...	...	...		...	...	...	...		...	...	...	...	
3313	Industrial process control equipment	...	...	...	...		...	...	...	...		...	...	...	...	
3320	Optical instruments & photographic equipment	10	10	11	12		400	376	439	504		5.3	4.6	5.3	5.5	
3330	Watches and clocks	...	...	...	...		...	...	...	...		...	...	...	...	
3410	Motor vehicles	17	17	17	20		5032	3979	1716	3485		123.6	107.2	95.5	110.5	
3420	Automobile bodies, trailers & semi-trailers	66	58	68	75		2697	2687	1802	2634		29.3	29.4	32.3	34.6	
3430	Parts/accessories for automobiles	96	112	110	110		4882	5178	3975	4404		55.2	61.6	55.6	58.7	
351	Building and repairing of ships and boats	7	5	11	10		321	341	341	394		3.2	4.3	6.0	5.2	
3511	Building and repairing of ships	...	...	...	...		...	...	...	...		...	...	...	...	
3512	Building/repairing of pleasure/sport. boats	...	...	...	...		...	...	...	...		...	...	...	...	
3520	Railway/tramway locomotives & rolling stock	...	...	...	...		...	...	...	...		...	...	...	...	
3530	Aircraft and spacecraft	8	9	10	12		648	572	618	766		16.5	17.9	20.8	24.7	
359	Transport equipment n.e.c.	28	32	37	38		2448	3461	2619	3298		31.9	43.1	43.4	47.9	
3591	Motorcycles	...	...	...	...		...	...	...	...		...	...	...	...	
3592	Bicycles and invalid carriages	...	...	...	...		...	...	...	...		...	...	...	...	
3599	Other transport equipment n.e.c.	...	...	...	...		...	...	...	...		...	...	...	...	
3610	Furniture	328	370	447	515		12363	13534	9879	15814		119.0	145.0	153.4	172.7	
369	Manufacturing n.e.c.	162	190	201	210		8834	8202	5257	7863		100.6	88.8	88.9	92.9	
3691	Jewellery and related articles	...	...	...	...		...	...	...	...		...	...	...	...	
3692	Musical instruments	...	...	...	...		...	...	...	...		...	...	...	...	
3693	Sports goods	...	...	...	...		...	...	...	...		...	...	...	...	
3694	Games and toys	...	...	...	...		...	...	...	...		...	...	...	...	
3699	Other manufacturing n.e.c.	...	...	...	...		...	...	...	...		...	...	...	...	
3710	Recycling of metal waste and scrap	...	...	...	...		...	...	...	...		...	...	...	...	
3720	Recycling of non-metal waste and scrap	...	...	...	...		...	...	...	...		...	...	...	...	
D	Total manufacturing	7257	7937	9135	9946		463203	483195	436785	504662		6315.5	7044.6	7470.2	7862.7	

Colombia

ISIC	Industry	Output at factor values (billions of Colombian Pesos) Note	2007	2008	2009	2010	Value added at factor values (billions of Colombian Pesos) Note	2007	2008	2009	2010	Gross fixed capital formation (billions of Colombian Pesos) 2009	2010
151	Processed meat,fish,fruit,vegetables,fats		7551.0	9747.4	9830.8	9876.8		2368.9	3139.9	3244.2	3054.2	...	...
1511	Processing/preserving of meat		...	...	...	...		...	...	...	...	...	...
1512	Processing/preserving of fish		...	...	...	...		...	...	...	...	...	...
1513	Processing/preserving of fruit & vegetables		...	...	...	...		...	...	...	...	...	...
1514	Vegetable and animal oils and fats		...	...	...	...		...	...	...	...	...	...
1520	Dairy products		4223.1	4992.6	5018.9	5252.1		1404.3	1845.8	1942.8	2235.1	...	...
153	Grain mill products; starches; animal feeds		6942.0	8721.6	8696.6	8517.8		1390.7	1839.6	1998.6	2037.5	...	...
1531	Grain mill products												
1532	Starches and starch products		...	...	...	...		...	...	...	...	...	...
1533	Prepared animal feeds		...	...	...	...		...	...	...	...	...	...
154	Other food products		12484.7	13214.5	14314.7	15271.2		5039.6	5482.0	5981.9	6207.1	...	...
1541	Bakery products		...	...	...	...		...	...	...	...	...	...
1542	Sugar		...	...	...	...		...	...	...	...	...	...
1543	Cocoa, chocolate and sugar confectionery		...	...	...	...		...	...	...	...	...	...
1544	Macaroni, noodles & similar products		...	...	...	...		...	...	...	...	...	...
1549	Other food products n.e.c.		...	...	...	...		...	...	...	...	...	...
155	Beverages		8098.3	9413.2	10104.4	9788.4		5456.2	6281.5	7027.1	6641.1	...	...
1551	Distilling, rectifying & blending of spirits												
1552	Wines		...	...	...	...		...	...	...	...	...	...
1553	Malt liquors and malt		...	...	...	...		...	...	...	...	...	...
1554	Soft drinks; mineral waters		...	...	...	...		...	...	...	...	...	...
1600	Tobacco products		753.2	802.3	750.0	684.4		502.7	541.9	549.9	500.3	...	...
171	Spinning, weaving and finishing of textiles		2477.2	2264.9	2145.2	2197.5		1114.1	954.0	930.8	787.0	...	...
1711	Textile fibre preparation; textile weaving		...	...	...	...		...	...	...	...	...	...
1712	Finishing of textiles		...	...	...	...		...	...	...	...	...	...
172	Other textiles		1057.0	1034.1	929.4	1099.1		436.8	453.5	414.6	437.5	...	...
1721	Made-up textile articles, except apparel		...	...	...	...		...	...	...	...	...	...
1722	Carpets and rugs												
1723	Cordage, rope, twine and netting		...	...	...	...		...	...	...	...	...	...
1729	Other textiles n.e.c.		...	...	...	...		...	...	...	...	...	...
1730	Knitted and crocheted fabrics and articles		1465.7	1445.6	1246.3	1322.5		548.4	634.9	536.7	469.8	...	...
1810	Wearing apparel, except fur apparel		4472.4	4699.7	4282.8	4852.8		2091.1	2219.5	2018.8	2104.3	...	...
1820	Dressing & dyeing of fur; processing of fur		...	...	...	...		...	...	...	...	...	...
191	Tanning, dressing and processing of leather		615.4	671.4	498.5	502.9		228.5	244.5	191.4	193.7	...	...
1911	Tanning and dressing of leather		...	...	...	...		...	...	...	...	...	...
1912	Luggage, handbags, etc.; saddlery & harness		...	...	...	...		...	...	...	...	...	...
1920	Footwear		756.0	746.9	779.0	867.4		362.0	342.8	361.1	370.1	...	...
2010	Sawmilling and planing of wood		135.3	141.2	156.6	177.1		40.2	44.3	54.5	55.9	...	...
202	Products of wood, cork, straw, etc.		550.2	497.8	507.1	546.9		280.0	246.7	245.8	259.5	...	...
2021	Veneer sheets, plywood, particle board, etc.		...	...	...	...		...	...	...	...	...	...
2022	Builders' carpentry and joinery		...	...	...	...		...	...	...	...	...	...
2023	Wooden containers		...	...	...	...		...	...	...	...	...	...
2029	Other wood products; articles of cork/straw		...	...	...	...		...	...	...	...	...	...
210	Paper and paper products		5593.1	5944.1	5609.6	5794.5		2211.1	2364.7	2276.7	2143.3	...	...
2101	Pulp, paper and paperboard		...	...	...	...		...	...	...	...	...	...
2102	Corrugated paper and paperboard		...	...	...	...		...	...	...	...	...	...
2109	Other articles of paper and paperboard		...	...	...	...		...	...	...	...	...	...
221	Publishing		1664.6	2013.7	2109.2	2087.6		1145.3	1386.4	1375.3	1444.1	...	...
2211	Publishing of books and other publications		...	...	...	...		...	...	...	...	...	...
2212	Publishing of newspapers, journals, etc.		...	...	...	...		...	...	...	...	...	...
2213	Publishing of recorded media		...	...	...	...		...	...	...	...	...	...
2219	Other publishing		...	...	...	...		...	...	...	...	...	...

continued

Colombia

ISIC	Industry	Output at factor values (billions of Colombian Pesos)				Value added at factor values (billions of Colombian Pesos)				Gross fixed capital formation (billions of Colombian Pesos)	
		2007	2008	2009	2010	2007	2008	2009	2010	2009	2010
222	Printing and related service activities	1799.0	1752.4	1891.1	2092.3	817.9	881.0	853.9	956.1	…	…
2221	Printing	…	…	…	…	…	…	…	…	…	…
2222	Service activities related to printing	…	…	…	…	…	…	…	…	…	…
2230	Reproduction of recorded media	…	…	…	…	…	…	…	…	…	…
2310	Coke oven products	…	65.4	…	246.7	…	29.4	…	120.6	…	…
2320	Refined petroleum products	17420.7	19909.2	15924.2	18632.2	9502.4	10047.3	8360.8	9737.4	…	…
2330	Processing of nuclear fuel	…	…	…	…	…	…	…	…	…	…
241	Basic chemicals	5957.5	6831.5	6236.7	7235.8	1717.2	2026.6	2085.5	2137.1	…	…
2411	Basic chemicals, except fertilizers	…	…	…	…	…	…	…	…	…	…
2412	Fertilizers and nitrogen compounds	…	…	…	…	…	…	…	…	…	…
2413	Plastics in primary forms; synthetic rubber	…	…	…	…	…	…	…	…	…	…
242	Other chemicals	10693.8	12222.0	12807.6	13451.9	5513.2	6488.4	6686.3	7187.4	…	…
2421	Pesticides and other agro-chemical products	…	…	…	…	…	…	…	…	…	…
2422	Paints, varnishes, printing ink and mastics	…	…	…	…	…	…	…	…	…	…
2423	Pharmaceuticals, medicinal chemicals, etc.	…	…	…	…	…	…	…	…	…	…
2424	Soap, cleaning & cosmetic preparations	…	…	…	…	…	…	…	…	…	…
2429	Other chemical products n.e.c.	…	…	…	…	…	…	…	…	…	…
2430	Man-made fibres	…	350.6	257.3	300.3	…	86.1	90.7	98.9	…	…
251	Rubber products	810.5	794.7	754.9	770.5	360.8	304.1	334.7	308.1	…	…
2511	Rubber tyres and tubes	…	…	…	…	…	…	…	…	…	…
2519	Other rubber products	…	…	…	…	…	…	…	…	…	…
2520	Plastic products	5850.7	6268.3	6138.3	6720.7	2434.3	2477.4	2668.4	2682.9	…	…
2610	Glass and glass products	1144.8	1197.1	1103.0	1258.6	623.2	659.8	598.3	656.3	…	…
269	Non-metallic mineral products n.e.c.	6472.4	7052.4	6742.8	6896.2	3915.3	4064.5	3983.1	3910.7	…	…
2691	Pottery, china and earthenware	…	…	…	…	…	…	…	…	…	…
2692	Refractory ceramic products	…	…	…	…	…	…	…	…	…	…
2693	Struct.non-refractory clay; ceramic products	…	…	…	…	…	…	…	…	…	…
2694	Cement, lime and plaster	…	…	…	…	…	…	…	…	…	…
2695	Articles of concrete, cement and plaster	…	…	…	…	…	…	…	…	…	…
2696	Cutting, shaping & finishing of stone	…	…	…	…	…	…	…	…	…	…
2699	Other non-metallic mineral products n.e.c.	…	…	…	…	…	…	…	…	…	…
2710	Basic iron and steel	7545.3	5959.0	5250.0	5865.3	4299.6	2487.9	2299.6	2910.5	…	…
2720	Basic precious and non-ferrous metals	1740.9	2031.8	2296.3	3668.4	383.7	292.4	231.6	242.8	…	…
273	Casting of metals	…	…	…	…	…	…	…	…	…	…
2731	Casting of iron and steel	…	…	…	…	…	…	…	…	…	…
2732	Casting of non-ferrous metals	…	…	…	…	…	…	…	…	…	…
281	Struct.metal products;tanks;steam generators	1087.4	1542.1	1540.0	1779.0	410.2	539.4	627.9	711.8	…	…
2811	Structural metal products	…	…	…	…	…	…	…	…	…	…
2812	Tanks, reservoirs and containers of metal	…	…	…	…	…	…	…	…	…	…
2813	Steam generators	…	…	…	…	…	…	…	…	…	…
289	Other metal products; metal working services	2071.3	2141.6	2025.4	2205.1	853.8	940.9	926.7	952.9	…	…
2891	Metal forging/pressing/stamping/roll-forming	…	…	…	…	…	…	…	…	…	…
2892	Treatment & coating of metals	…	…	…	…	…	…	…	…	…	…
2893	Cutlery, hand tools and general hardware	…	…	…	…	…	…	…	…	…	…
2899	Other fabricated metal products n.e.c.	…	…	…	…	…	…	…	…	…	…
291	General purpose machinery	1059.4	1200.5	1263.6	1528.7	461.5	532.1	584.5	674.7	…	…
2911	Engines & turbines (not for transport equipment)	…	…	…	…	…	…	…	…	…	…
2912	Pumps, compressors, taps and valves	…	…	…	…	…	…	…	…	…	…
2913	Bearings, gears, gearing & driving elements	…	…	…	…	…	…	…	…	…	…
2914	Ovens, furnaces and furnace burners	…	…	…	…	…	…	…	…	…	…
2915	Lifting and handling equipment	…	…	…	…	…	…	…	…	…	…
2919	Other general purpose machinery	…	…	…	…	…	…	…	…	…	…

292	Special purpose machinery	678.0	885.8	879.3	960.8	300.4	417.4	422.1	444.5
2921	Agricultural and forestry machinery	⋮	⋮	⋮	⋮	⋮	⋮	⋮	⋮
2922	Machine tools	⋮	⋮	⋮	⋮	⋮	⋮	⋮	⋮
2923	Machinery for metallurgy	⋮	⋮	⋮	⋮	⋮	⋮	⋮	⋮
2924	Machinery for mining & construction	⋮	⋮	⋮	⋮	⋮	⋮	⋮	⋮
2925	Food/beverage/tobacco processing machinery	⋮	⋮	⋮	⋮	⋮	⋮	⋮	⋮
2926	Machinery for textile, apparel and leather	⋮	⋮	⋮	⋮	⋮	⋮	⋮	⋮
2927	Weapons and ammunition	⋮	⋮	⋮	⋮	⋮	⋮	⋮	⋮
2929	Other special purpose machinery	⋮	⋮	⋮	⋮	⋮	⋮	⋮	⋮
2930	Domestic appliances n.e.c.	1135.1	1025.1	882.8	897.7	420.3	346.7	347.6	316.1
3000	Office, accounting and computing machinery	⋮	13.9	105.7	114.0	⋮	5.9	25.6	26.3
3110	Electric motors, generators and transformers	561.2	708.0	758.8	934.1	159.3	223.4	235.9	381.0
3120	Electricity distribution & control apparatus	282.6	311.4	369.1	470.9	112.3	141.4	178.8	207.6
3130	Insulated wire and cable	979.7	914.0	725.9	798.4	285.3	230.3	231.9	224.8
3140	Accumulators, primary cells and batteries	409.1	408.0	364.9	381.5	145.5	163.7	173.3	169.0
3150	Lighting equipment and electric lamps	185.0	241.0	236.8	184.9	67.3	92.9	90.7	69.9
3190	Other electrical equipment n.e.c.	475.4	373.1	313.0	352.3	210.7	179.3	155.2	150.2
3210	Electronic valves, tubes, etc.	45.1	45.1	38.1	42.4	25.6	25.3	18.5	22.3
3220	TV/radio transmitters; line comm. apparatus	85.5	⋮	15.0	15.8	32.8	⋮	7.8	8.5
3230	TV and radio receivers and associated goods	7.1	8.0	9.6	6.8	2.0	2.5	3.9	2.3
331	Medical, measuring, testing appliances, etc.	238.9	220.8	248.3	263.0	107.0	99.4	132.2	132.4
3311	Medical, surgical and orthopaedic equipment	⋮	⋮	⋮	⋮	⋮	⋮	⋮	⋮
3312	Measuring/testing/navigating appliances,etc.	⋮	⋮	⋮	⋮	⋮	⋮	⋮	⋮
3313	Industrial process control equipment	⋮	⋮	⋮	⋮	⋮	⋮	⋮	⋮
3320	Optical instruments & photographic equipment	38.0	35.2	37.5	35.6	26.3	25.0	24.2	20.8
3330	Watches and clocks	⋮	⋮	⋮	⋮	⋮	⋮	⋮	⋮
3410	Motor vehicles	5634.5	3500.0	2639.1	3587.6	1437.4	933.0	810.4	941.5
3420	Automobile bodies, trailers & semi-trailers	512.7	434.5	418.9	469.6	179.5	152.6	180.8	172.5
3430	Parts/accessories for automobiles	873.8	773.1	633.6	776.5	299.1	309.0	284.3	302.0
351	Building and repairing of ships and boats	34.4	40.4	59.7	65.9	11.4	13.0	25.0	29.8
3511	Building and repairing of ships	⋮	⋮	⋮	⋮	⋮	⋮	⋮	⋮
3512	Building/repairing of pleasure/sport. boats	⋮	⋮	⋮	⋮	⋮	⋮	⋮	⋮
3520	Railway/tramway locomotives & rolling stock	⋮	⋮	⋮	⋮	⋮	⋮	⋮	⋮
3530	Aircraft and spacecraft	255.2	293.6	402.9	481.1	107.6	114.9	189.0	232.9
359	Transport equipment n.e.c.	1285.9	1283.1	1133.0	1224.0	429.7	399.6	343.7	397.7
3591	Motorcycles	⋮	⋮	⋮	⋮	⋮	⋮	⋮	⋮
3592	Bicycles and invalid carriages	⋮	⋮	⋮	⋮	⋮	⋮	⋮	⋮
3599	Other transport equipment n.e.c.	⋮	⋮	⋮	⋮	⋮	⋮	⋮	⋮
3610	Furniture	1506.8	1710.7	1788.3	1991.2	633.4	763.2	806.9	840.9
369	Manufacturing n.e.c.	1473.1	1051.3	955.2	982.9	563.3	496.9	499.2	481.3
3691	Jewellery and related articles	⋮	⋮	⋮	⋮	⋮	⋮	⋮	⋮
3692	Musical instruments	⋮	⋮	⋮	⋮	⋮	⋮	⋮	⋮
3693	Sports goods	⋮	⋮	⋮	⋮	⋮	⋮	⋮	⋮
3694	Games and toys	⋮	⋮	⋮	⋮	⋮	⋮	⋮	⋮
3699	Other manufacturing n.e.c.	⋮	⋮	⋮	⋮	⋮	⋮	⋮	⋮
3710	Recycling of metal waste and scrap	⋮	⋮	⋮	⋮	⋮	⋮	⋮	⋮
3720	Recycling of non-metal waste and scrap	⋮	⋮	⋮	⋮	⋮	⋮	⋮	⋮
D	Total manufacturing	139189.8	149945.5	144225.9	156527.7	61469.4	65014.6	64669.3	67802.9

Colombia

- 326 -

Index numbers of industrial production
(2005=100)

ISIC	Industry	Note	1999	2000	2001	2002	2003	2004	2005	2006	2007	2008	2009	2010
15	Food and beverages	a/	92	91	93	94	98	102	100	110	116	117	116	121
16	Tobacco products		73	86	87	118	119	116	100	109	123	115	94	79
17	Textiles		85	102	100	92	96	103	100	109	118	111	97	103
18	Wearing apparel, fur		91	105	95	88	94	100	100	106	121	105	88	106
19	Leather, leather products and footwear		...	...	...	...	...	...	...	...	...	...	...	...
20	Wood products (excl. furniture)		106	105	90	78	87	101	100	113	139	124	106	107
21	Paper and paper products		78	95	93	96	96	97	100	106	114	119	114	117
22	Printing and publishing		101	109	108	100	94	97	100	105	118	126	122	117
23	Coke,refined petroleum products,nuclear fuel		...	...	...	...	...	...	...	...	...	...	...	...
24	Chemicals and chemical products		...	...	...	...	...	...	...	...	...	...	...	...
25	Rubber and plastics products		...	...	...	...	...	...	...	...	...	...	...	...
26	Non-metallic mineral products		...	...	...	...	...	...	...	...	...	...	...	...
27	Basic metals		...	...	...	...	...	...	...	...	...	...	...	...
28	Fabricated metal products		91	88	78	83	91	92	100	106	117	108	104	110
29	Machinery and equipment n.e.c.	b/	64	79	85	79	80	91	100	118	140	134	112	121
30	Office, accounting and computing machinery	b/	...	...	...	...	...	...	...	...	...	...	...	...
31	Electrical machinery and apparatus	c/	59	64	74	76	72	86	100	118	140	140	123	136
32	Radio,television and communication equipment	c/	...	...	...	...	...	...	...	...	...	...	...	...
33	Medical, precision and optical instruments		63	72	86	81	93	102	100	122	115	105	98	83
34	Motor vehicles, trailers, semi-trailers	d/	34	47	63	64	58	83	100	126	157	111	90	115
35	Other transport equipment	d/	...	...	...	...	...	...	...	...	...	...	...	...
36	Furniture; manufacturing n.e.c.		...	...	...	...	...	...	...	...	...	...	...	...
37	Recycling		...	...	...	...	...	...	...	...	...	...	...	...
D	Total manufacturing		80	88	89	89	91	96	100	110	121	118	112	117

a/ 15 excludes beverages.
b/ 29 includes 30.
c/ 31 includes 32.
d/ 34 includes 35.

Costa Rica

Supplier of information:
Banco Central de Costa Rica, San José.

Basic source of data:
Annual census/exhaustive survey; administrative source.

Major deviations from ISIC (Revision 2):
None reported.

Reference period:
Calendar year.

Scope:
All registered establishments.

Method of data collection:
Direct interview in the field and mail questionnaires.

Type of enumeration:
Not reported.

Adjusted for non-response:
Not reported.

Concepts and definitions of variables:
No deviations from the standard UN concepts and definitions are reported.

Related national publications:
None reported.

Costa Rica

ISIC	Industry	Note	Output 2007	Output 2008	Output 2009	Output 2010	Note	Value added 2007	Value added 2008	Value added 2009	Value added 2010	GFCF 2010
			(millions of Costa Rican Colones)					(millions of Costa Rican Colones)				(millions of Costa Rican Colones)
311/2	Food products		1734665	2118264	2307123	2466230		541077	636315	689556	760095	
3111	Slaughtering, preparing and preserving meat		418896	482463	498406	535200		113253	120427	124266	134755	
3112	Dairy products		328142	421034	496606	535278		78207	91388	111514	129586	
3113	Canning, preserving of fruits and vegetables		73945	89550	76854	81720		32143	38470	33409	35581	
3114	Canning, preserving and processing of fish		75679	86543	99262	106345		27611	30658	35933	39815	
3115	Vegetable and animal oils and fats		128987	165931	155797	157813		52187	67965	63717	63718	
3116	Grain mill products		224334	283295	325905	346443		43582	47985	55403	64961	
3117	Bakery products		99986	139191	153824	161054		46208	61642	67040	66345	
3118	Sugar factories and refineries		109285	124149	137877	147911		48749	66589	68494	74311	
3119	Cocoa, chocolate and sugar confectionery		21453	25158	29492	35497		7495	8543	10407	13869	
3121	Other food products		148936	167055	191412	211189		75530	84364	99726	116755	
3122	Prepared animal feeds		105023	133893	141688	147780		16112	18282	19646	20399	
313	Beverages	a/	284784	322813	349476	393078	a/	158458	178686	195252	233421	
3131	Distilling, rectifying and blending spirits		...	...	...	...		...	...	...	...	
3132	Wine industries		...	...	...	...		...	...	...	...	
3133	Malt liquors and malt		...	...	...	...		...	...	...	...	
3134	Soft drinks and carbonated waters		...	...	...	...		...	...	...	...	
314	Tobacco	a/	...	...	...	...	a/	...	...	...	...	
321	Textiles		55825	85921	59997	53497		20332	20718	21473	20048	
3211	Spinning, weaving and finishing textiles		13420	14058	14676	8883		4164	4077	4758	2942	
3212	Made-up textile goods excl. wearing apparel		9703	10810	10944	10715		3748	4163	4005	4496	
3213	Knitting mills	b/	32702	34053	34378	33899	b/	12421	12478	12710	12610	
3214	Carpets and rugs		...	...	...	...		...	...	...	...	
3215	Cordage, rope and twine	b/	...	...	...	...	b/	...	...	...	...	
3219	Other textiles		...	...	...	...		...	...	...	...	
322	Wearing apparel, except footwear		64897	72179	76877	85030		37166	41072	43331	49181	
323	Leather and fur products		14664	16310	14173	16130		5727	6194	5500	6198	
3231	Tanneries and leather finishing		8115	9129	6544	7922		2811	3009	2132	2574	
3232	Fur dressing and dyeing industries											
3233	Leather prods. excl. footwear, wearing apparel		6549	7181	7629	8209		2916	3185	3368	3624	
324	Footwear, except rubber or plastic		574	799	920	1050		259	364	417	494	
331	Wood products, except furniture		45773	44386	50745	49214		22607	22923	28958	30439	
3311	Sawmills, planing and other wood mills		32291	26055	20051	11469		13682	10740	8376	4709	
3312	Wooden and cane containers											
3319	Other wood and cork products		13483	18331	30694	37746		8926	12183	20582	25730	
332	Furniture and fixtures, excl. metal		19070	21923	21036	17837		8696	9885	9348	8580	
341	Paper and products		227178	229943	237116	298435		75549	73374	77681	97861	
3411	Pulp, paper and paperboard articles		175806	162568	166348	194025		57498	51162	53435	62340	
3412	Containers of paper and paperboard		51372	67375	70768	104410		18051	22212	24246	35520	
3419	Other pulp, paper and paperboard articles											
342	Printing and publishing		140430	152661	158118	171194		70386	75098	78460	86289	
351	Industrial chemicals		139738	157617	171456	174456		56925	61476	68417	73652	
3511	Basic chemicals excl. fertilizers		6344	7377	7518	10695		3340	3894	3886	5900	
3512	Fertilizers and pesticides		122130	136952	145945	142341		47693	50703	54929	54964	
3513	Synthetic resins and plastic materials		11264	13287	17993	21420		5893	6879	9602	12788	
352	Other chemicals		262084	284912	262224	264246		101289	107520	98730	103508	
3521	Paints, varnishes and lacquers		44404	51963	36399	24488		17983	20505	14358	9751	
3522	Drugs and medicines		91524	97544	97266	114695		35008	36214	35490	45925	
3523	Soap, cleaning preps., perfumes, cosmetics		70783	80650	84192	75384		26876	29898	31814	28589	
3529	Other chemical products		55373	54755	44367	49680		21422	20903	17068	19242	
353	Petroleum refineries		559360	818463	505151	586886		47403	94380	8464	85551	

Code	Industry	843	1226	1371	793	389	561	621	354
354	Misc. petroleum and coal products	86685	112446	105126	111865	35191	45171	42923	45621
355	Rubber products	79260	104883	98516	104627	31669	41694	39932	42159
3551	Tyres and tubes	7425	7563	6611	7238	3522	3477	2991	3462
3559	Other rubber products	71835	97320	91905	97389	28147	38217	36941	38697
356	Plastic products	338106	384426	362956	412470	110679	124818	118770	145035
361	Pottery, china and earthenware	20214	21544	14988	14468	9152	9152	5894	5377
362	Glass and products	45661	49541	47175	52922	18915	17072	21310	25438
369	Other non-metallic mineral products	192462	222764	209586	222749	86610	90113	95530	107300
3691	Structural clay products	4416	3716	4501	4019	1532	1153	1628	1508
3692	Cement, lime and plaster	111394	132966	134425	136537	54276	54091	65592	71925
3699	Other non-metallic mineral products	76652	86082	70659	82193	30801	34870	28309	33867
371	Iron and steel	108444	166091	121817	123142	16985	26189	18942	18851
372	Non-ferrous metals	32265	35185	30852	38765	14016	14831	13139	17101
381	Fabricated metal products	227599	226464	215333	271398	73588	70848	68845	86425
3811	Cutlery, hand tools and general hardware	3342	3950	4731	5635	1661	1963	2434	3257
3812	Furniture and fixtures primarily of metal	12910	14483	12464	14693	5483	5987	5231	6550
3813	Structural metal products	24034	24221	18491	24845	8184	8064	6214	8644
3819	Other fabricated metal products	187313	183811	179646	226224	58259	54834	54966	67974
382	Non-electrical machinery	69305	69524	81765	88499	32760	32971	39091	43554
3821 c/	Engines and turbines	17159	18682	23520	28494	10736	11408	14468	18053
3822 c/	Agricultural machinery and equipment	...	...	...	...	...	...	...	...
3823	Metal and wood working machinery	2808	3404	3604	4129	2077	2478	2640	3080
3824	Other special industrial machinery	...	...	...	...	...	...	...	...
3825	Office, computing and accounting machinery	...	...	...	...	...	...	...	...
3829	Other non-electrical machinery and equipment	49338	47439	54641	55876	19948	19084	21983	22421
383	Electrical machinery	262037	257360	181877	162472	121378	117264	78662	68172
3831	Electrical industrial machinery	29603	31042	31405	33209	20343	21272	21705	23157
3832 d/	Radio, television and communication equipment	231819	225719	149838	128600	100834	95798	56753	44801
3833 d/	Electrical appliances and housewares	...	...	...	...	...	...	...	...
3839	Other electrical apparatus and supplies	615	600	633	663	201	194	203	214
384	Transport equipment	32073	64714	47250	53922	14209	28661	21462	24382
3841	Shipbuilding and repairing	127	82	70	98	61	42	29	23
3842	Railroad equipment	5943	7269	5059	5878	3663	4391	2749	3348
3843	Motor vehicles	26002	57363	42121	47947	10484	24229	18684	21012
3844	Motorcycles and bicycles	...	...	...	...	...	...	...	...
3845 e/	Aircraft	...	...	...	...	...	...	...	...
3849 e/	Other transport equipment	...	...	...	...	...	...	...	...
385	Professional and scientific equipment	2068	1633	1525	1575	1064	840	775	798
3851	Prof. and scientific equipment n.e.c.	2068	1633	1525	1575	1064	840	775	798
3852	Photographic and optical goods	-	-	-	-	-	-	-	-
3853	Watches and clocks	-	-	-	-	-	-	-	-
390	Other manufacturing industries	34281	42645	46597	52861	12165	15283	16582	19783
3901	Jewellery and related articles	...	...	...	...	...	...	...	...
3902	Musical instruments	...	...	...	...	...	...	...	...
3903 f/	Sporting and athletic goods	34281	42645	46597	52861	12165	15283	16582	19783
3909 f/	Manufacturing industries, n.e.c.	...	...	...	...	...	...	...	...
3	Total manufacturing	5166202	6121992	5832984	6432084	1715205	1946019	1891507	2200713

a/ 313 includes 314.
b/ 3213 includes 3215.
c/ 3821 includes 3822.
d/ 3832 includes 3833.
e/ 3845 includes 3849.
f/ 3903 includes 3909.

Costa Rica

Index numbers of industrial production

ISIC Revision 3

(2005=100)

ISIC	Industry	Note	1999	2000	2001	2002	2003	2004	2005	2006	2007	2008	2009	2010
15	Food and beverages	a/	101	101	98	95	97	96	100	103	109	109	107	111
16	Tobacco products		...	...	...	...	...	...	...	...	...	...	...	...
17	Textiles		156	132	115	104	101	101	100	100	97	98	95	79
18	Wearing apparel, fur		106	98	91	95	89	95	100	95	100	101	101	107
19	Leather, leather products and footwear		...	...	...	...	...	...	...	...	...	...	...	...
20	Wood products (excl. furniture)		90	88	73	67	74	74	100	97	87	77	54	35
21	Paper and paper products		85	84	86	87	89	98	100	112	116	104	99	124
22	Printing and publishing		92	94	96	96	97	103	100	104	113	118	109	116
23	Coke,refined petroleum products,nuclear fuel		...	...	...	...	...	...	...	...	...	...	...	...
24	Chemicals and chemical products		...	...	...	...	...	...	...	...	...	...	...	...
25	Rubber and plastics products		...	...	...	...	...	...	...	...	...	...	...	...
26	Non-metallic mineral products		...	...	...	...	...	...	...	...	...	...	...	...
27	Basic metals		...	...	...	...	...	...	...	...	...	...	...	...
28	Fabricated metal products		87	88	90	94	98	89	100	108	118	105	89	107
29	Machinery and equipment n.e.c.		89	93	88	102	104	116	100	105	110	96	107	111
30	Office, accounting and computing machinery		...	...	...	...	...	...	...	...	...	...	...	...
31	Electrical machinery and apparatus	b/	104	97	82	87	86	93	100	103	96	94	76	83
32	Radio,television and communication equipment	b/	...	...	...	...	...	...	...	...	...	...	...	...
33	Medical, precision and optical instruments		...	...	...	...	...	...	...	...	...	...	...	...
34	Motor vehicles, trailers, semi-trailers	c/	124	108	88	98	78	92	100	201	230	297	285	299
35	Other transport equipment	c/	...	...	...	...	...	...	...	...	...	...	...	...
36	Furniture; manufacturing n.e.c.		...	...	...	...	...	...	...	...	...	...	...	...
37	Recycling		...	...	...	...	...	...	...	...	...	...	...	...
D	Total manufacturing		88	85	77	80	87	90	100	111	119	114	104	111

a/ 15 excludes beverages.
b/ 31 includes 32.
c/ 34 includes 35.

Croatia

Supplier of information:
Central Bureau of Statistics of the Republic of Croatia, Zagreb.

Basic source of data:
Survey on registered establishments.

Major deviations from ISIC (Revision 4):
None reported.

Reference period:
Fiscal year.

Scope:
All establishments.

Method of data collection:
Mail questionnaires.

Type of enumeration:
Complete enumeration.

Adjusted for non-response:
No.

Concepts and definitions of variables:
Number of employees is as of 31 March of the reference year.
Figures for wages and salaries were computed by UNIDO from the reported monthly average wages and salaries per employee.

Related national publications:
Persons in Employment by Sex and Economic Activities; Average Monthly Gross Earnings of Persons in Paid Employment; Statistical Report, all published by the Central Bureau of Statistics of the Republic of Croatia, Zagreb.

Croatia

ISIC	Industry	Number of establishments (number) Note	2007	2008	2009	2010	Number of employees (number) Note	2007	2008	2009	2010	Wages and salaries paid to employees (thousands of Croatian Kunas) Note	2007	2008	2009	2010
1010	Processing/preserving of meat	⋮	...	520	509	505	⋮	...	6876	6996	7022	⋮	...	3010349a/	3059762a/	2918979a/
1020	Processing/preserving of fish, etc.	⋮	...	78	87	90	⋮	...	1632	1228	1024	⋮	...	..a/	..a/	..a/
1030	Processing/preserving of fruit,vegetables	⋮	...	197	200	213	⋮	...	4326	1296	1250	⋮	...	..a/	..a/	..a/
1040	Vegetable and animal oils and fats	⋮	...	99	110	118	⋮	...	1134	1184	1200	⋮	...	..a/	..a/	..a/
1050	Dairy products	⋮	...	216	213	213	⋮	...	4213	4309	4017	⋮	...	..a/	..a/	..a/
106	Grain mill products,starches and starch products	⋮	...	177	168	168	⋮	...	2198	1099	966	⋮	...	..a/	..a/	..a/
1061	Grain mill products	⋮	...	170	160	158	⋮	...	2002	1076	958	⋮	...	..a/	..a/	..a/
1062	Starches and starch products	⋮	...	7	8	10	⋮	...	196	23	8	⋮	...	...	...	...
107	Other food products	⋮	...	1420	1503	1700	⋮	...	15871	20688	20470	⋮	...	..a/	..a/	..a/
1071	Bakery products	⋮	...	1020	1086	1169	⋮	...	9644	11180	11444	⋮	...	...	...	...
1072	Sugar	⋮	...	18	18	17	⋮	...	1288	1209	1012	⋮	...	...	...	...
1073	Cocoa, chocolate and sugar confectionery	⋮	...	34	34	36	⋮	...	2856	2628	2619	⋮	...	...	...	...
1074	Macaroni, noodles, couscous, etc.	⋮	...	85	87	84	⋮	...	237	191	210	⋮	...	...	...	...
1075	Prepared meals and dishes	⋮	...	1	2	5	⋮	...	...	1	...	⋮	...	...	...	...
1079	Other food products n.e.c.	⋮	...	262	276	282	⋮	...	1846	5479	5184	⋮	...	...	...	...
1080	Prepared animal feeds	⋮	...	116	116	107	⋮	...	1434	1405	1092	⋮	...	..a/	..a/	..a/
1101	Distilling, rectifying and blending of spirits	⋮	...	76	76	81	⋮	...	850	790	735	⋮	...	...	...	...
1102	Wines	⋮	...	220	247	270	⋮	...	1810	2207	2202	⋮	...	694710b/	710291b/	637781b/
1103	Malt liquors and malt	⋮	...	55	56	56	⋮	...	1643	1681	1433	⋮	...	..b/	..b/	..b/
1104	Soft drinks,mineral waters,other bottled waters	⋮	...	192	187	191	⋮	...	2389	2275	1725	⋮	...	..b/	..b/	..b/
1200	Tobacco products	⋮	...	14	14	12	⋮	...	863	741	792	⋮	...	109546	95705	105342
131	Spinning, weaving and finishing of textiles	⋮	...	154	153	146	⋮	...	2666	2232	1755	⋮	...	278213c/	257427c/	225900c/
1311	Preparation and spinning of textile fibres	⋮	...	45	44	41	⋮	...	870	675	475	⋮	...	...	...	...
1312	Weaving of textiles	⋮	...	67	65	61	⋮	...	1265	743	606	⋮	...	...	...	...
1313	Finishing of textiles	⋮	...	42	44	44	⋮	...	531	814	674	⋮	...	...	...	...
139	Other textiles	⋮	...	392	397	400	⋮	...	2620	2579	2447	⋮	...	..c/	..c/	..c/
1391	Knitted and crocheted fabrics	⋮	...	34	34	31	⋮	...	...	8	7	⋮	...	..c/	..c/	..c/
1392	Made-up textile articles, except apparel	⋮	...	232	234	241	⋮	...	1710	1742	1657	⋮	...	...	...	...
1393	Carpets and rugs	⋮	...	12	11	8	⋮	...	37	28	24	⋮	...	...	...	...
1394	Cordage, rope, twine and netting	⋮	...	17	18	18	⋮	...	89	150	145	⋮	...	...	...	...
1399	Other textiles n.e.c.	⋮	...	97	100	102	⋮	...	775	651	614	⋮	...	...	...	...
1410	Wearing apparel, except fur apparel	⋮	...	1464	1455	1448	⋮	...	19687	17719	15407	⋮	...	1007346d/	914610d/	779359d/
1420	Articles of fur	⋮	...	9	8	9	⋮	...	99	76	80	⋮	...	..d/	..d/	..d/
1430	Knitted and crocheted apparel	⋮	...	181	180	175	⋮	...	2780	2481	1953	⋮	...	..d/	..d/	..d/
151	Leather;luggage,handbags,saddlery,harness;fur	⋮	...	191	184	179	⋮	...	2850	2639	3061	⋮	...	381968e/	367795e/	390708e/
1511	Tanning/dressing of leather; dressing of fur	⋮	...	37	35	34	⋮	...	2330	222	200	⋮	...	..e/	..e/	..e/
1512	Luggage,handbags,etc.;saddlery/harness	⋮	...	154	149	145	⋮	...	520	2417	2861	⋮	...	...	...	...
1520	Footwear	⋮	...	270	264	250	⋮	...	5943	5609	5350	⋮	...	...	...	...
1610	Sawmilling and planing of wood	⋮	...	822	813	799	⋮	...	5192	5104	4713	⋮	...	649318f/	626607f/	571616f/
162	Wood products, cork, straw, plaiting materials	⋮	...	1173	1193	1213	⋮	...	7967	7102	6427	⋮	...	..f/	..f/	..f/

1621	Veneer sheets and wood-based panels	...	51	51	53	...	1393	1638	1562	...	...	...	...
1622	Builders' carpentry and joinery	...	662	671	676	...	4849	4063	3680	...	...	...	...
1623	Wooden containers	...	117	115	112	...	438	400	356	...	...	...	...
1629	Other wood products;articles of cork,straw	...	343	356	372	...	1287	1001	829	...	...	...	...
1701	Pulp, paper and paperboard	...	33	36	34	...	1078	1498	1381	...	309774g/	298920g/	254867g/
1702	Corrugated paper and paperboard	...	171	171	172	...	2590	2026	1188	...	...g/	...g/	...g/
1709	Other articles of paper and paperboard	...	147	151	153	...	747	837	1056	...	...g/	...g/	...g/
181	Printing and service activities related to printing	...	1886	1891	1964	...	6405	7193	6699	...	587623h/	649394h/	609051h/
1811	Printing	...	1244	1256	1265	...	5006	5799	5289	...	...	...	...
1812	Service activities related to printing	...	642	635	632	...	1399	1394	1410	...	...	...	...
1820	Reproduction of recorded media	...	70	69	67	...	99	120	110	...	...h/	...h/	...h/
1910	Coke oven products	...	-	-	-	...	-	-	-	...	493981i/	370080i/	500887i/
1920	Refined petroleum products	...	38	40	42	...	3583	2701	3563	...	...i/	...i/	...i/
201	Basic chemicals,fertilizers, etc.	...	131	129	129	...	4359	4544	4114	...	697710j/	678482j/	614211j/
2011	Basic chemicals	...	76	77	79	...	567	626	549	...	...	...	...
2012	Fertilizers and nitrogen compounds	...	17	18	19	...	2595	2654	2358	...	...	...	...
2013	Plastics and synthetic rubber in primary forms	...	38	34	31	...	1197	1264	1207	...	...	...	...
202	Other chemical products	...	461	459	468	...	3639	3323	3257	...	...j/	...j/	...j/
2021	Pesticides and other agrochemical products	...	10	10	10	...	360	319	342	...	...	...	...
2022	Paints,varnishes;printing ink and mastics	...	111	107	109	...	817	820	776	...	...	...	...
2023	Soap,cleaning and cosmetic preparations	...	215	217	220	...	1450	1757	1581	...	...	...	...
2029	Other chemical products n.e.c.	...	125	125	127	...	1012	427	558	...	...	...	...
2030	Man-made fibres	...	1	1	2	...	4	...	...	...	...j/	...j/	...j/
2100	Pharmaceuticals,medicinal chemicals, etc.	...	53	59	57	...	4953	4533	3919	...	727794	648400	575905
221	Rubber products	...	170	171	1380	...	786	1027	1023	...	558125k/	597454k/	529848k/
2211	Rubber tyres and tubes	...	35	34	33	...	163	119	113	...	...	...	...
2219	Other rubber products	...	135	137	133	...	623	908	910	...	...	...	...
2220	Plastics products	...	1184	1196	1214	...	7368	7566	6668	...	...k/	...k/	...k/
2310	Glass and glass products	...	128	128	135	...	2041	1882	1801	...	1295445m/	1216838m/	1054111m/
239	Non-metallic mineral products n.e.c.	...	1074	1087	1113	...	12731	12095	9823	...	...m/	...m/	...m/
2391	Refractory products	...	12	11	10	...	21	72	39	...	...	...	...
2392	Clay building materials	...	110	109	109	...	3743	2681	2187	...	...	...	...
2393	Other porcelain and ceramic products	...	116	118	120	...	811	684	466	...	...	...	...
2394	Cement, lime and plaster	...	32	30	29	...	2090	1946	1766	...	...	...	...
2395	Articles of concrete, cement and plaster	...	395	398	405	...	3757	3851	3141	...	...	...	...
2396	Cutting, shaping and finishing of stone	...	352	362	375	...	1823	1756	1635	...	...	...	...
2399	Other non-metallic mineral products n.e.c.	...	57	59	65	...	486	1105	589	...	...	...	...
2410	Basic iron and steel	...	48	52	42	...	2090	1870	1678	...	506113n/	465089n/	395559n/
2420	Basic precious and other non-ferrous metals	...	75	73	70	...	1663	1570	982	...	...n/	...n/	...n/
243	Casting of metals	...	113	113	108	...	3339	3192	2946	...	...n/	...n/	...n/
2431	Casting of iron and steel	...	58	57	53	...	2464	2496	2304	...	...	...	...
2432	Casting of non-ferrous metals	...	55	56	55	...	875	696	642	...	...	...	...
251	Struct.metal products, tanks, reservoirs	...	1422	1469	1533	...	14653	14067	13012	...	2076422p/	1960024p/	1812582p/
2511	Structural metal products	...	1294	1340	1397	...	12643	10962	10444	...	...	...	...
2512	Tanks, reservoirs and containers of metal	...	72	74	73	...	826	1745	1326	...	...	...	...

continued

Croatia

		Number of establishments					Number of employees					Wages and salaries paid to employees				
			(number)						(number)					(thousands of Croatian Kunas)			
ISIC	Industry	Note	2007	2008	2009	2010	Note	2007	2008	2009	2010	Note	2007	2008	2009	2010	
2513	Steam generators, excl. hot water boilers		...	56	55	53		...	1184	1360	1242		...	...	...	...	
2520	Weapons and ammunition		...	12	11	10		...	74	975	1055		...	...p/	...p/	...p/	
259	Other metal products;metal working services		...	2190	2191	2189		...	12557	10741	9970		...	...p/	...p/	...p/	
2591	Forging,pressing,stamping,roll-forming of metal		...	172	166	166		...	707	847	729		...	...	...	...	
2592	Treatment and coating of metals; machining		...	654	674	681		...	4941	4473	4280		...	...	...	...	
2593	Cutlery, hand tools and general hardware		...	326	317	315		...	2008	1416	1420		...	...	...	...	
2599	Other fabricated metal products n.e.c.		...	1038	1034	1027		...	4901	4005	3541		...	...	...	...	
2610	Electronic components and boards		...	162	166	168		...	2408	1481	1847		...	...	...	...	
2620	Computers and peripheral equipment		...	614	607	606		...	2012	1481	1389		...	897039q/	820438q/	496842q/	
2630	Communication equipment		...	141	141	136		...	2225	2212	810		...	...q/	...q/	...q/	
2640	Consumer electronics		...	4	4	4		...	...	32	13		...	...q/	...q/	...q/	
265	Measuring,testing equipment; watches, etc.		...	165	164	163		...	426	470	400		...	...q/	...q/	...q/	
2651	Measuring/testing/navigating equipment,etc.		...	152	151	151		...	402	450	379		...	...q/	...q/	...q/	
2652	Watches and clocks		...	13	13	12		...	24	20	21		...	...	...	...	
2660	Irradiation/electromedical equipment,etc.		...	13	13	14		...	...	205	123		...	...	...	...	
2670	Optical instruments and photographic equipment		...	189	195	196		...	546	284	389		...	...q/	...q/	...q/	
2680	Magnetic and optical media		...	4	4	4		...	...	...	...		...	...q/	...q/	...q/	
2710	Electric motors,generators,transformers,etc.		...	257	252	253		...	2751	5538	5337		...	...	...	...	
2720	Batteries and accumulators		...	27	26	23		...	82	57	57		...	608059r/	941254r/	858991r/	
273	Wiring and wiring devices		...	21	21	22		...	1086	1366	909		...	...r/	...r/	...r/	
2731	Fibre optic cables		...	-	-	-		...	-	-	-		...	...r/	...r/	...r/	
2732	Other electronic and electric wires and cables		...	20	20	22		...	1086	1366	909		...	...r/	...r/	...r/	
2733	Wiring devices		...	1	1	-		...	-	-	-		...	...	...	...	
2740	Electric lighting equipment		...	87	91	92		...	794	1044	651		...	...r/	...r/	...r/	
2750	Domestic appliances		...	78	78	77		...	1591	1195	902		...	...r/	...r/	...r/	
2790	Other electrical equipment		...	51	62	69		...	...	617	682		...	...r/	...r/	...r/	
281	General-purpose machinery		...	637	643	646		...	7576	7280	7040		...	...	...	...	
2811	Engines/turbines,excl.aircraft,vehicle engines		...	57	57	54		...	2466	2764	2362		...	1015348s/	1032620s/	890441s/	
2812	Fluid power equipment		...	5	5	8		...	...	64	65		...	...	...	...	
2813	Other pumps, compressors, taps and valves		...	96	95	93		...	789	910	753		...	...	...	...	
2814	Bearings, gears, gearing and driving elements		...	37	37	37		...	833	224	346		...	...	...	...	
2815	Ovens, furnaces and furnace burners		...	19	22	23		...	52	76	64		...	...	...	...	
2816	Lifting and handling equipment		...	110	111	112		...	917	855	812		...	...	...	...	
2817	Office machinery, excl.computers,etc.		...	23	23	23		...	65	58	103		...	...	...	...	
2818	Power-driven hand tools		...	...	1	1		...	3	28	28		...	...	...	...	
2819	Other general-purpose machinery		...	290	292	295		...	2451	2301	2507		...	...	...	...	
282	Special-purpose machinery		...	432	426	419		...	5017	5493	3711		...	...	...	...	
2821	Agricultural and forestry machinery		...	86	85	86		...	1380	1443	1119		...	...s/	...s/	...s/	
2822	Metal-forming machinery and machine tools		...	139	136	129		...	1225	851	709		...	...	...	...	
2823	Machinery for metallurgy		...	2	2	2		...	...	409	3		...	...	...	...	
2824	Mining, quarrying and construction machinery		...	36	35	36		...	95	1497	726		...	...	...	...	

Code	Description											
2825	Food/beverage/tobacco processing machinery	53	56	53	:	732	407	218	:	:	:	:
2826	Textile/apparel/leather production machinery	25	22	21	:	149	66	13	:	:	:	:
2829	Other special-purpose machinery	91	90	92	:	1436	820	923	:	349765t/	160875t/	200674t/
2910	Motor vehicles	29	29	29	:	721	292	278	:	..t/	..t/	..t/
2920	Automobile bodies, trailers and semi-trailers	33	34	34	:	410	342	216	:	..t/	..t/	..t/
2930	Parts and accessories for motor vehicles	123	124	124	:	2794	1220	1723	:	1185987u/	1334221u/	1090628u/
301	Building of ships and boats	447	468	513	:	11630	12200	11284	:	:	:	:
3011	Building of ships and floating structures	266	286	300	:	10883	11667	10833	:	..u/	..u/	..u/
3012	Building of pleasure and sporting boats	181	182	190	:	747	533	451	:	..u/	..u/	..u/
3020	Railway locomotives and rolling stock	14	12	12	:	719	2201	888	:	..u/	..u/	..u/
3030	Air and spacecraft and related machinery	11	11	11	:	-	45	45	:	..u/	..u/	..u/
3040	Military fighting vehicles	-	-	-	:	-	-	-	:	..u/	..u/	..u/
309	Transport equipment n.e.c.	30	29	29	:	163	35	40	:	:	:	:
3091	Motorcycles	4	4	6	:	6	2	1	:	:	:	:
3092	Bicycles and invalid carriages	24	23	21	:	154	31	35	:	:	:	:
3099	Other transport equipment n.e.c.	2	2	2	:	3	2	4	:	633780	532526	515747
3100	Furniture	1041	1086	1121	:	11906	10111	9835	:	:	:	:
321	Jewellery, bijouterie and related articles	134	134	137	:	223	202	194	:	120571v/	149715v/	135883v/
3211	Jewellery and related articles	105	102	104	:	209	182	171	:	..v/	..v/	..v/
3212	Imitation jewellery and related articles	29	32	33	:	14	20	23	:	..v/	..v/	..v/
3220	Musical instruments	20	20	20	:	31	24	23	:	..v/	..v/	..v/
3230	Sports goods	33	33	36	:	69	67	37	:	..v/	..v/	..v/
3240	Games and toys	62	61	62	:	125	183	175	:	..v/	..v/	..v/
3250	Medical and dental instruments and supplies	184	190	197	:	710	744	672	:	..v/	..v/	..v/
3290	Other manufacturing n.e.c.	283	282	284	:	561	791	785	:	1248457w/	727778w/	1248404w/
331	Repair of fabricated metal products/machinery	658	698	1047	:	11042	6183	8626	:	:	:	:
3311	Repair of fabricated metal products	3	6	6	:	:	131	1242	:	:	:	:
3312	Repair of machinery	47	74	100	:	:	549	626	:	:	:	:
3313	Repair of electronic and optical equipment	94	92	95	:	122	84	91	:	:	:	:
3314	Repair of electrical equipment	200	196	200	:	2994	268	248	:	:	:	:
3315	Repair of transport equip., excl. motor vehicles	313	329	339	:	7926	5150	6409	:	:	:	:
3319	Repair of other equipment	1	1	1	:	:	1	10	:	:	:	:
3320	Installation of industrial machinery/equipment	296	301	306	:	3316	1984	2552	:	..w/	..w/	..w/
C	Total manufacturing	23723	24035	24350	:	250736	238579	220999	:	19759000	18946990	17548205

a/ 1010 includes 1020, 1030, 1040, 1050, 106, 107 and 1080.
b/ 1101 includes 1102, 1103 and 1104.
c/ 131 includes 139.
d/ 1410 includes 1420 and 1430.
e/ 151 includes 1520.
f/ 1610 includes 162.
g/ 1701 includes 1702 and 1709.
h/ 181 includes 1820.
i/ 1910 includes 1920.
j/ 201 includes 202 and 2030.

k/ 221 includes 2220.
m/ 2310 includes 239.
n/ 2410 includes 2420 and 243.
p/ 251 includes 2520 and 259.
q/ 2610 includes 2620, 2630, 2640, 265, 2660, 2670 and 2680.
r/ 2710 includes 2720, 273, 2740, 2750 and 2790.
s/ 281 includes 282.
t/ 2910 includes 2920 and 2930.
u/ 301 includes 3020, 3030, 3040 and 309.
v/ 321 includes 3220, 3230, 3240, 3250 and 3290.

w/ 331 includes 3320.

Croatia

- 336 -

Output and Value added figures are not available (shown as "..."); only Gross fixed capital formation data (thousands of Croatian Kunas) are reported, for 2009 and 2010.

ISIC	Industry	Output Note	Output 2007	Output 2008	Output 2009	Output 2010	VA Note	VA 2007	VA 2008	VA 2009	VA 2010	GFCF Note	GFCF 2009	GFCF 2010
1010	Processing/preserving of meat		...	...	...	...		...	...	...	...		288233	205442
1020	Processing/preserving of fish, etc.		...	...	...	...		...	...	...	...		62312	17315
1030	Processing/preserving of fruit,vegetables		...	...	...	...		...	...	...	...		36309	9153
1040	Vegetable and animal oils and fats		...	...	...	...		...	...	...	...		162109	55414
1050	Dairy products		...	...	...	...		...	...	...	...		237954	364901
106	Grain mill products,starches and starch products		...	...	...	...		...	...	...	...		10557	32442
1061	Grain mill products		...	...	...	...		...	...	...	...		10557	32442
1062	Starches and starch products		...	...	...	...		...	...	...	...		-	-
107	Other food products		...	...	...	...		...	...	...	...		-	-
1071	Bakery products		...	...	...	...		...	...	...	...		481778	542123
1072	Sugar		...	...	...	...		...	...	...	...		108337	147468
1073	Cocoa, chocolate and sugar confectionery		...	...	...	...		...	...	...	...		100958	106420
1074	Macaroni, noodles, couscous, etc.		...	...	...	...		...	...	...	...		73518	128094
1075	Prepared meals and dishes		...	...	...	...		...	...	...	...		349	627
1079	Other food products n.e.c.		...	...	...	...		...	...	...	...		-	8309
1080	Prepared animal feeds		...	...	...	...		...	...	...	...		198616	151205
1101	Distilling, rectifying and blending of spirits		...	...	...	...		...	...	...	...		49213	32417
1102	Wines		...	...	...	...		...	...	...	...		5203	5344
1103	Malt liquors and malt		...	...	...	...		...	...	...	...		97350	114588
1104	Soft drinks,mineral waters,other bottled waters		...	...	...	...		...	...	...	...		241368	171018
1200	Tobacco products		...	...	...	...		...	...	...	...		163187	87713
131	Spinning, weaving and finishing of textiles		...	...	...	...		...	...	...	...		44701	32846
1311	Preparation and spinning of textile fibres		...	...	...	...		...	...	...	...		24770	11201
1312	Weaving of textiles		...	...	...	...		...	...	...	...		3447	7240
1313	Finishing of textiles		...	...	...	...		...	...	...	...		4587	2593
139	Other textiles		...	...	...	...		...	...	...	...		16736	1368
1391	Knitted and crocheted fabrics		...	...	...	...		...	...	...	...		20269	81812
1392	Made-up textile articles, except apparel		...	...	...	...		...	...	...	...		-	72975
1393	Carpets and rugs		...	...	...	...		...	...	...	...		12079	6059
1394	Cordage, rope, twine and netting		...	...	...	...		...	...	...	...		-	-
1399	Other textiles n.e.c.		...	...	...	...		...	...	...	...		3411	2778
1410	Wearing apparel, except fur apparel		...	...	...	...		...	...	...	...		4779	52132
1420	Articles of fur		...	...	...	...		...	...	...	...		75246	-
1430	Knitted and crocheted apparel		...	...	...	...		...	...	...	...		67496	81888
151	Leather;luggage,handbags,saddlery,harness;fur		...	...	...	...		...	...	...	...		10481	29644
1511	Tanning/dressing of leather; dressing of fur		...	...	...	...		...	...	...	...		907	-
1512	Luggage,handbags,etc.;saddlery/harness		...	...	...	...		...	...	...	...		9574	-
1520	Footwear		...	...	...	...		...	...	...	...		72365	57238
1610	Sawmilling and planing of wood		...	...	...	...		...	...	...	...		58316	42757
162	Wood products, cork, straw, plaiting materials		...	...	...	...		...	...	...	...		138409	191678

Code	Description		
1621	Veneer sheets and wood-based panels	34705	70600
1622	Builders' carpentry and joinery	61121	86924
1623	Wooden containers	10934	11320
1629	Other wood products;articles of cork,straw	31649	22834
1701	Pulp, paper and paperboard	38065	40778
1702	Corrugated paper and paperboard	35456	44877
1709	Other articles of paper and paperboard	43998	24459
181	Printing and service activities related to printing	221828	163053
1811	Printing	202060	157994
1812	Service activities related to printing	19768	5059
1820	Reproduction of recorded media	494	719
1910	Coke oven products	-	-
1920	Refined petroleum products	19674	29297
201	Basic chemicals,fertilizers, etc.	341136	349057
2011	Basic chemicals	45746	19523
2012	Fertilizers and nitrogen compounds	55178	147613
2013	Plastics and synthetic rubber in primary forms	240212	181921
202	Other chemical products	87730	69657
2021	Pesticides and other agrochemical products	25838	2823
2022	Paints,varnishes;printing ink and mastics	21176	19047
2023	Soap,cleaning and cosmetic preparations	32509	39204
2029	Other chemical products n.e.c.	8207	8583
2030	Man-made fibres	-	-
2100	Pharmaceuticals,medicinal chemicals, etc.	163394	249061
221	Rubber products	22038	25457
2211	Rubber tyres and tubes	659	-
2219	Other rubber products	21379	25457
2220	Plastics products	206554	146232
2310	Glass and glass products	86118	40008
239	Non-metallic mineral products n.e.c.	597128	240817
2391	Refractory products	1852	-
2392	Clay building materials	254275	23958
2393	Other porcelain and ceramic products	6097	9426
2394	Cement, lime and plaster	106127	114092
2395	Articles of concrete, cement and plaster	165353	55470
2396	Cutting, shaping and finishing of stone	38569	29398
2399	Other non-metallic mineral products n.e.c.	24855	8473
2410	Basic iron and steel	258321	121548
2420	Basic precious and other non-ferrous metals	9117	88597
243	Casting of metals	99605	31880
2431	Casting of iron and steel	83353	14420
2432	Casting of non-ferrous metals	16252	17460
251	Struct.metal products, tanks, reservoirs	293382	190338
2511	Structural metal products	212721	149978
2512	Tanks, reservoirs and containers of metal	33107	17738

continued

Croatia

ISIC Revision 4

ISIC	Industry	Output (thousands of Croatian Kunas)					Value added (thousands of Croatian Kunas)					Gross fixed capital formation (thousands of Croatian Kunas)		
		Note	2007	2008	2009	2010	Note	2007	2008	2009	2010	Note	2009	2010
2513	Steam generators, excl. hot water boilers		...	...	...	...		...	...	...	...		47554	22622
2520	Weapons and ammunition		...	...	...	...		...	...	...	...		40967	72011
259	Other metal products;metal working services		...	...	...	...		...	...	...	...		137977	173710
2591	Forging,pressing,stamping,roll-forming of metal		...	...	...	...		...	...	...	...		8910	615
2592	Treatment and coating of metals; machining		...	...	...	...		...	...	...	...		35532	60199
2593	Cutlery, hand tools and general hardware		...	...	...	...		...	...	...	...		30062	29020
2599	Other fabricated metal products n.e.c.		...	...	...	...		...	...	...	...		63473	83876
2610	Electronic components and boards		...	...	...	...		...	...	...	...		8046	7621
2620	Computers and peripheral equipment		...	...	...	...		...	...	...	...		16352	4955
2630	Communication equipment		...	...	...	...		...	...	...	...		56887	2646
2640	Consumer electronics		...	...	...	...		...	...	...	...		-	-
265	Measuring,testing equipment; watches, etc.		...	...	...	...		...	...	...	...		611	27658
2651	Measuring/testing/navigating equipment,etc.		...	...	...	...		...	...	...	...		611	27658
2652	Watches and clocks		...	...	...	...		...	...	...	...		-	-
2660	Irradiation/electromedical equipment,etc.		...	...	...	...		...	...	...	...		-	-
2670	Optical instruments and photographic equipment		...	...	...	...		...	...	...	...		4443	1356
2680	Magnetic and optical media		...	...	...	...		...	...	...	...		1382	782
2710	Electric motors,generators,transformers,etc.		...	...	...	...		...	...	...	...		-	-
2720	Batteries and accumulators		...	...	...	...		...	...	...	...		119701	103072
273	Wiring and wiring devices		...	...	...	...		...	...	...	...		15378	9345
2731	Fibre optic cables		...	...	...	...		...	...	...	...		58367	187672
2732	Other electronic and electric wires and cables		...	...	...	...		...	...	...	...		-	-
2733	Wiring devices		...	...	...	...		...	...	...	...		58367	186210
2740	Electric lighting equipment		...	...	...	...		...	...	...	...		-	1462
2750	Domestic appliances		...	...	...	...		...	...	...	...		26647	6583
2790	Other electrical equipment		...	...	...	...		...	...	...	...		15372	12767
281	General-purpose machinery		...	...	...	...		...	...	...	...		6993	13113
2811	Engines/turbines,excl.aircraft,vehicle engines		...	...	...	...		...	...	...	...		193311	114379
2812	Fluid power equipment		...	...	...	...		...	...	...	...		128638	64852
2813	Other pumps, compressors, taps and valves		...	...	...	...		...	...	...	...		2293	463
2814	Bearings, gears, gearing and driving elements		...	...	...	...		...	...	...	...		14315	4260
2815	Ovens, furnaces and furnace burners		...	...	...	...		...	...	...	...		13	547
2816	Lifting and handling equipment		...	...	...	...		...	...	...	...		-	999
2817	Office machinery, excl.computers,etc.		...	...	...	...		...	...	...	...		7114	11550
2818	Power-driven hand tools		...	...	...	...		...	...	...	...		1915	2160
2819	Other general-purpose machinery		...	...	...	...		...	...	...	...		-	-
282	Special-purpose machinery		...	...	...	...		...	...	...	...		39023	29548
2821	Agricultural and forestry machinery		...	...	...	...		...	...	...	...		67414	55795
2822	Metal-forming machinery and machine tools		...	...	...	...		...	...	...	...		20906	10250
2823	Machinery for metallurgy		...	...	...	...		...	...	...	...		4091	141
2824	Mining, quarrying and construction machinery		...	...	...	...		...	...	...	...		2078	-
			...	...	...	...		...	...	...	...		9547	15877

Code	Description		
2825	Food/beverage/tobacco processing machinery	3666	2007
2826	Textile/apparel/leather production machinery	16	-
2829	Other special-purpose machinery	27110	27503
2910	Motor vehicles	9002	3905
2920	Automobile bodies, trailers and semi-trailers	1582	2775
2930	Parts and accessories for motor vehicles	15920	11981
301	Building of ships and boats	128071	36421
3011	Building of ships and floating structures	125897	36033
3012	Building of pleasure and sporting boats	2174	388
3020	Railway locomotives and rolling stock	358047	13989
3030	Air and spacecraft and related machinery	-	311
3040	Military fighting vehicles	5930	1181
309	Transport equipment n.e.c.	-	-
3091	Motorcycles	5930	1181
3092	Bicycles and invalid carriages	-	-
3099	Other transport equipment n.e.c.	128776	67524
3100	Furniture	1929	1924
321	Jewellery, bijouterie and related articles	1929	1924
3211	Jewellery and related articles	-	-
3212	Imitation jewellery and related articles		
3220	Musical instruments	515	-
3230	Sports goods	1304	-
3240	Games and toys	12260	4995
3250	Medical and dental instruments and supplies	9327	3979
3290	Other manufacturing n.e.c.	69737	112724
331	Repair of fabricated metal products/machinery	670	6905
3311	Repair of fabricated metal products	3430	1779
3312	Repair of machinery	1334	635
3313	Repair of electronic and optical equipment	64303	1169
3314	Repair of electrical equipment	-	102178
3315	Repair of transport equip., excl. motor vehicles	16885	58
3319	Repair of other equipment		40246
3320	Installation of industrial machinery/equipment		
C	Total manufacturing	6400797	5162012

Croatia

ISIC Revision 4			Index numbers of industrial production (2005=100)											
ISIC	Industry	Note	1999	2000	2001	2002	2003	2004	2005	2006	2007	2008	2009	2010
10	Food products		71	71	76	83	86	91	100	107	111	113	108	108
11	Beverages		93	93	97	98	104	100	100	101	109	109	106	96
12	Tobacco products		88	88	99	96	100	105	100	92	97	105	78	91
13	Textiles		95	96	106	105	103	109	100	104	98	88	85	95
14	Wearing apparel		169	167	169	150	142	107	100	87	88	86	69	65
15	Leather and related products		137	132	144	121	112	110	100	130	156	163	129	167
16	Wood/wood products/cork,excl. furniture		81	91	87	88	86	95	100	107	114	116	112	96
17	Paper and paper products		73	74	92	96	94	95	100	108	116	114	129	149
18	Printing and reproduction of recorded media		46	48	55	66	80	86	100	107	123	133	126	120
19	Coke and refined petroleum products		101	106	100	101	108	106	100	87	95	77	84	74
20	Chemicals and chemical products		95	104	99	91	87	103	100	107	114	118	106	114
21	Pharmaceuticals,medicinal chemicals, etc.		91	102	91	112	97	98	100	79	74	87	50	66
22	Rubber and plastics products		75	68	75	81	86	88	100	98	96	94	92	90
23	Other non-metallic mineral products		68	71	75	86	93	94	100	110	114	111	99	79
24	Basic metals		74	77	80	72	76	96	100	104	103	113	85	89
25	Fabricated metal products, except machinery		63	64	69	76	89	93	100	108	125	131	99	86
26	Computer, electronic and optical products		111	115	87	93	104	88	100	90	99	88	79	79
27	Electrical equipment		70	64	72	75	86	86	100	92	97	89	85	78
28	Machinery and equipment n.e.c.		49	52	64	72	69	82	100	129	134	144	103	105
29	Motor vehicles, trailers and semi-trailers		40	50	68	69	76	92	100	120	133	121	108	83
30	Other transport equipment		69	63	94	92	79	94	100	101	99	106	88	69
31	Furniture		78	80	85	90	99	105	100	106	127	120	101	103
32	Other manufacturing		189	156	171	130	107	114	100	105	73	61	41	39
33	Repair and installation of machinery/equipment		57	88	82	84	85	91	100	126	144	136	148	166
C	Total manufacturing		78	80	85	88	91	94	100	104	110	111	99	97

Cyprus

Supplier of information:
Statistical Service, Ministry of Finance, Nicosia.

Basic source of data:
Industrial survey.

Major deviations from ISIC (Revision 4):
None reported.

Reference period:
Calendar year.

Scope:
All privately owned enterprises.

Method of data collection:
Direct interview in the field.

Type of enumeration:
Sample survey.

Adjusted for non-response:
Yes.

Concepts and definitions of variables:
Output includes revenues from non-industrial activities.

Related national publications:
Industrial Statistics (annual), published by the Statistical Service, Ministry of Finance, Nicosia.

Cyprus

ISIC	Industry	Number of enterprises (number) Note	2007	2008	2009	2010	Number of employees (number) Note	2007	2008	2009	2010	Wages and salaries paid to employees (thousands of Euros) Note	2007	2008	2009	2010
1010	Processing/preserving of meat		...	71	70	67		...	1367	1345	1310		...	21799	22192	22597
1020	Processing/preserving of fish, etc.		...	37a/	37a/	30a/		...	217a/	221a/	204a/		...	4219a/	4430a/	4400a/
1030	Processing/preserving of fruit,vegetables		...	41	45	35		...	684	708	754		...	14361	15030	16207
1040	Vegetable and animal oils and fats		...	...a/	...a/	...a/		...	...a/	...a/	...a/		...	...a/	...a/	...a/
1050	Dairy products		...	147	147	90		...	1563	1568	1535		...	36035	34843	33555
106	Grain mill products,starches and starch products		...	13	14	8		...	263	270	298		...	6420	7073	7842
1061	Grain mill products		...	13	14	8		...	263	270	298		...	6420	7073	7842
1062	Starches and starch products		...	-	-	-		...	-	-	-		...	-	-	-
107	Other food products		...	561	556	521		...	6429	6583	6636		...	85867	91315	94767
1071	Bakery products		...	447	447	416		...	5514	5716	5798		...	70740	76374	79414
1072	Sugar		...	-	-	-		...	-	-	-		...	-	-	-
1073	Cocoa, chocolate and sugar confectionery		...	53	52	29		...	203	188	191		...	4157	4028	4188
1074	Macaroni, noodles, couscous, etc.		...	22	19	24		...	148	116	119		...	1991	1762	1704
1075	Prepared meals and dishes		...	9	8	20		...	88	72	128		...	1065	953	1963
1079	Other food products n.e.c.		...	30	30	32		...	476	491	400		...	7914	8198	7498
1080	Prepared animal feeds		...	38	37	38		...	317	297	339		...	5684	5698	6711
1101	Distilling, rectifying and blending of spirits		...	15b/	15b/	15b/		...	216b/	191b/	672b/		...	5280b/	5075b/	18561b/
1102	Wines		...	43	44	46		...	745	768	253		...	18417	19126	5999
1103	Malt liquors and malt		...	...b/	...b/	...b/		...	...b/	...b/	...b/		...	...b/	...b/	...b/
1104	Soft drinks,mineral waters,other bottled waters		...	16	14	15		...	944	966	949		...	24505	25927	27600
1200	Tobacco products		...	3c/	3c/	3c/		...	66c/	75c/	78c/		...	1263c/	1480c/	1474c/
131	Spinning, weaving and finishing of textiles		...	27	27	25		...	48	57	64		...	863	1076	750
1311	Preparation and spinning of textile fibres		...	-	-	-		...	-	-	-		...	-	-	-
1312	Weaving of textiles		...	-	-	-		...	-	-	-		...	-	-	-
1313	Finishing of textiles		...	27d/	27d/	25d/		...	48d/	57d/	64d/		...	863d/	1076d/	750d/
139	Other textiles		...	...d/	...d/	...d/		...	...d/	...d/	...d/		...	...d/	...d/	...d/
1391	Knitted and crocheted fabrics		...	86	87	86		...	422	404	412		...	6007	5655	6003
1392	Made-up textile articles, except apparel		...	15e/	16e/	19e/		...	29e/	23e/	31e/		...	368e/	342e/	443e/
1393	Carpets and rugs		...	71	71	67		...	393	381	381		...	5639	5313	5560
1394	Cordage, rope, twine and netting		...	-	-	-		...	-	-	-		...	-	-	-
1399	Other textiles n.e.c.		...	...e/	...e/	...e/		...	...e/	...e/	...e/		...	...e/	...e/	...e/
1410	Wearing apparel, except fur apparel		...	395	385	230		...	897	750	607		...	12624	11709	9068
1420	Articles of fur		...	-	-	-		...	-	-	-		...	-	-	-
1430	Knitted and crocheted apparel		...	9	8	9		...	28	26	31		...	311	271	421
151	Leather;luggage,handbags,saddlery,harness;fur		...	19	19	14		...	32	32	21		...	445	409	248
1511	Tanning/dressing of leather; dressing of fur		...	19f/	19f/	14f/		...	32f/	32f/	21f/		...	445f/	409f/	248f/
1512	Luggage,handbags,etc.;saddlery/harness		...	...f/	...f/	...f/		...	...f/	...f/	...f/		...	...f/	...f/	...f/
1520	Footwear		...	40	30	24		...	140	93	66		...	2052	1468	769
1610	Sawmilling and planing of wood		...	976g/	992g/	5		...	2877g/	2717g/	26		...	51612g/	51362g/	375
162	Wood products, cork, straw, plaiting materials		...	...g/	...g/	1114		...	...g/	...g/	2640		...	...g/	...g/	48881

Code	Product									
1621	Veneer sheets and wood-based panels	3439	3520	3062	96	101	103	2	2	2
1622	Builders' carpentry and joinery	44575	47144	47864	2485	2561	2718	1083	962	943
1623	Wooden containers	109	334	306	12	26	26	5	…	…
1629	Other wood products;articles of cork,straw	758	334	306	47	26	26	24	24	27
1701	Pulp, paper and paperboard									
1702	Corrugated paper and paperboard	4756	4821	4691	212	218	216	10	10	10
1709	Other articles of paper and paperboard	8043	8119	8717	455	479	522	31	28	28
181	Printing and service activities related to printing	24233h/	26832h/	27235	1236h/	1381h/	1462	269h/	294h/	292
1811	Printing	22821	25959	26324	1146	1320	1398	234	267	267
1812	Service activities related to printing	1412	873	911	90	61	64	35	27	25
1820	Reproduction of recorded media	…h/	…h/	-	…h/	…h/	-	…h/	…h/	-
1910	Coke oven products	-	-	-	-	-	-	-	-	-
1920	Refined petroleum products	…c/	…c/	…c/	…c/	…c/	…c/	…c/	…c/	…c/
201	Basic chemicals,fertilizers, etc.	16504i/	15401i/	14870i/	832i/	776i/	777i/	58i/	54i/	54i/
2011	Basic chemicals	3197i/	3170i/	3241i/	124j/	127j/	126i/	11j/	10j/	10j/
2012	Fertilizers and nitrogen compounds	-	-	-	-	-	-	-	-	-
2013	Plastics and synthetic rubber in primary forms	-	-	-	-	-	-	-	-	-
202	Other chemical products	…i/	…i/	…i/	…i/	…i/	…i/	…i/	…i/	…i/
2021	Pesticides and other agrochemical products	2014	1940	1960	78	75	81	3	3	3
2022	Paints,varnishes;printing ink and mastics	6132	6222	5829	307	307	314	16	17	17
2023	Soap,cleaning and cosmetic preparations	5161	4069	3840	323	267	256	28	24	24
2029	Other chemical products n.e.c.	…i/	…i/	…i/	…i/	…i/	…i/	…i/	…i/	…i/
2030	Man-made fibres	-	-	-	-	-	-	-	-	-
2100	Pharmaceuticals,medicinal chemicals, etc.	25334	24563	22422	1122	1109	1108	7	9	9
221	Rubber products	154	388	395	10	24	26	6	9	9
2211	Rubber tyres and tubes	154k/	218	213	10k/	14	14	6k/	3	3
2219	Other rubber products	…k/	170	182	…k/	10	12	…k/	6	6
2220	Plastics products	24565	24083	22958	1287	1236	1218	74	62	62
2310	Glass and glass products	4228	4798	4176	285	305	268	57	71	67
239	Non-metallic mineral products n.e.c.	74665	74239	80465	2930	2920	3152	271	267	268
2391	Refractory products	285	4423m/	-	20	195m/	-	3	31m/	-
2392	Clay building materials	4286	…m/	4543	190	…m/	196	24	…m/	32
2393	Other porcelain and ceramic products	413	608	1330n/	26	22	48n/	28	37	41n/
2394	Cement, lime and plaster	15031	14911	17198	286	303	345	2	2	2
2395	Articles of concrete, cement and plaster	37980	37956	42834	1608	1619	1811	119	114	114
2396	Cutting, shaping and finishing of stone	14793	14363	14560	731	725	752	89	79	79
2399	Other non-metallic mineral products n.e.c.	1877	1978	…n/	69	56	…n/	6	4	…n/
2410	Basic iron and steel	8946p/	8332p/	9120p/	357p/	360p/	420p/	4p/	4p/	4p/
2420	Basic precious and other non-ferrous metals	…p/	…p/	…p/	…p/	…p/	…p/	…p/	…p/	…p/
243	Casting of metals	-	-	-	-	-	-	-	-	-
2431	Casting of iron and steel	-	-	-	-	-	-	-	-	-
2432	Casting of non-ferrous metals	-	-	-	-	-	-	-	-	-
251	Struct.metal products, tanks, reservoirs	50409	50757	50363	2891	2827	2796	932	812	771
2511	Structural metal products	49782	49194	47139	2854	2756	2647	921	799	758
2512	Tanks, reservoirs and containers of metal	627	1563	3224	37	71	149	11	13	13

continued

Cyprus

ISIC	Industry	Number of enterprises (number)					Number of employees (number)					Wages and salaries paid to employees (thousands of Euros)				
		Note	2007	2008	2009	2010	Note	2007	2008	2009	2010	Note	2007	2008	2009	2010
2513	Steam generators, excl. hot water boilers		…	-	-	-		…	-	-	-		…	-	-	-
2520	Weapons and ammunition		…	6	6	-		…	32	28	26		…	495	480	444
259	Other metal products;metal working services		…	320	319	306		…	968	989	904		…	18779	18767	17111
2591	Forging,pressing,stamping,roll-forming of metal		…	-	-	-		…	-	-	-		…	-	-	-
2592	Treatment and coating of metals; machining		…	138	139	135		…	253	263	190		…	5400	5422	4043
2593	Cutlery, hand tools and general hardware		…	34	33	25		…	111	116	96		…	2117	2091	1781
2599	Other fabricated metal products n.e.c.		…	148	147	146		…	604	610	618		…	11262	11254	11287
2610	Electronic components and boards		…	5q/	4r/	33s/		…	72q/	81r/	254s/		…	933q/	1229r/	4327s/
2620	Computers and peripheral equipment		…	-	-	-		…	-	-	-		…	-	-	-
2630	Communication equipment		…	-	-	-		…	-	-	-		…	-	-	-
2640	Consumer electronics		…	…q/	…r/	-		…	…q/	…r/	-		…	…q/	…r/	-
265	Measuring,testing equipment; watches, etc.		…	…q/	…r/	-		…	…q/	…r/	-		…	…q/	…r/	-
2651	Measuring/testing/navigating equipment,etc.		…	…q/	…r/	-		…	…q/	…r/	-		…	…q/	…r/	-
2652	Watches and clocks		…	…	…	-		…	…	…	-		…	…	…	-
2660	Irradiation/electromedical equipment,etc.		…	…q/	-	-		…	…q/	-	-		…	…q/	-	-
2670	Optical instruments and photographic equipment		…	-	-	-		…	-	-	-		…	-	-	-
2680	Magnetic and optical media		…	-	-	-		…	-	-	-		…	-	-	-
2710	Electric motors,generators,transformers,etc.		…	20	21	24		…	173	202	221		…	3541	4051	4287
2720	Batteries and accumulators		…	-	-	-		…	-	-	-		…	-	-	-
273	Wiring and wiring devices		…	34t/	34t/	-		…	187t/	178t/	-		…	3441t/	2891t/	-
2731	Fibre optic cables		…	-	-	-		…	-	-	-		…	-	-	-
2732	Other electronic and electric wires and cables		…	…	…	-		…	…	…	-		…	…	…	-
2733	Wiring devices		…	…	…	-		…	…	…	-		…	…	…	-
2740	Electric lighting equipment		…	…t/	…t/	…s/		…	…t/	…t/	…s/		…	…t/	…t/	…s/
2750	Domestic appliances		…	47	47	47		…	254	253	251		…	4153	4239	4053
2790	Other electrical equipment		…	-	-	-		…	-	-	-		…	-	-	-
281	General-purpose machinery		…	64u/	63u/	68u/		…	503u/	527u/	622u/		…	9369u/	10076u/	11651u/
2811	Engines/turbines,excl.aircraft,vehicle engines		…	-	-	-		…	-	-	-		…	-	-	-
2812	Fluid power equipment		…	3v/	3v/	4v/		…	30v/	29v/	34v/		…	541v/	614v/	668v/
2813	Other pumps, compressors, taps and valves		…	-	-	-		…	-	-	-		…	-	-	-
2814	Bearings, gears, gearing and driving elements		…	-	-	-		…	-	-	-		…	-	-	-
2815	Ovens, furnaces and furnace burners		…	-	-	-		…	-	-	-		…	-	-	-
2816	Lifting and handling equipment		…	3w/	3w/	40x/		…	14w/	15w/	419x/		…	257w/	244w/	7712x/
2817	Office machinery, excl.computers,etc.		…	-	-	-		…	-	-	-		…	-	-	-
2818	Power-driven hand tools		…	…w/	…w/	-		…	…w/	…w/	-		…	…w/	…w/	…w/
2819	Other general-purpose machinery		…	33	32	…x/		…	385	377	…x/		…	6808	7010	…x/
282	Special-purpose machinery		…	…u/	…u/	…u/		…	…u/	…u/	…u/		…	…u/	…u/	…u/
2821	Agricultural and forestry machinery		…	19	19	12		…	42	49	59		…	1171	1137	1113
2822	Metal-forming machinery and machine tools		…	…v/	…v/	…v/		…	…v/	…v/	…v/		…	…v/	…v/	…v/
2823	Machinery for metallurgy		…	3y/	3z/	4A/		…	14y/	19z/	56A/		…	273y/	300z/	1153A/
2824	Mining, quarrying and construction machinery		…	3	…z/	…A/		…	18	…z/	…A/		…	319	…z/	…A/

Code	Description			...A/			...A/			...A/
2825	Food/beverage/tobacco processing machinery	-	-	-	-	-	-	-	-	-
2826	Textile/apparel/leather production machinery	...y/	3	8	...y/	38	54	...y/	771	1005
2829	Other special-purpose machinery	-	-	-	-	-	-	-	-	-
2910	Motor vehicles	32	33	25	120	121	73	2381	2348	1725
2920	Automobile bodies, trailers and semi-trailers	60	59	59	88	90	74	1612	1972	1798
2930	Parts and accessories for motor vehicles	4	3	7	38	29	38	548	305	490
301	Building of ships and boats	-	-	-	-	-	-	-	-	-
3011	Building of ships and floating structures	4	3	7	38	29	38	548	305	490
3012	Building of pleasure and sporting boats	-	-	-	-	-	-	-	-	-
3020	Railway locomotives and rolling stock	-	-	-	-	-	-	-	-	-
3030	Air and spacecraft and related machinery	-	-	-	-	-	-	-	-	-
3040	Military fighting vehicles	-	-	-	-	-	-	-	-	-
309	Transport equipment n.e.c.	-	-	-	-	-	-	-	-	-
3091	Motorcycles	-	-	-	-	-	-	-	-	-
3092	Bicycles and invalid carriages	-	-	-	-	-	-	-	-	-
3099	Other transport equipment n.e.c.	373	375	366	1383	1301	1281	24354	23366	22535
3100	Furniture	150	159	181	362	351	318	6152	6010	5806
321	Jewellery, bijouterie and related articles	147	152	173	361	346	309	6115	5867	5664
3211	Jewellery and related articles	3	7	8	1	5	9	105B/	143	142
3212	Imitation jewellery and related articles	7B/	7B/	5	6B/	9B/	...	37	168B/	51
3220	Musical instruments	-	-	-	-	-	-	-	-	-
3230	Sports goods	...B/	...B/	4	...B/	...B/	9	...B/	...B/	141
3240	Games and toys	69	69	78	164	163	150	3074	3170	3448
3250	Medical and dental instruments and supplies	45	46	40	189	181	138	2516	2603	2189
3290	Other manufacturing n.e.c.	174	172	182	279	347	400	5889	8346	9978
331	Repair of fabricated metal products/machinery	16C/	14	10	18C/	68	71	452C/	1922	2175
3311	Repair of fabricated metal products	94	94	89	115	150	135	2521	3368	3159
3312	Repair of machinery	...C/	26D/	13	...C/	41D/	16	...C/	1074D/	582
3313	Repair of electronic and optical equipment	27	...D/	21	48	...D/	49	813	...D/	1244
3314	Repair of electrical equipment	37	38	45	98	88	125	2103	1982	2751
3315	Repair of transport equip., excl. motor vehicles	-	-	4	-	-	4	-	-	67
3319	Repair of other equipment	9	9	17	110	82	81	2079	1599	1553
3320	Installation of industrial machinery/equipment	...	...	...	...	...	...	...	...	...
C	Total manufacturing	5530	5576	5540	34148	33638	33352	632597	638092	639652

a/ 1020 includes 1040.
b/ 1101 includes 1103.
c/ 1200 includes 1920.
d/ 1312 includes 1313.
e/ 1391 includes 1399.
f/ 1511 includes 1512.
g/ 1610 includes 162.
h/ 181 includes 1820.
i/ 201 includes 202.
j/ 2011 includes 2029.

k/ 2211 includes 2219.
m/ 2391 includes 2392.
n/ 2393 includes 2399.
p/ 2410 includes 2420.
q/ 2610 includes 2640, 265 and 2660.
r/ 2610 includes 2630 and 265.
s/ 2610 includes 2740.
t/ 273 includes 2740.
u/ 281 includes 282.
v/ 2812 includes 2822.

w/ 2816 includes 2818.
x/ 2816 includes 2819.
y/ 2823 includes 2829.
z/ 2823 includes 2824.
A/ 2823 includes 2824 and 2825.
B/ 3220 includes 3240.
C/ 3311 includes 3313.
D/ 3313 includes 3314.

Cyprus

ISIC	Industry	Output at producers' prices (millions of Euros)					Value added at producers' prices (millions of Euros)					Gross fixed capital formation (millions of Euros)		
		Note	2007	2008	2009	2010	Note	2007	2008	2009	2010	Note	2009	2010
1010	Processing/preserving of meat		...	320.3	310.8	322.0		...	44.2	45.3	44.5		13.1	11.2
1020	Processing/preserving of fish, etc.		...	49.3a/	38.8a/	42.6a/		...	7.5a/	8.5a/	9.2a/		0.8a/	1.3a/
1030	Processing/preserving of fruit, vegetables		...	77.2	78.0	91.7		...	27.2	28.0	32.0		2.3	1.3
1040	Vegetable and animal oils and fats		...	...a/	...a/	...a/		...	...a/	...a/	...a/		...a/	...a/
1050	Dairy products		...	208.0	204.9	208.9		...	53.9	61.3	56.8		10.4	7.7
106	Grain mill products,starches and starch products		...	62.2	52.1	51.6		...	16.7	18.7	18.2		1.0	1.4
1061	Grain mill products		...	62.2	52.1	51.6		...	16.7	18.7	18.2		1.0	1.4
1062	Starches and starch products		...	-	-	-		...	-	-	-		-	-
107	Other food products		...	317.4	327.9	332.2		...	156.2	159.2	156.1		27.5	26.5
1071	Bakery products		...	258.0	269.3	273.6		...	119.3	133.4	131.5		19.6	19.8
1072	Sugar		...	-	-	-		...	-	-	-		-	-
1073	Cocoa, chocolate and sugar confectionery		...	9.5	10.1	10.3		...	5.8	5.8	5.4		0.2	-
1074	Macaroni, noodles, couscous, etc.		...	8.6	7.7	6.3		...	3.1	3.5	2.6		0.2	0.2
1075	Prepared meals and dishes		...	4.9	3.9	8.3		...	2.1	1.9	2.9		0.4	0.4
1079	Other food products n.e.c.		...	36.4	36.9	33.6		...	14.1	14.6	13.6		7.2	6.0
1080	Prepared animal feeds		...	90.6	87.9	106.8		...	11.7	14.0	15.6		7.6	1.6
1101	Distilling, rectifying and blending of spirits		...	33.0b/	29.9b/	66.5b/		...	19.9b/	18.7b/	38.3b/		0.7b/	1.2b/
1102	Wines		...	68.3	66.5	29.7		...	31.0	31.3	15.7		3.1	1.8
1103	Malt liquors and malt		...	...b/	...b/	...b/		...	...b/	...b/	...b/		...b/	...b/
1104	Soft drinks,mineral waters,other bottled waters		...	131.6	138.9	128.1		...	43.7	52.9	46.4		5.4	6.6
1200	Tobacco products		...	10.8c/	18.1c/	18.5c/		...	5.5c/	8.9c/	10.2c/		0.4c/	0.3c/
131	Spinning, weaving and finishing of textiles		...	4.7	5.3	2.5		...	1.9	2.3	1.0		0.2	0.1
1311	Preparation and spinning of textile fibres		...	-	-	-		...	-	-	-		-	-
1312	Weaving of textiles		...	-	-	-		...	-	-	-		-	-
1313	Finishing of textiles		...	4.7d/	5.3d/	2.5d/		...	1.9d/	2.3d/	1.0d/		0.2d/	0.1d/
139	Other textiles		...	...d/	...d/	...d/		...	...d/	...d/	...d/		...d/	...d/
1391	Knitted and crocheted fabrics		...	24.2	21.6	22.2		...	10.5	9.1	9.0		1.3	1.1
1392	Made-up textile articles, except apparel		...	1.0e/	0.9e/	1.8e/		...	0.6e/	0.6e/	1.1e/		-e/	1.1e/
1393	Carpets and rugs		...	23.1	20.7	20.3		...	9.9	8.5	7.9		1.3	1.1
1394	Cordage, rope, twine and netting		...	-	-	-		...	-	-	-		-	-
1399	Other textiles n.e.c.		...	...e/	...e/	...e/		...	...e/	...e/	...e/		...e/	...e/
1410	Wearing apparel, except fur apparel		...	40.1	33.4	24.9		...	17.5	16.1	12.1		1.4	-0.3
1420	Articles of fur		...	-	-	-		...	-	-	-		-	-
1430	Knitted and crocheted apparel		...	1.0	0.8	1.2		...	0.5	0.5	0.6		-	-
151	Leather;luggage,handbags,saddlery,harness;fur		...	1.5	1.1	0.7		...	0.9	0.6	0.3		-	-
1511	Tanning/dressing of leather; dressing of fur		...	1.5f/	1.1f/	0.7f/		...	0.9f/	0.6f/	0.3f/		-f/	-
1512	Luggage,handbags,etc.;saddlery/harness		...	...f/	...f/	...f/		...	...f/	...f/	...f/		...f/	...f/
1520	Footwear		...	6.1	3.9	2.5		...	2.9	1.8	1.1		0.3	0.1
1610	Sawmilling and planing of wood		...	221.2g/	193.5g/	1.7		...	89.8g/	80.6g/	1.0		7.3g/	-0.1
162	Wood products, cork, straw, plaiting materials		...	...g/	...g/	174.5		...	...g/	...g/	70.5		...g/	11.4

1621	Veneer sheets and wood-based panels	18.2	15.5	13.5	4.9	5.3	4.9	0.3	0.2
1622	Builders' carpentry and joinery	200.1	175.4	158.7	83.6	74.1	64.3	6.8	11.1
1623	Wooden containers	...	...	0.7	0.5	...	0.2	...	-
1629	Other wood products;articles of cork,straw	0.9	1.2	1.5	-	0.6	1.1	-	-
1701	Pulp, paper and paperboard	-	-	-	-	-	-	0.2	0.1
1702	Corrugated paper and paperboard	19.9	18.4	20.0	7.9	7.7	8.3	3.0	-1.3
1709	Other articles of paper and paperboard	43.7	37.5	37.2	18.3	14.3	13.5	5.1h/	4.1h/
181	Printing and service activities related to printing	121.3	105.0h/	103.6h/	53.1	46.6h/	44.7h/	4.8	3.3
1811	Printing	118.3	101.8	94.9	51.6	45.2	40.9	0.3	0.7
1812	Service activities related to printing	3.1	3.2	8.7	1.5	1.3	3.8	...h/	...h/
1820	Reproduction of recorded media	-	...h/	...h/	-	...h/	...h/		
1910	Coke oven products	...c/	...c/	...c/	...c/	...c/	...c/	...c/	...c/
1920	Refined petroleum products	-	-	-	-	-	-		
201	Basic chemicals,fertilizers, etc.	75.4i/	73.7i/	83.4i/	29.3i/	29.7i/	33.5i/	4.8i/	6.7i/
2011	Basic chemicals	17.9j/	16.5j/	18.2j/	8.1j/	8.4j/	9.3j/	2.0i/	0.8j/
2012	Fertilizers and nitrogen compounds	...i/	...i/	...i/	...i/	...i/	...i/	...i/	...i/
2013	Plastics and synthetic rubber in primary forms								
202	Other chemical products								
2021	Pesticides and other agrochemical products	5.3	6.5	7.4	2.4	3.0	3.7	0.1	0.8
2022	Paints,varnishes;printing ink and mastics	31.2	29.1	31.1	10.4	10.0	10.7	0.6	1.3
2023	Soap,cleaning and cosmetic preparations	21.0	21.6	26.6	8.4	8.2	9.8	2.1	3.7
2029	Other chemical products n.e.c.	...j/	...j/	...j/	...j/	...j/	...j/	...j/	...j/
2030	Man-made fibres	-	-	-	-	-	-	-	-
2100	Pharmaceuticals,medicinal chemicals, etc.	127.5	117.6	144.8	50.8	50.2	57.3	9.3	7.5
221	Rubber products	2.0	2.3	0.7k/	1.0	1.1	0.3k/	-	-
2211	Rubber tyres and tubes	1.3	1.7	1.7	0.6	0.8	-	-	-
2219	Other rubber products	0.7	0.6	0.6	0.4	0.4	...k/	-	-
2220	Plastics products	112.1	97.0	108.9	43.8	42.3	41.5	9.3	7.9
2310	Glass and glass products	23.4	24.6	20.9	8.9	9.7	9.1	4.1	1.9
239	Non-metallic mineral products n.e.c.	632.0	513.1	493.0	200.3	172.4	151.9	119.5	93.9
2391	Refractory products	-	32.2m/	1.0	-	17.4m/	0.4	3.5m/	-
2392	Clay building materials	46.9	...m/	28.6	24.4	...m/	14.2	...m/	2.1
2393	Other porcelain and ceramic products	18.1n/	1.4	1.1	4.3n/	0.9	0.6	-	-
2394	Cement, lime and plaster	128.2	103.7	94.1	42.4	41.8	34.2	92.1	79.0
2395	Articles of concrete, cement and plaster	361.8	278.6	266.7	99.0	78.3	70.9	14.8	9.5
2396	Cutting, shaping and finishing of stone	76.9	69.5	59.7	30.1	28.8	26.2	1.2	2.8
2399	Other non-metallic mineral products n.e.c.	...n/	27.6	41.9	...n/	5.1	5.5	7.9	0.4
2410	Basic iron and steel	90.8p/	60.7p/	71.7p/	29.1p/	24.8p/	29.0p/	1.2p/	0.7p/
2420	Basic precious and other non-ferrous metals	...p/	...p/	...p/	...p/	...p/	...p/	...p/	...p/
243	Casting of metals	-	-	-	-	-	-	-	-
2431	Casting of iron and steel	-	-	-	-	-	-	-	-
2432	Casting of non-ferrous metals	-	-	-	-	-	-	-	-
251	Struct.metal products, tanks, reservoirs	295.9	244.8	261.2	100.4	89.1	87.6	9.7	8.0
2511	Structural metal products	283.9	239.2	258.7	95.1	87.1	86.6	9.5	7.9
2512	Tanks, reservoirs and containers of metal	12.0	5.7	2.5	5.4	2.0	0.9	0.2	0.1

continued

Cyprus

ISIC	Industry	Output Note	2007	2008	2009	2010	VA Note	2007	2008	2009	2010	GFCF Note	2009	2010
			Output at producers' prices (millions of Euros)					**Value added at producers' prices (millions of Euros)**					**Gross fixed capital formation (millions of Euros)**	
2513	Steam generators, excl. hot water boilers		...	-	-	-		...	-	-	-		-	-
2520	Weapons and ammunition		...	7.0	5.5	8.6		...	1.8	1.5	1.7		0.1	-
259	Other metal products;metal working services		...	80.5	65.4	61.2		...	34.9	31.8	29.6		3.4	5.1
2591	Forging,pressing,stamping,roll-forming of metal		...	-	-	-		...	-	-	-		-	-
2592	Treatment and coating of metals; machining		...	14.2	14.4	13.3		...	8.2	8.6	7.2		0.9	0.2
2593	Cutlery, hand tools and general hardware		...	7.8	5.9	6.4		...	4.4	3.3	3.5		0.2	0.3
2599	Other fabricated metal products n.e.c.		...	58.6	45.1	41.5		...	22.3	20.0	18.9		2.4	4.6
2610	Electronic components and boards		...	59.4q/	59.3r/	91.8s/		...	4.5q/	4.6r/	10.8s/		5.3r/	4.5s/
2620	Computers and peripheral equipment		...	-	-	-		...	-	-	-			
2630	Communication equipment		...		...r/	-		...		...r/	-		...r/	
2640	Consumer electronics		...	...q/	...r/	-		...	...q/	...r/	-			
265	Measuring,testing equipment; watches, etc.		...	...q/	...r/	-		...	...q/	...r/	-		...r/	
2651	Measuring/testing/navigating equipment,etc.		...	...	...	-		...	...	...	-		...	
2652	Watches and clocks		...			-		...			-			
2660	Irradiation/electromedical equipment,etc.		...	...q/		-		...	...q/		-			
2670	Optical instruments and photographic equipment		...	-	-	-		...	-	-	-		-	
2680	Magnetic and optical media		...	-	-	-		...	-	-	-		-	
2710	Electric motors,generators,transformers,etc.		...	26.3	23.6	22.0		...	11.1	7.3	9.0		0.3	0.4
2720	Batteries and accumulators		...	-	-	-		...	-	-	-			
273	Wiring and wiring devices		...	15.3t/	14.7t/	-		...	5.7t/	5.3t/	-		0.5r/	
2731	Fibre optic cables		...	-	-	-		...	-	-	-			
2732	Other electronic and electric wires and cables		...	-	-	-		...	...	-	-			
2733	Wiring devices		...	...	...	-		...	...	...	-			
2740	Electric lighting equipment		...	...t/	...t/	...s/		...	...t/	...t/	...s/		...t/	...s/
2750	Domestic appliances		...	27.7	20.2	19.1		...	9.2	8.1	7.1		0.9	1.0
2790	Other electrical equipment		...	-	-	-		...	-	-	-		-	-
281	General-purpose machinery		...	46.1u/	45.1u/	56.0u/		...	20.4u/	21.1u/	26.1u/		5.0u/	5.7u/
2811	Engines/turbines,excl.aircraft,vehicle engines		...	-	-	-		...	-	-	-		-	-
2812	Fluid power equipment		...	4.1v/	3.8v/	1.9v/		...	1.7v/	1.5v/	0.8v/		0.4v/	1.2v/
2813	Other pumps, compressors, taps and valves		...	-	-	-		...	-	-	-		-	-
2814	Bearings, gears, gearing and driving elements		...	-	-	-		...	-	-	-		-	-
2815	Ovens, furnaces and furnace burners		...	-	-	-		...	-	-	-		-	-
2816	Lifting and handling equipment		...	1.2w/	0.9w/	32.4x/		...	0.6w/	0.4w/	13.6x/		-w/	0.5x/
2817	Office machinery, excl.computers,etc.		...	-	-	-		...	-	-	-		-	-
2818	Power-driven hand tools		...	...w/	...w/	-		...	...w/	...w/	-		...w/	
2819	Other general-purpose machinery		...	30.5	26.7	...x/		...	13.5	12.5	...x/		0.6	...x/
282	Special-purpose machinery		...	...u/	...u/	...u/		...	...u/	...u/	...u/		...u/	...u/
2821	Agricultural and forestry machinery		...	7.6	9.2	8.3		...	3.2	4.4	4.0		1.7	0.3
2822	Metal-forming machinery and machine tools		...	...v/	...v/	...v/		...	...v/	...v/	...v/		...v/	...v/
2823	Machinery for metallurgy		...	1.3v/	1.4z/	3.8A/		...	0.7y/	0.8z/	1.8A/		0.1z/	0.1A/
2824	Mining, quarrying and construction machinery		...	1.4	...z/	...A/		...	0.7	...z/	...A/		...z/	...A/

2825	Food/beverage/tobacco processing machinery	...	-	-	...A/	-	-	...A/	-	...A/
2826	Textile/apparel/leather production machinery	...	...y/	3.1	9.6	...y/	1.6	5.8	2.2	3.6
2829	Other special-purpose machinery	...	-	-	-	-	-	-	-	-
2910	Motor vehicles	...	11.4	11.7	8.2	4.5	4.9	3.0	0.5	-
2920	Automobile bodies, trailers and semi-trailers	...	5.6	6.7	5.9	2.7	3.2	3.0	0.3	0.2
2930	Parts and accessories for motor vehicles	...	2.5	1.7	2.8	1.0	0.5	1.1	0.7	0.4
301	Building of ships and boats	...	-	-	-	-	-	-	-	-
3011	Building of ships and floating structures	...	2.5	1.7	2.8	1.0	0.5	1.1	0.7	0.4
3012	Building of pleasure and sporting boats	...	-	-	-	-	-	-	-	-
3020	Railway locomotives and rolling stock	...	-	-	-	-	-	-	-	-
3030	Air and spacecraft and related machinery	...	-	-	-	-	-	-	-	-
3040	Military fighting vehicles	...	-	-	-	-	-	-	-	-
309	Transport equipment n.e.c.	...	-	-	-	-	-	-	-	-
3091	Motorcycles	...	-	-	-	-	-	-	-	-
3092	Bicycles and invalid carriages	...	-	-	-	-	-	-	-	-
3099	Other transport equipment n.e.c.	...	-	-	-	-	-	-	-	-
3100	Furniture	...	92.7	79.3	78.5	44.1	36.8	37.3	3.7	1.5
321	Jewellery, bijouterie and related articles	...	27.7	23.5	23.5	12.1	11.3	10.4	0.9	0.3
3211	Jewellery and related articles	...	27.6	23.1	22.9	12.1	11.2	10.1	0.8	0.3
3212	Imitation jewellery and related articles	...	0.1	0.4	0.6	0.1	0.2	0.3	-	-
3220	Musical instruments	...	0.5B/	0.5B/	0.1	0.1B/	0.3B/	0.1	-B/	...B/
3230	Sports goods	...	...B/	...B/	0.7	...B/	...B/	0.1	...B/	-
3240	Games and toys	...	8.6	8.5	8.0	5.2	4.9	5.0	0.8	1.5
3250	Medical and dental instruments and supplies	...	9.6	10.4	9.0	4.0	4.3	3.8	0.3	0.4
3290	Other manufacturing n.e.c.	...	27.5	31.9	34.0	12.9	17.1	18.3	1.2	0.7
331	Repair of fabricated metal products/machinery	...	-	-	-	-	-	-	-	-
3311	Repair of fabricated metal products	...	2.3C/	5.6	4.9	1.6C/	3.0	2.6	0.1	0.1
3312	Repair of machinery	...	8.1	10.3	11.0	4.1	6.1	5.4	0.6	0.3
3313	Repair of electronic and optical equipment	...	...C/	6.3D/	4.5	...C/	3.3D/	2.9	0.2D/	0.2
3314	Repair of electrical equipment	...	4.4	...D/	3.7	1.7	...D/	2.0	...D/	0.1
3315	Repair of transport equip., excl. motor vehicles	...	12.8	9.7	9.7	5.5	4.8	5.2	0.3	-
3319	Repair of other equipment	...	-	-	0.2	-	-	0.1	-	-
3320	Installation of industrial machinery/equipment	...	9.2	6.3	6.0	2.9	2.4	2.4	0.1	0.1
C	Total manufacturing	...	3669.1	3322.2	3409.3	1249.8	1211.0	1183.8	273.1	226.6

a/ 1020 includes 1040.
b/ 1101 includes 1103.
c/ 1200 includes 1920.
d/ 1312 includes 1313.
e/ 1391 includes 1399.
f/ 1511 includes 1512.
g/ 1610 includes 162.
h/ 181 includes 1820.
i/ 201 includes 202.
j/ 2011 includes 2029.

k/ 2211 includes 2219.
m/ 2391 includes 2392.
n/ 2393 includes 2399.
p/ 2410 includes 2420.
q/ 2610 includes 2640, 265 and 2660.
r/ 2610 includes 2630 and 265.
s/ 2610 includes 2740.
t/ 273 includes 2740.
u/ 281 includes 282.
v/ 2812 includes 2822.

w/ 2816 includes 2818.
x/ 2816 includes 2819.
y/ 2823 includes 2829.
z/ 2823 includes 2824.
A/ 2823 includes 2824 and 2825.
B/ 3220 includes 3240.
C/ 3311 includes 3313.
D/ 3313 includes 3314.

Cyprus

ISIC Revision 4 — Index numbers of industrial production (2005=100)

ISIC	Industry	Note	1999	2000	2001	2002	2003	2004	2005	2006	2007	2008	2009	2010
10	Food products	a/	...	...	...	...	...	...	100	93	96	98	94	93
11	Beverages	a/	...	...	...	...	...	...	...	...	...	...	...	...
12	Tobacco products	a/	...	...	...	...	...	...	...	...	...	...	...	...
13	Textiles	b/	...	...	...	...	...	...	100	96	88	76	60	54
14	Wearing apparel	b/	...	...	...	...	...	...	...	...	...	...	...	...
15	Leather and related products	b/	...	...	...	...	...	...	...	...	...	...	...	...
16	Wood/wood products/cork,excl. furniture	c/	...	...	...	...	...	...	100	100	116	123	115	88
17	Paper and paper products	c/	...	...	...	...	...	...	100	101	104	112	100	120
18	Printing and reproduction of recorded media	c/	...	...	...	...	...	...	...	...	...	...	...	...
19	Coke and refined petroleum products	d/	...	...	...	...	...	...	100	105	121	129	123	142
20	Chemicals and chemical products	d/	...	...	...	...	...	...	...	...	...	...	...	...
21	Pharmaceuticals,medicinal chemicals, etc.	d/	...	...	...	...	...	...	...	...	...	...	...	...
22	Rubber and plastics products		...	...	...	...	...	...	100	103	104	121	102	96
23	Other non-metallic mineral products		...	...	...	...	...	...	100	98	103	108	83	75
24	Basic metals	e/	...	...	...	...	...	...	100	109	117	120	102	93
25	Fabricated metal products, except machinery	e/	...	...	...	...	...	...	...	...	...	...	...	...
26	Computer, electronic and optical products	f/	...	...	...	...	...	...	100	129	154	191	179	230
27	Electrical equipment	f/	...	...	...	...	...	...	...	...	...	...	...	...
28	Machinery and equipment n.e.c.		...	...	...	...	...	...	100	109	100	102	88	96
29	Motor vehicles, trailers and semi-trailers	g/	...	...	...	...	...	...	100	110	113	107	114	70
30	Other transport equipment	g/	...	...	...	...	...	...	...	...	...	...	...	...
31	Furniture	h/	...	...	...	...	...	...	100	102	101	107	85	75
32	Other manufacturing	h/	...	...	...	...	...	...	...	...	...	...	...	...
33	Repair and installation of machinery/equipment	h/	...	...	...	...	...	...	...	...	...	...	...	...
C	Total manufacturing		...	96	101	101	99	101	100	99	104	109	96	93

a/ 10 includes 11 and 12.
b/ 13 includes 14 and 15.
c/ 17 includes 18.
d/ 19 includes 20 and 21.
e/ 24 includes 25.
f/ 26 includes 27.
g/ 29 includes 30.
h/ 31 includes 32 and 33.

Denmark

Supplier of information:
Danmarks Statistik, Copenhagen.
Industrial statistics for the OECD countries are compiled by the OECD secretariat, which supplies them to UNIDO.

Basic source of data:
Annual survey; tax register; business register.

Major deviations from ISIC (Revision 4):
Data have been converted from the national NACE equivalent system to ISIC (Revision 4) by the OECD.

Reference period:
Calendar year.

Scope:
All enterprises.

Method of data collection:
Not reported.

Type of enumeration:
Not reported.

Adjusted for non-response:
Not reported

Concepts and definitions of variables:
No deviations from the standard UN concepts and definitions are reported.

Related national publications:
None reported.

Denmark

ISIC Revision 4		Number of enterprises (number)					Number of employees (number)					Wages and salaries paid to employees (millions of Danish Kroner)				
ISIC	Industry	Note	2006	2007	2008	2009	Note	2006	2007	2008	2009	Note	2006	2007	2008	2009
1010	Processing/preserving of meat		...	...	147	145		...	...	17261	14873		...	...	5681	5764
1020	Processing/preserving of fish, etc.		...	...	119	117		...	...	4751	4140		...	...	1401	1319
1030	Processing/preserving of fruit,vegetables		...	...	51	54		...	...	2348	2167		...	...	702	723
1040	Vegetable and animal oils and fats		...	...	23	19		...	...	...	...		...	...	...	...
1050	Dairy products		...	...	75	69		...	...	...	...		...	...	...	...
106	Grain mill products,starches and starch products		...	...	22	22		...	...	874	868		...	...	330	337
1061	Grain mill products		...	...	15	15		...	...	594	575		...	...	227	226
1062	Starches and starch products		...	...	7	7		...	...	280	293		...	...	103	112
107	Other food products		...	...	1098	1049		...	...	36566	21135		...	...	6401	5267
1071	Bakery products		...	...	904	854		...	...	...	...		...	...	...	...
1072	Sugar		...	...	2	2		...	...	...	...		...	...	...	...
1073	Cocoa, chocolate and sugar confectionery		...	...	60	55		...	...	2962	2337		...	...	1061	771
1074	Macaroni, noodles, couscous, etc.		...	...	1	2		...	...	...	...		...	...	...	...
1075	Prepared meals and dishes		...	...	19	17		...	...	...	...		...	...	...	...
1079	Other food products n.e.c.		...	...	112	119		...	...	...	...		...	...	...	...
1080	Prepared animal feeds		...	...	67	63		...	...	3530	3184		...	...	1273	1239
1101	Distilling, rectifying and blending of spirits		...	...	106a/	99a/		...	...	4788a/	4254a/		...	...	1751a/	1628a/
1102	Wines		...	...	...a/	...a/		...	...	...a/	...a/		...	...	...a/	...a/
1103	Malt liquors and malt		...	...	...a/	...a/		...	...	...a/	...a/		...	...	...a/	...a/
1104	Soft drinks,mineral waters,other bottled waters		...	...	...a/	...a/		...	...	...a/	...a/		...	...	...a/	...a/
1200	Tobacco products		...	...	9	10		...	...	...	...		...	...	...	...
131	Spinning, weaving and finishing of textiles		...	...	106	90		...	...	674	424		...	...	204	161
1311	Preparation and spinning of textile fibres		...	...	8	5		...	...	...	...		...	...	...	...
1312	Weaving of textiles		...	...	19	16		...	...	...	...		...	...	...	...
1313	Finishing of textiles		...	...	79	69		...	...	...	252		...	...	...	...
139	Other textiles		...	...	314	306		...	...	4304	3154		...	...	1293	1108
1391	Knitted and crocheted fabrics		...	...	14	13		...	...	123	90		...	...	40	34
1392	Made-up textile articles, except apparel		...	...	209	203		...	...	2488	1681		...	...	691	564
1393	Carpets and rugs		...	...	17	16		...	...	732	131		...	...	251	40
1394	Cordage, rope, twine and netting		...	...	27	24		...	...	...	...		...	...	...	...
1399	Other textiles n.e.c.		...	...	47	50		...	...	...	...		...	...	...	...
1410	Wearing apparel, except fur apparel		...	...	353	324		...	...	1843	1201		...	...	541	436
1420	Articles of fur		...	...	26	31		...	...	40	23		...	...	7	6
1430	Knitted and crocheted apparel		...	...	30	21		...	...	232	219		...	...	78	71
151	Leather;luggage,handbags,saddlery,harness;fur		...	...	38	35		...	...	...	...		...	...	...	...
1511	Tanning/dressing of leather; dressing of fur		...	...	14	10		...	...	...	...		...	...	...	...
1512	Luggage,handbags,etc.;saddlery/harness		...	...	24	25		...	...	...	...		...	...	...	...
1520	Footwear		...	...	28	26		...	...	33	27		...	...	...	...
1610	Sawmilling and planing of wood		...	...	123	109		...	...	988	734		...	...	301	246
162	Wood products, cork, straw, plaiting materials		...	...	504	491		...	...	11293	8772		...	...	3738	2817

1621	Veneer sheets and wood-based panels	34	34	:	:	:	788	671	:	:	:	259	217
1622	Builders' carpentry and joinery	284	285	:	:	:	803	:	:	:	:	240	:
1623	Wooden containers	62	61	:	:	:	:	365	:	:	:	103	103
1629	Other wood products;articles of cork,straw	124	111	:	:	:	560	513	:	:	:	221	206
1701	Pulp, paper and paperboard	11	11	:	:	:	3668	2914	:	:	:	1326	1174
1702	Corrugated paper and paperboard	68	60	:	:	:	2636	2256	:	:	:	973	901
1709	Other articles of paper and paperboard	85	90	:	:	:	9594	6789	:	:	:	3299	2304
181	Printing and service activities related to printing	1063	992	:	:	:	7869	:	:	:	:	2767	:
1811	Printing	702	665	:	:	:	1725	:	:	:	:	532	:
1812	Service activities related to printing	361	327	:	:	:	448	:	:	:	:	132	:
1820	Reproduction of recorded media	40	36	:	:	:	:	:	:	:	:	:	:
1910	Coke oven products	-	-	:	:	:	-	-	:	:	:	-	-
1920	Refined petroleum products	4	4	:	:	:	:	:	:	:	:	:	:
201	Basic chemicals,fertilizers, etc.	60	54	:	:	:	4003	3836	:	:	:	1975	2054
2011	Basic chemicals	28	27	:	:	:	:	:	:	:	:	:	:
2012	Fertilizers and nitrogen compounds	7	6	:	:	:	:	234	:	:	:	:	101
2013	Plastics and synthetic rubber in primary forms	25	21	:	:	:	:	:	:	:	:	:	:
202	Other chemical products	185	192	:	:	:	:	:	:	:	:	:	:
2021	Pesticides and other agrochemical products	9	8	:	:	:	1557	1135	:	:	:	653	513
2022	Paints,varnishes;printing ink and mastics	38	41	:	:	:	1554	1461	:	:	:	531	511
2023	Soap,cleaning and cosmetic preparations	88	87	:	:	:	:	:	:	:	:	:	:
2029	Other chemical products n.e.c.	50	56	:	:	:	:	:	:	:	:	:	:
2030	Man-made fibres	3	3	:	:	:	:	:	:	:	:	:	:
2100	Pharmaceuticals,medicinal chemicals, etc.	74	83	:	:	:	16941	17368	:	:	:	8999	10060
221	Rubber products	74	70	:	:	:	875	651	:	:	:	284	228
2211	Rubber tyres and tubes	30	27	:	:	:	126	78	:	:	:	31	25
2219	Other rubber products	44	43	:	:	:	749	573	:	:	:	253	203
2220	Plastics products	517	509	:	:	:	17828	13910	:	:	:	6232	5523
2310	Glass and glass products	157	140	:	:	:	2378	1962	:	:	:	725	655
239	Non-metallic mineral products n.e.c.	455	441	:	:	:	15043	11145	:	:	:	5432	4538
2391	Refractory products	5	5	:	:	:	:	:	:	:	:	:	:
2392	Clay building materials	27	23	:	:	:	:	:	:	:	:	:	:
2393	Other porcelain and ceramic products	89	85	:	:	:	:	:	:	:	:	:	:
2394	Cement, lime and plaster	6	6	:	:	:	:	:	:	:	:	:	:
2395	Articles of concrete, cement and plaster	191	182	:	:	:	601	527	:	:	:	163	165
2396	Cutting, shaping and finishing of stone	103	99	:	:	:	:	:	:	:	:	:	:
2399	Other non-metallic mineral products n.e.c.	34	41	:	:	:	:	:	:	:	:	:	:
2410	Basic iron and steel	91	92	:	:	:	2894	2242	:	:	:	1000	787
2420	Basic precious and other non-ferrous metals	37	29	:	:	:	1607	1238	:	:	:	562	460
243	Casting of metals	61	52	:	:	:	1419	853	:	:	:	437	316
2431	Casting of iron and steel	28	20	:	:	:	:	537	:	:	:	:	:
2432	Casting of non-ferrous metals	33	32	:	:	:	:	316	:	:	:	199	117
251	Struct.metal products, tanks, reservoirs	579	595	:	:	:	11846	9443	:	:	:	4280	3797
2511	Structural metal products	522	532	:	:	:	1180	998	:	:	:	419	383
2512	Tanks, reservoirs and containers of metal	51	56	:	:	:	:	:	:	:	:	:	:

continued

Denmark

| | | Number of enterprises | | | | | Number of employees | | | | | Wages and salaries paid to employees | | | | |
| | | (number) | | | | | (number) | | | | | (millions of Danish Kroner) | | | | |
ISIC	Industry (ISIC Revision 4)	Note	2006	2007	2008	2009	Note	2006	2007	2008	2009	Note	2006	2007	2008	2009
2513	Steam generators, excl. hot water boilers		...	...	6	7		...	...	...	...		...	...	...	...
2520	Weapons and ammunition		...	...	11	9		...	...	...	...		...	...	...	...
259	Other metal products;metal working services		...	...	2671	2540		...	...	29152	...		...	...	9134	...
2591	Forging,pressing,stamping,roll-forming of metal		...	...	158	172		...	...	617	527		...	...	185	171
2592	Treatment and coating of metals; machining		...	...	1693	1580		...	...	13289	8786		...	...	3918	3150
2593	Cutlery, hand tools and general hardware		...	...	239	232		...	...	...	...		...	...	...	...
2599	Other fabricated metal products n.e.c.		...	...	581	556		...	...	...	...		...	...	...	...
2610	Electronic components and boards		...	...	94	93		...	...	2630	2111		...	...	893	780
2620	Computers and peripheral equipment		...	...	40	44		...	...	827	710		...	...	380	359
2630	Communication equipment		...	...	117	111		...	...	...	1819		...	...	...	832
2640	Consumer electronics		...	...	51	51		...	...	...	...		...	...	...	...
265	Measuring,testing equipment; watches, etc.		...	...	193	186		...	...	7218	6660		...	...	2867	3086
2651	Measuring/testing/navigating equipment,etc.		...	...	186	179		...	...	7184	6627		...	...	2855	3074
2652	Watches and clocks		...	...	7	7		...	...	34	33		...	...	12	12
2660	Irradiation/electromedical equipment,etc.		...	...	35	37		...	...	3667	3426		...	...	1575	1722
2670	Optical instruments and photographic equipment		...	...	31	28		...	...	559	440		...	...	224	208
2680	Magnetic and optical media		...	...	6	5		...	...	7	...		...	...	1	...
2710	Electric motors,generators,transformers,etc.		...	...	127	125		...	...	6217	4965		...	...	2132	2018
2720	Batteries and accumulators		...	...	4	4		...	...	13	...		...	...	3	...
273	Wiring and wiring devices		...	...	53	56		...	...	2489	2101		...	...	999	848
2731	Fibre optic cables		...	...	7	6		...	...	...	...		...	...	...	...
2732	Other electronic and electric wires and cables		...	...	28	32		...	...	1151	891		...	...	426	330
2733	Wiring devices		...	...	18	18		...	...	...	...		...	...	...	...
2740	Electric lighting equipment		...	...	126	110		...	...	2048	1475		...	...	684	559
2750	Domestic appliances		...	...	28	28		...	...	1058	764		...	...	336	292
2790	Other electrical equipment		...	...	106	115		...	...	1603	...		...	...	535	...
281	General-purpose machinery		...	...	866	854		...	...	52349	41444		...	...	19267	17487
2811	Engines/turbines,excl.aircraft,vehicle engines		...	...	107	111		...	...	17792	14375		...	...	6561	6632
2812	Fluid power equipment		...	...	44	44		...	...	3748	2783		...	...	1295	986
2813	Other pumps, compressors, taps and valves		...	...	76	76		...	...	13327	9843		...	...	4960	3883
2814	Bearings, gears, gearing and driving elements		...	...	29	29		...	...	832	641		...	...	297	253
2815	Ovens, furnaces and furnace burners		...	...	64	62		...	...	913	851		...	...	306	331
2816	Lifting and handling equipment		...	...	169	164		...	...	5939	4131		...	...	2138	1725
2817	Office machinery, excl.computers,etc.		...	...	7	3		...	...	...	...		...	...	...	...
2818	Power-driven hand tools		...	...	6	4		...	...	...	...		...	...	...	...
2819	Other general-purpose machinery		...	...	364	361		...	...	9616	8748		...	...	3643	3651
282	Special-purpose machinery		...	...	848	818		...	...	18876	14182		...	...	7114	5809
2821	Agricultural and forestry machinery		...	...	163	161		...	...	4251	2907		...	...	1423	1159
2822	Metal-forming machinery and machine tools		...	...	123	113		...	...	1381	1047		...	...	496	421
2823	Machinery for metallurgy		...	...	17	18		...	...	44	33		...	...	12	11
2824	Mining, quarrying and construction machinery		...	...	73	67		...	...	1945	1231		...	...	836	493

2825	Food/beverage/tobacco processing machinery	148	140	:	:	5010	4192	:	:	2006	1746
2826	Textile/apparel/leather production machinery	5	4	:	:	:	:	:	:	:	:
2829	Other special-purpose machinery	319	315	:	:	474	:	:	:	160	:
2910	Motor vehicles	16	19	:	:	2024	1289	:	:	701	468
2920	Automobile bodies, trailers and semi-trailers	82	79	:	:	3807	:	:	:	1203	:
2930	Parts and accessories for motor vehicles	71	74	:	:	:	3265	:	:	:	1429
301	Building of ships and boats	39	42	:	:	:	:	:	:	:	:
3011	Building of ships and floating structures	15	16	:	:	:	:	:	:	:	:
3012	Building of pleasure and sporting boats	24	26	:	:	:	:	:	:	:	:
3020	Railway locomotives and rolling stock	4	3	:	:	193	188	:	:	63	73
3030	Air and spacecraft and related machinery	30	25	:	:	:	:	:	:	:	:
3040	Military fighting vehicles	2	2	:	:	773	680	:	:	248	233
309	Transport equipment n.e.c.	55	58	:	:	:	:	:	:	:	:
3091	Motorcycles	2	2	:	:	631	:	:	:	210	:
3092	Bicycles and invalid carriages	43	44	:	:	:	78	:	:	:	28
3099	Other transport equipment n.e.c.	10	12	:	:	14168	10707	:	:	4682	3748
3100	Furniture	403	412	:	:	735	:	:	:	:	247
321	Jewellery, bijouterie and related articles	303	296	:	:	660	:	:	:	:	232
3211	Jewellery and related articles	259	254	:	:	82	75	:	:	18	16
3212	Imitation jewellery and related articles	44	42	:	:	202	175	:	:	55	57
3220	Musical instruments	40	43	:	:	:	:	:	:	:	:
3230	Sports goods	43	42	:	:	:	:	:	:	:	:
3240	Games and toys	66	73	:	:	4768	4189	:	:	1660	1564
3250	Medical and dental instruments and supplies	508	496	:	:	1317	:	:	:	360	:
3290	Other manufacturing n.e.c.	275	266	:	:	9336	6677	:	:	2828	2556
331	Repair of fabricated metal products/machinery	2143	2015	:	:	1794	1037	:	:	476	351
3311	Repair of fabricated metal products	884	722	:	:	3212	2220	:	:	937	820
3312	Repair of machinery	647	669	:	:	140	105	:	:	34	31
3313	Repair of electronic and optical equipment	47	48	:	:	1070	772	:	:	302	261
3314	Repair of electrical equipment	280	274	:	:	3037	2474	:	:	1061	1073
3315	Repair of transport equip., excl. motor vehicles	261	269	:	:	83	69	:	:	18	21
3319	Repair of other equipment	24	33	:	:	1739	1297	:	:	609	534
3320	Installation of industrial machinery/equipment	386	328	:	:	:	:	:	:	:	:
C	Total manufacturing	16676	16020	:	:	384794	303207	:	:	132088	119532

a/ 1101 includes 1102, 1103 and 1104.

Denmark

- 356 -

ISIC	Industry	Note	Output (millions of Danish Kroner)				Note	Value added at factor values (millions of Danish Kroner)				Note	Gross fixed capital formation (millions of Danish Kroner)	
			2006	2007	2008	2009		2006	2007	2008	2009		2008	2009
1010	Processing/preserving of meat		...	...	39377	40239		...	...	8794	8704		1570	1392
1020	Processing/preserving of fish, etc.		...	...	11394	10586		...	...	1997	2083		445	292
1030	Processing/preserving of fruit,vegetables		...	...	4633	4432		...	...	1161	1261		268	264
1040	Vegetable and animal oils and fats		...	...	...	...		...	...	...	...		...	...
1050	Dairy products		...	...	...	...		...	...	...	...		...	...
106	Grain mill products,starches and starch products		...	...	3097	2702		...	...	783	684		819	350
1061	Grain mill products		...	...	2053	1755		...	...	391	398		696	216
1062	Starches and starch products		...	...	1045	947		...	...	391	285		123	134
107	Other food products		...	...	30350	23202		...	...	9172	7926		1510	1104
1071	Bakery products		...	...	...	...		...	...	...	...		...	...
1072	Sugar		...	...	...	...		...	...	...	...		...	...
1073	Cocoa, chocolate and sugar confectionery		...	...	5096	3186		...	...	1483	1127		365	136
1074	Macaroni, noodles, couscous, etc.		...	...	...	...		...	...	...	...		...	...
1075	Prepared meals and dishes		...	...	...	...		...	...	...	...		...	...
1079	Other food products n.e.c.		...	...	...	...		...	...	...	...		...	...
1080	Prepared animal feeds		...	...	13371	11729		...	...	1953	1713		435	735
1101	Distilling, rectifying and blending of spirits		...	...	10758a/	9601a/		...	...	2672a/	3185a/		1158a/	650a/
1102	Wines		...	...	..a/	..a/		...	...	..a/	..a/		..a/	..a/
1103	Malt liquors and malt		...	...	..a/	..a/		...	...	..a/	..a/		..a/	..a/
1104	Soft drinks,mineral waters,other bottled waters		...	...	..a/	..a/		...	...	..a/	..a/		..a/	..a/
1200	Tobacco products		...	...	...	...		...	...	...	...		...	...
131	Spinning, weaving and finishing of textiles		...	...	919	701		...	...	341	222		39	35
1311	Preparation and spinning of textile fibres		...	...	...	...		...	...	...	...		...	...
1312	Weaving of textiles		...	...	...	...		...	...	...	...		...	...
1313	Finishing of textiles		...	...	...	321		...	...	...	113		...	26
139	Other textiles		...	...	5810	4699		...	...	1907	1538		291	114
1391	Knitted and crocheted fabrics		...	...	137	109		...	...	38	28		4	3
1392	Made-up textile articles, except apparel		...	...	2481	1943		...	...	962	690		69	42
1393	Carpets and rugs		...	...	1326	...		...	...	372	...		107	...
1394	Cordage, rope, twine and netting		...	...	...	158		...	...	...	49		...	4
1399	Other textiles n.e.c.		...	...	...	...		...	...	...	...		...	...
1410	Wearing apparel, except fur apparel		...	...	3149	2473		...	...	810	695		73	27
1420	Articles of fur		...	...	59	58		...	...	16	13		1	1
1430	Knitted and crocheted apparel		...	...	357	325		...	...	106	101		8	19
151	Leather;luggage,handbags,saddlery,harness;fur		...	...	...	...		...	...	...	...		...	...
1511	Tanning/dressing of leather; dressing of fur		...	...	...	...		...	...	...	...		...	...
1512	Luggage,handbags,etc.;saddlery/harness		...	...	25	25		...	...	5	6		1	1
1520	Footwear		...	...	...	...		...	...	...	...		...	...
1610	Sawmilling and planing of wood		...	...	1415	1113		...	...	374	300		82	85
162	Wood products, cork, straw, plaiting materials		...	...	14002	10504		...	...	5040	3583		737	392

1621	Veneer sheets and wood-based panels	1175	876	353	264	75	48
1622	Builders' carpentry and joinery	...	...	367	...	...	...
1623	Wooden containers	1013	420	...	141	58	...
1629	Other wood products;articles of cork,straw	...	...	292	...	...	33
1701	Pulp, paper and paperboard	1378	1386	1679	338	35	53
1702	Corrugated paper and paperboard	5123	4159	...	1481	300	156
1709	Other articles of paper and paperboard	3641	3356	1300	1249	166	197
181	Printing and service activities related to printing	11476	...	4635	...	816	...
1811	Printing	9966	8166	3905	3235	702	779
1812	Service activities related to printing	1511	...	729	...	113	...
1820	Reproduction of recorded media	418	...	156	...	16	...
1910	Coke oven products	-	...	-	...	-	-
1920	Refined petroleum products	...	...	...	...	...	...
201	Basic chemicals,fertilizers, etc.	10412	9438	4510	4260	561	418
2011	Basic chemicals	...	...	...	...	...	...
2012	Fertilizers and nitrogen compounds	...	...	...	211	...	23
2013	Plastics and synthetic rubber in primary forms	...	513	...	...	...	...
202	Other chemical products	...	...	...	...	...	...
2021	Pesticides and other agrochemical products	2870	...	552	...	350	98
2022	Paints,varnishes;printing ink and mastics	2445	2338	801	527	91	76
2023	Soap,cleaning and cosmetic preparations	...	2452	...	820	...	...
2029	Other chemical products n.e.c.	...	...	...	...	...	...
2030	Man-made fibres	...	...	...	...	...	...
2100	Pharmaceuticals,medicinal chemicals, etc.	47335	48767	20971	21090	1972	968
221	Rubber products	983	807	430	316	58	21
2211	Rubber tyres and tubes	160	112	59	39	6	2
2219	Other rubber products	823	695	371	276	52	18
2220	Plastics products	24221	19814	10340	9317	1696	2521
2310	Glass and glass products	3193	2423	1203	890	98	132
239	Non-metallic mineral products n.e.c.	22701	16781	9064	6678	1930	959
2391	Refractory products	...	...	...	...	...	...
2392	Clay building materials	...	...	...	...	...	...
2393	Other porcelain and ceramic products	...	...	...	...	...	...
2394	Cement, lime and plaster	...	...	...	...	...	...
2395	Articles of concrete, cement and plaster	632	582	254	251	42	17
2396	Cutting, shaping and finishing of stone	...	...	...	...	...	...
2399	Other non-metallic mineral products n.e.c.	...	...	...	...	...	...
2410	Basic iron and steel	7651	3634	1942	813	444	263
2420	Basic precious and other non-ferrous metals	3093	2180	761	436	107	45
243	Casting of metals	1521	1077	492	370	277	31
2431	Casting of iron and steel	...	635	...	213	...	21
2432	Casting of non-ferrous metals	...	442	...	157	...	10
251	Struct.metal products, tanks, reservoirs	...	...	...	...	...	...
2511	Structural metal products	16674	13595	6056	5081	740	585
2512	Tanks, reservoirs and containers of metal	1622	1221	576	461	47	13

continued

Denmark

ISIC	Industry	Output Note	Output 2006	Output 2007	Output 2008	Output 2009	VA Note	VA 2006	VA 2007	VA 2008	VA 2009	GFCF Note	GFCF 2008	GFCF 2009
			(millions of Danish Kroner)					(millions of Danish Kroner)					(millions of Danish Kroner)	
2513	Steam generators, excl. hot water boilers		...	...	...	...		...	...	...	...		...	...
2520	Weapons and ammunition		...	...	...	...		...	...	...	...		...	...
259	Other metal products;metal working services		...	...	32621	...		...	...	14075	...		2754	...
2591	Forging,pressing,stamping,roll-forming of metal		...	...	609	529		...	...	268	229		46	45
2592	Treatment and coating of metals; machining		...	...	13711	9684		...	...	6086	4282		1066	473
2593	Cutlery, hand tools and general hardware		...	...	...	...		...	...	...	...		...	...
2599	Other fabricated metal products n.e.c.		...	...	...	...		...	...	...	...		...	...
2610	Electronic components and boards		...	...	3188	3118		...	...	1153	1092		104	109
2620	Computers and peripheral equipment		...	...	1329	1238		...	...	444	442		40	34
2630	Communication equipment		...	...	...	2666		...	...	...	1153		...	45
2640	Consumer electronics		...	...	...	...		...	...	...	...		...	...
265	Measuring,testing equipment; watches, etc.		...	...	8982	9299		...	...	3876	4093		392	252
2651	Measuring/testing/navigating equipment,etc.		...	...	8938	9250		...	...	3858	4075		391	252
2652	Watches and clocks		...	...	44	48		...	...	18	17		1	1
2660	Irradiation/electromedical equipment,etc.		...	...	7240	6748		...	...	3294	3435		171	136
2670	Optical instruments and photographic equipment		...	...	999	768		...	...	268	234		13	15
2680	Magnetic and optical media		...	...	12	...		...	...	1	...		-	...
2710	Electric motors,generators,transformers,etc.		...	...	9165	7848		...	...	3349	2967		359	157
2720	Batteries and accumulators		...	...	12	...		...	...	6	...		3	...
273	Wiring and wiring devices		...	...	4509	3702		...	...	1771	1487		128	132
2731	Fibre optic cables		...	...	...	...		...	...	...	...		...	...
2732	Other electronic and electric wires and cables		...	...	2167	1633		...	...	658	516		63	51
2733	Wiring devices		...	...	...	...		...	...	...	...		...	...
2740	Electric lighting equipment		...	...	2494	1604		...	...	1013	607		84	36
2750	Domestic appliances		...	...	1484	1118		...	...	532	424		35	22
2790	Other electrical equipment		...	...	2033	...		...	...	837	...		57	...
281	General-purpose machinery		...	...	110694	99850		...	...	29552	25602		4446	2605
2811	Engines/turbines,excl.aircraft,vehicle engines		...	...	61461	61710		...	...	12204	12044		2124	1342
2812	Fluid power equipment		...	...	4809	2676		...	...	1781	999		394	137
2813	Other pumps, compressors, taps and valves		...	...	19461	15642		...	...	6805	5299		1010	438
2814	Bearings, gears, gearing and driving elements		...	...	1242	885		...	...	493	351		140	67
2815	Ovens, furnaces and furnace burners		...	...	1297	1264		...	...	435	485		38	39
2816	Lifting and handling equipment		...	...	7827	5244		...	...	2816	1900		356	216
2817	Office machinery, excl.computers,etc.		...	...	...	...		...	...	...	...		...	...
2818	Power-driven hand tools		...	...	...	...		...	...	...	...		...	...
2819	Other general-purpose machinery		...	...	14380	12361		...	...	4932	4497		378	366
282	Special-purpose machinery		...	...	28332	19974		...	...	10415	7142		1033	477
2821	Agricultural and forestry machinery		...	...	6629	4463		...	...	2103	1478		217	133
2822	Metal-forming machinery and machine tools		...	...	1920	1268		...	...	793	538		73	34
2823	Machinery for metallurgy		...	...	70	47		...	...	25	17		12	1
2824	Mining, quarrying and construction machinery		...	...	3373	1701		...	...	1564	582		283	51

Code		101	177	2142	2727	6161	7710
2825	Food/beverage/tobacco processing machinery	...	...	...	...	...	...
2826	Textile/apparel/leather production machinery						
2829	Other special-purpose machinery	...	19	...	245	...	715
2910	Motor vehicles	38	57	549	905	1757	2982
2920	Automobile bodies, trailers and semi-trailers	...	187	...	1802	...	4278
2930	Parts and accessories for motor vehicles	70	...	478	...	5942	...
301	Building of ships and boats	...	...	...	...	...	...
3011	Building of ships and floating structures	...	...	...	...	...	...
3012	Building of pleasure and sporting boats	...	...	...	...	...	...
3020	Railway locomotives and rolling stock	4	7	77	89	299	272
3030	Air and spacecraft and related machinery						
3040	Military fighting vehicles	10	19	323	333	863	983
309	Transport equipment n.e.c.	...	...	...	...	...	...
3091	Motorcycles	...	16	...	281	...	834
3092	Bicycles and invalid carriages	1	...	40	...	122	...
3099	Other transport equipment n.e.c.	372	622	5316	6746	14633	19044
3100	Furniture	25	...	406	...	1160	...
321	Jewellery, bijouterie and related articles	24	...	372	...	1059	...
3211	Jewellery and related articles	...	4	...	36	...	113
3212	Imitation jewellery and related articles	1	...	34	...	101	...
3220	Musical instruments	2	9	79	72	140	135
3230	Sports goods	...	...	...	...	...	...
3240	Games and toys	185	288	2474	2697	6408	6246
3250	Medical and dental instruments and supplies	...	86	...	565	...	1720
3290	Other manufacturing n.e.c.	257	368	3678	4406	9262	11541
331	Repair of fabricated metal products/machinery	48	78	583	815	1369	2009
3311	Repair of fabricated metal products	116	123	1211	1506	3195	3996
3312	Repair of machinery	...	4	51	60	128	130
3313	Repair of electronic and optical equipment	3	34	395	494	968	1192
3314	Repair of electrical equipment	69	127	1405	1504	3520	4150
3315	Repair of transport equip., excl. motor vehicles	1	1	32	27	83	63
3319	Repair of other equipment	28	42	743	878	1835	2111
3320	Installation of industrial machinery/equipment	...	...	...	...	...	...
C	Total manufacturing	24753	32523	185015	213849	568088	668785

a/ 1101 includes 1102, 1103 and 1104.

Denmark

ISIC Revision 4

Index numbers of industrial production
(2005=100)

ISIC	Industry	Note	1999	2000	2001	2002	2003	2004	2005	2006	2007	2008	2009	2010
10	Food products		...	99	99	100	103	100	100	101	100	99	93	96
11	Beverages		...	92	88	99	104	104	100	106	105	108	97	84
12	Tobacco products		...	129	118	121	122	107	100	103	94	85	77	78
13	Textiles		...	120	111	109	108	100	100	95	93	85	65	62
14	Wearing apparel		...	177	162	147	127	109	100	107	77	73	46	51
15	Leather and related products		...	963	703	636	637	128	100	117	110	71	205	248
16	Wood/wood products/cork,excl. furniture		...	94	87	87	85	95	100	115	109	95	68	71
17	Paper and paper products		...	113	110	108	102	101	100	108	104	96	84	72
18	Printing and reproduction of recorded media		...	106	104	100	95	100	100	101	104	99	59	61
19	Coke and refined petroleum products		...	...	...	...	...	...	...	...	...	...	...	...
20	Chemicals and chemical products		...	108	104	107	106	100	100	102	102	105	96	103
21	Pharmaceuticals,medicinal chemicals, etc.		...	85	101	104	99	85	100	99	93	85	85	93
22	Rubber and plastics products		...	92	94	93	93	93	100	102	105	108	74	75
23	Other non-metallic mineral products		...	94	95	91	93	93	100	108	105	107	75	74
24	Basic metals		...	149	136	104	111	102	100	104	113	115	71	79
25	Fabricated metal products, except machinery		...	95	96	102	104	104	100	105	112	113	86	80
26	Computer, electronic and optical products		...	105	110	108	107	100	100	111	119	108	89	105
27	Electrical equipment		...	88	89	90	84	98	100	109	110	113	76	86
28	Machinery and equipment n.e.c.		...	89	95	94	92	95	100	111	123	132	106	105
29	Motor vehicles, trailers and semi-trailers		...	109	114	102	107	100	100	108	99	90	52	59
30	Other transport equipment		...	76	81	87	74	76	100	83	64	69	66	47
31	Furniture		...	110	104	101	98	101	100	101	98	84	65	62
32	Other manufacturing		...	79	90	98	90	99	100	105	108	126	135	148
33	Repair and installation of machinery/equipment		...	91	99	109	100	91	100	120	114	128	116	120
C	Total manufacturing		...	98	100	100	99	97	100	106	107	106	88	90

Egypt

Supplier of information:
Central Agency for Public Mobilisation and Statistics (CAPMAS), Cairo.

Basic source of data:
Annual survey on registered establishments.

Major deviations from ISIC (Revision 4):
None reported.

Reference period:
Calendar year for private sector; fiscal year for public sector.

Scope:
Establishments with 10 or more employees.

Method of data collection:
Mail questionnaires.

Type of enumeration:
Complete enumeration.

Adjusted for non-response:
Yes.

Concepts and definitions of variables:
Wages and salaries includes employers' contributions (in respect of their employees) paid to social security, pension and insurance schemes as well as the benefits received by employees under these schemes and severance and termination pay.
Output excludes value of goods shipped in the same condition as received less the amount paid for these goods.

Related national publications:
Annual Bulletin on Industrial Production; Annual Bulletin on Industrial Statistics and Quarterly Bulletin on Industrial Statistics, all published by Central Agency for Public Mobilisation and Statistics, Cairo.

Egypt

ISIC	Industry	Number of establishments (number) Note	2007	2008	2009	2010	Number of persons engaged (number) Note	2007	2008	2009	2010	Wages and salaries paid to employees (millions of Egyptian Pounds) Note	2007	2008	2009	2010
1010	Processing/preserving of meat		...	...	...	35		...	...	...	9722		...	...	...	189.6
1020	Processing/preserving of fish, etc.		...	...	...	14		...	...	...	547		...	...	...	9.1
1030	Processing/preserving of fruit,vegetables		...	...	...	92		...	...	...	23443		...	...	...	327.2
1040	Vegetable and animal oils and fats		...	...	...	38		...	...	...	14432		...	...	...	252.1
1050	Dairy products		...	...	...	59		...	...	...	15451		...	...	...	317.8
106	Grain mill products,starches and starch products		...	...	...	197		...	...	...	22977		...	...	...	415.2
1061	Grain mill products		...	...	...	191		...	...	...	21216		...	...	...	369.2
1062	Starches and starch products		...	...	...	6		...	...	...	1761		...	...	...	45.9
107	Other food products		...	...	...	4360		...	...	...	107776		...	...	...	1643.9
1071	Bakery products		...	...	...	3983		...	...	...	68884		...	...	...	780.2
1072	Sugar		...	...	...	12		...	...	...	16425		...	...	...	503.7
1073	Cocoa, chocolate and sugar confectionery		...	...	...	80		...	...	...	8822		...	...	...	142.8
1074	Macaroni, noodles, couscous, etc.		...	...	...	85		...	...	...	3475		...	...	...	61.4
1075	Prepared meals and dishes		...	...	...	3		...	...	...	799		...	...	...	17.1
1079	Other food products n.e.c.		...	...	...	197		...	...	...	9371		...	...	...	138.7
1080	Prepared animal feeds		...	...	...	76		...	...	...	8297		...	...	...	126.1
1101	Distilling, rectifying and blending of spirits		...	...	...	1		...	...	...	531		...	...	...	15.2
1102	Wines		...	...	...	1		...	...	...	73		...	...	...	13.7
1103	Malt liquors and malt		...	...	...	1		...	...	...	286		...	...	...	10.7
1104	Soft drinks,mineral waters,other bottled waters		...	...	...	17		...	...	...	22406		...	...	...	766.2
1200	Tobacco products		...	...	...	29		...	...	...	14944		...	...	...	489.3
131	Spinning, weaving and finishing of textiles		...	...	...	394		...	...	...	98752		...	...	...	1645.6
1311	Preparation and spinning of textile fibres		...	...	...	110		...	...	...	59013		...	...	...	1017.3
1312	Weaving of textiles		...	...	...	235		...	...	...	36080		...	...	...	585.6
1313	Finishing of textiles		...	...	...	49		...	...	...	3659		...	...	...	42.8
139	Other textiles		...	...	...	192		...	...	...	32063		...	...	...	505.2
1391	Knitted and crocheted fabrics		...	...	...	30		...	...	...	1476		...	...	...	13.0
1392	Made-up textile articles, except apparel		...	...	...	118		...	...	...	12121		...	...	...	109.3
1393	Carpets and rugs		...	...	...	26		...	...	...	17436		...	...	...	368.4
1394	Cordage, rope, twine and netting		...	...	...	2		...	...	...	767		...	...	...	12.7
1399	Other textiles n.e.c.		...	...	...	16		...	...	...	263		...	...	...	1.8
1410	Wearing apparel, except fur apparel		...	...	...	411		...	...	...	101517		...	...	...	1271.3
1420	Articles of fur		...	...	...	...		...	...	...	...		...	...	...	...
1430	Knitted and crocheted apparel		...	...	...	28		...	...	...	1751		...	...	...	12.6
151	Leather;luggage,handbags,saddlery,harness;fur		...	...	...	73		...	...	...	1761		...	...	...	17.6
1511	Tanning/dressing of leather; dressing of fur		...	...	...	50		...	...	...	1331		...	...	...	13.5
1512	Luggage,handbags,etc.;saddlery/harness		...	...	...	23		...	...	...	430		...	...	...	4.1
1520	Footwear		...	...	...	77		...	...	...	3617		...	...	...	33.3
1610	Sawmilling and planing of wood		...	...	...	27		...	...	...	482		...	...	...	4.0
162	Wood products, cork, straw, plaiting materials		...	...	...	54		...	...	...	2564		...	...	...	42.5

Code	Description							
1621	Veneer sheets and wood-based panels	23.0	...	...	1320	...	16	...
1622	Builders' carpentry and joinery	8.1	...	...	658	...	26	...
1623	Wooden containers	...	...	...	...	...	...	...
1629	Other wood products;articles of cork,straw	11.5	...	...	586	...	12	...
1701	Pulp, paper and paperboard	193.2	...	...	9682	...	45	...
1702	Corrugated paper and paperboard	177.3	...	...	8961	...	66	...
1709	Other articles of paper and paperboard	114.1	...	...	5044	...	40	...
181	Printing and service activities related to printing	411.5	...	...	19799	...	165	...
1811	Printing	411.3	...	...	19766	...	164	...
1812	Service activities related to printing	0.2	...	...	33	...	1	...
1820	Reproduction of recorded media	0.5	...	...	58	...	1	...
1910	Coke oven products	149.7	...	...	3229	...	2	...
1920	Refined petroleum products	2775.2	...	...	35373	...	34	...
201	Basic chemicals,fertilizers, etc.	1447.6	...	...	29293	...	116	...
2011	Basic chemicals	461.9	...	...	11485	...	57	...
2012	Fertilizers and nitrogen compounds	967.9	...	...	16059	...	25	...
2013	Plastics and synthetic rubber in primary forms	17.8	...	...	1749	...	34	...
202	Other chemical products	515.0	...	...	25458	...	227	...
2021	Pesticides and other agrochemical products	27.8	...	...	1115	...	10	...
2022	Paints,varnishes;printing ink and mastics	192.1	...	...	9720	...	82	...
2023	Soap,cleaning and cosmetic preparations	207.1	...	...	11496	...	102	...
2029	Other chemical products n.e.c.	88.1	...	...	3127	...	33	...
2030	Man-made fibres	17.8	...	...	1224	...	16	...
2100	Pharmaceuticals,medicinal chemicals, etc.	1562.1	...	...	42314	...	57	...
221	Rubber products	297.3	...	...	11778	...	113	...
2211	Rubber tyres and tubes	117.7	...	...	3285	...	14	...
2219	Other rubber products	179.5	...	...	8493	...	99	...
2220	Plastics products	273.2	...	...	21838	...	252	...
2310	Glass and glass products	428.2	...	...	31806	...	46	...
239	Non-metallic mineral products n.e.c.	1483.3	...	...	68553	...	778	...
2391	Refractory products	14.7	...	...	818	...	9	...
2392	Clay building materials	608.7	...	...	42051	...	531	...
2393	Other porcelain and ceramic products	63.9	...	...	5335	...	13	...
2394	Cement, lime and plaster	576.7	...	...	10227	...	14	...
2395	Articles of concrete, cement and plaster	153.2	...	...	5935	...	80	...
2396	Cutting, shaping and finishing of stone	44.4	...	...	3055	...	95	...
2399	Other non-metallic mineral products n.e.c.	21.7	...	...	1132	...	36	...
2410	Basic iron and steel	1548.6	...	...	39976	...	81	...
2420	Basic precious and other non-ferrous metals	551.6	...	...	18155	...	23	...
243	Casting of metals	25.0	...	...	1658	...	11	...
2431	Casting of iron and steel	22.6	...	...	1447	...	7	...
2432	Casting of non-ferrous metals	2.4	...	...	211	...	4	...
251	Struct.metal products, tanks, reservoirs	247.2	...	...	13456	...	71	...
2511	Structural metal products	194.5	...	...	11835	...	52	...
2512	Tanks, reservoirs and containers of metal	52.7	...	...	1621	...	19	...

continued

Egypt

ISIC	Industry	Number of establishments (number)					Number of persons engaged (number)					Wages and salaries paid to employees (millions of Egyptian Pounds)				
		Note	2007	2008	2009	2010	Note	2007	2008	2009	2010	Note	2007	2008	2009	2010
2513	Steam generators, excl. hot water boilers		...	...	...	...		...	...	...	...		...	...	...	...
2520	Weapons and ammunition		...	...	...	1		...	...	...	2386		...	...	...	59.3
259	Other metal products;metal working services		...	...	...	357		...	...	...	20095		...	...	...	329.7
2591	Forging,pressing,stamping,roll-forming of metal		...	...	...	62		...	...	...	2373		...	...	...	26.0
2592	Treatment and coating of metals; machining		...	...	...	8		...	...	...	172		...	...	...	1.5
2593	Cutlery, hand tools and general hardware		...	...	...	19		...	...	...	3219		...	...	...	45.6
2599	Other fabricated metal products n.e.c.		...	...	...	268		...	...	...	14331		...	...	...	256.7
2610	Electronic components and boards		...	...	...	6		...	...	...	379		...	...	...	7.2
2620	Computers and peripheral equipment		...	...	...	8		...	...	...	1482		...	...	...	35.5
2630	Communication equipment		...	...	...	7		...	...	...	1169		...	...	...	20.8
2640	Consumer electronics		...	...	...	9		...	...	...	6074		...	...	...	122.1
265	Measuring,testing equipment; watches, etc.		...	...	...	8		...	...	...	3869		...	...	...	107.3
2651	Measuring/testing/navigating equipment,etc.		...	...	...	7		...	...	...	3831		...	...	...	107.0
2652	Watches and clocks		...	...	...	1		...	...	...	38		...	...	...	0.2
2660	Irradiation/electromedical equipment,etc.		...	...	...	3		...	...	...	456		...	...	...	3.2
2670	Optical instruments and photographic equipment		...	...	...	1		...	...	...	15		...	...	...	0.2
2680	Magnetic and optical media		...	...	...	2		...	...	...	171		...	...	...	0.9
2710	Electric motors,generators,transformers,etc.		...	...	...	55		...	...	...	9239		...	...	...	208.3
2720	Batteries and accumulators		...	...	...	7		...	...	...	3057		...	...	...	39.7
273	Wiring and wiring devices		...	...	...	27		...	...	...	4376		...	...	...	103.0
2731	Fibre optic cables		...	...	...	...		...	...	...	...		...	...	...	...
2732	Other electronic and electric wires and cables		...	...	...	25		...	...	...	4318		...	...	...	102.5
2733	Wiring devices		...	...	...	2		...	...	...	58		...	...	...	0.5
2740	Electric lighting equipment		...	...	...	27		...	...	...	3784		...	...	...	73.0
2750	Domestic appliances		...	...	...	58		...	...	...	24255		...	...	...	479.8
2790	Other electrical equipment		...	...	...	10		...	...	...	887		...	...	...	25.5
281	General-purpose machinery		...	...	...	94		...	...	...	20317		...	...	...	362.9
2811	Engines/turbines,excl.aircraft,vehicle engines		...	...	...	4		...	...	...	2568		...	...	...	58.5
2812	Fluid power equipment		...	...	...	1		...	...	...	130		...	...	...	3.1
2813	Other pumps, compressors, taps and valves		...	...	...	31		...	...	...	3305		...	...	...	61.0
2814	Bearings, gears, gearing and driving elements		...	...	...	1		...	...	...	11		...	...	...	-
2815	Ovens, furnaces and furnace burners		...	...	...	5		...	...	...	1912		...	...	...	30.3
2816	Lifting and handling equipment		...	...	...	9		...	...	...	1114		...	...	...	19.6
2817	Office machinery, excl.computers,etc.		...	...	...	2		...	...	...	1260		...	...	...	12.6
2818	Power-driven hand tools		...	...	...	1		...	...	...	26		...	...	...	0.2
2819	Other general-purpose machinery		...	...	...	40		...	...	...	9991		...	...	...	177.5
282	Special-purpose machinery		...	...	...	35		...	...	...	3780		...	...	...	80.4
2821	Agricultural and forestry machinery		...	...	...	16		...	...	...	815		...	...	...	14.5
2822	Metal-forming machinery and machine tools		...	...	...	...		...	...	...	...		...	...	...	...
2823	Machinery for metallurgy		...	...	...	...		...	...	...	...		...	...	...	...
2824	Mining, quarrying and construction machinery		...	...	...	5		...	...	...	1224		...	...	...	26.8

Code	Description					
2825	Food/beverage/tobacco processing machinery	…	…	…	…	…
2826	Textile/apparel/leather production machinery	3	48	…	…	0.5
2829	Other special-purpose machinery	11	1693	…	…	38.7
2910	Motor vehicles	56	20560	…	…	439.8
2920	Automobile bodies, trailers and semi-trailers	5	945	…	…	22.0
2930	Parts and accessories for motor vehicles	13	1866	…	…	32.0
301	Building of ships and boats	22	6764	…	…	204.5
3011	Building of ships and floating structures	20	6656	…	…	203.3
3012	Building of pleasure and sporting boats	2	108	…	…	1.1
3020	Railway locomotives and rolling stock	2	1282	…	…	41.0
3030	Air and spacecraft and related machinery	…	…	…	…	…
3040	Military fighting vehicles	3	895	…	…	7.9
309	Transport equipment n.e.c.	3	895	…	…	7.9
3091	Motorcycles	…	…	…	…	…
3092	Bicycles and invalid carriages	…	…	…	…	…
3099	Other transport equipment n.e.c.	…	…	…	…	…
3100	Furniture	164	14151	…	…	161.4
321	Jewellery, bijouterie and related articles	17	1270	…	…	17.5
3211	Jewellery and related articles	16	1248	…	…	17.4
3212	Imitation jewellery and related articles	1	22	…	…	0.1
3220	Musical instruments	1	10	…	…	0.1
3230	Sports goods	…	…	…	…	…
3240	Games and toys	6	306	…	…	2.4
3250	Medical and dental instruments and supplies	30	2285	…	…	25.5
3290	Other manufacturing n.e.c.	38	1938	…	…	22.9
331	Repair of fabricated metal products/machinery	6	677	…	…	13.4
3311	Repair of fabricated metal products	…	…	…	…	…
3312	Repair of machinery	5	473	…	…	8.9
3313	Repair of electronic and optical equipment	…	…	…	…	…
3314	Repair of electrical equipment	…	…	…	…	…
3315	Repair of transport equip., excl. motor vehicles	1	204	…	…	4.5
3319	Repair of other equipment	…	…	…	…	…
3320	Installation of industrial machinery/equipment	2	27	…	…	0.3
C	Total manufacturing	9400	1029814	…	…	23376.0

Egypt

- 366 -

ISIC	Industry	Output at producers' prices (millions of Egyptian Pounds)					Value added at producers' prices (millions of Egyptian Pounds)					Gross fixed capital formation (millions of Egyptian Pounds)		
		Note	2007	2008	2009	2010	Note	2007	2008	2009	2010	Note	2009	2010
1010	Processing/preserving of meat		...	...	...	2379.6		...	...	...	440.0		...	...
1020	Processing/preserving of fish, etc.		...	...	...	78.3		...	...	...	24.4		...	...
1030	Processing/preserving of fruit,vegetables		...	...	...	5431.2		...	...	...	1378.5		...	...
1040	Vegetable and animal oils and fats		...	...	...	5094.3		...	...	...	851.3		...	...
1050	Dairy products		...	...	...	6320.8		...	...	...	1897.1		...	...
106	Grain mill products,starches and starch products		...	...	...	10091.9		...	...	...	2205.6		...	...
1061	Grain mill products		...	...	...	9159.4		...	...	...	1624.2		...	...
1062	Starches and starch products		...	...	...	932.4		...	...	...	581.4		...	...
107	Other food products		...	...	...	17076.0		...	...	...	5288.0		...	...
1071	Bakery products		...	...	...	4622.7		...	...	...	1717.8		...	...
1072	Sugar		...	...	...	7458.7		...	...	...	2274.1		...	...
1073	Cocoa, chocolate and sugar confectionery		...	...	...	1404.0		...	...	...	374.4		...	...
1074	Macaroni, noodles, couscous, etc.		...	...	...	952.0		...	...	...	240.2		...	...
1075	Prepared meals and dishes		...	...	...	246.8		...	...	...	52.5		...	...
1079	Other food products n.e.c.		...	...	...	2391.7		...	...	...	629.0		...	...
1080	Prepared animal feeds		...	...	...	2575.7		...	...	...	742.1		...	...
1101	Distilling, rectifying and blending of spirits		...	...	...	157.4		...	...	...	121.7		...	...
1102	Wines		...	...	...	51.2		...	...	...	14.7		...	...
1103	Malt liquors and malt		...	...	...	596.6		...	...	...	235.9		...	...
1104	Soft drinks,mineral waters,other bottled waters		...	...	...	4747.6		...	...	...	1473.8		...	...
1200	Tobacco products		...	...	...	3963.3		...	...	...	3904.0		...	...
131	Spinning, weaving and finishing of textiles		...	...	...	6495.6		...	...	...	2368.4		...	...
1311	Preparation and spinning of textile fibres		...	...	...	4271.1		...	...	...	1431.8		...	...
1312	Weaving of textiles		...	...	...	2224.5		...	...	...	936.6		...	...
1313	Finishing of textiles		...	...	...	...		...	...	...	...		...	...
139	Other textiles		...	...	...	5414.7		...	...	...	1342.2		...	...
1391	Knitted and crocheted fabrics		...	...	...	126.6		...	...	...	36.2		...	...
1392	Made-up textile articles, except apparel		...	...	...	1298.6		...	...	...	304.0		...	...
1393	Carpets and rugs		...	...	...	3957.7		...	...	...	991.2		...	...
1394	Cordage, rope, twine and netting		...	...	...	24.5		...	...	...	8.5		...	...
1399	Other textiles n.e.c.		...	...	...	7.3		...	...	...	2.4		...	...
1410	Wearing apparel, except fur apparel		...	...	...	5740.8		...	...	...	2607.6		...	...
1420	Articles of fur		...	...	...	...		...	...	...	...		...	...
1430	Knitted and crocheted apparel		...	...	...	51.5		...	...	...	20.6		...	...
151	Leather;luggage,handbags,saddlery,harness;fur		...	...	...	193.1		...	...	...	45.1		...	...
1511	Tanning/dressing of leather; dressing of fur		...	...	...	163.1		...	...	...	38.2		...	...
1512	Luggage,handbags,etc.;saddlery/harness		...	...	...	30.0		...	...	...	6.9		...	...
1520	Footwear		...	...	...	231.8		...	...	...	135.8		...	...
1610	Sawmilling and planing of wood		...	...	...	34.2		...	...	...	11.9		...	...
162	Wood products, cork, straw, plaiting materials		...	...	...	299.3		...	...	...	105.0		...	...

Code	Description		
1621	Veneer sheets and wood-based panels	197.8	62.9
1622	Builders' carpentry and joinery	72.6	25.4
1623	Wooden containers	...	...
1629	Other wood products;articles of cork,straw	29.0	16.8
1701	Pulp, paper and paperboard	3559.9	991.7
1702	Corrugated paper and paperboard	2640.4	496.5
1709	Other articles of paper and paperboard	1116.6	340.4
181	Printing and service activities related to printing	2143.2	1099.7
1811	Printing	2143.2	1099.3
1812	Service activities related to printing	...	0.4
1820	Reproduction of recorded media	6.7	3.8
1910	Coke oven products	2017.4	302.6
1920	Refined petroleum products	86905.2	35027.5
201	Basic chemicals,fertilizers, etc.	14316.8	8315.6
2011	Basic chemicals	4517.2	1850.0
2012	Fertilizers and nitrogen compounds	9499.6	6395.9
2013	Plastics and synthetic rubber in primary forms	300.0	69.7
202	Other chemical products	9987.0	2826.6
2021	Pesticides and other agrochemical products	390.9	118.7
2022	Paints,varnishes;printing ink and mastics	2705.8	955.2
2023	Soap,cleaning and cosmetic preparations	5932.5	1487.1
2029	Other chemical products n.e.c.	957.8	265.6
2030	Man-made fibres	270.0	55.6
2100	Pharmaceuticals,medicinal chemicals, etc.	12176.5	5690.9
221	Rubber products	4094.8	1179.2
2211	Rubber tyres and tubes	1371.8	326.0
2219	Other rubber products	2723.0	853.2
2220	Plastics products	4539.8	923.5
2310	Glass and glass products	2730.4	1392.1
239	Non-metallic mineral products n.e.c.	26896.8	12246.7
2391	Refractory products	156.8	55.1
2392	Clay building materials	4906.9	1894.6
2393	Other porcelain and ceramic products	996.1	394.6
2394	Cement, lime and plaster	18923.6	9107.5
2395	Articles of concrete, cement and plaster	1417.4	566.4
2396	Cutting, shaping and finishing of stone	295.3	124.4
2399	Other non-metallic mineral products n.e.c.	200.7	103.9
2410	Basic iron and steel	32249.8	4831.7
2420	Basic precious and other non-ferrous metals	5462.9	1201.7
243	Casting of metals	261.9	60.4
2431	Casting of iron and steel	179.4	-13.5
2432	Casting of non-ferrous metals	82.5	73.9
251	Struct.metal products, tanks, reservoirs	2274.3	681.8
2511	Structural metal products	1838.3	532.4
2512	Tanks, reservoirs and containers of metal	436.0	149.4

continued

Egypt

ISIC	Industry	Output at producers' prices (millions of Egyptian Pounds)					Value added at producers' prices (millions of Egyptian Pounds)					Gross fixed capital formation (millions of Egyptian Pounds)		
		Note	2007	2008	2009	2010	Note	2007	2008	2009	2010	Note	2009	2010
2513	Steam generators, excl. hot water boilers													
2520	Weapons and ammunition					135.1					48.6			
259	Other metal products;metal working services					4560.9					1139.9			
2591	Forging,pressing,stamping,roll-forming of metal					917.1					200.9			
2592	Treatment and coating of metals; machining										2.6			
2593	Cutlery, hand tools and general hardware					330.4					89.2			
2599	Other fabricated metal products n.e.c.					3313.5					847.1			
2610	Electronic components and boards					81.4					20.0			
2620	Computers and peripheral equipment					835.5					99.4			
2630	Communication equipment					305.4					84.5			
2640	Consumer electronics					1166.9					348.3			
265	Measuring,testing equipment; watches, etc.					484.3					161.6			
2651	Measuring/testing/navigating equipment,etc.					483.2					161.2			
2652	Watches and clocks					1.1					0.3			
2660	Irradiation/electromedical equipment,etc.					64.8					45.0			
2670	Optical instruments and photographic equipment					1.2					0.4			
2680	Magnetic and optical media					7.8					5.0			
2710	Electric motors,generators,transformers,etc.					2233.8					666.8			
2720	Batteries and accumulators													
273	Wiring and wiring devices					2187.8					936.5			
2731	Fibre optic cables													
2732	Other electronic and electric wires and cables					2182.1					934.1			
2733	Wiring devices					5.7					2.4			
2740	Electric lighting equipment					487.0					158.1			
2750	Domestic appliances					6773.9					1830.0			
2790	Other electrical equipment					5628.9					272.2			
281	General-purpose machinery					3551.7					930.2			
2811	Engines/turbines,excl.aircraft,vehicle engines					150.8					74.1			
2812	Fluid power equipment										21.5			
2813	Other pumps, compressors, taps and valves					317.4					165.6			
2814	Bearings, gears, gearing and driving elements					1.3					0.2			
2815	Ovens, furnaces and furnace burners					157.1					31.6			
2816	Lifting and handling equipment					106.0					59.0			
2817	Office machinery, excl.computers,etc.					55.4					11.8			
2818	Power-driven hand tools					1.6					0.9			
2819	Other general-purpose machinery					2762.1					565.3			
282	Special-purpose machinery					531.6					279.1			
2821	Agricultural and forestry machinery					153.8					44.5			
2822	Metal-forming machinery and machine tools													
2823	Machinery for metallurgy													
2824	Mining, quarrying and construction machinery					90.7					48.5			

Code	Industry							
2825	Food/beverage/tobacco processing machinery	⋮	1.1	⋮	⋮	3.7	⋮	⋮
2826	Textile/apparel/leather production machinery	⋮	185.0	⋮	⋮	283.4	⋮	⋮
2829	Other special-purpose machinery	⋮	2070.9	⋮	⋮	8882.2	⋮	⋮
2910	Motor vehicles	⋮	41.9	⋮	⋮	238.2	⋮	⋮
2920	Automobile bodies, trailers and semi-trailers	⋮	114.0	⋮	⋮	488.2	⋮	⋮
2930	Parts and accessories for motor vehicles	⋮	⋮	⋮	⋮	⋮	⋮	⋮
301	Building of ships and boats	⋮	236.8	⋮	⋮	320.1	⋮	⋮
3011	Building of ships and floating structures	⋮	235.0	⋮	⋮	288.7	⋮	⋮
3012	Building of pleasure and sporting boats	⋮	1.8	⋮	⋮	31.4	⋮	⋮
3020	Railway locomotives and rolling stock	⋮	297.6	⋮	⋮	496.0	⋮	⋮
3030	Air and spacecraft and related machinery	⋮	⋮	⋮	⋮	⋮	⋮	⋮
3040	Military fighting vehicles	⋮	31.2	⋮	⋮	146.1	⋮	⋮
309	Transport equipment n.e.c.	⋮	31.2	⋮	⋮	146.1	⋮	⋮
3091	Motorcycles	⋮	⋮	⋮	⋮	⋮	⋮	⋮
3092	Bicycles and invalid carriages	⋮	⋮	⋮	⋮	⋮	⋮	⋮
3099	Other transport equipment n.e.c.	⋮	335.8	⋮	⋮	1130.0	⋮	⋮
3100	Furniture	⋮	74.9	⋮	⋮	2180.4	⋮	⋮
321	Jewellery, bijouterie and related articles	⋮	74.7	⋮	⋮	2180.0	⋮	⋮
3211	Jewellery and related articles	⋮	0.2	⋮	⋮	0.4	⋮	⋮
3212	Imitation jewellery and related articles	⋮	0.1	⋮	⋮	0.2	⋮	⋮
3220	Musical instruments	⋮	5.2	⋮	⋮	17.1	⋮	⋮
3230	Sports goods	⋮	64.8	⋮	⋮	205.4	⋮	⋮
3240	Games and toys	⋮	106.7	⋮	⋮	241.1	⋮	⋮
3250	Medical and dental instruments and supplies	⋮	9.9	⋮	⋮	-	⋮	⋮
3290	Other manufacturing n.e.c.	⋮	⋮	⋮	⋮	⋮	⋮	⋮
331	Repair of fabricated metal products/machinery	⋮	6.9	⋮	⋮	⋮	⋮	⋮
3311	Repair of fabricated metal products	⋮	⋮	⋮	⋮	⋮	⋮	⋮
3312	Repair of machinery	⋮	3.1	⋮	⋮	⋮	⋮	⋮
3313	Repair of electronic and optical equipment	⋮	⋮	⋮	⋮	⋮	⋮	⋮
3314	Repair of electrical equipment	⋮	⋮	⋮	⋮	⋮	⋮	⋮
3315	Repair of transport equip., excl. motor vehicles	⋮	0.5	⋮	⋮	0.5	⋮	⋮
3319	Repair of other equipment	⋮	⋮	⋮	⋮	⋮	⋮	⋮
3320	Installation of industrial machinery/equipment	⋮	⋮	⋮	⋮	⋮	⋮	⋮
C	Total manufacturing	⋮	113297.5	⋮	⋮	334058.5	⋮	⋮

Egypt

ISIC Revision 3

Index numbers of industrial production

(2005=100)

ISIC	Industry	Note	1999	2000	2001	2002	2003	2004	2005	2006	2007	2008	2009	2010
15	Food and beverages		148	166	119	107	95	95	100	100	116	121	111	131
16	Tobacco products		104	106	110	116	92	100	100	136	103	113	110	108
17	Textiles		144	127	113	120	135	112	100	100	100	109	95	124
18	Wearing apparel, fur		88	80	78	79	78	77	100	142	151	176	185	185
19	Leather, leather products and footwear		216	201	226	234	155	148	100	65	55	93	82	76
20	Wood products (excl. furniture)		396	400	194	251	137	95	100	147	223	404	383	209
21	Paper and paper products		65	71	75	77	85	89	100	114	125	142	108	119
22	Printing and publishing		49	53	54	57	52	100	100	131	149	98	81	90
23	Coke,refined petroleum products,nuclear fuel		90	62	69	64	108	88	100	232	281	286	165	205
24	Chemicals and chemical products		60	60	76	77	77	76	100	90	103	112	103	115
25	Rubber and plastics products		91	81	69	68	86	101	100	83	73	79	75	79
26	Non-metallic mineral products		83	69	70	79	83	82	100	130	148	187	202	194
27	Basic metals		102	107	95	99	138	110	100	127	135	110	118	102
28	Fabricated metal products		120	131	117	119	99	93	100	138	187	212	195	180
29	Machinery and equipment n.e.c.		126	103	95	99	90	97	100	106	96	176	177	180
30	Office, accounting and computing machinery		...	...	...	69	37	115	100	94	36	50	97	103
31	Electrical machinery and apparatus		81	79	74	75	78	87	100	95	110	147	163	125
32	Radio,television and communication equipment		...	...	...	143	85	140	100	85	163	168	72	135
33	Medical, precision and optical instruments		100	139	169	172	149	134	100	88	164	180	146	131
34	Motor vehicles, trailers, semi-trailers		...	...	...	180	144	82	100	133	126	175	166	203
35	Other transport equipment		...	...	...	38	139	113	100	61	36	56	58	34
36	Furniture; manufacturing n.e.c.		183	177	171	179	131	110	100	132	165	190	161	163
37	Recycling		...	...	...	...	...	...	...	...	...	...	...	...
D	Total manufacturing		91	87	85	91	86	91	100	115	125	130	120	130

Eritrea

Concepts and definitions of variables:

Number of employees includes temporary and contract workers.

Wages and salaries excludes remuneration for time not worked but includes employers' contributions paid to social security, pension and insurance schemes as well as the benefits received by employees under these schemes and severance and termination pay.

Output includes revenue from non-industrial activities.

Related national publications:

Report on Census of Manufacturing Establishments, Statistical Bulletin, published by the Ministry of Trade and Industry, Planning and Statistics Division, Asmara.

Supplier of information:

Ministry of Trade and Industry, Planning and Statistics Division, Asmara.

Basic source of data:

Census of the manufacturing industries.

Major deviations from ISIC (Revision 3):

None reported.

Reference period:

Calendar year.

Scope:

Establishments with 10 or more employees.

Method of data collection:

Direct interview in the field.

Type of enumeration:

Complete enumeration.

Adjusted for non-response:

No.

Eritrea

ISIC	Industry	Number of establishments (number)				Number of employees (number)				Wages and salaries paid to employees (thousands of Eritrean Nakfa)			
		2007	2008	2009	2010	2007	2008	2009	2010	2007	2008	2009	2010
151	Processed meat,fish,fruit,vegetables,fats	2	2	2	1	284	216	216	28	3918	2813	2796	434
1511	Processing/preserving of meat	1	1	1	-	187	179	195	-	2680	2263	2531	-
1512	Processing/preserving of fish	1	-	-	-	97	-	-	-	1238	-	-	-
1513	Processing/preserving of fruit & vegetables	-	-	-	-	-	-	-	-	-	-	-	-
1514	Vegetable and animal oils and fats	-	1	1	1	-	37	21	28	-	551	265	434
1520	Dairy products	5	5	5	5	222	227	220	221	3593	3505	3584	5543
153	Grain mill products; starches; animal feeds	5	5	5	5	601	515	481	472	8487	7777	8423	11534
1531	Grain mill products	2	2	2	2	501	430	401	410	7353	6746	7371	10442
1532	Starches and starch products	-	-	-	-	-	-	-	-	-	-	-	-
1533	Prepared animal feeds	3	3	3	3	100	85	80	62	1134	1031	1052	1092
154	Other food products	71	69	62	58	1203	1027	935	939	14094	12101	11687	13224
1541	Bakery products	66	65	58	54	979	904	790	784	11452	10243	9439	10765
1542	Sugar	-	-	-	-	-	-	-	-	-	-	-	-
1543	Cocoa, chocolate and sugar confectionery	1	1	1	1	37	37	38	36	343	341	403	519
1544	Macaroni, noodles & similar products	3	3	3	3	129	86	107	119	2164	1517	1845	1940
1549	Other food products n.e.c.	1	-	-	-	58	-	-	-	136	-	-	-
155	Beverages	22	20	21	19	1188	1112	1124	1280	26092	21864	22172	28718
1551	Distilling, rectifying & blending of spirits	3	3	2	2	140	88	76	98	1263	1239	1177	1168
1552	Wines	1	1	1	1	38	36	34	29	962	997	1477	1535
1553	Malt liquors and malt	2	2	2	2	463	449	449	415	14953	11287	11097	12923
1554	Soft drinks; mineral waters	16	14	16	14	547	539	565	738	8914	8340	8421	13092
1600	Tobacco products	1	1	1	1	45	45	42	43	3984	5138	7092	14230
171	Spinning, weaving and finishing of textiles	5	5	6	5	2212	2213	2103	2082	33728	43031	44004	48493
1711	Textile fibre preparation; textile weaving	-	-	-	-	-	-	-	-	-	-	-	-
1712	Finishing of textiles	5	5	6	5	2212	2213	2103	2082	33728	43031	44004	48493
172	Other textiles	-	-	-	-	-	-	-	-	-	-	-	-
1721	Made-up textile articles, except apparel	-	-	-	-	-	-	-	-	-	-	-	-
1722	Carpets and rugs	-	-	-	-	-	-	-	-	-	-	-	-
1723	Cordage, rope, twine and netting	-	-	-	-	-	-	-	-	-	-	-	-
1729	Other textiles n.e.c.	-	-	-	-	-	-	-	-	-	-	-	-
1730	Knitted and crocheted fabrics and articles	3	3	3	3	191	206	214	215	2581	2626	2801	3370
1810	Wearing apparel, except fur apparel	4	4	3	6	187	168	87	253	1761	1624	1437	3760
1820	Dressing & dyeing of fur; processing of fur	-	-	-	-	-	-	-	-	-	-	-	-
191	Tanning, dressing and processing of leather	6	6	6	6	321	310	351	367	5548	5503	5353	7196
1911	Tanning and dressing of leather	5	5	5	5	302	289	330	346	5358	5295	5118	6861
1912	Luggage, handbags, etc.; saddlery & harness	1	1	1	1	19	21	21	21	190	208	235	335
1920	Footwear	13	14	14	14	846	839	841	902	10469	10432	11097	13106
2010	Sawmilling and planing of wood	-	-	-	-	-	-	-	-	-	-	-	-
202	Products of wood, cork, straw, etc.	-	-	-	-	-	-	-	-	-	-	-	-
2021	Veneer sheets, plywood, particle board, etc.	-	-	-	-	-	-	-	-	-	-	-	-
2022	Builders carpentry and joinery	-	-	-	-	-	-	-	-	-	-	-	-
2023	Wooden containers	-	-	-	-	-	-	-	-	-	-	-	-
2029	Other wood products; articles of cork/straw	-	-	-	-	-	-	-	-	-	-	-	-
210	Paper and paper products	5	5	5	4	109	127	100	98	1075	1304	1157	905
2101	Pulp, paper and paperboard	2	2	2	2	54	60	42	43	396	531	570	519
2102	Corrugated paper and paperboard	1	1	1	-	13	15	13	-	298	263	266	-
2109	Other articles of paper and paperboard	2	2	2	2	42	52	45	55	381	510	321	386
221	Publishing	-	-	-	-	-	-	-	-	-	-	-	-
2211	Publishing of books and other publications	-	-	-	-	-	-	-	-	-	-	-	-
2212	Publishing of newspapers, journals, etc.	-	-	-	-	-	-	-	-	-	-	-	-
2213	Publishing of recorded media	-	-	-	-	-	-	-	-	-	-	-	-
2219	Other publishing	-	-	-	-	-	-	-	-	-	-	-	-

Code	Description	1	2	3	4	5	6	7	8	9	10	11	12	13	14	15	16
222	Printing and related service activities	8243	8014	6639	7610	505	505	442	459	9	9	8	8	9	9	8	8
2221	Printing	8243	8014	6639	7610	505	505	442	459	9	9	8	8	9	9	8	8
2222	Service activities related to printing	-	-	-	-	-	-	-	-	-	-	-	-	-	-	-	-
2230	Reproduction of recorded media	-	-	-	-	-	-	-	-	-	-	-	-	-	-	-	-
2310	Coke oven products	-	-	-	-	-	-	-	-	-	-	-	-	-	-	-	-
2320	Refined petroleum products	-	-	-	-	-	-	-	-	-	-	-	-	-	-	-	-
2330	Processing of nuclear fuel	-	-	-	-	-	-	-	-	-	-	-	-	-	-	-	-
241	Basic chemicals	835	771	672	666	25	25	26	27	2	2	2	2	2	2	2	2
2411	Basic chemicals, except fertilizers	835	771	672	666	25	25	26	27	2	2	2	2	2	2	2	2
2412	Fertilizers and nitrogen compounds	-	-	-	-	-	-	-	-	-	-	-	-	-	-	-	-
2413	Plastics in primary forms; synthetic rubber	-	-	-	-	-	-	-	-	-	-	-	-	-	-	-	-
242	Other chemicals	14110	13998	11658	10815	753	671	674	628	22	21	19	18	22	21	19	18
2421	Pesticides and other agro-chemical products	2080	1698	....	1601	83	82	90	91	4	4	3	3	4	4	3	3
2422	Paints, varnishes, printing ink and mastics	5245	4750	3779	3819	277	175	189	167	2	2	2	2	2	2	2	2
2423	Pharmaceuticals, medicinal chemicals, etc.	4014	3675	3296	2280	241	260	250	198	10	9	8	7	10	9	8	7
2424	Soap, cleaning & cosmetic preparations	2771	3875	2975	3115	152	154	145	172	6	6	6	6	6	6	6	6
2429	Other chemical products n.e.c.	-	-	-	-	-	-	-	-	-	-	-	-	-	-	-	-
2430	Man-made fibres	-	-	-	-	-	-	-	-	-	-	-	-	-	-	-	-
251	Rubber products	404	-	-	-	-	-	-	-	1	-	-	-	1	-	-	-
2511	Rubber tyres and tubes	404	-	-	-	-	-	-	-	1	-	-	-	1	-	-	-
2519	Other rubber products	-	-	-	-	-	-	-	-	-	-	-	-	-	-	-	-
2520	Plastic products	9087	7903	8026	5273	777	724	825	556	12	12	12	12	12	12	12	12
2610	Glass and glass products	688	612	564	719	39	52	51	63	2	3	3	3	2	3	3	3
269	Non-metallic mineral products n.e.c.	20224	21056	20008	20171	1200	1119	1039	1178	32	32	34	38	32	32	34	38
2691	Pottery, china and earthenware	-	-	-	-	-	-	-	-	-	-	-	-	-	-	-	-
2692	Refractory ceramic products	-	-	-	-	-	-	-	-	-	-	-	-	-	-	-	-
2693	Struct.non-refractory clay; ceramic products	4695	4518	4797	4630	323	352	335	409	13	13	13	15	13	13	13	15
2694	Cement, lime and plaster	4695	6610	6400	5199	290	277	230	190	3	3	3	3	3	3	3	3
2695	Articles of concrete, cement and plaster	3010	3317	2744	3628	185	152	164	223	9	10	11	11	9	10	11	11
2696	Cutting, shaping & finishing of stone	6267	5376	5084	4572	336	282	272	256	4	4	5	4	4	4	5	4
2699	Other non-metallic mineral products n.e.c.	1557	1235	984	2141	66	56	38	100	3	3	2	5	3	3	2	5
2710	Basic iron and steel	-	-	-	-	-	-	-	-	-	-	-	-	-	-	-	-
2720	Basic precious and non-ferrous metals	-	-	-	-	-	-	-	-	-	-	-	-	-	-	-	-
273	Casting of metals	-	-	-	-	-	-	-	-	-	-	-	-	-	-	-	-
2731	Casting of iron and steel	-	-	-	-	-	-	-	-	-	-	-	-	-	-	-	-
2732	Casting of non-ferrous metals	-	-	-	-	-	-	-	-	-	-	-	-	-	-	-	-
281	Struct.metal products;tanks;steam generators	938	1163	1207	1261	40	47	47	56	4	4	4	4	4	4	4	4
2811	Structural metal products	938	1163	1207	1261	40	47	47	56	4	4	4	4	4	4	4	4
2812	Tanks, reservoirs and containers of metal	-	-	-	-	-	-	-	-	-	-	-	-	-	-	-	-
2813	Steam generators	-	-	-	-	-	-	-	-	-	-	-	-	-	-	-	-
289	Other metal products; metal working services	4370	4205	3781	5323	309	291	223	364	9	9	9	11	9	9	9	11
2891	Metal forging/pressing/stamping/roll-forming	373	435	445	1445	19	21	22	93	1	1	1	3	1	1	1	3
2892	Treatment & coating of metals	-	-	-	-	-	-	-	-	-	-	-	-	-	-	-	-
2893	Cutlery, hand tools and general hardware	373	451	541	499	40	35	35	33	1	1	1	1	1	1	1	1
2899	Other fabricated metal products n.e.c.	3624	3319	2795	3379	250	235	166	238	7	7	7	7	7	7	7	7
291	General purpose machinery	882	938	917	997	60	64	72	74	1	1	1	1	1	1	1	1
2911	Engines & turbines (not for transport equipment)	-	-	-	-	-	-	-	-	-	-	-	-	-	-	-	-
2912	Pumps, compressors, taps and valves	882	938	917	997	60	64	72	74	1	1	1	1	1	1	1	1
2913	Bearings, gears, gearing & driving elements	-	-	-	-	-	-	-	-	-	-	-	-	-	-	-	-
2914	Ovens, furnaces and furnace burners	-	-	-	-	-	-	-	-	-	-	-	-	-	-	-	-
2915	Lifting and handling equipment	-	-	-	-	-	-	-	-	-	-	-	-	-	-	-	-
2919	Other general purpose machinery	-	-	-	-	-	-	-	-	-	-	-	-	-	-	-	-
292	Special purpose machinery	-	-	-	-	-	-	-	-	-	-	-	-	-	-	-	-
2921	Agricultural and forestry machinery	-	-	-	-	-	-	-	-	-	-	-	-	-	-	-	-
2922	Machine tools	-	-	-	-	-	-	-	-	-	-	-	-	-	-	-	-
2923	Machinery for metallurgy	-	-	-	-	-	-	-	-	-	-	-	-	-	-	-	-
2924	Machinery for mining & construction	-	-	-	-	-	-	-	-	-	-	-	-	-	-	-	-
2925	Food/beverage/tobacco processing machinery	-	-	-	-	-	-	-	-	-	-	-	-	-	-	-	-
2926	Machinery for textile, apparel and leather	-	-	-	-	-	-	-	-	-	-	-	-	-	-	-	-
2927	Weapons and ammunition	-	-	-	-	-	-	-	-	-	-	-	-	-	-	-	-
2929	Other special purpose machinery	-	-	-	-	-	-	-	-	-	-	-	-	-	-	-	-

continued

Eritrea

ISIC	Industry	Number of establishments (number)					Number of employees (number)					Wages and salaries paid to employees (thousands of Eritrean Nakfa)				
		Note	2007	2008	2009	2010	Note	2007	2008	2009	2010	Note	2007	2008	2009	2010
2930	Domestic appliances n.e.c.		-	-	-	-		-	-	-	-		-	-	-	-
3000	Office, accounting and computing machinery		-	-	-	-		-	-	-	-		-	-	-	-
3110	Electric motors, generators and transformers		-	-	-	-		-	-	-	-		-	-	-	-
3120	Electricity distribution & control apparatus		-	-	-	-		-	-	-	-		-	-	-	-
3130	Insulated wire and cable		-	-	-	-		-	-	-	-		-	-	-	-
3140	Accumulators, primary cells and batteries		-	-	-	-		-	-	-	-		-	-	-	-
3150	Lighting equipment and electric lamps		-	-	-	-		-	-	-	-		-	-	-	-
3190	Other electrical equipment n.e.c.		-	-	-	-		-	-	-	-		-	-	-	-
3210	Electronic valves, tubes, etc.		-	-	-	-		-	-	-	-		-	-	-	-
3220	TV/radio transmitters; line comm. apparatus		-	-	-	-		-	-	-	-		-	-	-	-
3230	TV and radio receivers and associated goods		-	-	-	-		-	-	-	-		-	-	-	-
331	Medical, measuring, testing appliances, etc.		-	-	-	-		-	-	-	-		-	-	-	-
3311	Medical, surgical and orthopaedic equipment		-	-	-	-		-	-	-	-		-	-	-	-
3312	Measuring/testing/navigating appliances,etc.		-	-	-	-		-	-	-	-		-	-	-	-
3313	Industrial process control equipment		-	-	-	-		-	-	-	-		-	-	-	-
3320	Optical instruments & photographic equipment		-	-	-	-		-	-	-	-		-	-	-	-
3330	Watches and clocks		-	-	-	-		-	-	-	-		-	-	-	-
3410	Motor vehicles		-	-	-	-		-	-	-	-		-	-	-	-
3420	Automobile bodies, trailers & semi-trailers		2	1	1	1		63	25	25	23		1097	231	238	381
3430	Parts/accessories for automobiles		4	4	4	3		64	69	66	39		2747	1528	1178	681
351	Building and repairing of ships and boats		-	-	-	-		-	-	-	-		-	-	-	-
3511	Building and repairing of ships		-	-	-	-		-	-	-	-		-	-	-	-
3512	Building/repairing of pleasure/sport. boats		-	-	-	-		-	-	-	-		-	-	-	-
3520	Railway/tramway locomotives & rolling stock		-	-	-	-		-	-	-	-		-	-	-	-
3530	Aircraft and spacecraft		-	-	-	-		-	-	-	-		-	-	-	-
359	Transport equipment n.e.c.		-	-	-	-		-	-	-	-		-	-	-	-
3591	Motorcycles		-	-	-	-		-	-	-	-		-	-	-	-
3592	Bicycles and invalid carriages		-	-	-	-		-	-	-	-		-	-	-	-
3599	Other transport equipment n.e.c.		-	-	-	-		-	-	-	-		-	-	-	-
3610	Furniture		28	28	31	31		2013	1968	2111	2309		30465	24016	34697	32498
369	Manufacturing n.e.c.		-	-	-	-		-	-	-	-		-	-	-	-
3691	Jewellery and related articles		-	-	-	-		-	-	-	-		-	-	-	-
3692	Musical instruments		-	-	-	-		-	-	-	-		-	-	-	-
3693	Sports goods		-	-	-	-		-	-	-	-		-	-	-	-
3694	Games and toys		-	-	-	-		-	-	-	-		-	-	-	-
3699	Other manufacturing n.e.c.		-	-	-	-		-	-	-	-		-	-	-	-
3710	Recycling of metal waste and scrap		-	-	-	-		-	-	-	-		-	-	-	-
3720	Recycling of non-metal waste and scrap		-	-	-	-		-	-	-	-		-	-	-	-
D	Total manufacturing	a/	274	265	261	255	a/	12975	12466	12414	12979	a/	202876	197165	216376	243450

a/ Sum of available data.

Eritrea

ISIC	Industry	Output at producers' prices (thousands of Eritrean Nakfa)					Value added at producers' prices (thousands of Eritrean Nakfa)					Gross fixed capital formation (thousands of Eritrean Nakfa)		
		Note	2007	2008	2009	2010	Note	2007	2008	2009	2010	Note	2009	2010
151	Processed meat,fish,fruit,vegetables,fats		41722	20811	28326	3465		4015	4187	13138	1780		74	-29
1511	Processing/preserving of meat		18700	12154	27899	-		5267	3780	13108	-		74	-
1512	Processing/preserving of fish		23022	-	-	-		-1252	-	-	-		-	-
1513	Processing/preserving of fruit & vegetables		-	-	-	-		-	-	-	-		-	-
1514	Vegetable and animal oils and fats		-	8657	427	3465		-	407	30	1780		-	-29
1520	Dairy products		85861	51196	41180	80379		16409	8594	7249	17137		-249	681
153	Grain mill products; starches; animal feeds		196284	146184	215501	195414		-239427	-207818	-201978	-223255		16991	9388
1531	Grain mill products		136929	102966	165452	161177		-265192	-218602	-214974	-230749		16890	9330
1532	Starches and starch products		59355	43217	50049	34237		25765	10783	12996	7494		101	58
1533	Prepared animal feeds		214447	192845	174776	167068		57945	45919	39905	38809		2329	807
154	Other food products		119082	100967	99200	97745		29263	21739	23324	24964		527	35
1541	Bakery products		4431	4790	5973	4391		1911	2289	2545	1939		-	-
1542	Sugar		-	-	-	-		-	-	-	-		-	-
1543	Cocoa, chocolate and sugar confectionery		90648	87089	69603	64932		27047	21890	14036	11906		1802	772
1544	Macaroni, noodles & similar products		-	-	-	-		-	-	-	-		-	-
1549	Other food products n.e.c.		285	-	-	-		-276	-	-	-		-	-
155	Beverages		444920	133026	584408	1111300		281137	54858	411584	836015		6195	1426
1551	Distilling, rectifying & blending of spirits		14104	16390	30026	34333		5881	10017	24703	27261		459	270
1552	Wines		5321	6897	4724	3653		3678	4713	3347	1833		6	-99
1553	Malt liquors and malt		373180	57536	489140	773724		246958	12170	349839	622090		5730	44
1554	Soft drinks; mineral waters		52315	52203	60518	299590		24620	27958	33695	184831		-	1211
1600	Tobacco products		37558	147511	127858	118759		18610	96332	83992	85171		603	145
171	Spinning, weaving and finishing of textiles		215702	204404	218883	264278		102032	72883	101907	126747		4326	14897
1711	Textile fibre preparation; textile weaving		215702	204404	218883	264278		102032	72883	101907	126747		4326	14897
1712	Finishing of textiles		-	-	-	-		-	-	-	-		-	-
172	Other textiles		-	-	-	-		-	-	-	-		-	-
1721	Made-up textile articles, except apparel		-	-	-	-		-	-	-	-		-	-
1722	Carpets and rugs		-	-	-	-		-	-	-	-		-	-
1723	Cordage, rope, twine and netting		-	-	-	-		-	-	-	-		-	-
1729	Other textiles n.e.c.		-	-	-	-		-	-	-	-		-	-
1730	Knitted and crocheted fabrics and articles		12373	16633	15229	21196		8276	13037	10133	15109		534	760
1810	Wearing apparel, except fur apparel		19996	22280	17039	37457		8272	7959	6392	16030		4	1526
1820	Dressing & dyeing of fur; processing of fur		-	-	-	-		-	-	-	-		-	-
191	Tanning, dressing and processing of leather		54887	65421	53412	66946		11685	13284	19288	22186		4746	3892
1911	Tanning and dressing of leather		54366	64743	52642	65206		11414	12976	18920	21428		4746	3892
1912	Luggage, handbags, etc.; saddlery & harness		521	678	770	1740		271	308	368	758		-	-
1920	Footwear		89705	90178	93221	101181		31162	34097	38273	38901		1526	2003
2010	Sawmilling and planing of wood		-	-	-	-		-	-	-	-		-	-
202	Products of wood, cork, straw, etc.		-	-	-	-		-	-	-	-		-	-
2021	Veneer sheets, plywood, particle board, etc.		-	-	-	-		-	-	-	-		-	-
2022	Builders' carpentry and joinery		-	-	-	-		-	-	-	-		-	-
2023	Wooden containers		-	-	-	-		-	-	-	-		-	-
2029	Other wood products; articles of cork/straw		-	-	-	-		-	-	-	-		-	-
210	Paper and paper products		3843	9174	8358	7993		321	4979	4319	4430		136	147
2101	Pulp, paper and paperboard		1464	2491	1666	1609		535	1240	510	438		16	-
2102	Corrugated paper and paperboard		1855	2476	2101	-		1230	1690	1583	-		-	-
2109	Other articles of paper and paperboard		524	4208	4591	6384		-1444	2050	2226	3992		120	147
221	Publishing		-	-	-	-		-	-	-	-		-	-
2211	Publishing of books and other publications		-	-	-	-		-	-	-	-		-	-
2212	Publishing of newspapers, journals, etc.		-	-	-	-		-	-	-	-		-	-
2213	Publishing of recorded media		-	-	-	-		-	-	-	-		-	-
2219	Other publishing		-	-	-	-		-	-	-	-		-	-

continued

Eritrea

ISIC	Industry	Output Note	Output 2007	2008	2009	2010	VA Note	VA 2007	2008	2009	2010	GFCF Note	GFCF 2009	2010
222	Printing and related service activities		73105	67592	100105	101738		32387	35326	49127	47860		2570	684
2221	Printing		73105	67592	100105	101738		32387	35326	49127	47860		2570	684
2222	Service activities related to printing		-	-	-	-		-	-	-	-		-	-
2230	Reproduction of recorded media		-	-	-	-		-	-	-	-		-	-
2310	Coke oven products		-	-	-	-		-	-	-	-		-	-
2320	Refined petroleum products		-	-	-	-		-	-	-	-		-	-
2330	Processing of nuclear fuel		-	-	-	-		-	-	-	-		-	-
241	Basic chemicals		4996	5330	6299	7552		3192	3233	3694	3427		83	57
2411	Basic chemicals, except fertilizers		4996	5330	6299	7552		3192	3233	3694	3427		83	57
2412	Fertilizers and nitrogen compounds		-	-	-	-		-	-	-	-		-	-
2413	Plastics in primary forms; synthetic rubber		-	-	-	-		-	-	-	-		-	-
242	Other chemicals		127499	129114	165580	181742		42212	44901	55349	80198		7299	7611
2421	Pesticides and other agro-chemical products		-	-	-	-		-	-	-	-		-	-
2422	Paints, varnishes, printing ink and mastics		29231	12773	26373	22425		12915	5443	12738	12043		1471	708
2423	Pharmaceuticals, medicinal chemicals, etc.		35603	36216	42916	57541		11416	3983	2140	22063		3277	4480
2424	Soap, cleaning & cosmetic preparations		51624	66140	77377	85545		12520	28104	28532	36245		2356	705
2429	Other chemical products n.e.c.		11042	13984	18914	16231		5361	7371	11939	9847		195	1718
2430	Man-made fibres		-	-	-	-		-	-	-	-		-	-
251	Rubber products		5884	-	-	-		3155	-	-	-		-	-
2511	Rubber tyres and tubes		5884	-	-	-		3155	-	-	-		-	-
2519	Other rubber products		-	-	-	-		-	-	-	-		-	-
2520	Plastic products		47526	47783	58832	60638		27003	27111	36559	37702		2433	1817
2610	Glass and glass products		9252	5592	6682	10536		3260	3027	2885	3970		328	15
269	Non-metallic mineral products n.e.c.		162535	120065	153965	187460		51468	33922	53969	75364		9377	-15562
2691	Pottery, china and earthenware		-	-	-	-		-	-	-	-		-	-
2692	Refractory ceramic products		-	-	-	-		-	-	-	-		-	-
2693	Struct.non-refractory clay; ceramic products		30781	6618	14022	21147		8369	2113	3506	9231		60	263
2694	Cement, lime and plaster		58012	64822	73008	78980		11777	16455	19849	25968		1824	1028
2695	Articles of concrete, cement and plaster		27154	15849	25260	24614		13659	6075	14720	13154		1699	-14114
2696	Cutting, shaping & finishing of stone		37014	29169	35482	44105		12955	7278	12465	14913		5833	-2749
2699	Other non-metallic mineral products n.e.c.		9574	3607	6193	18614		4707	2002	3429	12098		-39	10
2710	Basic iron and steel		-	-	-	-		-	-	-	-		-	-
2720	Basic precious and non-ferrous metals		-	-	-	-		-	-	-	-		-	-
273	Casting of metals		-	-	-	-		-	-	-	-		-	-
2731	Casting of iron and steel		-	-	-	-		-	-	-	-		-	-
2732	Casting of non-ferrous metals		-	-	-	-		-	-	-	-		-	-
281	Struct.metal products;tanks;steam generators		11559	6624	8414	7994		6872	3001	4408	3809		77	34
2811	Structural metal products		11559	6624	8414	7994		6872	3001	4408	3809		77	34
2812	Tanks, reservoirs and containers of metal		-	-	-	-		-	-	-	-		-	-
2813	Steam generators		-	-	-	-		-	-	-	-		-	-
289	Other metal products; metal working services		29112	19019	24877	29891		9348	9205	13239	14769		1908	14113
2891	Metal forging/pressing/stamping/roll-forming		328	1087	205	431		-514	384	-155	-120		-	28
2892	Treatment & coating of metals		-	-	-	-		-	-	-	-		-	-
2893	Cutlery, hand tools and general hardware		2966	1352	510	1610		1820	362	30	617		181	-
2899	Other fabricated metal products n.e.c.		25818	16580	24162	27850		8042	8458	13364	14272		1727	14085
291	General purpose machinery		11710	2553	2673	5357		4551	1622	-184	941		4	48
2911	Engines & turbines (not for transport equipment)		-	-	-	-		-	-	-	-		-	-
2912	Pumps, compressors, taps and valves		-	-	-	-		-	-	-	-		-	-
2913	Bearings, gears, gearing & driving elements		-	-	-	-		-	-	-	-		-	-
2914	Ovens, furnaces and furnace burners		11710	2553	2673	5357		4551	1622	-184	941		4	48
2915	Lifting and handling equipment		-	-	-	-		-	-	-	-		-	-
2919	Other general purpose machinery		-	-	-	-		-	-	-	-		-	-

292	Special purpose machinery										
2921	Agricultural and forestry machinery										
2922	Machine tools										
2923	Machinery for metallurgy										
2924	Machinery for mining & construction										
2925	Food/beverage/tobacco processing machinery										
2926	Machinery for textile, apparel and leather										
2927	Weapons and ammunition										
2929	Other special purpose machinery										
2930	Domestic appliances n.e.c.										
3000	Office, accounting and computing machinery										
3110	Electric motors, generators and transformers										
3120	Electricity distribution & control apparatus										
3130	Insulated wire and cable										
3140	Accumulators, primary cells and batteries										
3150	Lighting equipment and electric lamps										
3190	Other electrical equipment n.e.c.										
3210	Electronic valves, tubes, etc.										
3220	TV/radio transmitters; line comm. apparatus										
3230	TV and radio receivers and associated goods										
331	Medical, measuring, testing appliances, etc.										
3311	Medical, surgical and orthopaedic equipment										
3312	Measuring/testing/navigating appliances,etc.										
3313	Industrial process control equipment										
3320	Optical instruments & photographic equipment										
3330	Watches and clocks										
3410	Motor vehicles	6829	1588	1204	1911	1095	699	463	1194		-49
3420	Automobile bodies, trailers & semi-trailers	14285	10117	8392	6712	6501	3648	2663	2425		3
3430	Parts/accessories for automobiles										
351	Building and repairing of ships and boats										
3511	Building and repairing of ships										
3512	Building/repairing of pleasure/sport. boats										
3520	Railway/tramway locomotives & rolling stock										
3530	Aircraft and spacecraft										
359	Transport equipment n.e.c.										
3591	Motorcycles										
3592	Bicycles and invalid carriages										
3599	Other transport equipment n.e.c.	308100	258446	278253	366924	136151	138505	123285	204927	15778	14055
3610	Furniture										
369	Manufacturing n.e.c.										
3691	Jewellery and related articles										
3692	Musical instruments										
3693	Sports goods										
3694	Games and toys										
3699	Other manufacturing n.e.c.										
3710	Recycling of metal waste and scrap										
3720	Recycling of non-metal waste and scrap									77075	58466
D	Total manufacturing a/	2229690	1773486	2393467	3143891	867059	452511	879659	1455648		

a/ Sum of available data.

Estonia

Concepts and definitions of variables:
Number of employees includes home workers, paid working proprietors, seasonal workers, apprentices on the pay-roll, persons on strike or on short-term leave. Wages and salaries is compensation of employees.

Related national publications:
Statistical Yearbook of Estonia, published by Statistics Estonia, Tallinn.

Supplier of information:
Statistics Estonia, Tallinn.

Basic source of data:
Annual survey; administrative data; business register.

Major deviations from ISIC (Revision 4):
None reported.

Reference period:
Calendar year.

Scope:
All enterprises.

Method of data collection:
Mail questionnaires and online survey.

Type of enumeration:
Sample survey.

Adjusted for non-response:
Yes.

Estonia

ISIC Revision 4

Column groups: **Number of enterprises** (number) · **Number of employees** (thousands) · **Wages and salaries paid to employees** (thousands of Euros)

ISIC	Industry	Note	2007	2008	2009	2010	Note	2007	2008	2009	2010	Note	2007	2008	2009	2010
1010	Processing/preserving of meat	…	…	53	54	57	…	…	3.2	2.8	2.8	…	…	25156	23149	21564
1020	Processing/preserving of fish, etc.	…	…	59	56	58	…	…	2.1	1.8	1.8	…	…	14514	11747	12123
1030	Processing/preserving of fruit,vegetables	…	…	29	24	30	…	…	0.7	0.7	0.6	…	…	5989	5273	4689
1040	Vegetable and animal oils and fats	…	…	4	4	5	…	…	…	…	…	…	…	…	…	…
1050	Dairy products	…	…	31	28	27	…	…	2.3	2.2	2.2	…	…	22548	20522	20397
106	Grain mill products,starches and starch products	…	…	6	8	9	…	…	…	…	…	…	…	…	…	…
1061	Grain mill products	…	…	6	8	9	…	…	…	…	…	…	…	…	…	…
1062	Starches and starch products	…	…	-	-	-	…	…	-	-	-	…	…	-	-	-
107	Other food products	…	…	180	186	158	…	…	5.6	5.0	4.7	…	…	40456	37292	35911
1071	Bakery products	…	…	120	114	100	…	…	3.8	3.4	3.1	…	…	26185	23519	21897
1072	Sugar	…	…	-	-	-	…	…	-	-	-	…	…	-	-	-
1073	Cocoa, chocolate and sugar confectionery	…	…	3	12	6	…	…	…	…	…	…	…	…	…	…
1074	Macaroni, noodles, couscous, etc.	…	…	-	-	-	…	…	-	-	-	…	…	-	-	-
1075	Prepared meals and dishes	…	…	39	42	34	…	…	0.5	0.5	0.6	…	…	3087	3259	3786
1079	Other food products n.e.c.	…	…	18	18	18	…	…	…	…	…	…	…	…	…	…
1080	Prepared animal feeds	…	…	13	10	14	…	…	0.2	0.1	0.2	…	…	2128	1547	1689
1101	Distilling, rectifying and blending of spirits	…	…	6	5	4	…	…	0.4	0.4	0.3	…	…	4781	4723	4661
1102	Wines	…	…	6	5	5	…	…	…	…	…	…	…	…	…	…
1103	Malt liquors and malt	…	…	7	6	8	…	…	…	…	…	…	…	…	…	…
1104	Soft drinks,mineral waters,other bottled waters	…	…	14	14	14	…	…	0.5	0.5	0.4	…	…	5989	6142	4578
1200	Tobacco products	…	…	-	-	-	…	…	-	-	-	…	…	-	-	-
131	Spinning, weaving and finishing of textiles	…	…	30	31	32	…	…	2.3	1.0	1.0	…	…	14054	8155	6661
1311	Preparation and spinning of textile fibres	…	…	9	10	8	…	…	0.5	0.2	0.2	…	…	3579	2135	1547
1312	Weaving of textiles	…	…	8	10	9	…	…	…	…	…	…	…	…	…	…
1313	Finishing of textiles	…	…	13	11	15	…	…	…	…	…	…	…	…	…	…
139	Other textiles	…	…	140	160	150	…	…	3.9	3.3	3.4	…	…	27284	23194	25657
1391	Knitted and crocheted fabrics	…	…	3	2	-	…	…	…	…	…	…	…	…	…	…
1392	Made-up textile articles, except apparel	…	…	120	128	138	…	…	3.1	2.7	2.9	…	…	21640	18764	20844
1393	Carpets and rugs	…	…	10	6	5	…	…	0.4	0.3	0.3	…	…	3343	2493	2654
1394	Cordage, rope, twine and netting	…	…	2	2	2	…	…	…	…	…	…	…	…	…	…
1399	Other textiles n.e.c.	…	…	5	…	5	…	…	0.2	0.2	…	…	…	1265	914	…
1410	Wearing apparel, except fur apparel	…	…	353	311	310	…	…	8.5	7.0	6.2	…	…	49059	35567	31849
1420	Articles of fur	…	…	7	7	9	…	…	…	…	…	…	…	51	38	34
1430	Knitted and crocheted apparel	…	…	48	44	45	…	…	0.6	0.4	0.5	…	…	3049	2518	2853
151	Leather;luggage,handbags,saddlery,harness;fur	…	…	44	40	32	…	…	0.7	0.5	0.4	…	…	3637	2991	2578
1511	Tanning/dressing of leather; dressing of fur	…	…	8	6	2	…	…	…	0.1	…	…	…	…	799	…
1512	Luggage,handbags,etc.;saddlery/harness	…	…	36	34	30	…	…	…	…	…	…	…	…	2192	…
1520	Footwear	…	…	21	20	21	…	…	0.9	0.8	0.8	…	…	5873	4813	5022
1610	Sawmilling and planing of wood	…	…	417	393	374	…	…	4.8	3.7	4.0	…	…	39657	31285	34453
162	Wood products, cork, straw, plaiting materials	…	…	661	645	593	…	…	12.0	9.0	8.8	…	…	96973	68194	73975

1621	Veneer sheets and wood-based panels	15375	12853	14706	1.7	1.6	1.7	19	12	12
1622	Builders' carpentry and joinery	48298	45978	67555	5.6	5.8	8.0	450	443	375
1623	Wooden containers	6940	6353	9325	1.0	1.1	1.3	75	75	82
1629	Other wood products;articles of cork,straw	3361	3010	5388	0.5	0.5	1.0	117	115	124
1701	Pulp, paper and paperboard	5833	5624	…	0.5	0.5	0.5	4	3	4
1702	Corrugated paper and paperboard	4602	4621	5394	0.5	0.5	…	31	35	28
1709	Other articles of paper and paperboard	2883	5011	…	0.3	0.5	2.9	18	23	24
181	Printing and service activities related to printing	25304	24548	29783	2.7	2.5	…	263	279	308
1811	Printing	…	…	…	…	…	…	228	253	272
1812	Service activities related to printing	273	428	690	0.1	0.1	0.1	35	26	36
1820	Reproduction of recorded media	…	…	…	…	…	…	9	10	8
1910	Coke oven products	13107	11568	12098	-	-	-	-	-	-
1920	Refined petroleum products	10869	7912	9881	1.4	1.4	1.3	9	8	5
201	Basic chemicals,fertilizers, etc.	7499	…	3643	1.3	0.9	0.9	23	27	13
2011	Basic chemicals	…	940	…	0.8	…	0.3	14	15	7
2012	Fertilizers and nitrogen compounds	…	…	…	…	0.1	…	6	6	3
2013	Plastics and synthetic rubber in primary forms	12843	15633	6	0.9	1.4	…	3	6	3
202	Other chemical products	…	13	10092	…	…	0.7	60	45	57
2021	Pesticides and other agrochemical products	8789	8379	1905	0.6	0.6	0.2	3	3	1
2022	Paints,varnishes;printing ink and mastics	1556	1579	…	0.1	0.1	…	14	12	18
2023	Soap,cleaning and cosmetic preparations	…	5663	…	…	0.7	…	18	9	19
2029	Other chemical products n.e.c.	…	…	…	…	…	…	25	21	19
2030	Man-made fibres	4698	3943	3700	-	-	0.2	1	-	-
2100	Pharmaceuticals,medicinal chemicals, etc.	5553	3790	4940	0.3	0.2	0.5	14	15	12
221	Rubber products	…	…	1182	0.6	0.5	0.1	19	19	17
2211	Rubber tyres and tubes	…	…	3758	…	…	0.4	8	7	10
2219	Other rubber products	26651	27354	38174	…	3.0	4.1	11	12	7
2220	Plastics products	12832	11773	12840	2.7	1.0	1.1	156	160	130
2310	Glass and glass products	27413	29821	46771	1.1	3.0	4.3	52	37	17
239	Non-metallic mineral products n.e.c.	…	…	…	2.5	…	…	174	168	158
2391	Refractory products	…	…	703	…	…	0.1	1	1	1
2392	Clay building materials	333	435	…	…	0.1	…	11	12	6
2393	Other porcelain and ceramic products	…	…	…	0.1	…	3.0	12	11	12
2394	Cement, lime and plaster	17874	17269	31649	1.7	1.9	0.4	3	3	2
2395	Articles of concrete, cement and plaster	3489	3049	3803	0.3	0.3	0.1	76	71	67
2396	Cutting, shaping and finishing of stone	…	454	626	…	0.1	…	63	63	65
2399	Other non-metallic mineral products n.e.c.	…	…	307	…	…	0.1	8	7	5
2410	Basic iron and steel	1485	1598	1866	0.1	0.1	0.3	4	8	8
2420	Basic precious and other non-ferrous metals	…	…	2084	…	…	…	6	7	8
243	Casting of metals	923	997	1400	0.1	0.2	0.2	10	10	11
2431	Casting of iron and steel	…	…	…	0.1	…	0.1	3	3	4
2432	Casting of non-ferrous metals	…	…	684	…	…	…	7	7	7
251	Struct.metal products, tanks, reservoirs	66932	70590	84887	6.3	6.9	8.2	435	449	466
2511	Structural metal products	61248	67746	81161	5.8	6.6	7.8	424	437	450
2512	Tanks, reservoirs and containers of metal	…	2844	3726	…	0.3	0.4	11	12	13

continued

Estonia

ISIC	Industry	Number of enterprises (number)					Number of employees (thousands)					Wages and salaries paid to employees (thousands of Euros)				
		Note	2007	2008	2009	2010	Note	2007	2008	2009	2010	Note	2007	2008	2009	2010
2513	Steam generators, excl. hot water boilers		...	-	-	3		...	...	...	...		...	...	...	...
2520	Weapons and ammunition		...	-	-	2		...	-	-	...		...	-	-	...
259	Other metal products;metal working services		...	483	477	502		...	5.7	4.6	4.5		...	56332	41057	40911
2591	Forging,pressing,stamping,roll-forming of metal		...	33	36	48		...	0.2	0.2	0.3		...	1738	1387	2302
2592	Treatment and coating of metals; machining		...	262	256	246		...	2.8	2.1	2.3		...	28875	19634	22354
2593	Cutlery, hand tools and general hardware		...	23	19	22		...	0.4	0.3	0.2		...	3637	2269	2078
2599	Other fabricated metal products n.e.c.		...	165	166	186		...	2.3	2.0	1.7		...	22081	17767	14177
2610	Electronic components and boards		...	37	33	33		...	2.5	2.1	2.2		...	20714	16758	18117
2620	Computers and peripheral equipment		...	19	16	14		...	0.2	0.2	0.1		...	2000	1342	1006
2630	Communication equipment		...	15	14	14		...	3.2	...	2.3		...	25392	...	22670
2640	Consumer electronics		...	6	6	6		...	...	...	...		...	...	...	...
265	Measuring,testing equipment; watches, etc.		...	22	25	30		...	0.4	0.4	0.6		...	2793	3381	6165
2651	Measuring/testing/navigating equipment,etc.		...	21	25	28		...	0.4	0.4	...		...	...	3381	...
2652	Watches and clocks		...	1	-	2		...	...	-	...		...	...	-	...
2660	Irradiation/electromedical equipment,etc.		...	2	3	3		...	...	...	...		...	...	...	...
2670	Optical instruments and photographic equipment		...	10	8	5		...	...	...	...		...	...	...	...
2680	Magnetic and optical media		...	1	1	1		...	...	...	...		...	...	...	...
2710	Electric motors,generators,transformers,etc.		...	26	26	33		...	3.5	3.1	3.1		...	41165	33726	36088
2720	Batteries and accumulators		...	1	1	1		...	...	...	...		...	...	...	...
273	Wiring and wiring devices		...	12	13	11		...	0.6	0.5	0.3		...	5375	4563	3816
2731	Fibre optic cables		...	-	-	-		...	...	...	...		...	...	...	...
2732	Other electronic and electric wires and cables		...	9	10	8		...	-	...	...		...	-	...	...
2733	Wiring devices		...	3	3	3		...	0.6	...	0.3		...	5100	...	3533
2740	Electric lighting equipment		...	15	12	16		...	...	0.3	...		...	275	2576	282
2750	Domestic appliances		...	6	3	3		...	...	...	...		...	...	...	...
2790	Other electrical equipment		...	18	13	18		...	0.9	...	0.5		...	4269	...	2633
281	General-purpose machinery		...	85	80	50		...	3.0	2.1	1.6		...	32697	22324	15827
2811	Engines/turbines,excl.aircraft,vehicle engines		...	-	1	-		...	-	...	...		...	-	...	-
2812	Fluid power equipment		...	5	5	8		...	...	...	...		...	...	...	...
2813	Other pumps, compressors, taps and valves		...	3	4	1		...	0.1	0.1	...		...	914	620	...
2814	Bearings, gears, gearing and driving elements		...	1	-	-		...	...	-	-		...	-	...	...
2815	Ovens, furnaces and furnace burners		...	2	2	2		...	...	...	...		...	...	...	...
2816	Lifting and handling equipment		...	18	19	11		...	1.5	1.1	1.0		...	16949	12303	9984
2817	Office machinery, excl.computers,etc.		...	1	1	1		...	...	...	...		...	...	...	...
2818	Power-driven hand tools		...	-	-	-		...	-	...	-		...	-	-	-
2819	Other general-purpose machinery		...	55	48	27		...	1.1	0.7	...		...	11594	6794	...
282	Special-purpose machinery		...	59	63	78		...	1.9	1.6	1.6		...	22874	16297	17737
2821	Agricultural and forestry machinery		...	18	19	19		...	0.7	0.5	0.6		...	7848	5138	6244
2822	Metal-forming machinery and machine tools		...	10	11	10		...	0.2	0.1	...		...	3438	1956	...
2823	Machinery for metallurgy		...	1	1	1		...	...	...	...		...	...	...	...
2824	Mining, quarrying and construction machinery		...	11	7	11		...	0.2	...	0.2		...	2320	...	1757

Code	Activity									
2825	Food/beverage/tobacco processing machinery	9	7	5	0.3	0.3	0.2	4161	3304	2228
2826	Textile/apparel/leather production machinery	-	-	4	-	-	…	…	-	1
2829	Other special-purpose machinery	10	18	28	…	…	…	…	…	…
2910	Motor vehicles	3	4	2	…	…	…	…	…	…
2920	Automobile bodies, trailers and semi-trailers	33	30	24	3.0	2.3	2.4	29962	20349	23660
2930	Parts and accessories for motor vehicles	20	21	22	…	…	0.6	…	…	5927
301	Building of ships and boats	56	61	75	…	…	0.3	…	…	3232
3011	Building of ships and floating structures	21	24	36	0.5	0.3	0.3	3860	2288	2695
3012	Building of pleasure and sporting boats	35	37	39	…	…	…	…	…	…
3020	Railway locomotives and rolling stock	1	1	1	…	…	-	-	-	-
3030	Air and spacecraft and related machinery	1	-	-	-	…	-	-	-	-
3040	Military fighting vehicles	-	-	5	-	-	-	-	-	-
309	Transport equipment n.e.c.	1	3	5	-	…	…	…	…	…
3091	Motorcycles	-	2	2	…	…	-	-	-	-
3092	Bicycles and invalid carriages	1	1	2	-	…	…	-	-	-
3099	Other transport equipment n.e.c.	-	-	1	-	…	…	…	…	…
3100	Furniture	516	555	581	8.6	7.0	7.2	67734	50241	52805
321	Jewellery, bijouterie and related articles	34	39	37	0.3	0.2	…	1758	1521	1758
3211	Jewellery and related articles	34	37	37	0.3	…	-	1758	…	…
3212	Imitation jewellery and related articles	-	2	-	-	…	…	…	…	…
3220	Musical instruments	3	4	4	0.4	…	…	2844	…	…
3230	Sports goods	16	11	17	…	…	…	…	…	…
3240	Games and toys	6	5	10	1.0	0.9	0.8	9989	7912	8075
3250	Medical and dental instruments and supplies	70	70	67	0.6	0.7	0.6	5075	4793	4859
3290	Other manufacturing n.e.c.	51	52	65	…	…	…	…	…	…
331	Repair of fabricated metal products/machinery	339	351	427	3.4	3.2	3.4	38468	33240	33193
3311	Repair of fabricated metal products	40	30	33	0.2	0.1	0.1	3317	…	776
3312	Repair of machinery	133	147	182	1.0	1.0	1.2	11095	8877	10248
3313	Repair of electronic and optical equipment	25	23	18	0.1	0.1	0.1	518	415	…
3314	Repair of electrical equipment	42	41	30	0.4	0.3	0.2	3994	2895	1767
3315	Repair of transport equip., excl. motor vehicles	88	99	136	…	…	0.1	…	…	1026
3319	Repair of other equipment	11	11	28	…	…	0.4	…	…	4747
3320	Installation of industrial machinery/equipment	94	86	82	0.8	0.5	…	11677	6385	…
C	Total manufacturing	5478	5441	5468	119.7	97.5	94.5	1064889	835325	838144

Estonia

ISIC	Industry	Output (thousands of Euros) Note	2007	2008	2009	2010	Value added at factor values (thousands of Euros) Note	2007	2008	2009	2010	Gross fixed capital formation (thousands of Euros) Note	2009	2010
1010	Processing/preserving of meat		...	236563	217255	211607		...	47410	43594	43286		...	...
1020	Processing/preserving of fish, etc.		...	106694	95605	109978		...	25232	22861	26457		...	...
1030	Processing/preserving of fruit,vegetables		...	49174	40884	45340		...	12373	11619	11166		...	...
1040	Vegetable and animal oils and fats		...	...	...	...		...	...	...	...		...	...
1050	Dairy products		...	310157	257519	296396		...	54319	53187	47340		...	...
106	Grain mill products,starches and starch products		...	...	...	...		...	...	...	...		...	...
1061	Grain mill products		...	...	...	...		...	...	...	...		...	...
1062	Starches and starch products		...	-	-	-		...	...	...	...		...	...
107	Other food products		...	244398	227551	211070		...	76458	74547	66467		...	...
1071	Bakery products		...	126826	116006	107650		...	49148	45492	38896		...	...
1072	Sugar		...	-	-	-		...	-	-	-		...	...
1073	Cocoa, chocolate and sugar confectionery		...	...	...	...		...	...	...	...		...	...
1074	Macaroni, noodles, couscous, etc.		...	-	-	-		...	...	...	...		...	...
1075	Prepared meals and dishes		...	17563	18592	20836		...	7401	6966	7388		...	...
1079	Other food products n.e.c.		...	...	...	...		...	...	...	...		...	...
1080	Prepared animal feeds		...	43102	26268	29894		...	7791	4391	5092		...	...
1101	Distilling, rectifying and blending of spirits		...	39593	34857	30356		...	13402	11549	8608		...	...
1102	Wines		...	...	...	...		...	...	...	...		...	...
1103	Malt liquors and malt		...	...	...	...		...	...	...	...		...	...
1104	Soft drinks,mineral waters,other bottled waters		...	37529	36679	14777		...	14086	14572	9979		...	...
1200	Tobacco products		...	-	-	-		...	-	-	-		...	...
131	Spinning, weaving and finishing of textiles		...	55526	33183	27001		...	14265	7254	6296		...	...
1311	Preparation and spinning of textile fibres		...	15173	7280	8615		...	6257	2346	3161		...	...
1312	Weaving of textiles		...	...	...	...		...	...	...	...		...	...
1313	Finishing of textiles		...	...	...	...		...	...	...	...		...	...
139	Other textiles		...	184308	161959	182269		...	54740	46074	52148		...	...
1391	Knitted and crocheted fabrics		...	-	-	-		...	-	-	-		...	...
1392	Made-up textile articles, except apparel		...	158322	142395	160497		...	45134	39855	43692		...	...
1393	Carpets and rugs		...	15722	10456	13690		...	5784	4071	4739		...	...
1394	Cordage, rope, twine and netting		...	...	...	...		...	...	...	...		...	...
1399	Other textiles n.e.c.		...	6545	5215	...		...	1968	409	...		...	...
1410	Wearing apparel, except fur apparel		...	149854	104502	106361		...	73837	52152	52431		...	...
1420	Articles of fur		...	102	77	63		...	70	51	33		...	...
1430	Knitted and crocheted apparel		...	9568	8238	9482		...	5043	4257	4934		...	...
151	Leather;luggage,handbags,saddlery,harness;fur		...	13038	10219	8422		...	5861	5151	3682		...	...
1511	Tanning/dressing of leather; dressing of fur		...	...	2064	...		...	...	748	...		...	...
1512	Luggage,handbags,etc.;saddlery/harness		...	...	8155	...		...	...	4404	...		...	...
1520	Footwear		...	18349	12763	16894		...	8724	6602	8154		...	...
1610	Sawmilling and planing of wood		...	402880	333657	485966		...	71939	89892	122484		...	...
162	Wood products, cork, straw, plaiting materials		...	599555	396438	559707		...	176441	122813	164090		...	...

Code	Description					
1621	Veneer sheets and wood-based panels	104342	129105	22829	22446	35651
1622	Builders' carpentry and joinery	398189	349324	119675	84152	97908
1623	Wooden containers	73971	47525	25999	12105	15990
1629	Other wood products;articles of cork,straw	23053	33753	7938	4110	14541
1701	Pulp, paper and paperboard	78145	119610	...	14546	40083
1702	Corrugated paper and paperboard	39887	36234	10878	10303	11033
1709	Other articles of paper and paperboard	32537	24386	...	7727	-1479
181	Printing and service activities related to printing	178294	185965	65126	52548	61755
1811	Printing	151886	...	...	...	...
1812	Service activities related to printing	...	...	...	...	...
1820	Reproduction of recorded media	4461	3809	2525	300	1069
1910	Coke oven products	-	-	-	...	...
1920	Refined petroleum products	179176	180195	72342	47761	76202
201	Basic chemicals,fertilizers, etc.	173878	118300	58984	4282	21750
2011	Basic chemicals	56741	116271	10776	50867	26216
2012	Fertilizers and nitrogen compounds	...	...	...	19	...
2013	Plastics and synthetic rubber in primary forms	...	2525	13	33202	55303
202	Other chemical products	174818	204750	37810	3445	38448
2021	Pesticides and other agrochemical products	11613	32	4250	14201	...
2022	Paints,varnishes;printing ink and mastics	...	173010	...	...	3801
2023	Soap,cleaning and cosmetic preparations	61930	8413	...	...	-
2029	Other chemical products n.e.c.	-	...	...	...	...
2030	Man-made fibres	25712	61930	10290	8098	9159
2100	Pharmaceuticals,medicinal chemicals, etc.	22522	30463	8686	6602	11352
221	Rubber products	7350	16758	2352	...	...
2211	Rubber tyres and tubes	15173	...	6334	...	...
2219	Other rubber products	266767	171232	64186	43639	51796
2220	Plastics products	106994	110831	36232	33579	42291
2310	Glass and glass products	286874	149386	109755	35024	50345
239	Non-metallic mineral products n.e.c.	...	...	...	...	...
2391	Refractory products	1873	1202	1067	537	438
2392	Clay building materials	155593	1118	56217	19998	30330
2393	Other porcelain and ceramic products	18554	93319	7260	5311	8086
2394	Cement, lime and plaster	8398	19205	984	639	...
2395	Articles of concrete, cement and plaster	2710	3579	633	...	4794
2396	Cutting, shaping and finishing of stone	31023	27387	11268	11268	...
2399	Other non-metallic mineral products n.e.c.	9478	...	3573	3573	...
2410	Basic iron and steel	4442	2997	1956	...	907
2420	Basic precious and other non-ferrous metals	5036	2907	1617	1425	...
243	Casting of metals	552229	399881	143782	122896	118347
2431	Casting of iron and steel	532301	368330	137647	117802	109165
2432	Casting of non-ferrous metals	19928	16240	6136	5094	...

continued

Estonia

ISIC	Industry	Output (thousands of Euros)					Value added at factor values (thousands of Euros)					Gross fixed capital formation (thousands of Euros)		
		Note	2007	2008	2009	2010	Note	2007	2008	2009	2010	Note	2009	2010
2513	Steam generators, excl. hot water boilers		…	…	…	…		…	…	…	…		…	…
2520	Weapons and ammunition		…	-	-	…		…	-	-	…		…	…
259	Other metal products;metal working services		…	413623	211567	357743		…	106694	65337	96452		…	…
2591	Forging,pressing,stamping,roll-forming of metal		…	12309	9612	18269		…	2371	1579	4420		…	…
2592	Treatment and coating of metals; machining		…	272769	105397	230953		…	53999	23385	53549		…	…
2593	Cutlery, hand tools and general hardware		…	13543	8865	9006		…	5113	3406	4457		…	…
2599	Other fabricated metal products n.e.c.		…	115003	87693	99515		…	45211	36966	34025		…	…
2610	Electronic components and boards		…	184257	143290	174150		…	40239	28121	25857		…	…
2620	Computers and peripheral equipment		…	19717	9644	8045		…	2748	1048	1695		…	…
2630	Communication equipment		…	153081	…	627501		…	51085	…	66741		…	…
2640	Consumer electronics		…	…	…	…		…	…	…	…		…	…
265	Measuring,testing equipment; watches, etc.		…	13722	15460	60077		…	4544	7427	14187		…	…
2651	Measuring/testing/navigating equipment,etc.		…	…	15460	…		…	…	7427	…		…	…
2652	Watches and clocks		…	…	…	…		…	…	-	…		…	…
2660	Irradiation/electromedical equipment,etc.		…	…	…	…		…	…	…	…		…	…
2670	Optical instruments and photographic equipment		…	…	…	…		…	…	…	…		…	…
2680	Magnetic and optical media		…	…	…	…		…	…	…	…		…	…
2710	Electric motors,generators,transformers,etc.		…	341020	246718	281250		…	90039	66807	78192		…	…
2720	Batteries and accumulators		…	49321	32601	41709		…	8909	7088	9430		…	…
273	Wiring and wiring devices		…	…	…	…		…	…	…	…		…	…
2731	Fibre optic cables		…	…	…	-		…	…	…	-		…	…
2732	Other electronic and electric wires and cables		…	45192	…	37618		…	8251	…	8632		…	…
2733	Wiring devices		…	4129	…	4092		…	658	…	799		…	…
2740	Electric lighting equipment		…	…	18023	…		…	…	6155	…		…	…
2750	Domestic appliances		…	…	…	…		…	…	…	…		…	…
2790	Other electrical equipment		…	15371	…	13161		…	8417	…	5536		…	…
281	General-purpose machinery		…	148448	90346	74574		…	53079	34206	26612		…	…
2811	Engines/turbines,excl.aircraft,vehicle engines		…	…	…	-		…	…	…	-		…	…
2812	Fluid power equipment		…	-	…	-		…	-	…	-		…	…
2813	Other pumps, compressors, taps and valves		…	3534	3617	…		…	933	748	…		…	…
2814	Bearings, gears, gearing and driving elements		…	…	…	-		…	…	…	-		…	…
2815	Ovens, furnaces and furnace burners		…	…	…	-		…	…	…	-		…	…
2816	Lifting and handling equipment		…	76093	46758	43744		…	28044	18809	16652		…	…
2817	Office machinery, excl.computers,etc.		…	…	…	…		…	…	…	…		…	…
2818	Power-driven hand tools		…	…	…	…		…	…	…	…		…	…
2819	Other general-purpose machinery		…	51730	26843	…		…	18400	9766	…		…	…
282	Special-purpose machinery		…	143111	73997	115015		…	45767	24101	37516		…	…
2821	Agricultural and forestry machinery		…	59642	34851	49996		…	15754	9996	13591		…	…
2822	Metal-forming machinery and machine tools		…	30083	7522	…		…	7906	601	…		…	…
2823	Machinery for metallurgy		…	…	…	…		…	…	…	…		…	…
2824	Mining, quarrying and construction machinery		…	11964	…	10041		…	4263	…	3030		…	…

ISIC Revision 4

Code	Description							
2825	Food/beverage/tobacco processing machinery	:	16847	12514	9972	8123	5899	4169
2826	Textile/apparel/leather production machinery	:	–	–	47	–	–	4
2829	Other special-purpose machinery	:	:	:	:	:	:	:
2910	Motor vehicles	:	:	:	:	:	:	:
2920	Automobile bodies, trailers and semi-trailers	:	:	:	:	:	:	:
2930	Parts and accessories for motor vehicles	:	143552	96334	209371	57297	34947	66901
301	Building of ships and boats	:	21717	12693	47854	5867	5605	15315
3011	Building of ships and floating structures	:	:	:	28968	:	:	7790
3012	Building of pleasure and sporting boats	:	:	:	18886	:	:	7525
3020	Railway locomotives and rolling stock	:	:	:	:	:	:	:
3030	Air and spacecraft and related machinery	:	–	–	–	–	–	–
3040	Military fighting vehicles	:	–	:	:	:	:	–
309	Transport equipment n.e.c.	:	–	:	:	–	:	:
3091	Motorcycles	:	:	:	:	:	:	:
3092	Bicycles and invalid carriages	:	–	:	:	–	:	–
3099	Other transport equipment n.e.c.	:	:	:	:	:	:	:
3100	Furniture	:	360129	262587	322991	104630	80784	92842
321	Jewellery, bijouterie and related articles	:	10213	5579	:	3713	2537	2537
3211	Jewellery and related articles	:	10213	:	:	3713	:	:
3212	Imitation jewellery and related articles	:	–	:	–	:	:	–
3220	Musical instruments	:	17429	:	:	8187	:	:
3230	Sports goods	:	:	:	22	:	:	9
3240	Games and toys	:	49091	32646	38274	23622	15652	17408
3250	Medical and dental instruments and supplies	:	35848	31566	37988	10533	10641	11609
3290	Other manufacturing n.e.c.	:	193218	145808	154437	73383	56261	59745
331	Repair of fabricated metal products/machinery	:	:	:	:	:	:	:
3311	Repair of fabricated metal products	:	10430	:	3327	5873	:	1586
3312	Repair of machinery	:	41677	36347	34758	21711	17000	17465
3313	Repair of electronic and optical equipment	:	1138	2115	9321	684	869	3543
3314	Repair of electrical equipment	:	14610	11568	:	7516	4851	:
3315	Repair of transport equip., excl. motor vehicles	:	:	:	4059	:	:	2678
3319	Repair of other equipment	:	:	:	:	:	:	:
3320	Installation of industrial machinery/equipment	:	57610	26057	23400	18681	9651	7705
C	Total manufacturing	:	7492669	5442249	7029581	2153030	1582037	1903831

Estonia

Index numbers of industrial production

ISIC Revision 4

(2005=100)

ISIC	Industry	Note	1999	2000	2001	2002	2003	2004	2005	2006	2007	2008	2009	2010
10	Food products		…	83	90	90	92	96	100	105	105	103	94	96
11	Beverages		…	64	73	78	82	88	100	113	120	102	92	79
12	Tobacco products		…	…	…	…	…	…	…	…	…	…	…	…
13	Textiles		…	76	87	99	109	109	100	103	102	95	79	85
14	Wearing apparel		…	94	107	109	109	106	100	103	97	86	59	63
15	Leather and related products		…	207	176	177	183	111	100	101	93	86	63	72
16	Wood/wood products/cork,excl. furniture		…	56	64	71	77	90	100	106	102	84	62	83
17	Paper and paper products		…	65	71	86	82	89	100	126	144	127	100	122
18	Printing and reproduction of recorded media		…	45	55	64	77	88	100	111	124	132	116	138
19	Coke and refined petroleum products		…	87	81	89	88	104	100	108	142	137	110	118
20	Chemicals and chemical products		…	52	54	58	69	85	100	107	112	129	72	83
21	Pharmaceuticals,medicinal chemicals, etc.		…	68	61	80	71	97	100	108	109	124	110	137
22	Rubber and plastics products		…	45	60	67	88	91	100	133	136	115	78	96
23	Other non-metallic mineral products		…	51	55	61	71	81	100	118	130	99	63	71
24	Basic metals		…	41	63	82	141	110	100	102	163	143	75	112
25	Fabricated metal products, except machinery		…	44	53	57	72	80	100	121	131	135	93	100
26	Computer, electronic and optical products		…	56	33	38	46	67	100	111	127	141	130	319
27	Electrical equipment		…	26	29	38	42	69	100	124	148	171	119	131
28	Machinery and equipment n.e.c.		…	52	71	80	85	91	100	116	132	133	75	100
29	Motor vehicles, trailers and semi-trailers		…	59	75	84	85	94	100	110	133	142	91	185
30	Other transport equipment		…	…	…	…	47	160	100	87	118	110	88	98
31	Furniture		…	70	84	89	91	96	100	104	106	96	71	81
32	Other manufacturing		…	48	56	67	73	87	100	109	134	133	93	104
33	Repair and installation of machinery/equipment		…	62	62	67	80	88	100	104	118	125	88	86
C	Total manufacturing		…	61	67	73	80	89	100	111	117	112	83	103

Fiji

Supplier of information:
Bureau of Statistics, Suva.

Basic source of data:
Not reported.

Major deviations from ISIC (Revision 4):
Data for 2005-2007 were originally classified according to the 2004 Fiji Industrial Classification System; data as of 2008 were originally classified according to the 2010 Fiji Classification System.

Reference period:
Not reported.

Scope:
Not reported.

Method of data collection:
Not reported.

Type of enumeration:
Not reported.

Adjusted for non-response:
Not reported.

Concepts and definitions of variables:
No deviations from the standard UN concepts and definitions are reported.

Related national publications:
None reported.

Fiji

- 390 -

ISIC	Industry	Note	Number of establishments (number) 2006	2007	2008	2009	Note	Number of employees (number) 2006	2007	2008	2009	Note	Wages and salaries paid to employees (thousands of Fiji Dollars) 2006	2007	2008	2009
10	Food products		148	150	152	155		9272	8449	8591	8587		71182	70528	75859	72146
11	Beverages	a/	20	22	23	23		890	1230	1172a/	1177a/		13685	16116	24591a/	19359a/
12	Tobacco products	a/	…	…	…	…		68	68	…a/	…a/		827	828	…a/	…a/
13	Textiles		…	…	…	…		…	…	…	…		…	…	…	…
14	Wearing apparel		156	151	154	156		8204	6727	6760	6771		37892	35027	26508	29564
15	Leather and related products		8	8	8	8		926	922	919	921		7937	7153	7404	7412
16	Wood/wood products/cork,excl. furniture		17	17	17	17		848	986	1387	1393		12278	12130	12064	12335
17	Paper and paper products		15	14	14	14		635	842	842	845		5582	2659	1999	2734
18	Printing and reproduction of recorded media		43	45	36	42		377	416	472	472		3206	3574	3630	3666
19	Coke and refined petroleum products		…	…	…	…		…	…	…	…		…	…	…	…
20	Chemicals and chemical products		22	22	22	23		613	732	721	721		7734	9592	10250	10229
21	Pharmaceuticals,medicinal chemicals, etc.		…	…	…	…		…	…	…	…		…	…	…	…
22	Rubber and plastics products		21	23	22	22		405	406	405	403		2897	2664	2530	2550
23	Other non-metallic mineral products		21	19	19	20		461	393	388	388		4764	4452	2885	3236
24	Basic metals		4	3	3	3		148	86	86	86		1061	1756	1108	1156
25	Fabricated metal products, except machinery		45	43	44	41		1306	1237	1123	1121		9519	8306	7865	7868
26	Computer, electronic and optical products		…	…	…	…		…	…	…	…		…	…	…	…
27	Electrical equipment		19	10	11	9		188	178	191	188		1298	1251	745	741
28	Machinery and equipment n.e.c.		12	13	12	12		43	39	34	32		391	333	267	267
29	Motor vehicles, trailers and semi-trailers		8	8	8	7		88	71	92	93		835	489	686	686
30	Other transport equipment		7	8	7	7		165	165	185	184		1648	1235	1215	1215
31	Furniture		95	84	83	81		1188	914	913	917		8771	8255	6614	7152
32	Other manufacturing		27	28	26	25		160	167	208	206		1002	1079	1270	1260
33	Repair and installation of machinery/equipment		…	…	…	…		…	…	…	…		…	…	…	…
C	Total manufacturing	b/	688	668	661	665	b/	25985	24028	24489	24505	b/	192508	187429	187491	183576

a/ 11 includes 12.
b/ Sum of available data.

Fiji

ISIC	Industry	Output (thousands of Fiji Dollars)					Value added (thousands of Fiji Dollars)					Gross fixed capital formation (thousands of Fiji Dollars)		
		Note	2006	2007	2008	2009	Note	2006	2007	2008	2009	Note	2008	2009
10	Food products		797328	787973	807686	807198		177776	149414	162356	154525		14955	17588
11	Beverages		239445	270661	295144a/	298891a/		94573	103202	104958a/	97456a/		33168	29632
12	Tobacco products		7792	7852	...a/	...a/		1599	1724	...a/	...a/		...	...
13	Textiles		162631	158717	159247	160446		58652	59585	64072	68459		2805	4806
14	Wearing apparel		22224	22813	22223	23013		5383	6679	7030	8246		51	56
15	Leather and related products		90064	92287	111106	112721		33789	34113	36483	36847		19506	15777
16	Wood/wood products/cork,excl. furniture		69053	67860	70084	70084		16411	17279	20307	22525		864	2134
17	Paper and paper products		40198	43481	43986	44828		20169	20739	21185	21710		432	431
18	Printing and reproduction of recorded media		...	...	...	...		...	...	...	...		...	...
19	Coke and refined petroleum products		113477	108773	111852	115410		29299	27285	25861	31979		2375	2348
20	Chemicals and chemical products		...	...	...	...		...	...	...	...		...	...
21	Pharmaceuticals,medicinal chemicals, etc.		37936	34797	34543	34747		7543	6306	7012	7320		4208	3609
22	Rubber and plastics products		58711	61238	64569	65638		19001	17375	17804	21087		1776	1913
23	Other non-metallic mineral products		45462	47453	48547	48941		3617	3604	4123	3370		147	152
24	Basic metals		111753	111686	117983	119905		33571	31203	31345	40317		874	882
25	Fabricated metal products, except machinery		...	...	...	...		...	...	...	...		...	...
26	Computer, electronic and optical products		10299	11917	11672	11885		4949	4394	5674	4977		46	40
27	Electrical equipment		3766	2739	2454	2467		986	528	588	599		-	125
28	Machinery and equipment n.e.c.		4620	3645	3845	4351		1394	1078	1177	1495		-	-
29	Motor vehicles, trailers and semi-trailers		6108	4783	4899	5033		3467	2771	2899	2810		-	-
30	Other transport equipment		74973	78402	77400	80243		20662	19549	17218	16812		398	395
31	Furniture		18588	18025	18841	18834		5384	5266	5707	5970		3128	3264
32	Other manufacturing		...	...	...	...		...	...	...	...		...	...
33	Repair and installation of machinery/equipment		...	...	...	...		...	...	...	...		...	...
C	Total manufacturing	b/	1914427	1935104	2006082	2024634	b/	538225	512096	535800	546504	b/	84734	83150

a/ 11 includes 12.
b/ Sum of available data.

Fiji

Index numbers of industrial production

ISIC Revision 3

(2005=100)

ISIC	Industry	Note	1999	2000	2001	2002	2003	2004	2005	2006	2007	2008	2009	2010
15	Food and beverages		...	...	...	...	...	...	...	...	...	...	...	...
16	Tobacco products		...	...	...	...	...	...	...	...	...	...	...	...
17	Textiles		...	...	...	...	...	...	...	...	...	...	...	...
18	Wearing apparel, fur		...	...	...	...	...	...	100	97	97	88	91	94
19	Leather, leather products and footwear		...	...	...	...	...	...	100	90	114	99	112	111
20	Wood products (excl. furniture)		...	...	...	...	...	...	100	92	89	79	78	94
21	Paper and paper products		...	...	...	...	...	...	100	102	103	105	99	102
22	Printing and publishing		...	...	...	...	...	...	...	...	...	...	...	...
23	Coke,refined petroleum products,nuclear fuel		...	...	...	...	...	...	...	...	...	...	...	...
24	Chemicals and chemical products		...	...	...	...	...	...	100	100	97	88	100	115
25	Rubber and plastics products		...	...	...	...	...	...	100	108	102	104	98	98
26	Non-metallic mineral products		...	...	...	...	...	...	100	96	103	103	103	119
27	Basic metals		...	...	...	...	...	...	100	141	106	111	88	87
28	Fabricated metal products		...	...	...	...	...	...	100	112	98	84	97	98
29	Machinery and equipment n.e.c.		...	...	...	...	...	...	100	100	102	103	103	106
30	Office, accounting and computing machinery		...	...	...	...	...	...	...	...	...	...	...	...
31	Electrical machinery and apparatus		...	...	...	...	...	...	100	101	102	103	92	93
32	Radio,television and communication equipment		...	...	...	...	...	...	...	...	...	...	...	...
33	Medical, precision and optical instruments		...	...	...	...	...	...	...	...	...	...	...	...
34	Motor vehicles, trailers, semi-trailers		...	...	...	...	...	...	100	140	103	80	115	100
35	Other transport equipment		...	...	...	...	...	...	...	...	...	...	...	...
36	Furniture; manufacturing n.e.c.		...	...	...	...	...	...	...	...	...	...	...	...
37	Recycling		...	...	...	...	...	...	...	...	...	...	...	...
D	Total manufacturing		113	102	109	108	106	120	100	104	103	98	95	103

Finland

Supplier of information:
Statistics Finland, Helsinki.
Industrial statistics for the OECD countries are compiled by the OECD secretariat, which supplies them to UNIDO.

Basic source of data:
Annual survey; administrative data; business register. Annual survey; administrative data.

Major deviations from ISIC (Revision 4):
Data have been converted from the national NACE equivalent system to ISIC (Revision 4) by the OECD.

Reference period:
Calendar year.

Scope:
All enterprises.

Method of data collection:
Not reported.

Type of enumeration:
Not reported.

Adjusted for non-response:
Not reported.

Concepts and definitions of variables:
No deviations from the standard UN concepts and definitions are reported.

Related national publications:
None reported.

Finland

		Number of enterprises (number)					Number of employees (number)					Wages and salaries paid to employees (millions of Euros)				
ISIC	Industry	Note	2006	2007	2008	2009	Note	2006	2007	2008	2009	Note	2006	2007	2008	2009
1010	Processing/preserving of meat		...	...	204	203		...	...	...	...		...	...	...	...
1020	Processing/preserving of fish, etc.		...	...	147	142		...	...	778	853		...	...	18	21
1030	Processing/preserving of fruit,vegetables		...	...	168	167		...	...	2119	1732		...	...	61	50
1040	Vegetable and animal oils and fats		...	...	21	24		...	...	...	...		...	...	...	...
1050	Dairy products		...	...	52	53		...	...	...	...		...	...	...	...
106	Grain mill products,starches and starch products		...	...	75	71		...	...	554	430		...	...	23	18
1061	Grain mill products		...	...	69	66		...	...	494	380		...	...	22	16
1062	Starches and starch products		...	...	6	5		...	...	60	50		...	...	1	1
107	Other food products		...	...	984	955		...	...	...	...		...	...	...	...
1071	Bakery products		...	...	783	755		...	...	14775	14567		...	...	418	415
1072	Sugar		...	...	4	3		...	...	350	311		...	...	13	10
1073	Cocoa, chocolate and sugar confectionery		...	...	32	35		...	...	1711	1686		...	...	53	52
1074	Macaroni, noodles, couscous, etc.		...	...	1	1		...	...	...	...		...	...	...	...
1075	Prepared meals and dishes		...	...	49	50		...	...	1811	1778		...	...	52	51
1079	Other food products n.e.c.		...	...	115	111		...	...	1230	1252		...	...	41	45
1080	Prepared animal feeds		...	...	77	72		...	...	807	821		...	...	28	29
1101	Distilling, rectifying and blending of spirits		...	...	88a/	83a/		...	...	4146a/	3913a/		...	...	155a/	154a/
1102	Wines		...	...	...a/	...a/		...	...	...a/	...a/		...	...	155a/	154a/
1103	Malt liquors and malt		...	...	...a/	...a/		...	...	...a/	...a/		...	...	...a/	...a/
1104	Soft drinks,mineral waters,other bottled waters		...	...	...a/	...a/		...	...	...a/	...a/		...	...	...a/	...a/
1200	Tobacco products		...	...	1	1		...	...	...	...		...	...	...	...
131	Spinning, weaving and finishing of textiles		...	...	187	195		...	...	...	...		...	...	...	...
1311	Preparation and spinning of textile fibres		...	...	21	21		...	...	728	554		...	...	18	14
1312	Weaving of textiles		...	...	21	23		...	...	...	...		...	...	...	...
1313	Finishing of textiles		...	...	145	151		...	...	518	359		...	...	...	...
139	Other textiles		...	...	705	658		...	...	3820	3597		...	...	121	103
1391	Knitted and crocheted fabrics		...	...	18	14		...	...	114	70		...	...	3	2
1392	Made-up textile articles, except apparel		...	...	350	336		...	...	1433	1340		...	...	37	32
1393	Carpets and rugs		...	...	107	92		...	...	95	82		...	...	2	2
1394	Cordage, rope, twine and netting		...	...	19	18		...	...	131	139		...	...	3	4
1399	Other textiles n.e.c.		...	...	211	198		...	...	2047	1965		...	...	75	64
1410	Wearing apparel, except fur apparel		...	...	1029	998		...	...	...	...		...	...	...	...
1420	Articles of fur		...	...	45	42		...	...	100	90		...	...	2	2
1430	Knitted and crocheted apparel		...	...	95	92		...	...	259	241		...	...	6	6
151	Leather;luggage,handbags,saddlery,harness;fur		...	...	184	169		...	...	419	...		...	...	9	...
1511	Tanning/dressing of leather; dressing of fur		...	...	49	42		...	...	252	232		...	...	5	5
1512	Luggage,handbags,etc.;saddlery/harness		...	...	135	127		...	...	167	...		...	...	4	...
1520	Footwear		...	...	69	68		...	...	1548	1438		...	...	36	30
1610	Sawmilling and planing of wood		...	...	1007	952		...	...	9521	5635		...	...	292	155
162	Wood products, cork, straw, plaiting materials		...	...	1561	1439		...	...	18070	18786		...	...	492	489

Code	Description	(1)	(2)	(3)	(4)	(5)	(6)
1621	Veneer sheets and wood-based panels	37	34	4789	7140	147	195
1622	Builders' carpentry and joinery	864	834	11492	...	302	28
1623	Wooden containers	174	151	1209	1149	31	13
1629	Other wood products;articles of cork,straw	486	420	580	1286	...	...
1701	Pulp, paper and paperboard	64	68	27607	...	79	73
1702	Corrugated paper and paperboard	65	68	2333	2109	57	...
1709	Other articles of paper and paperboard	76	77	1732	...	...	...
181	Printing and service activities related to printing	1158	1137	11965	11185	377	345
1811	Printing	867	852	10977	10256	347	317
1812	Service activities related to printing	291	285	988	929	30	28
1820	Reproduction of recorded media	108	123	93	83	3	3
1910	Coke oven products	3	2	...	...	...	...
1920	Refined petroleum products	10	14	14646b/	8136	612b/	375
201	Basic chemicals,fertilizers, etc.	112	111	...b/	...	...	219
2011	Basic chemicals	59	60	4743	1051	...	44
2012	Fertilizers and nitrogen compounds	14	16	2606	2342	123	112
2013	Plastics and synthetic rubber in primary forms	39	35	...b/	...b/	...b/	...
202	Other chemical products	187	192	...b/	...	...	71
2021	Pesticides and other agrochemical products	2	2	...	...	...	...
2022	Paints,varnishes;printing ink and mastics	37	38	1862	...	...	...
2023	Soap,cleaning and cosmetic preparations	73	71	...	...	...	...
2029	Other chemical products n.e.c.	75	81	...b/	...	...	...
2030	Man-made fibres	2	2	...b/	...	65	60
2100	Pharmaceuticals,medicinal chemicals, etc.	29	31	1527	1371	118	81
221	Rubber products	75	65	3245	2842	...	...
2211	Rubber tyres and tubes	16	16	...	...	...	...
2219	Other rubber products	59	49	...	...	...	...
2220	Plastics products	602	580	13127	11944	428	392
2310	Glass and glass products	164	154	12867	11455	415	353
239	Non-metallic mineral products n.e.c.	699	697	...	42	...	2
2391	Refractory products	7	10	...	...	...	...
2392	Clay building materials	11	8	...	...	...	...
2393	Other porcelain and ceramic products	137	135	...	...	...	...
2394	Cement, lime and plaster	3	4	...	...	...	...
2395	Articles of concrete, cement and plaster	260	258	1657	1531	45	41
2396	Cutting, shaping and finishing of stone	252	251	...	...	...	...
2399	Other non-metallic mineral products n.e.c.	29	31	...	...	...	...
2410	Basic iron and steel	76	73	...	...	...	...
2420	Basic precious and other non-ferrous metals	20	26	3062	2752	102	71
243	Casting of metals	57	55	2170	1987	74	52
2431	Casting of iron and steel	26	26	892	765	28	19
2432	Casting of non-ferrous metals	31	29	...	...	...	...
251	Struct.metal products, tanks, reservoirs	1589	1574	15872	15544	505	466
2511	Structural metal products	1492	1472	12207	11923	362	326
2512	Tanks, reservoirs and containers of metal	74	72	1545	1443	49	45

Finland

		Number of enterprises (number)					Number of employees (number)					Wages and salaries paid to employees (millions of Euros)				
ISIC	Industry	Note	2006	2007	2008	2009	Note	2006	2007	2008	2009	Note	2006	2007	2008	2009
2513	Steam generators, excl. hot water boilers		...	...	23	30		...	...	2120	2178		...	...	94	95
2520	Weapons and ammunition		...	...	26	24		...	...	...	417		...	...	...	15
259	Other metal products;metal working services		...	...	3585	3486		...	...	...	27882		...	...	...	779
2591	Forging,pressing,stamping,roll-forming of metal		...	...	111	110		...	...	277	154		...	...	8	4
2592	Treatment and coating of metals; machining		...	...	2246	2206		...	...	21222	19036		...	...	627	516
2593	Cutlery, hand tools and general hardware		...	...	307	279		...	...	...	3038		...	...	...	94
2599	Other fabricated metal products n.e.c.		...	...	921	891		...	...	...	5654		...	...	...	166
2610	Electronic components and boards		...	...	168	156		...	...	2636	2273		...	...	87	69
2620	Computers and peripheral equipment		...	...	65	60		...	...	352	363		...	...	12	12
2630	Communication equipment		...	...	63	59		...	...	29552	27751		...	...	1777	1753
2640	Consumer electronics		...	...	24	23		...	...	161	147		...	...	5	5
265	Measuring,testing equipment; watches, etc.		...	...	231	220		...	...	5094	5162		...	...	202	200
2651	Measuring/testing/navigating equipment,etc.		...	...	231	218		...	...	5094	...		...	...	202	...
2652	Watches and clocks		...	...	-	2		...	...	-	...		...	...	-	...
2660	Irradiation/electromedical equipment,etc.		...	...	31	28		...	...	2528	2395		...	...	107	94
2670	Optical instruments and photographic equipment		...	...	13	17		...	...	45	46		...	...	2	2
2680	Magnetic and optical media		...	...	3	3		...	...	2	1		...	...	...	...
2710	Electric motors,generators,transformers,etc.		...	...	143	135		...	...	13863	13280		...	...	534	495
2720	Batteries and accumulators		...	...	6	7		...	...	35	57		...	...	1	2
273	Wiring and wiring devices		...	...	36	27		...	...	2501	1771		...	...	85	62
2731	Fibre optic cables		...	...	5	7		...	...	112	167		...	...	4	6
2732	Other electronic and electric wires and cables		...	...	25	14		...	...	1754	1017		...	...	58	37
2733	Wiring devices		...	...	6	6		...	...	635	587		...	...	22	19
2740	Electric lighting equipment		...	...	96	93		...	...	1558	1448		...	...	47	42
2750	Domestic appliances		...	...	40	42		...	...	1330	1203		...	...	42	38
2790	Other electrical equipment		...	...	135	141		...	...	2057	2216		...	...	64	61
281	General-purpose machinery		...	...	836	810		...	...	29220	28653		...	...	1121	1056
2811	Engines/turbines,excl.aircraft,vehicle engines		...	...	36	34		...	...	...	...		...	...	...	...
2812	Fluid power equipment		...	...	26	28		...	...	1170	...		...	...	37	...
2813	Other pumps, compressors, taps and valves		...	...	54	51		...	...	...	4344		...	...	...	160
2814	Bearings, gears, gearing and driving elements		...	...	42	41		...	...	2721	2462		...	...	94	80
2815	Ovens, furnaces and furnace burners		...	...	34	33		...	...	623	651		...	...	20	21
2816	Lifting and handling equipment		...	...	172	179		...	...	8149	8334		...	...	330	315
2817	Office machinery, excl.computers,etc.		...	...	5	4		...	...	...	...		...	...	...	...
2818	Power-driven hand tools		...	...	17	14		...	...	...	...		...	...	...	...
2819	Other general-purpose machinery		...	...	450	426		...	...	7713	7116		...	...	267	239
282	Special-purpose machinery		...	...	825	765		...	...	25825	24085		...	...	1006	855
2821	Agricultural and forestry machinery		...	...	174	153		...	...	4966	4558		...	...	174	137
2822	Metal-forming machinery and machine tools		...	...	92	89		...	...	2743	2253		...	...	98	71
2823	Machinery for metallurgy		...	...	14	16		...	...	60	59		...	...	2	2
2824	Mining, quarrying and construction machinery		...	...	116	106		...	...	5837	5563		...	...	228	188

- 397 -

2825	Food/beverage/tobacco processing machinery	81	77	⋮	733	730	⋮	24	23
2826	Textile/apparel/leather production machinery	30	22	⋮	31	31	⋮	1	1
2829	Other special-purpose machinery	318	302	⋮	11456	10892	⋮	479	434
2910	Motor vehicles	29	25	⋮	2360	2263	⋮	77	73
2920	Automobile bodies, trailers and semi-trailers	158	153	⋮	3991	3494	⋮	128	98
2930	Parts and accessories for motor vehicles	110	89	⋮	⋮	1674	⋮	⋮	44
301	Building of ships and boats	385	374	⋮	8730	⋮	⋮	297	⋮
3011	Building of ships and floating structures	126	115	⋮	5870	⋮	⋮	211	⋮
3012	Building of pleasure and sporting boats	259	259	⋮	2860	2318	⋮	86	59
3020	Railway locomotives and rolling stock	8	4	⋮	⋮	⋮	⋮	⋮	⋮
3030	Air and spacecraft and related machinery	5	4	⋮	⋮	⋮	⋮	⋮	⋮
3040	Military fighting vehicles	2	1	⋮	⋮	⋮	⋮	⋮	⋮
309	Transport equipment n.e.c.	32	31	⋮	298	275	⋮	8	8
3091	Motorcycles	3	3	⋮	⋮	⋮	⋮	⋮	⋮
3092	Bicycles and invalid carriages	12	13	⋮	119	115	⋮	3	4
3099	Other transport equipment n.e.c.	17	15	⋮	179	160	⋮	5	4
3100	Furniture	1175	1142	⋮	9937	8956	⋮	267	228
321	Jewellery, bijouterie and related articles	365	364	⋮	791	787	⋮	24	24
3211	Jewellery and related articles	332	331	⋮	⋮	⋮	⋮	⋮	⋮
3212	Imitation jewellery and related articles	33	33	⋮	⋮	⋮	⋮	⋮	⋮
3220	Musical instruments	77	76	⋮	85	74	⋮	2	2
3230	Sports goods	162	149	⋮	1087	983	⋮	31	28
3240	Games and toys	48	41	⋮	⋮	76	⋮	⋮	2
3250	Medical and dental instruments and supplies	508	488	⋮	⋮	1895	⋮	25	60
3290	Other manufacturing n.e.c.	201	210	⋮	921	791	⋮	25	22
331	Repair of fabricated metal products/machinery	1958	1895	⋮	9657	10171	⋮	318	340
3311	Repair of fabricated metal products	132	125	⋮	508	952	⋮	15	33
3312	Repair of machinery	1407	1347	⋮	7794	7934	⋮	261	269
3313	Repair of electronic and optical equipment	80	70	⋮	161	165	⋮	5	5
3314	Repair of electrical equipment	45	49	⋮	206	270	⋮	6	8
3315	Repair of transport equip., excl. motor vehicles	293	298	⋮	⋮	849	⋮	⋮	26
3319	Repair of other equipment	1	6	⋮	⋮	⋮	⋮	⋮	⋮
3320	Installation of industrial machinery/equipment	437	419	⋮	6451	5884	⋮	235	206
C	Total manufacturing	23781	22994	⋮	411237	381754	⋮	15037	13542

a/ 1101 includes 1102, 1103 and 1104.
b/ 201 includes 202 and 2030.

Finland

ISIC Revision 4		Output (millions of Euros)					Value added at factor values (millions of Euros)					Gross fixed capital formation (millions of Euros)		
ISIC	Industry	Note	2006	2007	2008	2009	Note	2006	2007	2008	2009	Note	2008	2009
1010	Processing/preserving of meat		:	:	:	:		:	:	:	:		:	:
1020	Processing/preserving of fish, etc.		:	:	154	177		:	:	34	36		5	9
1030	Processing/preserving of fruit,vegetables		:	:	483	379		:	:	132	106		28	17
1040	Vegetable and animal oils and fats		:	:	:	:		:	:	:	:		:	:
1050	Dairy products		:	:	:	:		:	:	:	:		:	:
106	Grain mill products,starches and starch products		:	:	270	175		:	:	62	43		13	6
1061	Grain mill products		:	:	247	159		:	:	57	41		13	6
1062	Starches and starch products		:	:	23	17		:	:	4	2		1	-
107	Other food products		:	:	2350	2275		:	:	779	778		79	111
1071	Bakery products		:	:	:	:		:	:	:	:		:	:
1072	Sugar		:	:	220	163		:	:	36	23		6	8
1073	Cocoa, chocolate and sugar confectionery		:	:	345	341		:	:	116	122		15	14
1074	Macaroni, noodles, couscous, etc.		:	:	:	:		:	:	:	:		:	:
1075	Prepared meals and dishes		:	:	310	315		:	:	95	95		10	14
1079	Other food products n.e.c.		:	:	437	431		:	:	125	117		12	50
1080	Prepared animal feeds		:	:	405	382		:	:	51	54		7	14
1101	Distilling, rectifying and blending of spirits		:	:	1172a/	1175a/		:	:	333a/	388a/		58a/	51a/
1102	Wines		:	:	...a/	...a/		:	:	...a/	...a/		...a/	...a/
1103	Malt liquors and malt		:	:	...a/	...a/		:	:	...a/	...a/		...a/	...a/
1104	Soft drinks,mineral waters,other bottled waters		:	:	...a/	...a/		:	:	...a/	...a/		...a/	...a/
1200	Tobacco products		:	:	:	:		:	:	:	:		:	:
131	Spinning, weaving and finishing of textiles		:	:	66	50		:	:	26	23		2	1
1311	Preparation and spinning of textile fibres		:	:	:	:		:	:	:	:		:	:
1312	Weaving of textiles		:	:	:	:		:	:	:	:		:	:
1313	Finishing of textiles		:	:	40	25		:	:	17	13		1	-
139	Other textiles		:	:	564	461		:	:	218	171		75	11
1391	Knitted and crocheted fabrics		:	:	15	6		:	:	6	2		1	-
1392	Made-up textile articles, except apparel		:	:	180	155		:	:	66	54		5	4
1393	Carpets and rugs		:	:	20	16		:	:	6	5		1	-
1394	Cordage, rope, twine and netting		:	:	16	16		:	:	6	7		-	1
1399	Other textiles n.e.c.		:	:	334	268		:	:	135	103		69	6
1410	Wearing apparel, except fur apparel		:	:	10	11		:	:	4	3		:	6
1420	Articles of fur		:	:	21	22		:	:	10	8		-	4
1430	Knitted and crocheted apparel		:	:	:	:		:	:	:	:		1	-
151	Leather;luggage,handbags,saddlery,harness;fur		:	:	35	21		:	:	17	7		3	-
1511	Tanning/dressing of leather; dressing of fur		:	:	21	:		:	:	9	:		2	1
1512	Luggage,handbags,etc.;saddlery/harness		:	:	14	21		:	:	8	7		1	-
1520	Footwear		:	:	153	131		:	:	65	53		7	7
1610	Sawmilling and planing of wood		:	:	3010	1606		:	:	384	213		150	77
162	Wood products, cork, straw, plaiting materials		:	:	2867	2785		:	:	801	614		130	64

1621	Veneer sheets and wood-based panels	803	1232	:	220	168	:	33	25
1622	Builders' carpentry and joinery	1813	..	:	495	..	:	82	..
1623	Wooden containers	190	143	:	62	50	:	11	8
1629	Other wood products;articles of cork,straw	61	..	:	24	..	:	3	..
1701	Pulp, paper and paperboard	14193	..	:	2615	..	:	739	..
1702	Corrugated paper and paperboard	395	330	:	140	117	:	13	13
1709	Other articles of paper and paperboard	331	..	:	86	..	:	29	..
181	Printing and service activities related to printing	1692	1441	:	664	554	:	93	58
1811	Printing	1595	1356	:	611	509	:	90	56
1812	Service activities related to printing	97	84	:	53	45	:	4	2
1820	Reproduction of recorded media	18	15	:	5	5	:	1	-
1910	Coke oven products	..	..	:	..	..	:	..	..
1920	Refined petroleum products	..	..	:	..	..	:	..	..
201	Basic chemicals,fertilizers, etc.	6338b/	3853	:	1606b/	879	:	296b/	209
2011	Basic chemicals	..	1909	:	..	569	:	..	98
2012	Fertilizers and nitrogen compounds	..	457	:	..	42	:	..	73
2013	Plastics and synthetic rubber in primary forms	2017	1487	:	317	268	:	81	37
202	Other chemical products	..b/	..	:	..b/	..	:	..b/	..
2021	Pesticides and other agrochemical products	..	..	:	..	..	:	..	..
2022	Paints,varnishes;printing ink and mastics	..	417	:	..	134	:	..	8
2023	Soap,cleaning and cosmetic preparations	..	..	:	..	..	:	..	..
2029	Other chemical products n.e.c.	..	..	:	..	..	:	..	..
2030	Man-made fibres	..b/	..	:	..b/	..	:	..b/	..
2100	Pharmaceuticals,medicinal chemicals, etc.	581	500	:	211	197	:	62	24
221	Rubber products	772	488	:	271	131	:	38	24
2211	Rubber tyres and tubes	..	..	:	..	..	:	..	..
2219	Other rubber products	..	..	:	..	..	:	..	..
2220	Plastics products	2557	2049	:	799	715	:	99	76
2310	Glass and glass products	..	..	:	..	..	:	..	..
239	Non-metallic mineral products n.e.c.	2702	1958	:	936	671	:	133	94
2391	Refractory products	..	12	:	..	4	:	..	-
2392	Clay building materials	..	..	:	..	..	:	..	..
2393	Other porcelain and ceramic products	..	..	:	..	..	:	..	..
2394	Cement, lime and plaster	..	..	:	..	..	:	..	..
2395	Articles of concrete, cement and plaster	200	166	:	81	68	:	10	6
2396	Cutting, shaping and finishing of stone	..	..	:	..	..	:	..	..
2399	Other non-metallic mineral products n.e.c.	..	..	:	..	..	:	..	..
2410	Basic iron and steel	..	..	:	..	..	:	..	..
2420	Basic precious and other non-ferrous metals	..	..	:	..	..	:	..	..
243	Casting of metals	469	266	:	177	100	:	32	11
2431	Casting of iron and steel	337	196	:	129	72	:	26	9
2432	Casting of non-ferrous metals	132	71	:	48	28	:	6	2
251	Struct.metal products, tanks, reservoirs	3249	2425	:	1002	793	:	113	81
2511	Structural metal products	2017	1532	:	722	547	:	96	71
2512	Tanks, reservoirs and containers of metal	295	200	:	102	70	:	7	4

continued

Finland

		Output (millions of Euros)					Value added at factor values (millions of Euros)					Gross fixed capital formation (millions of Euros)		
ISIC	Industry	Note	2006	2007	2008	2009	Note	2006	2007	2008	2009	Note	2008	2009
2513	Steam generators, excl. hot water boilers		...	...	937	693		...	...	179	175		10	6
2520	Weapons and ammunition		...	...		90		...	...	...	39			2
259	Other metal products;metal working services		...	...		3233		...	...	...	1316			231
2591	Forging,pressing,stamping,roll-forming of metal		...	...	44	17		...	...	18	8		4	1
2592	Treatment and coating of metals; machining		...	...	2915	2079		...	...	1234	839		200	186
2593	Cutlery, hand tools and general hardware		...	...		383		...	...	...	198			
2599	Other fabricated metal products n.e.c.		...	...		754		...	...	...	271			14
2610	Electronic components and boards		...	...	413	286		...	...	121	93		9	4
2620	Computers and peripheral equipment		...	...	67	62		...	...	17	16			1
2630	Communication equipment		...	...	20613	13906		...	...	5404	2055		210	128
2640	Consumer electronics		...	...	24	18		...	...	10	7		-	-
265	Measuring,testing equipment; watches, etc.		...	...	1044	894		...	...	394	342		26	29
2651	Measuring/testing/navigating equipment,etc.		...	...	1044			...	...	394			26	
2652	Watches and clocks		...	...	-			...	...	-			-	
2660	Irradiation/electromedical equipment,etc.		...	...	625	595		...	...	250	256			
2670	Optical instruments and photographic equipment		...	...	5	5		...	...	2	3		6	4
2680	Magnetic and optical media		...	...				...	...				1	-
2710	Electric motors,generators,transformers,etc.		...	...	3673	2713		...	...	1194	1005			50
2720	Batteries and accumulators		...	...	2	2		...	...	-1	-2		46	1
273	Wiring and wiring devices		...	...	693	411		...	...	161	98		-	20
2731	Fibre optic cables		...	...	14	27		...	...	2	8		25	1
2732	Other electronic and electric wires and cables		...	...	575	292		...	...	122	58		10	16
2733	Wiring devices		...	...	104	93		...	...	37	33		11	4
2740	Electric lighting equipment		...	...	268	182		...	...	106	85		4	4
2750	Domestic appliances		...	...	223	167		...	...	79	66		10	2
2790	Other electrical equipment		...	...	315	266		...	...	112	88		11	2
281	General-purpose machinery		...	...	8532	7622		...	...	2274	2018		266	192
2811	Engines/turbines,excl.aircraft,vehicle engines		...	...				...	...				8	15
2812	Fluid power equipment		...	...	184			...	...	61				
2813	Other pumps, compressors, taps and valves		...	...		665		...	...		248		5	
2814	Bearings, gears, gearing and driving elements		...	...	608	439		...	...	182	128			8
2815	Ovens, furnaces and furnace burners		...	...	120	99		...	...	34	32		48	86
2816	Lifting and handling equipment		...	...	2834	2471		...	...	669	616		2	1
2817	Office machinery, excl.computers,etc.		...	...				...	...				36	26
2818	Power-driven hand tools		...	...				...	...					
2819	Other general-purpose machinery		...	...	1521	1124		...	...	478	381		36	27
282	Special-purpose machinery		...	...	7546	4740		...	...	1907	1257		197	99
2821	Agricultural and forestry machinery		...	...	1587	876		...	...	352	151		23	9
2822	Metal-forming machinery and machine tools		...	...	522	263		...	...	148	88		13	10
2823	Machinery for metallurgy		...	...	16	11		...	...	5	5		-	-
2824	Mining, quarrying and construction machinery		...	...	2143	1145		...	...	528	270		48	31

Code							
2825	Food/beverage/tobacco processing machinery	122	89	44	39	2	1
2826	Textile/apparel/leather production machinery	5	4	2	2	-	-
2829	Other special-purpose machinery	3151	2353	830	704	111	49
2910	Motor vehicles	511	378	140	105	16	20
2920	Automobile bodies, trailers and semi-trailers	655	446	202	141	13	8
2930	Parts and accessories for motor vehicles	:	216	:	58	:	11
301	Building of ships and boats	1941	:	414	:	40	:
3011	Building of ships and floating structures	1517	:	277	:	26	:
3012	Building of pleasure and sporting boats	424	219	138	63	14	8
3020	Railway locomotives and rolling stock	:	:	:	:	:	:
3030	Air and spacecraft and related machinery	:	:	:	:	:	:
3040	Military fighting vehicles	32	28	13	11	1	1
309	Transport equipment n.e.c.	:	:	:	:	:	:
3091	Motorcycles	15	14	5	4	-	:
3092	Bicycles and invalid carriages	17	14	7	6	1	:
3099	Other transport equipment n.e.c.	1336	999	463	339	46	34
3100	Furniture	108	122	34	39	2	2
321	Jewellery, bijouterie and related articles	:	:	:	:	:	:
3211	Jewellery and related articles	:	:	:	:	:	:
3212	Imitation jewellery and related articles	8	7	3	3	-	-
3220	Musical instruments	132	119	51	45	3	2
3230	Sports goods	:	8	:	3	:	-
3240	Games and toys	:	251	:	109	:	6
3250	Medical and dental instruments and supplies	124	112	49	43	4	2
3290	Other manufacturing n.e.c.	1187	1229	538	540	54	33
331	Repair of fabricated metal products/machinery	65	116	27	53	2	8
3311	Repair of fabricated metal products	938	959	437	421	39	17
3312	Repair of machinery	23	23	9	10	4	1
3313	Repair of electronic and optical equipment	21	23	11	12	-	-
3314	Repair of electrical equipment	:	108	:	44	:	7
3315	Repair of transport equip., excl. motor vehicles	:	:	:	:	:	:
3319	Repair of other equipment	:	:	:	:	:	:
3320	Installation of industrial machinery/equipment	798	587	375	291	15	6
C	Total manufacturing	125890	93512	32089	22714	4156	3133

a/ 1101 includes 1102, 1103 and 1104.
b/ 201 includes 202 and 2030.

Finland

Index numbers of industrial production (2005=100)

ISIC Revision 4

ISIC	Industry	Note	1999	2000	2001	2002	2003	2004	2005	2006	2007	2008	2009	2010
10	Food products		...	93	96	99	101	102	100	100	101	101	99	103
11	Beverages		...	88	94	98	102	102	100	102	104	101	91	89
12	Tobacco products		...	...	...	...	...	...	...	...	...	...	...	...
13	Textiles		...	89	94	97	94	98	100	105	103	87	71	78
14	Wearing apparel		...	142	146	143	110	100	100	95	88	89	73	77
15	Leather and related products		...	125	120	123	112	109	100	106	113	114	101	126
16	Wood/wood products/cork,excl. furniture		...	90	90	92	96	99	100	105	104	87	68	78
17	Paper and paper products		...	106	99	103	106	113	100	115	116	108	88	98
18	Printing and reproduction of recorded media		...	98	101	101	99	103	100	106	106	100	84	82
19	Coke and refined petroleum products		...	...	...	...	...	...	...	...	...	...	...	...
20	Chemicals and chemical products		...	...	...	...	...	...	...	...	...	...	...	...
21	Pharmaceuticals,medicinal chemicals, etc.		...	...	...	...	...	...	...	...	...	...	...	...
22	Rubber and plastics products		...	...	...	...	...	...	...	...	...	...	...	...
23	Other non-metallic mineral products		...	86	84	84	86	92	100	105	110	104	78	86
24	Basic metals		...	100	101	102	105	109	100	103	95	91	70	91
25	Fabricated metal products, except machinery		...	94	98	96	95	96	100	108	117	123	85	88
26	Computer, electronic and optical products		...	...	...	...	...	...	...	...	...	...	...	...
27	Electrical equipment		...	...	...	...	...	...	...	...	...	...	...	...
28	Machinery and equipment n.e.c.		...	86	93	88	89	93	100	107	120	123	93	96
29	Motor vehicles, trailers and semi-trailers		...	92	95	100	94	96	100	113	108	107	69	74
30	Other transport equipment		...	100	104	103	96	91	100	131	134	130	99	80
31	Furniture		...	122	116	112	112	114	100	108	114	110	80	84
32	Other manufacturing		...	85	99	99	94	101	100	123	142	125	108	107
33	Repair and installation of machinery/equipment		...	109	113	105	103	103	100	113	117	119	96	97
C	Total manufacturing		...	91	91	93	93	99	100	109	115	117	93	98

France

Supplier of information:
Institut National de la Statistique et des Études Économiques, Paris.
Industrial statistics for the OECD countries are compiled by the OECD secretariat, which supplies them to UNIDO.

Basic source of data:
Annual survey; administrative data.

Major deviations from ISIC (Revision 4):
None reported.

Reference period:
Calendar year.

Scope:
All enterprises.

Method of data collection:
Not reported.

Type of enumeration:
Not reported.

Adjusted for non-response:
Not reported.

Concepts and definitions of variables:
No deviations from the standard UN concepts and definitions are reported.

Related national publications:
None reported.

France

- 404 -

ISIC	Industry	Number of enterprises (number)					Number of employees (thousands)					Wages and salaries paid to employees (millions of Euros)				
		Note	2006	2007	2008	2009	Note	2006	2007	2008	2009	Note	2006	2007	2008	2009
1010	Processing/preserving of meat		...	...	...	9460		...	...	...	136.2		...	...	...	3258
1020	Processing/preserving of fish, etc.		...	...	348	314		...	...	11.6	11.1		...	...	...	297
1030	Processing/preserving of fruit,vegetables		...	...	...	1147		...	...	...	25.9		...	...	...	764
1040	Vegetable and animal oils and fats		...	...	...	181		...	...	...	2.6		...	...	...	93
1050	Dairy products		...	...	...	1264		...	...	...	55.3		...	...	...	1631
106	Grain mill products,starches and starch products		...	...	451	487		...	...	13.5	13.8		...	...	...	495
1061	Grain mill products		...	...	...	481		...	...	...	9.0		...	...	...	299
1062	Starches and starch products		...	...	...	6		...	...	...	4.7		...	...	...	196
107	Other food products		...	...	45582	43775		...	...	258.3	272.8		...	...	...	6388
1071	Bakery products		...	...	...	39705		...	...	...	190.5		...	...	...	3828
1072	Sugar		...	...	...	23		...	...	...	6.2		...	...	...	238
1073	Cocoa, chocolate and sugar confectionery		...	...	873	826		...	...	20.1	17.8		...	...	...	547
1074	Macaroni, noodles, couscous, etc.		...	...	...	167		...	...	...	3.3		...	...	...	101
1075	Prepared meals and dishes		...	...	...	1039		...	...	...	21.7		...	...	...	544
1079	Other food products n.e.c.		...	...	...	2016		...	...	...	33.2		...	...	...	1129
1080	Prepared animal feeds		...	...	...	499		...	...	...	18.6		...	...	...	651
1101	Distilling, rectifying and blending of spirits		...	...	2725a/	2903a/		...	...	...	45.0a/		...	...	...	1745a/
1102	Wines		...	...	...a/	...a/		...	...	...	...a/		...	...	...	...a/
1103	Malt liquors and malt		...	...	...a/	...a/		...	...	...	...a/		...	...	...	...a/
1104	Soft drinks,mineral waters,other bottled waters		...	...	...a/	...a/		...	...	...	...a/		...	...	...	...a/
1200	Tobacco products		...	...	5	6		...	...	2.8	2.2		...	...	...	157
131	Spinning, weaving and finishing of textiles		...	...	1195	1106		...	...	18.8	16.6		...	...	...	489
1311	Preparation and spinning of textile fibres		...	...	264	245		...	...	4.4	4.1		...	...	...	103
1312	Weaving of textiles		...	...	397	305		...	...	8.5	6.9		...	...	...	217
1313	Finishing of textiles		...	...	534	556		...	...	6.0	5.6		...	...	...	169
139	Other textiles		...	...	2985	3020		...	...	35.0	32.4		...	...	...	900
1391	Knitted and crocheted fabrics		...	...	...	74		...	...	...	1.5		...	...	...	41
1392	Made-up textile articles, except apparel		...	...	...	1983		...	...	...	13.9		...	...	...	357
1393	Carpets and rugs		...	...	...	32		...	...	...	2.0		...	...	...	71
1394	Cordage, rope, twine and netting		...	...	...	107		...	...	...	1.0		...	...	...	24
1399	Other textiles n.e.c.		...	...	...	824		...	...	...	14.0		...	...	...	406
1410	Wearing apparel, except fur apparel		...	...	...	6380		...	...	...	40.2		...	...	...	1099
1420	Articles of fur		...	...	152	126		...	...	0.4	0.4		...	...	...	12
1430	Knitted and crocheted apparel		...	...	...	300		...	...	...	8.0		...	...	...	224
151	Leather;luggage,handbags,saddlery,harness;fur		...	...	1551	1423		...	...	18.3	17.1		...	...	...	452
1511	Tanning/dressing of leather; dressing of fur		...	...	197	130		...	...	2.0	1.9		...	...	...	50
1512	Luggage,handbags,etc.;saddlery/harness		...	...	1354	1293		...	...	16.3	15.2		...	...	...	403
1520	Footwear		...	...	394	333		...	...	7.3	8.2		...	...	...	210
1610	Sawmilling and planing of wood		...	...	3256	2951		...	...	10.7	18.7		...	...	...	519
162	Wood products, cork, straw, plaiting materials		...	...	5883	6270		...	...	50.4	49.7		...	...	...	1310

Code						
1621	Veneer sheets and wood-based panels	134	...	...	7.0	214
1622	Builders' carpentry and joinery	2860	...	...	23.8	608
1623	Wooden containers	1086	899	14.3	13.2	336
1629	Other wood products;articles of cork,straw	1891	2377	5.6	5.7	152
1701	Pulp, paper and paperboard	136	767	31.6	18.2	719
1702	Corrugated paper and paperboard	686	613	...	31.1	940
1709	Other articles of paper and paperboard	...	...	...	19.9	643
181	Printing and service activities related to printing	15848	14987	79.6	74.3	2367
1811	Printing	...	5722	...	56.1	1773
1812	Service activities related to printing	...	9265	...	18.1	594
1820	Reproduction of recorded media	385	379	1.9	2.2	79
1910	Coke oven products	88b/	98b/	17.5b/	15.9b/	969b/
1920	Refined petroleum products	...b/	...b/	...b/	...b/	...b/
201	Basic chemicals,fertilizers, etc.	856	792	66.4	68.5	3178
2011	Basic chemicals	...	439	...	53.3	2525
2012	Fertilizers and nitrogen compounds	...	114	...	4.4	171
2013	Plastics and synthetic rubber in primary forms	...	240	...	10.9	482
202	Other chemical products	1999	1961	88.6	84.4	3230
2021	Pesticides and other agrochemical products	100	90	5.4	5.4	238
2022	Paints,varnishes;printing ink and mastics	295	297	14.1	13.9	524
2023	Soap,cleaning and cosmetic preparations	1109	983	44.8	39.5	1365
2029	Other chemical products n.e.c.	...	590	...	25.6	1102
2030	Man-made fibres	18	18	...	1.2	45
2100	Pharmaceuticals,medicinal chemicals, etc.	475	859	84.2	78.7	3527
221	Rubber products	577	654	58.5	55.8	1942
2211	Rubber tyres and tubes	...	68	...	29.1	1106
2219	Other rubber products	...	586	...	26.7	835
2220	Plastics products	...	4041	...	142.5	4321
2310	Glass and glass products	7659	1247	84.2	42.3	1322
239	Non-metallic mineral products n.e.c.	62	7266	2.9	81.7	2694
2391	Refractory products	...	41	...	2.6	105
2392	Clay building materials	...	194	...	7.7	241
2393	Other porcelain and ceramic products	...	1757	...	8.2	230
2394	Cement, lime and plaster	...	77	...	6.0	272
2395	Articles of concrete, cement and plaster	...	2296	...	39.7	1278
2396	Cutting, shaping and finishing of stone	3151	2382	10.6	8.7	230
2399	Other non-metallic mineral products n.e.c.	...	517	...	8.7	338
2410	Basic iron and steel	...	378	...	37.5	1689
2420	Basic precious and other non-ferrous metals	473	459	29.1	29.2	864
243	Casting of metals	...	125	...	16.5	500
2431	Casting of iron and steel	...	334	...	12.7	364
2432	Casting of non-ferrous metals	4525	5807	70.8	87.7	2558
251	Struct.metal products, tanks, reservoirs	4361	5647	59.7	77.2	2223
2511	Structural metal products	113	127	9.9	9.4	297
2512	Tanks, reservoirs and containers of metal	...	...	...	...	...

continued

France

ISIC	Industry	Number of enterprises (number) Note	2006	2007	2008	2009	Number of employees (thousands) Note	2006	2007	2008	2009	Wages and salaries paid to employees (millions of Euros) Note	2006	2007	2008	2009
2513	Steam generators, excl. hot water boilers		...	...	51	33		...	...	1.2	1.2		...	...	...	38
2520	Weapons and ammunition		...	...	158	134		...	...	7.4	6.5		...	...	...	341
259	Other metal products;metal working services		...	...	14793	14713		...	...	247.4	229.9		...	...	...	7042
2591	Forging,pressing,stamping,roll-forming of metal		...	...	1665	1784		...	...	44.1	45.6		...	...	...	1394
2592	Treatment and coating of metals; machining		...	...		9054		...	...		105.6		...	...	...	3211
2593	Cutlery, hand tools and general hardware		...	...	2249	1905		...	...	34.3	30.6		...	...	...	955
2599	Other fabricated metal products n.e.c.		...	...		1969		...	...		48.1		...	...	...	1482
2610	Electronic components and boards		...	...		940		...	...		49.9		...	...	...	1860
2620	Computers and peripheral equipment		...	...	284	334		...	...	4.5	3.9		...	...	...	148
2630	Communication equipment		...	...	683	545		...	...	28.0	31.5		...	...	...	1320
2640	Consumer electronics		...	...	163	124		...	...	6.6	1.5		...	...	...	50
265	Measuring,testing equipment; watches, etc.		...	...	1187	1042		...	...	51.0	54.2		...	...	...	2432
2651	Measuring/testing/navigating equipment,etc.		...	...	1019	876		...	...	48.9	52.2		...	...	...	2369
2652	Watches and clocks		...	...	169	166		...	...	2.1	2.0		...	...	...	63
2660	Irradiation/electromedical equipment,etc.		...	...	97	97		...	...	4.5	4.3		...	...	...	231
2670	Optical instruments and photographic equipment		...	...	751	303		...	...	5.1	1.4		...	...	...	57
2680	Magnetic and optical media		...	...	12	21		...	...	0.1	0.2		...	...	...	6
2710	Electric motors,generators,transformers,etc.		...	...		708		...	...		51.6		...	...	...	1921
2720	Batteries and accumulators		...	...	31	29		...	...	4.9	4.3		...	...	...	155
273	Wiring and wiring devices		...	...	311	364		...	...	28.1	25.9		...	...	...	1016
2731	Fibre optic cables		...	...		21		...	...		1.3		...	...	...	59
2732	Other electronic and electric wires and cables		...	...		113		...	...		10.5		...	...	...	376
2733	Wiring devices		...	...		230		...	...		14.1		...	...	...	581
2740	Electric lighting equipment		...	...	833	819		...	...	13.2	16.6		...	...	...	617
2750	Domestic appliances		...	...		149		...	...		16.6		...	...	...	560
2790	Other electrical equipment		...	...	563	420		...	...	19.8	12.8		...	...	...	442
281	General-purpose machinery		...	...	4937	3444		...	...	142.9	134.2		...	...	...	4755
2811	Engines/turbines,excl.aircraft,vehicle engines		...	...	480	185		...	...		13.0		...	...	...	508
2812	Fluid power equipment		...	...		251		...	...	9.2	8.6		...	...	...	279
2813	Other pumps, compressors, taps and valves		...	...		267		...	...		27.7		...	...	...	1027
2814	Bearings, gears, gearing and driving elements		...	...	173	111		...	...	17.3	16.3		...	...	...	544
2815	Ovens, furnaces and furnace burners		...	...		107		...	...		3.3		...	...	...	163
2816	Lifting and handling equipment		...	...	953	688		...	...	23.5	21.3		...	...	...	720
2817	Office machinery, excl.computers,etc.		...	...		29		...	...		1.3		...	...	...	43
2818	Power-driven hand tools		...	...		15		...	...		0.6		...	...	...	23
2819	Other general-purpose machinery		...	...		1791		...	...		42.0		...	...	...	1448
282	Special-purpose machinery		...	...	2991	2690		...	...	69.1	61.6		...	...	...	2127
2821	Agricultural and forestry machinery		...	...	687	655		...	...	17.4	16.8		...	...	...	494
2822	Metal-forming machinery and machine tools		...	...		439		...	...		6.1		...	...	...	202
2823	Machinery for metallurgy		...	...		23		...	...		1.5		...	...	...	66
2824	Mining, quarrying and construction machinery		...	...		132		...	...		10.0		...	...	...	364

Code	Description					
2825	Food/beverage/tobacco processing machinery	703	578	12.5	10.6	361
2826	Textile/apparel/leather production machinery	:	114	:	3.4	124
2829	Other special-purpose machinery	:	749	13.2	13.2	516
2910	Motor vehicles	197	141	150.3	144.6	5805
2920	Automobile bodies, trailers and semi-trailers	1247	1092	27.6	24.7	693
2930	Parts and accessories for motor vehicles	:	564	:	64.9	2300
301	Building of ships and boats	541	491	20.7	19.6	707
3011	Building of ships and floating structures	:	138	:	11.2	491
3012	Building of pleasure and sporting boats	47	352	14.0	8.4	215
3020	Railway locomotives and rolling stock	167	50	91.5	14.0	647
3030	Air and spacecraft and related machinery	3	184	2.1	85.0	4310
3040	Military fighting vehicles	237	5	5.0	2.2	102
309	Transport equipment n.e.c.	56	210	2.1	4.8	153
3091	Motorcycles	:	74	:	1.8	68
3092	Bicycles and invalid carriages	:	104	:	1.9	55
3099	Other transport equipment n.e.c.	:	32	:	1.0	30
3100	Furniture	14200	12199	57.5	53.0	1464
321	Jewellery, bijouterie and related articles	4275	3745	9.3	7.9	259
3211	Jewellery and related articles	:	2357	:	6.4	217
3212	Imitation jewellery and related articles	798	1388	1.9	1.5	42
3220	Musical instruments	459	724	4.8	1.7	53
3230	Sports goods	489	369	2.2	4.4	157
3240	Games and toys	7719	3345	44.6	3.0	91
3250	Medical and dental instruments and supplies	:	7449	:	46.0	1545
3290	Other manufacturing n.e.c.	:	2040	:	8.7	264
331	Repair of fabricated metal products/machinery	13624	16310	77.5	113.1	3911
3311	Repair of fabricated metal products	:	1001	:	22.6	743
3312	Repair of machinery	:	9724	:	47.9	1687
3313	Repair of electronic and optical equipment	:	541	:	4.6	177
3314	Repair of electrical equipment	:	1834	:	15.8	552
3315	Repair of transport equip., excl. motor vehicles	:	2492	:	19.3	678
3319	Repair of other equipment	:	718	:	2.9	75
3320	Installation of industrial machinery/equipment	8941	8642	95.0	81.6	2886
C	Total manufacturing	211649	207040	3082.2	3053.7	103140

a/ 1101 includes 1102, 1103 and 1104.
b/ 1910 includes 1920.

France

ISIC	Industry	Note	Output (millions of Euros) 2006	2007	2008	2009	Note	Value added at factor values (millions of Euros) 2006	2007	2008	2009	Note	Gross fixed capital formation (millions of Euros) 2008	2009
1010	Processing/preserving of meat		...	...	...	29921		...	...	...	5570		...	...
1020	Processing/preserving of fish, etc.		...	...	2810	2709		...	...	556	560		...	...
1030	Processing/preserving of fruit,vegetables		...	...	...	7344		...	...	...	1550		...	...
1040	Vegetable and animal oils and fats		...	...	...	2865		...	...	...	323		...	...
1050	Dairy products		...	...	...	22255		...	...	...	3216		...	...
106	Grain mill products,starches and starch products		...	...	6584	6009		...	...	1144	1151		...	...
1061	Grain mill products		...	...	...	3655		...	...	...	621		...	...
1062	Starches and starch products		...	...	...	2354		...	...	...	530		...	...
107	Other food products		...	...	43069	40573		...	...	12477	12987		...	...
1071	Bakery products		...	...	...	16622		...	...	...	7280		...	...
1072	Sugar		...	...	...	3231		...	...	...	657		...	...
1073	Cocoa, chocolate and sugar confectionery		...	...	6662	5165		...	...	1473	1212		...	...
1074	Macaroni, noodles, couscous, etc.		...	...	...	831		...	...	...	245		...	...
1075	Prepared meals and dishes		...	...	...	4141		...	...	...	973		...	...
1079	Other food products n.e.c.		...	...	...	10584		...	...	...	2620		...	...
1080	Prepared animal feeds		...	...	...	9193		...	...	...	1402		...	...
1101	Distilling, rectifying and blending of spirits		...	...	22071a/	20866a/		...	...	5267a/	5007a/		...	...
1102	Wines		...	...	...a/	...a/		...	...	...a/	...a/		...	...
1103	Malt liquors and malt		...	...	...a/	...a/		...	...	...a/	...a/		...	...
1104	Soft drinks,mineral waters,other bottled waters		...	...	...a/	...a/		...	...	...a/	...a/		...	...
1200	Tobacco products		...	...	1405	1408		...	...	576	596		...	...
131	Spinning, weaving and finishing of textiles		...	...	3382	2308		...	...	871	599		...	...
1311	Preparation and spinning of textile fibres		...	...	887	472		...	...	199	116		...	...
1312	Weaving of textiles		...	...	1705	1206		...	...	413	274		...	...
1313	Finishing of textiles		...	...	790	630		...	...	259	209		...	...
139	Other textiles		...	...	5118	4235		...	...	1596	1393		...	...
1391	Knitted and crocheted fabrics		...	...	...	233		...	...	...	45		...	...
1392	Made-up textile articles, except apparel		...	...	...	1538		...	...	...	552		...	...
1393	Carpets and rugs		...	...	...	340		...	...	...	104		...	...
1394	Cordage, rope, twine and netting		...	...	...	117		...	...	...	37		...	...
1399	Other textiles n.e.c.		...	...	...	2007		...	...	...	654		...	...
1410	Wearing apparel, except fur apparel		...	...	...	5076		...	...	...	1870		...	...
1420	Articles of fur		...	...	71	43		...	...	22	19		...	...
1430	Knitted and crocheted apparel		...	...	...	879		...	...	...	362		...	...
151	Leather;luggage,handbags,saddlery,harness;fur		...	...	2111	1881		...	...	1048	1021		...	...
1511	Tanning/dressing of leather; dressing of fur		...	...	345	287		...	...	101	77		...	...
1512	Luggage,handbags,etc.;saddlery/harness		...	...	1766	1594		...	...	947	945		...	...
1520	Footwear		...	...	998	790		...	...	334	342		...	...
1610	Sawmilling and planing of wood		...	...	3625	2893		...	...	1050	859		...	...
162	Wood products, cork, straw, plaiting materials		...	...	8694	6988		...	...	2523	2161		...	...

Code	Description				
1621	Veneer sheets and wood-based panels	1419	⋮	⋮	285
1622	Builders' carpentry and joinery	3055	⋮	⋮	1027
1623	Wooden containers	1770	2393	753	591
1629	Other wood products;articles of cork,straw	744	933	278	259
1701	Pulp, paper and paperboard	6086	⋮	⋮	1123
1702	Corrugated paper and paperboard	5277	6248	1775	1677
1709	Other articles of paper and paperboard	3937	⋮	⋮	1202
181	Printing and service activities related to printing	10226	11915	4279	3682
1811	Printing	8045	⋮	⋮	2680
1812	Service activities related to printing	2181	319	71	1002
1820	Reproduction of recorded media	360	⋮	⋮	118
1910	Coke oven products	46793b/	66683b/	1632b/	2305b/
1920	Refined petroleum products	...b/	...b/	...b/	...b/
201	Basic chemicals,fertilizers, etc.	33531	40177	7375	5828
2011	Basic chemicals	25640	⋮	⋮	4821
2012	Fertilizers and nitrogen compounds	1652	⋮	⋮	232
2013	Plastics and synthetic rubber in primary forms	6240	⋮	8025	775
202	Other chemical products	23660	29825	625	6771
2021	Pesticides and other agrochemical products	2144	2103	1036	513
2022	Paints,varnishes;printing ink and mastics	3065	3564	3866	950
2023	Soap,cleaning and cosmetic preparations	10244	14182	⋮	3004
2029	Other chemical products n.e.c.	8208	317	40	2304
2030	Man-made fibres	269	⋮	⋮	54
2100	Pharmaceuticals,medicinal chemicals, etc.	28374	29571	9459	8728
221	Rubber products	6868	9529	3398	2848
2211	Rubber tyres and tubes	3722	⋮	⋮	1639
2219	Other rubber products	3146	⋮	⋮	1209
2220	Plastics products	23656	⋮	⋮	7499
2310	Glass and glass products	5776	⋮	6338	2135
239	Non-metallic mineral products n.e.c.	18871	20810	251	5960
2391	Refractory products	499	555	⋮	192
2392	Clay building materials	1243	⋮	⋮	565
2393	Other porcelain and ceramic products	656	⋮	⋮	273
2394	Cement, lime and plaster	2745	⋮	⋮	1069
2395	Articles of concrete, cement and plaster	10294	1085	527	2662
2396	Cutting, shaping and finishing of stone	795	⋮	⋮	374
2399	Other non-metallic mineral products n.e.c.	2639	⋮	⋮	825
2410	Basic iron and steel	15269	⋮	⋮	⋮
2420	Basic precious and other non-ferrous metals	⋮	5160	1557	2644
243	Casting of metals	3740	⋮	⋮	1286
2431	Casting of iron and steel	2302	⋮	⋮	796
2432	Casting of non-ferrous metals	1438	⋮	⋮	491
251	Struct.metal products, tanks, reservoirs	13773	12768	4002	4660
2511	Structural metal products	11702	10451	3284	3996
2512	Tanks, reservoirs and containers of metal	1872	2056	648	606

continued

France

ISIC Revision 4			Output (millions of Euros)					Value added at factor values (millions of Euros)					Gross fixed capital formation (millions of Euros)	
ISIC	Industry	Note	2006	2007	2008	2009	Note	2006	2007	2008	2009	Note	2008	2009
2513	Steam generators, excl. hot water boilers		...	...	261	199		...	...	70	58		...	...
2520	Weapons and ammunition		...	...	2108	1968		...	...	774	724		...	...
259	Other metal products;metal working services		...	...	37971	29546		...	...	13739	10937		...	...
2591	Forging,pressing,stamping,roll-forming of metal		...	...	8846	7115		...	...	2417	1975		...	...
2592	Treatment and coating of metals; machining		...	...	...	11350		...	...	...	4792		...	...
2593	Cutlery, hand tools and general hardware		...	...	4282	3253		...	...	1841	1437		...	...
2599	Other fabricated metal products n.e.c.		...	...	...	7829		...	...	...	2733		...	...
2610	Electronic components and boards		...	...	...	8292		...	...	...	2846		...	...
2620	Computers and peripheral equipment		...	...	1465	1187		...	...	298	268		...	...
2630	Communication equipment		...	...	7917	6186		...	...	1840	1188		...	...
2640	Consumer electronics		...	...	1034	205		...	...	458	68		...	...
265	Measuring,testing equipment; watches, etc.		...	...	9957	9805		...	...	4145	4046		...	...
2651	Measuring/testing/navigating equipment,etc.		...	...	9699	9567		...	...	4036	3939		...	...
2652	Watches and clocks		...	...	258	238		...	...	110	108		...	...
2660	Irradiation/electromedical equipment,etc.		...	...	1303	1200		...	...	456	464		...	...
2670	Optical instruments and photographic equipment		...	...	553	205		...	...	281	91		...	...
2680	Magnetic and optical media		...	...	15	21		...	...	6	9		...	...
2710	Electric motors,generators,transformers,etc.		...	...	...	9517		...	...	...	3223		...	...
2720	Batteries and accumulators		...	...	892	626		...	...	265	219		...	...
273	Wiring and wiring devices		...	...	6706	5505		...	...	1892	1840		...	...
2731	Fibre optic cables		...	...	...	578		...	...	...	164		...	...
2732	Other electronic and electric wires and cables		...	...	...	2717		...	...	...	700		...	...
2733	Wiring devices		...	...	...	2210		...	...	...	976		...	...
2740	Electric lighting equipment		...	...	1865	2458		...	...	727	988		...	...
2750	Domestic appliances		...	...	...	3095		...	...	...	1087		...	...
2790	Other electrical equipment		...	...	3938	1873		...	...	1331	722		...	...
281	General-purpose machinery		...	...	31612	25743		...	...	10219	8625		...	...
2811	Engines/turbines,excl.aircraft,vehicle engines		...	...	...	4387		...	...	...	1209		...	...
2812	Fluid power equipment		...	...	1597	1167		...	...	556	404		...	...
2813	Other pumps, compressors, taps and valves		...	...	...	5703		...	...	...	2075		...	...
2814	Bearings, gears, gearing and driving elements		...	...	3263	2382		...	...	1158	918		...	...
2815	Ovens, furnaces and furnace burners		...	...	...	882		...	...	...	231		...	...
2816	Lifting and handling equipment		...	...	5587	3845		...	...	1695	1208		...	...
2817	Office machinery, excl.computers,etc.		...	...	...	137		...	...	...	78		...	...
2818	Power-driven hand tools		...	...	...	99		...	...	...	44		...	...
2819	Other general-purpose machinery		...	...	...	7141		...	...	...	2459		...	...
282	Special-purpose machinery		...	...	15370	10755		...	...	4397	3255		...	...
2821	Agricultural and forestry machinery		...	...	4367	3482		...	...	1045	859		...	...
2822	Metal-forming machinery and machine tools		...	...	...	778		...	...	...	284		...	...
2823	Machinery for metallurgy		...	...	...	484		...	...	...	98		...	...
2824	Mining, quarrying and construction machinery		...	...	...	1760		...	...	...	559		...	...

Code	Description						
2825	Food/beverage/tobacco processing machinery	2059	1586	..	..	776	602
2826	Textile/apparel/leather production machinery	..	476	..	..	..	151
2829	Other special-purpose machinery	..	2189	..	..	..	703
2910	Motor vehicles	49186	36666	..	..	9356	6619
2920	Automobile bodies, trailers and semi-trailers	5467	3516	..	..	1444	1050
2930	Parts and accessories for motor vehicles	..	13922	..	..	..	3245
301	Building of ships and boats	5612	4881	..	..	1122	864
3011	Building of ships and floating structures	..	3910	..	..	..	606
3012	Building of pleasure and sporting boats	..	972	..	..	..	258
3020	Railway locomotives and rolling stock	4257	4405	..	..	1145	1173
3030	Air and spacecraft and related machinery	30713	29539	..	..	8677	7970
3040	Military fighting vehicles	578	844	..	..	185	330
309	Transport equipment n.e.c.	1089	744	..	..	254	193
3091	Motorcycles	488	303	..	..	90	58
3092	Bicycles and invalid carriages	..	305	..	..	..	92
3099	Other transport equipment n.e.c.	..	137	..	..	..	43
3100	Furniture	7933	6908	..	..	2699	2441
321	Jewellery, bijouterie and related articles	1736	1233	..	..	623	471
3211	Jewellery and related articles	..	1067	..	..	..	392
3212	Imitation jewellery and related articles	172	167	..	..	104	80
3220	Musical instruments	796	161	..	..	276	93
3230	Sports goods	368	727	..	..	119	240
3240	Games and toys	..	518	..	..	..	181
3250	Medical and dental instruments and supplies	5598	5893	..	..	2947	3010
3290	Other manufacturing n.e.c.	..	1077	..	..	..	424
331	Repair of fabricated metal products/machinery	11467	14436	..	..	5101	6636
3311	Repair of fabricated metal products	..	2702	..	..	..	1156
3312	Repair of machinery	..	5259	..	..	..	2761
3313	Repair of electronic and optical equipment	..	489	..	..	..	303
3314	Repair of electrical equipment	..	1749	..	..	..	907
3315	Repair of transport equip., excl. motor vehicles	..	3878	..	..	..	1360
3319	Repair of other equipment	..	360	..	..	..	149
3320	Installation of industrial machinery/equipment	14724	12292	..	..	5340	4414
C	Total manufacturing	816704	678510	..	..	203256	180452

a/ 1101 includes 1102, 1103 and 1104.
b/ 1910 includes 1920.

France

| ISIC Revision 4 | | | Index numbers of industrial production (2005=100) | | | | | | | | | | | |
ISIC	Industry	Note	1999	2000	2001	2002	2003	2004	2005	2006	2007	2008	2009	2010
10	Food products		101	100	101	102	100	101	100	101	103	104	102	102
11	Beverages		97	90	92	95	99	99	100	103	103	98	94	102
12	Tobacco products		159	144	143	147	142	105	100	94	97	96	84	83
13	Textiles		152	149	142	131	122	113	100	91	89	79	61	64
14	Wearing apparel		336	267	234	181	143	126	100	88	81	66	44	39
15	Leather and related products		176	162	152	136	119	112	100	92	90	87	80	88
16	Wood/wood products/cork, excl. furniture		93	100	100	97	96	100	100	104	104	97	83	82
17	Paper and paper products		100	102	99	99	99	100	100	98	98	93	83	85
18	Printing and reproduction of recorded media		107	111	110	105	103	102	100	97	95	88	81	79
19	Coke and refined petroleum products		97	101	102	96	101	102	100	97	97	99	85	77
20	Chemicals and chemical products		98	102	100	98	98	99	100	101	109	108	98	107
21	Pharmaceuticals, medicinal chemicals, etc.		65	70	79	84	89	95	100	108	112	111	112	116
22	Rubber and plastics products		89	94	95	95	95	99	100	98	99	91	77	83
23	Other non-metallic mineral products		96	99	98	97	95	99	100	104	106	101	84	86
24	Basic metals		102	108	104	105	102	105	100	102	101	95	68	79
25	Fabricated metal products, except machinery		94	100	100	99	97	101	100	102	105	100	76	80
26	Computer, electronic and optical products		88	101	99	95	98	103	100	103	101	100	91	91
27	Electrical equipment		112	118	119	111	101	98	100	107	112	113	89	96
28	Machinery and equipment n.e.c.		93	96	94	95	94	98	100	105	109	108	89	80
29	Motor vehicles, trailers and semi-trailers		83	89	96	97	96	102	100	105	109	108	74	69
30	Other transport equipment		98	95	99	94	95	94	100	104	89	78	61	114
31	Furniture		118	119	118	109	105	103	100	104	109	115	108	74
32	Other manufacturing		78	83	88	92	96	100	100	98	97	90	76	103
33	Repair and installation of machinery/equipment		99	102	104	102	94	95	100	105	98	104	99	102
C	Total manufacturing		98	101	101	100	98	100	100	100	101	103	99	89

- 413 -

Georgia

Supplier of information:
National Statistics Office of Georgia (GEOSTAT), Tbilisi.

Basic source of data:
Survey.

Major deviations from ISIC (Revision 3):
Data presented in ISIC (Revision 3) were originally classified according to the NACE (Revision 1.1).

Reference period:
Calendar year.

Scope:
All establishments.

Method of data collection:
Questionnaires; direct interview in the field.

Type of enumeration:
Sample survey.

Adjusted for non-response:
Yes.

Concepts and definitions of variables:
Output and value added are valued at basic prices.

Related national publications:
Entrepreneurship in Georgia; Statistical Yearbook, both published by National Statistics Office of Georgia, Tbilisi.

Georgia

ISIC	Industry	Number of establishments (number)					Number of employees (number)					Wages and salaries paid to employees (thousands of Georgian Lari)				
		Note	2007	2008	2009	2010	Note	2007	2008	2009	2010	Note	2007	2008	2009	2010
151	Processed meat,fish,fruit,vegetables,fats		112	99	204	217		3176	2438	3002	3516		9105	12696	12285	15296
1511	Processing/preserving of meat		38	32	60	82		1017	1121	1442	1729		5077	8226	7451	10320
1512	Processing/preserving of fish		6	5	18	13		104	...	134	129		186	...	677	853
1513	Processing/preserving of fruit & vegetables		55	54	100	105		1923	1079	1178	1480		3270	2909	2345	3379
1514	Vegetable and animal oils and fats		13	8	26	17		132	183	248	178		572	1433	1811	744
1520	Dairy products		54	52	85	85		1306	1359	1696	1570		6319	7973	9470	11113
153	Grain mill products; starches; animal feeds		107	100	178	171		2194	1724	2388	2339		7737	8041	11060	15054
1531	Grain mill products		104	97	176	167		2157	1700	2363	2294		7560	7848	10827	14692
1532	Starches and starch products		-	-	-	-		-	-	-	-		-	-	-	-
1533	Prepared animal feeds		3	3	2	4					45					362
154	Other food products		1045	1024	1386	1343		5134	5084	5678	7609		9639	12479	12744	20778
1541	Bakery products		939	943	1255	1210		3937	3747	4111	5900		5630	6907	8289	12749
1542	Sugar		5	4	5	4		513	693	583	461		3044	4485	2471	3390
1543	Cocoa, chocolate and sugar confectionery		6	3	14	17		25	27	63	240		65	81	144	2145
1544	Macaroni, noodles & similar products		21	16	27	30		86	69	245	381		141	163	775	1091
1549	Other food products n.e.c.		74	58	85	82		573	548	676	627		760	843	1065	1404
155	Beverages		392	373	471	432		7549	7420	6302	6848		36668	49263	44894	52715
1551	Distilling, rectifying & blending of spirits		28	28	46	37		1030	794	864	704		3186	3594	3622	3783
1552	Wines		137	128	184	180		3072	2566	2147	3406		9778	12145	10208	16063
1553	Malt liquors and malt		18	15	18	17		1769	1437	1131	966		10821	13442	12966	12586
1554	Soft drinks; mineral waters		209	202	223	198		1678	2623	2160	1772		12884	20082	18099	20283
1600	Tobacco products		13	10	10	10		500	500	529	493		5448	7160	6879	5782
171	Spinning, weaving and finishing of textiles		6	7	15	11		19	25	23	11		58	73	32	23
1711	Textile fibre preparation; textile weaving		6	6	14	11		19	25	23	11		58	73	32	23
1712	Finishing of textiles		-	1	-	-		-	-	-	-		-	-	-	-
172	Other textiles		23	20	44	42		70	110	119	287		225	567	546	1188
1721	Made-up textile articles, except apparel		18	15	34	32		62	100	98	248		208	509	420	1060
1722	Carpets and rugs		-	-	-	-		-	-	-	-		-	-	-	-
1723	Cordage, rope, twine and netting		-	-	-	-		-	-	-	-		-	-	-	-
1729	Other textiles n.e.c.		:	:	:	:		:	:	:	:		:	:	:	:
1730	Knitted and crocheted fabrics and articles		1	1	5	4		1	...	3	3			...	4	4
1810	Wearing apparel, except fur apparel		60	60	200	202		2184	2512	3849	3773		5501	7847	11633	14334
1820	Dressing & dyeing of fur; processing of fur		-	-	-	-		-	-	-	-		-	-	-	-
191	Tanning, dressing and processing of leather		17	15	17	16		62	59	86	128		123	132	218	784
1911	Tanning and dressing of leather		15	13	13	11		53	55	50	112		98	123	108	724
1912	Luggage, handbags, etc.; saddlery & harness		2	2	4	5		-	-	36	16		-	-	110	60
1920	Footwear		56	48	141	122		358	141	280	383		1027	233	441	875
2010	Sawmilling and planing of wood		294	234	342	231		1068	1180	1088	819		2266	5396	3789	3097
202	Products of wood, cork, straw, etc.		123	109	308	277		588	405	557	647		1200	1245	1736	3131
2021	Veneer sheets, plywood, particle board, etc.		4	3	7	8		103	...	18	36		212	...	50	93
2022	Builders' carpentry and joinery		94	87	242	224		422	336	413	508		881	1122	1444	2654
2023	Wooden containers		12	8	17	9		37	52	5	3		63	75	241	...
2029	Other wood products; articles of cork/straw		13	11	42	36		26	52	121	100		44	...	...	383
210	Paper and paper products		43	43	56	63		375	576	599	575		1002	2763	3009	3695
2101	Pulp, paper and paperboard		2	2	3	7										
2102	Corrugated paper and paperboard		12	12	14	11		221	320	299	286		752	2227	1888	2149
2109	Other articles of paper and paperboard		29	29	39	45		154	256	300	289		250	536	1122	1546
221	Publishing		177	176	311	310		1595	1665	2442	2629		5353	7548	9919	12206
2211	Publishing of books and other publications		45	48	109	110		281	383	664	615		898	1458	2477	3532
2212	Publishing of newspapers, journals, etc.		127	121	185	194		1218	1208	1703	1962		4117	5688	7058	8313
2213	Publishing of recorded media		1	1	1	-										
2219	Other publishing		4	6	16	6		96	74	62	52		338	402	348	361

Code	Description	A1	A2	A3	A4	B1	B2	B3	B4	C1	C2	C3	C4
222	Printing and related service activities	4063	6149	8162	9086	1297	1364	1523	1398	207	200	267	268
2221	Printing	4022	6035	8044	9026	1266	1324	1494	1382	199	192	247	243
2222	Service activities related to printing	41	114	119	60	31	40	29	16	8	8	20	25
2230	Reproduction of recorded media									1	1	4	4
2310	Coke oven products	-	-	-	-	-	-	-	-	-	-	-	-
2320	Refined petroleum products			212				41		4	8	8	7
2330	Processing of nuclear fuel												
241	Basic chemicals	19070	28526	21356	30117	3015	3082	3017	3198	25	24	31	30
2411	Basic chemicals, except fertilizers	:	:	:	:	:	:	:	:	:	:	:	:
2412	Fertilizers and nitrogen compounds	:	:	:	:	:	:	:	:	:	:	:	:
2413	Plastics in primary forms; synthetic rubber	6008	12095	18947	19006	1378	1882	2771	2654	78	80	105	106
242	Other chemicals												
2421	Pesticides and other agro-chemical products	115	1891	1974	1336	77	159	146	97	7	8	9	2
2422	Paints, varnishes, printing ink and mastics	5361	9566	14862	16041	1189	1638	2362	2401	59	59	70	68
2423	Pharmaceuticals, medicinal chemicals, etc.	240	257	489	1210	69	61	123	134	8	8	18	21
2424	Soap, cleaning & cosmetic preparations	292		1623	419	42		140	22	4	5	7	7
2429	Other chemical products n.e.c.												
2430	Man-made fibres	68		99	109	31		34	38	4	4	5	5
251	Rubber products												
2511	Rubber tyres and tubes	16428	13392	9925	9425	3098	1774	1933	1955	166	161	406	389
2519	Other rubber products	1766	2371	1838	2660	303	268	401	485	10	12	28	25
2520	Plastic products	25836	29646	28702	31817	5220	4707	5552	5649	387	387	654	621
2610	Glass and glass products	136		82	103	48		27	31	12	11	13	14
269	Non-metallic mineral products n.e.c.												
2691	Pottery, china and earthenware	786	1180	1065	670	365	448	475	276	13	13	28	20
2692	Refractory ceramic products	15928	15348	16008	13744	2451	1890	2138	1747	46	43	61	61
2693	Struct.non-refractory clay; ceramic products	8012	11823	10184	15392	1834	1839	2253	2902	176	182	315	314
2694	Cement, lime and plaster	811	1146	1330	1875	476	472	646	681	135	134	234	208
2695	Articles of concrete, cement and plaster									5	4	3	4
2696	Cutting, shaping & finishing of stone												
2699	Other non-metallic mineral products n.e.c.	26590	47310	50035	66579	7282	8520	8817	9355	11	14	12	12
2710	Basic iron and steel	2209	3246	2477	12569	628	625	538	550	2	2	3	5
2720	Basic precious and non-ferrous metals				2620				529	10	9	10	7
273	Casting of metals							529	529				
2731	Casting of iron and steel	4695	14852	9275	12107	723	1415	1579	1560	62	62	113	121
2732	Casting of non-ferrous metals	4602	14729	9268	12107	705	1398	1571	1560	61	61	112	121
281	Struct.metal products;tanks;steam generators												
2811	Structural metal products									1	1	1	1
2812	Tanks, reservoirs and containers of metal												
2813	Steam generators	5028	5043	5032	6510	1369	935	1014	1362	100	101	213	188
289	Other metal products; metal working services				2		6	6	1	1	6	6	
2891	Metal forging/pressing/stamping/roll-forming	513	758	283	439	167	147	116	273	20	18	43	40
2892	Treatment & coating of metals	76	61	85	77	30	28	19	21	5	5	8	6
2893	Cutlery, hand tools and general hardware	4438	4224	4648	5993	1172	760	873	1067	74	77	156	136
2899	Other fabricated metal products n.e.c.	5838	6271	4655	5670	620	598	528	686	33	39	61	70
291	General purpose machinery												
2911	Engines & turbines (not for transport equipment)												
2912	Pumps, compressors, taps and valves												
2913	Bearings, gears, gearing & driving elements												
2914	Ovens, furnaces and furnace burners												
2915	Lifting and handling equipment												
2919	Other general purpose machinery	886	1354	775	915	223	281	320	212	23	23	23	
292	Special purpose machinery	36	46	136	72	42	50	146	56	8	7	5	5
2921	Agricultural and forestry machinery	739		77	193	125		15	20	3	4	5	5
2922	Machine tools												
2923	Machinery for metallurgy												
2924	Machinery for mining & construction												
2925	Food/beverage/tobacco processing machinery												
2926	Machinery for textile, apparel and leather												
2927	Weapons and ammunition					1				1	1	1	1
2929	Other special purpose machinery	:	:	:	:	:	:	:	:	:	:	:	:

continued

Georgia

ISIC Revision 3

ISIC	Industry	Number of establishments (number)					Number of employees (number)					Wages and salaries paid to employees (thousands of Georgian Lari)				
		Note	2007	2008	2009	2010	Note	2007	2008	2009	2010	Note	2007	2008	2009	2010
2930	Domestic appliances n.e.c.		10	7	17	18		13	196	87	89		20	1142	751	743
3000	Office, accounting and computing machinery		-	-	-	-		-	-	-	-		-	-	-	-
3110	Electric motors, generators and transformers		15	14	19	22		853	287	257	784		3019	3201	3352	8348
3120	Electricity distribution & control apparatus		3	2	3	4		...	...	...	5		...	...	...	21
3130	Insulated wire and cable		1	1	2	1		...	...	...	...		...	...	...	...
3140	Accumulators, primary cells and batteries		3	2	2	2		7	...	...	...		...	...	...	...
3150	Lighting equipment and electric lamps		3	2	3	3		...	...	...	...		...	...	...	...
3190	Other electrical equipment n.e.c.		6	5	12	10		...	...	16	14		...	...	65	77
3210	Electronic valves, tubes, etc.		1	1	1	1		...	...	...	...		...	...	...	...
3220	TV/radio transmitters; line comm. apparatus		2	2	3	2		...	...	...	...		...	...	...	...
3230	TV and radio receivers and associated goods		1	1	...	...		...	...	...	...		...	...	...	...
331	Medical, measuring, testing appliances, etc.		15	14	16	19		251	220	196	205		650	664	662	882
3311	Medical, surgical and orthopaedic equipment		8	8	12	15		112	138	181	197		204	393	592	840
3312	Measuring/testing/navigating appliances,etc.		6	5	3	3		130	...	...	...		371	...	...	...
3313	Industrial process control equipment		1	1	1	...		...	...	...	...		...	...	...	...
3320	Optical instruments & photographic equipment		-	-	1	1		...	...	...	...		...	...	...	...
3330	Watches and clocks		-	-	-	-		-	-	-	-		-	-	-	-
3410	Motor vehicles		-	-	-	-		-	-	-	-		-	-	-	-
3420	Automobile bodies, trailers & semi-trailers		-	-	1	2		-	-	-	-		-	-	-	-
3430	Parts/accessories for automobiles		3	3	4	7		63	53	24	...		114	113	73	...
351	Building and repairing of ships and boats		6	7	6	7		328	288	136	111		1146	1859	975	625
3511	Building and repairing of ships		...	...	...	...		...	...	...	111		...	...	...	...
3512	Building/repairing of pleasure/sport. boats		...	...	...	...		...	...	...	...		...	...	...	...
3520	Railway/tramway locomotives & rolling stock		10	8	13	12		2512	2441	2829	2269		13954	18719	20281	16319
3530	Aircraft and spacecraft		2	2	3	5		...	...	...	...		...	...	...	...
359	Transport equipment n.e.c.		-	-	-	-		-	-	-	-		-	-	-	-
3591	Motorcycles		-	-	-	-		-	-	-	-		-	-	-	-
3592	Bicycles and invalid carriages		-	-	-	-		-	-	-	-		-	-	-	-
3599	Other transport equipment n.e.c.		-	-	-	-		-	-	-	-		-	-	-	-
3610	Furniture		181	195	441	406		903	779	905	1261		2424	2596	2227	6630
369	Manufacturing n.e.c.		19	19	64	55		277	217	187	167		...	1784	1055	906
3691	Jewellery and related articles		6	7	37	29		253	192	156	141		...	1739	987	832
3692	Musical instruments		-	-	-	...		-	-	-	...		...	...	...	...
3693	Sports goods		-	-	-	...		-	-	-	...		-	...	...	...
3694	Games and toys		1	1	6	5		...	...	2	...		...	...	2	...
3699	Other manufacturing n.e.c.		12	11	21	21		22	25	29	26		35	45	67	74
3710	Recycling of metal waste and scrap		4	3	2	2		...	...	...	...		...	...	...	...
3720	Recycling of non-metal waste and scrap		3	1	3	4		...	...	...	...		...	...	...	...
D	Total manufacturing		3934	3783	6330	5995		58305	56964	62994	67369		250042	348739	338382	412481

Georgia

ISIC	Industry	Note	Output (thousands of Georgian Lari)				Note	Value added (thousands of Georgian Lari)				Note	Gross fixed capital formation (thousands of Georgian Lari)	
			2007	2008	2009	2010		2007	2008	2009	2010		2009	2010
151	Processed meat,fish,fruit vegetables,fats		157613	120187	182687	216374		15710	28397	33373	42203		74382	80851
1511	Processing/preserving of meat		53814	66193	54739	85276		4897	15023	20574	27094		30252	28264
1512	Processing/preserving of fish		3202		7798	13104		503		2640	4453		1408	2837
1513	Processing/preserving of fruit & vegetables		88202	41741	64974	102652		9528	10481	5776	8598		22775	30524
1514	Vegetable and animal oils and fats		12396	11265	55177	15342		783	2654	4383	2058		19948	19226
1520	Dairy products		49053	64094	69364	89836		14873	19799	22482	21800		27808	21111
153	Grain mill products; starches; animal feeds		260537	176996	232897	323173		39110	17979	35113	62445		52724	55837
1531	Grain mill products		255314	174433	229859	321072		39060	17348	34530	61939		50608	54071
1532	Starches and starch products					2101					506			1766
1533	Prepared animal feeds													
154	Other food products		174968	135975	218047	300309		11603	13208	65569	56123		29630	49340
1541	Bakery products		67146	70955	78885	128748		8136	3684	17537	24752		355	19638
1542	Sugar		98837	57137	120933	120018		158	141	44203	26279		748	438
1543	Cocoa, chocolate and sugar confectionery		404	361	745	25071		158	325	121	127		1865	1913
1544	Macaroni, noodles & similar products		1184	1653	8317	10411		1255	1243	1827	1965		5782	5642
1549	Other food products n.e.c.		7397	5870	9167	16061		1896	7815	1881	3000		20882	21709
155	Beverages		391027	404509	404530	533034		114288	138549	128247	182154		260615	334079
1551	Distilling, rectifying & blending of spirits		35373	36574	65408	59294		7392	9430	21945	29472		25971	25130
1552	Wines		68333	87944	70802	107695		25548	43997	25648	43208		77959	101487
1553	Malt liquors and malt		96460	102915	103679	133557		25138	22137	20861	25653		63035	116563
1554	Soft drinks; mineral waters		190862	177077	164641	232489		56210	62984	59793	83820		93650	90899
1600	Tobacco products		83619	89537	94632	95081		26153	17778	22123	19930		13982	14467
171	Spinning, weaving and finishing of textiles		335	232	276	216		84	36	121	90		602	585
1711	Textile fibre preparation; textile weaving		335	226	276	216		84	34	121	90		602	585
1712	Finishing of textiles													
172	Other textiles		1803	2534	4849	6431		591	1032	1610	2478		962	1091
1721	Made-up textile articles, except apparel		1725	2374	3896	5791		539	923	1288	2165		608	763
1722	Carpets and rugs													
1723	Cordage, rope, twine and netting													
1729	Other textiles n.e.c.				72	53				8	10		6	7
1730	Knitted and crocheted fabrics and articles		18456	22592	38573	54445		8375	11903	19108	26894		23028	22772
1810	Wearing apparel, except fur apparel													
1820	Dressing & dyeing of fur; processing of fur													
191	Tanning, dressing and processing of leather		1013	712	955	4751		360	186	354	1737		501	2559
1911	Tanning and dressing of leather		836	641	430	4434		262	163	127	1587		407	2505
1912	Luggage, handbags, etc.; saddlery & harness				525	317				227	150		94	54
1920	Footwear		6033	1023	2725	4945		2105	375	912	1643		2309	2085
2010	Sawmilling and planing of wood		18565	17220	32093	13352		7089	5737	9398	5311		58190	11873
202	Products of wood, cork, straw, etc.		8999	9230	17030	13269		3838	3293	8158	5142		6094	10077
2021	Veneer sheets, plywood, particle board, etc.		1427		134	329		964		84	200		641	983
2022	Builders' carpentry and joinery		6398	8581	15764	10827		2539	2990	7518	4492		4469	8192
2023	Wooden containers		1030	544	133	125		296	244	29	13		12	3
2029	Other wood products; articles of cork/straw		143		1000	1988		39		528	438		972	899
210	Paper and paper products		12759	23559	21636	27632		3311	8431	6734	8925		6770	7410
2101	Pulp, paper and paperboard		7645	16844	11089	14076		1522	6947	3933	4832		3583	3612
2102	Corrugated paper and paperboard		5114	6715	10547	13556		1790	1484	2801	4093		3187	3798
2109	Other articles of paper and paperboard													
221	Publishing		43114	40048	47963	65454		18723	18869	22652	26444		10088	8485
2211	Publishing of books and other publications		12990	12705	20284	28864		5303	5704	9528	10414		5742	4053
2212	Publishing of newspapers, journals, etc.		26286	23636	24699	33935		11504	11049	11781	14642		2595	3009
2213	Publishing of recorded media													
2219	Other publishing		3838	3707	2858	2655		1917	2117	1340	1388		1739	1423

continued

Georgia

	ISIC Revision 3	Output (thousands of Georgian Lari)				Value added (thousands of Georgian Lari)				Gross fixed capital formation (thousands of Georgian Lari)	
ISIC	Industry	2007	2008	2009	2010	2007	2008	2009	2010	2009	2010
222	Printing and related service activities	38149	46117	59552	61512	14682	17129	23354	23441	19654	18614
2221	Printing	37409	45242	57737	61002	14411	1199	22653	23259	19459	18478
2222	Service activities related to printing	740	875	1815	510	270	561	701	182	195	137
2230	Reproduction of recorded media	...	...	...	...	...	...	...	...		
2310	Coke oven products	...	...	...	...	...	...	...	...		
2320	Refined petroleum products									1762	
2330	Processing of nuclear fuel	...	...	2639	...	-	-	1864	-		
241	Basic chemicals	162136	171005	150473	218619	35909	38400	11484	67371	44361	54396
2411	Basic chemicals, except fertilizers										
2412	Fertilizers and nitrogen compounds										
2413	Plastics in primary forms; synthetic rubber										
242	Other chemicals	43387	63688	93347	113552	20267	28426	45124	53518	42259	55186
2421	Pesticides and other agro-chemical products	401	8793	8746	6777	81	4002	2730	2048	5219	4118
2422	Paints, varnishes, printing ink and mastics	37937	49575	71382	90248	18491	22458	34825	41975	28967	29814
2423	Pharmaceuticals, medicinal chemicals, etc.	1267	1281	3020	12228	392	357	827	7129	1027	19927
2424	Soap, cleaning & cosmetic preparations	3770	...	10199	4299	1299	...	827	2366	7046	1328
2429	Other chemical products n.e.c.										
2430	Man-made fibres										
251	Rubber products	1572	...	1668	2250	133	...	476	634	336	370
2511	Rubber tyres and tubes										
2519	Other rubber products										
2520	Plastic products	85925	87536	82027	83454	27909	30332	18188	19314	39331	34720
2610	Glass and glass products	23786	22031	21186	18456	2107	4126	4805	6501	16979	21900
269	Non-metallic mineral products n.e.c.	341710	384250	258810	316926	118214	141686	42502	69063	257436	276549
2691	Pottery, china and earthenware	477	154	196	461	231	674	88	163	7	34
2692	Refractory ceramic products										
2693	Struct.non-refractory clay; ceramic products	4307	4100	3191	2359	1450	1887	1869	1039	4433	3532
2694	Cement, lime and plaster	248682	270995	164149	165520	88623	109201	13699	24696	205742	203348
2695	Articles of concrete, cement and plaster	83213	103559	82552	138811	25660	28163	23803	38407	42302	62813
2696	Cutting, shaping & finishing of stone	4410	5146	8507	9629	1793	2320	2940	4700	4273	6667
2699	Other non-metallic mineral products n.e.c.										
2710	Basic iron and steel	238805	460372	243522	590591	35135	170886	80255	200356	195958	276491
2720	Basic precious and non-ferrous metals	12503	14552	7769	215549	5095	5632	3647	98986	7364	28860
273	Casting of metals				6344				1916		6340
2731	Casting of iron and steel										
2732	Casting of non-ferrous metals										
281	Struct.metal products;tanks;steam generators	22629	36846	45483	49636	8538	12453	15966	18749	23362	21541
2811	Structural metal products	22557	35651	45455	49636	8514	11894	15953	18749	23362	21541
2813	Tanks, reservoirs and containers of metal / Steam generators										
289	Other metal products; metal working services	38877	33530	22388	36528	16547	12136	9323	14498	5346	9332
2891	Metal forging/pressing/stamping/roll-forming			160	48		54	54	8	15	20
2892	Treatment & coating of metals	2232	6484	1365	3917	1034	4326	529	1577	1215	709
2893	Cutlery, hand tools and general hardware	279	229	251	227	110	72	105	76	14	10
2899	Other fabricated metal products n.e.c.	36366	26817	20612	32336	15404	7738	8636	12838	4103	8592
291	General purpose machinery	21093	23959	22945	16598	13993	12563	9450	10125	5701	1555
2911	Engines & turbines (not for transport equipment)	...	...	...	...	...	...	...	...		
2912	Pumps, compressors, taps and valves	...	...	...	...	...	...	...	...		
2913	Bearings, gears, gearing & driving elements	-	-	-	-	-	-	-	-		
2914	Ovens, furnaces and furnace burners	-	-	-	-	-	-	-	-		
2915	Lifting and handling equipment	-	-	-	-	-	-	-	-		
2919	Other general purpose machinery	...	...	...	...	...	...	...	...		

292	Special purpose machinery	3194	6616	2936	3628	1384	1986	1688	2534	3249	2606
2921	Agricultural and forestry machinery	219	167	429	451	85	65	203	218	968	1082
2922	Machine tools	2454	...	193	370	1069	...	83	291	82	114
2923	Machinery for metallurgy	-	-	-	-	-	-	-	-	-	-
2924	Machinery for mining & construction	...	...	...	...	...	...	...	...	...	...
2925	Food/beverage/tobacco processing machinery	...	...	...	...	...	...	...	...	...	...
2926	Machinery for textile, apparel and leather	-	-	-	-	-	-	-	-	-	-
2927	Weapons and ammunition	...	...	...	...	...	...	...	...	...	...
2929	Other special purpose machinery	...	...	...	...	...	...	...	...	...	...
2930	Domestic appliances n.e.c.	683	4295	1758	2191	39	2269	705	997	18	40
3000	Office, accounting and computing machinery	-	-	-	-	-	-	-	-	-	-
3110	Electric motors, generators and transformers	10990	9248	7107	13544	3456	4307	4119	9968	3019	1262
3120	Electricity distribution & control apparatus	...	...	...	82	...	...	...	37	...	2
3130	Insulated wire and cable	...	...	...	...	...	...	...	...	...	...
3140	Accumulators, primary cells and batteries	...	...	...	...	...	...	...	...	...	...
3150	Lighting equipment and electric lamps	...	...	...	...	...	...	...	...	...	...
3190	Other electrical equipment n.e.c.	...	...	328	396	...	94	144	179	61	60
3210	Electronic valves, tubes, etc.	...	...	...	...	...	...	...	...	...	...
3220	TV/radio transmitters; line comm. apparatus	...	...	...	...	...	...	...	...	-	...
3230	TV and radio receivers and associated goods	...	...	...	...	...	...	...	...	-	...
331	Medical, measuring, testing appliances, etc.	2812	4775	2817	3973	1477	2994	1201	1603	1806	1758
3311	Medical, surgical and orthopaedic equipment	1301	2650	2513	3915	507	999	1008	1557	1774	1754
3312	Measuring/testing/navigating appliances,etc.	886	...	...	...	445	...	...	...	...	...
3313	Industrial process control equipment	...	...	...	...	...	...	...	...	...	...
3320	Optical instruments & photographic equipment	-	-	...	...	-	-	...	...	...	-
3330	Watches and clocks	-	-	-	-	-	-	-	-	-	...
3410	Motor vehicles	-	-	...	...	-	-	...	...	...	...
3420	Automobile bodies, trailers & semi-trailers	-	-	-	...	-	-	-	-	-	-
3430	Parts/accessories for automobiles	1146	925	634	-	212	215	241	...	172	...
351	Building and repairing of ships and boats	10305	7359	1284	2262	3362	2146	931	1095	5957	5377
3511	Building and repairing of ships	...	...	...	...	...	...	...	...	...	...
3512	Building/repairing of pleasure/sport. boats	...	...	...	...	...	...	...	...	...	...
3520	Railway/tramway locomotives & rolling stock	69394	102836	181257	120531	24846	53946	116643	49650	65047	81936
3530	Aircraft and spacecraft	...	...	...	...	...	...	...	...	...	...
359	Transport equipment n.e.c.	-	-	-	-	-	-	-	-	-	-
3591	Motorcycles	-	-	-	-	-	-	-	-	-	-
3592	Bicycles and invalid carriages	-	-	-	-	-	-	-	-	-	-
3599	Other transport equipment n.e.c.	-	-	-	-	-	-	-	-	-	-
3610	Furniture	18839	21110	17656	50261	6796	6149	5050	16059	4217	18962
369	Manufacturing n.e.c.	5081	4212	5843	4509	1329	2523	2896	1750	2392	438
3691	Jewellery and related articles	4549	3382	4858	3910	1230	2421	2741	1577	2339	410
3692	Musical instruments	-	-	-	-	-	-	-	...	-	-
3693	Sports goods	-	-	-	-	-	-	-	...	-	-
3694	Games and toys	...	...	44	...	...	...	25	...	...	...
3699	Other manufacturing n.e.c.	524	823	941	571	96	101	130	151	54	25
3710	Recycling of metal waste and scrap	...	...	...	...	...	...	...	...	...	...
3720	Recycling of non-metal waste and scrap	...	...	...	...	...	...	...	...	...	...
D	Total manufacturing	2532889	2804466	2822157	3723776	688336	972069	891867	1155462	1421309	1580427

Georgia

Index numbers of industrial production

(2005=100)

ISIC Revision 3

ISIC	Industry	Note	1999	2000	2001	2002	2003	2004	2005	2006	2007	2008	2009	2010
15	Food and beverages		...	...	...	...	...	...	...	...	...	...	...	...
16	Tobacco products		...	...	...	...	...	...	...	...	...	...	...	...
17	Textiles		...	...	...	...	...	...	...	...	...	...	...	...
18	Wearing apparel, fur		...	...	...	...	...	...	...	...	...	...	...	...
19	Leather, leather products and footwear		...	...	...	...	...	...	...	...	...	...	...	...
20	Wood products (excl. furniture)		...	...	...	...	...	...	...	...	...	...	...	...
21	Paper and paper products		...	...	...	...	...	...	...	...	...	...	...	...
22	Printing and publishing		...	...	...	...	...	...	...	...	...	...	...	...
23	Coke,refined petroleum products,nuclear fuel		...	...	...	...	...	...	...	...	...	...	...	...
24	Chemicals and chemical products		...	...	...	...	...	...	...	...	...	...	...	...
25	Rubber and plastics products		...	...	...	...	...	...	...	...	...	...	...	...
26	Non-metallic mineral products		...	...	...	...	...	...	...	...	...	...	...	...
27	Basic metals		...	...	...	...	...	...	...	...	...	...	...	...
28	Fabricated metal products		...	...	...	...	...	...	...	...	...	...	...	...
29	Machinery and equipment n.e.c.		...	...	...	...	...	...	...	...	...	...	...	...
30	Office, accounting and computing machinery		...	...	...	...	...	...	...	...	...	...	...	...
31	Electrical machinery and apparatus		...	...	...	...	...	...	...	...	...	...	...	...
32	Radio,television and communication equipment		...	...	...	...	...	...	...	...	...	...	...	...
33	Medical, precision and optical instruments		...	...	...	...	...	...	...	...	...	...	...	...
34	Motor vehicles, trailers, semi-trailers		...	...	...	...	...	...	...	...	...	...	...	...
35	Other transport equipment		...	...	...	...	...	...	...	...	...	...	...	...
36	Furniture; manufacturing n.e.c.		...	...	...	...	...	...	...	...	...	...	...	...
37	Recycling		...	...	...	...	...	...	...	...	...	...	...	...
D	Total manufacturing		...	40	39	53	65	71	100	136	146	136	119	141

Germany

Supplier of information:
Federal Statistical Office, Wiesbaden. Industrial statistics for the OECD countries are compiled by the OECD secretariat, which supplies them to UNIDO.

Basic source of data:
Annual survey.

Major deviations from ISIC (Revision 4):
Data have been converted from the national classification of economic activities, a NACE equivalent classification system, to ISIC (Revision 4) by the OECD.

Reference period:
Calendar year.

Scope:
Not reported.

Method of data collection:
Not reported.

Type of enumeration:
Not reported.

Adjusted for non-response:
Not reported.

Concepts and definitions of variables:
No deviations from the standard UN concepts and definitions are reported.

Related national publications:
None reported.

Germany

ISIC	Industry	Number of enterprises (number)					Number of employees (thousands)					Wages and salaries paid to employees (millions of Euros)				
		Note	2006	2007	2008	2009	Note	2006	2007	2008	2009	Note	2006	2007	2008	2009
1010	Processing/preserving of meat		...	...	11044	7521		...	...	180.1	157.7		...	...	3465	3096
1020	Processing/preserving of fish, etc.		...	...	233	233		...	...	9.3	8.2		...	...	240	219
1030	Processing/preserving of fruit,vegetables		...	...	646	754		...	...	29.3	29.9		...	...	844	878
1040	Vegetable and animal oils and fats		...	...	149	149		...	...	4.2	6.7		...	...	185	277
1050	Dairy products		...	...	401	420		...	...	38.1	35.8		...	...	1396	1311
106	Grain mill products,starches and starch products		...	...	579	411		...	...	13.6	13.1		...	...	488	487
1061	Grain mill products		...	...	563	392		...	...	11.0	10.4		...	...	366	363
1062	Starches and starch products		...	...	17	19		...	...	2.6	2.7		...	...	122	124
107	Other food products		...	...	15785	10469		...	...	442.7	416.4		...	...	8712	8380
1071	Bakery products		...	...	14464	9055		...	...	345.1	321.4		...	...	5375	5163
1072	Sugar		...	...	12	9		...	...	5.3	4.9		...	...	263	249
1073	Cocoa, chocolate and sugar confectionery		...	...	289	277		...	...	34.2	33.2		...	...	964	963
1074	Macaroni, noodles, couscous, etc.		...	...	104	168		...	...	2.7	2.7		...	...	69	73
1075	Prepared meals and dishes		...	...	194	182		...	...	6.6	9.2		...	...	176	248
1079	Other food products n.e.c.		...	...	721	778		...	...	48.9	45.0		...	...	1866	1683
1080	Prepared animal feeds		...	...	421	562		...	...	14.2	14.7		...	...	534	562
1101	Distilling, rectifying and blending of spirits		...	...	2296a/	2403a/		...	...	73.0a/	72.5a/		...	...	2641a/	2709a/
1102	Wines		...	...	...a/	...a/		...	...	...a/	...a/		...	...	...a/	...a/
1103	Malt liquors and malt		...	...	...a/	...a/		...	...	...a/	...a/		...	...	...a/	...a/
1104	Soft drinks,mineral waters,other bottled waters		...	...	...a/	...a/		...	...	...a/	...a/		...	...	...a/	...a/
1200	Tobacco products		...	...	31	22		...	...	10.5	10.2		...	...	576	573
131	Spinning, weaving and finishing of textiles		...	...	1427	1487		...	...	34.7	28.4		...	...	954	743
1311	Preparation and spinning of textile fibres		...	...	115	113		...	...	6.4	5.3		...	...	177	139
1312	Weaving of textiles		...	...	230	268		...	...	15.4	12.6		...	...	459	360
1313	Finishing of textiles		...	...	1082	1106		...	...	12.8	10.5		...	...	317	244
139	Other textiles		...	...	2297	2372		...	...	50.4	48.3		...	...	1454	1349
1391	Knitted and crocheted fabrics		...	...	131	142		...	...	3.7	3.5		...	...	103	97
1392	Made-up textile articles, except apparel		...	...	1091	1067		...	...	17.4	18.3		...	...	406	405
1393	Carpets and rugs		...	...	110	87		...	...	4.3	3.8		...	...	129	113
1394	Cordage, rope, twine and netting		...	...	...	...		...	...	...	...		...	...	...	...
1399	Other textiles n.e.c.		...	...	...	...		...	...	...	...		...	...	...	...
1410	Wearing apparel, except fur apparel		...	...	2184	2627		...	...	41.8	37.5		...	...	1186	1073
1420	Articles of fur		...	...	...	...		...	...	...	...		...	...	...	...
1430	Knitted and crocheted apparel		...	...	...	...		...	...	...	...		...	...	...	...
151	Leather;luggage,handbags,saddlery,harness;fur		...	...	671	661		...	...	7.9	6.7		...	...	190	167
1511	Tanning/dressing of leather; dressing of fur		...	...	101	92		...	...	2.5	2.1		...	...	74	61
1512	Luggage,handbags,etc.;saddlery/harness		...	...	570	569		...	...	5.4	4.6		...	...	116	105
1520	Footwear		...	...	328	355		...	...	9.9	9.5		...	...	264	243
1610	Sawmilling and planing of wood		...	...	2262	2674		...	...	23.0	24.3		...	...	618	608
162	Wood products, cork, straw, plaiting materials		...	...	9447	8969		...	...	100.1	89.7		...	...	2655	2464

1621	Veneer sheets and wood-based panels	524	551	14.6	16.0	203	207
1622	Builders' carpentry and joinery	1402	1514	51.4	59.9	6003	6467
1623	Wooden containers	279	307	11.4	11.9	803	785
1629	Other wood products;articles of cork,straw	260	284	12.3	12.3	1960	1989
1701	Pulp, paper and paperboard	1678	1754	38.9	41.3	331	335
1702	Corrugated paper and paperboard	1848	1902	53.7	55.5	756	744
1709	Other articles of paper and paperboard	1673	1684	45.4	45.6	675	699
181	Printing and service activities related to printing	4774	5012	154.1	160.6	12206	11982
1811	Printing	3808	3943	119.9	123.1	8601	8143
1812	Service activities related to printing	966	1069	34.1	37.5	3605	3840
1820	Reproduction of recorded media	200	207	6.0	6.4	369	375
1910	Coke oven products	1221b/	1240b/	19.0b/	19.6b/	79b/	86b/
1920	Refined petroleum products	...b/	...b/	...b/	...b/	...b/	...b/
201	Basic chemicals,fertilizers, etc.	9758	9349	176.2	170.8	1071	886
2011	Basic chemicals	4756	4272	86.3	77.1	553	448
2012	Fertilizers and nitrogen compounds	467	497	11.2	11.2	87	66
2013	Plastics and synthetic rubber in primary forms	4536	4581	78.6	82.5	431	373
202	Other chemical products	6005	5889	139.5	140.4	1996	1928
2021	Pesticides and other agrochemical products	135	123	3.2	3.0	69	48
2022	Paints,varnishes;printing ink and mastics	1751	1772	41.3	41.9	446	477
2023	Soap,cleaning and cosmetic preparations	1950	1814	46.9	46.0	703	770
2029	Other chemical products n.e.c.	2169	2181	48.2	49.4	778	633
2030	Man-made fibres	360	517	9.6	12.9	59	50
2100	Pharmaceuticals,medicinal chemicals, etc.	6184	6658	115.1	125.7	733	549
221	Rubber products	2835	3018	75.5	80.1	867	796
2211	Rubber tyres and tubes	1083	1090	24.5	26.3	254	232
2219	Other rubber products	1752	1928	51.0	53.8	613	564
2220	Plastics products	9608	9957	300.1	311.2	6383	6362
2310	Glass and glass products	1937	2030	57.4	60.6	1250	1210
239	Non-metallic mineral products n.e.c.	5423	5809	158.5	171.6	7382	8531
2391	Refractory products	273	297	7.1	7.6	94	85
2392	Clay building materials	450	492	13.2	14.1	243	291
2393	Other porcelain and ceramic products	612	696	20.9	22.8	883	716
2394	Cement, lime and plaster	553	542	12.2	12.3	81	72
2395	Articles of concrete, cement and plaster	2390	2380	68.2	68.3	2238	2065
2396	Cutting, shaping and finishing of stone	374	575	17.5	25.5	3355	4859
2399	Other non-metallic mineral products n.e.c.	770	828	19.4	21.0	488	444
2410	Basic iron and steel	5252	5803	127.5	130.4	1250	1202
2420	Basic precious and other non-ferrous metals	2527	2945	58.6	63.6	737	792
243	Casting of metals	2482	2959	71.6	79.7	790	809
2431	Casting of iron and steel	1442	1742	41.3	44.8	353	361
2432	Casting of non-ferrous metals	1041	1218	30.2	34.8	437	447
251	Struct.metal products, tanks, reservoirs	5392	5789	172.7	196.6	9060	10593
2511	Structural metal products	4374	4724	146.1	167.6	8592	10089
2512	Tanks, reservoirs and containers of metal	848	943	22.7	26.2	388	448

continued

Germany

ISIC Revision 4

ISIC	Industry	Number of enterprises (number)					Number of employees (thousands)					Wages and salaries paid to employees (millions of Euros)				
		Note	2006	2007	2008	2009	Note	2006	2007	2008	2009	Note	2006	2007	2008	2009
2513	Steam generators, excl. hot water boilers		...	...	56	80		...	...	2.8	3.9		...	...	121	171
2520	Weapons and ammunition		...	...	146	142		...	...	9.4	11.7		...	...	456	564
259	Other metal products;metal working services		...	...	28250	28181		...	...	606.5	559.2		...	...	19889	16867
2591	Forging,pressing,stamping,roll-forming of metal		...	...	1407	1414		...	...	107.7	101.5		...	...	3872	3304
2592	Treatment and coating of metals; machining		...	...	18549	18237		...	...	225.5	199.7		...	...	6324	4997
2593	Cutlery, hand tools and general hardware		...	...	4050	4034		...	...	134.5	133.4		...	...	4994	4564
2599	Other fabricated metal products n.e.c.		...	...	4244	4497		...	...	138.8	124.7		...	...	4700	4002
2610	Electronic components and boards		...	...	1511	1752		...	...	79.2	70.5		...	...	3741	2871
2620	Computers and peripheral equipment		...	...	1315	1434		...	...	31.2	20.1		...	...	1803	918
2630	Communication equipment		...	...	818	902		...	...	48.8	30.2		...	...	2527	1350
2640	Consumer electronics		...	...	111	188		...	...	13.1	14.6		...	...	614	673
265	Measuring,testing equipment; watches, etc.		...	...	2275	2657		...	...	109.2	128.2		...	...	4714	5486
2651	Measuring/testing/navigating equipment,etc.		...	...	2128	2488		...	...	105.4	124.5		...	...	4585	5358
2652	Watches and clocks		...	...	147	169		...	...	3.8	3.6		...	...	130	128
2660	Irradiation/electromedical equipment,etc.		...	...	474	376		...	...	11.8	11.5		...	...	533	532
2670	Optical instruments and photographic equipment		...	...	654	637		...	...	28.4	21.9		...	...	1248	971
2680	Magnetic and optical media		...	...	84	80		...	...	1.0	0.6		...	...	35	19
2710	Electric motors,generators,transformers,etc.		...	...	1580	1750		...	...	239.4	247.6		...	...	12564	11979
2720	Batteries and accumulators		...	...	53	55		...	...	6.0	6.1		...	...	257	264
273	Wiring and wiring devices		...	...	1515	1252		...	...	105.9	76.6		...	...	4079	2817
2731	Fibre optic cables		...	...	25	33		...	...	0.7	1.3		...	...	22	42
2732	Other electronic and electric wires and cables		...	...	310	375		...	...	21.2	20.3		...	...	771	705
2733	Wiring devices		...	...	1180	844		...	...	84.1	55.0		...	...	3286	2069
2740	Electric lighting equipment		...	...	848	752		...	...	39.2	36.8		...	...	1500	1443
2750	Domestic appliances		...	...	239	228		...	...	52.5	50.9		...	...	2296	2242
2790	Other electrical equipment		...	...	1178	1382		...	...	52.1	53.8		...	...	2040	2153
281	General-purpose machinery		...	...	8117	7731		...	...	645.9	608.8		...	...	28836	26491
2811	Engines/turbines,excl.aircraft,vehicle engines		...	...	206	213		...	...	111.4	110.7		...	...	5789	5634
2812	Fluid power equipment		...	...	263	303		...	...	33.8	41.3		...	...	1481	1715
2813	Other pumps, compressors, taps and valves		...	...	937	948		...	...	106.6	88.3		...	...	4823	3955
2814	Bearings, gears, gearing and driving elements		...	...	776	740		...	...	97.2	91.4		...	...	4167	3701
2815	Ovens, furnaces and furnace burners		...	...	377	385		...	...	14.3	12.7		...	...	567	531
2816	Lifting and handling equipment		...	...	1232	1101		...	...	74.7	69.0		...	...	3099	2684
2817	Office machinery, excl.computers,etc.		...	...	154	101		...	...	9.8	8.0		...	...	444	364
2818	Power-driven hand tools		...	...	237	212		...	...	11.3	10.5		...	...	509	455
2819	Other general-purpose machinery		...	...	3935	3728		...	...	186.8	176.9		...	...	7957	7452
282	Special-purpose machinery		...	...	8255	7376		...	...	436.9	409.5		...	...	18501	16779
2821	Agricultural and forestry machinery		...	...	710	677		...	...	32.2	31.2		...	...	1264	1210
2822	Metal-forming machinery and machine tools		...	...	2223	2045		...	...	116.8	109.7		...	...	5056	4321
2823	Machinery for metallurgy		...	...	237	150		...	...	11.2	9.6		...	...	642	582
2824	Mining, quarrying and construction machinery		...	...	441	327		...	...	43.5	41.4		...	...	1830	1748

2825	Food/beverage/tobacco processing machinery	546	482	23.1	26.2	1075	965
2826	Textile/apparel/leather production machinery	283	268	25.4	21.9	859	1076
2829	Other special-purpose machinery	3815	3427	184.8	169.4	6984	7667
2910	Motor vehicles	185	164	482.1	472.1	25028	26578
2920	Automobile bodies, trailers and semi-trailers	1255	1054	45.8	40.5	1297	1510
2930	Parts and accessories for motor vehicles	1232	1206	268.5	241.7	9911	11488
301	Building of ships and boats	307	246	22.0	18.9	838	872
3011	Building of ships and floating structures	55	80	16.9	15.3	703	706
3012	Building of pleasure and sporting boats	252	166	5.0	3.7	136	166
3020	Railway locomotives and rolling stock	69	88	16.4	19.3	946	799
3030	Air and spacecraft and related machinery	202	181	65.7	64.3	3958	3936
3040	Military fighting vehicles	:	:	:	:	:	:
309	Transport equipment n.e.c.	:	:	:	:	:	:
3091	Motorcycles	199	184	4.8	5.2	147	144
3092	Bicycles and invalid carriages	:	:	:	:	:	:
3099	Other transport equipment n.e.c.	8243	6458	144.3	129.4	3879	4338
3100	Furniture	2860	2567	11.1	11.1	215	244
321	Jewellery, bijouterie and related articles	2652	2372	9.8	10.0	195	220
3211	Jewellery and related articles	208	195	1.2	1.1	20	25
3212	Imitation jewellery and related articles	868	818	6.2	6.1	156	165
3220	Musical instruments	286	409	5.9	6.0	168	162
3230	Sports goods	610	529	13.2	11.9	340	365
3240	Games and toys	11878	9160	153.5	141.8	4597	4553
3250	Medical and dental instruments and supplies	1313	1570	27.0	27.2	761	785
3290	Other manufacturing n.e.c.	7113	6926	115.3	116.0	4646	4302
331	Repair of fabricated metal products/machinery	971	1017	16.2	12.3	447	596
3311	Repair of fabricated metal products	4487	4106	40.6	44.5	1634	1246
3312	Repair of machinery	340	451	9.7	8.2	557	557
3313	Repair of electronic and optical equipment	447	414	7.9	10.1	331	232
3314	Repair of electrical equipment	620	615	39.3	38.1	1623	1630
3315	Repair of transport equip., excl. motor vehicles	250	323	1.7	2.8	54	42
3319	Repair of other equipment	2658	2762	73.4	88.8	3907	3120
3320	Installation of industrial machinery/equipment	:	:	:	:	:	:
C	Total manufacturing	195442	179834	6938.6	6559.3	249901	268300

a/ 1101 includes 1102, 1103 and 1104.
b/ 1910 includes 1920.

Germany

ISIC	Industry	Output (millions of Euros)					Value added at factor values (millions of Euros)					Gross fixed capital formation (millions of Euros)		
		Note	2006	2007	2008	2009	Note	2006	2007	2008	2009	Note	2008	2009
1010	Processing/preserving of meat, etc.		...	...	37199	37093		...	...	6121	6189		645	692
1020	Processing/preserving of fish, etc.		...	...	2325	2077		...	...	364	342		55	36
1030	Processing/preserving of fruit,vegetables		...	...	8772	8557		...	...	1687	1711		243	204
1040	Vegetable and animal oils and fats		...	...	6404	4160		...	...	566	450		125	...
1050	Dairy products		...	...	24776	20308		...	...	2541	2498		440	458
106	Grain mill products,starches and starch products		...	...	6186	4939		...	...	1023	1005		231	158
1061	Grain mill products		...	...	4682	3565		...	...	669	709		159	112
1062	Starches and starch products		...	...	1504	1374		...	...	354	296		72	46
107	Other food products		...	...	47923	45505		...	...	14939	14475		1781	1895
1071	Bakery products		...	...	20563	19716		...	...	8658	8511		882	974
1072	Sugar		...	...	2952	2564		...	...	1111	748		104	58
1073	Cocoa, chocolate and sugar confectionery		...	...	7771	7775		...	...	1765	1778		336	273
1074	Macaroni, noodles, couscous, etc.		...	...	600	516		...	...	130	112		23	24
1075	Prepared meals and dishes		...	...	1467	2041		...	...	392	501		53	51
1079	Other food products n.e.c.		...	...	14569	12892		...	...	2882	2825		384	514
1080	Prepared animal feeds		...	...	7174	6606		...	...	1130	1242		139	139
1101	Distilling, rectifying and blending of spirits		...	...	20251a/	19520a/		...	...	4812a/	4843a/		1147a/	927a/
1102	Wines		...	...	...a/	...a/		...	...	...a/	...a/		...a/	...a/
1103	Malt liquors and malt		...	...	...a/	...a/		...	...	...a/	...a/		...a/	...a/
1104	Soft drinks,mineral waters,other bottled waters		...	...	...a/	...a/		...	...	...a/	...a/		...a/	...a/
1200	Tobacco products		...	...	13041	13071		...	...	966	1254		150	227
131	Spinning, weaving and finishing of textiles		...	...	4535	3275		...	...	1371	1016		162	114
1311	Preparation and spinning of textile fibres		...	...	1008	711		...	...	238	161		27	15
1312	Weaving of textiles		...	...	2186	1556		...	...	652	479		74	50
1313	Finishing of textiles		...	...	1341	1009		...	...	480	375		61	50
139	Other textiles		...	...	7425	6430		...	...	2360	2062		237	184
1391	Knitted and crocheted fabrics		...	...	597	544		...	...	142	133		24	11
1392	Made-up textile articles, except apparel		...	...	1979	2017		...	...	708	683		54	47
1393	Carpets and rugs		...	...	947	620		...	...	238	172		28	13
1394	Cordage, rope, twine and netting		...	...				...	...				5	4
1399	Other textiles n.e.c.		...	...				...	...				127	109
1410	Wearing apparel, except fur apparel		...	...	7727	6645		...	...	2075	1771		122	68
1420	Articles of fur		...	...				...	...				1	...
1430	Knitted and crocheted apparel		...	...				...	...				20	50
151	Leather;luggage,handbags,saddlery,harness;fur		...	...	981	855		...	...	299	282		27	17
1511	Tanning/dressing of leather; dressing of fur		...	...	479	308		...	...	109	88		10	4
1512	Luggage,handbags,etc.;saddlery/harness		...	...	502	547		...	...	190	195		17	13
1520	Footwear		...	...	1514	1321		...	...	481	399		117	95
1610	Sawmilling and planing of wood		...	...	5148	4785		...	...	1100	942		327	276
162	Wood products, cork, straw, plaiting materials		...	...	15802	14380		...	...	4546	4131		599	383

1621	Veneer sheets and wood-based panels	96	216	733	995	5522	4501
1622	Builders' carpentry and joinery	196	248	2443	2524	7508	7246
1623	Wooden containers	37	61	483	509	1569	1432
1629	Other wood products;articles of cork,straw	54	75	472	518	1204	1201
1701	Pulp, paper and paperboard	447	1094	3171	3198	15994	13415
1702	Corrugated paper and paperboard	415	476	3094	3394	11362	9845
1709	Other articles of paper and paperboard	278	342	2867	2850	9568	9189
181	Printing and service activities related to printing	970	1234	7265	8083	21241	20198
1811	Printing	826	1081	5741	6257	17680	16777
1812	Service activities related to printing	144	153	1525	1826	3562	3422
1820	Reproduction of recorded media	26	55	348	415	1076	1002
1910	Coke oven products	997b/	1164b/	2392b/	2572b/	108887b/	81382b/
1920	Refined petroleum products	...b/	...b/	...b/	...b/	...b/	...b/
201	Basic chemicals,fertilizers, etc.	3585	3781	18879	21602	79455	65000
2011	Basic chemicals	1729	1509	9067	9371	35548	31588
2012	Fertilizers and nitrogen compounds	69	192	1002	2356	4823	2845
2013	Plastics and synthetic rubber in primary forms	1787	2080	8810	9875	39083	30566
202	Other chemical products	1248	1503	10385	10853	37021	36101
2021	Pesticides and other agrochemical products	26	30	255	221	683	728
2022	Paints,varnishes;printing ink and mastics	182	256	3284	3275	10228	9383
2023	Soap,cleaning and cosmetic preparations	348	349	3045	2959	11339	12192
2029	Other chemical products n.e.c.	693	868	3801	4398	14771	13798
2030	Man-made fibres	103	93	527	735	3508	1930
2100	Pharmaceuticals,medicinal chemicals, etc.	1609	1862	15273	16365	39073	35875
221	Rubber products	432	651	4001	5040	14366	11084
2211	Rubber tyres and tubes	189	295	1352	1807	5716	4206
2219	Other rubber products	243	356	2649	3233	8650	6878
2220	Plastics products	1773	2262	15406	16910	51411	44957
2310	Glass and glass products	617	685	3204	3869	10497	9053
239	Non-metallic mineral products n.e.c.	1149	1491	9325	10582	30879	27804
2391	Refractory products	37	58	355	627	1730	1268
2392	Clay building materials	86	125	690	746	1978	1737
2393	Other porcelain and ceramic products	82	122	1006	1215	2447	2099
2394	Cement, lime and plaster	264	336	1284	1304	3717	3495
2395	Articles of concrete, cement and plaster	434	575	3930	3830	13070	12516
2396	Cutting, shaping and finishing of stone	55	87	703	1403	2844	1529
2399	Other non-metallic mineral products n.e.c.	193	188	1357	1457	5094	5159
2410	Basic iron and steel	1751	2186	8595	14002	62577	39916
2420	Basic precious and other non-ferrous metals	...	716	4072	4768	33311	21308
243	Casting of metals	541	853	3325	4646	14233	9325
2431	Casting of iron and steel	312	505	1878	2732	8637	5500
2432	Casting of non-ferrous metals	229	348	1447	1914	5596	3825
251	Struct.metal products, tanks, reservoirs	738	991	8497	9884	31215	25363
2511	Structural metal products	622	834	7004	8220	25820	20779
2512	Tanks, reservoirs and containers of metal	98	151	1157	1460	4593	3524

continued

Germany

ISIC	Industry	Output (millions of Euros)					Value added at factor values (millions of Euros)					Gross fixed capital formation (millions of Euros)		
		Note	2006	2007	2008	2009	Note	2006	2007	2008	2009	Note	2008	2009
2513	Steam generators, excl. hot water boilers		...	...	802	1061		...	...	204	336		7	18
2520	Weapons and ammunition		...	...	1838	2553		...	...	765	893		53	67
259	Other metal products;metal working services		...	...	86621	65973		...	...	33758	25886		4457	2848
2591	Forging,pressing,stamping,roll-forming of metal		...	...	19706	14211		...	...	6456	4585		838	614
2592	Treatment and coating of metals; machining		...	...	24632	18041		...	...	10972	8047		1741	1044
2593	Cutlery, hand tools and general hardware		...	...	18852	14967		...	...	8278	6687		915	609
2599	Other fabricated metal products n.e.c.		...	...	23431	18754		...	...	8053	6567		963	581
2610	Electronic components and boards		...	...	23880	15886		...	...	5474	4062		1846	1037
2620	Computers and peripheral equipment		...	...	9554	4717		...	...	2665	1295		107	58
2630	Communication equipment		...	...	10549	5643		...	...	3887	1958		211	107
2640	Consumer electronics		...	...	3226	2897		...	...	827	871		117	81
265	Measuring,testing equipment; watches, etc.		...	...	18795	18265		...	...	7840	7364		564	414
2651	Measuring/testing/navigating equipment,etc.		...	...	18228	17826		...	...	7630	7200		543	400
2652	Watches and clocks		...	...	567	438		...	...	210	164		21	14
2660	Irradiation/electromedical equipment,etc.		...	...	3130	2906		...	...	1223	1223		62	64
2670	Optical instruments and photographic equipment		...	...	5136	3363		...	...	2259	1357		211	143
2680	Magnetic and optical media		...	...	223	127		...	...	59	26		8	3
2710	Electric motors,generators,transformers,etc.		...	...	50284	47196		...	...	17295	17671		1184	1157
2720	Batteries and accumulators		...	...	2250	1779		...	...	448	357		32	44
273	Wiring and wiring devices		...	...	19151	11875		...	...	6733	4320		746	552
2731	Fibre optic cables		...	...	92	162		...	...	32	56		6	2
2732	Other electronic and electric wires and cables		...	...	5870	4507		...	...	1209	1126		201	181
2733	Wiring devices		...	...	13189	7206		...	...	5492	3137		539	369
2740	Electric lighting equipment		...	...	6061	5283		...	...	2450	2051		325	223
2750	Domestic appliances		...	...	10125	9419		...	...	3300	3270		479	311
2790	Other electrical equipment		...	...	9457	8394		...	...	3695	3416		307	285
281	General-purpose machinery		...	...	134976	106128		...	...	47587	37314		5896	3966
2811	Engines/turbines,excl.aircraft,vehicle engines		...	...	24088	21650		...	...	8019	6589		1452	934
2812	Fluid power equipment		...	...	6384	5069		...	...	2741	2091		399	247
2813	Other pumps, compressors, taps and valves		...	...	21486	16519		...	...	8001	6323		926	577
2814	Bearings, gears, gearing and driving elements		...	...	19150	14475		...	...	7272	5615		1186	791
2815	Ovens, furnaces and furnace burners		...	...	3155	2483		...	...	1005	809		61	45
2816	Lifting and handling equipment		...	...	18526	11919		...	...	5893	4163		472	303
2817	Office machinery, excl.computers,etc.		...	...	2354	1592		...	...	902	521		218	126
2818	Power-driven hand tools		...	...	2138	1637		...	...	948	705		85	83
2819	Other general-purpose machinery		...	...	37696	30786		...	...	12805	10498		1097	860
282	Special-purpose machinery		...	...	92324	67797		...	...	29857	22511		2589	1757
2821	Agricultural and forestry machinery		...	...	10607	7991		...	...	2658	2062		205	201
2822	Metal-forming machinery and machine tools		...	...	22577	15098		...	...	8010	5322		661	419
2823	Machinery for metallurgy		...	...	3877	3445		...	...	961	847		119	44
2824	Mining, quarrying and construction machinery		...	...	13614	9391		...	...	3818	2924		474	337

2825	Food/beverage/tobacco processing machinery	4291	4283	1596	1675	118	86
2826	Textile/apparel/leather production machinery	4260	2699	1320	836	109	52
2829	Other special-purpose machinery	33097	24889	11494	8845	904	618
2910	Motor vehicles	214927	172920	38464	29263	9467	7673
2920	Automobile bodies, trailers and semi-trailers	11365	6726	2590	1680	322	190
2930	Parts and accessories for motor vehicles	67236	49396	17556	12696	2460	1456
301	Building of ships and boats	6788	5093	1430	1040	122	81
3011	Building of ships and floating structures	5059	3947	948	783	77	33
3012	Building of pleasure and sporting boats	1729	1145	482	257	45	47
3020	Railway locomotives and rolling stock	4393	5190	1097	1304	90	84
3030	Air and spacecraft and related machinery	18617	18262	5733	5195	604	581
3040	Military fighting vehicles	...	...	...	...	9	13
309	Transport equipment n.e.c.	...	...	...	...	29	16
3091	Motorcycles	796	852	249	261	8	5
3092	Bicycles and invalid carriages	...	...	...	...	17	10
3099	Other transport equipment n.e.c.	...	...	...	...	5	2
3100	Furniture	22184	17588	6959	5972	564	422
321	Jewellery, bijouterie and related articles	1160	1015	453	388	26	29
3211	Jewellery and related articles	1061	950	409	357	24	26
3212	Imitation jewellery and related articles	99	65	43	31	2	2
3220	Musical instruments	559	453	294	254	28	12
3230	Sports goods	751	706	274	263	16	11
3240	Games and toys	2078	2245	695	988	200	178
3250	Medical and dental instruments and supplies	16991	16066	7924	7590	684	623
3290	Other manufacturing n.e.c.	3254	3119	1426	1236	138	104
331	Repair of fabricated metal products/machinery	21201	19991	6875	6571	405	441
3311	Repair of fabricated metal products	2999	1686	1005	606	49	51
3312	Repair of machinery	5089	5129	2120	2317	145	141
3313	Repair of electronic and optical equipment	1947	1794	584	412	25	23
3314	Repair of electrical equipment	1611	2064	425	499	17	42
3315	Repair of transport equip., excl. motor vehicles	9409	9142	2670	2647	161	181
3319	Repair of other equipment	147	177	72	91	6	3
3320	Installation of industrial machinery/equipment	13287	14374	4793	5146	170	185
C	Total manufacturing	1687997	1378217	453779	381548	62527	48500

a/ 1101 includes 1102, 1103 and 1104.
b/ 1910 includes 1920.

Germany

Index numbers of industrial production

ISIC Revision 4

(2005=100)

ISIC	Industry	Note	1999	2000	2001	2002	2003	2004	2005	2006	2007	2008	2009	2010
10	Food products		88	91	90	91	92	95	100	102	105	105	105	107
11	Beverages		110	107	108	108	107	102	100	102	97	95	92	93
12	Tobacco products		166	168	166	147	121	112	100	94	91	67	64	55
13	Textiles		116	118	114	108	104	104	100	100	101	96	77	87
14	Wearing apparel		179	163	152	130	115	109	100	88	81	69	59	59
15	Leather and related products		148	143	135	130	114	110	100	96	107	98	100	108
16	Wood/wood products/cork,excl. furniture		109	109	101	98	96	100	100	107	105	104	91	97
17	Paper and paper products		92	93	91	92	94	97	100	104	109	110	102	110
18	Printing and reproduction of recorded media		104	106	102	98	94	96	100	102	104	105	98	99
19	Coke and refined petroleum products		90	92	89	88	88	97	100	100	99	99	90	89
20	Chemicals and chemical products		91	94	91	94	93	97	100	104	106	102	87	102
21	Pharmaceuticals,medicinal chemicals, etc.		80	79	83	85	89	90	100	105	117	121	118	119
22	Rubber and plastics products		91	95	94	95	96	100	100	104	111	108	95	107
23	Other non-metallic mineral products		117	117	110	105	102	104	100	106	107	104	91	98
24	Basic metals		89	96	96	97	95	100	100	108	112	111	81	98
25	Fabricated metal products, except machinery		88	94	96	94	95	99	100	107	115	117	92	105
26	Computer, electronic and optical products		65	81	80	75	78	88	100	119	136	145	113	132
27	Electrical equipment		87	92	95	92	92	97	100	108	115	116	91	107
28	Machinery and equipment n.e.c.		86	92	93	91	90	96	100	108	119	125	92	102
29	Motor vehicles, trailers and semi-trailers		79	86	89	90	92	97	100	103	109	105	82	103
30	Other transport equipment		79	82	87	93	98	97	100	110	113	124	121	115
31	Furniture		128	127	121	104	99	99	100	107	109	108	92	94
32	Other manufacturing		87	92	94	95	97	100	100	107	112	113	104	112
33	Repair and installation of machinery/equipment		87	91	92	91	93	97	100	106	115	129	110	114
C	Total manufacturing		88	93	93	92	93	97	100	106	112	114	94	105

Hungary

Supplier of information:
Hungarian Central Statistical Office, Budapest.
Industrial statistics for the OECD countries are compiled by the OECD secretariat, which supplies them to UNIDO.

Basic source of data:
Annual structural business statistics surveys; administrative data.

Major deviations from ISIC (Revision 4):
None reported.

Reference period:
Calendar year.

Scope:
Enterprises with one or more employees.

Method of data collection:
Questionnaires are distributed by mail.

Type of enumeration:
Not reported.

Adjusted for non-response:
Not reported.

Concepts and definitions of variables:
No deviations from the standard UN concepts and definitions are reported.

Related national publications:
None reported.

Hungary

ISIC Revision 4		Number of enterprises (number)					Number of employees (number)					Wages and salaries paid to employees (billions of Hungarian Forints)				
ISIC	Industry	Note	2006	2007	2008	2009	Note	2006	2007	2008	2009	Note	2006	2007	2008	2009
1010	Processing/preserving of meat		...	...	592	575		...	...	29987	27640		...	...	56.3	56.5
1020	Processing/preserving of fish, etc.		...	...	13	10		...	...	57	76		...	...	0.1	0.1
1030	Processing/preserving of fruit,vegetables		...	...	491	493		...	...	8279	7678		...	...	15.8	15.1
1040	Vegetable and animal oils and fats		...	...	81	...		...	...	864	...		...	...	3.7	...
1050	Dairy products		...	...	100	98		...	...	7572	7255		...	...	19.1	18.6
106	Grain mill products,starches and starch products		...	...	150	137		...	...	3119	2942		...	...	8.0	7.8
1061	Grain mill products		...	...	146	130		...	...	2830	2630		...	...	6.4	5.9
1062	Starches and starch products		...	...	4	7		...	...	289	312		...	...	1.6	1.9
107	Other food products		...	...	2669	2653		...	...	38998	37564		...	...	66.9	63.3
1071	Bakery products		...	...	1819	1841		...	...	26973	26604		...	...	37.3	37.3
1072	Sugar		...	...	5	5		...	...	424	224		...	...	3.1	1.2
1073	Cocoa, chocolate and sugar confectionery		...	...	247	224		...	...	3361	2769		...	...	6.0	4.9
1074	Macaroni, noodles, couscous, etc.		...	...	241	234		...	...	1486	1514		...	...	1.7	1.8
1075	Prepared meals and dishes		...	...	36	31		...	...	1198	704		...	...	2.5	1.8
1079	Other food products n.e.c.		...	...	321	318		...	...	5556	5749		...	...	16.3	16.4
1080	Prepared animal feeds		...	...	196	182		...	...	4617	4263		...	...	13.5	12.8
1101	Distilling, rectifying and blending of spirits		...	...	2417a/	2370a/		...	...	13335a/	12494a/		...	...	37.3a/	36.0a/
1102	Wines		...	...	...a/	...a/		...	...	...a/	...a/		...	...	...a/	...a/
1103	Malt liquors and malt		...	...	...a/	...a/		...	...	...a/	...a/		...	...	...a/	...a/
1104	Soft drinks,mineral waters,other bottled waters		...	...	...a/	...a/		...	...	...a/	...a/		...	...	...a/	...a/
1200	Tobacco products		...	...	5	4		...	...	1055	1007		...	...	5.3	5.2
131	Spinning, weaving and finishing of textiles		...	...	217	191		...	...	3642	3025		...	...	6.7	5.9
1311	Preparation and spinning of textile fibres		...	...	45	42		...	...	1920	1677		...	...	3.6	3.3
1312	Weaving of textiles		...	...	40	39		...	...	1266	988		...	...	2.5	2.1
1313	Finishing of textiles		...	...	132	110		...	...	456	360		...	...	0.7	0.5
139	Other textiles		...	...	1053	965		...	...	6872	6236		...	...	9.3	8.5
1391	Knitted and crocheted fabrics		...	...	111	100		...	...	373	359		...	...	0.5	0.4
1392	Made-up textile articles, except apparel		...	...	394	361		...	...	4145	3586		...	...	5.1	4.4
1393	Carpets and rugs		...	...	39	34		...	...	362	292		...	...	0.5	0.3
1394	Cordage, rope, twine and netting		...	...	39	39		...	...	191	157		...	...	0.3	0.4
1399	Other textiles n.e.c.		...	...	470	431		...	...	1801	1842		...	...	3.0	2.9
1410	Wearing apparel, except fur apparel		...	...	3669	3221		...	...	28749	23100		...	...	34.2	28.8
1420	Articles of fur		...	...	78	77		...	...	69	51		...	...	0.1	0.1
1430	Knitted and crocheted apparel		...	...	339	277		...	...	3474	2895		...	...	4.0	3.4
151	Leather;luggage,handbags,saddlery,harness;fur		...	...	313	276		...	...	5765	3011		...	...	9.7	5.2
1511	Tanning/dressing of leather; dressing of fur		...	...	55	34		...	...	174	78		...	...	0.2	0.1
1512	Luggage,handbags,etc.;saddlery/harness		...	...	258	242		...	...	5591	2933		...	...	9.5	5.0
1520	Footwear		...	...	353	319		...	...	7427	6591		...	...	9.0	8.5
1610	Sawmilling and planing of wood		...	...	841	776		...	...	4799	3932		...	...	5.8	4.9
162	Wood products, cork, straw, plaiting materials		...	...	3209	3074		...	...	15056	12363		...	...	22.8	19.4

1621	Veneer sheets and wood-based panels	47	43	...	1547	1266	...	4.1	3.3
1622	Builders' carpentry and joinery	2138	2126	...	8689	7469	...	12.8	11.4
1623	Wooden containers	343	310	...	2855	2262	...	3.7	3.0
1629	Other wood products;articles of cork,straw	681	595	...	1965	1366	...	2.2	1.7
1701	Pulp, paper and paperboard	34	31	...	807	831	...	3.2	3.1
1702	Corrugated paper and paperboard	265	254	...	5502	5167	...	17.3	16.9
1709	Other articles of paper and paperboard	266	228	...	5595	5045	...	12.8	12.8
181	Printing and service activities related to printing	3984	3695	...	17152	15211	...	34.2	29.7
1811	Printing	1788	1668	...	12674	11448	...	27.1	23.8
1812	Service activities related to printing	2196	2027	...	4478	3763	...	7.1	5.9
1820	Reproduction of recorded media	173	148	...	406	348	...	0.9	0.8
1910	Coke oven products	3	3	...	791	757	...	3.1	2.6
1920	Refined petroleum products	7	8	...	5743	5624	...	44.5	44.2
201	Basic chemicals,fertilizers, etc.	217	192	...	8260	8045	...	34.5	34.9
2011	Basic chemicals	147	118	...	3041	2757	...	11.8	11.0
2012	Fertilizers and nitrogen compounds	13	20	...	602	856	...	2.9	3.0
2013	Plastics and synthetic rubber in primary forms	57	54	...	4617	4432	...	19.8	20.9
202	Other chemical products	425	373	...	5804	5344	...	19.3	16.5
2021	Pesticides and other agrochemical products	47	44	...	609	744	...	1.7	2.1
2022	Paints,varnishes;printing ink and mastics	57	53	...	1390	1397	...	4.9	4.7
2023	Soap,cleaning and cosmetic preparations	163	152	...	2817	2173	...	10.0	6.6
2029	Other chemical products n.e.c.	158	124	...	988	1030	...	2.6	3.1
2030	Man-made fibres	5	4	...	27	18	...	0.1	-
2100	Pharmaceuticals,medicinal chemicals, etc.	90	86	...	15927	15756	...	83.7	89.0
221	Rubber products	246	237	...	11124	8995	...	31.3	28.9
2211	Rubber tyres and tubes	58	49	...	3267	3353	...	12.8	14.0
2219	Other rubber products	188	188	...	7857	5642	...	18.5	14.9
2220	Plastics products	2083	1926	...	36327	32600	...	75.2	69.7
2310	Glass and glass products	352	340	...	4801	4157	...	10.3	10.4
239	Non-metallic mineral products n.e.c.	1949	1864	...	25637	20655	...	68.1	55.9
2391	Refractory products	35	35	...	1038	819	...	2.9	2.6
2392	Clay building materials	66	55	...	3299	2791	...	8.1	7.2
2393	Other porcelain and ceramic products	421	406	...	5561	4650	...	12.4	10.6
2394	Cement, lime and plaster	80	67	...	1389	1323	...	7.4	7.2
2395	Articles of concrete, cement and plaster	650	609	...	8583	7604	...	22.3	20.9
2396	Cutting, shaping and finishing of stone	597	599	...	1550	1435	...	1.7	1.6
2399	Other non-metallic mineral products n.e.c.	100	93	...	4217	2033	...	13.3	5.9
2410	Basic iron and steel	110	98	...	9078	8427	...	33.9	28.6
2420	Basic precious and other non-ferrous metals	37	...	...	7426	...	...	25.6	...
243	Casting of metals	192	181	...	5771	4827	...	13.1	10.9
2431	Casting of iron and steel	57	54	...	2020	1837	...	4.3	3.8
2432	Casting of non-ferrous metals	135	127	...	3751	2990	...	8.8	7.1
251	Struct.metal products, tanks, reservoirs	3530	3225	...	34169	29106	...	71.1	61.0
2511	Structural metal products	3166	2962	...	29520	25225	...	59.2	51.7
2512	Tanks, reservoirs and containers of metal	314	228	...	3823	3141	...	9.1	7.0

continued

Hungary

ISIC	Industry	Number of enterprises (number)					Number of employees (number)					Wages and salaries paid to employees (billions of Hungarian Forints)				
		Note	2006	2007	2008	2009	Note	2006	2007	2008	2009	Note	2006	2007	2008	2009
2513	Steam generators, excl. hot water boilers		...	...	50	35		...	...	826	740		...	...	2.8	2.3
2520	Weapons and ammunition		...	...	38	12		...	...	321	296		...	...	0.6	0.6
259	Other metal products;metal working services		...	...	5673	5346		...	...	39676	33723		...	...	80.7	73.1
2591	Forging,pressing,stamping,roll-forming of metal		...	...	192	175		...	...	3420	2066		...	...	6.3	5.0
2592	Treatment and coating of metals; machining		...	...	4054	3862		...	...	21871	18828		...	...	41.0	37.3
2593	Cutlery, hand tools and general hardware		...	...	650	624		...	...	5397	5194		...	...	13.4	13.0
2599	Other fabricated metal products n.e.c.		...	...	777	685		...	...	8988	7635		...	...	20.0	17.7
2610	Electronic components and boards		...	...	589	344		...	...	16130	15782		...	...	38.8	37.0
2620	Computers and peripheral equipment		...	...	238	193		...	...	10175	7984		...	...	28.7	24.4
2630	Communication equipment		...	...	745	439		...	...	21186	16413		...	...	61.3	49.1
2640	Consumer electronics		...	...	...	...		...	...	...	...		...	...	...	...
265	Measuring,testing equipment; watches, etc.		...	...	590	420		...	...	3980	3597		...	...	11.1	10.5
2651	Measuring/testing/navigating equipment,etc.		...	...	578	406		...	...	3959	3562		...	...	11.1	10.5
2652	Watches and clocks		...	...	12	14		...	...	21	35		...	...	-	0.1
2660	Irradiation/electromedical equipment,etc.		...	...	150	83		...	...	586	808		...	...	1.1	2.1
2670	Optical instruments and photographic equipment		...	...	98	99		...	...	1346	1240		...	...	3.1	3.1
2680	Magnetic and optical media		...	...	...	...		...	...	...	...		...	...	...	...
2710	Electric motors,generators,transformers,etc.		...	...	372	310		...	...	13483	12381		...	...	32.5	29.9
2720	Batteries and accumulators		...	...	18	16		...	...	1054	934		...	...	2.9	2.7
273	Wiring and wiring devices		...	...	64	60		...	...	8166	7243		...	...	18.6	18.8
2731	Fibre optic cables		...	...	...	...		...	...	...	...		...	...	...	...
2732	Other electronic and electric wires and cables		...	...	50	44		...	...	5125	4634		...	...	9.6	10.9
2733	Wiring devices		...	...	...	...		...	...	...	...		...	...	...	...
2740	Electric lighting equipment		...	...	152	139		...	...	17143	4065		...	...	50.2	8.0
2750	Domestic appliances		...	...	87	85		...	...	10698	9848		...	...	21.8	20.3
2790	Other electrical equipment		...	...	356	286		...	...	4681	3795		...	...	11.1	9.3
281	General-purpose machinery		...	...	3088	1848		...	...	30327	36636		...	...	81.7	109.7
2811	Engines/turbines,excl.aircraft,vehicle engines		...	...	75	59		...	...	2828	13055		...	...	10.2	47.2
2812	Fluid power equipment		...	...	42	51		...	...	939	972		...	...	3.1	3.3
2813	Other pumps, compressors, taps and valves		...	...	175	142		...	...	5536	5177		...	...	16.2	14.7
2814	Bearings, gears, gearing and driving elements		...	...	68	62		...	...	2221	1712		...	...	6.2	4.2
2815	Ovens, furnaces and furnace burners		...	...	43	44		...	...	446	334		...	...	0.9	0.6
2816	Lifting and handling equipment		...	...	657	330		...	...	5238	3901		...	...	12.5	9.3
2817	Office machinery, excl.computers,etc.		...	...	27	29		...	...	505	451		...	...	1.3	1.2
2818	Power-driven hand tools		...	...	21	17		...	...	1385	1411		...	...	3.9	4.0
2819	Other general-purpose machinery		...	...	1980	1114		...	...	11229	9623		...	...	27.5	25.1
282	Special-purpose machinery		...	...	1811	1112		...	...	19189	16192		...	...	46.0	39.3
2821	Agricultural and forestry machinery		...	...	427	175		...	...	5645	5234		...	...	12.6	10.6
2822	Metal-forming machinery and machine tools		...	...	322	204		...	...	2562	1653		...	...	6.1	3.7
2823	Machinery for metallurgy		...	...	15	9		...	...	453	128		...	...	1.2	0.3
2824	Mining, quarrying and construction machinery		...	...	91	67		...	...	2095	1758		...	...	5.4	4.6

2825	Food/beverage/tobacco processing machinery	⋮	288	222	⋮	3232	2936	⋮	⋮	8.3	7.7
2826	Textile/apparel/leather production machinery	⋮	77	35	⋮	621	302	⋮	⋮	1.1	0.6
2829	Other special-purpose machinery	⋮	591	400	⋮	4581	4181	⋮	⋮	11.4	11.8
2910	Motor vehicles	⋮	47	45	⋮	13062	11117	⋮	⋮	59.4	48.0
2920	Automobile bodies, trailers and semi-trailers	⋮	119	108	⋮	3066	2334	⋮	⋮	7.6	5.9
2930	Parts and accessories for motor vehicles	⋮	354	340	⋮	60937	50476	⋮	⋮	162.2	133.7
301	Building of ships and boats	⋮	127	106	⋮	336	258	⋮	⋮	0.5	0.4
3011	Building of ships and floating structures	⋮	31	28	⋮	56	61	⋮	⋮	0.1	0.1
3012	Building of pleasure and sporting boats	⋮	96	78	⋮	280	197	⋮	⋮	0.4	0.3
3020	Railway locomotives and rolling stock	⋮	76	47	⋮	7370	3061	⋮	⋮	22.0	11.1
3030	Air and spacecraft and related machinery	⋮	70	14	⋮	198	60	⋮	⋮	0.4	0.2
3040	Military fighting vehicles	⋮	-	-	⋮	-	-	⋮	⋮	-	-
309	Transport equipment n.e.c.	⋮	60	47	⋮	831	732	⋮	⋮	1.5	1.4
3091	Motorcycles	⋮	10	9	⋮	60	55	⋮	⋮	0.1	0.1
3092	Bicycles and invalid carriages	⋮	35	27	⋮	726	647	⋮	⋮	1.3	1.3
3099	Other transport equipment n.e.c.	⋮	15	11	⋮	45	30	⋮	⋮	0.1	-
3100	Furniture	⋮	3466	2923	⋮	20203	17709	⋮	⋮	29.3	26.8
321	Jewellery, bijouterie and related articles	⋮	782	816	⋮	880	819	⋮	⋮	1.2	1.1
3211	Jewellery and related articles	⋮	418	452	⋮	711	706	⋮	⋮	1.1	1.0
3212	Imitation jewellery and related articles	⋮	364	364	⋮	169	113	⋮	⋮	0.2	0.1
3220	Musical instruments	⋮	132	94	⋮	109	138	⋮	⋮	0.2	0.2
3230	Sports goods	⋮	126	111	⋮	1167	1087	⋮	⋮	2.4	2.1
3240	Games and toys	⋮	183	168	⋮	1413	2413	⋮	⋮	2.7	5.1
3250	Medical and dental instruments and supplies	⋮	1810	1670	⋮	8346	8002	⋮	⋮	15.9	17.0
3290	Other manufacturing n.e.c.	⋮	736	795	⋮	2616	2541	⋮	⋮	3.8	3.8
331	Repair of fabricated metal products/machinery	⋮	1875	4510	⋮	9536	14764	⋮	⋮	28.3	43.5
3311	Repair of fabricated metal products	⋮	24	364	⋮	40	200	⋮	⋮	0.1	0.3
3312	Repair of machinery	⋮	1532	2730	⋮	4697	5205	⋮	⋮	13.2	13.7
3313	Repair of electronic and optical equipment	⋮	83	306	⋮	558	605	⋮	⋮	1.2	1.8
3314	Repair of electrical equipment	⋮	147	888	⋮	1029	961	⋮	⋮	1.9	1.9
3315	Repair of transport equip., excl. motor vehicles	⋮	45	157	⋮	3080	7664	⋮	⋮	11.7	25.7
3319	Repair of other equipment	⋮	44	65	⋮	132	129	⋮	⋮	0.2	0.2
3320	Installation of industrial machinery/equipment	⋮	1356	1351	⋮	4678	4450	⋮	⋮	12.3	11.7
C	Total manufacturing	⋮	56346	52710	⋮	726043	637558	⋮	⋮	1778.7	1614.9

a/ 1101 includes 1102, 1103 and 1104.

ISIC Revision 4

ISIC	Industry	Output — Note	Output 2006	Output 2007	Output 2008	Output 2009	Value added — Note	VA 2006	VA 2007	VA 2008	VA 2009	GFCF — Note	GFCF 2008	GFCF 2009
			(billions of Hungarian Forints)					(billions of Hungarian Forints)					(billions of Hungarian Forints)	
1010	Processing/preserving of meat		...	...	585.9	584.5		...	...	87.6	105.5		13.2	14.6
1020	Processing/preserving of fish, etc.		...	...	0.5	0.8		...	...	0.1	0.2		-	-
1030	Processing/preserving of fruit,vegetables		...	...	192.7	181.5		...	...	41.2	46.0		7.7	11.0
1040	Vegetable and animal oils and fats		...	...	130.5	...		...	...	26.2	...		3.9	7.7
1050	Dairy products		...	...	252.3	222.1		...	...	40.4	44.2		8.0	7.7
106	Grain mill products,starches and starch products		...	...	168.4	151.2		...	...	29.7	38.3		7.9	7.0
1061	Grain mill products		...	...	100.7	82.0		...	...	18.1	14.7		4.4	5.0
1062	Starches and starch products		...	...	67.7	69.1		...	...	11.6	23.6		3.5	2.0
107	Other food products		...	...	491.8	481.2		...	...	129.5	139.7		23.9	27.8
1071	Bakery products		...	...	207.7	201.8		...	...	70.0	72.9		9.0	11.5
1072	Sugar		...	...	17.3	23.0		...	...	-3.2	4.2		0.8	0.5
1073	Cocoa, chocolate and sugar confectionery		...	...	39.9	39.1		...	...	11.5	10.5		2.9	1.9
1074	Macaroni, noodles, couscous, etc.		...	...	26.7	26.7		...	...	6.1	6.4		1.1	4.1
1075	Prepared meals and dishes		...	...	24.1	17.1		...	...	4.9	4.7		0.3	0.5
1079	Other food products n.e.c.		...	...	176.0	173.4		...	...	40.2	41.1		9.8	9.3
1080	Prepared animal feeds		...	...	196.1	190.5		...	...	29.2	35.4		5.8	...
1101	Distilling, rectifying and blending of spirits		...	...	476.9a/	430.2a/		...	...	117.3a/	102.9a/		22.2a/	23.5a/
1102	Wines		...	...	...a/	...a/		...	...	...a/	...a/		...a/	...a/
1103	Malt liquors and malt		...	...	...a/	...a/		...	...	...a/	...a/		...a/	...a/
1104	Soft drinks,mineral waters,other bottled waters		...	...	...a/	...a/		...	...	...a/	...a/		...a/	...a/
1200	Tobacco products		...	...	168.9	159.3		...	...	16.4	15.0		2.3	1.6
131	Spinning, weaving and finishing of textiles		...	...	41.0	34.2		...	...	11.1	10.5		3.8	1.7
1311	Preparation and spinning of textile fibres		...	...	19.6	17.2		...	...	5.5	6.0		2.5	0.9
1312	Weaving of textiles		...	...	16.6	13.8		...	...	4.3	3.6		1.0	0.5
1313	Finishing of textiles		...	...	4.7	3.2		...	...	1.3	0.8		0.3	0.2
139	Other textiles		...	...	48.3	41.2		...	...	16.4	14.7		1.7	2.0
1391	Knitted and crocheted fabrics		...	...	1.9	1.7		...	...	0.6	0.8		2.0	0.7
1392	Made-up textile articles, except apparel		...	...	26.0	20.0		...	...	9.1	7.3		0.7	0.7
1393	Carpets and rugs		...	...	1.3	0.9		...	...	0.8	0.5		1.0	-
1394	Cordage, rope, twine and netting		...	...	1.4	1.5		...	...	0.6	0.4		-	0.1
1399	Other textiles n.e.c.		...	...	17.6	17.2		...	...	5.3	5.7		0.1	0.5
1410	Wearing apparel, except fur apparel		...	...	119.4	90.6		...	...	55.9	45.6		2.8	3.5
1420	Articles of fur		...	...	0.4	0.4		...	...	0.2	0.2		-	0.1
1430	Knitted and crocheted apparel		...	...	11.2	10.1		...	...	8.4	7.2		0.5	0.4
151	Leather;luggage,handbags,saddlery,harness;fur		...	...	75.5	37.5		...	...	15.1	9.7		0.9	1.9
1511	Tanning/dressing of leather; dressing of fur		...	...	0.9	0.4		...	...	0.2	0.1		-	-
1512	Luggage,handbags,etc.;saddlery/harness		...	...	74.6	37.1		...	...	15.0	9.6		0.9	1.9
1520	Footwear		...	...	43.4	39.3		...	...	13.3	13.7		1.1	0.8
1610	Sawmilling and planing of wood		...	...	45.9	36.3		...	...	12.1	9.2		2.4	2.4
162	Wood products, cork, straw, plaiting materials		...	...	193.4	147.0		...	...	51.3	39.4		18.3	6.9

1621	Veneer sheets and wood-based panels	60.7	37.2	10.3	5.9	12.6	1.4
1622	Builders' carpentry and joinery	88.7	77.6	27.1	23.2	4.0	4.3
1623	Wooden containers	31.0	22.1	9.3	6.8	1.4	1.0
1629	Other wood products;articles of cork,straw	13.1	10.1	4.6	3.6	0.3	0.3
1701	Pulp, paper and paperboard	37.4	46.1	6.2	6.6	28.2	37.2
1702	Corrugated paper and paperboard	156.8	147.1	38.0	34.2	15.4	5.7
1709	Other articles of paper and paperboard	86.4	88.0	36.4	39.0	10.4	6.3
181	Printing and service activities related to printing	211.7	184.4	71.5	59.2	17.6	12.3
1811	Printing	172.7	154.4	55.9	46.9	16.2	11.0
1812	Service activities related to printing	39.0	30.0	15.6	12.2	1.4	1.3
1820	Reproduction of recorded media	5.4	3.6	1.9	1.3	0.2	0.1
1910	Coke oven products	91.1	69.6	5.7	4.3	0.5	0.1
1920	Refined petroleum products	1968.9	1596.1	386.1	319.0	45.6	29.8
201	Basic chemicals,fertilizers, etc.	748.0	582.8	129.3	81.3	68.6	38.7
2011	Basic chemicals	121.4	113.8	38.1	40.4	15.7	11.0
2012	Fertilizers and nitrogen compounds	57.1	41.1	20.0	10.1	1.2	1.1
2013	Plastics and synthetic rubber in primary forms	569.4	427.9	71.2	30.8	51.7	26.6
202	Other chemical products	214.1	163.8	55.3	45.4	10.2	4.3
2021	Pesticides and other agrochemical products	25.7	14.9	7.8	4.2	0.7	1.3
2022	Paints,varnishes;printing ink and mastics	38.0	35.0	10.1	9.9	2.1	0.8
2023	Soap,cleaning and cosmetic preparations	102.3	89.8	30.7	25.0	5.8	1.6
2029	Other chemical products n.e.c.	48.1	24.1	6.6	6.3	1.6	0.7
2030	Man-made fibres	0.2	0.2	0.1	0.1	-	0.1
2100	Pharmaceuticals,medicinal chemicals, etc.	550.9	620.1	243.1	271.2	49.3	62.1
221	Rubber products	239.1	219.5	68.5	73.9	32.1	15.9
2211	Rubber tyres and tubes	115.2	114.3	28.5	38.6	24.3	12.3
2219	Other rubber products	123.8	105.2	40.0	35.3	7.9	3.6
2220	Plastics products	636.5	590.2	161.6	163.8	43.4	38.1
2310	Glass and glass products	79.0	85.9	22.5	24.1	7.0	6.4
239	Non-metallic mineral products n.e.c.	607.8	431.4	202.7	142.9	90.4	43.3
2391	Refractory products	17.6	14.6	6.2	5.0	1.2	0.4
2392	Clay building materials	61.4	35.7	23.7	10.8	23.4	5.5
2393	Other porcelain and ceramic products	77.4	61.1	40.1	32.0	12.8	7.3
2394	Cement, lime and plaster	93.3	75.2	35.2	27.4	22.6	20.4
2395	Articles of concrete, cement and plaster	227.2	182.9	61.7	53.0	20.0	8.0
2396	Cutting, shaping and finishing of stone	12.0	11.0	3.6	3.2	0.3	0.3
2399	Other non-metallic mineral products n.e.c.	118.7	51.0	32.2	11.3	10.2	1.2
2410	Basic iron and steel	411.6	188.6	95.3	15.5	51.5	14.2
2420	Basic precious and other non-ferrous metals	290.1	…	58.2	…	11.5	…
243	Casting of metals	102.2	80.2	24.5	21.3	4.6	7.5
2431	Casting of iron and steel	23.5	17.2	6.2	5.0	0.8	5.6
2432	Casting of non-ferrous metals	78.7	63.0	18.3	16.2	3.8	1.9
251	Struct.metal products, tanks, reservoirs	471.4	332.6	147.8	108.3	17.9	15.2
2511	Structural metal products	405.9	283.2	126.4	91.4	14.9	12.8
2512	Tanks, reservoirs and containers of metal	54.6	42.9	17.4	13.5	2.8	2.1

continued

Hungary

ISIC	Industry	Output (billions of Hungarian Forints)					Value added at factor values (billions of Hungarian Forints)					Gross fixed capital formation (billions of Hungarian Forints)		
		Note	2006	2007	2008	2009	Note	2006	2007	2008	2009	Note	2008	2009
2513	Steam generators, excl. hot water boilers		...	...	10.9	6.5		...	...	4.0	3.4		0.2	0.3
2520	Weapons and ammunition		...	...	3.4	3.9		...	...	1.0	1.2		0.3	0.4
259	Other metal products;metal working services		...	...	526.6	426.0		...	...	174.3	145.4		33.0	21.8
2591	Forging,pressing,stamping,roll-forming of metal		...	...	52.4	34.6		...	...	14.4	8.3		4.8	1.5
2592	Treatment and coating of metals; machining		...	...	237.5	191.6		...	...	90.4	78.0		16.5	11.8
2593	Cutlery, hand tools and general hardware		...	...	81.7	70.9		...	...	27.9	26.2		4.3	3.3
2599	Other fabricated metal products n.e.c.		...	...	155.1	128.9		...	...	41.5	32.9		7.5	5.2
2610	Electronic components and boards		...	...	441.4	366.9		...	...	80.7	78.2		17.5	15.6
2620	Computers and peripheral equipment		...	...	555.5	399.9		...	...	71.6	53.9		5.4	3.3
2630	Communication equipment		...	...	1764.3	1486.0		...	...	204.5	154.9		36.3	11.5
2640	Consumer electronics		...	...	...	...		...	...	...	...			
265	Measuring,testing equipment; watches, etc.		...	...	63.4	55.4		...	...	23.6	22.0		3.1	2.6
2651	Measuring/testing/navigating equipment,etc.		...	...	63.0	55.1		...	...	23.5	21.9		3.1	2.6
2652	Watches and clocks		...	...	0.4	0.3		...	...	0.1	0.1		-	-
2660	Irradiation/electromedical equipment,etc.		...	...	3.9	9.7		...	...	1.8	4.0		0.1	0.3
2670	Optical instruments and photographic equipment		...	...	12.8	12.0		...	...	...	...			
2680	Magnetic and optical media		...	...	...	...		...	...	5.7	5.1		0.7	1.0
2710	Electric motors,generators,transformers,etc.		...	...	248.1	222.8		...	...	68.3	62.1		...	...
2720	Batteries and accumulators		...	...	107.4	72.2		...	...	19.7	5.0		12.5	15.2
273	Wiring and wiring devices		...	...	187.2	151.5		...	...	34.2	37.4		1.6	0.2
2731	Fibre optic cables		...	...	...	...		...	...	...	...		4.7	7.2
2732	Other electronic and electric wires and cables		...	...	130.5	104.8		...	...	18.8	19.1		...	...
2733	Wiring devices		...	...	...	...		...	...	...	...		2.0	1.3
2740	Electric lighting equipment		...	...	521.2	51.0		...	...	258.8	21.3		...	...
2750	Domestic appliances		...	...	235.0	211.2		...	...	52.9	51.0		16.4	1.8
2790	Other electrical equipment		...	...	88.8	70.3		...	...	25.1	21.1		6.9	6.9
281	General-purpose machinery		...	...	571.7	1077.7		...	...	180.6	515.8		3.4	2.4
2811	Engines/turbines,excl.aircraft,vehicle engines		...	...	59.4	621.7		...	...	23.9	375.6		30.6	32.9
2812	Fluid power equipment		...	...	19.2	16.0		...	...	6.2	5.6		2.5	12.0
2813	Other pumps, compressors, taps and valves		...	...	128.8	127.1		...	...	34.2	34.0		0.8	0.9
2814	Bearings, gears, gearing and driving elements		...	...	35.3	23.5		...	...	12.8	9.7		6.5	7.0
2815	Ovens, furnaces and furnace burners		...	...	5.1	4.1		...	...	1.8	1.3		3.3	0.5
2816	Lifting and handling equipment		...	...	71.0	45.2		...	...	22.7	16.3		0.3	0.2
2817	Office machinery, excl.computers,etc.		...	...	5.5	4.7		...	...	1.8	1.5		2.9	1.9
2818	Power-driven hand tools		...	...	58.4	54.9		...	...	14.9	11.2		0.1	0.3
2819	Other general-purpose machinery		...	...	189.2	180.4		...	...	62.3	60.7		2.8	2.3
282	Special-purpose machinery		...	...	321.3	241.6		...	...	99.8	80.9		11.5	7.8
2821	Agricultural and forestry machinery		...	...	126.3	97.4		...	...	32.5	25.1		12.5	10.7
2822	Metal-forming machinery and machine tools		...	...	34.1	17.7		...	...	14.6	7.7		4.0	4.0
2823	Machinery for metallurgy		...	...	5.4	0.8		...	...	2.1	0.3		1.6	1.0
2824	Mining, quarrying and construction machinery		...	...	37.9	21.0		...	...	8.5	7.6		1.8	1.2

Code		...			...			...		
2825	Food/beverage/tobacco processing machinery	...	49.2	48.9	...	17.3	18.8	...	2.4	1.8
2826	Textile/apparel/leather production machinery	...	4.9	2.7	...	1.7	1.0	...	0.3	0.1
2829	Other special-purpose machinery	...	63.5	53.0	...	23.1	20.5	...	2.3	2.5
2910	Motor vehicles	...	2097.3	1472.9	...	344.4	278.9	...	75.7	102.0
2920	Automobile bodies, trailers and semi-trailers	...	78.2	42.8	...	18.3	9.4	...	3.4	1.1
2930	Parts and accessories for motor vehicles	...	1888.4	1474.2	...	420.5	308.5	...	100.2	68.9
301	Building of ships and boats	...	2.4	2.1	...	0.7	0.7	...	0.1	0.1
3011	Building of ships and floating structures	...	0.4	0.8	...	0.1	0.1	...	-	-
3012	Building of pleasure and sporting boats	...	2.0	1.3	...	0.7	0.6	...	-	-
3020	Railway locomotives and rolling stock	...	110.8	70.9	...	44.0	27.1	...	7.7	5.0
3030	Air and spacecraft and related machinery	...	2.6	2.5	...	0.9	0.8	...	0.1	0.1
3040	Military fighting vehicles	...	-	-	...	-	-	...	-	-
309	Transport equipment n.e.c.	...	17.9	21.3	...	3.0	3.4	...	0.3	0.4
3091	Motorcycles	...	0.7	0.6	...	0.3	0.2	...	-	0.1
3092	Bicycles and invalid carriages	...	16.7	20.5	...	2.6	3.1	...	0.3	0.4
3099	Other transport equipment n.e.c.	...	0.6	0.2	...	0.2	0.1	...	-	-
3100	Furniture	...	199.9	155.8	...	53.7	49.2	...	11.7	6.4
321	Jewellery, bijouterie and related articles	...	5.9	6.5	...	2.6	2.6	...	0.3	0.2
3211	Jewellery and related articles	...	5.0	5.9	...	2.1	2.3	...	0.3	0.2
3212	Imitation jewellery and related articles	...	0.9	0.6	...	0.5	0.3	...	-	-
3220	Musical instruments	...	0.7	0.7	...	0.3	0.3	...	-	0.1
3230	Sports goods	...	28.6	22.5	...	7.9	5.7	...	0.5	0.3
3240	Games and toys	...	18.1	22.6	...	7.2	10.3	...	3.7	4.4
3250	Medical and dental instruments and supplies	...	95.2	97.3	...	35.4	39.5	...	8.6	13.2
3290	Other manufacturing n.e.c.	...	23.6	23.3	...	8.0	7.6	...	1.6	1.1
331	Repair of fabricated metal products/machinery	...	105.7	155.1	...	49.7	68.3	...	2.4	4.4
3311	Repair of fabricated metal products	...	0.3	1.8	...	0.1	0.9	...	-	-
3312	Repair of machinery	...	48.3	57.1	...	21.7	24.8	...	1.2	1.4
3313	Repair of electronic and optical equipment	...	4.4	5.7	...	1.9	2.8	...	0.1	0.1
3314	Repair of electrical equipment	...	9.6	9.4	...	4.2	3.4	...	0.2	0.3
3315	Repair of transport equip., excl. motor vehicles	...	41.5	80.1	...	21.2	36.1	...	0.8	2.6
3319	Repair of other equipment	...	1.6	1.0	...	0.7	0.3	...	0.1	-
3320	Installation of industrial machinery/equipment	...	77.8	63.1	...	30.4	26.5	...	2.8	2.7
C	Total manufacturing	...	21822.6	18335.9	...	4848.7	4330.5	...	1055.4	838.4

a/ 1101 includes 1102, 1103 and 1104.

Hungary

Index numbers of industrial production

(2005=100)

ISIC Revision 4		Note	1999	2000	2001	2002	2003	2004	2005	2006	2007	2008	2009	2010
ISIC	Industry													
10	Food products		...	105	104	107	106	106	100	100	94	89	89	88
11	Beverages		...	106	103	103	103	97	100	107	112	97	96	94
12	Tobacco products		...	418	476	423	373	187	100	109	127	126	50	63
13	Textiles		...	151	131	122	105	111	100	94	75	71	55	64
14	Wearing apparel		...	117	133	127	124	114	100	97	88	66	55	48
15	Leather and related products		...	152	152	145	112	95	100	135	203	210	148	142
16	Wood/wood products/cork,excl. furniture		...	85	88	95	98	104	100	98	95	110	85	100
17	Paper and paper products		...	91	92	97	101	98	100	107	113	105	102	129
18	Printing and reproduction of recorded media		...	85	93	89	94	91	100	102	102	101	92	99
19	Coke and refined petroleum products		...	87	85	87	81	90	100	98	103	100	90	92
20	Chemicals and chemical products		...	88	85	87	87	89	100	100	106	100	83	95
21	Pharmaceuticals,medicinal chemicals, etc.		...	81	78	77	94	101	100	113	108	116	116	123
22	Rubber and plastics products		...	70	80	88	91	95	100	118	132	133	105	125
23	Other non-metallic mineral products		...	84	88	90	92	89	100	107	132	138	104	94
24	Basic metals		...	90	87	91	98	105	100	115	108	103	54	65
25	Fabricated metal products, except machinery		...	81	89	80	92	100	100	108	122	130	90	96
26	Computer, electronic and optical products		...	46	41	44	66	84	100	117	134	131	112	137
27	Electrical equipment		...	67	101	111	81	95	100	106	109	104	82	72
28	Machinery and equipment n.e.c.		...	57	69	91	87	92	100	110	128	144	131	187
29	Motor vehicles, trailers and semi-trailers		...	67	70	72	82	87	100	122	141	141	100	119
30	Other transport equipment		...	50	59	74	89	105	100	97	123	167	101	107
31	Furniture		...	81	97	117	90	98	100	114	125	153	112	101
32	Other manufacturing		...	84	87	96	80	84	100	126	135	166	199	244
33	Repair and installation of machinery/equipment		...	72	91	80	87	106	100	106	116	149	178	144
C	Total manufacturing		...	73	76	79	85	93	100	111	120	119	98	109

India

Supplier of information:
Central Statistics Office, Ministry of Statistics and Programme Implementation, Industrial Statistics Wing, Kolkata.

Basic source of data:
Annual survey of registered establishments.

Major deviations from ISIC (Revision 4):
Data were originally classified according to the National Industrial Classification 2008, which was based on ISIC Revision 4.

Reference period:
From 1 April of the year indicated to 31 March of the following year. However, individual factory returns for an accounting year ending on any day during the reference period are accepted.

Scope:
Manufacturing units using power and employing 10 or more workers on any day of the reference period and those without power and employing 20 or more workers. Four provinces excluded from the survey are: Arunachal Pradesh, Lakshadweep, Mizoram and Sikkim.

Method of data collection:
The survey is carried out by mail and field contacts.

Type of enumeration:
Sample survey.

Adjusted for non-response:
Yes.

Concepts and definitions of variables:
Wages and salaries is compensation of employees.

Related national publications:
Annual Survey of Industries, published by the Central Statistics Office, Ministry of Statistics and Programme Implementation, Industrial Statistics Wing, Kolkata.

India

ISIC	Industry	Number of establishments (number) Note	2006	2007	2008	2009	Number of employees (thousands) Note	2006	2007	2008	2009	Wages and salaries paid to employees (billions of Indian Rupees) Note	2006	2007	2008	2009
1010	Processing/preserving of meat		...	...	90	85		...	...	14.5	15.0		...	...	1.3	1.4
1020	Processing/preserving of fish, etc.		...	...	352	359		...	...	33.0	37.5		...	...	1.9	2.4
1030	Processing/preserving of fruit,vegetables		...	...	709	832		...	...	44.7	54.4		...	...	3.0	3.7
1040	Vegetable and animal oils and fats		...	...	2429	2421		...	...	105.4	105.2		...	...	7.2	8.2
1050	Dairy products		...	...	1100	1112		...	...	102.0	109.7		...	...	13.2	16.5
106	Grain mill products,starches and starch products		...	...	14053	14067		...	...	335.5	338.8		...	...	15.5	17.5
1061	Grain mill products		...	...	13464	13397		...	...	318.8	318.8		...	...	14.3	15.9
1062	Starches and starch products		...	...	589	670		...	...	16.7	20.0		...	...	1.2	1.5
107	Other food products		...	...	6578	6681		...	...	759.8	768.0		...	...	49.5	56.3
1071	Bakery products		...	...	993	1056		...	...	60.2	61.0		...	...	5.0	5.1
1072	Sugar		...	...	733	744		...	...	261.7	259.8		...	...	25.7	28.7
1073	Cocoa, chocolate and sugar confectionery		...	...	456	466		...	...	28.0	29.3		...	...	2.6	2.7
1074	Macaroni, noodles, couscous, etc.		...	...	61	51		...	...	3.7	3.6		...	...	0.2	0.4
1075	Prepared meals and dishes		...	...	45	139		...	...	5.7	18.8		...	...	0.8	2.0
1079	Other food products n.e.c.		...	...	4290	4225		...	...	400.5	395.5		...	...	15.2	17.4
1080	Prepared animal feeds		...	...	547	606		...	...	28.2	30.7		...	...	2.3	2.9
1101	Distilling, rectifying and blending of spirits		...	...	291	296		...	...	43.3	42.5		...	...	4.1	4.7
1102	Wines		...	...	79	69		...	...	8.2	6.6		...	...	1.1	0.6
1103	Malt liquors and malt		...	...	96	117		...	...	24.2	27.3		...	...	2.7	3.2
1104	Soft drinks,mineral waters,other bottled waters		...	...	896	834		...	...	47.8	55.0		...	...	5.6	6.8
1200	Tobacco products		...	...	3280	3120		...	...	449.4	417.2		...	...	12.1	13.0
131	Spinning, weaving and finishing of textiles		...	...	9617	9874		...	...	1088.1	1107.7		...	...	76.9	86.3
1311	Preparation and spinning of textile fibres		...	...	4082	4432		...	...	611.2	671.3		...	...	40.2	48.8
1312	Weaving of textiles		...	...	2420	2313		...	...	226.0	188.7		...	...	18.2	17.4
1313	Finishing of textiles		...	...	3115	3129		...	...	251.0	247.7		...	...	18.5	20.1
139	Other textiles		...	...	3742	3470		...	...	305.6	271.6		...	...	21.2	21.4
1391	Knitted and crocheted fabrics		...	...	1310	736		...	...	135.6	67.6		...	...	8.6	5.6
1392	Made-up textile articles, except apparel		...	...	766	822		...	...	64.3	83.1		...	...	4.8	6.6
1393	Carpets and rugs		...	...	354	355		...	...	28.6	24.2		...	...	2.2	1.8
1394	Cordage, rope, twine and netting		...	...	603	638		...	...	35.8	47.5		...	...	2.2	3.1
1399	Other textiles n.e.c.		...	...	709	919		...	...	41.2	49.2		...	...	3.4	4.4
1410	Wearing apparel, except fur apparel		...	...	3959	3760		...	...	622.9	641.8		...	...	44.5	48.2
1420	Articles of fur		...	...	44	14		...	...	2.9	0.7		...	...	0.4	0.1
1430	Knitted and crocheted apparel		...	...	1758	2370		...	...	169.5	220.2		...	...	10.0	14.6
151	Leather;luggage,handbags,saddlery,harness;fur		...	...	1228	1514		...	...	69.9	86.8		...	...	5.0	6.4
1511	Tanning/dressing of leather; dressing of fur		...	...	789	987		...	...	33.2	38.9		...	...	2.5	2.7
1512	Luggage,handbags,etc.;saddlery/harness		...	...	439	527		...	...	36.8	47.9		...	...	2.5	3.7
1520	Footwear		...	...	1331	1307		...	...	179.8	167.1		...	...	10.3	13.2
1610	Sawmilling and planing of wood		...	...	1127	1100		...	...	9.1	8.5		...	...	0.5	0.4
162	Wood products, cork, straw, plaiting materials		...	...	1976	2275		...	...	57.5	65.4		...	...	4.1	4.6

Code	Description											
1621	Veneer sheets and wood-based panels	...	1355	1518	...	...	40.9	42.3	...	...	2.8	2.8
1622	Builders' carpentry and joinery	...	171	151	...	...	6.0	5.7	...	...	0.5	0.6
1623	Wooden containers	...	201	209	...	...	4.7	5.8	...	...	0.3	0.5
1629	Other wood products;articles of cork,straw	...	249	397	...	...	5.9	11.6	...	...	0.4	0.8
1701	Pulp, paper and paperboard	...	887	921	...	...	87.4	97.7	...	...	9.5	12.6
1702	Corrugated paper and paperboard	...	2859	2906	...	...	81.5	84.6	...	...	5.2	6.6
1709	Other articles of paper and paperboard	...	891	771	...	...	60.3	44.4	...	...	6.2	5.0
181	Printing and service activities related to printing	...	3272	3160	...	...	127.2	130.4	...	...	15.5	17.5
1811	Printing	...	2790	2776	...	...	113.1	122.0	...	...	14.2	16.5
1812	Service activities related to printing	...	482	384	...	...	14.1	8.4	...	...	1.3	1.0
1820	Reproduction of recorded media	...	18	14	...	...	0.7	2.2	...	...	0.1	0.6
1910	Coke oven products	...	515	550	...	...	39.6	29.8	...	...	4.4	5.5
1920	Refined petroleum products	...	438	617	...	...	73.0	92.5	...	...	25.3	28.9
201	Basic chemicals,fertilizers, etc.	...	3229	3220	...	...	231.1	232.4	...	...	51.7	53.6
2011	Basic chemicals	...	2316	2332	...	...	132.8	130.8	...	...	19.5	22.3
2012	Fertilizers and nitrogen compounds	...	542	573	...	...	66.2	65.8	...	...	23.4	20.9
2013	Plastics and synthetic rubber in primary forms	...	371	315	...	...	32.1	35.9	...	...	8.7	10.4
202	Other chemical products	...	5137	5125	...	...	321.6	334.2	...	...	41.6	40.1
2021	Pesticides and other agrochemical products	...	498	459	...	...	43.3	48.1	...	...	7.1	8.2
2022	Paints,varnishes;printing ink and mastics	...	911	901	...	...	36.3	43.2	...	...	5.9	7.8
2023	Soap,cleaning and cosmetic preparations	...	1246	1323	...	...	89.8	98.2	...	...	11.3	10.9
2029	Other chemical products n.e.c.	...	2482	2442	...	...	152.3	144.7	...	...	17.2	13.2
2030	Man-made fibres	...	90	72	...	...	25.2	19.3	...	...	5.4	3.9
2100	Pharmaceuticals,medicinal chemicals, etc.	...	3420	3477	...	...	378.4	414.0	...	...	61.2	76.6
221	Rubber products	...	1977	2084	...	...	148.7	172.5	...	...	17.9	26.4
2211	Rubber tyres and tubes	...	555	529	...	...	79.5	90.5	...	...	11.7	17.6
2219	Other rubber products	...	1422	1555	...	...	69.2	82.0	...	...	6.2	8.8
2220	Plastics products	...	6357	6260	...	...	279.1	302.1	...	...	23.3	32.0
2310	Glass and glass products	...	622	596	...	...	58.3	55.9	...	...	6.3	6.1
239	Non-metallic mineral products n.e.c.	...	15965	16874	...	...	710.8	733.2	...	...	54.4	62.8
2391	Refractory products	...	820	904	...	...	56.2	58.4	...	...	5.1	6.9
2392	Clay building materials	...	5888	6237	...	...	267.0	294.3	...	...	7.6	9.2
2393	Other porcelain and ceramic products	...	629	698	...	...	52.1	52.8	...	...	4.4	5.7
2394	Cement, lime and plaster	...	970	984	...	...	126.6	118.3	...	...	21.4	23.6
2395	Articles of concrete, cement and plaster	...	1812	1928	...	...	72.2	81.4	...	...	5.5	7.4
2396	Cutting, shaping and finishing of stone	...	5187	5416	...	...	101.2	93.2	...	...	6.0	5.9
2399	Other non-metallic mineral products n.e.c.	...	659	707	...	...	35.5	34.8	...	...	4.4	4.1
2410	Basic iron and steel	...	4167	4575	...	...	599.7	599.0	...	...	111.6	100.7
2420	Basic precious and other non-ferrous metals	...	1144	1243	...	...	86.1	87.0	...	...	20.1	20.2
243	Casting of metals	...	3345	3102	...	...	209.6	205.5	...	...	21.6	22.7
2431	Casting of iron and steel	...	2923	2690	...	...	186.3	183.8	...	...	19.4	20.2
2432	Casting of non-ferrous metals	...	422	412	...	...	23.3	21.7	...	...	2.2	2.4
251	Struct.metal products, tanks, reservoirs	...	2994	3046	...	...	221.8	239.9	...	...	32.5	33.9
2511	Structural metal products	...	1811	1822	...	...	137.6	131.6	...	...	15.4	14.8
2512	Tanks, reservoirs and containers of metal	...	826	927	...	...	35.9	55.3	...	...	3.9	6.7

continued

India

		Number of establishments (number)					Number of employees (thousands)					Wages and salaries paid to employees (billions of Indian Rupees)				
ISIC	Industry	Note	2006	2007	2008	2009	Note	2006	2007	2008	2009	Note	2006	2007	2008	2009
2513	Steam generators, excl. hot water boilers		...	...	357	297		...	...	48.2	53.0		...	...	13.2	12.4
2520	Weapons and ammunition		...	...	40	75		...	...	2.1	3.8		...	...	0.2	0.3
259	Other metal products;metal working services		...	...	6739	7733		...	...	279.5	311.2		...	...	26.0	33.3
2591	Forging,pressing,stamping,roll-forming of metal		...	...	699	917		...	...	49.2	53.0		...	...	5.2	6.0
2592	Treatment and coating of metals; machining		...	...	1087	1404		...	...	31.7	32.9		...	...	2.8	3.5
2593	Cutlery, hand tools and general hardware		...	...	1083	1360		...	...	53.3	60.5		...	...	6.4	8.0
2599	Other fabricated metal products n.e.c.		...	...	3870	4052		...	...	145.3	164.7		...	...	11.6	15.8
2610	Electronic components and boards		...	...	758	702		...	...	70.3	86.1		...	...	12.4	14.9
2620	Computers and peripheral equipment		...	...	158	128		...	...	19.7	21.9		...	...	3.7	5.4
2630	Communication equipment		...	...	251	212		...	...	38.3	85.5		...	...	13.5	19.9
2640	Consumer electronics		...	...	245	234		...	...	26.9	30.7		...	...	4.5	6.1
265	Measuring,testing equipment; watches, etc.		...	...	542	467		...	...	45.6	...		...	...	8.3	9.5
2651	Measuring/testing/navigating equipment,etc.		...	...	413	342		...	...	35.6	...		...	...	7.2	7.0
2652	Watches and clocks		...	...	129	125		...	...	10.0	10.3		...	...	1.1	2.6
2660	Irradiation/electromedical equipment,etc.		...	...	69	65		...	...	3.4	5.2		...	...	0.5	1.6
2670	Optical instruments and photographic equipment		...	...	61	64		...	...	3.5	2.6		...	...	0.4	0.4
2680	Magnetic and optical media		...	...	20	5		...	...	1.2	1.8		...	...	0.2	0.2
2710	Electric motors,generators,transformers,etc.		...	...	2078	2245		...	...	164.2	181.7		...	...	29.8	35.5
2720	Batteries and accumulators		...	...	307	337		...	...	30.0	50.2		...	...	4.4	7.8
273	Wiring and wiring devices		...	...	1012	1054		...	...	67.7	87.8		...	...	9.0	11.5
2731	Fibre optic cables		...	...	115	112		...	...	9.7	17.2		...	...	1.4	3.0
2732	Other electronic and electric wires and cables		...	...	585	579		...	...	37.0	42.5		...	...	4.2	4.8
2733	Wiring devices		...	...	312	363		...	...	21.0	28.1		...	...	3.4	3.8
2740	Electric lighting equipment		...	...	466	383		...	...	40.8	38.6		...	...	3.9	4.5
2750	Domestic appliances		...	...	658	633		...	...	37.2	43.5		...	...	4.3	6.0
2790	Other electrical equipment		...	...	730	835		...	...	40.0	40.0		...	...	4.3	5.2
281	General-purpose machinery		...	...	4473	4481		...	...	448.5	313.3		...	...	63.6	67.4
2811	Engines/turbines,excl.aircraft,vehicle engines		...	...	402	456		...	...	...	57.7		...	...	8.9	24.7
2812	Fluid power equipment		...	...	433	447		...	...	29.9	29.4		...	...	5.1	4.3
2813	Other pumps, compressors, taps and valves		...	...	869	842		...	...	60.5	54.9		...	...	10.1	10.4
2814	Bearings, gears, gearing and driving elements		...	...	610	622		...	...	53.9	51.2		...	...	8.3	8.9
2815	Ovens, furnaces and furnace burners		...	...	98	120		...	...	6.4	8.5		...	...	1.3	1.5
2816	Lifting and handling equipment		...	...	310	379		...	...	21.1	29.5		...	...	4.3	5.5
2817	Office machinery, excl.computers, etc.		...	...	25	54		...	...	1.0	1.2		...	...	0.2	0.2
2818	Power-driven hand tools		...	...	81	62		...	...	3.0	1.7		...	...	0.4	0.2
2819	Other general-purpose machinery		...	...	1645	1499		...	...	113.8	79.0		...	...	25.0	11.8
282	Special-purpose machinery		...	...	4443	4529		...	...	262.6	245.6		...	...	48.4	50.7
2821	Agricultural and forestry machinery		...	...	735	797		...	...	51.6	56.7		...	...	10.0	11.0
2822	Metal-forming machinery and machine tools		...	...	718	801		...	...	34.3	31.1		...	...	10.0	11.0
2823	Machinery for metallurgy		...	...	148	112		...	...	7.7	5.3		...	...	5.5	6.9
2824	Mining, quarrying and construction machinery		...	...	434	417		...	...	34.6	35.7		...	...	7.2	7.5

Code	Description									
2825	Food/beverage/tobacco processing machinery	⋮	486	473	⋮	27.6	25.2	⋮	4.7	3.8
2826	Textile/apparel/leather production machinery	⋮	726	712	⋮	32.2	28.3	⋮	4.2	3.9
2829	Other special-purpose machinery	⋮	1196	1217	⋮	74.5	63.4	⋮	16.0	16.7
2910	Motor vehicles	⋮	154	136	⋮	112.7	113.0	⋮	32.9	37.1
2920	Automobile bodies, trailers and semi-trailers	⋮	481	438	⋮	39.4	43.3	⋮	3.4	4.1
2930	Parts and accessories for motor vehicles	⋮	3026	3612	⋮	356.5	462.2	⋮	44.0	64.5
301	Building of ships and boats	⋮	83	80	⋮	26.1	28.0	⋮	4.6	7.3
3011	Building of ships and floating structures	⋮	73	75	⋮	22.6	27.9	⋮	4.0	7.3
3012	Building of pleasure and sporting boats	⋮	10	5	⋮	3.5	0.1	⋮	0.6	-
3020	Railway locomotives and rolling stock	⋮	298	297	⋮	26.6	28.0	⋮	3.1	4.5
3030	Air and spacecraft and related machinery	⋮	54	57	⋮	6.2	3.2	⋮	1.6	0.6
3040	Military fighting vehicles	⋮	40	35	⋮	1.2	1.0	⋮	0.1	0.1
309	Transport equipment n.e.c.	⋮	1376	1335	⋮	158.3	161.2	⋮	19.7	24.0
3091	Motorcycles	⋮	747	684	⋮	125.7	129.9	⋮	17.1	20.9
3092	Bicycles and invalid carriages	⋮	591	607	⋮	29.3	29.6	⋮	2.2	2.9
3099	Other transport equipment n.e.c.	⋮	38	44	⋮	3.3	1.7	⋮	0.4	0.2
3100	Furniture	⋮	948	1071	⋮	40.0	50.0	⋮	5.3	8.2
321	Jewellery, bijouterie and related articles	⋮	1037	825	⋮	135.5	118.4	⋮	14.7	13.7
3211	Jewellery and related articles	⋮	975	761	⋮	133.0	115.1	⋮	14.5	13.5
3212	Imitation jewellery and related articles	⋮	62	64	⋮	2.6	3.3	⋮	0.2	0.2
3220	Musical instruments	⋮	21	21	⋮	0.5	1.0	⋮	-	0.2
3230	Sports goods	⋮	115	142	⋮	7.6	7.2	⋮	0.5	0.5
3240	Games and toys	⋮	131	91	⋮	4.0	2.9	⋮	0.3	0.2
3250	Medical and dental instruments and supplies	⋮	349	284	⋮	26.2	25.5	⋮	3.7	3.3
3290	Other manufacturing n.e.c.	⋮	761	672	⋮	51.0	47.9	⋮	3.7	4.0
331	Repair of fabricated metal products/machinery	⋮	689	444	⋮	25.0	26.8	⋮	5.0	5.5
3311	Repair of fabricated metal products	⋮	121	88	⋮	2.7	5.2	⋮	0.2	0.8
3312	Repair of machinery	⋮	238	156	⋮	11.4	7.4	⋮	2.5	2.1
3313	Repair of electronic and optical equipment	⋮	14	20	⋮	0.3	0.3	⋮	0.1	-
3314	Repair of electrical equipment	⋮	134	39	⋮	3.5	1.1	⋮	0.5	0.2
3315	Repair of transport equip., excl. motor vehicles	⋮	160	104	⋮	6.1	11.0	⋮	1.5	2.1
3319	Repair of other equipment	⋮	22	37	⋮	0.9	1.8	⋮	0.2	0.2
3320	Installation of industrial machinery/equipment	⋮	110	50	⋮	8.5	7.0	⋮	1.4	1.2
C	Total manufacturing	⋮	145332	148668	⋮	10847.9	11307.8	⋮	1187.8	1347.2

India

			Output at producers' prices (billions of Indian Rupees)					Value added at producers' prices (billions of Indian Rupees)					Gross fixed capital formation (billions of Indian Rupees)	
ISIC	Industry	Note	2006	2007	2008	2009	Note	2006	2007	2008	2009	Note	2008	2009
1010	Processing/preserving of meat		...	...	66.1	67.7		...	...	8.5	9.4		1.3	1.4
1020	Processing/preserving of fish, etc.		...	...	72.9	89.0		...	...	7.4	9.1		0.8	1.6
1030	Processing/preserving of fruit,vegetables		...	...	57.2	66.1				6.7	11.2		6.1	6.2
1040	Vegetable and animal oils and fats				1188.6	1009.4				64.9	55.6		18.6	27.7
1050	Dairy products				426.5	518.5				41.3	49.8		16.7	31.3
106	Grain mill products,starches and starch products				910.2	1040.1				86.5	87.2		25.2	25.2
1061	Grain mill products				880.3	991.3				82.3	79.8		23.2	22.3
1062	Starches and starch products				29.9	48.7				4.1	7.4		2.0	2.9
107	Other food products				897.0	1210.1				147.7	197.2		52.9	61.0
1071	Bakery products				119.5	124.0				22.7	23.8		5.2	4.9
1072	Sugar		...		386.4	600.9		...		42.7	75.3		30.5	37.2
1073	Cocoa, chocolate and sugar confectionery				56.2	58.0				15.3	16.5		2.9	2.7
1074	Macaroni, noodles, couscous, etc.				6.3	12.6				1.4	3.7		1.7	1.9
1075	Prepared meals and dishes				4.5	29.9				1.7	9.1		0.4	2.9
1079	Other food products n.e.c.				324.1	384.8				63.9	68.8		12.3	11.5
1080	Prepared animal feeds				103.9	130.1				7.7	12.9		1.4	1.5
1101	Distilling, rectifying and blending of spirits				123.2	122.9				34.3	30.9		10.0	8.7
1102	Wines				25.9	22.3				9.1	10.6		2.1	1.4
1103	Malt liquors and malt				65.5	82.0				15.3	20.5		6.6	4.6
1104	Soft drinks,mineral waters,other bottled waters		...		116.6	108.7		...		45.7	24.3		14.7	19.5
1200	Tobacco products				201.9	221.7				93.2	74.9		4.7	7.0
131	Spinning, weaving and finishing of textiles				1358.9	1620.8				213.7	288.7		104.7	125.8
1311	Preparation and spinning of textile fibres				821.0	1062.2				118.9	187.3		63.4	84.5
1312	Weaving of textiles				289.9	294.4				53.3	56.6		22.7	12.3
1313	Finishing of textiles				248.1	264.3				41.5	44.8		18.6	29.0
139	Other textiles				358.1	356.3				63.4	62.5		21.3	17.9
1391	Knitted and crocheted fabrics				141.3	87.9				26.0	15.2		9.3	3.0
1392	Made-up textile articles, except apparel				99.9	124.8				14.5	20.8		5.1	7.4
1393	Carpets and rugs		...		36.7	39.9		...		5.0	5.0		1.8	1.5
1394	Cordage, rope, twine and netting				26.7	34.9				8.2	7.8		1.9	1.9
1399	Other textiles n.e.c.				53.4	68.7				9.7	13.7		3.2	4.1
1410	Wearing apparel, except fur apparel				400.1	453.2				98.3	99.2		18.7	13.1
1420	Articles of fur				2.3	1.2				0.7	0.5		0.1	0.6
1430	Knitted and crocheted apparel				135.2	182.7				23.7	35.1		5.5	7.1
151	Leather;luggage,handbags,saddlery,harness;fur				94.1	113.3				13.4	18.6		3.9	5.4
1511	Tanning/dressing of leather; dressing of fur				58.2	67.7				7.3	9.5		2.3	3.8
1512	Luggage,handbags,etc.;saddlery/harness				36.0	45.6				6.0	9.1		1.6	1.6
1520	Footwear		...		151.7	192.3		...		26.3	34.5		10.0	8.8
1610	Sawmilling and planing of wood				13.9	10.9				0.9	0.8		0.4	0.1
162	Wood products, cork, straw, plaiting materials				71.0	95.2				9.2	14.5		4.8	6.2

Code	Description						
1621	Veneer sheets and wood-based panels	54.8	66.6	6.7	11.6	3.6	5.2
1622	Builders' carpentry and joinery	5.6	7.9	1.3	1.7	0.4	0.3
1623	Wooden containers	4.9	6.2	-0.5	-1.6	0.1	0.4
1629	Other wood products;articles of cork,straw	5.7	14.5	1.8	2.8	0.7	0.4
1701	Pulp, paper and paperboard	182.7	218.7	39.3	30.9	29.1	45.8
1702	Corrugated paper and paperboard	92.5	129.8	17.4	24.5	6.8	9.1
1709	Other articles of paper and paperboard	135.5	94.5	28.8	20.6	29.0	13.0
181	Printing and service activities related to printing	193.0	203.8	45.6	57.8	22.3	13.0
1811	Printing	179.5	189.5	43.0	54.8	20.5	12.3
1812	Service activities related to printing	13.5	14.3	2.6	3.0	1.8	0.7
1820	Reproduction of recorded media	2.0	9.2	0.8	3.6	0.3	0.5
1910	Coke oven products	151.5	117.3	30.6	22.3	6.6	10.6
1920	Refined petroleum products	4657.4	5278.2	734.1	681.3	108.8	273.7
201	Basic chemicals,fertilizers, etc.	1837.5	1702.9	316.9	367.3	158.1	79.1
2011	Basic chemicals	527.1	619.4	105.0	148.4	68.1	38.6
2012	Fertilizers and nitrogen compounds	832.4	600.5	116.0	85.8	23.2	23.4
2013	Plastics and synthetic rubber in primary forms	478.0	483.0	95.9	133.1	66.8	17.1
202	Other chemical products	959.6	1005.8	228.9	260.1	63.6	50.0
2021	Pesticides and other agrochemical products	157.6	219.4	34.8	58.8	9.2	10.3
2022	Paints,varnishes;printing ink and mastics	156.6	197.5	33.9	44.0	5.1	5.9
2023	Soap,cleaning and cosmetic preparations	347.4	292.2	98.9	79.4	13.0	14.9
2029	Other chemical products n.e.c.	298.0	296.7	61.3	77.9	36.3	19.0
2030	Man-made fibres	96.8	82.4	12.2	16.7	6.9	3.2
2100	Pharmaceuticals,medicinal chemicals, etc.	1020.0	1116.3	350.8	383.1	86.9	87.3
221	Rubber products	376.9	455.8	87.4	103.1	29.5	46.1
2211	Rubber tyres and tubes	283.3	326.4	70.4	79.6	20.2	39.6
2219	Other rubber products	93.5	129.5	16.9	23.5	9.4	6.5
2220	Plastics products	616.7	803.3	121.9	145.3	50.5	50.9
2310	Glass and glass products	92.8	89.6	21.4	24.7	20.9	9.6
239	Non-metallic mineral products n.e.c.	1121.3	1187.6	392.1	436.4	188.3	164.8
2391	Refractory products	73.7	108.7	18.9	34.2	5.6	5.7
2392	Clay building materials	53.3	48.5	17.2	18.6	4.2	4.7
2393	Other porcelain and ceramic products	68.2	79.1	16.7	20.3	9.1	7.0
2394	Cement, lime and plaster	651.0	661.8	267.3	281.4	148.8	132.2
2395	Articles of concrete, cement and plaster	87.7	131.4	16.4	37.7	6.0	6.7
2396	Cutting, shaping and finishing of stone	112.5	92.5	34.1	23.4	13.7	4.1
2399	Other non-metallic mineral products n.e.c.	74.7	65.6	21.6	20.7	0.9	4.4
2410	Basic iron and steel	3608.3	3969.5	625.4	720.7	451.0	560.1
2420	Basic precious and other non-ferrous metals	728.4	663.5	146.0	99.4	38.6	125.1
243	Casting of metals	519.0	447.6	77.5	84.0	38.6	41.4
2431	Casting of iron and steel	483.3	410.4	72.0	75.5	33.5	38.7
2432	Casting of non-ferrous metals	35.7	37.2	5.5	8.5	5.1	2.7
251	Struct.metal products, tanks, reservoirs	552.0	607.7	111.2	148.3	33.6	26.8
2511	Structural metal products	351.7	333.5	55.0	70.0	19.2	17.8
2512	Tanks, reservoirs and containers of metal	67.0	102.9	11.7	18.8	6.8	3.6

continued

India

- 448 -

ISIC	Industry	Output at producers' prices (billions of Indian Rupees)					Value added at producers' prices (billions of Indian Rupees)					Gross fixed capital formation (billions of Indian Rupees)		
		Note	2006	2007	2008	2009	Note	2006	2007	2008	2009	Note	2008	2009
2513	Steam generators, excl. hot water boilers		...	...	133.2	171.3		...	...	44.5	59.5		7.7	5.4
2520	Weapons and ammunition		...	...	2.9	5.7		...	...	0.7	1.7		0.3	0.4
259	Other metal products;metal working services		...	...	446.1	474.3		...	...	85.9	105.9		42.9	25.5
2591	Forging,pressing,stamping,roll-forming of metal		...	...	126.0	94.6		...	...	23.1	15.3		20.0	4.2
2592	Treatment and coating of metals; machining		...	...	37.8	44.2		...	...	8.2	10.7		2.8	2.2
2593	Cutlery, hand tools and general hardware		...	...	71.1	98.7		...	...	16.6	34.6		4.6	4.2
2599	Other fabricated metal products n.e.c.		...	...	211.1	236.8		...	...	38.1	45.3		15.5	14.9
2610	Electronic components and boards		...	...	150.7	207.3		...	...	34.8	51.6		9.6	8.9
2620	Computers and peripheral equipment		...	...	112.0	134.6		...	...	19.1	25.5		2.8	2.3
2630	Communication equipment		...	...	232.5	254.1		...	...	70.3	45.7		12.0	13.8
2640	Consumer electronics		...	...	224.5	284.5		...	...	29.1	42.4		8.0	14.2
265	Measuring,testing equipment; watches, etc.		...	...	83.8	90.6		...	...	27.4	31.8		4.3	3.3
2651	Measuring/testing/navigating equipment,etc.		...	...	71.5	61.8		...	...	21.3	20.9		4.1	2.9
2652	Watches and clocks		...	...	12.2	28.7		...	...	6.1	10.9		0.2	0.4
2660	Irradiation/electromedical equipment,etc.		...	...	9.3	22.1		...	...	2.2	7.4		0.7	1.6
2670	Optical instruments and photographic equipment		...	...	4.6	3.6		...	...	1.8	1.4		0.1	0.2
2680	Magnetic and optical media		...	...	2.1	11.1		...	...	0.5	6.5		-	0.6
2710	Electric motors,generators,transformers,etc.		...	...	648.1	657.9		...	...	135.4	142.7		26.1	23.0
2720	Batteries and accumulators		...	...	99.5	159.7		...	...	23.3	45.3		14.1	10.5
273	Wiring and wiring devices		...	...	283.9	358.7		...	...	41.3	58.8		15.9	12.0
2731	Fibre optic cables		...	...	34.6	72.5		...	...	3.0	8.2		3.6	2.1
2732	Other electronic and electric wires and cables		...	...	194.9	209.5		...	...	21.3	27.4		8.7	6.8
2733	Wiring devices		...	...	54.4	76.7		...	...	16.9	23.2		3.5	3.2
2740	Electric lighting equipment		...	...	65.6	67.0		...	...	13.5	15.3		4.3	5.4
2750	Domestic appliances		...	...	110.8	193.2		...	...	25.1	37.5		9.5	7.1
2790	Other electrical equipment		...	...	102.0	89.1		...	...	21.2	14.6		4.3	5.1
281	General-purpose machinery		...	...	910.1	961.2		...	...	266.3	266.2		44.4	45.7
2811	Engines/turbines,excl.aircraft,vehicle engines		...	...	142.8	320.1		...	...	35.0	110.0		10.1	14.9
2812	Fluid power equipment		...	...	77.1	73.7		...	...	24.1	17.4		5.2	3.6
2813	Other pumps, compressors, taps and valves		...	...	148.0	136.5		...	...	32.6	37.6		5.9	4.7
2814	Bearings, gears, gearing and driving elements		...	...	114.1	119.4		...	...	27.2	35.0		8.5	8.9
2815	Ovens, furnaces and furnace burners		...	...	21.1	27.6		...	...	5.7	6.0		1.0	2.0
2816	Lifting and handling equipment		...	...	75.3	97.5		...	...	8.9	19.7		2.7	3.4
2817	Office machinery, excl.computers,etc.		...	...	2.4	2.3		...	...	0.6	0.5		0.2	0.5
2818	Power-driven hand tools		...	...	5.7	1.7		...	...	1.1	0.5		0.2	0.1
2819	Other general-purpose machinery		...	...	323.5	182.3		...	...	131.0	39.5		10.5	8.0
282	Special-purpose machinery		...	...	791.7	737.3		...	...	157.1	176.3		42.0	40.0
2821	Agricultural and forestry machinery		...	...	198.3	245.3		...	...	35.1	51.6		7.5	10.8
2822	Metal-forming machinery and machine tools		...	...	59.2	44.9		...	...	14.1	9.9		6.0	5.6
2823	Machinery for metallurgy		...	...	19.4	10.9		...	...	2.0	2.3		2.3	2.4
2824	Mining, quarrying and construction machinery		...	...	119.5	130.4		...	...	27.4	31.6		5.6	4.8

Code	Description						
2825	Food/beverage/tobacco processing machinery	56.9	76.4	12.4	19.6	3.1	2.0
2826	Textile/apparel/leather production machinery	54.2	43.8	13.9	10.7	2.5	2.1
2829	Other special-purpose machinery	194.7	275.2	54.7	48.3	15.0	12.3
2910	Motor vehicles	1249.1	954.2	185.9	130.6	127.4	75.6
2920	Automobile bodies, trailers and semi-trailers	49.6	45.3	10.2	10.0	10.5	3.5
2930	Parts and accessories for motor vehicles	1053.5	750.1	235.2	137.9	71.5	83.4
301	Building of ships and boats	85.6	83.9	34.1	30.3	20.0	30.6
3011	Building of ships and floating structures	85.5	75.4	34.1	27.7	19.8	30.6
3012	Building of pleasure and sporting boats	0.1	8.5	-	2.6	0.2	-
3020	Railway locomotives and rolling stock	77.6	53.6	23.2	11.1	3.9	3.7
3030	Air and spacecraft and related machinery	3.2	11.5	1.3	3.8	2.9	0.8
3040	Military fighting vehicles	0.4	0.4	0.1	0.1	0.1	-
309	Transport equipment n.e.c.	643.2	520.8	130.6	96.2	17.8	16.1
3091	Motorcycles	569.2	454.4	121.6	88.6	16.8	14.4
3092	Bicycles and invalid carriages	69.9	62.0	8.3	7.0	1.0	1.5
3099	Other transport equipment n.e.c.	4.1	4.4	0.6	0.7	0.1	0.1
3100	Furniture	92.2	60.9	18.0	12.3	2.4	4.6
321	Jewellery, bijouterie and related articles	1538.5	572.4	51.3	28.4	3.7	3.4
3211	Jewellery and related articles	1535.8	571.0	50.6	27.9	3.6	3.3
3212	Imitation jewellery and related articles	2.7	1.4	0.7	0.5	0.1	0.1
3220	Musical instruments	1.4	0.4	0.4	0.1	-	-
3230	Sports goods	7.5	7.6	1.6	1.6	0.3	0.4
3240	Games and toys	3.6	4.9	1.2	0.9	0.3	0.5
3250	Medical and dental instruments and supplies	36.0	36.8	12.7	14.2	2.5	2.6
3290	Other manufacturing n.e.c.	56.1	73.0	14.0	14.4	4.2	3.3
331	Repair of fabricated metal products/machinery	75.5	65.6	14.9	19.5	1.6	1.8
3311	Repair of fabricated metal products	18.2	2.8	4.1	0.6	-	0.1
3312	Repair of machinery	12.6	11.1	5.0	4.2	0.3	0.6
3313	Repair of electronic and optical equipment	0.4	0.4	0.1	0.1	-	-
3314	Repair of electrical equipment	2.1	10.7	0.4	1.4	0.9	0.9
3315	Repair of transport equip., excl. motor vehicles	40.3	40.0	5.0	13.0	-	0.1
3319	Repair of other equipment	1.9	0.6	0.4	0.3		
3320	Installation of industrial machinery/equipment	14.4	18.5	3.0	4.3	1.0	1.6
C	Total manufacturing	35597.4	31325.2	6592.6	5876.6	2211.2	2443.6

India

Index numbers of industrial production

ISIC Revision 3			(2005=100)									
ISIC	Industry	Note	1999	2000	2001	2002	2003	2004	2005	2006	2007	2008	2009	2010
15	Food and beverages		63	69	72	83	86	88	100	116	130	120	118	126
16	Tobacco products		149	136	110	99	90	99	100	102	97	102	101	103
17	Textiles		78	81	82	85	84	92	100	108	115	111	118	125
18	Wearing apparel, fur		49	59	50	43	55	88	100	120	131	118	120	125
19	Leather, leather products and footwear		94	104	110	107	102	110	100	114	121	115	116	126
20	Wood products (excl. furniture)		127	131	116	96	102	94	100	118	139	145	150	147
21	Paper and paper products		74	67	69	74	85	94	100	104	106	111	114	124
22	Printing and publishing		...	...	...	...	...	...	...	...	...	...	...	...
23	Coke,refined petroleum products,nuclear fuel		71	80	82	86	91	99	100	112	119	123	121	121
24	Chemicals and chemical products		69	74	76	78	85	99	100	109	117	114	120	122
25	Rubber and plastics products		58	62	79	90	92	89	100	107	121	127	149	165
26	Non-metallic mineral products		76	75	76	80	83	93	100	111	121	125	135	140
27	Basic metals		65	66	69	75	82	87	100	115	135	138	140	153
28	Fabricated metal products		65	77	70	72	72	90	100	120	129	129	143	164
29	Machinery and equipment n.e.c.		55	55	49	56	62	79	100	120	147	136	157	203
30	Office, accounting and computing machinery		30	22	20	35	48	69	100	107	113	102	106	101
31	Electrical machinery and apparatus		39	41	43	50	64	86	100	113	319	454	393	404
32	Radio,television and communication equipment		69	97	124	65	67	81	100	255	492	592	659	743
33	Medical, precision and optical instruments		68	77	87	88	93	105	100	110	117	126	106	113
34	Motor vehicles, trailers, semi-trailers		53	48	49	59	72	91	100	125	137	125	163	212
35	Other transport equipment		55	57	62	70	79	87	100	115	112	116	148	183
36	Furniture; manufacturing n.e.c.		...	...	...	...	...	...	...	...	...	...	...	...
37	Recycling		...	...	...	...	...	...	...	...	...	...	...	...
D	Total manufacturing		65	68	70	75	80	91	100	115	136	139	146	159

Iran (Islamic Republic of)

Supplier of information:
Statistical Centre of Iran, Teheran.

Basic source of data:
Census; sample survey.

Major deviations from ISIC (Revision 3):
None reported.

Reference period:
Fiscal year.

Scope:
Establishments with 10 or more persons engaged.

Method of data collection:
Direct interview in the field.

Type of enumeration:
Complete enumeration.

Adjusted for non-response:
Yes.

Concepts and definitions of variables:
Wages and salaries includes employers' contributions paid to social security, pension and insurance schemes as well as the benefits received by employees under these schemes and severance and termination pay.

Related national publications:
Survey results of manufacturing establishments with 10 to 49 workers; Survey results of manufacturing establishments with 50 workers and more, both published by the Statistical Centre of Iran, Teheran.

Iran (Islamic Republic of)

ISIC	Industry	Number of establishments (number)					Number of employees (number)					Wages and salaries paid to employees (billions of Iranian Rials)				
		Note	2006	2007	2008	2009	Note	2006	2007	2008	2009	Note	2006	2007	2008	2009
151	Processed meat,fish,fruit,vegetables,fats		722	825	887	848		46912	52463	58803	57017		1812	2180	3056	3346
1511	Processing/preserving of meat		315	344	375	362		16965	19813	22574	23017		565	731	1017	1228
1512	Processing/preserving of fish		51	67	84	80		3998	4908	5402	4897		184	185	290	270
1513	Processing/preserving of fruit & vegetables		308	358	362	339		15654	17250	17987	17651		485	612	793	924
1514	Vegetable and animal oils and fats		48	56	66	67		10295	10492	12840	11412		578	653	956	924
1520	Dairy products		233	259	323	317		20446	23541	29925	30996		899	1145	1761	2196
153	Grain mill products; starches; animal feeds		445	448	484	483		14645	14911	15927	15396		548	638	802	938
1531	Grain mill products		326	318	338	335		10090	10167	10846	10444		354	425	531	615
1532	Starches and starch products		26	30	30	28		1248	1369	1410	1253		48	60	69	91
1533	Prepared animal feeds		93	100	116	120		3307	3375	3671	3699		146	153	201	232
154	Other food products		1208	1124	1192	1115		69239	65528	73309	68266		2750	2991	3837	4228
1541	Bakery products		478	438	456	431		19588	18834	24580	24608		689	803	1192	1465
1542	Sugar		73	71	89	81		23196	18639	19009	15925		1173	1119	1283	1204
1543	Cocoa, chocolate and sugar confectionery		73	76	89	94		6225	7179	6345	5729		198	273	285	318
1544	Macaroni, noodles & similar products		135	129	120	101		3324	3410	3384	3242		103	120	154	165
1549	Other food products n.e.c.		449	410	438	408		16906	17465	19991	18762		588	676	924	1076
155	Beverages		97	111	131	121		12111	12578	14100	12173		644	735	1123	1003
1551	Distilling, rectifying & blending of spirits		9	9	11	9		233	310	505	377		9	16	33	35
1552	Wines		-	-	-	-		-	-	-	-		-	-	-	-
1553	Malt liquors and malt		5	7	9	10		701	721	950	1198		51	58	69	101
1554	Soft drinks; mineral waters		83	95	111	102		11177	11547	12645	10598		584	662	1021	867
1600	Tobacco products		2	2	2	2		5779	6847	6568	7905		275	591	963	1280
171	Spinning, weaving and finishing of textiles		747	685	693	639		68487	64614	66672	63968		2588	2818	3505	3614
1711	Textile fibre preparation; textile weaving		645	594	597	542		64558	60821	62658	59533		2445	2661	3321	3365
1712	Finishing of textiles		102	92	96	97		3929	3793	4014	4435		142	157	184	249
172	Other textiles		716	605	604	600		29061	26750	28836	28446		959	1061	1361	1556
1721	Made-up textile articles, except apparel		67	74	73	70		4944	4957	4852	4438		177	199	252	251
1722	Carpets and rugs		628	506	502	501		23317	20577	22512	22614		756	814	1043	1225
1723	Cordage, rope, twine and netting		4	5	7	6		368	400	422	367		12	18	21	20
1729	Other textiles n.e.c.		17	20	22	23		432	817	1050	1027		14	29	45	60
1730	Knitted and crocheted fabrics and articles		55	47	37	46		1378	1152	1078	1132		41	40	52	53
1810	Wearing apparel, except fur apparel		173	165	193	166		6317	6820	9280	7727		202	236	369	402
1820	Dressing & dyeing of fur; processing of fur		-	-	-	-		-	-	-	-		-	-	-	-
191	Tanning, dressing and processing of leather		92	108	103	105		2658	3161	3228	3311		83	122	141	157
1911	Tanning and dressing of leather		86	103	96	96		2521	3036	3031	3130		79	118	135	149
1912	Luggage, handbags, etc.; saddlery & harness		6	5	7	9		137	125	197	181		4	4	6	8
1920	Footwear		193	138	153	121		6046	5322	5815	4835		171	178	244	231
2010	Sawmilling and planing of wood		11	16	29	29		2006	1930	2101	2194		117	125	164	181
202	Products of wood, cork, straw, etc.		117	121	127	110		5037	5393	5970	4813		227	275	372	341
2021	Veneer sheets, plywood, particle board, etc.		57	60	60	50		3809	4101	4675	3625		191	231	316	285
2022	Builders' carpentry and joinery		34	37	42	38		825	834	830	787		25	29	36	37
2023	Wooden containers		11	11	12	10		202	207	211	167		6	7	8	8
2029	Other wood products; articles of cork/straw		15	13	13	12		201	251	254	234		6	9	11	11
210	Paper and paper products		295	318	367	360		17331	18365	21197	21971		877	1046	1292	1614
2101	Pulp, paper and paperboard		54	61	87	90		6006	5951	7322	7144		433	495	583	675
2102	Corrugated paper and paperboard		167	172	192	181		6870	7407	8091	8175		289	358	447	539
2109	Other articles of paper and paperboard		74	85	88	89		4455	5007	5784	6652		154	192	262	400
221	Publishing		83	74	77	71		7183	7305	6969	6586		428	479	547	618
2211	Publishing of books and other publications		37	29	32	28		2667	2598	3100	2220		128	134	239	191
2212	Publishing of newspapers, journals, etc.		42	40	39	38		4437	4626	3752	4273		296	342	302	422
2213	Publishing of recorded media		-	-	-	-		-	-	-	-		-	-	-	-
2219	Other publishing		4	5	6	5		79	81	117	93		4	4	6	6

Code	Description												
222	Printing and related service activities	304	336	214	186	5274	5600	5183	5356	179	204	230	230
2221	Printing	274	310	185	172	4677	4934	4190	4819	137	154	153	199
2222	Service activities related to printing	30	26	29	15	596	666	993	537	42	50	77	31
2230	Reproduction of recorded media	15	16	2	2	260	248	68	72	3	2	1	-
2310	Coke oven products	-	-	-	-	-	-	-	-	-	-	-	-
2320	Refined petroleum products	12	23	12	7	281	356	305	193	10	9	6	3
2330	Processing of nuclear fuel	3698	3867	2971	2411	26215	25874	17123	15385	134	141	131	122
241	Basic chemicals	7116	5298	3010	2365	50962	43787	30215	27651	344	363	390	327
2411	Basic chemicals, except fertilizers	1999	1583	885	621	16045	15223	11062	9439	196	205	202	181
2412	Fertilizers and nitrogen compounds	1440	1193	604	499	10024	8592	5772	5262	51	50	95	58
2413	Plastics in primary forms; synthetic rubber	3677	2522	1521	1245	24893	19972	13381	12950	97	108	92	88
242	Other chemicals	4700	3861	3162	2579	52525	51104	47058	45931	621	633	580	547
2421	Pesticides and other agro-chemical products	94	76	76	87	1472	1529	1527	1673	28	29	25	23
2422	Paints, varnishes, printing ink and mastics	534	441	381	300	7919	7478	7508	6895	178	174	165	142
2423	Pharmaceuticals, medicinal chemicals, etc.	2411	1934	1641	1214	22225	21121	19287	18551	170	176	155	145
2424	Soap, cleaning & cosmetic preparations	1290	1061	804	663	15111	15146	13304	12367	146	156	148	151
2429	Other chemical products n.e.c.	371	349	260	316	5798	5730	5433	6445	99	98	88	86
2430	Man-made fibres	345	265	215	197	3626	3673	2333	2466	20	18	13	19
251	Rubber products	1544	1456	1230	960	17986	19224	17003	17807	123	129	125	127
2511	Rubber tyres and tubes	1230	1187	1028	736	12469	13527	11880	11918	28	27	28	29
2519	Other rubber products	313	270	202	225	5517	5697	5123	5889	95	102	97	98
2520	Plastic products	2482	2061	1492	1198	41020	41230	34790	32051	952	1063	931	885
2610	Glass and glass products	1271	990	719	624	16712	16298	14431	13735	140	134	130	128
269	Non-metallic mineral products n.e.c.	11393	9966	7747	6031	155432	160656	140713	136295	3275	3520	3212	3468
2691	Pottery, china and earthenware	721	670	563	438	11793	11719	12294	11466	71	72	75	64
2692	Refractory ceramic products	317	265	212	137	3767	3464	2869	2523	31	34	28	30
2693	Struct.non-refractory clay; ceramic products	3954	3654	2607	2239	66214	70420	61730	63640	1442	1490	1405	1733
2694	Cement, lime and plaster	3678	2730	2375	1706	29558	28283	23036	20442	175	177	164	147
2695	Articles of concrete, cement and plaster	1200	1163	904	664	18718	19045	16514	14376	458	529	415	343
2696	Cutting, shaping & finishing of stone	543	519	455	359	10264	10889	11084	11169	622	691	692	750
2699	Other non-metallic mineral products n.e.c.	981	966	633	488	15118	16836	13187	12679	476	526	434	401
2710	Basic iron and steel	9184	6823	5308	4121	70920	59530	47408	43866	268	280	227	197
2720	Basic precious and non-ferrous metals	2227	1898	1902	1749	19507	19842	17623	17119	185	189	164	144
273	Casting of metals	1189	1073	820	684	14657	15981	13856	13463	204	217	207	199
2731	Casting of iron and steel	1010	897	680	574	12127	13760	11825	11299	167	179	161	157
2732	Casting of non-ferrous metals	179	176	141	109	2530	2220	2031	2164	37	38	45	42
281	Struct.metal products;tanks;steam generators	2983	2429	1659	1373	40184	39153	32624	26645	494	482	448	361
2811	Structural metal products	1841	1415	903	611	27208	25923	19467	14350	367	353	317	235
2812	Tanks, reservoirs and containers of metal	1072	949	755	758	12234	12161	13102	12172	125	127	130	124
2813	Steam generators	70	65	2	4	742	1069	55	123	2	2	1	2
289	Other metal products; metal working services	2743	2804	1887	1652	38380	44341	38931	42317	756	855	836	947
2891	Metal forging/pressing/stamping/roll-forming	56	85	73	51	990	1414	1413	1565	37	39	38	42
2892	Treatment & coating of metals	484	461	371	341	7504	7795	7928	8712	197	224	232	277
2893	Cutlery, hand tools and general hardware	211	224	178	145	3840	4196	4085	4015	66	75	69	74
2899	Other fabricated metal products n.e.c.	1992	2035	1264	1115	26046	30936	25505	28025	456	517	498	554
291	General purpose machinery	2765	2578	2155	1615	35818	36762	34352	33684	466	468	449	443
2911	Engines & turbines (not for transport equipment)	661	604	545	368	5301	5103	4179	3961	23	22	19	14
2912	Pumps, compressors, taps and valves	699	493	493	349	9775	10385	9187	8051	149	155	142	142
2913	Bearings, gears, gearing & driving elements	100	95	82	72	1459	1541	1344	1493	35	38	36	34
2914	Ovens, furnaces and furnace burners	149	151	120	82	2286	2532	1951	1997	28	33	27	28
2915	Lifting and handling equipment	302	305	253	172	4395	4720	4593	3929	69	67	66	62
2919	Other general purpose machinery	854	755	661	571	12602	12481	13098	14253	162	153	159	163
292	Special purpose machinery	1892	1728	1509	1298	25641	26218	25752	25221	380	430	408	418
2921	Agricultural and forestry machinery	638	583	529	474	6925	6930	7174	6966	84	89	87	83
2922	Machine tools	342	298	252	239	4610	5014	5043	4817	84	91	85	81
2923	Machinery for metallurgy	21	20	17	16	304	324	308	342	6	6	5	7
2924	Machinery for mining & construction	326	411	382	248	4810	5466	5249	4508	49	65	62	57
2925	Food/beverage/tobacco processing machinery	217	186	135	133	3603	3751	3416	3601	82	87	78	85
2926	Machinery for textile, apparel and leather	102	67	63	55	1175	1235	1323	1320	11	16	21	23
2927	Weapons and ammunition	-	-	-	-	-	-	-	-	-	-	-	-
2929	Other special purpose machinery	246	163	130	133	4214	3498	3239	3667	64	76	70	82

continued

Iran (Islamic Republic of)

ISIC Revision 3

		Number of establishments (number)					Number of employees (number)					Wages and salaries paid to employees (billions of Iranian Rials)				
ISIC	Industry	Note	2006	2007	2008	2009	Note	2006	2007	2008	2009	Note	2006	2007	2008	2009
2930	Domestic appliances n.e.c.		234	225	243	230		21170	21772	23787	23067		906	975	1483	1424
3000	Office, accounting and computing machinery		31	32	38	37		2468	2673	5980	5819		100	146	474	490
3110	Electric motors, generators and transformers		83	78	91	88		9147	8910	13212	12611		512	600	1194	1260
3120	Electricity distribution & control apparatus		148	156	178	175		11219	11706	13110	13575		525	573	768	891
3130	Insulated wire and cable		106	110	126	127		9063	9618	10859	10400		430	525	723	767
3140	Accumulators, primary cells and batteries		11	11	14	12		4131	5321	4214	4139		194	261	427	482
3150	Lighting equipment and electric lamps		62	60	69	67		4233	4966	6453	5528		171	203	312	324
3190	Other electrical equipment n.e.c.		47	50	43	48		7907	8528	9988	10752		341	460	555	929
3210	Electronic valves, tubes, etc.		30	30	33	32		1066	1133	1277	1236		45	51	75	88
3220	TV/radio transmitters; line comm. apparatus		13	18	24	24		4009	3932	4040	3526		260	275	275	304
3230	TV and radio receivers and associated goods		26	25	26	24		3575	3064	3380	3137		195	178	232	252
331	Medical, measuring, testing appliances, etc.		138	143	153	155		9960	10899	11645	12407		378	522	675	812
3311	Medical, surgical and orthopaedic equipment		105	107	112	112		5868	5979	6637	6698		213	255	333	404
3312	Measuring/testing/navigating appliances,etc.		31	33	36	38		4004	4312	4677	5378		162	203	305	378
3313	Industrial process control equipment		2	3	5	5		88	608	331	331		4	65	37	30
3320	Optical instruments & photographic equipment		12	12	10	10		652	757	621	628		52	58	62	78
3330	Watches and clocks		8	8	7	7		543	548	325	318		15	17	12	18
3410	Motor vehicles		23	34	36	37		53038	56947	64940	67328		5259	7171	9468	11182
3420	Automobile bodies, trailers & semi-trailers		49	47	48	42		4590	4653	4627	4620		228	265	227	265
3430	Parts/accessories for automobiles		650	669	685	667		60907	65590	75568	74873		2949	3805	5125	5848
351	Building and repairing of ships and boats		26	30	46	35		6687	4895	6419	4746		471	351	490	413
3511	Building and repairing of ships		6	8	18	13		5980	4098	4892	3750		448	319	394	330
3512	Building/repairing of pleasure/sport. boats		20	22	28	22		707	797	1527	996		23	32	96	82
3520	Railway/tramway locomotives & rolling stock		20	17	19	17		3864	3474	3834	3819		168	174	360	226
3530	Aircraft and spacecraft		2	3	2	2		3172	3230	3199	2831		235	293	358	417
359	Transport equipment n.e.c.		113	128	126	119		7853	6223	6287	6054		323	269	370	401
3591	Motorcycles		98	111	110	102		7148	5449	5518	5344		293	231	271	286
3592	Bicycles and invalid carriages		9	9	9	10		438	454	477	489		16	14	72	91
3599	Other transport equipment n.e.c.		6	8	7	7		267	320	292	221		14	23	27	24
3610	Furniture		323	281	316	297		12479	12343	13046	12843		465	549	717	849
369	Manufacturing n.e.c.		138	166	191	185		4778	5555	6855	6346		159	205	285	307
3691	Jewellery and related articles		15	14	14	12		415	493	505	501		12	17	22	24
3692	Musical instruments		2	1	1	1		42	18	13	14		2	1		1
3693	Sports goods		6	5	4	4		175	185	282	277		6	7	8	10
3694	Games and toys		6	4	6	7		128	245	441	179		6	7	13	8
3699	Other manufacturing n.e.c.		109	142	166	161		4018	4614	5614	5375		135	173	241	264
3710	Recycling of metal waste and scrap		-	1	2	2			11	86	63		-	-	10	-
3720	Recycling of non-metal waste and scrap		10	11	11	8		185	256	217	179		4	7	7	6
D	Total manufacturing		16058	15881	17076	16134		1060589	1093454	1253624	1242981		56060	68611	91747	105655

Iran (Islamic Republic of)

ISIC Revision 3		Output at producers' prices (billions of Iranian Rials)					Value added at producers' prices (billions of Iranian Rials)					Gross fixed capital formation (billions of Iranian Rials)		
ISIC	Industry	Note	2006	2007	2008	2009	Note	2006	2007	2008	2009	Note	2008	2009
151	Processed meat,fish,fruit,vegetables,fats		26857	36959	51111	60745		7111	9307	10097	13164		969	1078
1511	Processing/preserving of meat		6951	9313	12731	14619		1816	2339	2644	3286		238	624
1512	Processing/preserving of fish		1404	1857	1756	1941		471	636	583	628		96	35
1513	Processing/preserving of fruit & vegetables		6414	8207	9246	10713		1843	2678	3188	3202		241	128
1514	Vegetable and animal oils and fats		12088	17582	27379	33472		2981	3655	3682	6048		395	291
1520	Dairy products		15090	20261	30588	31573		3446	3656	5614	5955		977	1092
153	Grain mill products; starches; animal feeds		6159	9003	11266	15155		2019	2511	2781	3060		474	553
1531	Grain mill products		2150	3352	3351	8945		964	1339	1385	1884		374	518
1532	Starches and starch products		494	637	702	666		213	215	246	208		6	-76
1533	Prepared animal feeds		3515	5014	7212	5544		843	957	1151	968		95	111
154	Other food products		20978	21222	28009	30235		7816	7155	9262	10572		2068	1851
1541	Bakery products		4126	4365	6766	7294		1648	1751	2649	3056		375	181
1542	Sugar		9126	7641	7587	8897		3326	2192	2154	2536		893	791
1543	Cocoa, chocolate and sugar confectionery		1383	1759	2082	2223		479	603	651	852		152	222
1544	Macaroni, noodles & similar products		906	1191	1460	1100		321	400	505	405		101	25
1549	Other food products n.e.c.		5437	6268	10115	10720		2042	2209	3303	3723		547	633
155	Beverages		4632	5624	7568	9441		2066	2509	2988	3425		1100	1196
1551	Distilling, rectifying & blending of spirits		77	138	272	337		37	44	111	116		381	3
1552	Wines		446	690	1436	2331		204	344	556	808		106	430
1553	Malt liquors and malt		4109	4796	5861	6773		1825	2121	2321	2502		613	762
1554	Soft drinks; mineral waters		1832	2089	3060	3565		1008	1175	1488	2164		20	192
1600	Tobacco products		16116	19536	22361	22646		5210	6194	7075	7396		1213	1336
171	Spinning, weaving and finishing of textiles		15621	19044	21720	21532		4936	5916	6728	6940		1169	1306
1711	Textile fibre preparation; textile weaving		495	492	641	1114		274	278	346	456		44	30
1712	Finishing of textiles		9540	9726	11187	11851		3411	3175	3969	3972		731	569
172	Other textiles		1579	1634	2096	1936		636	517	704	704		27	54
1721	Made-up textile articles, except apparel		7808	7798	8684	9443		2721	2571	3129	3108		698	493
1722	Carpets and rugs		79	114	122	104		25	29	43	29		-1	6
1723	Cordage, rope, twine and netting		74	180	285	369		29	58	93	131		7	16
1729	Other textiles n.e.c.		252	281	256	245		106	105	123	100		15	2
1730	Knitted and crocheted fabrics and articles		904	1195	1752	1812		420	562	749	889		-55	94
1810	Wearing apparel, except fur apparel		-	-	-	-		-	-	-	-		-	-
1820	Dressing & dyeing of fur; processing of fur		-	-	-	-		-	-	-	-		-	-
191	Tanning, dressing and processing of leather		1395	1841	1228	1959		415	469	306	570		30	81
1911	Tanning and dressing of leather		1369	1823	1212	1925		408	463	300	554		17	59
1912	Luggage, handbags, etc.; saddlery & harness		26	18	16	35		7	6	6	15		13	22
1920	Footwear		1203	1213	1525	1307		451	383	544	464		78	53
2010	Sawmilling and planing of wood		185	303	449	562		124	190	238	377		5	3
202	Products of wood, cork, straw, etc.		2258	3274	3296	2669		851	945	1222	1033		107	84
2021	Veneer sheets, plywood, particle board, etc.		2049	3035	2992	2428		757	850	1099	932		96	83
2022	Builders' carpentry and joinery		140	152	221	152		71	65	90	66		10	-
2023	Wooden containers		37	40	26	42		11	12	9	14		-	1
2029	Other wood products; articles of cork/straw		32	46	57	48		12	17	23	21		1	-
210	Paper and paper products		6807	8220	10733	10302		2238	2743	3487	3594		402	292
2101	Pulp, paper and paperboard		2338	2507	3670	3047		1003	972	1404	1181		132	77
2102	Corrugated paper and paperboard		3055	3694	4752	4362		791	1057	1299	1270		200	323
2109	Other articles of paper and paperboard		1414	2019	2311	2892		444	714	784	1143		69	-109
221	Publishing		1352	1363	1837	1960		752	689	849	943		151	144
2211	Publishing of books and other publications		571	545	961	889		332	280	543	424		52	2
2212	Publishing of newspapers, journals, etc.		766	799	859	1056		411	399	296	511		99	142
2213	Publishing of recorded media		-	-	-	-		-	-	-	-		-	-
2219	Other publishing		15	19	17	16		9	10	10	9		-	-

continued

Iran (Islamic Republic of)

		Output at producers' prices (billions of Iranian Rials)					Value added at producers' prices (billions of Iranian Rials)					Gross fixed capital formation (billions of Iranian Rials)		
ISIC	Industry (ISIC Revision 3)	Note	2006	2007	2008	2009	Note	2006	2007	2008	2009	Note	2008	2009
222	Printing and related service activities		967	1665	1906	2638		484	643	586	869		135	111
2221	Printing		922	1508	1779	2488		459	585	540	825		134	108
2222	Service activities related to printing		45	157	127	150		25	58	47	44		1	4
2230	Reproduction of recorded media		57	36	129	68		22	15	89	26		-	-
2310	Coke oven products		102	76	120	111		34	31	31	15		2	2
2320	Refined petroleum products		56535	69826	113018	501113		30118	36076	49257	43398		6187	1636
2330	Processing of nuclear fuel												-	-
241	Basic chemicals		68649	111516	148761	153094		29337	49281	53278	67570		27259	18145
2411	Basic chemicals, except fertilizers		13963	28395	54019	55686		6956	13907	17179	26739		4158	11488
2412	Fertilizers and nitrogen compounds		3351	5413	12247	10418		2209	3846	9500	7882		3399	643
2413	Plastics in primary forms; synthetic rubber		51335	77708	82495	86991		20172	31528	26598	32948		19702	6014
242	Other chemicals		28290	33626	42980	49606		9987	11221	14891	19285		1252	1448
2421	Pesticides and other agro-chemical products		1308	954	1497	1593		382	358	319	572		28	47
2422	Paints, varnishes, printing ink and mastics		3799	4771	5468	6604		1037	1392	1399	1765		85	138
2423	Pharmaceuticals, medicinal chemicals, etc.		11817	15505	20192	24369		4663	6121	8417	10868		624	888
2424	Soap, cleaning & cosmetic preparations		8662	9369	12302	13244		3124	2387	3869	4974		324	178
2429	Other chemical products n.e.c.		2704	3027	3522	3795		781	962	886	1106		191	197
2430	Man-made fibres		2567	2313	3350	2722		682	415	478	602		66	57
251	Rubber products		8064	9444	11063	11853		3196	3693	3599	4431		407	274
2511	Rubber tyres and tubes		6455	8216	9641	10023		2416	3061	3005	3763		322	232
2519	Other rubber products		1609	1228	1422	1830		780	632	594	668		85	41
2520	Plastic products		12543	15943	20155	20540		4087	4833	6351	7410		1220	1107
2610	Glass and glass products		4122	4839	7028	7949		1854	2207	3238	3865		858	2882
269	Non-metallic mineral products n.e.c.		37522	48423	66833	74574		21403	27799	39496	44833		9309	8736
2691	Pottery, china and earthenware		1463	1979	2064	2647		873	1201	1164	1430		252	200
2692	Refractory ceramic products		1009	1071	1828	2019		350	397	711	850		88	20
2693	Struct.non-refractory clay; ceramic products		9705	13030	18444	18432		5808	7811	11222	10833		1559	2576
2694	Cement, lime and plaster		13285	16618	24821	30293		9212	11380	17850	22102		6469	5258
2695	Articles of concrete, cement and plaster		4628	6538	8204	7514		2148	3026	3762	3462		454	251
2696	Cutting, shaping & finishing of stone		2583	3759	3490	3717		997	1568	1475	1690		154	81
2699	Other non-metallic mineral products n.e.c.		4849	5428	7981	9952		2015	2417	3312	4466		332	350
2710	Basic iron and steel		84423	125136	174422	141385		31628	49792	57771	41084		12418	13174
2720	Basic precious and non-ferrous metals		31510	35629	36366	41283		12345	13292	10401	10425		1390	802
273	Casting of metals		4099	5482	7067	6701		1832	2213	2725	2673		241	197
2731	Casting of iron and steel		3235	4446	6048	5583		1531	1910	2224	2092		209	189
2732	Casting of non-ferrous metals		863	1036	1019	1118		301	303	501	580		32	8
281	Struct.metal products;tanks;steam generators		9488	17128	21205	21695		3651	8471	6954	7782		847	955
2811	Structural metal products		5668	12315	14655	14933		1723	6523	4671	4922		584	391
2812	Tanks, reservoirs and containers of metal		3788	4787	6207	6250		1913	1942	2115	2644		261	306
2813	Steam generators		32	26	388	512		15	6	168	216		1	258
289	Other metal products; metal working services		15350	18814	28084	23333		5167	6100	7900	7092		945	1678
2891	Metal forging/pressing/stamping/roll-forming		965	1559	3213	1660		294	337	647	285		61	22
2892	Treatment & coating of metals		2786	3241	3067	3238		1114	1144	1025	1212		80	138
2893	Cutlery, hand tools and general hardware		736	836	1222	1285		341	390	501	433		37	36
2899	Other fabricated metal products n.e.c.		10863	13178	20582	17150		3418	4229	5727	5161		767	1482
291	General purpose machinery		12980	15848	24168	26159		4848	5921	7510	8890		545	456
2911	Engines & turbines (not for transport equipment)		4000	5803	8540	11146		1503	2052	2424	3648		57	120
2912	Pumps, compressors, taps and valves		2645	2709	5579	5261		949	1049	1800	1926		268	169
2913	Bearings, gears, gearing & driving elements		247	306	442	437		141	151	222	209		10	11
2914	Ovens, furnaces and furnace burners		461	650	977	858		216	351	337	262		9	26
2915	Lifting and handling equipment		1021	1186	1673	1753		391	455	571	663		42	-1
2919	Other general purpose machinery		4607	5195	6956	6703		1648	1863	2157	2181		160	130

Code	Description										
292	Special purpose machinery	10509	15951	15592	12416	3750	5776	5444	4091	1050	176
2921	Agricultural and forestry machinery	4774	5537	5745	4266	1427	1696	1964	1432	175	76
2922	Machine tools	1152	1312	2191	1999	617	553	914	729	8	20
2923	Machinery for metallurgy	40	67	192	475	28	28	108	124	1	1
2924	Machinery for mining & construction	2805	7199	4276	2635	888	2700	1408	754	795	39
2925	Food/beverage/tobacco processing machinery	768	891	1418	1290	327	349	513	442	43	23
2926	Machinery for textile, apparel and leather	281	250	399	338	157	118	180	131	21	4
2927	Weapons and ammunition	-	-	-	-	-	-	-	480	7	-
2929	Other special purpose machinery	689	695	1372	1413	307	332	357	4279	618	13
2930	Domestic appliances n.e.c.	7567	10898	12870	12508	3083	3612	3845	2158	492	390
3000	Office, accounting and computing machinery	587	896	3557	4712	312	372	1670	6628	460	211
3110	Electric motors, generators and transformers	5355	7050	14830	15041	1579	2208	5644	3026	171	457
3120	Electricity distribution & control apparatus	3491	4414	6119	8328	1562	1778	2078	3580	250	114
3130	Insulated wire and cable	8723	10680	12377	12377	2392	2638	3021	727	242	411
3140	Accumulators, primary cells and batteries	1718	2900	2708	2717	436	596	904	876	43	97
3150	Lighting equipment and electric lamps	868	1294	2518	2356	391	1268	1547	2905	168	39
3190	Other electrical equipment n.e.c.	4284	5137	6841	9490	1128	114	141	170	12	138
3210	Electronic valves, tubes, etc.	228	354	402	520	106	1022	711	820	31	16
3220	TV/radio transmitters; line comm. apparatus	1708	2106	2439	2711	667	514	831	809	124	30
3230	TV and radio receivers and associated goods	1987	1884	2587	2626	604					71
331	Medical, measuring, testing appliances, etc.	2130	2997	4727	6613	1045	1226	1898	2360	91	176
3311	Medical, surgical and orthopaedic equipment	1115	1421	2089	2625	580	646	897	983	59	71
3312	Measuring/testing/navigating appliances,etc.	1005	1329	2513	3894	460	482	930	1323	31	104
3313	Industrial process control equipment	11	247	125	94	5	98	71	55	2	1
3320	Optical instruments & photographic equipment	384	468	493	1130	138	200	190	425	8	-
3330	Watches and clocks	73	94	65	220	24	35	30	29		1
3410	Motor vehicles	126040	134955	194346	217139	36035	34568	42540	54755	1514	3023
3420	Automobile bodies, trailers & semi-trailers	2353	3227	3422	3001	614	1165	1052	772	138	16
3430	Parts/accessories for automobiles	30306	36421	51840	60768	10952	11538	14703	19169	1593	846
351	Building and repairing of ships and boats	4402	3067	7163	7469	1804	938	1491	1610	109	33
3511	Building and repairing of ships	4285	2777	6197	7040	1746	820	1099	1492	45	36
3512	Building/repairing of pleasure/sport. boats	116	291	966	428	58	118	392	118	64	-3
3520	Railway/tramway locomotives & rolling stock	674	701	910	701	326	413	376	424	74	74
3530	Aircraft and spacecraft	457	587	738	1189	385	497	629	840	-	28
359	Transport equipment n.e.c.	4288	3685	4510	4214	2289	1022	1210	694	32	80
3591	Motorcycles	4039	3447	4022	3904	2137	911	964	576	27	72
3592	Bicycles and invalid carriages	118	111	273	218	69	48	116	70	5	5
3599	Other transport equipment n.e.c.	132	127	215	93	84	63	131	47	-	1
3610	Furniture	3003	3385	4724	4284	1197	1273	1718	1598	62	139
369	Manufacturing n.e.c.	1039	1529	2290	3271	448	548	749	868	205	99
3691	Jewellery and related articles	63	70	142	1041	29	36	56	243	45	4
3692	Musical instruments	12	5	6	5	4	2	11	1	-	-
3693	Sports goods	20	22	24	26	11	12	11	13	-	-
3694	Games and toys	20	22	66	54	7	14	20	20	36	95
3699	Other manufacturing n.e.c.	923	1410	2052	2145	397	484	661	591	124	1
3710	Recycling of metal waste and scrap	-	3	13	68	-	1	6	23	1	
3720	Recycling of non-metal waste and scrap	34	66	54	42	12	27	17	14		
D	Total manufacturing	715033	912603	1250545	1686758	269400	338159	408649	441575	78855	66949

Iran (Islamic Republic of)

ISIC Revision 3 — Index numbers of industrial production (2005=100)

ISIC	Industry	Note	1999	2000	2001	2002	2003	2004	2005	2006	2007	2008	2009	2010
15	Food and beverages	a/	40	42	40	48	54	56	100	99	110	…	…	…
16	Tobacco products		…	…	…	…	…	…	…	…	…	…	…	…
17	Textiles		92	88	86	94	93	92	100	96	104	…	…	…
18	Wearing apparel, fur		…	…	…	…	…	…	…	…	…	…	…	…
19	Leather, leather products and footwear		…	…	…	…	…	…	…	…	…	…	…	…
20	Wood products (excl. furniture)		…	…	…	…	…	…	…	…	…	…	…	…
21	Paper and paper products		…	…	…	…	…	…	…	…	…	…	…	…
22	Printing and publishing		…	…	…	…	…	…	…	…	…	…	…	…
23	Coke, refined petroleum products, nuclear fuel		…	…	…	…	…	…	…	…	…	…	…	…
24	Chemicals and chemical products		54	55	59	63	71	78	100	113	127	…	…	…
25	Rubber and plastics products		…	…	…	…	…	…	…	…	…	…	…	…
26	Non-metallic mineral products		67	71	79	88	97	100	100	110	125	…	…	…
27	Basic metals		…	…	…	…	…	…	…	…	…	…	…	…
28	Fabricated metal products		67	70	78	96	102	113	100	97	102	…	…	…
29	Machinery and equipment n.e.c.	b/	54	55	57	70	79	96	100	101	133	…	…	…
30	Office, accounting and computing machinery	b/	…	…	…	…	…	…	…	…	…	…	…	…
31	Electrical machinery and apparatus	c/	31	35	37	69	94	102	100	104	118	…	…	…
32	Radio, television and communication equipment	c/	…	…	…	…	…	…	…	…	…	…	…	…
33	Medical, precision and optical instruments		…	…	…	…	…	…	…	…	…	…	…	…
34	Motor vehicles, trailers, semi-trailers	d/	…	…	…	…	…	82	100	128	111	…	…	…
35	Other transport equipment	d/	…	…	…	…	…	…	…	…	…	…	…	…
36	Furniture; manufacturing n.e.c.		…	…	…	…	…	…	…	…	…	…	…	…
37	Recycling		…	…	…	…	…	…	…	…	…	…	…	…
D	Total manufacturing		45	51	58	69	87	89	100	109	121	…	…	…

a/ 15 excludes beverages.
b/ 29 includes 30.
c/ 31 includes 32.
d/ 34 includes 35.

- 459 -

Ireland

Supplier of information:
Irish Central Statistics Office, Dublin.
Industrial statistics for the OECD countries are compiled by the OECD secretariat, which supplies them to UNIDO.

Basic source of data:
Annual services inquiry; sample survey; business registers.

Major deviations from ISIC (Revision 4):
None reported.

Reference period:
Calendar year.

Scope:
Not reported.

Method of data collection:
Not reported.

Type of enumeration:
Not reported.

Adjusted for non-response:
Not reported.

Concepts and definitions of variables:
No deviations from the standard UN concepts and definitions are reported.

Related national publications:
None reported.

Ireland

ISIC	Industry	Number of enterprises (number)					Number of employees (number)					Wages and salaries paid to employees (millions of Euros)				
		Note	2006	2007	2008	2009	Note	2006	2007	2008	2009	Note	2006	2007	2008	2009
1010	Processing/preserving of meat		...	...	133	125		...	...	12454	11812		...	...	373	332
1020	Processing/preserving of fish, etc.		...	...	68	65		...	...	1793	1743		...	...	46	46
1030	Processing/preserving of fruit,vegetables		...	...	...	...		...	...	...	...		...	...	...	...
1040	Vegetable and animal oils and fats		...	...	...	...		...	...	...	...		...	...	...	...
1050	Dairy products		...	...	59	57		...	...	5012	4901		...	...	212	208
106	Grain mill products,starches and starch products		...	...	7	...		...	...	254	...		...	...	11	...
1061	Grain mill products		...	...	...	...		...	...	...	...		...	...	...	...
1062	Starches and starch products		...	...	...	...		...	...	...	...		...	...	...	...
107	Other food products		...	...	251	234		...	...	12061	11813		...	...	486	463
1071	Bakery products		...	...	...	...		...	...	...	...		...	...	...	...
1072	Sugar		...	...	-	-		...	...	-	...		...	...	-	-
1073	Cocoa, chocolate and sugar confectionery		...	...	...	19		...	...	...	2133		...	...	...	87
1074	Macaroni, noodles, couscous, etc.		...	...	...	...		...	...	...	...		...	...	...	...
1075	Prepared meals and dishes		...	...	...	14		...	...	...	734		...	...	...	20
1079	Other food products n.e.c.		...	...	...	...		...	...	...	...		...	...	...	...
1080	Prepared animal feeds		...	...	58	55		...	...	2174	2104		...	...	70	68
1101	Distilling, rectifying and blending of spirits		...	...	34a/	27a/		...	...	4260a/	3905a/		...	...	230a/	212a/
1102	Wines		...	...	...a/	...a/		...	...	...a/	...a/		...	...	...a/	...a/
1103	Malt liquors and malt		...	...	...a/	...a/		...	...	...a/	...a/		...	...	...a/	...a/
1104	Soft drinks,mineral waters,other bottled waters		...	...	...a/	...a/		...	...	...a/	...a/		...	...	...a/	...a/
1200	Tobacco products		...	...	...	...		...	...	...	...		...	...	...	...
131	Spinning, weaving and finishing of textiles		...	...	26	22		...	...	896	1302		...	...	22	34
1311	Preparation and spinning of textile fibres		...	...	...	...		...	...	...	...		...	...	...	...
1312	Weaving of textiles		...	...	...	...		...	...	...	...		...	...	...	...
1313	Finishing of textiles		...	...	8	7		...	...	67	73		...	...	2	2
139	Other textiles		...	...	118	105		...	...	1388	1146		...	...	40	32
1391	Knitted and crocheted fabrics		...	...	-	-		...	...	-	-		...	...	-	-
1392	Made-up textile articles, except apparel		...	...	83	77		...	...	808	731		...	...	10	...
1393	Carpets and rugs		...	...	5	...		...	...	164	...		...	...	21	19
1394	Cordage, rope, twine and netting		...	...	9	...		...	...	114	...		...	...	6	...
1399	Other textiles n.e.c.		...	...	21	16		...	...	302	190		...	...	4	6
1410	Wearing apparel, except fur apparel		...	...	77b/	66b/		...	...	1715b/	1389b/		...	...	37b/	30b/
1420	Articles of fur		...	...	..b/	..b/		...	...	..b/	..b/		...	...	..b/	..b/
1430	Knitted and crocheted apparel		...	...	..b/	..b/		...	...	..b/	..b/		...	...	..b/	..b/
151	Leather;luggage,handbags,saddlery,harness;fur		...	...	...	...		...	...	...	...		...	...	...	...
1511	Tanning/dressing of leather; dressing of fur		...	...	16c/	7		...	...	163c/	61		...	...	4c/	1
1512	Luggage,handbags,etc.;saddlery/harness		...	...	...	...		...	...	...	...		...	...	...	...
1520	Footwear		...	...	..c/	7		...	...	..c/	80		...	...	..c/	2
1610	Sawmilling and planing of wood		...	...	34	29		...	...	1069	980		...	...	33	25
162	Wood products, cork, straw, plaiting materials		...	...	280	251		...	...	4589	3476		...	...	145	100

Code	Description						
1621	Veneer sheets and wood-based panels	13	11	729	654	30	23
1622	Builders' carpentry and joinery	⋮	180	⋮	2082	⋮	59
1623	Wooden containers	38	⋮	562	⋮	14	⋮
1629	Other wood products;articles of cork,straw	8	7	85	73	3	2
1701	Pulp, paper and paperboard	38	34	1820	1444	74	60
1702	Corrugated paper and paperboard	77	69	1407	1241	51	43
1709	Other articles of paper and paperboard	344	320	5132	4657	185	168
181	Printing and service activities related to printing	⋮	⋮	⋮	⋮	⋮	⋮
1811	Printing	⋮	⋮	⋮	⋮	⋮	⋮
1812	Service activities related to printing	11	11	1049	1225	50	66
1820	Reproduction of recorded media	⋮	⋮	⋮	⋮	⋮	⋮
1910	Coke oven products	-	-	-	-	-	-
1920	Refined petroleum products	⋮	⋮	⋮	⋮	⋮	⋮
201	Basic chemicals,fertilizers, etc.	63	45	4141	1614	233	75
2011	Basic chemicals	29	21	3320	930	201	48
2012	Fertilizers and nitrogen compounds	14	11	366	313	15	14
2013	Plastics and synthetic rubber in primary forms	20	13	455	371	17	14
202	Other chemical products	⋮	⋮	⋮	⋮	⋮	⋮
2021	Pesticides and other agrochemical products	14	12	418	347	16	14
2022	Paints,varnishes;printing ink and mastics	22	24	2412	2378	122	108
2023	Soap,cleaning and cosmetic preparations	⋮	⋮	⋮	⋮	⋮	⋮
2029	Other chemical products n.e.c.	⋮	⋮	⋮	⋮	⋮	⋮
2030	Man-made fibres	61	66	14611	16570	789	982
2100	Pharmaceuticals,medicinal chemicals, etc.	28	25	884	778	28	25
221	Rubber products	⋮	⋮	⋮	⋮	⋮	⋮
2211	Rubber tyres and tubes	4	4	29	28	1	⋮
2219	Other rubber products	24	21	855	750	27	24
2220	Plastics products	239	214	7937	7379	256	243
2310	Glass and glass products	344	309	8227	6632	328	250
239	Non-metallic mineral products n.e.c.	⋮	⋮	⋮	⋮	⋮	⋮
2391	Refractory products	⋮	⋮	⋮	⋮	⋮	⋮
2392	Clay building materials	⋮	⋮	⋮	⋮	⋮	⋮
2393	Other porcelain and ceramic products	⋮	⋮	⋮	⋮	⋮	⋮
2394	Cement, lime and plaster	⋮	⋮	⋮	⋮	⋮	⋮
2395	Articles of concrete, cement and plaster	107	94	1231	996	42	30
2396	Cutting, shaping and finishing of stone	⋮	⋮	⋮	⋮	⋮	⋮
2399	Other non-metallic mineral products n.e.c.	⋮	⋮	⋮	⋮	⋮	⋮
2410	Basic iron and steel	⋮	⋮	⋮	⋮	⋮	⋮
2420	Basic precious and other non-ferrous metals	23	19	176	127	6	4
243	Casting of metals	⋮	⋮	⋮	⋮	⋮	⋮
2431	Casting of iron and steel	14	14	⋮	97	⋮	3
2432	Casting of non-ferrous metals	⋮	5	⋮	30	⋮	1
251	Struct.metal products, tanks, reservoirs	274	235	4938	3960	177	134
2511	Structural metal products	⋮	⋮	⋮	⋮	⋮	⋮
2512	Tanks, reservoirs and containers of metal	⋮	⋮	⋮	⋮	⋮	⋮

continued

Ireland

ISIC Revision 4		Number of enterprises (number)					Number of employees (number)					Wages and salaries paid to employees (millions of Euros)				
ISIC	Industry	Note	2006	2007	2008	2009	Note	2006	2007	2008	2009	Note	2006	2007	2008	2009
2513	Steam generators, excl. hot water boilers		...	...	...	...		...	...	...	...		...	...	...	...
2520	Weapons and ammunition		...	...	-	-		...	...	-	-		...	...	-	-
259	Other metal products;metal working services		...	...	...	...		...	...	...	...		...	...	...	...
2591	Forging,pressing,stamping,roll-forming of metal		...	...	...	...		...	...	...	...		...	...	...	...
2592	Treatment and coating of metals; machining		...	...	231	194		...	...	3044	2418		...	...	106	90
2593	Cutlery, hand tools and general hardware		...	...	...	...		...	...	...	...		...	...	...	...
2599	Other fabricated metal products n.e.c.		...	...	...	...		...	...	...	...		...	...	...	...
2610	Electronic components and boards		...	...	...	...		...	...	...	...		...	...	...	...
2620	Computers and peripheral equipment		...	...	22	19		...	...	10607	8119		...	...	427	375
2630	Communication equipment		...	...	...	12		...	...	...	469		...	...	...	21
2640	Consumer electronics		...	...	7	6		...	...	746	471		...	...	28	16
265	Measuring,testing equipment; watches, etc.		...	...	...	...		...	...	...	...		...	...	...	...
2651	Measuring/testing/navigating equipment,etc.		...	...	35	37		...	...	1262	1416		...	...	59	63
2652	Watches and clocks		...	...	...	...		...	...	...	...		...	...	...	...
2660	Irradiation/electromedical equipment,etc.		...	...	...	...		...	...	...	...		...	...	...	...
2670	Optical instruments and photographic equipment		...	...	11	10		...	...	1929	1667		...	...	73	59
2680	Magnetic and optical media		...	...	...	...		...	...	...	...		...	...	...	...
2710	Electric motors,generators,transformers,etc.		...	...	55	...		...	...	1666	...		...	...	59	...
2720	Batteries and accumulators		...	...	4	4		...	...	105	78		...	...	4	2
273	Wiring and wiring devices		...	...	...	...		...	...	...	...		...	...	...	...
2731	Fibre optic cables		...	...	23	20		...	...	748	542		...	...	31	17
2732	Other electronic and electric wires and cables		...	...	11	10		...	...	593	401		...	...	27	14
2733	Wiring devices		...	...	...	10		...	...	...	141		...	...	...	3
2740	Electric lighting equipment		...	...	...	...		...	...	...	...		...	...	...	...
2750	Domestic appliances		...	...	...	...		...	...	...	...		...	...	...	...
2790	Other electrical equipment		...	...	16	14		...	...	1337	738		...	...	44	25
281	General-purpose machinery		...	...	197	175		...	...	8049	7245		...	...	300	274
2811	Engines/turbines,excl.aircraft,vehicle engines		...	...	...	...		...	...	...	...		...	...	...	...
2812	Fluid power equipment		...	...	10	11		...	...	558	491		...	...	20	17
2813	Other pumps, compressors, taps and valves		...	...	19	17		...	...	1143	1011		...	...	41	38
2814	Bearings, gears, gearing and driving elements		...	...	...	...		...	...	...	...		...	...	...	...
2815	Ovens, furnaces and furnace burners		...	...	9	6		...	...	485	333		...	...	...	...
2816	Lifting and handling equipment		...	...	39	36		...	...	1766	1514		...	...	19	12
2817	Office machinery, excl.computers,etc.		...	...	11	...		...	...	160	...		...	...	63	56
2818	Power-driven hand tools		...	...	...	...		...	...	...	...		...	...	6	...
2819	Other general-purpose machinery		...	...	...	...		...	...	...	...		...	...	...	...
282	Special-purpose machinery		...	...	142	138		...	...	3468	3072		...	...	114	103
2821	Agricultural and forestry machinery		...	...	42	38		...	...	1022	862		...	...	33	29
2822	Metal-forming machinery and machine tools		...	...	36	37		...	...	578	608		...	...	19	20
2823	Machinery for metallurgy		...	...	...	...		...	...	...	...		...	...	...	...
2824	Mining, quarrying and construction machinery		...	...	-	...		...	...	-	...		...	...	-	...

Code	Description						
2825	Food/beverage/tobacco processing machinery	11	11	311	282	13	13
2826	Textile/apparel/leather production machinery	:	:	:	:	:	:
2829	Other special-purpose machinery	:	5	:	154	:	4
2910	Motor vehicles	17	9	517	300	33	26
2920	Automobile bodies, trailers and semi-trailers	:	:	:	:	:	:
2930	Parts and accessories for motor vehicles	:	:	:	:	:	:
301	Building of ships and boats	:	:	:	:	:	:
3011	Building of ships and floating structures	:	:	:	:	:	:
3012	Building of pleasure and sporting boats	:	:	:	:	:	:
3020	Railway locomotives and rolling stock	151	101	2781	2015	16	14
3030	Air and spacecraft and related machinery	-	-	:	-	-	:
3040	Military fighting vehicles	:	:	:	:	:	:
309	Transport equipment n.e.c.	:	:	:	:	:	:
3091	Motorcycles	:	:	:	:	:	:
3092	Bicycles and invalid carriages	:	-	:	-	:	:
3099	Other transport equipment n.e.c.	:	:	:	:	:	:
3100	Furniture	76	34	1200	910	29	25
321	Jewellery, bijouterie and related articles	:	:	:	:	:	:
3211	Jewellery and related articles	:	:	:	:	:	:
3212	Imitation jewellery and related articles	:	:	:	:	:	:
3220	Musical instruments	:	2	:	52	:	7
3230	Sports goods	:	:	:	:	:	:
3240	Games and toys	728	762	19627	20107	81	81
3250	Medical and dental instruments and supplies	78	64	1978	1605	141	117
3290	Other manufacturing n.e.c.	:	:	:	:	:	:
331	Repair of fabricated metal products/machinery	4	2	93	52	11	10
3311	Repair of fabricated metal products	22	14	593	392	74	56
3312	Repair of machinery	2	2	50	40	8	6
3313	Repair of electronic and optical equipment	14	13	342	289	14	12
3314	Repair of electrical equipment	:	33	:	805	:	29
3315	Repair of transport equip., excl. motor vehicles	:	1	:	27	:	4
3319	Repair of other equipment	24	38	584	751	30	27
3320	Installation of industrial machinery/equipment	:	:	:	:	:	:
C	Total manufacturing	7641	6863	193418	172727	4989	4449

a/ 1101 includes 1102, 1103 and 1104.
b/ 1410 includes 1420 and 1430.
c/ 151 includes 1520.

Ireland

			Output (millions of Euros)					Value added at factor values (millions of Euros)					Gross fixed capital formation (millions of Euros)	
ISIC	Industry	Note	2006	2007	2008	2009	Note	2006	2007	2008	2009	Note	2008	2009
1010	Processing/preserving of meat		...	...	4097	3791		...	...	645	561		84	51
1020	Processing/preserving of fish, etc.		...	...	360	384		...	...	78	90		16	3
1030	Processing/preserving of fruit,vegetables		...	...	...	...		...	...	...	...		...	...
1040	Vegetable and animal oils and fats		...	...	...	...		...	...	...	...		...	...
1050	Dairy products		...	...	3290	2750		...	...	544	314		103	101
106	Grain mill products,starches and starch products		...	...	122	...		...	...	25	...		2	...
1061	Grain mill products		...	...	...	...		...	...	...	...		...	...
1062	Starches and starch products		...	...	...	...		...	...	...	...		...	...
107	Other food products		...	...	9119	8893		...	...	3308	3342		116	88
1071	Bakery products		...	...	...	...		...	...	...	...		...	...
1072	Sugar		...	...	-	-		...	...	-	-		-	-
1073	Cocoa, chocolate and sugar confectionery		...	...	...	378		...	...	...	152		...	22
1074	Macaroni, noodles, couscous, etc.		...	...	...	...		...	...	...	...		...	...
1075	Prepared meals and dishes		...	...	...	117		...	...	...	23		...	2
1079	Other food products n.e.c.		...	...	...	...		...	...	...	...		...	...
1080	Prepared animal feeds		...	...	1003	1017		...	...	155	158		37	17
1101	Distilling, rectifying and blending of spirits		...	...	2774a/	2341a/		...	...	444a/	443a/		77a/	62a/
1102	Wines		...	...	...a/	...a/		...	...	...a/	...a/		...a/	...a/
1103	Malt liquors and malt		...	...	...a/	...a/		...	...	...a/	...a/		...a/	...a/
1104	Soft drinks,mineral waters,other bottled waters		...	...	...a/	...a/		...	...	...a/	...a/		...a/	...a/
1200	Tobacco products		...	...	...	...		...	...	...	...		...	...
131	Spinning, weaving and finishing of textiles		...	...	105	132		...	...	41	50		5	2
1311	Preparation and spinning of textile fibres		...	...	...	...		...	...	...	...		...	...
1312	Weaving of textiles		...	...	...	...		...	...	...	2		...	...
1313	Finishing of textiles		...	...	5	7		...	...	3	2		-	-
139	Other textiles		...	...	151	115		...	...	55	41		3	2
1391	Knitted and crocheted fabrics		...	...	-	-		...	...	-	-		-	-
1392	Made-up textile articles, except apparel		...	...	78	67		...	...	31	24		2	1
1393	Carpets and rugs		...	...	27	...		...	...	4	...		-	...
1394	Cordage, rope, twine and netting		...	...	10	22		...	...	5	9		1	...
1399	Other textiles n.e.c.		...	...	35	22		...	...	15	9		2b/	-
1410	Wearing apparel, except fur apparel		...	...	118b/	104b/		...	...	49b/	41b/		2b/	1b/
1420	Articles of fur		...	...	...b/	...b/		...	...	...b/	...b/		...b/	...b/
1430	Knitted and crocheted apparel		...	...	...b/	...b/		...	...	...b/	...b/		...b/	...b/
151	Leather;luggage,handbags,saddlery,harness;fur		...	...	15c/	7		...	...	...	3		1c/	-
1511	Tanning/dressing of leather; dressing of fur		...	...	...	...		...	...	...	...		...	...
1512	Luggage,handbags,etc.;saddlery/harness		...	...	...	...		...	...	...	...		...	...
1520	Footwear		...	...	...c/	17		...	...	...	5		...c/	-
1610	Sawmilling and planing of wood		...	...	278	182		...	...	46	22		12	3
162	Wood products, cork, straw, plaiting materials		...	...	668	470		...	...	213	-3		38	17

Code	Description					
1621	Veneer sheets and wood-based panels	224	166	52	31	21 / 6
1622	Builders' carpentry and joinery	..	226	..	71	.. / 8
1623	Wooden containers	60	..	21	..	2 / ..
1629	Other wood products;articles of cork,straw	14	11	6	4	1 / 1
1701	Pulp, paper and paperboard	306	217	104	77	17 / 4
1702	Corrugated paper and paperboard	231	185	76	61	6 / 2
1709	Other articles of paper and paperboard	625	559	296	261	46 / 23
181	Printing and service activities related to printing	..	..	..	..	.. / ..
1811	Printing	..	..	..	..	.. / ..
1812	Service activities related to printing	1025	984	204	201	11 / 2
1820	Reproduction of recorded media	-	-	-	-	- / -
1910	Coke oven products	..	..	..	..	.. / ..
1920	Refined petroleum products	5347	589	2500	117	219 / 25
201	Basic chemicals,fertilizers, etc.	4764	234	2335	102	212 / 19
2011	Basic chemicals	395	238	109	-13	5 / 4
2012	Fertilizers and nitrogen compounds	188	117	57	28	2 / 2
2013	Plastics and synthetic rubber in primary forms	..	..	..	..	.. / ..
202	Other chemical products	..	..	..	..	.. / ..
2021	Pesticides and other agrochemical products	93	78	28	23	2 / 2
2022	Paints,varnishes;printing ink and mastics	978	1207	290	457	31 / 17
2023	Soap,cleaning and cosmetic preparations	..	..	..	..	.. / ..
2029	Other chemical products n.e.c.	..	..	..	..	.. / ..
2030	Man-made fibres	26384	34649	9756	13075	720 / 768
2100	Pharmaceuticals,medicinal chemicals, etc.	164	142	24	29	2 / 2
221	Rubber products	5	4	2	2	- / -
2211	Rubber tyres and tubes	160	138	21	27	2 / 2
2219	Other rubber products	1268	1082	421	352	43 / 25
2220	Plastics products	..	..	..	..	.. / ..
2310	Glass and glass products	2151	1485	765	458	193 / 261
239	Non-metallic mineral products n.e.c.	..	..	..	..	.. / ..
2391	Refractory products	..	..	..	..	.. / ..
2392	Clay building materials	..	..	..	..	.. / ..
2393	Other porcelain and ceramic products	..	..	..	..	.. / ..
2394	Cement, lime and plaster	..	..	..	..	.. / ..
2395	Articles of concrete, cement and plaster	179	114	64	41	14 / 5
2396	Cutting, shaping and finishing of stone	..	..	..	..	.. / ..
2399	Other non-metallic mineral products n.e.c.	..	..	..	..	.. / ..
2410	Basic iron and steel	..	..	..	..	.. / ..
2420	Basic precious and other non-ferrous metals	31	14	10	5	- / -
243	Casting of metals	..	..	..	..	.. / ..
2431	Casting of iron and steel	..	11	..	4	.. / -
2432	Casting of non-ferrous metals	..	3	..	1	.. / -
251	Struct.metal products, tanks, reservoirs	901	532	246	147	14 / 13
2511	Structural metal products	..	..	..	..	.. / ..
2512	Tanks, reservoirs and containers of metal	..	..	..	..	.. / ..

continued

Ireland

ISIC Revision 4		Output (millions of Euros)					Value added at factor values (millions of Euros)					Gross fixed capital formation (millions of Euros)		
ISIC	Industry	Note	2006	2007	2008	2009	Note	2006	2007	2008	2009	Note	2008	2009
2513	Steam generators, excl. hot water boilers		...	...	...	...		...	...	...	...		...	...
2520	Weapons and ammunition		...	...	-	-		...	...	-	-		-	-
259	Other metal products;metal working services		...	...	...	...		...	...	...	...		-	-
2591	Forging,pressing,stamping,roll-forming of metal		...	...	...	...		...	...	...	...		...	...
2592	Treatment and coating of metals; machining		...	...	378	283		...	...	172	133		9	5
2593	Cutlery, hand tools and general hardware		...	...	...	...		...	...	...	...		...	...
2599	Other fabricated metal products n.e.c.		...	...	...	...		...	...	...	...		...	...
2610	Electronic components and boards		...	...	...	...		...	...	...	...		...	...
2620	Computers and peripheral equipment		...	...	15148	13558		...	...	1881	1067		47	44
2630	Communication equipment		...	...	197	182		...	...	76	20		...	...
2640	Consumer electronics		...	...	359	165		...	...	108	53		2	4
265	Measuring,testing equipment; watches, etc.		...	...	...	327		...	...	...	130		6	8
2651	Measuring/testing/navigating equipment,etc.		...	...	...	...		...	...	...	...		...	7
2652	Watches and clocks		...	...	...	...		...	...	...	...		...	...
2660	Irradiation/electromedical equipment,etc.		...	...	...	...		...	...	...	...		...	...
2670	Optical instruments and photographic equipment		...	...	...	...		...	...	...	...		...	...
2680	Magnetic and optical media		...	...	272	246		...	...	146	76		9	12
2710	Electric motors,generators,transformers,etc.		...	...	314	...		...	...	85	...		...	...
2720	Batteries and accumulators		...	...	17	9		...	...	5	3		7	...
273	Wiring and wiring devices		...	...	283	173		...	...	63	48		1	-
2731	Fibre optic cables		...	...	...	-		...	...	...	...		2	2
2732	Other electronic and electric wires and cables		...	...	262	161		...	...	52	42		...	...
2733	Wiring devices		...	...	...	13		...	...	...	6		2	1
2740	Electric lighting equipment		...	...	...	...		...	...	...	...		...	1
2750	Domestic appliances		...	...	...	...		...	...	...	...		...	...
2790	Other electrical equipment		...	...	262	99		...	...	76	46		14	1
281	General-purpose machinery		...	...	1891	1550		...	...	752	571		55	52
2811	Engines/turbines,excl.aircraft,vehicle engines		...	...	...	...		...	...	...	...		...	...
2812	Fluid power equipment		...	...	97	73		...	...	29	21		2	1
2813	Other pumps, compressors, taps and valves		...	...	232	194		...	...	104	71		12	7
2814	Bearings, gears, gearing and driving elements		...	...	84	61		...	...	29	19		...	...
2815	Ovens, furnaces and furnace burners		...	...	434	353		...	...	169	148		...	...
2816	Lifting and handling equipment		...	...	...	...		...	...	...	...		2	1
2817	Office machinery, excl.computers,etc.		...	...	25	...		...	...	11	...		4	5
2818	Power-driven hand tools		...	...	...	...		...	...	...	...		-	...
2819	Other general-purpose machinery		...	...	750	678		...	...	341	249		...	...
282	Special-purpose machinery		...	...	189	138		...	...	64	38		28	15
2821	Agricultural and forestry machinery		...	...	65	75		...	...	32	31		13	3
2822	Metal-forming machinery and machine tools		...	...	...	...		...	...	...	...		4	7
2823	Machinery for metallurgy		...	...	-	-		...	...	-	-		-	-
2824	Mining, quarrying and construction machinery		...	...	...	...		...	...	...	...		...	...

Code	Industry						
2825	Food/beverage/tobacco processing machinery	53	50	14	13	1	1
2826	Textile/apparel/leather production machinery	...	...	...	...	...	...
2829	Other special-purpose machinery	...	20	...	3	...	-
2910	Motor vehicles	80	37	22	2	3	1
2920	Automobile bodies, trailers and semi-trailers	...	...	...	...	...	...
2930	Parts and accessories for motor vehicles	...	...	...	...	...	...
301	Building of ships and boats	...	...	...	...	...	...
3011	Building of ships and floating structures	...	...	...	...	...	...
3012	Building of pleasure and sporting boats	...	...	...	...	...	...
3020	Railway locomotives and rolling stock	468	344	218	178	10	6
3030	Air and spacecraft and related machinery	-	-	-	-	-	-
3040	Military fighting vehicles	...	...	...	...	...	...
309	Transport equipment n.e.c.	...	...	...	...	...	...
3091	Motorcycles	...	...	...	...	-	...
3092	Bicycles and invalid carriages	-	...	-	...	...	...
3099	Other transport equipment n.e.c.	...	...	...	...	...	...
3100	Furniture	346	181	151	76	6	40
321	Jewellery, bijouterie and related articles	...	...	...	...	...	...
3211	Jewellery and related articles	...	...	...	...	...	...
3212	Imitation jewellery and related articles	...	...	...	...	...	...
3220	Musical instruments	...	5	...	2	...	-
3230	Sports goods	...	...	...	...	...	...
3240	Games and toys	5414	5682	2344	2613	200	183
3250	Medical and dental instruments and supplies	...	...	...	...	...	...
3290	Other manufacturing n.e.c.	256	190	117	95	8	5
331	Repair of fabricated metal products/machinery	16	8	7	4	-	...
3311	Repair of fabricated metal products	97	46	39	18	1	1
3312	Repair of machinery	10	7	6	4	-	-
3313	Repair of electronic and optical equipment	42	40	20	24	1	2
3314	Repair of electrical equipment	...	86	...	43	...	2
3315	Repair of transport equip., excl. motor vehicles	...	3	...	1	1	-
3319	Repair of other equipment	96	112	47	58	...	1
3320	Installation of industrial machinery/equipment	...	...	...	...	...	...
C	Total manufacturing	99637	93747	30517	28408	2553	2051

a/ 1101 includes 1102, 1103 and 1104.
b/ 1410 includes 1420 and 1430.
c/ 151 includes 1520.

Ireland

Index numbers of industrial production

ISIC Revision 4

ISIC	Industry	Note	(2005=100)											
			1999	2000	2001	2002	2003	2004	2005	2006	2007	2008	2009	2010
10	Food products		77	78	84	87	93	100	100	98	101	99	95	97
11	Beverages		82	93	94	97	95	90	100	122	121	112	107	116
12	Tobacco products	a/	114	135	129	120	105	98	100	91	98	86	62	59
13	Textiles		190	175	198	152	125	117	100	91	89	88	69	65
14	Wearing apparel		259	173	169	96	105	113	100	64	40	33	32	29
15	Leather and related products		479	455	394	403	272	183	100	94	114	122	122	112
16	Wood/wood products/cork,excl. furniture		77	74	68	77	80	93	100	109	102	74	49	48
17	Paper and paper products		101	103	106	104	100	107	100	98	99	92	71	67
18	Printing and reproduction of recorded media		120	106	103	97	93	90	100	98	107	101	88	83
19	Coke and refined petroleum products	a/	...	...	...	...	...	...	...	...	...	...	...	...
20	Chemicals and chemical products		110	110	114	123	123	113	100	111	122	118	106	123
21	Pharmaceuticals,medicinal chemicals, etc.		60	68	84	105	109	99	100	103	110	106	127	151
22	Rubber and plastics products		108	111	110	100	107	106	100	102	105	95	75	78
23	Other non-metallic mineral products		83	91	92	89	93	95	100	101	105	87	52	44
24	Basic metals		109	112	100	98	93	88	100	105	120	122	74	87
25	Fabricated metal products, except machinery		99	108	99	97	98	106	100	101	110	105	66	68
26	Computer, electronic and optical products		62	85	79	65	81	93	100	110	116	117	83	61
27	Electrical equipment		44	62	74	80	82	93	100	108	103	95	90	51
28	Machinery and equipment n.e.c.		116	121	114	115	119	106	100	113	119	110	83	95
29	Motor vehicles, trailers and semi-trailers	b/	87	108	112	98	96	101	100	101	119	110	83	95
30	Other transport equipment	b/	...	...	...	...	...	...	...	...	107	115	74	79
31	Furniture	a/	...	...	...	...	...	...	...	...	...	...	...	...
32	Other manufacturing		37	52	70	70	86	89	100	96	103	113	112	135
33	Repair and installation of machinery/equipment		45	62	81	78	92	92	100	110	111	128	121	111
C	Total manufacturing		65	74	83	90	95	96	100	103	109	106	102	110

a/ 12 includes 19 and 31.
b/ 29 includes 30.

Israel

Supplier of information:
Central Bureau of Statistics, Jerusalem.

Basic source of data:
Annual manufacturing survey; administrative data.

Major deviations from ISIC (Revision 3):
None reported.

Reference period:
Calendar year.

Scope:
All establishments.

Method of data collection:
Collection of balance sheets and profit-and-loss statements from income tax authorities.

Type of enumeration:
Sample survey.

Adjusted for non-response:
Yes.

Concepts and definitions of variables:
Wages and salaries is compensation of employees.
Output is valued at basic prices.
Value added is valued at basic prices.

Related national publications:
Manufacturing Survey, published by the Central Bureau of Statistics, Jerusalem.

Israel

ISIC	Industry	Est. Note	Est. 2006	Est. 2007	Est. 2008	Est. 2009	Eng. Note	Eng. 2006	Eng. 2007	Eng. 2008	Eng. 2009	Wages 2006	Wages 2007	Wages 2008	Wages 2009
			(number)					**(thousands)**				**(millions of Israeli New Sheqalim)**			
151	Processed meat,fish,fruit,vegetables,fats		293	263	264	354		12.6	12.3	13.1	13.2	1391	1393	1510	1533
1511	Processing/preserving of meat		...	...	...	...		...	...	...	...	...	...	...	...
1512	Processing/preserving of fish		...	...	...	...		...	...	...	...	...	...	...	...
1513	Processing/preserving of fruit & vegetables		...	...	...	...		...	...	...	...	...	...	...	...
1514	Vegetable and animal oils and fats		...	...	...	...		...	...	...	...	...	...	...	...
1520	Dairy products		...	...	...	...		...	...	...	...	...	...	...	...
153	Grain mill products; starches; animal feeds		116	85	101	121		6.4	5.4	5.7	6.9	1069	985	1088	1035
1531	Grain mill products		78	116	103	72		1.5	1.6	1.6	1.7	223	243	264	262
1532	Starches and starch products		...	...	...	...		...	...	...	...	...	...	...	...
1533	Prepared animal feeds		...	...	...	...		...	...	...	...	...	...	...	...
154	Other food products		1992	1990	2082	1985		28.8	30.8	32.0	35.4	2289	2507	2637	3006
1541	Bakery products		...	...	...	...		...	...	...	...	...	...	...	...
1542	Sugar		...	...	...	...		...	...	...	...	...	...	...	...
1543	Cocoa, chocolate and sugar confectionery		...	...	...	...		...	...	...	...	...	...	...	...
1544	Macaroni, noodles & similar products		...	...	...	...		...	...	...	...	...	...	...	...
1549	Other food products n.e.c.		...	...	...	...		...	...	...	...	...	...	...	...
155	Beverages	a/	181	293	292	310	a/	6.7	4.5	4.3	4.5	814	647	692	688
1551	Distilling, rectifying & blending of spirits		...	...	...	...		...	...	...	...	...	...	...	...
1552	Wines		...	...	...	...		...	...	...	...	...	...	...	...
1553	Malt liquors and malt		...	...	...	...		...	...	...	...	...	...	...	...
1554	Soft drinks; mineral waters		...	...	...	...		...	...	...	...	...	...	...	...
1600	Tobacco products	a/	...	...	...	...	a/	...	...	...	...	...	...	...	...
171	Spinning, weaving and finishing of textiles	b/	119	103	89	88	b/	4.1	3.6	3.5	2.9	512	475	446	365
1711	Textile fibre preparation; textile weaving		...	...	...	...		...	...	...	...	...	...	...	...
1712	Finishing of textiles		...	...	...	...		...	...	...	...	...	...	...	...
172	Other textiles	c/	250	255	237	226	c/	3.4	3.1	2.9	2.5	325	310	290	261
1721	Made-up textile articles, except apparel		...	...	...	...		...	...	...	...	...	...	...	...
1722	Carpets and rugs		...	...	...	...		...	...	...	...	...	...	...	...
1723	Cordage, rope, twine and netting	b/	...	...	...	...	b/	...	...	...	...	...	...	...	...
1729	Other textiles n.e.c.		...	...	...	...		...	...	...	...	...	...	...	...
1730	Knitted and crocheted fabrics and articles		61	44	50	44		3.6	3.0	2.9	2.4	377	338	335	260
1810	Wearing apparel, except fur apparel		902	891	979	701		6.3	6.3	6.4	4.9	404	427	434	376
1820	Dressing & dyeing of fur; processing of fur	d/	...	...	...	...	d/	...	...	...	...	...	...	...	...
191	Tanning, dressing and processing of leather	d/	239	256	187	174	d/	1.5	1.8	1.6	1.5	120	136	124	118
1911	Tanning and dressing of leather		...	...	...	...		...	...	...	...	...	...	...	...
1912	Luggage, handbags, etc.; saddlery & harness		...	...	...	...		...	...	...	...	...	...	...	...
1920	Footwear		...	...	...	...		...	...	...	...	...	...	...	...
2010	Sawmilling and planing of wood	e/	155	156	100	91	e/	1.0	1.1	1.1	1.2	87	94	93	93
202	Products of wood, cork, straw, etc.	f/	40	45	44	34	f/	1.0	1.1	0.8	0.7	105	120	82	79
2021	Veneer sheets, plywood, particle board, etc.	e/	738	818	538	660	e/	3.3	3.8	3.7	4.0	310	339	387	391
2022	Builders' carpentry and joinery		...	...	...	...		...	...	...	...	...	...	...	...
2023	Wooden containers		...	...	...	...		...	...	...	...	...	...	...	...
2029	Other wood products; articles of cork/straw		...	...	...	...		...	...	...	...	...	...	...	...
210	Paper and paper products		285	286	266	282		9.6	10.1	9.2	8.8	1131	1183	1183	1069
2101	Pulp, paper and paperboard		...	...	...	...		...	...	...	...	...	...	...	...
2102	Corrugated paper and paperboard		...	...	...	...		...	...	...	...	...	...	...	...
2109	Other articles of paper and paperboard		...	...	...	...		...	...	...	...	...	...	...	...
221	Publishing		765	783	625	624		13.5	13.0	12.3	13.2	1381	1300	1461	1418
2211	Publishing of books and other publications		...	...	...	...		...	...	...	...	...	...	...	...
2212	Publishing of newspapers, journals, etc.		...	...	...	...		...	...	...	...	...	...	...	...
2213	Publishing of recorded media		...	...	...	...		...	...	...	...	...	...	...	...
2219	Other publishing		...	...	...	...		...	...	...	...	...	...	...	...

Code	Industry		1619	1700	1630	1596		11.5	12.2	12.0	10.3		1119	1380	1263	1036
222	Printing and related service activities	g/	...	...	...	...	g/	...	...	...	...	g/	...	...	...	...
2221	Printing		...	...	...	...		...	...	...	...		...	...	...	...
2222	Service activities related to printing	g/	...	...	...	...	g/	...	...	...	...	g/	...	...	...	...
2230	Reproduction of recorded media	h/	...	...	...	...	h/	...	...	...	...	h/	...	...	...	...
2310	Coke oven products	h/	...	...	...	...	h/	...	...	...	...	h/	...	...	...	...
2320	Refined petroleum products	h/	...	...	...	...	h/	...	...	...	...	h/	...	...	...	...
2330	Processing of nuclear fuel	h/	...	...	...	...	h/	...	...	...	...	h/	...	...	...	...
241	Basic chemicals	i/	90	82	96	114	i/	4.7	4.2	4.3	4.8	i/	1371	1297	1398	1514
2411	Basic chemicals, except fertilizers	i/	...	...	...	...	i/	...	...	...	...	i/	...	...	...	...
2412	Fertilizers and nitrogen compounds		34	34	25	35		3.5	3.9	3.6	3.7		888	995	948	946
2413	Plastics in primary forms; synthetic rubber	h/	349	413	396	372	h/	18.2	19.4	20.4	21.8	h/	3224	3633	4026	4237
242	Other chemicals		...	...	...	...		...	...	...	...		...	...	...	...
2421	Pesticides and other agro-chemical products		...	...	...	...		...	...	...	...		...	...	...	...
2422	Paints, varnishes, printing ink and mastics		...	...	...	...		...	...	...	...		...	...	...	...
2423	Pharmaceuticals, medicinal chemicals, etc.		...	...	...	...		...	...	...	...		...	...	...	...
2424	Soap, cleaning & cosmetic preparations		...	...	...	...		...	...	...	...		...	...	...	...
2429	Other chemical products n.e.c.		...	...	...	...		...	...	...	...		...	...	...	...
2430	Man-made fibres	h/	54	69	58	67	h/	2.4	2.6	2.2	2.0	h/	277	330	303	257
251	Rubber products		...	...	...	...		...	...	...	...		...	...	...	...
2511	Rubber tyres and tubes	j/	...	...	...	...	j/	...	...	...	...	j/	...	...	...	...
2519	Other rubber products	j/	...	...	...	...	j/	...	...	...	...	j/	...	...	...	...
2520	Plastic products		482	461	656	774		16.8	18.0	19.6	20.7		2113	2276	2494	2578
2610	Glass and glass products	j/	147	163	248	229	j/	2.7	2.8	2.6	2.1	j/	290	336	310	259
269	Non-metallic mineral products n.e.c.		...	...	...	...		...	...	...	...		...	...	...	...
2691	Pottery, china and earthenware		...	...	...	...		...	...	...	...		...	...	...	...
2692	Refractory ceramic products		...	...	...	...		...	...	...	...		...	...	...	...
2693	Struct.non-refractory clay; ceramic products	j/	166	104	110	119	j/	3.8	4.1	4.4	4.2	j/	653	718	783	740
2694	Cement, lime and plaster	k/	...	...	...	...	k/	...	...	...	...	k/	...	...	...	...
2695	Articles of concrete, cement and plaster	k/	596	665	632	543	k/	2.9	2.9	2.9	3.1	k/	306	280	320	362
2696	Cutting, shaping & finishing of stone	m/	...	...	...	...	m/	...	...	...	...	m/	...	...	...	...
2699	Other non-metallic mineral products n.e.c.	m/	91	152	182	165	m/	2.5	3.0	3.0	2.8	m/	375	444	436	392
2710	Basic iron and steel		28	77	82	65		1.2	1.3	1.5	1.4		157	174	195	179
2720	Basic precious and non-ferrous metals		116	113	40	36		1.7	1.9	1.6	1.4		239	250	237	173
273	Casting of metals		...	...	...	...		...	...	...	...		...	...	...	...
2731	Casting of iron and steel		...	...	...	...		...	...	...	...		...	...	...	...
2732	Casting of non-ferrous metals		...	...	...	...		...	...	...	...		...	...	...	...
281	Struct.metal products;tanks;steam generators		911	888	991	823		9.9	9.6	11.6	11.1		945	1027	1229	1249
2811	Structural metal products		...	...	...	...		...	...	...	...		...	...	...	...
2812	Tanks, reservoirs and containers of metal		...	...	...	...		...	...	...	...		...	...	...	...
2813	Steam generators		...	...	...	...		...	...	...	...		...	...	...	...
289	Other metal products; metal working services		3762	3866	4389	3661		34.1	39.0	36.8	32.8		3689	4433	4397	3881
2891	Metal forging/pressing/stamping/roll-forming		...	...	...	...		...	...	...	...		...	...	...	...
2892	Treatment & coating of metals		...	...	...	...		...	...	...	...		...	...	...	...
2893	Cutlery, hand tools and general hardware		...	...	...	...		...	...	...	...		...	...	...	...
2899	Other fabricated metal products n.e.c.		218	368	200	307		8.7	9.4	10.0	10.6		1512	1702	1848	2012
291	General purpose machinery		...	...	...	...		...	...	...	...		...	...	...	...
2911	Engines & turbines (not for transport equipment)		...	...	...	...		...	...	...	...		...	...	...	...
2912	Pumps, compressors, taps and valves		...	...	...	...		...	...	...	...		...	...	...	...
2913	Bearings, gears, gearing & driving elements		...	...	...	...		...	...	...	...		...	...	...	...
2914	Ovens, furnaces and furnace burners		...	...	...	...		...	...	...	...		...	...	...	...
2915	Lifting and handling equipment		...	...	...	...		...	...	...	...		...	...	...	...
2919	Other general purpose machinery		207	300	363	379		4.1	5.3	5.5	7.3		686	851	1002	1222
292	Special purpose machinery		...	...	...	...		...	...	...	...		...	...	...	...
2921	Agricultural and forestry machinery		...	...	...	...		...	...	...	...		...	...	...	...
2922	Machine tools		...	...	...	...		...	...	...	...		...	...	...	...
2923	Machinery for metallurgy		...	...	...	...		...	...	...	...		...	...	...	...
2924	Machinery for mining & construction		...	...	...	...		...	...	...	...		...	...	...	...
2925	Food/beverage/tobacco processing machinery		...	...	...	...		...	...	...	...		...	...	...	...
2926	Machinery for textile, apparel and leather		...	...	...	...		...	...	...	...		...	...	...	...
2927	Weapons and ammunition		...	...	...	...		...	...	...	...		...	...	...	...
2929	Other special purpose machinery		...	...	...	...		...	...	...	...		...	...	...	...

continued

Israel

ISIC	Industry	Number of establishments (number) — Note	2006	2007	2008	2009	Number of persons engaged (thousands) — Note	2006	2007	2008	2009	Wages and salaries paid to employees (millions of Israeli New Sheqalim) — Note	2006	2007	2008	2009
2930	Domestic appliances n.e.c.	n/	73	73	81	99	n/	2.9	3.4	3.8	3.8	n/	422	483	652	835
3000	Office, accounting and computing machinery	n/	...	...	...	...	n/	...	...	...	...	n/	...	...	...	...
3110	Electric motors, generators and transformers		157	157	185	192		1.9	2.3	2.3	2.3		275	326	360	340
3120	Electricity distribution & control apparatus	p/	189	206	195	189	p/	3.4	3.8	3.5	3.7	p/	438	459	454	471
3130	Insulated wire and cable	q/	32	36	37	45	q/	2.1	2.1	2.1	2.0	q/	345	332	320	301
3140	Accumulators, primary cells and batteries	q/	...	...	...	...	q/	...	...	...	...	q/	...	...	...	...
3150	Lighting equipment and electric lamps	p/	...	...	...	...	p/	...	...	...	...	p/	...	...	...	...
3190	Other electrical equipment n.e.c.	p/	...	...	...	...	p/	...	...	...	...	p/	...	...	...	...
3210	Electronic valves, tubes, etc.		93	97	117	183		17.1	19.4	22.5	22.0		3057	3669	3787	3496
3220	TV/radio transmitters; line comm. apparatus	r/	139	116	144	142	r/	15.1	14.9	16.4	16.7	r/	4339	4544	4727	4816
3230	TV and radio receivers and associated goods	r/	...	...	...	...	r/	...	...	...	...	r/	...	...	...	...
331	Medical, measuring, testing appliances, etc.	s/	279	368	388	356	s/	29.5	32.8	33.9	32.1	s/	8125	9020	8620	8457
3311	Medical, surgical and orthopaedic equipment		...	...	...	...		...	...	...	...		...	...	...	...
3312	Measuring/testing/navigating appliances,etc.		...	...	...	...		...	...	...	...		...	...	...	...
3313	Industrial process control equipment		...	...	...	...		...	...	...	...		...	...	...	...
3320	Optical instruments & photographic equipment		16	32	32	21		2.6	2.7	2.8	3.1		633	650	773	830
3330	Watches and clocks	s/	...	...	...	...	s/	...	...	...	...	s/	...	...	...	...
3410	Motor vehicles	t/	106	121	106	130	t/	3.2	3.7	4.6	5.0	t/	594	482	596	645
3420	Automobile bodies, trailers & semi-trailers	t/	...	...	...	...	t/	...	...	...	...	t/	...	...	...	...
3430	Parts/accessories for automobiles	t/	...	...	...	...	t/	...	...	...	...	t/	...	...	...	...
351	Building and repairing of ships and boats	u/	...	...	...	...	u/	...	...	...	...	u/	...	...	...	...
3511	Building and repairing of ships		...	...	...	...		...	...	...	...		...	...	...	...
3512	Building/repairing of pleasure/sport. boats		...	...	...	...		...	...	...	...		...	...	...	...
3520	Railway/tramway locomotives & rolling stock	u/	30	39	31	28	u/	13.1	15.0	14.9	15.3	u/	3862	3953	3853	4041
3530	Aircraft and spacecraft	u/	...	...	...	...	u/	...	...	...	...	u/	...	...	...	...
359	Transport equipment n.e.c.	u/	...	...	...	...	u/	...	...	...	...	u/	...	...	...	...
3591	Motorcycles		...	...	...	...		...	...	...	...		...	...	...	...
3592	Bicycles and invalid carriages		...	...	...	...		...	...	...	...		...	...	...	...
3599	Other transport equipment n.e.c.		...	...	...	...		...	...	...	...		...	...	...	...
3610	Furniture		3700	3634	3679	3603		13.2	13.6	17.4	17.0		1138	1216	1335	1376
369	Manufacturing n.e.c.		1046	1124	1315	1097		7.8	7.0	6.4	6.3		584	573	489	510
3691	Jewellery and related articles		...	...	...	...		...	...	...	...		...	...	...	...
3692	Musical instruments		...	...	...	...		...	...	...	...		...	...	...	...
3693	Sports goods		...	...	...	...		...	...	...	...		...	...	...	...
3694	Games and toys		...	...	...	...		...	...	...	...		...	...	...	...
3699	Other manufacturing n.e.c.		...	...	...	...		...	...	...	...		...	...	...	...
3710	Recycling of metal waste and scrap		...	...	...	...		...	...	...	...		...	...	...	...
3720	Recycling of non-metal waste and scrap		...	...	...	...		...	...	...	...		...	...	...	...
D	Total manufacturing		20944	21842	22365	21136		346.3	364.4	376.4	375.9		53030	57274	59206	59040

a/ 155 includes 1600.
b/ 171 includes 1722.
c/ 172 excludes 1722.
d/ 191 includes 1820.
e/ 2010 includes 2021.
f/ 202 excludes 2021.
g/ 222 includes 2230.
h/ 2413 includes 2310, 2320, 2330 and 2430.
i/ 2411 includes 2412.
j/ 2691 includes 2610 and 2693.

k/ 2694 includes 2695.
m/ 2696 includes 2699.
n/ 2930 includes 3000.
p/ 3120 includes 3150 and 3190.
q/ 3130 includes 3140.
r/ 3220 includes 3230.
s/ 331 includes 3330.
t/ 3420 includes 3410 and 3430.
u/ 3520 includes 351, 3530 and 359.

Israel

ISIC	Industry	Note	Output 2006	Output 2007	Output 2008	Output 2009	Note	Value added 2006	Value added 2007	Value added 2008	Value added 2009	Note	GFCF 2008	GFCF 2009
			(millions of Israeli New Sheqalim)					(millions of Israeli New Sheqalim)					(millions of Israeli New Sheqalim)	
151	Processed meat,fish,fruit,vegetables,fats		10902	11998	13340	13942		1973	2167	2216	2590		346	381
1511	Processing/preserving of meat		...	...	...	...		...	...	...	...		...	...
1512	Processing/preserving of fish		...	...	...	...		...	...	...	...		...	...
1513	Processing/preserving of fruit & vegetables		...	...	...	...		...	...	...	...		...	...
1514	Vegetable and animal oils and fats		6723	6917	7799	7882		1957	1783	2049	2234		261	240
1520	Dairy products		4160	5663	6917	5886		540	672	808	914		90	91
153	Grain mill products; starches; animal feeds		...	...	...	...		...	...	...	...		...	...
1531	Grain mill products		...	...	...	...		...	...	...	...		...	...
1532	Starches and starch products		...	...	...	...		...	...	...	...		...	...
1533	Prepared animal feeds		9472	10890	12625	12912		3378	3635	4387	4588		818	579
154	Other food products		...	...	...	...		...	...	...	...		...	...
1541	Bakery products		...	...	...	...		...	...	...	...		...	...
1542	Sugar		...	...	...	...		...	...	...	...		...	...
1543	Cocoa, chocolate and sugar confectionery		...	...	...	...		...	...	...	...		...	...
1544	Macaroni, noodles & similar products		...	...	...	...		...	...	...	...		...	...
1549	Other food products n.e.c.	a/	4506	4519	4379	4207	a/	1514	1546	1500	1485		405a/	312a/
155	Beverages		...	...	...	...		...	...	...	...		...	...
1551	Distilling, rectifying & blending of spirits		...	...	...	...		...	...	...	...		...	...
1552	Wines		...	...	...	...		...	...	...	...		...	...
1553	Malt liquors and malt		...	...	...	...		...	...	...	...		...	...
1554	Soft drinks; mineral waters	a/	...	...	...	...	a/	...	...	...	...		...a/	...a/
1600	Tobacco products	b/	3296	3023	2794	2340	b/	918	773	718	426		96b/	41b/
171	Spinning, weaving and finishing of textiles		...	...	...	...		...	...	...	...		...	...
1711	Textile fibre preparation; textile weaving		...	...	...	...		...	...	...	...		...	...
1712	Finishing of textiles	c/	1808	1761	1612	1522		476c/	559c/	481c/	493		36c/	17c/
172	Other textiles		...	...	...	...		...	...	...	...		...	...
1721	Made-up textile articles, except apparel	b/	...	...	...	...	b/	...	...	...	...		...b/	...b/
1722	Carpets and rugs		...	...	...	...		...	...	...	...		...	...
1723	Cordage, rope, twine and netting		1643	1324	1235	1276		535	367	310	513		26	26
1729	Other textiles n.e.c.		1857	1910	1752	1615		545	572	557	485		36	34
1730	Knitted and crocheted fabrics and articles		...	...	...	...		...	...	...	...		...	...
1810	Wearing apparel, except fur apparel	d/	464	574	507	475	d/	153	215	203	211		...d/	...d/
1820	Dressing & dyeing of fur; processing of fur	d/	...	...	...	...	d/	...	...	...	...		15d/	13d/
191	Tanning, dressing and processing of leather		...	...	...	...		...	...	...	...		...	...
1911	Tanning and dressing of leather		...	...	...	...		...	...	...	...		...	...
1912	Luggage, handbags, etc.; saddlery & harness		348	411	404	388		108	154	160	177		11	12
1920	Footwear		701	850	741	645	e/	177	189	148	142		27e/	35e/
2010	Sawmilling and planing of wood	e/	1087	1205	1425	1461		367f/	425f/	562f/	559		98f/	59f/
202	Products of wood, cork, straw, etc.	f/	...	...	...	...	e/	...	...	...	...		...e/	...e/
2021	Veneer sheets, plywood, particle board, etc.	e/	...	...	...	...		...	...	...	...		...	...
2022	Builders' carpentry and joinery		...	...	...	...		...	...	...	...		...	...
2023	Wooden containers		...	...	...	...		...	...	...	...		...	...
2029	Other wood products; articles of cork/straw		6157	6636	6354	5883		1726	1854	1885	1842		571	766
210	Paper and paper products		...	...	...	...		...	...	...	...		...	...
2101	Pulp, paper and paperboard		...	...	...	...		...	...	...	...		...	...
2102	Corrugated paper and paperboard		...	...	...	...		...	...	...	...		...	...
2109	Other articles of paper and paperboard		4217	4095	3976	4538		1745	1613	1214	1581		93	86
221	Publishing		...	...	...	...		...	...	...	...		...	...
2211	Publishing of books and other publications		...	...	...	...		...	...	...	...		...	...
2212	Publishing of newspapers, journals, etc.		...	...	...	...		...	...	...	...		...	...
2213	Publishing of recorded media		...	...	...	...		...	...	...	...		...	...
2219	Other publishing		...	...	...	...		...	...	...	...		...	...

continued

Israel

ISIC	Industry	Output Note	Output 2006	Output 2007	Output 2008	Output 2009	VA Note	VA 2006	VA 2007	VA 2008	VA 2009	GFCF 2008	GFCF 2009
			(millions of Israeli New Sheqalim)					(millions of Israeli New Sheqalim)				(millions of Israeli New Sheqalim)	
222	Printing and related service activities	g/	4160	4575	4604	3979	g/	1783	1983	1991	1642	481g/	269g/
2221	Printing		...	...	...	...		...	...	...	...	...g/	...g/
2222	Service activities related to printing		...	...	...	...		...	...	...	...		
2230	Reproduction of recorded media	g/	...	...	...	...	g/	...	...	...	...	...g/	...g/
2310	Coke oven products	h/	...	...	...	...		...	...	...	...	...h/	...h/
2320	Refined petroleum products	h/	...	...	...	...	h/	...	...	...	...	...h/	...h/
2330	Processing of nuclear fuel	h/	...	...	...	...	h/	...	...	...	...	...h/	...h/
241	Basic chemicals												
2411	Basic chemicals, except fertilizers	i/	8338	7910	11331	6876	i/	2908	2582	3632	2039	657i/	702i/
2412	Fertilizers and nitrogen compounds	i/					i/					...i/	...i/
2413	Plastics in primary forms; synthetic rubber	i/	34953	38941	48429	37356	i/	3777	4062	2173	3625	963h/	1229h/
242	Other chemicals	h/	27735	29671	35423	30889	h/	11519	11386	15083	12281	1491	1972
2421	Pesticides and other agro-chemical products												
2422	Paints, varnishes, printing ink and mastics												
2423	Pharmaceuticals, medicinal chemicals, etc.												
2424	Soap, cleaning & cosmetic preparations												
2429	Other chemical products n.e.c.												
2430	Man-made fibres	h/					h/					...h/	...h/
251	Rubber products		1292	1502	1269	1100		376	464	413	361	43	27
2511	Rubber tyres and tubes												
2519	Other rubber products												
2520	Plastic products		12737	13456	12947	13271		3980	3988	3756	4408	1011	704
2610	Glass and glass products	j/	1350	1628	1536	1269	j/	444	578	564	451	52j/	144j/
269	Non-metallic mineral products n.e.c.												
2691	Pottery, china and earthenware												
2692	Refractory ceramic products	j/					j/						
2693	Struct.non-refractory clay; ceramic products	j/					j/						
2694	Cement, lime and plaster	k/	4726	5329	5671	5623	k/	1103	1393	1492	1525	183k/	160k/
2695	Articles of concrete, cement and plaster	k/					k/					...k/	...k/
2696	Cutting, shaping & finishing of stone	m/	1472	1671	1777	1706	m/	475	507	551	642	73m/	83m/
2699	Other non-metallic mineral products n.e.c.	m/					m/					...m/	...m/
2710	Basic iron and steel		4278	5548	6366	4283		676	909	835	569	121	177
2720	Basic precious and non-ferrous metals		1713	1828	1553	1239		340	349	294	275	87	32
273	Casting of metals												
2731	Casting of iron and steel		962	1001	842	512		...	365	303	221	47	30
2732	Casting of non-ferrous metals												
281	Struct.metal products;tanks;steam generators		4374	5230	5681	5301		1290	1479	1600	1724	507	196
2811	Structural metal products												
2812	Tanks, reservoirs and containers of metal												
2813	Steam generators												
289	Other metal products; metal working services		14299	17230	16660	12552		5829	7417	7147	5527	1211	525
2891	Metal forging/pressing/stamping/roll-forming												
2892	Treatment & coating of metals												
2893	Cutlery, hand tools and general hardware												
2899	Other fabricated metal products n.e.c.												
291	General purpose machinery		5421	6540	7655	7433		2102	2304	3193	2774	152	129
2911	Engines & turbines (not for transport equipment)												
2912	Pumps, compressors, taps and valves												
2913	Bearings, gears, gearing & driving elements												
2914	Ovens, furnaces and furnace burners												
2915	Lifting and handling equipment												
2919	Other general purpose machinery												

Code	Description						note						
292	Special purpose machinery	3483	5215	4937	4043		535	1457	1878	1407		228	102
2921	Agricultural and forestry machinery	...	...	...	...		...	...	...	...		...	...
2922	Machine tools	...	...	...	...		...	...	...	...		...	...
2923	Machinery for metallurgy	...	...	...	...		...	...	...	...		...	...
2924	Machinery for mining & construction	...	...	...	...		...	...	...	...		...	...
2925	Food/beverage/tobacco processing machinery	...	...	...	...		...	...	...	...		...	...
2926	Machinery for textile, apparel and leather	...	...	...	...		...	...	...	...		...	...
2927	Weapons and ammunition	...	...	...	...		...	...	...	...		...	...
2929	Other special purpose machinery	2189	2710	2489	2757	n/	456	990	612	630		198n/	129n/
2930	Domestic appliances n.e.c.	...	...	...	...	n/	...	...	...	...		..n/	..n/
3000	Office, accounting and computing machinery	1149	1254	1381	1377		430	512	543	518		32	38
3110	Electric motors, generators and transformers	1956	2631	1903	2008		620	789	713	647		60p/	34p/
3120	Electricity distribution & control apparatus	2405	2088	1912	1573	p/	564	523	385	423		38q/	36q/
3130	Insulated wire and cable	...	...	...	...	q/	...	...	...	...		..q/	..q/
3140	Accumulators, primary cells and batteries	...	...	...	...	q/	...	...	...	...		..p/	..p/
3150	Lighting equipment and electric lamps	...	...	...	...	p/	...	...	...	...		..p/	..p/
3190	Other electrical equipment n.e.c.	...	...	...	...	p/	...	...	...	...		..p/	..p/
3210	Electronic valves, tubes, etc.	10669	11741	11699	19837	r/	5429	5848	5329	12473		4964	1078
3220	TV/radio transmitters; line comm. apparatus	16551	16613	16700	15485	r/	5889	5282	5139	4811		562r/	1291r/
3230	TV and radio receivers and associated goods	29901	33845	30233	27951	s/	11148	13196	11155	10852		1079s/	944s/
331	Medical, measuring, testing appliances, etc.	...	...	...	...		...	...	...	...		...	...
3311	Medical, surgical and orthopaedic equipment	...	...	...	...		...	...	...	...		...	...
3312	Measuring/testing/navigating appliances,etc.	...	...	...	...		...	...	...	...		...	...
3313	Industrial process control equipment	2261	2291	2637	2736		849	885	1023	1216		83	151
3320	Optical instruments & photographic equipment	...	...	...	...	s/	...	...	...	...		..s/	..s/
3330	Watches and clocks	...	...	...	...	t/	...	...	...	...		..t/	..t/
3410	Motor vehicles	2394	3090	4037	5145	t/	965	929	1266	1600		86t/	82t/
3420	Automobile bodies, trailers & semi-trailers	...	...	...	...	t/	...	...	...	...		..t/	..t/
3430	Parts/accessories for automobiles	...	...	...	...	u/	...	...	...	...		..u/	..u/
351	Building and repairing of ships and boats	...	...	...	...		...	...	...	...		...	...
3511	Building and repairing of ships	...	...	...	...		...	...	...	...		...	...
3512	Building/repairing of pleasure/sport. boats	...	...	...	...	u/	...	...	...	...		...	...
3520	Railway/tramway locomotives & rolling stock	9911	12798	10104	9906	u/	4572	5178	4338	4486		658u/	553u/
3530	Aircraft and spacecraft	...	...	...	...	u/	...	...	...	...		..u/	..u/
359	Transport equipment n.e.c.	...	...	...	...		...	...	...	...		...	...
3591	Motorcycles	...	...	...	...		...	...	...	...		...	...
3592	Bicycles and invalid carriages	...	...	...	...		...	...	...	...		...	...
3599	Other transport equipment n.e.c.	...	...	...	...		...	...	...	...		...	...
3610	Furniture	5518	5552	5476	5469		1677	1711	1821	2012		215	208
369	Manufacturing n.e.c.	3015	2655	2241	2200		908	743	659	669		47	63
3691	Jewellery and related articles	...	...	...	...		...	...	...	...		...	...
3692	Musical instruments	...	...	...	...		...	...	...	...		...	...
3693	Sports goods	...	...	...	...		...	...	...	...		...	...
3694	Games and toys	...	...	...	...		...	...	...	...		...	...
3699	Other manufacturing n.e.c.	...	...	...	...		...	...	...	...		...	...
3710	Recycling of metal waste and scrap	...	...	...	...		...	...	...	...		...	...
3720	Recycling of non-metal waste and scrap	...	...	...	...		...	...	...	...		...	...
D	Total manufacturing	281333	312297	333747	305114		89584	97512	101539	101837		18613	14279

a/ 155 includes 1600.
b/ 171 includes 1722.
c/ 172 excludes 1722.
d/ 191 includes 1820.
e/ 2010 includes 2021.
f/ 202 excludes 2021.
g/ 222 includes 2230.
h/ 2413 includes 2310, 2320, 2330 and 2430.
i/ 2411 includes 2412.
j/ 2691 includes 2610 and 2693.

k/ 2694 includes 2695.
m/ 2696 includes 2699.
n/ 2930 includes 3000.
p/ 3120 includes 3150 and 3190.
q/ 3130 includes 3140.
r/ 3220 includes 3230.
s/ 331 includes 3330.
t/ 3420 includes 3410 and 3430.
u/ 3520 includes 351, 3530 and 359.

Israel

Index numbers of industrial production

ISIC Revision 3

(2005=100)

ISIC	Industry	Note	1999	2000	2001	2002	2003	2004	2005	2006	2007	2008	2009	2010
15	Food and beverages	a/	103	103	102	100	98	100	100	102	105	103	102	105
16	Tobacco products	a/	...	...	...	...	...	...	...	...	...	...	...	...
17	Textiles		124	118	107	103	99	100	100	104	98	96	83	86
18	Wearing apparel, fur		...	...	...	...	...	...	...	...	...	...	...	...
19	Leather, leather products and footwear		...	...	...	...	...	...	...	...	...	...	...	...
20	Wood products (excl. furniture)		...	...	...	...	...	...	...	...	...	...	...	...
21	Paper and paper products		103	103	99	99	96	96	100	102	106	105	104	109
22	Printing and publishing		104	103	100	96	93	98	100	104	104	101	91	89
23	Coke,refined petroleum products,nuclear fuel	b/	64	66	70	81	85	96	100	124	122	162	149	177
24	Chemicals and chemical products	b/	...	...	...	...	...	...	...	...	...	...	...	...
25	Rubber and plastics products		70	73	75	81	86	91	100	105	114	122	107	124
26	Non-metallic mineral products		136	125	116	110	104	96	100	104	113	111	98	100
27	Basic metals		119	121	112	102	91	98	100	100	107	99	82	93
28	Fabricated metal products		88	96	92	91	90	95	100	112	115	116	94	110
29	Machinery and equipment n.e.c.		116	131	121	113	109	101	100	107	118	136	130	130
30	Office, accounting and computing machinery		...	...	...	...	...	...	...	...	...	...	...	...
31	Electrical machinery and apparatus		...	...	...	...	...	...	...	...	...	...	...	...
32	Radio,television and communication equipment		...	...	...	...	...	...	...	...	...	...	...	...
33	Medical, precision and optical instruments		...	...	...	...	...	...	...	...	...	...	...	...
34	Motor vehicles, trailers, semi-trailers		...	...	...	...	...	...	...	...	...	...	...	...
35	Other transport equipment		...	...	...	...	...	...	...	...	...	...	...	...
36	Furniture; manufacturing n.e.c.		...	...	...	...	...	...	...	...	...	...	...	...
37	Recycling		...	...	...	...	...	...	...	...	...	...	...	...
D	Total manufacturing		88	97	92	90	90	96	100	110	115	124	117	126

a/ 15 includes 16.
b/ 23 includes 24.

Italy

Supplier of information:
Istituto Nazionale di Statistica (National Institute of Statistics), Rome.
Industrial statistics for the OECD countries are compiled by the OECD secretariat, which supplies them to UNIDO.

Basic source of data:
Annual surveys; administrative data.

Major deviations from ISIC (Revision 4):
Data have been converted from the national NACE equivalent system to ISIC (Revision 4) by the OECD.

Reference period:
Calendar year.

Scope:
All enterprises.

Method of data collection:
Not reported.

Type of enumeration:
Not reported.

Adjusted for non-response:
Not reported.

Concepts and definitions of variables:
No deviations from the standard UN concepts and definitions are reported.

Related national publications:
None reported.

Italy

		Number of enterprises (number)					Number of employees (thousands)					Wages and salaries paid to employees (millions of Euros)				
ISIC	Industry	Note	2006	2007	2008	2009	Note	2006	2007	2008	2009	Note	2006	2007	2008	2009
1010	Processing/preserving of meat		...	...	3559	3495		...	...	53.0	53.0		...	...	1257	1297
1020	Processing/preserving of fish, etc.		...	...	442	419		...	...	5.4	4.8		...	...	118	114
1030	Processing/preserving of fruit,vegetables		...	...	1877	1808		...	...	27.3	27.0		...	...	599	612
1040	Vegetable and animal oils and fats		...	...	3614	3449		...	...	6.3	5.8		...	...	152	158
1050	Dairy products		...	...	3295	3141		...	...	37.1	37.1		...	...	991	1009
106	Grain mill products,starches and starch products		...	...	1213	1126		...	...	7.8	6.9		...	...	221	203
1061	Grain mill products		...	...	1188	1098		...	...	6.5	6.2		...	...	171	178
1062	Starches and starch products		...	...	25	28		...	...	1.4	0.7		...	...	50	25
107	Other food products		...		42970	41010		...		155.2	176.2		...		3492	3973
1071	Bakery products		...		32603	30993		...		86.4	106.3		...		1599	2012
1072	Sugar		...		26	13		...		1.7	1.5		...		46	43
1073	Cocoa, chocolate and sugar confectionery		...		818	822		...		19.8	19.1		...		595	595
1074	Macaroni, noodles, couscous, etc.		...		4807	4555		...		19.1	21.2		...		489	541
1075	Prepared meals and dishes		...		1096	1129		...		7.1	6.7		...		159	159
1079	Other food products n.e.c.		...		3620	3498		...		21.1	21.4		...		604	623
1080	Prepared animal feeds		...		579	542		...		7.6	7.2		...		243	247
1101	Distilling, rectifying and blending of spirits		...		2813a/	2758a/		...		34.7a/	32.5a/		...		1108a/	1036a/
1102	Wines		...		...a/	...a/		...		...a/	...a/		...		...a/	...a/
1103	Malt liquors and malt		...		...a/	...a/		...		...a/	...a/		...		...a/	...a/
1104	Soft drinks,mineral waters,other bottled waters		...		...a/	...a/		...		...a/	...a/		...		...a/	...a/
1200	Tobacco products		...		...	3		...		...	1.1		...		...	47
131	Spinning, weaving and finishing of textiles		...		7614	7037		...		97.8	88.7		...		2191	1955
1311	Preparation and spinning of textile fibres		...		2493	2246		...		25.7	21.8		...		521	424
1312	Weaving of textiles		...		2479	2385		...		39.7	38.1		...		967	876
1313	Finishing of textiles		...		2642	2406		...		32.4	28.8		...		703	654
139	Other textiles		...		10737	10219		...		53.6	50.6		...		1111	1086
1391	Knitted and crocheted fabrics		...		1275	1078		...		6.6	6.0		...		137	125
1392	Made-up textile articles, except apparel		...		5230	5039		...		16.9	16.4		...		306	327
1393	Carpets and rugs		...		155	157		...		1.9	1.6		...		42	32
1394	Cordage, rope, twine and netting		...		191	191		...		1.2	1.1		...		22	22
1399	Other textiles n.e.c.		...		3886	3754		...		27.1	25.5		...		604	581
1410	Wearing apparel, except fur apparel		...		31192	28806		...		184.0	166.9		...		3275	3058
1420	Articles of fur		...		1107	1023		...		1.3	1.2		...		21	18
1430	Knitted and crocheted apparel		...		5150	4828		...		33.5	31.0		...		602	565
151	Leather;luggage,handbags,saddlery,harness;fur		...		7554	7080		...		48.3	44.7		...		1079	1016
1511	Tanning/dressing of leather; dressing of fur		...		2133	2011		...		23.3	21.2		...		567	499
1512	Luggage,handbags,etc.;saddlery/harness		...		5421	5069		...		25.0	23.5		...		512	517
1520	Footwear		...		9639	9025		...		80.2	74.6		...		1589	1349
1610	Sawmilling and planing of wood		...		5526	5852		...		15.9	14.9		...		318	280
162	Wood products, cork, straw, plaiting materials		...		31170	28435		...		88.3	82.6		...		1753	1653

1621	Veneer sheets and wood-based panels	…	2141	2281	…	13.9	12.7	…	322	288	…
1622	Builders' carpentry and joinery	…	20664	19282	…	50.4	50.0	…	968	958	…
1623	Wooden containers	…	1336	1172	…	8.8	8.0	…	164	160	…
1629	Other wood products;articles of cork,straw	…	7029	5700	…	15.1	11.9	…	300	247	…
1701	Pulp, paper and paperboard	…	261	258	…	14.6	14.0	…	452	418	…
1702	Corrugated paper and paperboard	…	1285	1242	…	23.6	23.0	…	616	601	…
1709	Other articles of paper and paperboard	…	2539	2664	…	32.9	32.9	…	905	886	…
181	Printing and service activities related to printing	…	17837	16901	…	84.3	82.3	…	2111	2057	…
1811	Printing	…	13482	12764	…	67.5	65.1	…	1704	1652	…
1812	Service activities related to printing	…	4355	4137	…	16.7	17.2	…	406	406	…
1820	Reproduction of recorded media	…	423	378	…	0.9	1.0	…	32	29	…
1910	Coke oven products	…	7	6	…	0.3	0.3	…	7	11	…
1920	Refined petroleum products	…	346	324	…	15.6	15.4	…	666	664	…
201	Basic chemicals,fertilizers, etc.	…	1049	1040	…	41.3	39.7	…	1483	1441	…
2011	Basic chemicals	…	484	499	…	24.7	23.7	…	920	886	…
2012	Fertilizers and nitrogen compounds	…	167	164	…	2.6	2.5	…	84	83	…
2013	Plastics and synthetic rubber in primary forms	…	398	377	…	14.0	13.5	…	479	472	…
202	Other chemical products	…	3607	3468	…	68.9	66.5	…	2341	2169	…
2021	Pesticides and other agrochemical products	…	53	56	…	2.1	2.1	…	83	81	…
2022	Paints,varnishes;printing ink and mastics	…	951	916	…	20.6	20.2	…	673	666	…
2023	Soap,cleaning and cosmetic preparations	…	1431	1405	…	27.0	25.8	…	917	812	…
2029	Other chemical products n.e.c.	…	1172	1091	…	19.2	18.4	…	668	610	…
2030	Man-made fibres	…	41	39	…	3.7	3.3	…	111	77	…
2100	Pharmaceuticals,medicinal chemicals, etc.	…	528	498	…	67.5	65.1	…	3068	2932	…
221	Rubber products	…	1615	1559	…	43.6	41.5	…	1217	1113	…
2211	Rubber tyres and tubes	…	157	143	…	13.0	12.6	…	450	434	…
2219	Other rubber products	…	1458	1416	…	30.6	28.8	…	767	679	…
2220	Plastics products	…	10005	9557	…	138.3	133.1	…	3431	3342	…
2310	Glass and glass products	…	4699	4544	…	37.5	35.8	…	991	929	…
239	Non-metallic mineral products n.e.c.	…	20357	19548	…	172.3	163.4	…	4512	4183	…
2391	Refractory products	…	128	124	…	2.6	2.6	…	78	73	…
2392	Clay building materials	…	951	919	…	38.5	35.6	…	1214	1007	…
2393	Other porcelain and ceramic products	…	3325	3054	…	13.8	12.4	…	316	245	…
2394	Cement, lime and plaster	…	242	227	…	11.2	10.7	…	390	366	…
2395	Articles of concrete, cement and plaster	…	4134	3927	…	53.0	50.5	…	1345	1268	…
2396	Cutting, shaping and finishing of stone	…	10363	10141	…	39.6	38.9	…	808	883	…
2399	Other non-metallic mineral products n.e.c.	…	1214	1156	…	13.7	12.7	…	362	341	…
2410	Basic iron and steel	…		2006	…		78.2	…		2134	…
2420	Basic precious and other non-ferrous metals	…	679	763	…	21.5	20.6	…	655	586	…
243	Casting of metals	…	1225	1184	…	32.7	30.5	…	909	729	…
2431	Casting of iron and steel	…	212	205	…	11.9	11.2	…	357	267	…
2432	Casting of non-ferrous metals	…	1013	979	…	20.8	19.3	…	552	462	…
251	Struct.metal products, tanks, reservoirs	…	37440	36394	…	174.1	173.7	…	3906	3878	…
2511	Structural metal products	…	36542	35532	…	155.6	156.3	…	3367	3410	…
2512	Tanks, reservoirs and containers of metal	…	762	725	…	15.5	14.5	…	436	364	…

continued

Italy

ISIC Revision 4		Number of enterprises (number)					Number of employees (thousands)					Wages and salaries paid to employees (millions of Euros)				
ISIC	Industry	Note	2006	2007	2008	2009	Note	2006	2007	2008	2009	Note	2006	2007	2008	2009
2513	Steam generators, excl. hot water boilers		...	...	136	137		...	...	3.0	2.9		...	...	103	104
2520	Weapons and ammunition		...	...	237	245		...	...	6.8	6.9		...	...	236	248
259	Other metal products;metal working services		...	...	44867	40823		...	...	352.8	321.0		...	...	8889	7352
2591	Forging,pressing,stamping,roll-forming of metal		...	...	1810	1708		...	...	43.0	40.4		...	...	1217	1010
2592	Treatment and coating of metals; machining		...	...	23205	20313		...	...	154.1	134.9		...	...	3631	2849
2593	Cutlery, hand tools and general hardware		...	...	5110	5018		...	...	51.5	48.4		...	...	1431	1202
2599	Other fabricated metal products n.e.c.		...	...	14742	13784		...	...	104.3	97.3		...	...	2610	2291
2610	Electronic components and boards		...	...	2487	2370		...	...	39.6	36.8		...	...	1078	992
2620	Computers and peripheral equipment		...	...	1127	963		...	...	7.5	7.1		...	...	228	204
2630	Communication equipment		...	...	1043	964		...	...	27.9	25.3		...	...	952	865
2640	Consumer electronics		...	...	247	230		...	...	3.2	2.8		...	...	83	68
265	Measuring,testing equipment; watches, etc.		...	...	1067	1004		...	...	24.7	23.0		...	...	835	776
2651	Measuring/testing/navigating equipment,etc.		...	...	968	904		...	...	24.0	22.2		...	...	818	759
2652	Watches and clocks		...	...	99	100		...	...	0.7	0.7		...	...	17	18
2660	Irradiation/electromedical equipment,etc.		...	...	651	687		...	...	12.5	12.2		...	...	412	378
2670	Optical instruments and photographic equipment		...	...	184	156		...	...	2.4	2.1		...	...	68	58
2680	Magnetic and optical media		...	...	45	37		...	...	0.4	0.3		...	...	10	7
2710	Electric motors,generators,transformers,etc.		...	...	3015	2852		...	...	52.2	49.7		...	...	1523	1432
2720	Batteries and accumulators		...	...	78	78		...	...	2.7	2.7		...	...	80	72
273	Wiring and wiring devices		...	...	1087	1020		...	...	19.9	18.8		...	...	535	484
2731	Fibre optic cables		...	...	31	34		...	...	1.5	1.3		...	...	62	49
2732	Other electronic and electric wires and cables		...	...	626	568		...	...	11.4	11.0		...	...	293	278
2733	Wiring devices		...	...	430	418		...	...	7.0	6.5		...	...	180	156
2740	Electric lighting equipment		...	...	1666	1588		...	...	16.8	16.1		...	...	436	400
2750	Domestic appliances		...	...	584	556		...	...	49.6	42.7		...	...	1342	1137
2790	Other electrical equipment		...	...	2802	3126		...	...	29.8	30.3		...	...	767	763
281	General-purpose machinery		...	...	10545	10582		...	...	251.1	249.8		...	...	7818	7370
2811	Engines/turbines,excl.aircraft,vehicle engines		...	...	272	263		...	...	17.0	17.4		...	...	672	689
2812	Fluid power equipment		...	...	263	259		...	...	15.1	14.8		...	...	498	445
2813	Other pumps, compressors, taps and valves		...	...	1530	1573		...	...	39.8	42.6		...	...	1171	1203
2814	Bearings, gears, gearing and driving elements		...	...	769	778		...	...	28.4	27.3		...	...	849	682
2815	Ovens, furnaces and furnace burners		...	...	451	485		...	...	12.3	12.0		...	...	382	342
2816	Lifting and handling equipment		...	...	1752	1780		...	...	35.7	34.0		...	...	1055	952
2817	Office machinery, excl.computers,etc.		...	...	304	347		...	...	1.4	1.6		...	...	35	46
2818	Power-driven hand tools		...	...	52	44		...	...	0.7	0.6		...	...	20	13
2819	Other general-purpose machinery		...	...	5152	5053		...	...	100.5	99.5		...	...	3138	2998
282	Special-purpose machinery		...	...	13379	13490		...	...	197.8	189.3		...	...	6044	5204
2821	Agricultural and forestry machinery		...	...	2003	1994		...	...	30.2	29.3		...	...	824	721
2822	Metal-forming machinery and machine tools		...	...	2143	2106		...	...	43.1	41.0		...	...	1412	1162
2823	Machinery for metallurgy		...	...	1737	1792		...	...	18.0	17.7		...	...	543	540
2824	Mining, quarrying and construction machinery		...	...	1208	1222		...	...	22.7	21.6		...	...	662	510

Code	Description													
2825	Food/beverage/tobacco processing machinery	:	2315	2323	:	:	:	26.9	26.3	:	:	:	805	772
2826	Textile/apparel/leather production machinery	:	1229	1200	:	:	:	16.3	14.6	:	:	:	460	357
2829	Other special-purpose machinery	:	2744	2853	:	:	:	40.6	38.8	:	:	:	1337	1141
2910	Motor vehicles	:	86	105	:	:	:	68.4	68.3	:	:	:	1848	1606
2920	Automobile bodies, trailers and semi-trailers	:	548	618	:	:	:	16.1	14.7	:	:	:	433	346
2930	Parts and accessories for motor vehicles	:	1626	1531	:	:	:	95.9	89.7	:	:	:	2614	2210
301	Building of ships and boats	:	1991	1875	:	:	:	32.8	29.4	:	:	:	920	821
3011	Building of ships and floating structures	:	910	935	:	:	:	19.5	18.0	:	:	:	571	517
3012	Building of pleasure and sporting boats	:	1081	940	:	:	:	13.3	11.4	:	:	:	349	304
3020	Railway locomotives and rolling stock	:	161	164	:	:	:	33.0	34.1	:	:	:	1195	1172
3030	Air and spacecraft and related machinery	:	:	:	:	:	:	:	:	:	:	:	:	:
3040	Military fighting vehicles	:	:	:	:	:	:	:	:	:	:	:	:	:
309	Transport equipment n.e.c.	:	927	917	:	:	:	20.9	20.2	:	:	:	585	525
3091	Motorcycles	:	411	412	:	:	:	15.0	14.3	:	:	:	433	384
3092	Bicycles and invalid carriages	:	474	463	:	:	:	5.4	5.5	:	:	:	139	131
3099	Other transport equipment n.e.c.	:	42	42	:	:	:	0.4	0.4	:	:	:	13	9
3100	Furniture	:	23761	21825	:	:	:	152.7	142.0	:	:	:	3250	3039
321	Jewellery, bijouterie and related articles	:	9488	8880	:	:	:	26.3	24.2	:	:	:	508	442
3211	Jewellery and related articles	:	7989	7417	:	:	:	24.3	22.2	:	:	:	470	399
3212	Imitation jewellery and related articles	:	1499	1463	:	:	:	1.9	2.0	:	:	:	38	43
3220	Musical instruments	:	642	601	:	:	:	1.5	1.4	:	:	:	30	29
3230	Sports goods	:	671	642	:	:	:	5.6	5.4	:	:	:	137	142
3240	Games and toys	:	478	448	:	:	:	3.1	3.0	:	:	:	65	67
3250	Medical and dental instruments and supplies	:	16370	17423	:	:	:	42.7	43.7	:	:	:	990	1008
3290	Other manufacturing n.e.c.	:	3622	3581	:	:	:	17.0	16.6	:	:	:	360	357
331	Repair of fabricated metal products/machinery	:	28992	28573	:	:	:	78.6	70.9	:	:	:	1940	1649
3311	Repair of fabricated metal products	:	2002	2097	:	:	:	5.3	4.4	:	:	:	131	96
3312	Repair of machinery	:	16948	16743	:	:	:	37.9	37.7	:	:	:	930	839
3313	Repair of electronic and optical equipment	:	5123	5134	:	:	:	12.6	11.2	:	:	:	313	296
3314	Repair of electrical equipment	:	2044	1874	:	:	:	6.5	5.5	:	:	:	146	129
3315	Repair of transport equip., excl. motor vehicles	:	2475	2261	:	:	:	15.8	11.7	:	:	:	410	280
3319	Repair of other equipment	:	400	464	:	:	:	0.5	0.4	:	:	:	10	9
3320	Installation of industrial machinery/equipment	:	9023	8630	:	:	:	47.3	44.7	:	:	:	1316	1265
C	Total manufacturing	:	459728	439112	:	:	:	3741.4	3582.6	:	:	:	97841	90678

a/ 1101 includes 1102, 1103 and 1104.

Italy

ISIC Revision 4		Output (millions of Euros)					Value added at factor values (millions of Euros)					Gross fixed capital formation (millions of Euros)		
ISIC	Industry	Note	2006	2007	2008	2009	Note	2006	2007	2008	2009	Note	2008	2009
1010	Processing/preserving of meat		…	…	18228	19211		…	…	2444	2281		363	461
1020	Processing/preserving of fish, etc.		…	…	1975	2009		…	…	270	296		42	60
1030	Processing/preserving of fruit,vegetables		…	…	8526	8919		…	…	1376	1314		510	351
1040	Vegetable and animal oils and fats		…	…	5673	4881		…	…	579	520		308	128
1050	Dairy products		…	…	16269	14936		…	…	2210	2744		651	448
106	Grain mill products,starches and starch products		…	…	6868	4325		…	…	801	664		577	129
1061	Grain mill products		…	…	6064	3857		…	…	630	547		550	100
1062	Starches and starch products		…	…	805	468		…	…	171	117		27	29
107	Other food products		…	…	34749	34411		…	…	8695	9315		1643	2711
1071	Bakery products		…	…	10882	11867		…	…	3871	4271		597	1522
1072	Sugar		…	…	544	397		…	…	3	-14		51	62
1073	Cocoa, chocolate and sugar confectionery		…	…	6822	6392		…	…	1394	1276		356	381
1074	Macaroni, noodles, couscous, etc.		…	…	6289	6563		…	…	1303	1409		183	346
1075	Prepared meals and dishes		…	…	1653	1383		…	…	367	388		68	39
1079	Other food products n.e.c.		…	…	8559	7809		…	…	1758	1986		389	362
1080	Prepared animal feeds		…	…	5704	4784		…	…	589	627		180	74
1101	Distilling, rectifying and blending of spirits		…	…	16466 a/	14475 a/		…	…	2664 a/	2701 a/		755 a/	677 a/
1102	Wines		…	…	…a/	…a/		…	…	…a/	…a/		…a/	…a/
1103	Malt liquors and malt		…	…	…a/	…a/		…	…	…a/	…a/		…a/	…a/
1104	Soft drinks,mineral waters,other bottled waters		…	…	…a/	…a/		…	…	…a/	…a/		…a/	…a/
1200	Tobacco products		…	…	…	509		…	…	…	274		…	18
131	Spinning, weaving and finishing of textiles		…	…	14734	11467		…	…	3881	3015		769	446
1311	Preparation and spinning of textile fibres		…	…	4212	3079		…	…	976	703		141	206
1312	Weaving of textiles		…	…	7049	5759		…	…	1714	1385		313	117
1313	Finishing of textiles		…	…	3473	2630		…	…	1191	927		315	124
139	Other textiles		…	…	9696	9619		…	…	2207	2340		353	353
1391	Knitted and crocheted fabrics		…	…	1331	842		…	…	348	246		40	45
1392	Made-up textile articles, except apparel		…	…	2815	3420		…	…	596	720		62	79
1393	Carpets and rugs		…	…	323	223		…	…	67	58		14	6
1394	Cordage, rope, twine and netting		…	…	204	195		…	…	47	44		2	9
1399	Other textiles n.e.c.		…	…	5023	4938		…	…	1149	1272		237	213
1410	Wearing apparel, except fur apparel		…	…	28130	24124		…	…	6596	5496		499	474
1420	Articles of fur		…	…	211	149		…	…	46	40		1	3
1430	Knitted and crocheted apparel		…	…	4955	4402		…	…	1203	1092		144	115
151	Leather;luggage,handbags,saddlery,harness;fur		…	…	12627	9382		…	…	2340	1863		320	345
1511	Tanning/dressing of leather; dressing of fur		…	…	6471	4867		…	…	1061	911		169	163
1512	Luggage,handbags,etc.;saddlery/harness		…	…	6157	4515		…	…	1280	952		151	182
1520	Footwear		…	…	14355	11046		…	…	3361	2507		296	266
1610	Sawmilling and planing of wood		…	…	2996	2757		…	…	620	635		156	152
162	Wood products, cork, straw, plaiting materials		…	…	13875	12095		…	…	4151	3493		618	596

Code	Description								
1621	Veneer sheets and wood-based panels	:	3168	2556	:	685	567	155	143
1622	Builders' carpentry and joinery	:	6933	6382	:	2415	2089	329	341
1623	Wooden containers	:	1545	1386	:	382	317	41	62
1629	Other wood products;articles of cork,straw	:	2230	1772	:	669	519	93	50
1701	Pulp, paper and paperboard	:	5665	4481	:	877	948	213	153
1702	Corrugated paper and paperboard	:	6007	5192	:	1340	1279	254	239
1709	Other articles of paper and paperboard	:	9477	8453	:	2132	1376	503	390
181	Printing and service activities related to printing	:	14138	11513	:	4540	3884	591	546
1811	Printing	:	11278	9630	:	3707	3132	369	416
1812	Service activities related to printing	:	2860	1883	:	833	752	222	130
1820	Reproduction of recorded media	:	391	462	:	85	59	4	4
1910	Coke oven products	:	118	202	:	45	40	5	14
1920	Refined petroleum products	:	44590	23768	:	2599	1145	1174	991
201	Basic chemicals,fertilizers, etc.	:	22724	17111	:	2605	2229	1025	911
2011	Basic chemicals	:	13088	10284	:	1317	1023	743	591
2012	Fertilizers and nitrogen compounds	:	1674	1172	:	264	162	19	18
2013	Plastics and synthetic rubber in primary forms	:	7961	5655	:	1024	1044	264	302
202	Other chemical products	:	27797	20933	:	5527	5424	867	671
2021	Pesticides and other agrochemical products	:	1034	1020	:	221	220	22	34
2022	Paints,varnishes;printing ink and mastics	:	6577	5633	:	1499	1539	244	176
2023	Soap,cleaning and cosmetic preparations	:	10775	8156	:	2280	2130	354	217
2029	Other chemical products n.e.c.	:	9410	6125	:	1527	1535	246	244
2030	Man-made fibres	:	1101	752	:	116	83	21	11
2100	Pharmaceuticals,medicinal chemicals, etc.	:	24990	22837	:	7123	7232	1018	874
221	Rubber products	:	8889	6647	:	2230	1936	370	256
2211	Rubber tyres and tubes	:	3434	2376	:	728	691	135	130
2219	Other rubber products	:	5455	4271	:	1503	1245	235	126
2220	Plastics products	:	29491	25627	:	7228	6959	1442	1085
2310	Glass and glass products	:	7100	5587	:	2100	1737	526	472
239	Non-metallic mineral products n.e.c.	:	37151	30578	:	9684	8329	2084	1337
2391	Refractory products	:	598	480	:	175	145	17	7
2392	Clay building materials	:	7519	5728	:	2243	1782	544	259
2393	Other porcelain and ceramic products	:	1464	1154	:	518	417	119	50
2394	Cement, lime and plaster	:	4117	3086	:	1096	905	341	220
2395	Articles of concrete, cement and plaster	:	13147	10956	:	2870	2553	693	374
2396	Cutting, shaping and finishing of stone	:	6700	5990	:	1944	1740	233	370
2399	Other non-metallic mineral products n.e.c.	:	3606	3185	:	838	789	138	57
2410	Basic iron and steel	:	:	25539	:	:	3262	:	2071
2420	Basic precious and other non-ferrous metals	:	14078	8821	:	1253	1015	517	226
243	Casting of metals	:	8164	4778	:	1799	1266	425	314
2431	Casting of iron and steel	:	3390	1793	:	803	505	199	117
2432	Casting of non-ferrous metals	:	4774	2985	:	996	761	226	198
251	Struct.metal products, tanks, reservoirs	:	30804	27182	:	8335	8553	1380	1089
2511	Structural metal products	:	26128	23585	:	7253	7535	1151	957
2512	Tanks, reservoirs and containers of metal	:	3705	2703	:	930	809	217	121

continued

Italy

ISIC Revision 4		Output (millions of Euros)					Value added at factor values (millions of Euros)					Gross fixed capital formation (millions of Euros)		
ISIC	Industry	Note	2006	2007	2008	2009	Note	2006	2007	2008	2009	Note	2008	2009
2513	Steam generators, excl. hot water boilers		...	...	970	895		...	...	151	209		12	11
2520	Weapons and ammunition		...	...	1869	2211		...	...	542	546		54	37
259	Other metal products;metal working services		...	...	67430	45668		...	...	19793	14297		3497	2542
2591	Forging,pressing,stamping,roll-forming of metal		...	...	14364	8687		...	...	3449	2386		797	468
2592	Treatment and coating of metals; machining		...	...	23671	14031		...	...	7687	5136		1224	697
2593	Cutlery, hand tools and general hardware		...	...	8382	6044		...	...	2940	2295		562	463
2599	Other fabricated metal products n.e.c.		...	...	21014	16907		...	...	5717	4480		914	914
2610	Electronic components and boards		...	...	6276	4633		...	...	2107	1818		308	190
2620	Computers and peripheral equipment		...	...	1808	2386		...	...	419	380		23	25
2630	Communication equipment		...	...	6660	5425		...	...	1560	1382		139	86
2640	Consumer electronics		...	...	739	576		...	...	121	119		11	7
265	Measuring,testing equipment; watches, etc.		...	...	4897	4276		...	...	1649	1463		121	76
2651	Measuring/testing/navigating equipment,etc.		...	...	4645	4097		...	...	1598	1431		116	75
2652	Watches and clocks		...	...	252	179		...	...	51	32		5	-
2660	Irradiation/electromedical equipment,etc.		...	...	3164	2428		...	...	881	778		86	89
2670	Optical instruments and photographic equipment		...	...	502	391		...	...	148	135		8	10
2680	Magnetic and optical media		...	...	64	59		...	...	21	13		1	2
2710	Electric motors,generators,transformers,etc.		...	...	12684	10101		...	...	3674	3020		294	351
2720	Batteries and accumulators		...	...	744	752		...	...	160	152		43	18
273	Wiring and wiring devices		...	...	7112	4366		...	...	1191	934		166	124
2731	Fibre optic cables		...	...	384	206		...	...	79	70		9	8
2732	Other electronic and electric wires and cables		...	...	5399	3151		...	...	704	538		100	71
2733	Wiring devices		...	...	1330	1010		...	...	408	326		57	45
2740	Electric lighting equipment		...	...	3710	2946		...	...	983	804		96	74
2750	Domestic appliances		...	...	10705	8051		...	...	2304	2099		331	248
2790	Other electrical equipment		...	...	5898	5291		...	...	1846	1636		153	142
281	General-purpose machinery		...	...	64482	51562		...	...	17286	15179		2084	1321
2811	Engines/turbines,excl.aircraft,vehicle engines		...	...	7032	6929		...	...	1775	1714		220	131
2812	Fluid power equipment		...	...	4164	3075		...	...	1245	1027		148	108
2813	Other pumps, compressors, taps and valves		...	...	11447	9090		...	...	3038	2775		305	298
2814	Bearings, gears, gearing and driving elements		...	...	6227	3665		...	...	1718	1114		346	125
2815	Ovens, furnaces and furnace burners		...	...	3135	2373		...	...	623	618		45	26
2816	Lifting and handling equipment		...	...	8638	6481		...	...	2166	1784		282	102
2817	Office machinery, excl.computers,etc.		...	...	212	239		...	...	71	89		17	15
2818	Power-driven hand tools		...	...	176	62		...	...	45	24		11	1
2819	Other general-purpose machinery		...	...	23452	19649		...	...	6607	6034		712	514
282	Special-purpose machinery		...	...	49500	34318		...	...	12273	8774		1612	1133
2821	Agricultural and forestry machinery		...	...	8123	5328		...	...	1772	1294		388	171
2822	Metal-forming machinery and machine tools		...	...	9668	6622		...	...	2689	1839		184	179
2823	Machinery for metallurgy		...	...	6035	4615		...	...	1388	968		366	156
2824	Mining, quarrying and construction machinery		...	...	7456	3450		...	...	1448	801		190	222

Code	Description	5930	5859	1754	1365	114	141
2825	Food/beverage/tobacco processing machinery	5930	5859	1754	1365	114	141
2825	Food/beverage/tobacco processing machinery	2857	1928	700	554	120	36
2826	Textile/apparel/leather production machinery	9431	6517	2522	1953	250	229
2829	Other special-purpose machinery	30147	22220	3863	3503	1615	1171
2910	Motor vehicles	3760	2223	766	521	69	63
2920	Automobile bodies, trailers and semi-trailers	19758	14804	4418	3579	981	443
2930	Parts and accessories for motor vehicles	9898	7356	1991	1332	276	156
301	Building of ships and boats	5499	4806	1127	874	148	93
3011	Building of ships and floating structures	4399	2550	864	457	128	63
3012	Building of pleasure and sporting boats	:	:	:	:	:	:
3020	Railway locomotives and rolling stock	8452	8329	2548	2433	283	319
3030	Air and spacecraft and related machinery	:	:	:	:	:	:
3040	Military fighting vehicles	4976	4457	1132	919	253	190
309	Transport equipment n.e.c.	3502	3078	825	666	209	130
3091	Motorcycles	1348	1313	282	234	41	60
3092	Bicycles and invalid carriages	127	66	25	20	4	1
3099	Other transport equipment n.e.c.	25362	21131	6546	5748	874	801
3100	Furniture	4929	3348	1080	832	109	94
321	Jewellery, bijouterie and related articles	4580	3012	983	739	101	77
3211	Jewellery and related articles	349	336	98	93	9	17
3212	Imitation jewellery and related articles	161	152	48	57	6	12
3220	Musical instruments	1285	1213	335	315	47	28
3230	Sports goods	646	668	150	153	39	19
3240	Games and toys	6697	7067	2464	2296	340	225
3250	Medical and dental instruments and supplies	2618	2527	785	782	168	134
3290	Other manufacturing n.e.c.	11486	7850	4331	3382	696	1241
331	Repair of fabricated metal products/machinery	647	413	258	194	31	12
3311	Repair of fabricated metal products	5826	4109	2291	1866	449	936
3312	Repair of machinery	1705	1303	679	583	74	41
3313	Repair of electronic and optical equipment	864	584	331	244	30	16
3314	Repair of electrical equipment	2370	1362	749	472	111	231
3315	Repair of transport equip., excl. motor vehicles	74	79	23	24	2	5
3319	Repair of other equipment	9405	7259	2710	2429	294	133
3320	Installation of industrial machinery/equipment	:	:	:	:	:	:
C	Total manufacturing	948298	742725	211745	180257	38364	31024

a/ 1101 includes 1102, 1103 and 1104.

Italy

Index numbers of industrial production

ISIC Revision 4

(2005=100)

ISIC	Industry	Note	1999	2000	2001	2002	2003	2004	2005	2006	2007	2008	2009	2010
10	Food products		90	91	95	96	98	99	100	101	102	102	101	103
11	Beverages		90	95	99	101	103	100	100	105	107	105	105	106
12	Tobacco products		...	...	...	...	...	...	...	...	...	...	...	...
13	Textiles		120	121	119	113	110	105	100	100	97	85	67	76
14	Wearing apparel		123	124	128	117	112	112	100	112	127	133	127	133
15	Leather and related products		151	149	141	129	124	111	100	99	96	88	76	76
16	Wood/wood products/cork,excl. furniture		85	94	94	97	98	101	100	99	96	88	76	76
17	Paper and paper products		89	91	92	95	95	99	100	101	99	86	67	66
18	Printing and reproduction of recorded media		97	96	94	93	95	99	100	103	106	100	90	95
19	Coke and refined petroleum products		94	92	94	93	95	96	100	95	92	95	85	85
20	Chemicals and chemical products		100	103	99	100	96	100	100	99	100	95	86	89
21	Pharmaceuticals,medicinal chemicals, etc.		100	98	97	104	103	105	100	104	108	101	88	95
22	Rubber and plastics products		105	111	109	105	105	105	100	107	107	103	103	104
23	Other non-metallic mineral products		96	101	103	102	102	101	100	102	99	101	83	86
24	Basic metals		92	99	95	94	95	100	100	99	99	93	71	72
25	Fabricated metal products, except machinery		94	97	100	98	101	102	100	107	107	101	71	85
26	Computer, electronic and optical products		141	140	129	116	111	109	100	100	107	103	73	78
27	Electrical equipment		117	125	115	108	108	106	100	104	103	95	86	92
28	Machinery and equipment n.e.c.		97	102	103	102	98	106	100	107	105	97	69	79
29	Motor vehicles, trailers and semi-trailers		127	131	122	114	108	108	100	106	110	107	71	83
30	Other transport equipment		128	133	118	114	106	107	100	107	117	113	74	88
31	Furniture		102	108	110	106	102	103	100	112	120	126	110	101
32	Other manufacturing		111	112	114	106	101	101	100	97	101	104	88	88
33	Repair and installation of machinery/equipment		103	105	103	100	101	103	100	107	102	89	75	88
C	Total manufacturing		103	107	106	104	102	103	100	103	106	103	83	89

Japan

Concepts and definitions of variables:

Number of employees includes all employees with contracts of more than one month, temporary employees provided by employment agencies and employees working for 18 days or more in two consecutive months.

Wages and salaries relates to total cash payments, including basic wages, bonuses and other premiums, allowances and employees' retirement and termination allowances.

Value added is output less the value of raw materials, fuels and electricity consumed, the cost of contract and commission work done by others, value of excise taxes and depreciation. It is valued at basic prices.

Related national publications:
None reported.

Supplier of information:
Ministry of Economy, Trade and Industry (METI), Tokyo.
Industrial statistics for the OECD countries are compiled by the OECD secretariat, which supplies them to UNIDO.

Basic source of data:
Manufacturing census; survey.

Major deviations from ISIC (Revision 4):
None reported.

Reference period:
Calendar year.

Scope:
Census covers all establishments in years where the last digit is 0, 3, 5 or 8. In other years, only those establishments with four or more persons engaged are covered. Data on investment cover establishments with 10 or more persons engaged in 2001 and earlier, and 30 or more persons engaged from 2002 onwards. Data on wages cover establishments with 30 or more persons engaged

Method of data collection:
Questionnaires are distributed and collected by enumerators.

Type of enumeration:
Not reported.

Adjusted for non-response:
No.

Japan

ISIC	Industry	Note	Establishments (number)				Note	Number of employees (thousands)				Note	Wages and salaries paid to employees (billions of Japanese Yen)			
			2007	2008	2009	2010		2007	2008	2009	2010		2007	2008	2009	2010
1010	Processing/preserving of meat		:	:	:	:		:	64	66	65		:	145	150	151
1020	Processing/preserving of fish, etc.		:	:	:	:		:	169	166	164		:	229	228	228
1030	Processing/preserving of fruit,vegetables		:	:	:	:		:	87	86	84		:	126	125	125
1040	Vegetable and animal oils and fats		:	:	:	:		:	9	8	8		:	37	35	35
1050	Dairy products		:	:	:	:		:	38	39	39		:	132	136	138
106	Grain mill products,starches and starch products		:	:	:	:		:	17	17	18		:	43	43	44
1061	Grain mill products		:	:	:	:		:	15	15	16		:	32	32	32
1062	Starches and starch products		:	:	:	:		:	3	3	3		:	11	12	11
107	Other food products		:	:	:	:		:	729	739	743		:	1483	1497	1539
1071	Bakery products		:	:	:	:		:	227	229	227		:	476	482	491
1072	Sugar		:	:	:	:		:	4	4	4		:	17	17	17
1073	Cocoa, chocolate and sugar confectionery		:	:	:	:		:	42	44	46		:	112	114	122
1074	Macaroni, noodles, couscous, etc.		:	:	:	:		:	53	53	54		:	79	81	85
1075	Prepared meals and dishes		:	:	:	:		:	47	50	51		:	106	109	116
1079	Other food products n.e.c.		:	:	:	:		:	356	359	361		:	692	694	709
1080	Prepared animal feeds		:	:	:	:		:	14	14	14		:	27	27	27
1101	Distilling, rectifying and blending of spirits		:	:	:	:		:	12	12	12		:	34	33	34
1102	Wines		:	:	:	:		:	23	22	21		:	37	35	34
1103	Malt liquors and malt		:	:	:	:		:	5	5	5		:	30	32	31
1104	Soft drinks,mineral waters,other bottled waters		:	:	:	:		:	27	26	26		:	98	94	94
1200	Tobacco products		:	:	:	:		:	3	3	3		:	25	24	22
131	Spinning, weaving and finishing of textiles		:	:	:	:		:	71	63	59		:	138	114	107
1311	Preparation and spinning of textile fibres		:	:	:	:		:	13	11	11		:	22	19	19
1312	Weaving of textiles		:	:	:	:		:	27	23	21		:	45	34	32
1313	Finishing of textiles		:	:	:	:		:	31	29	27		:	71	61	56
139	Other textiles		:	:	:	:		:	87	81	78		:	142	128	125
1391	Knitted and crocheted fabrics		:	:	:	:		:	6	5	5		:	9	8	7
1392	Made-up textile articles, except apparel		:	:	:	:		:	38	36	36		:	41	38	37
1393	Carpets and rugs		:	:	:	:		:	5	4	4		:	14	11	12
1394	Cordage, rope, twine and netting		:	:	:	:		:	6	6	6		:	8	9	8
1399	Other textiles n.e.c.		:	:	:	:		:	31	29	28		:	70	62	61
1410	Wearing apparel, except fur apparel		:	:	:	:		:	144	129	123		:	154	138	132
1420	Articles of fur		:	:	:	:		:	:	:	:		:	:	-	:
1430	Knitted and crocheted apparel		:	:	:	:		:	17	16	14		:	25	22	21
151	Leather;luggage,handbags,saddlery,harness;fur		:	:	:	:		:	15	14	13		:	16	15	14
1511	Tanning/dressing of leather; dressing of fur		:	:	:	:		:	3	2	2		:	3	2	2
1512	Luggage,handbags,etc.;saddlery/harness		:	:	:	:		:	13	11	11		:	13	12	12
1520	Footwear		:	:	:	:		:	18	16	15		:	29	24	22
1610	Sawmilling and planing of wood		:	:	:	:		:	44	42	38		:	39	34	36
162	Wood products, cork, straw, plaiting materials		:	:	:	:		:	99	89	85		:	151	128	128

Code	Description				:				:	:	:
1621	Veneer sheets and wood-based panels	43	45	51	:	21	19	18	:	:	:
1622	Builders' carpentry and joinery	59	59	71	:	44	39	37	:	:	:
1623	Wooden containers	11	9	11	:	12	11	11	:	:	:
1629	Other wood products;articles of cork, straw	15	15	18	:	23	21	20	:	:	:
1701	Pulp, paper and paperboard	195	200	221	:	43	40	39	:	:	:
1702	Corrugated paper and paperboard	218	214	216	:	94	92	91	:	:	:
1709	Other articles of paper and paperboard	139	141	154	:	57	54	52	:	:	:
181	Printing and service activities related to printing	728	746	788	:	315	303	294	:	:	:
1811	Printing	623	635	662	:	255	249	243	:	:	:
1812	Service activities related to printing	105	112	125	:	60	55	51	:	:	:
1820	Reproduction of recorded media	19	20	18	:	5	6	5	:	:	:
1910	Coke oven products	8	8	8	:	1	2	1	:	:	:
1920	Refined petroleum products	111	116	112	:	22	22	22	:	:	:
201	Basic chemicals,fertilizers, etc.	664	655	692	:	119	120	118	:	:	:
2011	Basic chemicals	442	438	473	:	83	81	80	:	:	:
2012	Fertilizers and nitrogen compounds	13	12	13	:	4	4	4	:	:	:
2013	Plastics and synthetic rubber in primary forms	209	204	206	:	32	34	34	:	:	:
202	Other chemical products	493	479	516	:	118	117	117	:	:	:
2021	Pesticides and other agrochemical products	20	21	22	:	4	4	4	:	:	:
2022	Paints,varnishes;printing ink and mastics	96	90	109	:	23	21	22	:	:	:
2023	Soap,cleaning and cosmetic preparations	172	165	171	:	44	47	47	:	:	:
2029	Other chemical products n.e.c.	205	204	215	:	46	46	45	:	:	:
2030	Man-made fibres	39	44	40	:	9	9	8	:	:	:
2100	Pharmaceuticals,medicinal chemicals, etc.	459	455	448	:	87	90	90	:	:	:
221	Rubber products	380	360	398	:	109	104	106	:	:	:
2211	Rubber tyres and tubes	124	112	121	:	22	22	23	:	:	:
2219	Other rubber products	256	248	277	:	87	82	83	:	:	:
2220	Plastics products	1076	1026	1121	:	409	388	391	:	:	:
2310	Glass and glass products	196	189	220	:	51	46	46	:	:	:
239	Non-metallic mineral products n.e.c.	406	408	468	:	211	195	188	:	:	:
2391	Refractory products	31	29	35	:	9	8	9	:	:	:
2392	Clay building materials	36	40	46	:	15	13	12	:	:	:
2393	Other porcelain and ceramic products	88	83	98	:	32	29	29	:	:	:
2394	Cement, lime and plaster	35	37	40	:	8	8	8	:	:	:
2395	Articles of concrete, cement and plaster	109	115	127	:	94	88	83	:	:	:
2396	Cutting, shaping and finishing of stone	9	14	15	:	21	19	17	:	:	:
2399	Other non-metallic mineral products n.e.c.	97	89	106	:	32	30	31	:	:	:
2410	Basic iron and steel	715	751	842	:	153	150	147	:	:	:
2420	Basic precious and other non-ferrous metals	283	272	309	:	65	63	64	:	:	:
243	Casting of metals	285	261	318	:	98	89	92	:	:	:
2431	Casting of iron and steel	168	154	189	:	53	49	51	:	:	:
2432	Casting of non-ferrous metals	117	107	129	:	44	40	41	:	:	:
251	Struct.metal products, tanks, reservoirs	425	414	453	:	178	165	160	:	:	:
2511	Structural metal products	316	327	357	:	163	151	143	:	:	:
2512	Tanks, reservoirs and containers of metal	...	-	...	:	...	...	...	:	:	:

continued

Japan

ISIC	Industry	Establishments (number)					Number of employees (thousands)					Wages and salaries paid to employees (billions of Japanese Yen)				
		Note	2007	2008	2009	2010	Note	2007	2008	2009	2010	Note	2007	2008	2009	2010
2513	Steam generators, excl. hot water boilers		...	...	...	...		...	15	14	17		...	96	87	108
2520	Weapons and ammunition		...	...	...	...		...	6	7	7		...	40	44	44
259	Other metal products;metal working services		...	...	...	...		...	469	424	423		...	1146	960	983
2591	Forging,pressing,stamping,roll-forming of metal		...	...	...	...		...	105	96	98		...	308	261	274
2592	Treatment and coating of metals; machining		...	...	...	...		...	109	97	99		...	244	198	204
2593	Cutlery, hand tools and general hardware		...	...	...	...		...	55	50	48		...	169	137	137
2599	Other fabricated metal products n.e.c.		...	...	...	...		...	200	181	177		...	425	364	368
2610	Electronic components and boards		...	...	...	...		...	452	416	406		...	2086	1767	1817
2620	Computers and peripheral equipment		...	...	...	...		...	68	62	58		...	335	292	277
2630	Communication equipment		...	...	...	...		...	59	58	62		...	317	284	325
2640	Consumer electronics		...	...	...	...		...	49	46	44		...	249	224	239
265	Measuring,testing equipment; watches, etc.		...	...	...	...		...	92	83	83		...	365	302	301
2651	Measuring/testing/navigating equipment,etc.		...	...	...	...		...	83	76	75		...	328	275	271
2652	Watches and clocks		...	...	...	...		...	9	7	8		...	37	27	31
2660	Irradiation/electromedical equipment,etc.		...	...	...	...		...	41	37	40		...	201	171	194
2670	Optical instruments and photographic equipment		...	...	...	...		...	49	45	42		...	170	154	145
2680	Magnetic and optical media		...	...	...	...		...	5	4	3		...	26	18	17
2710	Electric motors,generators,transformers,etc.		...	...	...	...		...	146	144	141		...	556	528	533
2720	Batteries and accumulators		...	...	...	...		...	19	20	20		...	92	93	106
273	Wiring and wiring devices		...	...	...	...		...	48	46	45		...	206	181	189
2731	Fibre optic cables		...	...	...	...		...	4	4	4		...	24	19	22
2732	Other electronic and electric wires and cables		...	...	...	...		...	25	24	23		...	117	102	104
2733	Wiring devices		...	...	...	...		...	20	18	19		...	65	60	62
2740	Electric lighting equipment		...	...	...	...		...	37	34	35		...	151	132	137
2750	Domestic appliances		...	...	...	...		...	83	81	81		...	317	302	309
2790	Other electrical equipment		...	...	...	...		...	81	79	80		...	268	257	268
281	General-purpose machinery		...	...	...	...		...	461	429	419		...	1913	1693	1689
2811	Engines/turbines,excl.aircraft,vehicle engines		...	...	...	...		...	50	50	44		...	243	237	208
2812	Fluid power equipment		...	...	...	...		...	33	30	31		...	119	103	111
2813	Other pumps, compressors, taps and valves		...	...	...	...		...	53	51	52		...	215	203	210
2814	Bearings, gears, gearing and driving elements		...	...	...	...		...	68	65	67		...	322	269	293
2815	Ovens, furnaces and furnace burners		...	...	...	...		...	4	3	3		...	13	13	12
2816	Lifting and handling equipment		...	...	...	...		...	52	47	45		...	200	162	155
2817	Office machinery, excl.computers,etc.		...	...	...	...		...	52	45	44		...	239	196	196
2818	Power-driven hand tools		...	...	...	...		...	...	...	...		...	-	...	...
2819	Other general-purpose machinery		...	...	...	...		...	149	137	133		...	562	512	503
282	Special-purpose machinery		...	...	...	...		...	509	456	456		...	1727	1393	1438
2821	Agricultural and forestry machinery		...	...	...	...		...	29	28	30		...	109	95	106
2822	Metal-forming machinery and machine tools		...	...	...	...		...	136	116	111		...	459	352	323
2823	Machinery for metallurgy		...	...	...	...		...	4	3	3		...	13	8	8
2824	Mining, quarrying and construction machinery		...	...	...	...		...	47	42	45		...	183	154	163

Code	Description						
2825	Food/beverage/tobacco processing machinery	155	137	139	55	52	50
2826	Textile/apparel/leather production machinery	38	37	49	12	12	14
2829	Other special-purpose machinery	644	609	774	201	202	230
2910	Motor vehicles	1049	1067	1257	159	163	171
2920	Automobile bodies, trailers and semi-trailers	51	59	75	13	15	17
2930	Parts and accessories for motor vehicles	2888	2711	3152	635	629	661
301	Building of ships and boats	207	180	194	49	46	47
3011	Building of ships and floating structures	207	180	194	49	46	47
3012	Building of pleasure and sporting boats	84	82	72	…	…	…
3020	Railway locomotives and rolling stock	202	199	222	20	19	17
3030	Air and spacecraft and related machinery	-	…	…	37	36	37
3040	Military fighting vehicles	43	39	40	13	13	13
309	Transport equipment n.e.c.	…	…	…	…	…	…
3091	Motorcycles	25	20	24	7	7	7
3092	Bicycles and invalid carriages	18	19	17	6	6	6
3099	Other transport equipment n.e.c.	162	160	174	77	81	90
3100	Furniture	10	11	13	7	7	8
321	Jewellery, bijouterie and related articles	10	11	13	7	7	8
3211	Jewellery and related articles	…	…	…	…	…	…
3212	Imitation jewellery and related articles	28	45	49	8	10	10
3220	Musical instruments	33	31	31	13	13	13
3230	Sports goods	9	15	21	8	9	11
3240	Games and toys	162	153	151	50	50	50
3250	Medical and dental instruments and supplies	152	151	169	64	66	69
3290	Other manufacturing n.e.c.	…	…	…	…	…	…
331	Repair of fabricated metal products/machinery	…	…	…	…	…	…
3311	Repair of fabricated metal products	…	…	…	…	…	…
3312	Repair of machinery	…	…	…	…	…	…
3313	Repair of electronic and optical equipment	…	…	…	…	…	…
3314	Repair of electrical equipment	…	…	…	…	…	…
3315	Repair of transport equip., excl. motor vehicles	…	…	…	…	…	…
3319	Repair of other equipment	…	…	…	…	…	…
3320	Installation of industrial machinery/equipment	…	…	…	…	…	…
C	Total manufacturing	24017	23521	26269	7263	7339	7724

Japan

ISIC Revision 4			Output (billions of Japanese Yen)					Value added (billions of Japanese Yen)					Gross fixed capital formation (billions of Japanese Yen)	
ISIC	Industry	Note	2007	2008	2009	2010	Note	2007	2008	2009	2010	Note	2009	2010
1010	Processing/preserving of meat		...	2033	1942	1893		...	445	452	443		34	30
1020	Processing/preserving of fish, etc.		...	3198	3045	2933		...	1060	1015	994		46	44
1030	Processing/preserving of fruit,vegetables		...	1123	1119	1089		...	486	494	481		31	24
1040	Vegetable and animal oils and fats		...	1062	810	742		...	239	160	166		21	18
1050	Dairy products		...	2263	2342	2396		...	627	662	729		71	71
106	Grain mill products,starches and starch products		...	1639	1578	1406		...	320	326	302		23	22
1061	Grain mill products		...	1355	1266	1156		...	259	242	234		12	16
1062	Starches and starch products		...	284	312	250		...	62	84	68		11	6
107	Other food products		...	13208	13067	13040		...	5671	5656	5695		397	383
1071	Bakery products		...	3120	3119	3129		...	1658	1661	1677		128	86
1072	Sugar		...	274	280	271		...	93	95	87		9	19
1073	Cocoa, chocolate and sugar confectionery		...	1273	1266	1275		...	582	599	621		43	44
1074	Macaroni, noodles, couscous, etc.		...	910	920	917		...	359	349	356		25	43
1075	Prepared meals and dishes		...	975	983	978		...	328	350	367		27	35
1079	Other food products n.e.c.		...	6655	6499	6471		...	2650	2600	2587		165	156
1080	Prepared animal feeds		...	1358	1220	1121		...	198	207	200		23	13
1101	Distilling, rectifying and blending of spirits		...	1130	1021	1014		...	421	376	371		21	15
1102	Wines		...	523	497	475		...	261	247	235		25	9
1103	Malt liquors and malt		...	1920	2095	2002		...	483	608	599		36	39
1104	Soft drinks,mineral waters,other bottled waters		...	1980	2198	2243		...	842	875	984		70	61
1200	Tobacco products		...	2318	2263	2098		...	430	464	417		68	97
131	Spinning, weaving and finishing of textiles		...	1097	849	814		...	473	362	358		25	14
1311	Preparation and spinning of textile fibres		...	184	141	145		...	71	51	58		4	3
1312	Weaving of textiles		...	456	336	316		...	193	140	139		6	4
1313	Finishing of textiles		...	457	372	354		...	208	171	160		15	7
139	Other textiles		...	1570	1311	1279		...	582	511	486		30	26
1391	Knitted and crocheted fabrics		...	135	110	103		...	49	39	35		2	2
1392	Made-up textile articles, except apparel		...	542	449	455		...	211	183	176		4	5
1393	Carpets and rugs		...	169	133	133		...	40	31	35		2	1
1394	Cordage, rope, twine and netting		...	90	84	81		...	41	38	36		2	1
1399	Other textiles n.e.c.		...	634	536	509		...	240	219	204		19	17
1410	Wearing apparel, except fur apparel		...	1158	1011	938		...	586	522	489		11	9
1420	Articles of fur		...	...	...	...		...	-	...	...		-	-
1430	Knitted and crocheted apparel		...	178	151	138		...	76	64	58		3	2
151	Leather;luggage,handbags,saddlery,harness;fur		...	260	207	193		...	98	78	76		1	1
1511	Tanning/dressing of leather; dressing of fur		...	63	47	45		...	21	16	15		-	-
1512	Luggage,handbags,etc.;saddlery/harness		...	198	160	149		...	77	63	61		1	-
1520	Footwear		...	271	228	209		...	105	92	83		2	2
1610	Sawmilling and planing of wood		...	861	714	716		...	314	265	272		10	9
162	Wood products, cork, straw, plaiting materials		...	2048	1646	1655		...	728	589	590		26	24

Code	Description	(1)	(2)	(3)	(4)	(5)	(6)	(7)	(8)
1621	Veneer sheets and wood-based panels	620	491	486	173	136	146	12	9
1622	Builders' carpentry and joinery	958	777	795	349	283	272	9	12
1623	Wooden containers	192	146	147	77	61	63	2	1
1629	Other wood products;articles of cork,straw	277	231	227	129	109	108	3	1
1701	Pulp, paper and paperboard	3614	3080	3144	935	941	928	242	106
1702	Corrugated paper and paperboard	2347	2237	2238	831	791	822	60	70
1709	Other articles of paper and paperboard	1575	1418	1405	610	540	539	47	52
181	Printing and service activities related to printing	6616	6061	5907	2890	2669	2581	162	137
1811	Printing	5800	5379	5277	2389	2251	2198	134	120
1812	Service activities related to printing	816	682	630	501	418	383	28	18
1820	Reproduction of recorded media	347	297	242	226	181	168	6	6
1910	Coke oven products	325	363	292	-4	9	4	19	11
1920	Refined petroleum products	13600	9639	14500	907	729	1171	202	356
201	Basic chemicals,fertilizers, etc.	14380	10494	12383	3501	2900	3680	699	612
2011	Basic chemicals	9843	6767	8251	2548	1926	2518	466	393
2012	Fertilizers and nitrogen compounds	338	317	285	89	71	79	6	6
2013	Plastics and synthetic rubber in primary forms	4199	3410	3847	864	903	1082	227	213
202	Other chemical products	6463	5663	6038	2553	2386	2681	188	190
2021	Pesticides and other agrochemical products	294	256	253	128	113	106	11	27
2022	Paints,varnishes;printing ink and mastics	1341	1094	1267	381	381	485	28	22
2023	Soap,cleaning and cosmetic preparations	2453	2377	2446	1304	1289	1352	54	52
2029	Other chemical products n.e.c.	2375	1936	2072	741	603	739	94	90
2030	Man-made fibres	432	379	402	126	99	132	50	22
2100	Pharmaceuticals,medicinal chemicals, etc.	6964	7236	7177	4128	4106	4043	267	231
221	Rubber products	3263	2419	2809	1248	949	1125	114	119
2211	Rubber tyres and tubes	1327	968	1184	448	371	451	59	67
2219	Other rubber products	1937	1450	1626	801	578	673	55	52
2220	Plastics products	11462	9512	10376	4160	3577	4021	432	393
2310	Glass and glass products	2264	1615	2059	1151	740	1059	251	234
239	Non-metallic mineral products n.e.c.	5493	4559	4615	2380	1935	2008	176	181
2391	Refractory products	286	206	241	122	73	104	9	5
2392	Clay building materials	225	179	169	106	86	79	8	4
2393	Other porcelain and ceramic products	605	429	513	303	202	269	35	41
2394	Cement, lime and plaster	589	528	519	169	143	163	61	54
2395	Articles of concrete, cement and plaster	2480	2212	2082	1019	919	879	26	30
2396	Cutting, shaping and finishing of stone	352	308	285	219	191	177	5	3
2399	Other non-metallic mineral products n.e.c.	957	697	806	441	321	337	32	44
2410	Basic iron and steel	20301	13234	15235	4726	1839	2877	1069	878
2420	Basic precious and other non-ferrous metals	6157	4085	5870	927	785	1186	215	230
243	Casting of metals	2867	1891	2151	1087	778	935	87	72
2431	Casting of iron and steel	1591	1104	1224	621	473	543	48	42
2432	Casting of non-ferrous metals	1276	786	928	466	305	391	39	30
251	Struct.metal products, tanks, reservoirs	5618	5100	4624	1950	1830	1717	93	108
2511	Structural metal products	4790	4245	3693	1646	1470	1315	67	63
2512	Tanks, reservoirs and containers of metal	...	...	...	...	...	...	-	-

continued

Japan

ISIC	Industry	Output (billions of Japanese Yen)					Value added (billions of Japanese Yen)					Gross fixed capital formation (billions of Japanese Yen)		
		Note	2007	2008	2009	2010	Note	2007	2008	2009	2010	Note	2009	2010
2513	Steam generators, excl. hot water boilers			828	855	932			303	360	402		27	45
2520	Weapons and ammunition			523	516	439			166	139	113		27	16
259	Other metal products;metal working services			10521	7722	8291			4631	3325	3652		320	243
2591	Forging,pressing,stamping,roll-forming of metal			2944	2142	2491			1051	743	927		122	106
2592	Treatment and coating of metals; machining			1980	1402	1512			1048	716	796		50	38
2593	Cutlery, hand tools and general hardware			1138	737	800			645	410	451		30	22
2599	Other fabricated metal products n.e.c.			4459	3441	3487			1888	1456	1478		118	77
2610	Electronic components and boards			19247	13803	15485			5898	4055	5591		1322	1018
2620	Computers and peripheral equipment			4458	3383	3543			1103	986	1196		75	86
2630	Communication equipment			3722	2706	2974			1151	895	1007		46	46
2640	Consumer electronics			2718	2402	2883			670	620	753		52	43
265	Measuring,testing equipment; watches, etc.			2553	1804	2001			1092	750	863		51	41
2651	Measuring/testing/navigating equipment,etc.			2276	1623	1760			1032	712	786		42	33
2652	Watches and clocks			277	182	241			60	38	76		9	8
2660	Irradiation/electromedical equipment,etc.			1694	1172	1488			729	434	580		40	67
2670	Optical instruments and photographic equipment			2819	1958	1846			573	366	385		52	38
2680	Magnetic and optical media			350	177	191			126	58	76		19	16
2710	Electric motors,generators,transformers,etc.			4380	3678	3753			1528	1284	1363		120	88
2720	Batteries and accumulators			1081	930	965			299	268	263		102	117
273	Wiring and wiring devices			2715	1792	2030			573	407	508		67	54
2731	Fibre optic cables			172	157	172			65	53	58		7	7
2732	Other electronic and electric wires and cables			2044	1242	1429			338	215	289		38	35
2733	Wiring devices			498	392	429			170	139	161		22	12
2740	Electric lighting equipment			1319	1013	1170			466	330	409		43	32
2750	Domestic appliances			3428	3140	3392			1418	1353	1535		71	68
2790	Other electrical equipment			2585	2035	2286			1028	763	876		92	69
281	General-purpose machinery			16758	12475	12582			6173	4615	4959		498	366
2811	Engines/turbines,excl.aircraft,vehicle engines			2532	2233	1911			865	672	685		112	63
2812	Fluid power equipment			1172	673	962			467	268	390		31	24
2813	Other pumps, compressors, taps and valves			1798	1527	1476			656	560	575		53	38
2814	Bearings, gears, gearing and driving elements			2241	1455	1876			859	501	685		96	64
2815	Ovens, furnaces and furnace burners			223	227	187			70	77	72		2	3
2816	Lifting and handling equipment			2222	1449	1318			815	568	479		36	27
2817	Office machinery, excl.computers,etc.			1987	1387	1402			489	352	392		70	59
2818	Power-driven hand tools												-	
2819	Other general-purpose machinery			4583	3524	3450			1950	1618	1682		97	88
282	Special-purpose machinery			17723	10725	12798			6512	3943	4871		368	289
2821	Agricultural and forestry machinery			968	811	915			292	258	314		17	18
2822	Metal-forming machinery and machine tools			3938	2054	2293			1590	845	1026		83	50
2823	Machinery for metallurgy			173	68	54			78	33	20		2	1
2824	Mining, quarrying and construction machinery			3199	1623	2153			932	445	571		73	37

Code	Description							
2825	Food/beverage/tobacco processing machinery	1283	988	1119	554	420	471	17	29
2826	Textile/apparel/leather production machinery	336	192	282	156	83	131	7	6
2829	Other special-purpose machinery	7826	4988	5981	2910	1859	2338	168	149
2910	Motor vehicles	23508	16503	18577	4851	3704	3920	483	253
2920	Automobile bodies, trailers and semi-trailers	591	377	363	168	107	119	13	8
2930	Parts and accessories for motor vehicles	27190	20029	24113	8697	6151	7810	1078	772
301	Building of ships and boats	2960	2764	2860	930	742	881	129	97
3011	Building of ships and floating structures	2960	2764	2860	930	742	881	129	97
3012	Building of pleasure and sporting boats	557	635	639	177	232	248	13	18
3020	Railway locomotives and rolling stock	1446	1189	1247	544	451	510	48	39
3030	Air and spacecraft and related machinery	-	-	-	-	-	-	-	-
3040	Military fighting vehicles	512	386	404	207	148	167	14	11
309	Transport equipment n.e.c.	-	-	-	-	-	-	-	-
3091	Motorcycles	316	261	283	147	95	108	8	8
3092	Bicycles and invalid carriages	196	125	121	60	54	59	5	2
3099	Other transport equipment n.e.c.	1593	1259	1247	680	521	509	23	22
3100	Furniture	:::	:::	:::	:::	:::	:::	-	1
321	Jewellery, bijouterie and related articles	181	138	147	68	51	58	-	-
3211	Jewellery and related articles	181	138	147	68	51	58	:::	1
3212	Imitation jewellery and related articles	210	184	145	121	113	64	10	5
3220	Musical instruments	273	243	268	133	121	139	4	5
3230	Sports goods	363	246	120	67	81	55	6	4
3240	Games and toys	1193	1166	1137	656	653	602	57	46
3250	Medical and dental instruments and supplies	1954	1523	1584	705	600	627	42	36
3290	Other manufacturing n.e.c.	:::	:::	:::	:::	:::	:::	:::	:::
331	Repair of fabricated metal products/machinery	:::	:::	:::	:::	:::	:::	:::	:::
3311	Repair of fabricated metal products	:::	:::	:::	:::	:::	:::	:::	:::
3312	Repair of machinery	:::	:::	:::	:::	:::	:::	:::	:::
3313	Repair of electronic and optical equipment	:::	:::	:::	:::	:::	:::	:::	:::
3314	Repair of electrical equipment	:::	:::	:::	:::	:::	:::	:::	:::
3315	Repair of transport equip., excl. motor vehicles	:::	:::	:::	:::	:::	:::	:::	:::
3319	Repair of other equipment	:::	:::	:::	:::	:::	:::	:::	:::
3320	Installation of industrial machinery/equipment	:::	:::	:::	:::	:::	:::	:::	:::
C	Total manufacturing	316409	246667	270832	100919	80074	90411	10638	8935

Japan

Index numbers of industrial production

ISIC Revision 4

ISIC	Industry	Note	(2005=100)											
			1999	2000	2001	2002	2003	2004	2005	2006	2007	2008	2009	2010
10	Food products		...	...	...	...	101	101	100	99	99	96	95	94
11	Beverages		...	...	...	...	99	102	100	98	103	107	113	116
12	Tobacco products		...	...	...	...	...	...	...	...	...	...	...	...
13	Textiles		...	...	...	...	110	106	100	97	93	86	68	70
14	Wearing apparel		...	...	...	...	125	112	100	94	86	78	68	64
15	Leather and related products		...	...	...	...	109	107	100	93	91	80	62	60
16	Wood/wood products/cork,excl. furniture		...	...	...	...	104	103	100	99	94	83	70	73
17	Paper and paper products		...	...	...	...	98	99	100	101	101	100	86	89
18	Printing and reproduction of recorded media		...	...	...	...	100	99	100	105	108	108	106	109
19	Coke and refined petroleum products		...	...	...	...	100	98	100	98	98	96	90	91
20	Chemicals and chemical products		...	...	...	...	98	99	100	100	101	95	85	92
21	Pharmaceuticals,medicinal chemicals, etc.		...	...	...	...	...	...	...	...	...	...	...	...
22	Rubber and plastics products		...	...	...	...	97	99	100	102	103	99	80	90
23	Other non-metallic mineral products		...	...	...	...	100	100	100	101	102	97	77	85
24	Basic metals		...	...	...	...	97	101	100	103	106	102	74	93
25	Fabricated metal products, except machinery		...	...	...	...	101	101	100	99	97	95	78	83
26	Computer, electronic and optical products		...	...	...	...	91	98	100	113	121	115	91	111
27	Electrical equipment		...	...	...	...	93	99	100	105	104	104	82	97
28	Machinery and equipment n.e.c.		...	...	...	...	82	95	100	106	109	101	60	83
29	Motor vehicles, trailers and semi-trailers		...	...	...	...	93	97	100	108	114	113	75	96
30	Other transport equipment		...	...	...	...	65	84	100	87	92	91	82	86
31	Furniture		...	...	...	...	100	103	100	99	96	91	82	86
32	Other manufacturing		...	...	...	...	99	95	100	99	96	83	70	70
33	Repair and installation of machinery/equipment		...	...	...	...	99	95	100	123	144	151	41	43
C	Total manufacturing		...	...	...	...	94	99	100	105	107	104	81	95

Jordan

Supplier of information:
Department of Statistics, Amman.

Basic source of data:
Annual industrial survey.

Major deviations from ISIC (Revision 3):
None reported.

Reference period:
Fiscal year.

Scope:
All establishments.

Method of data collection:
Direct interview in the field.

Type of enumeration:
Sample survey.

Adjusted for non-response:
Yes.

Concepts and definitions of variables:
Output refers to gross output.
Value added refers to total value added.

Related national publications:
Industry Survey (annual); Statistical Yearbook, both published by the Department of Statistics, Amman.

Jordan

ISIC Revision 3		Number of establishments (number)					Number of employees (number)					Wages and salaries paid to employees (thousands of Jordanian Dinars)				
ISIC	Industry	Note	2007	2008	2009	2010	Note	2007	2008	2009	2010	Note	2007	2008	2009	2010
151	Processed meat,fish,fruit,vegetables,fats		189	165	182	138		6078	6271	6513	6725		18539	24464	32863	29249
1511	Processing/preserving of meat		14	14	16	13		3687	4000	3934	4064		10181	14904	22917	17228
1512	Processing/preserving of fish		-	-	-	-		-	-	-	-		-	-	-	-
1513	Processing/preserving of fruit & vegetables		24	24	31	34		1014	1013	1557	1589		2596	3606	6004	7726
1514	Vegetable and animal oils and fats		151	127	135	91		1377	1258	1022	1072		5762	5954	3942	4295
1520	Dairy products		534	522	451	446		4191	4122	4008	3674		8659	9255	12033	11879
153	Grain mill products; starches; animal feeds		254	256	246	230		2003	2073	2035	2289		5837	7715	6465	7517
1531	Grain mill products		96	100	100	96		1128	1217	1233	1416		3662	4735	4129	4517
1532	Starches and starch products		-	-	-	-		-	-	-	-		-	-	-	-
1533	Prepared animal feeds		158	156	146	134		875	856	802	873		2175	2980	2336	3000
154	Other food products		2553	2407	2428	2410		16487	17069	19132	18939		32894	39810	51151	51739
1541	Bakery products		1955	1912	1920	1917		12434	12608	14071	13539		23664	27788	35756	34713
1542	Sugar		-	-	-	-		-	-	-	-		-	-	-	-
1543	Cocoa, chocolate and sugar confectionery		84	81	61	63		1379	1661	1704	1847		3221	4580	5339	6388
1544	Macaroni, noodles & similar products		-	-	-	-		-	-	-	-		-	-	-	-
1549	Other food products n.e.c.		514	414	447	430		2674	2800	3357	3553		6009	7442	10056	10638
155	Beverages		76	108	138	137		3931	3745	3968	4741		15348	20457	22173	25490
1551	Distilling, rectifying & blending of spirits		6	5	8	7		367	338	383	597		1882	2287	4413	3903
1552	Wines		-	-	-	-		-	-	-	-		-	-	-	-
1553	Malt liquors and malt		-	-	-	-		-	-	-	-		-	-	-	-
1554	Soft drinks; mineral waters		70	103	130	130		3564	3407	3585	4144		13466	18170	17760	21587
1600	Tobacco products		10	13	14	12		1464	1417	1573	1577		5958	8793	9658	8689
171	Spinning, weaving and finishing of textiles		22	15	19	11		367	466	430	402		1643	3177	2202	2284
1711	Textile fibre preparation; textile weaving		22	15	19	11		367	466	430	402		1643	3177	2202	2284
1712	Finishing of textiles		-	-	-	-		-	-	-	-		-	-	-	-
172	Other textiles		600	636	602	689		2376	2257	2061	2329		4571	4962	6149	6538
1721	Made-up textile articles, except apparel		471	513	482	565		1054	1012	1036	1290		931	1006	1544	1713
1722	Carpets and rugs		24	22	25	24		785	790	625	642		2690	3083	2869	3085
1723	Cordage, rope, twine and netting		-	-	-	-		-	-	-	-		-	-	-	-
1729	Other textiles n.e.c.		105	101	95	100		537	455	400	397		950	873	1736	1740
1730	Knitted and crocheted fabrics and articles		103	101	100	98		959	1000	1054	1066		1144	2393	2756	2603
1810	Wearing apparel, except fur apparel		2073	2040	2077	2087		25524	22410	29460	33683		47386	65317	72044	76805
1820	Dressing & dyeing of fur; processing of fur		-	-	-	-		-	-	-	-		-	-	-	-
191	Tanning, dressing and processing of leather		78	80	83	83		400	458	456	448		653	815	584	498
1911	Tanning and dressing of leather		27	30	31	31		156	171	182	197		407	495	352	285
1912	Luggage, handbags, etc.; saddlery & harness		51	50	52	52		244	287	274	251		246	320	232	213
1920	Footwear		189	109	109	105		939	783	775	727		2062	2144	2224	3329
2010	Sawmilling and planing of wood		35	33	47	39		457	500	738	644		818	1409	795	1131
202	Products of wood, cork, straw, etc.		1218	1200	1178	1189		3383	3775	3553	3482		4582	5160	5267	4437
2021	Veneer sheets, plywood, particle board, etc.		-	-	-	-		-	-	-	-		-	-	-	-
2022	Builders' carpentry and joinery		1062	1044	1019	1010		2524	2952	2700	2681		3098	3831	3654	3180
2023	Wooden containers		35	33	29	32		217	278	296	258		358	435	370	213
2029	Other wood products; articles of cork/straw		121	123	130	147		642	545	557	543		1126	894	1243	1044
210	Paper and paper products		98	87	78	98		3469	3765	3699	3660		14254	15869	16851	18743
2101	Pulp, paper and paperboard		11	10	7	10		649	694	676	629		2076	2447	1889	2118
2102	Corrugated paper and paperboard		50	49	44	60		1228	1387	1293	1194		4287	2965	4777	5854
2109	Other articles of paper and paperboard		37	28	27	28		1592	1684	1730	1837		7891	10457	10185	10771
221	Publishing		76	118	105	102		3308	3216	3023	3131		15674	17835	19646	21852
2211	Publishing of books and other publications		-	-	-	-		-	-	-	-		-	-	-	-
2212	Publishing of newspapers, journals, etc.		-	-	-	-		-	-	-	-		-	-	-	-
2213	Publishing of recorded media		76	118	105	102		3308	3216	3023	3131		15674	17835	19646	21852
2219	Other publishing		-	-	-	-		-	-	-	-		-	-	-	-

Code	Description	C1	C2	C3	C4	C5	C6	C7	C8	C9	C10	C11	C12
222	Printing and related service activities	11793	13344	12000	9825	3480	3616	3601	3301	492	500	477	467
2221	Printing	11402	12855	11575	9246	3220	3357	3393	3074	451	458	429	425
2222	Service activities related to printing	391	489	425	579	260	259	208	227	41	42	48	42
2230	Reproduction of recorded media	–	–	–	–	–	–	–	–	–	–	–	–
2310	Coke oven products	–	–	–	–	–	–	–	–	–	–	–	–
2320	Refined petroleum products	29968	28201	32261	22837	3506	3501	3346	3176	1	1	1	1
2330	Processing of nuclear fuel	–	–	–	–	–	–	–	–	–	–	–	–
241	Basic chemicals	32079	29459	30421	22095	3773	3889	3493	3641	55	56	55	46
2411	Basic chemicals, except fertilizers	9101	9327	9470	7711	1005	1126	1076	1166	22	23	21	21
2412	Fertilizers and nitrogen compounds	19682	16856	18049	11752	1810	1686	1493	1484	10	9	9	8
2413	Plastics in primary forms; synthetic rubber	3296	3276	2902	2632	958	1077	924	991	23	24	25	17
242	Other chemicals	98081	71139	77206	62090	11659	10922	11272	10713	215	206	230	232
2421	Pesticides and other agro-chemical products	1962	1533	1586	1121	314	318	342	274	6	5	5	4
2422	Paints, varnishes, printing ink and mastics	8778	7264	7517	5597	1997	1679	1600	1685	64	66	76	73
2423	Pharmaceuticals, medicinal chemicals, etc.	72146	48869	53682	45159	5430	5215	5737	5654	29	28	28	32
2424	Soap, cleaning & cosmetic preparations	14014	12618	13105	9163	3546	3332	3237	2888	107	99	112	114
2429	Other chemical products n.e.c.	1181	855	1316	1050	372	378	356	212	9	8	9	9
2430	Man-made fibres	625	534	691	588	150	163	206	203	22	22	24	24
251	Rubber products	412	368	528	429	89	95	135	127	9	9	10	10
2511	Rubber tyres and tubes	213	166	163	159	61	68	71	76	13	13	10	14
2519	Other rubber products	23868	23318	17998	12486	6008	5607	5007	4805	247	233	244	255
2520	Plastic products	2525	1877	2636	2091	947	724	923	856	35	30	33	31
2610	Glass and glass products	56712	50329	59488	46891	14792	16245	18460	18040	2432	2526	2606	2501
269	Non-metallic mineral products n.e.c.	775	511	818	535	361	389	391	306	18	25	18	23
2691	Pottery, china and earthenware	1726	1637	2980	2312	883	888	959	1001	19	24	15	27
2692	Refractory ceramic products	19618	16540	20428	12976	1545	1864	1979	1826	21	22	21	20
2693	Struct.non-refractory clay; ceramic products	21234	17684	19481	17317	7020	7409	8049	8120	1488	1529	1497	1521
2694	Cement, lime and plaster	11563	13249	14513	12666	4699	5354	6765	6476	880	1000	971	900
2695	Articles of concrete, cement and plaster	1796	708	1268	1085	284	341	317	311	6	6	4	10
2696	Cutting, shaping & finishing of stone	15859	14651	15103	10999	2145	2233	2252	2176	20	21	22	28
2699	Other non-metallic mineral products n.e.c.	3172	2943	3776	3240	939	833	1082	1097	22	21	5	20
2710	Basic iron and steel	1236	1328	2032	1358	702	729	525	525	5	6	72	72
2720	Basic precious and non-ferrous metals	1236	1328	2032	1358	702	729	525	525	72	74	73	72
273	Casting of metals	1236	1328	2032	1358	702	729	525	525	72	74	73	72
2731	Casting of iron and steel	–	–	–	–	–	–	–	–	–	–	–	–
2732	Casting of non-ferrous metals	–	–	–	–	–	–	–	–	–	–	–	–
281	Struct.metal products;tanks;steam generators	26022	26015	20443	12636	10562	10294	9782	9260	3422	3439	3425	3427
2811	Structural metal products	25701	25708	19982	12405	10265	10038	9500	9049	3314	3330	3322	3323
2812	Tanks, reservoirs and containers of metal	321	307	461	231	297	256	282	211	108	109	103	104
2813	Steam generators	16510	17585	14026	8847	5430	5628	5477	5172	1015	1021	1036	1016
289	Other metal products; metal working services	2442	3611	3051	2212	2034	2084	2000	1802	615	618	648	644
2891	Metal forging/pressing/stamping/roll-forming	1881	1510	1407	1196	501	552	528	545	114	117	125	124
2892	Treatment & coating of metals	12187	12464	9568	5439	2895	2992	2949	2825	286	286	263	248
2893	Cutlery, hand tools and general hardware	10579	8360	7360	6017	1976	1983	1929	1853	45	47	53	56
2899	Other fabricated metal products n.e.c.	–	–	–	–	–	–	–	–	–	–	–	–
291	General purpose machinery	–	–	–	–	–	–	–	–	–	–	–	–
2911	Engines & turbines (not for transport equipment)	–	–	–	–	–	–	–	–	–	–	–	–
2912	Pumps, compressors, taps and valves	–	–	–	–	–	–	–	–	–	–	–	–
2913	Bearings, gears, gearing & driving elements	1709	1384	2203	1708	319	417	421	451	18	29	22	28
2914	Ovens, furnaces and furnace burners	8870	6976	5157	4309	1657	1566	1508	1402	27	24	25	28
2915	Lifting and handling equipment	2997	2779	2827	2100	1030	1012	1182	985	142	210	191	196
2919	Other general purpose machinery	439	470	642	488	278	319	396	338	50	81	72	71
292	Special purpose machinery	366	366	763	202	128	128	186	97	7	11	15	9
2921	Agricultural and forestry machinery	–	–	–	–	–	–	–	–	–	–	–	–
2922	Machine tools	1132	853	771	704	390	343	371	328	67	91	85	89
2923	Machinery for metallurgy	191	271	271	75	67	78	99	58	5	8	6	11
2924	Machinery for mining & construction	–	–	–	–	–	–	–	–	–	–	–	–
2925	Food/beverage/tobacco processing machinery	–	–	–	–	–	–	–	–	–	–	–	–
2926	Machinery for textile, apparel and leather	869	689	380	631	167	144	130	164	13	19	13	16
2927	Weapons and ammunition	–	–	–	–	–	–	–	–	–	–	–	–
2929	Other special purpose machinery												

continued

Jordan

ISIC	Industry	Number of establishments (number) 2007	2008	2009	2010	Number of employees (number) 2007	2008	2009	2010	Wages and salaries paid to employees (thousands of Jordanian Dinars) 2007	2008	2009	2010
2930	Domestic appliances n.e.c.	62	64	54	53	1311	1390	1462	1594	3553	5402	8453	6593
3000	Office, accounting and computing machinery	-	-	-	-	-	-	-	-	-	-	-	-
3110	Electric motors, generators and transformers	7	6	6	6	210	204	192	190	637	549	512	626
3120	Electricity distribution & control apparatus	36	37	35	32	532	672	518	541	1293	2109	1391	2727
3130	Insulated wire and cable	4	6	4	6	2535	2627	2491	2510	5821	7383	7509	7481
3140	Accumulators, primary cells and batteries												
3150	Lighting equipment and electric lamps	39	31	35	41	764	856	974	961	2089	2801	2826	4458
3190	Other electrical equipment n.e.c.	-	-	-	-	-	-	-	-	-	-	-	-
3210	Electronic valves, tubes, etc.	-	-	-	-	-	-	-	-	-	-	-	-
3220	TV/radio transmitters; line comm. apparatus	-	-	-	-	-	-	-	-	-	-	-	-
3230	TV and radio receivers and associated goods	-	-	-	-	-	-	-	-	-	-	-	-
331	Medical, measuring, testing appliances, etc.	253	215	201	207	1373	1302	1084	1046	3307	3648	2862	3680
3311	Medical, surgical and orthopaedic equipment	253	215	201	207	1373	1302	1084	1046	3307	3648	2862	3680
3312	Measuring/testing/navigating appliances,etc.	-	-	-	-	-	-	-	-	-	-	-	-
3313	Industrial process control equipment	-	-	-	-	-	-	-	-	-	-	-	-
3320	Optical instruments & photographic equipment	-	-	-	-	-	-	-	-	-	-	-	-
3330	Watches and clocks	-	-	-	-	-	-	-	-	-	-	-	-
3410	Motor vehicles	-	-	-	-	-	-	-	-	-	-	-	-
3420	Automobile bodies, trailers & semi-trailers	191	199	190	176	1465	1471	1445	1477	4254	4892	3908	3207
3430	Parts/accessories for automobiles	39	41	32	33	743	688	681	675	1786	2084	1426	2025
351	Building and repairing of ships and boats	9	13	9	9	199	1211	1166	1249	1964	14322	10823	11668
3511	Building and repairing of ships	-	-	-	-	-	-	-	-	-	-	-	-
3512	Building/repairing of pleasure/sport. boats	9	13	9	9	199	1211	1166	1249	1964	14322	10823	11668
3520	Railway/tramway locomotives & rolling stock	-	-	-	-	-	-	-	-	-	-	-	-
3530	Aircraft and spacecraft	-	-	-	-	-	-	-	-	-	-	-	-
359	Transport equipment n.e.c.	-	-	-	-	-	-	-	-	-	-	-	-
3591	Motorcycles	-	-	-	-	-	-	-	-	-	-	-	-
3592	Bicycles and invalid carriages	-	-	-	-	-	-	-	-	-	-	-	-
3599	Other transport equipment n.e.c.	-	-	-	-	-	-	-	-	-	-	-	-
3610	Furniture	3337	3374	3402	3400	12513	13044	12583	12390	22428	27667	25441	26466
369	Manufacturing n.e.c.	201	206	199	191	1279	1234	1172	1080	2664	3230	2352	2728
3691	Jewellery and related articles	115	116	114	113	534	468	556	591	955	1078	901	705
3692	Musical instruments	-	-	-	-	-	-	-	-	-	-	-	-
3693	Sports goods	-	-	-	-	-	-	-	-	-	-	-	-
3694	Games and toys	-	-	-	-	-	-	-	-	-	-	-	-
3699	Other manufacturing n.e.c.	86	90	85	78	745	766	616	489	1709	2152	1451	2023
3710	Recycling of metal waste and scrap	-	-	-	-	-	-	-	-	-	-	-	-
3720	Recycling of non-metal waste and scrap	-	-	-	-	-	-	-	-	-	-	-	-
D	Total manufacturing	20643	20575	20399	20249	163996	166563	173625	178329	453918	601930	622226	676468

a/ Sum of available data.

Jordan

ISIC	Industry	Note	Output at producers' prices (thousands of Jordanian Dinars)				Note	Value added at producers' prices (thousands of Jordanian Dinars)				Note	Gross fixed capital formation (thousands of Jordanian Dinars)	
			2007	2008	2009	2010		2007	2008	2009	2010		2009	2010
151	Processed meat,fish,fruit,vegetables,fats		346410	559401	631966	689002		84824	129209	166527	177457		35162	18087
1511	Processing/preserving of meat		196903	311768	333653	370443		42726	64061	73992	80143		30920	14461
1512	Processing/preserving of fish		41978	55983	79359	84436		11125	14236	20980	18289		1557	2889
1513	Processing/preserving of fruit & vegetables		107529	191650	218954	234123		30973	50912	71555	79025		2685	737
1514	Vegetable and animal oils and fats		114356	123742	144451	160536		24657	25088	45523	53303		937	2852
1520	Dairy products		166590	202977	199692	204216		23875	35212	38111	30358		11254	4615
153	Grain mill products; starches; animal feeds		94042	103838	106365	101126		10674	14641	17029	20162		6427	4562
1531	Grain mill products		-	-	-	-		-	-	-	-		4827	53
1532	Starches and starch products		72548	99139	93327	103090		13201	20571	21082	10196		25426	10389
1533	Prepared animal feeds		335209	395496	478415	528664		98954	112047	140485	143149		11600	2405
154	Other food products		198039	215957	279469	284670		58629	67588	81418	80993		5228	5024
1541	Bakery products		43706	61589	72815	90911		11380	13967	15469	17326		8598	2960
1542	Sugar		-	-	-	-		-	-	-	-		-	-
1543	Cocoa, chocolate and sugar confectionery		93464	117950	126131	153083		28945	30492	43598	44830		13174	8875
1544	Macaroni, noodles & similar products		221531	256056	295296	357056		97210	114709	138193	172050		1192	849
1549	Other food products n.e.c.		34930	41042	68622	89529		23716	27768	45741	60381		-	-
155	Beverages		-	-	-	-		-	-	-	-		-	-
1551	Distilling, rectifying & blending of spirits		-	-	-	-		-	-	-	-		-	-
1552	Wines		-	-	-	-		-	-	-	-		-	-
1553	Malt liquors and malt		186601	215014	226674	267527		73494	86941	92452	111669		11982	8026
1554	Soft drinks; mineral waters		295316	320360	553613	607621		187995	203845	432822	432822		884	9811
1600	Tobacco products		11445	16284	21628	20347		5602	6726	7909	10660		..	539
171	Spinning, weaving and finishing of textiles		11445	16284	21628	20347		5602	6726	7909	10660		290	539
1711	Textile fibre preparation; textile weaving		-	-	-	-		-	-	-	-		16	191
1712	Finishing of textiles		-	-	-	-		-	-	-	-		-	7
172	Other textiles		50850	52386	52325	60601		21476	22701	23414	21065		274	182
1721	Made-up textile articles, except apparel		7707	9789	11268	12562		3538	4423	4765	5162		13	2
1722	Carpets and rugs		39041	37940	31634	38523		15487	15210	15471	11341		95	95
1723	Cordage, rope, twine and netting		4102	4657	9423	9516		2451	3068	3178	4562		-	-
1729	Other textiles n.e.c.		7083	7559	8457	11741		2964	2919	3441	5866		-	-
1730	Knitted and crocheted fabrics and articles		373561	475763	530251	570824		185783	243498	298930	357005		4019	1436
1810	Wearing apparel, except fur apparel		3072	5111	3949	4049		1086	1727	1329	1997		250	40
1820	Dressing & dyeing of fur; processing of fur		1729	3337	1915	2026		506	833	423	1105		87	38
191	Tanning, dressing and processing of leather		-	-	-	-		-	-	-	-		-	-
1911	Tanning and dressing of leather		1343	1774	2034	2023		580	894	906	892		163	260
1912	Luggage, handbags, etc.; saddlery & harness		20458	23541	23364	17522		7798	9241	9661	9791		1	-
1920	Footwear		11785	13914	15369	16436		2256	2663	9685	10081		540	68
2010	Sawmilling and planing of wood		35635	43599	33888	37160		16121	17568	13533	12366		348	68
202	Products of wood, cork, straw, etc.		28438	33470	25059	26471		12803	14473	10208	8302		170	-
2021	Veneer sheets, plywood, particle board, etc.		2363	3887	1388	2210		614	722	556	505		22	-
2022	Builders' carpentry and joinery		4834	6242	7441	8479		2704	2373	2769	3559		-	-
2023	Wooden containers		-	-	-	-		-	-	-	-		-	-
2029	Other wood products; articles of cork/straw		-	-	-	-		-	-	-	-		-	-
210	Paper and paper products		183573	219757	220011	220989		57620	76045	80377	63903		11380	11864
2101	Pulp, paper and paperboard		34307	41919	33512	37937		9532	11382	8298	8495		473	103
2102	Corrugated paper and paperboard		69063	80808	73950	77116		27324	33611	29467	23124		1920	1457
2109	Other articles of paper and paperboard		80203	97030	112549	105936		20764	31052	42612	32284		8987	10304
221	Publishing		99825	106068	102787	113345		63124	66491	61279	60077		1619	3833
2211	Publishing of books and other publications		99825	106068	102787	113345		63124	66491	61279	60077		1619	3833
2212	Publishing of newspapers, journals, etc.		-	-	-	-		-	-	-	-		-	-
2213	Publishing of recorded media		-	-	-	-		-	-	-	-		-	-
2219	Other publishing		-	-	-	-		-	-	-	-		-	-

continued

Jordan

ISIC	Industry	Output Note	2007	2008	2009	2010	VA Note	2007	2008	2009	2010	GFCF Note	2009	2010
			Output at producers' prices (thousands of Jordanian Dinars)					Value added at producers' prices (thousands of Jordanian Dinars)					Gross fixed capital formation (thousands of Jordanian Dinars)	
222	Printing and related service activities		72141	78620	94015	90336		30107	34658	34740	38876		7787	1517
2221	Printing		69423	76412	90393	87596		28673	33621	33311	37569		5915	1517
2222	Service activities related to printing		2718	2208	3622	2740		1434	1037	1429	1307		1872	-
2230	Reproduction of recorded media		-	-	-	-		-	-	-	-		-	-
2310	Coke oven products		-	-	-	-		-	-	-	-		-	-
2320	Refined petroleum products		1802698	2309685	1893738	2473472		109234	181510	185102	218757		31889	49467
2330	Processing of nuclear fuel		-	-	-	-		-	-	-	-		-	-
241	Basic chemicals		397955	793478	566543	577948		129053	260679	209102	244980		27042	28808
2411	Basic chemicals, except fertilizers		117186	230521	243823	237214		61269	115000	119732	117900		3283	1513
2412	Fertilizers and nitrogen compounds		250167	527606	290575	307294		59156	133309	77927	118787		20918	25912
2413	Plastics in primary forms; synthetic rubber		30602	35351	32145	33440		8628	12370	11443	8293		2841	1383
242	Other chemicals		639462	700894	736025	964620		253728	274990	319306	409226		27605	30934
2421	Pesticides and other agro-chemical products		20620	24957	22529	26685		6492	8554	6685	8083		1380	550
2422	Paints, varnishes, printing ink and mastics		108161	123912	119399	139541		25115	29400	30720	37171		2042	861
2423	Pharmaceuticals, medicinal chemicals, etc.		369966	403727	442200	591352		172449	186111	225855	301172		22162	24878
2424	Soap, cleaning & cosmetic preparations		125123	127469	133094	184826		44631	43062	50313	55553		1626	3801
2429	Other chemical products n.e.c.		15592	20829	18803	22216		5041	7863	5733	7247		395	844
2430	Man-made fibres		-	-	-	-		-	-	-	-		-	-
251	Rubber products		4857	6349	5771	8191		1433	1999	2325	3854		84	4
2511	Rubber tyres and tubes		4008	5390	4119	5007		985	1435	1404	1840		68	2
2519	Other rubber products		849	959	1652	3184		448	564	921	2014		16	2
2520	Plastic products		199367	259850	304032	322752		54375	75466	84610	95420		12460	7136
2610	Glass and glass products		14828	19454	14346	15349		6647	9196	6285	6198		325	43
269	Non-metallic mineral products n.e.c.		706677	826283	703211	667287		334560	415786	359564	318670		66236	30057
2691	Pottery, china and earthenware		4094	6846	4115	4378		2348	4577	2236	2696		48	73
2692	Refractory ceramic products		-	-	-	-		-	-	-	-		-	-
2693	Struct.non-refractory clay; ceramic products		17907	16063	9262	9842		8317	7037	2335	3542		537	96
2694	Cement, lime and plaster		331195	396557	345932	294812		210890	264868	231056	188485		14268	25973
2695	Articles of concrete, cement and plaster		254101	282060	243914	252386		80278	94069	85916	88899		50356	3303
2696	Cutting, shaping & finishing of stone		91092	115795	93658	97911		29724	41943	36351	33248		816	663
2699	Other non-metallic mineral products n.e.c.		8288	8962	6330	7958		3003	3272	1670	1800		211	-51
2710	Basic iron and steel		395387	473630	343147	353287		110684	148738	137603	130581		7514	10814
2720	Basic precious and non-ferrous metals		63295	60678	42856	52707		26858	25532	15672	18600		735	1141
273	Casting of metals		16821	18923	19673	25510		8235	10128	10779	7232		191	-708
2731	Casting of iron and steel		16821	18923	19673	25510		8235	10128	10779	7232		191	-708
2732	Casting of non-ferrous metals		-	-	-	-		-	-	-	-		-	-
281	Struct.metal products;tanks;steam generators		124389	178948	203557	186978		42318	69896	73304	66983		7450	1529
2811	Structural metal products		122486	175855	201224	184603		41497	68593	72533	66094		7446	1529
2812	Tanks, reservoirs and containers of metal		1903	3093	2333	2375		821	1303	771	889		4	-
2813	Steam generators		-	-	-	-		-	-	-	-		-	-
289	Other metal products; metal working services		179790	204396	187997	279450		74972	73024	71369	87593		9408	2988
2891	Metal forging/pressing/stamping/roll-forming		-	-	-	-		-	-	-	-		-	-
2892	Treatment & coating of metals		11341	15106	19256	18464		6337	8419	9995	8295		1220	-
2893	Cutlery, hand tools and general hardware		21921	21366	19681	20517		10090	10098	6853	6416		126	19
2899	Other fabricated metal products n.e.c.		146528	167924	149060	240469		58545	54507	54521	72882		8062	2969
291	General purpose machinery		63484	75532	76135	85708		21022	27245	32482	35138		1087	2778
2911	Engines & turbines (not for transport equipment)		-	-	-	-		-	-	-	-		-	-
2912	Pumps, compressors, taps and valves		-	-	-	-		-	-	-	-		-	-
2913	Bearings, gears, gearing & driving elements		-	-	-	-		-	-	-	-		-	-
2914	Ovens, furnaces and furnace burners		-	-	-	-		-	-	-	-		-	-
2915	Lifting and handling equipment		16671	17928	17026	19459		3207	3525	4216	7341		135	41
2919	Other general purpose machinery		46813	57604	59109	66249		17815	23720	28266	27797		952	2737

ISIC	Category	(1)	(2)	(3)	(4)	(5)	(6)	(7)	(8)	(9)	(10)
292	Special purpose machinery	39251	48440	41231	43542	15492	17324	15121	17433	348	142
2921	Agricultural and forestry machinery	16868	21473	17257	17548	4221	7183	3865	3966	111	4
2922	Machine tools	5015	4583	5153	4699	3039	1162	3046	2357	-	-
2923	Machinery for metallurgy	7780	9556	9804	9237	4095	4976	4754	4121	47	52
2924	Machinery for mining & construction	3849	5149	5423	6832	1907	1238	1559	4334	1	1
2925	Food/beverage/tobacco processing machinery	-	-	-	-	-	-	-	-	-	-
2926	Machinery for textile, apparel and leather	5739	7679	3594	5226	2230	2765	1897	2655	189	85
2927	Weapons and ammunition										
2929	Other special purpose machinery										
2930	Domestic appliances n.e.c.	47493	91802	84236	75598	16647	30993	25898	33922	...	257
3000	Office, accounting and computing machinery	16693	18598	20127	21856	4242	2327	2971	2934	142	690
3110	Electric motors, generators and transformers	19023	24852	24907	30907	7782	9915	16755	18903	259	801
3120	Electricity distribution & control apparatus	250449	291253	214496	179204	53629	61139	40649	35810	9948	104186
3130	Insulated wire and cable										
3140	Accumulators, primary cells and batteries	28361	38262	40269	42195	10327	14813	18580	19796	347	251
3150	Lighting equipment and electric lamps										
3190	Other electrical equipment n.e.c.										
3210	Electronic valves, tubes, etc.										
3220	TV/radio transmitters; line comm. apparatus										
3230	TV and radio receivers and associated goods										
331	Medical, measuring, testing appliances, etc.	19028	19838	22081	24702	7341	8801	12934	13678	494	1309
3311	Medical, surgical and orthopaedic equipment										
3312	Measuring/testing/navigating appliances,etc.	19028	19838	22081	24702	7341	8801	12934	13678	494	1309
3313	Industrial process control equipment										
3320	Optical instruments & photographic equipment										
3330	Watches and clocks										
3410	Motor vehicles	26790	30230	26428	23474	6926	8906	8301	7667	526	132
3420	Automobile bodies, trailers & semi-trailers	13647	14871	18559	12809	3943	4189	8424	5269	140	63
3430	Parts/accessories for automobiles										
351	Building and repairing of ships and boats	6577	57382	52521	54810	3059	33024	36535	37748	4746	3748
3511	Building and repairing of ships	6577	57382	52521	54810	3059	33024	36535	37748	4746	3748
3512	Building/repairing of pleasure/sport. boats										
3520	Railway/tramway locomotives & rolling stock										
3530	Aircraft and spacecraft										
359	Transport equipment n.e.c.										
3591	Motorcycles										
3592	Bicycles and invalid carriages										
3599	Other transport equipment n.e.c.										
3610	Furniture	139092	172783	171108	190375	63405	78172	72859	73312	7414	7586
369	Manufacturing n.e.c.	30424	47974	52910	80315	16490	15434	12204	15551	459	308
3691	Jewellery and related articles	14215	26503	39550	63141	6642	4488	7623	11685	235	235
3692	Musical instruments										
3693	Sports goods										
3694	Games and toys	16209	21471	13360	17174	9848	10946	4581	3866	224	73
3699	Other manufacturing n.e.c.										
3710	Recycling of metal waste and scrap										
3720	Recycling of non-metal waste and scrap										
D	Total manufacturing	7594678 a/	9685019	9275381	10503491 a/	2293854 a/	2963553	2851871	3526081 a/	329585 a/	358934

a/ Sum of available data.

Jordan

Index numbers of industrial production

ISIC Revision 3

(2005=100)

ISIC	Industry	Note	1999	2000	2001	2002	2003	2004	2005	2006	2007	2008	2009	2010
15	Food and beverages		81	80	81	90	73	84	100	105	98	104	127	128
16	Tobacco products		33	44	57	70	77	85	100	112	125	125	120	129
17	Textiles		159	139	96	117	128	126	100	116	129	111	124	130
18	Wearing apparel, fur		123	108	87	83	71	91	100	105	94	105	100	96
19	Leather, leather products and footwear		252	286	229	216	211	241	100	119	14	90	151	29
20	Wood products (excl. furniture)		318	222	720	420	142	222	100	96	100	101	103	106
21	Paper and paper products		77	75	76	78	71	89	100	106	114	106	87	81
22	Printing and publishing		129	103	101	86	75	86	100	103	105	86	112	99
23	Coke,refined petroleum products,nuclear fuel		77	85	85	86	88	94	100	96	93	93	84	80
24	Chemicals and chemical products		76	80	89	85	81	94	100	108	107	111	113	115
25	Rubber and plastics products		76	60	89	102	79	82	100	91	103	80	96	87
26	Non-metallic mineral products		66	64	74	78	78	88	100	106	107	110	100	83
27	Basic metals		64	60	75	72	78	86	100	83	89	84	76	73
28	Fabricated metal products		55	61	86	78	75	90	100	112	149	151	154	155
29	Machinery and equipment n.e.c.		100	88	80	63	76	92	100	178	221	297	277	179
30	Office, accounting and computing machinery		...	...	...	...	...	...	...	...	...	...	...	...
31	Electrical machinery and apparatus		47	49	53	57	58	82	100	107	128	139	141	87
32	Radio,television and communication equipment		31	35	32	33	55	81	100	183	170	84	46	9
33	Medical, precision and optical instruments		173	152	141	198	159	121	100	72	47	36	119	68
34	Motor vehicles, trailers, semi-trailers		68	69	57	90	92	94	100	85	86	73	76	44
35	Other transport equipment		...	...	...	...	...	...	...	...	...	...	...	...
36	Furniture; manufacturing n.e.c.		76	69	75	69	73	83	100	105	125	120	119	158
37	Recycling		...	...	...	...	...	...	...	...	...	...	...	...
D	Total manufacturing		67	72	82	87	79	90	100	106	109	110	111	105

Kenya

Concepts and definitions of variables:
Output and value added are valued at basic prices.

Related national publications:
Statistical Abstract (annual); Economic Survey Report, both published by the Kenya National Bureau of Statistics, Nairobi.

Supplier of information:
Kenya National Bureau of Statistics, Nairobi.

Basic source of data:
Annual enumeration of employed and self-employed persons survey; monthly survey of industrial production.

Major deviations from ISIC (Revision 3):
Data for number of establishments and number of employees were originally classified according to ISIC (Revision 2).

Reference period:
Calendar year.

Scope:
All establishments with four or more persons engaged.

Method of data collection:
The survey is conducted by mail questionnaire, followed by interviews of field enumerators.

Type of enumeration:
Complete enumeration for number of establishments, number of employees and wages and salaries; sample survey for output and value added.

Adjusted for non-response:
Yes.

Kenya

ISIC	Industry	Number of establishments (number) 2007	2008	2009	2010	Note	Number of employees (number) 2007	2008	2009	2010	Note	Wages and salaries paid to employees (millions of Kenyan Shillings) 2007	2008	2009	2010	Note
151	Processed meat,fish,fruit,vegetables,fats	...	...	...	...		...	...	...	...		4044.3	3927.1	4604.4	5267.9	
1511	Processing/preserving of meat	...	...	...	...		...	...	...	...		...	...	...	...	
1512	Processing/preserving of fish	...	...	...	...		...	...	...	...		...	...	...	...	
1513	Processing/preserving of fruit & vegetables	...	...	...	...		...	...	...	...		...	...	...	...	
1514	Vegetable and animal oils and fats	...	...	...	...		...	...	...	...		...	...	...	...	
1520	Dairy products	...	...	...	...		...	...	...	...		1631.6	1500.2	1776.7	1959.7	
153	Grain mill products; starches; animal feeds	...	...	...	...		...	...	...	...		1925.0	1920.6	2300.3	2527.3	
1531	Grain mill products	...	...	...	...		...	...	...	...		...	...	...	...	
1532	Starches and starch products	...	...	...	...		...	...	...	...		...	...	...	...	
1533	Prepared animal feeds	...	...	...	...		...	...	...	...		...	...	...	...	
154	Other food products	...	...	...	...		...	...	...	...		5238.0	5503.0	6624.0	7667.9	
1541	Bakery products	...	...	...	...		...	...	...	...		808.9	817.0	1031.7	1119.5	
1542	Sugar	...	...	...	...		...	...	...	...		2794.1	2901.9	3467.5	3825.8	
1543	Cocoa, chocolate and sugar confectionery	...	...	...	...		...	...	...	...		516.1	415.7	585.5	899.4	
1544	Macaroni, noodles & similar products	...	...	...	...		...	...	...	...		92.2	116.3	140.3	170.8	
1549	Other food products n.e.c.	...	...	...	...		...	...	...	...		1026.8	1252.1	1398.9	1652.3	
155	Beverages	...	...	...	...		...	...	...	...		4086.1	4463.2	5437.3	6086.6	
1551	Distilling, rectifying & blending of spirits	...	...	...	...		...	...	...	...		...	...	...	...	
1552	Wines	...	...	...	...		...	...	...	...		...	...	...	...	
1553	Malt liquors and malt	...	...	...	...		...	...	...	...		...	...	...	...	
1554	Soft drinks; mineral waters	...	...	...	...		...	...	...	...		350.5	395.9	483.2	546.3	
1600	Tobacco products	...	...	...	...		...	...	...	...		617.7	1750.4	2018.1	2280.8	
171	Spinning, weaving and finishing of textiles	...	...	...	...		...	...	...	...		...	...	...	...	
1711	Textile fibre preparation; textile weaving	...	...	...	...		...	...	...	...		...	...	...	...	
1712	Finishing of textiles	...	...	...	...		...	...	...	...		...	...	...	...	
172	Other textiles	...	...	...	...		...	...	...	...		...	...	...	...	
1721	Made-up textile articles, except apparel	...	...	...	...		...	...	...	...		...	...	...	...	
1722	Carpets and rugs	...	...	...	...		...	...	...	...		...	...	...	...	
1723	Cordage, rope, twine and netting	...	...	...	...		...	...	...	...		...	...	...	...	
1729	Other textiles n.e.c.	...	...	...	...		...	...	...	...		...	...	...	...	
1730	Knitted and crocheted fabrics and articles	...	...	...	...		...	...	...	...		...	...	...	...	
1810	Wearing apparel, except fur apparel	...	...	...	...		...	...	...	...		2651.9	2654.1	3081.9	3451.5	
1820	Dressing & dyeing of fur; processing of fur	...	...	...	...		...	...	...	...		...	...	...	...	
191	Tanning, dressing and processing of leather	...	...	...	...		...	...	...	...		455.4	469.6	589.6	658.6	
1911	Tanning and dressing of leather	...	...	...	...		...	...	...	...		...	...	...	...	
1912	Luggage, handbags, etc.; saddlery & harness	...	...	...	...		...	...	...	...		...	...	...	...	
1920	Footwear	...	...	...	...		...	...	...	...		...	...	...	...	
2010	Sawmilling and planing of wood	...	...	...	...		...	...	...	...		1473.3	1472.2	1782.7	1978.2	
202	Products of wood, cork, straw, etc.	...	...	...	...		...	...	...	...		...	...	...	...	
2021	Veneer sheets, plywood, particle board, etc.	...	...	...	...		...	...	...	...		...	...	...	...	
2022	Builders' carpentry and joinery	...	...	...	...		...	...	...	...		...	...	...	...	
2023	Wooden containers	...	...	...	...		...	...	...	...		...	...	...	...	
2029	Other wood products; articles of cork/straw	...	...	...	...		...	...	...	...		...	...	...	...	
210	Paper and paper products	...	...	...	...		...	...	...	...		2534.4	2556.4	3079.5	3414.2	
2101	Pulp, paper and paperboard	...	...	...	...		...	...	...	...		...	...	...	...	
2102	Corrugated paper and paperboard	...	...	...	...		...	...	...	...		...	...	...	...	
2109	Other articles of paper and paperboard	...	...	...	...		...	...	...	...		...	...	...	...	
221	Publishing	...	...	...	...		...	...	...	...		2699.4	2637.1	3104.7	3384.0	
2211	Publishing of books and other publications	...	...	...	...		...	...	...	...		...	...	...	...	
2212	Publishing of newspapers, journals, etc.	...	...	...	...		...	...	...	...		...	...	...	...	
2213	Publishing of recorded media	...	...	...	...		...	...	...	...		...	...	...	...	
2219	Other publishing	...	...	...	...		...	...	...	...		...	...	...	...	

Code	Description					Note
222	Printing and related service activities					
2221	Printing					
2222	Service activities related to printing					
2230	Reproduction of recorded media					
2310	Coke oven products	71.3	81.6	103.2	118.3	
2320	Refined petroleum products					
2330	Processing of nuclear fuel	6264.5	6292.2	7615.0	8374.4	
241	Basic chemicals					
2411	Basic chemicals, except fertilizers					
2412	Fertilizers and nitrogen compounds					
2413	Plastics in primary forms; synthetic rubber					
242	Other chemicals					
2421	Pesticides and other agro-chemical products					
2422	Paints, varnishes, printing ink and mastics					
2423	Pharmaceuticals, medicinal chemicals, etc.					
2424	Soap, cleaning & cosmetic preparations					
2429	Other chemical products n.e.c.					
2430	Man-made fibres	4123.9	4049.5	4732.7	5204.8	a/
251	Rubber products					
2511	Rubber tyres and tubes					
2519	Other rubber products					
2520	Plastic products	3297.3	3315.5	4019.0	4504.5	a/
2610	Glass and glass products					
269	Non-metallic mineral products n.e.c.					
2691	Pottery, china and earthenware					
2692	Refractory ceramic products					
2693	Struct.non-refractory clay; ceramic products					
2694	Cement, lime and plaster					
2695	Articles of concrete, cement and plaster					
2696	Cutting, shaping & finishing of stone					
2699	Other non-metallic mineral products n.e.c.					
2710	Basic iron and steel	4452.5	4508.1	5449.0	6046.5	b/
2720	Basic precious and non-ferrous metals					b/
273	Casting of metals					b/
2731	Casting of iron and steel					
2732	Casting of non-ferrous metals					
281	Struct.metal products;tanks;steam generators					b/
2811	Structural metal products					
2812	Tanks, reservoirs and containers of metal					
2813	Steam generators					
289	Other metal products; metal working services					b/
2891	Metal forging/pressing/stamping/roll-forming					
2892	Treatment & coating of metals					
2893	Cutlery, hand tools and general hardware					
2899	Other fabricated metal products n.e.c.	1906.3	1935.3	2297.2	2641.7	c/
291	General purpose machinery					
2911	Engines & turbines (not for transport equipment)					
2912	Pumps, compressors, taps and valves					
2913	Bearings, gears, gearing & driving elements					
2914	Ovens, furnaces and furnace burners					
2915	Lifting and handling equipment					
2919	Other general purpose machinery					
292	Special purpose machinery					c/
2921	Agricultural and forestry machinery					
2922	Machine tools					
2923	Machinery for metallurgy					
2924	Machinery for mining & construction					
2925	Food/beverage/tobacco processing machinery					
2926	Machinery for textile, apparel and leather					
2927	Weapons and ammunition					
2929	Other special purpose machinery					

continued

Kenya

ISIC	Industry	Number of establishments (number) Note	2007	2008	2009	2010	Number of employees (number) Note	2007	2008	2009	2010	Wages and salaries paid to employees (millions of Kenyan Shillings) Note	2007	2008	2009	2010
2930	Domestic appliances n.e.c.											c/				
3000	Office, accounting and computing machinery											c/				
3110	Electric motors, generators and transformers											c/				
3120	Electricity distribution & control apparatus											c/				
3130	Insulated wire and cable											c/				
3140	Accumulators, primary cells and batteries											c/				
3150	Lighting equipment and electric lamps											c/				
3190	Other electrical equipment n.e.c.											c/				
3210	Electronic valves, tubes, etc.											c/				
3220	TV/radio transmitters; line comm. apparatus											c/				
3230	TV and radio receivers and associated goods											c/				
331	Medical, measuring, testing appliances, etc.															
3311	Medical, surgical and orthopaedic equipment															
3312	Measuring/testing/navigating appliances,etc.															
3313	Industrial process control equipment															
3320	Optical instruments & photographic equipment															
3330	Watches and clocks											c/				
3410	Motor vehicles											d/	1852.9	1711.4	1982.5	2213.8
3420	Automobile bodies, trailers & semi-trailers											d/				
3430	Parts/accessories for automobiles											d/				
351	Building and repairing of ships and boats															
3511	Building and repairing of ships											d/				
3512	Building/repairing of pleasure/sport. boats															
3520	Railway/tramway locomotives & rolling stock											d/				
3530	Aircraft and spacecraft											d/				
359	Transport equipment n.e.c.											d/				
3591	Motorcycles															
3592	Bicycles and invalid carriages															
3599	Other transport equipment n.e.c.															
3610	Furniture												2902.4	2859.1	3389.4	3855.7
369	Manufacturing n.e.c.															
3691	Jewellery and related articles															
3692	Musical instruments															
3693	Sports goods															
3694	Games and toys															
3699	Other manufacturing n.e.c.															
3710	Recycling of metal waste and scrap															
3720	Recycling of non-metal waste and scrap															
D	Total manufacturing		4843	4961	4960	5553		268873	264065	266429	274284	e/	52578.4	54002.4	64470.5	72182.7

a/ 251 includes 2520.
b/ 2710 includes 2720, 273, 281 and 289.
c/ 291 includes 292, 2930, 3000, 3110, 3120, 3130, 3140, 3150, 3190, 3210, 3220, 3230, 331, 3320, 3330.
d/ 3410 includes 3420, 3430, 351, 3520, 3530 and 359.
e/ Sum of available data.

Kenya

ISIC Revision 3		Output (millions of Kenyan Shillings)					Value added (millions of Kenyan Shillings)					Gross fixed capital formation (millions of Kenyan Shillings)		
ISIC / Industry		Note	2007	2008	2009	2010	Note	2007	2008	2009	2010	Note	2009	2010
151	Processed meat,fish,fruit,vegetables,fats		61626.2	68084.0	85774.1	87317.0		12907.2	14297.6	18012.6	18336.6			
1511	Processing/preserving of meat													
1512	Processing/preserving of fish													
1513	Processing/preserving of fruit & vegetables													
1514	Vegetable and animal oils and fats		7595.6	8091.3	9421.8	9809.7		1974.9	2103.7	2449.7	2550.5			
1520	Dairy products		66242.9	75924.6	87846.5	78601.7		13911.0	15944.2	18447.8	16506.4			
153	Grain mill products; starches; animal feeds													
1531	Grain mill products													
1532	Starches and starch products													
1533	Prepared animal feeds													
154	Other food products		59113.0					10904.8	8232.4	9752.9	10483.4			
1541	Bakery products		17423.1	20332.3	21501.2	23779.2		3658.8	4269.8	4515.2	4993.6			
1542	Sugar		19562.0	18869.7	24941.4	26141.6		4108.7	3962.6	5237.7	5489.7			
1543	Cocoa, chocolate and sugar confectionery		10321.8	8314.2	11710.7	17989.0		3137.3						
1544	Macaroni, noodles & similar products		2027.5	2558.6	3085.7	3758.2								
1549	Other food products n.e.c.		9778.6	11924.8	13322.9	15736.0								
155	Beverages		36958.5	44269.7	48172.1	54266.1		15153.0	18150.6	19750.6	22249.1			
1551	Distilling, rectifying & blending of spirits													
1552	Wines													
1553	Malt liquors and malt													
1554	Soft drinks; mineral waters		7910.1	7851.5	8199.6	9975.9		2847.6	2826.5	2951.9	3591.3			
1600	Tobacco products	a/	12660.4	11822.7	9898.6	10572.8		3073.9	2573.6	2748.9	2788.7			
171	Spinning, weaving and finishing of textiles													
1711	Textile fibre preparation; textile weaving													
1712	Finishing of textiles													
172	Other textiles	a/												
1721	Made-up textile articles, except apparel													
1722	Carpets and rugs													
1723	Cordage, rope, twine and netting													
1729	Other textiles n.e.c.													
1730	Knitted and crocheted fabrics and articles	a/	10048.8	12141.5	9792.7	10304.5	a/	2612.7	3156.8	2546.1	2679.2			
1810	Wearing apparel, except fur apparel	b/	13427.7	14687.4	13898.9	18898.7	b/	3491.2	3818.7	3613.7	4913.7			
1820	Dressing & dyeing of fur; processing of fur	b/					b/							
191	Tanning, dressing and processing of leather		4049.9											
1911	Tanning and dressing of leather													
1912	Luggage, handbags, etc.; saddlery & harness													
1920	Footwear													
2010	Sawmilling and planing of wood	c/	2484.7	2484.7	2920.6	2859.0	c/	1391.5	1635.5	1601.0	1913.1			
202	Products of wood, cork, straw, etc.	c/					c/							
2021	Veneer sheets, plywood, particle board, etc.													
2022	Builders' carpentry and joinery													
2023	Wooden containers													
2029	Other wood products; articles of cork/straw													
210	Paper and paper products		28748.8	41333.5	27662.0	26606.7		7474.7	10746.7	7192.1	6917.7			
2101	Pulp, paper and paperboard													
2102	Corrugated paper and paperboard													
2109	Other articles of paper and paperboard													
221	Publishing	d/	15839.1	12458.0	16903.6	18766.9	d/	4910.1	3862.0	5240.1	5817.8			
2211	Publishing of books and other publications													
2212	Publishing of newspapers, journals, etc.													
2213	Publishing of recorded media													
2219	Other publishing													

continued

Kenya

ISIC	ISIC Revision 3 Industry	Output Note	Output (millions of Kenyan Shillings) 2007	2008	2009	2010	Value added Note	Value added (millions of Kenyan Shillings) 2007	2008	2009	2010	GFCF Note	Gross fixed capital formation (millions of Kenyan Shillings) 2009	2010
222	Printing and related service activities	d/					d/							
2221	Printing													
2222	Service activities related to printing													
2230	Reproduction of recorded media	d/					d/							
2310	Coke oven products	e/	77643.4	114857.9	77920.4	103924.6	d/							
2320	Refined petroleum products	e/						22060.2e/	31277.7	15459.3	16175.3			
2330	Processing of nuclear fuel	e/						...e/						
241	Basic chemicals		27195.6	32217.0	35868.0	41602.3		9790.4	11598.1	12912.5	14976.8			
2411	Basic chemicals, except fertilizers													
2412	Fertilizers and nitrogen compounds													
2413	Plastics in primary forms; synthetic rubber													
242	Other chemicals													
2421	Pesticides and other agro-chemical products													
2422	Paints, varnishes, printing ink and mastics													
2423	Pharmaceuticals, medicinal chemicals, etc.													
2424	Soap, cleaning & cosmetic preparations													
2429	Other chemical products n.e.c.													
2430	Man-made fibres													
251	Rubber products		19179.8	17844.4	21329.2	22752.9		5753.9	5353.3	6398.8	6825.9			
2511	Rubber tyres and tubes													
2519	Other rubber products													
2520	Plastic products		7128.1											
2610	Glass and glass products	f/	37285.9	52361.3	62752.1	67453.1	f/	24608.7	34558.4	41416.4	44519.0			
269	Non-metallic mineral products n.e.c.	f/					f/							
2691	Pottery, china and earthenware													
2692	Refractory ceramic products													
2693	Struct.non-refractory clay; ceramic products													
2694	Cement, lime and plaster													
2695	Articles of concrete, cement and plaster													
2696	Cutting, shaping & finishing of stone													
2699	Other non-metallic mineral products n.e.c.													
2710	Basic iron and steel	g/	21365.7	22697.7	24091.0	25827.7	g/	8759.9	9306.1	9877.3	10589.4			
2720	Basic precious and non-ferrous metals	g/					g/							
273	Casting of metals	g/					g/							
2731	Casting of iron and steel													
2732	Casting of non-ferrous metals													
281	Struct.metal products;tanks;steam generators	g/					g/							
2811	Structural metal products													
2812	Tanks, reservoirs and containers of metal													
2813	Steam generators													
289	Other metal products; metal working services	g/					g/							
2891	Metal forging/pressing/stamping/roll-forming													
2892	Treatment & coating of metals													
2893	Cutlery, hand tools and general hardware													
2899	Other fabricated metal products n.e.c.													
291	General purpose machinery	h/	8826.5	7969.3	8226.2	8303.1	h/	3177.5	2868.9	2961.4	2989.1			
2911	Engines & turbines (not for transport equipment)													
2912	Pumps, compressors, taps and valves													
2913	Bearings, gears, gearing & driving elements													
2914	Ovens, furnaces and furnace burners													
2915	Lifting and handling equipment													
2919	Other general purpose machinery													

Code	Description	Notes	C1	C2	C3	C4	C5	C6	C7	C8
292	Special purpose machinery	h/	...	...	...	...	...	...	...	...
2921	Agricultural and forestry machinery		...	...	...	...	...	...	...	...
2922	Machine tools		...	...	...	...	...	...	...	...
2923	Machinery for metallurgy		...	...	...	...	...	...	...	...
2924	Machinery for mining & construction		...	...	...	...	...	...	...	...
2925	Food/beverage/tobacco processing machinery		...	...	...	...	...	...	...	...
2926	Machinery for textile, apparel and leather		...	...	...	...	...	...	...	...
2927	Weapons and ammunition		...	...	...	...	...	...	...	...
2929	Other special purpose machinery		...	...	...	...	...	...	...	...
2930	Domestic appliances n.e.c.	h/	...	...	...	...	...	...	...	...
3000	Office, accounting and computing machinery	h/	...	...	...	...	...	...	...	...
3110	Electric motors, generators and transformers		...	...	...	...	...	...	...	...
3120	Electricity distribution & control apparatus		...	...	...	...	...	...	...	...
3130	Insulated wire and cable		...	...	...	...	...	...	...	...
3140	Accumulators, primary cells and batteries		...	...	...	...	...	...	...	...
3150	Lighting equipment and electric lamps		...	...	...	...	...	...	...	...
3190	Other electrical equipment n.e.c.		...	...	...	...	...	...	...	...
3210	Electronic valves, tubes, etc.		...	...	...	...	...	...	...	...
3220	TV/radio transmitters; line comm. apparatus		...	...	...	...	...	...	...	...
3230	TV and radio receivers and associated goods		...	...	...	...	...	...	...	...
331	Medical, measuring, testing appliances, etc.		...	...	...	...	...	...	...	...
3311	Medical, surgical and orthopaedic equipment		...	...	...	...	...	...	...	...
3312	Measuring/testing/navigating appliances,etc.		...	...	...	...	...	...	...	...
3313	Industrial process control equipment		...	...	...	...	...	...	...	...
3320	Optical instruments & photographic equipment		...	...	...	...	...	...	...	...
3330	Watches and clocks		...	...	...	...	...	...	...	...
3410	Motor vehicles	i/	3372.9	3738.9	3502.3	3060.3	21047.9	24316.0	23169.3	19576.6
3420	Automobile bodies, trailers & semi-trailers	i/	...	...	...	...	...	...	...	...
3430	Parts/accessories for automobiles	i/	...	...	...	...	...	...	...	...
351	Building and repairing of ships and boats	i/	...	...	...	...	...	...	...	...
3511	Building and repairing of ships		...	...	...	...	...	...	...	...
3512	Building/repairing of pleasure/sport. boats		...	...	...	...	...	...	...	...
3520	Railway/tramway locomotives & rolling stock	i/	...	...	...	...	...	...	...	...
3530	Aircraft and spacecraft	i/	...	...	...	...	...	...	...	...
359	Transport equipment n.e.c.	i/	...	...	...	...	...	...	...	...
3591	Motorcycles		...	...	...	...	...	...	...	...
3592	Bicycles and invalid carriages		...	...	...	...	...	...	...	...
3599	Other transport equipment n.e.c.		...	...	...	...	...	...	...	...
3610	Furniture	j/	5594.6	4219.2	3289.8	2549.9	13645.4	10290.7	8024.0	6219.4
369	Manufacturing n.e.c.	j/	...	...	...	...	...	...	...	...
3691	Jewellery and related articles		...	...	...	...	...	...	...	...
3692	Musical instruments		...	...	...	...	...	...	...	...
3693	Sports goods		...	...	...	...	...	...	...	...
3694	Games and toys		...	...	...	...	...	...	...	...
3699	Other manufacturing n.e.c.		...	...	...	...	...	...	...	...
3710	Recycling of metal waste and scrap		...	...	...	...	...	...	...	...
3720	Recycling of non-metal waste and scrap		...	...	...	...	...	...	...	...
D	Total manufacturing	k/	252122.4	234555.5	228304.1	190496.9	719939.8	659846.1	640289.3	551126.9

a/ 171 includes 172 and 1730.
b/ 1810 includes 1820.
c/ 2010 includes 202.
d/ 221 includes 222 and 2230.
e/ 2310 includes 2320 and 2330.
f/ 2610 includes 269.
g/ 2710 includes 2720, 273, 281 and 289.
h/ 291 includes 292, 2930 and 3000.
i/ 3410 includes 3420, 3430, 351, 3520, 3530 and 359.
j/ 3610 includes 369.

k/ Sum of available data.

Kenya

Index numbers of industrial production

ISIC Revision 3

(2005=100)

ISIC	Industry	Note	1999	2000	2001	2002	2003	2004	2005	2006	2007	2008	2009	2010
15	Food and beverages	a/	87	85	85	90	90	99	100	101	114	110	114	124
16	Tobacco products		99	82	80	63	65	73	100	140	166	166	150	156
17	Textiles		122	119	118	124	109	92	100	105	107	101	120	127
18	Wearing apparel, fur		57	62	64	66	70	70	100	141	147	159	122	124
19	Leather, leather products and footwear		42	47	51	70	69	64	100	107	106	108	163	213
20	Wood products (excl. furniture)		210	192	183	152	131	103	100	102	101	113	96	113
21	Paper and paper products		56	60	62	63	85	79	100	97	94	122	100	97
22	Printing and publishing		111	101	101	104	102	101	100	68	70	57	50	44
23	Coke,refined petroleum products,nuclear fuel		65	70	78	73	91	104	100	108	131	140	152	161
24	Chemicals and chemical products		...	...	...	...	...	...	...	...	...	...	...	...
25	Rubber and plastics products		...	...	...	...	...	...	...	...	...	...	...	...
26	Non-metallic mineral products		...	...	...	...	...	...	...	...	...	...	...	...
27	Basic metals		...	...	...	...	...	...	...	...	...	...	...	...
28	Fabricated metal products		105	92	92	94	92	96	100	109	122	124	120	136
29	Machinery and equipment n.e.c.		97	98	101	98	99	101	100	102	94	84	88	71
30	Office, accounting and computing machinery		...	...	...	...	...	...	...	...	...	...	...	...
31	Electrical machinery and apparatus		70	70	74	77	81	96	100	91	67	52	50	51
32	Radio,television and communication equipment		...	...	...	...	...	...	...	...	...	...	...	...
33	Medical, precision and optical instruments		...	...	...	...	...	...	...	...	...	...	...	...
34	Motor vehicles, trailers, semi-trailers		...	...	...	...	...	...	...	...	...	...	...	...
35	Other transport equipment		37	25	22	49	50	114	100	131	134	113	107	115
36	Furniture; manufacturing n.e.c.		...	...	...	...	...	...	...	...	...	...	...	...
37	Recycling		...	...	...	...	...	...	...	...	...	...	...	...
D	Total manufacturing		85	84	85	86	87	93	100	106	113	113	118	126

a/ 15 excludes beverages.

Kuwait

Supplier of information:
Central Statistical Bureau, Kuwait City.

Basic source of data:
Annual survey.

Major deviations from ISIC (Revision 3):
None reported.

Reference period:
Calendar year.

Scope:
All establishments.

Method of data collection:
Direct interview in the field.

Type of enumeration:
Sample survey.

Adjusted for non-response:
Yes.

Concepts and definitions of variables:
Wages and salaries is compensation of employees.
Output refers to gross output.
Value added refers to total value added.

Related national publications:
Annual Survey of Establishments (Industry), published by the Central Statistical Office, Kuwait City.

Kuwait

ISIC	Industry	Number of establishments (number)					Number of employees (number)					Wages and salaries paid to employees (millions of Kuwaiti Dinars)				
		Note	2007	2008	2009	2010	Note	2007	2008	2009	2010	Note	2007	2008	2009	2010
151	Processed meat,fish,fruit,vegetables,fats		16	15	16	17		2113	2248	2224	2163		6.8	6.9	6.2	6.7
1511	Processing/preserving of meat		...	...	...	...		...	...	...	...		...	...	...	...
1512	Processing/preserving of fish		...	...	...	...		...	...	...	...		...	...	...	...
1513	Processing/preserving of fruit & vegetables		...	...	...	...		...	...	...	...		...	...	...	...
1514	Vegetable and animal oils and fats		...	...	...	...		...	...	...	...		...	...	...	...
1520	Dairy products		4	4	4	4		1550	1603	2652	2712		4.4	4.3	11.9	13.3
153	Grain mill products; starches; animal feeds		...	...	...	...		...	...	...	...		...	...	...	...
1531	Grain mill products		11	11	11	11		1939	2269	2341	2437		8.9	11.9	10.0	13.4
1532	Starches and starch products		...	...	...	...		...	...	...	...		...	...	...	...
1533	Prepared animal feeds		...	...	...	...		...	...	...	...		...	...	...	...
154	Other food products		...	...	...	...		...	...	...	...		...	...	...	...
1541	Bakery products		599	606	613	615		9941	11087	11720	11995		22.5	23.8	26.4	28.2
1542	Sugar		...	...	...	...		...	...	...	...		...	...	...	...
1543	Cocoa, chocolate and sugar confectionery		...	...	...	...		...	...	...	...		...	...	...	...
1544	Macaroni, noodles & similar products		...	...	...	...		...	...	...	...		...	...	...	...
1549	Other food products n.e.c.		...	...	...	...		...	...	...	...		...	...	...	...
155	Beverages		6	6	6	6		3179	3215	3128	3204		8.0	9.3	10.3	12.7
1551	Distilling, rectifying & blending of spirits		...	...	...	...		...	...	...	...		...	...	...	...
1552	Wines		...	...	...	...		...	...	...	...		...	...	...	...
1553	Malt liquors and malt		...	...	...	...		...	...	...	...		...	...	...	...
1554	Soft drinks; mineral waters		...	...	...	...		...	...	...	...		...	...	...	...
1600	Tobacco products		...	...	...	...		...	...	...	...		...	...	...	...
171	Spinning, weaving and finishing of textiles		-	-	-	-		-	-	-	-		-	-	-	-
1711	Textile fibre preparation; textile weaving		-	-	-	-		-	-	-	-		-	-	-	-
1712	Finishing of textiles		...	...	...	...		...	...	...	...		...	...	...	...
172	Other textiles		295	293	294	293		2008	2056	2200	1967		3.9	4.0	4.1	4.0
1721	Made-up textile articles, except apparel		...	...	...	...		...	...	...	...		...	...	...	...
1722	Carpets and rugs		...	...	...	...		...	...	...	...		...	...	...	...
1723	Cordage, rope, twine and netting		...	...	...	...		...	...	...	...		...	...	...	...
1729	Other textiles n.e.c.		...	...	...	...		...	...	...	...		...	...	...	...
1730	Knitted and crocheted fabrics and articles		...	...	...	...		...	...	...	...		...	...	...	...
1810	Wearing apparel, except fur apparel		2550	2550	2546	2548		14047	13429	14000	14565		22.8	22.9	24.4	26.1
1820	Dressing & dyeing of fur; processing of fur		-	-	-	-		-	-	-	-		-	-	-	-
191	Tanning, dressing and processing of leather		...	...	...	...		...	...	...	...		...	...	...	...
1911	Tanning and dressing of leather		3	3	3	3		113	142	118	117		0.2	0.3	0.3	0.3
1912	Luggage, handbags, etc.; saddlery & harness		2	2	2	2		85	95	112	112		0.3	0.3	0.3	0.3
1920	Footwear		...	...	...	...		...	...	...	...		...	...	...	...
2010	Sawmilling and planing of wood		...	...	...	...		...	...	...	...		...	...	...	...
202	Products of wood, cork, straw, etc.		...	...	...	...		...	...	...	...		...	...	...	...
2021	Veneer sheets, plywood, particle board, etc.		...	...	...	...		...	...	...	...		...	...	...	...
2022	Builders' carpentry and joinery		111	113	119	116		1117	1152	1211	1209		2.2	2.2	2.3	2.4
2023	Wooden containers		...	...	...	...		...	...	...	...		...	...	...	...
2029	Other wood products; articles of cork/straw		...	...	...	...		...	...	...	...		...	...	...	...
210	Paper and paper products		...	...	...	...		...	...	...	...		...	...	...	...
2101	Pulp, paper and paperboard		30	32	31	31		1981	2045	2137	2335		6.8	5.7	6.8	7.6
2102	Corrugated paper and paperboard		...	...	...	...		...	...	...	...		...	...	...	...
2109	Other articles of paper and paperboard		...	...	...	...		...	...	...	...		...	...	...	...
221	Publishing		...	...	...	...		...	...	...	...		...	...	...	...
2211	Publishing of books and other publications		22	28	24	24		2551	3921	3670	3251		16.1	29.6	29.5	27.4
2212	Publishing of newspapers, journals, etc.		...	...	...	...		...	...	...	...		...	...	...	...
2213	Publishing of recorded media		...	...	...	...		...	...	...	...		...	...	...	...
2219	Other publishing		...	...	...	...		...	...	...	...		...	...	...	...

Code	Description	75	74	73	72	2419	2605	2435	2469				
222	Printing and related service activities									7.7	8.9	7.9	8.3
2221	Printing												
2222	Service activities related to printing	-	-	-	-					-	-	-	-
2230	Reproduction of recorded media	1	1	1	1				154	-	-	-	1.3
2310	Coke oven products					4765	4850	4964	5105	173.7	173.6	202.1	221.4
2320	Refined petroleum products					2865	3307	3731	3867				
2330	Processing of nuclear fuel	15	15	15	15					51.2	62.8	72.7	70.4
241	Basic chemicals												
2411	Basic chemicals, except fertilizers												
2412	Fertilizers and nitrogen compounds					1524	1626	1667	1645	6.6	6.9	6.7	7.2
2413	Plastics in primary forms; synthetic rubber	24	24	25	22								
242	Other chemicals												
2421	Pesticides and other agro-chemical products												
2422	Paints, varnishes, printing ink and mastics												
2423	Pharmaceuticals, medicinal chemicals, etc.												
2424	Soap, cleaning & cosmetic preparations												
2429	Other chemical products n.e.c.												
2430	Man-made fibres	3	3	3	3	238	336	344	315	0.6	0.8	0.7	0.7
251	Rubber products	38	37	37	37					9.8	13.1	13.4	12.5
2511	Rubber tyres and tubes					3806	3942	4276	4049				
2519	Other rubber products	42	43	43	43	863	947	980	996	2.6	2.8	3.0	3.1
2520	Plastic products	157	154	157	158	9557	9305	9217	9395	30.9	31.8	31.9	34.3
2610	Glass and glass products												
269	Non-metallic mineral products n.e.c.												
2691	Pottery, china and earthenware												
2692	Refractory ceramic products												
2693	Struct.non-refractory clay; ceramic products												
2694	Cement, lime and plaster												
2695	Articles of concrete, cement and plaster												
2696	Cutting, shaping & finishing of stone	5	5	5	5	785	698	762	817	5.2	5.5	4.4	4.8
2699	Other non-metallic mineral products n.e.c.	3	3	3	3	429	439	396	363	1.1	0.6	0.8	0.8
2710	Basic iron and steel	1	1	1	1	7	7	6	7				
2720	Basic precious and non-ferrous metals												
273	Casting of metals												
2731	Casting of iron and steel												
2732	Casting of non-ferrous metals	726	728	727	728	10936	11137	9811	9643	25.6	26.6	25.8	25.5
281	Struct.metal products;tanks;steam generators												
2811	Structural metal products												
2812	Tanks, reservoirs and containers of metal	165	165	166	166	1852	2036	2197	2222	7.3	7.1	7.6	8.1
2813	Steam generators												
289	Other metal products; metal working services												
2891	Metal forging/pressing/stamping/roll-forming												
2892	Treatment & coating of metals												
2893	Cutlery, hand tools and general hardware												
2899	Other fabricated metal products n.e.c.	54	54	56	57	2164	1251	1042	1413	5.5	3.7	2.7	3.6
291	General purpose machinery												
2911	Engines & turbines (not for transport equipment)												
2912	Pumps, compressors, taps and valves												
2913	Bearings, gears, gearing & driving elements												
2914	Ovens, furnaces and furnace burners												
2915	Lifting and handling equipment												
2919	Other general purpose machinery	5	5	5	4	4349	4359	4360	3037	9.0	9.1	9.2	7.4
292	Special purpose machinery												
2921	Agricultural and forestry machinery												
2922	Machine tools												
2923	Machinery for metallurgy												
2924	Machinery for mining & construction												
2925	Food/beverage/tobacco processing machinery												
2926	Machinery for textile, apparel and leather												
2927	Weapons and ammunition												
2929	Other special purpose machinery												

continued

Kuwait

ISIC	Industry	Number of establishments (number)					Number of employees (number)					Wages and salaries paid to employees (millions of Kuwaiti Dinars)				
		Note	2007	2008	2009	2010	Note	2007	2008	2009	2010	Note	2007	2008	2009	2010
2930	Domestic appliances n.e.c.		3	3	3	3		89	92	82	75		0.2	0.2	0.2	0.2
3000	Office, accounting and computing machinery		:	-	-	:		:	-	-	:		:	-	-	:
3110	Electric motors, generators and transformers		-	-	-	:		-	-	-	:		-	-	-	:
3120	Electricity distribution & control apparatus		10	11	11	11		2394	2528	2757	2849		9.4	9.3	10.7	10.9
3130	Insulated wire and cable		1	1	1	1		624	545	562	563		3.5	5.1	5.0	6.5
3140	Accumulators, primary cells and batteries		-	-	-	-		-	-	-	-		-	-	-	-
3150	Lighting equipment and electric lamps															
3190	Other electrical equipment n.e.c.		-	-	-	:		-	-	-	:		-	-	-	:
3210	Electronic valves, tubes, etc.		:	:	:	:		:	:	:	:		:	:	:	:
3220	TV/radio transmitters; line comm. apparatus		-	-	-	:		-	-	-	:		-	-	-	:
3230	TV and radio receivers and associated goods		-	-	-	:		-	-	-	:		-	-	-	:
331	Medical, measuring, testing appliances, etc.		8	8	7	7		5613	6137	5990	5606		18.4	21.1	20.0	26.3
3311	Medical, surgical and orthopaedic equipment		:	:	:	:		:	:	:	:		:	:	:	:
3312	Measuring/testing/navigating appliances,etc.		:	:	:	:		:	:	:	:		:	:	:	:
3313	Industrial process control equipment		:	:	:	:		:	:	:	:		:	:	:	:
3320	Optical instruments & photographic equipment		:	:	:	:		:	:	:	:		:	:	:	:
3330	Watches and clocks															
3410	Motor vehicles		-	-	-	:		-	-	-	:		-	-	-	:
3420	Automobile bodies, trailers & semi-trailers		6	8	8	8		324	380	339	322		1.3	1.3	1.0	1.1
3430	Parts/accessories for automobiles		1	1	1	1		54	54	50	50		0.1	0.1	0.1	0.1
351	Building and repairing of ships and boats		17	17	17	17		3805	4611	5586	5589		14.8	22.0	20.6	21.2
3511	Building and repairing of ships		:	:	:	:		:	:	:	:		:	:	:	:
3512	Building/repairing of pleasure/sport. boats		:	:	:	:		:	:	:	:		:	:	:	:
3520	Railway/tramway locomotives & rolling stock		-	-	-	:		-	-	-	:		-	-	-	:
3530	Aircraft and spacecraft		-	-	-	:		-	-	-	:		-	-	-	:
359	Transport equipment n.e.c.		-	-	-	:		-	-	-	:		-	-	-	:
3591	Motorcycles															
3592	Bicycles and invalid carriages		:	:	:	:		:	:	:	:		:	:	:	:
3599	Other transport equipment n.e.c.		:	:	:	:		:	:	:	:		:	:	:	:
3610	Furniture		374	373	370	372		5451	5684	5552	5686		11.6	12.1	13.0	13.3
369	Manufacturing n.e.c.		88	89	82	84		899	1019	815	824		1.7	1.8	1.5	1.7
3691	Jewellery and related articles		:	:	:	:		:	:	:	:		:	:	:	:
3692	Musical instruments		:	:	:	:		:	:	:	:		:	:	:	:
3693	Sports goods		:	:	:	:		:	:	:	:		:	:	:	:
3694	Games and toys		:	:	:	:		:	:	:	:		:	:	:	:
3699	Other manufacturing n.e.c.		:	:	:	:		:	:	:	:		:	:	:	:
3710	Recycling of metal waste and scrap		1	1	1	1		159	191	209	572		1.2	1.2	1.0	1.0
3720	Recycling of non-metal waste and scrap		2	2	1	2		133	139	127	211		0.7	0.9	0.6	1.0
D	Total manufacturing	a/	5474	5489	5495	5500	a/	106728	111487	113770	113911	a/	502.9	549.6	594.8	635.3

a/ Sum of available data.

Kuwait

ISIC	Industry	Note	Output at producers' prices (millions of Kuwaiti Dinars)				Note	Value added at producers' prices (millions of Kuwaiti Dinars)				Note	Gross fixed capital formation (millions of Kuwaiti Dinars)	
			2007	2008	2009	2010		2007	2008	2009	2010		2009	2010
151	Processed meat,fish,fruit,vegetables,fats		43.0	45.8	40.9	47.7		12.0	12.6	11.0	14.1		-0.8	2.0
1511	Processing/preserving of meat		...	...	...	...		...	...	...	...		...	...
1512	Processing/preserving of fish		...	...	...	...		...	...	...	...		...	...
1513	Processing/preserving of fruit & vegetables		...	...	...	...		...	...	...	...		...	...
1514	Vegetable and animal oils and fats		33.6	35.7	79.6	84.2		11.1	11.9	24.3	28.7		1.0	10.9
1520	Dairy products		70.4	74.9	97.3	106.7		2.6	2.0	5.8	10.8		4.8	-4.9
153	Grain mill products; starches; animal feeds		...	...	...	...		...	...	...	...		...	...
1531	Grain mill products		...	...	...	...		...	...	...	...		...	...
1532	Starches and starch products		...	...	...	...		...	...	...	...		...	...
1533	Prepared animal feeds		122.3	156.0	160.3	161.9		36.0	35.7	43.3	44.5		8.6	17.2
154	Other food products		...	...	...	...		...	...	...	...		...	...
1541	Bakery products		...	...	...	...		...	...	...	...		...	...
1542	Sugar		...	...	...	...		...	...	...	...		...	...
1543	Cocoa, chocolate and sugar confectionery		...	...	...	...		...	...	...	...		...	...
1544	Macaroni, noodles & similar products		...	...	...	...		...	...	...	...		...	...
1549	Other food products n.e.c.		69.6	77.5	101.8	112.0		22.2	24.2	24.5	28.2		9.1	2.4
155	Beverages		...	...	...	...		...	...	...	...		...	...
1551	Distilling, rectifying & blending of spirits		...	...	...	...		...	...	...	...		...	...
1552	Wines		-	-	-	...		-	-	-	...		-	...
1553	Malt liquors and malt		-	-	-	...		-	-	-	...		-	...
1554	Soft drinks; mineral waters		...	...	...	...		...	...	...	...		...	...
1600	Tobacco products		-	-	-	...		-	-	-	...		-	...
171	Spinning, weaving and finishing of textiles													
1711	Textile fibre preparation; textile weaving		-	-	-	...		-	-	-	...		-	...
1712	Finishing of textiles		20.1	22.9	23.0	22.4		8.0	8.6	8.4	8.5		-	0.5
172	Other textiles		...	...	...	...		...	...	...	...		...	...
1721	Made-up textile articles, except apparel		...	...	...	...		...	...	...	...		...	...
1722	Carpets and rugs		...	...	...	...		...	...	...	...		...	...
1723	Cordage, rope, twine and netting		...	...	...	...		...	...	...	...		...	...
1729	Other textiles n.e.c.		-	-	-	...		-	-	-	...		-	...
1730	Knitted and crocheted fabrics and articles		65.8	67.5	76.0	81.0		42.0	41.9	45.4	49.3		-	-
1810	Wearing apparel, except fur apparel		-	-	-	...		...	...	...	...		0.1	-0.1
1820	Dressing & dyeing of fur; processing of fur		1.3	1.0	1.2	1.4		-	0.2	0.4	0.5		...	...
191	Tanning, dressing and processing of leather		...	...	...	...		...	...	...	...		...	...
1911	Tanning and dressing of leather		...	...	...	...		...	...	...	...		...	...
1912	Luggage, handbags, etc.; saddlery & harness		1.7	1.6	1.7	1.7		0.8	0.7	0.6	0.7		1.7	0.1
1920	Footwear		-	-	-	...		-	-	-	...		-	-
2010	Sawmilling and planing of wood		17.4	16.6	15.6	16.3		5.7	5.0	5.2	5.7		-0.7	0.2
202	Products of wood, cork, straw, etc.		...	...	...	...		...	...	...	...		...	...
2021	Veneer sheets, plywood, particle board, etc.		...	...	...	...		...	...	...	...		...	...
2022	Builders' carpentry and joinery		...	...	...	...		...	...	...	...		...	...
2023	Wooden containers		...	...	...	...		...	...	...	...		...	...
2029	Other wood products; articles of cork/straw		55.2	64.9	67.0	76.5		14.7	15.7	18.6	21.5		1.6	6.1
210	Paper and paper products		...	...	...	...		...	...	...	...		...	...
2101	Pulp, paper and paperboard		...	...	...	...		...	...	...	...		...	...
2102	Corrugated paper and paperboard		...	...	...	...		...	...	...	...		...	...
2109	Other articles of paper and paperboard		64.6	84.6	76.9	72.7		31.8	34.5	29.5	27.5		8.5	7.9
221	Publishing		...	...	...	...		...	...	...	...		...	...
2211	Publishing of books and other publications		...	...	...	...		...	...	...	...		...	...
2212	Publishing of newspapers, journals, etc.		...	...	...	...		...	...	...	...		...	...
2213	Publishing of recorded media		...	...	...	...		...	...	...	...		...	...
2219	Other publishing		...	...	...	...		...	...	...	...		...	...

continued

Kuwait

ISIC	Industry	Note	Output at producers' prices (millions of Kuwaiti Dinars)				Note	Value added at producers' prices (millions of Kuwaiti Dinars)				Note	Gross fixed capital formation (millions of Kuwaiti Dinars)	
			2007	2008	2009	2010		2007	2008	2009	2010		2009	2010
222	Printing and related service activities													
2221	Printing		32.3	40.1	36.5	36.9		13.5	17.1	15.1	15.2		12.2	4.1
2222	Service activities related to printing		…	…	…	…		…	…	…	…		…	…
2230	Reproduction of recorded media		…	-	-	…		…	…	…	…		…	…
2310	Coke oven products					26.3					16.5		-	0.3
2320	Refined petroleum products		9777.3	9553.5	8621.3	10936.6		906.6	837.8	810.2	1078.1		222.6	393.8
2330	Processing of nuclear fuel		-	-	-	…		-	-	-	…		-	-
241	Basic chemicals													
2411	Basic chemicals, except fertilizers		570.2	601.2	476.5	1055.4		280.3	303.7	170.4	183.6		-4.7	21.5
2412	Fertilizers and nitrogen compounds		…	…	…	…		…	…	…	…		…	…
2413	Plastics in primary forms; synthetic rubber		…	…	…	…		…	…	…	…		…	…
242	Other chemicals													
2421	Pesticides and other agro-chemical products		57.4	62.9	55.3	56.2		19.4	19.5	17.3	18.5		0.8	3.1
2422	Paints, varnishes, printing ink and mastics		…	…	…	…		…	…	…	…		…	…
2423	Pharmaceuticals, medicinal chemicals, etc.		…	…	…	…		…	…	…	…		…	…
2424	Soap, cleaning & cosmetic preparations		…	…	…	…		…	…	…	…		…	…
2429	Other chemical products n.e.c.		…	…	…	…		…	…	…	…		…	…
2430	Man-made fibres		…	-	-	…		…	…	…	…		-	…
251	Rubber products		-	-	-	…							-	…
2511	Rubber tyres and tubes		4.8	6.8	6.9	7.2		1.3	1.8	1.9	1.6		0.3	0.4
2519	Other rubber products		…	…	…	…		…	…	…	…		…	…
2520	Plastic products		102.4	116.1	105.2	114.2		29.3	32.0	32.8	32.4		6.7	5.5
2610	Glass and glass products		18.0	20.3	21.1	20.3		6.9	8.0	9.5	9.5		1.8	1.7
269	Non-metallic mineral products n.e.c.		310.8	363.9	333.3	332.1		109.0	106.0	100.3	102.7		59.0	39.0
2691	Pottery, china and earthenware		…	…	…	…		…	…	…	…		…	…
2692	Refractory ceramic products		…	…	…	…		…	…	…	…		…	…
2693	Struct.non-refractory clay; ceramic products		…	…	…	…		…	…	…	…		…	…
2694	Cement, lime and plaster		…	…	…	…		…	…	…	…		…	…
2695	Articles of concrete, cement and plaster		…	…	…	…		…	…	…	…		…	…
2696	Cutting, shaping & finishing of stone		…	…	…	…		…	…	…	…		…	…
2699	Other non-metallic mineral products n.e.c.		…	…	…	…		…	…	…	…		…	…
2710	Basic iron and steel		137.3	218.9	28.5	76.8		23.3	3.8	-28.9	10.0		-46.9	51.0
2720	Basic precious and non-ferrous metals		12.2	11.1	10.3	10.8		2.5	1.8	2.6	2.7		4.0	2.2
273	Casting of metals													
2731	Casting of iron and steel		0.1		0.1	0.1		-	-	-	-		-	-
2732	Casting of non-ferrous metals		…	…	…	…		…	…	…	…		…	…
281	Struct.metal products;tanks;steam generators		169.7	174.0	154.5	141.4		55.4	57.0	46.8	43.1		5.3	-0.2
2811	Structural metal products		…	…	…	…		…	…	…	…		…	…
2812	Tanks, reservoirs and containers of metal		…	…	…	…		…	…	…	…		…	…
2813	Steam generators		…	…	…	…		…	…	…	…		…	…
289	Other metal products; metal working services													
2891	Metal forging/pressing/stamping/roll-forming		63.2	82.2	74.2	93.7		14.5	13.6	16.6	22.1		15.3	17.1
2892	Treatment & coating of metals		…	…	…	…		…	…	…	…		…	…
2893	Cutlery, hand tools and general hardware		…	…	…	…		…	…	…	…		…	…
2899	Other fabricated metal products n.e.c.		…	…	…	…		…	…	…	…		…	…
291	General purpose machinery		27.0	30.8	26.2	27.8		9.5	7.1	5.6	8.4		-2.0	1.3
2911	Engines & turbines (not for transport equipment)		…	…	…	…		…	…	…	…		…	…
2912	Pumps, compressors, taps and valves		…	…	…	…		…	…	…	…		…	…
2913	Bearings, gears, gearing & driving elements		…	…	…	…		…	…	…	…		…	…
2914	Ovens, furnaces and furnace burners		…	…	…	…		…	…	…	…		…	…
2915	Lifting and handling equipment		…	…	…	…		…	…	…	…		…	…
2919	Other general purpose machinery		…	…	…	…		…	…	…	…		…	…

292	Special purpose machinery	15.5	15.8	16.2	15.6	11.1	11.4	11.5	9.0	3.4	3.7
2921	Agricultural and forestry machinery	...	...	...	...	...	...	...	...	...	...
2922	Machine tools	...	...	...	...	...	...	...	...	...	...
2923	Machinery for metallurgy	...	...	...	...	...	...	...	...	...	...
2924	Machinery for mining & construction	...	...	...	...	...	...	...	...	...	...
2925	Food/beverage/tobacco processing machinery	...	...	...	...	...	...	...	...	...	...
2926	Machinery for textile, apparel and leather	...	...	...	...	...	...	...	...	...	...
2927	Weapons and ammunition	1.2	1.2	1.0	1.1	0.5	0.4	0.4	0.4	-0.1	0.2
2929	Other special purpose machinery	...	...	...	...	...	...	...	...	...	...
2930	Domestic appliances n.e.c.	-	-	-	-	-	-	-	-	-	-
3000	Office, accounting and computing machinery	-	-	-	-	-	-	-	-	-	-
3110	Electric motors, generators and transformers	61.4	59.2	81.5	88.7	24.9	23.0	28.8	26.0	9.6	22.6
3120	Electricity distribution & control apparatus	90.9	114.5	68.2	92.3	27.0	25.7	17.2	14.0	-11.6	2.6
3130	Insulated wire and cable	-	-	-	-	-	-	-	-	-	-
3140	Accumulators, primary cells and batteries	-	-	-	-	-	-	-	-	-	-
3150	Lighting equipment and electric lamps	-	-	-	-	-	-	-	-	-	-
3190	Other electrical equipment n.e.c.	-	-	-	-	-	-	-	-	-	-
3210	Electronic valves, tubes, etc.	...	...	...	...	...	...	...	...	...	...
3220	TV/radio transmitters; line comm. apparatus	...	...	...	...	...	...	...	...	...	...
3230	TV and radio receivers and associated goods	53.8	55.4	45.0	69.6	24.9	29.5	29.1	34.3	4.7	7.9
331	Medical, measuring, testing appliances, etc.	...	...	...	...	...	...	...	...	...	...
3311	Medical, surgical and orthopaedic equipment	-	-	-	-	-	-	-	-	-	-
3312	Measuring/testing/navigating appliances,etc.	...	...	...	...	...	...	...	...	...	...
3313	Industrial process control equipment	-	-	-	-	-	-	-	-	-	-
3320	Optical instruments & photographic equipment	-	-	-	-	-	-	-	-	-	-
3330	Watches and clocks	-	-	-	-	-	-	-	-	-	-
3410	Motor vehicles	14.6	11.8	6.3	6.7	3.1	3.3	2.0	1.9	-1.6	-0.3
3420	Automobile bodies, trailers & semi-trailers	0.5	0.5	0.5	0.8	0.2	0.2	0.2	0.3	-	0.1
3430	Parts/accessories for automobiles	46.6	77.0	66.7	55.1	22.5	28.4	27.4	30.1	3.6	3.0
351	Building and repairing of ships and boats	-	-	-	-	-	-	-	-	-	-
3511	Building and repairing of ships	-	-	-	-	-	-	-	-	-	-
3512	Building/repairing of pleasure/sport. boats	-	-	-	-	-	-	-	-	-	-
3520	Railway/tramway locomotives & rolling stock	-	-	-	-	-	-	-	-	-	-
3530	Aircraft and spacecraft	-	-	-	-	-	-	-	-	-	-
359	Transport equipment n.e.c.	...	...	...	...	...	...	...	...	...	...
3591	Motorcycles	...	...	...	...	...	...	...	...	...	...
3592	Bicycles and invalid carriages	...	...	...	...	...	...	...	...	...	...
3599	Other transport equipment n.e.c.	23.5	19.6	12.6	18.7	5.1	4.6	3.5	4.0	1.4	-1.0
3610	Furniture	60.5	66.7	61.1	66.7	21.3	22.0	24.0	25.2	...	...
369	Manufacturing n.e.c.	...	...	...	...	...	...	...	...	...	...
3691	Jewellery and related articles	...	...	...	...	...	...	...	...	...	...
3692	Musical instruments	...	...	...	...	...	...	...	...	...	...
3693	Sports goods	...	...	...	...	...	...	...	...	...	...
3694	Games and toys	...	...	...	...	...	...	...	...	...	...
3699	Other manufacturing n.e.c.	...	...	...	...	...	...	...	...	...	...
3710	Recycling of metal waste and scrap	9.5	15.6	10.9	12.1	1.8	0.6	-1.4	1.0	-0.3	0.9
3720	Recycling of non-metal waste and scrap	2.7	3.0	2.7	3.9	2.0	2.2	2.1	2.5	0.4	0.4
D	Total manufacturing	12228.3 a/	12370.9	11063.7	14151.5 a/	1803.0	1753.5	1561.9	1933.1 a/	318.0	622.9

a/ Sum of available data.

Kyrgyzstan

Supplier of information:
National Statistical Committee of the Kyrgyz Republic, Bishkek.

Basic source of data:
Annual industrial survey.

Major deviations from ISIC (Revision 3):
Data collected under the national classification system have been reclassified by the national authorities to correspond with ISIC (Revision 3).

Reference period:
Calendar year.

Scope:
All establishments.

Method of data collection:
Direct interview in the field.

Type of enumeration:
Complete enumeration.

Adjusted for non-response:
Yes.

Concepts and definitions of variables:
No deviations from the standard UN concepts and definitions are reported.

Related national publications:
None reported.

Kyrgyzstan

ISIC	Industry	Number of establishments (number)					Number of employees (number)					Wages and salaries paid to employees (thousands of Kyrgyzstan Soms)				
		Note	2007	2008	2009	2010	Note	2007	2008	2009	2010	Note	2007	2008	2009	2010
151	Processed meat,fish,fruit,vegetables,fats		93	86	77	69		1127	1222	1371	1173		40308	54270	63291	70818
1511	Processing/preserving of meat		37	31	30	27		444	540	640	629		26747	36332	46578	53791
1512	Processing/preserving of fish		4	4	6	5		38	35	60	72		686	835	1250	1562
1513	Processing/preserving of fruit & vegetables		43	41	33	28		582	598	637	434		11895	15969	13917	13573
1514	Vegetable and animal oils and fats		9	10	8	9		63	49	34	38		979	1133	1546	1892
1520	Dairy products		35	41	42	43		2179	2212	2015	1950		165165	191167	211001	193898
153	Grain mill products; starches; animal feeds		104	98	92	79		1427	1351	1373	1434		34627	49600	58985	62146
1531	Grain mill products		80	77	73	64		1278	1261	1300	1376		30215	46713	56569	59157
1532	Starches and starch products		2	2	2	2		77	58	42	31		2626	2462	1818	2449
1533	Prepared animal feeds		22	19	17	13		72	32	31	27		1786	425	599	541
154	Other food products		124	112	108	110		4595	3806	3365	3152		205417	192097	190135	198261
1541	Bakery products		92	84	81	81		2004	1819	1623	1629		43989	60922	68169	66241
1542	Sugar		8	7	7	8		1960	1485	1222	1044		141220	113914	103947	108988
1543	Cocoa, chocolate and sugar confectionery		8	5	5	3		181	101	57	19		9776	3747	1906	728
1544	Macaroni, noodles & similar products		8	9	7	7		103	90	171	202		1595	2335	5316	10358
1549	Other food products n.e.c.		8	7	8	11		347	311	292	258		8838	11178	10797	11946
155	Beverages		93	96	90	86		4526	4082	3470	3753		183349	214651	226800	276187
1551	Distilling, rectifying & blending of spirits		31	36	26	23		1777	1432	1164	1394		67395	71250	88343	108507
1552	Wines		22	21	19	17		304	313	232	204		7096	5169	6728	6972
1553	Malt liquors and malt		10	9	10	12		424	426	999	1100		23229	28189	49897	62195
1554	Soft drinks; mineral waters		30	30	35	34		2021	1911	1075	1055		85629	110043	81833	98514
1600	Tobacco products		14	3	3	4		707	578	474	521		101453	105452	116901	142351
171	Spinning, weaving and finishing of textiles		58	43	42	39		3227	2603	1938	1891		96241	90505	63612	72001
1711	Textile fibre preparation; textile weaving		52	38	36	34		2759	2224	1618	1534		75580	66173	40545	51752
1712	Finishing of textiles		6	6	6	5		468	379	320	357		20661	24331	23067	20248
172	Other textiles		12	11	12	17		220	222	459	455		4736	6612	12304	24437
1721	Made-up textile articles, except apparel		4	2	6	7		13	5	78	159		216	156	1172	6645
1722	Carpets and rugs		6	6	6	5		116	100	86	50		1370	1310	1053	1448
1723	Cordage, rope, twine and netting		-	-	-	-		-	-	-	-		-	-	-	-
1729	Other textiles n.e.c.		2	3	3	5		91	117	295	246		3150	5146	10079	16345
1730	Knitted and crocheted fabrics and articles		11	13	14	16		380	399	383	419		12230	15806	20039	25708
1810	Wearing apparel, except fur apparel		77	72	61	55		1661	1686	1095	904		28567	44361	38486	43047
1820	Dressing & dyeing of fur; processing of fur		3	2	3	4		52	40	38	40		662	746	712	1063
191	Tanning, dressing and processing of leather		5	5	7	5		185	191	186	110		5257	6419	7271	6233
1911	Tanning and dressing of leather		4	3	5	4		151	159	159	87		4474	5740	6582	5450
1912	Luggage, handbags, etc.; saddlery & harness		1	2	2	1		34	32	27	23		782	678	689	782
1920	Footwear		11	13	10	11		162	149	119	121		2547	2962	2316	2508
2010	Sawmilling and planing of wood		39	37	36	36		356	388	364	411		4073	5856	7185	12122
202	Products of wood, cork, straw, etc.		34	30	26	22		586	391	269	211		17486	13917	8470	5419
2021	Veneer sheets, plywood, particle board, etc.		-	-	-	-		-	-	-	-		-	-	-	-
2022	Builders' carpentry and joinery		23	20	17	16		528	353	243	185		16568	13408	8116	5160
2023	Wooden containers		-	-	-	-		-	-	-	-		-	-	-	-
2029	Other wood products; articles of cork/straw		11	10	9	6		58	38	26	6		918	509	354	259
210	Paper and paper products		19	22	20	17		721	694	640	679		36180	43617	47083	46462
2101	Pulp, paper and paperboard		2	2	2	2		37	24	25	25		504	706	1031	1239
2102	Corrugated paper and paperboard		5	4	4	4		444	442	416	424		28725	34572	38491	36181
2109	Other articles of paper and paperboard		12	16	14	11		240	228	199	230		6952	8339	7560	9042
221	Publishing		129	129	129	139		1285	1264	1222	1257		55082	65073	70263	89589
2211	Publishing of books and other publications		25	25	19	22		170	144	124	219		4768	6273	5938	9768
2212	Publishing of newspapers, journals, etc.		98	101	108	113		1098	1112	1088	1013		49604	57954	63572	76298
2213	Publishing of recorded media		-	-	-	-		-	-	-	-		-	-	-	-
2219	Other publishing		6	3	2	3		17	8	10	23		709	846	752	3523

222	Printing and related service activities	107	94	103	102	1797	1697	1486	1294	92004	101513	91077	97552
2221	Printing	103	89	98	96	1773	1683	1486	1279	91437	101160	91077	97552
2222	Service activities related to printing	4	5	5	6	24	14		15	567	353		
2230	Reproduction of recorded media	1	1	1	1	7	6	5	4	44	68	78	397
2310	Coke oven products	4	4		7	275	256	379	323	108466	77355	88856	106689
2320	Refined petroleum products	1	1		1	807	858	825	603	57211	85758	123341	98390
2330	Processing of nuclear fuel	19	21	18	17	1704	1489	1179	996	95621	111908	93341	64142
241	Basic chemicals	19	21	18	17	1704	1489	1179	996	95621	111908	93341	64142
2411	Basic chemicals, except fertilizers												
2412	Fertilizers and nitrogen compounds												
2413	Plastics in primary forms; synthetic rubber	54	53	47	44	639	615	604	523	16363	21699	29481	28218
242	Other chemicals												
2421	Pesticides and other agro-chemical products	10	11	8	8	147	129	126	92	2803	4103	7122	5033
2422	Paints, varnishes, printing ink and mastics	34	32	30	30	360	357	343	290	9677	11600	15066	15001
2423	Pharmaceuticals, medicinal chemicals, etc.	8	8	7	4	110	106	116	112	3263	4936	5770	5807
2424	Soap, cleaning & cosmetic preparations	2	2	2	2	22	23	19	29	620	1060	1523	2377
2429	Other chemical products n.e.c.												
2430	Man-made fibres									1498	1597	1282	1294
251	Rubber products	6	6	6	4	88	66	42	44	389	1597	1282	
2511	Rubber tyres and tubes	1				26		42		1109			
2519	Other rubber products	5	6	6	4	62	66		44	55158	67954	68736	63299
2520	Plastic products	93	118	148	129	1589	1558	1322	968	147882	152795	33525	39804
2610	Glass and glass products	7	6	6	6	1565	1407	384	411	569346	651331	577439	660323
269	Non-metallic mineral products n.e.c.	155	184	187	187	8969	8322	7202	6807				
2691	Pottery, china and earthenware		7	7	5		90	105	38	136921	2858	3386	1802
2692	Refractory ceramic products	35	51	57	55	2777	2267	1569	1375	247902	109468	54262	52450
2693	Struct.non-refractory clay; ceramic products	6	7	10	13	2040	1607	1976	2038	157467	249731	254091	296898
2694	Cement, lime and plaster	82	95	89	90	3340	3650	2686	2601	19140	257164	223312	266891
2695	Articles of concrete, cement and plaster	13	11	13	14	454	405	499	499	7917	21601	27907	25996
2696	Cutting, shaping & finishing of stone	19	13	11	10	358	303	367	367		10509	14481	16285
2699	Other non-metallic mineral products n.e.c.												
2710	Basic iron and steel	8	9	9	8	5561	4424	4246	4577	2130999	2401734	3189387	3561326
2720	Basic precious and non-ferrous metals	15	13	11	16	270	203	91	181	4439	2163	2142	6453
273	Casting of metals	15	13	11	16	270	203	91	181	4439	2163	2142	6453
2731	Casting of iron and steel												
2732	Casting of non-ferrous metals												
281	Struct.metal products;tanks;steam generators	52	64	57	46	1082	1198	963	846	39644	58501	61261	60956
2811	Structural metal products	49	62	54	43	1003	1106	878	771	36251	53328	56181	55685
2812	Tanks, reservoirs and containers of metal	3	2	3	3	79	92	85	75	3393	5173	5081	5271
2813	Steam generators	39	41	39	32	1119	921	751	627	42848	46267	44068	41966
289	Other metal products; metal working services	3	3	3	2	68	76	68	55	4012	4718	4112	4047
2891	Metal forging/pressing/stamping/roll-forming	3	2	2	3	11	18	16	224	636	867	970	21238
2892	Treatment & coating of metals	11	12	12	8	335	261	136	75	9355	8637	7561	3972
2893	Cutlery, hand tools and general hardware	24	24	22	19	705	566	531	273	28846	32046	31424	12710
2899	Other fabricated metal products n.e.c.	24	25	24	25	307	287	234	215	8974	11392	12142	11474
291	General purpose machinery	2	2	3	3	7	13	15	3	578	226	252	86
2911	Engines & turbines (not for transport equipment)	7	7	7	8	111	88	70	69	2365	2748	2808	2736
2912	Pumps, compressors, taps and valves	2	1	7	1	42	30	12	7	1381	928	362	184
2913	Bearings, gears, gearing & driving elements	2	2	1		3	3			17	70		
2914	Ovens, furnaces and furnace burners	1	3	3	4	5	12	12	13	85	468	820	1001
2915	Lifting and handling equipment	10	10	8	9	139	141	125	123	4549	6952	7900	7466
2919	Other general purpose machinery	82	81	78	69	3001	2807	2608	2264	219433	283432	271007	268106
292	Special purpose machinery	54	58	52	46	450	454	400	401	14865	16097	15852	23007
2921	Agricultural and forestry machinery	6	4	5	4	29	24	25	27	1246	1197	1853	1942
2922	Machine tools												
2923	Machinery for metallurgy	8	6	8	7	643	572	592	342	49657	58216	49328	40934
2924	Machinery for mining & construction	5	4	4	3	134	56	52	31	4273	2839	2623	1545
2925	Food/beverage/tobacco processing machinery												
2926	Machinery for textile, apparel and leather	4	4	4	4	1398	1411	1315	1253	127625	177146	176512	178955
2927	Weapons and ammunition	5	5	5	5	347	290	224	210	21768	27937	24839	21724
2929	Other special purpose machinery												

continued

Kyrgyzstan

ISIC	Industry		Number of establishments (number)					Number of employees (number)					Wages and salaries paid to employees (thousands of Kyrgyzstan Soms)			
		Note	2007	2008	2009	2010	Note	2007	2008	2009	2010	Note	2007	2008	2009	2010
2930	Domestic appliances n.e.c.		9	7	8	9		336	290	160	146		11399	13705	6794	10218
3000	Office, accounting and computing machinery		16	9	6	5		86	77	42	16		2673	3717	3156	606
3110	Electric motors, generators and transformers		9	14	16	13		274	279	251	225		13472	19080	12518	20971
3120	Electricity distribution & control apparatus		5	4	4	5		529	558	248	287		19988	24716	...	13259
3130	Insulated wire and cable		1	2	1	1		79	127	81	94		2435	4147	4097	3836
3140	Accumulators, primary cells and batteries		5	3	2	2		53	41	18	6		1257	1334	462	177
3150	Lighting equipment and electric lamps		2	2	2	2		-	-	-	-		-	-	-	-
3190	Other electrical equipment n.e.c.		7	6	5	4		3719	3407	2442	2940		240456	277755	202410	272056
3210	Electronic valves, tubes, etc.		5	4	5	3		54	35	28	18		1519	1995	1690	1648
3220	TV/radio transmitters; line comm. apparatus		5	3	3	4		253	216	176	164		18298	17949	15664	17160
3230	TV and radio receivers and associated goods		4	6	6	5		37	35	23	30		944	907	944	1342
331	Medical, measuring, testing appliances, etc.		13	14	14	14		63	136	81	54		2114	3067	3227	2966
3311	Medical, surgical and orthopaedic equipment		3	3	3	4		221	225	249	255		13008	14583	23238	28180
3312	Measuring/testing/navigating appliances,etc.		4	7	7	7		145	143	179	179		10623	11139	16504	18886
3313	Industrial process control equipment		6	4	4	7		32	67	60	66		1891	3181	6046	8652
3320	Optical instruments & photographic equipment		2	1	-	3		44	15	10	10		494	263	689	643
3330	Watches and clocks		-	-	-	-		36	31	-	-		1484	1500	-	-
3410	Motor vehicles		1	1	1	1		8	...	...	...		234	...	...	...
3420	Automobile bodies, trailers & semi-trailers		-	-	-	-		-	-	-	4		-	-	-	-
3430	Parts/accessories for automobiles		2	2	2	2		465	520	490	401		27994	53758	40756	44777
351	Building and repairing of ships and boats		1	1	3	4		1	...	...	...		14	...	...	...
3511	Building and repairing of ships		1	1	3	4		1	...	...	...		14	...	...	...
3512	Building/repairing of pleasure/sport. boats		-	-	-	-		-	-	-	-		-	-	-	-
3520	Railway/tramway locomotives & rolling stock		1	1	1	1		...	...	...	...		...	...	...	...
3530	Aircraft and spacecraft		2	3	2	3		8	10	6	6		316	986	999	379
359	Transport equipment n.e.c.		-	-	-	-		109	156	130	154		4948	11452	16921	18106
3591	Motorcycles		-	-	-	-		-	-	-	-		-	-	-	-
3592	Bicycles and invalid carriages		-	-	-	-		-	-	-	-		-	-	-	-
3599	Other transport equipment n.e.c.		-	-	-	-		-	-	-	-		-	-	-	-
3610	Furniture		34	38	42	47		1013	986	889	772		27998	37256	41889	32769
369	Manufacturing n.e.c.		14	17	19	16		666	609	531	242		8826	10868	10676	9447
3691	Jewellery and related articles		8	11	11	8		376	372	357	80		4869	7093	6024	3706
3692	Musical instruments		-	-	-	-		-	-	-	-		-	-	-	-
3693	Sports goods		-	-	-	-		-	-	-	-		-	-	-	-
3694	Games and toys		1	1	-	-		5	3	-	-		115	124	-	-
3699	Other manufacturing n.e.c.		5	5	8	8		285	234	174	162		3842	3651	4652	5741
3710	Recycling of metal waste and scrap		7	4	3	2		96	36	3	3		1573	559	142	85
3720	Recycling of non-metal waste and scrap		1	3	2	2		4	9	4	36		21	138	108	341
D	Total manufacturing		1674	1679	1661	1592		60286	55181	46954	45017		4984282	5678046	6402728	6860994

Kyrgyzstan

Output at producers' prices and Value added in millions of Kyrgyzstan Soms; Gross fixed capital formation in millions of Kyrgyzstan Soms.

ISIC Revision 3		Output at producers' prices (millions of Kyrgyzstan Soms)					Value added (millions of Kyrgyzstan Soms)					Gross fixed capital formation (millions of Kyrgyzstan Soms)		
ISIC	Industry	Note	2007	2008	2009	2010	Note	2007	2008	2009	2010	Note	2009	2010
151	Processed meat,fish,fruit,vegetables,fats		615.2	1051.2	1263.5	1488.6		204.3	545.6	404.2	835.7		...	...
1511	Processing/preserving of meat		274.0	454.3	870.2	1012.6		86.3	161.3	278.1	485.0		...	...
1512	Processing/preserving of fish		46.0	34.2	41.5	89.4		3.1	-0.3	15.8	9.7		...	...
1513	Processing/preserving of fruit & vegetables		121.5	345.6	200.5	121.4		60.4	138.0	110.3	40.9		...	...
1514	Vegetable and animal oils and fats		173.7	217.1	151.3	265.2		54.5	...	...	...		...	...
1520	Dairy products		2405.6	2832.0	3082.5	3092.2		462.0	958.7	965.1	903.4		...	...
153	Grain mill products; starches; animal feeds		1483.1	1954.4	2347.8	2966.1		866.7	604.3	959.6	777.4		...	...
1531	Grain mill products		1421.1	1880.3	2146.6	2628.3		824.3	569.6	898.9	748.2		...	...
1532	Starches and starch products		61.9	74.1	201.2	188.4		42.4	34.7	60.7	25.8		...	...
1533	Prepared animal feeds		-	-	-	149.4		-	-	-	3.5		...	...
154	Other food products		2921.3	4023.8	4502.9	4934.4		772.7	1052.3	1463.8	1346.0		...	...
1541	Bakery products		2094.6	3228.8	3605.3	3652.5		608.0	809.4	1218.9	828.7		...	...
1542	Sugar		527.7	381.3	344.6	537.2		93.3	134.4	119.7	235.9		...	...
1543	Cocoa, chocolate and sugar confectionery		37.5	16.2	16.2	16.4		17.5	15.6	12.8	16.4		...	...
1544	Macaroni, noodles & similar products		95.4	197.9	306.0	429.9		19.7	29.7	29.2	152.7		...	...
1549	Other food products n.e.c.		166.0	199.7	230.6	308.2		34.3	63.2	83.2	112.4		...	...
155	Beverages		2027.8	2566.7	2824.5	3286.6		596.9	921.0	862.0	1260.8		...	...
1551	Distilling, rectifying & blending of spirits		905.1	1272.3	1316.2	1515.8		222.5	350.1	374.5	605.1		...	...
1552	Wines		71.8	74.4	78.3	58.8		26.0	28.9	22.8	21.1		...	...
1553	Malt liquors and malt		202.6	236.8	429.9	531.1		102.1	108.5	148.2	138.7		...	...
1554	Soft drinks; mineral waters		848.3	983.2	1000.7	1181.0		246.2	433.5	316.5	495.9		...	...
1600	Tobacco products		1065.2	1042.5	1309.1	1390.5		373.8	490.6	359.3	456.9		...	...
171	Spinning, weaving and finishing of textiles		784.6	711.1	563.8	670.8		213.4	343.2	210.7	177.1		...	...
1711	Textile fibre preparation; textile weaving		725.3	647.8	495.8	627.5		205.1	321.2	170.2	156.0		...	...
1712	Finishing of textiles		59.3	63.3	68.0	43.3		8.3	22.0	40.5	21.0		...	...
172	Other textiles		131.5	112.6	169.4	224.8		41.3	38.3	73.0	92.5		...	...
1721	Made-up textile articles, except apparel		43.9	16.8	48.1	71.8		10.0	6.7	34.1	39.6		...	...
1722	Carpets and rugs		73.6	73.0	76.4	108.6		27.2	23.1	22.0	28.5		...	...
1723	Cordage, rope, twine and netting		-	-	-	-		-	-	-	-		...	...
1729	Other textiles n.e.c.		14.1	22.8	44.9	44.5		4.1	8.4	16.9	24.4		...	...
1730	Knitted and crocheted fabrics and articles		89.2	152.8	207.0	460.8		35.1	56.1	49.5	136.8		...	...
1810	Wearing apparel, except fur apparel		3174.9	4849.3	3556.2	5138.6		970.9	1852.7	1708.4	1139.3		...	...
1820	Dressing & dyeing of fur; processing of fur		14.0	11.6	22.4	13.7		4.8	3.7	17.3	7.9		...	...
191	Tanning, dressing and processing of leather		58.9	64.9	85.6	104.3		17.9	15.9	30.4	26.8		...	...
1911	Tanning and dressing of leather		46.3	60.6	58.4	92.6		13.1	10.8	13.4	25.9		...	...
1912	Luggage, handbags, etc.; saddlery & harness		12.5	...	27.2	11.7		4.8	5.2	16.9	0.9		...	...
1920	Footwear		66.0	119.8	120.2	...		13.7	12.6	15.6	18.6		...	...
2010	Sawmilling and planing of wood		28.5	40.2	83.4	54.3		19.7	26.6	54.8	27.3		...	...
202	Products of wood, cork, straw, etc.		105.8	104.0	163.2	190.3		38.1	43.9	53.5	54.2		...	...
2021	Veneer sheets, plywood, particle board, etc.		88.6	89.2	81.1	103.6		33.0	39.0	27.5	34.8		...	...
2022	Builders' carpentry and joinery		-	-	-	-		-	-	-	-		...	...
2023	Wooden containers		17.2	14.8	82.2	86.7		5.1	4.9	26.0	16.5		...	...
2029	Other wood products; articles of cork/straw		-	-	-	-		-	-	-	-		...	...
210	Paper and paper products		254.9	258.2	262.9	453.7		68.5	87.9	87.0	195.9		...	...
2101	Pulp, paper and paperboard		4.0	6.7	2.7	7.8		0.5	2.4	1.3	2.8		...	...
2102	Corrugated paper and paperboard		213.1	208.4	223.7	272.7		54.5	66.9	68.9	125.1		...	...
2109	Other articles of paper and paperboard		37.7	43.0	36.5	173.2		13.5	18.6	16.8	68.1		...	...
221	Publishing		243.7	271.5	287.9	405.5		83.3	90.9	137.8	168.6		...	...
2211	Publishing of books and other publications		42.8	48.3	53.9	110.6		10.5	15.4	26.0	35.5		...	...
2212	Publishing of newspapers, journals, etc.		196.5	220.7	230.9	281.9		69.0	74.8	110.3	130.5		...	...
2213	Publishing of recorded media		-	-	-	-		-	-	-	-		...	...
2219	Other publishing		4.3	2.4	3.1	12.6		3.8	0.7	1.5	2.5		...	...

continued

Kyrgyzstan

ISIC	Industry	Note	Output at producers' prices (millions of Kyrgyzstan Soms) 2007	2008	2009	2010	Note	Value added (millions of Kyrgyzstan Soms) 2007	2008	2009	2010	Note	Gross fixed capital formation (millions of Kyrgyzstan Soms) 2009	2010
222	Printing and related service activities		537.1	708.3	676.5	644.2		198.6	272.9	276.9	302.5		...	...
2221	Printing		534.6	703.2	672.6	641.9		195.1	270.7	274.8	301.5		...	...
2222	Service activities related to printing		2.5	5.0	3.9	2.2		3.5	2.3	2.1	1.0		...	...
2230	Reproduction of recorded media		1.5	0.9	0.9	1.3		0.3	0.1	0.2	0.8		...	...
2310	Coke oven products		-	-	-	-		-	-	-	-		...	...
2320	Refined petroleum products		560.4	754.8	553.3	764.6		208.3	407.8	171.0	386.6		...	...
2330	Processing of nuclear fuel		187.3	323.1	844.6	485.5		105.1	154.2	215.5	164.2		...	...
241	Basic chemicals		338.6	404.4	108.5	188.3		116.5	82.9	33.6	61.8		...	...
2411	Basic chemicals, except fertilizers		338.6	404.4	108.5	188.3		116.5	82.9	33.6	61.8		...	...
2412	Fertilizers and nitrogen compounds		-	-	-	-		-	-	-	-		...	...
2413	Plastics in primary forms; synthetic rubber		-	-	-	-		-	-	-	-		...	...
242	Other chemicals		286.6	326.1	437.8	436.3		84.2	133.4	176.5	151.0		...	...
2421	Pesticides and other agro-chemical products		-	-	-	-		-	-	-	-		...	...
2422	Paints, varnishes, printing ink and mastics		138.0	158.2	153.1	172.2		24.4	113.2	37.3	33.8		...	...
2423	Pharmaceuticals, medicinal chemicals, etc.		83.1	89.7	178.0	158.4		24.1	-16.2	69.6	80.6		...	...
2424	Soap, cleaning & cosmetic preparations		62.3	72.3	96.1	94.8		31.1	34.6	59.6	31.6		...	...
2429	Other chemical products n.e.c.		3.2	5.9	10.6	10.9		...	1.7	9.9	5.0		...	...
2430	Man-made fibres		-	-	-	-		-	-	-	-		...	...
251	Rubber products		51.6	30.1	36.8	40.1		13.8	11.0	14.8	12.9		...	...
2511	Rubber tyres and tubes		0.7	...	36.8	...							...	...
2519	Other rubber products		50.9	30.1	...	40.1		13.8	11.0	14.8	12.9		...	...
2520	Plastic products		1218.2	1229.7	1080.3	1181.8		471.6	418.3	391.9	352.3		...	...
2610	Glass and glass products		1618.9	1574.3	89.9	163.4		666.7	763.4	28.2	53.2		...	...
269	Non-metallic mineral products n.e.c.		5818.7	7354.5	5465.0	6147.9		1703.9	2485.1	1989.8	1865.7		...	...
2691	Pottery, china and earthenware		-	-	-	-		-	-	-	-		...	...
2692	Refractory ceramic products		-	-	17.7	13.4		-	8.6	6.8	3.4		...	...
2693	Struct.non-refractory clay; ceramic products		531.8	400.0	238.9	228.1		272.1	173.3	102.1	93.2		...	...
2694	Cement, lime and plaster		3657.3	4010.6	2284.5	2999.8		756.7	1466.0	982.7	815.9		...	...
2695	Articles of concrete, cement and plaster		1367.3	2710.1	2694.7	2750.4		624.0	695.5	790.3	886.8		...	...
2696	Cutting, shaping & finishing of stone		86.2	98.1	105.8	99.3		37.6	46.2	59.1	38.8		...	...
2699	Other non-metallic mineral products n.e.c.		176.0	135.6	123.4	56.9		6.6	95.4	48.8	27.6		...	...
2710	Basic iron and steel		-	-	-	-		-	-	-	-		...	...
2720	Basic precious and non-ferrous metals		16502.9	35521.8	46566.0	63511.8		4398.0	12100.3	16588.2	26304.7		...	...
273	Casting of metals		55.1	24.6	29.0	254.3		23.5	17.8	17.1	51.9		...	...
2731	Casting of iron and steel		55.1	24.6	29.0	254.3		23.5	17.8	17.1	51.9		...	...
2732	Casting of non-ferrous metals		-	-	-	-		-	-	-	-		...	...
281	Struct.metal products;tanks;steam generators		338.7	498.0	856.5	710.4		140.5	208.5	286.5	236.0		...	...
2811	Structural metal products		287.8	428.5	767.6	626.5		106.5	184.6	250.1	195.8		...	...
2812	Tanks, reservoirs and containers of metal		-	-	-	-		-	-	-	-		...	...
2813	Steam generators		50.9	69.5	88.9	83.9		34.0	23.9	36.4	40.2		...	...
289	Other metal products; metal working services		391.2	314.6	289.0	252.3		55.8	80.4	101.9	81.7		...	...
2891	Metal forging/pressing/stamping/roll-forming		125.9	105.2	117.8	102.1		15.1	15.9	36.5	31.1		...	...
2892	Treatment & coating of metals		4.9	8.9	12.5	24.9		2.1	2.9	10.5	8.5		...	...
2893	Cutlery, hand tools and general hardware		88.8	93.1	46.9	39.5		24.8	27.5	21.6	11.7		...	...
2899	Other fabricated metal products n.e.c.		171.6	107.4	111.7	85.8		13.9	34.1	33.3	30.3		...	...
291	General purpose machinery		121.1	158.5	163.2	157.0		38.0	38.1	52.4	20.2		...	...
2911	Engines & turbines (not for transport equipment)		17.2	7.9	6.5	1.3		5.5	1.1	1.4	0.2		...	...
2912	Pumps, compressors, taps and valves		11.5	10.9	12.9	17.7		2.0	4.3	4.5	6.2		...	...
2913	Bearings, gears, gearing & driving elements		1.3	1.8	0.5	0.4		...	0.1	0.1	0.3		...	...
2914	Ovens, furnaces and furnace burners		...	...	0.6	0.8		...	...	...	...		...	...
2915	Lifting and handling equipment		0.1	3.4	3.6	3.7		0.1	0.4	2.6	2.6		...	...
2919	Other general purpose machinery		91.0	134.5	139.0	133.0		30.3	32.1	43.2	10.5		...	...

ISIC Revision 3

Code	Industry	1	2	3	4	5	6	7	8
292	Special purpose machinery	324.1	261.1	433.1	450.0	709.6	736.6	819.4	799.1
2921	Agricultural and forestry machinery	18.4	13.6	16.4	22.0	72.5	48.0	45.6	31.4
2922	Machine tools	6.4	7.7	...	...	9.1	11.1	5.6	5.1
2923	Machinery for metallurgy	53.7	57.5	76.0	76.7	91.2	91.2	182.2	180.2
2924	Machinery for mining & construction	0.7	1.6	2.3	5.7	2.3	4.0	6.5	6.6
2925	Food/beverage/tobacco processing machinery	-	-	-	-	-	-	-	-
2926	Machinery for textile, apparel and leather	222.2	153.7	290.4	307.3	493.2	525.0	506.9	522.6
2927	Weapons and ammunition	22.7	26.9	39.9	31.7	41.2	57.1	72.5	53.3
2929	Other special purpose machinery	9.9	12.4	9.5	19.8	31.3	24.2	56.6	36.3
2930	Domestic appliances n.e.c.	1.6	10.8	10.1	0.7	5.8	15.5	13.9	15.3
3000	Office, accounting and computing machinery	-	32.9	33.8	30.3	98.0	88.4	90.8	75.0
3110	Electric motors, generators and transformers	49.8	48.7	83.7	40.7	187.1	149.0	294.8	176.4
3120	Electricity distribution & control apparatus	56.8	0.9	8.6	0.6	3.1	1.7	49.9	1.4
3130	Insulated wire and cable	2.1	4.5	1.3	0.3	3.5	7.2	2.6	2.0
3140	Accumulators, primary cells and batteries	1.5	314.3	520.7	366.4	961.2	787.1	1015.6	769.9
3150	Lighting equipment and electric lamps	418.8	1.8	3.5	2.2	7.9	4.8	6.4	4.4
3190	Other electrical equipment n.e.c.	5.2	34.7	37.8	34.4	83.6	77.1	89.7	80.5
3210	Electronic valves, tubes, etc.	40.1	14.8	21.3	6.5	31.5	53.3	16.1	14.0
3220	TV/radio transmitters; line comm. apparatus	7.9	19.4	23.9	1.4	58.9	44.3	31.7	2.5
3230	TV and radio receivers and associated goods	33.1	67.3	31.3	19.4	76.5	120.4	53.7	35.6
331	Medical, measuring, testing appliances, etc.	41.0	28.5	18.6	17.6	46.2	51.9	30.4	32.0
3311	Medical, surgical and orthopaedic equipment	26.3	38.1	12.5	1.5	29.6	67.3	22.8	-
3312	Measuring/testing/navigating appliances,etc.	14.3	0.7	0.3	0.2	0.8	1.2	0.4	1.9
3313	Industrial process control equipment	0.3	-	3.5	-	-	-	7.0	6.8
3320	Optical instruments & photographic equipment	-	-	-	-	-	-	-	-
3330	Watches and clocks	-	-	-	-	-	-	-	0.1
3410	Motor vehicles	-	...	...	45.9	0.4	0.4	-	-
3420	Automobile bodies, trailers & semi-trailers	0.2	195.8	100.0	-	-	-	-	0.2
3430	Parts/accessories for automobiles	102.0	4.0	0.4	1.4	284.3	413.2	345.8	205.5
351	Building and repairing of ships and boats	...	4.0	0.4	1.4	...	...	...	0.2
3511	Building and repairing of ships	...	0.9	2.1	1.1	1.4	1.2	2.9	1.6
3512	Building/repairing of pleasure/sport. boats	-	11.7	17.6	5.7	28.7	21.0	25.2	15.5
3520	Railway/tramway locomotives & rolling stock	1.0	0.1	-	-	0.5	0.5	-	-
3530	Aircraft and spacecraft	16.2	-	-	-	-	-	-	-
359	Transport equipment n.e.c.	0.1	-	-	-	-	-	-	-
3591	Motorcycles	-	-	-	-	-	-	-	-
3592	Bicycles and invalid carriages	-	0.1	0.1	-	0.5	-	-	-
3599	Other transport equipment n.e.c.	0.1	254.1	135.5	98.9	474.7	522.4	420.5	327.8
3610	Furniture	192.9	79.7	228.2	49.2	27.4	96.5	673.9	127.7
369	Manufacturing n.e.c.	10.8	71.3	227.8	49.8	14.1	80.5	664.0	115.5
3691	Jewellery and related articles	5.6	-	-	-	-	-	-	-
3692	Musical instruments	-	-	0.1	-0.6	13.2	16.1	0.3	0.6
3693	Sports goods	-	8.4	0.4	9.0	86.6	7.6	9.5	11.5
3694	Games and toys	5.2	1.6	0.6	9.0	86.6	7.6	37.7	47.0
3699	Other manufacturing n.e.c.	24.7	8.4	0.4	-0.6	13.2	16.1	9.5	11.5
3710	Recycling of metal waste and scrap	0.8	1.6	0.6	9.0	86.6	7.6	37.7	47.0
3720	Recycling of non-metal waste and scrap	0.8	0.1	2.0	0.4	1.8	0.4	1.8	0.4
D	Total manufacturing	39011.2	29668.8	26027.4	14208.5	102990.0	85708.1	73446.3	46243.3

Kyrgyzstan

Index numbers of industrial production

ISIC Revision 3

(2005=100)

ISIC	Industry	Note	1999	2000	2001	2002	2003	2004	2005	2006	2007	2008	2009	2010
15	Food and beverages	a/	...	87	82	89	96	101	100	108	113	115	127	124
16	Tobacco products	a/	...	...	...	...	...	...	...	...	...	...	...	...
17	Textiles	b/	...	48	56	65	63	88	100	119	151	168	117	168
18	Wearing apparel, fur	b/	...	...	...	...	...	...	...	...	...	...	...	...
19	Leather, leather products and footwear		...	...	...	...	...	...	...	...	...	...	...	...
20	Wood products (excl. furniture)		...	39	88	105	97	98	100	147	196	288	401	467
21	Paper and paper products		...	...	...	...	...	...	...	...	...	...	...	...
22	Printing and publishing		...	...	...	...	...	...	...	...	...	...	...	...
23	Coke,refined petroleum products,nuclear fuel		...	...	...	...	...	...	...	...	...	...	...	...
24	Chemicals and chemical products		...	42	45	75	81	115	100	89	126	132	75	91
25	Rubber and plastics products		...	...	...	...	...	...	...	...	...	...	...	...
26	Non-metallic mineral products		...	79	79	77	94	118	100	102	118	104	64	90
27	Basic metals	c/	...	139	158	110	138	131	100	64	64	102	92	98
28	Fabricated metal products	c/	...	...	...	...	...	...	...	...	...	...	...	...
29	Machinery and equipment n.e.c.		...	94	107	101	100	107	100	105	77	76	64	59
30	Office, accounting and computing machinery	d/	...	96	112	120	146	138	100	97	85	128	109	148
31	Electrical machinery and apparatus	d/	...	...	...	...	...	...	...	...	...	...	...	...
32	Radio,television and communication equipment	d/	...	...	...	...	...	...	...	...	...	...	...	...
33	Medical, precision and optical instruments	d/	...	...	...	...	...	...	...	...	...	...	...	...
34	Motor vehicles, trailers, semi-trailers	e/	...	52	100	117	85	97	100	54	55	63	27	53
35	Other transport equipment	e/	...	...	...	...	...	...	...	...	...	...	...	...
36	Furniture; manufacturing n.e.c.		...	...	...	...	...	...	...	...	...	...	...	...
37	Recycling		...	...	...	...	...	...	...	...	...	...	...	...
D	Total manufacturing		...	77	84	75	101	112	100	83	81	54	50	55

a/ 15 includes 16.
b/ 17 includes 18.
c/ 27 includes 28.
d/ 30 includes 31, 32 and 33.
e/ 34 includes 35.

Latvia

Supplier of information:
Central Statistical Bureau of Latvia, Riga.

Basic source of data:
Survey; administrative source.

Major deviations from ISIC (Revision 4):
None reported.

Reference period:
Calendar year.

Scope:
Privately owned enterprises only.

Method of data collection:
Online survey.

Type of enumeration:
Sample survey.

Adjusted for non-response:
Yes.

Concepts and definitions of variables:
Wages and salaries excludes payments in kind and housing and family allowances paid directly by the employer.

Related national publications:
Statistical Yearbook, published by the Central Statistical Bureau of Latvia, Riga.

Latvia

ISIC Revision 4

Number of enterprises (number) · Number of employees (number) · Wages and salaries paid to employees (thousands of Latvian Lats)

ISIC	Industry	Ent. Note	Ent. 2007	Ent. 2008	Ent. 2009	Ent. 2010	Emp. Note	Emp. 2007	Emp. 2008	Emp. 2009	Emp. 2010	Wages Note	Wages 2007	Wages 2008	Wages 2009	Wages 2010
1010	Processing/preserving of meat		124	128	128	137		5138	6144	5168	4928		20171	24788	19496	17039
1020	Processing/preserving of fish, etc.		107	108	96	111		6203	6000	4725	5007		13508	18284	12507	12978
1030	Processing/preserving of fruit,vegetables		29	35	33	41		772	736	644	665		2907	3661	3186	...
1040	Vegetable and animal oils and fats		5	5	7	7		223	246	210	201		471	1011	993	...
1050	Dairy products		49	43	44	47		3993	3719	3165	3024		18470	20991	16401	15375
106	Grain mill products,starches and starch products		29	25	23	27		676	573	420	376		3892	3949	2785	...
1061	Grain mill products		28	24	22	26		631	527	378	348		...	...	...	...
1062	Starches and starch products		1	1	1	1		45	46	42	28		...	...	...	...
107	Other food products		325	315	303	344		10560	9556	8407	8465		35145	40029	33081	31218
1071	Bakery products		240	227	223	251		7582	7016	6395	6345		...	25805	22891	21048
1072	Sugar		2	2	2	-		419	142	48	-		...	...	...	...
1073	Cocoa, chocolate and sugar confectionery		16	18	20	26		828	812	685	869		4011	4664	3438	...
1074	Macaroni, noodles, couscous, etc.		1	1	-	2		...	...	...	1		...	...	...	...
1075	Prepared meals and dishes		23	20	14	20		764	502	427	477		1976	1269	1020	1083
1079	Other food products n.e.c.		43	47	44	45		967	1084	851	772		...	...	...	...
1080	Prepared animal feeds		14	16	14	20		457	456	397	398		1825	2035	1839	1747
1101	Distilling, rectifying and blending of spirits		11	10	10	10		1089	940	834	770		8455	7105	5578	4892
1102	Wines		-	-	-	4		-	-	-	3		...	...	...	...
1103	Malt liquors and malt		20	17	18	16		1618	1141	845	815	2	...	8579	6672	6404
1104	Soft drinks,mineral waters,other bottled waters		22	20	22	23		1108	1094	926	775		...	8026	6415	5096
1200	Tobacco products		2	2	2	1		311	334	258	12		...	...	...	...
131	Spinning, weaving and finishing of textiles		66	57	61	69		1435	960	377	376		4817	3297	...	...
1311	Preparation and spinning of textile fibres		30	21	14	14		794	413	69	63		...	1545	1123	1060
1312	Weaving of textiles		17	18	21	23		621	527	282	284		1873	1717	894	909
1313	Finishing of textiles		19	18	26	31		20	20	26	29		...	35	207	122
139	Other textiles		177	183	217	264		3043	2653	2079	1949		10156	10924	7418	7018
1391	Knitted and crocheted fabrics		33	31	47	76		865	728	545	532		...	...	...	...
1392	Made-up textile articles, except apparel		93	92	94	105		1487	1315	973	869		3603	4381	2619	2166
1393	Carpets and rugs		2	-	-	-		2	-	-	-		...	...	...	...
1394	Cordage, rope, twine and netting		10	9	11	11		423	384	360	349		...	...	...	...
1399	Other textiles n.e.c.		39	51	65	72		266	226	201	199		1134	977	649	553
1410	Wearing apparel, except fur apparel		812	775	845	835		11033	9559	7491	7845		28950	29201	18320	19300
1420	Articles of fur		20	10	8	10		21	22	15	10		25	30	16	11
1430	Knitted and crocheted apparel		129	96	100	99		2263	2128	1824	1750		6384	6860	5093	4990
151	Leather;luggage,handbags,saddlery,harness;fur		51	46	42	43		356	321	235	209		...	...	463	375
1512	Luggage,handbags,etc.;saddlery/harness		9	9	9	6		83	71	61	50		...	...	...	...
1511	Tanning/dressing of leather; dressing of fur		42	37	33	36		273	250	174	159		546	599	...	...
1520	Footwear		29	19	15	15		207	149	131	145		514	424	306	395
1610	Sawmilling and planing of wood		1005	943	860	892		18599	14944	11447	12516		55120	49585	34027	38148
162	Wood products, cork, straw, plaiting materials		621	634	685	762		11672	10667	7890	8441		48790	50721	32475	34927

Code	Description	1	2	3	4	5	6	7	8	9	10	11	12
1621	Veneer sheets and wood-based panels	24	25	25	27	4516	4690	2558	2641	30211	33442	17072	19025
1622	Builders' carpentry and joinery	364	379	381	402	4274	3447	2715	2850	3114	3749	4779	9337
1623	Wooden containers	87	93	103	137	1456	1451	1348	1689	...	...	...	...
1629	Other wood products;articles of cork,straw	146	137	176	196	1426	1079	1269	1261	...	...	...	...
1701	Pulp, paper and paperboard	3	2	3	2	171	146	137	140	4406	4569	3470	3779
1702	Corrugated paper and paperboard	41	41	42	38	886	804	666	698	...	...	...	...
1709	Other articles of paper and paperboard	37	38	42	48	710	684	620	645	17312	20914	12185	10605
181	Printing and service activities related to printing	399	443	422	426	4384	4406	3061	2767	16321	19413	11423	10013
1811	Printing	280	308	294	292	4007	3865	2689	2422	990	1501	762	592
1812	Service activities related to printing	119	135	128	134	377	541	372	345	269	168	64	38
1820	Reproduction of recorded media	32	33	27	25	85	54	41	30	-	-	61	-
1910	Coke oven products	-	-	-	-	-	-	-	-	...	...	...	70
1920	Refined petroleum products	3	3	4	5	31	9	12	12	2273	...	...	3311
201	Basic chemicals,fertilizers, etc.	30	40	39	52	575	699	661	798	...	...	...	2476
2011	Basic chemicals	25	33	25	33	501	623	563	624	...	257	404	...
2012	Fertilizers and nitrogen compounds	4	6	10	15	72	69	89	142	...	...	...	...
2013	Plastics and synthetic rubber in primary forms	1	1	4	4	2	7	9	32	8039	10508	7851	8262
202	Other chemical products	72	82	84	109	1839	1906	1695	1726	...	...	...	...
2021	Pesticides and other agrochemical products	4	5	5	6	23	23	23	28	...	3381	2154	2392
2022	Paints,varnishes;printing ink and mastics	14	14	14	24	464	558	465	537	4929	5402	4184	4152
2023	Soap,cleaning and cosmetic preparations	29	35	36	45	1032	997	883	837	1338	...	...	1663
2029	Other chemical products n.e.c.	25	28	29	34	320	328	324	324	...	...	...	...
2030	Man-made fibres	1	1	1	2	137	128	94	98	...	...	...	...
2100	Pharmaceuticals,medicinal chemicals, etc.	23	23	21	27	2000	1990	1748	1713	1273	1386	931	1007
221	Rubber products	19	23	19	19	306	293	188	224	317	334	258	240
2211	Rubber tyres and tubes	6	9	7	5	59	56	50	50	957	1052	672	767
2219	Other rubber products	13	14	12	14	247	237	138	173	18175	17653	5973	9127
2220	Plastics products	202	207	101	209	4338	3921	1496	2504	8591	8999	6611	7080
2310	Glass and glass products	39	42	43	46	1827	1551	1245	1240	26653	30172	17122	15380
239	Non-metallic mineral products n.e.c.	379	402	386	372	5187	5169	3308	3165	2167	2546	...	25
2391	Refractory products	3	2	3	4	21	9	13	14	390	395	238	169
2392	Clay building materials	10	11	7	6	290	209	187	159	...	...	...	...
2393	Other porcelain and ceramic products	50	47	55	52	251	329	328	299	...	...	...	...
2394	Cement, lime and plaster	5	7	3	1	3599	3594	2082	1919	19334	20934	9636	8384
2395	Articles of concrete, cement and plaster	174	195	176	164	487	514	412	457	981	1068	696	563
2396	Cutting, shaping and finishing of stone	129	130	132	133	68	101	76	68	...	...	650	...
2399	Other non-metallic mineral products n.e.c.	8	10	10	11	471	413	210	247	...	...	...	...
2410	Basic iron and steel	13	19	17	20	413	407	286	281	3134	2749	2739	...
2420	Basic precious and other non-ferrous metals	7	8	7	5	111	65	38	17	1279	1540	993	...
243	Casting of metals	5	5	5	3	48	42	36	20	...	...	...	...
2431	Casting of iron and steel	2	1	2	1	17	21	19	17	...	...	...	...
2432	Casting of non-ferrous metals	3	4	3	2	31	21	17	3	20530	26890	16307	15014
251	Struct.metal products, tanks, reservoirs	302	348	337	340	4923	5452	3819	3790	19404	24911	14425	13531
2511	Structural metal products	280	324	311	314	4577	4977	3378	3374	1127	1979	1882	-
2512	Tanks, reservoirs and containers of metal	22	24	26	26	346	475	441	416	...	...	...	...

Latvia

ISIC Revision 4

ISIC	Industry	Note	Number of enterprises (number)				Note	Number of employees (number)				Note	Wages and salaries paid to employees (thousands of Latvian Lats)			
			2007	2008	2009	2010		2007	2008	2009	2010		2007	2008	2009	2010
2513	Steam generators, excl. hot water boilers		-	-	-	-		-	-	-	-		-	-	-	-
2520	Weapons and ammunition		1	1	1	2		13	13	8	24		...	...	...	...
259	Other metal products;metal working services		384	399	398	421		5434	5040	3674	3882		18402	21130	13470	...
2591	Forging,pressing,stamping,roll-forming of metal		20	23	23	23		219	208	132	130		...	...	...	...
2592	Treatment and coating of metals; machining		159	172	171	190		1239	1258	1010	1245		4417	4915	3395	3777
2593	Cutlery, hand tools and general hardware		41	31	28	24		930	822	571	546		...	...	...	...
2599	Other fabricated metal products n.e.c.		164	173	176	184		3046	2752	1961	1961		10106	12289	7784	7766
2610	Electronic components and boards		14	13	12	18		446	442	321	364		...	...	...	1634
2620	Computers and peripheral equipment		14	21	20	22		38	70	62	72		...	...	162	195
2630	Communication equipment		17	16	17	20		524	467	330	323		3551	3412	...	1804
2640	Consumer electronics		7	5	5	4		272	239	146	77		989	983	523	...
265	Measuring,testing equipment; watches, etc.		27	27	28	33		656	395	372	326		3462	2162	2133	...
2651	Measuring/testing/navigating equipment,etc.		27	27	28	31		654	395	371	323		3462	2162	2133	...
2652	Watches and clocks		-	-	-	2		-	-	-	2		...	...	...	...
2660	Irradiation/electromedical equipment,etc.		2	1	1	1		16	7	3	2		...	...	...	...
2670	Optical instruments and photographic equipment		5	4	5	5		92	98	68	75		...	...	...	...
2680	Magnetic and optical media		-	-	-	-		-	-	-	-		-	-	-	-
2710	Electric motors,generators,transformers,etc.		14	16	17	23		2047	2095	1435	1245		13580	13692	7876	7017
2720	Batteries and accumulators		1	2	1	1		1	4	3	1		...	...	...	1
273	Wiring and wiring devices		13	15	15	12		1243	1097	770	716		5324	6101	5012	...
2731	Fibre optic cables		3	3	3	3		152	152	131	138		...	...	...	...
2732	Other electronic and electric wires and cables		5	5	5	3		700	522	351	316		...	...	...	...
2733	Wiring devices		5	7	7	6		391	423	288	261		...	...	...	...
2740	Electric lighting equipment		12	17	13	17		230	231	92	84		...	940	293	239
2750	Domestic appliances		3	3	5	2		31	31	22	10		...	...	51	...
2790	Other electrical equipment		8	8	8	11		67	86	60	64		...	...	233	256
281	General-purpose machinery		67	72	66	78		3641	3022	1607	1602		14431	14646	7033	...
2811	Engines/turbines,excl.aircraft,vehicle engines		2	2	2	1		19	24	8	5		...	...	...	...
2812	Fluid power equipment		5	6	5	6		258	268	202	176		1381	1612	1135	1229
2813	Other pumps, compressors, taps and valves		3	3	6	6		44	38	47	43		...	...	...	...
2814	Bearings, gears, gearing and driving elements		2	2	3	7		617	521	362	393		...	...	...	1404
2815	Ovens, furnaces and furnace burners		2	3	3	2		141	176	16	17		...	...	...	...
2816	Lifting and handling equipment		11	16	11	10		271	332	243	210		1597	1824	1333	1217
2817	Office machinery, excl.computers,etc.		3	1	1	2		58	35	36	31		...	...	...	...
2818	Power-driven hand tools		4	3	2	2		1384	767	9	9		...	...	...	...
2819	Other general-purpose machinery		35	36	33	42		849	861	684	718		3521	4163	2637	3246
282	Special-purpose machinery		51	58	51	51		1656	1575	1112	1152		6705	7604	5096	6030
2821	Agricultural and forestry machinery		13	15	13	12		829	800	599	603		3379	4072	2759	3128
2822	Metal-forming machinery and machine tools		20	21	20	20		580	540	303	321		1862	1754	810	1141
2823	Machinery for metallurgy		1	1	1	-		6	1	1	-		...	...	...	...
2824	Mining, quarrying and construction machinery		3	1	-	-		4	1	-	-		...	...	-	-

2825	Food/beverage/tobacco processing machinery	5	7	5	5	30	39	25	26	:	:	38	:
2826	Textile/apparel/leather production machinery	1	1	1	-	3	3	1	-	:	:	:	:
2829	Other special-purpose machinery	8	12	11	14	204	191	183	202	:	:	:	:
2910	Motor vehicles	4	3	3	4	188	169	106	102	1946	:	:	:
2920	Automobile bodies, trailers and semi-trailers	8	10	9	7	543	523	259	223	5535	:	3932	4960
2930	Parts and accessories for motor vehicles	13	16	18	18	612	744	525	658	:	6862	:	:
301	Building of ships and boats	24	31	32	37	1037	1047	963	847	:	:	:	:
3011	Building of ships and floating structures	5	6	9	11	826	831	842	723	1322	:	501	472
3012	Building of pleasure and sporting boats	19	25	23	26	211	216	121	123	8222	:	:	:
3020	Railway locomotives and rolling stock	8	5	5	5	1990	1811	1268	1139	:	:	:	:
3030	Air and spacecraft and related machinery	1	1	1	2	5	5	5	13	-	:	-	-
3040	Military fighting vehicles	-	-	1	1	-	4	4	-	:	-	-	-
309	Transport equipment n.e.c.	2	2	3	1	14	4	-	-	-	:	-	-
3091	Motorcycles	-	-	-	-	-	-	2	-	:	-	-	-
3092	Bicycles and invalid carriages	2	2	1	1	10	4	2	-	:	-	-	-
3099	Other transport equipment n.e.c.	-	-	:	-	-	-	-	-	-	:	-	-
3100	Furniture	637	689	662	601	10198	8284	6531	5794	32311	28785	19523	15830
321	Jewellery, bijouterie and related articles	123	117	144	139	168	153	163	152	360	367	312	217
3211	Jewellery and related articles	114	111	122	112	162	148	151	127	:	:	:	:
3212	Imitation jewellery and related articles	9	6	22	26	6	5	12	25	:	:	:	:
3220	Musical instruments	17	17	14	17	56	60	40	51	111	:	79	:
3230	Sports goods	23	26	22	40	578	483	400	413	1746	1759	1248	1183
3240	Games and toys	87	81	70	70	636	689	583	545	1955	2271	1714	1350
3250	Medical and dental instruments and supplies	80	88	127	144	1143	985	712	990	3514	3640	2812	3344
3290	Other manufacturing n.e.c.	395	449	480	494	4729	6129	5635	5031	20556	32005	29366	25770
331	Repair of fabricated metal products/machinery	15	24	24	22	180	188	142	58	686	762	498	:
3311	Repair of fabricated metal products	197	206	214	224	1224	1183	1108	1032	4457	5139	3676	:
3312	Repair of machinery	21	25	27	25	119	104	104	107	434	398	436	388
3313	Repair of electronic and optical equipment	37	43	54	63	554	576	554	527	3726	:	4463	4148
3314	Repair of electrical equipment	110	139	149	148	2577	4044	3693	3284	:	:	:	17354
3315	Repair of transport equip., excl. motor vehicles	15	12	12	12	75	34	34	23	73	:	75	66
3319	Repair of other equipment	20	29	31	34	148	183	145	164	458	884	819	841
3320	Installation of industrial machinery/equipment	:	:	:	:	:	:	:	:	:	:	:	:
C	Total manufacturing	7339	7491	7521	7873	151312	139314	107985	107422	577821	634111	443399	428416

Latvia

ISIC	Industry	Note	Output at producers' prices (thousands of Latvian Lats)				Note	Value added at factor values (thousands of Latvian Lats)				Note	Gross fixed capital formation (thousands of Latvian Lats)	
			2007	2008	2009	2010		2007	2008	2009	2010		2009	2010
1010	Processing/preserving of meat		227442	255553	203351	210124		51186	48169	37560	44467		4317	4818
1020	Processing/preserving of fish, etc.		114119	136684	95658	102220		30646	39446	20805	27767		3837	5524
1030	Processing/preserving of fruit, vegetables		28056	27964	25020	...		11066	8940	6469	...		1067	...
1040	Vegetable and animal oils and fats		10163	17752	13123	...		1979	3504	-1274	...		725	...
1050	Dairy products		229992	234373	169149	201623		43587	42275	32432	36408		5178	6329
106	Grain mill products, starches and starch products		46621	54903	40220	...		11037	9623	7240	...		1311	...
1061	Grain mill products		...	...	...	...		...	...	...	...		...	...
1062	Starches and starch products		...	...	...	...		...	...	...	...		...	...
107	Other food products		225656	229202	205984	221110		77671	81247	72759	60203		...	...
1071	Bakery products		...	135157	121761	114208		...	49644	43679	41194		13115	5691
1072	Sugar		...	...	...	...		...	...	...	-		6724	3377
1073	Cocoa, chocolate and sugar confectionery		30272	30126	33336	...		8981	7915	8618	...		2663	...
1074	Macaroni, noodles, couscous, etc.		...	...	...	...		...	...	-	...		-	...
1075	Prepared meals and dishes		15607	13287	10225	11778		3880	3129	2611	2561		130	560
1079	Other food products n.e.c.		...	...	...	34987		...	...	...	9828		...	1174
1080	Prepared animal feeds		27972	35112	30252	27985		5792	7288	6665	5868		788	1625
1101	Distilling, rectifying and blending of spirits		...	130766	105664	95229		...	19682	17317	21251		1517	696
1102	Wines		...	...	...	23		...	...	...	2		...	11
1103	Malt liquors and malt		90044	72633	57267	58803		33073	17013	10289	8511		2193	1537
1104	Soft drinks,mineral waters,other bottled waters		...	57384	47544	34974		33073	20172	11288	9609		1576	540
1200	Tobacco products		...	...	...	...		...	...	...	...		...	...
131	Spinning, weaving and finishing of textiles		28953	18592	8555	10774		8434	3843	2922	3283		1192	70
1311	Preparation and spinning of textile fibres		...	6085	931	561		...	1590	501	312		18	10
1312	Weaving of textiles		15574	12275	7469	9684		3237	2151	2383	2860		1168	50
1313	Finishing of textiles		...	232	156	529		...	103	38	111		6	10
139	Other textiles		65879	58030	38033	41820		23882	20178	13532	14729		5274	2114
1391	Knitted and crocheted fabrics		...	...	...	...		...	...	...	...		...	...
1392	Made-up textile articles, except apparel		23204	22653	12270	11665		7659	7114	4387	4294		680	183
1393	Carpets and rugs		...	...	...	...		...	...	...	...		-	...
1394	Cordage, rope, twine and netting		8346	...	...	...		2260	...	...	...			
1399	Other textiles n.e.c.		...	3748	2339	2614		...	1574	1110	1021		170	781
1410	Wearing apparel, except fur apparel		116671	103794	63711	79815		51415	46186	26161	33660		3668	4487
1420	Articles of fur		117	75	51	33		52	38	26	16		-	...
1430	Knitted and crocheted apparel		26990	24890	19655	21311		10978	10534	7489	8310		368	551
151	Leather;luggage,handbags,saddlery,harness;fur		...	...	...	...		...	...	...	...		29	53
1511	Tanning/dressing of leather; dressing of fur		...	...	2064	2639		...	...	523	561		...	...
1512	Luggage,handbags,etc.;saddlery/harness		2215	2073	...	...		1074	995	...	...		...	...
1520	Footwear		2006	1213	970	1175		1223	819	649	910		4	23
1610	Sawmilling and planing of wood		700715	477884	362807	558128		177624	99642	85191	144754		21498	38341
162	Wood products, cork, straw, plaiting materials		393996	398639	281380	393364		110351	112010	70873	127627		24969	34127

1621	Veneer sheets and wood-based panels	227928	260003	213969	137555	61789	72047	30581	81812	17065	12488
1622	Builders' carpentry and joinery	57094	52002	59623	62704	13053	12050	18008	15041	…	3875
1623	Wooden containers	…	…	…	…	…	…	…	…	2100	…
1629	Other wood products;articles of cork,straw	…	…	…	…	…	…	…	…	…	…
1701	Pulp, paper and paperboard	39407	38769	36409	28137	9818	10199	8173	8295	1306	1904
1702	Corrugated paper and paperboard	…	…	…	…	…	…	…	…	…	…
1709	Other articles of paper and paperboard	…	…	…	…	…	…	…	…	…	…
181	Printing and service activities related to printing	135079	134900	104397	95834	42915	50208	23967	28931	3078	14880
1811	Printing	118470	121830	96610	82693	38580	45879	21127	26627	2731	14363
1812	Service activities related to printing	16609	13071	7787	13140	4335	4329	2840	2304	347	517
1820	Reproduction of recorded media	1903	791	1116	619	995	-572	190	643	774	40
1910	Coke oven products	…	-	-	-	…	168	…	172	81	16
1920	Refined petroleum products	17533	…	420	…	7246	…	…	14147	…	7708
201	Basic chemicals,fertilizers, etc.	…	…	35835	…	…	292	433	12442	259	6621
2011	Basic chemicals	…	1970	29161	3362	…	…	…	…	…	…
2012	Fertilizers and nitrogen compounds	…	…	…	…	…	…	…	…	…	…
2013	Plastics and synthetic rubber in primary forms	47156	90510	91029	68900	18087	23909	17769	31890	1993	2612
202	Other chemical products	…	…	…	…	…	…	…	…	…	…
2021	Pesticides and other agrochemical products	…	34753	28322	22400	9481	8405	4925	6178	1158	1464
2022	Paints,varnishes;printing ink and mastics	18817	20996	19404	14630	…	8342	5421	8120	548	449
2023	Soap,cleaning and cosmetic preparations	10838	…	42554	…	4030	…	…	17364	…	665
2029	Other chemical products n.e.c.	…	…	…	…	…	…	…	…	…	…
2030	Man-made fibres	…	…	…	…	…	…	…	…	…	…
2100	Pharmaceuticals,medicinal chemicals, etc.	…	…	…	…	…	…	…	…	…	…
221	Rubber products	15441	10422	9567	5302	3048	3315	1502	2244	111	87
2211	Rubber tyres and tubes	7805	2074	2223	1074	922	501	276	662	69	42
2219	Other rubber products	7636	8348	7344	4228	2126	2814	1226	1582	283	7831
2220	Plastics products	169613	142928	94679	52855	46537	33441	11797	19791	11460	10585
2310	Glass and glass products	58160	63608	56578	42377	17088	16739	9779	18712	9420	38134
239	Non-metallic mineral products n.e.c.	276330	247061	141073	113775	90687	60409	26874	30398	96030	2
2391	Refractory products	8651	12363	…	4420	4905	4420	4905	…	…	…
2392	Clay building materials	1953	1849	1637	1172	744	696	215	454	79	68
2393	Other porcelain and ceramic products	…	…	…	…	…	…	…	…	…	…
2394	Cement, lime and plaster	204668	170006	79798	75546	71762	46212	21366	21563	11289	8320
2395	Articles of concrete, cement and plaster	6839	7844	4271	3489	2344	2738	906	1422	333	574
2396	Cutting, shaping and finishing of stone	…	7352	…	…	1469	1469	1469	…	950	…
2399	Other non-metallic mineral products n.e.c.	…	…	…	…	22758	…	22758	…	4997	…
2410	Basic iron and steel	55953	50723	56625	…	9376	10279	…	4465	2344	…
2420	Basic precious and other non-ferrous metals	…	…	…	…	…	…	…	…	…	…
243	Casting of metals	…	…	…	…	…	…	…	…	…	…
2431	Casting of iron and steel	…	…	…	…	…	…	…	…	…	…
2432	Casting of non-ferrous metals	…	…	…	…	…	…	…	…	…	…
251	Struct.metal products, tanks, reservoirs	176237	188685	108160	136704	55957	58157	28734	32640	6587	8017
2511	Structural metal products	165626	174918	95344	121165	51567	52521	24037	27512	5606	7495
2512	Tanks, reservoirs and containers of metal	10611	13767	12817	…	4390	5636	4697	…	982	…

continued

Latvia

ISIC	Industry	Output at producers' prices (thousands of Latvian Lats)					Value added at factor values (thousands of Latvian Lats)					Gross fixed capital formation (thousands of Latvian Lats)		
		Note	2007	2008	2009	2010	Note	2007	2008	2009	2010	Note	2009	2010
2513	Steam generators, excl. hot water boilers		-	-	-	-		-	-	-	-		-	-
2520	Weapons and ammunition		..	..	..	..		..	..	..	..		..	..
259	Other metal products;metal working services		129856	137946	83337	..		51811	49830	28555	..		5509	..
2591	Forging,pressing,stamping,roll-forming of metal		..	..	..	..		..	..	..	..		..	..
2592	Treatment and coating of metals; machining		28827	34960	20467	29777		13199	13674	8055	11250		1223	2049
2593	Cutlery, hand tools and general hardware		..	..	..	..		..	..	..	..		..	..
2599	Other fabricated metal products n.e.c.		78793	85131	49331	59959		27827	28647	14667	17377		3550	4757
2610	Electronic components and boards		..	..	..	..		..	..	..	..		..	..
2620	Computers and peripheral equipment		..	..	1126	9485		..	..	283	4526		..	473
2630	Communication equipment		26427	17108	2134	1920		7235	5192	983	433		37	44
2640	Consumer electronics		4528	3428	..	..		2114	1970	..	..		..	..
265	Measuring,testing equipment; watches, etc.		16199	14309	9358	8147		7531	6518	3376	3394		196	..
2651	Measuring/testing/navigating equipment,etc.		16199	14309	..	..		7531	6518	..	..		282	293
2652	Watches and clocks		..	..	..	..		..	..	..	..		282	..
2660	Irradiation/electromedical equipment,etc.		-	-	-	-		-	-	-	-		..	..
2670	Optical instruments and photographic equipment		..	..	..	..		..	..	..	..		..	..
2680	Magnetic and optical media		-	-	-	-		-	-	-	-		..	..
2710	Electric motors,generators,transformers,etc.		55847	55856	27682	34371		24564	21976	8967	10517		425	2294
2720	Batteries and accumulators		..	..	..	9		..	..	..	8		..	8
273	Wiring and wiring devices		38046	36411	27103	..		13874	12585	8901	..		..	..
2731	Fibre optic cables		..	..	..	..		..	..	..	..		..	..
2732	Other electronic and electric wires and cables		..	..	..	..		..	..	..	..		..	..
2733	Wiring devices		..	..	..	..		..	..	..	..		..	..
2740	Electric lighting equipment		..	4975	2114	2114		..	1210	446	346		137	52
2750	Domestic appliances		..	..	343	..		..	..	73	..		56	52
2790	Other electrical equipment		..	..	1482	1857		..	..	629	867		11	52
281	General-purpose machinery		79035	81881	37529	..		30624	32129	16003	..		2053	..
2811	Engines/turbines,excl.aircraft,vehicle engines		..	..	..	..		..	..	..	..		..	..
2812	Fluid power equipment		..	..	..	..		..	..	..	..		..	..
2813	Other pumps, compressors, taps and valves		7390	7953	3724	6743		3238	4221	1265	3065		97	124
2814	Bearings, gears, gearing and driving elements		..	..	..	..		..	..	..	..		..	..
2815	Ovens, furnaces and furnace burners		..	..	..	8726		..	..	..	3396		..	1879
2816	Lifting and handling equipment		10893	12200	9095	8325		3315	3959	3318	3773		326	689
2817	Office machinery, excl.computers,etc.		..	..	..	..		..	..	..	..		..	..
2818	Power-driven hand tools		..	..	..	..		..	..	..	..		..	..
2819	Other general-purpose machinery		20765	28340	15426	22155		8320	11922	7585	9411		1577	786
282	Special-purpose machinery		34146	34002	20959	25288		14676	14202	10141	10686		2389	915
2821	Agricultural and forestry machinery		14232	16201	11586	13186		6685	6729	5644	5328		1720	177
2822	Metal-forming machinery and machine tools		11651	8023	4351	6172		4576	4172	1640	2466		173	502
2823	Machinery for metallurgy		..	..	..	-		..	..	..	-		..	..
2824	Mining, quarrying and construction machinery		..	..	..	-		..	..	..	-		-	-

2825	Food/beverage/tobacco processing machinery	:	:	:	:	:	:	:	:	:	:
2826	Textile/apparel/leather production machinery	:	:	:	:	:	:	:	:	:	:
2829	Other special-purpose machinery	:	:	:	:	:	:	:	:	:	:
2910	Motor vehicles	29820	:	:	:	6228	:	:	:	:	:
2920	Automobile bodies, trailers and semi-trailers	40103	22118	39002	:	12529	7267	13510	:	1110	1884
2930	Parts and accessories for motor vehicles	52028	:	:	:	16034	:	:	:	:	:
301	Building of ships and boats	:	:	:	:	:	:	:	:	:	:
3011	Building of ships and floating structures	6817	:	2535	2156	2417	1294	835	:	121	239
3012	Building of pleasure and sporting boats	:	:	:	:	:	:	:	:	:	:
3020	Railway locomotives and rolling stock	42198	:	:	:	13163	:	:	:	:	:
3030	Air and spacecraft and related machinery	-	-	-	-	-	-	-	-	-	-
3040	Military fighting vehicles	-	-	-	-	-	-	-	-	-	-
309	Transport equipment n.e.c.	-	-	-	-	-	-	-	-	-	-
3091	Motorcycles	-	-	-	-	-	-	-	-	-	-
3092	Bicycles and invalid carriages	-	-	-	-	-	-	-	-	-	-
3099	Other transport equipment n.e.c.	184737	144220	108388	106208	60740	45062	33237	29532	3869	3382
3100	Furniture	1824	1584	1221	1138	533	521	247	463	68	43
321	Jewellery, bijouterie and related articles	:	:	:	981	:	:	:	395	:	35
3211	Jewellery and related articles	:	:	:	:	:	:	:	:	:	:
3212	Imitation jewellery and related articles	:	:	:	:	:	:	:	:	:	:
3220	Musical instruments	:	:	:	:	:	183	248	:	6	:
3230	Sports goods	7220	1040	1069	3546	2920	2893	2012	1743	20	79
3240	Games and toys	10299	6294	3497	8800	5168	5562	3404	3265	189	274
3250	Medical and dental instruments and supplies	22258	11821	7646	16806	8099	7737	5492	8197	868	1199
3290	Other manufacturing n.e.c.	139086	171202	141923	138481	54351	68360	57201	58390	21044	8773
331	Repair of fabricated metal products/machinery	2841	3175	2481	:	1025	1125	945	:	62	:
3311	Repair of fabricated metal products	42164	37963	28398	:	17871	15040	11964	:	:	1100
3312	Repair of machinery	5099	5610	4837	5545	1309	2149	1161	1113	124	77
3313	Repair of electronic and optical equipment	25865	27024	20073	:	7994	9135	7916	:	391	127
3314	Repair of electrical equipment	:	:	82172	:	:	:	35408	:	:	7386
3315	Repair of transport equip., excl. motor vehicles	:	:	628	:	:	:	:	:	:	:
3319	Repair of other equipment	:	:	:	:	:	:	:	:	:	:
3320	Installation of industrial machinery/equipment	4480	4597	4426	6738	1384	1657	1468	1178	160	174
C	Total manufacturing	4844235	4725077	3371431	4050111	1440357	1317906	868386	1091552	292682	292600

Latvia

Index numbers of industrial production

ISIC Revision 4

(2005=100)

ISIC	Industry	Note	1999	2000	2001	2002	2003	2004	2005	2006	2007	2008	2009	2010
10	Food products		...	79	86	88	88	94	100	105	104	103	90	90
11	Beverages		...	...	...	...	...	...	...	...	...	...	...	...
12	Tobacco products		...	...	...	...	...	...	...	...	...	...	...	...
13	Textiles		...	142	157	96	99	89	100	117	122	105	58	72
14	Wearing apparel		...	75	77	96	89	95	100	98	96	86	56	65
15	Leather and related products		...	...	...	...	...	...	...	...	...	...	...	...
16	Wood/wood products/cork,excl. furniture		...	63	67	72	90	96	100	97	92	80	82	109
17	Paper and paper products		...	78	87	98	98	97	100	107	120	112	103	118
18	Printing and reproduction of recorded media		...	55	60	65	72	76	100	108	100	98	78	95
19	Coke and refined petroleum products		...	...	...	...	...	...	...	...	...	...	...	...
20	Chemicals and chemical products		...	67	89	85	83	88	100	127	119	135	136	145
21	Pharmaceuticals,medicinal chemicals, etc.		...	64	69	74	62	82	100	126	124	124	103	100
22	Rubber and plastics products		...	31	35	50	68	83	100	111	127	110	77	85
23	Other non-metallic mineral products		...	45	64	63	69	83	100	110	91	78	47	55
24	Basic metals		...	67	80	93	97	103	100	103	105	99	89	106
25	Fabricated metal products, except machinery		...	55	65	75	79	88	100	118	140	151	92	118
26	Computer, electronic and optical products		...	46	37	47	99	103	100	124	120	159	112	142
27	Electrical equipment		...	56	76	102	104	88	100	109	121	110	68	93
28	Machinery and equipment n.e.c.		...	45	55	64	74	86	100	116	122	135	87	102
29	Motor vehicles, trailers and semi-trailers		...	33	27	48	63	55	100	151	202	203	99	168
30	Other transport equipment		...	145	132	130	102	65	100	98	100	113	58	89
31	Furniture		...	51	64	69	74	83	100	107	98	70	57	56
32	Other manufacturing		...	53	53	55	66	90	100	150	151	128	115	124
33	Repair and installation of machinery/equipment		...	108	118	146	144	158	100	74	92	140	104	94
C	Total manufacturing		...	67	75	80	87	93	100	106	107	103	82	96

Liechtenstein

Supplier of information:
Office of Statistics, Vaduz.

Basic source of data:
Annual survey on registered establishments.

Major deviations from ISIC (Revision 4):
None reported.

Reference period:
Calendar year.

Scope:
All establishments.

Method of data collection:
Mail questionnaires.

Type of enumeration:
Complete enumeration.

Adjusted for non-response:
No.

Concepts and definitions of variables:
Number of persons engaged excludes unpaid family workers.

Related national publications:
Beschäftigungsstatistik, published by the Office of Statistics, Vaduz.

Liechtenstein

ISIC	Industry	Number of establishments					Number of persons engaged					Wages and salaries (Swiss Francs)				
		Note	(number) 2007	2008	2009	2010	Note	(number) 2007	2008	2009	2010	Note	2007	2008	2009	2010
10	Food products		18	17	18	17		1972	1852	1857	1824		…	…	…	…
11	Beverages		3	3	3	3		16	19	18	23		…	…	…	…
12	Tobacco products		-	-	-	-		-	-	-	-		…	…	…	…
13	Textiles		6	5	5	6		116	90	80	71		…	…	…	…
14	Wearing apparel		5	4	4	5		8	8	6	11		…	…	…	…
15	Leather and related products		-	-	1	1		-	-	1	1		…	…	…	…
16	Wood/wood products/cork,excl. furniture		44	45	44	43		255	257	268	267		…	…	…	…
17	Paper and paper products		1	1	1	-		2	2	2	-		…	…	…	…
18	Printing and reproduction of recorded media		21	21	20	22		182	185	179	184		…	…	…	…
19	Coke and refined petroleum products		-	-	-	-		-	-	-	-		…	…	…	…
20	Chemicals and chemical products		2	2	2	2		81	90	81	88		…	…	…	…
21	Pharmaceuticals,medicinal chemicals, etc.		1	1	1	1		9	9	9	15		…	…	…	…
22	Rubber and plastics products		5	6	4	5		55	58	50	50		…	…	…	…
23	Other non-metallic mineral products		11	12	12	12		715	749	753	795		…	…	…	…
24	Basic metals		3	3	3	3		10	11	12	12		…	…	…	…
25	Fabricated metal products, except machinery		60	59	57	59		1207	1158	1054	1137		…	…	…	…
26	Computer, electronic and optical products		16	17	17	17		365	384	478	478		…	…	…	…
27	Electrical equipment		7	7	9	7		356	346	323	304		…	…	…	…
28	Machinery and equipment n.e.c.		34	35	33	34		3413	3488	3012	2975		…	…	…	…
29	Motor vehicles, trailers and semi-trailers		6	6	6	6		1324	1362	1338	1479		…	…	…	…
30	Other transport equipment		1	1	1	1		24	22	25	24		…	…	…	…
31	Furniture		3	4	4	4		102	108	105	105		…	…	…	…
32	Other manufacturing		43	44	44	45		986	1041	1040	1124		…	…	…	…
33	Repair and installation of machinery/equipment		8	7	8	8		90	117	91	98		…	…	…	…
C	Total manufacturing		298	300	297	301		11288	11356	10782	11065		…	…	…	…

Lithuania

Concepts and definitions of variables:
Output includes revenue from non-industrial activities.
Value added includes cost of non-industrial activities.

Related national publications:
None reported.

Supplier of information:
Statistics Lithuania, Vilnius.

Basic source of data:
Annual survey; administrative data.

Major deviations from ISIC (Revision 4):
None reported.

Reference period:
Calendar year.

Scope:
All registered enterprises.

Method of data collection:
Mail questionnaires, online survey and administrative data.

Type of enumeration:
Complete enumeration.

Adjusted for non-response:
Yes.

Lithuania

ISIC	Industry	Number of enterprises (number)				Note	Number of employees (number)				Note	Wages and salaries paid to employees (thousands of Lithuanian Litas)				Note
		2007	2008	2009	2010		2007	2008	2009	2010		2007	2008	2009	2010	
1010	Processing/preserving of meat	196	176	184	189		10512	9624	8918	8387		141981	154879	120696	109770	
1020	Processing/preserving of fish, etc.	69	66	63	69		4545	4529	4220	4495		76165	88026	80617	88702	
1030	Processing/preserving of fruit, vegetables	192	215	207	203		826	1021	939	857		12646	17573	16532	14259	
1040	Vegetable and animal oils and fats	9	9	9	8		143	172	181	167		2924	3826	4863	4507	
1050	Dairy products	69	69	44	40		9241	8625	8095	7627		200161	228031	189179	178187	
106	Grain mill products, starches and starch products	87	82	61	55		1624	1088	966	969		30522	26495	24153	25209	
1061	Grain mill products	86	81	60	54		1575	1043	941	958		29881	25851	23661	25032	
1062	Starches and starch products	1	1	1	1		49	45	25	11		641	644	492	177	
107	Other food products	513	502	489	529		17300	16267	14772	14392		257199	300992	268094	257313	
1071	Bakery products	419	409	389	421		12306	11923	10998	10454		152755	188666	172743	158603	
1072	Sugar	3	2	2	2		943	617	574	552		24876	21498	16263	16655	
1073	Cocoa, chocolate and sugar confectionery	22	17	17	14		2377	2115	1743	1615		54995	64576	55592	53413	
1074	Macaroni, noodles, couscous, etc.	4	4	7	7		86	91	100	101		1354	1592	1705	1728	
1075	Prepared meals and dishes	24	30	29	34		614	703	589	629		8047	9590	8203	8183	
1079	Other food products n.e.c.	41	40	45	51		974	818	768	1041		15172	15071	13588	18731	
1080	Prepared animal feeds	22	25	24	24		1763	1854	1795	1719		53826	66696	61224	61844	
1101	Distilling, rectifying and blending of spirits	3	3	6	4		633	547	713	614		21175	19775	17253	20952	
1102	Wines	4	6	6	5		758	875	662	445		16235	20008	14976	9080	
1103	Malt liquors and malt	63	62	55	56		2428	2409	2160	2029		75022	89901	74109	71449	
1104	Soft drinks, mineral waters, other bottled waters	30	29	31	28		926	852	695	635		14833	17057	13363	14372	
1200	Tobacco products	1	2	1	1		482	473	454	424		24177	28657	29394	29391	
131	Spinning, weaving and finishing of textiles	105	98	84	78		7507	4445	3262	2855		134209	102556	64166	58649	
1311	Preparation and spinning of textile fibres	47	42	37	35		1872	1627	1353	1259		32883	33228	24646	24798	
1312	Weaving of textiles	34	33	27	26		5232	2350	1287	1005		94109	59593	28500	22675	
1313	Finishing of textiles	24	23	20	17		403	468	622	591		7217	9735	11020	11176	
139	Other textiles	549	585	393	422		5132	5059	4200	4095		86783	97420	69737	72208	
1391	Knitted and crocheted fabrics	154	152	99	105		187	179	228	234		3207	3136	3180	4156	
1392	Made-up textile articles, except apparel	337	372	232	240		3669	3470	2775	2642		57971	64007	43348	41633	
1393	Carpets and rugs	3	3	3	3		44	43	34	33		852	935	611	480	
1394	Cordage, rope, twine and netting	9	9	8	10		687	689	562	602		14059	15382	11194	13195	
1399	Other textiles n.e.c.	46	49	51	64		545	678	601	584		10694	13960	11404	12744	
1410	Wearing apparel, except fur apparel	2158	2194	1752	1627		26458	22384	18462	17581		337409	322019	235299	229704	
1420	Articles of fur	45	41	37	39		291	231	178	152		2732	3156	1923	1588	
1430	Knitted and crocheted apparel	102	98	87	71		2867	2492	1992	1871		35621	39585	26780	26529	
151	Leather;luggage,handbags,saddlery,harness;fur	116	122	96	89		913	770	504	400		10056	9443	5561	5471	
1511	Tanning/dressing of leather; dressing of fur	13	14	12	11		350	294	229	190		4908	4606	2941	3440	
1512	Luggage,handbags,etc.;saddlery/harness	103	108	84	78		563	476	275	210		5149	4836	2620	2032	
1520	Footwear	45	41	33	32		721	653	606	585		10960	11654	9575	9830	
1610	Sawmilling and planing of wood	800	740	680	624		13625	10994	8703	8635		173071	171323	112748	119263	
162	Wood products, cork, straw, plaiting materials	3503	3620	2302	2134		14904	13063	10992	9882		249956	258856	188583	160457	

1621	Veneer sheets and wood-based panels	40	32	39	28	2991	2197	2282	1449	74001	63911	67391	45916
1622	Builders' carpentry and joinery	2626	2763	1531	1347	7518	6961	5210	4539	120904	137167	81368	68364
1623	Wooden containers	101	111	116	116	2459	2415	2216	2394	29432	35860	24556	27755
1629	Other wood products;articles of cork,straw	736	714	616	643	1936	1490	1284	1500	25619	21918	15268	18422
1701	Pulp, paper and paperboard	9	8	8	11	449	418	234	313	13604	13949	5670	7880
1702	Corrugated paper and paperboard	32	38	34	36	1359	1800	1676	1659	30481	46655	44214	45362
1709	Other articles of paper and paperboard	68	60	49	49	1589	1087	852	1274	29049	24039	18370	32129
181	Printing and service activities related to printing	332	370	349	360	4035	4255	3787	3430	79491	97814	76398	63764
1811	Printing	187	208	206	202	3484	3775	3340	2952	68939	87221	67069	54098
1812	Service activities related to printing	145	162	143	158	551	480	447	478	10552	10593	9330	9666
1820	Reproduction of recorded media	15	11	8	7	32	31	33	27	213	663	393	313
1910	Coke oven products	-	-	-	-	-	-	-	-	-	-	-	-
1920	Refined petroleum products	6	5	6	6	3536	3303	2704	2287	165902	174364	166191	136478
201	Basic chemicals,fertilizers, etc.	26	21	23	24	4175	4231	3955	3548	174639	208217	171757	149389
2011	Basic chemicals	15	10	10	12	573	586	583	560	20435	20756	22026	23884
2012	Fertilizers and nitrogen compounds	5	6	8	7	3063	3082	2870	2563	131916	160176	127914	105514
2013	Plastics and synthetic rubber in primary forms	6	5	5	5	539	563	502	425	22288	27285	21817	19991
202	Other chemical products	64	71	71	65	1076	1138	1056	966	21608	27392	23706	22110
2021	Pesticides and other agrochemical products	-	2	1	2	-	10	8	11	-	415	170	214
2022	Paints,varnishes;printing ink and mastics	28	31	31	28	417	463	415	377	8535	10240	7540	6685
2023	Soap,cleaning and cosmetic preparations	17	18	20	17	468	452	393	349	8094	9254	7516	7237
2029	Other chemical products n.e.c.	19	20	19	18	191	213	240	229	4979	7482	8480	7974
2030	Man-made fibres	2	2	2	2	472	362	475	444	11427	28550	11315	10829
2100	Pharmaceuticals,medicinal chemicals, etc.	16	18	17	16	798	777	732	674	25641	29547	26343	26312
221	Rubber products	30	28	30	28	433	366	279	495	7382	6314	3731	8739
2211	Rubber tyres and tubes	11	8	11	8	94	68	80	75	2150	1698	1459	1413
2219	Other rubber products	19	20	19	20	339	298	199	420	5232	4616	2271	7326
2220	Plastics products	341	350	343	335	9473	8942	7132	6502	201569	226950	158045	141115
2310	Glass and glass products	79	84	77	78	2226	1982	1408	1231	54759	55533	28692	24571
239	Non-metallic mineral products n.e.c.	908	938	823	838	9366	9229	6529	6101	224468	246017	142867	124530
2391	Refractory products	8	6	5	5	205	64	32	43	5503	2124	1144	1232
2392	Clay building materials	19	21	20	16	1004	987	669	551	21240	23115	13582	9418
2393	Other porcelain and ceramic products	194	199	178	175	671	628	526	492	6605	30597	5034	4889
2394	Cement, lime and plaster	3	3	3	2	824	832	647	519	25155	6605	23195	17388
2395	Articles of concrete, cement and plaster	200	221	172	160	4931	4962	3101	2972	134316	145182	71630	63064
2396	Cutting, shaping and finishing of stone	466	469	429	468	1168	1205	1138	1028	10414	12908	10589	8777
2399	Other non-metallic mineral products n.e.c.	18	19	16	12	563	551	416	496	21539	25487	17694	19762
2410	Basic iron and steel	23	27	23	20	414	725	612	656	8034	19330	16229	17513
2420	Basic precious and other non-ferrous metals	3	2	1	1	71	28	16	21	774	649	234	266
243	Casting of metals	18	14	12	10	745	641	290	212	17217	16446	7609	4940
2431	Casting of iron and steel	10	9	8	5	639	562	225	147	15552	15013	6576	3749
2432	Casting of non-ferrous metals	8	5	4	5	106	79	65	65	1665	1433	1034	1191
251	Struct.metal products, tanks, reservoirs	260	297	304	277	7955	8435	5488	4980	195975	231204	108473	93513
2511	Structural metal products	232	267	273	250	5539	6049	4041	3683	123171	150388	73147	60506
2512	Tanks, reservoirs and containers of metal	28	30	31	27	2416	2386	1447	1297	72805	80815	35326	33006

continued

Lithuania

ISIC	Industry	Number of enterprises (number)					Number of employees (number)					Wages and salaries paid to employees (thousands of Lithuanian Litas)				
		Note	2007	2008	2009	2010	Note	2007	2008	2009	2010	Note	2007	2008	2009	2010
2513	Steam generators, excl. hot water boilers		-	-	-	-		-	-	-	-		-	-	-	-
2520	Weapons and ammunition		2	2	2	2		77	80	83	79		1921	2344	2270	2038
259	Other metal products;metal working services		1260	1238	949	867		8980	7671	6080	6010		168341	164615	111723	114992
2591	Forging,pressing,stamping,roll-forming of metal		52	46	42	42		771	694	517	545		15165	16064	10041	11641
2592	Treatment and coating of metals; machining		174	183	160	153		1839	1582	1163	1148		37528	34821	22339	21694
2593	Cutlery, hand tools and general hardware		799	785	536	479		696	570	485	504		12481	10971	8192	8039
2599	Other fabricated metal products n.e.c.		235	224	211	193		5674	4825	3915	3813		103166	102758	71151	73619
2610	Electronic components and boards		27	22	24	20		1111	609	611	537		22960	14530	14071	13224
2620	Computers and peripheral equipment		19	20	21	21		321	429	289	230		5450	8928	5689	4268
2630	Communication equipment		23	24	17	21		616	729	695	886		18916	25036	22066	31314
2640	Consumer electronics		15	15	13	15		1210	886	744	786		22400	33748	14633	16160
265	Measuring;testing equipment; watches, etc.		42	47	41	40		819	957	795	700		20961	26511	21088	19952
2651	Measuring/testing/navigating equipment,etc.		40	45	39	39		818	955	794	700		20955	26499	21086	19952
2652	Watches and clocks		2	2	2	1		1	2	1	-		6	11	2	-
2660	Irradiation/electromedical equipment,etc.		5	5	5	6		26	17	15	95		264	217	137	1832
2670	Optical instruments and photographic equipment		8	10	10	13		229	230	214	256		10641	12009	11726	15720
2680	Magnetic and optical media		1	1	1	1		49	75	69	62		1044	1854	1101	1209
2710	Electric motors,generators,transformers,etc.		45	43	42	43		1544	1571	1320	1374		34213	43559	31341	33834
2720	Batteries and accumulators		2	4	2	1		56	73	18	4		2215	3152	1265	34
273	Wiring and wiring devices		13	15	13	13		650	860	433	489		9335	15840	6034	8141
2731	Fibre optic cables		-	-	-	-		-	-	-	-		-	-	-	-
2732	Other electronic and electric wires and cables		4	4	4	5		352	378	227	306		5186	6864	3230	5185
2733	Wiring devices		9	11	9	8		298	482	206	183		4149	8976	2804	2956
2740	Electric lighting equipment		10	11	15	16		228	270	281	331		3560	5510	4592	6213
2750	Domestic appliances		17	14	14	13		2028	1869	1189	1093		39531	40499	21611	21255
2790	Other electrical equipment		8	8	7	8		67	50	58	30		851	1401	1937	550
281	General-purpose machinery		87	94	94	90		4583	4126	3738	3747		104871	116319	91798	92311
2811	Engines/turbines,excl.aircraft,vehicle engines		2	3	2	3		182	312	212	139		4125	6905	4507	1646
2812	Fluid power equipment		5	3	4	4		183	174	152	18		4102	4757	3276	269
2813	Other pumps, compressors, taps and valves		3	5	4	5		309	467	305	428		6751	10855	6282	10925
2814	Bearings, gears, gearing and driving elements		11	10	9	9		240	195	140	123		3519	3618	1967	1591
2815	Ovens, furnaces and furnace burners		5	4	5	5		340	316	505	539		7400	7909	11547	11897
2816	Lifting and handling equipment		9	11	14	13		189	166	297	237		3826	3640	4947	5070
2817	Office machinery, excl.computers,etc.		3	3	3	4		442	557	502	453		6563	16663	15530	14407
2818	Power-driven hand tools		1	1	1	1		3	3	2	2		16	20	6	4
2819	Other general-purpose machinery		48	54	52	46		2695	1936	1623	1808		68569	61952	43736	46502
282	Special-purpose machinery		61	70	64	59		1434	1742	1339	1165		27959	38334	24761	22963
2821	Agricultural and forestry machinery		17	17	11	10		576	491	351	343		9806	10690	6632	6609
2822	Metal-forming machinery and machine tools		19	24	21	23		301	285	193	157		4379	4428	2607	2000
2823	Machinery for metallurgy		-	1	2	2		-	27	23	18		-	889	475	438
2824	Mining, quarrying and construction machinery		2	2	3	2		63	406	370	357		1312	9128	7631	8392

Code													
2825	Food/beverage/tobacco processing machinery	8	7	6	6	147	125	114	111	3513	3460	2840	2108
2826	Textile/apparel/leather production machinery	1	1	2	1	14	12	25	17	291	298	522	317
2829	Other special-purpose machinery	14	18	19	15	333	396	263	162	8658	9441	4054	3099
2910	Motor vehicles	5	7	5	5	227	224	96	86	4625	6137	2085	1377
2920	Automobile bodies, trailers and semi-trailers	13	15	15	13	848	980	567	505	22421	30960	13859	14499
2930	Parts and accessories for motor vehicles	22	18	13	13	2646	1708	1085	698	49415	41373	24076	16115
301	Building of ships and boats	28	32	32	36	2218	2342	1871	520	76459	100239	77310	53600
3011	Building of ships and floating structures	21	24	22	17	2024	2141	1708	334	71062	94304	73196	47627
3012	Building of pleasure and sporting boats	7	8	10	19	194	201	163	186	5397	5934	4114	5973
3020	Railway locomotives and rolling stock	1	1	1	1	65	76	65	59	3543	4274	3345	3269
3030	Air and spacecraft and related machinery	3	4	4	3	311	285	267	261	6628	7846	7188	6446
3040	Military fighting vehicles	-	-	-	-	-	-	-	-	-	-	-	-
309	Transport equipment n.e.c.	10	10	5	4	920	922	565	518	21349	23643	13649	10992
3091	Motorcycles	-	-	-	-	-	-	-	-	-	-	-	-
3092	Bicycles and invalid carriages	6	6	3	2	893	902	553	484	21126	23384	13540	10714
3099	Other transport equipment n.e.c.	4	4	2	2	27	20	12	34	223	259	109	277
3100	Furniture	1159	1310	1146	1122	23927	23968	19041	19047	424857	510830	340781	360723
321	Jewellery, bijouterie and related articles	523	566	479	528	1056	915	715	608	15866	16907	14286	8630
3211	Jewellery and related articles	492	502	414	453	845	593	449	431	13318	10888	8485	6240
3212	Imitation jewellery and related articles	31	64	65	75	211	322	266	177	2548	6019	5801	2390
3220	Musical instruments	4	3	2	2	15	14	4	4	238	257	26	26
3230	Sports goods	33	37	32	35	125	125	178	155	1681	2193	2461	2217
3240	Games and toys	14	15	15	15	194	166	118	103	2195	2528	1658	1547
3250	Medical and dental instruments and supplies	185	201	223	230	2359	2395	2462	2438	46512	53036	48859	47580
3290	Other manufacturing n.e.c.	101	96	101	102	1318	1318	1274	1249	30176	32517	26820	24939
331	Repair of fabricated metal products/machinery	636	640	576	606	7815	7759	7321	6700	199298	229196	203990	181489
3311	Repair of fabricated metal products	31	32	23	22	399	414	87	84	11644	11983	1268	1265
3312	Repair of machinery	283	271	257	269	3403	3012	2337	2053	85344	81507	53345	43834
3313	Repair of electronic and optical equipment	20	20	20	17	40	48	60	48	347	462	712	628
3314	Repair of electrical equipment	188	191	145	167	158	133	378	385	1970	1685	8806	15390
3315	Repair of transport equip., excl. motor vehicles	105	120	122	122	3768	4110	4427	4094	99572	133001	139530	120031
3319	Repair of other equipment	9	6	9	9	47	42	32	36	421	559	329	342
3320	Installation of industrial machinery/equipment	37	41	40	33	708	717	531	367	15945	19948	14198	8636
C	Total manufacturing	15332	15768	12847	12487	240583	222335	184858	174828	4646538	5167850	3821498	3626587

Lithuania

ISIC	Industry	Output at factor values (thousands of Lithuanian Litas)				Note	Value added at factor values (thousands of Lithuanian Litas)				Note	Gross fixed capital formation (thousands of Lithuanian Litas)		Note
		2007	2008	2009	2010		2007	2008	2009	2010		2009	2010	
1010	Processing/preserving of meat	1706405	2046876	1684306	1593913		278522	285091	260961	206769		50785	32720	
1020	Processing/preserving of fish, etc.	751483	822867	821908	1021070		153161	102026	172463	175520		37903	35725	
1030	Processing/preserving of fruit,vegetables	159660	186848	177104	161990		34459	35061	39063	38417		6580	4227	
1040	Vegetable and animal oils and fats	67065	75868	72496	83412		8353	5210	5590	7972		2587	6329	
1050	Dairy products	2800252	2913996	2266152	2766402		612002	381588	492850	449555		79460	45596	
106	Grain mill products,starches and starch products	302671	355135	294072	389774		58568	52607	76346	63770		9366	26552	
1061	Grain mill products	299402	351974	291713	389662		57926	51978	74684	64149		8313	26552	
1062	Starches and starch products	3268	3160	2359	111		642	630	1662	...		1053	-	
107	Other food products	1886535	1853030	1674036	1663105		589690	550937	507624	472545		72343	76791	
1071	Bakery products	768059	923125	803519	742896		281903	326963	316750	250455		31081	29407	
1072	Sugar	338061	203961	232401	238193		128483	38858	12329	51940		11475	11124	
1073	Cocoa, chocolate and sugar confectionery	565579	492509	417843	397281		120146	123439	117512	105254		18850	28471	
1074	Macaroni, noodles, couscous, etc.	14176	19699	19916	21809		5779	7361	7401	7316		740	464	
1075	Prepared meals and dishes	51189	63963	47812	58402		19227	20438	18588	17399		5136	1955	
1079	Other food products n.e.c.	149470	149773	152547	204523		34151	33879	35043	40181		5061	5372	
1080	Prepared animal feeds	1016321	1140755	990879	1086838		178012	121799	199002	174822		43933	39139	
1101	Distilling, rectifying and blending of spirits	248437	228411	191405	207033		87860	69077	60627	28032		8424	14174	
1102	Wines	245864	231317	172291	146145		54329	35470	35493	22447		4203	3218	
1103	Malt liquors and malt	942984	1063751	862024	862980		360858	349734	293582	243733		46346	33478	
1104	Soft drinks,mineral waters,other bottled waters	149836	141759	107695	139020		36882	34786	34664	32606		7072	6341	
1200	Tobacco products	114788	127801	127717	122787		73328	84840	92600	85543		10465	19544	
131	Spinning, weaving and finishing of textiles	560058	417113	284377	319371		192417	133915	89029	96893		21708	9096	
1311	Preparation and spinning of textile fibres	179969	169589	127082	151666		60621	60613	45079	50264		6457	2581	
1312	Weaving of textiles	332418	215834	117758	120038		116570	62515	24884	27018		8322	4468	
1313	Finishing of textiles	47671	31691	39537	47667		15226	10787	19066	19611		6929	2047	
139	Other textiles	543421	556891	456993	548839		171584	178182	152810	171224		12565	20476	
1391	Knitted and crocheted fabrics	23590	22739	22338	30771		7302	6675	5730	8093		441	287	
1392	Made-up textile articles, except apparel	344383	327377	250335	270740		107333	105143	81254	82364		7389	9676	
1393	Carpets and rugs	4323	5009	3806	3360		1260	1661	1629	570		15	58	
1394	Cordage, rope, twine and netting	57959	99251	79466	100419		22760	30748	24280	31165		3405	2617	
1399	Other textiles n.e.c.	113165	102515	101046	143550		32928	33954	39916	49032		1315	7839	
1410	Wearing apparel, except fur apparel	1219756	1113052	801541	863083		550111	482914	361284	376224		17237	23052	
1420	Articles of fur	16557	9864	3830	5478		5332	2873	317	1446		167	107	
1430	Knitted and crocheted apparel	134708	143463	94374	102197		53830	58502	36260	41257		2500	2648	
151	Leather;luggage,handbags,saddlery,harness;fur	49479	48387	30084	36875		13199	19633	9003	8186		2150	11872	
1511	Tanning/dressing of leather; dressing of fur	27258	22915	22738	29415		3369	11319	5531	4929		1978	11429	
1512	Luggage,handbags,etc.;saddlery/harness	22220	19472	7346	7460		9831	8314	3472	3257		172	442	
1520	Footwear	45697	39604	33009	39702		17763	18343	14813	15884		323	1128	
1610	Sawmilling and planing of wood	1411932	1088620	832450	1123442		315573	219459	201112	270783		38022	50422	
162	Wood products, cork, straw, plaiting materials	1849752	1641822	1349207	1342887		506837	475191	377773	349544		61221	97776	

1621	Veneer sheets and wood-based panels	649811	665742	550983	153632	149766	200115	117732	33312	50846
1622	Builders' carpentry and joinery	790808	431885	435415	240896	226533	111318	130916	16342	25740
1623	Wooden containers	247832	176223	239392	67786	61502	42853	62190	7685	10594
1629	Other wood products;articles of cork,straw	161300	75358	117098	44523	37390	23487	38705	3882	10597
1701	Pulp, paper and paperboard	142936	65360	130206	38214	34668	18733	20640	5614	4588
1702	Corrugated paper and paperboard	288976	352592	408038	45972	103993	101965	112705	52852	14208
1709	Other articles of paper and paperboard	219538	139280	270162	79662	50081	54330	87442	6767	26575
181	Printing and service activities related to printing	559830	439387	459304	181909	209047	129245	140255	20836	21215
1811	Printing	481847	371944	384625	154976	176753	109357	118990	18469	19450
1812	Service activities related to printing	77983	67443	74678	26933	32293	19888	21265	2367	1764
1820	Reproduction of recorded media	2142	1273	1392	580	1343	549	375	23	3
1910	Coke oven products	-	-	-	-	-	-	-	-	-
1920	Refined petroleum products	8871944	10699473	15329908	316132	-73905	304594	622723	187516	48409
201	Basic chemicals,fertilizers, etc.	4771938	3484874	5070283	817037	859151	359419	896844	165621	102403
2011	Basic chemicals	2758497	166345	193060	53923	50389	76210	77882	11881	7937
2012	Fertilizers and nitrogen compounds	139943	1922265	2463827	622221	743417	127937	607381	143709	90280
2013	Plastics and synthetic rubber in primary forms	1873499	1396264	2413396	140893	65345	155272	211580	10032	4186
202	Other chemical products	259084	610052	569880	54316	71797	78188	75959	5976	8866
2021	Pesticides and other agrochemical products	-	1125	1227	-	784	508	460	24	14
2022	Paints,varnishes;printing ink and mastics	85140	70501	86770	22844	24325	24479	28417	1675	2396
2023	Soap,cleaning and cosmetic preparations	45020	47113	48248	15832	4334	15378	15911	1037	547
2029	Other chemical products n.e.c.	128924	491313	433635	15639	42354	37823	31171	3240	5909
2030	Man-made fibres	109302	71643	120123	22117	33746	9428	22492	7351	423
2100	Pharmaceuticals,medicinal chemicals, etc.	159483	185430	223565	54561	48311	86545	91089	7293	30782
221	Rubber products	47105	28025	69667	15006	12741	5397	20910	223	12271
2211	Rubber tyres and tubes	10918	9459	16428	4070	3418	1911	3175	64	313
2219	Other rubber products	36186	18566	53239	10936	9323	3486	17735	159	11958
2220	Plastics products	2464755	1598883	1810431	493705	437073	377168	383898	72256	87236
2310	Glass and glass products	433553	189329	203118	128729	115089	45790	51345	5232	7831
239	Non-metallic mineral products n.e.c.	1798612	767601	915154	698566	559243	226225	228059	238639	52242
2391	Refractory products	41239	8122	10424	13365	-379	782	2664	1	41
2392	Clay building materials	87051	43220	46118	39851	35217	19293	15802	2579	2114
2393	Other porcelain and ceramic products	26849	15916	18107	10358	12062	8362	9574	509	746
2394	Cement, lime and plaster	286954	173521	177818	103164	113089	58863	31244	136413	7897
2395	Articles of concrete, cement and plaster	1010308	382226	472890	358490	297215	90830	114563	91549	17225
2396	Cutting, shaping and finishing of stone	62993	42150	41401	23102	26553	17867	14903	2416	679
2399	Other non-metallic mineral products n.e.c.	283218	102446	148397	150235	75485	30228	39309	5172	23540
2410	Basic iron and steel	64267	147181	189527	14181	39607	12190	23293	1393	2396
2420	Basic precious and other non-ferrous metals	13412	7138	20398	1559	3091	573	1947	-	5
243	Casting of metals	53250	18833	15473	24043	16272	5171	5630	364	1986
2431	Casting of iron and steel	46807	16501	11995	20568	14142	4043	3975	349	1878
2432	Casting of non-ferrous metals	6443	2332	3478	3475	2130	1128	1655	14	108
251	Struct.metal products, tanks, reservoirs	1348463	596351	645897	397487	418886	189481	199846	21080	17310
2511	Structural metal products	968135	400434	409318	277598	282886	124638	123469	9840	11885
2512	Tanks, reservoirs and containers of metal	380328	195917	236579	119890	136000	64842	76377	11240	5425

continued

Lithuania

ISIC Revision 4		Output at factor values (thousands of Lithuanian Litas)					Value added at factor values (thousands of Lithuanian Litas)					Gross fixed capital formation (thousands of Lithuanian Litas)		
ISIC	Industry	Note	2007	2008	2009	2010	Note	2007	2008	2009	2010	Note	2009	2010
2513	Steam generators, excl. hot water boilers		-	-	-	-		-	-	-	-		-	-
2520	Weapons and ammunition		4101	12316	9963	14510		-3110	2645	2811	6116		322	-
259	Other metal products;metal working services		1101403	918714	632483	759617		318018	307698	186558	234215		51048	33938
2591	Forging,pressing,stamping,roll-forming of metal		77606	67605	36214	72875		22363	34673	14301	22567		14050	6081
2592	Treatment and coating of metals; machining		217826	188710	108620	138658		64502	57112	20630	38599		4498	4308
2593	Cutlery, hand tools and general hardware		74910	66318	43125	46454		26603	24927	16445	15835		1618	3851
2599	Other fabricated metal products n.e.c.		731061	596081	444524	501630		204551	190986	135183	157214		30881	19698
2610	Electronic components and boards		97632	69950	90268	107821		17181	21303	28631	24329		1163	1938
2620	Computers and peripheral equipment		54279	51524	28557	19742		10835	15942	8034	6906		896	783
2630	Communication equipment		126541	111554	94243	187703		40759	49745	38789	58659		3591	19261
2640	Consumer electronics		294899	365798	228845	329732		36847	68370	17366	36072		547	3039
265	Measuring,testing equipment; watches, etc.		104905	121272	80924	103292		52187	54963	36273	53680		2742	3666
2651	Measuring/testing/navigating equipment,etc.		104584	121142	80812	103292		52100	54902	36208	53680		2742	3666
2652	Watches and clocks		321	129	111	-		86	61	65	-		-	-
2660	Irradiation/electromedical equipment,etc.		1284	888	555	5300		566	289	74	2358		27	3
2670	Optical instruments and photographic equipment		53662	68653	57593	82468		28467	28424	35678	41470		6231	2869
2680	Magnetic and optical media		14502	20988	10025	9995		3787	7325	4278	4475		98	9
2710	Electric motors,generators,transformers,etc.		210117	271493	167611	208601		64958	66188	44801	61274		6506	3452
2720	Batteries and accumulators		10104	21321	468	544		4742	8812	214	121		5064	-
273	Wiring and wiring devices		112962	124808	24416	51991		24224	38841	7750	15316		526	869
2731	Fibre optic cables		-	-	-	-		-	-	-	-		-	-
2732	Other electronic and electric wires and cables		95966	58937	15581	42264		14960	14060	2334	10163		205	381
2733	Wiring devices		16995	65870	8835	9727		9265	24781	5416	5154		321	488
2740	Electric lighting equipment		51413	65200	69421	96297		8073	15771	8343	19268		981	1451
2750	Domestic appliances		376304	312107	140640	168066		72716	65978	27394	47195		1370	3021
2790	Other electrical equipment		6262	12363	13589	2966		1973	1285	2500	500		129	18
281	General-purpose machinery		771458	708055	469396	617773		251035	227736	172096	222513		55827	36009
2811	Engines/turbines,excl.aircraft,vehicle engines		11551	18615	12227	4473		8862	10981	8241	3675		310	96
2812	Fluid power equipment		22990	23857	20712	2085		8561	8317	7282	458		28	137
2813	Other pumps, compressors, taps and valves		38981	44149	20185	51115		14013	18899	10335	22345		539	3457
2814	Bearings, gears, gearing and driving elements		15237	11874	6321	8550		7370	4955	3236	3187		1337	945
2815	Ovens, furnaces and furnace burners		37787	45228	32549	45169		14499	16385	14248	17809		2534	1059
2816	Lifting and handling equipment		29234	25090	24394	35211		11345	8227	9821	10497		9498	2439
2817	Office machinery, excl.computers,etc.		191957	225252	146481	139115		34573	31960	15783	32586		1185	3561
2818	Power-driven hand tools		21	32	16	21		22	23	8	15		-	-
2819	Other general-purpose machinery		423700	313957	206512	332033		151791	127988	103141	131939		40396	24316
282	Special-purpose machinery		134529	182712	108896	121906		51068	69912	42127	45381		6974	10462
2821	Agricultural and forestry machinery		60057	60553	37232	39472		21799	20526	13679	15327		1301	5826
2822	Metal-forming machinery and machine tools		18536	16056	7195	7624		7713	6807	3092	2960		236	987
2823	Machinery for metallurgy		-	10201	4428	5264		-	1993	1782	1287		116	31
2824	Mining, quarrying and construction machinery		4310	50144	42682	49472		1164	20861	16762	17437		4499	2725

Code											
2825	Food/beverage/tobacco processing machinery	12749	13594	5932	6058	4861	5314	1929	2639	145	496
2826	Textile/apparel/leather production machinery	702	625	1172	791	433	410	799	557	7	-
2829	Other special-purpose machinery	38175	31538	10256	13226	15097	14000	4084	5174	670	398
2910	Motor vehicles	66146	49109	9449	18244	9905	5065	2263	2844	298	21
2920	Automobile bodies, trailers and semi-trailers	409333	439943	124128	311325	79222	79547	17444	78177	2746	4726
2930	Parts and accessories for motor vehicles	289843	126162	47207	41229	70042	39331	28223	25935	2957	3526
301	Building of ships and boats	297387	342461	231443	188439	128928	163975	118983	108398	3526	1276
3011	Building of ships and floating structures	254836	309149	210865	157678	113725	153106	115291	99151	2909	1054
3012	Building of pleasure and sporting boats	42550	33312	20578	30762	15202	10869	3692	9247	617	221
3020	Railway locomotives and rolling stock	39785	53217	22259	26748	6657	9851	6947	8213	1178	386
3030	Air and spacecraft and related machinery	53279	70837	60402	55584	17891	19028	16404	12793	326	1214
3040	Military fighting vehicles	-	-	-	-	-	-	-	-	-	2107
309	Transport equipment n.e.c.	194576	190223	118742	162471	36701	42714	21806	19463	549	-
3091	Motorcycles	-	-	-	-	-	-	-	-	-	1917
3092	Bicycles and invalid carriages	192775	188875	118333	161216	35931	42356	21780	19042	549	190
3099	Other transport equipment n.e.c.	1802	1348	409	1255	770	358	26	421	-	130420
3100	Furniture	2670073	2974569	2270633	2610390	820146	593078	622008	711304	54233	130420
321	Jewellery, bijouterie and related articles	126052	165735	117276	76784	33438	44295	27686	25396	1788	1348
3211	Jewellery and related articles	116853	89507	66552	66724	27429	30375	21168	20666	1309	1205
3212	Imitation jewellery and related articles	9199	76228	50724	10060	6009	13920	6518	4730	479	143
3220	Musical instruments	771	552	129	115	350	335	82	90	82	82
3230	Sports goods	9081	24262	24429	14209	1821	3601	5302	7407	215	232
3240	Games and toys	8309	9201	5708	5786	3376	3197	2273	2491	131	100
3250	Medical and dental instruments and supplies	230254	252800	240770	244762	109383	125302	123308	105456	13696	20426
3290	Other manufacturing n.e.c.	125041	137410	122596	113393	61317	63280	47209	47068	17443	10922
331	Repair of fabricated metal products/machinery	965009	1201949	1021365	801660	359204	431193	265590	286518	26562	15969
3311	Repair of fabricated metal products	41824	46023	12905	17569	20617	25640	1977	1868	156	127
3312	Repair of machinery	313949	278108	149213	131775	139697	132193	71421	58617	3594	2865
3313	Repair of electronic and optical equipment	1817	4317	3026	4309	981	2633	1464	1598	17	412
3314	Repair of electrical equipment	13165	13013	24809	38482	5577	4663	13337	20731	2688	555
3315	Repair of transport equip., excl. motor vehicles	590827	857206	829449	606988	190962	264682	176430	202859	20078	11890
3319	Repair of other equipment	3427	3282	1963	2537	1369	1382	961	845	28	120
3320	Installation of industrial machinery/equipment	118587	110581	56144	50661	37381	41391	18729	17579	1752	1086
C	Total manufacturing	46962138	57260341	39431230	48688994	10496485	9353883	7506231	8657605	1605920	1313794

Lithuania

Index numbers of industrial production

ISIC Revision 4

(2005=100)

ISIC	Industry	Note	1999	2000	2001	2002	2003	2004	2005	2006	2007	2008	2009	2010
10	Food products		…	80	75	77	88	93	100	111	126	121	112	111
11	Beverages		…	89	97	99	95	89	100	106	122	122	108	109
12	Tobacco products		…	68	73	65	54	60	100	150	169	181	157	160
13	Textiles		…	93	100	106	89	99	100	110	115	92	73	84
14	Wearing apparel		…	103	103	110	117	107	100	102	95	81	61	74
15	Leather and related products		…	177	136	157	120	72	100	90	113	101	64	96
16	Wood/wood products/cork,excl. furniture		…	48	45	69	84	87	100	105	114	103	82	91
17	Paper and paper products		…	62	62	83	85	91	100	135	142	133	130	184
18	Printing and reproduction of recorded media		…	85	86	104	109	111	100	114	123	131	90	99
19	Coke and refined petroleum products		…	52	77	72	77	96	100	91	66	104	93	96
20	Chemicals and chemical products		…	76	66	86	89	87	100	127	195	181	181	199
21	Pharmaceuticals,medicinal chemicals, etc.		…	90	115	96	86	101	100	127	135	109	122	195
22	Rubber and plastics products		…	29	34	44	72	81	100	119	117	110	87	105
23	Other non-metallic mineral products		…	47	43	51	67	76	100	135	137	112	59	68
24	Basic metals		…	177	149	146	95	79	100	90	129	235	211	221
25	Fabricated metal products, except machinery		…	31	34	38	60	83	100	130	164	117	69	80
26	Computer, electronic and optical products		…	47	52	62	84	100	100	99	91	79	89	97
27	Electrical equipment		…	40	51	73	78	94	100	102	113	114	69	94
28	Machinery and equipment n.e.c.		…	77	59	72	83	74	100	128	142	221	160	183
29	Motor vehicles, trailers and semi-trailers		…	41	38	47	78	107	100	110	127	110	31	53
30	Other transport equipment		…	60	64	63	68	88	100	101	108	126	101	100
31	Furniture		…	36	39	55	67	90	100	131	151	169	131	143
32	Other manufacturing		…	65	55	75	86	92	100	108	160	202	181	170
33	Repair and installation of machinery/equipment		…	95	61	61	55	74	100	124	138	146	132	145
C	Total manufacturing		…	62	69	74	82	92	100	108	110	117	99	107

Luxembourg

Supplier of information:
Service central de la statistique et des études économiques (STATEC), Luxembourg. Industrial statistics for the OECD countries are compiled by the OECD secretariat, which supplies them to UNIDO.

Basic source of data:
Annual sample survey; administrative source.

Major deviations from ISIC (Revision 4):
None reported.

Reference period:
Calendar year.

Scope:
All enterprises included in the business register.

Method of data collection:
Not reported.

Type of enumeration:
Not reported.

Adjusted for non-response:
Yes.

Concepts and definitions of variables:
No deviations from the standard UN concepts and definitions are reported.

Related national publications:
None reported.

Luxembourg

ISIC	Industry	Number of enterprises (number)					Number of employees (number)					Wages and salaries paid to employees (millions of Euros)				
		Note	2006	2007	2008	2009	Note	2006	2007	2008a/	2009a/	Note	2006	2007	2008a/	2009a/
10	Food products		...	...	147	141		...	...	2612	2439		...	...	67	62
11	Beverages		...	...	28	29		...	...	514	510		...	...	21	21
12	Tobacco products		...	...	1	1		...	...	-	-		...	...	-	-
13	Textiles		...	...	22	23		...	...	-	-		...	...	-	-
14	Wearing apparel		...	...	17	16		...	...	-	-		...	...	-	-
15	Leather and related products		...	...	-	-		...	...	-	-		...	...	-	-
16	Wood/wood products/cork,excl. furniture		...	...	23	21		...	...	636	616		...	...	23	21
17	Paper and paper products		...	...	3	3		...	...	-	-		...	...	-	-
18	Printing and reproduction of recorded media		...	...	99	105		...	...	1020	912		...	...	44	41
19	Coke and refined petroleum products		...	...	-	-		...	...	-	-		...	...	-	-
20	Chemicals and chemical products		...	...	16	17		...	...	-	-		...	...	-	-
21	Pharmaceuticals,medicinal chemicals, etc.		...	...	1	1		...	...	-	-		...	...	-	-
22	Rubber and plastics products		...	...	26	26		...	...	-	-		...	...	-	-
23	Other non-metallic mineral products		...	...	40	40		...	...	-	-		...	...	-	-
24	Basic metals		...	...	7	8		...	...	67	55		...	...	2	2
25	Fabricated metal products, except machinery		...	...	193	204		...	...	-	-		...	...	-	-
26	Computer, electronic and optical products		...	...	10	10		...	...	3577	3623		...	...	140	122
27	Electrical equipment		...	...	16	17		...	...	-	-		...	...	-	-
28	Machinery and equipment n.e.c.		...	...	26	25		...	...	-	-		...	...	-	-
29	Motor vehicles, trailers and semi-trailers		...	...	11	11		...	...	491	409		...	...	14	12
30	Other transport equipment		...	...	1	1		...	...	-	-		...	...	-	-
31	Furniture		...	...	40	40		...	...	182	175		...	...	6	5
32	Other manufacturing		...	...	77	79		...	...	484	497		...	...	14	15
33	Repair and installation of machinery/equipment		...	...	57	56		...	...	420	434		...	...	22	19
C	Total manufacturing		...	...	861	874		...	...	35861	34574		...	...	1581	1480

a/ Data are aggregated from incomplete 3- and/or 4-digit level of ISICs.

Luxembourg

ISIC	Industry	Note	Output (millions of Euros) 2006	2007	2008a/	2009a/	Note	Value added at factor values (millions of Euros) 2006	2007	2008a/	2009a/	Note	Gross fixed capital formation (millions of Euros) 2008a/	2009a/
10	Food products		...	...	176	169		...	...	96	94		16	8
11	Beverages		...	...	139	153		...	...	50	55		6	7
12	Tobacco products		...	...	...	...		...	...	...	...		...	...
13	Textiles		...	...	-	-		...	...	-	-		-	-
14	Wearing apparel		...	...	-	-		...	...	-	-		-	-
15	Leather and related products		...	...	174	162		...	...	41	41		4	17
16	Wood/wood products/cork,excl. furniture		...	...	...	...		...	...	...	...		...	...
17	Paper and paper products		...	...	141	123		...	...	70	58		7	4
18	Printing and reproduction of recorded media		...	...	...	...		...	...	...	...		...	...
19	Coke and refined petroleum products		...	...	-	-		...	...	-	-		-	-
20	Chemicals and chemical products		...	...	...	...		...	...	...	...		...	...
21	Pharmaceuticals,medicinal chemicals, etc.		...	...	...	...		...	...	...	...		...	...
22	Rubber and plastics products		...	...	7	6		...	...	4	3		-	-
23	Other non-metallic mineral products		...	...	...	...		...	...	...	...		...	...
24	Basic metals		...	...	-	-		...	...	-	-		-	-
25	Fabricated metal products, except machinery		...	...	698	500		...	...	213	178		17	10
26	Computer, electronic and optical products		...	...	-	-		...	...	-	-		-	-
27	Electrical equipment		...	...	-	-		...	...	-	-		-	-
28	Machinery and equipment n.e.c.		...	...	-	-		...	...	-	-		-	-
29	Motor vehicles, trailers and semi-trailers		...	...	133	78		...	...	40	21		1	1
30	Other transport equipment		...	...	-	-		...	...	-	-		-	-
31	Furniture		...	...	20	19		...	...	8	9		-	-
32	Other manufacturing		...	...	37	39		...	...	19	21		3	2
33	Repair and installation of machinery/equipment		...	...	230	137		...	...	54	35		6	4
C	Total manufacturing		...	...	14375	7837		...	...	5422	1127		520	338

a/ Data are aggregated from incomplete 3- and/or 4-digit level of ISICs.

Luxembourg

Index numbers of industrial production

ISIC Revision 4

(2005=100)

ISIC	Industry	Note	1999	2000	2001	2002	2003	2004	2005	2006	2007	2008	2009	2010
10	Food products		...	...	...	...	...	...	100	102	109	106	108	...
11	Beverages		...	...	...	...	...	...	...	...	...	...	...	...
12	Tobacco products		...	...	...	...	...	...	...	...	...	...	...	...
13	Textiles		...	...	...	...	...	...	...	...	...	...	...	...
14	Wearing apparel		...	...	...	...	...	...	...	...	...	...	...	...
15	Leather and related products		...	...	...	...	...	...	...	...	...	...	...	...
16	Wood/wood products/cork,excl. furniture		...	...	...	...	...	...	100	98	105	85	84	...
17	Paper and paper products		...	...	...	...	...	...	...	...	...	...	...	...
18	Printing and reproduction of recorded media		...	...	...	...	...	...	...	...	...	...	...	...
19	Coke and refined petroleum products		...	...	...	...	...	...	...	...	...	...	...	...
20	Chemicals and chemical products		...	...	...	...	...	...	...	...	...	...	...	...
21	Pharmaceuticals,medicinal chemicals, etc.		...	...	...	...	...	...	...	...	...	...	...	...
22	Rubber and plastics products		...	...	...	...	...	...	...	...	...	...	...	...
23	Other non-metallic mineral products		...	...	...	...	...	...	...	...	...	...	...	...
24	Basic metals		...	...	...	...	...	...	...	...	...	...	...	...
25	Fabricated metal products, except machinery		...	...	...	...	...	...	100	107	99	98	77	...
26	Computer, electronic and optical products		...	...	...	...	...	...	...	...	...	...	...	...
27	Electrical equipment		...	...	...	...	...	...	...	...	...	...	...	...
28	Machinery and equipment n.e.c.		...	...	...	...	...	...	100	95	106	101	71	...
29	Motor vehicles, trailers and semi-trailers		...	...	...	...	...	...	...	...	...	...	...	...
30	Other transport equipment		...	...	...	...	...	...	...	...	...	...	...	...
31	Furniture		...	...	...	...	...	...	...	...	...	...	...	...
32	Other manufacturing		...	...	...	...	...	...	...	...	...	...	...	...
33	Repair and installation of machinery/equipment		...	...	...	...	...	...	...	...	...	...	...	...
C	Total manufacturing		...	79	83	87	92	98	100	102	101	96	80	88

Malaysia

Supplier of information:
Department of Statistics, Putrajaya.

Basic source of data:
Annual survey; census/exhaustive survey (every five years).

Major deviations from ISIC (Revision 4):
The data presented in ISIC (Revision 4) were originally classified according to the Malaysia Standard Industrial Classification 2008, which conforms closely with ISIC (Revision 4).

Reference period:
Calendar year; however, data given for a financial year are accepted and incorporated into the calendar year which adheres to the major part of the financial year.

Scope:
All registered establishments engaged in manufacturing activities.

Method of data collection:
The annual survey is conducted by mail and e-mail questionnaire and direct interview in the field.

Type of enumeration:
Sample survey for 2009; complete enumeration for 2010.

Adjusted for non-response:
Yes.

Concepts and definitions of variables:
Wages and salaries excludes housing and family allowances paid directly by the employer and payments in kind.
Output is at basic prices.
Value added excludes net change between the beginning and end of the year in the stocks of fuels and materials and supplies (deductible). It is at basic prices.

Related national publications:
Report on the Annual Survey of Manufacturing Industries 2010 (Reference year 2009); Economic Census 2011 of Manufacturing Industries (Reference year 2010, both published by the Department of Statistics, Putrajaya.

Malaysia

		Number of establishments (number)					Number of employees (thousands)					Wages and salaries paid to employees (millions of Malaysian Ringgits)				
ISIC	Industry	Note	2007	2008	2009	2010	Note	2007	2008	2009	2010	Note	2007	2008	2009	2010
1010	Processing/preserving of meat		…	…	78	114		…	…	9.1	8.2		…	…	184.5	185.9
1020	Processing/preserving of fish, etc.		…	…	313	516		…	…	11.6	15.3		…	…	147.5	223.0
1030	Processing/preserving of fruit,vegetables		…	…	104	242		…	…	3.0	4.0		…	…	52.7	68.4
1040	Vegetable and animal oils and fats		…	…	502	497		…	…	54.9	52.6		…	…	1120.3	1117.3
1050	Dairy products		…	…	61	91		…	…	11.2	13.4		…	…	492.6	423.0
106	Grain mill products,starches and starch products		…	…	291	282		…	…	7.7	12.4		…	…	173.3	236.0
1061	Grain mill products		…	…	279	265		…	…	7.2	12.0		…	…	163.9	228.5
1062	Starches and starch products		…	…	12	17		…	…	0.5	0.4		…	…	9.4	7.5
107	Other food products		…	…	2932	4099		…	…	67.8	78.6		…	…	1251.1	1513.5
1071	Bakery products		…	…	1688	2232		…	…	34.0	36.3		…	…	551.9	596.6
1072	Sugar		…	…	12	12		…	…	1.8	1.9		…	…	66.1	80.2
1073	Cocoa, chocolate and sugar confectionery		…	…	83	103		…	…	8.6	8.6		…	…	194.5	203.2
1074	Macaroni, noodles, couscous, etc.		…	…	354	347		…	…	5.5	6.1		…	…	82.4	91.0
1075	Prepared meals and dishes		…	…	53	181		…	…	2.2	3.2		…	…	50.8	71.2
1079	Other food products n.e.c.		…	…	742	1224		…	…	15.8	22.6		…	…	305.4	471.2
1080	Prepared animal feeds		…	…	71	89		…	…	4.9	5.7		…	…	112.2	245.3
1101	Distilling, rectifying and blending of spirits		…	…	28	29		…	…	0.5	0.4		…	…	10.3	11.6
1102	Wines		…	…a/	9a/	15a/		…	…	0.9a/	0.7a/		…	…	44.4a/	48.5a/
1103	Malt liquors and malt		…	…a/	…a/	…a/		…	…	…a/	…a/		…	…	…a/	…a/
1104	Soft drinks,mineral waters,other bottled waters		…	…	204	254		…	…	7.7	10.7		…	…	168.8	290.6
1200	Tobacco products		…	…	99	63		…	…	3.1	2.5		…	…	140.5	114.1
131	Spinning, weaving and finishing of textiles		…	…	276	351		…	…	22.1	16.6		…	…	396.9	306.0
1311	Preparation and spinning of textile fibres		…	…	55	46		…	…	4.1	3.5		…	…	62.7	59.5
1312	Weaving of textiles		…	…	93	78		…	…	10.3	7.9		…	…	176.0	142.0
1313	Finishing of textiles		…	…	128	227		…	…	7.7	5.2		…	…	158.2	104.5
139	Other textiles		…	…	488	629		…	…	11.9	13.3		…	…	208.0	241.8
1391	Knitted and crocheted fabrics		…	…	62	72		…	…	3.7	4.2		…	…	70.9	80.7
1392	Made-up textile articles, except apparel		…	…	247	357		…	…	2.9	4.9		…	…	45.7	93.2
1393	Carpets and rugs		…	…	13	35		…	…	0.8	1.1		…	…	14.1	16.3
1394	Cordage, rope, twine and netting		…	…	19	15		…	…	1.1	0.9		…	…	16.8	15.6
1399	Other textiles n.e.c.		…	…	147	150		…	…	3.4	2.3		…	…	60.6	36.0
1410	Wearing apparel, except fur apparel		…	…	5623	9067		…	…	51.3	53.5		…	…	751.2	786.5
1420	Articles of fur		…	…	6	20		…	…	0.1	0.2		…	…	2.1	2.7
1430	Knitted and crocheted apparel		…	…	12	34		…	…	1.0	0.8		…	…	13.7	12.8
151	Leather;luggage,handbags,saddlery,harness;fur		…	…	53	74		…	…	2.0	1.9		…	…	30.5	31.1
1511	Tanning/dressing of leather; dressing of fur		…	…	5	4		…	…	0.3	0.3		…	…	3.6	3.6
1512	Luggage,handbags,etc.;saddlery/harness		…	…	48	70		…	…	1.8	1.7		…	…	26.9	27.4
1520	Footwear		…	…	276	308		…	…	7.7	6.3		…	…	118.4	116.7
1610	Sawmilling and planing of wood		…	…	654	569		…	…	33.0	32.1		…	…	523.6	522.6
162	Wood products, cork, straw, plaiting materials		…	…	952	990		…	…	76.9	79.6		…	…	1079.2	1194.9

ISIC Revision 4

1621	Veneer sheets and wood-based panels	184	196	58.4	60.7	776.7	864.4
1622	Builders' carpentry and joinery	392	361	12.8	10.4	215.7	182.6
1623	Wooden containers	66	103	2.4	3.3	42.9	58.9
1629	Other wood products;articles of cork,straw	310	330	3.3	5.3	44.0	88.9
1701	Pulp, paper and paperboard	105	175	6.9	9.5	170.0	231.4
1702	Corrugated paper and paperboard	258	243	18.5	28.7	400.5	585.0
1709	Other articles of paper and paperboard	258	472	13.4	15.6	271.8	322.1
181	Printing and service activities related to printing	1830	2956	35.9	54.1	746.5	1200.5
1811	Printing	1262	2083	22.7	40.9	461.0	929.0
1812	Service activities related to printing	568	873	13.3	13.1	285.5	271.5
1820	Reproduction of recorded media	3	5	0.2	0.1	3.2	1.4
1910	Coke oven products	…	…	…	…	…	…
1920	Refined petroleum products	28	77	6.3	7.7	407.6	427.0
201	Basic chemicals,fertilizers, etc.	365	437	36.4	40.2	1896.6	1887.9
2011	Basic chemicals	127	151	21.8	22.4	1286.8	1186.3
2012	Fertilizers and nitrogen compounds	62	131	3.3	3.9	176.0	135.9
2013	Plastics and synthetic rubber in primary forms	176	155	11.4	13.9	433.8	565.7
202	Other chemical products	627	624	35.4	36.5	1056.1	1057.6
2021	Pesticides and other agrochemical products	24	31	2.3	5.3	59.7	133.9
2022	Paints,varnishes;printing ink and mastics	155	189	8.3	10.4	288.9	365.5
2023	Soap,cleaning and cosmetic preparations	157	182	10.7	10.9	267.9	258.3
2029	Other chemical products n.e.c.	291	222	14.1	10.0	439.6	299.9
2030	Man-made fibres	5	6	0.6	0.2	22.8	8.2
2100	Pharmaceuticals,medicinal chemicals, etc.	156	207	10.6	10.3	241.2	247.9
221	Rubber products	526	554	83.3	85.9	1476.7	1823.1
2211	Rubber tyres and tubes	58	92	7.2	8.7	206.4	290.4
2219	Other rubber products	468	462	76.1	77.2	1270.3	1532.8
2220	Plastics products	1464	1456	114.6	114.9	2550.3	2544.4
2310	Glass and glass products	283	318	11.9	14.9	310.5	593.8
239	Non-metallic mineral products n.e.c.	1059	1141	65.3	61.7	1659.2	1583.1
2391	Refractory products	59	47	2.1	1.4	34.2	27.0
2392	Clay building materials	164	156	21.2	17.4	467.0	368.3
2393	Other porcelain and ceramic products	112	88	7.2	5.4	164.7	112.9
2394	Cement, lime and plaster	53	82	6.2	6.6	247.5	252.5
2395	Articles of concrete, cement and plaster	406	539	21.3	23.2	546.3	574.5
2396	Cutting, shaping and finishing of stone	105	115	1.6	2.0	31.3	39.6
2399	Other non-metallic mineral products n.e.c.	160	114	5.7	5.7	168.3	208.4
2410	Basic iron and steel	648	629	37.7	36.7	1149.0	1755.6
2420	Basic precious and other non-ferrous metals	282	325	17.1	23.9	447.0	593.4
243	Casting of metals	244	215	8.1	9.0	173.4	209.9
2431	Casting of iron and steel	209	183	6.3	6.5	143.8	167.0
2432	Casting of non-ferrous metals	35	32	1.9	2.5	29.6	42.9
251	Struct.metal products, tanks, reservoirs	1760	2474	30.4	32.8	706.3	691.4
2511	Structural metal products	1669	2382	22.9	26.1	501.2	522.3
2512	Tanks, reservoirs and containers of metal	89	88	6.7	6.0	182.3	151.1

continued

Malaysia

ISIC	Industry	Number of establishments (number)					Number of employees (thousands)					Wages and salaries paid to employees (millions of Malaysian Ringgits)				
		Note	2007	2008	2009	2010	Note	2007	2008	2009	2010	Note	2007	2008	2009	2010
2513	Steam generators, excl. hot water boilers		…	…	2b/	4b/		…	…	0.9b/	0.7b/		…	…	22.8b/	18.0b/
2520	Weapons and ammunition		…	…	..b/	..b/		…	…	..b/	..b/		…	…	..b/	..b/
259	Other metal products;metal working services		…	…	1396	1605		…	…	73.0	73.4		…	…	1663.6	1770.5
2591	Forging,pressing,stamping,roll-forming of metal		…	…	170	150		…	…	17.6	12.9		…	…	343.1	291.0
2592	Treatment and coating of metals; machining		…	…	118	124		…	…	6.7	7.1		…	…	139.6	164.3
2593	Cutlery, hand tools and general hardware		…	…	248	339		…	…	6.0	7.4		…	…	118.1	174.5
2599	Other fabricated metal products n.e.c.		…	…	860	992		…	…	42.7	46.0		…	…	1062.8	1140.8
2610	Electronic components and boards		…	…	337	366		…	…	183.6	182.5		…	…	5434.0	5755.1
2620	Computers and peripheral equipment		…	…	56	85		…	…	58.1	64.0		…	…	1473.7	1315.9
2630	Communication equipment		…	…	38	55		…	…	24.7	27.3		…	…	537.7	701.3
2640	Consumer electronics		…	…	149	90		…	…	42.6	40.2		…	…	1069.5	1172.3
265	Measuring,testing equipment; watches, etc.		…	…	39	58		…	…	12.7	9.9		…	…	223.1	252.1
2651	Measuring/testing/navigating equipment,etc.		…	…	29	47		…	…	5.9	3.8		…	…	60.8	92.2
2652	Watches and clocks		…	…	10	11		…	…	6.8	6.1		…	…	162.3	159.9
2660	Irradiation/electromedical equipment,etc.		…	…	11	18		…	…	7.4	9.2		…	…	197.4	249.2
2670	Optical instruments and photographic equipment		…	…	10	10		…	…	12.9	13.4		…	…	311.8	234.8
2680	Magnetic and optical media		…	…	8	5		…	…	1.1	1.1		…	…	39.4	47.1
2710	Electric motors,generators,transformers,etc.		…	…	228	246		…	…	32.7	32.4		…	…	734.1	781.9
2720	Batteries and accumulators		…	…	18	21		…	…	2.4	2.5		…	…	56.9	57.0
273	Wiring and wiring devices		…	…	141	137		…	…	20.0	16.4		…	…	427.8	384.6
2731	Fibre optic cables		…	…	5	7		…	…	0.4	1.6		…	…	13.6	38.9
2732	Other electronic and electric wires and cables		…	…	122	109		…	…	19.2	13.8		…	…	406.2	325.5
2733	Wiring devices		…	…	14	21		…	…	0.4	1.0		…	…	8.0	20.2
2740	Electric lighting equipment		…	…	40	52		…	…	2.9	4.4		…	…	76.8	97.6
2750	Domestic appliances		…	…	78	93		…	…	9.9	9.8		…	…	240.4	300.9
2790	Other electrical equipment		…	…	75	151		…	…	3.6	6.0		…	…	72.5	120.0
281	General-purpose machinery		…	…	534	614		…	…	36.1	40.6		…	…	1027.2	1254.9
2811	Engines/turbines,excl.aircraft,vehicle engines		…	…	18c/	25		…	…	0.8c/	0.2		…	…	22.1c/	4.2
2812	Fluid power equipment		…	…	..c/	7		…	…	..c/	0.2		…	…	..c/	9.7
2813	Other pumps, compressors, taps and valves		…	…	65	66		…	…	7.5	6.6		…	…	281.5	243.1
2814	Bearings, gears, gearing and driving elements		…	…	85	64		…	…	4.7	2.6		…	…	125.2	61.5
2815	Ovens, furnaces and furnace burners		…	…	3	8		…	…	0.4	0.4		…	…	8.0	12.1
2816	Lifting and handling equipment		…	…	62	51		…	…	3.5	3.9		…	…	103.9	93.4
2817	Office machinery, excl.computers, etc.		…	…	4	14		…	…	1.5	1.2		…	…	24.0	20.8
2818	Power-driven hand tools		…	…	6	14		…	…	1.3	1.7		…	…	38.9	54.5
2819	Other general-purpose machinery		…	…	291	365		…	…	16.3	23.8		…	…	423.6	755.6
282	Special-purpose machinery		…	…	679	668		…	…	27.0	30.3		…	…	685.7	721.0
2821	Agricultural and forestry machinery		…	…	78	65		…	…	2.3	1.7		…	…	51.4	45.9
2822	Metal-forming machinery and machine tools		…	…	278	324		…	…	14.5	17.9		…	…	380.1	412.3
2823	Machinery for metallurgy		…	…	19	14		…	…	0.3	0.3		…	…	5.6	7.6
2824	Mining, quarrying and construction machinery		…	…	53	47		…	…	1.6	1.4		…	…	64.8	49.3

Code							
2825	Food/beverage/tobacco processing machinery	25	30	0.8	0.9	21.7	23.9
2826	Textile/apparel/leather production machinery	13	15	0.2	0.7	4.5	18.3
2829	Other special-purpose machinery	213	173	7.3	7.4	157.5	163.7
2910	Motor vehicles	28	37	24.7	27.4	736.3	877.9
2920	Automobile bodies, trailers and semi-trailers	73	99	3.6	4.5	89.7	113.8
2930	Parts and accessories for motor vehicles	283	375	30.1	41.8	690.1	936.5
301	Building of ships and boats	137	264	14.1	18.0	546.4	515.7
3011	Building of ships and floating structures	117	236	13.8	17.2	542.7	496.2
3012	Building of pleasure and sporting boats	20	28	0.2	0.8	3.8	19.5
3020	Railway locomotives and rolling stock	12d/	16d/	4.1d/	5.1d/	110.8d/	177.5d/
3030	Air and spacecraft and related machinery	...d/	...d/	...d/	...d/	...d/	...d/
3040	Military fighting vehicles	...d/	...d/	...d/	...d/	...d/	...d/
309	Transport equipment n.e.c.	66	89	9.6	12.3	237.4	295.1
3091	Motorcycles	43	55	6.7	8.1	175.4	210.2
3092	Bicycles and invalid carriages	23e/	31	2.9e/	4.1	62.0e/	82.7
3099	Other transport equipment n.e.c.	...e/	3	...e/	0.1	...e/	2.2
3100	Furniture	1928	1932	81.8	78.7	1293.5	1340.9
321	Jewellery, bijouterie and related articles	326	232	4.7	3.3	111.4	74.8
3211	Jewellery and related articles	306	211	4.6	3.1	108.9	71.3
3212	Imitation jewellery and related articles	20	21	0.1	0.2	2.4	3.5
3220	Musical instruments	3	6	-	-	0.2	0.4
3230	Sports goods	19	26	1.5	1.5	27.8	39.2
3240	Games and toys	21	22	4.2	4.7	65.2	78.5
3250	Medical and dental instruments and supplies	95	159	4.0	3.8	70.3	79.7
3290	Other manufacturing n.e.c.	566	574	13.2	13.2	244.5	242.4
331	Repair of fabricated metal products/machinery	267	894	5.0	12.5	189.7	288.3
3311	Repair of fabricated metal products	45	71	0.5	0.9	14.4	20.4
3312	Repair of machinery	137	630f/	1.1	5.9f/	22.8	118.0f/
3313	Repair of electronic and optical equipment	...f/	...f/	...f/	...f/	...f/	...f/
3314	Repair of electrical equipment	20	64	0.3	0.6	6.7	12.3
3315	Repair of transport equip., excl. motor vehicles	45	86	2.8	4.5	141.8	125.3
3319	Repair of other equipment	20	43	0.2	0.6	4.0	12.4
3320	Installation of industrial machinery/equipment	12	23	0.1	0.5	2.3	11.8
C	Total manufacturing	30607g/	39669g/	1672.4g/	1782.0g/	39397.5g/	43744.8g/

a/ 1102 includes 1103.
b/ 2513 includes 2520.
c/ 2811 includes 2812.
d/ 3020 includes 3030 and 3040.
e/ 3092 includes 3099.
f/ 3312 includes 3313.
g/ Sum of available data.

Malaysia

ISIC	Industry	Output Note	2007	2008	2009	2010	Value added Note	2007	2008	2009	2010	GFCF Note	2009	2010
			(millions of Malaysian Ringgits)					(millions of Malaysian Ringgits)					(millions of Malaysian Ringgits)	
1010	Processing/preserving of meat		...	...	2672	2665		...	...	346	373		65	88
1020	Processing/preserving of fish, etc.		...	...	2143	2824		...	...	318	573		52	73
1030	Processing/preserving of fruit,vegetables		...	...	618	707		...	...	115	135		18	26
1040	Vegetable and animal oils and fats		...	...	86298	103516		...	...	7431	9649		1422	881
1050	Dairy products		...	...	5630	6317		...	...	995	1012		338	93
106	Grain mill products,starches and starch products		...	...	4523	4380		...	...	549	700		-12	104
1061	Grain mill products		...	...	4419	4300		...	...	533	685		-14	100
1062	Starches and starch products		...	...	103	80		...	...	17	14		2	3
107	Other food products		...	...	16960	21470		...	...	3834	4806		425	776
1071	Bakery products		...	...	4834	5322		...	...	1400	1529		219	258
1072	Sugar		...	...	2719	3580		...	...	534	665		-19	139
1073	Cocoa, chocolate and sugar confectionery		...	...	4472	5816		...	...	598	733		51	95
1074	Macaroni, noodles, couscous, etc.		...	...	761	884		...	...	191	218		31	50
1075	Prepared meals and dishes		...	...	938	1049		...	...	255	258		16	20
1079	Other food products n.e.c.		...	...	3236	4818		...	...	856	1405		127	216
1080	Prepared animal feeds		...	...	4258	4765		...	...	393	623		16	43
1101	Distilling, rectifying and blending of spirits		...	...	220	216		...	...	53	56		5	-
1102	Wines		...	...	1429a/	1880a/		...	...	760a/	826a/		-a/	38a/
1103	Malt liquors and malt		...	...	...a/	...a/		...	...	...a/	...a/		...a/	...a/
1104	Soft drinks,mineral waters,other bottled waters		...	...	2968	4356		...	...	448	680		36	279
1200	Tobacco products		...	...	2178	2162		...	...	823	988		180	25
131	Spinning, weaving and finishing of textiles		...	...	5008	4739		...	...	1191	1083		80	105
1311	Preparation and spinning of textile fibres		...	...	699	746		...	...	169	192		9	32
1312	Weaving of textiles		...	...	2809	2929		...	...	620	650		36	-1
1313	Finishing of textiles		...	...	1500	1065		...	...	401	240		36	74
139	Other textiles		...	...	1852	1918		...	...	445	501		51	48
1391	Knitted and crocheted fabrics		...	...	750	822		...	...	150	142		16	7
1392	Made-up textile articles, except apparel		...	...	535	620		...	...	121	209		9	9
1393	Carpets and rugs		...	...	168	160		...	...	43	43		14	1
1394	Cordage, rope, twine and netting		...	...	135	129		...	...	36	34		3	24
1399	Other textiles n.e.c.		...	...	264	187		...	...	94	73		9	7
1410	Wearing apparel, except fur apparel		...	...	4371	4634		...	...	1219	1404		26	43
1420	Articles of fur		...	...	22	20		...	...	7	10		1	-
1430	Knitted and crocheted apparel		...	...	80	82		...	...	22	20		1	-
151	Leather;luggage,handbags,saddlery,harness;fur		...	...	211	216		...	...	59	63		13	3
1511	Tanning/dressing of leather; dressing of fur		...	...	40	37		...	...	3	3		1	1
1512	Luggage,handbags,etc.;saddlery/harness		...	...	170	179		...	...	57	60		12	2
1520	Footwear		...	...	818	772		...	...	228	239		32	11
1610	Sawmilling and planing of wood		...	...	4372	5238		...	...	833	1070		19	75
162	Wood products, cork, straw, plaiting materials		...	...	12036	13631		...	...	2553	3576		487	-34

1621	Veneer sheets and wood-based panels	9976	11255	2053	2948	449	-69
1622	Builders' carpentry and joinery	1523	1414	340	341	26	26
1623	Wooden containers	215	517	69	130	3	4
1629	Other wood products;articles of cork,straw	322	444	92	158	8	5
1701	Pulp, paper and paperboard	2215	2415	513	629	94	132
1702	Corrugated paper and paperboard	4000	5122	859	1316	267	270
1709	Other articles of paper and paperboard	3134	3702	701	832	71	168
181	Printing and service activities related to printing	4343	7238	1418	2574	165	261
1811	Printing	2808	5675	900	2041	115	228
1812	Service activities related to printing	1535	1563	518	533	50	34
1820	Reproduction of recorded media	26	21	7	4	2	-
1910	Coke oven products	91938	113003	20962	29889	380	4624
1920	Refined petroleum products	51546	56560	12870	15480	1780	2062
201	Basic chemicals,fertilizers, etc.	31406	34391	9039	11922	1282	1703
2011	Basic chemicals	4500	3068	914	715	226	32
2012	Fertilizers and nitrogen compounds	15640	19102	2916	2843	272	328
2013	Plastics and synthetic rubber in primary forms	11132	16322	2567	3328	149	298
202	Other chemical products	890	1421	173	351	3	12
2021	Pesticides and other agrochemical products	3141	3905	790	854	58	62
2022	Paints,varnishes;printing ink and mastics	2500	3313	652	736	41	39
2023	Soap,cleaning and cosmetic preparations	4603	7683	951	1387	47	185
2029	Other chemical products n.e.c.	575	326	98	24	14	5
2030	Man-made fibres	2022	2720	746	885	195	137
2100	Pharmaceuticals,medicinal chemicals, etc.	24335	32140	4642	5689	659	752
221	Rubber products	2770	2948	470	534	77	93
2211	Rubber tyres and tubes	21566	29192	4172	5155	582	660
2219	Other rubber products	21816	23027	5413	5853	637	695
2220	Plastics products	3645	5265	919	1664	62	1914
2310	Glass and glass products	19289	19905	5452	5296	765	870
239	Non-metallic mineral products n.e.c.	211	221	65	72	-7	8
2391	Refractory products	3180	2492	1113	892	171	292
2392	Clay building materials	1048	649	387	208	165	12
2393	Other porcelain and ceramic products	5631	5920	1841	1984	304	257
2394	Cement, lime and plaster	6942	7801	1484	1562	77	220
2395	Articles of concrete, cement and plaster	230	287	80	94	3	11
2396	Cutting, shaping and finishing of stone	2047	2536	482	484	53	70
2399	Other non-metallic mineral products n.e.c.	30070	28599	3507	4554	1030	448
2410	Basic iron and steel	13351	16023	1607	2278	20	406
2420	Basic precious and other non-ferrous metals	1168	1490	346	439	42	61
243	Casting of metals	956	1133	283	347	36	38
2431	Casting of iron and steel	212	357	63	92	6	23
2432	Casting of non-ferrous metals	...	...	...	...	...	...
251	Struct.metal products, tanks, reservoirs	6716	6097	1545	1653	225	224
2511	Structural metal products	4151	4309	1024	1204	167	167
2512	Tanks, reservoirs and containers of metal	2139	1593	437	385	55	54

continued

Malaysia

ISIC	Industry	Output Note	Output 2007	Output 2008	Output 2009	Output 2010	VA Note	VA 2007	VA 2008	VA 2009	VA 2010	GFCF Note	GFCF 2009	GFCF 2010
			(millions of Malaysian Ringgits)					(millions of Malaysian Ringgits)					(millions of Malaysian Ringgits)	
2513	Steam generators, excl. hot water boilers		...	...	426b/	195b/		...	...	85b/	64b/		3b/	3b/
2520	Weapons and ammunition		...	...	...b/	...b/		...	...	...b/	...b/		...b/	...b/
259	Other metal products;metal working services		...	...	16990	18648		...	...	4082	4338		489	374
2591	Forging,pressing,stamping,roll-forming of metal		...	...	2461	2028		...	...	714	569		89	51
2592	Treatment and coating of metals; machining		...	...	1602	1696		...	...	575	460		29	-
2593	Cutlery, hand tools and general hardware		...	...	985	1501		...	...	245	441		35	56
2599	Other fabricated metal products n.e.c.		...	...	11942	13424		...	...	2548	2868		336	266
2610	Electronic components and boards		...	...	75172	90910		...	...	13893	18003		1091	6270
2620	Computers and peripheral equipment		...	...	38411	30114		...	...	5696	5567		1255	2226
2630	Communication equipment		...	...	10308	11421		...	...	1941	1977		129	144
2640	Consumer electronics		...	...	31175	40260		...	...	3528	5290		1006	724
265	Measuring,testing equipment; watches, etc.		...	...	1697	2506		...	...	463	558		35	118
2651	Measuring/testing/navigating equipment,etc.		...	...	438	1061		...	...	129	259		9	81
2652	Watches and clocks		...	...	1260	1444		...	...	334	298		26	38
2660	Irradiation/electromedical equipment,etc.		...	...	1365	1517		...	...	571	596		120	65
2670	Optical instruments and photographic equipment		...	...	2713	2966		...	...	543	452		115	112
2680	Magnetic and optical media		...	...	391	1045		...	...	104	148		24	21
2710	Electric motors,generators,transformers,etc.		...	...	6527	6863		...	...	1528	1433		139	109
2720	Batteries and accumulators		...	...	697	684		...	...	152	183		12	35
273	Wiring and wiring devices		...	...	7487	8681		...	...	830	1114		154	156
2731	Fibre optic cables		...	...	165	266		...	...	42	76		5	9
2732	Other electronic and electric wires and cables		...	...	7247	8254		...	...	761	995		147	173
2733	Wiring devices		...	...	74	160		...	...	27	43		2	-26
2740	Electric lighting equipment		...	...	731	816		...	...	206	244		48	42
2750	Domestic appliances		...	...	3649	4025		...	...	763	627		93	151
2790	Other electrical equipment		...	...	640	828		...	...	148	251		13	6
281	General-purpose machinery		...	...	12836	13814		...	...	2777	3065		-1258	-214
2811	Engines/turbines,excl.aircraft,vehicle engines		...	...	230c/	27		...	...	48c/	9		12c/	-
2812	Fluid power equipment		...	...	...c/	209		...	...	...c/	31		...c/	-
2813	Other pumps, compressors, taps and valves		...	...	3070	2551		...	...	502	459		-1577	-718
2814	Bearings, gears, gearing and driving elements		...	...	1137	777		...	...	383	363		33	47
2815	Ovens, furnaces and furnace burners		...	...	126	62		...	...	23	25		10	1
2816	Lifting and handling equipment		...	...	1250	1056		...	...	272	195		33	25
2817	Office machinery, excl.computers,etc.		...	...	249	283		...	...	46	50		2	3
2818	Power-driven hand tools		...	...	660	934		...	...	108	108		22	27
2819	Other general-purpose machinery		...	...	6114	7915		...	...	1395	1825		207	401
282	Special-purpose machinery		...	...	5392	6457		...	...	1590	1864		161	114
2821	Agricultural and forestry machinery		...	...	383	743		...	...	107	109		20	7
2822	Metal-forming machinery and machine tools		...	...	2723	3096		...	...	849	971		82	31
2823	Machinery for metallurgy		...	...	35	46		...	...	13	14		2	-
2824	Mining, quarrying and construction machinery		...	...	843	614		...	...	209	166		14	26

Code	Description	120	120	37	46	3	4
2825	Food/beverage/tobacco processing machinery	30	166	12	56	-	20
2826	Textile/apparel/leather production machinery	1259	1672	364	502	40	26
2829	Other special-purpose machinery	20014	22506	2749	3503	181	461
2910	Motor vehicles	1036	980	248	254	98	11
2920	Automobile bodies, trailers and semi-trailers	7613	10855	2013	2764	213	232
2930	Parts and accessories for motor vehicles	12505	8369	2521	1312	757	309
301	Building of ships and boats	12485	8266	2515	1287	757	305
3011	Building of ships and floating structures	21	102	7	24	-	3
3012	Building of pleasure and sporting boats	...	...	...	...	...	...
3020	Railway locomotives and rolling stock	831d/	2389d/	234d/	597d/	41d/	18d/
3030	Air and spacecraft and related machinery	...d/	...d/	...d/	...d/	...d/	...d/
3040	Military fighting vehicles	...d/	...d/	...d/	...d/	...d/	...d/
309	Transport equipment n.e.c.	3908	4843	871	930	78	61
3091	Motorcycles	2760	3411	614	623	34	46
3092	Bicycles and invalid carriages	1148e/	1407	258e/	302	44e/	15
3099	Other transport equipment n.e.c.	...e/	25	...e/	5	...e/	-
3100	Furniture	9682	10292	2423	2882	160	181
321	Jewellery, bijouterie and related articles	3465	2508	345	211	17	10
3211	Jewellery and related articles	3459	2480	341	206	17	10
3212	Imitation jewellery and related articles	6	28	3	5	-	-
3220	Musical instruments	1	3	51	57	14	19
3230	Sports goods	213	237	110	131	6	11
3240	Games and toys	285	340	206	175	25	24
3250	Medical and dental instruments and supplies	507	438	717	723	53	89
3290	Other manufacturing n.e.c.	1926	2148	379	628	10	56
331	Repair of fabricated metal products/machinery	1878	2428	25	52	3	5
3311	Repair of fabricated metal products	69	111	39	...	5	...
3312	Repair of machinery	101	574f/	...	217f/	...	14f/
3313	Repair of electronic and optical equipment	...f/	...f/	...	...f/	...	...f/
3314	Repair of electrical equipment	23	64	10	315	2	36
3315	Repair of transport equip., excl. motor vehicles	1664	1619	300	23	-	-
3319	Repair of other equipment	20	61	5	21	-	-
3320	Installation of industrial machinery/equipment	8	121	3	...	...	...
C	Total manufacturing	730043g/	836494g/	138481g/	170673g/	15094g/	279941g/

a/ 1102 includes 1103.
b/ 2513 includes 2520.
c/ 2811 includes 2812.
d/ 3020 includes 3030 and 3040.
e/ 3092 includes 3099.
f/ 3312 includes 3313.
g/ Sum of available data.

Malaysia

Index numbers of industrial production

ISIC Revision 3

(2005=100)

ISIC	Industry	Note	1999	2000	2001	2002	2003	2004	2005	2006	2007	2008	2009	2010
15	Food and beverages		62	71	76	80	90	93	100	105	111	122	123	129
16	Tobacco products		64	113	106	95	99	103	100	96	99	94	88	88
17	Textiles		125	127	121	116	111	104	100	97	95	103	88	88
18	Wearing apparel, fur		107	129	112	101	103	85	100	115	113	103	80	83
19	Leather, leather products and footwear		31	57	80	83	58	87	100	63	56	65	84	88
20	Wood products (excl. furniture)		87	91	92	87	87	98	100	101	99	97	63	64
21	Paper and paper products		64	73	75	84	91	93	100	113	129	124	84	94
22	Printing and publishing		...	...	...	...	...	...	100	112	129	116	102	112
23	Coke,refined petroleum products,nuclear fuel		63	76	93	88	89	90	100	108	111	116	131	145
24	Chemicals and chemical products		67	72	73	73	84	94	100	106	107	117	117	114
25	Rubber and plastics products		58	68	60	63	79	90	100	106	107	102	101	116
26	Non-metallic mineral products		68	82	89	94	103	98	100	119	125	127	122	132
27	Basic metals		90	94	94	96	107	106	100	103	105	115	99	122
28	Fabricated metal products		54	72	75	76	81	105	100	106	123	119	92	111
29	Machinery and equipment n.e.c.		71	103	106	113	119	115	100	122	138	146	145	166
30	Office, accounting and computing machinery		129	169	147	114	101	93	100	98	107	111	88	118
31	Electrical machinery and apparatus		56	79	65	71	78	93	100	131	133	126	85	68
32	Radio,television and communication equipment		57	80	66	72	80	96	100	109	116	118	90	131
33	Medical, precision and optical instruments		83	95	76	82	89	103	100	109	103	98	81	104
34	Motor vehicles, trailers, semi-trailers		59	71	84	89	84	92	100	100	110	102	129	115
35	Other transport equipment		...	...	...	...	...	97	100	96	94	115	104	128
36	Furniture; manufacturing n.e.c.		...	...	...	...	...	...	100	91	95	123	88	144
37	Recycling		...	...	...	...	...	...	100	94	89	77	58	64
D	Total manufacturing		62	77	72	76	83	95	100	109	112	112	101	112

Mauritius

Supplier of information:
Central Statistical Office, Port-Louis.

Basic source of data:
Annual sample survey; administrative source (quarterly)

Major deviations from ISIC (Revision 3):
Data are collected under the National Classification of Industrial Activities (NSIC) and correspond approximately with ISIC (Revision 3).

Reference period:
Calendar year.

Scope:
Establishments with 10 or more persons engaged.

Method of data collection:
Mail questionnaires.

Type of enumeration:
Sample survey; however, data for number of establishments and number of employees are a result of complete enumeration.

Adjusted for non-response:
Yes.

Concepts and definitions of variables:
Output is at basic prices.
Value added is at basic prices.

Related national publications:
Digest of Industrial Statistics; Digest of Labour Statistics, both published by the Central Statistical Office, Port-Louis.

Mauritius

ISIC Revision 3		Number of establishments (number)					Number of employees (number)					Wages and salaries paid to employees (millions of Mauritian Rupees)				
ISIC	Industry	Note	2007	2008	2009	2010	Note	2007	2008	2009	2010	Note	2007	2008	2009	2010
151	Processed meat,fish,fruit,vegetables,fats	a/	115	116	116	110	a/	11109	10894	11090	10636	a/	1902.6	2704.8	2494.0	2493.5
1511	Processing/preserving of meat		...	...	...	...		...	...	...	...		...	...	...	...
1512	Processing/preserving of fish		...	...	...	...		...	...	...	...		...	...	...	...
1513	Processing/preserving of fruit & vegetables		...	...	...	...		...	...	...	...		...	...	...	...
1514	Vegetable and animal oils and fats		...	...	...	...		...	...	...	...		...	...	...	...
1520	Dairy products		...	...	...	...		...	...	...	...		...	...	...	...
153	Grain mill products; starches; animal feeds		...	...	...	...		...	...	...	...		...	...	...	...
1531	Grain mill products	a/	...	...	...	...	a/	...	...	...	...	a/	...	...	...	...
1532	Starches and starch products	a/	...	...	...	...	a/	...	...	...	...	a/	...	...	...	...
1533	Prepared animal feeds		...	...	...	...		...	...	...	...		...	...	...	...
154	Other food products	a/	...	...	...	...	a/	...	...	...	...	a/	...	...	...	...
1541	Bakery products		...	...	...	...		...	...	...	...		...	...	...	...
1542	Sugar		...	...	...	...		...	...	...	...		...	...	...	...
1543	Cocoa, chocolate and sugar confectionery		...	...	...	...		...	...	...	...		...	...	...	...
1544	Macaroni, noodles & similar products		...	...	...	...		...	...	...	...		...	...	...	...
1549	Other food products n.e.c.		...	...	...	...		...	...	...	...		...	...	...	...
155	Beverages	b/	16	16	16	16	b/	2703	2698	2576	2562	b/	1226.3	1359.0	1478.7	1543.5
1551	Distilling, rectifying & blending of spirits		...	...	...	...		...	...	...	...		...	...	...	...
1552	Wines		...	...	...	...		...	...	...	...		...	...	...	...
1553	Malt liquors and malt		...	...	...	...		...	...	...	...		...	...	...	...
1554	Soft drinks; mineral waters		...	...	...	...		...	...	...	...		...	...	...	...
1600	Tobacco products	b/	...	...	...	...	b/	...	...	...	...	b/	...	...	...	...
171	Spinning, weaving and finishing of textiles		...	...	...	...		...	...	...	...		...	...	...	...
1711	Textile fibre preparation; textile weaving	c/	55	52	45	41	c/	7122	6974	5601	5296	c/	959.9	1140.8	1075.2	1172.4
1712	Finishing of textiles		...	...	...	...		...	...	...	...		...	...	...	...
172	Other textiles	c/	...	...	...	...	c/	...	...	...	...	c/	...	...	...	...
1721	Made-up textile articles, except apparel		...	...	...	...		...	...	...	...		...	...	...	...
1722	Carpets and rugs		...	...	...	...		...	...	...	...		...	...	...	...
1723	Cordage, rope, twine and netting		...	...	...	...		...	...	...	...		...	...	...	...
1729	Other textiles n.e.c.		...	...	...	...		...	...	...	...		...	...	...	...
1730	Knitted and crocheted fabrics and articles	c/	...	...	...	...	c/	...	...	...	...	c/	...	...	...	...
1810	Wearing apparel, except fur apparel	d/	229	233	204	182	d/	51149	50924	42355	41192	d/	5728.6	6512.6	7021.1	7302.9
1820	Dressing & dyeing of fur; processing of fur	d/	...	...	...	...	d/	...	...	...	...	d/	...	...	...	...
191	Tanning, dressing and processing of leather	e/	16	17	17	14	e/	962	1022	931	732	e/	121.6	116.0	80.3	95.8
1911	Tanning and dressing of leather		...	...	...	...		...	...	...	...		...	...	...	...
1912	Luggage, handbags, etc.; saddlery & harness	e/	...	...	...	...	e/	...	...	...	...	e/	...	...	...	...
1920	Footwear	e/	...	...	...	...	e/	...	...	...	...	e/	...	...	...	...
2010	Sawmilling and planing of wood		...	...	...	...		...	...	...	...		...	...	...	...
202	Products of wood, cork, straw, etc.	f/	11	14	15	15	f/	599	613	586	563	f/	94.0	69.2	60.1	71.1
2021	Veneer sheets, plywood, particle board, etc.	f/	...	...	...	...	f/	...	...	...	...	f/	...	...	...	...
2022	Builders' carpentry and joinery		...	...	...	...		...	...	...	...		...	...	...	...
2023	Wooden containers		...	...	...	...		...	...	...	...		...	...	...	...
2029	Other wood products; articles of cork/straw		...	...	...	...		...	...	...	...		...	...	...	...
210	Paper and paper products		...	...	...	...		...	...	...	...		...	...	...	...
2101	Pulp, paper and paperboard		19	19	18	17		624	672	645	652		157.9	174.6	219.2	261.0
2102	Corrugated paper and paperboard		...	...	...	...		...	...	...	...		...	...	...	...
2109	Other articles of paper and paperboard		...	...	...	...		...	...	...	...		...	...	...	...
221	Publishing	g/	46	46	43	44	g/	2765	2860	2506	2736	g/	786.6	870.9	920.8	937.3
2211	Publishing of books and other publications		...	...	...	...		...	...	...	...		...	...	...	...
2212	Publishing of newspapers, journals, etc.		...	...	...	...		...	...	...	...		...	...	...	...
2213	Publishing of recorded media		...	...	...	...		...	...	...	...		...	...	...	...
2219	Other publishing		...	...	...	...		...	...	...	...		...	...	...	...

Code	Description																
222	Printing and related service activities																
2221	Printing																
2222	Service activities related to printing	g/					g/					g/				
2230	Reproduction of recorded media	g/	37	37	36	33	g/	2319	2244	2357	2293	g/	507.8	605.8	604.7	627.0
2310	Coke oven products	h/					h/					h/				
2320	Refined petroleum products	h/					h/					h/				
2330	Processing of nuclear fuel	h/					h/					h/				
241	Basic chemicals																
2411	Basic chemicals, except fertilizers																
2412	Fertilizers and nitrogen compounds																
2413	Plastics in primary forms; synthetic rubber	h/					h/					h/				
242	Other chemicals																
2421	Pesticides and other agro-chemical products																
2422	Paints, varnishes, printing ink and mastics																
2423	Pharmaceuticals, medicinal chemicals, etc.																
2424	Soap, cleaning & cosmetic preparations																
2429	Other chemical products n.e.c.	h/					h/					h/				
2430	Man-made fibres	i/	83	84	80	72	i/	3902	3982	3819	3520	i/	207.2	1091.0	1082.9	1185.8
251	Rubber products																
2511	Rubber tyres and tubes	i/					i/					i/				
2519	Other rubber products	i/					i/					i/				
2520	Plastic products	i/					i/					i/				
2610	Glass and glass products																
269	Non-metallic mineral products n.e.c.																
2691	Pottery, china and earthenware																
2692	Refractory ceramic products																
2693	Struct.non-refractory clay; ceramic products																
2694	Cement, lime and plaster																
2695	Articles of concrete, cement and plaster	j/					j/					j/				
2696	Cutting, shaping & finishing of stone	j/					j/					j/				
2699	Other non-metallic mineral products n.e.c.	j/	6	5	5	4	j/	443	395	388	225	j/	80.2	97.7	69.5	70.0
2710	Basic iron and steel																
2720	Basic precious and non-ferrous metals																
273	Casting of metals																
2731	Casting of iron and steel																
2732	Casting of non-ferrous metals	k/	42	45	45	49	k/	2476	2591	2539	2638	k/	557.4	476.7	461.0	463.3
281	Struct.metal products;tanks;steam generators																
2811	Structural metal products	k/					k/					k/				
2812	Tanks, reservoirs and containers of metal																
2813	Steam generators	k/					k/					k/				
289	Other metal products; metal working services																
2891	Metal forging/pressing/stamping/roll-forming																
2892	Treatment & coating of metals																
2893	Cutlery, hand tools and general hardware																
2899	Other fabricated metal products n.e.c.	m/	14	14	10	9	m/	598	495	451	435	m/	207.1	258.3	339.8	296.8
291	General purpose machinery	m/					m/					m/				
2911	Engines & turbines (not for transport equipment)																
2912	Pumps, compressors, taps and valves	m/					m/					m/				
2913	Bearings, gears, gearing & driving elements																
2914	Ovens, furnaces and furnace burners																
2915	Lifting and handling equipment																
2919	Other general purpose machinery																
292	Special purpose machinery																
2921	Agricultural and forestry machinery																
2922	Machine tools																
2923	Machinery for metallurgy																
2924	Machinery for mining & construction																
2925	Food/beverage/tobacco processing machinery																
2926	Machinery for textile, apparel and leather																
2927	Weapons and ammunition																
2929	Other special purpose machinery																

continued

Mauritius

Columns grouped as: **Number of establishments (number)**, **Number of employees (number)**, **Wages and salaries paid to employees (millions of Mauritian Rupees)**.

ISIC	Industry	Est. Note	Est. 2007	Est. 2008	Est. 2009	Est. 2010	Emp. Note	Emp. 2007	Emp. 2008	Emp. 2009	Emp. 2010	Wage Note	Wage 2007	Wage 2008	Wage 2009	Wage 2010
2930	Domestic appliances n.e.c.	m/	…	…	…	…	m/	…	…	…	…	m/	…	…	…	…
3000	Office, accounting and computing machinery	m/	…	…	…	…	m/	…	…	…	…	m/	…	…	…	…
3110	Electric motors, generators and transformers	n/	19	21	19	13	n/	667	777	757	588	n/	142.1	168.7	195.2	131.2
3120	Electricity distribution & control apparatus	n/	…	…	…	…	n/	…	…	…	…	n/	…	…	…	…
3130	Insulated wire and cable	n/	…	…	…	…	n/	…	…	…	…	n/	…	…	…	…
3140	Accumulators, primary cells and batteries	n/	…	…	…	…	n/	…	…	…	…	n/	…	…	…	…
3150	Lighting equipment and electric lamps	n/	…	…	…	…	n/	…	…	…	…	n/	…	…	…	…
3190	Other electrical equipment n.e.c.	n/	…	…	…	…	n/	…	…	…	…	n/	…	…	…	…
3210	Electronic valves, tubes, etc.	n/	…	…	…	…	n/	…	…	…	…	n/	…	…	…	…
3220	TV/radio transmitters; line comm. apparatus	n/	…	…	…	…	n/	…	…	…	…	n/	…	…	…	…
3230	TV and radio receivers and associated goods	n/	…	…	…	…	n/	…	…	…	…	n/	…	…	…	…
331	Medical, measuring, testing appliances, etc.	p/	15	15	15	13	p/	1706	1832	1579	1453	p/	79.1	299.1	231.3	224.6
3311	Medical, surgical and orthopaedic equipment		…	…	…	…		…	…	…	…		…	…	…	…
3312	Measuring/testing/navigating appliances,etc.		…	…	…	…		…	…	…	…		…	…	…	…
3313	Industrial process control equipment		…	…	…	…		…	…	…	…		…	…	…	…
3320	Optical instruments & photographic equipment	p/	…	…	…	…	p/	…	…	…	…	p/	…	…	…	…
3330	Watches and clocks	p/	…	…	…	…	p/	…	…	…	…	p/	…	…	…	…
3410	Motor vehicles	q/	9	9	10	8	q/	460	465	512	501	q/	236.0	61.3	70.9	67.0
3420	Automobile bodies, trailers & semi-trailers	q/	…	…	…	…	q/	…	…	…	…	q/	…	…	…	…
3430	Parts/accessories for automobiles	q/	…	…	…	…	q/	…	…	…	…	q/	…	…	…	…
351	Building and repairing of ships and boats	q/	…	…	…	…	q/	…	…	…	…	q/	…	…	…	…
3511	Building and repairing of ships		…	…	…	…		…	…	…	…		…	…	…	…
3512	Building/repairing of pleasure/sport. boats		…	…	…	…		…	…	…	…		…	…	…	…
3520	Railway/tramway locomotives & rolling stock		…	…	…	…		…	…	…	…		…	…	…	…
3530	Aircraft and spacecraft	q/	…	…	…	…	q/	…	…	…	…	q/	…	…	…	…
359	Transport equipment n.e.c.	q/	…	…	…	…	q/	…	…	…	…	q/	…	…	…	…
3591	Motorcycles	q/	…	…	…	…	q/	…	…	…	…	q/	…	…	…	…
3592	Bicycles and invalid carriages		…	…	…	…		…	…	…	…		…	…	…	…
3599	Other transport equipment n.e.c.		…	…	…	…		…	…	…	…		…	…	…	…
3610	Furniture		32	32	31	33		960	944	845	956	r/	1012.3	822.5	923.9	991.8
369	Manufacturing n.e.c.		64	66	64	55		3463	3432	3943	2841	r/				
3691	Jewellery and related articles	s/	41	45	41	32	s/	2150	2139	1797	1577	s/	…	…	…	…
3692	Musical instruments	s/	23	21	23	21	s/	1313	1293	2146	1189	s/	…	…	…	…
3693	Sports goods	s/	…	…	…	…	s/	…	…	…	…	s/	…	…	…	…
3694	Games and toys	s/	…	…	…	…	s/	…	…	…	…	s/	…	…	…	…
3699	Other manufacturing n.e.c.	s/	…	…	…	…	s/	…	…	…	…	s/	…	…	…	…
3710	Recycling of metal waste and scrap		…	…	…	…		…	…	…	…		…	…	…	…
3720	Recycling of non-metal waste and scrap		…	…	…	…		…	…	…	…		30.0	31.0	37.0	39.0
D	Total manufacturing		828	841	789	728		94027	93814	83480	79819		14786.0	16860.1	17365.9	17974.3

a/ 151 includes 1520, 153 and 154.
b/ 155 includes 1600.
c/ 171 includes 172 and 1730.
d/ 1810 includes 1820.
e/ 191 includes 1920.
f/ 2010 includes 202.
g/ 221 includes 222 and 2230.
h/ 2310 includes 2320, 2330, 241, 242 and 2430.
i/ 251 includes 2520, 2610 and 269.
j/ 2710 includes 2720 and 273.
k/ 281 includes 289.
m/ 291 includes 292, 2930 and 3000.
n/ 3110 includes 3120, 3130, 3140, 3150, 3190, 3210, 3220 and 3230.
p/ 331 includes 3320 and 3330.
q/ 3410 includes 3420, 3430, 351, 3520 and 359.
r/ 3610 includes 369.
s/ 3692 includes 3693, 3694 and 3699.

Mauritius

All monetary figures in millions of Mauritian Rupees. Output, Value added and Gross fixed capital formation (GFCF). A dotted entry (..) indicates data not available.

ISIC	Industry	Output Note	Output 2007	Output 2008	Output 2009	Output 2010	VA Note	VA 2007	VA 2008	VA 2009	VA 2010	GFCF Note	GFCF 2009	GFCF 2010
151	Processed meat,fish,fruit,vegetables,fats	a/	24946.7	38375.6	35598.1	35680.0	a/	8806.2	10377.4	10044.2	10057.7		..	..
1511	Processing/preserving of meat		..	..	..	..		..	..	..	..		..	..
1512	Processing/preserving of fish		..	..	..	..		..	..	..	..		..	..
1513	Processing/preserving of fruit & vegetables		..	..	..	..		..	..	..	..		..	..
1514	Vegetable and animal oils and fats	a/	..	..	..	..	a/	..	..	..	..		..	..
1520	Dairy products	a/	..	..	..	..	a/	..	..	..	..		..	..
153	Grain mill products; starches; animal feeds	a/	..	..	..	..	a/	..	..	..	..		..	..
1531	Grain mill products		..	..	..	..		..	..	..	..		..	..
1532	Starches and starch products		..	..	..	..		..	..	..	..		..	..
1533	Prepared animal feeds		..	..	..	..		..	..	..	..		..	..
154	Other food products		..	..	..	..		..	..	..	..		..	..
1541	Bakery products		..	..	..	..		..	..	..	..		..	..
1542	Sugar		..	..	..	..		..	..	..	..		..	..
1543	Cocoa, chocolate and sugar confectionery		..	..	..	..		..	..	..	..		..	..
1544	Macaroni, noodles & similar products		..	..	..	..		..	..	..	..		..	..
1549	Other food products n.e.c.	b/	8021.5	9984.2	10372.6	11093.3	b/	4595.0	5723.3	5938.1	6339.6		..	..
155	Beverages		..	..	..	..		..	..	..	..		..	..
1551	Distilling, rectifying & blending of spirits		..	..	..	..		..	..	..	..		..	..
1552	Wines		..	..	..	..		..	..	..	..		..	..
1553	Malt liquors and malt		..	..	..	..		..	..	..	..		..	..
1554	Soft drinks; mineral waters		..	..	..	..		..	..	..	..		..	..
1600	Tobacco products	b/	6444.7	6538.3	5833.8	6109.1	b/	2431.6	2363.3	2098.7	2207.3		..	..
171	Spinning, weaving and finishing of textiles	c/	..	..	..	..	c/	..	..	..	..		..	..
1711	Textile fibre preparation; textile weaving		..	..	..	..		..	..	..	..		..	..
1712	Finishing of textiles		..	..	..	..		..	..	..	..		..	..
172	Other textiles	c/	..	..	..	..	c/	..	..	..	..		..	..
1721	Made-up textile articles, except apparel		..	..	..	..		..	..	..	..		..	..
1722	Carpets and rugs		..	..	..	..		..	..	..	..		..	..
1723	Cordage, rope, twine and netting		..	..	..	..		..	..	..	..		..	..
1729	Other textiles n.e.c.		..	..	..	..		..	..	..	..		..	..
1730	Knitted and crocheted fabrics and articles	c/	..	..	..	..	c/	..	..	..	..		..	..
1810	Wearing apparel, except fur apparel	d/	30186.5	26332.3	26895.2	26053.8	d/	12260.6	10629.0	10838.8	10525.6		..	..
1820	Dressing & dyeing of fur; processing of fur	d/	917.1	557.7	383.5	431.5	d/	350.4	207.9	134.9	149.8		..	..
191	Tanning, dressing and processing of leather	e/	..	..	..	..	e/	..	..	..	..		..	..
1911	Tanning and dressing of leather		..	..	..	..		..	..	..	..		..	..
1912	Luggage, handbags, etc.: saddlery & harness		..	..	..	..		..	..	..	..		..	..
1920	Footwear	e/	..	..	..	..	e/	..	..	..	..		..	..
2010	Sawmilling and planing of wood	f/	835.0	664.1	634.9	700.5	f/	297.0	205.3	194.6	216.0		..	..
202	Products of wood, cork, straw, etc.		..	..	..	..		..	..	..	..		..	..
2021	Veneer sheets, plywood, particle board, etc.		..	..	..	..		..	..	..	..		..	..
2022	Builders' carpentry and joinery		..	..	..	..		..	..	..	..		..	..
2023	Wooden containers		..	..	..	..		..	..	..	..		..	..
2029	Other wood products; articles of cork/straw	f/	580.8	652.5	810.1	1043.9	f/	200.1	229.7	283.3	357.9		..	..
210	Paper and paper products		..	..	..	..		..	..	..	..		..	..
2101	Pulp, paper and paperboard		..	..	..	..		..	..	..	..		..	..
2102	Corrugated paper and paperboard		..	..	..	..		..	..	..	..		..	..
2109	Other articles of paper and paperboard	g/	3332.3	3748.8	3847.3	4103.5	g/	1747.4	1928.1	1980.0	2111.9		..	..
221	Publishing		..	..	..	..		..	..	..	..		..	..
2211	Publishing of books and other publications		..	..	..	..		..	..	..	..		..	..
2212	Publishing of newspapers, journals, etc.		..	..	..	..		..	..	..	..		..	..
2213	Publishing of recorded media		..	..	..	..		..	..	..	..		..	..
2219	Other publishing		..	..	..	..		..	..	..	..		..	..

continued

Mauritius

ISIC	Industry	Note	Output (millions of Mauritian Rupees) 2007	2008	2009	2010	Note	Value added (millions of Mauritian Rupees) 2007	2008	2009	2010	Gross fixed capital formation (millions of Mauritian Rupees) 2009	2010
222	Printing and related service activities	g/	...	...	...	...	g/	...	...	...	...	...	...
2221	Printing		...	...	...	...		...	...	...	...	...	...
2222	Service activities related to printing		...	...	...	...		...	...	...	...	...	...
2230	Reproduction of recorded media	g/	...	...	...	...	g/	...	...	...	...	...	...
2310	Coke oven products	h/	...	...	...	...	h/	...	...	...	...	...	...
2320	Refined petroleum products	h/	4697.6	61416.5	5817.7	6221.6	h/	1518.9	1964.2	1938.1	2052.7	...	...
2330	Processing of nuclear fuel	h/	...	...	...	...	h/	...	...	...	...	...	...
241	Basic chemicals		...	...	...	...		...	...	...	...	...	...
2411	Basic chemicals, except fertilizers	h/	...	...	...	...	h/	...	...	...	...	...	...
2412	Fertilizers and nitrogen compounds		...	...	...	...		...	...	...	...	...	...
2413	Plastics in primary forms; synthetic rubber		...	...	...	...		...	...	...	...	...	...
242	Other chemicals		...	...	...	...		...	...	...	...	...	...
2421	Pesticides and other agro-chemical products		...	...	...	...		...	...	...	...	...	...
2422	Paints, varnishes, printing ink and mastics		...	...	...	...		...	...	...	...	...	...
2423	Pharmaceuticals, medicinal chemicals, etc.		...	...	...	...		...	...	...	...	...	...
2424	Soap, cleaning & cosmetic preparations	h/	...	...	...	...	h/	...	...	...	...	...	...
2429	Other chemical products n.e.c.		...	...	...	...		...	...	...	...	...	...
2430	Man-made fibres	h/	...	...	...	...	h/	...	...	...	...	...	...
251	Rubber products	i/	8046.8	10319.0	9740.5	10797.8	i/	2761.9	3482.2	3289.4	3640.9	...	...
2511	Rubber tyres and tubes		...	...	...	...		...	...	...	...	...	...
2519	Other rubber products		...	...	...	...		...	...	...	...	...	...
2520	Plastic products	i/	...	...	...	...	i/	...	...	...	...	...	...
2610	Glass and glass products	i/	...	...	...	...	i/	...	...	...	...	...	...
269	Non-metallic mineral products n.e.c.	i/	...	...	...	...	i/	...	...	...	...	...	...
2691	Pottery, china and earthenware		...	...	...	...		...	...	...	...	...	...
2692	Refractory ceramic products		...	...	...	...		...	...	...	...	...	...
2693	Struct.non-refractory clay; ceramic products		...	...	...	...		...	...	...	...	...	...
2694	Cement, lime and plaster		...	...	...	...		...	...	...	...	...	...
2695	Articles of concrete, cement and plaster		...	...	...	...		...	...	...	...	...	...
2696	Cutting, shaping & finishing of stone		...	...	...	...		...	...	...	...	...	...
2699	Other non-metallic mineral products n.e.c.		...	...	...	...		...	...	...	...	...	...
2710	Basic iron and steel	j/	1025.9	1375.8	934.9	969.0	j/	234.1	313.9	213.3	221.1	...	...
2720	Basic precious and non-ferrous metals	j/	...	...	...	...	j/	...	...	...	...	...	...
273	Casting of metals	j/	...	...	...	...	j/	...	...	...	...	...	...
2731	Casting of iron and steel		...	...	...	...		...	...	...	...	...	...
2732	Casting of non-ferrous metals		...	...	...	...		...	...	...	...	...	...
281	Struct.metal products;tanks;steam generators	k/	4339.4	2735.5	2510.8	2540.2	k/	1798.0	1134.0	1037.7	1053.9	...	...
2811	Structural metal products		...	...	...	...		...	...	...	...	...	...
2812	Tanks, reservoirs and containers of metal		...	...	...	...		...	...	...	...	...	...
2813	Steam generators		...	...	...	...		...	...	...	...	...	...
289	Other metal products; metal working services	k/	...	...	...	...	k/	...	...	...	...	...	...
2891	Metal forging/pressing/stamping/roll-forming		...	...	...	...		...	...	...	...	...	...
2892	Treatment & coating of metals		...	...	...	...		...	...	...	...	...	...
2893	Cutlery, hand tools and general hardware		...	...	...	...		...	...	...	...	...	...
2899	Other fabricated metal products n.e.c.		...	...	...	...		...	...	...	...	...	...
291	General purpose machinery	m/	940.3	1113.0	1378.1	1225.2	m/	302.8	363.7	454.6	404.2	...	...
2911	Engines & turbines (not for transport equipment)		...	...	...	...		...	...	...	...	...	...
2912	Pumps, compressors, taps and valves		...	...	...	...		...	...	...	...	...	...
2913	Bearings, gears, gearing & driving elements		...	...	...	...		...	...	...	...	...	...
2914	Ovens, furnaces and furnace burners		...	...	...	...		...	...	...	...	...	...
2915	Lifting and handling equipment		...	...	...	...		...	...	...	...	...	...
2919	Other general purpose machinery		...	...	...	...		...	...	...	...	...	...

Code	Description	Note	1	2	3	4	5	6	7	8	9	10
292	Special purpose machinery	m/										
2921	Agricultural and forestry machinery											
2922	Machine tools											
2923	Machinery for metallurgy											
2924	Machinery for mining & construction											
2925	Food/beverage/tobacco processing machinery											
2926	Machinery for textile, apparel and leather											
2927	Weapons and ammunition											
2929	Other special purpose machinery											
2930	Domestic appliances n.e.c.	m/										
3000	Office, accounting and computing machinery	m/			306.5	429.9	390.4	331.6	1423.8	1828.0	1716.2	1436.2
3110	Electric motors, generators and transformers	n/										
3120	Electricity distribution & control apparatus	n/										
3130	Insulated wire and cable	n/										
3140	Accumulators, primary cells and batteries	n/										
3150	Lighting equipment and electric lamps	n/										
3190	Other electrical equipment n.e.c.	n/										
3210	Electronic valves, tubes, etc.	n/										
3220	TV/radio transmitters; line comm. apparatus	n/										
3230	TV and radio receivers and associated goods	n/										
331	Medical, measuring, testing appliances, etc.	p/			287.5	328.6	447.9	327.5	781.4p/	886.6p/		450.1p/
3311	Medical, surgical and orthopaedic equipment											
3312	Measuring/testing/navigating appliances, etc.											
3313	Industrial process control equipment											
3320	Optical instruments & photographic equipment	p/							..p/	..p/		
3330	Watches and clocks	p/			115.5	118.8	107.6	270.3	356.2	366.3	331.8	998.8
3410	Motor vehicles	q/										
3420	Automobile bodies, trailers & semi-trailers	q/										
3430	Parts/accessories for automobiles	q/										
351	Building and repairing of ships and boats	q/										
3511	Building and repairing of ships											
3512	Building/repairing of pleasure/sport. boats											
3520	Railway/tramway locomotives & rolling stock	q/										
3530	Aircraft and spacecraft	q/										
359	Transport equipment n.e.c.	q/										
3591	Motorcycles											
3592	Bicycles and invalid carriages											
3599	Other transport equipment n.e.c.											
3610	Furniture	r/			1550.9	1511.4	1425.3	3113.2	4088.3	3889.7	3730.0	6957.3
369	Manufacturing n.e.c.	r/										
3691	Jewellery and related articles											
3692	Musical instruments											
3693	Sports goods											
3694	Games and toys											
3699	Other manufacturing n.e.c.											
3710	Recycling of metal waste and scrap	s/			56.7	58.4	51.3	62.7	143.7	148.0	130.0	159.0
3720	Recycling of non-metal waste and scrap	s/										
D	Total manufacturing		7013.0	5161.0	41655.7	40892.8	41344.7	41409.3	113762.9	111876.1	169833.7	115771.9

a/ 151 includes 1520, 153 and 154.
b/ 155 includes 1600.
c/ 171 includes 172 and 1730.
d/ 1810 includes 1820.
e/ 191 includes 1920.
f/ 2010 includes 202.
g/ 221 includes 222 and 2230.
h/ 2310 includes 2320, 2330, 241, 242 and 2430.
i/ 251 includes 2520, 2610 and 269.
j/ 2710 includes 2720 and 273.
k/ 281 includes 289.
m/ 291 includes 292, 2930 and 3000.
n/ 3110 includes 3120, 3130, 3140, 3150, 3190, 3210, 3220 and 3230.
p/ 331 includes 3320 and 3330.
q/ 3410 includes 3420, 3430, 351, 3520, 3530 and 359.
r/ 3610 includes 369.
s/ 3710 includes 3720.

Mauritius

Index numbers of industrial production

ISIC Revision 3

(2005=100)

ISIC	Industry	Note	1999	2000	2001	2002	2003	2004	2005	2006	2007	2008	2009	2010
15	Food and beverages	a/	59	76	84	84	91	97	100	109	108	118	126	130
16	Tobacco products		...	...	...	...	...	...	...	...	...	...	...	...
17	Textiles		84	92	111	124	121	114	100	99	113	105	85	90
18	Wearing apparel, fur		155	163	165	146	132	117	100	102	107	109	113	111
19	Leather, leather products and footwear		92	93	92	90	118	116	100	107	154	153	108	157
20	Wood products (excl. furniture)		...	...	...	...	...	...	...	...	...	...	...	...
21	Paper and paper products		118	130	126	101	104	95	100	98	102	97	117	155
22	Printing and publishing		86	95	99	93	106	108	100	93	91	96	102	108
23	Coke,refined petroleum products,nuclear fuel													
24	Chemicals and chemical products		120	129	130	132	156	127	100	98	116	126	126	129
25	Rubber and plastics products		...	...	...	...	...	...	...	...	...	...	...	...
26	Non-metallic mineral products		86	93	101	120	122	112	100	96	104	101	94	102
27	Basic metals		94	99	104	122	111	136	100	135	94	99	84	88
28	Fabricated metal products	b/	32	33	33	35	43	76	100	116	123	126	131	129
29	Machinery and equipment n.e.c.	b/	...	...	...	...	...	...	...	...	...	...	...	...
30	Office, accounting and computing machinery		...	...	...	...	...	...	...	...	...	...	...	...
31	Electrical machinery and apparatus	c/	136	153	160	118	104	128	100	117	150	184	354	159
32	Radio,television and communication equipment	c/	...	...	...	...	...	...	...	...	...	...	...	...
33	Medical, precision and optical instruments		...	42	42	44	39	68	100	135	152	186	116	109
34	Motor vehicles, trailers, semi-trailers	d/	...	65	68	72	68	74	100	138	157	175	170	194
35	Other transport equipment	d/	...	...	...	...	...	...	...	...	...	...	...	...
36	Furniture; manufacturing n.e.c.		...	...	...	...	...	...	...	...	...	...	...	...
37	Recycling		...	...	...	...	...	...	...	...	...	...	...	...
D	Total manufacturing		98	107	112	109	109	108	100	104	105	109	111	114

a/ 15 excludes beverages.
b/ 28 includes 29.
c/ 31 includes 32.
d/ 34 includes 35.

Mexico

Concepts and definitions of variables:
Number of employees covers all permanent and temporary employees who, in the course of the reference year, worked within or outside the establishment, and who were managed or supervised by the establishment.
Wages and salaries covers all wages and salaries that the company has paid to staff during the reference year, as well as money in the form of social security benefits, employers' social security contributions and profit-sharing.
Output refers to gross output.

Related national publications:
None reported.

Supplier of information:
Instituto Nacional de Estadística y Geografía (INEGI), Aguascalientes.

Basic source of data:
Annual and monthly industrial survey; economic census.

Major deviations from ISIC (Revision 3):
Data presented in ISIC (Revision 3) were originally classified according to the North American Industry Classification System (NAICS).

Reference period:
Calendar year.

Scope:
Not reported.

Method of data collection:
The inquiry is conducted by mail and interviews.

Type of enumeration:
Not reported.

Adjusted for non-response:
No.

Mexico

ISIC	Industry	Est. Note	Est. 2007	Est. 2008	Est. 2009	Est. 2010	Emp. Note	Emp. 2007	Emp. 2008	Emp. 2009	Emp. 2010	Wage Note	Wage 2007	Wage 2008	Wage 2009	Wage 2010
				(number)					**(thousands)**					**(millions of Mexican Pesos)**		
151	Processed meat,fish,fruit,vegetables,fats		...		130545a/	130548a/		...	307.5a/	611.5a/	609.1a/		...	33098a/	42034a/	43917a/
1511	Processing/preserving of meat		...	141	138	138		...	55.1	55.8	55.9		...	4324	4587	4890
1512	Processing/preserving of fish		...	49	65	65		...	7.4	9.0	7.9		...	271	323	279
1513	Processing/preserving of fruit & vegetables		...	56	88	88		...	29.7	35.3	35.3		...	2449	2694	2921
1514	Vegetable and animal oils and fats		...	31	33	33		...	8.4	8.4	8.6		...	1261	1319	1416
1520	Dairy products		...	...	...a/	...a/		...	...a/	...a/	...a/		...	...a/	...a/	...a/
153	Grain mill products; starches; animal feeds		...	...	...a/	...a/		...	...a/	...a/	...a/		...	...a/	...a/	...a/
1531	Grain mill products		...					...					...			
1532	Starches and starch products		...	8	9	9		...	2.1	2.4	2.4		...	532	676	711
1533	Prepared animal feeds		...	117	114	114		...	10.7	10.4	10.5		...	597	484	490
154	Other food products		...	...	...a/	...a/		...	...a/	...a/	...a/		...	...a/	...a/	...a/
1541	Bakery products		...					...					...			
1542	Sugar		...	58	58	58		...	28.5	28.3	28.7		...	4805	4818	5241
1543	Cocoa, chocolate and sugar confectionery		...	65	87	87		...	24.5	31.0	31.6		...	2077	2450	2706
1544	Macaroni, noodles & similar products		...					...					...			
1549	Other food products n.e.c.		...	160	192	192		...	28.7	32.0	32.2		...	1944	2366	2522
155	Beverages		...		13187	13181		...	83.4	123.7	120.7		...	11485	12204	11920
1551	Distilling, rectifying & blending of spirits		...	35	55	55		...	4.5	6.1	6.1		...	401	635	537
1552	Wines		...	11	9	9		...	2.1	1.8	1.9		...	350	277	274
1553	Malt liquors and malt		...	13	14	14		...	13.6	12.2	11.4		...	2308	1935	1615
1554	Soft drinks; mineral waters		...	89	97	97		...	63.2	53.0	52.1		...	8427	6877	7020
1600	Tobacco products		...	7	9	9		...	2.6	2.8	2.8		...	430	411	416
171	Spinning, weaving and finishing of textiles		...	216	264	264		...	48.6	62.1	63.5		...	4349	4627	5078
1711	Textile fibre preparation; textile weaving		...	191	216	216		...	44.5	51.3	52.0		...	4018	3862	4201
1712	Finishing of textiles		...	25	48	48		...	4.1	10.7	11.5		...	331	765	877
172	Other textiles		...	110	163	163		...	15.6	20.3	20.2		...	1005	1314	1361
1721	Made-up textile articles, except apparel		...	36	54	54		...	7.0	9.6	9.5		...	377	493	492
1722	Carpets and rugs		...	5	5	5		...	1.1	0.9	0.8		...	156	135	130
1723	Cordage, rope, twine and netting		...	16	19	19		...	1.9	1.5	1.5		...	115	111	115
1729	Other textiles n.e.c.		...					...					...			
1730	Knitted and crocheted fabrics and articles		...					...					...			
1810	Wearing apparel, except fur apparel		...	499	861	861		...	64.4	162.2	163.1		...	4016	9339	9859
1820	Dressing & dyeing of fur; processing of fur		...	...b/	...b/	...b/		...	...b/	...b/	...b/		...	...b/	...b/	...b/
191	Tanning, dressing and processing of leather		...	135b/	182b/	182b/		...	8.8b/	13.5b/	15.0b/		...	360b/	646b/	833b/
1911	Tanning and dressing of leather		...					...					...			
1912	Luggage, handbags, etc.; saddlery & harness		...					...					...			
1920	Footwear		...	239	280	280		...	41.4	46.1	48.3		...	2922	2997	3360
2010	Sawmilling and planing of wood		...	90	93	92		...	3.7	3.6	3.6		...	200	199	229
202	Products of wood, cork, straw, etc.		...	154	246	246		...	9.6	13.1	12.9		...	634	926	914
2021	Veneer sheets, plywood, particle board, etc.		...					...					...			
2022	Builders' carpentry and joinery		...	56	75	75		...	2.9	4.1	3.9		...	203	338	324
2023	Wooden containers		...	62	125	125		...	2.3	4.3	4.5		...	162	286	324
2029	Other wood products; articles of cork/straw		...					...					...			
210	Paper and paper products		...	238	325	325		...	55.9	69.3	71.5		...	6946	8473	9350
2101	Pulp, paper and paperboard		...	54	64	64		...	17.2	20.5	20.5		...	2388	2972	3201
2102	Corrugated paper and paperboard		...	184c/	261c/	261c/		...	38.8c/	48.8c/	51.1c/		...	4558c/	5501c/	6149c/
2109	Other articles of paper and paperboard		...	...c/	...c/	...c/		...	...c/	...c/	...c/		...	...c/	...c/	...c/
221	Publishing		...					...					...			
2211	Publishing of books and other publications		...					...					...			
2212	Publishing of newspapers, journals, etc.		...					...					...			
2213	Publishing of recorded media		...					...					...			
2219	Other publishing		...					...					...			

ISIC Revision 3

ISIC	Description														
222	Printing and related service activities	3023	2837	2287	:	:	:	31.5	32.4	22.7	:	:	:	246	246	149
2221	Printing	:	:	:	:	:	:	:	:	:	:	:	:	:	:	:
2222	Service activities related to printing	:	:	:	:	:	:	:	:	:	:	:	:	:	:	:
2230	Reproduction of recorded media	9954	9617	9956	:	:	:	28.7	28.1	28.5	:	:	:	56	56	58
2310	Coke oven products	:	:	:	:	:	:	:	:	:	:	:	:	:	:	:
2320	Refined petroleum products	:	:	:	:	:	:	:	:	:	:	:	:	:	:	:
2330	Processing of nuclear fuel	11834	11379	11051	:	:	:	36.7	36.6	35.7	:	:	:	137	137	128
241	Basic chemicals	:	:	:	:	:	:	:	:	:	:	:	:	:	:	:
2411	Basic chemicals, except fertilizers	528	441	537	:	:	:	2.9	2.9	1.6	:	:	:	14	14	12
2412	Fertilizers and nitrogen compounds	:	:	:	:	:	:	:	:	:	:	:	:	:	:	:
2413	Plastics in primary forms; synthetic rubber	:	:	:	:	:	:	:	:	:	:	:	:	:	:	:
242	Other chemicals	200	177	381	:	:	:	2.7	2.6	2.5	:	:	:	21	21	19
2421	Pesticides and other agro-chemical products	1531	1416	1301	:	:	:	9.3	9.1	9.3	:	:	:	64	64	53
2422	Paints, varnishes, printing ink and mastics	11545	10910	11874	:	:	:	49.4	50.1	48.6	:	:	:	115	115	98
2423	Pharmaceuticals, medicinal chemicals, etc.	6029	5466	5031	:	:	:	31.6	30.1	29.9	:	:	:	81	81	73
2424	Soap, cleaning & cosmetic preparations	1591	1616	1686	:	:	:	10.6	10.7	8.8	:	:	:	83	83	67
2429	Other chemical products n.e.c.	1294	1182	1150	:	:	:	12.1	12.1	10.2	:	:	:	60	60	46
2430	Man-made fibres	2974	2628	2651	:	:	:	26.1	23.9	15.7	:	:	:	139	139	91
251	Rubber products	994	898	1379	:	:	:	5.6	5.4	5.0	:	:	:	11	11	10
2511	Rubber tyres and tubes	1980	1730	1272	:	:	:	20.5	18.5	10.8	:	:	:	128	128	81
2519	Other rubber products	11975	10533	6950	:	:	:	143.9	132.7	75.9	:	:	:	832	832	476
2520	Plastic products	3337	3126	2888	:	:	:	29.7	28.8	27.1	:	:	:	106	106	68
2610	Glass and glass products	2055d/	1797d/	2051d/	:	:	:	24.4d/	23.4d/	20.3d/	:	:	:	105d/	105d/	86d/
269	Non-metallic mineral products n.e.c.	...d/	...d/	...d/	:	:	:	...d/	...d/	...d/	:	:	:	...d/	...d/	...d/
2691	Pottery, china and earthenware	...d/	...d/	...d/	:	:	:	...d/	...d/	...d/	:	:	:	...d/	...d/	...d/
2692	Refractory ceramic products	...d/	...d/	...d/	:	:	:	...d/	...d/	...d/	:	:	:	...d/	...d/	...d/
2693	Struct.non-refractory clay; ceramic products	612	547	718	:	:	:	4.7	4.7	4.7	:	:	:	51	51	52
2694	Cement, lime and plaster	5354	5206	5433	:	:	:	24.7	25.2	25.3	:	:	:	392	392	311
2695	Articles of concrete, cement and plaster	924	851	643	:	:	:	9.4	9.1	7.2	:	:	:	116	116	78
2696	Cutting, shaping & finishing of stone	9192	8248	7959	:	:	:	40.4	39.6	35.2	:	:	:	125	125	81
2699	Other non-metallic mineral products n.e.c.	2417	2436	2076	:	:	:	17.3	17.2	13.9	:	:	:	66	66	41
2710	Basic iron and steel	1355	1355	909	:	:	:	14.8	13.3	9.3	:	:	:	130	130	93
2720	Basic precious and non-ferrous metals	803	766	598	:	:	:	9.5	8.5	6.5	:	:	:	73	73	51
273	Casting of metals	552	468	311	:	:	:	5.3	4.7	2.8	:	:	:	57	57	42
2731	Casting of iron and steel	:	:	:	:	:	:	:	:	:	:	:	:	:	:	:
2732	Casting of non-ferrous metals	:	:	:	:	:	:	:	:	:	:	:	:	:	:	:
281	Struct.metal products;tanks;steam generators	7222	7128	917	:	:	:	113.3	115.6	10.9	:	:	:	53052	53068	66
2811	Structural metal products	1453	1357	1223	:	:	:	14.0	14.2	10.0	:	:	:	96	96	96
2812	Tanks, reservoirs and containers of metal	:	:	:	:	:	:	:	:	:	:	:	:	:	:	:
2813	Steam generators	:	:	:	:	:	:	:	:	:	:	:	:	:	:	:
289	Other metal products; metal working services	:	:	:	:	:	:	:	:	:	:	:	:	:	:	:
2891	Metal forging/pressing/stamping/roll-forming	990	890	550	:	:	:	8.0	7.0	3.2	:	:	:	79	79	33
2892	Treatment & coating of metals	723	692	458	:	:	:	13.3	12.9	11.2	:	:	:	45	45	30
2893	Cutlery, hand tools and general hardware	9880	8795	4447	:	:	:	75.3	71.2	34.0	:	:	:	437	437	201
2899	Other fabricated metal products n.e.c.	8017	7093	4430	:	:	:	54.9	50.1	32.8	:	:	:	328	328	207
291	General purpose machinery	:	:	28	:	:	:	:	:	0.4	:	:	:	:	:	9
2911	Engines & turbines (not for transport equipment)	:	:	:	:	:	:	:	:	:	:	:	:	:	:	:
2912	Pumps, compressors, taps and valves	:	:	:	:	:	:	:	:	:	:	:	:	:	:	:
2913	Bearings, gears, gearing & driving elements	1101	974	527	:	:	:	6.9	6.3	3.4	:	:	:	40	40	28
2914	Ovens, furnaces and furnace burners	1085	955	956	:	:	:	9.5	8.8	8.3	:	:	:	65	65	44
2915	Lifting and handling equipment	:	:	:	:	:	:	:	:	:	:	:	:	:	:	:
2919	Other general purpose machinery	:	:	:	:	:	:	:	:	:	:	:	:	:	:	:
292	Special purpose machinery	:	:	:	:	:	:	:	:	:	:	:	:	:	:	:
2921	Agricultural and forestry machinery	864	812	570	:	:	:	7.9	7.7	5.6	:	:	:	28	28	27
2922	Machine tools	592	532	427	:	:	:	3.4	3.1	2.4	:	:	:	37	37	27
2923	Machinery for metallurgy	1312	1023	1026	:	:	:	8.3	6.9	5.2	:	:	:	27	27	14
2924	Machinery for mining & construction	599	574	489	:	:	:	3.8	3.7	3.1	:	:	:	27	27	20
2925	Food/beverage/tobacco processing machinery	27	28	5	:	:	:	0.3	0.3	0.1	:	:	:	8	8	5
2926	Machinery for textile, apparel and leather	:	:	498	:	:	:	:	:	2.9	:	:	:	:	:	32
2927	Weapons and ammunition	:	:	:	:	:	:	:	:	:	:	:	:	:	:	:
2929	Other special purpose machinery	:	:	:	:	:	:	:	:	:	:	:	:	:	:	:

continued

Mexico

ISIC	Industry	Number of establishments (number)					Number of employees (thousands)					Wages and salaries paid to employees (millions of Mexican Pesos)				
		Note	2007	2008	2009	2010	Note	2007	2008	2009	2010	Note	2007	2008	2009	2010
2930	Domestic appliances n.e.c.		…	…	…	…		…	…	…	…		…	…	…	…
3000	Office, accounting and computing machinery		…	10	37	37		…	2.1	34.2	36.7		…	95	2979	3404
3110	Electric motors, generators and transformers		…	35	109	109		…	15.7	48.4	50.7		…	1892	5684	6180
3120	Electricity distribution & control apparatus		…	37	88	88		…	24.2	47.0	52.1		…	2381	4022	4844
3130	Insulated wire and cable		…	50e/	149e/	149e/		…	15.8e/	42.6e/	44.9e/		…	1606e/	4918e/	5330e/
3140	Accumulators, primary cells and batteries		…	…e/	…e/	…e/		…	…e/	…e/	…e/		…	…e/	…e/	…e/
3150	Lighting equipment and electric lamps		…	24	47	47		…	4.1	13.0	12.9		…	316	1482	1529
3190	Other electrical equipment n.e.c.		…	…e/	…e/	…e/		…	…e/	…e/	…e/		…	…e/	…e/	…e/
3210	Electronic valves, tubes, etc.		…	…	…	…		…	…	…	…		…	…	…	…
3220	TV/radio transmitters; line comm. apparatus		…	15	221	221		…	1.5	99.3	109.2		…	252	10283	11896
3230	TV and radio receivers and associated goods		…	5	58	58		…	2.5	43.8	44.1		…	201	5144	5544
331	Medical, measuring, testing appliances, etc.		…	5	50	50		…		40.7	42.5		…		4731	5071
3311	Medical, surgical and orthopaedic equipment		…		44	44		…		10.6	11.6		…		1268	1481
3312	Measuring/testing/navigating appliances, etc.		…	…	…	…		…	…	…	…		…	…	…	…
3313	Industrial process control equipment		…	…	…	…		…	…	…	…		…	…	…	…
3320	Optical instruments & photographic equipment		…	…	…	…		…	…	…	…		…	…	…	…
3330	Watches and clocks		…	3	13	13		…	1.8	5.3	5.9		…	365	946	1093
3410	Motor vehicles		…	21	29	29		…	45.8	43.1	49.7		…	11587	10690	12561
3420	Automobile bodies, trailers & semi-trailers		…	43	59	59		…	9.6	10.0	10.9		…	994	1087	1203
3430	Parts/accessories for automobiles		…	224	669	669		…	129.4	334.6	384.4		…	14386	32709	38805
351	Building and repairing of ships and boats		…	7	15	15		…	1.5	3.8	3.5		…	277	455	412
3511	Building and repairing of ships		…	…	…	…		…	…	…	…		…	…	…	…
3512	Building/repairing of pleasure/sport. boats		…	…	…	…		…	…	…	…		…	…	…	…
3520	Railway/tramway locomotives & rolling stock		…	8	10	10		…	2.1	3.8	3.9		…	536	501	514
3530	Aircraft and spacecraft		…		35	35		…		10.2	10.8		…		1048	1127
359	Transport equipment n.e.c.		…	…	…	…		…	…	…	…		…	…	…	…
3591	Motorcycles		…		9	9		…		2.6	2.5		…		328	349
3592	Bicycles and invalid carriages		…	16	11	11		…	3.7	1.8	1.6		…	417	186	164
3599	Other transport equipment n.e.c.		…	…	…	…		…	…	…	…		…	…	…	…
3610	Furniture		…	195	366	366		…	25.6	45.5	46.5		…	2164	3845	4252
369	Manufacturing n.e.c.		…	…	…	…		…	…	…	…		…	…	…	…
3691	Jewellery and related articles		…	251	530	529		…	26.7	128.5	134.8		…	2901	13084	14976
3692	Musical instruments		…	50	75	74		…	2.0	4.8	4.6		…	132	301	315
3693	Sports goods		…	…	…	…		…	…	…	…		…	…	…	…
3694	Games and toys		…	20	46	46		…	0.5	3.7	3.7		…	31	320	342
3699	Other manufacturing n.e.c.		…	30	46	46		…	2.5	7.8	9.3		…	187	545	711
3710	Recycling of metal waste and scrap		…	…	…	…		…	…	…	…		…	…	…	…
3720	Recycling of non-metal waste and scrap		…	…	…	…		…	…	…	…		…	…	…	…
D	Total manufacturing		…	6626	205855	205834		…	1515.6	2924.4	3044.9		…	198740	299102	327324

a/ 151 includes 1520, 153 and 154.
b/ 191 includes 1820.
c/ 2102 includes 2109.
d/ 2691 includes 2692 and 2693.
e/ 3130 includes 3140 and 3190.

Mexico

ISIC	Industry	Note	Output (billions of Mexican Pesos)				Note	Value added (billions of Mexican Pesos)				Note	Gross fixed capital formation (billions of Mexican Pesos)	
	ISIC Revision 3		2007	2008	2009	2010		2007	2008	2009	2010		2009	2010
151	Processed meat,fish,fruit,vegetables,fats		112.2	551.3a/	682.2a/	709.7a/		25.8	176.0a/	236.9a/	247.7a/		12.5a/	10.6a/
1511	Processing/preserving of meat		48.8	54.1	65.1	68.4		11.2	12.0	17.7	18.7		1.9	1.2
1512	Processing/preserving of fish		7.0	7.7	9.2	9.2		1.5	1.7	2.2	2.3		0.2	0.2
1513	Processing/preserving of fruit & vegetables		26.4	30.3	38.5	38.0		9.3	10.6	14.4	13.9		0.7	0.9
1514	Vegetable and animal oils and fats		30.0	43.0	43.8	43.5		3.9	6.7	6.6	6.2		0.6	0.4
1520	Dairy products		94.8	...a/	...a/	...a/		30.3	...a/	...a/	...a/		...a/	...a/
153	Grain mill products; starches; animal feeds		91.1	...a/	...a/	...a/		17.8	...a/	...a/	...a/		...	...
1531	Grain mill products		37.9	...	...	...		9.0	...	...	...		0.7	0.2
1532	Starches and starch products		10.9	11.6	14.9	14.9		3.2	3.4	6.0	5.7		0.3	0.6
1533	Prepared animal feeds		42.3	50.4	53.5	51.9		5.5	6.7	9.0	8.7		...	...a/
154	Other food products		195.1	...a/	...a/	...a/		89.0	...a/	...a/	...a/		...	...
1541	Bakery products		53.7	32.0	35.9	48.6		23.8	9.7	11.9	16.5		0.7	0.8
1542	Sugar		34.9	28.5	37.6	40.6		11.3	12.1	16.5	17.4		0.8	1.2
1543	Cocoa, chocolate and sugar confectionery		26.4	...	...	...		11.6	...	...	...		...	...
1544	Macaroni, noodles & similar products		80.1	75.2	87.0	94.7		42.3	40.5	44.8	48.5		1.9	1.8
1549	Other food products n.e.c.		193.2	194.2	227.8	232.7		79.6	76.9	100.5	102.1		5.8	5.9
155	Beverages		19.1	15.9	17.5	17.6		10.7	8.1	8.9	8.7		0.6	0.5
1551	Distilling, rectifying & blending of spirits		...	4.0	4.0	4.0		...	1.6	1.8	1.8		-	-
1552	Wines		62.9	61.8	69.7	69.9		27.6	25.2	28.0	27.8		1.8	1.1
1553	Malt liquors and malt		111.1	112.4	125.3	130.4		41.3	42.0	55.3	57.6		3.3	4.1
1554	Soft drinks; mineral waters		27.6	33.0	38.3	39.8		22.8	27.2	31.3	32.6		0.4	0.6
1600	Tobacco products		27.9	33.4	41.7	47.3		8.6	10.4	13.5	15.4		0.5	1.0
171	Spinning, weaving and finishing of textiles		27.2	30.2	36.5	41.3		8.2	9.5	11.6	13.2		0.4	0.9
1711	Textile fibre preparation; textile weaving		0.7	3.2	5.2	6.0		0.4	0.9	1.9	2.2		-	0.1
1712	Finishing of textiles		16.1	10.2	10.4	11.4		4.4	2.8	3.5	3.8		0.2	0.2
172	Other textiles		7.7	4.8	5.4	5.7		2.0	1.5	1.9	2.0		0.1	-
1721	Made-up textile articles, except apparel		1.0	0.8	0.7	0.8		0.3	0.3	0.3	0.3		-	-
1722	Carpets and rugs		6.4	0.9	0.6	0.7		0.4	0.3	0.2	0.2		-	-
1723	Cordage, rope, twine and netting		6.5	...	...	...		1.7	...	...	...		...	...
1729	Other textiles n.e.c.		...	...	...	...		2.5	...	...	...		...	...
1730	Knitted and crocheted fabrics and articles		23.4	29.1	53.1	56.1		7.8	10.5	23.3	24.3		0.3	0.5
1810	Wearing apparel, except fur apparel		...b/	...b/	...b/	...b/		...b/	...b/	...b/	...b/		...b/	...b/
1820	Dressing & dyeing of fur; processing of fur		7.3	6.4b/	9.6b/	9.4b/		1.1b/	1.1b/	2.1b/	2.8b/		0.1b/	0.2b/
191	Tanning, dressing and processing of leather		...	...	...	...		...	...	...	...		...	...
1911	Tanning and dressing of leather		6.0	...	...	...		1.0	...	...	...		0.2	0.2
1912	Luggage, handbags, etc.; saddlery & harness		13.7	13.5	19.9	22.7		4.4	4.3	6.2	6.9		...	0.2
1920	Footwear		1.3	1.1	1.3	1.2		0.5	0.4	0.5	0.5		...	...
2010	Sawmilling and planing of wood		6.7	6.6	7.8	8.3		1.8	1.7	2.2	2.2		0.1	0.2
202	Products of wood, cork, straw, etc.		2.8	...	1.3	...		0.7	...	...	...		...	...
2021	Veneer sheets, plywood, particle board, etc.		1.8	1.7	2.2	2.3		0.5	0.5	0.7	0.7		...	...
2022	Builders' carpentry and joinery		1.9	1.7	2.4	2.7		0.5	0.4	0.7	0.7		...	...
2023	Wooden containers		0.3	...	...	...		0.1	...	...	...		...	...
2029	Other wood products; articles of cork/straw		...	...	...	...		...	...	...	...		...	...
210	Paper and paper products		96.6	98.7	122.6	134.8		28.8	27.6	35.9	38.5		2.8	3.2
2101	Pulp, paper and paperboard		32.3	38.2	47.8	52.0		8.2	9.4	12.8	13.2		1.5	1.4
2102	Corrugated paper and paperboard		38.1	60.5c/	74.8c/	82.8c/		11.3c/	18.1c/	23.0c/	25.3c/		1.3c/	1.8c/
2109	Other articles of paper and paperboard		26.2	...c/	...c/	...c/		9.3	...c/	...c/	...c/		...c/	...c/
221	Publishing		...	...	...	...		...	...	...	...		...	...
2211	Publishing of books and other publications		...	...	...	...		...	...	...	...		...	...
2212	Publishing of newspapers, journals, etc.		...	...	...	...		...	...	...	...		...	...
2213	Publishing of recorded media		...	...	...	...		...	...	...	...		...	...
2219	Other publishing		...	...	...	...		...	...	...	...		...	...

continued

Mexico

ISIC	Industry	Output Note	Output (billions of Mexican Pesos) 2007	2008	2009	2010	Value added Note	Value added (billions of Mexican Pesos) 2007	2008	2009	2010	Gross fixed capital formation (billions of Mexican Pesos) 2009	2010
222	Printing and related service activities		15.6	16.2	20.1	21.0		6.1	6.5	7.1	7.3	0.4	1.1
2221	Printing		15.6	…	…	…		6.1	…	…	…	…	…
2222	Service activities related to printing		…	…	…	…		…	…	…	…	…	…
2230	Reproduction of recorded media		…	…	…	…		…	…	…	…	…	…
2310	Coke oven products		…	…	…	…		…	…	…	…	…	…
2320	Refined petroleum products		337.4	396.3	551.5	626.2		81.9	96.6	172.2	189.2	56.9	10.5
2330	Processing of nuclear fuel		…	…	…	…		…	…	…	…	…	…
241	Basic chemicals		336.0	350.9	301.7	306.7		68.3	74.9	48.3	51.8	9.1	45.5
2411	Basic chemicals, except fertilizers		284.7	…	…	…		63.7	…	…	…	…	…
2412	Fertilizers and nitrogen compounds		4.4	8.0	9.9	12.6		1.2	2.2	2.0	2.6	-	-
2413	Plastics in primary forms; synthetic rubber		46.8	…	…	…		3.5	…	…	…	…	…
242	Other chemicals		246.0	…	…	…		102.2	…	…	…	…	…
2421	Pesticides and other agro-chemical products		7.8	8.0	8.8	9.5		2.8	2.8	2.9	3.1	-	0.1
2422	Paints, varnishes, printing ink and mastics		25.7	17.8	21.2	24.8		7.1	4.7	5.6	6.7	0.1	0.2
2423	Pharmaceuticals, medicinal chemicals, etc.		119.9	124.8	118.2	118.8		58.6	60.0	54.5	54.9	3.1	2.0
2424	Soap, cleaning & cosmetic preparations		75.7	79.6	88.1	88.2		28.7	29.6	36.6	36.0	2.5	2.7
2429	Other chemical products n.e.c.		16.9	19.9	21.1	21.0		5.0	6.1	7.0	7.0	0.1	0.2
2430	Man-made fibres		10.9	60.3	67.7	80.4		2.4	5.7	12.7	15.4	0.5	0.6
251	Rubber products		8.6	18.8	23.3	29.3		2.4	6.0	8.2	10.5	1.0	0.7
2511	Rubber tyres and tubes		8.6	8.8	9.9	12.3		2.4	2.5	3.4	4.3	0.6	0.5
2519	Other rubber products			10.0	13.4	17.0			3.6	4.8	6.2	0.3	0.2
2520	Plastic products		85.3	78.3	128.0	147.6		23.3	20.1	36.5	42.2	3.8	4.2
2610	Glass and glass products		30.2	30.8	36.0	38.5		10.9	11.5	12.8	13.2	0.9	0.7
269	Non-metallic mineral products n.e.c.		109.7	…	…	…		57.1	…	…	…	…	…
2691	Pottery, china and earthenware		3.8	18.4 d/	19.9 d/	21.2 d/		2.0	6.8 d/	6.8 d/	7.4 d/	0.3 d/	0.3 d/
2692	Refractory ceramic products		1.9	…d/	…d/	…d/		0.5	…d/	…d/	…d/	…d/	…d/
2693	Struct.non-refractory clay; ceramic products		12.8	…	…	…		4.8	…	…	…	…	…
2694	Cement, lime and plaster		57.7	5.5	5.3	5.9		37.7	2.1	2.1	2.4	0.5	0.1
2695	Articles of concrete, cement and plaster		24.5	77.6	75.7	73.2		9.0	44.8	38.1	36.1	1.6	2.0
2696	Cutting, shaping & finishing of stone		1.4	…	…	…		0.5	…	…	…	…	…
2699	Other non-metallic mineral products n.e.c.		7.6	5.0	6.6	7.0		2.5	2.0	2.5	2.6	0.1	0.1
2710	Basic iron and steel		185.7	218.3	203.2	250.0		49.3	57.5	69.5	84.8	5.6	8.1
2720	Basic precious and non-ferrous metals		102.7	95.2	90.5	116.0		24.7	22.2	18.1	21.7	1.3	2.2
273	Casting of metals		…	10.5	13.8	15.8		…	3.4	5.0	5.7	0.7	1.0
2731	Casting of iron and steel		…	8.5	9.7	10.6		…	2.6	3.1	3.3	0.7	0.9
2732	Casting of non-ferrous metals		…	2.0	4.1	5.2		…	0.8	1.8	2.4	-	-
281	Struct.metal products;tanks;steam generators		15.0	11.2	32.8	29.1		4.3	3.1	13.0	12.1		
2811	Structural metal products		9.4	19.9	25.5	25.2		2.6	4.9	6.9	6.9	0.2	0.2
2812	Tanks, reservoirs and containers of metal		5.6	…	…	…		1.7	…	…	…	0.6	0.5
2813	Steam generators		…	…	…	…		…	…	…	…	…	…
289	Other metal products; metal working services		68.4	…	…	…		18.2	…	…	…	…	…
2891	Metal forging/pressing/stamping/roll-forming		4.4	4.7	9.7	10.6		1.2	1.3	2.6	2.7	0.1	0.2
2892	Treatment & coating of metals		18.2	…	…	…		3.1	…	…	…	…	…
2893	Cutlery, hand tools and general hardware		10.7	8.8	10.6	11.6		3.6	2.9	3.7	4.1	0.3	0.3
2899	Other fabricated metal products n.e.c.		35.1	56.6	73.3	81.8		10.3	16.4	24.4	26.8	1.1	1.3
291	General purpose machinery		49.4	44.6	66.0	78.3		16.9	14.8	31.2	37.4	0.9	1.0
2911	Engines & turbines (not for transport equipment)		9.9	…	…	…		1.5	…	…	…	…	…
2912	Pumps, compressors, taps and valves		12.2	…	…	…		4.8	…	…	…	…	…
2913	Bearings, gears, gearing & driving elements		0.8	0.4	…	…		0.4	0.1	…	…	…	…
2914	Ovens, furnaces and furnace burners		…	…	…	…		…	…	…	…	…	…
2915	Lifting and handling equipment		3.2	2.6	4.1	4.3		1.3	1.0	1.9	2.0	-	0.1
2919	Other general purpose machinery		23.3	12.8	12.2	16.2		8.8	5.2	5.6	7.5	-	-

Code											
292	Special purpose machinery	20.3				8.1	2.4	2.9	3.0	0.2	0.2
2921	Agricultural and forestry machinery	6.3	8.1	8.9	9.1	1.7	1.0	1.4	1.6	-	-
2922	Machine tools	4.2	2.6	3.5	3.9	1.8					
2923	Machinery for metallurgy	5.9	6.3	7.6	9.5	2.6	2.9	3.1	3.9	0.1	0.2
2924	Machinery for mining & construction	2.2	2.5	3.2	3.3	1.1	1.3	1.6	1.6	0.1	0.1
2925	Food/beverage/tobacco processing machinery		-	0.2	0.1		-	0.1	0.1		
2926	Machinery for textile, apparel and leather	-				1.4	1.4				
2927	Weapons and ammunition		3.7								
2929	Other special purpose machinery	1.7				0.8					
2930	Domestic appliances n.e.c.	33.2				9.6	0.3	6.1	6.6	0.6	0.7
3000	Office, accounting and computing machinery	9.8	5.4	20.2	22.2	1.0				0.8	0.9
3110	Electric motors, generators and transformers	7.5	29.1	44.9	49.0	2.7	9.0	18.9	20.0	0.8	0.9
3120	Electricity distribution & control apparatus	14.9	32.0	46.5	52.2	4.4	9.4	14.1	16.3	1.5	2.1
3130	Insulated wire and cable	23.3	40.0e/	51.7e/	59.1e/	5.8	11.4e/	19.7e/	22.6e/	0.9e/	1.0e/
3140	Accumulators, primary cells and batteries	8.7	...e/	...e/	...e/	2.7	...e/	...e/	...e/	...e/	...e/
3150	Lighting equipment and electric lamps	3.4	3.5	6.8	7.0	0.9	1.1	3.0	3.1	0.6	0.6
3190	Other electrical equipment n.e.c.	44.1	...e/	...e/	...e/	12.9	...e/	...e/	...e/	...e/	...e/
3210	Electronic valves, tubes, etc.	7.2	7.1	32.4	36.5	2.0	2.0	20.3	22.5	0.6	0.6
3220	TV/radio transmitters; line comm. apparatus	1.7	2.6	14.5	15.2	0.5	0.9	8.8	9.2	0.1	0.1
3230	TV and radio receivers and associated goods	9.4	4.5	15.8	16.9	2.8	1.2	8.8	9.2	0.7	0.7
331	Medical, measuring, testing appliances, etc.	6.5				2.7		2.7	3.2		
3311	Medical, surgical and orthopaedic equipment	4.8				2.2					
3312	Measuring/testing/navigating appliances,etc.	1.7				0.5					
3313	Industrial process control equipment										
3320	Optical instruments & photographic equipment	0.8	3.3	5.9	6.5	0.2	1.0	3.3	3.7	0.1	0.1
3330	Watches and clocks										
3410	Motor vehicles	422.1	393.7	382.2	500.7	99.7	86.8	72.1	94.4	5.2	6.5
3420	Automobile bodies, trailers & semi-trailers	8.6	8.2	9.1	10.0	2.4	2.4	3.4	3.8	0.2	0.2
3430	Parts/accessories for automobiles	112.6	198.9	323.4	393.9	33.0	57.4	113.0	135.2	6.8	8.2
351	Building and repairing of ships and boats	0.7	1.4	2.4	2.0	0.4	0.9	1.3	1.1	0.1	0.1
3511	Building and repairing of ships	0.7				0.4					
3512	Building/repairing of pleasure/sport. boats						0.8				
3520	Railway/tramway locomotives & rolling stock	2.2	2.3	5.9	5.5	0.8		2.1	1.9	0.2	0.2
3530	Aircraft and spacecraft			7.7	7.8			2.7	2.7		
359	Transport equipment n.e.c.	2.0				0.6	0.7	0.7	0.8		
3591	Motorcycles		2.3	1.4	1.6						
3592	Bicycles and invalid carriages	2.0		1.6	1.7	0.6	0.7	0.7	0.7		
3599	Other transport equipment n.e.c.										
3610	Furniture	13.9	14.1	21.2	22.6	4.2	4.2	8.1	8.6	0.2	0.3
369	Manufacturing n.e.c.	12.2	18.2	48.0	52.2	3.8	6.5	25.0	27.1	0.7	1.5
3691	Jewellery and related articles	1.2	1.0	1.6	1.7	0.4	0.3	0.7	0.7		
3692	Musical instruments	0.2	0.2	0.9	0.9	0.1	0.1	0.5	0.5		
3693	Sports goods	1.2	1.3	3.4	4.3	0.4	0.4	1.1	1.5	-	
3694	Games and toys	9.6				3.0					
3699	Other manufacturing n.e.c.										
3710	Recycling of metal waste and scrap										
3720	Recycling of non-metal waste and scrap									133.9	132.4
D	Total manufacturing	3279.5	3557.0	4318.5	4824.9	994.6	1053.4	1431.6	1572.3	133.9	132.4

a/ 151 includes 1520, 153 and 154.
b/ 191 includes 1820.
c/ 2102 includes 2109.
d/ 2691 includes 2692 and 2693.
e/ 3130 includes 3140 and 3190.

Mexico

Index numbers of industrial production

ISIC Revision 3

ISIC	Industry	Note	(2005=100)											
			1999	2000	2001	2002	2003	2004	2005	2006	2007	2008	2009	2010
15	Food and beverages	a/	85	89	90	92	93	97	100	103	105	107	107	108
16	Tobacco products	a/	...	...	...	...	...	...	...	...	...	...	...	...
17	Textiles	b/	124	129	116	109	101	103	100	101	97	95	86	92
18	Wearing apparel, fur	b/	...	...	...	...	...	...	...	...	...	...	...	...
19	Leather, leather products and footwear		...	...	...	...	...	...	...	...	...	...	...	...
20	Wood products (excl. furniture)		...	...	...	...	...	...	...	...	...	...	...	...
21	Paper and paper products	c/	96	99	96	95	95	97	100	106	108	112	109	116
22	Printing and publishing	c/	...	...	...	...	...	...	...	...	...	...	...	...
23	Coke,refined petroleum products,nuclear fuel	d/	93	96	93	93	94	98	100	103	105	103	99	99
24	Chemicals and chemical products	d/	...	...	...	...	...	...	...	...	...	...	...	...
25	Rubber and plastics products	d/	...	...	...	...	...	...	...	...	...	...	...	...
26	Non-metallic mineral products		85	89	86	89	90	94	100	107	109	105	96	100
27	Basic metals		89	92	85	87	91	94	100	104	102	101	84	95
28	Fabricated metal products	e/	95	107	101	97	92	95	100	112	115	113	88	113
29	Machinery and equipment n.e.c.	e/	...	...	...	...	...	...	...	...	...	...	...	...
30	Office, accounting and computing machinery	e/	...	...	...	...	...	...	...	...	...	...	...	...
31	Electrical machinery and apparatus	e/	...	...	...	...	...	...	...	...	...	...	...	...
32	Radio,television and communication equipment	e/	...	...	...	...	...	...	...	...	...	...	...	...
33	Medical, precision and optical instruments	e/	...	...	...	...	...	...	...	...	...	...	...	...
34	Motor vehicles, trailers, semi-trailers	e/	...	...	...	...	...	...	...	...	...	...	...	...
35	Other transport equipment	e/	...	...	...	...	...	...	...	...	...	...	...	...
36	Furniture; manufacturing n.e.c.		...	...	...	...	...	...	...	...	...	...	...	...
37	Recycling		...	...	...	...	...	...	...	...	...	...	...	...
D	Total manufacturing		93	99	95	94	93	97	100	106	108	107	96	106

a/ 15 includes 16.
b/ 17 includes 18.
c/ 21 includes 22.
d/ 23 includes 24 and 25.
e/ 28 includes 29, 30, 31, 32, 33, 34 and 35.

Morocco

Supplier of information:
Haut Commissariat au Plan, Direction de la Statistique, Rabat.

Basic source of data:
Annual industrial survey.

Major deviations from ISIC (Revision 3):
Data collected under the national classification system have been reclassified by UNIDO to correspond with ISIC (Revision 3).

Reference period:
Fiscal year.

Scope:
Enterprises with 10 or more employees or a turnover of more than 100,000 dirhams per year.

Method of data collection:
Direct interview in the field.

Type of enumeration:
Complete enumeration.

Adjusted for non-response:
Yes.

Concepts and definitions of variables:
Wages and salaries is compensation of employees.

Related national publications:
None reported.

Morocco

ISIC	Industry	Number of enterprises (number)				Number of employees (number)				Wages and salaries paid to employees (millions of Moroccan Dirhams)			
		Note / 2007	2008	2009	2010	Note / 2007	2008	2009	2010	Note / 2007	2008	2009	2010
151	Processed meat,fish,fruit,vegetables,fats	545	554	551	...	30964	52608	48050	50791	1780.5	1939.2	2022.7	2133.6
1511	Processing/preserving of meat	54	53	53	...	2404	2514	3075	3814	104.8	101.9	137.9	188.8
1512	Processing/preserving of fish	193	195	180	...	17496	37003	31512	34146	1037.9	1112.1	1110.9	1231.7
1513	Processing/preserving of fruit & vegetables	117	122	117	...	5717	7279	7440	6749	217.7	256.1	237.7	263.6
1514	Vegetable and animal oils and fats	181	184	201	...	5347	5812	6023	6082	420.0	469.2	536.2	449.5
1520	Dairy products	80	82	83	...	8316	10632	11507	11802	865.0	1091.2	1311.7	1349.9
153	Grain mill products; starches; animal feeds	204	215	210	...	8813	9600	10001	11221	543.2	593.2	590.8	661.7
1531	Grain mill products	168	175	174	...	6616	7187	7583	8219	357.3	391.4	406.4	460.6
1532	Starches and starch products	5	6	5	...	113	121	122	123	24.5	20.6	21.0	21.0
1533	Prepared animal feeds	31	34	31	...	2084	2292	2296	2879	161.4	181.2	163.3	180.1
154	Other food products	1167	1151	1139	...	20195	20688	21110	22327	1748.5	1538.4	1521.9	1530.8
1541	Bakery products	1062	1048	1034	...	10976	11707	11805	12322	466.1	373.1	407.8	448.4
1542	Sugar	5	16	4	...	3112	2692	2566	2647	627.3	674.0	593.1	537.6
1543	Cocoa, chocolate and sugar confectionery	17	4	16	...	1243	1225	1226	1997	90.2	91.7	99.3	134.4
1544	Macaroni, noodles & similar products	15	16	19	...	502	1081	1363	841	25.1	60.8	68.3	52.5
1549	Other food products n.e.c.	68	67	66	...	4362	3983	4150	4520	539.9	338.7	353.4	358.0
155	Beverages	27	28	26	...	5858	7451	8614	7958	604.4	849.8	895.9	942.6
1551	Distilling, rectifying & blending of spirits	5	5	5	...	140	158	150	64	28.3	30.6	30.3	5.6
1552	Wines	4	4	3	...	849	647	750	822	58.2	69.2	67.4	136.9
1553	Malt liquors and malt	3	3	3	...	900	772	1182	921	132.9	137.9	139.7	138.9
1554	Soft drinks; mineral waters	15	16	15	...	3969	5874	6532	6151	384.9	612.2	658.5	661.2
1600	Tobacco products	1	1	1	...	1481	1510	1385	1385	369.3	286.7	373.1	375.9
171	Spinning, weaving and finishing of textiles	239	245	231	...	19901	19483	17673	18444	887.1	964.6	895.9	819.7
1711	Textile fibre preparation; textile weaving	156	158	151	...	13684	12597	11551	12676	667.0	683.0	639.8	590.5
1712	Finishing of textiles	83	87	80	...	6217	6886	6122	5768	220.1	281.6	256.1	229.2
172	Other textiles	197	218	207	...	8199	10221	8171	8559	363.7	468.5	319.3	344.8
1721	Made-up textile articles, except apparel	45	73	74	...	2780	5116	4518	4936	107.4	189.0	181.7	208.2
1722	Carpets and rugs	20	23	18	...	2030	1969	1023	992	154.2	172.9	48.6	48.1
1723	Cordage, rope, twine and netting	5	5	5	...	446	469	464	428	15.7	15.0	15.3	15.0
1729	Other textiles n.e.c.	127	117	110	...	2943	2667	2166	2203	86.5	91.6	73.6	73.5
1730	Knitted and crocheted fabrics and articles	92	78	79	...	7841	6849	6664	7023	251.6	251.7	238.1	259.6
1810	Wearing apparel, except fur apparel	872	832	786	...	149477	144535	129244	129508	4497.7	4624.2	4084.0	4007.2
1820	Dressing & dyeing of fur; processing of fur	...	...	...	...	...	...	...	...	...	...	...	...
191	Tanning, dressing and processing of leather	99	93	92	...	2894	2632	2858	2776	117.4	110.8	121.0	122.6
1911	Tanning and dressing of leather	58	58	59	...	1437	1411	1448	1434	66.2	65.9	72.6	69.8
1912	Luggage, handbags, etc.; saddlery & harness	41	35	33	...	1457	1221	1410	1342	51.1	44.9	48.4	52.8
1920	Footwear	244	231	237	...	13977	13984	14220	14655	498.0	502.0	532.7	591.8
2010	Sawmilling and planing of wood	67	67	71	...	1136	1323	1246	1205	32.9	37.0	37.2	36.0
202	Products of wood, cork, straw, etc.	423	411	424	...	8033	7815	7878	7796	348.5	360.2	362.3	356.3
2021	Veneer sheets, plywood, particle board, etc.	4	4	4	...	1107	788	884	853	80.3	76.5	56.5	64.9
2022	Builders' carpentry and joinery	361	356	362	...	4751	5029	4758	4782	163.1	186.8	203.6	203.2
2023	Wooden containers	22	19	20	...	994	980	1146	1193	65.1	57.1	57.1	55.8
2029	Other wood products; articles of cork/straw	36	32	38	...	1181	1018	1090	968	39.9	39.8	45.1	32.4
210	Paper and paper products	82	77	74	...	4585	4511	4841	4475	403.9	386.8	403.1	393.9
2101	Pulp, paper and paperboard	14	10	9	...	2065	1084	1122	1180	245.4	86.5	85.9	92.9
2102	Corrugated paper and paperboard	44	42	44	...	1866	2575	2803	2621	110.5	244.4	266.6	264.9
2109	Other articles of paper and paperboard	24	25	21	...	654	852	916	674	48.0	55.9	50.6	36.1
221	Publishing	39	29	49	...	2075	1923	2160	2316	127.8	118.5	140.4	152.5
2211	Publishing of books and other publications	8	9	10	...	537	559	511	495	27.3	29.0	31.2	26.8
2212	Publishing of newspapers, journals, etc.	10	11	10	...	1216	1304	1313	1316	82.7	87.5	88.1	89.5
2213	Publishing of recorded media	1	2	2	...	3	26	33	34	0.1	1.0	2.1	2.1
2219	Other publishing	20	7	27	...	319	34	303	471	17.7	1.0	19.0	34.1

Code	Description	1	2	3	4	5	6	7	8	9	10	11
222	Printing and related service activities	481.6	444.6	436.7	418.3	6844	7133	6881	7242	433	443	455
2221	Printing	480.1	443.1	417.3	416.0	6815	6894	6850	7211	430	426	453
2222	Service activities related to printing	1.5	1.5	19.4	2.3	29	239	31	31	3	17	2
2230	Reproduction of recorded media											
2310	Coke oven products	13.1	16.1	15.2	12.4	120	141	145	114	2	2	2
2320	Refined petroleum products	502.1	440.9	455.7	457.6	2696	2871	2485	2677	26	25	14
2330	Processing of nuclear fuel											
241	Basic chemicals	3200.0	2387.6	2373.3	1952.0	8143	9061	11002	10786	44	48	51
2411	Basic chemicals, except fertilizers	3070.2	2069.0	2075.7	183.5	1217	7701	9273	9562	23	30	31
2412	Fertilizers and nitrogen compounds	125.6	179.3	167.6	1635.3	5903	398	734	336	8	6	8
2413	Plastics in primary forms; synthetic rubber	3018.4	139.2	130.1	133.2	1023	962	995	888	13	12	12
242	Other chemicals	11.7	2695.1	2429.5	2069.0	12938	14276	15386	16977	182	194	198
2421	Pesticides and other agro-chemical products	489.1	23.5	23.4	20.7	167	165	159	108	5	5	5
2422	Paints, varnishes, printing ink and mastics	1831.7	382.6	357.1	329.8	2790	2968	3060	3882	51	54	51
2423	Pharmaceuticals, medicinal chemicals, etc.	501.8	1648.4	1439.8	1226.0	6386	7175	7648	8224	36	38	39
2424	Soap, cleaning & cosmetic preparations	184.2	473.8	461.9	375.1	2508	2745	3101	3234	53	57	60
2429	Other chemical products n.e.c.	5.3	166.8	147.3	117.5	1087	1223	1418	1529	37	40	43
2430	Man-made fibres	56.3	5.5	10.7	12.4	302	251	137	157	2	2	2
251	Rubber products	3.7	46.1	41.6	43.8	789	822	1705	1519	26	27	32
2511	Rubber tyres and tubes	52.6	3.7	4.2	3.6	67	81	88	88	3	4	4
2519	Other rubber products	760.7	42.5	37.4	40.2	722	741	1625	1431	23	23	28
2520	Plastic products	129.7	781.7	740.4	646.0	11649	12489	12622	12296	250	261	261
2610	Glass and glass products	2936.7	115.4	113.5	107.9	1463	1926	1553	2113	38	36	36
269	Non-metallic mineral products n.e.c.	123.6	2706.0	2605.2	2401.8	28677	32717	32718	34927	722	738	750
2691	Pottery, china and earthenware	339.8	116.9	112.1	97.4	1357	1558	1580	1637	15	17	17
2692	Refractory ceramic products	207.7	323.3	327.1	315.1	5112	5062	4668	4651	30	28	31
2693	Struct.non-refractory clay; ceramic products	753.0	180.5	175.6	162.8	4186	5312	4430	5932	83	84	81
2694	Cement, lime and plaster	804.2	683.9	655.5	666.5	2665	2460	2499	2727	26	23	19
2695	Articles of concrete, cement and plaster	82.3	739.0	680.6	581.5	10239	12305	14061	14486	365	375	382
2696	Cutting, shaping & finishing of stone	626.1	77.5	74.2	73.1	2675	2608	2592	2714	177	180	188
2699	Other non-metallic mineral products n.e.c.	551.6	585.1	580.1		2443	3412	2888	2780	26	31	32
2710	Basic iron and steel	150.1	422.3	376.2	260.9	2761	3793	4492	6159	66	64	68
2720	Basic precious and non-ferrous metals	70.6	137.2	120.9	110.7	1271	1425	1625	2420	29	27	32
273	Casting of metals	66.2	88.3	46.2	50.0	785	791	1303	1033	20	20	18
2731	Casting of iron and steel	4.3	84.5	42.4	46.9	686	674	1186	912	15	15	13
2732	Casting of non-ferrous metals	959.5	3.8	3.8	3.1	99	117	117	121	5	5	5
281	Struct.metal products;tanks;steam generators	861.7	1413.0	821.3	746.0	11687	13076	14653	14839	401	416	426
2811	Structural metal products	86.0	1317.1	727.3	640.8	9789	10730	12237	12585	371	385	398
2812	Tanks, reservoirs and containers of metal	11.9	83.0	90.9	102.1	1758	2228	2230	2057	22	24	22
2813	Steam generators	907.6	12.9	3.1	3.1	140	118	186	197	8	7	6
289	Other metal products; metal working services	137.0	812.6	752.1	678.7	10460	11944	11718	13016	470	485	494
2891	Metal forging/pressing/stamping/roll-forming	187.5	129.4	122.1	94.3	966	1664	1312	1144	15	14	14
2892	Treatment & coating of metals	37.6	174.0	150.4	140.9	3447	3497	3684	3906	293	310	315
2893	Cutlery, hand tools and general hardware	545.5	36.5	33.8	66.6	1244	643	683	735	27	21	22
2899	Other fabricated metal products n.e.c.	285.2	472.7	445.8	377.0	4803	6140	6039	7231	135	140	143
291	General purpose machinery	4.1	4.6	4.6	3.9	4199	4020	4514	4200	114	120	125
2911	Engines & turbines (not for transport equipment)	106.8	119.3	112.0	102.2	145	170	161	149	18	19	18
2912	Pumps, compressors, taps and valves	19.8	17.7	13.6	13.8	1458	1500	1657	1517	22	22	24
2913	Bearings, gears, gearing & driving elements	0.4	0.2	0.2	0.2	335	335	413	409	22	28	27
2914	Ovens, furnaces and furnace burners	48.7	47.6	37.9	33.8	15	12	12	20	1	1	
2915	Lifting and handling equipment	105.4	105.4	99.2	85.2	413	463	511	461	10	11	10
2919	Other general purpose machinery	73.3	79.9	74.3	54.1	1833	1540	1760	1644	41	39	45
292	Special purpose machinery	46.4	51.0	48.3	27.5	882	1067	1164	1126	59	54	57
2921	Agricultural and forestry machinery	12.5	10.5	9.2	9.7	324	505	556	525	18	18	11
2922	Machine tools	6.7	7.1	2.0	2.0	245	234	237	254	22	17	20
2923	Machinery for metallurgy	3.3	4.1	6.7	7.1	25	26	8			1	
2924	Machinery for mining & construction	1.1	1.4	2.0	2.0	153	154	151	176	6	4	5
2925	Food/beverage/tobacco processing machinery							93	89			7
2926	Machinery for textile, apparel and leather	3.3	5.5	6.1	5.9	27	27	17	17	2	2	2
2927	Weapons and ammunition											
2929	Other special purpose machinery					108	121	102	65	10	12	11

continued

Morocco

ISIC	Industry	Number of enterprises (number)					Number of employees (number)					Wages and salaries paid to employees (millions of Moroccan Dirhams)				
		Note	2007	2008	2009	2010	Note	2007	2008	2009	2010	Note	2007	2008	2009	2010
2930	Domestic appliances n.e.c.		23	21	19	...		1270	1257	1213	1263		91.5	95.2	92.8	92.2
3000	Office, accounting and computing machinery		6	5	5	...		109	182	176	72		...	...	...	4.4
3110	Electric motors, generators and transformers		35	39	37	...		938	870	818	1518		38.8	38.0	39.6	85.5
3120	Electricity distribution & control apparatus		38	38	38	...		5845	6033	4438	4057		392.7	428.6	343.5	313.3
3130	Insulated wire and cable		9	8	11	...		1252	1165	1461	1577		147.8	142.3	191.0	192.3
3140	Accumulators, primary cells and batteries		5	6	5	...		676	1037	807	792		55.1	85.1	55.6	58.3
3150	Lighting equipment and electric lamps		40	38	40	...		1568	1501	1670	1594		71.1	72.4	83.7	81.0
3190	Other electrical equipment n.e.c.		46	43	43	...		30534	31620	30778	37364		1336.1	1445.4	1417.4	1914.2
3210	Electronic valves, tubes, etc.		9	9	9	...		5579	4611	3700	4415		508.0	473.5	380.5	417.5
3220	TV/radio transmitters; line comm. apparatus		1	2	2	...		47	348	309	237		2.4	1.1	1.4	1.2
3230	TV and radio receivers and associated goods		2	1	1	...		49	13	16	16					
331	Medical, measuring, testing appliances, etc.		26	24	24	...		950	1023	1777	1245		82.6	86.1	189.9	95.4
3311	Medical, surgical and orthopaedic equipment		15	13	13	...		329	292	318	275		12.5	12.9	13.1	10.8
3312	Measuring/testing/navigating appliances,etc.		11	11	11	...		621	731	1459	970		70.1	73.2	176.8	84.7
3313	Industrial process control equipment															
3320	Optical instruments & photographic equipment		7	7	7	...		69	37	...	33		2.4	0.9	...	0.5
3330	Watches and clocks		...	...	...	...										
3410	Motor vehicles		6	7	7	...		2134	2552	3891	4182		227.8	314.3	356.0	359.2
3420	Automobile bodies, trailers & semi-trailers		52	47	49	...		2607	2456	2321	2726		169.3	159.6	107.8	143.3
3430	Parts/accessories for automobiles		30	31	34	...		1673	1331	1478	2024		106.7	95.1	105.0	108.2
351	Building and repairing of ships and boats		34	33	29	...		1035	1160	892	749		94.1	101.8	85.9	77.1
3511	Building and repairing of ships		31	30	27	...		745	914	764	640		83.6	90.4	79.1	71.7
3512	Building/repairing of pleasure/sport. boats		3	3	2	...		290	246	128	109		10.4	11.4	6.8	5.4
3520	Railway/tramway locomotives & rolling stock		1	2	2	...		534	603	488	519		28.4	47.1	43.1	45.8
3530	Aircraft and spacecraft		14	19	23	...		1731	2856	2934	3391		138.4	214.3	245.2	280.9
359	Transport equipment n.e.c.		13	11	11	...		500	488	460	392		46.2	52.2	51.9	48.4
3591	Motorcycles		8	6	7	...		341	355	328	325		41.1	47.1	46.5	45.9
3592	Bicycles and invalid carriages		2	2	2	...		70	69	73	9		3.1	3.1	3.4	0.4
3599	Other transport equipment n.e.c.		3	3	2	...		89	64	59	58		2.0	2.0	2.0	2.1
3610	Furniture		150	123	128	...		4103	4514	5402	6859		271.8	278.6	427.1	546.0
369	Manufacturing n.e.c.		53	52	48	...		2129	2146	2091	1957		121.2	124.6	125.6	132.3
3691	Jewellery and related articles		13	12	13	...		962	1007	1167	1152		50.1	56.2	64.4	69.6
3692	Musical instruments															
3693	Sports goods		2	2	2	...		14	21	15	19		0.3	0.4	0.4	0.7
3694	Games and toys		3	3	3	...		140	123	147	92		6.0	6.4	6.2	5.8
3699	Other manufacturing n.e.c.		35	35	30	...		1013	995	762	694		64.8	61.6	54.4	56.2
3710	Recycling of metal waste and scrap		...	1	1	...		50	56	44	25		1.1	1.1	1.2	1.5
3720	Recycling of non-metal waste and scrap		...	...	...	...										
D	Total manufacturing	a/	7863	7841	7854	...	a/	464793	501427	488725	510958	a/	27655.7	30208.2	31411.9	33305.8

a/ Sum of available data.

Morocco

		Output at factor values (millions of Moroccan Dirhams)					Value added at factor values (millions of Moroccan Dirhams)					Gross fixed capital formation (millions of Moroccan Dirhams)	
ISIC	Industry (ISIC Revision 3)	Note	2007	2008	2009	2010	Note	2007	2008	2009	2010	Note	2009	2010
151	Processed meat,fish,fruit,vegetables,fats		21258	23787	23145	24380		3914	4335	4866	5165		:	1006
1511	Processing/preserving of meat		1105	1171	1713	2866		219	186	255	333		:	103
1512	Processing/preserving of fish		8708	9557	8986	9343		1946	2015	2279	2687		:	444
1513	Processing/preserving of fruit & vegetables		2918	3062	2681	3034		584	652	577	673		:	140
1514	Vegetable and animal oils and fats		8527	9998	9765	9137		1166	1481	1754	1472		:	321
1520	Dairy products		9607	11564	12797	13568		2179	2734	3396	3458		:	1212
153	Grain mill products; starches; animal feeds		19283	22322	20482	23375		2033	2192	2009	2260		:	737
1531	Grain mill products		14180	15546	14833	16248		1379	1548	1350	1333		:	652
1532	Starches and starch products		147	202	191	219		66	48	53	56		:	8
1533	Prepared animal feeds		4956	6573	5457	6907		588	595	606	871		:	77
154	Other food products		13024	15455	11936	16388		4264	4031	4128	4402		:	802
1541	Bakery products		1872	2181	2518	2615		769	706	794	840		:	138
1542	Sugar		6396	9001	4932	8977		1941	2094	2050	2126		:	426
1543	Cocoa, chocolate and sugar confectionery		615	666	767	988		183	185	211	300		:	66
1544	Macaroni, noodles & similar products		502	945	998	867		83	168	185	130		:	41
1549	Other food products n.e.c.		3639	2663	2721	2941		1288	877	889	1007		:	131
155	Beverages		5765	7308	7852	8785		2874	3513	3868	4182		:	845
1551	Distilling, rectifying & blending of spirits		86	80	67			80					:	113
1552	Wines		650	704	759	1434		299	353	357	501		:	84
1553	Malt liquors and malt		1810	1958	1992	2001		1344	1378	1428	1497		:	647
1554	Soft drinks; mineral waters		3218	4566	5033	5301		1150	1782	1996	2170		:	
1600	Tobacco products		7378	5782	8281	8235		7139	5602	8133	9450		:	175
171	Spinning, weaving and finishing of textiles		6010	6700	5781	5461		1647	1646	1683	1529		:	207
1711	Textile fibre preparation; textile weaving		5044	5291	4639	4532		1321	1223	1337	1113		:	159
1712	Finishing of textiles		966	1409	1142	930		326	423	346	416		:	48
172	Other textiles		2061	2826	1821	2072		667	746	467	554		:	65
1721	Made-up textile articles, except apparel		581	1257	996	1334		190	271	238	339		:	42
1722	Carpets and rugs		876	943	283	236		304	318	81	72		:	11
1723	Cordage, rope, twine and netting		123	132	108	108		22	24	23	20		:	2
1729	Other textiles n.e.c.		482	493	434	393		151	132	126	123		:	10
1730	Knitted and crocheted fabrics and articles		1145	1094	938	1090		372	344	340	359		:	15
1810	Wearing apparel, except fur apparel		15631	15722	13109	13948		6339	6355	5477	5556		:	465
1820	Dressing & dyeing of fur; processing of fur												:	
191	Tanning, dressing and processing of leather		546	515	553	608		169	160	163	197		:	11
1911	Tanning and dressing of leather		372	368	408	447		99	100	108	129		:	5
1912	Luggage, handbags, etc.; saddlery & harness		174	147	145	160		70	60	55	68		:	6
1920	Footwear		1950	1951	2065	2292		761	747	765	1006		:	136
2010	Sawmilling and planing of wood		443	473	368	334		96	91	92	87		:	6
202	Products of wood, cork, straw, etc.		2951	2906	2475	2681		694	704	589	600		:	72
2021	Veneer sheets, plywood, particle board, etc.		908	846	502	654		229	201	92	97		:	40
2022	Builders' carpentry and joinery		1106	1225	1131	1217		258	304	302	313		:	15
2023	Wooden containers		673	587	567	590		134	129	116	128		:	13
2029	Other wood products; articles of cork/straw		263	248	274	221		72	71	79	62		:	4
210	Paper and paper products		4144	3982	3789	4680		1132	965	864	1249		:	173
2101	Pulp, paper and paperboard		2655	1075	983	1643		760	224	119	481		:	34
2102	Corrugated paper and paperboard		1080	2353	2241	2446		286	636	617	663		:	92
2109	Other articles of paper and paperboard		409	555	565	591		87	105	129	105		:	47
221	Publishing		434	414	633	711		212	196	235	260		:	143
2211	Publishing of books and other publications		124	153	165	163		36	42	47	46		:	4
2212	Publishing of newspapers, journals, etc.		236	248	374	377		143	150	152	154		:	121
2213	Publishing of recorded media		-	5	11	11			2	5	5		:	1
2219	Other publishing		74	7	84	160		32	2	32	55		:	17

continued

Morocco

ISIC	Industry	Note	Output 2007	Output 2008	Output 2009	Output 2010	Note	Value added 2007	Value added 2008	Value added 2009	Value added 2010	Note	GFCF 2009	GFCF 2010
			(millions of Moroccan Dirhams)					(millions of Moroccan Dirhams)					(millions of Moroccan Dirhams)	
222	Printing and related service activities		2468	2475	2467	2635		694	718	718	812		…	148
2221	Printing		2445	2381	2457	2624		682	679	714	810		…	147
2222	Service activities related to printing		22	94	10	11		11	39	3	3		…	-
2230	Reproduction of recorded media		…	153	223	60		…	…	…	…		…	
2310	Coke oven products		77	…	…	…		45	71	91	23		…	3
2320	Refined petroleum products		28458	32235	18844	35219		2096	1026	2787	4368		…	1857
2330	Processing of nuclear fuel		…	…	…	…		…	…	…	…		…	
241	Basic chemicals		20178	40220	16252	34846		7576	8344	3010	9448		…	1990
2411	Basic chemicals, except fertilizers		17372	38303	13124	30992		6618	7900	2403	8550		…	1501
2412	Fertilizers and nitrogen compounds		…	240	1749	2337		537	1	196	582		…	457
2413	Plastics in primary forms; synthetic rubber		1514	1677	1378	1516		421	443	411	316		…	32
242	Other chemicals		12511	14860	15042	19256		4552	5635	5976	7718		…	940
2421	Pesticides and other agro-chemical products		136	107	101	110		54	60	58	29		…	3
2422	Paints, varnishes, printing ink and mastics		2617	3080	3241	4880		785	786	806	1187		…	247
2423	Pharmaceuticals, medicinal chemicals, etc.		5025	6337	6452	8528		2507	3200	3610	4799		…	466
2424	Soap, cleaning & cosmetic preparations		3962	4453	4381	4487		935	1338	1212	1299		…	204
2429	Other chemical products n.e.c.		772	883	867	1251		271	252	289	403		…	20
2430	Man-made fibres		21	20	15	15		16	13	4	4		…	1
251	Rubber products		234	233	240	198		68	62	78	51		…	20
2511	Rubber tyres and tubes		17	25	20	23		8	7	6	7		…	2
2519	Other rubber products		217	208	220	175		60	55	72	44		…	18
2520	Plastic products		6362	7356	6553	6678		1393	1582	1795	1577		…	271
2610	Glass and glass products		690	745	772	929		300	319	315	359		…	171
269	Non-metallic mineral products n.e.c.		26108	25969	26770	27827		9053	9669	11152	12813		…	3997
2691	Pottery, china and earthenware		629	664	461	674		273	300	415	319		…	233
2692	Refractory ceramic products		2489	2781	2628	3192		565	682	778	737		…	185
2693	Struct.non-refractory clay; ceramic products		1144	1357	1398	1545		354	421	479	503		…	444
2694	Cement, lime and plaster		10643	10914	12005	12376		5844	5813	7009	7330		…	2436
2695	Articles of concrete, cement and plaster		6867	7661	7820	7707		1279	1641	1686	1832		…	404
2696	Cutting, shaping & finishing of stone		2695	628	614	602		154	142	149	162		…	26
2699	Other non-metallic mineral products n.e.c.		1640	1964	1843	1731		584	671	736	…		…	269
2710	Basic iron and steel		10086	14260	12057	13936		1836	2413	1670	1481		…	580
2720	Basic precious and non-ferrous metals		2171	1901	1499	2537		475	271	571	595		…	48
273	Casting of metals		304	322	459	544		97	98	153	133		…	23
2731	Casting of iron and steel		292	310	448	533		92	95	149	130		…	23
2732	Casting of non-ferrous metals		12	12	11	10		4	3	4	3		…	-
281	Struct.metal products;tanks;steam generators		5846	6289	6214	6107		1404	1599	2157	1701		…	311
2811	Structural metal products		5161	5619	5533	5315		1155	1397	1929	1473		…	261
2812	Tanks, reservoirs and containers of metal		668	655	630	736		244	198	206	209		…	22
2813	Steam generators		17	16	51	56		5	5	22	19		…	28
289	Other metal products; metal working services		6357	7835	6463	7430		1554	1781	1439	1833		…	
2891	Metal forging/pressing/stamping/roll-forming		616	851	688	537		161	215	197	188		…	2168
2892	Treatment & coating of metals		729	765	796	816		224	244	273	288		…	13
2893	Cutlery, hand tools and general hardware		425	201	177	162		135	61	55	55		…	111
2899	Other fabricated metal products n.e.c.		4588	6018	4801	5915		1034	1262	914	1301		…	24
291	General purpose machinery		1176	1305	1377	1325		411	471	468	507		…	2020
2911	Engines & turbines (not for transport equipment)		11	14	20	11		5	5	7	8		…	37
2912	Pumps, compressors, taps and valves		384	446	431	391		164	184	170	156		…	
2913	Bearings, gears, gearing & driving elements		52	52	67	96		21	21	23	22		…	11
2914	Ovens, furnaces and furnace burners		1	1	1	2		-	-	-	1		…	-
2915	Lifting and handling equipment		190	223	265	250		75	84	103	92		…	1
2919	Other general purpose machinery		537	569	593	574		145	177	165	227		…	24

Code										
292	Special purpose machinery	221	467	433	340	168	199	188	114	128
2921	Agricultural and forestry machinery	125	370	319	253	...	161	149	85	124
2922	Machine tools	37	39	46	42	15	13	16	18	3
2923	Machinery for metallurgy	8	9	-	...	5	5	8	...	...
2924	Machinery for mining & construction	22	20	22	15	7	6	5	4	-
2925	Food/beverage/tobacco processing machinery	...	...	23	18	...	...	...	2	-
2926	Machinery for textile, apparel and leather	10	8	5	4	3	4	2	...	-
2927	Weapons and ammunition	...	...	...	...	...	...	...	...	-
2929	Other special purpose machinery	18	21	19	9	8	9	7	4	...
2930	Domestic appliances n.e.c.	1098	727	648	614	256	558	245	214	12
3000	Office, accounting and computing machinery	96	273	126	27	36	60	52	10	15
3110	Electric motors, generators and transformers	199	312	277	430	56	65	80	156	86
3120	Electricity distribution & control apparatus	1877	2167	1589	1626	642	672	576	587	87
3130	Insulated wire and cable	2899	1829	2908	3374	403	303	512	520	29
3140	Accumulators, primary cells and batteries	426	1640	348	359	152	309	183	165	15
3150	Lighting equipment and electric lamps	375	433	445	431	111	125	175	151	624
3190	Other electrical equipment n.e.c.	12570	11428	10334	13417	2449	2156	2087	3165	298
3210	Electronic valves, tubes, etc.	1192	1212	761	1100	577	575	266	922	...
3220	TV/radio transmitters; line comm. apparatus	7	271	249	228	4	149	165	109	1
3230	TV and radio receivers and associated goods	11	2	2	2	3	1	2	1	
331	Medical, measuring, testing appliances, etc.	898	1116	2262	854	228	241	556	200	48
3311	Medical, surgical and orthopaedic equipment	46	48	66	44	18	9	22	17	3
3312	Measuring/testing/navigating appliances,etc.	852	1067	2196	809	209	232	534	184	45
3313	Industrial process control equipment	...	4	...	...	...	...	...	...	...
3320	Optical instruments & photographic equipment	7	...	...	4	4	1	...	1	
3330	Watches and clocks	...	...	...	...	...	...	...	...	121
3410	Motor vehicles	3754	5369	5158	5214	544	705	981	1011	40
3420	Automobile bodies, trailers & semi-trailers	2331	2409	1537	1950	592	630	310	449	30
3430	Parts/accessories for automobiles	547	412	492	565	165	136	165	173	
351	Building and repairing of ships and boats	297	283	278	...	133	131	139	102	2
3511	Building and repairing of ships	239	246	219	198	119	126	108	9	-
3512	Building/repairing of pleasure/sport. boats	58	37	59	48	14	6	32	84	10
3520	Railway/tramway locomotives & rolling stock	311	481	167	170	136	205	78	610	161
3530	Aircraft and spacecraft	1670	2404	2333	2762	296	579	548	84	5
359	Transport equipment n.e.c.	330	386	359	293	119	137	128	81	5
3591	Motorcycles	305	360	334	279	112	130	122	1	-
3592	Bicycles and invalid carriages	15	14	15	2	5	4	5	2	
3599	Other transport equipment n.e.c.	10	12	11	12	2	4	2	...	104
3610	Furniture	1511	1724	2840	3018	518	569	702	957	56
369	Manufacturing n.e.c.	936	899	927	884	224	234	261	252	51
3691	Jewellery and related articles	520	505	499	492	94	107	136	135	...
3692	Musical instruments	...	4	...	...	...	1	1	...	2
3693	Sports goods	3	...	5	6	1	1	1	28	3
3694	Games and toys	49	47	46	60	20	19	17	89	
3699	Other manufacturing n.e.c.	365	343	377	325	109	106	108	...	
3710	Recycling of metal waste and scrap	...	...	...	...	...	...	...	...	
3720	Recycling of non-metal waste and scrap	34	33	33	35	2	3	3	5	-
D	Total manufacturing	268275 a/	315258	266244 a/	326090	73882	77507	78079	94451 a/	20509 a/

a/ Sum of available data.

Morocco

- 588 -

ISIC	Industry	Note	1999	2000	2001	2002	2003	2004	2005	2006	2007	2008	2009	2010
15	Food and beverages		...	...	...	...	...	...	...	...	...	...	...	...
16	Tobacco products		79	80	84	88	90	95	100	105	119	125	...	...
17	Textiles		93	88	97	100	96	96	100	109	109	107	134	138
18	Wearing apparel, fur		80	97	94	94	93	94	100	97	101	102	106	106
19	Leather, leather products and footwear		93	90	97	96	99	96	100	99	96	102	102	107
20	Wood products (excl. furniture)		84	114	104	101	101	111	100	89	94	88	84	86
21	Paper and paper products		53	63	66	69	81	95	100	89	94	110	102	105
22	Printing and publishing		74	75	73	81	88	85	100	120	126	122	122	123
23	Coke,refined petroleum products,nuclear fuel		102	93	97	94	68	92	100	100	106	105	104	104
24	Chemicals and chemical products		79	80	82	88	89	96	100	105	113	114	91	99
25	Rubber and plastics products		72	86	80	87	83	99	100	102	101	105	107	113
26	Non-metallic mineral products		71	71	76	83	91	95	100	112	133	151	148	148
27	Basic metals		59	65	67	77	92	91	100	106	114	120	120	119
28	Fabricated metal products		72	78	85	85	83	94	100	105	113	105	108	101
29	Machinery and equipment n.e.c.		78	91	84	87	97	100	100	103	109	112	117	120
30	Office, accounting and computing machinery		...	...	...	...	...	...	100	105	111	124	113	117
31	Electrical machinery and apparatus		73	81	81	88	94	97	100	99	104	106	104	...
32	Radio,television and communication equipment		94	56	84	82	95	94	100	173	179	180	180	104
33	Medical, precision and optical instruments		53	70	57	79	71	98	100	98	88	92	91	177
34	Motor vehicles, trailers, semi-trailers		96	93	98	99	88	89	100	139	171	174	173	89
35	Other transport equipment		94	88	110	106	119	99	100	106	108	112	106	189
36	Furniture; manufacturing n.e.c.		...	...	...	...	...	...	...	...	...	...	...	105
37	Recycling		...	...	...	...	...	...	...	...	...	...	...	...
D	Total manufacturing		78	82	85	88	91	95	100	105	110	112	113	115

Index numbers of industrial production (2005=100)

ISIC Revision 3

Myanmar

Supplier of information:
Central Statistical Organization, Nay Pyi Taw.

Basic source of data:
Administrative data.

Major deviations from ISIC (Revision 3):
Data were originally compiled according to the national classification system (MSIC).

Reference period:
Fiscal year.

Scope:
All government-owned enterprises.

Method of data collection:
Mail questionnaires.

Type of enumeration:
Not reported.

Adjusted for non-response:
No.

Concepts and definitions of variables:
No deviations from the standard UN concepts and definitions are reported.

Related national publications:
Statistical Yearbook (annual); Selected Monthly Economic Indicator, both published by the Central Statistical Organization, Nay Pyi Taw.

Myanmar

Column groups: **Number of enterprises (number)** · **Number of employees (number)** · **Wages and salaries (millions of Myanmar Kyats)**

ISIC	Industry (ISIC Revision 3)	Note	2007	2008	2009	2010	Note	2007	2008	2009	2010	Note	2007	2008	2009	2010
151	Processed meat,fish,fruit,vegetables,fats		…	…	…	…		…	…	…	…		…	…	…	…
1511	Processing/preserving of meat		…	…	…	…		…	…	…	…		…	…	…	…
1512	Processing/preserving of fish		…	…	…	…		…	…	…	…		…	…	…	…
1513	Processing/preserving of fruit & vegetables		…	…	…	…		…	…	…	…		…	…	…	…
1514	Vegetable and animal oils and fats		…	…	…	…		…	…	…	…		…	…	…	…
1520	Dairy products		…	…	…	…		…	…	…	…		…	…	…	…
153	Grain mill products; starches; animal feeds		…	…	…	…		…	…	…	…		…	…	…	…
1531	Grain mill products		…	…	…	…		…	…	…	…		…	…	…	…
1532	Starches and starch products		…	…	…	…		…	…	…	…		…	…	…	…
1533	Prepared animal feeds		…	…	…	…		…	…	…	…		…	…	…	…
154	Other food products		…	…	…	…		…	…	…	…		…	…	…	…
1541	Bakery products		…	…	…	…		…	…	…	…		…	…	…	…
1542	Sugar		…	…	…	…		463	463	414	336		…	…	…	…
1543	Cocoa, chocolate and sugar confectionery		…	…	…	…		109	109	67	82		…	…	…	…
1544	Macaroni, noodles & similar products		…	…	…	…		290	261	198	95		…	…	…	…
1549	Other food products n.e.c.		…	…	…	…		343	308	320	389		…	…	…	…
155	Beverages		…	…	…	…		…	…	…	…		…	…	…	…
1551	Distilling, rectifying & blending of spirits		…	…	…	…		421	363	342	134		…	…	…	…
1552	Wines		…	…	…	…		…	…	…	…		…	…	…	…
1553	Malt liquors and malt		…	…	…	…		…	…	…	…		…	…	…	…
1554	Soft drinks; mineral waters		…	…	…	…		659	655	615	366		…	…	…	…
1600	Tobacco products		…	…	…	…		939	768	595	…		…	…	…	…
171	Spinning, weaving and finishing of textiles		…	…	…	…		…	…	…	…		…	…	…	…
1711	Textile fibre preparation; textile weaving		…	…	…	…		…	…	…	…		…	…	…	…
1712	Finishing of textiles		…	…	…	…		…	…	…	…		…	…	…	…
172	Other textiles		…	…	…	…		…	…	…	…		…	…	…	…
1721	Made-up textile articles, except apparel		…	…	…	…		…	…	…	…		…	…	…	…
1722	Carpets and rugs		…	…	…	…		…	…	…	…		…	…	…	…
1723	Cordage, rope, twine and netting		…	…	…	…		…	…	…	…		…	…	…	…
1729	Other textiles n.e.c.		…	…	…	…		…	…	…	…		…	…	…	…
1730	Knitted and crocheted fabrics and articles		…	…	…	…		…	…	…	…		…	…	…	…
1810	Wearing apparel, except fur apparel		…	…	…	…		…	…	…	…		…	…	…	…
1820	Dressing & dyeing of fur; processing of fur		…	…	…	…		…	…	…	…		…	…	…	…
191	Tanning, dressing and processing of leather		2	2	2	…		273	…	240	240		…	…	…	…
1911	Tanning and dressing of leather		…	…	…	…		…	…	…	…		…	…	…	…
1912	Luggage, handbags, etc.; saddlery & harness		…	…	…	…		…	…	…	…		…	…	…	…
1920	Footwear		3	3	2	2		…	…	…	…		…	…	…	…
2010	Sawmilling and planing of wood		97	97	96	96		1055	804	556	550		…	…	…	…
202	Products of wood, cork, straw, etc.		…	…	…	…		…	…	…	…		…	…	…	…
2021	Veneer sheets, plywood, particle board, etc.		5	5	5	6		…	…	…	…		…	…	…	…
2022	Builders' carpentry and joinery		…	…	…	…		…	…	…	…		…	…	…	…
2023	Wooden containers		1	1	1	1		218	117	31	…		…	…	…	…
2029	Other wood products; articles of cork/straw		…	…	…	…		…	…	…	…		…	…	…	…
210	Paper and paper products		…	…	…	…		…	…	…	…		…	…	…	…
2101	Pulp, paper and paperboard		5	5	5	6		4178	1970	1878	2246		…	…	…	…
2102	Corrugated paper and paperboard		…	…	…	…		…	…	…	…		…	…	…	…
2109	Other articles of paper and paperboard		1	1	1	1		191	142	139	90		…	…	…	…
221	Publishing		…	…	…	…		…	…	…	…		…	…	…	…
2211	Publishing of books and other publications		…	…	…	…		…	…	…	…		…	…	…	…
2212	Publishing of newspapers, journals, etc.		…	…	…	…		…	…	…	…		…	…	…	…
2213	Publishing of recorded media		…	…	…	…		…	…	…	…		…	…	…	…
2219	Other publishing		…	…	…	…		…	…	…	…		…	…	…	…

222	Printing and related service activities								
2221	Printing								
2222	Service activities related to printing								
2230	Reproduction of recorded media								
2310	Coke oven products								
2320	Refined petroleum products								
2330	Processing of nuclear fuel	5	5	5	6	1049	1068	1093	1124
241	Basic chemicals	3	3	3	1	68	126	146	300
2411	Basic chemicals, except fertilizers	3	3	3	5	779	766	676	683
2412	Fertilizers and nitrogen compounds								
2413	Plastics in primary forms; synthetic rubber								
242	Other chemicals								
2421	Pesticides and other agro-chemical products	1	1	1	1	50	55	60	79
2422	Paints, varnishes, printing ink and mastics	1	1	1	1	1733	1885	1803	1620
2423	Pharmaceuticals, medicinal chemicals, etc.	1	1	1	1	713	890	1042	1168
2424	Soap, cleaning & cosmetic preparations								
2429	Other chemical products n.e.c.								
2430	Man-made fibres								
251	Rubber products	2	2	2	1	190	105	109	289
2511	Rubber tyres and tubes								
2519	Other rubber products	2	1	1	1	515	609	679	387
2520	Plastic products								
2610	Glass and glass products								
269	Non-metallic mineral products n.e.c.								
2691	Pottery, china and earthenware								
2692	Refractory ceramic products								
2693	Struct.non-refractory clay; ceramic products								
2694	Cement, lime and plaster								
2695	Articles of concrete, cement and plaster								
2696	Cutting, shaping & finishing of stone								
2699	Other non-metallic mineral products n.e.c.								
2710	Basic iron and steel								
2720	Basic precious and non-ferrous metals								
273	Casting of metals								
2731	Casting of iron and steel								
2732	Casting of non-ferrous metals								
281	Struct.metal products;tanks;steam generators								
2811	Structural metal products								
2812	Tanks, reservoirs and containers of metal								
2813	Steam generators								
289	Other metal products; metal working services								
2891	Metal forging/pressing/stamping/roll-forming								
2892	Treatment & coating of metals								
2893	Cutlery, hand tools and general hardware	3	3	3	2	572	630	750	717
2899	Other fabricated metal products n.e.c.								
291	General purpose machinery								
2911	Engines & turbines (not for transport equipment)								
2912	Pumps, compressors, taps and valves								
2913	Bearings, gears, gearing & driving elements								
2914	Ovens, furnaces and furnace burners								
2915	Lifting and handling equipment								
2919	Other general purpose machinery								
292	Special purpose machinery								
2921	Agricultural and forestry machinery								
2922	Machine tools								
2923	Machinery for metallurgy								
2924	Machinery for mining & construction								
2925	Food/beverage/tobacco processing machinery								
2926	Machinery for textile, apparel and leather								
2927	Weapons and ammunition								
2929	Other special purpose machinery								

continued

Myanmar

ISIC	Industry	Number of enterprises (number)				Note	Number of employees (number)				Note	Wages and salaries (millions of Myanmar Kyats)				Note
		2007	2008	2009	2010		2007	2008	2009	2010		2007	2008	2009	2010	
2930	Domestic appliances n.e.c.	…	…	…	…		…	…	…	…		…	…	…	…	
3000	Office, accounting and computing machinery	…	…	…	…		…	…	…	…		…	…	…	…	
3110	Electric motors, generators and transformers	…	…	…	…		…	…	…	…		…	…	…	…	
3120	Electricity distribution & control apparatus	…	…	…	…		…	…	…	…		…	…	…	…	
3130	Insulated wire and cable	…	…	…	…		…	…	…	…		…	…	…	…	
3140	Accumulators, primary cells and batteries	…	…	…	…		…	…	…	…		…	…	…	…	
3150	Lighting equipment and electric lamps	…	…	…	…		…	…	…	…		…	…	…	…	
3190	Other electrical equipment n.e.c.	1	1	1	1		45	44	44	61		…	…	…	…	
3210	Electronic valves, tubes, etc.	…	…	…	…		…	…	…	…		…	…	…	…	
3220	TV/radio transmitters; line comm. apparatus	…	…	…	…		…	…	…	…		…	…	…	…	
3230	TV and radio receivers and associated goods	…	…	…	…		…	…	…	…		…	…	…	…	
331	Medical, measuring, testing appliances, etc.	…	…	…	…		…	…	…	…		…	…	…	…	
3311	Medical, surgical and orthopaedic equipment	…	…	…	…		…	…	…	…		…	…	…	…	
3312	Measuring/testing/navigating appliances,etc.	…	…	…	…		…	…	…	…		…	…	…	…	
3313	Industrial process control equipment	…	…	…	…		…	…	…	…		…	…	…	…	
3320	Optical instruments & photographic equipment	…	…	…	…		…	…	…	…		…	…	…	…	
3330	Watches and clocks	…	…	…	…		…	…	…	…		…	…	…	…	
3410	Motor vehicles	…	…	…	…		…	…	…	…		…	…	…	…	
3420	Automobile bodies, trailers & semi-trailers	…	…	…	…		…	…	…	…		…	…	…	…	
3430	Parts/accessories for automobiles	…	…	…	…		…	…	…	…		…	…	…	…	
351	Building and repairing of ships and boats	…	…	…	…		…	…	…	…		…	…	…	…	
3511	Building and repairing of ships	…	…	…	…		…	…	…	…		…	…	…	…	
3512	Building/repairing of pleasure/sport. boats	…	…	…	…		…	…	…	…		…	…	…	…	
3520	Railway/tramway locomotives & rolling stock	…	…	…	…		…	…	…	…		…	…	…	…	
3530	Aircraft and spacecraft	…	…	…	…		…	…	…	…		…	…	…	…	
359	Transport equipment n.e.c.	…	…	…	…		…	…	…	…		…	…	…	…	
3591	Motorcycles	2	2	2	2		1070	821	932	940		…	…	…	…	
3592	Bicycles and invalid carriages	…	…	…	…		…	…	…	…		…	…	…	…	
3599	Other transport equipment n.e.c.	…	…	…	…		…	…	…	…		…	…	…	…	
3610	Furniture	…	2	2	2		…	490	408	362		…	…	…	…	
369	Manufacturing n.e.c.	…	…	…	…		…	…	…	…		…	…	…	…	
3691	Jewellery and related articles	…	…	…	…		…	…	…	…		…	…	…	…	
3692	Musical instruments	…	…	…	…		…	…	…	…		…	…	…	…	
3693	Sports goods	…	…	…	…		…	…	…	…		…	…	…	…	
3694	Games and toys	…	…	…	…		…	…	…	…		…	…	…	…	
3699	Other manufacturing n.e.c.	…	…	…	…		…	…	…	…		…	…	…	…	
3710	Recycling of metal waste and scrap	…	…	…	…		…	…	…	…		…	…	…	…	
3720	Recycling of non-metal waste and scrap	…	…	…	…		…	…	…	…		…	…	…	…	
D	Total manufacturing	…	…	…	…		…	…	…	…		…	…	…	…	

Myanmar

ISIC	Industry	Note	Output at producers' prices (millions of Myanmar Kyats)				Note	Value added (millions of Myanmar Kyats)				Note	Gross fixed capital formation (millions of Myanmar Kyats)	
	ISIC Revision 3		2007	2008	2009	2010		2007	2008	2009	2010		2009	2010
151	Processed meat,fish,fruit,vegetables,fats													
1511	Processing/preserving of meat													
1512	Processing/preserving of fish													
1513	Processing/preserving of fruit & vegetables													
1514	Vegetable and animal oils and fats													
1520	Dairy products													
153	Grain mill products; starches; animal feeds													
1531	Grain mill products													
1532	Starches and starch products													
1533	Prepared animal feeds													
154	Other food products													
1541	Bakery products		2373	2601	1632	1378							15	2930
1542	Sugar		526	366	322	245							1193	1255
1543	Cocoa, chocolate and sugar confectionery		337	369	462	722							487	687
1544	Macaroni, noodles & similar products		539	856	961	835							8434	6387
1549	Other food products n.e.c.													
155	Beverages		8866	9123	4781	2676							4062	2253
1551	Distilling, rectifying & blending of spirits													
1552	Wines		7223	7129	4936	4697							5957	5866
1553	Malt liquors and malt		15010	15687	833								-	
1554	Soft drinks; mineral waters													
1600	Tobacco products													
171	Spinning, weaving and finishing of textiles													
1711	Textile fibre preparation; textile weaving													
1712	Finishing of textiles													
172	Other textiles													
1721	Made-up textile articles, except apparel													
1722	Carpets and rugs													
1723	Cordage, rope, twine and netting													
1729	Other textiles n.e.c.													
1730	Knitted and crocheted fabrics and articles													
1810	Wearing apparel, except fur apparel		1425	-	-	-								
1820	Dressing & dyeing of fur; processing of fur			1524	1639	1451							883	501
191	Tanning, dressing and processing of leather												4705	3274
1911	Tanning and dressing of leather													
1912	Luggage, handbags, etc.; saddlery & harness		35	3270	3907	3243								
1920	Footwear													
2010	Sawmilling and planing of wood													
202	Products of wood, cork, straw, etc.													
2021	Veneer sheets, plywood, particle board, etc.													
2022	Builders' carpentry and joinery													
2023	Wooden containers			261									76	
2029	Other wood products; articles of cork/straw		534											
210	Paper and paper products		17497	32946	12285	20354							74864	78398
2101	Pulp, paper and paperboard													
2102	Corrugated paper and paperboard		1456	1456	1488	736							896	968
2109	Other articles of paper and paperboard													
221	Publishing													
2211	Publishing of books and other publications													
2212	Publishing of newspapers, journals, etc.													
2213	Publishing of recorded media													
2219	Other publishing													

continued

Myanmar

ISIC Revision 3		Output at producers' prices (millions of Myanmar Kyats)					Value added (millions of Myanmar Kyats)					Gross fixed capital formation (millions of Myanmar Kyats)		
ISIC	Industry	Note	2007	2008	2009	2010	Note	2007	2008	2009	2010	Note	2009	2010
222	Printing and related service activities		...	...	...	...		...	...	...	...		...	...
2221	Printing		...	...	...	...		...	...	...	...		...	...
2222	Service activities related to printing		...	...	...	...		...	...	...	...		...	...
2230	Reproduction of recorded media		...	...	...	...		...	...	...	...		...	...
2310	Coke oven products		...	...	...	...		...	...	...	...		...	...
2320	Refined petroleum products		159112	147529	139947	180947		...	...	...	...		208	90
2330	Processing of nuclear fuel													
241	Basic chemicals													
2411	Basic chemicals, except fertilizers		1146	1124	849	659		...	...	...	...		3168	3366
2412	Fertilizers and nitrogen compounds		39577	38211	25119	12706		...	...	...	...		34614	19739
2413	Plastics in primary forms; synthetic rubber		...	...	...	...		...	...	...	...		...	...
242	Other chemicals													
2421	Pesticides and other agro-chemical products													
2422	Paints, varnishes, printing ink and mastics		772	593	667	92		...	...	...	...		1180	14
2423	Pharmaceuticals, medicinal chemicals, etc.		10060	11263	11346	10581		...	...	...	...		1622	5077
2424	Soap, cleaning & cosmetic preparations		37413	41403	38970	27606		...	...	...	...		2015	1018
2429	Other chemical products n.e.c.													
2430	Man-made fibres		...	...	...	...		...	...	...	...		...	...
251	Rubber products													
2511	Rubber tyres and tubes		...	...	...	...		...	...	...	...		...	...
2519	Other rubber products		1609	6436	6020	6431		...	...	...	...		1186	1221
2520	Plastic products		9539	10683	11352	10441		...	...	...	...		1087	461
2610	Glass and glass products		...	...	...	...		...	...	...	...		...	...
269	Non-metallic mineral products n.e.c.													
2691	Pottery, china and earthenware													
2692	Refractory ceramic products													
2693	Struct.non-refractory clay; ceramic products													
2694	Cement, lime and plaster													
2695	Articles of concrete, cement and plaster													
2696	Cutting, shaping & finishing of stone													
2699	Other non-metallic mineral products n.e.c.													
2710	Basic iron and steel													
2720	Basic precious and non-ferrous metals													
273	Casting of metals													
2731	Casting of iron and steel													
2732	Casting of non-ferrous metals													
281	Struct.metal products;tanks;steam generators													
2811	Structural metal products													
2812	Tanks, reservoirs and containers of metal													
2813	Steam generators													
289	Other metal products; metal working services													
2891	Metal forging/pressing/stamping/roll-forming													
2892	Treatment & coating of metals													
2893	Cutlery, hand tools and general hardware													
2899	Other fabricated metal products n.e.c.			2094	2234	2317								
291	General purpose machinery		...	...	...	...		...	...	...	...		6295	7528
2911	Engines & turbines (not for transport equipment)													
2912	Pumps, compressors, taps and valves													
2913	Bearings, gears, gearing & driving elements													
2914	Ovens, furnaces and furnace burners													
2915	Lifting and handling equipment													
2919	Other general purpose machinery													

Code	Description							
292	Special purpose machinery							
2921	Agricultural and forestry machinery							
2922	Machine tools							
2923	Machinery for metallurgy							
2924	Machinery for mining & construction							
2925	Food/beverage/tobacco processing machinery							
2926	Machinery for textile, apparel and leather							
2927	Weapons and ammunition							
2929	Other special purpose machinery							
2930	Domestic appliances n.e.c.							
3000	Office, accounting and computing machinery							
3110	Electric motors, generators and transformers							
3120	Electricity distribution & control apparatus							
3130	Insulated wire and cable							
3140	Accumulators, primary cells and batteries						155	885
3150	Lighting equipment and electric lamps		553	776	768			
3190	Other electrical equipment n.e.c.							
3210	Electronic valves, tubes, etc.							
3220	TV/radio transmitters; line comm. apparatus							
3230	TV and radio receivers and associated goods							
331	Medical, measuring, testing appliances, etc.							
3311	Medical, surgical and orthopaedic equipment							
3312	Measuring/testing/navigating appliances,etc.							
3313	Industrial process control equipment							
3320	Optical instruments & photographic equipment							
3330	Watches and clocks							
3410	Motor vehicles							
3420	Automobile bodies, trailers & semi-trailers							
3430	Parts/accessories for automobiles							
351	Building and repairing of ships and boats							
3511	Building and repairing of ships							
3512	Building/repairing of pleasure/sport. boats							
3520	Railway/tramway locomotives & rolling stock							
3530	Aircraft and spacecraft							
359	Transport equipment n.e.c.	2721	2455	2124	2309		7475	8314
3591	Motorcycles							
3592	Bicycles and invalid carriages							
3599	Other transport equipment n.e.c.							
3610	Furniture							
369	Manufacturing n.e.c.							
3691	Jewellery and related articles							
3692	Musical instruments							
3693	Sports goods		1195	1182	1892			
3694	Games and toys						2518	6156
3699	Other manufacturing n.e.c.							
3710	Recycling of metal waste and scrap							
3720	Recycling of non-metal waste and scrap							
D	Total manufacturing							

Netherlands

Supplier of information:
Central Bureau of Statistics, Voorburg.
Industrial statistics for the OECD countries are compiled by the OECD secretariat, which supplies them to UNIDO.

Basic source of data:
Survey on annual production statistics; survey on investment; annual census; VAT register.

Major deviations from ISIC (Revision 3):
Data presented by OECD in accordance with ISIC (Revision 3) were originally classified according to a classification system compatible with NACE (Revision 1).

Reference period:
Calendar year.

Scope:
All enterprises.

Method of data collection:
Not reported.

Type of enumeration:
Enterprises with 20 or more employees are completely enumerated, while smaller enterprises are surveyed through sampling.

Adjusted for non-response:
Yes.

Concepts and definitions of variables:
Number of employees is not converted to full time equivalent.
Wages and salaries includes gratuities, tips, severance payments, workplace and performance bonuses, ex-gratia payments, thirteenth month pay and seniority attendance.
Output is gross output. It excludes income from sales of capital assets produced on own accounts.
Value added refers to the national accounting concept.
Gross fixed capital formation is defined as the value of fixed assets purchased or constructed by the unit's own labour force for its own use, during the reference year. Major additions, alterations and improvements to fixed assets carried out by third parties are included. Transactions in fixed assets includes land, buildings, site preparation and other construction work, land which is not used for the establishment's business, transport equipment, machinery and other equipment, as well as additions, alterations and improvements which prolong the service life or increase productive capacity of capital goods. Fixed assets are valued at acquisition costs, including transportation costs and costs of installation, taxes and insurance for goods in transit.

Related national publications:
Summary of Manufacturing Industries (annual), published by Central Bureau of Statistics, Voorburg.

Netherlands

		Number of enterprises (number)					Number of employees (number)					Wages and salaries paid to employees (millions of Euros)				
ISIC	Industry	Note	2005	2006	2007	2008	Note	2005	2006	2007	2008	Note	2005	2006	2007	2008
151	Processed meat,fish,fruit,vegetables,fats		1015	985	930	925		33592	34311	34661	34670		...	1067	...	...
1511	Processing/preserving of meat		735	710	635	647		19075	18750	18578	18253		587	517	572	565
1512	Processing/preserving of fish		120	115	130	122		3263	3626	3215	3743		77	92	...	...
1513	Processing/preserving of fruit & vegetables		135	135	135	126		9060	9812	10258	10299		325	333	350	371
1514	Vegetable and animal oils and fats		25	25	30	30		2194	2123	2610	2375		...	125	111	106
1520	Dairy products		255	255	260	255		10260	10642	11265	11635		457	434	447	494
153	Grain mill products; starches; animal feeds		280	275	300	287		10605	11520	10742	11066		457	460	465	451
1531	Grain mill products		80	80	95	91		1249	1496	1373	1309		...	53	52	52
1532	Starches and starch products		10	15	10	11		2264	2203	1745	2084		...	103	85	84
1533	Prepared animal feeds		185	180	195	185		7092	7821	7624	7673		292	304	329	314
154	Other food products		2910	2850	2570	2504		56799	59263	57504	56568		1552	1591	1594	1624
1541	Bakery products		2620	2565	2260	2196		37417	39528	38478	38223		760	752	791	867
1542	Sugar		5	5	5	2		...	...	...	...		...	...	...	...
1543	Cocoa, chocolate and sugar confectionery		135	135	130	128		6333	6239	6331	6303		245	240	255	265
1544	Macaroni, noodles & similar products		5	5	10	10		...	113	117	54		...	2	...	...
1549	Other food products n.e.c.		150	145	165	168		...	...	...	...		...	...	...	...
155	Beverages		130	140	155	154		7720	6144	8566	8297		338	379	353	335
1551	Distilling, rectifying & blending of spirits		30	30	35	37		...	...	...	...		...	...	...	...
1552	Wines		25	30	30	36		...	...	117	...		...	...	...	...
1553	Malt liquors and malt		50	55	55	61		...	3525	...	5804		...	...	...	...
1554	Soft drinks; mineral waters		20	20	20	20		1956	1710	1690	1694		88	88	...	...
1600	Tobacco products		20	20	20	18		4292	4494	3805	3964		...	196	...	...
171	Spinning, weaving and finishing of textiles		285	315	295	293		3445	3422	3204	3130		114	...	112	101
1711	Textile fibre preparation; textile weaving		70	75	75	69		1713	1848	1742	1685		61	...	60	53
1712	Finishing of textiles		215	240	220	224		1732	1574	1462	1445		54	52	52	48
172	Other textiles		955	1030	975	1011		8838	8962	8865	8944		289	273	275	279
1721	Made-up textile articles, except apparel		705	740	695	700		4204	4341	4524	4377		104	104	100	113
1722	Carpets and rugs		65	70	70	72		2478	2616	2387	2600		105	96	103	94
1723	Cordage, rope, twine and netting		35	35	30	28		240	230	232	240		...	8	5	4
1729	Other textiles n.e.c.		150	185	180	211		1916	1774	1722	1726		...	65	67	69
1730	Knitted and crocheted fabrics and articles		65	60	50	46		346	305	277	281		9	...	11	9
1810	Wearing apparel, except fur apparel		1510	1265	1320	1339		3083	2681a/	2850a/	2642a/		82a/	72a/	84a/	...a/
1820	Dressing & dyeing of fur; processing of fur		10	10	10	8		13	...a/	...a/	...a/		...a/	...a/	...a/	...a/
191	Tanning, dressing and processing of leather		210	140	205	194		719	936	940	1010		21	...	21	25
1911	Tanning and dressing of leather		45	30	35	32		296	346	357	466		10	9	9	12
1912	Luggage, handbags, etc.; saddlery & harness		165	110	170	162		423	590	583	544		11	9	13	14
1920	Footwear		105	75	110	100		783	825	847	808		30	27	26	21
2010	Sawmilling and planing of wood		190	190	215	226		1055	1416	1510	1611		33	34	40	42
202	Products of wood, cork, straw, etc.		1785	1815	1700	1731		15981	16272	16606	16253		479	...	533	535
2021	Veneer sheets, plywood, particle board, etc.		25	25	25	26		241	263	254	364		5	...	...	12
2022	Builders' carpentry and joinery		1095	1120	1045	1084		11856	12171	12533	12508		363	357	410	416
2023	Wooden containers		140	145	150	148		2011	2129	2113	1974		62	61	65	67
2029	Other wood products; articles of cork/straw		525	525	480	473		1873	1709	1706	1407		49	46	...	39
210	Paper and paper products		435	425	425	409		22059	21580	19753	19614		844	837	830	786
2101	Pulp, paper and paperboard		85	85	95	81		6189	5861	5234	4724		262	262	246	...
2102	Corrugated paper and paperboard		195	190	190	186		8670	8631	7904	8272		300	301	310	313
2109	Other articles of paper and paperboard		155	150	140	142		7200	7088	6615	6618		281	273	274	...
221	Publishing		2780	2855	2995	3054		34421	35183	34812	34844		1315	1310	1382	1464
2211	Publishing of books and other publications		1170	1190	1300	1324		8826	9813	9172	7709		319	374	355	320
2212	Publishing of newspapers, journals, etc.		1080	1135	1160	1179		24121	24091	24405	25754		955	893	991	1097
2213	Publishing of recorded media		430	435	465	474		687	644	700	737		17	16	18	23
2219	Other publishing		100	95	75	77		787	636	535	644		25	26	19	24

ISIC Revision 3

222	Printing and related service activities	3425	3400	3720	3700	34577	34947	34889	33822	1178	1133	1107	1114
2221	Printing	2595	2580	2880	2855	28960	29149	29306	28282	1007	...	952	926
2222	Service activities related to printing	830	820	840	845	5617	5798	5582	5540	170	...	155	189
2230	Reproduction of recorded media	225	230	225	245	1258	1101	1121	873	41	37	38	20
2310	Coke oven products	-	5	5	-	-	6589b/	6556b/	7324	-	...	410b/	...
2320	Refined petroleum products	30	30	30	38	...	...b/	...b/	...	...	...	...b/	...
2330	Processing of nuclear fuel	-	-	5	3	...	...b/	...b/	...	...	...	...b/	...
241	Basic chemicals	240	260	305	304	26111	24670	23799	26463	1476	1558	1517	1573
2411	Basic chemicals, except fertilizers	120	125	135	133	...	14173	13801	15014	...	...	...	890
2412	Fertilizers and nitrogen compounds	25	25	30	29	1915	1531	1621	1596	87	84	90	94
2413	Plastics in primary forms; synthetic rubber	100	115	135	142	...	8967	8377	9853	...	...	...	589
242	Other chemicals	475	530	575	583	36070	35305	34651	34942	1536	1584	1608	1572
2421	Pesticides and other agro-chemical products	15	20	15	22	604	545	455	427	...	27	24	22
2422	Paints, varnishes, printing ink and mastics	105	110	120	112	6699	5691	5571	6093	287	295	338	292
2423	Pharmaceuticals, medicinal chemicals, etc.	125	145	155	159	16335	17283	17318	16382	696	714	771	753
2424	Soap, cleaning & cosmetic preparations	130	145	155	163	4915	4139	4306	4593	...	144	147	145
2429	Other chemical products n.e.c.	100	110	130	127	7517	7647	7001	7447	358	405	328	360
2430	Man-made fibres	20	25	30	28	2720	2779	2730	2742	137	140	142	136
251	Rubber products	100	80	95	95	3362	3221	3244	3478	111	111	121	134
2511	Rubber tyres and tubes	15	15	15	16	...	...	...	...	...	52	60	62
2519	Other rubber products	80	65	80	79	...	...	...	...	...	59	61	72
2520	Plastic products	1080	930	1140	1161	28673	29109	28852	29308	944	1005	1004	1031
2610	Glass and glass products	470	485	510	534	5648	5735	5434	5286	208	234	209	213
269	Non-metallic mineral products n.e.c.	1145	1135	1230	1183	21931	22045	22381	22456	784	825	848	863
2691	Pottery, china and earthenware	215	210	240	240	...	...	...	...	...	...	...	...
2692	Refractory ceramic products	10	10	10	8	...	...	280	359	...	...	13	17
2693	Struct.non-refractory clay; ceramic products	55	55	60	51	...	...	...	...	...	...	...	...
2694	Cement, lime and plaster	5	5	5	6	...	...	...	...	...	...	...	...
2695	Articles of concrete, cement and plaster	455	440	470	441	12878	12781	12824	13028	463	480	500	513
2696	Cutting, shaping & finishing of stone	335	340	360	358	2006	2033	2229	1974	66	59	71	60
2699	Other non-metallic mineral products n.e.c.	65	75	90	79	2462	2585	2686	2692	95	117	109	115
2710	Basic iron and steel	75	85	95	103	...	12381	12508	13177	616	609	640	625
2720	Basic precious and non-ferrous metals	70	80	85	93	5830	4982	4508	5534	241	250	235	243
273	Casting of metals	115	120	120	119	...	3620	3659	3818	119	120	112	123
2731	Casting of iron and steel	25	30	30	33	...	...	...	...	...	...	...	67
2732	Casting of non-ferrous metals	95	95	90	86	1697	...	...	...	...	...	...	57
281	Struct.metal products;tanks;steam generators	2150	2310	2245	2307	42375	45151	45217	45355	1478	1530	1602	3365c/
2811	Structural metal products	2005	2165	2100	2166	36464	37612	37702	37495	1246	1288	1364	1396
2812	Tanks, reservoirs and containers of metal	135	135	135	132	5176	6765	6695	6997	198	200	198	230
2813	Steam generators	10	10	10	9	735	774	820	863	34	42	40	...
289	Other metal products; metal working services	4975	5515	5405	5791	44132	47733	50413	50472	1502	1554	1631	...c/
2891	Metal forging/pressing/stamping/roll-forming	455	510	525	535	8208	8863	9124	9605	287	298	310	314
2892	Treatment & coating of metals	3495	3890	3750	4078	19986	21677	22872	22574	639	661	731	742
2893	Cutlery, hand tools and general hardware	315	340	370	368	4261	4348	4494	4668	153	160	156	...
2899	Other fabricated metal products n.e.c.	710	775	760	810	11677	12845	13923	13625	424	435	434	477
291	General purpose machinery	2445	2485	2415	2508	48207	50069	52203	54095	1814	1906	2048	2125
2911	Engines & turbines (not for transport equipment)	320	320	335	344	4126	3993	4210	4774	150	156	173	183
2912	Pumps, compressors, taps and valves	295	305	285	294	9230	9698	9989	10136	372	379	398	424
2913	Bearings, gears, gearing & driving elements	55	55	55	53	1754	1833	1859	1239	71	74	73	45
2914	Ovens, furnaces and furnace burners	40	35	40	41	723	1132	699	1245	26	53	34	56
2915	Lifting and handling equipment	415	425	395	414	12285	12696	13009	13695	454	489	513	548
2919	Other general purpose machinery	1310	1345	1310	1362	20088	20718	22436	23006	741	755	858	869
292	Special purpose machinery	1895	1945	1965	2013	33182	...	36225	38092	1339	...	1523	1589
2921	Agricultural and forestry machinery	905	920	985	1014	7965	8666	9278	9634	233	274	293	313
2922	Machine tools	165	195	190	210	2219	2345	...	...	...	89	...	...
2923	Machinery for metallurgy	15	20	20	18	...	227	228	223	...	8	9	11
2924	Machinery for mining & construction	95	95	85	84	1437	1815	1571	1894	54	69	48	81
2925	Food/beverage/tobacco processing machinery	245	240	235	236	7882	7997	7737	7897	318	339	327	318
2926	Machinery for textile, apparel and leather	60	60	55	59	875	865	811	439	39	38	32	11
2927	Weapons and ammunition	5	5	10	7	1	...	...	...	...	...	...	...
2929	Other special purpose machinery	405	410	390	385	...	12934	14068	15268	...	645	715	741

continued

Netherlands

ISIC Revision 3

ISIC	Industry	Number of enterprises (number)					Number of employees (number)					Wages and salaries paid to employees (millions of Euros)				
		Note	2005	2006	2007	2008	Note	2005	2006	2007	2008	Note	2005	2006	2007	2008
2930	Domestic appliances n.e.c.		100	95	95	90		1987	...	4007	3089		61	...	184	275
3000	Office, accounting and computing machinery		200	205	200	199		...	5101	4743	4509		227	219	...	202
3110	Electric motors, generators and transformers		250	250	275	319		3437	3900	4165	4862		128	164	163	205
3120	Electricity distribution & control apparatus		120	120	105	108		3648	3627	3795	3811		138	120	136	146
3130	Insulated wire and cable		60	55	45	53		2455	2597	2466	2661		109	99	99	108
3140	Accumulators, primary cells and batteries		15	15	10	11		192	159	163	130		9	7	10	6
3150	Lighting equipment and electric lamps		300	280	260	258		2236	2300	2335	6912		73	64	339	340
3190	Other electrical equipment n.e.c.		295	280	240	262		4105	4333	4508	4452		174	180	202	196
3210	Electronic valves, tubes, etc.		195	215	215	211		3448	...	9212	9230		141	230	504	548
3220	TV/radio transmitters; line comm. apparatus		70	75	80	89		842	944	1058	1422		26	31	38	50
3230	TV and radio receivers and associated goods		120	130	130	127		...	...	6782	878		...	...	39	36
331	Medical, measuring, testing appliances, etc.		1970	2120	2010	2011		23316	22502	26230	26868		...	...	502	1104
3311	Medical, surgical and orthopaedic equipment		1425	1530	1450	1424		11144	10735	14514	14854		333	303	...	578
3312	Measuring/testing/navigating appliances,etc.		420	455	430	447		10805	10224	10169	10213		427	439	...	464
3313	Industrial process control equipment		125	135	130	140		1367	1543	1547	1801		...	...	58	61
3320	Optical instruments & photographic equipment		120	130	130	139		1843	1844	1839	1847		...	...	63	71
3330	Watches and clocks		35	35	35	37		128	120	127	139		4	3	6	3
3410	Motor vehicles		110	120	110	110		9640	9168	9059	9645		424	493	381	285
3420	Automobile bodies, trailers & semi-trailers		410	430	465	457		8062	8230	8343	8312		249	270	270	...
3430	Parts/accessories for automobiles		95	105	120	124		4577	4625	4982	4995		165	167	188	...
351	Building and repairing of ships and boats		1580	1320	1590	1635		11948	12073	12689	13601		496	480	608	599
3511	Building and repairing of ships		560	475	540	555		6995	7268	7638	8419		341	319	389	382
3512	Building/repairing of pleasure/sport. boats		1020	845	1050	1080		4953	4805	5051	5182		155	160	218	217
3520	Railway/tramway locomotives & rolling stock		15	15	15	21		...	...	...	...		17	17	...	...
3530	Aircraft and spacecraft		80	70	80	84		...	...	...	...		...	...	...	...
359	Transport equipment n.e.c.		165	140	155	148		5061	5118	5230	5288		203	230	224	226
3591	Motorcycles		35	25	30	30		375	329	302	...		95	88	...	...
3592	Bicycles and invalid carriages		90	75	85	79		...	1950	...	2103		...	11	...	...
3599	Other transport equipment n.e.c.		40	35	40	39		394	...	169	140		15	62	...	...
3610	Furniture		5220	5645	5345	5540		23752	22391	23175	22795		689	667	679	711
369	Manufacturing n.e.c.		2020	2170	1900	1946		4947	5298	5427	5199		179	165	180	178
3691	Jewellery and related articles		675	715	660	685		700	862	836	728		24	21	30	26
3692	Musical instruments		235	245	245	243		435	459	421	426		14	10	10	11
3693	Sports goods		135	150	140	151		539	785	776	786		22	18	20	24
3694	Games and toys		305	310	255	239		692	713	748	714		28	17	33	23
3699	Other manufacturing n.e.c.		670	750	600	628		2581	2479	2646	2545		90	100	88	94
3710	Recycling of metal waste and scrap		50	60	70	75		475	483	493	546		17	20	19	18
3720	Recycling of non-metal waste and scrap		160	180	175	184		2373	2614	2627	2658		83	89	97	103
D	Total manufacturing		45630	46620	46590	47600		725287	735826	734211	742552		27087	27693	28176	29049

a/ 1810 includes 1820.
b/ 2310 includes 2320 and 2330.
c/ 281 includes 289.

Netherlands

ISIC	Industry	Note	Output (millions of Euros)				Note	Value added at factor values (millions of Euros)				Note	Gross fixed capital formation (millions of Euros)	
			2005	2006	2007	2008		2005	2006	2007	2008		2007	2008
151	Processed meat,fish,fruit,vegetables,fats		...	14817	...	...		...	2234	...	...		336	381
1511	Processing/preserving of meat		7986	7854	8695	8920		1196	1076	1236	1141		142	149
1512	Processing/preserving of fish		643	767	...	...		131	183	...	...		14	34
1513	Processing/preserving of fruit & vegetables		2796	2982	3843	4012		672	669	834	861		129	165
1514	Vegetable and animal oils and fats		..a/	3213	3759	4872		...	307	266	201		50	34
1520	Dairy products		6485	6901	8329	9146		861	888	1043	956		270	192
153	Grain mill products; starches; animal feeds		6127	6461	7301	7734		993	940	999	1021		164	182
1531	Grain mill products		...	577	653	756		615	112	113	119		24	26
1532	Starches and starch products		...	1173	989	1142		...	209	197	243		22	47
1533	Prepared animal feeds		4445	4711	5659	5836		...	620	689	659		118	109
154	Other food products		12133	12028	12985	13647		3814	3923	4017	3827		469	465
1541	Bakery products		2941	2853	3076	3418		1410	1375	1453	1604		60	79
1542	Sugar		...	...	...	...		687	665	655	626		1	-
1543	Cocoa, chocolate and sugar confectionery		3583	...	...	...		...	1	1	...		157	128
1544	Macaroni, noodles & similar products		...	8	...	...		...	...	...	...		...	...
1549	Other food products n.e.c.		3459	4174	4250	4375		999	1156	1135	1143		280	196
155	Beverages		...	...	...	...		...	...	...	...		...	...
1551	Distilling, rectifying & blending of spirits		...	...	...	...		...	...	...	...		2	2
1552	Wines		...	...	...	...		...	...	...	...		...	...
1553	Malt liquors and malt		955	1007	...	...		219	233	...	...		47	40
1554	Soft drinks; mineral waters		...	5509	...	...		...	1976	...	...		80	122
1600	Tobacco products		566	...	601	551		195	...	203	188		18	22
171	Spinning, weaving and finishing of textiles		306	...	341	290		94	94	106	90		11	10
1711	Textile fibre preparation; textile weaving		260	264	260	262		100	...	97	99		11	11
1712	Finishing of textiles		1830	1903	2030	1887		543	554	592	548		7	11
172	Other textiles		470	530	534	552		174	182	185	189		57	38
1721	Made-up textile articles, except apparel		940	966	1101	968		229	233	260	224		18	14
1722	Carpets and rugs		...	32	24	15		...	14	7	6		25	11
1723	Cordage, rope, twine and netting		37	375	371	353		13	125	140	128		1	6
1729	Other textiles n.e.c.		...	...	43	34		...	...	16	17		14	1
1730	Knitted and crocheted fabrics and articles		519a/	532a/	578a/	...		138a/	133a/	166a/	6a/		1	6a/
1810	Wearing apparel, except fur apparel		..a/	..a/	..a/	...		..a/	..a/	..a/	..a/		12	..a/
1820	Dressing & dyeing of fur; processing of fur		...	...	...	146		...	...	...	...		-	5
191	Tanning, dressing and processing of leather		144	87	199	65		38	14	56	43		2	2
1911	Tanning and dressing of leather		70	...	71	81		16	...	12	16		1	3
1912	Luggage, handbags, etc.; saddlery & harness		74	141	128	112		22	49	44	27		7	5
1920	Footwear		159	235	132	280		58	73	47	42		26	14
2010	Sawmilling and planing of wood		171	...	273	2956		60	...	76	87		128	102
202	Products of wood, cork, straw, etc.		2555	...	3005	91		862	...	958	953		2	5
2021	Veneer sheets, plywood, particle board, etc.		36	1958	2241	2225		10	639	734	751		89	70
2022	Builders' carpentry and joinery		1859	432	488	419		645	100	120	124		26	16
2023	Wooden containers		379	241	...	222		103	89	...	53		12	11
2029	Other wood products; articles of cork/straw		281	5781	5892	5589		103	...	...	...		195	188
210	Paper and paper products		5521	...	...	...		1597	1620	1615	1476		59	49
2101	Pulp, paper and paperboard		1915	2040	2072	2092		487	531	530	...		79	59
2102	Corrugated paper and paperboard		1841	1934	2040	...		554	527	548	570		58	80
2109	Other articles of paper and paperboard		1765	1807	1855	...		556	563	536	...		66	73
221	Publishing		7294	7463	7855	7258		2722	2804	2995	2984		25	20
2211	Publishing of books and other publications		1846	2101	2025	1837		717	840	872	740		36	47
2212	Publishing of newspapers, journals, etc.		5171	5083	5589	5127		1926	1881	2051	2141		2	3
2213	Publishing of recorded media		168	151	146	172		34	38	40	54		3	3
2219	Other publishing		110	128	95	121		44	44	32	49		...	...

continued

Netherlands

ISIC	Industry	Output (millions of Euros)					Value added at factor values (millions of Euros)					Gross fixed capital formation (millions of Euros)		
		Note	2005	2006	2007	2008	Note	2005	2006	2007	2008	Note	2007	2008
222	Printing and related service activities		5103	5029	5384	5261		2020	1938	1938	1917		250	337
2221	Printing		4511	...	4812	4638		1752	...	1677	1610		214	302
2222	Service activities related to printing		592	...	572	623		268	...	261	307		36	35
2230	Reproduction of recorded media		272	227	233	106		53	50	67	39		3	3
2310	Coke oven products		-	...	...	...		-	...	...	...		...	...
2320	Refined petroleum products		...	...	34696b/	...		...	...	2245b/	...		573b/	766
2330	Processing of nuclear fuel		...	...	...b/	...		...	...	...b/	...		...b/	-
241	Basic chemicals		32826	35545	38611	38988		6633	5027	5338	5233		758	934
2411	Basic chemicals, except fertilizers		...	...	...	28260		...	...	...	...		...	...
2412	Fertilizers and nitrogen compounds		1407	1601	1708	2718		364	259	363	759		...	...
2413	Plastics in primary forms; synthetic rubber		...	...	...	8010		...	...	...	...		143	104
242	Other chemicals		11217	11507	12497	12833		3568	3214	3359	3625		397	400
2421	Pesticides and other agro-chemical products		...	275	235	249		...	73	69	92		5	6
2422	Paints, varnishes, printing ink and mastics		1826	1940	2160	1952		557	604	677	612		45	35
2423	Pharmaceuticals, medicinal chemicals, etc.		5329	5317	5810	5543		1765	1414	1392	1668		159	183
2424	Soap, cleaning & cosmetic preparations		...	1256	1366	1328		...	315	362	368		26	54
2429	Other chemical products n.e.c.		2484	2720	2927	3760		805	807	860	886		163	123
2430	Man-made fibres		1009	1105	1096	875		334	370	402	316		80	...
251	Rubber products		584	534	611	670		216	189	229	249		29	32
2511	Rubber tyres and tubes		...	229	261	286		...	84	109	115		...	...
2519	Other rubber products		...	304	350	384		...	105	120	135		...	...
2520	Plastic products		5782	6258	6627	6582		1771	1891	1928	1941		323	239
2610	Glass and glass products		1037	1159	1142	1104		376	444	450	441		49	62
269	Non-metallic mineral products n.e.c.		4632	5118	5701	6123		1593	1791	1842	1916		250	254
2691	Pottery, china and earthenware		...	...	...	...		...	...	...	...		...	...
2692	Refractory ceramic products		...	...	82	101		...	...	18	22		...	2
2693	Struct.non-refractory clay; ceramic products		...	...	...	...		...	...	...	...		...	...
2694	Cement, lime and plaster		2821	3065	3380	3808		877	981	1047	1114		117	147
2695	Articles of concrete, cement and plaster		274	246	395	266		116	110	135	109		11	12
2696	Cutting, shaping & finishing of stone		645	834	890	970		197	278	240	270		27	41
2699	Other non-metallic mineral products n.e.c.		...	...	...	...		...	...	...	...		...	...
2710	Basic iron and steel		4365	4449	5136	5249		1565	1385	1587	1180		92	92
2720	Basic precious and non-ferrous metals		2145	2884	3068	2659		452	549	629	396		76	76
273	Casting of metals		610	639	694	692		189	192	183	198		26	21
2731	Casting of iron and steel		...	...	...	381		...	...	...	94		13	11
2732	Casting of non-ferrous metals		...	...	...	311		...	...	...	104		14	9
281	Struct.metal products;tanks;steam generators		7963	8718	9895	20934c/		2389	2608	2931	6506c/		...	270
2811	Structural metal products		6612	7138	8281	8861		1988	2161	2463	2594		219	239
2812	Tanks, reservoirs and containers of metal		1159	1286	1328	1469		356	383	407	487		182	28
2813	Steam generators		193	294	286	...c/		45	64	62	...c/		...	3
289	Other metal products; metal working services		7519	8365	9434	...c/		2757	2986	3295	...c/		420	467
2891	Metal forging/pressing/stamping/roll-forming		1625	1847	2177	2233		508	553	648	638		90	54
2892	Treatment & coating of metals		2789	3115	3698	3718		1186	1295	1468	1465		207	216
2893	Cutlery, hand tools and general hardware		597	610	636	...		253	282	285	...		29	30
2899	Other fabricated metal products n.e.c.		2508	2793	2924	3489		811	856	894	961		95	167
291	General purpose machinery		9168	10678	12634	12465		3154	3396	3827	3973		283	310
2911	Engines & turbines (not for transport equipment)		807	1123	1437	1118		288	302	351	384		42	37
2912	Pumps, compressors, taps and valves		2026	2232	2786	2840		697	765	809	938		66	72
2913	Bearings, gears, gearing & driving elements		360	437	488	251		119	134	134	90		13	14
2914	Ovens, furnaces and furnace burners		125	335	174	287		39	92	59	75		3	13
2915	Lifting and handling equipment		2576	2946	3408	3519		853	888	1016	998		60	67
2919	Other general purpose machinery		3274	3607	4342	4450		1159	1215	1458	1489		100	107

Code	Description																		
292	Special purpose machinery	7960	1320	10887	2065	10232	2253	2458	420	3022	616	2906	552	47	9	236	68		
2921	Agricultural and forestry machinery	1629	415	2065				137		616		552		9		68	14		
2922	Machine tools	33		35		41		18		16		15		11		1	1		
2923	Machinery for metallurgy	256	452	316		616		92		95		198		35		9			
2924	Machinery for mining & construction	1387	1528	1590		1656		490		579		603		5		32			
2925	Food/beverage/tobacco processing machinery	190	192	182		52		59		61		18				2			
2926	Machinery for textile, apparel and leather															-			
2927	Weapons and ammunition																		
2929	Other special purpose machinery	5549		6045		4963	1374	115		1476	397	1312	448			109			
2930	Domestic appliances n.e.c.	329		1154		1122		356		397		256				59			
3000	Office, accounting and computing machinery	1246	1372					346											
3110	Electric motors, generators and transformers	586	921	1068		1309		228	330	300		398		15					
3120	Electricity distribution & control apparatus	698	644	808		811		279	236	302		306		13		12			
3130	Insulated wire and cable	667	787	877		924		173	175	207		229				30			
3140	Accumulators, primary cells and batteries	54	58	67		61		22	19	19		21		44		30			
3150	Lighting equipment and electric lamps	363	363	1400		1354		121	113	477		483		39		44			
3190	Other electrical equipment n.e.c.	887	994	1121		1089		294	304	310		330		80					
3210	Electronic valves, tubes, etc.	638	962	1889		1777		230	282	578		312		3		86			
3220	TV/radio transmitters; line comm. apparatus	140	173	154		227		51	64	60		69		3					
3230	TV and radio receivers and associated goods			291		263				80		75				5			
331	Medical, measuring, testing appliances, etc.	1419	1284	3071		6319		668	613	968		2082		96		148			
3311	Medical, surgical and orthopaedic equipment	2110	2271			3672		868	862			1151		52		97			
3312	Measuring/testing/navigating appliances,etc.					2369						830		40		43			
3313	Industrial process control equipment			250		278			93	93		101		3		8			
3320	Optical instruments & photographic equipment	250		320		361			145	145		159		13		17			
3330	Watches and clocks	25	19	42		15		8	7	15		5				1			
3410	Motor vehicles	5890	6529	7457				1476	1904	2055						137			
3420	Automobile bodies, trailers & semi-trailers	1483	1664	1900		1926		385	428	456		462		51		32			
3430	Parts/accessories for automobiles	979	1061	1341				280	331	374						54			
351	Building and repairing of ships and boats	3356	3954	5253		5932		835	889	1224		1179							
3511	Building and repairing of ships	2477	2862	3712		4397		604	593	825		793		31		46			
3512	Building/repairing of pleasure/sport. boats	879	1093	1542		1535		231	295	399		386							
3520	Railway/tramway locomotives & rolling stock	126	94	94				42	41										
3530	Aircraft and spacecraft	871	970	988		1057		333	349	337		362		31		40			
359	Transport equipment n.e.c.	695	739					188	187					10		11			
3591	Motorcycles		75						20					1		2			
3592	Bicycles and invalid carriages		585						141					7		8			
3599	Other transport equipment n.e.c.	71	79					22	26					1		1			
3610	Furniture	3444	3357	3673		3758		1163	1119	1217		1262		138		156			
369	Manufacturing n.e.c.	918	975	1017		1031		312	327	321		343		110					
3691	Jewellery and related articles	116	111	148		134		40	44	52		50		8		2			
3692	Musical instruments	65	45	42		47		25	19	19		25		2		1			
3693	Sports goods	109	106	104		107		38	38	38		34		5		3			
3694	Games and toys	121	98	123		133		38	30	40		39		1		3			
3699	Other manufacturing n.e.c.	507	615	601		611		163	196	172		196		94		147			
3710	Recycling of metal waste and scrap	371	401	504		455		48	76	85		55		7		7			
3720	Recycling of non-metal waste and scrap	744	948	998		1216		203	218	233		235		57		68			
D	Total manufacturing	228640	254285	275049		288700		57637	60128	63658		62624		7703		8055			

a/ 1810 includes 1820.
b/ 2310 includes 2320 and 2330.
c/ 281 includes 289.

Netherlands

Index numbers of industrial production

ISIC Revision 3

(2005=100)

ISIC	Industry	Note	1999	2000	2001	2002	2003	2004	2005	2006	2007	2008	2009	2010
15	Food and beverages		91	93	93	93	94	96	100	103	105	:	:	:
16	Tobacco products		93	97	97	113	104	99	100	99	96	:	:	:
17	Textiles		117	121	124	119	115	101	100	104	108	85	:	:
18	Wearing apparel, fur		128	144	130	124	119	92	100	113	118	:	:	:
19	Leather, leather products and footwear		107	104	95	89	94	100	100	95	92	:	:	:
20	Wood products (excl. furniture)		106	106	107	93	96	99	100	102	102	:	:	:
21	Paper and paper products		88	91	87	92	93	98	100	101	99	:	:	:
22	Printing and publishing		111	112	110	106	101	99	100	101	103	:	:	:
23	Coke,refined petroleum products,nuclear fuel		69	80	76	90	93	99	100	99	109	:	:	:
24	Chemicals and chemical products		72	75	84	93	93	99	100	105	107	102	:	:
25	Rubber and plastics products		92	94	93	97	93	96	100	104	106	:	:	:
26	Non-metallic mineral products		99	104	104	98	92	99	100	103	103	:	:	:
27	Basic metals		83	87	86	88	91	103	100	98	103	100	:	:
28	Fabricated metal products		89	96	97	94	91	94	100	102	104	:	:	:
29	Machinery and equipment n.e.c.		78	93	93	90	89	98	100	106	114	:	:	:
30	Office, accounting and computing machinery	a/	103	133	111	93	94	97	100	103	111	:	:	:
31	Electrical machinery and apparatus	a/	:	:	:	:	:	:	:	:	:	:	:	:
32	Radio,television and communication equipment	a/	:	:	:	:	:	:	:	:	:	:	:	:
33	Medical, precision and optical instruments	a/	:	:	:	:	:	:	:	:	:	:	:	:
34	Motor vehicles, trailers, semi-trailers		97	98	103	100	99	100	100	103	110	:	:	:
35	Other transport equipment		97	96	110	104	99	99	100	103	105	:	:	:
36	Furniture; manufacturing n.e.c.	b/	101	102	99	99	99	99	100	102	105	:	:	:
37	Recycling	b/	:	:	:	:	:	:	:	:	:	:	:	:
D	Total manufacturing		90	96	96	96	95	98	100	103	106	105	:	:

a/ 30 includes 31, 32 and 33.
b/ 36 includes 37.

New Zealand

Supplier of information:
Statistics New Zealand, Wellington.
Industrial statistics for the OECD countries are compiled by the OECD secretariat, which supplies them to UNIDO.

Basic source of data:
Annual enterprise survey.

Major deviations from ISIC (Revision 4):
None reported.

Reference period:
Fiscal year beginning 1 April of the year indicated.

Scope:
Enterprises with paid employees.

Method of data collection:
Not reported.

Type of enumeration:
Not reported.

Adjusted for non-response:
Not reported.

Concepts and definitions of variables:
No deviations from the standard UN concepts and definitions are reported.

Related national publications:
None reported.

New Zealand

		Number of enterprises (number)					Number of employees (number)					Wages and salaries paid to employees (millions of New Zealand Dollars)				
ISIC	Industry	Note	2006	2007	2008	2009	Note	2006	2007	2008	2009	Note	2006	2007	2008	2009
1010	Processing/preserving of meat		266	256	267	270		30870	31100	31690	31010		...	2988a/	3287a/	3245a/
1020	Processing/preserving of fish, etc.		121	112	115	104		7330	7310	6740	7030		...	..a/	..a/	..a/
1030	Processing/preserving of fruit,vegetables		121	120	121	118		5200	5110	4850	4650		...	..a/	..a/	..a/
1040	Vegetable and animal oils and fats		49	41	43	40		400	270	250	240		...	..a/	..a/	..a/
1050	Dairy products		76	74	74	92		13320	11540	10540	10980		...	..a/	..a/	..a/
106	Grain mill products,starches and starch products		...	...	...	...		...	...	...	...		...	..a/	..a/	..a/
1061	Grain mill products		34	30	31	33		770	800	790	810		...	...	...	...
1062	Starches and starch products		...	...	...	...		...	...	...	...		...	...	...	...
107	Other food products		...	...	...	...		...	...	...	...		...	..a/	..a/	..a/
1071	Bakery products		1187	1207	1215	1215		12660	14060	14220	13650		...	...	...	...
1072	Sugar		5	6	4	4		210	220	230	230		...	...	...	...
1073	Cocoa, chocolate and sugar confectionery		85	88	97	96		2020	2070	1850	1660		...	...	...	...
1074	Macaroni, noodles, couscous, etc.		...	...	...	...		...	...	...	...		...	...	...	...
1075	Prepared meals and dishes		...	...	...	...		...	...	...	...		...	...	...	...
1079	Other food products n.e.c.		364	380	390	392		5900	6330	6600	6320		...	...	...	...
1080	Prepared animal feeds		80	82	80	84		600	620	710	730		...	...	...	...
1101	Distilling, rectifying and blending of spirits		25	27	27	26		590	520	540	530		...	..a/	..a/	..a/
1102	Wines		258	281	290	319		4590	4770	5070	5220		...	382b/	409b/	418b/
1103	Malt liquors and malt		46	47	39	39		1500	1470	1440	1490		...	..b/	..b/	..b/
1104	Soft drinks,mineral waters,other bottled waters		77	81	85	86		1850	2010	2040	2080		...	..b/	..b/	..b/
1200	Tobacco products		2	1	2	1		420	130	130	150		...	..b/	..b/	..b/
131	Spinning, weaving and finishing of textiles		83	79	78	72		2240	2790	2590	2140		...	240c/	211c/	235c/
1311	Preparation and spinning of textile fibres		...	...	...	...		...	...	...	...		...	...	...	...
1312	Weaving of textiles		...	...	...	...		...	...	...	...		...	...	...	...
1313	Finishing of textiles		145	132	130	135		870	860	860	830		...	...	...	...
139	Other textiles		...	...	...	...		...	...	...	...		...	...	...	...
1391	Knitted and crocheted fabrics		69	66	66	67		1010	1040	1020	800		...	..c/	..c/	..c/
1392	Made-up textile articles, except apparel		509	508	500	496		2170	2120	2130	1970		...	...	...	...
1393	Carpets and rugs		27	27	22	23		1470	620	750	640		...	...	...	...
1394	Cordage, rope, twine and netting		21	19	18	17		180	190	180	190		...	...	...	...
1399	Other textiles n.e.c.		...	...	...	...		...	...	...	...		...	...	...	...
1410	Wearing apparel, except fur apparel		1005	978	943	912		6470	5970	5490	4580		...	156d/	155d/	160d/
1420	Articles of fur		...	...	...	...		...	...	...	...		...	..d/	..d/	..d/
1430	Knitted and crocheted apparel		...	...	...	...		...	...	...	...		...	..d/	..d/	..d/
151	Leather;luggage,handbags,etc.;saddlery,harness;fur		...	...	...	...		...	...	...	...		...	..d/	..d/	..d/
1511	Tanning/dressing of leather; dressing of fur		122	115	115	111		1700	1470	1380	1260		...	74e/	59e/	73e/
1512	Luggage,handbags,etc.;saddlery/harness		...	...	...	...		...	...	...	...		...	...	...	...
1520	Footwear		37	34	32	30		610	550	420	370		...	..e/	..e/	..e/
1610	Sawmilling and planing of wood		566	555	538	509		9880	9960	9300	7870		...	796f/	812f/	790f/
162	Wood products, cork, straw, plaiting materials		...	...	...	...		...	...	...	...		...	..f/	..f/	..f/

Code	Product	A1	A2	A3	A4	B1	B2	B3	B4	C1	C2	C3	C4	D1	D2	D3
1621	Veneer sheets and wood-based panels	48	43	43	47	2860	2800	2640	2290	...	...	...	...	...	...	...
1622	Builders' carpentry and joinery	1289	1258	1243	1172	6710	6640	6610	5310	...	...	...	...	...	...	...
1623	Wooden containers	429	415	404	387	1940	2090	2080	1860	...	...	...	...	...	...	...
1629	Other wood products;articles of cork,straw	17	17	17	15	2940	2690	2630	2430	...	...	...	...	412g/	382g/	392g/
1701	Pulp, paper and paperboard	39	37	35	35	2000	2080	1930	2100	...	...	...	...	..g/	..g/	..g/
1702	Corrugated paper and paperboard	52	49	44	43	1160	1100	1020	890	...	...	...	...	..g/	..g/	..g/
1709	Other articles of paper and paperboard	1432	1404	1384	1359	12280	11180	10930	9950	...	...	...	...	470h/	490h/	466h/
181	Printing and service activities related to printing	1145	1117	1112	1082	11180	10070	9900	9020	...	...	...	...	...	...	...
1811	Printing	287	287	272	277	1100	1110	1030	930	...	...	...	...	...	...	...
1812	Service activities related to printing	57	68	79	83	70	65	95	120	...	...	...	...	..h/	..h/	..h/
1820	Reproduction of recorded media	...	...	...	...	...	...	...	...	...	...	...	...	198i/	201i/	202i/
1910	Coke oven products	...	...	...	...	...	...	...	...	...	...	...	...	..i/	..i/	...
1920	Refined petroleum products	33	47	43	38	2080	2150	1880	1800	...	...	...	...	430j/	434j/	403j/
201	Basic chemicals,fertilizers, etc.	145	146	145	128	3060	3010	2990	3070	...	...	...	...	...	...	...
2011	Basic chemicals	35	33	35	32	410	430	410	440	...	...	...	...	...	...	...
2012	Fertilizers and nitrogen compounds	60	65	63	56	1470	1490	1450	1520	...	...	...	...	...	...	...
2013	Plastics and synthetic rubber in primary forms	50	48	47	40	1180	1090	1130	1110	...	...	...	...	..j/	..j/	..j/
202	Other chemical products	290	288	298	287	5170	5110	4720	4440	...	...	...	...	...	...	...
2021	Pesticides and other agrochemical products	12	11	12	11	150	230	140	150	...	...	...	...	...	...	...
2022	Paints,varnishes;printing ink and mastics	95	82	83	80	2560	2360	2400	2310	...	...	...	...	...	...	...
2023	Soap,cleaning and cosmetic preparations	130	138	143	137	1800	1810	1550	1450	...	...	...	...	...	...	...
2029	Other chemical products n.e.c.	53	57	60	59	660	710	630	530	...	...	...	...	...	...	...
2030	Man-made fibres	...	...	...	...	...	...	...	...	...	...	...	...	91	100	91
2100	Pharmaceuticals,medicinal chemicals, etc.	105	105	105	104	2360	2190	2060	1950	...	...	...	...	...	...	...
221	Rubber products	69	71	67	69	840	845	805	715	...	...	...	...	549k/	491k/	516k/
2211	Rubber tyres and tubes	12	11	10	12	70	85	75	75	...	...	...	...	...	...	...
2219	Other rubber products	57	60	57	57	770	760	730	640	...	...	...	...	..k/	..k/	..k/
2220	Plastics products	587	593	580	570	10860	10840	10380	9650	...	...	...	...	423m/	471m/	480m/
2310	Glass and glass products	144	145	147	147	1260	1200	2050	1860	...	...	...	...	..m/	..m/	..m/
239	Non-metallic mineral products n.e.c.	...	...	...	...	...	...	...	...	...	...	...	...	...	...	...
2391	Refractory products	...	...	...	...	...	...	...	...	...	...	...	...	...	...	...
2392	Clay building materials	11	12	10	9	160	150	140	40	...	...	...	...	...	...	...
2393	Other porcelain and ceramic products	162	146	139	137	480	400	380	370	...	...	...	...	...	...	...
2394	Cement, lime and plaster	18	17	20	19	430	420	1080	1060	...	...	...	...	...	...	...
2395	Articles of concrete, cement and plaster	329	336	317	312	5280	5310	4740	4440	...	...	...	...	...	...	...
2396	Cutting, shaping and finishing of stone	138	140	137	144	730	710	620	580	...	...	...	...	...	...	...
2399	Other non-metallic mineral products n.e.c.	114	112	118	117	1890	1900	1950	1730	...	...	...	...	339n/	358n/	385n/
2410	Basic iron and steel	49	47	51	54	2790	2720	2890	2660	...	...	...	...	..n/	..n/	..n/
2420	Basic precious and other non-ferrous metals	67	68	67	67	1030	900	910	820	...	...	...	...	..n/	..n/	..n/
243	Casting of metals	39	40	40	40	740	650	640	580	...	...	...	...	...	...	...
2431	Casting of iron and steel	28	28	27	27	290	250	270	240	...	...	...	...	...	...	...
2432	Casting of non-ferrous metals	...	...	...	...	...	...	...	...	...	...	...	...	...	...	...
251	Struct.metal products, tanks, reservoirs	1169	1150	1133	1104	10560	11100	11220	10550	...	...	...	...	1054p/	1083p/	1070p/
2511	Structural metal products	41	41	37	38	900	910	660	610	...	...	...	...	...	...	...
2512	Tanks, reservoirs and containers of metal	...	...	...	...	...	...	...	...	...	...	...	...	...	...	...

continued

New Zealand

ISIC	Industry	Number of enterprises (number)				Number of employees (number)				Wages and salaries paid to employees (millions of New Zealand Dollars)			
		2006	2007	2008	2009	2006	2007	2008	2009	2006	2007	2008	2009
2513	Steam generators, excl. hot water boilers	...	...	...	...	...	...	...	...	...	...	...	...
2520	Weapons and ammunition	...	...	...	...	...	...	...	...	...	...	...	...
259	Other metal products;metal working services	...	...	...	...	...	...	...	...	...	...p/	...p/	...p/
2591	Forging,pressing,stamping,roll-forming of metal	29	30	32	28	130	150	170	160	...	...p/	...p/	...p/
2592	Treatment and coating of metals; machining	322	327	319	316	1560	1570	1560	1330	...	...	...	...
2593	Cutlery, hand tools and general hardware	...	...	...	...	...	...	...	...	...	...	...	...
2599	Other fabricated metal products n.e.c.	1892	1895	1843	1773	11270	10900	11050	10470	...	...	...	...
2610	Electronic components and boards	44	45	43	38	95	85	95	110	...	...	...	...
2620	Computers and peripheral equipment	34	35	39	35	800	820	800	850	...	263q/	252q/	285q/
2630	Communication equipment	253	245	248	238	2880	2930	2990	2500	...	...q/	...q/	...q/
2640	Consumer electronics	...	...	...	...	...	...	...	...	...	...q/	...q/	...q/
265	Measuring,testing equipment; watches, etc.	76	80	69	72	1000	940	710	560	...	...q/	...q/	...q/
2651	Measuring/testing/navigating equipment,etc.	...	...	...	...	...	...	...	...	...	...q/	...q/	...q/
2652	Watches and clocks	...	...	...	...	...	...	...	...	...	...	...	...
2660	Irradiation/electromedical equipment,etc.	...	...	...	...	...	...	...	...	...	...	...	...
2670	Optical instruments and photographic equipment	22	22	24	26	200	210	210	200	...	...q/	...q/	...q/
2680	Magnetic and optical media	...	...	...	...	...	...	...	...	...	...q/	...q/	...q/
2710	Electric motors,generators,transformers,etc.	...	...	...	...	...	...	...	...	...	...	...	...
2720	Batteries and accumulators	...	...	...	...	...	...	...	...	...	320r/	321r/	271r/
273	Wiring and wiring devices	...	...	...	...	...	...	...	...	...	...r/	...r/	...r/
2731	Fibre optic cables	...	...	...	...	...	...	...	...	...	...r/	...r/	...r/
2732	Other electronic and electric wires and cables	8	9	9	10	650	650	640	640	...	...	...	...
2733	Wiring devices	...	...	...	...	...	...	...	...	...	...	...	...
2740	Electric lighting equipment	72	69	68	64	490	470	470	410	...	...r/	...r/	...r/
2750	Domestic appliances	46	48	48	60	3100	2950	2570	2290	...	...r/	...r/	...r/
2790	Other electrical equipment	188	197	208	210	2290	2660	2720	2790	...	...r/	...r/	...r/
281	General-purpose machinery	...	...	...	...	...	...	...	...	...	...	...	...
2811	Engines/turbines,excl.aircraft,vehicle engines	33	33	32	35	310	350	330	320	...	720s/	742s/	810s/
2812	Fluid power equipment	...	...	...	...	...	...	...	...	...	...	...	...
2813	Other pumps, compressors, taps and valves	...	...	...	...	...	...	...	...	...	...	...	...
2814	Bearings, gears, gearing and driving elements	...	...	...	...	...	...	...	...	...	...	...	...
2815	Ovens, furnaces and furnace burners	...	...	...	...	...	...	...	...	...	...	...	...
2816	Lifting and handling equipment	67	65	62	61	1090	1020	1010	950	...	...	...	...
2817	Office machinery, excl.computers, etc.	...	...	...	...	...	...	...	...	...	...	...	...
2818	Power-driven hand tools	260	255	242	246	1420	1450	1310	1180	...	...	...	...
2819	Other general-purpose machinery	1862	1943	2056	2075	9510	9530	10110	9950	...	...	...	...
282	Special-purpose machinery	...	...	...	...	...	...	...	...	...	...	...	...
2821	Agricultural and forestry machinery	241	238	239	236	2480	2370	2570	2650	...	...s/	...s/	...s/
2822	Metal-forming machinery and machine tools	...	...	...	...	...	...	...	...	...	...	...	...
2823	Machinery for metallurgy	...	...	...	...	...	...	...	...	...	...	...	...
2824	Mining, quarrying and construction machinery	27	26	25	24	280	270	290	300	...	...	...	...

ISIC	Industry	(1)	(2)	(3)	(4)	(5)	(6)	(7)	(8)	(9)	(10)	(11)
2825	Food/beverage/tobacco processing machinery	...	...	...	...	...	...	...	...	...	...	...
2826	Textile/apparel/leather production machinery	...	...	...	...	...	...	...	...	...	...	...
2829	Other special-purpose machinery	75	84	92	100	610	590	630	630	...	...	...
2910	Motor vehicles	45	50	55	58	110	110	100	110	129t/	147t/	161t/
2920	Automobile bodies, trailers and semi-trailers	271	271	272	265	2030	1910	2050	1970	...t/	...t/	...t/
2930	Parts and accessories for motor vehicles	326	311	302	287	2010	1650	1580	1510	520u/	603u/	576u/
301	Building of ships and boats	780	768	748	745	4410	4490	4930	4510	...	...	...
3011	Building of ships and floating structures	58	50	48	47	720	650	630	590	...	...	...
3012	Building of pleasure and sporting boats	722	718	700	698	3690	3840	4300	3920	...u/	...u/	...u/
3020	Railway locomotives and rolling stock	4	2	2	2	530	450	440	460	...u/	...u/	...u/
3030	Air and spacecraft and related machinery	166	189	209	222	1730	1760	1840	1910	...u/	...u/	...u/
3040	Military fighting vehicles	...	...	...	...	...	...	...	...	...u/	...u/	...u/
309	Transport equipment n.e.c.	...	...	...	...	...	...	...	...	...	...	...
3091	Motorcycles	...	...	...	...	...	...	...	...	...	...	...
3092	Bicycles and invalid carriages	52	43	43	48	260	260	310	230	...	...	...
3099	Other transport equipment n.e.c.	...	...	...	...	...	...	...	...	269	287	270
3100	Furniture	1787	1712	1636	1564	8480	8160	7360	6350	212v/	230v/	260v/
321	Jewellery, bijouterie and related articles	...	...	...	...	...	...	...	...	...	...	...
3211	Jewellery and related articles	388	381	384	381	800	790	790	760	...	...	...
3212	Imitation jewellery and related articles	...	...	...	...	...	...	...	...	...v/	...v/	...v/
3220	Musical instruments	207	204	200	193	590	570	480	490	...v/	...v/	...v/
3230	Sports goods	...	...	...	...	...	...	...	...	...v/	...v/	...v/
3240	Games and toys	234	245	242	235	1780	2170	2390	2490	...v/	...v/	...v/
3250	Medical and dental instruments and supplies	466	437	434	404	1950	2000	2070	1820	...v/	...v/	...v/
3290	Other manufacturing n.e.c.	...	...	...	...	...	...	...	...	130w/	143w/	155w/
331	Repair of fabricated metal products/machinery	...	...	...	...	...	...	...	...	...	...	...
3311	Repair of fabricated metal products	742	753	764	780	2660	2870	2980	3020	...	...	...
3312	Repair of machinery	...	...	...	...	...	...	...	...	...	...	...
3313	Repair of electronic and optical equipment	...	...	...	...	...	...	...	...	...	...	...
3314	Repair of electrical equipment	...	...	...	...	...	...	...	...	...	...	...
3315	Repair of transport equip., excl. motor vehicles	418	412	400	366	510	500	530	480	...	...	...
3319	Repair of other equipment	...	...	...	...	...	...	...	...	...w/	...w/	...w/
3320	Installation of industrial machinery/equipment	...	...	...	...	...	...	...	...	...	...	...
C	Total manufacturing	...	...	...	...	...	...	...	...	11166	11670	11712

a/ 1010 includes 1020, 1030, 1040, 1050, 106, 107 and 1080.
b/ 1101 includes 1102, 1103, 1104 and 1200.
c/ 131 includes 139.
d/ 1410 includes 1420 and 1430.
e/ 151 includes 1520.
f/ 1610 includes 162.
g/ 1701 includes 1702 and 1709.
h/ 181 includes 1820.
i/ 1910 includes 1920.
j/ 201 includes 202 and 2030.

k/ 221 includes 2220.
m/ 2310 includes 239.
n/ 2410 includes 2420 and 243.
p/ 251 includes 2520 and 259.
q/ 2610 includes 2620, 2630, 2640, 265, 2660, 2670 and 2680.
r/ 2710 includes 2720, 273, 2740, 2750 and 2790.
s/ 281 includes 282.
t/ 2910 includes 2920 and 2930.
u/ 301 includes 3020, 3030, 3040 and 309.
v/ 321 includes 3220, 3230, 3240, 3250 and 3290.

w/ 331 includes 3320.

New Zealand

ISIC Revision 4			Output (millions of New Zealand Dollars)					Value added (millions of New Zealand Dollars)					Gross fixed capital formation (millions of New Zealand Dollars)		
ISIC	Industry	Note	2006	2007	2008	2009	Note	2006	2007	2008	2009	Note	2008	2009
10	Food products		...	24669	29810	30799		...	4975	5461	7304		851	1102
11	Beverages		...	4655a/	4248a/	4279a/		...	2567a/	2076a/	1990a/		419a/	353a/
12	Tobacco products			...a/	...a/	...a/			...a/	...a/	...a/		...a/	...a/
13	Textiles		...	1759	1627	1430		...	383	361	321		40	-7
14	Wearing apparel		...	559	542	530		...	226	237	229		17	6
15	Leather and related products		...	370	343	375		...	90	85	105		6	2
16	Wood/wood products/cork,excl. furniture		...	4738	4956	4350		...	1300	1389	1133		114	232
17	Paper and paper products		...	2984	2946	3048		...	737	810	709		21	130
18	Printing and reproduction of recorded media		...	1800	1840	1661		...	768	749	661		113	49
19	Coke and refined petroleum products		...	8538	8282	10279		...	3373	3379	3310		242	246
20	Chemicals and chemical products		...	3169	3372	3519		...	939	968	694		137	218
21	Pharmaceuticals,medicinal chemicals, etc.		...	467	520	418		...	154	155	141		12	11
22	Rubber and plastics products		...	2625	2454	2533		...	857	790	855		92	103
23	Other non-metallic mineral products		...	2599	2669	2562		...	1018	1101	1004		178	194
24	Basic metals		...	4158	4203	4392		...	1176	1084	1002		92	79
25	Fabricated metal products, except machinery		...	5469	5435	5610		...	1851	1787	1937		156	122
26	Computer, electronic and optical products		...	1152	1107	1144		...	294	392	373		29	37
27	Electrical equipment		...	1824	1939	1488		...	538	554	347		38	9
28	Machinery and equipment n.e.c.		...	2902	3234	3426		...	1199	1265	1339		76	93
29	Motor vehicles, trailers and semi-trailers		...	483	550	712		...	197	209	248		15	33
30	Other transport equipment		...	1584	1974	1842		...	760	866	903		52	37
31	Furniture		...	1232	1187	1040		...	438	455	389		28	11
32	Other manufacturing		...	882	846	1051		...	411	394	517		33	27
33	Repair and installation of machinery/equipment		...	507	569	561		...	248	275	280		15	12
C	Total manufacturing		...	79124	84655	87049		...	24501	24840	25791		2774	3097

a/ 11 includes 12.

New Zealand

Index numbers of industrial production

(2005=100)

ISIC	Industry	Note	1999	2000	2001	2002	2003	2004	2005	2006	2007	2008	2009	2010
10	Food products	a/	74	75	77	79	93	99	100	104	100	102	100	96
11	Beverages	a/	...	...	...	...	...	...	...	...	...	...	...	...
12	Tobacco products	a/	...	...	...	...	...	...	...	...	...	...	...	...
13	Textiles	b/	121	119	107	102	106	98	100	98	101	98	92	90
14	Wearing apparel	b/	...	...	...	...	...	...	...	...	...	...	...	...
15	Leather and related products	b/	...	...	...	...	...	...	...	...	...	...	...	...
16	Wood/wood products/cork,excl. furniture	c/	75	87	90	87	94	93	100	100	98	98	92	93
17	Paper and paper products	c/	...	...	...	...	...	...	...	...	...	...	...	...
18	Printing and reproduction of recorded media		91	93	91	96	94	97	100	98	91	91	86	80
19	Coke and refined petroleum products	d/	94	95	100	101	100	96	100	100	96	96	91	93
20	Chemicals and chemical products	d/	...	...	...	...	...	...	...	...	...	...	...	...
21	Pharmaceuticals,medicinal chemicals, etc.	d/	...	...	...	...	...	...	...	...	...	...	...	...
22	Rubber and plastics products	d/	...	...	...	...	...	...	...	...	...	...	...	...
23	Other non-metallic mineral products		71	76	77	78	84	92	100	100	103	109	101	85
24	Basic metals	e/	73	81	81	86	94	101	100	99	95	92	82	73
25	Fabricated metal products, except machinery	e/	...	...	...	...	...	...	...	...	...	...	...	...
26	Computer, electronic and optical products	f/	82	84	90	91	93	96	100	102	96	105	97	81
27	Electrical equipment	f/	...	...	...	...	...	...	...	...	...	...	...	...
28	Machinery and equipment n.e.c.	f/	...	...	...	...	...	...	...	...	...	...	...	...
29	Motor vehicles, trailers and semi-trailers	f/	...	...	...	...	...	...	...	...	...	...	...	...
30	Other transport equipment	f/	...	...	...	...	...	...	...	...	...	...	...	...
31	Furniture	g/	83	91	90	89	96	99	100	98	95	88	78	73
32	Other manufacturing	g/	...	...	...	...	...	...	...	...	...	...	...	...
33	Repair and installation of machinery/equipment		...	...	...	...	...	...	...	...	...	...	...	...
C	Total manufacturing		81	84	86	87	95	97	100	101	98	99	94	88

ISIC Revision 4

a/ 10 includes 11 and 12.
b/ 13 includes 14 and 15.
c/ 16 includes 17.
d/ 19 includes 20, 21 and 22.
e/ 24 includes 25.
f/ 26 includes 27, 28, 29 and 30.
g/ 31 includes 32.

Norway

Supplier of information:
Statistics Norway, Oslo.
Industrial statistics for the OECD countries are compiled by the OECD secretariat, which supplies them to UNIDO.

Basic source of data:
Annual industrial inquiry.

Major deviations from ISIC (Revision 3):
Data presented in ISIC (Revision 3) were originally classified according to the NACE (Revision 1).

Reference period:
Calendar year.

Scope:
All enterprises.

Method of data collection:
Not reported.

Type of enumeration:
Not reported.

Adjusted for non-response:
Not reported.

Concepts and definitions of variables:
Number of establishments refers to local kind-of-activity units.
Number of employees is calculated as the average number of employees throughout the year, whether full- or part-time; homeworkers are not included.
Wages and salaries comprises all payments, whether in cash or in kind, made by the employer in connection with work done, to all persons included in the count of employees (also employed outworkers). It includes taxes, social insurance and pension contributions payable by the employee, but deducted by the employer. Bonuses, production awards, holiday allowances and wages paid during periods of sickness, military leave or other absences and commission earned by salesmen and representatives are also included. Fees paid to shareholders committees are included to some extend.
Output refers to gross output, excluding all subsidies and including all indirect taxes exept VAT. Included are the values of all goods produced on own account, repair work for others, mounting or installation of own products and merchandise, contract work, other work, own-account investment work, own-account repair work, rental receipts and gross profit of goods sold in the same condition as purchased.
Value added is value of output, less cost of goods and services consumed. It includes subsidies, less indirect taxes (except VAT) and investment levy.
Gross fixed capital formation is defined as the acquisition of fixed durable assets, new and used, with an expected productive life of more than one year, including own-account investment work less receipts from sales of fixed durable assets.

Related national publications:
Industristatistikk (annual), published by Statistics Norway, Oslo.

Norway

Values: ".." = not available/confidential; "-" = nil. The three metric groups each have an (empty) Note column in the original. Wages and salaries are in millions of Norwegian Kroner.

ISIC	Industry	Ent. 2005	Ent. 2006	Ent. 2007	Ent. 2008	Empl. 2005	Empl. 2006	Empl. 2007	Empl. 2008	Wages 2005	Wages 2006	Wages 2007	Wages 2008
		(number)				(number)				(millions of Norwegian Kroner)			
151	Processed meat,fish,fruit,vegetables,fats	975	956	895	901	23985	23330	22978	23373	7666	7920	7731	8050
1511	Processing/preserving of meat	314	312	312	310	12899	12892	12739	13347	4110	4299	4205	4379
1512	Processing/preserving of fish	567	542	483	483	8771	8170	7928	8000	2599	2721	2690	2877
1513	Processing/preserving of fruit & vegetables	64	68	65	70	1340	1362	1385	1037	437	462	416	354
1514	Vegetable and animal oils and fats	30	34	35	38	975	906	926	989	520	439	419	441
1520	Dairy products	48	50	59	62	6338	6378	6266	6311	2130	2226	2217	2398
153	Grain mill products; starches; animal feeds	131	129	122	126	..	..	2399	2496	..	..	1060	1118
1531	Grain mill products	41	40	40	41	..	..	600	561	..	..	244	229
1532	Starches and starch products	1	-	-	-	..	..	..	..	..	..	..	..
1533	Prepared animal feeds	89	89	82	85	1741	1727	1799	1935	687	766	816	888
154	Other food products	778	783	777	820	12756	12428	12410	12807	3457	3740	3878	3993
1541	Bakery products	658	652	638	680	8316	8403	8860	8921	1986	2256	2406	2488
1542	Sugar	1	1	1	1	..	..	..	..	..	..	..	..
1543	Cocoa, chocolate and sugar confectionery	16	20	25	26	2352	1885	1485	1825	706	692	707	691
1544	Macaroni, noodles & similar products	3	3	3	3	27	..	..	..	8	..	..	..
1549	Other food products n.e.c.	101	107	110	110	2061	..	2043	2044	757	..	760	811
155	Beverages	67	75	69	73	4942	4702	..	..	1763	1795	..	..
1551	Distilling, rectifying & blending of spirits	2	3	3	4	..	..	..	..	..	..	..	..
1552	Wines	4	6	6	6	..	199	209	..	..	113	119	..
1553	Malt liquors and malt	17	18	16	18	..	..	..	..	..	..	..	..
1554	Soft drinks; mineral waters	44	48	44	45	2875	2684	2596	2561	1068	1067	1063	1044
1600	Tobacco products	1	1	1	1	1794	1818	1817	1785	569	615	657	658
171	Spinning, weaving and finishing of textiles	103	104	114	119	739	723	757	771	202	212	218	218
1711	Textile fibre preparation; textile weaving	61	56	51	54	549	528	511	528	143	145	143	145
1712	Finishing of textiles	42	48	63	65	190	195	246	243	58	68	75	73
172	Other textiles	494	473	436	469	2489	2572	2713	2618	707	784	846	841
1721	Made-up textile articles, except apparel	302	314	289	314	1052	1148	1144	1135	296	342	350	359
1722	Carpets and rugs	10	10	10	11	33	34	34	32	8	10	11	9
1723	Cordage, rope, twine and netting	83	76	72	74	988	998	1096	1101	288	314	348	361
1729	Other textiles n.e.c.	99	73	65	70	416	392	439	350	115	119	136	112
1730	Knitted and crocheted fabrics and articles	88	86	73	87	390	372	352	282	99	101	108	88
1810	Wearing apparel, except fur apparel	545	554	555	621	948	1004	1208	1259	247	286	360	377
1820	Dressing & dyeing of fur; processing of fur	38	36	33	32	108	114	115	86	26	26	26	22
191	Tanning, dressing and processing of leather	43	34	31	36	135	138	..	..	41	40	..	..
1911	Tanning and dressing of leather	4	4	4	5	116	113	..	..	35	34	..	..
1912	Luggage, handbags, etc.; saddlery & harness	39	30	27	31	19	25	24	115	6	6	8	36
1920	Footwear	21	18	14	12	151	137	126	101	37	32	34	25
2010	Sawmilling and planing of wood	767	757	717	761	4200	4225	4338	4183	1281	1326	1430	1397
202	Products of wood, cork, straw, etc.	1257	1234	1086	1118	10334	10920	11388	11165	3121	3395	3718	3712
2021	Veneer sheets, plywood, particle board, etc.	26	26	24	27	1020	1103	1181	1192	355	394	430	454
2022	Builders' carpentry and joinery	793	779	706	711	8490	8960	9372	9180	2551	2773	3056	3034
2023	Wooden containers	78	80	74	75	331	..	380	362	86	..	115	109
2029	Other wood products; articles of cork/straw	360	349	282	305	493	..	455	431	129	..	116	115
210	Paper and paper products	105	99	94	94	7069	6240	5648	5242	2604	2517	2250	2130
2101	Pulp, paper and paperboard	26	23	24	23	4579	4059	3590	3293	1804	1773	1498	1416
2102	Corrugated paper and paperboard	29	27	26	24	1673	1542	1420	1317	543	511	505	465
2109	Other articles of paper and paperboard	50	49	44	47	817	639	638	632	258	233	247	249
221	Publishing	1509	1505	1463	1934	16595	16633	16601	16504	7171	7574	7874	7528
2211	Publishing of books and other publications	437	431	405	560	2909	2924	2943	2746	1308	1366	1403	1289
2212	Publishing of newspapers, journals, etc.	597	603	600	663	12951	12941	12885	13038	5586	5931	6182	5969
2213	Publishing of recorded media	194	193	196	389	185	217	209	189	63	72	77	74
2219	Other publishing	281	278	262	322	550	551	564	531	214	205	213	195

222	Printing and related service activities	1606	1524	1362	1418	7927	7905	7634	7575	2847	2924	3025	2988
2221	Printing	889	860	763	793	6215	6232	5979	6055	2303	2364	2445	2441
2222	Service activities related to printing	717	664	599	625	1712	1673	1655	1520	545	558	580	548
2230	Reproduction of recorded media	78	69	62	68	106	98	88	72	32	32	31	21
2310	Coke oven products	2	1	1	-	...	...	...	-	...	...	...	-
2320	Refined petroleum products	9	11	10	9	...	...	...	...	...	...	...	...
2330	Processing of nuclear fuel	-	-	-	-	-	-	-	-	-	-	-	-
241	Basic chemicals	71	68	73	76	7548	7345	7564	...	3920	3690	3956	...
2411	Basic chemicals, except fertilizers	48	46	52	55	5300	5114	5418	...	2575	2474	2687	...
2412	Fertilizers and nitrogen compounds	11	11	11	11	937	939	909	...	710	558	605	...
2413	Plastics in primary forms; synthetic rubber	12	11	10	10	1311	1292	1237	942	635	658	664	461
242	Other chemicals	185	183	187	186	5897	6096	5963	...	2661	2822	2831	...
2421	Pesticides and other agro-chemical products	3	7	6	4	...	1	3	...	...	...	...	...
2422	Paints, varnishes, printing ink and mastics	34	35	33	29	1061	1077	1089	1132	505	505	515	576
2423	Pharmaceuticals, medicinal chemicals, etc.	35	34	32	35	3061	3080	3017	3028	1357	1480	1513	1428
2424	Soap, cleaning & cosmetic preparations	59	57	63	63	926	953	976	918	329	368	366	358
2429	Other chemical products n.e.c.	54	50	53	55	848	985	878	952	470	469	437	424
2430	Man-made fibres	-	-	-	-	-	-	-	-	-	-	-	-
251	Rubber products	52	49	46	48	621	693	709	775	228	267	266	316
2511	Rubber tyres and tubes	18	16	13	14	137	151	125	135	46	51	42	49
2519	Other rubber products	34	33	33	34	484	542	584	640	183	216	224	267
2520	Plastic products	373	365	345	360	4628	4604	4861	4811	1555	1622	1720	1830
2610	Glass and glass products	122	123	114	115	1968	2014	2000	2027	689	730	744	788
269	Non-metallic mineral products n.e.c.	653	634	600	636	8477	8907	9296	9891	3170	3505	3878	4294
2691	Pottery, china and earthenware	172	160	137	152	619	570	541	...	178	179	164	...
2692	Refractory ceramic products	7	7	8	8	11	13	15	20	4	5	4	8
2693	Struct.non-refractory clay; ceramic products	4	4	3	2	51	42	40	...	18	17	18	...
2694	Cement, lime and plaster	6	6	8	8	479	452	509	...	219	202	240	...
2695	Articles of concrete, cement and plaster	262	261	258	265	4273	4669	5010	5244	1583	1854	2094	2209
2696	Cutting, shaping & finishing of stone	176	168	160	171	723	682	692	712	219	228	251	262
2699	Other non-metallic mineral products n.e.c.	26	28	26	30	2321	2479	2489	2864	949	1021	1107	1402
2710	Basic iron and steel	88	78	68	64	2818	2739	2686	2743	1119	1115	1154	1138
2720	Basic precious and non-ferrous metals	29	29	28	26	6980	7394	7046	8527	3086	3740	4356	4319
273	Casting of metals	50	47	48	46	1489	1513	1620	1672	530	575	614	659
2731	Casting of iron and steel	19	19	21	21	958	945	1046	1088	356	381	415	454
2732	Casting of non-ferrous metals	31	28	27	25	531	568	574	584	174	195	200	205
281	Struct.metal products;tanks;steam generators	561	536	527	531	7561	8176	8852	9083	2582	3030	3379	3592
2811	Structural metal products	525	503	497	501	7094	7635	8309	8538	2413	2850	3154	3358
2812	Tanks, reservoirs and containers of metal	31	28	25	25	330	344	307	316	115	119	123	128
2813	Steam generators	5	5	5	5	137	197	236	229	54	61	102	106
289	Other metal products; metal working services	1826	1898	1938	2062	10803	11472	12654	13215	3738	4275	4856	5123
2891	Metal forging/pressing/stamping/roll-forming	31	34	34	42	179	189	228	233	59	60	73	81
2892	Treatment & coating of metals	1250	1338	1411	1519	5331	5827	6686	7398	1881	2215	2587	2900
2893	Cutlery, hand tools and general hardware	137	114	103	109	1230	1405	1379	1358	420	521	551	525
2899	Other fabricated metal products n.e.c.	408	412	390	392	4063	4051	4361	4226	1378	1479	1645	1617
291	General purpose machinery	1248	1192	1138	1213	13469	13662	14354	15985	5488	6114	7038	7857
2911	Engines & turbines (not for transport equipment)	93	90	88	94	3580	3838	3929	4369	1657	1850	2188	2291
2912	Pumps, compressors, taps and valves	134	112	95	100	2406	2366	2448	2979	1078	1160	1325	1583
2913	Bearings, gears, gearing & driving elements	11	9	11	12	239	251	312	341	93	102	127	151
2914	Ovens, furnaces and furnace burners	24	20	18	17	253	264	297	295	94	101	127	134
2915	Lifting and handling equipment	212	193	184	199	2782	2783	3136	3669	1053	1286	1541	1822
2919	Other general purpose machinery	774	768	742	791	4209	4160	4232	4332	1512	1614	1731	1876
292	Special purpose machinery	1216	1182	1128	1225	7748	8109	9504	10727	3523	4107	4798	5904
2921	Agricultural and forestry machinery	611	605	557	615	1469	1384	1470	1505	517	563	556	579
2922	Machine tools	86	87	90	86	701	676	703	618	269	274	297	262
2923	Machinery for metallurgy	8	8	7	9	12	37	665	...	3	14	325	...
2924	Machinery for mining & construction	169	168	169	203	1812	2181	2646	3388	1107	1431	1772	2357
2925	Food/beverage/tobacco processing machinery	151	128	124	118	695	669	728	721	245	278	297	321
2926	Machinery for textile, apparel and leather	28	18	16	17	38	25	20	...	10	7	7	...
2927	Weapons and ammunition	43	42	42	45	1842	1922	2037	2330	872	1000	955	1266
2929	Other special purpose machinery	120	126	123	132	1179	1215	1235	1374	501	541	589	670

continued

Norway

ISIC Revision 3

Number of enterprises — (number); Number of employees — (number); Wages and salaries paid to employees — (millions of Norwegian Kroner)

ISIC	Industry	Note	Ent 2005	Ent 2006	Ent 2007	Ent 2008	Note	Emp 2005	Emp 2006	Emp 2007	Emp 2008	Note	Wages 2005	Wages 2006	Wages 2007	Wages 2008
2930	Domestic appliances n.e.c.		60	49	48	55		1118	1150	1180	1123		365	411	437	410
3000	Office, accounting and computing machinery		38	24	15	16		180	164	120	103		94	97	65	49
3110	Electric motors, generators and transformers		62	54	47	45		1069	1107	1081	1156		457	509	540	565
3120	Electricity distribution & control apparatus		93	91	89	93		1429	1526	1654	1711		515	580	672	698
3130	Insulated wire and cable		18	18	14	18		1372	1542	1634	1720		652	775	907	901
3140	Accumulators, primary cells and batteries		5	5	3	2		...	...	...	...		...	...	...	...
3150	Lighting equipment and electric lamps		61	57	49	53	1	1052	963	941	916		379	379	359	344
3190	Other electrical equipment n.e.c.		250	237	215	220		1306	1410	1399	...		509	596	623	...
3210	Electronic valves, tubes, etc.		69	55	51	51		1936	1994	2174	2289		738	829	940	958
3220	TV/radio transmitters; line comm. apparatus		30	27	29	30		1667	1416	1324	944		968	962	679	470
3230	TV and radio receivers and associated goods		47	53	49	58		342	426	494	518		121	162	197	207
331	Medical, measuring, testing appliances, etc.		552	569	562	578		7893	8416	8896	9231		3570	4203	4595	5001
3311	Medical, surgical and orthopaedic equipment		391	392	384	395		2117	2188	2230	2230		783	859	875	907
3312	Measuring/testing/navigating appliances,etc.		130	145	146	151		3581	4007	4174	4417		1724	2125	2204	2589
3313	Industrial process control equipment		31	32	32	32		2195	2221	2492	2584		1062	1219	1516	1505
3320	Optical instruments & photographic equipment		13	14	15	16		112	99	104	104		42	39	42	41
3330	Watches and clocks		7	5	3	7		13	13	9	12		3	2	3	4
3410	Motor vehicles		7	7	7	8		258	240	275	288		66	93	106	103
3420	Automobile bodies, trailers & semi-trailers		73	68	61	66		1199	1153	1115	1103		373	384	390	396
3430	Parts/accessories for automobiles		67	60	53	58		3312	3237	3380	3292		1237	1268	1324	1400
351	Building and repairing of ships and boats		1104	1079	1071	1165		28130	32293	34998	36775		12973	15880	16963	18178
3511	Building and repairing of ships		680	644	633	672		26691	30749	33281	35184		12496	15344	16347	17623
3512	Building/repairing of pleasure/sport. boats		424	435	438	493		1439	1544	1717	1591		477	535	616	555
3520	Railway/tramway locomotives & rolling stock		11	13	13	14		330	1093	1083	1206		128	427	465	493
3530	Aircraft and spacecraft		30	31	30	30		1172	2395	2309	2269		509	1204	1112	1180
359	Transport equipment n.e.c.		27	23	22	25		308	296	281	250		95	97	95	82
3591	Motorcycles		1	-	1	1		...	...	...	...		...	...	...	...
3592	Bicycles and invalid carriages		17	15	14	16		...	270	...	...		...	...	...	...
3599	Other transport equipment n.e.c.		9	8	7	8		...	26	28	27		...	...	...	...
3610	Furniture		1151	1129	1064	1168		8062	8102	8107	7929		2465	2594	2610	2627
369	Manufacturing n.e.c.		636	610	577	643		2034	1989	1986	1851		637	660	665	627
3691	Jewellery and related articles		223	218	211	241		633	621	594	589		174	174	172	175
3692	Musical instruments		37	43	42	49		28	28	31	28		8	8	7	7
3693	Sports goods		56	58	51	52		712	709	709	595		255	268	275	224
3694	Games and toys		40	31	23	24		44	30	17	21		14	9	5	7
3699	Other manufacturing n.e.c.		280	260	250	277		617	601	635	618		186	201	205	214
3710	Recycling of metal waste and scrap		68	72	63	66		700	726	859	984		274	304	342	400
3720	Recycling of non-metal waste and scrap		68	65	58	60		292	375	447	528		103	134	171	222
D	Total manufacturing		19686	19298	18422	19894		247215	255276	263005	270620		94064	104211	110750	115516

Norway

ISIC	Industry	Output (millions of Norwegian Kroner)					Value added at factor values (millions of Norwegian Kroner)					Gross fixed capital formation (millions of Norwegian Kroner)		
		Note	2005	2006	2007	2008	Note	2005	2006	2007	2008	Note	2007	2008
151	Processed meat,fish,fruit,vegetables,fats		71793	67015	69915	73956		12635	12298	12939	14574		2011	2803
1511	Processing/preserving of meat		42372	34060	36044	36726		6258	5587	7031	8477		813	1063
1512	Processing/preserving of fish		23011	26509	27068	29429		4387	4885	4091	4339		955	1154
1513	Processing/preserving of fruit & vegetables		2751	2962	3114	2953		832	814	889	721		103	279
1514	Vegetable and animal oils and fats		3659	3484	3690	4848		1159	1011	928	1037		141	308
1520	Dairy products		14648	15200	16838	16540		3145	3100	4271	3738		560	708
153	Grain mill products; starches; animal feeds		...	...	15191	17096		...	...	2226	2259		799	612
1531	Grain mill products		...	...	2309	2470		...	...	532	582		119	94
1532	Starches and starch products		9374	11239	12883	14627		1511	1605	1694	1677		680	518
1533	Prepared animal feeds		14260	15819	16692	17479		5673	6103	6392	6444		681	879
154	Other food products		6254	7252	8041	8460		2884	3051	3323	3347		308	373
1541	Bakery products		3691	3894	3866	3987		1286	1415	1474	1396		119	140
1542	Sugar		-	...	...	...		-	...	...	...		...	...
1543	Cocoa, chocolate and sugar confectionery		4298	...	4771	5026		1495	...	1590	1699		255	368
1544	Macaroni, noodles & similar products		17	...	...	...		9	...	...	...		...	...
1549	Other food products n.e.c.		12881	13423	...	...		3032	3094	...	...		...	...
155	Beverages		...	542	672	...		...	215	208	...		17	...
1551	Distilling, rectifying & blending of spirits		...	2	...	...		...	1	...	...		...	...
1552	Wines		8628	8951	9272	9971		1735	1795	2524	1863		212	242
1553	Malt liquors and malt		3687	3927	3940	4356		1064	1083	1200	1076		174	270
1554	Soft drinks; mineral waters		...	...	...	...		...	...	...	...		...	...
1600	Tobacco products		738	795	783	808		297	328	302	299		20	29
171	Spinning, weaving and finishing of textiles		486	483	467	511		203	216	192	196		13	25
1711	Textile fibre preparation; textile weaving		252	312	316	298		95	112	111	104		7	4
1712	Finishing of textiles		2990	3367	3878	3663		1080	1227	1448	1405		169	155
172	Other textiles		1250	1401	1582	1529		461	535	615	611		29	27
1721	Made-up textile articles, except apparel		22	25	30	30		14	14	16	15		...	...
1722	Carpets and rugs		1276	1462	1727	1673		445	508	626	646		127	117
1723	Cordage, rope, twine and netting		441	480	540	432		158	170	191	133		13	12
1729	Other textiles n.e.c.		347	408	370	400		135	134	135	114		11	4
1730	Knitted and crocheted fabrics and articles		1258	1603	2086	2233		474	578	782	818		76	66
1810	Wearing apparel, except fur apparel		151	170	127	115		52	40	12	24		1	1
1820	Dressing & dyeing of fur; processing of fur		183	162	...	172		50	48	...	45		...	4
191	Tanning, dressing and processing of leather		147	130	...	...		37	35	16	...		...	...
1911	Tanning and dressing of leather		36	31	36	...		13	13	16	...		...	...
1912	Luggage, handbags, etc.; saddlery & harness		...	...	205	189		48	39	55	42		...	1
1920	Footwear		185	175	...	...		...	...	...	...		10	...
2010	Sawmilling and planing of wood		9875	9446	10260	8620		1923	2263	3082	2082		600	699
202	Products of wood, cork, straw, etc.		13411	15156	17694	16590		4639	5270	5895	5563		572	746
2021	Veneer sheets, plywood, particle board, etc.		1968	2248	2556	2504		551	666	709	609		137	72
2022	Builders' carpentry and joinery		10436	11899	13930	12904		3739	4201	4781	4555		398	447
2023	Wooden containers		449	631	631	633		137	...	204	203		19	47
2029	Other wood products; articles of cork/straw		557	...	576	549		211	...	201	195		18	180
210	Paper and paper products		15691	15843	16568	16619		3891	4169	3802	3116		1004	698
2101	Pulp, paper and paperboard		12522	12904	13431	13595		2812	3216	2749	2155		860	604
2102	Corrugated paper and paperboard		2150	2087	2213	2072		686	612	683	611		80	53
2109	Other articles of paper and paperboard		1019	852	924	951		394	340	370	350		64	42
221	Publishing		27541	29254	30791	30381		11391	12034	12624	12248		502	516
2211	Publishing of books and other publications		5462	5891	6139	5871		2517	2614	2728	2585		84	37
2212	Publishing of newspapers, journals, etc.		20743	21898	23272	23056		8493	8954	9496	9218		397	460
2213	Publishing of recorded media		460	490	497	561		103	130	123	139		4	7
2219	Other publishing		876	976	882	892		278	336	277	308		17	13

continued

Norway

ISIC	Industry		Output (millions of Norwegian Kroner)					Value added at factor values (millions of Norwegian Kroner)					Gross fixed capital formation (millions of Norwegian Kroner)	
		Note	2005	2006	2007	2008	Note	2005	2006	2007	2008	Note	2007	2008
222	Printing and related service activities		11171	11383	12067	12255		4563	4689	4901	4759		561	377
2221	Printing		9170	9345	9932	10100		3720	3852	4015	3855		487	324
2222	Service activities related to printing		2001	2038	2135	2155		842	838	887	904		75	52
2230	Reproduction of recorded media		82	86	90	71		50	49	45	35		3	2
2310	Coke oven products		:	:	:	:		:	:	:	:			
2320	Refined petroleum products		:	:	:	:		:	:	:	:			
2330	Processing of nuclear fuel		:	:	:	:		:	:	:	:			
241	Basic chemicals		34437	34708	39879	:		8868	10300	10968	:		3193	
2411	Basic chemicals, except fertilizers		22769	20936	25318	:		7373	8358	8788	:		2634	
2412	Fertilizers and nitrogen compounds		5506	6008	6805	:		660	767	778	:		399	
2413	Plastics in primary forms; synthetic rubber		6161	7765	7756	6860		834	1177	1401	691		160	259
242	Other chemicals		13880	16259	16668	:		6170	7753	7728	:		616	
2421	Pesticides and other agro-chemical products		:	14	10	:		:	4	:	:			
2422	Paints, varnishes, printing ink and mastics		2416	2664	3013	3053		803	868	903	1001		39	61
2423	Pharmaceuticals, medicinal chemicals, etc.		7445	8614	8396	7749		3809	4959	4705	3895		320	260
2424	Soap, cleaning & cosmetic preparations		2123	2301	2272	2435		756	811	714	772		71	72
2429	Other chemical products n.e.c.		1896	2666	2977	3601		803	1111	1405	1947		185	192
2430	Man-made fibres		:	:	:	:		:	:	:	:			
251	Rubber products		711	886	938	1358		356	440	427	507			
2511	Rubber tyres and tubes		159	179	180	224		67	73	74	72		43	33
2519	Other rubber products		552	707	757	1134		288	366	354	435		6	9
2520	Plastic products		7225	7710	9078	9741		2412	2552	2922	3011		38	24
2610	Glass and glass products		2711	3056	3334	3333		1052	1129	1255	1310		431	459
269	Non-metallic mineral products n.e.c.		15847	18173	22234	24297		5526	6154	7435	7871		3848	1671
2691	Pottery, china and earthenware		580	618	850	:		258	258	313	:		258	220
2692	Refractory ceramic products		11	12	14	21		5	4	4	7		12	18
2693	Struct.non-refractory clay; ceramic products		74	75	82	:		18	17	21	:		2	
2694	Cement, lime and plaster		1156	1357	1719	:		494	543	694	:		187	44
2695	Articles of concrete, cement and plaster		8778	10317	12436	13001		2951	3440	4140	4150		681	902
2696	Cutting, shaping & finishing of stone		792	867	973	1000		321	349	392	401		37	
2699	Other non-metallic mineral products n.e.c.		4456	4928	6160	8011		1479	1543	1871	2407		2926	748
2710	Basic iron and steel		10685	10869	13119	17551		2505	2439	3753	6428		319	623
2720	Basic precious and non-ferrous metals		40165	55612	73108	51864		9439	12624	13531	8507		1822	2061
273	Casting of metals		1868	2256	2727	2694		803	873	998	935		225	183
2731	Casting of iron and steel		1237	1378	1611	1726		569	596	646	627		145	135
2732	Casting of non-ferrous metals		630	879	1116	967		235	276	352	309		81	49
281	Struct.metal products;tanks;steam generators		9727	11667	14265	15063		3581	4336	5465	5448		323	387
2811	Structural metal products		9081	10828	13327	14074		3335	4098	5109	5067		288	364
2812	Tanks, reservoirs and containers of metal		419	477	576	608		163	194	208	226		26	16
2813	Steam generators		227	362	363	382		82	43	148	155		9	6
289	Other metal products; metal working services		14036	16475	19814	21275		5862	6972	8107	8394		740	904
2891	Metal forging/pressing/stamping/roll-forming		215	235	263	290		87	83	111	113		9	8
2892	Treatment & coating of metals		6612	7857	9577	11141		2872	3485	4222	4657		387	465
2893	Cutlery, hand tools and general hardware		1610	2103	2257	2154		690	862	935	865		32	30
2899	Other fabricated metal products n.e.c.		5599	6280	7717	7689		2213	2542	2839	2759		312	400
291	General purpose machinery		27379	34122	39731	48470		8183	10148	12178	14628		1214	1475
2911	Engines & turbines (not for transport equipment)		7970	10527	12842	16649		1962	2367	2795	3861		301	318
2912	Pumps, compressors, taps and valves		8833	10490	10683	11846		2335	2849	3577	4008		439	553
2913	Bearings, gears, gearing & driving elements		457	534	708	895		155	168	232	268		39	50
2914	Ovens, furnaces and furnace burners		458	512	537	541		131	150	232	206		8	7
2915	Lifting and handling equipment		4227	5818	8089	10628		1444	2115	2589	3266		207	266
2919	Other general purpose machinery		5433	6241	6873	7910		2157	2500	2750	3018		220	281

292	Special purpose machinery	14545	23651	34373	42540	4843	7141	9583	12702	494	817
2921	Agricultural and forestry machinery	2260	2349	2606	2805	815	752	814	961	63	74
2922	Machine tools	927	996	1154	1011	453	469	556	456	47	115
2923	Machinery for metallurgy	14	26	1719	...	5	15	418	...	19	19
2924	Machinery for mining & construction	4671	11190	18956	25230	1265	2651	4327	6627	152	189
2925	Food/beverage/tobacco processing machinery	1062	1126	1377	1377	376	488	479	526	18	27
2926	Machinery for textile, apparel and leather	46	23	23	...	23	14	13	...	129	...
2927	Weapons and ammunition	3100	4039	5053	6267	1277	1646	1984	2208	66	342
2929	Other special purpose machinery	2464	3902	3485	3967	627	1106	992	1243	76	53
2930	Domestic appliances n.e.c.	1471	1689	1818	1678	576	615	616	535	5	68
3000	Office, accounting and computing machinery	502	559	649	554	121	101	123	163	57	2
3110	Electric motors, generators and transformers	2108	2557	2418	3204	593	815	744	684	37	66
3120	Electricity distribution & control apparatus	1896	2329	2868	3023	804	970	1219	1210	162	45
3130	Insulated wire and cable	3856	5046	6068	6066	1221	1427	1936	2073	42	240
3140	Accumulators, primary cells and batteries	22	23	3	3	1	1	-22	...	52	...
3150	Lighting equipment and electric lamps	1425	1404	1444	1351	575	588	575	567	761	37
3190	Other electrical equipment n.e.c.	1992	2387	2659	...	737	826	987	...	71	...
3210	Electronic valves, tubes, etc.	3315	4113	4537	5875	1113	1464	1655	1895	18	402
3220	TV/radio transmitters; line comm. apparatus	4820	4882	5292	2872	1742	1383	1975	759	...	44
3230	TV and radio receivers and associated goods	549	752	920	1080	219	300	371	437	...	116
331	Medical, measuring, testing appliances, etc.	14658	17663	21057	23172	5408	6266	7657	8445	289	349
3311	Medical, surgical and orthopaedic equipment	2970	3297	3555	3212	1334	1397	1400	1391	79	75
3312	Measuring/testing/navigating appliances, etc.	6541	8217	9836	11573	2638	2850	3709	4307	156	183
3313	Industrial process control equipment	5148	6149	7666	8387	1436	2018	2547	2747	55	90
3320	Optical instruments & photographic equipment	141	122	155	146	56	64	87	72	5	4
3330	Watches and clocks	8	6	7	10	3	3	4	6	-	-
3410	Motor vehicles	386	735	688	592	44	127	115	96	43	5
3420	Automobile bodies, trailers & semi-trailers	1871	2062	2311	2150	560	541	574	542	15	36
3430	Parts/accessories for automobiles	5036	5380	6089	6044	1820	1753	1799	1760	278	188
351	Building and repairing of ships and boats	59777	84442	100849	101791	17245	22296	24029	26353	4626	3030
3511	Building and repairing of ships	57399	81776	97701	99179	16528	21487	23079	25599	4505	2938
3512	Building/repairing of pleasure/sport. boats	2378	2664	3148	2613	717	810	950	755	121	93
3520	Railway/tramway locomotives & rolling stock	497	1236	1300	1154	268	604	602	609	26	37
3530	Aircraft and spacecraft	2378	4203	4255	4753	1019	1500	1259	1799	798	794
359	Transport equipment n.e.c.	415	430	413	412	161	169	135	135	6	13
3591	Motorcycles	389	389	...	...	...	159	...	...	...	...
3592	Bicycles and invalid carriages	40	40	42	43	10	10	6	7	-	-
3599	Other transport equipment n.e.c.	...	...	...	...	...	...	...	...	400	...
3610	Furniture	10308	10884	11883	11738	3860	4223	4572	4121	400	428
369	Manufacturing n.e.c.	2243	2442	2450	2573	894	970	946	1040	85	54
3691	Jewellery and related articles	584	610	616	678	255	257	263	282	6	16
3692	Musical instruments	31	35	34	32	14	18	18	18	...	...
3693	Sports goods	872	972	928	897	296	347	287	354	45	21
3694	Games and toys	54	33	22	19	26	19	10	7	2	1
3699	Other manufacturing n.e.c.	702	791	849	947	301	331	369	383	33	17
3710	Recycling of metal waste and scrap	2231	2771	3933	4897	579	836	934	806	266	292
3720	Recycling of non-metal waste and scrap	611	769	992	1176	176	252	315	350	89	95
D	Total manufacturing	535472	617354	711801	733489	158372	181847	202842	208723	29735	33268

Norway

Index numbers of industrial production

ISIC Revision 3

(2005=100)

ISIC	Industry	Note	1999	2000	2001	2002	2003	2004	2005	2006	2007	2008	2009	2010
15	Food and beverages	a/	112	110	109	107	103	103	100	101	102	102	...	...
16	Tobacco products	a/	...	...	...	...	...	...	...	...	...	...	...	...
17	Textiles	b/	151	138	131	120	103	99	100	110	106	88	...	...
18	Wearing apparel, fur	b/	...	...	...	...	...	...	...	...	...	...	...	...
19	Leather, leather products and footwear	b/	...	...	...	...	...	...	...	...	...	...	...	...
20	Wood products (excl. furniture)		99	101	97	95	88	93	100	100	103	91	...	...
21	Paper and paper products		105	108	103	96	98	102	100	92	88	82	...	...
22	Printing and publishing		99	97	98	95	95	96	100	101	102	102	...	...
23	Coke,refined petroleum products,nuclear fuel	c/	92	92	92	91	94	96	100	101	103	101	...	...
24	Chemicals and chemical products	c/	...	...	...	...	...	...	...	...	...	...	...	...
25	Rubber and plastics products		141	127	125	120	99	102	100	102	104	102	...	...
26	Non-metallic mineral products		106	103	100	104	96	95	100	109	113	113	...	...
27	Basic metals		96	97	93	91	92	101	100	102	103	100	...	...
28	Fabricated metal products		105	99	101	101	95	94	100	112	122	133	...	...
29	Machinery and equipment n.e.c.		98	95	97	96	92	93	100	107	119	139	...	...
30	Office, accounting and computing machinery	d/	110	107	104	101	92	94	100	102	108	116	...	...
31	Electrical machinery and apparatus	d/	...	...	...	...	...	...	...	...	...	...	...	...
32	Radio,television and communication equipment	d/	...	...	...	...	...	...	...	...	...	...	...	...
33	Medical, precision and optical instruments	d/	...	...	...	...	...	...	...	...	...	...	...	...
34	Motor vehicles, trailers, semi-trailers		120	112	112	113	101	93	100	110	118	125	...	...
35	Other transport equipment		102	94	95	103	97	95	100	119	130	150	...	...
36	Furniture; manufacturing n.e.c.	e/	117	107	99	97	92	98	100	98	100	95	...	...
37	Recycling	e/	...	...	...	...	...	...	...	...	...	...	...	...
D	Total manufacturing		105	102	101	100	96	97	100	104	109	112	...	...

a/ 15 includes 16.
b/ 17 includes 18 and 19.
c/ 23 includes 24.
d/ 30 includes 31, 32 and 33.
e/ 36 includes 37.

- 621 -

Oman

Concepts and definitions of variables:
No deviations from the standard UN concepts and definitions are reported.

Related national publications:
Industrial Statistical Book; Features of the Manufacturing Sector of Large and Medium Industries; Annual Industrial Report, all published by the Industrial Information Department, Ministry of Commerce and Industry, Muscat.

Supplier of information:
Ministry of Commerce and Industry, Muscat.

Basic source of data:
Annual survey.

Major deviations from ISIC (Revision 3):
None reported.

Reference period:
Calendar year.

Scope:
Establishments with 10 or more employees.

Method of data collection:
Not reported.

Type of enumeration:
Complete enumeration.

Adjusted for non-response:
No.

Oman

ISIC Revision 3 — Number of establishments (number) · Number of employees (number) · Wages and salaries paid to employees (thousands of Omani Rials)

ISIC	Industry	Est. Note	Est. 2007	Est. 2008	Est. 2009	Est. 2010	Emp. Note	Emp. 2007	Emp. 2008	Emp. 2009	Emp. 2010	Wage Note	Wage 2007	Wage 2008	Wage 2009	Wage 2010
151	Processed meat,fish,fruit,vegetables,fats		29	32	31	29		2985	3148	2759	2690		8355	11376	9254	11013
1511	Processing/preserving of meat		4	5	4	4		575	617	794	680		1682	2887	2371	2796
1512	Processing/preserving of fish		15	15	16	15		1014	922	891	804		1912	2160	2004	2197
1513	Processing/preserving of fruit & vegetables		8	10	9	8		882	1104	531	548		2127	3263	1576	1647
1514	Vegetable and animal oils and fats		2	2	2	2		514	505	543	658		2633	3066	3302	4374
1520	Dairy products		3	3	4	5		890	889	1529	1604		1788	2019	3668	4264
153	Grain mill products; starches; animal feeds		7	7	7	7		518	572	620	637		3087	3494	4104	4519
1531	Grain mill products		3	3	3	3		319	368	394	442		2221	2471	2964	3553
1532	Starches and starch products		…	…	…	…		…	…	…	…		…	…	…	…
1533	Prepared animal feeds		4	4	4	4		199	204	226	195		866	1023	1139	966
154	Other food products		39	42	45	45		3249	3939	4214	4249		7317	9131	10836	12651
1541	Bakery products		30	32	34	34		2674	3267	3218	2995		5704	6978	7007	7909
1542	Sugar		…	…	…	…		…	…	…	…		…	…	…	…
1543	Cocoa, chocolate and sugar confectionery		1	1	1	1		135	145	171	303		344	447	606	797
1544	Macaroni, noodles & similar products		1	1	1	1		20	70	78	100		40	172	457	621
1549	Other food products n.e.c.		7	8	9	9		420	457	747	851		1229	1534	2766	3324
155	Beverages		19	20	23	29		1810	2130	2183	2625		5463	6917	7771	10303
1551	Distilling, rectifying & blending of spirits		…	…	…	…		…	…	…	…		…	…	…	…
1552	Wines		…	…	…	…		…	…	…	…		…	…	…	…
1553	Malt liquors and malt		…	…	…	…		…	…	…	…		…	…	…	…
1554	Soft drinks; mineral waters		19	20	23	29		1810	2130	2183	2625		5463	6917	7771	10303
1600	Tobacco products		…	…	…	…		…	…	…	…		…	…	…	…
171	Spinning, weaving and finishing of textiles		2	2	2	2		244	234	239	241		873	944	921	1045
1711	Textile fibre preparation; textile weaving		1	1	1	1		179	168	175	181		499	511	517	641
1712	Finishing of textiles		1	1	1	1		65	66	64	60		373	432	404	404
172	Other textiles		2	2	1	2		24	24	9	15		66	69	18	47
1721	Made-up textile articles, except apparel		1	1	1	1		8	8	9	8		24	24	18	24
1722	Carpets and rugs		1	1	…	1		16	16	…	7		42	45	…	22
1723	Cordage, rope, twine and netting		…	…	…	…		…	…	…	…		…	…	…	…
1729	Other textiles n.e.c.		…	…	…	…		…	…	…	…		…	…	…	…
1730	Knitted and crocheted fabrics and articles		…	…	…	…		…	…	…	…		…	…	…	…
1810	Wearing apparel, except fur apparel		3	4	4	3		679	633	789	689		763	789	870	781
1820	Dressing & dyeing of fur; processing of fur		…	…	…	…		…	…	…	…		…	…	…	…
191	Tanning, dressing and processing of leather		…	…	…	…		…	…	…	…		…	…	…	…
1911	Tanning and dressing of leather		…	…	…	…		…	…	…	…		…	…	…	…
1912	Luggage, handbags, etc.; saddlery & harness		…	…	…	…		…	…	…	…		…	…	…	…
1920	Footwear		3	3	3	2		160	177	181	126		365	430	404	270
2010	Sawmilling and planing of wood		…	…	…	…		…	…	…	…		…	…	…	…
202	Products of wood, cork, straw, etc.		10	9	12	10		1837	1933	1860	1880		3758	4727	4543	4248
2021	Veneer sheets, plywood, particle board, etc.		…	…	…	1		…	…	…	808		…	…	…	1842
2022	Builders' carpentry and joinery		10	9	12	10		1837	1933	1860	808		3758	4727	4543	1842
2023	Wooden containers		…	…	…	…		…	…	…	…		…	…	…	…
2029	Other wood products; articles of cork/straw		…	…	…	…		…	…	…	…		…	…	…	…
210	Paper and paper products		13	12	14	12		769	764	806	648		1921	2204	2405	2008
2101	Pulp, paper and paperboard		1	…	3	4		55	…	82	153		118	…	122	293
2102	Corrugated paper and paperboard		6	6	6	5		461	502	530	380		1216	1557	1710	1361
2109	Other articles of paper and paperboard		6	6	5	3		253	262	194	115		587	647	573	354
221	Publishing		9	10	9	6		615	570	672	596		2170	2597	3237	3004
2211	Publishing of books and other publications		5	6	4	3		276	228	203	196		813	926	882	598
2212	Publishing of newspapers, journals, etc.		3	3	3	2		319	327	446	391		1328	1651	2314	2385
2213	Publishing of recorded media		1	1	1	1		20	15	11	9		29	21	23	21
2219	Other publishing		…	1	1	1		…	…	12	9		…	…	18	21

Code	Description	(1)	(2)	(3)	(4)	(5)	(6)	(7)	(8)	(9)	(10)	(11)	(12)
222	Printing and related service activities	2466	2452	2185	1674	994	920	843	716	23	22	19	18
2221	Printing	2466	2452	2185	1674	994	920	843	716	23	22	19	18
2222	Service activities related to printing	34	31	47	45	24	24	35	35	1	1	1	1
2230	Reproduction of recorded media	19144	26844	15220	17589	2426	2122	2120	2224	17	16	17	13
2310	Coke oven products	...	...	...	...	...	...	...	...	...	...	...	...
2320	Refined petroleum products	...	...	...	...	...	...	...	...	...	...	...	...
2330	Processing of nuclear fuel	...	...	...	...	...	...	...	...	...	...	...	...
241	Basic chemicals	15805	15730	11940	15607	2106	1998	1653	1423	28	24	23	18
2411	Basic chemicals, except fertilizers	3900	3681	2814	1828	769	693	685	520	21	18	17	13
2412	Fertilizers and nitrogen compounds	8550	8696	5571	4939	926	889	525	475	5	4	3	3
2413	Plastics in primary forms; synthetic rubber	3355	3354	3555	8840	411	416	443	428	2	2	3	2
242	Other chemicals	7613	8851	7331	6387	1903	2180	1888	1510	24	25	23	24
2421	Pesticides and other agro-chemical products	129	...	...	...	33	...	...	...	1	1	1	1
2422	Paints, varnishes, printing ink and mastics	2893	2792	2300	1849	539	530	453	363	7	7	7	6
2423	Pharmaceuticals, medicinal chemicals, etc.	2013	3389	2820	2239	666	909	841	481	7	4	4	4
2424	Soap, cleaning & cosmetic preparations	1667	1165	1283	1684	487	450	380	487	3	7	6	8
2429	Other chemical products n.e.c.	910	1505	928	616	178	291	214	179	8	7	6	6
2430	Man-made fibres	...	...	...	...	...	...	...	...	5	5	4	...
251	Rubber products	370	...	...	...	116	94	100	91	5	4	4	4
2511	Rubber tyres and tubes	159	...	...	...	55	46	49	56	4	3	3	3
2519	Other rubber products	211	...	...	...	61	48	51	35	1	1	1	1
2520	Plastic products	10061	...	...	...	3873	3219	2925	2975	45	44	41	41
2610	Glass and glass products	3370	...	...	...	836	840	843	649	12	13	14	10
269	Non-metallic mineral products n.e.c.	42928	38881	30962	24688	11968	12120	9906	8862	153	141	121	99
2691	Pottery, china and earthenware	868	619	589	505	219	262	263	216	2	2	2	1
2692	Refractory ceramic products	2352	2281	1882	1122	321	339	315	192	1	2	2	1
2693	Struct.non-refractory clay; ceramic products	34	...	...	...	19	...	...	...	2	...	...	...
2694	Cement, lime and plaster	12809	11309	9632	7194	1351	1265	1209	935	8	8	8	7
2695	Articles of concrete, cement and plaster	6343	6444	5120	5200	2242	2270	2185	2254	51	46	40	33
2696	Cutting, shaping & finishing of stone	11645	9351	7622	6180	4451	4135	3514	3251	22	20	18	15
2699	Other non-metallic mineral products n.e.c.	8877	8878	6118	4487	3365	3849	2420	2014	68	64	52	42
2710	Basic iron and steel	6503	6545	5192	6741	1445	1592	1521	1089	6	9	6	6
2720	Basic precious and non-ferrous metals	13617	7190	4000	5347	1847	1619	658	659	6	3	2	3
273	Casting of metals	7190	7059	2679	167	2169	1475	1436	60	4	3	4	2
2731	Casting of iron and steel	7059	4419	2636	133	2137	1446	1417	42	3	2	3	1
2732	Casting of non-ferrous metals	132	53	43	33	32	29	19	18	1	1	1	...
281	Struct.metal products;tanks;steam generators	13065	15296	12573	12691	5166	4958	4612	4856	41	35	35	35
2811	Structural metal products	12781	14676	12266	11879	5060	4703	4424	4572	38	32	33	34
2812	Tanks, reservoirs and containers of metal	285	620	306	812	106	255	188	284	3	3	2	1
2813	Steam generators	...	...	...	...	...	...	...	...	...	...	...	...
289	Other metal products; metal working services	8956	7382	4132	4922	2163	2035	1435	1733	15	18	17	18
2891	Metal forging/pressing/stamping/roll-forming	2048	309	731	861	590	169	376	501	5	4	5	8
2892	Treatment & coating of metals	20	20	20	...	16	...	16	...	1	1	1	...
2893	Cutlery, hand tools and general hardware	6888	7073	3381	4061	1557	1866	1043	1232	9	14	11	10
2899	Other fabricated metal products n.e.c.	1164	1719	1570	935	282	421	429	314	6	8	6	6
291	General purpose machinery	798	756	792	548	138	145	151	134	1	1	1	1
2911	Engines & turbines (not for transport equipment)	141	126	107	117	42	41	38	45	1	1	1	1
2912	Pumps, compressors, taps and valves	...	...	...	...	...	...	...	...	3	3	3	2
2913	Bearings, gears, gearing & driving elements	...	...	...	...	...	...	...	...	...	...	...	...
2914	Ovens, furnaces and furnace burners	225	838	672	270	102	235	240	135	2	4	4	...
2915	Lifting and handling equipment	1716	1066	1146	814	335	178	181	171	4	3	3	3
2919	Other general purpose machinery	457	...	59	90	138	13	19	22	1	3	3	3
292	Special purpose machinery	44	63	...	...	11	...	...	...	1	1	1	1
2921	Agricultural and forestry machinery	...	...	...	...	...	...	...	...	1	1	1	...
2922	Machine tools	911	674	832	522	125	97	94	72	1	1	1	1
2923	Machinery for metallurgy	...	...	...	...	...	...	...	...	...	...	...	...
2924	Machinery for mining & construction	...	...	...	...	...	...	...	...	...	...	...	...
2925	Food/beverage/tobacco processing machinery	303	329	254	202	61	68	68	77	1	1	1	1
2926	Machinery for textile, apparel and leather	...	...	...	...	...	...	...	...	...	...	...	...
2927	Weapons and ammunition	...	...	...	...	...	...	...	...	...	...	...	...
2929	Other special purpose machinery	...	...	...	...	...	...	...	...	...	...	...	...

continued

Oman

		Number of establishments					Number of employees					Wages and salaries paid to employees				
			(number)					(number)					(thousands of Omani Rials)			
ISIC	Industry	Note	2007	2008	2009	2010	Note	2007	2008	2009	2010	Note	2007	2008	2009	2010
2930	Domestic appliances n.e.c.		2	2	2	3		169	202	213	276		610	883	716	1025
3000	Office, accounting and computing machinery		...	...	...	...		...	...	...	...		...	...	...	...
3110	Electric motors, generators and transformers		...	...	...	...		...	...	...	...		...	...	...	...
3120	Electricity distribution & control apparatus		8	10	11	11		523	697	857	877		1695	2695	3156	3588
3130	Insulated wire and cable		1	1	1	2		569	627	609	734		1877	4470	3314	6017
3140	Accumulators, primary cells and batteries		2	2	2	2		448	462	406	397		1135	1226	1190	1196
3150	Lighting equipment and electric lamps		1	1	2	2		35	31	90	80		102	86	229	254
3190	Other electrical equipment n.e.c.		...	...	...	...		...	...	...	...		...	...	...	...
3210	Electronic valves, tubes, etc.		...	...	...	...		...	...	...	...		...	...	...	...
3220	TV/radio transmitters; line comm. apparatus		...	...	...	...		...	...	...	...		...	...	...	...
3230	TV and radio receivers and associated goods		...	...	...	1		...	...	...	26		...	...	...	172
331	Medical, measuring, testing appliances, etc.		...	...	...	...		...	...	...	...		...	...	...	...
3311	Medical, surgical and orthopaedic equipment		...	...	...	...		...	...	...	...		...	...	...	...
3312	Measuring/testing/navigating appliances,etc.		...	...	...	...		...	...	...	...		...	...	...	...
3313	Industrial process control equipment		...	...	...	...		...	...	...	...		...	...	...	...
3320	Optical instruments & photographic equipment		...	...	...	...		...	...	...	...		...	...	...	...
3330	Watches and clocks		1	...	1	1		70	85	90	118		600	549	637	987
3410	Motor vehicles		1	1	1	1		36	43	36	43		47	50	50	50
3420	Automobile bodies, trailers & semi-trailers		...	1	3	3		...	46	104	420		...	89	213	988
3430	Parts/accessories for automobiles		2	1	1	1		100	41	...	73		192	74	...	256
351	Building and repairing of ships and boats		...	...	...	...		...	...	...	...		...	...	...	...
3511	Building and repairing of ships		...	1	1	2		...	36	32	32		...	50	46	57
3512	Building/repairing of pleasure/sport. boats		...	1	1	2		...	36	32	32		...	50	46	57
3520	Railway/tramway locomotives & rolling stock		...	...	...	...		...	...	...	...		...	...	...	...
3530	Aircraft and spacecraft		...	...	...	...		...	...	...	...		...	...	...	...
359	Transport equipment n.e.c.		...	...	...	...		...	...	...	...		...	...	...	...
3591	Motorcycles		...	...	...	...		...	...	...	...		...	...	...	...
3592	Bicycles and invalid carriages		...	...	...	...		...	...	...	...		...	...	...	...
3599	Other transport equipment n.e.c.		...	...	...	...		...	...	...	...		...	...	...	...
3610	Furniture		16	17	19	19		2741	2911	3034	3331		6030	6619	6806	9672
369	Manufacturing n.e.c.		8	7	6	6		435	406	377	438		1252	894	939	1228
3691	Jewellery and related articles		3	3	3	2		109	100	104	40		286	327	355	242
3692	Musical instruments		...	...	...	...		...	...	...	...		...	...	...	...
3693	Sports goods		...	...	...	...		...	...	...	...		...	...	...	...
3694	Games and toys		1	...	...	...		22	...	...	...		132	...	...	...
3699	Other manufacturing n.e.c.		4	4	3	4		304	306	273	398		834	567	584	986
3710	Recycling of metal waste and scrap		1	1	1	1		29	29	32	35		108	124	104	105
3720	Recycling of non-metal waste and scrap		...	...	...	...		...	...	...	...		...	...	...	...
D	Total manufacturing	a/	483	532	574	598	a/	46302	51214	57536	61341	a/	156515	172280	211324	235591

a/ Sum of available data.

Oman

ISIC	Industry	Output at producers' prices (millions of Omani Rials)					Value added at producers' prices (millions of Omani Rials)					Gross fixed capital formation (millions of Omani Rials)		
		Note	2007	2008	2009	2010	Note	2007	2008	2009	2010	Note	2009	2010
151	Processed meat,fish,fruit,vegetables,fats		114.4	168.4	120.4	134.0		28.0	45.6	45.4	36.4		51.5	73.3
1511	Processing/preserving of meat		15.7	22.3	18.8	22.6		5.9	11.1	10.1	12.5		10.0	35.0
1512	Processing/preserving of fish		26.8	21.2	18.6	24.6		7.9	6.6	8.8	4.9		17.3	15.2
1513	Processing/preserving of fruit & vegetables		14.8	26.2	12.0	10.9		5.6	14.5	6.1	5.3		8.6	7.6
1514	Vegetable and animal oils and fats		57.1	98.6	71.0	75.9		8.7	13.5	20.4	13.7		15.6	15.6
1520	Dairy products		74.2	158.2	112.6	118.6		17.2	21.8	35.7	24.9		10.1	10.2
153	Grain mill products; starches; animal feeds		55.1	85.1	85.8	77.2		10.1	14.6	29.6	20.2		31.1	27.7
1531	Grain mill products		38.0	57.9	55.4	50.0		8.6	11.1	20.8	15.0		18.4	19.4
1532	Starches and starch products		17.1	27.3	30.4	27.2		1.5	3.5	8.8	5.2		12.6	8.3
1533	Prepared animal feeds		65.7	77.9	102.8	107.2		26.6	27.0	46.1	44.9		45.8	51.8
154	Other food products		44.6	50.3	54.8	60.0		19.1	15.8	23.3	29.9		25.7	30.9
1541	Bakery products		4.3	6.0	6.6	8.1		2.0	2.8	3.0	3.6		2.1	2.4
1542	Sugar		0.5	0.6	6.9	8.1		0.4	0.2	1.9	1.8		4.6	6.6
1543	Cocoa, chocolate and sugar confectionery		...	...	...	...		...	...	...	...		...	...
1544	Macaroni, noodles & similar products		16.2	21.0	34.5	31.1		5.2	8.2	17.9	9.6		13.4	11.9
1549	Other food products n.e.c.		...	...	...	...		...	...	...	...		...	...
155	Beverages		...	...	...	...		...	...	...	...		...	...
1551	Distilling, rectifying & blending of spirits		...	...	...	...		...	...	...	...		...	...
1552	Wines		...	...	...	...		...	...	...	...		...	...
1553	Malt liquors and malt		51.4	57.8	59.6	64.4		24.5	21.5	24.9	27.5		20.4	18.1
1554	Soft drinks; mineral waters		...	...	...	...		...	...	...	...		...	...
1600	Tobacco products		3.3	4.4	3.7	13.0		0.8	2.0	1.5	8.3		11.5	4.8
171	Spinning, weaving and finishing of textiles		0.9	1.6	1.0	9.7		-0.4	0.5	0.3	7.1		10.3	3.6
1711	Textile fibre preparation; textile weaving		2.4	2.9	2.7	3.3		1.3	1.5	1.2	1.2		1.2	1.1
1712	Finishing of textiles		0.3	0.4	0.1	0.2		0.2	0.3	...	0.1		...	...
172	Other textiles		0.2	0.1	0.1	0.1		0.1	...	...	...		...	...
1721	Made-up textile articles, except apparel		0.2	0.3	0.1	0.1		0.1	0.3	...	0.1		...	...
1722	Carpets and rugs		...	...	...	...		...	...	...	...		...	...
1723	Cordage, rope, twine and netting		...	...	...	...		...	...	...	...		...	...
1729	Other textiles n.e.c.		...	...	...	...		...	...	...	...		...	...
1730	Knitted and crocheted fabrics and articles		2.6	3.5	3.1	4.1		1.6	2.1	2.0	2.1		1.7	0.9
1810	Wearing apparel, except fur apparel		...	...	...	...		...	...	...	...		...	...
1820	Dressing & dyeing of fur; processing of fur		...	...	...	...		...	...	...	...		...	...
191	Tanning, dressing and processing of leather		...	...	...	...		...	...	...	...		...	...
1911	Tanning and dressing of leather		...	...	...	...		...	...	...	...		...	...
1912	Luggage, handbags, etc.; saddlery & harness		3.1	3.8	2.9	1.9		1.1	1.6	1.2	0.3		0.6	1.0
1920	Footwear		...	...	...	6.5		...	...	...	4.6		...	2.2
2010	Sawmilling and planing of wood		13.5	19.1	23.0	16.9		7.7	10.8	13.0	12.4		5.2	2.4
202	Products of wood, cork, straw, etc.		13.5	19.1	23.0	16.9		7.7	10.8	13.0	12.4		5.2	...
2021	Veneer sheets, plywood, particle board, etc.		...	...	...	...		...	...	...	...		...	...
2022	Builders' carpentry and joinery		...	...	...	...		...	...	...	...		...	...
2023	Wooden containers		...	...	...	...		...	...	...	...		...	...
2029	Other wood products; articles of cork/straw		21.2	30.9	26.4	33.1		1.7	10.1	9.5	19.1		17.0	9.9
210	Paper and paper products		0.3	1.2	1.2	3.4		-0.6	0.6	0.6	1.5		1.1	0.4
2101	Pulp, paper and paperboard		...	...	...	...		...	...	...	...		...	...
2102	Corrugated paper and paperboard		15.9	23.2	20.3	14.6		2.3	6.2	7.2	4.8		13.7	7.7
2109	Other articles of paper and paperboard		5.0	7.7	4.9	15.1		...	4.0	1.8	12.8		2.2	1.7
221	Publishing		11.5	16.5	14.5	12.1		7.2	10.7	8.9	5.7		12.9	12.0
2211	Publishing of books and other publications		4.4	4.3	4.3	3.6		2.3	2.3	2.2	2.0		2.6	1.4
2212	Publishing of newspapers, journals, etc.		7.0	12.1	9.9	8.4		4.9	8.4	6.4	3.6		10.1	10.4
2213	Publishing of recorded media		0.1	0.1	0.1	0.1		...	...	...	0.1		0.1	0.1
2219	Other publishing		...	...	0.2	...		...	...	0.2	...		...	...

continued

Oman

		Output at producers' prices (millions of Omani Rials)					Value added at producers' prices (millions of Omani Rials)					Gross fixed capital formation (millions of Omani Rials)		
ISIC	**Industry**	Note	2007	2008	2009	2010	Note	2007	2008	2009	2010	Note	2009	2010
222	Printing and related service activities		10.3	12.4	11.8	13.5		5.8	7.3	6.3	7.4		17.1	305.6
2221	Printing		10.3	12.4	11.8	13.5		5.8	7.3	6.3	7.4		17.1	305.6
2222	Service activities related to printing		-	-	-	-		-	-	-	-		…	…
2230	Reproduction of recorded media		0.2	0.2	0.7	0.4		0.2	0.1	0.5	0.2		…	…
2310	Coke oven products		…	…	…	…		…	…	…	…		…	…
2320	Refined petroleum products		2231.8	4145.9	2633.4	3280.3		648.4	1122.9	680.2	940.2		1107.8	1276.5
2330	Processing of nuclear fuel		…	…	…	…		…	…	…	…		…	…
241	Basic chemicals		…	…	…	…		…	…	…	…		…	…
2411	Basic chemicals, except fertilizers		203.5	323.0	618.3	527.4		130.3	172.1	466.9	357.1		815.5	597.0
2412	Fertilizers and nitrogen compounds		18.8	38.9	117.4	124.7		12.1	20.4	90.9	87.1		238.9	49.4
2413	Plastics in primary forms; synthetic rubber		118.6	167.1	387.9	280.8		98.2	136.9	347.0	248.2		459.4	437.5
242	Other chemicals		66.1	117.0	112.9	121.9		20.0	14.8	29.0	21.8		117.2	110.1
2421	Pesticides and other agro-chemical products		81.5	90.0	102.3	88.8		33.7	40.2	42.3	38.6		43.2	32.6
2422	Paints, varnishes, printing ink and mastics		-	-	-	1.2		-	-	-	0.3		-	-
2423	Pharmaceuticals, medicinal chemicals, etc.		21.9	32.7	32.6	33.9		8.3	16.0	20.5	18.3		5.4	6.3
2424	Soap, cleaning & cosmetic preparations		30.5	30.6	30.6	24.4		14.3	13.2	10.1	7.9		24.4	12.8
2429	Other chemical products n.e.c.		18.4	17.2	18.1	20.1		7.9	7.0	6.5	8.6		12.5	12.5
2430	Man-made fibres		10.8	9.6	20.9	9.3		3.1	4.1	5.3	3.6		0.8	0.9
251	Rubber products		…	…	…	…		…	…	…	…		…	…
2511	Rubber tyres and tubes		1.6	2.0	2.3	1.4		0.9	1.4	1.6	0.6		0.2	53.0
2519	Other rubber products		0.9	0.9	1.0	1.1		0.4	0.4	0.5	0.5		-	52.5
2520	Plastic products		0.6	1.1	1.3	0.3		0.6	1.0	1.1	0.2		0.2	0.5
2610	Glass and glass products		85.4	111.9	103.1	119.2		26.9	34.7	42.5	49.9		50.4	64.5
269	Non-metallic mineral products n.e.c.		23.4	40.1	30.1	28.7		11.8	18.0	17.7	18.4		22.6	162.2
2691	Pottery, china and earthenware		251.1	356.9	397.4	382.5		165.0	224.4	260.8	259.2		335.3	315.2
2692	Refractory ceramic products		2.2	2.6	2.7	2.5		1.7	2.0	2.1	1.7		4.7	4.8
2693	Struct.non-refractory clay; ceramic products		8.8	11.2	14.5	17.3		5.3	6.9	8.5	11.1		17.4	18.0
2694	Cement, lime and plaster		…	0.1	0.1	0.1		…	…	…	0.1		…	…
2695	Articles of concrete, cement and plaster		121.2	168.9	174.3	132.4		90.3	117.9	129.8	98.2		180.4	161.2
2696	Cutting, shaping & finishing of stone		31.5	46.1	56.4	51.7		13.2	21.9	31.1	29.7		39.5	23.3
2699	Other non-metallic mineral products n.e.c.		36.4	53.0	66.3	74.0		27.4	35.0	48.0	57.3		35.3	43.3
2710	Basic iron and steel		51.0	75.0	83.2	104.4		27.1	40.6	41.3	61.2		58.0	64.6
2720	Basic precious and non-ferrous metals		162.8	245.7	158.1	224.7		33.6	23.3	24.9	36.2		67.6	65.9
273	Casting of metals		47.9	61.7	304.6	364.3		23.3	35.3	182.7	220.7		883.8	784.0
2731	Casting of iron and steel		1.0	11.9	13.1	41.3		0.3	8.6	11.1	35.8		2.5	11.5
2732	Casting of non-ferrous metals		0.4	11.2	12.4	40.6		0.2	8.4	10.7	35.5		2.3	11.3
281	Struct.metal products;tanks;steam generators		0.5	0.7	0.7	0.8		0.2	0.2	0.4	0.3		0.2	0.2
2811	Structural metal products		73.1	76.2	98.0	163.8		35.1	40.2	48.7	128.3		18.6	16.3
2812	Tanks, reservoirs and containers of metal		69.6	73.7	95.5	162.2		33.3	39.2	46.9	127.5		15.1	15.7
2813	Steam generators		3.5	2.4	2.5	1.6		1.7	1.0	1.8	0.8		3.6	0.6
289	Other metal products; metal working services		30.8	33.0	46.0	62.1		13.8	13.8	28.0	40.6		17.5	18.2
2891	Metal forging/pressing/stamping/roll-forming		-	-	-	-		-	-	-	-		…	…
2892	Treatment & coating of metals		6.8	7.6	4.6	11.2		2.9	2.1	2.1	5.6		1.1	3.8
2893	Cutlery, hand tools and general hardware		-	0.2	0.2	0.2		-	0.1	-	0.1		…	…
2899	Other fabricated metal products n.e.c.		23.9	25.2	41.4	50.7		10.9	11.7	25.9	34.9		16.3	14.4
291	General purpose machinery		19.2	21.6	17.5	11.4		9.2	13.5	7.0	5.3		…	…
2911	Engines & turbines (not for transport equipment)		1.0	1.3	0.9	1.5		0.3	1.1	0.2	0.3		8.8	1.2
2912	Pumps, compressors, taps and valves		16.1	14.0	10.8	8.4		8.3	7.8	6.2	4.3		0.1	0.1
2913	Bearings, gears, gearing & driving elements		…	…	…	…		…	…	…	…		0.7	0.5
2914	Ovens, furnaces and furnace burners		…	…	…	…		…	…	…	…		…	…
2915	Lifting and handling equipment		…	…	…	…		…	…	…	…		…	…
2919	Other general purpose machinery		2.1	6.3	5.8	1.5		0.7	4.6	0.6	0.8		8.0	0.6

Code	Description	(1)	(2)	(3)	(4)	(5)	(6)	(7)	(8)	(9)	(10)
292	Special purpose machinery	5.5	10.7	4.7	7.1	4.5	8.6	3.3	5.6	5.6	7.1
2921	Agricultural and forestry machinery	0.5	0.3	0.2	0.8	0.3	0.1	0.1	0.8	1.2	1.0
2922	Machine tools	4.7	9.1	3.1	0.1	4.2	7.6	2.2	4.0	4.1	1.2
2923	Machinery for metallurgy	0.3	1.2	1.4	5.0	-	0.9	1.1	0.9	0.2	4.6
2924	Machinery for mining & construction										
2925	Food/beverage/tobacco processing machinery				1.1						0.2
2926	Machinery for textile, apparel and leather										
2927	Weapons and ammunition	-									
2929	Other special purpose machinery	5.0	7.3	4.9	6.9	2.1	2.7	1.1	3.3	1.8	2.3
2930	Domestic appliances n.e.c.										
3000	Office, accounting and computing machinery									4.3	4.4
3110	Electric motors, generators and transformers	25.5	38.6	34.1	36.7	8.6	12.6	11.5	14.2	20.7	36.4
3120	Electricity distribution & control apparatus	215.7	308.9	148.9	212.2	27.8	27.3	13.8	30.3	4.9	4.8
3130	Insulated wire and cable	20.1	21.6	11.1	16.2	6.5	4.8	5.2	5.7	0.1	0.1
3140	Accumulators, primary cells and batteries	0.6	0.6	9.4	9.9	0.2	0.2	3.3	3.1		
3150	Lighting equipment and electric lamps										
3190	Other electrical equipment n.e.c.										
3210	Electronic valves, tubes, etc.										1.7
3220	TV/radio transmitters; line comm. apparatus										
3230	TV and radio receivers and associated goods										
331	Medical, measuring, testing appliances, etc.										
3311	Medical, surgical and orthopaedic equipment										
3312	Measuring/testing/navigating appliances, etc.										
3313	Industrial process control equipment	5.5	8.5	7.1	11.3	3.0	4.9	4.5	9.5	2.8	1.9
3320	Optical instruments & photographic equipment		0.1		0.1		0.1		0.1		
3330	Watches and clocks	0.1	0.1	0.5	3.6	0.1	-0.1	0.4	1.4	0.7	2.7
3410	Motor vehicles	0.5	0.2		0.8	0.3	0.2		0.3		2.4
3420	Automobile bodies, trailers & semi-trailers		0.3	3.8	0.2		0.2	3.7	0.1	0.3	0.3
3430	Parts/accessories for automobiles		0.3	3.8	0.2		0.2	3.7	0.1	0.3	0.3
351	Building and repairing of ships and boats										
3511	Building and repairing of ships										
3512	Building/repairing of pleasure/sport. boats										
3520	Railway/tramway locomotives & rolling stock										
3530	Aircraft and spacecraft										
359	Transport equipment n.e.c.										
3591	Motorcycles										
3592	Bicycles and invalid carriages	46.8	59.9	36.6	58.9	25.4	31.0	11.6	28.2	6.6	10.7
3599	Other transport equipment n.e.c.	12.2	5.6	6.4	8.1	6.7	3.4	2.4	2.7	1.2	4.8
3610	Furniture	4.5	1.9	2.7	1.7	3.3	1.7	0.3	0.1	0.1	0.3
369	Manufacturing n.e.c.										
3691	Jewellery and related articles	0.1				0.1					
3692	Musical instruments										
3693	Sports goods	7.6	3.7	3.7	6.4	3.4	1.6	2.0	2.7	1.1	4.5
3694	Games and toys										
3699	Other manufacturing n.e.c.										
3710	Recycling of metal waste and scrap	1.8	3.0	1.5	2.2	0.2	0.5	0.3	0.3	0.3	0.3
3720	Recycling of non-metal waste and scrap										
D	Total manufacturing	3979.0 a/	6623.9	5360.5	6273.8 a/	1350.6	2020.2	2100.0	2450.3 a/	3648.2	3998.2 a/

a/ Sum of available data.

Oman

Index numbers of industrial production

ISIC Revision 3 — (2005=100)

ISIC	Industry	Note	1999	2000	2001	2002	2003	2004	2005	2006	2007	2008	2009	2010
15	Food and beverages		...	...	...	...	...	...	...	...	...	...	...	...
16	Tobacco products		...	...	...	...	...	...	...	...	...	...	...	...
17	Textiles		...	...	...	...	...	...	...	...	...	...	...	...
18	Wearing apparel, fur		...	...	...	...	...	...	...	...	...	...	...	...
19	Leather, leather products and footwear		...	...	...	...	...	...	...	...	...	...	...	...
20	Wood products (excl. furniture)		...	...	...	...	...	...	...	...	...	...	...	...
21	Paper and paper products		...	...	...	...	...	...	...	...	...	...	...	...
22	Printing and publishing		...	...	...	...	...	...	...	...	...	...	...	...
23	Coke,refined petroleum products,nuclear fuel		...	...	...	...	...	...	...	...	...	...	...	...
24	Chemicals and chemical products		...	...	...	...	...	...	...	...	...	...	...	...
25	Rubber and plastics products		...	...	...	...	...	...	...	...	...	...	...	...
26	Non-metallic mineral products		...	...	...	...	...	...	...	...	...	...	...	...
27	Basic metals		...	...	...	...	...	...	...	...	...	...	...	...
28	Fabricated metal products		...	...	...	...	...	...	...	...	...	...	...	...
29	Machinery and equipment n.e.c.		...	...	...	...	...	...	...	...	...	...	...	...
30	Office, accounting and computing machinery		...	...	...	...	...	...	...	...	...	...	...	...
31	Electrical machinery and apparatus		...	...	...	...	...	...	...	...	...	...	...	...
32	Radio,television and communication equipment		...	...	...	...	...	...	...	...	...	...	...	...
33	Medical, precision and optical instruments		...	...	...	...	...	...	...	...	...	...	...	...
34	Motor vehicles, trailers, semi-trailers		...	...	...	...	...	...	...	...	...	...	...	...
35	Other transport equipment		...	...	...	...	...	...	...	...	...	...	...	...
36	Furniture; manufacturing n.e.c.		...	...	...	...	...	...	...	...	...	...	...	...
37	Recycling		...	...	...	...	...	...	...	...	...	...	...	...
D	Total manufacturing		33	55	77	88	91	92	100	110	124	137	153	...

Palestine

Concepts and definitions of variables:
Wages and salaries is compensation of employees.

Related national publications:
Economic Surveys Series, published by the Palestinian Central Bureau of Statistics, Ramallah.

Supplier of information:
Palestinian Central Bureau of Statistics, Ramallah.

Basic source of data:
Survey.

Major deviations from ISIC (Revision 4):
None reported.

Reference period:
Calendar year.

Scope:
All privately owned enterprises.

Method of data collection:
Direct interview in the field.

Type of enumeration:
Sample survey.

Adjusted for non-response:
Yes.

Palestine

ISIC Revision 4

ISIC	Industry	Number of enterprises					Number of persons engaged					Wages and salaries paid to employees				
		Note	(number) 2007	2008	2009	2010	Note	(number) 2007	2008	2009	2010	Note	(thousands of US Dollars) 2007	2008	2009	2010
10	Food products		...	...	...	2020		...	...	...	9913		...	...	...	38896
11	Beverages		...	...	...	44		...	...	...	339		...	...	...	1492
12	Tobacco products		...	...	...	18		...	...	...	192		...	...	...	3796
13	Textiles		...	...	...	385		...	...	...	1246		...	...	...	4268
14	Wearing apparel		...	...	...	1858		...	...	...	11216		...	...	...	38860
15	Leather and related products		...	...	...	423		...	...	...	1995		...	...	...	7144
16	Wood/wood products/cork,excl. furniture		...	...	...	536		...	...	...	1748		...	...	...	4166
17	Paper and paper products		...	...	...	85		...	...	...	921		...	...	...	5685
18	Printing and reproduction of recorded media		...	...	...	220		...	...	...	1121		...	...	...	5637
19	Coke and refined petroleum products		...	...	...	23		...	...	...	122		...	...	...	629
20	Chemicals and chemical products		...	...	...	138		...	...	...	903		...	...	...	4253
21	Pharmaceuticals,medicinal chemicals, etc.		...	...	...	7		...	...	...	686		...	...	...	6572
22	Rubber and plastics products		...	...	...	176		...	...	...	1492		...	...	...	6794
23	Other non-metallic mineral products		...	...	...	1727		...	...	...	10953		...	...	...	50793
24	Basic metals		...	...	...	30		...	...	...	196		...	...	...	838
25	Fabricated metal products, except machinery		...	...	...	4107		...	...	...	8181		...	...	...	21204
26	Computer, electronic and optical products		...	...	...	59		...	...	...	170		...	...	...	466
27	Electrical equipment		...	...	...	57		...	...	...	280		...	...	...	1283
28	Machinery and equipment n.e.c.		...	...	...	40		...	...	...	254		...	...	...	1878
29	Motor vehicles, trailers and semi-trailers		...	...	...	19		...	...	...	124		...	...	...	484
30	Other transport equipment		...	...	...	4		...	...	...	12		...	...	...	20
31	Furniture		...	...	...	2676		...	...	...	7759		...	...	...	28040
32	Other manufacturing		...	...	...	62		...	...	...	280		...	...	...	1130
33	Repair and installation of machinery/equipment		...	...	...	167		...	...	...	332		...	...	...	535
C	Total manufacturing		...	...	...	14882		...	...	...	60436		...	...	...	234864

Palestine

ISIC	Industry	Output (millions of US Dollars)					Value added (millions of US Dollars)					Gross fixed capital formation (millions of US Dollars)		
		Note	2007	2008	2009	2010	Note	2007	2008	2009	2010	Note	2009	2010
10	Food products		…	…	…	606.3		…	…	…	259.9		…	5.7
11	Beverages		…	…	…	18.7		…	…	…	7.4		…	-
12	Tobacco products		…	…	…	110.7		…	…	…	102.9		…	1.0
13	Textiles		…	…	…	44.5		…	…	…	13.5		…	0.2
14	Wearing apparel		…	…	…	136.0		…	…	…	89.2		…	1.5
15	Leather and related products		…	…	…	50.3		…	…	…	28.0		…	0.6
16	Wood/wood products/cork,excl. furniture		…	…	…	41.0		…	…	…	21.0		…	0.3
17	Paper and paper products		…	…	…	54.4		…	…	…	19.0		…	-1.4
18	Printing and reproduction of recorded media		…	…	…	62.2		…	…	…	42.9		…	15.4
19	Coke and refined petroleum products		…	…	…	6.1		…	…	…	1.9		…	-
20	Chemicals and chemical products		…	…	…	39.9		…	…	…	14.7		…	0.4
21	Pharmaceuticals,medicinal chemicals, etc.		…	…	…	42.7		…	…	…	27.3		…	4.5
22	Rubber and plastics products		…	…	…	68.9		…	…	…	26.0		…	0.9
23	Other non-metallic mineral products		…	…	…	385.3		…	…	…	166.5		…	14.6
24	Basic metals		…	…	…	15.2		…	…	…	6.7		…	0.1
25	Fabricated metal products, except machinery		…	…	…	269.0		…	…	…	121.7		…	1.1
26	Computer, electronic and optical products		…	…	…	2.1		…	…	…	1.3		…	-
27	Electrical equipment		…	…	…	9.4		…	…	…	4.1		…	0.1
28	Machinery and equipment n.e.c.		…	…	…	12.6		…	…	…	4.6		…	-
29	Motor vehicles, trailers and semi-trailers		…	…	…	5.5		…	…	…	4.2		…	-
30	Other transport equipment		…	…	…	0.1		…	…	…	-		…	4.9
31	Furniture		…	…	…	234.3		…	…	…	108.8		…	0.2
32	Other manufacturing		…	…	…	20.4		…	…	…	10.5		…	0.1
33	Repair and installation of machinery/equipment		…	…	…	3.2		…	…	…	2.0		…	…
C	Total manufacturing		…	…	…	2238.7		…	…	…	1083.8		…	50.4

Palestine

Index numbers of industrial production

ISIC Revision 4

(2005=100)

ISIC	Industry	Note	1999	2000	2001	2002	2003	2004	2005	2006	2007	2008	2009	2010
10	Food products		...	...	...	...	...	...	...	...	...	...	...	...
11	Beverages		...	...	...	...	...	...	...	...	...	...	...	...
12	Tobacco products		...	...	...	...	...	...	...	...	...	...	...	...
13	Textiles		...	...	...	...	...	...	...	...	...	...	...	...
14	Wearing apparel		...	...	...	...	...	...	...	...	...	...	...	...
15	Leather and related products		...	...	...	...	...	...	...	...	...	...	...	...
16	Wood/wood products/cork,excl. furniture		...	...	...	...	...	...	...	...	...	...	...	...
17	Paper and paper products		...	...	...	...	...	...	...	...	...	...	...	...
18	Printing and reproduction of recorded media		...	...	...	...	...	...	...	...	...	...	...	...
19	Coke and refined petroleum products		...	...	...	...	...	...	...	...	...	...	...	...
20	Chemicals and chemical products		...	...	...	...	...	...	...	...	...	...	...	...
21	Pharmaceuticals,medicinal chemicals, etc.		...	...	...	...	...	...	...	...	...	...	...	...
22	Rubber and plastics products		...	...	...	...	...	...	...	...	...	...	...	...
23	Other non-metallic mineral products		...	...	...	...	...	...	...	...	...	...	...	...
24	Basic metals		...	...	...	...	...	...	...	...	...	...	...	...
25	Fabricated metal products, except machinery		...	...	...	...	...	...	...	...	...	...	...	...
26	Computer, electronic and optical products		...	...	...	...	...	...	...	...	...	...	...	...
27	Electrical equipment		...	...	...	...	...	...	...	...	...	...	...	...
28	Machinery and equipment n.e.c.		...	...	...	...	...	...	...	...	...	...	...	...
29	Motor vehicles, trailers and semi-trailers		...	...	...	...	...	...	...	...	...	...	...	...
30	Other transport equipment		...	...	...	...	...	...	...	...	...	...	...	...
31	Furniture		...	...	...	...	...	...	...	...	...	...	...	...
32	Other manufacturing		...	...	...	...	...	...	...	...	...	...	...	...
33	Repair and installation of machinery/equipment		...	...	...	...	...	...	...	...	...	...	...	...
C	Total manufacturing		...	85	84	69	83	94	100	85	89	91	91	87

Peru

Supplier of information:
Instituto Nacional de Estadística e Informática (INEI), Lima.

Basic source of data:
Survey.

Major deviations from ISIC (Revision 3):
None reported.

Reference period:
Calendar year.

Scope:
Establishments with five or more persons engaged.

Method of data collection:
Mail questionnaires and online survey.

Type of enumeration:
Sample survey.

Adjusted for non-response:
No.

Concepts and definitions of variables:
Wages and salaries is compensation of employees.
Output is at basic prices.
Value added is at basic prices

Related national publications:
Oferta y Demanda Global 1991-2007; Encuesta Nacional de Hogares (ENAHO); both published by Instituto Nacional de Estadística e Informática (INEI), Lima.

Peru

ISIC	Industry	Establishments (number) Note	2007	2008	2009	2010	Number of persons engaged (thousands) Note	2007	2008	2009	2010	Wages and salaries paid to employees (millions of Peruvian New Soles) Note	2007	2008	2009	2010
151	Processed meat,fish,fruit,vegetables,fats							203.1a/					2308.8a/			
1511	Processing/preserving of meat															
1512	Processing/preserving of fish															
1513	Processing/preserving of fruit & vegetables															
1514	Vegetable and animal oils and fats															
1520	Dairy products							17.6 ...a/					209.4 ...a/			
153	Grain mill products; starches; animal feeds															
1531	Grain mill products												...a/			
1532	Starches and starch products															
1533	Prepared animal feeds															
154	Other food products							...a/					...a/			
1541	Bakery products															
1542	Sugar															
1543	Cocoa, chocolate and sugar confectionery															
1544	Macaroni, noodles & similar products															
1549	Other food products n.e.c.															
155	Beverages							20.2b/					644.4b/			
1551	Distilling, rectifying & blending of spirits															
1552	Wines															
1553	Malt liquors and malt															
1554	Soft drinks; mineral waters															
1600	Tobacco products							...b/					...b/			
171	Spinning, weaving and finishing of textiles							154.5c/					647.8c/			
1711	Textile fibre preparation; textile weaving															
1712	Finishing of textiles															
172	Other textiles							...c/					...c/			
1721	Made-up textile articles, except apparel															
1722	Carpets and rugs															
1723	Cordage, rope, twine and netting															
1729	Other textiles n.e.c.															
1730	Knitted and crocheted fabrics and articles							...c/					...c/			
1810	Wearing apparel, except fur apparel							198.6d/					751.9d/			
1820	Dressing & dyeing of fur; processing of fur							...d/					...d/			
191	Tanning, dressing and processing of leather							8.6					26.0			
1911	Tanning and dressing of leather															
1912	Luggage, handbags, etc.; saddlery & harness															
1920	Footwear							47.6					50.6			
2010	Sawmilling and planing of wood															
202	Products of wood, cork, straw, etc.															
2021	Veneer sheets, plywood, particle board, etc.															
2022	Builders' carpentry and joinery															
2023	Wooden containers															
2029	Other wood products; articles of cork/straw															
210	Paper and paper products							7.6					141.5			
2101	Pulp, paper and paperboard															
2102	Corrugated paper and paperboard															
2109	Other articles of paper and paperboard															
221	Publishing							50.9e/					342.5e/			
2211	Publishing of books and other publications															
2212	Publishing of newspapers, journals, etc.															
2213	Publishing of recorded media															
2219	Other publishing															

222	Printing and related service activities	..e/	..e/
2221	Printing		
2222	Service activities related to printing	..e/	..e/
2230	Reproduction of recorded media	270.6f/	2.6f/
2310	Coke oven products	..f/	..f/
2320	Refined petroleum products	..f/	..f/
2330	Processing of nuclear fuel	283.5	5.3
241	Basic chemicals		
2411	Basic chemicals, except fertilizers		
2412	Fertilizers and nitrogen compounds		
2413	Plastics in primary forms; synthetic rubber	730.8	26.8
242	Other chemicals		
2421	Pesticides and other agro-chemical products		
2422	Paints, varnishes, printing ink and mastics		
2423	Pharmaceuticals, medicinal chemicals, etc.		
2424	Soap, cleaning & cosmetic preparations		
2429	Other chemical products n.e.c.		
2430	Man-made fibres	379.8g/	19.9g/
251	Rubber products		
2511	Rubber tyres and tubes	..g/	..g/
2519	Other rubber products	500.3h/	50.4h/
2520	Plastic products	..h/	..h/
2610	Glass and glass products		
269	Non-metallic mineral products n.e.c.		
2691	Pottery, china and earthenware		
2692	Refractory ceramic products		
2693	Struct.non-refractory clay; ceramic products		
2694	Cement, lime and plaster		
2695	Articles of concrete, cement and plaster		
2696	Cutting, shaping & finishing of stone		
2699	Other non-metallic mineral products n.e.c.		
2710	Basic iron and steel	263.6	6.8
2720	Basic precious and non-ferrous metals	295.8	4.8
273	Casting of metals		
2731	Casting of iron and steel		
2732	Casting of non-ferrous metals	413.1i/	87.4i/
281	Struct.metal products;tanks;steam generators		
2811	Structural metal products		
2812	Tanks, reservoirs and containers of metal		
2813	Steam generators	..j/	..j/
289	Other metal products; metal working services		
2891	Metal forging/pressing/stamping/roll-forming		
2892	Treatment & coating of metals		
2893	Cutlery, hand tools and general hardware		
2899	Other fabricated metal products n.e.c.	173.4/	36.2/
291	General purpose machinery		
2911	Engines & turbines (not for transport equipment)		
2912	Pumps, compressors, taps and valves		
2913	Bearings, gears, gearing & driving elements		
2914	Ovens, furnaces and furnace burners		
2915	Lifting and handling equipment		
2919	Other general purpose machinery		
292	Special purpose machinery		
2921	Agricultural and forestry machinery		
2922	Machine tools		
2923	Machinery for metallurgy		
2924	Machinery for mining & construction	..j/	..j/
2925	Food/beverage/tobacco processing machinery		
2926	Machinery for textile, apparel and leather		
2927	Weapons and ammunition		
2929	Other special purpose machinery		

continued

Peru

ISIC Revision 3			Establishments (number)					Number of persons engaged (thousands)					Wages and salaries paid to employees (millions of Peruvian New Soles)				
ISIC	Industry		Note	2007	2008	2009	2010	Note	2007	2008	2009	2010	Note	2007	2008	2009	2010
2930	Domestic appliances n.e.c.			…	…	…	…		..j/	…	…	…		..j/	…	…	…
3000	Office, accounting and computing machinery			…	…	…	…		…	…	…	…		…	…	…	…
3110	Electric motors, generators and transformers			…	…	…	…		9.7k/	…	…	…		430.3k/	…	…	…
3120	Electricity distribution & control apparatus			…	…	…	…		..k/	…	…	…		..k/	…	…	…
3130	Insulated wire and cable			…	…	…	…		..k/	…	…	…		..k/	…	…	…
3140	Accumulators, primary cells and batteries			…	…	…	…		..k/	…	…	…		..k/	…	…	…
3150	Lighting equipment and electric lamps			…	…	…	…		..k/	…	…	…		..k/	…	…	…
3190	Other electrical equipment n.e.c.			…	…	…	…		..k/	…	…	…		..k/	…	…	…
3210	Electronic valves, tubes, etc.			…	…	…	…		…	…	…	…		…	…	…	…
3220	TV/radio transmitters; line comm. apparatus			…	…	…	…		…	…	…	…		…	…	…	…
3230	TV and radio receivers and associated goods			…	…	…	…		…	…	…	…		…	…	…	…
331	Medical, measuring, testing appliances, etc.			…	…	…	…		…	…	…	…		…	…	…	…
3311	Medical, surgical and orthopaedic equipment			…	…	…	…		…	…	…	…		…	…	…	…
3312	Measuring/testing/navigating appliances,etc.			…	…	…	…		…	…	…	…		…	…	…	…
3313	Industrial process control equipment			…	…	…	…		…	…	…	…		…	…	…	…
3320	Optical instruments & photographic equipment			…	…	…	…		…	…	…	…		…	…	…	…
3330	Watches and clocks			…	…	…	…		…	…	…	…		…	…	…	…
3410	Motor vehicles			…	…	…	…		8.8m/	…	…	…		211.1m/	…	…	…
3420	Automobile bodies, trailers & semi-trailers			…	…	…	…		..m/	…	…	…		..m/	…	…	…
3430	Parts/accessories for automobiles			…	…	…	…		..m/	…	…	…		..m/	…	…	…
351	Building and repairing of ships and boats			…	…	…	…		..m/	…	…	…		..m/	…	…	…
3511	Building and repairing of ships			…	…	…	…		…	…	…	…		…	…	…	…
3512	Building/repairing of pleasure/sport. boats			…	…	…	…		…	…	…	…		…	…	…	…
3520	Railway/tramway locomotives & rolling stock			…	…	…	…		..m/	…	…	…		..m/	…	…	…
3530	Aircraft and spacecraft			…	…	…	…		..m/	…	…	…		..m/	…	…	…
359	Transport equipment n.e.c.			…	…	…	…		..m/	…	…	…		..m/	…	…	…
3591	Motorcycles			…	…	…	…		…	…	…	…		…	…	…	…
3592	Bicycles and invalid carriages			…	…	…	…		…	…	…	…		…	…	…	…
3599	Other transport equipment n.e.c.			…	…	…	…		…	…	…	…		…	…	…	…
3610	Furniture			…	…	…	…		161.3	…	…	…		393.1	…	…	…
369	Manufacturing n.e.c.			…	…	…	…		45.0	…	…	…		257.5	…	…	…
3691	Jewellery and related articles			…	…	…	…		…	…	…	…		…	…	…	…
3692	Musical instruments			…	…	…	…		…	…	…	…		…	…	…	…
3693	Sports goods			…	…	…	…		…	…	…	…		…	…	…	…
3694	Games and toys			…	…	…	…		…	…	…	…		…	…	…	…
3699	Other manufacturing n.e.c.			…	…	…	…		…	…	…	…		…	…	…	…
3710	Recycling of metal waste and scrap			…	…	…	…		…	…	…	…		…	…	…	…
3720	Recycling of non-metal waste and scrap			…	…	…	…		…	…	…	…		…	…	…	…
D	Total manufacturing			…	…	…	…		1173.6	…	…	…		9725.8	…	…	…

a/ 151 includes 153 and 154.
b/ 155 includes 1600.
c/ 171 includes 172 and 1730.
d/ 1810 includes 1820.
e/ 221 includes 222 and 2230.
f/ 2310 includes 2320 and 2330.
g/ 251 includes 2520.
h/ 2610 includes 269.
i/ 281 includes 289.
j/ 291 includes 292 and 2930.

k/ 3110 includes 3120, 3130, 3140, 3150 and 3190.
m/ 3410 includes 3420, 3430, 351, 3520, 3530 and 359.

Peru

| | | | Output | | | | | Value added | | | | | Gross fixed capital formation | |
| | | | (millions of Peruvian New Soles) | | | | | (millions of Peruvian New Soles) | | | | | (millions of Peruvian New Soles) | |
ISIC	Industry	Note	2007	2008	2009	2010	Note	2007	2008	2009	2010	Note	2009	2010
151	Processed meat,fish,fruit,vegetables,fats		25565.5	30120.5	30111.5	30262.7		8127.0	9179.0	8571.1	8626.6		...	...
1511	Processing/preserving of meat		11255.9	14023.9	15461.8	16745.9		2274.7	2662.9	2935.9	3478.1		...	...
1512	Processing/preserving of fish		4794.4	5611.4	5276.6	3814.1		1979.6	2312.5	2125.7	1532.5		...	...
1513	Processing/preserving of fruit & vegetables		2204.1	2725.4	2397.4	2435.5		709.0	876.5	771.0	798.8		...	...
1514	Vegetable and animal oils and fats		7311.1	7759.8	6975.7	7267.2		3163.7	3327.2	2738.6	2817.1		...	...
1520	Dairy products		3177.9	3825.5	3714.7	4239.5		846.4	1019.3	989.6	1129.3		...	...
153	Grain mill products; starches; animal feeds		7002.5	9294.3	8809.3	9034.4		998.3	1144.3	1079.0	1093.8		...	...
1531	Grain mill products		4856.3	6471.9	5841.3	5775.8		714.7	785.8	709.3	703.5		...	...
1532	Starches and starch products		141.0	140.5	125.3	146.0		60.9	60.7	54.1	63.2		...	...
1533	Prepared animal feeds		2005.1	2681.8	2842.7	3112.6		222.7	297.7	315.6	327.1		...	...
154	Other food products		8363.1	8862.8	9571.4	10765.3		2904.3	3097.9	3335.3	3656.9		...	...
1541	Bakery products		3541.3	3832.4	4084.7	4101.8		1626.7	1760.4	1876.3	1883.1		...	...
1542	Sugar		1726.7	1595.8	1993.8	2680.0		437.1	407.1	508.6	683.7		...	...
1543	Cocoa, chocolate and sugar confectionery		1431.2	1593.1	1595.7	1797.2		283.4	315.4	316.0	343.5		...	...
1544	Macaroni, noodles & similar products		618.5	711.4	717.8	742.9		186.3	214.3	216.2	222.9		...	...
1549	Other food products n.e.c.		1045.3	1130.3	1179.4	1443.4		370.7	400.7	418.1	523.7		...	...
155	Beverages		5977.0	6965.5	7391.0	8289.0		2002.6	2330.4	2467.6	2767.6		...	...
1551	Distilling, rectifying & blending of spirits		229.8	241.6	216.8	232.3		76.9	83.6	75.0	80.3		...	...
1552	Wines		303.7	391.3	356.2	377.3		83.9	110.1	100.3	106.8		...	...
1553	Malt liquors and malt		3225.0	3723.9	3788.0	4100.6		1166.6	1311.2	1333.8	1447.5		...	...
1554	Soft drinks; mineral waters		2219.5	2608.7	3030.0	3578.7		675.1	825.5	958.8	1133.0		...	...
1600	Tobacco products		...	...	...	...		...	...	...	...		...	...
171	Spinning, weaving and finishing of textiles		4540.5	4395.4	3402.0	4218.0		1227.4	1199.8	907.9	1121.4		...	...
1711	Textile fibre preparation; textile weaving		4362.1	4221.2	3265.8	4045.7		1203.4	1176.1	889.3	1098.0		...	...
1712	Finishing of textiles		178.3	174.2	136.1	172.3		24.0	23.7	18.5	23.4		...	...
172	Other textiles		1724.3	1494.2	1012.2	1492.1		492.9	432.3	290.3	426.0		...	...
1721	Made-up textile articles, except apparel		221.1	217.3	179.4	219.8		70.3	69.9	57.2	70.1		...	...
1722	Carpets and rugs		348.7	343.3	283.5	347.6		95.7	95.2	78.1	95.8		...	...
1723	Cordage, rope, twine and netting		296.8	239.9	140.4	236.8		114.0	93.2	54.5	92.0		...	...
1729	Other textiles n.e.c.		857.8	693.8	409.0	688.0		212.9	174.1	100.5	168.2		...	...
1730	Knitted and crocheted fabrics and articles		3112.2	2574.3	1979.0	2285.8		1195.6	999.8	764.0	882.4		...	...
1810	Wearing apparel, except fur apparel		7432.6	7322.0	5214.1	8291.6		2988.2	2943.6	2096.2	3333.4		...	...
1820	Dressing & dyeing of fur; processing of fur		39.8	36.8	37.1	41.7		10.4	9.6	9.7	10.9		...	...
191	Tanning, dressing and processing of leather		236.2	244.3	276.1	301.1		51.5	53.4	61.0	66.4		...	...
1911	Tanning and dressing of leather		192.3	179.5	182.3	204.5		40.8	37.8	38.4	43.1		...	...
1912	Luggage, handbags, etc.; saddlery & harness		43.9	64.8	93.8	96.6		10.7	15.6	22.6	23.3		...	...
1920	Footwear		190.3	326.6	499.0	510.2		67.1	115.2	176.0	180.0		...	...
2010	Sawmilling and planing of wood		872.5	823.6	602.1	623.5		348.1	328.4	240.1	248.6		...	...
202	Products of wood, cork, straw, etc.		848.3	843.9	656.4	758.3		310.4	311.2	242.1	283.4		...	...
2021	Veneer sheets, plywood, particle board, etc.		121.5	137.7	109.9	155.9		57.6	65.3	52.1	74.0		...	...
2022	Builders' carpentry and joinery		450.7	430.2	340.9	373.1		149.0	142.2	112.7	123.3		...	...
2023	Wooden containers		34.1	34.2	25.4	28.3		12.6	12.6	9.4	10.4		...	...
2029	Other wood products; articles of cork/straw		242.0	241.9	180.3	201.0		91.2	91.1	67.9	75.7		...	...
210	Paper and paper products		4549.9	6001.6	5244.5	6182.4		1714.7	2261.8	1961.3	2315.3		...	...
2101	Pulp, paper and paperboard		1814.3	2025.0	1917.7	2234.2		604.0	663.4	628.2	724.4		...	...
2102	Corrugated paper and paperboard		470.3	500.6	496.0	600.1		169.6	177.6	176.0	214.2		...	...
2109	Other articles of paper and paperboard		2265.3	3476.0	2830.9	3348.1		941.1	1420.8	1157.1	1376.7		...	...
221	Publishing		1493.9	1626.8	1945.6	2269.9		623.0	678.3	810.7	946.6		...	...
2211	Publishing of books and other publications		485.0	517.4	628.3	723.5		193.8	207.2	251.6	289.7		...	...
2212	Publishing of newspapers, journals, etc.		755.6	805.0	952.3	1125.1		334.9	357.6	423.0	499.8		...	...
2213	Publishing of recorded media		7.3	7.6	9.1	10.3		3.6	3.7	4.5	5.1		...	...
2219	Other publishing		246.0	296.9	356.0	411.0		90.7	109.8	131.6	152.0		...	...

continued

Peru

ISIC	Industry	Output (millions of Peruvian New Soles) Note	2007	2008	2009	2010	Value added (millions of Peruvian New Soles) Note	2007	2008	2009	2010	Gross fixed capital formation (millions of Peruvian New Soles) Note	2009	2010
222	Printing and related service activities		2533.2	3057.7	2733.4	3336.7		994.6	1203.3	1075.6	1313.0		...	...
2221	Printing		2320.2	2800.6	2503.9	3056.5		899.4	1088.1	972.9	1187.6		...	...
2222	Service activities related to printing		213.0	257.1	229.6	280.2		95.1	115.1	102.8	125.5		...	...
2230	Reproduction of recorded media		...	...	...	...		...	...	...	...		...	...
2310	Coke oven products													
2320	Refined petroleum products		17078.9	19103.4	22553.2	26535.6		2775.3	3104.3	3664.9	4312.0		...	...
2330	Processing of nuclear fuel													
241	Basic chemicals		3529.4	3348.8	2467.4	2760.0		1618.2	1548.2	1146.2	1282.1		...	...
2411	Basic chemicals, except fertilizers		2147.4	2334.6	1813.9	2011.3		1040.0	1126.3	875.1	970.3		...	...
2412	Fertilizers and nitrogen compounds		1176.3	768.5	450.5	589.3		495.3	322.9	189.3	247.6		...	...
2413	Plastics in primary forms; synthetic rubber		205.7	245.7	202.9	159.3		82.9	99.0	81.8	64.2		...	...
242	Other chemicals		9421.5	11104.7	10891.7	11607.1		3855.9	4514.8	4419.3	4698.4		...	...
2421	Pesticides and other agro-chemical products		555.5	848.0	680.8	808.8		208.8	318.7	255.5	304.0		...	...
2422	Paints, varnishes, printing ink and mastics		1332.7	1653.6	1712.8	1828.9		530.1	657.7	681.2	727.4		...	...
2423	Pharmaceuticals, medicinal chemicals, etc.		2071.0	2387.3	2459.2	2345.5		980.4	1112.0	1145.5	1091.8		...	...
2424	Soap, cleaning & cosmetic preparations		3105.6	3578.9	3670.6	3911.1		1071.5	1234.8	1266.4	1349.4		...	...
2429	Other chemical products n.e.c.		2356.8	2636.9	2368.4	2712.7		1065.2	1191.6	1070.3	1225.8		...	...
2430	Man-made fibres		292.8	289.9	272.7	279.4		150.3	148.8	139.9	143.4		...	...
251	Rubber products		999.1	929.0	856.9	1045.7		302.6	281.4	259.5	316.7		...	...
2511	Rubber tyres and tubes		753.6	699.5	646.5	789.0		229.5	213.0	196.9	240.3		...	...
2519	Other rubber products		245.5	229.5	210.4	256.6		73.1	68.3	62.6	76.4		...	...
2520	Plastic products		2695.7	2881.1	2734.3	3305.3		897.3	958.5	909.7	1099.6		...	...
2610	Glass and glass products		1704.1	2592.4	2438.1	3147.9		616.1	937.2	881.4	1138.0		...	...
269	Non-metallic mineral products n.e.c.		7139.0	9028.9	9142.8	11098.3		3380.7	4258.8	4336.3	5253.7		...	...
2691	Pottery, china and earthenware		856.9	1066.3	823.1	1025.0		347.2	432.1	333.6	415.4		...	...
2692	Refractory ceramic products		444.1	688.1	746.9	914.5		234.1	362.6	393.6	481.9		...	...
2693	Struct.non-refractory clay; ceramic products		1648.9	1958.8	2015.5	2708.4		720.9	856.0	880.8	1183.6		...	...
2694	Cement, lime and plaster		2809.9	3200.1	3365.1	3991.8		1471.1	1675.4	1761.7	2089.4		...	...
2695	Articles of concrete, cement and plaster		1145.2	1816.7	1918.8	2122.5		509.6	807.6	853.0	943.6		...	...
2696	Cutting, shaping & finishing of stone		108.5	137.7	141.0	171.1		42.3	53.7	55.0	66.8		...	...
2699	Other non-metallic mineral products n.e.c.		125.4	161.3	132.5	165.0		55.5	71.4	58.6	73.0		...	...
2710	Basic iron and steel		4584.7	5128.2	3597.2	3766.7		1788.0	2000.0	1402.9	1469.0		...	...
2720	Basic precious and non-ferrous metals		19188.8	17858.3	13881.7	17826.6		2509.7	2396.5	1658.9	2201.1		...	...
273	Casting of metals		1483.5	1698.3	2261.3	2551.0		548.7	671.4	866.4	965.0		...	...
2731	Casting of iron and steel		385.8	785.2	872.0	923.4		176.7	359.6	399.4	422.9		...	...
2732	Casting of non-ferrous metals		1097.6	913.1	1389.2	1627.6		372.0	311.8	467.0	542.1		...	...
281	Struct.metal products;tanks;steam generators		2126.7	3111.0	1550.6	2003.8		923.6	1350.3	1368.3	1761.4		...	...
2811	Structural metal products		1799.3	2680.7	1232.8	1580.8		776.9	1157.5	1225.8	1571.8		...	...
2812	Tanks, reservoirs and containers of metal		308.1	404.9	298.3	397.5		136.2	179.0	131.9	175.8		...	...
2813	Steam generators		19.3	25.4	19.6	25.5		10.5	13.8	10.6	13.8		...	...
289	Other metal products; metal working services		3458.7	4086.3	3005.8	3814.1		1414.9	1678.2	1235.5	1573.2		...	...
2891	Metal forging/pressing/stamping/roll-forming		96.4	119.6	91.1	117.0		48.2	59.8	45.6	58.5		...	...
2892	Treatment & coating of metals		936.1	1161.1	832.6	1083.1		481.5	597.1	428.2	557.1		...	...
2893	Cutlery, hand tools and general hardware		174.6	180.5	166.7	221.1		82.4	85.2	78.7	104.3		...	...
2899	Other fabricated metal products n.e.c.		2251.5	2625.2	1915.4	2392.9		802.9	936.1	683.0	853.3		...	...
291	General purpose machinery		194.6	134.6	95.4	112.3		86.7	59.2	42.0	48.7		...	...
2911	Engines & turbines (not for transport equipment)		1.3	0.8	0.4	-		0.7	0.4	0.2	-		...	...
2912	Pumps, compressors, taps and valves		78.2	85.3	59.8	76.0		30.7	33.5	23.5	29.9		...	...
2913	Bearings, gears, gearing & driving elements		9.8	10.1	7.4	7.8		4.0	4.1	3.0	3.1		...	...
2914	Ovens, furnaces and furnace burners		3.6	3.7	2.7	2.8		2.3	2.4	1.7	1.8		...	...
2915	Lifting and handling equipment		30.2	31.2	21.9	22.8		16.7	17.2	12.1	12.6		...	...
2919	Other general purpose machinery		71.5	3.5	3.2	2.8		32.4	1.6	1.5	1.3		...	...

292	Special purpose machinery	95.2	99.4	122.9	103.9	235.1	242.2	306.1	265.3
2921	Agricultural and forestry machinery	8.7	8.4	12.0	11.6	24.8	23.8	33.9	32.9
2922	Machine tools	7.8	7.5	10.5	10.2	14.8	14.2	19.9	19.3
2923	Machinery for metallurgy	0.5	0.5	0.6	0.6	0.9	0.8	1.2	1.1
2924	Machinery for mining & construction	54.3	60.3	67.9	50.4	112.1	124.5	140.1	104.1
2925	Food/beverage/tobacco processing machinery	2.6	2.5	3.4	3.3	6.2	6.0	8.1	7.9
2926	Machinery for textile, apparel and leather	2.0	1.9	2.6	2.5	5.2	5.0	6.8	6.6
2927	Weapons and ammunition	4.7	4.3	6.1	6.0	10.0	9.3	13.1	12.9
2929	Other special purpose machinery	14.6	14.0	19.8	19.2	61.0	58.5	83.0	80.5
2930	Domestic appliances n.e.c.	232.6	206.3	305.5	238.8	624.3	558.8	827.3	646.6
3000	Office, accounting and computing machinery	19.0	18.5	26.3	25.5	48.0	46.6	66.3	64.3
3110	Electric motors, generators and transformers	78.3	53.3	72.5	71.0	217.0	147.9	201.0	196.9
3120	Electricity distribution & control apparatus	47.3	27.5	42.7	36.2	166.3	96.8	149.9	127.1
3130	Insulated wire and cable	320.4	274.3	382.9	413.0	1052.9	908.3	1268.2	1367.8
3140	Accumulators, primary cells and batteries	69.2	58.9	67.1	61.6	171.8	146.5	166.7	153.1
3150	Lighting equipment and electric lamps	11.5	10.7	13.4	14.3	32.7	30.4	38.1	40.8
3190	Other electrical equipment n.e.c.	38.6	37.7	48.5	52.3	102.0	99.6	128.0	138.1
3210	Electronic valves, tubes, etc.	3.8	3.1	4.4	4.5	12.8	10.3	15.0	15.3
3220	TV/radio transmitters; line comm. apparatus	12.7	9.8	8.3	8.5	51.7	39.7	33.6	34.4
3230	TV and radio receivers and associated goods	16.7	15.2	22.0	22.6	62.7	51.1	73.9	75.8
331	Medical, measuring, testing appliances, etc.	…	…	…	…	…	…	…	…
3311	Medical, surgical and orthopaedic equipment	…	…	…	…	…	…	…	…
3312	Measuring/testing/navigating appliances,etc.	…	…	…	…	…	…	…	…
3313	Industrial process control equipment	…	…	…	…	…	…	…	…
3320	Optical instruments & photographic equipment	…	…	…	…	…	…	…	…
3330	Watches and clocks	57.9	21.1	20.6	12.5	241.8	88.2	86.0	52.3
3410	Motor vehicles	349.8	326.0	326.5	222.5	1309.5	1204.0	1222.1	833.1
3420	Automobile bodies, trailers & semi-trailers	746.6	438.4	385.7	284.4	2036.4	1195.8	1052.2	1222.1
3430	Parts/accessories for automobiles	594.7	349.1	307.7	226.3	1613.7	947.4	835.0	1052.2
351	Building and repairing of ships and boats	151.9	89.3	78.0	58.2	422.6	248.4	217.1	835.0
3511	Building and repairing of ships	…	…	…	…	…	…	…	217.1
3512	Building/repairing of pleasure/sport. boats	…	…	…	…	…	…	…	5.4
3520	Railway/tramway locomotives & rolling stock	3.0	1.8	1.6	1.2	10.4	6.1	5.4	6.9
3530	Aircraft and spacecraft	2.6	1.5	1.3	1.0	13.2	7.8	6.9	5.0
359	Transport equipment n.e.c.	111.6	66.9	60.4	45.5	434.5	260.2	232.5	174.8
3591	Motorcycles	61.0	36.9	31.0	22.6	217.5	131.4	110.5	80.6
3592	Bicycles and invalid carriages	17.0	10.2	12.1	10.0	52.0	31.4	37.2	30.5
3599	Other transport equipment n.e.c.	33.6	19.8	17.2	12.9	165.0	97.4	84.8	63.6
3610	Furniture	753.1	629.5	577.8	443.4	2717.1	2271.3	2084.8	1599.8
369	Manufacturing n.e.c.	1188.5	1188.5	1215.1	1201.6	2804.3	2739.0	2813.0	2811.3
3691	Jewellery and related articles	24.1	50.2	65.2	96.7	76.6	159.2	206.7	306.4
3692	Musical instruments	4.7	4.5	4.6	4.5	19.5	18.7	19.0	18.6
3693	Sports goods	9.0	8.5	8.6	8.5	42.6	40.7	41.3	40.4
3694	Games and toys	105.1	101.1	102.8	100.4	238.7	229.6	233.3	228.0
3699	Other manufacturing n.e.c.	1040.9	1024.1	1033.9	991.5	2426.9	2290.8	2312.7	2217.8
3710	Recycling of metal waste and scrap	…	…	…	…	…	…	…	…
3720	Recycling of non-metal waste and scrap	…	…	…	…	…	…	…	…
D	Total manufacturing	58817.7	50897.2	54920.6	49034.8	195100.0	169099.2	179887.8	160939.5

Peru

Index numbers of industrial production

ISIC Revision 3

(2005=100)

ISIC	Industry	Note	1999	2000	2001	2002	2003	2004	2005	2006	2007	2008	2009	2010
15	Food and beverages		84	87	84	88	89	94	100	108	119	130	130	135
16	Tobacco products		:	:	:	:	:	:	:	:	:	:	:	:
17	Textiles		55	61	58	72	79	94	100	99	104	87	68	81
18	Wearing apparel, fur		69	80	80	84	93	98	100	98	106	103	72	114
19	Leather, leather products and footwear		270	309	230	170	137	123	100	71	83	117	162	166
20	Wood products (excl. furniture)		65	72	74	96	88	97	100	98	91	84	63	69
21	Paper and paper products		47	59	59	63	64	81	100	112	128	176	144	174
22	Printing and publishing		46	50	61	75	81	89	100	105	113	131	127	146
23	Coke,refined petroleum products,nuclear fuel		80	79	82	83	81	86	100	98	102	106	136	155
24	Chemicals and chemical products		75	78	80	83	85	91	100	114	132	144	134	144
25	Rubber and plastics products		71	77	84	90	90	93	100	106	117	123	117	140
26	Non-metallic mineral products		65	68	67	74	79	88	100	114	133	158	156	190
27	Basic metals		89	93	97	94	97	98	100	104	97	106	88	85
28	Fabricated metal products		70	78	78	81	89	89	100	119	141	173	148	193
29	Machinery and equipment n.e.c.		143	161	164	138	114	94	100	105	133	140	97	103
30	Office, accounting and computing machinery		:	:	:	:	:	:	:	:	:	:	:	:
31	Electrical machinery and apparatus		111	118	107	98	93	112	100	125	154	149	119	153
32	Radio,television and communication equipment		:	:	:	:	:	:	:	:	:	:	:	:
33	Medical, precision and optical instruments		:	:	:	:	:	:	:	:	:	:	:	:
34	Motor vehicles, trailers, semi-trailers		92	105	105	65	72	87	100	111	155	225	213	269
35	Other transport equipment		27	48	50	69	70	71	100	143	211	298	356	588
36	Furniture; manufacturing n.e.c.		78	77	76	79	80	96	100	109	141	158	157	174
37	Recycling		:	:	:	:	:	:	:	:	:	:	:	:
D	Total manufacturing		74	79	79	84	87	93	100	108	119	130	121	137

Philippines

Supplier of information:
National Statistics Office, Manila.

Basic source of data:
Census; survey.

Major deviations from ISIC (Revision 4):
None reported.

Reference period:
Calendar year.

Scope:
Establishments with 20 or more persons engaged.

Method of data collection:
The inquiry is carried out through personal visits.

Type of enumeration:
Sample survey.

Adjusted for non-response:
Not reported.

Concepts and definitions of variables:
No deviations from the standard UN concepts and definitions are reported.

Related national publications:
None reported.

Philippines

ISIC	Industry		Number of establishments (number)					Number of employees (thousands)					Wages and salaries paid to employees (millions of Philippine Pesos)			
		Note	2006	2007	2008	2009	Note	2006	2007	2008	2009	Note	2006	2007	2008	2009
1010	Processing/preserving of meat		72	...	69	...		12.2	...	11.0	...		2515	...	2415	...
1020	Processing/preserving of fish, etc.		93	...	91	...		25.3	...	26.8	...		2066	...	1839	...
1030	Processing/preserving of fruit,vegetables		65	...	67	...		17.5	...	26.0	...		4305	...	5850	...
1040	Vegetable and animal oils and fats		74	...	66	...		10.7	...	9.5	...		1220	...	1073	...
1050	Dairy products		18	...	26	...		4.8	...	7.5	...		2424	...	4409	...
106	Grain mill products,starches and starch products		68	...	60	...		4.7	...	5.2	...		593	...	752	...
1061	Grain mill products		62	...	51	...		3.8	...	4.1	...		467	...	608	...
1062	Starches and starch products		6	...	9	...		0.9	...	1.1	...		126	...	144	...
107	Other food products		437	...	397	...		54.6	...	49.2	...		8730	...	8881	...
1071	Bakery products		268	...	242	...		29.1	...	29.5	...		3322	...	4865	...
1072	Sugar		25	...	27	...		10.7	...	9.5	...		2000	...	2009	...
1073	Cocoa, chocolate and sugar confectionery		32	...	33	...		3.5	...	3.3	...		798	...	643	...
1074	Macaroni, noodles, couscous, etc.		39	...	27	...		5.7	...	1.8	...		487	...	164	...
1075	Prepared meals and dishes		...a/	...	...a/	...		...a/	...	...a/	...		...a/	...	...a/	...
1079	Other food products n.e.c.		73a/	...	68a/	...		5.6a/	...	5.2a/	...		2123a/	...	1200a/	...
1080	Prepared animal feeds		82	...	82	...		6.3	...	6.8	...		964	...	1235	...
1101	Distilling, rectifying and blending of spirits		17	...	10	...		2.1	...	1.4	...		441	...	361	...
1102	Wines		4	...	3	...		0.2	...	0.1	...		11	...	7	...
1103	Malt liquors and malt		5	...	5	...		3.2	...	2.2	...		1198	...	1077	...
1104	Soft drinks,mineral waters,other bottled waters		60	...	54	...		9.1	...	9.5	...		2676	...	3009	...
1200	Tobacco products		18	...	18	...		8.8	...	9.5	...		2360	...	2213	...
131	Spinning, weaving and finishing of textiles		64	...	55	...		8.2	...	6.0	...		1194	...	786	...
1311	Preparation and spinning of textile fibres		64b/	...	55b/	...		8.2b/	...	6.0b/	...		1194b/	...	786b/	...
1312	Weaving of textiles		...b/	...	...b/	...		...b/	...	...b/	...		...b/	...	...b/	...
1313	Finishing of textiles		...b/	...	...b/	...		...b/	...	...b/	...		...b/	...	...b/	...
139	Other textiles		112	...	107	...		16.5	...	10.8	...		1969	...	1400	...
1391	Knitted and crocheted fabrics		22	...	18	...		2.6	...	0.8	...		240	...	93	...
1392	Made-up textile articles, except apparel		29	...	31	...		6.9	...	4.6	...		619	...	601	...
1393	Carpets and rugs		7	...	5	...		0.8	...	0.5	...		139	...	95	...
1394	Cordage, rope, twine and netting		16	...	17	...		2.5	...	2.4	...		339	...	298	...
1399	Other textiles n.e.c.		38	...	36	...		3.8	...	2.4	...		632	...	313	...
1410	Wearing apparel, except fur apparel		517	...	382	...		139.5	...	102.2	...		14719	...	10130	...
1420	Articles of fur		3	...	...	...		1.2	...	...	...		188	...	...	...
1430	Knitted and crocheted apparel		27	...	19	...		4.2	...	3.6	...		482	...	484	...
151	Leather;luggage,handbags,saddlery,harness;fur		31	...	32	...		7.2	...	6.2	...		871	...	817	...
1511	Tanning/dressing of leather; dressing of fur		3	...	4	...		0.1	...	0.2	...		12	...	13	...
1512	Luggage,handbags,etc.;saddlery/harness		28	...	28	...		7.1	...	6.1	...		859	...	804	...
1520	Footwear		86	...	68	...		8.4	...	7.4	...		617	...	580	...
1610	Sawmilling and planing of wood		28	...	23	...		1.7	...	1.7	...		138	...	147	...
162	Wood products, cork, straw, plaiting materials		131	...	115	...		21.8	...	17.2	...		2082	...	2004	...

Code	Description											
1621	Veneer sheets and wood-based panels	32	...	35	...	9.3	...	8.6	...	801	...	877
1622	Builders' carpentry and joinery	15	...	20	...	7.8	...	5.6	...	896	...	873
1623	Wooden containers	...c/	...	...c/	...	...c/	...	...c/	...	...c/	...	...c/
1629	Other wood products;articles of cork,straw	84c/	...	60c/	...	4.6c/	...	3.1c/	...	385c/	...	254c/
1701	Pulp, paper and paperboard	106d/	...	108d/	...	14.5d/	...	13.1d/	...	1818d/	...	2194d/
1702	Corrugated paper and paperboard	...d/	...	...d/	...	...d/	...	...d/	...	...d/	...	...d/
1709	Other articles of paper and paperboard	61	...	50	...	6.8	...	5.2	...	1355	...	932
181	Printing and service activities related to printing	225	...	215	...	11.5	...	11.0	...	1500	...	1482
1811	Printing	205	...	199	...	10.4	...	10.0	...	1370	...	1379
1812	Service activities related to printing	20	...	16	...	1.1	...	1.0	...	130	...	103
1820	Reproduction of recorded media	3	...	...	...	0.1	...	...	...	38	...	...
1910	Coke oven products	...	...	...	...	...	...	...	...	...	...	...
1920	Refined petroleum products	6	...	8	...	0.7	...	1.8	...	658	...	1988
201	Basic chemicals,fertilizers, etc.	105	...	88	...	9.3	...	8.2	...	2235	...	2305
2011	Basic chemicals	65	...	65	...	5.5	...	5.6	...	1507	...	1647
2012	Fertilizers and nitrogen compounds	9	...	7	...	1.5	...	1.2	...	363	...	381
2013	Plastics and synthetic rubber in primary forms	31	...	16	...	2.4	...	1.4	...	365	...	277
202	Other chemical products	146	...	141	...	15.9	...	15.6	...	4773	...	5063
2021	Pesticides and other agrochemical products	7	...	7	...	1.1	...	1.2	...	367	...	589
2022	Paints,varnishes;printing ink and mastics	51	...	55	...	5.6	...	4.1	...	1224	...	858
2023	Soap,cleaning and cosmetic preparations	55	...	53	...	6.2	...	7.6	...	2435	...	2902
2029	Other chemical products n.e.c.	33	...	26	...	3.0	...	2.7	...	747	...	714
2030	Man-made fibres	...	...	...	...	...	...	...	...	...	...	...
2100	Pharmaceuticals,medicinal chemicals, etc.	61	...	54	...	15.4	...	14.0	...	6973	...	5469
221	Rubber products	72	...	72	...	9.8	...	9.1	...	1503	...	1543
2211	Rubber tyres and tubes	20	...	20	...	3.4	...	3.8	...	780	...	894
2219	Other rubber products	52	...	52	...	6.3	...	5.3	...	723	...	649
2220	Plastics products	314	...	310	...	32.5	...	34.3	...	4497	...	5551
2310	Glass and glass products	34	...	33	...	4.9	...	4.6	...	1168	...	1232
239	Non-metallic mineral products n.e.c.	159	...	142	...	23.9	...	18.3	...	4502	...	4372
2391	Refractory products	6	...	3	...	0.7	...	0.3	...	91	...	67
2392	Clay building materials	13	...	10	...	2.3	...	1.8	...	272	...	243
2393	Other porcelain and ceramic products	30	...	23	...	9.3	...	5.0	...	848	...	731
2394	Cement, lime and plaster	21	...	21	...	4.7	...	4.6	...	2404	...	2439
2395	Articles of concrete, cement and plaster	63	...	65	...	5.0	...	4.8	...	616	...	665
2396	Cutting, shaping and finishing of stone	8	...	7	...	0.4	...	0.3	...	27	...	21
2399	Other non-metallic mineral products n.e.c.	18	...	13	...	1.6	...	1.5	...	244	...	206
2410	Basic iron and steel	140	...	122	...	16.0	...	13.9	...	2517	...	3015
2420	Basic precious and other non-ferrous metals	22	...	23	...	3.5	...	3.4	...	1012	...	1131
243	Casting of metals	33	...	39	...	4.1	...	3.8	...	763	...	727
2431	Casting of iron and steel	14	...	20	...	1.0	...	1.1	...	117	...	168
2432	Casting of non-ferrous metals	19	...	19	...	3.2	...	2.7	...	646	...	559
251	Struct.metal products, tanks, reservoirs	...	...	...	...	...	...	...	...	...	...	...
2511	Structural metal products	90	...	54	...	7.0	...	5.1	...	731	...	635
2512	Tanks, reservoirs and containers of metal	16	...	14	...	0.8	...	1.0	...	95	...	121

continued

Philippines

- 644 -

ISIC	Industry	Number of establishments (number)				Number of employees (thousands)				Wages and salaries paid to employees (millions of Philippine Pesos)			
		2006	2007	2008	2009	2006	2007	2008	2009	2006	2007	2008	2009
2513	Steam generators, excl. hot water boilers	...	...	...	...	...	...	...	...	...	...	...	...
2520	Weapons and ammunition	5e/	...	6e/	...	1.1e/	...	0.9e/	...	157e/	...	134e/	...
259	Other metal products;metal working services	223	...	231	...	25.0	...	24.8	...	3578	...	3750	...
2591	Forging,pressing,stamping,roll-forming of metal	51	...	58	...	9.8	...	6.8	...	1419	...	1257	...
2592	Treatment and coating of metals; machining	15	...	16	...	...	...	...	...	...	...	...	...
2593	Cutlery, hand tools and general hardware	22	...	20	...	1.5	...	2.3	...	186	...	265	...
2599	Other fabricated metal products n.e.c.	135	...	137	...	1.4	...	1.7	...	198	...	208	...
2610	Electronic components and boards	158	...	149	...	12.3	...	14.0	...	1775	...	2020	...
2620	Computers and peripheral equipment	52	...	40	...	140.4	...	136.7	...	29307	...	27464	...
2630	Communication equipment	...	...	...	...	65.5	...	45.4	...	9750	...	7920	...
2640	Consumer electronics	26	...	26	...	...	...	...	...	...	...	...	...
265	Measuring,testing equipment; watches, etc.	17	...	14	...	8.4	...	6.5	...	1050	...	1043	...
2651	Measuring/testing/navigating equipment,etc.	11	...	10	...	6.5	...	4.5	...	1238	...	847	...
2652	Watches and clocks	6	...	4	...	2.7	...	1.0	...	820	...	152	...
2660	Irradiation/electromedical equipment,etc.	..f/	...	..f/	...	3.7	...	3.5	...	418	...	695	...
2670	Optical instruments and photographic equipment	...	...	...	...	...	...	...	...	...	...	...	...
2680	Magnetic and optical media	...	...	..f/	...	..f/	...	..f/	...	..f/	...	..f/	...
2710	Electric motors,generators,transformers,etc.	39	...	34	...	4.3	...	5.3	...	623	...	1403	...
2720	Batteries and accumulators	6	...	6	...	0.7	...	0.7	...	221	...	156	...
273	Wiring and wiring devices	36	...	36	...	4.6	...	7.2	...	620	...	1125	...
2731	Fibre optic cables	..g/	...	..g/	...	..g/	...	..g/	...	..g/	...	..g/	...
2732	Other electronic and electric wires and cables	..g/	...	..g/	...	..g/	...	..g/	...	..g/	...	..g/	...
2733	Wiring devices	36g/	...	36g/	...	4.6g/	...	7.2g/	...	620g/	...	1125g/	...
2740	Electric lighting equipment	27	...	22	...	3.9	...	4.7	...	566	...	806	...
2750	Domestic appliances	27	...	24	...	3.9	...	3.4	...	992	...	1148	...
2790	Other electrical equipment	23	...	16	...	10.2	...	3.2	...	1459	...	680	...
281	General-purpose machinery	...	...	...	...	...	...	...	...	...	...	...	...
2811	Engines/turbines,excl.aircraft,vehicle engines	4	...	3	...	0.9	...	0.9	...	195	...	244	...
2812	Fluid power equipment	...	...	...	...	...	...	...	...	...	...	...	...
2813	Other pumps, compressors, taps and valves	9	...	11	...	1.0	...	0.8	...	138	...	126	...
2814	Bearings, gears, gearing and driving elements	5	...	5	...	0.7	...	0.8	...	191	...	193	...
2815	Ovens, furnaces and furnace burners	...	...	...	...	...	...	...	...	...	...	...	...
2816	Lifting and handling equipment	5	...	5	...	0.3	...	0.3	...	38	...	59	...
2817	Office machinery, excl.computers,etc.	8	...	6	...	5.0	...	1.1	...	944	...	195	...
2818	Power-driven hand tools	...	...	...	...	...	...	...	...	...	...	...	...
2819	Other general-purpose machinery	31	...	32	...	2.4	...	2.7	...	628	...	716	...
282	Special-purpose machinery	...	...	74	...	...	...	10.1	...	...	...	1599	...
2821	Agricultural and forestry machinery	9	...	11	...	0.4	...	0.5	...	34	...	51	...
2822	Metal-forming machinery and machine tools	16	...	20	...	1.3	...	1.4	...	170	...	153	...
2823	Machinery for metallurgy	10	...	14	...	1.1	...	1.8	...	169	...	366	...
2824	Mining, quarrying and construction machinery	...	...	4	...	...	...	0.6	...	...	...	133	...

Code	Description						
2825	Food/beverage/tobacco processing machinery	5	8	0.3	0.3	37	56
2826	Textile/apparel/leather production machinery	...	3	7.0	0.4	1061	30
2829	Other special-purpose machinery	11	14	5.6	5.1	2177	810
2910	Motor vehicles	16	15	1.6	4.9	177	2260
2920	Automobile bodies, trailers and semi-trailers	16	19	52.3	1.1	7540	119
2930	Parts and accessories for motor vehicles	97	97	4.7	57.1	688	10691
301	Building of ships and boats	31	31h/	...	6.8h/	...	2646h/
3011	Building of ships and floating structures	...	28	...	6.6	...	2627
3012	Building of pleasure and sporting boats	...	3	...	0.2	...	19
3020	Railway locomotives and rolling stock	8	6	3.9	2.9	1882	2174
3030	Air and spacecraft and related machinery	...e/	...e/	...e/	...e/	...e/	...e/
3040	Military fighting vehicles	...	...	...	...	...	...
309	Transport equipment n.e.c.	12	14	3.4	5.4	944	1181
3091	Motorcycles	5	...	1.2	...	130	...
3092	Bicycles and invalid carriages	...	...	...	...	...	...
3099	Other transport equipment n.e.c.	240	211	31.0	22.8	3132	2532
3100	Furniture	41	44	3.4	3.3	260	269
321	Jewellery, bijouterie and related articles	19	22	1.3	1.6	103	127
3211	Jewellery and related articles	22	22	2.1	1.7	157	142
3212	Imitation jewellery and related articles	...	...	...	...	...	...
3220	Musical instruments	13	12	4.7	3.8	602	601
3230	Sports goods	13	15	1.8	2.2	191	247
3240	Games and toys	49f/	50f/	15.3f/	13.7f/	2536f/	2299f/
3250	Medical and dental instruments and supplies	69	66	5.6	5.0	688	679
3290	Other manufacturing n.e.c.	...	...	...	...	...	...
331	Repair of fabricated metal products/machinery	97i/	82i/	6.2i/	4.0l/	830l/	527l/
3311	Repair of fabricated metal products	...i/	...i/	...i/	...i/	...i/	...i/
3312	Repair of machinery	...	...	...	...	...	...
3313	Repair of electronic and optical equipment	...	...	...	...	...	...
3314	Repair of electrical equipment	..h/	..h/	...	..h/	...	..h/
3315	Repair of transport equip., excl. motor vehicles	...	...	...	...	...	...
3319	Repair of other equipment	...	...	...	...	...	...
3320	Installation of industrial machinery/equipment	...	...	...	...	...	...
C	Total manufacturing	5160 j/	4725 j/	989.4 j/	887.0 j/	164705 j/	166311 j/

a/ 1079 includes 1075.
b/ 1311 includes 1312 and 1313.
c/ 1629 includes 1623.
d/ 1701 includes 1702.
e/ 2520 includes 3040.
f/ 3250 includes 2670.
g/ 2733 includes 2731 and 2732.
h/ 301 includes 3315.
i/ 3311 includes 3312.
j/ Total manufacturing includes publishing.

Philippines

ISIC	Industry	Note	Output at producers' prices (millions of Philippine Pesos)				Note	Value added at producers' prices (millions of Philippine Pesos)				Note	Gross fixed capital formation (millions of Philippine Pesos)	
			2006	2007	2008	2009		2006	2007	2008	2009		2008	2009
1010	Processing/preserving of meat		39033	...	44052	...		6817	...	9210	...		442	...
1020	Processing/preserving of fish, etc.		31202	...	35925	...		5119	...	6615	...		629	...
1030	Processing/preserving of fruit,vegetables		45642	...	76767	...		10467	...	19156	...		4122	...
1040	Vegetable and animal oils and fats		55079	...	65475	...		7936	...	9834	...		670	...
1050	Dairy products		64715	...	134810	...		17700	...	37415	...		3689	...
106	Grain mill products,starches and starch products		19396	...	36274	...		3234	...	9445	...		433	...
1061	Grain mill products		17800	...	33658	...		2949	...	8956	...		413	...
1062	Starches and starch products		1596	...	2616	...		285	...	489	...		20	...
107	Other food products		115406	...	120315	...		36744	...	33016	...		5112	...
1071	Bakery products		37376	...	59770	...		9259	...	13587	...		1925	...
1072	Sugar		25260	...	26581	...		12592	...	12505	...		2616	...
1073	Cocoa, chocolate and sugar confectionery		9498	...	8879	...		2235	...	1610	...		93	...
1074	Macaroni, noodles, couscous, etc.		6827	...	4445	...		1619	...	861	...		64	...
1075	Prepared meals and dishes		...a/	...	...a/	...		...a/	...	...a/	...		...a/	...
1079	Other food products n.e.c.		36445a/	...	20640a/	...		11039a/	...	4453a/	...		414a/	...
1080	Prepared animal feeds		35150	...	55751	...		4161	...	14673	...		553	...
1101	Distilling, rectifying and blending of spirits		18067	...	14139	...		5441	...	3292	...		1075	...
1102	Wines		100	...	59	...		17	...	20	...		1	...
1103	Malt liquors and malt		25300	...	21682	...		15691	...	10543	...		1015	...
1104	Soft drinks,mineral waters,other bottled waters		42725	...	56517	...		14114	...	18994	...		1057	...
1200	Tobacco products		64729	...	73565	...		22301	...	35365	...		904	...
131	Spinning, weaving and finishing of textiles		10444	...	8070	...		1920	...	1571	...		185	...
1311	Preparation and spinning of textile fibres		10444b/	...	8070b/	...		1920b/	...	1571b/	...		185b/	...
1312	Weaving of textiles		...b/	...	...b/	...		...b/	...	...b/	...		...b/	...
1313	Finishing of textiles		...b/	...	...b/	...		...b/	...	...b/	...		...b/	...
139	Other textiles		13627	...	10402	...		4484	...	2705	...		154	...
1391	Knitted and crocheted fabrics		1311	...	868	...		574	...	287	...		1	...
1392	Made-up textile articles, except apparel		3913	...	4736	...		844	...	1166	...		50	...
1393	Carpets and rugs		517	...	480	...		182	...	161	...		1	...
1394	Cordage, rope, twine and netting		2248	...	2929	...		679	...	692	...		75	...
1399	Other textiles n.e.c.		5638	...	1389	...		2205	...	399	...		27	...
1410	Wearing apparel, except fur apparel		60548	...	45316	...		21989	...	15451	...		1267	...
1420	Articles of fur		1089	...	...	...		259	...	...	...		35	...
1430	Knitted and crocheted apparel		3176	...	2003	...		755	...	752	...			...
151	Leather;luggage;handbags;saddlery;harness;fur		10176	...	10996	...		2329	...	4156	...		212	...
1511	Tanning/dressing of leather; dressing of fur		111	...	95	...		26	...	21	...		1	...
1512	Luggage,handbags,etc.;saddlery/harness		10065	...	10901	...		2303	...	4135	...		211	...
1520	Footwear		4555	...	4057	...		1255	...	1359	...		80	...
1610	Sawmilling and planing of wood		1295	...	1317	...		400	...	414	...		22	...
162	Wood products, cork, straw, plaiting materials		23669	...	25966	...		2405	...	4992	...		420	...

Code	Industry									
1621	Veneer sheets and wood-based panels	5543	...	6770	...	1632	...	1671	...	171
1622	Builders' carpentry and joinery	14937	...	16668	...	-25	...	2816	...	238
1623	Wooden containers	...c/	...	...c/	...	...c/	...	...c/	...	...c/
1629	Other wood products;articles of cork,straw	3189c/	...	2528c/	...	798c/	...	505c/	...	11c/
1701	Pulp, paper and paperboard	35219d/	...	39017d/	...	5797d/	...	8279d/	...	554d/
1702	Corrugated paper and paperboard	...d/	...	...d/	...	...d/	...	...d/	...	...d/
1709	Other articles of paper and paperboard	16510	...	14202	...	2944	...	2752	...	165
181	Printing and service activities related to printing	11911	...	11354	...	3831	...	3063	...	343
1811	Printing	11383	...	10421	...	3629	...	2725	...	277
1812	Service activities related to printing	528	...	933	...	202	...	338	...	66
1820	Reproduction of recorded media	272	...	...	...	64	...	...	...	...
1910	Coke oven products	...	...	...	...	...	...	...	...	...
1920	Refined petroleum products	399533	...	460965	...	64187	...	174861	...	1762
201	Basic chemicals,fertilizers, etc.	58702	...	71908	...	9648	...	14243	...	4906
2011	Basic chemicals	33679	...	46176	...	6902	...	7612	...	3290
2012	Fertilizers and nitrogen compounds	13499	...	16449	...	1117	...	5404	...	315
2013	Plastics and synthetic rubber in primary forms	11524	...	9283	...	1629	...	1227	...	1301
202	Other chemical products	81534	...	104849	...	17430	...	22604	...	2662
2021	Pesticides and other agrochemical products	7133	...	6725	...	2781	...	2309	...	218
2022	Paints,varnishes;printing ink and mastics	21789	...	25987	...	4377	...	4180	...	326
2023	Soap,cleaning and cosmetic preparations	44190	...	59067	...	8058	...	12531	...	1906
2029	Other chemical products n.e.c.	8422	...	13070	...	2214	...	3584	...	212
2030	Man-made fibres	...	...	...	...	...	...	...	...	...
2100	Pharmaceuticals,medicinal chemicals, etc.	53962	...	41909	...	16980	...	10461	...	667
221	Rubber products	17652	...	22669	...	4518	...	4913	...	1118
2211	Rubber tyres and tubes	11196	...	16362	...	2168	...	3046	...	586
2219	Other rubber products	6456	...	6307	...	2350	...	1867	...	532
2220	Plastics products	50984	...	55127	...	12930	...	15433	...	1647
2310	Glass and glass products	10034	...	13451	...	3334	...	3665	...	553
239	Non-metallic mineral products n.e.c.	69994	...	77734	...	20684	...	27602	...	3579
2391	Refractory products	380	...	363	...	90	...	45	...	9
2392	Clay building materials	3140	...	2413	...	955	...	818	...	-
2393	Other porcelain and ceramic products	11001	...	11620	...	232	...	2464	...	612
2394	Cement, lime and plaster	43214	...	52378	...	15416	...	21804	...	2819
2395	Articles of concrete, cement and plaster	6598	...	9013	...	1799	...	2035	...	88
2396	Cutting, shaping and finishing of stone	169	...	102	...	64	...	31	...	1
2399	Other non-metallic mineral products n.e.c.	5492	...	1845	...	2128	...	405	...	50
2410	Basic iron and steel	79584	...	92594	...	12452	...	18570	...	4861
2420	Basic precious and other non-ferrous metals	113350	...	91196	...	19141	...	12371	...	1335
243	Casting of metals	10079	...	11857	...	3125	...	2160	...	895
2431	Casting of iron and steel	734	...	1098	...	255	...	459	...	9
2432	Casting of non-ferrous metals	9345	...	10759	...	2870	...	1701	...	886
251	Struct.metal products, tanks, reservoirs	...	...	...	...	...	...	...	...	30
2511	Structural metal products	5067	...	3619	...	1401	...	1166	...	13
2512	Tanks, reservoirs and containers of metal	798	...	923	...	200	...	235	...	...

continued

Philippines

ISIC Revision 4		Output at producers' prices (millions of Philippine Pesos)					Value added at producers' prices (millions of Philippine Pesos)					Gross fixed capital formation (millions of Philippine Pesos)		
ISIC	Industry	Note	2006	2007	2008	2009	Note	2006	2007	2008	2009	Note	2008	2009
2513	Steam generators, excl. hot water boilers		...	...	...	...		...	...	...	...		...	...
2520	Weapons and ammunition		923e/	...	921e/	...		424e/	...	623e/	...		27e/	...
259	Other metal products;metal working services		49315	...	48636	...		9823	...	11368	...		1724	...
2591	Forging,pressing,stamping,roll-forming of metal		21377	...	21006	...		3858	...	3846	...		602	...
2592	Treatment and coating of metals; machining		2810	...	2143	...		1113	...	697	...		46	...
2593	Cutlery, hand tools and general hardware		2228	...	2263	...		430	...	523	...		439	...
2599	Other fabricated metal products n.e.c.		22900	...	23224	...		4422	...	6302	...		637	...
2610	Electronic components and boards		484625	...	462869	...		116851	...	89317	...		22829	...
2620	Computers and peripheral equipment		246206	...	153932	...		41433	...	32795	...		8564	...
2630	Communication equipment		...	...	...	...		...	...	...	...		...	...
2640	Consumer electronics		28329	...	16105	...		7794	...	2110	...		630	...
265	Measuring,testing equipment; watches, etc.		...	...	...	...		...	...	...	...		...	...
2651	Measuring/testing/navigating equipment,etc.		21521	...	5213	...		4068	...	1901	...		145	...
2652	Watches and clocks		19432	...	3840	...		2836	...	1046	...		104	...
2660	Irradiation/electromedical equipment,etc.		2089	...	1373	...		1232	...	855	...		41	...
2670	Optical instruments and photographic equipment		...	...	...	...		...	...	...	...		...	...
2680	Magnetic and optical media		...f/	...	...f/	...		...f/	...	...f/	...		...f/	...
2710	Electric motors,generators,transformers,etc.		17730	...	45859	...		4758	...	10797	...		510	...
2720	Batteries and accumulators		2553	...	1239	...		848	...	437	...		11	...
273	Wiring and wiring devices		23442	...	37407	...		2960	...	11030	...		249	...
2731	Fibre optic cables		...g/	...	...g/	...		...g/	...	...g/	...		...g/	...
2732	Other electronic and electric wires and cables		...g/	...	...g/	...		...g/	...	...g/	...		...g/	...
2733	Wiring devices		23442g/	...	37407g/	...		2960g/	...	11030g/	...		249g/	...
2740	Electric lighting equipment		4717	...	5455	...		1508	...	1382	...		342	...
2750	Domestic appliances		17002	...	17194	...		6985	...	3464	...		217	...
2790	Other electrical equipment		25350	...	5393	...		9915	...	883	...		820	...
281	General-purpose machinery		...	...	...	...		...	...	...	...		...	...
2811	Engines/turbines,excl.aircraft,vehicle engines		1380	...	1751	...		750	...	667	...		80	...
2812	Fluid power equipment		...	...	...	...		...	...	...	...		...	...
2813	Other pumps, compressors, taps and valves		2578	...	2691	...		956	...	717	...		21	...
2814	Bearings, gears, gearing and driving elements		1260	...	1211	...		698	...	288	...		13	...
2815	Ovens, furnaces and furnace burners		...	...	...	...		...	...	...	...		...	...
2816	Lifting and handling equipment		392	...	409	...		91	...	126	...		7	...
2817	Office machinery, excl.computers,etc.		51196	...	4788	...		5346	...	606	...		54	...
2818	Power-driven hand tools		...	...	...	...		...	...	...	...		...	...
2819	Other general-purpose machinery		14870	...	11780	...		4024	...	2433	...		538	...
282	Special-purpose machinery		...	...	20161	...		...	...	6527	...		504	...
2821	Agricultural and forestry machinery		412	...	935	...		167	...	371	...		1	...
2822	Metal-forming machinery and machine tools		3049	...	897	...		748	...	373	...		70	...
2823	Machinery for metallurgy		1538	...	2733	...		430	...	812	...		142	...
2824	Mining, quarrying and construction machinery		...	...	2052	...		...	...	332	...		138	...

Code	Industry	(1)	(2)	(3)	(4)	(5)
2825	Food/beverage/tobacco processing machinery	357	471	168	173	3
2826	Textile/apparel/leather production machinery	...	129	...	48	-
2829	Other special-purpose machinery	27946	12944	5829	4418	150
2910	Motor vehicles	67129	58731	9841	18632	540
2920	Automobile bodies, trailers and semi-trailers	2212	1528	789	242	10
2930	Parts and accessories for motor vehicles	108046	118613	17996	23880	9516
301	Building of ships and boats	18975	31196h/	2393	7716h/	6643h/
3011	Building of ships and floating structures	...	31155	...	7696	6636
3012	Building of pleasure and sporting boats	...	41	...	20	7
3020	Railway locomotives and rolling stock	13301	11419	3553	3788	247
3030	Air and spacecraft and related machinery	...e/	...e/	...e/	...e/	...e/
3040	Military fighting vehicles	...	...	...	...	...
309	Transport equipment n.e.c.	25593	30061	3460	7988	718
3091	Motorcycles	1011	...	130	...	...
3092	Bicycles and invalid carriages	...	...	...	...	...
3099	Other transport equipment n.e.c.	...	...	...	...	...
3100	Furniture	21457	18827	6982	5190	192
321	Jewellery, bijouterie and related articles	1543	1514	511	596	20
3211	Jewellery and related articles	391	703	145	277	4
3212	Imitation jewellery and related articles	1152	811	366	319	16
3220	Musical instruments	4052	3985	1016	1000	74
3230	Sports goods	1614	1700	359	522	27
3240	Games and toys	23128f/	25419f/	5914f/	6220f/	1585f/
3250	Medical and dental instruments and supplies	3647	5351	1395	1705	185
3290	Other manufacturing n.e.c.	...	...	...	...	...
331	Repair of fabricated metal products/machinery	5174i/	3177i/	2248i/	1403i/	76i/
3311	Repair of fabricated metal products	...i/	...i/	...i/	...i/	...i/
3312	Repair of machinery	...	...	...	...	...
3313	Repair of electronic and optical equipment	...	...	...	...	...
3314	Repair of electrical equipment	...h/	...h/	...	...h/	...h/
3315	Repair of transport equip., excl. motor vehicles	...	...	...	...	...
3319	Repair of other equipment	...	...	...	...	...
3320	Installation of industrial machinery/equipment	...	...	...	...	...
C	Total manufacturing	3039650 j/	3133217 j/	672931 j/	826582 j/	105914 j/

a/ 1079 includes 1075.
b/ 1311 includes 1312 and 1313.
c/ 1629 includes 1623.
d/ 1701 includes 1702.
e/ 2520 includes 3040.
f/ 3250 includes 2670.
g/ 2733 includes 2731 and 2732.
h/ 301 includes 3315.
i/ 3311 includes 3312.
j/ Total manufacturing includes publishing.

Philippines

Index numbers of industrial production

ISIC Revision 3

(2005=100)

ISIC	Industry	Note	1999	2000	2001	2002	2003	2004	2005	2006	2007	2008	2009	2010
15	Food and beverages	a/	...	93	94	95	95	89	100	103	98	99	95	101
16	Tobacco products		...	339	306	324	157	120	100	72	49	50	52	27
17	Textiles		...	69	64	77	90	88	100	90	55	43	37	40
18	Wearing apparel, fur		...	181	173	175	139	96	100	80	64	74	49	37
19	Leather, leather products and footwear		...	1648	1597	1532	832	100	100	103	109	130	71	79
20	Wood products (excl. furniture)		...	114	122	111	180	181	100	71	77	84	70	77
21	Paper and paper products		...	141	109	94	86	96	100	102	101	96	84	96
22	Printing and publishing		...	119	117	92	101	122	100	104	92	79	75	76
23	Coke,refined petroleum products,nuclear fuel		...	141	138	112	118	93	100	93	92	84	62	86
24	Chemicals and chemical products		...	135	119	102	90	93	100	97	95	97	88	89
25	Rubber and plastics products		...	86	68	64	73	94	100	90	97	100	101	118
26	Non-metallic mineral products		...	95	81	101	97	99	100	86	83	88	97	107
27	Basic metals		...	94	85	77	100	127	100	136	111	102	92	114
28	Fabricated metal products		...	75	86	98	92	95	100	100	108	113	105	122
29	Machinery and equipment n.e.c.		...	146	194	160	188	189	100	51	48	28	25	36
30	Office, accounting and computing machinery		...	...	...	...	...	...	...	...	...	...	...	...
31	Electrical machinery and apparatus		...	131	110	112	93	105	100	...	...	...	...	...
32	Radio,television and communication equipment		...	...	...	...	...	...	100	60	57	57	52	77
33	Medical, precision and optical instruments		...	...	...	...	...	...	...	...	...	...	...	...
34	Motor vehicles, trailers, semi-trailers		...	...	...	...	...	...	...	...	...	...	...	...
35	Other transport equipment		...	87	83	86	81	86	100	86	89	80	78	104
36	Furniture; manufacturing n.e.c.		...	...	...	...	...	...	...	...	...	...	...	...
37	Recycling		...	...	...	...	...	...	...	...	...	...	...	...
D	Total manufacturing		92	105	103	97	97	98	100	90	86	86	76	94

a/ 15 excludes beverages.

Poland

Supplier of information:
Central Statistical Office of Poland, Warsaw.
Industrial statistics for the OECD countries are compiled by the OECD secretariat, which supplies them to UNIDO.

Basic source of data:
Annual surveys.

Major deviations from ISIC (Revision 4):
None reported.

Reference period:
Calendar year.

Scope:
All enterprises.

Method of data collection:
Not reported.

Type of enumeration:
Not reported.

Adjusted for non-response:
Not reported.

Concepts and definitions of variables:
No deviations from the standard UN concepts and definitions are reported.

Related national publications:
None reported.

Poland

ISIC	Industry	Number of enterprises (number)					Number of employees (thousands)					Wages and salaries paid to employees (millions of Polish Zlotys)				
		Note	2006	2007	2008	2009	Note	2006	2007	2008	2009	Note	2006	2007	2008	2009
1010	Processing/preserving of meat		...	...	3283	2921		...	...	118.4	116.6		...	...	3008	3066
1020	Processing/preserving of fish, etc.		...	...	410	337		...	...	15.9	16.8		...	...	439	467
1030	Processing/preserving of fruit,vegetables		...	...	1078	984		...	...	35.2	33.7		...	...	1157	1144
1040	Vegetable and animal oils and fats		...	...	113	107		...	...	3.5	3.5		...	...	173	165
1050	Dairy products		...	...	718	656		...	...	41.0	41.3		...	...	1429	1463
106	Grain mill products,starches and starch products		...	...	914	775		...	...	10.5	10.6		...	...	371	396
1061	Grain mill products		...	...	897	757		...	...	...	...		...	...		
1062	Starches and starch products		...	...	17	18		...	...	...	...		...	...		
107	Other food products		...	...	8190	7422		...	...	146.0	147.9		...	...	3973	4207
1071	Bakery products		...	...	6283	5830		...	...	86.9	90.2		...	...	1717	1920
1072	Sugar		...	...	32	15		...	...	6.9	5.5		...	...	338	278
1073	Cocoa, chocolate and sugar confectionery		...	...	385	334		...	...	19.4	19.7		...	...	655	693
1074	Macaroni, noodles, couscous, etc.		...	...	483	377		...	...	19.4	19.7		...	...	655	693
1075	Prepared meals and dishes		...	...	188	174		...	...	2.5	2.4		...	...	54	64
1079	Other food products n.e.c.		...	...	819	692		...	...	25.2	25.1		...	...	1101	1133
1080	Prepared animal feeds		...	...	461	404		...	...	...	...		...	...		
1101	Distilling, rectifying and blending of spirits		...	...	870a/	626a/		...	...	32.4a/	29.7a/		...	...	1611a/	1583a/
1102	Wines		...	...	...a/	...a/		...	...	...a/	...a/		...	...	...a/	...a/
1103	Malt liquors and malt		...	...	...a/	...a/		...	...	...a/	...a/		...	...	...a/	...a/
1104	Soft drinks,mineral waters,other bottled waters		...	...	...a/	...a/		...	...	...a/	...a/		...	...	...a/	...a/
1200	Tobacco products		...	...	23	22		...	...	7.2	6.5		...	...	417	422
131	Spinning, weaving and finishing of textiles		...	...	1196	1156		...	...	18.8	15.9		...	...	512	424
1311	Preparation and spinning of textile fibres		...	...	128	100		...	...	4.5	3.6		...	...	132	106
1312	Weaving of textiles		...	...	173	152		...	...	7.9	6.2		...	...	221	162
1313	Finishing of textiles		...	...	895	904		...	...	6.5	6.2		...	...	159	156
139	Other textiles		...	...	2786	2716		...	...	34.8	33.7		...	...	875	827
1391	Knitted and crocheted fabrics		...	...	269	215		...	...	3.8	3.5		...	...	103	92
1392	Made-up textile articles, except apparel		...	...	1770	1742		...	...	18.4	17.7		...	...	423	398
1393	Carpets and rugs		...	...	68	58		...	...	1.4	1.1		...	...	44	35
1394	Cordage, rope, twine and netting		...	...	130	126		...	...	1.3	1.3		...	...	38	37
1399	Other textiles n.e.c.		...	...	549	575		...	...	9.9	10.1		...	...	267	265
1410	Wearing apparel, except fur apparel		...	...	15686	13593		...	...	115.0	97.4		...	...	2025	1754
1420	Articles of fur		...	...	381	436		...	...	0.7	...		...	...	10	...
1430	Knitted and crocheted apparel		...	...	1884	1165		...	...	13.5	...		...	...	267	...
151	Leather;luggage,handbags,saddlery,harness;fur		...	...	1349	974		...	...	7.4	6.6		...	...	153	138
1511	Tanning/dressing of leather; dressing of fur		...	...	423	216		...	...	2.4	2.1		...	...	57	51
1512	Luggage,handbags,etc.;saddlery/harness		...	...	926	758		...	...	5.0	4.5		...	...	96	87
1520	Footwear		...	...	2515	2019		...	...	18.4	17.4		...	...	380	361
1610	Sawmilling and planing of wood		...	...	4990	4740		...	...	28.1	27.3		...	...	607	566
162	Wood products, cork, straw, plaiting materials		...	...	14493	11509		...	...	86.8	79.5		...	...	2162	1993

1621	Veneer sheets and wood-based panels	...	219	201	...	...	12.5	12.0	...	...	472	428	...
1622	Builders' carpentry and joinery	...	7506	6169	...	...	45.4	42.1	...	...	1083	1018	...
1623	Wooden containers	...	2019	1631	...	...	10.9	9.5	...	...	232	201	...
1629	Other wood products;articles of cork,straw	...	4749	3508	...	...	18.0	15.8	...	...	375	346	...
1701	Pulp, paper and paperboard	...	108	137	...	...	6.5	6.5	...	...	335	345	...
1702	Corrugated paper and paperboard	...	1116	1207	...	...	23.4	24.4	...	...	820	853	...
1709	Other articles of paper and paperboard	...	806	1140	...	...	16.6	18.3	...	...	583	653	...
181	Printing and service activities related to printing	...	10553	8186	...	...	34.7	32.2	...	...	1145	1121	...
1811	Printing	...	7017	5133	...	...	30.0	27.6	...	...	1025	1001	...
1812	Service activities related to printing	...	3536	3053	...	...	4.6	4.6	...	...	119	120	...
1820	Reproduction of recorded media	...	245	244	...	...	0.7	0.9	...	...	32	44	...
1910	Coke oven products	...	26	19	...	...	16.4b/	6.7	...	...	1157b/	348	...
1920	Refined petroleum products	...	132	147	...	...	..b/	9.2	...	...	..b/	768	...
201	Basic chemicals,fertilizers, etc.	...	617	738	...	...	32.2	31.1	...	...	1533	1519	...
2011	Basic chemicals	...	319	415	...	...	8.5	8.4	...	...	431	418	...
2012	Fertilizers and nitrogen compounds	...	82	90	...	...	...	...	...	...	...	...	...
2013	Plastics and synthetic rubber in primary forms	...	216	233	...	...	38.0	37.6	...	...	1602	1647	...
202	Other chemical products	...	1421	1432	...	...	0.8	0.8	...	...	43	40	...
2021	Pesticides and other agrochemical products	...	47	44	...	...	5.8	5.7	...	...	284	282	...
2022	Paints,varnishes;printing ink and mastics	...	288	295	...	...	22.7	22.5	...	...	940	987	...
2023	Soap,cleaning and cosmetic preparations	...	712	713	...	...	8.6	8.7	...	...	335	338	...
2029	Other chemical products n.e.c.	...	374	380	...	...	1.2	0.9	...	...	46	34	...
2030	Man-made fibres	...	15	15	...	...	24.0	24.8	...	...	1414	1561	...
2100	Pharmaceuticals,medicinal chemicals, etc.	...	236	261	...	...	34.6	32.8	...	...	1327	1233	...
221	Rubber products	...	772	774	...	...	10.5	10.0	...	...	542	499	...
2211	Rubber tyres and tubes	...	137	139	...	...	24.1	22.7	...	...	786	735	...
2219	Other rubber products	...	635	635	...	...	120.3	119.5	...	...	3762	3746	...
2220	Plastics products	...	8093	7190	...	...	93.9	89.9	...	...	3423	3264	...
2310	Glass and glass products	...	1257	1114	...	...	2.9	2.7	...	...	112	101	...
239	Non-metallic mineral products n.e.c.	...	9603	8808	...	...	14.7	13.3	...	...	550	479	...
2391	Refractory products	...	73	73	...	...	6.7	6.6	...	...	422	414	...
2392	Clay building materials	...	466	393	...	...	...	...	...	...	185	201	...
2393	Other porcelain and ceramic products	...	571	527	...	...	8.7	8.7	...	...	310	301	...
2394	Cement, lime and plaster	...	80	74	...	...	7.1	7.6	...	...	1709	1541	...
2395	Articles of concrete, cement and plaster	...	4705	4081	...	...	...	...	...	...	...	...	...
2396	Cutting, shaping and finishing of stone	...	3436	3393	...	...	...	...	...	...	...	...	...
2399	Other non-metallic mineral products n.e.c.	...	272	267	...	...	...	...	...	...	...	...	...
2410	Basic iron and steel	...	371	357	...	...	...	...	...	...	...	...	...
2420	Basic precious and other non-ferrous metals	...	141	167	...	...	35.9	33.4	...	...	767	605	...
243	Casting of metals	...	433	423	...	...	21.2	18.0	...	...	569	439	...
2431	Casting of iron and steel	...	204	195	...	...	16.0	13.5	...	...	198	167	...
2432	Casting of non-ferrous metals	...	229	228	...	...	5.2	4.6	...	...	3479	3383	...
251	Struct.metal products, tanks, reservoirs	...	5218	6106	...	...	96.5	93.4	...	...	2682	2552	...
2511	Structural metal products	...	4571	5336	...	...	74.9	72.0	...	...	553	534	...
2512	Tanks, reservoirs and containers of metal	...	527	682	...	...	16.1	16.1	...	...			...

continued

Poland

ISIC	Industry	Number of enterprises (number)					Number of employees (thousands)					Wages and salaries paid to employees (millions of Polish Zlotys)				
		Note	2006	2007	2008	2009	Note	2006	2007	2008	2009	Note	2006	2007	2008	2009
2513	Steam generators, excl. hot water boilers		…	…	120	88		…	…	5.5	5.4		…	…	244	297
2520	Weapons and ammunition		…	…	25	41		…	…	6.4	6.1		…	…	221	215
259	Other metal products;metal working services		…	…	24652	22592		…	…	143.8	136.6		…	…	4491	4270
2591	Forging,pressing,stamping,roll-forming of metal		…	…	566	638		…	…	9.8	8.8		…	…	331	284
2592	Treatment and coating of metals; machining		…	…	17385	15932		…	…	57.9	55.5		…	…	1659	1589
2593	Cutlery, hand tools and general hardware		…	…	823	937		…	…	14.0	13.6		…	…	502	461
2599	Other fabricated metal products n.e.c.		…	…	5878	5085		…	…	62.1	58.7		…	…	1999	1936
2610	Electronic components and boards		…	…	435	387		…	…	21.3	15.6		…	…	669	486
2620	Computers and peripheral equipment		…	…	433	703		…	…	7.2	6.9		…	…	290	277
2630	Communication equipment		…	…	483	268		…	…	12.0	12.2		…	…	521	508
2640	Consumer electronics		…	…	133	236		…	…	10.8	11.3		…	…	374	364
265	Measuring,testing equipment; watches, etc.		…	…	451	665		…	…	11.2	10.9		…	…	425	428
2651	Measuring/testing/navigating equipment,etc.		…	…	443	625		…	…	…	10.7		…	…	…	418
2652	Watches and clocks		…	…	8	40		…	…	…	0.1		…	…	…	9
2660	Irradiation/electromedical equipment,etc.		…	…	75	76		…	…	…	0.6		…	…	…	26
2670	Optical instruments and photographic equipment		…	…	116	328		…	…	1.2	1.7		…	…	50	58
2680	Magnetic and optical media		…	…	20	15		…	…	…	0.1		…	…	…	3
2710	Electric motors,generators,transformers,etc.		…	…	611	773		…	…	28.4	27.7		…	…	1151	1127
2720	Batteries and accumulators		…	…	82	71		…	…	2.2	2.1		…	…	105	106
273	Wiring and wiring devices		…	…	199	186		…	…	9.1	10.1		…	…	270	277
2731	Fibre optic cables		…	…	3	10		…	…	0.5	0.5		…	…	18	17
2732	Other electronic and electric wires and cables		…	…	95	116		…	…	6.1	7.2		…	…	176	191
2733	Wiring devices		…	…	101	60		…	…	2.5	2.4		…	…	75	70
2740	Electric lighting equipment		…	…	740	693		…	…	16.4	15.1		…	…	567	530
2750	Domestic appliances		…	…	145	227		…	…	27.4	26.9		…	…	959	980
2790	Other electrical equipment		…	…	594	300		…	…	10.9	10.0		…	…	438	393
281	General-purpose machinery		…	…	2065	2717		…	…	79.4	76.7		…	…	3323	3149
2811	Engines/turbines,excl.aircraft,vehicle engines		…	…	193	118		…	…	20.6	19.8		…	…	981	980
2812	Fluid power equipment		…	…	50	87		…	…	2.2	2.1		…	…	87	85
2813	Other pumps, compressors, taps and valves		…	…	163	237		…	…	8.0	7.9		…	…	317	289
2814	Bearings, gears, gearing and driving elements		…	…	118	112		…	…	12.2	11.0		…	…	483	394
2815	Ovens, furnaces and furnace burners		…	…	230	185		…	…	4.0	3.4		…	…	158	130
2816	Lifting and handling equipment		…	…	201	548		…	…	8.6	9.0		…	…	344	352
2817	Office machinery, excl.computers,etc.		…	…	33	39		…	…	0.7	0.7		…	…	38	40
2818	Power-driven hand tools		…	…	85	106		…	…	1.3	1.1		…	…	41	34
2819	Other general-purpose machinery		…	…	992	1285		…	…	21.9	21.7		…	…	875	845
282	Special-purpose machinery		…	…	2274	2045		…	…	69.4	65.8		…	…	2638	2427
2821	Agricultural and forestry machinery		…	…	762	503		…	…	17.8	16.2		…	…	624	541
2822	Metal-forming machinery and machine tools		…	…	263	183		…	…	9.4	7.9		…	…	334	273
2823	Machinery for metallurgy		…	…	46	37		…	…	4.4	3.8		…	…	199	166
2824	Mining, quarrying and construction machinery		…	…	305	277		…	…	17.6	18.4		…	…	691	728

2825	Food/beverage/tobacco processing machinery	189	368	6.6	6.7	260	271
2826	Textile/apparel/leather production machinery	90	86	1.1	1.1	35	38
2829	Other special-purpose machinery	619	591	12.6	11.6	425	480
2910	Motor vehicles	74	90	35.2	32.9	1771	1884
2920	Automobile bodies, trailers and semi-trailers	312	268	10.0	8.9	273	356
2930	Parts and accessories for motor vehicles	1180	982	106.1	102.1	3556	3763
301	Building of ships and boats	827	920	23.9	17.3	850	1183
3011	Building of ships and floating structures	617	537	20.2	13.7	742	1037
3012	Building of pleasure and sporting boats	210	383	3.7	3.6	109	145
3020	Railway locomotives and rolling stock	71	233	9.0	…	…	386
3030	Air and spacecraft and related machinery	49	48	14.8	15.2	588	580
3040	Military fighting vehicles	-	1	-	…	…	-
309	Transport equipment n.e.c.	310	225	6.2	…	…	168
3091	Motorcycles	29	28	0.4	0.4	10	14
3092	Bicycles and invalid carriages	209	142	5.0	4.7	129	135
3099	Other transport equipment n.e.c.	72	55	0.8	…	…	19
3100	Furniture	10790	14692	145.1	148.0	3818	3816
321	Jewellery, bijouterie and related articles	2561	2889	5.2	4.5	112	106
3211	Jewellery and related articles	2340	2608	…	4.2	107	…
3212	Imitation jewellery and related articles	221	281	…	0.3	5	…
3220	Musical instruments	123	276	0.3	0.4	10	9
3230	Sports goods	287	298	1.7	1.5	37	42
3240	Games and toys	656	637	2.8	2.8	75	65
3250	Medical and dental instruments and supplies	5923	4596	15.1	14.5	449	488
3290	Other manufacturing n.e.c.	4388	4609	15.2	14.0	335	334
331	Repair of fabricated metal products/machinery	22482	18200	77.6	67.6	2809	3046
3311	Repair of fabricated metal products	1567	1104	7.2	5.4	263	270
3312	Repair of machinery	11333	8328	37.0	30.4	1253	1450
3313	Repair of electronic and optical equipment	3013	2597	5.1	4.9	233	179
3314	Repair of electrical equipment	2461	2656	6.0	6.2	233	221
3315	Repair of transport equip., excl. motor vehicles	3864	3143	22.0	20.2	815	918
3319	Repair of other equipment	244	372	0.4	0.5	12	7
3320	Installation of industrial machinery/equipment	3567	3444	18.1	18.0	734	740
C	Total manufacturing	189636	175758	2331.3	2227.5	75438	78435

a/ 1101 includes 1102, 1103 and 1104.
b/ 1910 includes 1920.

Poland

ISIC	Industry	Output (millions of Polish Zlotys)					Value added at factor values (millions of Polish Zlotys)					Gross fixed capital formation (millions of Polish Zlotys)		
		Note	2006	2007	2008	2009	Note	2006	2007	2008	2009	Note	2008	2009
1010	Processing/preserving of meat		...	...	36843	39418		...	...	4897	4937		1385	1069
1020	Processing/preserving of fish, etc.		...	...	4623	5456		...	...	1000	1229		202	176
1030	Processing/preserving of fruit,vegetables		...	...	11849	11824		...	...	2845	3121		818	604
1040	Vegetable and animal oils and fats		...	...	4621	4689		...	...	813	755		162	86
1050	Dairy products		...	...	19548	19996		...	...	3215	3810		887	713
106	Grain mill products,starches and starch products		...	...	6101	5917		...	...	1047	1212		278	176
1061	Grain mill products		...	...	...	...		...	...	...	...		...	...
1062	Starches and starch products		...	...	...	...		...	...	...	...		...	...
107	Other food products		...	...	35541	37344		...	...	11487	12811		2766	2468
1071	Bakery products		...	...	12730	13115		...	...	3856	4366		659	703
1072	Sugar		...	...	3824	4448		...	...	1956	2261		340	232
1073	Cocoa, chocolate and sugar confectionery		...	...	6226	7116		...	...	1942	2191		710	711
1074	Macaroni, noodles, couscous, etc.		...	...	1106	1138		...	...	282	335		64	60
1075	Prepared meals and dishes		...	...	613	708		...	...	111	142		142	28
1079	Other food products n.e.c.		...	...	11043	10817		...	...	3340	3515		851	735
1080	Prepared animal feeds		...	...	...	...		...	...	...	...		...	...
1101	Distilling, rectifying and blending of spirits		...	...	29028a/	30799a/		...	...	7499a/	8757a/		1759a/	861a/
1102	Wines		...	...	...a/	...a/		...	...	...a/	...a/		...a/	...a/
1103	Malt liquors and malt		...	...	...a/	...a/		...	...	...a/	...a/		...a/	...a/
1104	Soft drinks,mineral waters,other bottled waters		...	...	...a/	...a/		...	...	...a/	...a/		...a/	...a/
1200	Tobacco products		...	...	12359	12416		...	...	1167	1526		536	665
131	Spinning, weaving and finishing of textiles		...	...	2704	2539		...	...	975	810		176	98
1311	Preparation and spinning of textile fibres		...	...	646	502		...	...	240	207		42	21
1312	Weaving of textiles		...	...	1051	831		...	...	397	280		65	28
1313	Finishing of textiles		...	...	1007	1206		...	...	339	322		70	49
139	Other textiles		...	...	5270	5435		...	...	1770	1834		316	214
1391	Knitted and crocheted fabrics		...	...	648	616		...	...	206	188		58	28
1392	Made-up textile articles, except apparel		...	...	2606	2778		...	...	861	901		122	88
1393	Carpets and rugs		...	...	203	179		...	...	84	71		18	3
1394	Cordage, rope, twine and netting		...	...	284	279		...	...	97	97		19	30
1399	Other textiles n.e.c.		...	...	1528	1583		...	...	523	578		98	64
1410	Wearing apparel, except fur apparel		...	...	7377	6282		...	...	3428	2930		298	238
1420	Articles of fur		...	...	130	...		...	...	30	...		4	...
1430	Knitted and crocheted apparel		...	...	1557	...		...	...	604	...		105	...
151	Leather;luggage,handbags,saddlery,harness;fur		...	...	1081	958		...	...	299	281		26	21
1511	Tanning/dressing of leather; dressing of fur		...	...	368	360		...	...	108	109		13	10
1512	Luggage,handbags,etc.;saddlery/harness		...	...	712	599		...	...	191	172		13	12
1520	Footwear		...	...	1998	1905		...	...	760	734		91	75
1610	Sawmilling and planing of wood		...	...	4899	4254		...	...	1278	1177		314	229
162	Wood products, cork, straw, plaiting materials		...	...	20430	18151		...	...	5701	5310		1539	954

1621	Veneer sheets and wood-based panels	7146	6611	1846	1690	569	362
1622	Builders' carpentry and joinery	8282	7441	2477	2361	592	388
1623	Wooden containers	2055	1576	530	455	145	58
1629	Other wood products;articles of cork,straw	2947	2523	848	804	234	145
1701	Pulp, paper and paperboard	5915	6408	1540	1809	946	824
1702	Corrugated paper and paperboard	7846	7530	2316	2180	659	723
1709	Other articles of paper and paperboard	5006	5926	1715	2140	537	533
181	Printing and service activities related to printing	9457	8624	3260	2788	803	829
1811	Printing	8228	7580	2865	2468	745	763
1812	Service activities related to printing	1228	1044	394	321	58	66
1820	Reproduction of recorded media	223	279	100	117	23	14
1910	Coke oven products	66614b/	5384	157b/	995	4477b/	248
1920	Refined petroleum products	...b/	55539	...b/	-499	...b/	6002
201	Basic chemicals,fertilizers, etc.	24192	21445	5756	4453	2369	1740
2011	Basic chemicals	6644	4082	1910	557	307	406
2012	Fertilizers and nitrogen compounds	16492	17285	4981	5170	1093	882
2013	Plastics and synthetic rubber in primary forms	341	306	131	101	46	13
202	Other chemical products	...	...	...	...	...	...
2021	Pesticides and other agrochemical products	2929	2991	816	798	163	124
2022	Paints,varnishes;printing ink and mastics	9958	10579	3133	3349	564	606
2023	Soap,cleaning and cosmetic preparations	3264	3409	902	921	320	138
2029	Other chemical products n.e.c.	292	278	105	140	5	2
2030	Man-made fibres	...	...	...	...	...	...
2100	Pharmaceuticals,medicinal chemicals, etc.	10382	11492	4674	4728	658	575
221	Rubber products	10526	10807	3060	3431	1548	611
2211	Rubber tyres and tubes	5084	5307	1423	1669	1210	360
2219	Other rubber products	5442	5501	1638	1762	338	250
2220	Plastics products	33981	33903	9772	10391	3227	2322
2310	Glass and glass products	33371	29458	12961	10952	4236	2536
239	Non-metallic mineral products n.e.c.	...	...	...	...	...	...
2391	Refractory products	920	778	270	218	68	142
2392	Clay building materials	4522	3755	1957	1527	504	154
2393	Other porcelain and ceramic products	7124	6291	3458	3015	1169	2110
2394	Cement, lime and plaster	1768	1902	491	518	145	212
2395	Articles of concrete, cement and plaster	2824	2708	953	872	662	112
2396	Cutting, shaping and finishing of stone	...	...	...	...	...	...
2399	Other non-metallic mineral products n.e.c.	32932	18918	6854	3037	2318	100
2410	Basic iron and steel	4918	4419	1485	1302	314	1290
2420	Basic precious and other non-ferrous metals	3501	3111	1096	883	133	984
243	Casting of metals	1417	1308	389	419	181	227
2431	Casting of iron and steel	...	...	...	...	...	...
2432	Casting of non-ferrous metals	...	...	...	...	...	...
251	Struct.metal products, tanks, reservoirs	22947	21436	7967	7812	1548	...
2511	Structural metal products	17727	16027	6080	5801	1200	...
2512	Tanks, reservoirs and containers of metal	4028	4138	1311	1349	229	...

continued

Poland

ISIC Revision 4

ISIC	Industry	Output (millions of Polish Zlotys)					Value added at factor values (millions of Polish Zlotys)					Gross fixed capital formation (millions of Polish Zlotys)		
		Note	2006	2007	2008	2009	Note	2006	2007	2008	2009	Note	2008	2009
2513	Steam generators, excl. hot water boilers		...	...	1192	1271		...	...	576	662		119	80
2520	Weapons and ammunition		...	...	1996	1619		...	...	516	515		48	25
259	Other metal products;metal working services		...	...	34466	30911		...	...	11818	10969		2528	2124
2591	Forging,pressing,stamping,roll-forming of metal		...	...	3206	2507		...	...	728	621		269	196
2592	Treatment and coating of metals; machining		...	...	13067	11294		...	...	4522	3987		793	715
2593	Cutlery, hand tools and general hardware		...	...	2413	2180		...	...	1219	1094		243	205
2599	Other fabricated metal products n.e.c.		...	...	15780	14930		...	...	5349	5268		1223	1008
2610	Electronic components and boards		...	...	7145	6261		...	...	1301	1108		228	222
2620	Computers and peripheral equipment		...	...	2012	1981		...	...	633	711		247	191
2630	Communication equipment		...	...	4319	4886		...	...	1229	971		130	95
2640	Consumer electronics		...	...	10594	13206		...	...	1105	1336		176	186
265	Measuring,testing equipment; watches, etc.		...	...	2231	2188		...	...	1004	983		269	193
2651	Measuring/testing/navigating equipment,etc.		...	...	...	2147		...	...	...	962		...	192
2652	Watches and clocks		...	...	...	40		...	...	...	21		...	1
2660	Irradiation/electromedical equipment,etc.		...	...	...	109		...	...	...	42		...	6
2670	Optical instruments and photographic equipment		...	...	281	479		...	...	101	157		17	20
2680	Magnetic and optical media		...	...	...	21		...	...	...	7		...	-
2710	Electric motors,generators,transformers,etc.		...	...	7379	6966		...	...	2650	2693		443	424
2720	Batteries and accumulators		...	...	1127	1113		...	...	264	277		48	64
273	Wiring and wiring devices		...	...	2239	2348		...	...	570	615		136	93
2731	Fibre optic cables		...	...	99	98		...	...	30	30		8	-
2732	Other electronic and electric wires and cables		...	...	1639	1851		...	...	368	434		102	74
2733	Wiring devices		...	...	501	399		...	...	172	152		25	18
2740	Electric lighting equipment		...	...	4227	4462		...	...	1493	1682		303	151
2750	Domestic appliances		...	...	14837	17623		...	...	3063	3215		906	502
2790	Other electrical equipment		...	...	3091	2520		...	...	1323	1241		215	97
281	General-purpose machinery		...	...	23993	23517		...	...	7580	8112		1896	1037
2811	Engines/turbines,excl.aircraft,vehicle engines		...	...	10202	11054		...	...	2606	3158		840	400
2812	Fluid power equipment		...	...	460	453		...	...	197	198		50	13
2813	Other pumps, compressors, taps and valves		...	...	1717	1598		...	...	652	653		99	68
2814	Bearings, gears, gearing and driving elements		...	...	2702	2098		...	...	911	863		346	141
2815	Ovens, furnaces and furnace burners		...	...	939	750		...	...	293	299		79	39
2816	Lifting and handling equipment		...	...	1872	2004		...	...	729	783		100	76
2817	Office machinery, excl.computers,etc.		...	...	190	191		...	...	98	94		17	16
2818	Power-driven hand tools		...	...	190	165		...	...	83	72		10	7
2819	Other general-purpose machinery		...	...	5720	5204		...	...	2010	1992		355	278
282	Special-purpose machinery		...	...	15932	13637		...	...	5696	5265		805	656
2821	Agricultural and forestry machinery		...	...	4808	3884		...	...	1477	1321		218	197
2822	Metal-forming machinery and machine tools		...	...	1723	1244		...	...	710	553		114	55
2823	Machinery for metallurgy		...	...	695	485		...	...	314	261		34	8
2824	Mining, quarrying and construction machinery		...	...	4801	4332		...	...	1673	1651		212	224

2825	Food/beverage/tobacco processing machinery	1341	1443	516	574	65	47
2826	Textile/apparel/leather production machinery	140	138	63	64	11	6
2829	Other special-purpose machinery	2424	2110	943	842	149	118
2910	Motor vehicles	45727	45270	6562	6724	1257	1846
2920	Automobile bodies, trailers and semi-trailers	3217	2107	811	527	223	111
2930	Parts and accessories for motor vehicles	36617	37764	8744	9171	2346	1952
301	Building of ships and boats	6469	5168	2117	2140	210	187
3011	Building of ships and floating structures	5677	4483	1837	1895	135	132
3012	Building of pleasure and sporting boats	791	685	280	245	75	55
3020	Railway locomotives and rolling stock	2531	...	881	...	81	...
3030	Air and spacecraft and related machinery	2034	2604	911	1262	294	377
3040	Military fighting vehicles	...	...	-	...	-	...
309	Transport equipment n.e.c.	1303	...	381	...	36	36
3091	Motorcycles	152	85	40	17	-	11
3092	Bicycles and invalid carriages	1034	1110	294	311	33	68
3099	Other transport equipment n.e.c.	117	...	47	...	2	2
3100	Furniture	26399	28400	7608	8401	1845	1402
321	Jewellery, bijouterie and related articles	1093	1117	336	414	44	73
3211	Jewellery and related articles	...	1075	...	400	...	72
3212	Imitation jewellery and related articles	...	42	...	14	1	1
3220	Musical instruments	64	65	17	22	2	3
3230	Sports goods	242	219	89	97	11	25
3240	Games and toys	414	427	152	180	21	31
3250	Medical and dental instruments and supplies	3217	2624	1278	1026	163	133
3290	Other manufacturing n.e.c.	2798	2845	764	845	119	119
331	Repair of fabricated metal products/machinery	17167	13051	6980	6138	641	480
3311	Repair of fabricated metal products	1570	1084	616	522	47	34
3312	Repair of machinery	7900	5558	3324	2656	325	204
3313	Repair of electronic and optical equipment	1456	1467	490	783	57	33
3314	Repair of electrical equipment	1389	1198	563	531	31	32
3315	Repair of transport equip., excl. motor vehicles	4778	3610	1969	1599	178	172
3319	Repair of other equipment	73	132	19	46	3	4
3320	Installation of industrial machinery/equipment	4495	4229	1723	1708	240	240
C	Total manufacturing	804496	772630	200935	197883	54020	44809

a/ 1101 includes 1102, 1103 and 1104.
b/ 1910 includes 1920.

Poland

Index numbers of industrial production

ISIC Revision 4

(2005=100)

ISIC	Industry	Note	1999	2000	2001	2002	2003	2004	2005	2006	2007	2008	2009	2010
10	Food products		...	...	...	...	...	...	100	109	116	116	123	131
11	Beverages		...	...	...	...	...	...	100	105	114	120	128	119
12	Tobacco products		...	...	...	...	...	...	100	96	101	68	66	64
13	Textiles		...	...	...	...	...	...	100	110	121	111	105	113
14	Wearing apparel		...	...	...	...	...	...	100	105	108	103	92	92
15	Leather and related products		...	...	...	...	...	...	100	106	126	114	102	111
16	Wood/wood products/cork,excl. furniture		...	...	...	...	...	...	100	106	121	117	116	128
17	Paper and paper products		...	...	...	...	...	...	100	105	116	111	116	136
18	Printing and reproduction of recorded media		...	...	...	...	...	...	100	116	126	124	131	147
19	Coke and refined petroleum products		...	...	...	...	...	...	100	112	111	116	111	107
20	Chemicals and chemical products		...	...	...	...	...	...	100	111	118	112	107	120
21	Pharmaceuticals,medicinal chemicals, etc.		...	...	...	...	...	...	100	111	120	138	148	157
22	Rubber and plastics products		...	...	...	...	...	...	100	116	130	137	134	155
23	Other non-metallic mineral products		...	...	...	...	...	...	100	120	135	137	128	150
24	Basic metals		...	...	...	...	...	...	100	115	124	118	89	108
25	Fabricated metal products, except machinery		...	...	...	...	...	...	100	118	140	147	139	158
26	Computer, electronic and optical products		...	...	...	...	...	...	100	145	180	193	215	316
27	Electrical equipment		...	...	...	...	...	...	100	118	155	178	191	220
28	Machinery and equipment n.e.c.		...	...	...	...	...	...	100	118	139	150	138	136
29	Motor vehicles, trailers and semi-trailers		...	...	...	...	...	...	100	122	140	148	131	151
30	Other transport equipment		...	...	...	...	...	...	100	111	114	123	119	105
31	Furniture		...	...	...	...	...	...	100	113	122	122	119	113
32	Other manufacturing		...	...	...	...	...	...						
33	Repair and installation of machinery/equipment		...	...	...	...	...	...	...	...	...	...	...	...
C	Total manufacturing		...	...	...	...	...	...	100	114	127	131	126	141

Portugal

Supplier of information:
National Institute of Statistics, Lisbon.
Industrial statistics for the OECD countries are compiled by the OECD secretariat, which supplies them to UNIDO.

Basic source of data:
Annual survey; administrative data.

Major deviations from ISIC (Revision 4):
None reported.

Reference period:
Calendar year.

Scope:
All enterprises.

Method of data collection:
Not reported.

Type of enumeration:
Not reported.

Adjusted for non-response:
Not reported.

Concepts and definitions of variables:
No deviations from the standard UN concepts and definitions are reported.

Related national publications:
None reported.

Portugal

ISIC	Industry	Number of enterprises (number)					Number of employees (number)					Wages and salaries paid to employees (millions of Euros)				
		Note	2006	2007	2008	2009	Note	2006	2007	2008	2009	Note	2006	2007	2008	2009
1010	Processing/preserving of meat		...	...	633	619		...	...	16699	16494		...	...	176	176
1020	Processing/preserving of fish, etc.		...	...	211	191		...	...	6619	6566		...	...	70	72
1030	Processing/preserving of fruit,vegetables		...	...	228	221		...	...	...	3559		...	...	...	46
1040	Vegetable and animal oils and fats		...	...	500	495		...	...	2034	2110		...	...	29	31
1050	Dairy products		...	...	439	430		...	...	7056	6765		...	...	102	103
106	Grain mill products,starches and starch products		...	...	299	256		...	...	1849	1719		...	...	28	27
1061	Grain mill products		...	...	294	251		...	...	1731	1597		...	...	25	24
1062	Starches and starch products		...	...	5	5		...	...	118	122		...	...	3	3
107	Other food products		...	...	7448	7089		...	...	52692	52385		...	...	500	515
1071	Bakery products		...	...	6861	6508		...	...	44815	44384		...	...	372	379
1072	Sugar		...	...	5	6		...	...	735	710		...	...	15	14
1073	Cocoa, chocolate and sugar confectionery		...	...	134	122		...	...	1168	1082		...	...	12	12
1074	Macaroni, noodles, couscous, etc.		...	...	14	8		...	...	361	362		...	...	5	5
1075	Prepared meals and dishes		...	...	40	54		...	...	431	799		...	...	4	8
1079	Other food products n.e.c.		...	...	394	391		...	...	5182	5048		...	...	92	96
1080	Prepared animal feeds		...	...	128	125		...	...	...	3528		...	...	...	53
1101	Distilling, rectifying and blending of spirits		...	...	949a/	1035a/		...	...	13805a/	13584a/		...	...	245a/	229a/
1102	Wines		...	...	...a/	...a/		...	...	...a/	...a/		...	...	...a/	...a/
1103	Malt liquors and malt		...	...	...a/	...a/		...	...	...a/	...a/		...	...	...a/	...a/
1104	Soft drinks,mineral waters,other bottled waters		...	...	...a/	...a/		...	...	...a/	...a/		...	...	...a/	...a/
1200	Tobacco products		...	...	4	4		...	...	...	...		...	...	...	...
131	Spinning, weaving and finishing of textiles		...	...	960	905		...	...	25130	22637		...	...	252	229
1311	Preparation and spinning of textile fibres		...	...	156	144		...	...	4713	3865		...	...	49	39
1312	Weaving of textiles		...	...	311	293		...	...	11029	9761		...	...	112	101
1313	Finishing of textiles		...	...	493	468		...	...	9388	9011		...	...	91	89
139	Other textiles		...	...	2937	2715		...	...	28945	24826		...	...	281	242
1391	Knitted and crocheted fabrics		...	...	288	270		...	...	3651	3269		...	...	39	36
1392	Made-up textile articles, except apparel		...	...	1080	1005		...	...	11453	9904		...	...	106	92
1393	Carpets and rugs		...	...	167	147		...	...	1726	1385		...	...	16	13
1394	Cordage, rope, twine and netting		...	...	49	42		...	...	2936	2354		...	...	33	26
1399	Other textiles n.e.c.		...	...	1353	1251		...	...	9179	7914		...	...	88	75
1410	Wearing apparel, except fur apparel		...	...	10399	9251		...	...	101665	88910		...	...	739	665
1420	Articles of fur		...	...	31	29		...	...	105	114		...	...	1	1
1430	Knitted and crocheted apparel		...	...	860	770		...	...	9258	8492		...	...	77	73
151	Leather;luggage,handbags,saddlery,harness;fur		...	...	487	439		...	...	3689	3336		...	...	37	35
1511	Tanning/dressing of leather; dressing of fur		...	...	129	118		...	...	2255	2058		...	...	27	25
1512	Luggage,handbags,etc.;saddlery/harness		...	...	358	321		...	...	1434	1278		...	...	10	9
1520	Footwear		...	...	2560	2374		...	...	41280	39594		...	...	335	326
1610	Sawmilling and planing of wood		...	...	897	822		...	...	7498	6458		...	...	68	60
162	Wood products, cork, straw, plaiting materials		...	...	6415	5857		...	...	31493	27240		...	...	327	290

ISIC Revision 4

ISIC	Description						
1621	Veneer sheets and wood-based panels	49	47	2275	1828	39	32
1622	Builders' carpentry and joinery	4188	3810	14148	12710	115	103
1623	Wooden containers	162	156	1211	1178	11	11
1629	Other wood products;articles of cork,straw	2016	1844	13859	11524	162	144
1701	Pulp, paper and paperboard	55	50	5489	5307	74	71
1702	Corrugated paper and paperboard	306	282	...	...	...	...
1709	Other articles of paper and paperboard	192	190	...	...	...	...
181	Printing and service activities related to printing	3297	3200	20684	19695	267	260
1811	Printing	1657	1673	14805	14270	205	200
1812	Service activities related to printing	1640	1527	5879	5425	63	59
1820	Reproduction of recorded media	64	62	183	192	3	3
1910	Coke oven products	-	-	-	-	-	-
1920	Refined petroleum products	1	1	...	...	...	...
201	Basic chemicals,fertilizers, etc.	237	226	4579	4152	119	115
2011	Basic chemicals	124	120	1903	696	46	17
2012	Fertilizers and nitrogen compounds	21	28	...	...	...	...
2013	Plastics and synthetic rubber in primary forms	92	78	9016	8302	160	151
202	Other chemical products	623	592	...	...	7	7
2021	Pesticides and other agrochemical products	7	5	335	274	7	7
2022	Paints,varnishes;printing ink and mastics	150	148	4242	3878	81	74
2023	Soap,cleaning and cosmetic preparations	202	194	2710	2518	44	42
2029	Other chemical products n.e.c.	264	245	1729	1632	28	28
2030	Man-made fibres	16	16	462	438	9	8
2100	Pharmaceuticals,medicinal chemicals, etc.	16	15	667	...	19	75
221	Rubber products	220	154	4763	4563	77	49
2211	Rubber tyres and tubes	119	55	2421	2417	48	26
2219	Other rubber products	101	99	2342	2146	29	260
2220	Plastics products	1016	988	19821	18435	277	112
2310	Glass and glass products	517	496	7007	6833	114	555
239	Non-metallic mineral products n.e.c.	4566	4282	46767	42659	598	4
2391	Refractory products	22	19	300	313	3	...
2392	Clay building materials	276	259	7919	...	109	52
2393	Other porcelain and ceramic products	1145	1052	13208	1682	146	131
2394	Cement, lime and plaster	37	37	1725	8764	52	123
2395	Articles of concrete, cement and plaster	794	730	9023	12214	130	17
2396	Cutting, shaping and finishing of stone	2197	2095	13133	1145	133	...
2399	Other non-metallic mineral products n.e.c.	95	90	1459	...	26	32
2410	Basic iron and steel	78	80	...	...	...	...
2420	Basic precious and other non-ferrous metals	111	100	2416	2155	37	54
243	Casting of metals	224	212	4704	3861	65	34
2431	Casting of iron and steel	51	41	3039	2314	46	...
2432	Casting of non-ferrous metals	173	171	1665	1547	20	20
251	Struct.metal products, tanks, reservoirs	5901	5603	36487	38931	481	...
2511	Structural metal products	5761	5456	...	35885	428	...
2512	Tanks, reservoirs and containers of metal	122	127	2218	2348	37	...

continued

Portugal

ISIC	Industry	Number of enterprises (number)					Number of employees (number)					Wages and salaries paid to employees (millions of Euros)				
		Note	2006	2007	2008	2009	Note	2006	2007	2008	2009	Note	2006	2007	2008	2009
2513	Steam generators, excl. hot water boilers		…	…	18	20		…	…		698		…	…		16
2520	Weapons and ammunition		…	…	9	9		…	…		…		…	…		
259	Other metal products;metal working services		…	…	8667	7977		…	…	51520	…		…	…		
2591	Forging,pressing,stamping,roll-forming of metal		…	…	1017	914		…	…	2956	…		…	…	640	
2592	Treatment and coating of metals; machining		…	…	3622	3340		…	…	16036	14435		…	…	26	
2593	Cutlery, hand tools and general hardware		…	…	1862	1701		…	…	16753	15668		…	…	185	171
2599	Other fabricated metal products n.e.c.		…	…	2166	2022		…	…	15775	15808		…	…	238	216
2610	Electronic components and boards		…	…	106	91		…	…	4192	3247		…	…	191	188
2620	Computers and peripheral equipment		…	…	53	50		…	…	817	865		…	…	71	44
2630	Communication equipment		…	…	80	72		…	…	913	1127		…	…	14	16
2640	Consumer electronics		…	…	44	38		…	…	2969	3507		…	…	21	21
265	Measuring,testing equipment; watches, etc.		…	…	85	82		…	…	869	787		…	…	51	60
2651	Measuring/testing/navigating equipment,etc.		…	…	64	62		…	…	638	585		…	…	12	11
2652	Watches and clocks		…	…	21	20		…	…	231	202		…	…	9	9
2660	Irradiation/electromedical equipment,etc.		…	…	6	7		…	…	16	21		…	…	2	2
2670	Optical instruments and photographic equipment		…	…	15	15		…	…	532	529		…	…		
2680	Magnetic and optical media		…	…	-	-		…	…		-		…	…	8	8
2710	Electric motors,generators,transformers,etc.		…	…	271	271		…	…	5389	5990		…	…	-	-
2720	Batteries and accumulators		…	…	4	4		…	…	689	592		…	…	113	121
273	Wiring and wiring devices		…	…	48	44		…	…	3121	3414		…	…	13	12
2731	Fibre optic cables		…	…	-	-		…	…		-		…	…	56	61
2732	Other electronic and electric wires and cables		…	…	24	23		…	…	2483	2886		…	…	-	-
2733	Wiring devices		…	…	24	21		…	…	638	528		…	…	48	51
2740	Electric lighting equipment		…	…	273	249		…	…	2532	2329		…	…	8	10
2750	Domestic appliances		…	…	89	78		…	…	3812	3592		…	…	33	31
2790	Other electrical equipment		…	…	171	160		…	…	3138	2795		…	…	52	49
281	General-purpose machinery		…	…	1104	981		…	…	13653	10595		…	…	44	37
2811	Engines/turbines,excl.aircraft,vehicle engines		…	…	46	33		…	…	267	266		…	…	204	154
2812	Fluid power equipment		…	…	20	14		…	…	61	39		…	…	6	5
2813	Other pumps, compressors, taps and valves		…	…	85	77		…	…	3834	2255		…	…	1	…
2814	Bearings, gears, gearing and driving elements		…	…	22	21		…	…	633	556		…	…	60	33
2815	Ovens, furnaces and furnace burners		…	…	46	35		…	…	321	248		…	…	11	9
2816	Lifting and handling equipment		…	…	149	145		…	…	2243	1944		…	…	5	4
2817	Office machinery, excl.computers,etc.		…	…	10	5		…	…	42	15		…	…	35	31
2818	Power-driven hand tools		…	…	16	11		…	…	61	36		…	…	1	…
2819	Other general-purpose machinery		…	…	710	640		…	…	6191	5236		…	…	86	71
282	Special-purpose machinery		…	…	808	759		…	…	11681	10228		…	…	169	149
2821	Agricultural and forestry machinery		…	…	106	100		…	…	1283	1351		…	…	16	17
2822	Metal-forming machinery and machine tools		…	…	119	125		…	…	1670	1498		…	…	24	22
2823	Machinery for metallurgy		…	…	27	22		…	…	220	121		…	…	3	1
2824	Mining, quarrying and construction machinery		…	…	103	83		…	…	1322	906		…	…	18	12

Code	Item												
2825	Food/beverage/tobacco processing machinery	…	109	102	…	…	2226	1695	…	…	…	37	27
2826	Textile/apparel/leather production machinery	…	51	48	…	…	1270	1071	…	…	…	19	17
2829	Other special-purpose machinery	…	293	279	…	…	3690	3586	…	…	…	53	53
2910	Motor vehicles	…	27	27	…	…	5893	5130	…	…	…	109	102
2920	Automobile bodies, trailers and semi-trailers	…	201	203	…	…	3550	3207	…	…	…	46	41
2930	Parts and accessories for motor vehicles	…	320	310	…	…	27071	23037	…	…	…	387	332
301	Building of ships and boats	…	184	161	…	…	3320	2574	…	…	…	59	47
3011	Building of ships and floating structures	…	121	115	…	…	2670	2321	…	…	…	52	44
3012	Building of pleasure and sporting boats	…	63	46	…	…	650	253	…	…	…	7	3
3020	Railway locomotives and rolling stock	…	4	4	…	…	1730	1739	…	…	…	33	34
3030	Air and spacecraft and related machinery	…	15	14	…	…	…	…	…	…	…	…	…
3040	Military fighting vehicles	…	2	1	…	…	1642	1449	…	…	…	18	17
309	Transport equipment n.e.c.	…	64	58	…	…	901	789	…	…	…	6	5
3091	Motorcycles	…	18	19	…	…	561	481	…	…	…	10	9
3092	Bicycles and invalid carriages	…	37	29	…	…	180	179	…	…	…	3	3
3099	Other transport equipment n.e.c.	…	9	10	…	…	…	…	…	…	…	326	310
3100	Furniture	…	6390	5719	…	…	38792	35509	…	…	…	25	22
321	Jewellery, bijouterie and related articles	…	1144	1074	…	…	2785	2571	…	…	…	24	22
3211	Jewellery and related articles	…	954	866	…	…	2565	2334	…	…	…	1	1
3212	Imitation jewellery and related articles	…	190	208	…	…	220	237	…	…	…	1	1
3220	Musical instruments	…	34	27	…	…	114	127	…	…	…	3	3
3230	Sports goods	…	69	62	…	…	255	285	…	…	…	4	4
3240	Games and toys	…	69	71	…	…	499	513	…	…	…	53	54
3250	Medical and dental instruments and supplies	…	923	901	…	…	4281	4298	…	…	…	54	54
3290	Other manufacturing n.e.c.	…	1337	1237	…	…	5983	5851	…	…	…	172	198
331	Repair of fabricated metal products/machinery	…	2677	2800	…	…	11717	13160	…	…	…	9	16
3311	Repair of fabricated metal products	…	211	219	…	…	878	1039	…	…	…	84	96
3312	Repair of machinery	…	1869	1891	…	…	6475	7254	…	…	…	2	3
3313	Repair of electronic and optical equipment	…	63	72	…	…	136	195	…	…	…	9	9
3314	Repair of electrical equipment	…	204	226	…	…	626	748	…	…	…	67	73
3315	Repair of transport equip., excl. motor vehicles	…	262	303	…	…	3467	3743	…	…	…	1	1
3319	Repair of other equipment	…	68	89	…	…	135	181	…	…	…	79	90
3320	Installation of industrial machinery/equipment	…	330	374	…	…	3289	3853	…	…	…	…	…
C	Total manufacturing	…	79589	74234	…	…	758280	703895	…	…	…	9025	8508

a/ 1101 includes 1102, 1103 and 1104.

Portugal

ISIC	Industry	Output Note	Output (millions of Euros) 2006	2007	2008	2009	Value added at factor values Note	VA (millions of Euros) 2006	2007	2008	2009	GFCF Note	Gross fixed capital formation (millions of Euros) 2008	2009
1010	Processing/preserving of meat		...	...	1824	1809		...	...	326	344		136	129
1020	Processing/preserving of fish, etc.		...	...	780	733		...	...	150	145		57	54
1030	Processing/preserving of fruit,vegetables		...	...	...	532		...	...	...	114		...	108
1040	Vegetable and animal oils and fats		...	...	1059	811		...	...	90	92		46	37
1050	Dairy products		...	...	1663	1451		...	...	297	281		83	40
106	Grain mill products,starches and starch products		...	...	649	483		...	...	93	79		14	14
1061	Grain mill products		...	...	616	456		...	...	84	72		14	13
1062	Starches and starch products		...	...	33	27		...	...	9	7		1	1
107	Other food products		...	...	2864	2850		...	...	943	985		209	206
1071	Bakery products		...	...	1490	1468		...	...	605	632		138	136
1072	Sugar		...	...	316	308		...	...	39	35		6	6
1073	Cocoa, chocolate and sugar confectionery		...	...	63	63		...	...	24	24		4	7
1074	Macaroni, noodles, couscous, etc.		...	...	95	85		...	...	20	20		10	9
1075	Prepared meals and dishes		...	...	28	45		...	...	9	15		3	6
1079	Other food products n.e.c.		...	...	872	882		...	...	247	261		49	42
1080	Prepared animal feeds		...	...	...	1085		...	...	...	142		...	50
1101	Distilling, rectifying and blending of spirits		...	...	2757a/	2689a/		...	...	663a/	691a/		246a/	177a/
1102	Wines		...	...	...a/	...a/		...	...	...a/	...a/		...a/	...a/
1103	Malt liquors and malt		...	...	...a/	...a/		...	...	...a/	...a/		...a/	...a/
1104	Soft drinks,mineral waters,other bottled waters		...	...	...a/	...a/		...	...	...a/	...a/		...a/	...a/
1200	Tobacco products		...	...	...	...		...	...	...	...		...	...
131	Spinning, weaving and finishing of textiles		...	...	1254	1049		...	...	390	332		68	70
1311	Preparation and spinning of textile fibres		...	...	259	190		...	...	71	52		11	8
1312	Weaving of textiles		...	...	614	511		...	...	177	148		24	26
1313	Finishing of textiles		...	...	381	347		...	...	143	133		34	36
139	Other textiles		...	...	1694	1383		...	...	471	398		103	70
1391	Knitted and crocheted fabrics		...	...	350	317		...	...	73	66		19	9
1392	Made-up textile articles, except apparel		...	...	542	460		...	...	153	131		20	15
1393	Carpets and rugs		...	...	78	51		...	...	25	16		4	1
1394	Cordage, rope, twine and netting		...	...	253	169		...	...	62	53		19	16
1399	Other textiles n.e.c.		...	...	472	386		...	...	158	133		40	29
1410	Wearing apparel, except fur apparel		...	...	2845	2369		...	...	1047	894		101	75
1420	Articles of fur		...	...	2	3		...	...	1	1		-	-
1430	Knitted and crocheted apparel		...	...	330	301		...	...	108	109		17	13
151	Leather;luggage,handbags,saddlery,harness;fur		...	...	235	213		...	...	61	59		7	6
1511	Tanning/dressing of leather; dressing of fur		...	...	197	178		...	...	44	44		6	4
1512	Luggage,handbags,etc.;saddlery/harness		...	...	38	35		...	...	16	15		1	2
1520	Footwear		...	...	1735	1617		...	...	543	523		84	58
1610	Sawmilling and planing of wood		...	...	456	347		...	...	130	104		59	72
162	Wood products, cork, straw, plaiting materials		...	...	2725	1981		...	...	635	498		180	98

1621	Veneer sheets and wood-based panels	…	445	308	…	92	65	…	4	23
1622	Builders' carpentry and joinery	…	608	489	…	203	173	…	30	38
1623	Wooden containers	…	80	67	…	22	22	…	6	6
1629	Other wood products;articles of cork,straw	…	1593	1116	…	318	238	…	59	113
1701	Pulp, paper and paperboard	…	…	…	…	…	…	…	…	…
1702	Corrugated paper and paperboard	…	604	562	…	161	174	…	54	49
1709	Other articles of paper and paperboard	…	…	…	…	540	518	…	127	207
181	Printing and service activities related to printing	…	1241	1195	…	418	404	…	102	158
1811	Printing	…	958	932	…	122	114	…	25	50
1812	Service activities related to printing	…	283	264	…	3	6	…	-	-
1820	Reproduction of recorded media	…	13	16	…	-	-	…	…	…
1910	Coke oven products	…	-	-	…	-	-	…	…	…
1920	Refined petroleum products	…	2333	1421	…	412	231	…	330	288
201	Basic chemicals,fertilizers, etc.	…	637	…	…	166	…	…	…	128
2011	Basic chemicals	…	…	143	…	…	4	…	20	…
2012	Fertilizers and nitrogen compounds	…	…	…	…	…	…	…	…	…
2013	Plastics and synthetic rubber in primary forms	…	1508	1455	…	340	352	…	80	68
202	Other chemical products	…	101	70	…	18	16	…	8	7
2021	Pesticides and other agrochemical products	…	637	550	…	167	158	…	27	19
2022	Paints,varnishes;printing ink and mastics	…	377	343	…	103	102	…	13	17
2023	Soap,cleaning and cosmetic preparations	…	393	492	…	53	76	…	33	25
2029	Other chemical products n.e.c.	…	124	92	…	14	22	…	3	3
2030	Man-made fibres	…	208	…	…	84	…	…	3	…
2100	Pharmaceuticals,medicinal chemicals, etc.	…	…	…	…	…	…	…	…	60
221	Rubber products	…	684	653	…	256	255	…	50	52
2211	Rubber tyres and tubes	…	534	530	…	209	208	…	45	46
2219	Other rubber products	…	150	123	…	47	47	…	5	6
2220	Plastics products	…	2229	1944	…	555	557	…	135	242
2310	Glass and glass products	…	913	834	…	340	336	…	87	153
239	Non-metallic mineral products n.e.c.	…	3958	3440	…	1333	1202	…	261	405
2391	Refractory products	…	14	14	…	7	6	…	2	2
2392	Clay building materials	…	646	…	…	219	…	…	…	109
2393	Other porcelain and ceramic products	…	491	…	…	226	…	…	…	42
2394	Cement, lime and plaster	…	838	694	…	319	293	…	39	51
2395	Articles of concrete, cement and plaster	…	1140	1109	…	261	264	…	81	114
2396	Cutting, shaping and finishing of stone	…	632	555	…	236	212	…	47	62
2399	Other non-metallic mineral products n.e.c.	…	197	126	…	65	46	…	11	25
2410	Basic iron and steel	…	…	…	…	…	…	…	…	…
2420	Basic precious and other non-ferrous metals	…	466	270	…	79	54	…	12	14
243	Casting of metals	…	364	296	…	116	95	…	20	44
2431	Casting of iron and steel	…	242	156	…	78	55	…	14	33
2432	Casting of non-ferrous metals	…	122	140	…	37	40	…	6	11
251	Struct.metal products, tanks, reservoirs	…	…	2769	…	…	877	…	162	173
2511	Structural metal products	…	2776	2346	…	827	764	…	144	…
2512	Tanks, reservoirs and containers of metal	…	247	257	…	69	73	…	15	16

continued

Portugal

ISIC	Industry	Output (millions of Euros) Note	2006	2007	2008	2009	Value added at factor values (millions of Euros) Note	2006	2007	2008	2009	Gross fixed capital formation (millions of Euros) Note	2008	2009
2513	Steam generators, excl. hot water boilers		…	…	…	167		…	…	…	40		…	3
2520	Weapons and ammunition		…	…	…	…		…	…	…	…		…	…
259	Other metal products;metal working services		…	…	3279	…		…	…	1226	…		264	…
2591	Forging,pressing,stamping,roll-forming of metal		…	…	175	…		…	…	50	…		11	…
2592	Treatment and coating of metals; machining		…	…	837	714		…	…	362	323		82	50
2593	Cutlery, hand tools and general hardware		…	…	978	828		…	…	422	377		83	79
2599	Other fabricated metal products n.e.c.		…	…	1289	1109		…	…	392	370		87	91
2610	Electronic components and boards		…	…	1394	470		…	…	208	45		61	5
2620	Computers and peripheral equipment		…	…	119	216		…	…	26	44		2	2
2630	Communication equipment		…	…	131	150		…	…	49	43		4	7
2640	Consumer electronics		…	…	514	709		…	…	104	121		21	23
265	Measuring,testing equipment; watches, etc.		…	…	53	46		…	…	20	16		2	3
2651	Measuring/testing/navigating equipment,etc.		…	…	48	41		…	…	18	13		2	3
2652	Watches and clocks		…	…	5	5		…	…	3	3		1	1
2660	Irradiation/electromedical equipment,etc.		…	…	1	2		…	…	1	1		1	1
2670	Optical instruments and photographic equipment		…	…	24	26		…	…	9	11		4	1
2680	Magnetic and optical media		…	…	-	-		…	…	-	-		-	-
2710	Electric motors,generators,transformers,etc.		…	…	1374	1862		…	…	277	329		117	44
2720	Batteries and accumulators		…	…	78	62		…	…	24	16		3	3
273	Wiring and wiring devices		…	…	745	634		…	…	134	131		31	20
2731	Fibre optic cables		…	…	-	-		…	…	-	1		-	-
2732	Other electronic and electric wires and cables		…	…	691	582		…	…	113	105		26	18
2733	Wiring devices		…	…	55	51		…	…	21	26		5	2
2740	Electric lighting equipment		…	…	175	143		…	…	68	54		9	10
2750	Domestic appliances		…	…	450	427		…	…	117	128		28	28
2790	Other electrical equipment		…	…	293	205		…	…	91	62		30	12
281	General-purpose machinery		…	…	1669	936		…	…	447	297		83	43
2811	Engines/turbines,excl.aircraft,vehicle engines		…	…	105	53		…	…	17	11		9	1
2812	Fluid power equipment		…	…	3	2		…	…	1	1		-	-
2813	Other pumps, compressors, taps and valves		…	…	668	250		…	…	156	74		21	9
2814	Bearings, gears, gearing and driving elements		…	…	58	42		…	…	21	18		7	1
2815	Ovens, furnaces and furnace burners		…	…	21	13		…	…	8	5		1	-
2816	Lifting and handling equipment		…	…	249	162		…	…	65	47		9	6
2817	Office machinery, excl.computers,etc.		…	…	1	…		…	…	…	…		-	-
2818	Power-driven hand tools		…	…	3	1		…	…	1	1		1	-
2819	Other general-purpose machinery		…	…	561	413		…	…	176	139		34	25
282	Special-purpose machinery		…	…	894	801		…	…	328	265		52	45
2821	Agricultural and forestry machinery		…	…	85	85		…	…	30	31		6	3
2822	Metal-forming machinery and machine tools		…	…	117	100		…	…	44	39		5	8
2823	Machinery for metallurgy		…	…	15	6		…	…	6	3		1	-
2824	Mining, quarrying and construction machinery		…	…	99	64		…	…	37	26		8	7

Code	Activity						
2825	Food/beverage/tobacco processing machinery	183	120	70	50	7	6
2826	Textile/apparel/leather production machinery	69	52	37	28	9	8
2829	Other special-purpose machinery	326	375	105	89	16	13
2910	Motor vehicles	2342	1758	297	271	115	121
2920	Automobile bodies, trailers and semi-trailers	261	190	78	62	12	16
2930	Parts and accessories for motor vehicles	3308	2759	694	600	163	87
301	Building of ships and boats	285	163	86	59	15	7
3011	Building of ships and floating structures	238	148	73	55	10	6
3012	Building of pleasure and sporting boats	47	15	13	5	5	1
3020	Railway locomotives and rolling stock	101	95	41	48	10	5
3030	Air and spacecraft and related machinery	:	:	:	:	:	:
3040	Military fighting vehicles	119	101	35	29	8	4
309	Transport equipment n.e.c.	31	24	11	10	5	2
3091	Motorcycles	72	66	19	16	3	2
3092	Bicycles and invalid carriages	16	12	4	3	-	1
3099	Other transport equipment n.e.c.	1554	1353	535	492	187	124
3100	Furniture	132	144	36	40	5	4
321	Jewellery, bijouterie and related articles	129	140	35	39	5	3
3211	Jewellery and related articles	3	4	1	1	-	-
3212	Imitation jewellery and related articles	3	4	1	2	-	-
3220	Musical instruments	17	19	4	6	1	1
3230	Sports goods	14	16	6	7	1	-
3240	Games and toys	292	285	117	120	19	12
3250	Medical and dental instruments and supplies	311	269	100	93	17	29
3290	Other manufacturing n.e.c.	:	:	:	:	:	:
331	Repair of fabricated metal products/machinery	833	961	314	361	36	39
3311	Repair of fabricated metal products	37	79	21	29	2	2
3312	Repair of machinery	351	404	140	162	18	25
3313	Repair of electronic and optical equipment	5	8	3	4	-	1
3314	Repair of electrical equipment	26	27	14	15	1	3
3315	Repair of transport equip., excl. motor vehicles	410	437	135	149	14	8
3319	Repair of other equipment	4	6	2	3	-	-
3320	Installation of industrial machinery/equipment	531	730	154	180	28	22
C	Total manufacturing	78956	65803	18962	16687	5491	4787

a/ 1101 includes 1102, 1103 and 1104.

Portugal

Index numbers of industrial production

ISIC Revision 4

(2005=100)

ISIC	Industry	Note	1999	2000	2001	2002	2003	2004	2005	2006	2007	2008	2009	2010
10	Food products		...	90	93	96	96	100	100	104	110	109	113	116
11	Beverages		...	89	92	91	98	95	100	105	106	101	105	103
12	Tobacco products		...	79	86	93	91	95	100	100	98	92	92	88
13	Textiles		...	129	130	125	118	113	100	95	90	82	76	79
14	Wearing apparel		...	124	128	119	114	108	100	100	101	92	84	84
15	Leather and related products		...	154	150	137	120	110	100	96	91	84	69	70
16	Wood/wood products/cork,excl. furniture		...	156	127	147	179	147	100	100	104	97	85	88
17	Paper and paper products		...	66	79	97	98	101	100	101	103	103	108	111
18	Printing and reproduction of recorded media		...	119	118	115	107	103	100	102	99	98	90	86
19	Coke and refined petroleum products		...	83	89	90	93	93	100	100	96	92	80	88
20	Chemicals and chemical products		...	81	80	92	98	99	100	99	104	94	81	96
21	Pharmaceuticals,medicinal chemicals, etc.		...	119	106	108	100	104	100	107	107	115	111	106
22	Rubber and plastics products		...	76	80	85	91	93	100	102	111	101	101	110
23	Other non-metallic mineral products		...	105	106	106	100	102	100	98	102	94	82	80
24	Basic metals		...	100	96	97	96	99	100	111	114	118	127	145
25	Fabricated metal products, except machinery		...	99	103	110	108	104	100	111	113	115	104	103
26	Computer, electronic and optical products		...	88	89	83	87	90	100	108	113	122	51	45
27	Electrical equipment		...	248	210	169	154	146	100	102	99	96	84	82
28	Machinery and equipment n.e.c.		...	112	113	111	107	103	100	100	101	99	95	93
29	Motor vehicles, trailers and semi-trailers		...	143	159	166	141	125	100	114	110	97	58	59
30	Other transport equipment		...	...	...	...	...	...	...	...	...	...	...	...
31	Furniture		...	143	159	166	141	125	100	94	90	83	68	77
32	Other manufacturing		...	95	103	140	127	119	100	105	94	81	59	63
33	Repair and installation of machinery/equipment		...	...	...	...	...	...	...	...	...	...	...	...
C	Total manufacturing		...	110	110	112	110	107	100	103	104	100	90	92

Qatar

Supplier of information:
Qatar Statistics Authority, Doha.

Basic source of data:
Annual industrial survey.

Major deviations from ISIC (Revision 3):
None reported.

Reference period:
Calendar year.

Scope:
All establishments.

Method of data collection:
Direct interview in the field, mail questionnaires and online survey.

Type of enumeration:
Complete enumeration for large establishments; sample survey for small establishments.

Adjusted for non-response:
No.

Concepts and definitions of variables:
No deviations from the standard UN concepts and definitions are reported.

Related national publications:
Annual Statistical Abstract, published by Qatar Statistics Authority, Doha.

Qatar

ISIC Revision 3

ISIC	Industry	Number of establishments (number)				Number of persons engaged (number)				Wages and salaries paid to employees (millions of Qatari Riyals)			
		2007	2008	2009	2010	2007	2008	2009	2010	2007	2008	2009	2010
15	Food and beverages	238	226	243	193	4747	4756	5879	5651	117	128	177	175
16	Tobacco products	...	...	...	...	...	...	...	...	...	...	...	...
17	Textiles	38	34	21	26	422	459	470	454	9	11	12	10
18	Wearing apparel, fur	1112	1104	1112	941	8448	7283	7306	6761	137	131	139	121
19	Leather, leather products and footwear	3	2	3	5	104	101	143	133	2	2	4	3
20	Wood products (excl. furniture)	207	220	210	125	8146	9457	7208	6620	162	214	171	188
21	Paper and paper products	8	8	9	6	362	382	544	378	8	9	13	9
22	Printing and publishing	53	58	54	55	3463	3949	4033	3489	186	252	230	211
23	Coke,refined petroleum products,nuclear fuel	8	10	9	5	2473	2699	2580	2153	480	665	1001	937
24	Chemicals and chemical products	35	36	38	27	4949	5256	5479	5118	610	594	668	1055
25	Rubber and plastics products	29	38	36	45	3924	5142	4424	3356	106	161	178	133
26	Non-metallic mineral products	177	188	188	119	20009	23536	24610	25090	509	666	1022	916
27	Basic metals	9	13	11	11	2506	3486	3399	4813	309	435	322	533
28	Fabricated metal products	479	496	505	385	18411	21934	23078	23078	340	575	570	699
29	Machinery and equipment n.e.c.	11	16	19	15	706	1060	1033	859	50	27	49	30
30	Office, accounting and computing machinery	...	...	...	...	...	...	...	...	...	...	...	...
31	Electrical machinery and apparatus	7	15	24	29	233	761	874	724	11	32	29	40
32	Radio,television and communication equipment	...	...	...	...	...	...	...	...	...	...	...	...
33	Medical, precision and optical instruments	-	2	2	2	-	58	40	61	-	5	2	2
34	Motor vehicles, trailers, semi-trailers	4	4	5	7	227	273	116	366	5	7	2	23
35	Other transport equipment	7	6	5	5	36	42	73	50	1	1	2	3
36	Furniture; manufacturing n.e.c.	235	219	225	179	3155	3006	3374	3105	75	80	102	94
37	Recycling	3	3	5	7	127	127	254	320	4	4	8	19
D	Total manufacturing	2663	2698	2724	2187	82448	93767	94917	92579	3122	3999	4702	5203

Qatar

ISIC Revision 3			Output at producers' prices (millions of Qatari Riyals)					Value added at producers' prices (millions of Qatari Riyals)					Gross fixed capital formation (millions of Qatari Riyals)		
ISIC	Industry	Note	2007	2008	2009	2010	Note	2007	2008	2009	2010	Note	2009	2010
15	Food and beverages		937	1198	1326	1294		301	312	550	466		...	...
16	Tobacco products		...	...	...	...		...	...	...	...		...	...
17	Textiles		32	67	66	89		14	19	29	47		...	...
18	Wearing apparel, fur		668	407	560	493		372	243	344	233		...	...
19	Leather, leather products and footwear		12	12	41	30		5	2	22	17		...	...
20	Wood products (excl. furniture)		1171	1313	1107	651		511	565	505	352		...	...
21	Paper and paper products		150	61	110	66		77	24	58	37		...	...
22	Printing and publishing		957	794	1055	902		722	473	725	637		...	...
23	Coke,refined petroleum products,nuclear fuel		18615	21181	12508	31039		11778	7935	5058	13690		...	...
24	Chemicals and chemical products		9844	15506	10535	14925		7661	12290	6355	9119		...	...
25	Rubber and plastics products		746	1671	1639	972		171	468	724	389		...	...
26	Non-metallic mineral products		7785	22424	13589	9344		2215	8464	5565	3402		...	...
27	Basic metals		7187	8619	7302	10809		4012	4781	4831	6479		...	...
28	Fabricated metal products		2278	3306	5016	4455		871	1726	2228	1689		...	...
29	Machinery and equipment n.e.c.		100	97	3523	496		57	56	3354	193		...	...
30	Office, accounting and computing machinery		...	...	...	...		...	...	...	...		...	...
31	Electrical machinery and apparatus		143	210	461	388		67	70	187	249		...	...
32	Radio,television and communication equipment		...	...	...	...		...	...	...	...		...	...
33	Medical, precision and optical instruments		-	21	15	11		-	15	3	2		...	...
34	Motor vehicles, trailers, semi-trailers		35	31	19	82		18	18	6	58		...	...
35	Other transport equipment		4	2	8	17		2	1	4	11		...	...
36	Furniture; manufacturing n.e.c.		449	378	517	515		216	222	304	280		...	...
37	Recycling		19	14	62	39		8	3	18	30		...	...
D	Total manufacturing		51132	77312	59459	76617		29079	37687	30871	37380		...	...

Qatar

- 674 -

Index numbers of industrial production

ISIC Revision 3

(2005=100)

ISIC	Industry	Note	1999	2000	2001	2002	2003	2004	2005	2006	2007	2008	2009	2010
15	Food and beverages		...	...	...	...	...	...	...	...	...	...	...	
16	Tobacco products		...	...	...	...	...	...	...	...	...	...	...	
17	Textiles		...	...	...	...	...	...	...	...	...	...	...	
18	Wearing apparel, fur		...	...	...	...	...	...	...	...	...	...	...	
19	Leather, leather products and footwear		...	...	...	...	...	...	...	...	...	...	...	
20	Wood products (excl. furniture)		...	...	...	...	...	...	...	...	...	...	...	
21	Paper and paper products		...	...	...	...	...	...	...	...	...	...	...	
22	Printing and publishing		...	...	...	...	...	...	...	...	...	...	...	
23	Coke,refined petroleum products,nuclear fuel		...	...	...	...	...	...	...	...	...	...	...	
24	Chemicals and chemical products		...	...	...	...	...	...	...	...	...	...	...	
25	Rubber and plastics products		...	...	...	...	...	...	...	...	...	...	...	
26	Non-metallic mineral products		...	...	...	...	...	...	...	...	...	...	...	
27	Basic metals		...	...	...	...	...	...	...	...	...	...	...	
28	Fabricated metal products		...	...	...	...	...	...	...	...	...	...	...	
29	Machinery and equipment n.e.c.		...	...	...	...	...	...	...	...	...	...	...	
30	Office, accounting and computing machinery		...	...	...	...	...	...	...	...	...	...	...	
31	Electrical machinery and apparatus		...	...	...	...	...	...	...	...	...	...	...	
32	Radio,television and communication equipment		...	...	...	...	...	...	...	...	...	...	...	
33	Medical, precision and optical instruments		...	...	...	...	...	...	...	...	...	...	...	
34	Motor vehicles, trailers, semi-trailers		...	...	...	...	...	...	...	...	...	...	...	
35	Other transport equipment		...	...	...	...	...	...	...	...	...	...	...	
36	Furniture; manufacturing n.e.c.		...	...	...	...	...	...	...	...	...	...	...	
37	Recycling		...	...	...	...	...	...	...	...	...	...	...	
D	Total manufacturing		70	64	73	81	87	92	100	105	112	133	151	185

Republic of Moldova

Supplier of information:
National Bureau of Statistics of the Republic of Moldova, Chisinau.

Basic source of data:
Not reported.

Major deviations from ISIC (Revision 3):
None reported.

Reference period:
Calendar year.

Scope:
All self-sustained establishments. Data exclude the area of the left bank of the Dniester and the town of Bender.

Method of data collection:
Not reported.

Type of enumeration:
Not reported.

Adjusted for non-response:
Not reported.

Concepts and definitions of variables:
No deviations from the standard UN concepts and definitions are reported.

Related national publications:
None reported.

Republic of Moldova

ISIC	Industry (ISIC Revision 3)	Number of establishments (number)					Number of employees (number)					Wages and salaries paid to employees (thousands of Moldovan Lei)				
		Note	2007	2008	2009	2010	Note	2007	2008	2009	2010	Note	2007	2008	2009	2010
151	Processed meat,fish,fruit,vegetables,fats		46	46	61	72		8659	8595	7524	7642		192532	234534	197930	219772
1511	Processing/preserving of meat		15	17	25	34		2434	2486	2294	2984		55894	66437	64375	84304
1512	Processing/preserving of fish		2	2	1	3		235	363	281	219		4293	7230	6016	4194
1513	Processing/preserving of fruit & vegetables		27	25	31	29		4779	4619	3859	3433		92057	107242	75638	81474
1514	Vegetable and animal oils and fats		2	2	4	6		1211	1127	1090	1006		40288	53625	51902	49801
1520	Dairy products		13	12	16	14		3571	3429	3038	3073		96425	116664	117931	129609
153	Grain mill products; starches; animal feeds		13	11	14	15		1421	1268	962	888		20780	26849	18565	20189
1531	Grain mill products		10	8	13	13		1116	981	886	688		13158	17446	15995	13419
1532	Starches and starch products		-	-	-	-		...	...	...	...		...	...	...	...
1533	Prepared animal feeds		3	3	1	2		305	287	76	200		7622	9403	2570	6770
154	Other food products		69	66	51	57		9846	9150	9226	9589		267786	292309	284256	295221
1541	Bakery products		55	51	36	39		5922	5717	6274	6904		149896	164632	183296	203301
1542	Sugar		6	4	5	6		2228	1723	1269	833		58710	59784	39737	31256
1543	Cocoa, chocolate and sugar confectionery		3	4	3	4		1397	1439	1393	1391		53104	60428	53717	56528
1544	Macaroni, noodles & similar products		3	3	3	3		41	110	104	107		496	1959	2025	2154
1549	Other food products n.e.c.		2	2	4	5		...	...	...	...		...	...	...	...
155	Beverages		162	147	111	88		14931	13742	11653	10703		286866	333100	275723	287318
1551	Distilling, rectifying & blending of spirits		17	17	18	16		...	...	...	...		...	...	...	...
1552	Wines		127	114	80	61		9881	8862	7640	6924		137032	163808	140102	144570
1553	Malt liquors and malt		5	5	3	3		...	...	...	...		...	...	...	...
1554	Soft drinks; mineral waters		13	11	10	8		...	...	...	...		...	...	...	...
1600	Tobacco products		7	6	4	6		1467	1329	1200	1205		51580	53260	62483	73464
171	Spinning, weaving and finishing of textiles		5	5	3	3		...	...	...	...		...	...	...	...
1711	Textile fibre preparation; textile weaving		3	3	2	2		...	...	...	...		...	...	...	...
1712	Finishing of textiles		2	2	1	1		...	...	...	...		...	...	...	...
172	Other textiles		5	4	4	5		...	...	...	...		...	...	...	...
1721	Made-up textile articles, except apparel		1	1	1	2		...	...	...	...		...	...	...	...
1722	Carpets and rugs		2	2	2	2		...	...	...	...		...	...	...	...
1723	Cordage, rope, twine and netting		-	-	-	-		...	...	...	...		...	...	...	...
1729	Other textiles n.e.c.		2	1	-	1		...	...	...	...		...	...	...	...
1730	Knitted and crocheted fabrics and articles		3	3	4	4		...	...	...	...		...	...	...	...
1810	Wearing apparel, except fur apparel		43	46	53	48		...	...	...	...		...	...	...	...
1820	Dressing & dyeing of fur; processing of fur		1	1	-	-		...	...	...	...		...	...	...	...
191	Tanning, dressing and processing of leather		4	5	6	5		...	...	...	...		...	...	...	...
1911	Tanning and dressing of leather		1	1	1	1		...	...	...	...		...	...	...	...
1912	Luggage, handbags, etc.; saddlery & harness		3	4	5	4		...	...	...	...		...	...	...	...
1920	Footwear		8	8	7	10		...	...	...	...		...	...	...	...
2010	Sawmilling and planing of wood		3	2	4	4		...	...	...	...		...	...	...	...
202	Products of wood, cork, straw, etc.		9	8	5	9		...	...	...	...		...	...	...	...
2021	Veneer sheets, plywood, particle board, etc.		-	-	-	-		...	...	...	...		...	...	...	...
2022	Builders' carpentry and joinery		7	6	4	7		...	...	...	...		...	...	...	...
2023	Wooden containers		2	2	1	1		...	...	...	...		...	...	...	...
2029	Other wood products; articles of cork/straw		...	...	...	1		...	...	...	...		...	...	...	...
210	Paper and paper products		15	16	12	16		1610	1345	893	860		46512	39021	28631	25597
2101	Pulp, paper and paperboard		1	1	1	1		...	...	...	...		...	...	...	...
2102	Corrugated paper and paperboard		9	9	4	7		...	...	...	...		...	...	...	...
2109	Other articles of paper and paperboard		5	6	7	9		...	...	...	...		...	...	...	...
221	Publishing		2	3	5	6		...	...	...	...		...	...	...	...
2211	Publishing of books and other publications		1	2	4	4		...	...	...	...		...	...	...	...
2212	Publishing of newspapers, journals, etc.		1	1	1	1		...	...	...	...		...	...	...	...
2213	Publishing of recorded media		...	...	...	...		...	...	...	...		...	...	...	...
2219	Other publishing		...	...	...	1		...	...	...	...		...	...	...	...

Code	Description	23	24		
222	Printing and related service activities	:	:	20	27
2221	Printing	:	:	20	26
2222	Service activities related to printing	:	:	-	1
2230	Reproduction of recorded media	:	:	:	:
2310	Coke oven products	1	1	-	-
2320	Refined petroleum products	1	1	1	1
2330	Processing of nuclear fuel	-	-	-	-
241	Basic chemicals	2	3	1	2
2411	Basic chemicals, except fertilizers	1	1	1	-
2412	Fertilizers and nitrogen compounds	-	-	-	:
2413	Plastics in primary forms; synthetic rubber	1	2	1	2
242	Other chemicals	12	14	17	21
2421	Pesticides and other agro-chemical products	3	3	4	5
2422	Paints, varnishes, printing ink and mastics	7	7	8	11
2423	Pharmaceuticals, medicinal chemicals, etc.	2	3	4	3
2424	Soap, cleaning & cosmetic preparations	1	1	1	2
2429	Other chemical products n.e.c.	-	-	1	-
2430	Man-made fibres	-	-	-	-
251	Rubber products	:	:	1	:
2511	Rubber tyres and tubes	:	:	:	:
2519	Other rubber products	22	28	39	49
2520	Plastic products	5	6	6	5
2610	Glass and glass products	29	31	30	33
269	Non-metallic mineral products n.e.c.	1	1	1	-
2691	Pottery, china and earthenware	-	-	-	-
2692	Refractory ceramic products	4	4	4	3
2693	Struct.non-refractory clay; ceramic products	3	3	2	3
2694	Cement, lime and plaster	19	21	23	26
2695	Articles of concrete, cement and plaster	2	2	1	2
2696	Cutting, shaping & finishing of stone	:	:	:	:
2699	Other non-metallic mineral products n.e.c.	-	-	-	-
2710	Basic iron and steel	-	-	-	-
2720	Basic precious and non-ferrous metals	4	5	7	9
273	Casting of metals	:	5	7	9
2731	Casting of iron and steel	-	-	-	-
2732	Casting of non-ferrous metals	20	20	19	31
281	Struct.metal products;tanks;steam generators	17	17	17	29
2811	Structural metal products	3	3	2	2
2812	Tanks, reservoirs and containers of metal	-	-	-	-
2813	Steam generators	18	16	15	15
289	Other metal products; metal working services	1	1	1	-
2891	Metal forging/pressing/stamping/roll-forming	2	2	3	3
2892	Treatment & coating of metals	2	2	1	1
2893	Cutlery, hand tools and general hardware	11	11	10	11
2899	Other fabricated metal products n.e.c.	10	10	11	12
291	General purpose machinery	1	1	1	1
2911	Engines & turbines (not for transport equipment)	3	3	3	4
2912	Pumps, compressors, taps and valves	2	2	2	1
2913	Bearings, gears, gearing & driving elements	2	2	2	1
2914	Ovens, furnaces and furnace burners	2	2	3	3
2915	Lifting and handling equipment	2	2	3	3
2919	Other general purpose machinery	22	19	10	10
292	Special purpose machinery	15	12	5	4
2921	Agricultural and forestry machinery	3	3	1	2
2922	Machine tools	-	-	-	-
2923	Machinery for metallurgy	1	1	1	1
2924	Machinery for mining & construction	3	3	3	2
2925	Food/beverage/tobacco processing machinery	1	1	1	:
2926	Machinery for textile, apparel and leather	-	-	-	:
2927	Weapons and ammunition	:	:	:	:
2929	Other special purpose machinery	1	1	1	2

continued

Republic of Moldova

ISIC	Industry	Number of establishments (number)					Number of employees (number)					Wages and salaries paid to employees (thousands of Moldovan Lei)				
		Note	2007	2008	2009	2010	Note	2007	2008	2009	2010	Note	2007	2008	2009	2010
2930	Domestic appliances n.e.c.		2	2	2	1										
3000	Office, accounting and computing machinery		2	3	2	1		397	390	338	190		11973	17033	12659	10287
3110	Electric motors, generators and transformers		3	2	2	1										
3120	Electricity distribution & control apparatus		3	3	3	2										
3130	Insulated wire and cable		2	2	3	2										
3140	Accumulators, primary cells and batteries		1	2	2	2										
3150	Lighting equipment and electric lamps		1	1	-	-										
3190	Other electrical equipment n.e.c.		1	1	3	4										
3210	Electronic valves, tubes, etc.															
3220	TV/radio transmitters; line comm. apparatus		1	1	1	1										
3230	TV and radio receivers and associated goods		1	1	2	2										
331	Medical, measuring, testing appliances, etc.		7	7	8	10										
3311	Medical, surgical and orthopaedic equipment		1	1	1	2										
3312	Measuring/testing/navigating appliances,etc.		4	4	6	7										
3313	Industrial process control equipment		2	2	1	1										
3320	Optical instruments & photographic equipment		-	-	-	-										
3330	Watches and clocks															
3410	Motor vehicles		-	-	-	-										
3420	Automobile bodies, trailers & semi-trailers		-	-	-	-										
3430	Parts/accessories for automobiles		-	-	-	-										
351	Building and repairing of ships and boats		-	-	-	-										
3511	Building and repairing of ships		-	-	-	-										
3512	Building/repairing of pleasure/sport. boats		-	-	-	-										
3520	Railway/tramway locomotives & rolling stock		1	1	1	1										
3530	Aircraft and spacecraft															
359	Transport equipment n.e.c.															
3591	Motorcycles					1										
3592	Bicycles and invalid carriages															
3599	Other transport equipment n.e.c.					1										
3610	Furniture		21	21	26	33										
369	Manufacturing n.e.c.		3	2	2	3										
3691	Jewellery and related articles		1	1	1	1										
3692	Musical instruments		-	-	-	-										
3693	Sports goods															
3694	Games and toys		1	1	1	2										
3699	Other manufacturing n.e.c.		1	1	1											
3710	Recycling of metal waste and scrap		5	4	4	4										
3720	Recycling of non-metal waste and scrap															
D	Total manufacturing		630	618	595	644		97229	93366	81572	77495		2383524	2734564	2302914	2476235

Republic of Moldova

		Output at producers' prices (thousands of Moldovan Lei)					Value added (thousands of Moldovan Lei)					Gross fixed capital formation (thousands of Moldovan Lei)		
ISIC	Industry (ISIC Revision 3)	Note	2007	2008	2009	2010	Note	2007	2008	2009	2010	Note	2009	2010
151	Processed meat,fish,fruit,vegetables,fats		3399821	3888289	2997897	3652769	a/	2381455	2768848	2516020	3085999		…	…
1511	Processing/preserving of meat		1123692	1467662	1296083	1473746		…	…	…	…		…	…
1512	Processing/preserving of fish		68267	87577	82302	139507		…	…	…	…		…	…
1513	Processing/preserving of fruit & vegetables	a/	1277845	1148384	802429	1042797		…	…	…	…		…	…
1514	Vegetable and animal oils and fats	a/	930017	1184666	817084	996719		…	…	…	…		…	…
1520	Dairy products		1027618	1192415	1043040	1248493		…	…	…	…		…	…
153	Grain mill products; starches; animal feeds	a/	233462	302190	241417	310493		…	…	…	…		…	…
1531	Grain mill products		189928	221024	142073	150802		…	…	…	…		…	…
1532	Starches and starch products		43007	80496	99343	158479		…	…	…	…		…	…
1533	Prepared animal feeds		…	…	…	…		…	…	…	…		…	…
154	Other food products		1987001	2700903	2028626	3025446		…	…	…	…		…	…
1541	Bakery products		1056085	1266793	1185311	1371965		…	…	…	…		…	…
1542	Sugar		442834	876866	340497	1058026		…	…	…	…		…	…
1543	Cocoa, chocolate and sugar confectionery		405438	467749	419128	481330		…	…	…	…		…	…
1544	Macaroni, noodles & similar products		23336	36466	36914	39027		…	…	…	…		…	…
1549	Other food products n.e.c.		59308	53029	46776	75098		…	…	…	…		…	…
155	Beverages	a/	3304565	3697594	2945705	3500414		…	…	…	…		…	…
1551	Distilling, rectifying & blending of spirits		527786	556424	487154	529502		…	…	…	…		…	…
1552	Wines		1767710	2211131	1676290	2023118		…	…	…	…		…	…
1553	Malt liquors and malt		695186	596115	527405	623939		…	…	…	…		…	…
1554	Soft drinks; mineral waters		313883	333924	254857	323855	b/	78305	76335	108840	152319		…	…
1600	Tobacco products		368047	352573	499264	685524	b/	264682	249712	232021	280644		…	…
171	Spinning, weaving and finishing of textiles		124375	96496	75364	89549		…	…	…	…		…	…
1711	Textile fibre preparation; textile weaving		119907	89595	66652	77879		…	…	…	…		…	…
1712	Finishing of textiles		4468	6901	8712	11670		…	…	…	…		…	…
172	Other textiles		499619	476501	345229	382539		…	…	…	…		…	…
1721	Made-up textile articles, except apparel		17413	21184	40084	31687		…	…	…	…		…	…
1722	Carpets and rugs		474871	448083	300620	345084		…	…	…	…		…	…
1723	Cordage, rope, twine and netting		7251	7177	4512	5768		…	…	…	…		…	…
1729	Other textiles n.e.c.		…	…	…	…		…	…	…	…		…	…
1730	Knitted and crocheted fabrics and articles		46839	53082	66970	76141		…	…	…	…		…	…
1810	Wearing apparel, except fur apparel		895604	900613	799634	920609	c/	543958	611142	636007	713261		…	…
1820	Dressing & dyeing of fur; processing of fur		1587	2287	872	917		…	…	…	…		…	…
191	Tanning, dressing and processing of leather		87050	111359	65360	75644		…	…	…	…		…	…
1911	Tanning and dressing of leather		29796	35315	6647	…		…	…	…	…		…	…
1912	Luggage, handbags, etc.; saddlery & harness		57254	76044	58713	75644		…	…	…	…		…	…
1920	Footwear		173562	188714	168774	257415	d/	154715	165579	122989	152098		…	…
2010	Sawmilling and planing of wood		58519	99458	76611	56800		…	…	…	…		…	…
202	Products of wood, cork, straw, etc.		90845	99748	98212	98235		…	…	…	…		…	…
2021	Veneer sheets, plywood, particle board, etc.		63124	66024	68987	57227		…	…	…	…		…	…
2022	Builders' carpentry and joinery		20136	21367	13680	21155		…	…	…	…		…	…
2023	Wooden containers		7585	12357	15545	19250		…	…	…	…		…	…
2029	Other wood products; articles of cork/straw		…	…	…	…		…	…	…	…		…	…
210	Paper and paper products		595819	415814	296660	317019	e/	220571	260201	234273	263973		…	…
2101	Pulp, paper and paperboard		345968	109437	2252	838		…	…	…	…		…	…
2102	Corrugated paper and paperboard		85100	116209	109846	168118		…	…	…	…		…	…
2109	Other articles of paper and paperboard		164751	190168	184563	148063	e/	97399	134053	97965	102487		…	…
221	Publishing	f/	214667	212202	159772	222778	f/	88121	69222	54053	59913	f/	28426	37774
2211	Publishing of books and other publications		125097	114698	55942	91090		…	…	…	…		…	…
2212	Publishing of newspapers, journals, etc.		86537	93329	87831	94913		…	…	…	…		…	…
2213	Publishing of recorded media		363	95	77	-		…	…	…	…		…	…
2219	Other publishing		2670	4080	15922	36775		…	…	…	…		…	…

continued

Republic of Moldova

ISIC	Industry	Out. Note	Output 2007	2008	2009	2010	VA Note	Value added 2007	2008	2009	2010	GFCF Note	GFCF 2009	2010
			(thousands of Moldovan Lei)					(thousands of Moldovan Lei)					(thousands of Moldovan Lei)	
222	Printing and related service activities	f/	328998	383376	351650	396432	f/							
2221	Printing		323689	377641	342311	383523								
2222	Service activities related to printing		5309	5735	9339	12909								
2230	Reproduction of recorded media	f/	811	...	887	-	f/							
2310	Coke oven products													
2320	Refined petroleum products	g/	52152	37259	43588	75900	g/							
2330	Processing of nuclear fuel	g/					g/							
241	Basic chemicals		30277	49087	53971	65206								
2411	Basic chemicals, except fertilizers	g/	6940	7415	7951	12515	g/							
2412	Fertilizers and nitrogen compounds													
2413	Plastics in primary forms; synthetic rubber		23337	41672	46020	52691								
242	Other chemicals		348884	474911	538051	693132		100690	131116	155068	195810			
2421	Pesticides and other agro-chemical products	g/	1062	1286	1528	4004	g/							
2422	Paints, varnishes, printing ink and mastics		162382	252627	228030	276043								
2423	Pharmaceuticals, medicinal chemicals, etc.		105528	141412	252672	341644								
2424	Soap, cleaning & cosmetic preparations		55570	49756	35130	40699								
2429	Other chemical products n.e.c.		24342	29830	20690	30742								
2430	Man-made fibres						g/							
251	Rubber products		9443	4969	4274	6373								
2511	Rubber tyres and tubes	h/	...	...	1904	2413	h/							
2519	Other rubber products		9443	4969	2370	3960								
2520	Plastic products		1008242	1029112	763786	939329								
2610	Glass and glass products	h/	707969	785240	633597	751127	h/	278607	234997	183999	212016			
269	Non-metallic mineral products n.e.c.		2569054	2892378	1521402	1693834		1019760	1052336	598506	663265			
2691	Pottery, china and earthenware	i/	9023	2702	2195	1943	i/							
2692	Refractory ceramic products													
2693	Struct.non-refractory clay; ceramic products	i/	226272	210799	120279	131398	i/							
2694	Cement, lime and plaster		1366994	1631048	551618	531111								
2695	Articles of concrete, cement and plaster		897105	995727	813690	987032								
2696	Cutting, shaping & finishing of stone		44670	49000	32802	40829								
2699	Other non-metallic mineral products n.e.c.		24990	3102	818	1521								
2710	Basic iron and steel													
2720	Basic precious and non-ferrous metals	j/	151133	209802	147571	241166	j/	55187	72836	48585	78977			
273	Casting of metals		151125	209802	147571	241166								
2731	Casting of iron and steel	j/					j/							
2732	Casting of non-ferrous metals	j/					j/							
281	Struct.metal products;tanks;steam generators	k/	424020	498330	329744	335931	k/	144933	245698	215313	229995	k/	639562	770425
2811	Structural metal products		385832	442866	306677	309260								
2812	Tanks, reservoirs and containers of metal		38188	55464	23066	26671								
2813	Steam generators													
289	Other metal products; metal working services	k/	208625	217995	156653	227377	k/					k/		
2891	Metal forging/pressing/stamping/roll-forming		4286	358	168	486								
2892	Treatment & coating of metals		19760	17158	23268	38838								
2893	Cutlery, hand tools and general hardware		40737	44326	10877	14595								
2899	Other fabricated metal products n.e.c.		143842	156153	122340	173458								
291	General purpose machinery	m/	239460	266078	172203	272588	m/	183072	237968	193855	240745	m/	1075258	1551269
2911	Engines & turbines (not for transport equipment)		9914	13238	15124	11907								
2912	Pumps, compressors, taps and valves		104354	112222	56297	114845								
2913	Bearings, gears, gearing & driving elements		1114	1470	660	506								
2914	Ovens, furnaces and furnace burners		13337	9944	8223	13400								
2915	Lifting and handling equipment		41337	50211	46559	69538								
2919	Other general purpose machinery		69404	78993	45340	62392								

Code	Description					fn					fn		
292	Special purpose machinery	236504	273547	170668	205795								
2921	Agricultural and forestry machinery	174402	174540	112766	127455								
2922	Machine tools	20103	18318	5556	4905								
2923	Machinery for metallurgy	6193	8130	3030	10214								
2924	Machinery for mining & construction	12587	17846	15826	27446								
2925	Food/beverage/tobacco processing machinery	5982	8425	842	1177								
2926	Machinery for textile, apparel and leather			8267	9923								
2927	Weapons and ammunition	17237	22565	24381	24675								
2929	Other special purpose machinery	38603	23723	17480	23851							211758	255085
2930	Domestic appliances n.e.c.	29544	38108	25225	25225	m/	27063	37310	19133	15126	m/	504015	517734
3000	Office, accounting and computing machinery	46073	59530	31430	35621								
3110	Electric motors, generators and transformers	32913	35736	23962	30566	n/	74813 n/	182035 n/			n/		
3120	Electricity distribution & control apparatus	23763	94858	132793	132033	n/					n/		
3130	Insulated wire and cable	4482	2535	2116	2123	n/					n/		
3140	Accumulators, primary cells and batteries	3317	37203	35512	48527	n/					n/		
3150	Lighting equipment and electric lamps	27962	348	257		n/					n/		
3190	Other electrical equipment n.e.c.	388	15229	16531	16531								
3210	Electronic valves, tubes, etc.	22507	27271	6008	31647	p/	19391 p/	39993 p/			p/	240322	269495
3220	TV/radio transmitters; line comm. apparatus	26841		32928		p/					p/		
3230	TV and radio receivers and associated goods		349493			q/	174440	183920	119123	161522	q/	301086	384538
331	Medical, measuring, testing appliances, etc.	326927	28097	184321	248793								
3311	Medical, surgical and orthopaedic equipment	25316	273330	22379	25869								
3312	Measuring/testing/navigating appliances,etc.	215205	48066	151325	182603								
3313	Industrial process control equipment	86406	2179	10617	40321	q/					q/		
3320	Optical instruments & photographic equipment	1807		2414	2496	q/			22462	23015	q/		
3330	Watches and clocks							16878					
3410	Motor vehicles					r/	14190				s/	1311277	1890504
3420	Automobile bodies, trailers & semi-trailers					r/							
3430	Parts/accessories for automobiles					r/					s/		
351	Building and repairing of ships and boats					r/							
3511	Building and repairing of ships										s/		
3512	Building/repairing of pleasure/sport. boats	5952	11058	1309	20706	r/					s/		
3520	Railway/tramway locomotives & rolling stock	2940	7054	2131	2943	r/					s/		
3530	Aircraft and spacecraft	25	19007	13212	13215								
359	Transport equipment n.e.c.												
3591	Motorcycles	25	19007	13212	13215								
3592	Bicycles and invalid carriages												
3599	Other transport equipment n.e.c.					t/	205144	239862	254619	267480			
3610	Furniture	567396	640273	555264	615399	t/							
369	Manufacturing n.e.c.	54396	47442	52998	57783								
3691	Jewellery and related articles	35345	31266	20312	15521								
3692	Musical instruments	1601	1239	1086	4683								
3693	Sports goods	13358	11778	25207	30529								
3694	Games and toys	4092	3159	6393	7050								
3699	Other manufacturing n.e.c.	749075	725538	173635	650570	u/	173695	83906	27162	98019			
3710	Recycling of metal waste and scrap	769	3827	1851	1689	u/							
3720	Recycling of non-metal waste and scrap												
D	Total manufacturing	21390252	24045451	18080229	22784950		6300191	7093947	6390778	7618917		4311704	5676824

a/ 151 includes 1520, 153, 154 and 155.
b/ 171 includes 172 and 1730.
c/ 1810 includes 1820.
d/ 191 includes 1920.
e/ 2010 includes 202.
f/ 221 includes 222 and 2230.
g/ 2310 includes 2320, 2330, 241, 242 and 2430.
h/ 251 includes 2520.
i/ 2610 includes 269.
j/ 2710 includes 2720 and 273.

k/ 281 includes 289.
m/ 291 includes 292 and 2930.
n/ 3110 includes 3120, 3130, 3140, 3150 and 3190.
p/ 3210 includes 3220 and 3230.
q/ 331 includes 3320 and 3330.
r/ 3410 includes 3420, 3430, 351, 3520, 3530 and 359.
s/ 351 includes 3420, 3430, 3520, 3530 and 359.
t/ 3610 includes 369.
u/ 3710 includes 3720.

Republic of Moldova

ISIC Revision 3

Index numbers of industrial production

(2005=100)

ISIC	Industry	Note	1999	2000	2001	2002	2003	2004	2005	2006	2007	2008	2009	2010
15	Food and beverages		48	55	65	76	90	95	100	82	75	82	68	76
16	Tobacco products		180	169	164	110	110	105	100	78	72	62	73	76
17	Textiles		41	55	70	81	90	102	100	121	133	123	92	93
18	Wearing apparel, fur		54	68	77	80	81	95	100	104	100	123	75	91
19	Leather, leather products and footwear		36	43	43	57	69	86	100	103	107	111	64	82
20	Wood products (excl. furniture)		62	107	155	158	125	116	100	104	91	112	75	75
21	Paper and paper products		14	24	33	43	78	84	100	89	104	75	55	73
22	Printing and publishing		44	56	62	67	89	89	100	90	84	79	59	62
23	Coke,refined petroleum products,nuclear fuel		..	..	..	..	..	..	..	..	..	..	..	58
24	Chemicals and chemical products		60	60	76	82	66	78	100	112	123	134	123	143
25	Rubber and plastics products		14	27	31	52	77	85	100	124	130	131	96	97
26	Non-metallic mineral products		29	49	53	67	73	83	100	112	120	114	70	76
27	Basic metals		50	51	67	52	61	67	100	122	125	162	123	138
28	Fabricated metal products		36	40	41	50	71	88	100	117	126	117	81	80
29	Machinery and equipment n.e.c.		46	62	76	84	99	110	100	101	102	99	61	76
30	Office, accounting and computing machinery		..	..	..	..	..	..	..	..	..	..	..	..
31	Electrical machinery and apparatus		99	95	89	88	120	179	100	103	84	144	155	151
32	Radio,television and communication equipment		81	77	79	138	165	170	100	95	107	98	99	96
33	Medical, precision and optical instruments		87	77	74	85	116	119	100	174	224	219	108	141
34	Motor vehicles, trailers, semi-trailers		..	..	..	..	..	..	..	..	..	..	..	..
35	Other transport equipment		..	..	..	..	..	..	..	..	..	..	..	..
36	Furniture; manufacturing n.e.c.		..	..	..	..	..	..	..	..	..	..	..	..
37	Recycling		..	..	..	..	..	..	..	..	..	..	..	..
D	Total manufacturing		47	56	64	73	86	94	100	94	92	93	72	80

Romania

Supplier of information:
National Commission for Statistics, Bucharest.

Basic source of data:
Annual survey; administrative source.

Major deviations from ISIC (Revision 4):
The data presented in ISIC (Revision 4) were originally classified according to NACE (Revision 2).

Reference period:
Calendar year.

Scope:
All registered enterprises.

Method of data collection:
Mail questionnaires.

Type of enumeration:
Sample survey.

Adjusted for non-response:
Yes.

Concepts and definitions of variables:
Wages and salaries excludes payments in kind.
Output data refers to turnover.

Related national publications:
Annuaire Statistique de la Roumanie, published by the National Institute of Statistics, Bucharest.

Romania

		Number of enterprises (number)					Number of employees (number)					Wages and salaries paid to employees (millions of Romanian Lei)				
ISIC	Industry	Note	2007	2008	2009	2010	Note	2007	2008	2009	2010	Note	2007	2008	2009	2010
1010	Processing/preserving of meat		945	950	880	844		174344a/	43295	40320	40957		2477.0a/	769.4	637.8	735.2
1020	Processing/preserving of fish, etc.		36	40	35	31		..a/	1581	1365	1384		..a/	25.6	18.9	20.1
1030	Processing/preserving of fruit,vegetables		297	287	272	270		..a/	5265	5613	5240		..a/	109.0	104.6	103.8
1040	Vegetable and animal oils and fats		255	248	217	178		..a/	3850	3337	2936		..a/	111.4	84.8	85.6
1050	Dairy products		711	676	642	565		..a/	17595	16369	14882		..a/	362.2	298.9	282.1
106	Grain mill products,starches and starch products		1471	1320	1114	965		..a/	13066	12265	12086		..a/	227.3	193.8	188.6
1061	Grain mill products		1450	1292	1090	942		...	12632	11830	11628		...	215.3	183.5	178.4
1062	Starches and starch products		21	28	24	23		...	434	435	458		...	12.0	10.3	10.2
107	Other food products		5539	5329	5393	5135		..a/	86735	83323	82348		..a/	1347.8	1075.5	1055.9
1071	Bakery products		4714	4503	4564	4396		...	69571	67591	66584		...	923.2	732.4	733.7
1072	Sugar		17	20	17	20		...	2118	2065	2028		...	63.6	52.5	50.5
1073	Cocoa, chocolate and sugar confectionery		248	243	266	247		...	6780	6294	6997		...	183.8	161.3	139.5
1074	Macaroni, noodles, couscous, etc.		72	80	80	76		...	903	929	941		...	16.3	15.0	15.2
1075	Prepared meals and dishes		12	14	38	48		...	119	274	292		...	1.4	1.7	2.5
1079	Other food products n.e.c.		476	469	428	348		...	7244	6170	5506		...	159.5	112.6	114.5
1080	Prepared animal feeds		135	144	164	138		..a/	2209	2233	1832		..a/	68.7	40.2	36.4
1101	Distilling, rectifying and blending of spirits		240	201	169	140		31864b/	4415	3773	2718		785.0b/	76.6	63.4	53.5
1102	Wines		195	216	216	208		..b/	5553	4448	3719		..b/	...	...	...
1103	Malt liquors and malt		52	44	42	42		..b/	7331	6870	6220		..b/	...	...	...
1104	Soft drinks,mineral waters,other bottled waters		485	498	517	412		..b/	14172	11376	10555		..b/	401.4	309.1	311.6
1200	Tobacco products		31	20	18	16		1818	1618	1591	1520					
131	Spinning, weaving and finishing of textiles		390	372	328	291		40238c/	15681	11402	10677		542.0c/	278.7	178.5	179.9
1311	Preparation and spinning of textile fibres		108	102	81	71		...	5177	4415	4403		...	93.1	72.1	76.8
1312	Weaving of textiles		157	151	129	115		...	6938	4945	4505		...	124.1	76.4	74.9
1313	Finishing of textiles		125	119	118	105		...	3566	2042	1769		...	61.5	30.0	28.2
139	Other textiles		1491	1417	1323	1219		..c/	20143	16855	17086		..c/	317.5	220.8	239.2
1391	Knitted and crocheted fabrics		21	29	25	25		...	318	216	290		...	4.6	3.1	3.9
1392	Made-up textile articles, except apparel		1099	1027	959	851		...	15093	12776	13180		...	236.2	162.6	182.2
1393	Carpets and rugs		41	41	33	28		...	799	502	421		...	13.0	6.6	6.2
1394	Cordage, rope, twine and netting		29	28	33	29		...	396	349	302		...	7.6	5.7	5.5
1399	Other textiles n.e.c.		301	292	273	286		...	3537	3012	2893		...	56.1	42.8	41.4
1410	Wearing apparel, except fur apparel		5703	5408	4947	4159		247584d/	188441	153299	141445		2988.0d/	2631.8	1801.0	1768.5
1420	Articles of fur		85	78	65	56		..d/	548	285	245		..d/	6.7	2.9	2.0
1430	Knitted and crocheted apparel		515	470	420	356		..d/	18640	14347	12857		..d/	264.3	181.9	183.4
151	Leather;luggage,handbags,saddlery,harness;fur		439	409	381	342		87182e/	7983	6156	6234		1066.0e/	125.6	81.5	94.2
1511	Tanning/dressing of leather; dressing of fur		84	77	73	56		..e/	883	573	491		...	14.5	9.0	6.8
1512	Luggage,handbags,etc.;saddlery/harness		355	332	308	286		...	7100	5583	5743		...	111.1	72.5	87.4
1520	Footwear		1644	1553	1408	1249		..e/	64726	53239	51343		..e/	932.7	661.7	666.5
1610	Sawmilling and planing of wood		4250	4337	3808	3422		78107f/	39419	30311	28246		852.0f/	428.6	284.0	273.1
162	Wood products, cork, straw, plaiting materials		3148	3670	2591	2388		..f/	33584	26175	25310		..f/	548.2	386.2	390.3

Code	Industry												
1621	Veneer sheets and wood-based panels	240	228	164	152	...	8242	6549	6729	...	171.3	129.2	143.6
1622	Builders' carpentry and joinery	1879	2451	1699	1532	...	17599	13547	12555	...	276.6	189.5	171.9
1623	Wooden containers	200	218	186	181	...	1789	1344	1526	...	21.9	15.9	17.2
1629	Other wood products;articles of cork,straw	829	773	542	523	...	5954	4735	4500	...	78.4	51.6	57.6
1701	Pulp, paper and paperboard	42	43	46	63	17452g/	3316	2466	2179	316.0g/	...	...	49.4
1702	Corrugated paper and paperboard	374	372	379	332	..g/	7088	5894	5329	..g/	90.7	65.6	97.0
1709	Other articles of paper and paperboard	442	402	384	365	..g/	4985	4456	4483	..g/	...	...	73.0
181	Printing and service activities related to printing	2181	2328	2187	1979	19014h/	20200	18502	16851	365.0h/	467.4	346.8	312.4
1811	Printing	1584	1657	1632	1506	...	17635	16141	14744	...	416.3	299.5	271.7
1812	Service activities related to printing	597	671	555	473	...	2565	2361	2107	...	51.1	47.3	40.7
1820	Reproduction of recorded media	162	149	139	109	..h/	482	443	364	..h/	10.5	7.4	6.3
1910	Coke oven products	7	5	7	9	6571i/	49	40	46	...	...	...	0.5
1920	Refined petroleum products	35	37	49	51	..i/	4959	4232	3896	953.0i/	...	...	...
201	Basic chemicals,fertilizers, etc.	331	344	322	323	35975i/	23771	21536	21134	..i/	778.3	549.2	593.0
2011	Basic chemicals	211	216	212	217	...	15130	13485	12921	...	196.3	134.3	375.5
2012	Fertilizers and nitrogen compounds	23	26	27	23	...	6579	6424	6568	...	301.3	229.0	160.3
2013	Plastics and synthetic rubber in primary forms	97	102	83	83	..i/	2062	1627	1645	...	149.1	103.7	57.2
202	Other chemical products	707	706	665	615	...	10613	9244	8663	...	110.6	89.6	214.2
2021	Pesticides and other agrochemical products	25	51	31	30	...	458	483	477	...	...	...	...
2022	Paints,varnishes;printing ink and mastics	197	204	226	207	...	4998	4216	3799	...	41.6	35.7	96.9
2023	Soap,cleaning and cosmetic preparations	238	228	216	204	...	3198	2910	2913	...	...	...	91.0
2029	Other chemical products n.e.c.	247	223	192	174	...	1959	1635	1474	...	...	...	26.3
2030	Man-made fibres	17	16	13	11	9946	1031	845	918	344.0	...	...	...
2100	Pharmaceuticals,medicinal chemicals, etc.	131	138	133	135	51320k/	9415	9008	8836	892.0k/	343.2	296.6	314.3
221	Rubber products	400	482	352	302	...	13382	12010	12427	...	342.0	279.3	319.8
2211	Rubber tyres and tubes	96	196	82	74	...	6404	6513	6650	...	199.1	173.7	203.1
2219	Other rubber products	304	286	270	228	..k/	6978	5497	5777	..k/	142.9	105.6	116.7
2220	Plastics products	2536	2721	2988	2657	58903m/	40922	36104	33785	1217.0m/	776.5	575.5	578.0
2310	Glass and glass products	597	604	580	481	..m/	9290	7175	6590	..m/	176.6	116.0	107.5
239	Non-metallic mineral products n.e.c.	2558	2692	2638	2289	...	47524	39062	34048	...	1249.7	885.5	806.7
2391	Refractory products	41	39	31	33	...	1328	970	960	...	25.1	16.4	17.7
2392	Clay building materials	318	324	259	201	...	6703	4252	3404	...	143.0	83.9	71.8
2393	Other porcelain and ceramic products	228	206	192	165	...	7807	6183	5913	...	159.6	105.1	114.5
2394	Cement, lime and plaster	74	80	75	66	...	4026	3791	3516	...	232.0	183.5	165.5
2395	Articles of concrete, cement and plaster	1320	1440	1418	1205	...	21413	18372	15298	...	549.7	399.2	344.5
2396	Cutting, shaping and finishing of stone	482	511	546	513	...	3300	2914	2588	...	49.4	35.4	33.3
2399	Other non-metallic mineral products n.e.c.	95	92	117	106	...	2947	2580	2369	...	90.9	62.0	59.4
2410	Basic iron and steel	222	216	205	203	58243n/	38206	31721	27745	1679.0n/	1194.6	1024.8	864.0
2420	Basic precious and other non-ferrous metals	70	68	72	67	..n/	8116	5948	5708	..n/	377.8	200.6	199.3
243	Casting of metals	228	229	221	193	..n/	6401	4720	4294	..n/	132.6	81.3	77.6
2431	Casting of iron and steel	141	146	143	65	...	4236	2874	2175	...	...	...	...
2432	Casting of non-ferrous metals	87	83	78	128	...	2165	1846	2119	...	...	...	...
251	Struct.metal products, tanks, reservoirs	4356	4478	4419	3576	112005p/	65648	52825	44810	2087.0p/	1335.6	889.0	766.5
2511	Structural metal products	4213	4330	4271	3435	...	57364	46270	39362	...	1100.8	739.9	640.5
2512	Tanks, reservoirs and containers of metal	119	126	120	121	...	5835	4301	3935	...	146.4	83.8	84.7

continued

Romania

| ISIC Revision 4 | | Number of enterprises | | | | | Number of employees | | | | | Wages and salaries paid to employees | | | | |
| | | | (number) | | | | | (number) | | | | | (millions of Romanian Lei) | | | |
ISIC	Industry	Note	2007	2008	2009	2010	Note	2007	2008	2009	2010	Note	2007	2008	2009	2010
2513	Steam generators, excl. hot water boilers		24	22	28	20		...	2449	2254	1513		...	88.4	65.3	41.3
2520	Weapons and ammunition		28	25	23	18		...p/	...q/	...q/	...q/		...p/	...q/	...q/	...q/
259	Other metal products;metal working services		2445	2568	2564	2320		...p/	48660	39145	37355		...p/	1067.9	731.4	741.1
2591	Forging,pressing,stamping,roll-forming of metal		201	211	205	194		...	5013	3881	3437		...	122.7	80.3	73.9
2592	Treatment and coating of metals; machining		1076	1175	1286	1123		...	15557	13645	12884		...	337.9	237.6	234.9
2593	Cutlery, hand tools and general hardware		280	279	265	248		...	6832	4902	4739		...	159.2	98.9	99.8
2599	Other fabricated metal products n.e.c.		888	903	808	755		...	21258q/	16717q/	16295q/		...	448.1q/	314.6q/	332.5q/
2610	Electronic components and boards		185	198	167	167		29568r/	10925	8125	9450		721.0r/	295.6	183.5	233.5
2620	Computers and peripheral equipment		442	455	391	319		...r/	3756	3617	3607		...r/	109.1	70.7	75.8
2630	Communication equipment		106	114	102	87		...r/	3806	4542	4099		...r/	...	...	...
2640	Consumer electronics		10	27	28	21		...r/	381	217	269		...r/	6.7	2.9	...
265	Measuring,testing equipment; watches, etc.		189	205	202	191		...r/	6229	6075	5991		...r/	...	...	...
2651	Measuring/testing/navigating equipment,etc.		189	205	202	191		...r/	6229	6075	5991		...r/	...	162.5	183.5
2652	Watches and clocks							...	...	...	27		...	...	...	...
2660	Irradiation/electromedical equipment,etc.		22	42	51	59		...r/	570	498	462		...r/	11.9	8.7	7.5
2670	Optical instruments and photographic equipment		167	171	150	142		...r/	1238	988	968		...r/	24.6	16.2	15.1
2680	Magnetic and optical media		2	1	1	2		...r/	8	8	9		...r/	...	...	...
2710	Electric motors,generators,transformers,etc.		382	382	331	304		49701s/	16541	14417	13677		931.0s/	377.2	294.3	...
2720	Batteries and accumulators		10	10	10	6		...s/	774	769	747		...s/	...	...	...
273	Wiring and wiring devices		56	62	63	60		...s/	5511	4128	4323		...s/	136.2	93.1	107.6
2731	Fibre optic cables		4	4	5	6		...	114	91	52		...	...	...	1.6
2732	Other electronic and electric wires and cables		42	45	39	35		...s/	4351	3161	3145		...s/	117.3	74.1	85.0
2733	Wiring devices		10	13	19	19		...	1046	876	1126		...	18.9	...	21.0
2740	Electric lighting equipment		128	137	125	102		...s/	9664	3752	2767		...s/	184.7	77.7	62.3
2750	Domestic appliances		77	70	75	69		...s/	10595	8555	8576		...s/	...	...	...
2790	Other electrical equipment		144	152	127	132		...s/	5546	5173	6045		...s/	117.7	96.1	127.6
281	General-purpose machinery		831	870	857	827		74560t/	35394	29881	27522		1595.0t/	973.6	693.9	682.8
2811	Engines/turbines,excl.aircraft,vehicle engines		60	44	69	80		...	8757	8322	7681		...	291.7	222.0	...
2812	Fluid power equipment		...	...	...	...		...	...	...	413		...	...	...	6.9
2813	Other pumps, compressors, taps and valves		108	110	107	117		...	5170	3659	3295		...	...	...	...
2814	Bearings, gears, gearing and driving elements		61	63	63	59		...	9528	7478	6629		...	258.0	164.7	167.9
2815	Ovens, furnaces and furnace burners		19	26	30	33		...	559	579	735		...	23.7	20.8	27.4
2816	Lifting and handling equipment		272	304	270	240		...	6539	5500	4629		...	162.4	118.1	102.5
2817	Office machinery, excl.computers,etc.		43	40	31	35		...	270	661	708		...	...	...	...
2818	Power-driven hand tools		39	33	22	20		...	838	657	730		...	23.4	...	...
2819	Other general-purpose machinery		229	250	265	243		...	3733	3025	2702		...	90.8	61.7	58.5
282	Special-purpose machinery		578	611	591	557		...t/	33599	27204	23380		...t/	874.1	583.1	344.9
2821	Agricultural and forestry machinery		84	82	65	68		...t/	3455	2473	2081		...	73.1	42.5	38.1
2822	Metal-forming machinery and machine tools		125	150	163	151		...	5551	4452	4140		...	145.5	97.3	92.0
2823	Machinery for metallurgy		25	25	24	22		...	6258	4821	3473		...	165.9	97.2	69.4
2824	Mining, quarrying and construction machinery		73	78	75	70		...	10953	1039	914		...	304.6	17.1	...

2825	Food/beverage/tobacco processing machinery	88	90	96	80	...	1209	621	629	...	22.5	12.2	13.0
2826	Textile/apparel/leather production machinery	37	31	23	24	...	939	4596	4603	...	21.4	110.3	113.8
2829	Other special-purpose machinery	146	155	145	142	...	5234	9202	7540	...	141.1	206.5	...
2910	Motor vehicles	27	35	29	28	105175u/	18350	17355	17464	2289.0u/	...	...	...
2920	Automobile bodies, trailers and semi-trailers	62	82	85	75	...u/	2401	1818	1620	...u/	...	...	...
2930	Parts and accessories for motor vehicles	398	424	398	359	...u/	92416	89971	97072	...u/	2211.2	1896.6	2242.7
301	Building of ships and boats	138	256	341	316	39920v/	23236	22237	17410	1038.0v/	817.2	628.9	560.6
3011	Building of ships and floating structures	90	203	295	276	...	22916	21983	17196	...	812.5	626.1	558.1
3012	Building of pleasure and sporting boats	48	53	46	40	...	320	254	214	...	4.7	2.8	2.5
3020	Railway locomotives and rolling stock	78	68	63	58	...v/	13828w/	10799w/	8713w/	...v/	378.0w/	259.2w/	213.2w/
3030	Air and spacecraft and related machinery	23	20	18	21	...v/	3053	4238	3528	...v/	127.6	124.6	121.2
3040	Military fighting vehicles	...	1	1	2	...v/	...w/	...w/	...w/	...v/	...w/	...w/	...w/
309	Transport equipment n.e.c.	15	15	16	20	...v/	900	838	927	...v/	14.9	12.9	16.6
3091	Motorcycles	3	2	2	2	...	3	3	3	...	...	...	...
3092	Bicycles and invalid carriages	11	12	14	17	...	884	835	924	...	14.7	...	16.6
3099	Other transport equipment n.e.c.	1	1	...	1	...	13	...	...	...	...	...	...
3100	Furniture	4278	4472	4449	3763	86829	80376	65041	59810	1147.0	1277.3	863.8	810.4
321	Jewellery, bijouterie and related articles	380	387	400	350	14876x/	2375	2256	2193	199.0x/	...	29.4	29.9
3211	Jewellery and related articles	332	336	343	311	...	2018	1928	1850	...	...	...	...
3212	Imitation jewellery and related articles	48	51	57	39	...	357	328	343	...	...	...	...
3220	Musical instruments	43	36	39	45	...x/	1019	857	912	...x/	15.7	12.3	14.1
3230	Sports goods	56	52	49	46	...x/	1333	1361	1446	...x/	29.2	24.9	29.1
3240	Games and toys	111	106	103	96	...x/	1384	1225	1342	...x/	17.7	14.0	18.1
3250	Medical and dental instruments and supplies	611	650	821	747	...x/	3381	3872	3616	...x/	51.9	48.5	46.7
3290	Other manufacturing n.e.c.	654	691	656	585	...x/	5370	4571	4226	...x/	...	...	57.0
331	Repair of fabricated metal products/machinery	825	1087	1541	1641	35497y/	34111	27705	24324	798.0y/	944.8	571.8	529.5
3311	Repair of fabricated metal products	44	70	81	87	...	3420	1602	1073	...	127.5	23.7	14.6
3312	Repair of machinery	218	347	653	682	...	6105	5712	6181	...	169.2	132.8	155.7
3313	Repair of electronic and optical equipment	15	39	144	195	...	138	413	604	...	2.0	3.4	8.3
3314	Repair of electrical equipment	32	72	171	191	...	2065	1842	1671	...	...	49.2	...
3315	Repair of transport equip., excl. motor vehicles	512	531	433	387	...	22251	17915	14593	...	...	...	...
3319	Repair of other equipment	4	28	59	99	...	132	221	202	...	1.4	...	3.3
3320	Installation of industrial machinery/equipment	286	306	373	345	...y/	3333	3080	2907	...y/	83.5	71.2	61.0
C	Total manufacturing	57240	58505	55989	50066	1466692	1391311	1185201	1118703	25281.0	29161.8	21468.2	21538.7

a/ 1010 includes 1020, 1030, 1040, 1050, 106, 107 and 1080.
b/ 1101 includes 1102, 1103 and 1104.
c/ 131 includes 139.
d/ 1410 includes 1420 and 1430.
e/ 151 includes 1520.
f/ 1610 includes 162.
g/ 1701 includes 1702 and 1709.
h/ 181 includes 1820.
i/ 1910 includes 1920.
j/ 201 includes 202 and 2030.
k/ 221 includes 2220.
m/ 2310 includes 239.
n/ 2410 includes 2420 and 243.
p/ 251 includes 2520 and 259.
q/ 2599 includes 2520.
r/ 2610 includes 2620, 2630, 2640, 265, 2660, 2670 and 2680.
s/ 2710 includes 2720, 273, 2740, 2750 and 2790.
t/ 281 includes 282.
u/ 2910 includes 2920 and 2930.
v/ 301 includes 3020, 3030, 3040 and 309.
w/ 3020 includes 3040.
x/ 321 includes 3220, 3230, 3240, 3250 and 3290.
y/ 331 includes 3320.

Romania

ISIC	Industry	Output at factor values (millions of Romanian Lei)					Value added at factor values (millions of Romanian Lei)					Gross fixed capital formation (millions of Romanian Lei)		
		Note	2007	2008	2009	2010	Note	2007	2008	2009	2010	Note	2009	2010
1010	Processing/preserving of meat		24287.0a/	9123.3	9658.7	9929.3		4392.0a/	1637.0	1657.1	1586.6		...	...
1020	Processing/preserving of fish, etc.		...a/	249.6	312.5	305.6		...a/	62.6	58.8	59.6		...	...
1030	Processing/preserving of fruit,vegetables		...a/	1287.9	1621.7	1583.9		...a/	301.6	290.2	349.7		...	...
1040	Vegetable and animal oils and fats		...a/	2058.1	1543.6	2218.0		...a/	403.7	251.6	361.6		...	...
1050	Dairy products		...a/	3870.8	3742.3	3721.2		...a/	730.0	690.9	749.0		...	...
106	Grain mill products,starches and starch products		...a/	2725.7	2277.7	2538.5		...a/	511.0	492.6	497.2		...	...
1061	Grain mill products		...	2574.0	2131.5	2390.7		...	500.6	474.9	448.4		...	...
1062	Starches and starch products		...	151.7	146.2	147.8		...	10.4	17.7	48.8		...	...
107	Other food products		...a/	10599.0	10288.5	10217.5		...a/	2570.1	2654.2	2512.2		...	...
1071	Bakery products		...	5672.1	5204.3	5233.9		...	1580.6	1627.2	1429.7		...	...
1072	Sugar		...	1226.1	1399.5	1292.4		...	158.4	186.1	96.6		...	...
1073	Cocoa, chocolate and sugar confectionery		...	1801.2	1884.6	1853.7		...	386.4	409.2	488.7		...	...
1074	Macaroni, noodles, couscous, etc.		...	145.1	140.4	136.5		...	30.3	34.2	37.0		...	...
1075	Prepared meals and dishes		...	10.2	19.4	22.2		...	2.0	3.1	4.6		...	...
1079	Other food products n.e.c.		...a/	1744.3	1640.3	1678.8		...a/	412.4	394.4	455.6		...	...
1080	Prepared animal feeds		...	857.5	932.3	800.6		...	79.7	155.5	119.1		...	...
1101	Distilling, rectifying and blending of spirits		9670.0b/	1148.5	1144.3	797.1		2530.0b/	256.3	332.9	455.3		...	...
1102	Wines		...b/	907.2	776.3	781.4		...b/	...	...	...		...	...
1103	Malt liquors and malt		...b/	4014.2	3729.9	3889.5		...b/	...	...	...		...	...
1104	Soft drinks,mineral waters,other bottled waters		...b/	4557.2	4354.1	4210.5		...b/	1210.5	1139.0	1058.1		...	...
1200	Tobacco products		3395.0	4135.6	2390.4	2165.6			...	...	...		...	...
131	Spinning, weaving and finishing of textiles		2942.0c/	1786.7	1641.2	1894.3		747.0c/	627.3	443.7	494.8		...	...
1311	Preparation and spinning of textile fibres		...	883.8	952.5	1128.4		...	206.9	226.4	250.2		...	...
1312	Weaving of textiles		...	629.0	546.7	589.1		...	301.5	142.6	175.6		...	...
1313	Finishing of textiles		...	273.9	142.0	176.8		...	118.9	74.7	69.0		...	...
139	Other textiles		...c/	1566.8	1393.2	1650.5		...c/	447.9	405.2	461.3		...	...
1391	Knitted and crocheted fabrics		...	15.5	12.1	11.6		...	9.1	5.7	5.4		...	...
1392	Made-up textile articles, except apparel		...	1166.1	979.0	1086.7		...	309.7	273.7	332.3		...	...
1393	Carpets and rugs		...	36.7	27.2	25.6		...	14.5	22.7	16.1		...	...
1394	Cordage, rope, twine and netting		...	79.5	51.4	51.4		...	17.0	10.7	11.4		...	...
1399	Other textiles n.e.c.		...	269.0	323.5	475.2		...	97.6	92.4	96.1		...	...
1410	Wearing apparel, except fur apparel		8526.0d/	8158.9	7095.9	7286.9		3520.0d/	3708.5	3077.4	3113.6		...	...
1420	Articles of fur		...d/	19.4	12.4	9.7		...d/	9.2	3.9	3.2		...	...
1430	Knitted and crocheted apparel		...d/	767.7	710.7	694.4		...d/	389.7	332.8	346.8		...	...
151	Leather;luggage,handbags,saddlery,harness;fur		3465.0e/	468.9	383.3	441.6		1329.0e/	192.6	161.7	175.0		...	...
1511	Tanning/dressing of leather; dressing of fur		...	162.5	108.7	124.1		...	32.8	21.0	19.1		...	...
1512	Luggage,handbags,etc.;saddlery/harness		...	306.4	274.6	317.5		...	159.8	140.7	155.9		...	...
1520	Footwear		...e/	3058.7	2910.2	3330.4		...e/	1222.2	1167.1	1195.0		...	...
1610	Sawmilling and planing of wood		7743.0f/	4105.4	3274.5	3598.6		1614.0f/	1000.2	876.4	859.9		...	...
162	Wood products, cork, straw, plaiting materials		...f/	4468.7	4413.9	5488.1		...f/	1092.2	1080.8	1341.3		...	...

1621	Veneer sheets and wood-based panels	…	…	506.3	429.6	358.9	…	2462.0	1896.4	1821.2	…
1622	Builders' carpentry and joinery	…	…	666.4	516.6	554.9	…	2398.0	2003.1	1954.2	…
1623	Wooden containers	…	…	42.0	35.2	51.3	…	180.1	151.1	214.3	…
1629	Other wood products;articles of cork,straw	…	…	126.6	99.4	127.1	…	448.0	363.3	479.0	…
1701	Pulp, paper and paperboard	…	…	157.3	…	…	545.0g/	797.8	726.8	770.1	2617.0g/
1702	Corrugated paper and paperboard	…	…	264.1	…	…	..g/	1234.4	1057.4	1187.0	..g/
1709	Other articles of paper and paperboard	…	…	182.1	149.4	157.3	..g/	793.3	668.8	646.9	..g/
181	Printing and service activities related to printing	…	…	869.7	940.2	1076.3	763.0h/	2802.3	2753.8	2967.0	2332.0h/
1811	Printing	…	…	773.0	824.6	936.0	…	2578.4	2489.9	2677.2	…
1812	Service activities related to printing	…	…	96.7	115.6	140.3	…	223.9	263.9	289.8	…
1820	Reproduction of recorded media	…	…	19.7	27.2	29.1	..h/	65.7	78.0	87.9	..h/
1910	Coke oven products	…	…	2.0	…	…	…	11.1	7.0	9.3	..i/
1920	Refined petroleum products	…	…	1630.2	…	…	…	13771.2	10767.5	15116.3	10889.0i/
201	Basic chemicals,fertilizers, etc.	…	…	1026.2	1323.7	1372.6	1534.0j/	7056.6	6050.1	7879.4	9449.0j/
2011	Basic chemicals	…	…	464.8	279.7	547.4	..j/	1683.4	1494.6	2160.4	..j/
2012	Fertilizers and nitrogen compounds	…	…	139.2	…	…	…	1282.9	1141.5	1370.1	…
2013	Plastics and synthetic rubber in primary forms	…	…	568.7	712.7	642.3	..j/	2389.2	2944.4	3105.3	…
202	Other chemical products	…	…	…	…	…	…	201.5	197.0	179.7	…
2021	Pesticides and other agrochemical products	…	…	284.3	319.5	311.0	…	1165.5	1173.6	1278.0	…
2022	Paints,varnishes;printing ink and mastics	…	…	232.1	317.6	260.7	…	629.0	977.1	1034.5	…
2023	Soap,cleaning and cosmetic preparations	…	…	52.3	75.6	70.6	…	393.2	596.7	613.1	…
2029	Other chemical products n.e.c.	…	…	…	…	…	…	398.4	261.5	243.3	…
2030	Man-made fibres	…	…	1255.4	836.1	802.3	699.0	2967.9	2348.4	1855.5	1769.0
2100	Pharmaceuticals,medicinal chemicals, etc.	…	…	1377.8	1038.9	746.5	1842.0k/	5628.8	4252.0	4931.3	…
221	Rubber products	…	…	1059.0	811.5	503.6	…	4374.7	3327.5	3975.1	9119.0k/
2211	Rubber tyres and tubes	…	…	318.8	227.4	242.9	…	1254.1	924.5	956.2	…
2219	Other rubber products	…	…	1529.5	1605.7	1052.3	..k/	7339.9	6889.5	7687.2	..k/
2220	Plastics products	…	…	305.1	301.4	391.8	3736.0m/	1120.1	1087.2	1311.5	11353.0m/
2310	Glass and glass products	…	…	3406.5	3620.1	4481.7	..m/	9232.1	9509.9	13032.2	..m/
239	Non-metallic mineral products n.e.c.	…	…	38.9	24.4	24.4	…	107.1	95.6	166.2	…
2391	Refractory products	…	…	258.9	231.7	368.4	…	629.4	593.8	747.6	…
2392	Clay building materials	…	…	207.9	187.7	197.1	…	567.6	495.4	553.5	…
2393	Other porcelain and ceramic products	…	…	1475.8	1625.7	1822.2	…	2652.5	3029.1	4077.3	…
2394	Cement, lime and plaster	…	…	1072.9	1195.4	1657.4	…	4171.2	4334.7	6134.0	…
2395	Articles of concrete, cement and plaster	…	…	83.1	81.4	102.0	…	222.3	265.0	286.5	…
2396	Cutting, shaping and finishing of stone	…	…	269.0	273.8	310.2	…	882.0	696.3	1067.1	…
2399	Other non-metallic mineral products n.e.c.	…	…	…	…	…	…	…	…	…	…
2410	Basic iron and steel	…	…	1407.8	360.6	3872.6	3679.0n/	13042.1	9002.9	17523.7	19854.0n/
2420	Basic precious and other non-ferrous metals	…	…	777.8	287.6	683.6	..n/	3023.7	2121.0	3794.4	..n/
243	Casting of metals	…	…	182.1	162.2	221.7	…	897.5	602.4	808.4	…
2431	Casting of iron and steel	…	…	…	…	…	…	246.3	254.1	369.8	…
2432	Casting of non-ferrous metals	…	…	…	…	…	…	651.2	348.3	438.6	…
251	Struct.metal products, tanks, reservoirs	3118.2p/	…	1620.5	1937.1	2455.7	3191.0p/	6245.1	6703.1	8583.8	11640.0p/
2511	Structural metal products	…	…	1367.8	1636.4	2066.2	…	5527.2	5959.4	7511.0	…
2512	Tanks, reservoirs and containers of metal	…	…	196.6	196.1	261.0	…	564.3	557.7	841.8	…

continued

Romania

ISIC	Industry	Output at factor values (millions of Romanian Lei)				Value added at factor values (millions of Romanian Lei)				Gross fixed capital formation (millions of Romanian Lei)	
	ISIC Revision 4	2007	2008	2009	2010	2007	2008	2009	2010	2009	2010
2513	Steam generators, excl. hot water boilers	...	231.0	186.0	153.6	...	128.5	104.6	56.1	...	...
2520	Weapons and ammunition	...p/	...q/	...q/	...q/	...p/	...	...q/	...q/	...p/	...
259	Other metal products;metal working services	...p/	6304.8	5076.1	5967.9	...p/	1960.2	1439.0	1655.0	...p/	...
2591	Forging,pressing,stamping,roll-forming of metal	...	1073.4	974.5	1144.7	...	253.5	203.6	187.5	...	...
2592	Treatment and coating of metals; machining	...	1450.6	1160.2	1523.2	...	603.5	454.1	529.0	...	...
2593	Cutlery, hand tools and general hardware	...	622.4	456.8	574.5	...	223.1	155.7	172.3	...	...
2599	Other fabricated metal products n.e.c.	...	3158.4q/	2484.6q/	2725.5q/	...	880.1q/	625.6q/	766.2q/	...	...
2610	Electronic components and boards	5373.0r/	1021.6	793.2	1150.3	1417.0r/	439.2	372.7	458.0	8923.4r/	...
2620	Computers and peripheral equipment	...r/	1549.0	1272.6	1806.1	...r/	246.3	344.6	266.9	...	...
2630	Communication equipment	...r/	2631.2	5117.2	7445.7	...r/	...	...	...	...r/	...
2640	Consumer electronics	...r/	156.2	37.8	41.7	...r/	13.4	7.1	...	...r/	...
265	Measuring,testing equipment; watches, etc.	...r/	1231.7	1300.0	1496.6	...r/	...	...	...	...r/	...
2651	Measuring/testing/navigating equipment,etc.	...r/	1231.7	1300.0	1496.6	...r/	...	394.3	485.0	...r/	...
2652	Watches and clocks	...	...	...	...	...	...	...	...	...	...
2660	Irradiation/electromedical equipment,etc.	...r/	71.9	59.5	53.8	...r/	27.9	24.9	24.6	...r/	...
2670	Optical instruments and photographic equipment	...r/	98.9	66.7	61.4	...r/	49.2	30.3	30.3	...r/	...
2680	Magnetic and optical media	...r/	...	0.9	0.8	...r/	...	...	...	...r/	...
2710	Electric motors,generators,transformers,etc.	7351.0s/	2868.3	2527.1	3029.0	1696.0s/	617.2	600.0	...	2823.9s/	...
2720	Batteries and accumulators	...s/	238.6	256.3	342.7	...s/	...	225.5	323.3	...s/	...
273	Wiring and wiring devices	...s/	2287.3	1679.7	2456.0	...s/	343.5	...	...	...s/	...
2731	Fibre optic cables	...	109.5	64.2	9.5	...	...	...	2.0	...s/	...
2732	Other electronic and electric wires and cables	...	2066.0	1429.4	2231.4	...	315.7	159.1	258.6	...s/	...
2733	Wiring devices	...	111.8	186.1	215.1	...	27.8	...	62.7	...	...
2740	Electric lighting equipment	...s/	753.6	591.9	676.0	...s/	...	...	149.7	...s/	...
2750	Domestic appliances	...s/	2318.1	1979.9	2300.5	...s/	250.4	155.5	...	...s/	...
2790	Other electrical equipment	...s/	849.0	942.4	1383.6	...s/	...	...	575.2	...s/	...
281	General-purpose machinery	7121.0t/	5221.1	4449.1	4950.3	2073.0t/	229.3	252.0	365.1	13161.5t/	...
2811	Engines/turbines,excl.aircraft,vehicle engines	...	1556.9	1546.2	1742.4	...	1725.4	1496.8	1868.6	...	...
2812	Fluid power equipment	...	...	...	...	...	517.2	430.8	15.6	...	...
2813	Other pumps, compressors, taps and valves	...	569.9	386.9	376.6	...	...	...	...	...	...
2814	Bearings, gears, gearing and driving elements	...	1306.7	1005.7	1190.1	...	484.6	454.3	476.9	...	...
2815	Ovens, furnaces and furnace burners	...	102.6	105.1	128.0	...	35.0	42.7	53.6	...	...
2816	Lifting and handling equipment	...	824.1	583.9	566.5	...	276.0	216.1	196.5	...	...
2817	Office machinery, excl.computers,etc.	...	20.7	106.5	104.1	...	...	...	...	...	...
2818	Power-driven hand tools	...	217.0	187.3	284.5	...	59.0	144.0	...	...	...
2819	Other general-purpose machinery	...	623.2	527.5	558.1	...	173.0	...	153.0	...	...
282	Special-purpose machinery	...	3904.6	3195.0	3256.4	...	1549.1	1117.6	641.6	...	...
2821	Agricultural and forestry machinery	...t/	469.0	478.7	622.1	...t/	139.9	93.9	108.5	...t/	...
2822	Metal-forming machinery and machine tools	...	584.1	469.1	427.7	...	234.6	193.4	191.4	...	...
2823	Machinery for metallurgy	...	477.4	329.5	204.8	...	191.9	141.1	66.7	...	...
2824	Mining, quarrying and construction machinery	...	1663.5	154.1	151.9	...	586.3	38.4	...	...	...

Code		...	...	...	...	...	...	...	...	...
2825	Food/beverage/tobacco processing machinery	...	129.7	29.6	38.3	...	62.3	13.1	16.9	...
2826	Textile/apparel/leather production machinery	...	61.0	533.7	511.3	...	24.8	226.2	216.8	...
2829	Other special-purpose machinery	18450.0u/	519.9	1200.3	1300.3	4952.0u/	309.3	411.5	...	19089.0u/
2910	Motor vehicles	...u/	8598.2	9322.0	12087.1	...u/	...	...	...	...u/
2920	Automobile bodies, trailers and semi-trailers	...u/	397.4	243.8	242.8	...u/	3684.5	3770.8	4740.7	...u/
2930	Parts and accessories for motor vehicles	...u/	12548.8	15326.7	20389.3	1318.0v/	956.1	927.2	1305.5	2187.3v/
301	Building of ships and boats	5083.0v/	3883.8	4289.8	3845.2	...	947.7	920.4	1298.4	...
3011	Building of ships and floating structures	...	3826.7	4259.1	3813.9	...	8.4	6.8	7.1	...
3012	Building of pleasure and sporting boats	...v/	57.1	30.7	31.3	...v/	...	...	...	...v/
3020	Railway locomotives and rolling stock	...v/	2409.3w/	2039.1w/	1245.8w/	...v/	799.2w/	661.9w/	483.8w/	...v/
3030	Air and spacecraft and related machinery	...v/	356.3	470.6	494.3	...v/	146.2	229.5	231.1	...v/
3040	Military fighting vehicles	...v/	...w/	...w/	...w/	...v/	38.5	34.6	50.0	...v/
309	Transport equipment n.e.c.	...v/	135.6	167.5	393.9	...	...	...	...	...
3091	Motorcycles	...	0.1	0.1	0.1	...	38.2	...	49.9	...
3092	Bicycles and invalid carriages	...	133.6	167.4	393.8	...	...	...	...	...
3099	Other transport equipment n.e.c.	...	1.9	...	...	...	...	...	...	...
3100	Furniture	6027.0	6716.5	5968.3	6213.4	1612.0	1905.1	1779.4	1635.6	3012.4
321	Jewellery, bijouterie and related articles	976.0x/	135.9	146.0	138.1	304.0x/	...	53.3	60.2	...
3211	Jewellery and related articles	...	116.9	126.3	115.7	...	22.7	...	...	...
3212	Imitation jewellery and related articles	...x/	19.0	19.7	22.4	...x/	23.7	22.7	26.9	...
3220	Musical instruments	...x/	54.9	48.9	59.9	...x/	46.8	47.1	56.9	...
3230	Sports goods	...x/	83.3	98.9	113.0	...x/	31.3	37.9	43.7	...
3240	Games and toys	...x/	116.6	107.7	107.4	...x/	110.4	114.8	129.1	...
3250	Medical and dental instruments and supplies	...x/	237.1	280.2	285.3	...x/	...	128.2	128.2	...
3290	Other manufacturing n.e.c.	2759.0y/	500.7	382.1	428.9	1101.0y/	1310.4	999.2	961.0	1020.6y/
331	Repair of fabricated metal products/machinery	...	2768.8	2298.2	2209.2	...	148.3	44.4	59.0	...
3311	Repair of fabricated metal products	...	225.8	98.9	147.7	...	237.4	229.3	264.4	...
3312	Repair of machinery	...	588.5	604.7	637.2	...	6.0	8.5	23.4	...
3313	Repair of electronic and optical equipment	...	...	40.5	86.5	...	...	80.7	...	...
3314	Repair of electrical equipment	...	235.8	217.1	179.9	...	...	...	...	...
3315	Repair of transport equip., excl. motor vehicles	...	1688.4	1313.6	1139.7	...	6.6	6.6	11.0	...
3319	Repair of other equipment	...y/	11.3	23.4	18.2	...	153.0	165.5	163.5	...y/
3320	Installation of industrial machinery/equipment	...	480.1	766.4	780.0	...y/	...	...	...	...
C	Total manufacturing	192190.0	232406.1	203740.9	231822.8	44594.0	56977.4	48567.8	53823.4	53336.3

a/ 1010 includes 1020, 1030, 1040, 1050, 106, 107 and 1080.
b/ 1101 includes 1102, 1103 and 1104.
c/ 131 includes 139.
d/ 1410 includes 1420 and 1430.
e/ 151 includes 1520.
f/ 1610 includes 162.
g/ 1701 includes 1702 and 1709.
h/ 181 includes 1820.
i/ 1910 includes 1920.
j/ 201 includes 202 and 2030.

k/ 221 includes 2220.
l/ 2310 includes 239.
m/ 2410 includes 2420 and 243.
n/ 251 includes 2520 and 259.
o/ 2599 includes 2520.
p/ 2610 includes 2620, 2630, 2640, 265, 2660, 2670 and 2680.
q/ 2710 includes 2720, 273, 2740, 2750 and 2790.
r/ 281 includes 282.
s/ 2910 includes 2920 and 2930.
t/ 301 includes 3020, 3030, 3040 and 309.
u/ 2910 includes 2920 and 2930.
v/ 301 includes 3020, 3030, 3040 and 309.

w/ 3020 includes 3040.
x/ 321 includes 3220, 3230, 3240, 3250 and 3290.
y/ 331 includes 3320.

Romania

Index numbers of industrial production

ISIC Revision 4

ISIC	Industry	Note	1999	2000	2001	2002	2003	2004	2005 (2005=100)	2006	2007	2008	2009	2010
10	Food products		...	96	94	90	97	102	100	105	129	136	135	126
11	Beverages		...	82	103	129	118	102	100	117	123	139	129	121
12	Tobacco products		...	92	114	103	97	108	100	92	116	141	141	114
13	Textiles		...	117	115	116	122	120	100	95	101	93	72	78
14	Wearing apparel		...	111	127	131	126	120	100	101	89	71	53	53
15	Leather and related products		...	106	110	114	117	115	100	102	96	83	65	68
16	Wood/wood products/cork,excl. furniture		...	93	74	65	67	89	100	122	133	123	145	163
17	Paper and paper products		...	87	96	104	107	103	100	112	120	113	101	102
18	Printing and reproduction of recorded media		...	45	73	56	75	89	100	102	97	121	128	116
19	Coke and refined petroleum products		...	73	80	92	83	88	100	97	95	95	84	74
20	Chemicals and chemical products		...	113	110	91	90	102	100	104	105	122	102	112
21	Pharmaceuticals,medicinal chemicals, etc.		...	97	64	72	93	80	100	98	108	126	105	113
22	Rubber and plastics products		...	72	83	84	105	110	100	128	162	179	167	179
23	Other non-metallic mineral products		...	102	102	103	101	109	100	115	147	166	115	109
24	Basic metals		...	83	91	104	89	99	100	101	103	87	56	71
25	Fabricated metal products, except machinery		...	144	128	120	112	107	100	126	147	170	148	136
26	Computer, electronic and optical products		...	148	133	111	128	150	100	134	131	137	104	104
27	Electrical equipment		...	83	88	86	91	100	100	134	141	156	181	238
28	Machinery and equipment n.e.c.		...	134	154	142	120	124	100	106	135	130	107	101
29	Motor vehicles, trailers and semi-trailers		...	49	47	53	61	76	100	114	139	143	158	204
30	Other transport equipment		...	94	93	89	103	97	100	113	128	129	107	71
31	Furniture		...	81	79	83	84	84	100	114	117	113	97	95
32	Other manufacturing		...	144	160	175	146	108	100	106	116	84	74	66
33	Repair and installation of machinery/equipment		...	96	109	108	116	109	100	104	111	91	92	100
C	Total manufacturing		...	97	101	102	100	104	100	113	126	130	122	129

Russian Federation

Supplier of information:
Federal State Statistics Service (Rosstat), Moscow.

Basic source of data:
Survey on registered enterprises.

Major deviations from ISIC (Revision 3):
Data originally classified according to OKVED were harmonized with ISIC (Revision 3).

Reference period:
Calendar year.

Scope:
All registered enterprises.

Method of data collection:
Mail questionnaires; administrative sources; e-mail questionnaires.

Type of enumeration:
Complete enumeration for large and medium enterprises. Sample survey for small enterprises.

Adjusted for non-response:
No.

Concepts and definitions of variables:
Wages and salaries was computed by UNIDO from reported monthly average of wages and salaries per employee.
Output includes revenue from non-industrial activities and is reported at basic prices.
Value added includes cost of non-industrial activities and is reported at basic prices.

Related national publications:
Monthly reports "Social and economic situation in Russia", published by Rosstat, Moscow.

Russian Federation

ISIC	Industry	Enterprises Note	Ent. 2007	Ent. 2008	Ent. 2009	Ent. 2010	Employees Note	Emp. 2007	Emp. 2008	Emp. 2009	Emp. 2010	Wages Note	Wag. 2007	Wag. 2008	Wag. 2009	Wag. 2010
			(number)					(thousands)					(millions of Russian Roubles)			
151	Processed meat,fish,fruit,vegetables,fats		23169a/	23494a/	24821a/	...		374	362	363	365		47859	58873	66066	74904
1511	Processing/preserving of meat		...	...	...	...		250	234	238	233		31942	37405	42531	43802
1512	Processing/preserving of fish		...	...	...	...		50	53	54	61		6713	8451	9291	15245
1513	Processing/preserving of fruit & vegetables		...	...	...	...		32	33	30	31		4541	5729	5879	6746
1514	Vegetable and animal oils and fats		...a/	...a/	...a/	...		41	41	40	40		4663	7289	8366	9111
1520	Dairy products		...a/	...a/	...a/	...		203	186	175	175		24060	28286	29711	33717
153	Grain mill products; starches; animal feeds		...a/	...a/	...a/	...		105	110	100	97		11588	16146	16409	17931
1531	Grain mill products		...a/	...a/	...a/	...		65	72	62	59		6368	9535	9003	9738
1532	Starches and starch products		...a/	...a/	...a/	...		7	6	7	6		616	880	971	1011
1533	Prepared animal feeds		...a/	...a/	...a/	...		33	31	31	32		4606	5731	6435	7182
154	Other food products		...a/	...a/	...a/	...		569	553	522	509		68775	83582	91723	95641
1541	Bakery products		...	...	...	...		375	350	338	335		41181	49001	54442	57308
1542	Sugar		...	...	...	...		52	49	45	41		5122	5986	6769	6160
1543	Cocoa, chocolate and sugar confectionery		...	...	...	...		78	86	76	71		13772	16470	17558	17685
1544	Macaroni, noodles & similar products		...	...	...	...		24	22	17	16		2851	3345	3068	3490
1549	Other food products n.e.c.		...	...	...	...		40	48	45	45		5852	8783	9886	10997
155	Beverages		...	...	...	...		192	188	170	161		36295	43236	42324	45103
1551	Distilling, rectifying & blending of spirits		...	...	...	...		80	74	65	58		11737	13175	12496	12297
1552	Wines		...	...	...	...		21	21	19	19		2656	3321	3167	3459
1553	Malt liquors and malt		...	...	...	...		54	52	47	45		13511	15575	15617	16518
1554	Soft drinks; mineral waters		...	...	...	...		38	41	39	38		8390	11165	11045	12828
1600	Tobacco products		61	65	47	...		13	13	12	11		4892	5731	6135	6458
171	Spinning, weaving and finishing of textiles		3712b/	3867b/	4230b/	...		126	105	87	81		10198	11078	9893	10055
1711	Textile fibre preparation; textile weaving		...	...	...	...		120	100	83	77		9665	10492	9413	9606
1712	Finishing of textiles		...	...	...	...		6	5	4	4		534	586	480	449
172	Other textiles		...	...b/	...b/	...		53	49	43	50		4672	5635	5408	7201
1721	Made-up textile articles, except apparel		...	...	...	...		22	20	17	19		1639	2040	1898	2275
1722	Carpets and rugs		...	...	...	...		3	2	2	2		134	151	216	230
1723	Cordage, rope, twine and netting		...	...	...	...		7	7	6	8		690	827	695	1240
1729	Other textiles n.e.c.		...	...	...	...		22	20	19	22		2210	2616	2599	3456
1730	Knitted and crocheted fabrics and articles		...b/	...b/	...b/	...		19	17	17	16		1727	2003	2003	2055
1810	Wearing apparel, except fur apparel		6860c/	7281c/	7583c/	...		225	213	182	180		16864	20156	18191	20968
1820	Dressing & dyeing of fur; processing of fur		...c/	...c/	...c/	...		7	8	7	6		602	889	929	884
191	Tanning, dressing and processing of leather		1206d/	1213d/	1302d/	...		23	21	18	17		2465	2790	2561	2497
1911	Tanning and dressing of leather		...d/	...	...	...		11	8	8	7		1181	1193	1117	1241
1912	Luggage, handbags, etc.; saddlery & harness		...	...d/	...	...		12	13	10	9		1285	1596	1443	1256
1920	Footwear		...	...	...d/	...		56	51	40	41		4686	5545	4420	5311
2010	Sawmilling and planing of wood		11458e/	13075e/	14829e/	...		131	144	125	117		12672	16775	14667	16148
202	Products of wood, cork, straw, etc.		...e/	...e/	...e/	...		209	183	152	147		23347	27560	21630	24122
2021	Veneer sheets, plywood, particle board, etc.		...	...	...	...		103	77	60	58		13689	14272	10067	11480
2022	Builders' carpentry and joinery		...	...	...	...		87	85	75	71		8348	11405	9703	10482
2023	Wooden containers		...	...	...	...		11	9	9	8		785	921	849	913
2029	Other wood products; articles of cork/straw		...	...	...	...		9	11	8	10		526	961	1010	1246
210	Paper and paper products		1693	1772	2043	...		132	124	115	112		20951	25073	23920	27654
2101	Pulp, paper and paperboard		...	...	...	...		76	67	58	57		12929	14454	13673	15388
2102	Corrugated paper and paperboard		...	...	...	...		34	36	34	32		5072	6325	6211	7009
2109	Other articles of paper and paperboard		...	...	...	...		21	22	22	24		2949	4294	4036	5257
221	Publishing		17783f/	19320f/	21885f/	...		144	136	131	149		27235	33714	30587	37134
2211	Publishing of books and other publications		...	...	...	...		21	23	22	28		4579	6273	5668	7643
2212	Publishing of newspapers, journals, etc.		...	...	...	...		118	107	103	118		21780	25714	23408	28412
2213	Publishing of recorded media		...	...	...	...		-	-	-	-		10	11	37	41
2219	Other publishing		...	...	...	...		5	6	6	3		867	1696	1474	1038

ISIC	Industry											
222	Printing and related service activities	22769	22027	25506	17768	102	115	137	123	...f/	...f/	...f/
2221	Printing	20698	20215	23771	16498	93	105	127	114			
2222	Service activities related to printing	2071	1812	1736	1220	9	9	10	-	...f/	...f/	...f/
2230	Reproduction of recorded media	321	335	281	65	1	2	2		762g/	780g/	666g/
2310	Coke oven products	5029	5074	5220	4648	16	17	19	20	...g/	...g/	...g/
2320	Refined petroleum products	49283	45755	45255	41343	93	94	101	114	...g/	...g/	...g/
2330	Processing of nuclear fuel h/									5525i/	5696i/	6016i/
241	Basic chemicals	70916	64154	65950	56033	255	269	289	304			
2411	Basic chemicals, except fertilizers	30395	27845	27951	22113	114	121	129	129			
2412	Fertilizers and nitrogen compounds	20398	18682	18884	16104	66	72	75	81			
2413	Plastics in primary forms; synthetic rubber	20123	17627	19116	17815	74	77	85	95	...i/	...i/	...i/
242	Other chemicals	42263	36929	38784	32062	166	161	186	191			
2421	Pesticides and other agro-chemical products	374	355	357	204	2	2	2	2			
2422	Paints, varnishes, printing ink and mastics	5333	4332	4651	3614	24	23	28	26			
2423	Pharmaceuticals, medicinal chemicals, etc.	18378	15873	17149	14044	71	71	84	85			
2424	Soap, cleaning & cosmetic preparations	9098	8080	8145	7158	35	31	34	38			
2429	Other chemical products n.e.c.	9080	8280	8460	7042	34	33	38	40	...i/	...i/	...i/
2430	Man-made fibres	1895	1781	2004	1684	11	11	14	16			
251	Rubber products	12914	11934	15754	14744	65	72	91	110	6950j/	8261j/	9786j/
2511	Rubber tyres and tubes	6285	6337	7776	7763	29	34	41	50			
2519	Other rubber products	6629	5598	7978	6981	36	38	50	60	...j/	...j/	...j/
2520	Plastic products	33470	31178	31874	23185	180	188	204	175	9601k/	11470k/	13431k/
2610	Glass and glass products	14705	13510	14783	10757	67	73	81	76	...k/	...k/	...k/
269	Non-metallic mineral products n.e.c.	107260	101306	122305	96114	494	523	616	599			
2691	Pottery, china and earthenware	5181	4429	4873	3983	24	24	29	29			
2692	Refractory ceramic products	5899	4754	6091	5396	26	26	32	35			
2693	Struct.non-refractory clay; ceramic products	14009	14064	18750	14288	78	91	109	102			
2694	Cement, lime and plaster	12026	10974	14448	11512	49	50	60	61			
2695	Articles of concrete, cement and plaster	56222	54898	63513	50376	256	268	312	304			
2696	Cutting, shaping & finishing of stone	1974	1974	1887	712	11	11	12	5			
2699	Other non-metallic mineral products n.e.c.	11949	10584	12744	9847	51	54	63	62			
2710	Basic iron and steel	94962	83653	93986	80877	324	339	377	394	1565m/	1836m/	2045m/
2720	Basic precious and non-ferrous metals	45760	42327	48063	44722	137	143	170	180	...m/	...m/	...m/
273	Casting of metals	9036	7249	9579	7316	46	46	57	54	...m/	...m/	...m/
2731	Casting of iron and steel	7962	6319	8742	6652	41	41	52	49			
2732	Casting of non-ferrous metals											
281	Struct.metal products;tanks;steam generators	48061	41261	47561	35807	215	215	241	233	11671n/	13706n/	16726n/
2811	Structural metal products	31371	27491	34088	25333	145	149	172	165			
2812	Tanks, reservoirs and containers of metal	5687	4968	5167	4341	30	31	32	33			
2813	Steam generators	10771	8802	8308	6134	39	35	38	36	...n/	...n/	...n/
289	Other metal products; metal working services	48586	40364	47199	38810	248	255	285	293			
2891	Metal forging/pressing/stamping/roll-forming	7555	6116	8356	6612	37	39	46	44			
2892	Treatment & coating of metals	16279	13206	13553	10814	83	80	82	83			
2893	Cutlery, hand tools and general hardware	7277	6203	7695	6871	40	45	53	58			
2899	Other fabricated metal products n.e.c.	17475	14839	17594	14513	87	91	104	109	14452p/	16382p/	20405p/
291	General purpose machinery	124292	113924	133751	106659	464	492	589	583			
2911	Engines & turbines (not for transport equipment)	17722	16502	19014	17388	61	64	78	88			
2912	Pumps, compressors, taps and valves	28307	24903	27246	23108	117	119	131	135			
2913	Bearings, gears, gearing & driving elements	6288	5681	7582	6388	32	36	48	50			
2914	Ovens, furnaces and furnace burners	2481	2326	2657	2293	12	13	15	15			
2915	Lifting and handling equipment	15509	14544	20701	17120	67	77	102	105			
2919	Other general purpose machinery	53984	49967	56549	40186	174	181	216	189	...p/	...p/	...p/
292	Special purpose machinery	70737	63910	79804	65289	340	374	453	472			
2921	Agricultural and forestry machinery	8729	9766	11459	11281	61	77	91	117			
2922	Machine tools	6176	5175	8202	7067	35	34	52	54			
2923	Machinery for metallurgy	13320	11313	13485	9660	51	54	61	51			
2924	Machinery for mining & construction	21771	19784	28417	23482	102	116	148	153			
2925	Food/beverage/tobacco processing machinery	2349	2202	2550	2131	12	14	16	18			
2926	Machinery for textile, apparel and leather	474	376	491	582	3	4	4	6			
2927	Weapons and ammunition											
2929	Other special purpose machinery	17918	15293	15201	11090	75	76	80	73			

h/

continued

Russian Federation

ISIC Revision 3 — Number of enterprises (number) / Number of employees (thousands) / Wages and salaries paid to employees (millions of Russian Roubles)

ISIC	Industry	Ent. Note	Ent. 2007	Ent. 2008	Ent. 2009	Ent. 2010	Emp. Note	Emp. 2007	Emp. 2008	Emp. 2009	Emp. 2010	Wage Note	Wage 2007	Wage 2008	Wage 2009	Wage 2010
2930	Domestic appliances n.e.c.		...p/	...p/	...	...		53	46	35	36		7374	7773	6120	7386
3000	Office, accounting and computing machinery		1567	1701	1284	...		23	24	20	17		3752	5165	4777	5652
3110	Electric motors, generators and transformers		4715q/	5365q/	6809q/	...		117	112	101	89		19007	23027	20688	21587
3120	Electricity distribution & control apparatus		...q/	...q/	...q/	...		95	102	89	80		15676	22362	19071	19177
3130	Insulated wire and cable		...q/	...q/	...q/	...		43	42	34	32		8003	9473	7214	8201
3140	Accumulators, primary cells and batteries		...q/	...q/	...q/	...		16	15	13	12		2089	2488	2354	2629
3150	Lighting equipment and electric lamps		...q/	...q/	...q/	...		26	27	20	20		2556	3338	2832	3001
3190	Other electrical equipment n.e.c.		...q/	...q/	...q/	...	h/	111	110	89	83	h/	15441	19477	15720	18159
3210	Electronic valves, tubes, etc.	h/	2203r/	2484r/	2116r/	...		...	...	...	...	h/	...	...	...	...
3220	TV/radio transmitters; line comm. apparatus		...r/	...r/	...r/	...		...	...	...	...	h/	...	...	...	...
3230	TV and radio receivers and associated goods	h/	...r/	...r/	...r/	...	h/	...	...	...	...	h/	...	...	...	...
331	Medical, measuring, testing appliances, etc.		4216s/	4419s/	5054s/	...		263	271	262	250		44497	57774	58450	64896
3311	Medical, surgical and orthopaedic equipment		...	...	...	...		49	45	41	38		8187	9672	9916	10338
3312	Measuring/testing/navigating appliances,etc.		...	...	...	...		208	221	217	210		34920	46400	47592	53695
3313	Industrial process control equipment		...	...	...	...		6	5	3	2		1389	1702	943	863
3320	Optical instruments & photographic equipment		...s/	...s/	...s/	...		22	20	21	18		3592	3550	3923	4280
3330	Watches and clocks		...s/	...s/	...s/	...		5	5	3	2		614	693	546	399
3410	Motor vehicles	h/	1599t/	1715t/	1723t/	...		280	280	237	213	h/	48927	60231	44880	50479
3420	Automobile bodies, trailers & semi-trailers		...t/	...t/	...t/	...		24	26	19	16		3639	4775	2747	3094
3430	Parts/accessories for automobiles		...t/	...t/	...t/	...		177	174	136	120		23350	27631	...	21217
351	Building and repairing of ships and boats	h/	2424u/	2607u/	2801u/	...		...	...	...	...		...	...	...	...
3511	Building and repairing of ships	h/	...u/	...u/	...u/	...		...	...	...	...		...	...	...	...
3512	Building/repairing of pleasure/sport. boats	h/	...u/	...u/	...u/	...		...	...	...	...		...	...	...	...
3520	Railway/tramway locomotives & rolling stock		...u/	...u/	...u/	...		...	...	...	...		...	...	...	...
3530	Aircraft and spacecraft	h/	...u/	...u/	...u/	...	h/	201	208	205	217	h/	35377	46844	46471	57148
359	Transport equipment n.e.c.		...u/	...u/	...u/	...		...	...	...	...		432	400	239	81
3591	Motorcycles		...	...	...	...		4	3	2	1		168	108	78	-
3592	Bicycles and invalid carriages		...	...	...	...		2	1	1	1		109	81	74	131
3599	Other transport equipment n.e.c.		...	...	...	...		1	1	1	-		155	212	87	95
3610	Furniture		9320v/	10467v/	12746v/	...		160	186	162	169		17321	25677	21657	24433
369	Manufacturing n.e.c.		...v/	...v/	...v/	...		92	82	74	72		12465	13597	12594	13697
3691	Jewellery and related articles		...	...	...	...		44	37	33	33		7448	7688	6480	7640
3692	Musical instruments		...	...	...	...		1	1	1	1		106	193	131	139
3693	Sports goods		...	...	...	...		1	1	1	1		443	686	629	738
3694	Games and toys		...	...	...	...		4	5	4	4		139	686	629	738
3699	Other manufacturing n.e.c.		...	...	...	...		13	10	8	8		1133	1105	1213	1249
3710	Recycling of metal waste and scrap		5088w/	5226w/	4104w/	...		30	29	28	26		3334	3924	4141	3930
3720	Recycling of non-metal waste and scrap		...w/	...w/	...w/	...		58	51	42	42		7789	9086	7626	8288
								10	12	8	9		1168	1708	1246	1524
D	Total manufacturing		147906	162451	182705	...		9259	9126	8118	7810		1430951	1757713	1615502	1788008

a/ 151 includes 1520, 153, 154 and 155.
b/ 171 includes 172 and 1730.
c/ 1810 includes 1820.
d/ 191 includes 1920.
e/ 2010 includes 202.
f/ 221 includes 222 and 2230.
g/ 2310 includes 2320 and 2330.
h/ Data suppressed due to confidentiality rules.
i/ 241 includes 242 and 2430.
j/ 251 includes 2520.

k/ 2610 includes 269.
m/ 2710 includes 2720 and 273.
n/ 281 includes 289.
p/ 291 includes 292 and 2930.
q/ 3110 includes 3120, 3130, 3140, 3150 and 3190.
r/ 3210 includes 3220 and 3230.
s/ 331 includes 3320 and 3330.
t/ 3410 includes 3420 and 3430.
u/ 351 includes 3520, 3530 and 359.
v/ 3610 includes 369.

w/ 3710 includes 3720.

Russian Federation

ISIC	Industry	Output Note	Output (millions of Russian Roubles)				Value added Note	Value added (millions of Russian Roubles)				GFCF Note	Gross fixed capital formation (millions of Russian Roubles)	
			2007	2008	2009	2010		2007	2008	2009	2010		2009	2010
151	Processed meat,fish,fruit,vegetables,fats		794378	1005221	1028549	...		224075	286124	289420	310048		...	...
1511	Processing/preserving of meat		432848	546863	581668	657124		102504	140469	142818	168185		...	...
1512	Processing/preserving of fish		141051	164859	153262	159548		84679	96462	87994	86081		...	...
1513	Processing/preserving of fruit & vegetables		78522	88878	97738	106334		18732	19674	22321	26682		...	...
1514	Vegetable and animal oils and fats		141957	204621	195881	236146		18160	29519	36287	29099		...	...
1520	Dairy products		352368	418698	437857	515317		64942	84592	100621	100847		...	...
153	Grain mill products; starches; animal feeds		189129	260965	242370	308930		35040	48416	50163	74258		...	...
1531	Grain mill products		...	...	...	...		...	...	...	...		...	...
1532	Starches and starch products		56952	76075	90721	153578		5457	7505	13530	35963		...	...
1533	Prepared animal feeds		605157	732844	856514	871840		178418	233710	288748	243394		...	...
154	Other food products		219430	277656	297958	309737		85548	114679	131315	131128		...	...
1541	Bakery products		114287	126813	140896	149331		28332	36685	44120	39415		...	...
1542	Sugar		...	...	...	...		...	...	...	...		...	...
1543	Cocoa, chocolate and sugar confectionery		...	...	...	...		...	...	...	...		...	...
1544	Macaroni, noodles & similar products		...	...	...	...		...	...	...	...		...	...
1549	Other food products n.e.c.		571758	638910	629878	618484		182137	206774	226909	202089		...	...
155	Beverages		...	...	...	...		...	...	...	...		...	...
1551	Distilling, rectifying & blending of spirits		...	...	...	...		...	...	...	...		...	...
1552	Wines		...	...	...	...		...	...	...	...		...	...
1553	Malt liquors and malt		105424	124535	150845	165648		30381	40754	48121	68382		...	...
1554	Soft drinks; mineral waters		115211	125529	117374	144731		36487	40780	38708	43821		...	...
1600	Tobacco products		...	...	...	...		...	...	...	...		...	...
171	Spinning, weaving and finishing of textiles	a/	...	...	...	...	a/	...	...	...	...		...	...
1711	Textile fibre preparation; textile weaving		...	...	...	...		...	...	...	...		...	...
1712	Finishing of textiles		...	...	...	...		...	...	...	...		...	...
172	Other textiles	a/	...	...	...	...	a/	...	...	...	...		...	...
1721	Made-up textile articles, except apparel		...	...	...	...		...	...	...	...		...	...
1722	Carpets and rugs		...	...	...	...		...	...	...	...		...	...
1723	Cordage, rope, twine and netting		...	...	...	...		...	...	...	...		...	...
1729	Other textiles n.e.c.		...	...	...	...		...	...	...	...		...	...
1730	Knitted and crocheted fabrics and articles		108063	108711	86994	93654		49511	56120	44634	44574		...	...
1810	Wearing apparel, except fur apparel	b/	41669	47910	45100	55577	b/	14587	18597	16113	18936		...	...
1820	Dressing & dyeing of fur; processing of fur	b/	...	...	...	...	b/	...	...	...	...		...	...
191	Tanning, dressing and processing of leather	c/	...	...	...	...	c/	...	...	...	...		...	...
1911	Tanning and dressing of leather		...	...	...	...		...	...	...	...		...	...
1912	Luggage, handbags, etc.; saddlery & harness		...	...	...	...		...	...	...	...		...	...
1920	Footwear	c/	...	...	...	...	c/	...	...	...	...		...	...
2010	Sawmilling and planing of wood		131649	130746	132344	140845		51717	47349	50222	54082		...	...
202	Products of wood, cork, straw, etc.		192681	228447	176474	215603		73895	80666	65737	93024		...	...
2021	Veneer sheets, plywood, particle board, etc.		...	...	...	...		...	...	...	...		...	...
2022	Builders' carpentry and joinery		...	...	...	...		...	...	...	...		...	...
2023	Wooden containers		...	...	...	...		...	...	...	...		...	...
2029	Other wood products; articles of cork/straw		294636	317069	319501	380070		76995	79849	91024	114916		...	...
210	Paper and paper products		155472	187399	138467	142289		82098	100028	72582	78048		...	...
2101	Pulp, paper and paperboard		...	...	...	...		...	...	...	...		...	...
2102	Corrugated paper and paperboard		...	...	...	...		...	...	...	...		...	...
2109	Other articles of paper and paperboard		...	...	...	...		...	...	...	...		...	...
221	Publishing		...	...	...	...		...	...	...	...		...	...
2211	Publishing of books and other publications		...	...	...	...		...	...	...	...		...	...
2212	Publishing of newspapers, journals, etc.		...	...	...	...		...	...	...	...		...	...
2213	Publishing of recorded media		...	...	...	...		...	...	...	...		...	...
2219	Other publishing		...	...	...	...		...	...	...	...		...	...

continued

Russian Federation

- 698 -

ISIC	Industry	Output (millions of Russian Roubles)					Value added (millions of Russian Roubles)					Gross fixed capital formation (millions of Russian Roubles)		
		Note	2007	2008	2009	2010	Note	2007	2008	2009	2010	Note	2009	2010
222	Printing and related service activities		123163	145522	119495	135516		41716	50298	35562	51065		...	...
2221	Printing		...	...	...	...		...	...	...	...		...	...
2222	Service activities related to printing		...	...	...	...		...	...	...	...		...	...
2230	Reproduction of recorded media		12841	13922	3759	3559		3736	6397	1812	1767		...	...
2310	Coke oven products		51956	83406	47985	92373		12134	13041	8656	18667		...	...
2320	Refined petroleum products		2951643	3907341	3336609	4050905	d/	887774	1230219	864622	1083702		...	...
2330	Processing of nuclear fuel	d/	...	...	...	...		...	...	...	...		...	...
241	Basic chemicals		1015925	1369985	1111107	1405216		310137	515395	367488	434759		...	...
2411	Basic chemicals, except fertilizers		...	...	...	...		...	...	...	...		...	...
2412	Fertilizers and nitrogen compounds		...	...	...	...		...	...	...	...		...	...
2413	Plastics in primary forms; synthetic rubber		...	...	...	...		...	...	...	...		...	...
242	Other chemicals		315633	423982	411780	501367		89444	121466	125254	150902		...	...
2421	Pesticides and other agro-chemical products		...	...	...	...		...	...	...	...		...	...
2422	Paints, varnishes, printing ink and mastics		50501	62395	60462	67021		18390	26069	22483	23482		...	...
2423	Pharmaceuticals, medicinal chemicals, etc.		94604	111071	130994	185397		37209	45864	54944	70785		...	...
2424	Soap, cleaning & cosmetic preparations		91489	113932	121669	114276		23083	35857	35635	36034		...	...
2429	Other chemical products n.e.c.		79038	136583	98655	134673		10763	13677	12192	20601		...	...
2430	Man-made fibres		14168	14046	11487	14146		2550	2060	2938	3581		...	...
251	Rubber products	e/	426703	523480	419766	521248	e/	104002	130082	122744	140184		...	...
2511	Rubber tyres and tubes		...	...	...	...		...	...	...	...		...	...
2519	Other rubber products		...	...	...	...		...	...	...	...		...	...
2520	Plastic products	e/	...	...	...	...	e/	...	...	...	...		...	...
2610	Glass and glass products		114383	125057	100793	120266		44035	45734	23767	37346		...	...
269	Non-metallic mineral products n.e.c.		820128	984937	674259	738594		323366	360924	215995	226176		...	...
2691	Pottery, china and earthenware		...	...	...	...		...	...	...	...		...	...
2692	Refractory ceramic products		...	...	...	...		...	...	...	...		...	...
2693	Struct.non-refractory clay; ceramic products		216463	242093	148970	154183		110562	112724	41801	35306		...	...
2694	Cement, lime and plaster		...	...	...	...		...	...	...	...		...	...
2695	Articles of concrete, cement and plaster		...	...	...	...		...	...	...	...		...	...
2696	Cutting, shaping & finishing of stone		...	...	...	...		...	...	...	...		...	...
2699	Other non-metallic mineral products n.e.c.		...	...	...	...		...	...	...	...		...	...
2710	Basic iron and steel		1606795	1988794	1276339	1820309		475804	565718	282146	394773		...	...
2720	Basic precious and non-ferrous metals		1275211	1303207	1031212	1319369		493134	391391	315277	458218		...	...
273	Casting of metals		22548	34545	24297	35912		5202	7461	4855	8549		...	...
2731	Casting of iron and steel		...	...	...	...		...	...	...	...		...	...
2732	Casting of non-ferrous metals		...	...	...	...		...	...	...	...		...	...
281	Struct.metal products;tanks;steam generators		262549	326063	248232	301760		78976	90686	70199	93467		...	...
2811	Structural metal products		...	...	...	...		...	...	...	...		...	...
2812	Tanks, reservoirs and containers of metal		...	...	...	...		...	...	...	...		...	...
2813	Steam generators		...	...	...	...		...	...	...	...		...	...
289	Other metal products; metal working services		223099	273379	190963	248564		53051	71931	54912	68960		...	...
2891	Metal forging/pressing/stamping/roll-forming		...	...	...	...		...	...	...	...		...	...
2892	Treatment & coating of metals		...	...	...	...		...	...	...	...		...	...
2893	Cutlery, hand tools and general hardware		...	...	...	...		...	...	...	...		...	...
2899	Other fabricated metal products n.e.c.		...	...	...	...		...	...	...	...		...	...
291	General purpose machinery		512015	648755	501205	584926		185124	251856	191343	219556		...	...
2911	Engines & turbines (not for transport equipment)		...	...	...	...		...	...	...	...		...	...
2912	Pumps, compressors, taps and valves		...	...	...	...		...	...	...	...		...	...
2913	Bearings, gears, gearing & driving elements		...	...	...	...		...	...	...	...		...	...
2914	Ovens, furnaces and furnace burners		...	...	...	...		...	...	...	...		...	...
2915	Lifting and handling equipment		...	...	...	...		...	...	...	...		...	...
2919	Other general purpose machinery		...	...	...	...		...	...	...	...		...	...

ISIC Revision 3

292	Special purpose machinery		331436	426032	286191	315677		114439	150095	96946	107369
2921	Agricultural and forestry machinery										
2922	Machine tools										
2923	Machinery for metallurgy										
2924	Machinery for mining & construction										
2925	Food/beverage/tobacco processing machinery										
2926	Machinery for textile, apparel and leather										
2927	Weapons and ammunition	d/					d/				
2929	Other special purpose machinery		63087	78072	76319	85086		11253	12300	14192	14705
2930	Domestic appliances n.e.c.		56493	51199	42029	55407		13403	12432	12289	18100
3000	Office, accounting and computing machinery										
3110	Electric motors, generators and transformers		190701	216564	180024	220265		60453	72189	60575	79061
3120	Electricity distribution & control apparatus		115476	115495	75121	122159		18623	19349	7951	16945
3130	Insulated wire and cable										
3140	Accumulators, primary cells and batteries	f/					f/				
3150	Lighting equipment and electric lamps	f/					f/				
3190	Other electrical equipment n.e.c.	f/	103277	123270	105513	132465	f/	31694	40573	37925	47991
3210	Electronic valves, tubes, etc.	d/					d/				
3220	TV/radio transmitters; line comm. apparatus	d/					d/				
3230	TV and radio receivers and associated goods	d/	189055	221924	212941	253926	d/	84506	105383	95565	113162
331	Medical, measuring, testing appliances, etc.										
3311	Medical, surgical and orthopaedic equipment										
3312	Measuring/testing/navigating appliances,etc.										
3313	Industrial process control equipment		13256	18680	18717	22469		6484	9436	8274	9680
3320	Optical instruments & photographic equipment	g/					g/				
3330	Watches and clocks	g/					g/				
3410	Motor vehicles	h/	850120	961414	521295	915085	h/	151454	137259	68771	120284
3420	Automobile bodies, trailers & semi-trailers	h/					h/				
3430	Parts/accessories for automobiles										
351	Building and repairing of ships and boats	d/					d/				
3511	Building and repairing of ships	d/					d/				
3512	Building/repairing of pleasure/sport. boats	d/					d/				
3520	Railway/tramway locomotives & rolling stock		179107	241539	179503	258333		47798	65738	47632	69445
3530	Aircraft and spacecraft	d/					d/				
359	Transport equipment n.e.c.	d/					d/				
3591	Motorcycles										
3592	Bicycles and invalid carriages										
3599	Other transport equipment n.e.c.										
3610	Furniture		132558	166073	141950	159163		35567	45548	43065	48763
369	Manufacturing n.e.c.		138217	170414	145177	171641		44110	58935	59483	64582
3691	Jewellery and related articles		109855	132405	112945	133513		35670	46809	49120	53681
3692	Musical instruments										
3693	Sports goods										
3694	Games and toys										
3699	Other manufacturing n.e.c.		193192	226274	147831	212707		29223	36605	27781	37686
3710	Recycling of metal waste and scrap		9753	13866	9393	11308		2543	5358	3123	3334
3720	Recycling of non-metal waste and scrap										
D	Total manufacturing		16531566	20191423	16759591	20461516		5027649	6172342	4913884	5827824

a/ 171 includes 172 and 1730.
b/ 1810 includes 1820.
c/ 191 includes 1920.
d/ Data suppressed due to confidentiality rules.
e/ 251 includes 2520.
f/ 3190 includes 3140 and 3150.
g/ 3320 includes 3330.
h/ 3410 includes 3420.

Russian Federation

ISIC Revision 3 — Index numbers of industrial production (2005=100)

ISIC	Industry	Note	1999	2000	2001	2002	2003	2004	2005	2006	2007	2008	2009	2010
15	Food and beverages		69	71	77	83	89	94	100	108	117	119	118	125
16	Tobacco products		70	85	90	96	94	94	100	102	98	101	100	97
17	Textiles		68	85	92	92	92	92	100	114	113	100	84	97
18	Wearing apparel, fur		87	107	116	110	112	102	100	110	109	110	91	100
19	Leather, leather products and footwear		66	71	81	90	100	100	100	122	125	124	124	148
20	Wood products (excl. furniture)		68	77	75	78	86	93	100	104	112	112	89	99
21	Paper and paper products		63	73	78	83	89	95	100	106	111	111	110	117
22	Printing and publishing		64	78	87	89	96	99	100	108	120	120	94	100
23	Coke,refined petroleum products,nuclear fuel		83	85	87	91	94	96	100	107	110	113	112	118
24	Chemicals and chemical products		74	85	85	86	90	96	100	105	112	107	99	114
25	Rubber and plastics products		56	70	72	72	76	86	100	121	152	187	163	198
26	Non-metallic mineral products		71	78	81	82	88	95	100	114	124	120	87	96
27	Basic metals		71	82	84	88	94	97	100	109	110	103	89	99
28	Fabricated metal products		46	53	64	68	73	78	100	114	135	149	123	140
29	Machinery and equipment n.e.c.		68	72	76	70	83	100	100	112	142	141	97	108
30	Office, accounting and computing machinery		27	25	29	37	48	78	100	141	206	163	103	123
31	Electrical machinery and apparatus		53	67	76	75	83	97	100	123	133	122	81	100
32	Radio,television and communication equipment		...	...	...	...	...	...	100	...	...	...	...	...
33	Medical, precision and optical instruments		16	27	29	21	45	59	100	113	119	112	76	97
34	Motor vehicles, trailers, semi-trailers		82	87	88	86	91	100	100	115	134	133	60	103
35	Other transport equipment		96	109	67	67	80	90	100	100	105	106	76	87
36	Furniture; manufacturing n.e.c.		56	63	69	72	81	91	100	111	121	127	96	115
37	Recycling		73	82	84	89	94	97	100	107	107	98	83	94
D	Total manufacturing		67	74	75	76	84	93	100	108	120	120	102	114

Senegal

Supplier of information:
Agence Nationale de la Statistique et de la Démographie, Dakar.

Basic source of data:
Annual survey; administrative source.

Major deviations from ISIC (Revision 3):
None reported.

Reference period:
Calendar year.

Scope:
All establishments.

Method of data collection:
Mail questionnaires.

Type of enumeration:
Sample survey.

Adjusted for non-response:
Yes.

Concepts and definitions of variables:
No deviations from the standard UN concepts and definitions are reported.

Related national publications:
None reported.

Senegal

ISIC	Industry	Number of establishments (number)					Employees (number)					Wages and salaries (West African CFA Francs)				
		Note	2007	2008	2009	2010	Note	2007	2008	2009	2010	Note	2007	2008	2009	2010
151	Processed meat,fish,fruit,vegetables,fats		47	48	46	46		…	…	…	…		…	…	…	…
1511	Processing/preserving of meat		4	5	5	5		…	…	…	…		…	…	…	…
1512	Processing/preserving of fish		33	34	33	33		…	…	…	…		…	…	…	…
1513	Processing/preserving of fruit & vegetables		6	5	5	5		…	…	…	…		…	…	…	…
1514	Vegetable and animal oils and fats		4	4	3	3		…	…	…	…		…	…	…	…
1520	Dairy products		13	13	14	14		…	…	…	…		…	…	…	…
153	Grain mill products; starches; animal feeds		5	5	5	5		…	…	…	…		…	…	…	…
1531	Grain mill products		5	5	5	5		…	…	…	…		…	…	…	…
1532	Starches and starch products		…	…	…	…		…	…	…	…		…	…	…	…
1533	Prepared animal feeds		…	…	…	…		…	…	…	…		…	…	…	…
154	Other food products		230	256	252	253		…	…	…	…		…	…	…	…
1541	Bakery products		189	213	210	211		…	…	…	…		…	…	…	…
1542	Sugar		1	1	1	1		…	…	…	…		…	…	…	…
1543	Cocoa, chocolate and sugar confectionery		4	4	4	4		…	…	…	…		…	…	…	…
1544	Macaroni, noodles & similar products		36	38	37	37		…	…	…	…		…	…	…	…
1549	Other food products n.e.c.		17	17	17	17		…	…	…	…		…	…	…	…
155	Beverages		2	2	2	2		…	…	…	…		…	…	…	…
1551	Distilling, rectifying & blending of spirits		2	2	2	2		…	…	…	…		…	…	…	…
1552	Wines		2	2	2	2		…	…	…	…		…	…	…	…
1553	Malt liquors and malt		13	13	13	13		…	…	…	…		…	…	…	…
1554	Soft drinks; mineral waters		2	2	2	2		…	…	…	…		…	…	…	…
1600	Tobacco products		11	11	11	11		…	…	…	…		…	…	…	…
171	Spinning, weaving and finishing of textiles		11	11	11	11		…	…	…	…		…	…	…	…
1711	Textile fibre preparation; textile weaving		11	11	11	11		…	…	…	…		…	…	…	…
1712	Finishing of textiles		…	…	…	…		…	…	…	…		…	…	…	…
172	Other textiles		10	10	9	9		…	…	…	…		…	…	…	…
1721	Made-up textile articles, except apparel		…	…	…	…		…	…	…	…		…	…	…	…
1722	Carpets and rugs		…	…	…	…		…	…	…	…		…	…	…	…
1723	Cordage, rope, twine and netting		1	1	1	1		…	…	…	…		…	…	…	…
1729	Other textiles n.e.c.		9	9	8	8		…	…	…	…		…	…	…	…
1730	Knitted and crocheted fabrics and articles		…	…	…	…		…	…	…	…		…	…	…	…
1810	Wearing apparel, except fur apparel		17	17	17	17		…	…	…	…		…	…	…	…
1820	Dressing & dyeing of fur; processing of fur		…	…	…	…		…	…	…	…		…	…	…	…
191	Tanning, dressing and processing of leather		3	3	3	3		…	…	…	…		…	…	…	…
1911	Tanning and dressing of leather		3	3	3	3		…	…	…	…		…	…	…	…
1912	Luggage, handbags, etc.; saddlery & harness		…	…	…	…		…	…	…	…		…	…	…	…
1920	Footwear		9	9	9	9		…	…	…	…		…	…	…	…
2010	Sawmilling and planing of wood		6	6	6	6		…	…	…	…		…	…	…	…
202	Products of wood, cork, straw, etc.		10	10	10	10		…	…	…	…		…	…	…	…
2021	Veneer sheets, plywood, particle board, etc.		…	…	…	…		…	…	…	…		…	…	…	…
2022	Builders' carpentry and joinery		…	…	…	…		…	…	…	…		…	…	…	…
2023	Wooden containers		10	10	10	10		…	…	…	…		…	…	…	…
2029	Other wood products; articles of cork/straw		12	13	13	13		…	…	…	…		…	…	…	…
210	Paper and paper products		…	…	…	…		…	…	…	…		…	…	…	…
2101	Pulp, paper and paperboard		12	13	13	13		…	…	…	…		…	…	…	…
2102	Corrugated paper and paperboard		…	…	…	…		…	…	…	…		…	…	…	…
2109	Other articles of paper and paperboard		12	13	13	13		…	…	…	…		…	…	…	…
221	Publishing		11	14	16	16		…	…	…	…		…	…	…	…
2211	Publishing of books and other publications		3	4	4	4		…	…	…	…		…	…	…	…
2212	Publishing of newspapers, journals, etc.		8	8	9	9		…	…	…	…		…	…	…	…
2213	Publishing of recorded media		…	…	…	…		…	…	…	…		…	…	…	…
2219	Other publishing		-	2	3	3		…	…	…	…		…	…	…	…

Code	Activity				
222	Printing and related service activities	70	72	74	74
2221	Printing	70	72	74	74
2222	Service activities related to printing				
2230	Reproduction of recorded media				
2310	Coke oven products				
2320	Refined petroleum products	1	1	1	1
2330	Processing of nuclear fuel	1	1	1	1
241	Basic chemicals	2	2	2	2
2411	Basic chemicals, except fertilizers				
2412	Fertilizers and nitrogen compounds	2	2	2	2
2413	Plastics in primary forms; synthetic rubber				
242	Other chemicals	52	52	52	51
2421	Pesticides and other agro-chemical products	2	2	2	2
2422	Paints, varnishes, printing ink and mastics	8	8	8	8
2423	Pharmaceuticals, medicinal chemicals, etc.	6	6	6	6
2424	Soap, cleaning & cosmetic preparations	25	25	24	24
2429	Other chemical products n.e.c.	11	11	12	11
2430	Man-made fibres				
251	Rubber products	4	4	4	4
2511	Rubber tyres and tubes	4	4	4	4
2519	Other rubber products				
2520	Plastic products	35	37	34	35
2610	Glass and glass products	1	1	1	1
269	Non-metallic mineral products n.e.c.	15	16	16	16
2691	Pottery, china and earthenware				
2692	Refractory ceramic products				
2693	Struct.non-refractory clay; ceramic products				
2694	Cement, lime and plaster	7	9	9	9
2695	Articles of concrete, cement and plaster				
2696	Cutting, shaping & finishing of stone	8	7	7	7
2699	Other non-metallic mineral products n.e.c.				
2710	Basic iron and steel	21	21	21	21
2720	Basic precious and non-ferrous metals	7	8	8	8
273	Casting of metals	7	7	7	7
2731	Casting of iron and steel				
2732	Casting of non-ferrous metals				
281	Struct.metal products;tanks;steam generators	38	39	38	38
2811	Structural metal products	37	38	37	37
2812	Tanks, reservoirs and containers of metal	1	1	1	1
2813	Steam generators	-	-	-	-
289	Other metal products; metal working services	-			
2891	Metal forging/pressing/stamping/roll-forming				
2892	Treatment & coating of metals				
2893	Cutlery, hand tools and general hardware				
2899	Other fabricated metal products n.e.c.				
291	General purpose machinery	-	-		
2911	Engines & turbines (not for transport equipment)				
2912	Pumps, compressors, taps and valves				
2913	Bearings, gears, gearing & driving elements				
2914	Ovens, furnaces and furnace burners				
2915	Lifting and handling equipment				
2919	Other general purpose machinery				
292	Special purpose machinery	1	1	1	1
2921	Agricultural and forestry machinery	1	1	1	1
2922	Machine tools				
2923	Machinery for metallurgy				
2924	Machinery for mining & construction				
2925	Food/beverage/tobacco processing machinery				
2926	Machinery for textile, apparel and leather				
2927	Weapons and ammunition				
2929	Other special purpose machinery				

continued

Senegal

ISIC	Industry	Number of establishments (number)					Employees (number)					Wages and salaries (West African CFA Francs)				
		Note	2007	2008	2009	2010	Note	2007	2008	2009	2010	Note	2007	2008	2009	2010
2930	Domestic appliances n.e.c.		2	2	2	2		...	...	...	...		...	...	...	...
3000	Office, accounting and computing machinery		2	2	2	2		...	...	...	...		...	...	...	...
3110	Electric motors, generators and transformers		...	...	...	...		...	...	...	...		...	...	...	...
3120	Electricity distribution & control apparatus		1	1	1	1		...	...	...	...		...	...	...	...
3130	Insulated wire and cable		...	...	...	...		...	...	...	...		...	...	...	...
3140	Accumulators, primary cells and batteries		2	2	2	2		...	...	...	...		...	...	...	...
3150	Lighting equipment and electric lamps															
3190	Other electrical equipment n.e.c.		1	1	1	1		...	...	...	...		...	...	...	...
3210	Electronic valves, tubes, etc.		1	1	1	1		...	...	...	...		...	...	...	...
3220	TV transmitters; line comm. apparatus		1	1	1	1		...	...	...	...		...	...	...	...
3230	TV and radio receivers and associated goods		...	...	...	...		...	...	...	...		...	...	...	...
331	Medical, measuring, testing appliances, etc.		-	-	-	-		...	...	...	...		...	...	...	...
3311	Medical, surgical and orthopaedic equipment		...	...	...	...		...	...	...	...		...	...	...	...
3312	Measuring/testing/navigating appliances,etc.		...	...	...	...		...	...	...	...		...	...	...	...
3313	Industrial process control equipment		...	...	...	...		...	...	...	...		...	...	...	...
3320	Optical instruments & photographic equipment		12	12	13	13		...	...	...	...		...	...	...	...
3330	Watches and clocks		1	1	1	1		...	...	...	...		...	...	...	...
3410	Motor vehicles		1	1	1	1		...	...	...	...		...	...	...	...
3420	Automobile bodies, trailers & semi-trailers		...	...	...	...		...	...	...	...		...	...	...	...
3430	Parts/accessories for automobiles		...	...	...	...		...	...	...	...		...	...	...	...
351	Building and repairing of ships and boats		9	11	10	10		...	...	...	...		...	...	...	...
3511	Building and repairing of ships		6	8	8	8		...	...	...	...		...	...	...	...
3512	Building/repairing of pleasure/sport. boats		3	3	2	2		...	...	...	...		...	...	...	...
3520	Railway/tramway locomotives & rolling stock		1	1	1	1		...	...	...	...		...	...	...	...
3530	Aircraft and spacecraft		...	...	...	...		...	...	...	...		...	...	...	...
359	Transport equipment n.e.c.		2	1	1	1		...	...	...	...		...	...	...	...
3591	Motorcycles		2	1	1	1		...	...	...	...		...	...	...	...
3592	Bicycles and invalid carriages		...	...	...	...		...	...	...	...		...	...	...	...
3599	Other transport equipment n.e.c.		...	...	...	...		...	...	...	...		...	...	...	...
3610	Furniture		...	...	...	...		...	...	...	...		...	...	...	...
369	Manufacturing n.e.c.		-	-	-	-		...	...	...	...		...	...	...	...
3691	Jewellery and related articles		...	...	...	...		...	...	...	...		...	...	...	...
3692	Musical instruments		...	...	...	...		...	...	...	...		...	...	...	...
3693	Sports goods		...	...	...	...		...	...	...	...		...	...	...	...
3694	Games and toys		...	...	...	...		...	...	...	...		...	...	...	...
3699	Other manufacturing n.e.c.		...	...	...	...		...	...	...	...		...	...	...	...
3710	Recycling of metal waste and scrap															
3720	Recycling of non-metal waste and scrap		...	...	...	...		...	...	...	...		...	...	...	...
D	Total manufacturing		685	723	718	719		...	...	...	...		...	...	...	...

Senegal

ISIC	Industry	Output at producers' prices (millions of West African CFA Francs)					Value added at producers' prices (millions of West African CFA Francs)					Gross fixed capital formation (millions of West African CFA Francs)
		Note	2007	2008	2009	2010	Note	2007	2008	2009	2010	Note
151	Processed meat,fish,fruit,vegetables,fats		225747	214752	204883	208050		23994	18380	15995	20041	
1511	Processing/preserving of meat		5877	6090	5364	6026		1927	2011	1079	1664	
1512	Processing/preserving of fish		99593	93786	87017	88154		8689	6867	3435	5432	
1513	Processing/preserving of fruit & vegetables		11024	11824	15449	15308		2845	2957	3504	3437	
1514	Vegetable and animal oils and fats		109253	103051	97053	98562		10533	6545	7977	9509	
1520	Dairy products		53695	51120	20888	38582		6758	4650	-10770	9096	
153	Grain mill products; starches; animal feeds		109425	133915	115020	117036		17735	18840	25995	18825	
1531	Grain mill products		109425	133915	115020	117036		17735	18840	25995	18825	
1532	Starches and starch products		...	...	...	...		...	...	...	...	
1533	Prepared animal feeds		170909	180169	177716	187957		51356	50495	48183	52229	
154	Other food products		29236	35468	33856	35989		4184	4669	4104	4374	
1541	Bakery products		53377	49151	45583	52864		28109	27976	25773	32152	
1542	Sugar		11156	11808	11759	9109		3496	3932	3993	3227	
1543	Cocoa, chocolate and sugar confectionery		...	...	...	...		...	...	...	...	
1544	Macaroni, noodles & similar products		77140	83742	86518	89995		15567	13918	14313	12476	
1549	Other food products n.e.c.		51037	52769	55116	63442		12175	9763	9575	10902	
155	Beverages		...	...	...	...		...	...	...	...	
1551	Distilling, rectifying & blending of spirits		7310	7769	9117	8801		1110	1149	1216	1315	
1552	Wines		444	510	487	491		123	133	131	122	
1553	Malt liquors and malt		43284	44491	45511	54151		10943	8481	8229	9465	
1554	Soft drinks; mineral waters		34175	54187	61100	65426		2315	9226	12775	11295	
1600	Tobacco products		9294	8941	10140	8362		1880	2389	2147	2342	
171	Spinning, weaving and finishing of textiles		9294	8941	10140	8362		1880	2389	2147	2342	
1711	Textile fibre preparation; textile weaving		...	...	...	...		...	...	...	...	
1712	Finishing of textiles		13030	12956	13152	15131		3368	3363	2627	2722	
172	Other textiles		...	...	...	...		...	...	...	...	
1721	Made-up textile articles, except apparel		...	...	...	...		...	...	...	...	
1722	Carpets and rugs		121	128	135	142		21	22	23	24	
1723	Cordage, rope, twine and netting		12909	12829	13017	14989		3348	3341	2604	2697	
1729	Other textiles n.e.c.		...	...	...	...		...	...	...	...	
1730	Knitted and crocheted fabrics and articles		1702	1926	1848	1946		670	699	683	710	
1810	Wearing apparel, except fur apparel		...	...	...	...		...	...	...	...	
1820	Dressing & dyeing of fur; processing of fur		5280	5170	3185	4021		878	567	691	525	
191	Tanning, dressing and processing of leather		5280	5170	3185	4021		878	567	691	525	
1911	Tanning and dressing of leather		...	...	...	...		...	...	...	...	
1912	Luggage, handbags, etc.; saddlery & harness		2663	2582	2710	2780		623	385	405	413	
1920	Footwear		22082	35712	33741	34731		3750	4099	4965	4886	
2010	Sawmilling and planing of wood		546	711	731	769		75	80	80	84	
202	Products of wood, cork, straw, etc.		...	...	...	...		...	...	...	...	
2021	Veneer sheets, plywood, particle board, etc.		...	...	...	...		...	...	...	...	
2022	Builders' carpentry and joinery		...	...	...	...		...	...	...	...	
2023	Wooden containers		546	711	731	769		75	80	80	84	
2029	Other wood products; articles of cork/straw		27771	29662	30384	32864		4808	6017	6457	7144	
210	Paper and paper products		...	...	...	...		...	...	...	...	
2101	Pulp, paper and paperboard		...	...	...	...		...	...	...	...	
2102	Corrugated paper and paperboard		27771	29662	30384	32864		4808	6017	6457	7144	
2109	Other articles of paper and paperboard		...	...	...	...		...	...	...	...	
221	Publishing		3808	3845	4783	4710		1422	1416	1491	1695	
2211	Publishing of books and other publications		608	547	612	711		261	158	192	305	
2212	Publishing of newspapers, journals, etc.		3200	3165	3840	3650		1161	1237	1279	1368	
2213	Publishing of recorded media		-	134	331	349		-	20	21	22	
2219	Other publishing		...	...	...	...		...	...	...	...	

continued

Senegal

ISIC	Industry	Output at producers' prices (millions of West African CFA Francs)					Value added at producers' prices (millions of West African CFA Francs)					Gross fixed capital formation (millions of West African CFA Francs)
		Note	2007	2008	2009	2010	Note	2007	2008	2009	2010	Note
222	Printing and related service activities		22877	20680	21922	20620		6097	5884	6146	5227	
2221	Printing		22877	20680	21922	20620		6097	5884	6146	5227	
2222	Service activities related to printing		...	...	...	...		...	...	...	...	
2230	Reproduction of recorded media		...	...	...	...		...	...	...	...	
2310	Coke oven products											
2320	Refined petroleum products		258184	386639	210482	239380		27755	16542	11300	5950	
2330	Processing of nuclear fuel											
241	Basic chemicals		82728	124316	116742	124029		23526	30988	26694	29880	
2411	Basic chemicals, except fertilizers		82728	124316	116742	124029		23526	30988	26694	29880	
2412	Fertilizers and nitrogen compounds		...	...	...	...		...	...	...	...	
2413	Plastics in primary forms; synthetic rubber		...	...	...	...		...	...	...	...	
242	Other chemicals		115131	114660	109864	107350		23659	22889	26442	26383	
2421	Pesticides and other agro-chemical products		6839	6267	7470	5185		2244	1749	1639	1437	
2422	Paints, varnishes, printing ink and mastics		9459	8666	8778	8986		2037	1897	1976	2254	
2423	Pharmaceuticals, medicinal chemicals, etc.		25689	25622	24836	27934		6253	6127	6638	7587	
2424	Soap, cleaning & cosmetic preparations		62244	62542	57601	55238		10419	10418	13800	12326	
2429	Other chemical products n.e.c.		10900	11564	11179	10007		2706	2698	2389	2780	
2430	Man-made fibres		...	...	...	...		...	...	...	...	
251	Rubber products		595	594	613	640		125	90	92	113	
2511	Rubber tyres and tubes		595	594	613	640		125	90	92	113	
2519	Other rubber products		...	...	...	...		...	...	...	...	
2520	Plastic products		62593	61928	60801	66145		10464	10086	11871	12140	
2610	Glass and glass products		553	582	614	646		101	106	112	118	
269	Non-metallic mineral products n.e.c.		185634	186775	208624	245712		58302	67844	79726	98621	
2691	Pottery, china and earthenware		...	...	...	...		...	...	...	...	
2692	Refractory ceramic products		...	...	...	...		...	...	...	...	
2693	Struct.non-refractory clay; ceramic products		...	...	...	...		...	...	...	...	
2694	Cement, lime and plaster		158837	172344	192026	224954		55288	64425	75653	93071	
2695	Articles of concrete, cement and plaster		26797	14430	16599	20758		3013	3419	4073	5550	
2696	Cutting, shaping & finishing of stone		...	...	...	...		...	...	...	...	
2699	Other non-metallic mineral products n.e.c.		...	...	...	...		...	...	...	...	
2710	Basic iron and steel		...	...	...	...		...	...	...	...	
2720	Basic precious and non-ferrous metals		57135	43906	45315	45889		4943	6437	7140	6982	
273	Casting of metals		2285	2107	2944	4188		530	413	549	655	
2731	Casting of iron and steel		2285	2107	2944	4188		530	413	549	655	
2732	Casting of non-ferrous metals		...	...	...	...		...	...	...	...	
281	Struct.metal products;tanks;steam generators		17240	9828	9861	8945		1349	1156	1587	1317	
2811	Structural metal products		17235	9815	9861	8945		1348	1156	1587	1318	
2812	Tanks, reservoirs and containers of metal		...	...	...	...		...	...	...	...	
2813	Steam generators		5	13	-	-		-	1	-1	-1	
289	Other metal products; metal working services		-	-	-	-		-	-	-	-	
2891	Metal forging/pressing/stamping/roll-forming		...	...	...	...		...	...	...	...	
2892	Treatment & coating of metals		...	...	...	...		...	...	...	...	
2893	Cutlery, hand tools and general hardware		...	...	...	...		...	...	...	...	
2899	Other fabricated metal products n.e.c.		...	...	...	...		...	...	...	...	
291	General purpose machinery		-	-	-	-		-	-	-	-	
2911	Engines & turbines (not for transport equipment)		...	...	...	...		...	...	...	...	
2912	Pumps, compressors, taps and valves		...	...	...	...		...	...	...	...	
2913	Bearings, gears, gearing & driving elements		...	...	...	...		...	...	...	...	
2914	Ovens, furnaces and furnace burners		...	...	...	...		...	...	...	...	
2915	Lifting and handling equipment		...	...	...	...		...	...	...	...	
2919	Other general purpose machinery		...	...	...	...		...	...	...	...	

292	Special purpose machinery	3506	2488	3513	2116	491	387	443	457
2921	Agricultural and forestry machinery	3506	2488	3513	2116	491	387	443	457
2922	Machine tools	…	…	…	…	…	…	…	…
2923	Machinery for metallurgy	…	…	…	…	…	…	…	…
2924	Machinery for mining & construction	…	…	…	…	…	…	…	…
2925	Food/beverage/tobacco processing machinery	…	…	…	…	…	…	…	…
2926	Machinery for textile, apparel and leather	…	…	…	…	…	…	…	…
2927	Weapons and ammunition	…	…	…	…	…	…	…	…
2929	Other special purpose machinery	3944	4153	4382	4612	208	219	232	244
2930	Domestic appliances n.e.c.	690	705	740	779	125	119	128	129
3000	Office, accounting and computing machinery	…	…	…	…	…	…	…	…
3110	Electric motors, generators and transformers	1407	1481	1563	1645	358	377	398	419
3120	Electricity distribution & control apparatus	…	…	…	…	…	…	…	…
3130	Insulated wire and cable	5593	4547	4569	4693	915	1061	1272	1171
3140	Accumulators, primary cells and batteries	8505	9232	6856	7437	1067	1049	1093	1464
3150	Lighting equipment and electric lamps	242	255	269	283	61	65	68	72
3190	Other electrical equipment n.e.c.	…	…	…	…	…	…	…	…
3210	Electronic valves, tubes, etc.	…	…	…	…	…	…	…	…
3220	TV/radio transmitters; line comm. apparatus	…	…	…	…	…	…	…	…
3230	TV and radio receivers and associated goods	-	-	-	-	-	-	-	-
331	Medical, measuring, testing appliances, etc.	-	-	-	-	-	-	-	-
3311	Medical, surgical and orthopaedic equipment	…	…	…	…	…	…	…	…
3312	Measuring/testing/navigating appliances,etc.	…	…	…	…	…	…	…	…
3313	Industrial process control equipment	2151	1672	1764	1684	501	542	569	617
3320	Optical instruments & photographic equipment	345	459	316	297	91	132	101	168
3330	Watches and clocks	686	1203	2014	2945	139	346	1429	1368
3410	Motor vehicles	…	…	…	…	…	…	…	…
3420	Automobile bodies, trailers & semi-trailers	…	…	…	…	…	…	…	…
3430	Parts/accessories for automobiles	9683	14914	13248	14070	2958	4850	3897	4172
351	Building and repairing of ships and boats	1843	2742	2521	2781	471	460	482	578
3511	Building and repairing of ships	7840	12171	10727	11289	2486	4390	3415	3594
3512	Building/repairing of pleasure/sport. boats	292	307	324	341	144	152	160	169
3520	Railway/tramway locomotives & rolling stock	…	…	…	…	…	…	…	…
3530	Aircraft and spacecraft	73	53	56	59	-23	6	7	7
359	Transport equipment n.e.c.	73	53	56	59	-23	6	7	7
3591	Motorcycles	…	…	…	…	…	…	…	…
3592	Bicycles and invalid carriages	…	…	…	…	…	…	…	…
3599	Other transport equipment n.e.c.	-	-	-	-	-	-	-	-
3610	Furniture	…	…	…	…	…	…	…	…
369	Manufacturing n.e.c.	…	…	…	…	…	…	…	…
3691	Jewellery and related articles	…	…	…	…	…	…	…	…
3692	Musical instruments	…	…	…	…	…	…	…	…
3693	Sports goods	…	…	…	…	…	…	…	…
3694	Games and toys	…	…	…	…	…	…	…	…
3699	Other manufacturing n.e.c.	…	…	…	…	…	…	…	…
3710	Recycling of metal waste and scrap	…	…	…	…	…	…	…	…
3720	Recycling of non-metal waste and scrap	…	…	…	…	…	…	…	…
D	Total manufacturing	1573236	1781902	1562793	1690312	295694	302112	302755	340749

Senegal

Index numbers of industrial production

ISIC Revision 3

(2005=100)

ISIC	Industry	Note	1999	2000	2001	2002	2003	2004	2005	2006	2007	2008	2009	2010
15	Food and beverages	a/	69	65	62	67	72	93	100	118	128	106	114	114
16	Tobacco products	a/	...	...	...	...	...	...	...	...	...	...	...	...
17	Textiles	b/	156	150	188	95	135	108	100	94	103	50	74	33
18	Wearing apparel, fur	b/	...	...	...	...	...	...	...	...	...	...	...	...
19	Leather, leather products and footwear	b/	...	...	...	...	...	...	...	...	...	...	...	...
20	Wood products (excl. furniture)		130	138	124	173	148	148	100	108	6	8	58	87
21	Paper and paper products		73	78	70	105	82	70	100	73	78	99	99	99
22	Printing and publishing		...	...	...	...	...	...	...	...	...	...	...	...
23	Coke,refined petroleum products,nuclear fuel	c/	75	96	80	117	109	110	100	54	64	58	59	59
24	Chemicals and chemical products	c/	...	...	...	...	...	...	...	...	...	...	...	...
25	Rubber and plastics products	c/	...	...	...	...	...	...	...	...	...	...	...	...
26	Non-metallic mineral products		...	...	...	...	...	...	...	...	...	...	...	...
27	Basic metals		...	...	...	...	...	...	...	...	...	...	...	...
28	Fabricated metal products	d/	172	173	67	109	112	111	100	97	94	83	77	92
29	Machinery and equipment n.e.c.	d/	...	...	...	...	...	...	...	...	...	...	...	...
30	Office, accounting and computing machinery	d/	...	...	...	...	...	...	...	...	...	...	...	...
31	Electrical machinery and apparatus	d/	...	...	...	...	...	...	...	...	...	...	...	...
32	Radio,television and communication equipment	d/	...	...	...	...	...	...	...	...	...	...	...	...
33	Medical, precision and optical instruments	d/	...	...	...	...	...	...	...	...	...	...	...	...
34	Motor vehicles, trailers, semi-trailers	d/	...	...	...	...	...	...	...	...	...	...	...	...
35	Other transport equipment	d/	...	...	...	...	...	...	...	...	...	...	...	...
36	Furniture; manufacturing n.e.c.		...	111	120	87	83	93	100	89	86	91	96	94
37	Recycling		...	...	...	...	...	...	...	...	...	...	...	...
D	Total manufacturing		...	70	70	85	85	98	100	95	105	92	100	102

a/ 15 includes 16.
b/ 17 includes 18 and 19.
c/ 23 includes 24 and 25.
d/ 28 includes 29, 30, 31, 32, 33, 34 and 35.

Serbia

Supplier of information:
Statistical Office of the Republic of Serbia, Belgrade.

Basic source of data:
Annual survey; administrative source.

Major deviations from ISIC (Revision 4):
Data presented in ISIC (Revision 4) were originally classified according to NACE (Revision 2).

Reference period:
Calendar year.

Scope:
All enterprises, excluding Kosovo and Metohia.

Method of data collection:
Data for output and value added are derived from the financial statements of the National Bank of Serbia; other data are collected by mail questionnaires.

Type of enumeration:
Complete enumeration for large and medium enterprises; sample survey for small enterprises with less than 50 employees.

Adjusted for non-response:
Yes.

Concepts and definitions of variables:
Output refers to gross output at basic prices.
Value added refers to total value added at basic prices.

Related national publications:
System of National Accounts of the Republic of Serbia; Statistical Release: Gross domestic product of the Republic of Serbia, both published by the Statistical Office of the Republic of Serbia, Belgrade.

Serbia

ISIC Revision 4

ISIC	Industry	Output (billions of Serbian Dinars) Note	2007	2008	2009	2010	Value added (billions of Serbian Dinars) Note	2007	2008	2009	2010	Gross fixed capital formation (billions of Serbian Dinars) Note	2009	2010
10	Food products		289.6	339.0	373.5	388.5		69.5	83.4	90.8	96.0		…	…
11	Beverages		87.9	102.8	76.4	78.1		20.7	24.8	27.4	26.3		…	…
12	Tobacco products		23.5	25.6	27.8	27.6		6.5	7.5	6.4	6.8		…	…
13	Textiles		13.0	14.9	15.7	16.3		3.6	4.7	5.1	5.2		…	…
14	Wearing apparel		29.3	33.2	29.1	33.8		10.6	13.3	12.3	12.9		…	…
15	Leather and related products		12.5	13.4	12.4	17.1		5.0	5.3	4.9	5.1		…	…
16	Wood/wood products/cork, excl. furniture		25.7	32.7	29.4	32.6		6.0	7.8	7.4	6.9		…	…
17	Paper and paper products		32.7	37.8	40.6	46.4		7.9	9.5	12.2	12.4		…	…
18	Printing and reproduction of recorded media		25.0	26.9	26.4	28.4		8.3	8.5	8.4	9.0		…	…
19	Coke and refined petroleum products		74.9	96.4	71.2	128.9		16.2	18.4	18.9	29.3		…	…
20	Chemicals and chemical products		56.0	61.5	78.9	106.7		13.5	12.8	12.8	16.7		…	…
21	Pharmaceuticals, medicinal chemicals, etc.		71.3	77.8	34.7	35.8		16.4	15.2	17.2	14.4		…	…
22	Rubber and plastics products		75.8	81.8	72.4	91.0		20.4	23.0	24.5	25.1		…	…
23	Other non-metallic mineral products		59.9	68.6	61.8	62.7		20.4	22.4	22.8	21.7		…	…
24	Basic metals		119.9	142.2	96.7	151.1		17.7	17.6	5.2	6.3		…	…
25	Fabricated metal products, except machinery		91.2	114.4	101.3	110.7		25.2	31.4	31.9	33.4		…	…
26	Computer, electronic and optical products		31.3	35.4	32.9	32.0		11.6	13.3	11.3	10.9		…	…
27	Electrical equipment		37.7	44.7	42.3	49.1		9.8	12.8	12.0	13.1		…	…
28	Machinery and equipment n.e.c.		34.2	41.1	36.3	39.1		10.5	12.7	13.0	12.6		…	…
29	Motor vehicles, trailers and semi-trailers		29.2	39.2	32.3	36.2		6.0	10.8	6.6	6.8		…	…
30	Other transport equipment		5.7	9.8	9.0	8.1		2.2	2.7	3.3	2.3		…	…
31	Furniture		24.3	28.4	27.7	30.2		7.3	8.5	8.9	9.6		…	…
32	Other manufacturing		14.3	16.8	14.3	15.9		4.9	5.8	5.6	5.8		…	…
33	Repair and installation of machinery/equipment		2.7	3.7	3.0	3.2		1.0	1.2	1.3	1.2		…	…
C	Total manufacturing		1267.6	1488.2	1346.1	1569.5		321.2	373.6	370.3	389.9		108.4	94.8

Serbia

ISIC	Industry	Note	1999	2000	2001	2002	2003	2004	2005	2006	2007	2008	2009	2010
	ISIC Revision 4								**Index numbers of industrial production** (2005=100)					
10	Food products		...	87	85	93	88	93	100	103	108	108	101	103
11	Beverages		...	98	96	100	110	106	100	115	122	120	105	103
12	Tobacco products		...	86	79	94	89	87	100	111	109	108	106	114
13	Textiles		...	176	188	157	108	108	100	99	80	66	45	51
14	Wearing apparel		...	255	265	193	126	119	100	94	95	89	68	68
15	Leather and related products		...	196	199	150	119	100	100	99	97	94	77	76
16	Wood/wood products/cork,excl. furniture		...	278	227	156	111	129	100	98	121	100	57	45
17	Paper and paper products		...	115	114	118	104	107	100	97	107	110	105	116
18	Printing and reproduction of recorded media		...	113	103	101	100	107	100	107	119	125	133	144
19	Coke and refined petroleum products		...	41	66	85	85	103	100	103	100	98	89	86
20	Chemicals and chemical products		...	64	75	74	77	101	100	99	116	111	82	100
21	Pharmaceuticals,medicinal chemicals, etc.		...	59	61	65	87	90	100	120	112	129	108	107
22	Rubber and plastics products		...	71	81	88	87	92	100	96	103	104	84	85
23	Other non-metallic mineral products		...	109	113	114	100	102	100	107	107	101	81	82
24	Basic metals		...	58	52	57	58	82	100	123	120	124	89	107
25	Fabricated metal products, except machinery		...	103	88	90	87	97	100	104	113	124	101	108
26	Computer, electronic and optical products		...	279	234	352	268	158	100	53	46	45	35	25
27	Electrical equipment		...	100	95	100	94	103	100	99	126	129	116	132
28	Machinery and equipment n.e.c.		...	129	129	132	115	192	100	83	84	102	74	66
29	Motor vehicles, trailers and semi-trailers		...	82	70	82	75	80	100	92	90	76	46	44
30	Other transport equipment		...	213	165	165	133	114	100	97	146	227	216	179
31	Furniture		...	116	125	115	116	110	100	170	177	198	124	127
32	Other manufacturing		...	173	172	201	145	127	100	89	120	78	81	66
33	Repair and installation of machinery/equipment		...	135	132	126	123	114	100	85	85	76	77	72
C	Total manufacturing		...	94	95	97	93	101	100	105	109	111	93	96

Singapore

Supplier of information:
Research and Statistics Unit, Economic Development Board, Singapore.

Basic source of data:
Annual census of manufacturing activities.

Major deviations from ISIC (Revision 4):
None reported.

Reference period:
Calendar year.

Scope:
All establishments.

Method of data collection:
The census was based on information obtained through mail questionnaires and online surveys.

Type of enumeration:
Sample survey.

Adjusted for non-response:
Yes.

Concepts and definitions of variables:
Number of persons engaged excludes unpaid family workers.
Wages and salaries is compensation of employees.
Output refers to gross output at basic prices.
Value added refers to total value added at basic prices.

Related national publications:
Report on the Census of Manufacturing Activities, published by the Economic Development Board, Singapore.

Singapore

ISIC	Industry		Number of establishments (number)					Number of persons engaged (number)					Wages and salaries paid to employees (millions of Singapore Dollars)				
		Note	2007	2008	2009	2010	Note	2007	2008	2009	2010	Note	2007	2008	2009	2010
1010	Processing/preserving of meat		64	68	71	77		2143	2475	2792	2845		53	62	70	74
1020	Processing/preserving of fish, etc.		36	40	40	38		1462	1372	1380	1298		34	32	33	37
1030	Processing/preserving of fruit,vegetables		10	10	11	11		223	255	265	286		6	7	7	8
1040	Vegetable and animal oils and fats		14	14	15	13		791	801	852	817		35	36	41	42
1050	Dairy products		10	14	14	13		1419	1667	2096	1711		53	68	101	77
106	Grain mill products,starches and starch products	a/	…	…	…	…	a/	…	…	…	…	a/	…	…	…	…
1061	Grain mill products	a/	…	…	…	…	a/	…	…	…	…	a/	…	…	…	…
1062	Starches and starch products	a/	…	…	…	…	a/	…	…	…	…	a/	…	…	…	…
107	Other food products		583	613	666	652		13829	14918	16587	16797		360	403	433	453
1071	Bakery products	a/	256	272	289	286	a/	5961	6641	7458	7331	a/	125	146	162	164
1072	Sugar		…	…	…	…		…	…	…	…		…	…	…	…
1073	Cocoa, chocolate and sugar confectionery		12	11	10	10		486	481	468	496		22	26	24	23
1074	Macaroni, noodles, couscous, etc.		49	45	53	48		904	1073	1266	1248		19	24	27	26
1075	Prepared meals and dishes		100	107	137	140		2102	2339	2855	3033		45	52	59	70
1079	Other food products n.e.c.	a/	166	178	177	168	a/	4376	4384	4540	4689	a/	149	155	161	170
1080	Prepared animal feeds	a/	…	…	…	…	a/	…	…	…	…	a/	…	…	…	…
1101	Distilling, rectifying and blending of spirits	b/	21	22	28	28	b/	1892	1868	2012	1847	b/	94	107	107	109
1102	Wines	b/	…	…	…	…	b/	…	…	…	…	b/	…	…	…	…
1103	Malt liquors and malt	b/	…	…	…	…	b/	…	…	…	…	b/	…	…	…	…
1104	Soft drinks,mineral waters,other bottled waters	b/	…	…	…	…	b/	…	…	…	…	b/	…	…	…	…
1200	Tobacco products	a/	…	…	…	…	a/	…	…	…	…	a/	…	…	…	…
131	Spinning, weaving and finishing of textiles	c/	…	…	…	…	c/	…	…	…	…	c/	…	…	…	…
1311	Preparation and spinning of textile fibres		…	…	…	…		…	…	…	…		…	…	…	…
1312	Weaving of textiles		…	…	…	…		…	…	…	…		…	…	…	…
1313	Finishing of textiles		…	…	…	…		…	…	…	…		…	…	…	…
139	Other textiles		102	101	105	94		1176	912	808	492		24	21	18	12
1391	Knitted and crocheted fabrics	c/	…	…	…	…	c/	…	…	…	…	c/	…	…	…	…
1392	Made-up textile articles, except apparel		80	88	93	87		666	641	623	388		13	14	13	9
1393	Carpets and rugs		…	…	…	…		…	…	…	…		…	…	…	…
1394	Cordage, rope, twine and netting		…	…	…	…		…	…	…	…		…	…	…	…
1399	Other textiles n.e.c.	c/	22	13	12	7	c/	510	271	185	104	c/	11	7	5	3
1410	Wearing apparel, except fur apparel	d/	494	505	502	461	d/	6912	5317	3373	2959	d/	138	110	83	67
1420	Articles of fur	d/	…	…	…	…	d/	…	…	…	…	d/	…	…	…	…
1430	Knitted and crocheted apparel	d/	…	…	…	…	d/	…	…	…	…	d/	…	…	…	…
151	Leather;luggage,handbags,saddlery,harness;fur		24	22	14	12		1034	841	416	431		34	30	14	15
1511	Tanning/dressing of leather; dressing of fur		…	…	…	…		…	…	…	…		…	…	…	…
1512	Luggage,handbags,etc.;saddlery/harness		…	…	…	…		…	…	…	…		…	…	…	…
1520	Footwear		20	15	17	13		163	98	118	124		2	2	2	2
1610	Sawmilling and planing of wood		…	…	…	…		…	…	…	…		…	…	…	…
162	Wood products, cork, straw, plaiting materials	e/	106	119	121	116	e/	1896	2030	1886	1987	e/	46	48	51	50

ISIC	Industry	Note												
1621	Veneer sheets and wood-based panels	e/	30	30	31	30	716	696	663	615	18	16	18	15
1622	Builders' carpentry and joinery		42	48	46	48	862	1036	838	863	22	26	23	25
1623	Wooden containers		34	41	44	38	318	298	385	509	6	7	10	9
1629	Other wood products;articles of cork,straw	e/	...	...	...	...	...	...	...	...	...	...	...	...
1701	Pulp, paper and paperboard	f/	87	81	86	83	3668	3468	3222	3202	121	119	116	122
1702	Corrugated paper and paperboard		32	24	26	26	790	694	757	799	31	29	32	35
1709	Other articles of paper and paperboard	f/	849	854	848	826	16514	16873	16258	15851	705	736	664	728
181	Printing and service activities related to printing		734	759	754	735	15121	15668	15174	14778	664	708	629	696
1811	Printing		115	95	94	91	1393	1205	1084	1073	41	29	35	32
1812	Service activities related to printing		12	12	12	10	1463	1635	1517	1381	63	70	63	54
1820	Reproduction of recorded media		...	...	...	...	...	...	...	...	...	...	...	...
1910	Coke oven products		16	16	14	14	3093	3185	3421	3645	406	427	426	512
1920	Refined petroleum products		77	83	87	85	7128	7094	7081	6910	564	633	633	666
201	Basic chemicals,fertilizers, etc.		28	31	32	27	2000	2092	2042	2049	126	148	136	142
2011	Basic chemicals		...	...	...	...	...	...	...	...	...	...	...	...
2012	Fertilizers and nitrogen compounds	g/	49	52	55	58	5128	5002	5039	4861	439	484	497	524
2013	Plastics and synthetic rubber in primary forms	g/	182	186	196	191	9340	9713	9668	9652	632	659	652	702
202	Other chemical products	h/	...	...	...	...	...	...	...	...	...	...	...	...
2021	Pesticides and other agrochemical products		37	35	37	35	2199	2266	2273	2227	121	129	137	135
2022	Paints,varnishes;printing ink and mastics		50	52	54	53	1422	1597	1695	1584	109	109	110	123
2023	Soap,cleaning and cosmetic preparations		95	99	105	103	5719	5850	5700	5841	402	422	405	443
2029	Other chemical products n.e.c.	h/	...	...	...	...	...	...	...	...	...	...	...	...
2030	Man-made fibres	h/	45	46	46	45	4221	4139	4856	5363	305	345	425	486
2100	Pharmaceuticals,medicinal chemicals, etc.		47	47	48	49	2858	2697	2542	2944	109	109	97	121
221	Rubber products	i/	...	...	...	...	...	...	...	...	...	...	...	...
2211	Rubber tyres and tubes	i/	47	47	48	49	2858	2697	2542	2944	109	109	97	121
2219	Other rubber products	i/	294	292	310	295	14421	13207	11337	11029	435	404	357	370
2220	Plastics products		45	35	41	42	1439	1077	1203	1187	44	33	34	37
2310	Glass and glass products		92	104	104	101	3926	4625	5133	4972	145	152	156	163
239	Non-metallic mineral products n.e.c.	j/	...	...	...	...	...	...	...	...	...	...	...	...
2391	Refractory products		...	...	...	...	...	...	...	...	...	...	...	...
2392	Clay building materials	j/	...	...	...	...	...	...	...	...	...	...	...	...
2393	Other porcelain and ceramic products	j/	17	19	19	19	1398	1777	1886	2031	61	66	68	76
2394	Cement, lime and plaster		21	23	23	26	189	241	289	422	4	5	7	8
2395	Articles of concrete, cement and plaster		54	62	62	56	2339	2607	2958	2519	80	81	82	79
2396	Cutting, shaping and finishing of stone	i/	24	33	30	30	2200	2571	2388	2475	104	107	103	102
2399	Other non-metallic mineral products n.e.c.		...	...	...	...	...	...	...	...	...	...	...	...
2410	Basic iron and steel	k/	...	...	...	...	...	...	...	...	...	...	...	...
2420	Basic precious and other non-ferrous metals	k/	...	...	...	...	...	...	...	...	...	...	...	...
243	Casting of metals	k/	...	...	...	...	...	...	...	...	...	...	...	...
2431	Casting of iron and steel		...	...	...	...	...	...	...	...	...	...	...	...
2432	Casting of non-ferrous metals		...	...	...	...	...	...	...	...	...	...	...	...
251	Struct.metal products, tanks, reservoirs		425	415	445	457	11866	13145	14745	16196	314	375	440	491
2511	Structural metal products		404	390	418	429	11085	11931	13473	14780	284	333	387	438
2512	Tanks, reservoirs and containers of metal		9	14	16	17	573	812	826	954	19	25	28	32

continued

Singapore

ISIC	Industry	Note	Number of establishments (number) 2007	2008	2009	2010	Note	Number of persons engaged (number) 2007	2008	2009	2010	Note	Wages and salaries paid to employees (millions of Singapore Dollars) 2007	2008	2009	2010
2513	Steam generators, excl. hot water boilers		12	11	11	11		208	402	446	462		11	17	26	21
2520	Weapons and ammunition	m/	...	...	...	...	m/	...	...	...	...	m/	...	...	...	...
259	Other metal products;metal working services		798	795	820	812		30184	28433	25511	25010		1047	1018	913	960
2591	Forging,pressing,stamping,roll-forming of metal		65	50	61	54		6894	5373	4615	4140		240	200	162	163
2592	Treatment and coating of metals; machining		149	150	143	139		4414	4323	3438	3870		130	132	105	125
2593	Cutlery, hand tools and general hardware	m/	22	17	17	19	m/	670	450	405	434	m/	23	17	15	16
2599	Other fabricated metal products n.e.c.	n/	562	578	599	600	n/	18206	18287	17053	16566	n/	653	669	632	656
2610	Electronic components and boards		159	155	156	151		73545	70820	61570	65508		3436	3317	2926	3243
2620	Computers and peripheral equipment		22	21	24	25		17786	16597	14762	15578		799	798	721	715
2630	Communication equipment		19	24	28	27		4565	4577	2990	3094		280	279	179	191
2640	Consumer electronics		11	11	6	6		2336	1997	1640	1008		101	97	79	50
265	Measuring,testing equipment; watches, etc.		62	72	78	72		5070	5319	4917	5084		246	273	264	294
2651	Measuring/testing/navigating equipment,etc.		...	...	...	...		...	...	...	...		...	...	...	...
2652	Watches and clocks		...	...	...	...		...	...	...	...		...	...	...	...
2660	Irradiation/electromedical equipment,etc.	n/	...	...	...	...	n/	...	...	...	...	n/	...	...	...	...
2670	Optical instruments and photographic equipment		14	13	14	14		1839	2196	2029	2006		80	89	80	86
2680	Magnetic and optical media	n/	...	...	...	...	n/	...	...	...	...	n/	...	...	...	...
2710	Electric motors,generators,transformers,etc.		146	143	161	160		4102	4199	4070	3939		152	164	177	171
2720	Batteries and accumulators		6	7	7	9		633	901	945	1031		36	55	60	67
273	Wiring and wiring devices		37	35	33	35		1727	1641	1355	1464		67	64	55	58
2731	Fibre optic cables		...	...	...	...		...	...	...	...		...	...	...	...
2732	Other electronic and electric wires and cables		...	...	...	...		...	...	...	...		...	...	...	...
2733	Wiring devices		...	...	...	...		...	...	...	...		...	...	...	...
2740	Electric lighting equipment		9	12	15	14		208	229	193	189		9	8	8	7
2750	Domestic appliances		7	8	8	7		1432	699	694	86		40	39	39	3
2790	Other electrical equipment		17	14	26	22		773	841	994	1000		32	38	41	49
281	General-purpose machinery		381	380	437	435		13770	14137	14154	14698		583	622	624	677
2811	Engines/turbines,excl.aircraft,vehicle engines		10	10	12	11		461	443	551	676		32	35	38	48
2812	Fluid power equipment		38	39	50	52		514	561	780	980		26	31	43	47
2813	Other pumps, compressors, taps and valves		...	...	...	...		...	...	...	...		...	...	...	...
2814	Bearings, gears, gearing and driving elements		15	13	13	14		1588	1462	1349	1361		60	56	50	55
2815	Ovens, furnaces and furnace burners		...	...	...	...		...	...	...	...		...	...	...	...
2816	Lifting and handling equipment		112	126	145	149		4920	5015	5035	5293		233	249	238	263
2817	Office machinery, excl.computers,etc.		...	...	...	...		...	...	...	...		...	...	...	...
2818	Power-driven hand tools		...	...	...	...		...	...	...	...		...	...	...	...
2819	Other general-purpose machinery		206	192	217	209		6287	6656	6439	6388		232	251	255	264
282	Special-purpose machinery		990	960	985	975		38729	45608	40862	41169		1643	1905	1741	1937
2821	Agricultural and forestry machinery		...	...	...	...		...	...	...	...		...	...	...	...
2822	Metal-forming machinery and machine tools		655	581	594	581		13035	12209	10213	9611		455	421	334	350
2823	Machinery for metallurgy		...	...	...	...		...	...	...	...		...	...	...	...
2824	Mining, quarrying and construction machinery		127	163	174	178		16147	23749	22197	21613		746	1004	977	1020

Code	Description	f/	17	16	19	18	f/	199	192	192	190	f/	7	7	7	8
2825	Food/beverage/tobacco processing machinery		...	...	...	...		...	...	...	...		...	...	...	...
2826	Textile/apparel/leather production machinery	p/	191	200	198	198	p/	9348	9458	8260	9755	p/	435	472	422	558
2829	Other special-purpose machinery	p/	...	...	...	...	p/	...	...	...	...	p/	...	...	...	...
2910	Motor vehicles	q/	29	28	31	34	q/	751	598	676	705	q/	20	16	16	18
2920	Automobile bodies, trailers and semi-trailers		31	28	43	43		2618	2468	2267	2009		122	122	118	114
2930	Parts and accessories for motor vehicles	q/	...	...	...	...	q/	...	...	...	...	q/	...	...	...	...
301	Building of ships and boats		474	826	985	984		47931	71362	72432	64306		1178	1647	1609	1537
3011	Building of ships and floating structures		447	790	951	950		46947	69818	71458	63154		1155	1600	1583	1507
3012	Building of pleasure and sporting boats		27	36	34	34		984	1544	974	1152		23	48	26	31
3020	Railway locomotives and rolling stock	r/	59	64	65	65	r/	18639	18777	18529	18581	r/	1184	1214	1185	1218
3030	Air and spacecraft and related machinery	r/	9	7	7	8	r/	2084	2300	2314	2773	r/	127	133	139	190
3040	Military fighting vehicles	r/	...	...	...	...	r/	...	...	...	...	r/	...	...	...	...
309	Transport equipment n.e.c.		...	...	...	...		...	...	...	...		...	...	...	...
3091	Motorcycles		...	...	...	...		...	...	...	...		...	...	...	...
3092	Bicycles and invalid carriages		...	...	...	...		...	...	...	...		...	...	...	...
3099	Other transport equipment n.e.c.		528	548	615	620		5438	7177	8413	8574		124	174	203	230
3100	Furniture		99	107	117	112		613	852	807	850		14	27	22	27
321	Jewellery, bijouterie and related articles		...	...	...	...		...	...	...	...		...	...	...	...
3211	Jewellery and related articles		...	...	...	...		...	...	...	...		...	...	...	...
3212	Imitation jewellery and related articles		...	...	...	...		...	...	...	...		...	...	...	...
3220	Musical instruments	s/	...	...	...	...	s/	...	...	...	...	s/	...	...	...	...
3230	Sports goods	s/	...	...	...	...	s/	...	...	...	...	s/	...	...	...	...
3240	Games and toys	s/	72	79	86	81	s/	7041	7456	7762	7892	s/	257	281	307	326
3250	Medical and dental instruments and supplies	s/	224	277	300	303	s/	1951	2603	3436	4117	s/	56	72	102	129
3290	Other manufacturing n.e.c.		...	...	...	...		...	...	...	...		...	...	...	...
331	Repair of fabricated metal products/machinery		...	...	...	...		...	...	...	...		...	...	...	...
3311	Repair of fabricated metal products		...	...	...	...		...	...	...	...		...	...	...	...
3312	Repair of machinery		...	...	...	...		...	...	...	...		...	...	...	...
3313	Repair of electronic and optical equipment		...	...	...	...		...	...	...	...		...	...	...	...
3314	Repair of electrical equipment		...	...	...	...		...	...	...	...		...	...	...	...
3315	Repair of transport equip., excl. motor vehicles		...	...	...	...		...	...	...	...		...	...	...	...
3319	Repair of other equipment		...	...	...	...		...	...	...	...		...	...	...	...
3320	Installation of industrial machinery/equipment		252	255	352	294		4425	6690	7534	6305		107	159	186	155
C	Total manufacturing	t/	8166	8640	9296	9090	t/	404057	435154	417569	414176	t/	16597	17736	16950	17987

a/ 1079 includes 1061, 1062, 1072, 1080 and 1200.
b/ 1101 includes 1102, 1103 and 1104.
c/ 1399 includes 131 and 1391.
d/ 1410 includes 1420 and 1430.
e/ 1629 includes 1610 and 1621.
f/ 1709 includes 1701.
g/ 2013 includes 2012.
h/ 2029 includes 2021 and 2030.
i/ 2219 includes 2211.
j/ 2399 includes 2391, 2393 and 2394.

k/ 2410 includes 2420 and 243.
m/ 2599 includes 2520.
n/ 2610 includes 2660 and 2680.
p/ 2829 includes 2826.
q/ 2930 includes 2910.
r/ 309 includes 3020 and 3040.
s/ 3290 includes 3220, 3230 and 3240.
t/ Sum of available data.

Singapore

ISIC	Industry	Note	Output 2007	Output 2008	Output 2009	Output 2010	Note	Value added 2007	Value added 2008	Value added 2009	Value added 2010	Note	GFCF 2009	GFCF 2010
			(millions of Singapore Dollars)					(millions of Singapore Dollars)					(millions of Singapore Dollars)	
1010	Processing/preserving of meat		359	462	523	529		88	115	142	131		17	10
1020	Processing/preserving of fish, etc.		208	197	207	203		52	49	57	53		13	7
1030	Processing/preserving of fruit,vegetables		30	34	36	37		10	12	12	12		1	3
1040	Vegetable and animal oils and fats		689	946	818	727		88	94	143	99		20	5
1050	Dairy products		557	928	865	947		120	147	233	191		15	18
106	Grain mill products,starches and starch products		...	...	...	...		...	...	...	...		...	...
1061	Grain mill products	a/	...	...	...	...	a/	...	...	...	...	a/	...	...
1062	Starches and starch products	a/	...	...	...	...	a/	...	...	...	...	a/	...	...
107	Other food products		3200	3734	3607	3915		717	855	999	974		168	194
1071	Bakery products		573	714	705	759		198	248	253	257		39	51
1072	Sugar	a/	...	...	...	...	a/	...	...	...	...	a/	...	...
1073	Cocoa, chocolate and sugar confectionery		464	587	563	668		64	51	54	58		9	6
1074	Macaroni, noodles, couscous, etc.		101	133	152	144		29	38	48	43		6	6
1075	Prepared meals and dishes		223	264	296	339		86	99	109	134		10	16
1079	Other food products n.e.c.	a/	1838	2035	1891	2005	a/	340	420	534	481	a/	103	114
1080	Prepared animal feeds	a/	...	...	...	...	a/	...	...	...	...	a/	...	...
1101	Distilling, rectifying and blending of spirits	b/	665	694	739	993	b/	194	208	237	404	b/	31	54
1102	Wines	b/	...	...	...	...	b/	...	...	...	...	b/	...	...
1103	Malt liquors and malt	b/	...	...	...	...	b/	...	...	...	...	b/	...	...
1104	Soft drinks,mineral waters,other bottled waters	b/	...	...	...	...	b/	...	...	...	...	b/	...	...
1200	Tobacco products	a/	...	...	...	...	a/	...	...	...	...	a/	...	...
131	Spinning, weaving and finishing of textiles	c/	...	...	...	...	c/	...	...	...	...	c/	...	...
1311	Preparation and spinning of textile fibres		...	...	...	...		...	...	...	...		...	...
1312	Weaving of textiles		...	...	...	...		...	...	...	...		...	...
1313	Finishing of textiles		...	...	...	...		...	...	...	...		...	...
139	Other textiles	c/	142	144	91	54	c/	36	31	21	18	c/	5	-
1391	Knitted and crocheted fabrics		...	...	...	...		...	...	...	...		...	...
1392	Made-up textile articles, except apparel		46	62	47	32		20	20	17	13		4	-
1393	Carpets and rugs		...	...	...	...		...	...	...	...		...	...
1394	Cordage, rope, twine and netting		...	...	...	...		...	...	...	...		...	...
1399	Other textiles n.e.c.		96	82	43	22		16	12	4	5		-	-
1410	Wearing apparel, except fur apparel	c/	721	562	663	601	c/	219	164	126	114	c/	3	3
1420	Articles of fur	d/	...	...	...	...	d/	...	...	...	...	d/	...	...
1430	Knitted and crocheted apparel	d/	...	...	...	...	d/	...	...	...	...	d/	...	...
151	Leather;luggage,handbags,saddlery,harness;fur	d/	238	205	80	93	d/	57	50	23	30	d/	1	1
1511	Tanning/dressing of leather; dressing of fur		...	...	...	...		...	...	...	...		...	...
1512	Luggage,handbags,etc.;saddlery/harness		...	...	...	...		...	...	...	...		...	...
1520	Footwear		9	7	9	6		3	2	2	2		-	-
1610	Sawmilling and planing of wood	e/	...	...	...	...	e/	...	...	...	...	e/	...	...
162	Wood products, cork, straw, plaiting materials		255	288	267	242		70	70	77	81		2	5

1621	Veneer sheets and wood-based panels	e/	...	...	...	...	e/	...	...	...	...	...	...
1622	Builders' carpentry and joinery		111	101	101	71		32	30	26	27	1	2
1623	Wooden containers		95	123	105	119		27	31	33	41	1	3
1629	Other wood products;articles of cork,straw	e/	50	64	61	52	e/	11	15	12	12	-	-
1701	Pulp, paper and paperboard		...	...	...	...		...	...	...	...	...	...
1702	Corrugated paper and paperboard	f/	812	859	778	860	f/	205	203	210	215	17	26
1709	Other articles of paper and paperboard	f/	224	223	222	249	f/	44	47	37	53	2	2
181	Printing and service activities related to printing		2730	2786	2383	2501		1292	1143	1328	1265	83	87
1811	Printing		2623	2722	2303	2436		1234	1091	1292	1227	83	86
1812	Service activities related to printing		107	64	80	64		59	51	36	37	1	1
1820	Reproduction of recorded media		256	267	202	138		97	91	104	75	5	3
1910	Coke oven products		...	...	...	...		...	...	...	...	...	...
1920	Refined petroleum products		48040	59945	35383	42318		1770	1116	743	1272	1208	670
201	Basic chemicals,fertilizers, etc.		29418	28534	21786	31371		3505	1652	569	2552	1211	4771
2011	Basic chemicals	g/	1180	1332	1151	1333	g/	423	425	434	465	146	324
2012	Fertilizers and nitrogen compounds	g/	...	...	...	...	g/	...	...	...	...	...	...
2013	Plastics and synthetic rubber in primary forms		28237	27202	20635	30037		3083	1227	135	2087	1066	4447
202	Other chemical products		5830	6314	5868	6700		1590	1873	1572	2207	139	126
2021	Pesticides and other agrochemical products	h/	1005	1061	976	965	h/	240	265	248	279	12	34
2022	Paints,varnishes;printing ink and mastics		611	765	945	886		183	273	212	234	6	9
2023	Soap,cleaning and cosmetic preparations	h/	4214	4488	3948	4849	h/	1167	1334	1112	1695	120	83
2029	Other chemical products n.e.c.	h/	...	...	...	...	h/	...	...	...	...	...	...
2030	Man-made fibres		21207	17635	17822	18956		12633	9016	7829	8598	405	865
2100	Pharmaceuticals,medicinal chemicals, etc.		515	522	440	534		184	170	191	230	21	15
221	Rubber products		...	...	...	...		...	...	...	...	...	...
2211	Rubber tyres and tubes	i/	515	522	440	534	i/	184	170	191	230	21	15
2219	Other rubber products	i/	2136	1969	1669	1801	i/	641	557	586	573	64	65
2220	Plastics products		326	222	212	260		159	83	104	118	88	45
2310	Glass and glass products		1580	1930	1775	1587		347	400	414	357	37	27
239	Non-metallic mineral products n.e.c.	i/	...	...	...	...	i/	...	...	...	...	...	...
2391	Refractory products		...	...	...	...		...	...	...	...	...	...
2392	Clay building materials	j/	...	...	...	...	j/	...	...	...	...	...	...
2393	Other porcelain and ceramic products	j/	...	...	...	...	j/	...	...	...	...	...	...
2394	Cement, lime and plaster	j/	1076	1341	1198	1038	j/	208	183	215	149	22	14
2395	Articles of concrete, cement and plaster		18	19	20	33		6	7	7	15	-	-
2396	Cutting, shaping and finishing of stone	j/	486	571	557	515	j/	133	210	192	193	15	13
2399	Other non-metallic mineral products n.e.c.		1345	1674	1013	1141		319	169	266	165	23	21
2410	Basic iron and steel	k/	...	...	...	...	k/	...	...	...	...	...	...
2420	Basic precious and other non-ferrous metals	k/	...	...	...	...	k/	...	...	...	...	...	...
243	Casting of metals	k/	...	...	...	...	k/	...	...	...	...	...	...
2431	Casting of iron and steel		...	...	...	...		...	...	...	...	...	...
2432	Casting of non-ferrous metals		...	...	...	...		...	...	...	...	...	...
251	Struct.metal products, tanks, reservoirs		1658	2339	2301	2444		639	748	686	917	153	137
2511	Structural metal products		1432	2057	2025	2167		565	639	586	811	149	133
2512	Tanks, reservoirs and containers of metal		150	195	171	196		30	64	69	72	3	3

continued

Singapore

ISIC	Industry	Output Note	Output 2007	Output 2008	Output 2009	Output 2010	VA Note	Value added 2007	Value added 2008	Value added 2009	Value added 2010	GFCF Note	GFCF 2009	GFCF 2010
			(millions of Singapore Dollars)					(millions of Singapore Dollars)					(millions of Singapore Dollars)	
2513	Steam generators, excl. hot water boilers		75	88	105	81		44	32	46	34		1	1
2520	Weapons and ammunition	m/	...	...	...	...	m/	...	...	...	...	m/	...	...
259	Other metal products;metal working services		7462	7429	6606	6780		1803	1810	1582	1691		188	172
2591	Forging,pressing,stamping,roll-forming of metal		1387	1182	881	908		331	249	206	211		54	26
2592	Treatment and coating of metals; machining		540	528	415	454		242	248	197	231		24	14
2593	Cutlery, hand tools and general hardware		154	139	113	114		71	69	54	52		2	2
2599	Other fabricated metal products n.e.c.	m/	5382	5581	5197	5305	m/	1159	1245	1125	1197	m/	108	130
2610	Electronic components and boards	n/	53264	50271	46642	66397	n/	12998	10718	9207	13931	n/	2955	5421
2620	Computers and peripheral equipment		21123	22304	26519	30005		2649	3571	3805	5463		261	259
2630	Communication equipment		3663	1635	943	935		577	241	250	281		12	14
2640	Consumer electronics		954	976	919	953		145	127	104	64		2	20
265	Measuring,testing equipment; watches, etc.		2256	2386	2160	2375		599	608	617	756		25	37
2651	Measuring/testing/navigating equipment,etc.		...	...	...	...		...	...	...	...		...	...
2652	Watches and clocks		...	...	...	...		...	...	...	...		...	...
2660	Irradiation/electromedical equipment,etc.		...	...	...	...		...	...	...	...		...	...
2670	Optical instruments and photographic equipment	n/	472	472	500	549	n/	172	177	203	219	n/	14	11
2680	Magnetic and optical media	n/	...	...	...	...	n/	...	...	...	...	n/	...	...
2710	Electric motors,generators,transformers,etc.		1583	1675	1344	1239		320	355	319	297		17	22
2720	Batteries and accumulators		252	233	270	385		73	62	81	127		33	62
273	Wiring and wiring devices		722	741	515	552		135	132	95	102		19	9
2731	Fibre optic cables		...	...	...	...		...	...	...	...		...	...
2732	Other electronic and electric wires and cables		...	...	...	...		...	...	...	...		...	...
2733	Wiring devices		...	...	...	...		...	...	...	...		...	...
2740	Electric lighting equipment		48	50	48	26		10	11	15	14		...	...
2750	Domestic appliances		323	337	292	19		103	111	71	6		-	2
2790	Other electrical equipment		212	237	236	293		63	67	72	87		-	-
281	General-purpose machinery		3925	4080	3470	4389		1353	1200	1161	1138		15	3
2811	Engines/turbines,excl.aircraft,vehicle engines		198	185	191	197		107	89	86	97		137	189
2812	Fluid power equipment		212	225	293	274		43	53	79	94		6	15
2813	Other pumps, compressors, taps and valves		...	...	...	...		...	...	...	...		7	6
2814	Bearings, gears, gearing and driving elements		280	227	197	265		126	85	79	87		...	...
2815	Ovens, furnaces and furnace burners		...	...	...	...		...	...	...	...		10	16
2816	Lifting and handling equipment		1055	1227	1144	1219		374	317	351	398		...	...
2817	Office machinery, excl.computers,etc.		...	...	...	...		...	...	...	...		28	10
2818	Power-driven hand tools		...	...	...	...		...	...	...	...		...	...
2819	Other general-purpose machinery		2180	2216	1645	2434		703	656	565	462		87	141
282	Special-purpose machinery		14446	15514	14633	16418		3100	3647	3677	4570		234	316
2821	Agricultural and forestry machinery		...	...	...	...		...	...	...	...		...	...
2822	Metal-forming machinery and machine tools		1746	1494	1127	1417		722	573	432	533		34	55
2823	Machinery for metallurgy		...	...	...	...		...	...	...	...		...	...
2824	Mining, quarrying and construction machinery		9960	11471	11553	9648		1578	2294	2747	2850		151	169

Code	Description	(1)	(2)	(3)	(4)	(5)	(6)	(7)	(8)	(9)	(10)	Note
2825	Food/beverage/tobacco processing machinery	33	38	42	28	9	9	12	7	1	1	
2826	Textile/apparel/leather production machinery	2707	2510	1912	5325	790	771	486	1179	47	91	p/
2829	Other special-purpose machinery	...	...	...	...	...	...	...	...	...	...	p/
2910	Motor vehicles	81	92	85	135	28	24	23	33	2	2	q/
2920	Automobile bodies, trailers and semi-trailers	710	555	490	585	170	135	159	150	15	15	
2930	Parts and accessories for motor vehicles	6956	8726	8502	7336	2298	3183	2993	2906	239	201	q/
301	Building of ships and boats	6747	8409	8279	7165	2269	3118	2938	2853	234	196	
3011	Building of ships and floating structures	209	317	223	170	30	65	54	52	5	6	
3012	Building of pleasure and sporting boats	...	...	...	...	...	...	...	...	...	...	
3020	Railway locomotives and rolling stock	6796	7178	6895	7280	2716	2802	2701	2791	294	232	r/
3030	Air and spacecraft and related machinery	...	...	...	...	...	...	...	...	...	...	
3040	Military fighting vehicles	733	836	619	1032	214	256	237	338	38	84	r/
309	Transport equipment n.e.c.	...	...	...	...	...	...	...	...	...	...	r/
3091	Motorcycles	...	...	...	...	...	...	...	...	...	...	
3092	Bicycles and invalid carriages	...	...	...	...	...	...	...	...	...	...	
3099	Other transport equipment n.e.c.	619	832	1033	1113	189	260	336	368	34	6	
3100	Furniture	450	618	595	700	21	44	35	46	2	1	
321	Jewellery, bijouterie and related articles	...	...	...	...	...	...	...	...	...	...	
3211	Jewellery and related articles	...	...	...	...	...	...	...	...	...	...	
3212	Imitation jewellery and related articles	...	...	...	...	...	...	...	...	...	...	
3220	Musical instruments	...	...	...	...	...	...	...	...	...	...	s/
3230	Sports goods	...	...	...	...	...	...	...	...	...	...	s/
3240	Games and toys	2558	2460	2769	3283	980	956	1034	1379	77	106	s/
3250	Medical and dental instruments and supplies	256	301	342	532	83	96	123	181	188	123	
3290	Other manufacturing n.e.c.	...	...	...	...	...	...	...	...	...	...	s/
331	Repair of fabricated metal products/machinery	...	...	...	...	...	...	...	...	...	...	
3311	Repair of fabricated metal products	...	...	...	...	...	...	...	...	...	...	
3312	Repair of machinery	...	...	...	...	...	...	...	...	...	...	
3313	Repair of electronic and optical equipment	...	...	...	...	...	...	...	...	...	...	
3314	Repair of electrical equipment	...	...	...	...	...	...	...	...	...	...	
3315	Repair of transport equip., excl. motor vehicles	...	...	...	...	...	...	...	...	...	...	
3319	Repair of other equipment	367	527	600	533	144	222	275	238	6	9	
3320	Installation of industrial machinery/equipment											
C	Total manufacturing	253381	263886	226784	273050	56021	47252	48514	57880	8540	14480	t/

a/ 1079 includes 1061, 1062, 1072, 1080 and 1200.
b/ 1101 includes 1102, 1103 and 1104.
c/ 1399 includes 131 and 1391.
d/ 1410 includes 1420 and 1430.
e/ 1629 includes 1610 and 1621.
f/ 1709 includes 1701.
g/ 2013 includes 2012.
h/ 2029 includes 2021 and 2030.
i/ 2219 includes 2211.
j/ 2399 includes 2391, 2393 and 2394.

k/ 2410 includes 2420 and 243.
m/ 2599 includes 2520.
n/ 2610 includes 2660 and 2680.
p/ 2829 includes 2826.
q/ 2930 includes 2910.
r/ 309 includes 3020 and 3040.
s/ 3290 includes 3220, 3230 and 3240.
t/ Sum of available data.

Singapore

Index numbers of industrial production

(2005=100)

ISIC Revision 4

ISIC	Industry	Note	1999	2000	2001	2002	2003	2004	2005	2006	2007	2008	2009	2010
10	Food products	a/	89	91	95	92	92	93	100	104	116	125	119	127
11	Beverages	a/	...	...	...	...	...	...	...	...	...	...	...	...
12	Tobacco products	a/	...	...	...	...	...	...	...	...	...	...	...	...
13	Textiles		205	240	204	147	154	132	100	84	70	65	53	44
14	Wearing apparel		151	172	145	126	123	120	100	90	79	57	36	21
15	Leather and related products		103	119	111	95	86	96	100	100	100	85	53	54
16	Wood/wood products/cork,excl. furniture		100	106	92	77	85	100	100	113	106	94	72	74
17	Paper and paper products		91	89	83	89	89	94	100	103	112	110	104	116
18	Printing and reproduction of recorded media		107	122	106	97	97	98	100	104	107	103	88	90
19	Coke and refined petroleum products		84	77	77	78	82	92	100	97	97	98	83	83
20	Chemicals and chemical products		63	70	73	91	95	100	100	105	112	106	101	123
21	Pharmaceuticals,medicinal chemicals, etc.		36	37	41	61	69	89	100	127	124	115	129	198
22	Rubber and plastics products		102	126	94	103	96	94	100	100	100	92	77	86
23	Other non-metallic mineral products		146	147	110	111	101	115	100	96	85	71	67	68
24	Basic metals		77	81	82	84	72	86	100	118	107	130	109	121
25	Fabricated metal products, except machinery		123	133	108	105	96	101	100	108	111	105	94	108
26	Computer, electronic and optical products		69	88	71	75	79	91	100	107	110	103	94	125
27	Electrical equipment		91	99	87	90	88	92	100	115	116	114	121	173
28	Machinery and equipment n.e.c.		63	80	67	68	68	82	100	128	153	149	131	180
29	Motor vehicles, trailers and semi-trailers		...	...	...	...	...	...	...	...	...	...	...	...
30	Other transport equipment		54	54	67	73	69	83	100	125	146	158	149	146
31	Furniture		166	149	149	118	110	102	100	126	125	140	151	166
32	Other manufacturing		71	77	85	96	95	95	100	92	111	108	109	121
33	Repair and installation of machinery/equipment		...	...	...	...	...	...	...	...	...	...	...	...
C	Total manufacturing		70	81	72	78	80	91	100	112	119	114	109	141

a/ 10 includes 11 and 12.

Slovakia

Concepts and definitions of variables:
No deviations from the standard UN concepts and definitions are reported.

Related national publications:
None reported.

Supplier of information:
Statistical Office of the Slovak Republic, Bratislava.
Industrial statistics for the OECD countries are compiled by the OECD secretariat, which supplies them to UNIDO.

Basic source of data:
Business surveys.

Major deviations from ISIC (Revision 4):
Data have been converted from the national NACE equivalent system to ISIC (Revision 4) by the OECD.

Reference period:
Calendar year.

Scope:
All enterprises.

Method of data collection:
Not reported.

Type of enumeration:
Not reported.

Adjusted for non-response:
Not reported.

Slovakia

ISIC Revision 4

ISIC	Industry	Number of enterprises (number)					Number of employees (number)					Wages and salaries paid to employees (millions of Euros)				
		Note	2006	2007	2008	2009	Note	2006	2007	2008	2009	Note	2006	2007	2008	2009
1010	Processing/preserving of meat		...	...	72	89		...	...	8355	6830		...	...	56	47
1020	Processing/preserving of fish, etc.		...	...	8	10		...	...	789	697		...	...	6	6
1030	Processing/preserving of fruit,vegetables		...	...	35	...		...	...	1081	...		...	...	7	6
1040	Vegetable and animal oils and fats		...	...	7	...		...	...	989	...		...	...	10	...
1050	Dairy products		...	...	38	58		...	...	3346	3408		...	...	30	31
106	Grain mill products,starches and starch products		...	...	31	...		...	...	887	...		...	...	10	...
1061	Grain mill products		...	...	...	25		...	...	...	...		...	...	...	...
1062	Starches and starch products		...	...	...	...		...	...	...	557		...	...	...	5
107	Other food products		...	...	407	367		...	...	16809	15834		...	...	122	121
1071	Bakery products		...	...	292	267		...	...	11660	11083		...	...	74	77
1072	Sugar		...	...	...	3		...	...	...	335		...	...	...	5
1073	Cocoa, chocolate and sugar confectionery		...	...	16	16		...	...	1448	1477		...	...	13	14
1074	Macaroni, noodles, couscous, etc.		...	...	22	22		...	...	581	548		...	...	4	4
1075	Prepared meals and dishes		...	...	...	...		...	...	...	...		...	...	...	...
1079	Other food products n.e.c.		...	...	...	...		...	...	...	...		...	...	...	...
1080	Prepared animal feeds		...	...	60	59		...	...	1387	1123		...	...	12	9
1101	Distilling, rectifying and blending of spirits		...	...	...	...		...	...	...	...		...	...	...	...
1102	Wines		...	...	206a/	180a/		...	...	6289a/	6156a/		...	...	62a/	62a/
1103	Malt liquors and malt		...	...	...a/	...a/		...	...	...a/	...a/		...	...	...a/	...a/
1104	Soft drinks,mineral waters,other bottled waters		...	...	...a/	...a/		...	...	...a/	...a/		...	...	...a/	...a/
1200	Tobacco products		...	...	...a/	...a/		...	...	...a/	...a/		...	...	...a/	...a/
131	Spinning, weaving and finishing of textiles		...	...	8	...		...	...	2643	...		...	...	53	...
1311	Preparation and spinning of textile fibres		...	...	182b/	30		...	...	6809b/	1542		...	...	43b/	13
1312	Weaving of textiles		...	...	12	10		...	...	1851	1114		...	...	14	10
1313	Finishing of textiles		...	...	9	...		...	...	152	...		...	...	1	...
139	Other textiles		...	...	..b/	117		...	...	..b/	3724		...	...	...	...
1391	Knitted and crocheted fabrics		...	...	6	...		...	...	406	...		...	...	..b/	24
1392	Made-up textile articles, except apparel		...	...	84	66		...	...	2356	1921		...	...	3	...
1393	Carpets and rugs		...	...	...	...		...	...	301	282		...	...	12	10
1394	Cordage, rope, twine and netting		...	...	7	8		...	...	...	...		...	...	2	2
1399	Other textiles n.e.c.		...	...	56	...		...	...	1250	...		...	...	8	...
1410	Wearing apparel, except fur apparel		...	...	...	325		...	...	...	13902		...	...	...	73
1420	Articles of fur		...	...	6	5		...	...	60	40		...	...	...	...
1430	Knitted and crocheted apparel		...	...	45	38		...	...	4497	3368		...	...	22	17
151	Leather;luggage,handbags,saddlery,harness;fur		...	...	23	25		...	...	1278	1034		...	...	8	7
1511	Tanning/dressing of leather; dressing of fur		...	...	4	4		...	...	320	265		...	...	3	2
1512	Luggage,handbags,etc.;saddlery/harness		...	...	19	21		...	...	958	769		...	...	5	4
1520	Footwear		...	...	92	106		...	...	10841	9711		...	...	59	59
1610	Sawmilling and planing of wood		...	...	438	533		...	...	7075	5897		...	...	45	36
162	Wood products, cork, straw, plaiting materials		...	...	478	432		...	...	8530	7057		...	...	54	50

Code	Description	(1)	(2)	(3)	(4)	(5)	(6)
1621	Veneer sheets and wood-based panels	55	13	2188	1598	18	15
1622	Builders' carpentry and joinery	212	213	3827	3543	23	24
1623	Wooden containers	81	76	1262	891	7	6
1629	Other wood products;articles of cork,straw	130	130	1253	1025	7	6
1701	Pulp, paper and paperboard	15	16	2925	2533	36	34
1702	Corrugated paper and paperboard	50	46	2242	1959	20	19
1709	Other articles of paper and paperboard	54	79	2907	2958	28	31
181	Printing and service activities related to printing	245	319c/	6225	6171c/	55	57c/
1811	Printing	169	193	5491	5275	50	47
1812	Service activities related to printing	76	...c/	734	...c/	6	...
1820	Reproduction of recorded media	25	...	67	...	1	...c/
1910	Coke oven products	-	-	-	-	-	-
1920	Refined petroleum products	55	55	6643	6438	74	69
201	Basic chemicals,fertilizers, etc.	55	...	...	...	74	69
2011	Basic chemicals	...	...	3029	3036	32	32
2012	Fertilizers and nitrogen compounds	15	15	2045	2110	18	20
2013	Plastics and synthetic rubber in primary forms	113	73	4	9	...	...
202	Other chemical products	...	5	...	...	...	...
2021	Pesticides and other agrochemical products	4	19	509	519	4	5
2022	Paints,varnishes;printing ink and mastics	21	15	1054	823	9	8
2023	Soap,cleaning and cosmetic preparations	46	34	478	759	5	7
2029	Other chemical products n.e.c.	42	6	1480	930	13	12
2030	Man-made fibres	7	...	2603	...	29	...
2100	Pharmaceuticals,medicinal chemicals, etc.	21	51	7171	6571	73	68
221	Rubber products	44	21	...	...	45	41
2211	Rubber tyres and tubes	19	30	3422	3293	28	26
2219	Other rubber products	25	536	3749	3278	171	174
2220	Plastics products	484	58	21159	19879	...	47
2310	Glass and glass products	327	295	4902	4902	145	138
239	Non-metallic mineral products n.e.c.	15	12	14316	12637	25	19
2391	Refractory products	17	17	3010	2256	12	11
2392	Clay building materials	...	...	1404	1118	...	...
2393	Other porcelain and ceramic products	9	9	2745	2584	41	40
2394	Cement, lime and plaster	53	58	...	...	...	...
2395	Articles of concrete, cement and plaster	...	...	355	525	2	4
2396	Cutting, shaping and finishing of stone	...	...	...	...	...	...
2399	Other non-metallic mineral products n.e.c.	...	...	...	...	...	...
2410	Basic iron and steel	...	42	4930	3552	43	33
2420	Basic precious and other non-ferrous metals	...	16	1796	...	16	14
243	Casting of metals	46	26	...	1612	...	...
2431	Casting of iron and steel	13	...	3134	1940	27	19
2432	Casting of non-ferrous metals	33	...	...	...	...	...
251	Struct.metal products, tanks, reservoirs	420	400	11728	10299	99	93
2511	Structural metal products	51	56	3058	2457	26	22
2512	Tanks, reservoirs and containers of metal						

continued

Slovakia

ISIC	Industry	Number of enterprises (number)					Number of employees (number)					Wages and salaries paid to employees (millions of Euros)				
		Note	2006	2007	2008	2009	Note	2006	2007	2008	2009	Note	2006	2007	2008	2009
2513	Steam generators, excl. hot water boilers		...	...	...	...		...	...	...	...		...	...	...	...
2520	Weapons and ammunition		...	...	...	...		...	...	...	...		...	...	...	...
259	Other metal products;metal working services		...	...	1165	1037		...	...	26552	20620		...	...	220	174
2591	Forging,pressing,stamping,roll-forming of metal		...	...	21	31		...	...	2119	1270		...	...	20	13
2592	Treatment and coating of metals; machining		...	...	702	588		...	...	10823	7919		...	...	86	65
2593	Cutlery, hand tools and general hardware		...	...	139	119		...	...	2476	1597		...	...	19	13
2599	Other fabricated metal products n.e.c.		...	...	303	299		...	...	11134	9834		...	...	95	84
2610	Electronic components and boards		...	...	84	49		...	...	7535	7977		...	...	56	62
2620	Computers and peripheral equipment		...	...	32	37		...	...	1058	974		...	...	8	9
2630	Communication equipment		...	...	23	28		...	...	1604	1630		...	...	12	13
2640	Consumer electronics		...	...	20	20		...	...	9305	8360		...	...	79	78
265	Measuring,testing equipment; watches, etc.		...	...	72	55		...	...	2257	2299		...	...	20	22
2651	Measuring/testing/navigating equipment,etc.		...	...	...	55		...	...	...	2299		...	...	...	22
2652	Watches and clocks		...	...	...	-		...	...	...	-		...	...	...	-
2660	Irradiation/electromedical equipment,etc.		...	...	10	17		...	...	86	122		...	...	1	1
2670	Optical instruments and photographic equipment		...	...	3	6		...	...	6	80		...	...	...	1
2680	Magnetic and optical media		...	...	3	4		...	...	...	...		...	...	...	...
2710	Electric motors,generators,transformers,etc.		...	...	90	82		...	...	9544	8425		...	...	87	86
2720	Batteries and accumulators		...	...	6	7		...	...	16	58		...	...	...	1
273	Wiring and wiring devices		...	...	46	70		...	...	8116	4776		...	...	50	36
2731	Fibre optic cables		...	...	3	9		...	...	142	158		...	...	2	2
2732	Other electronic and electric wires and cables		...	...	35	31		...	...	7773	4228		...	...	46	31
2733	Wiring devices		...	...	8	30		...	...	201	390		...	...	2	3
2740	Electric lighting equipment		...	...	38	35		...	...	5912	5248		...	...	46	43
2750	Domestic appliances		...	...	17	18		...	...	3258	2771		...	...	28	25
2790	Other electrical equipment		...	...	160	138		...	...	5107	4090		...	...	43	38
281	General-purpose machinery		...	...	312	405		...	...	27452	22442		...	...	264	218
2811	Engines/turbines,excl.aircraft,vehicle engines		...	...	10	8		...	...	771	366		...	...	6	3
2812	Fluid power equipment		...	...	7	17		...	...	630	466		...	...	4	3
2813	Other pumps, compressors, taps and valves		...	...	20	28		...	...	6333	4966		...	...	55	47
2814	Bearings, gears, gearing and driving elements		...	...	27	29		...	...	12837	10449		...	...	132	104
2815	Ovens, furnaces and furnace burners		...	...	9	20		...	...	513	609		...	...	5	6
2816	Lifting and handling equipment		...	...	70	66		...	...	2042	1742		...	...	20	17
2817	Office machinery, excl.computers,etc.		...	...	...	9		...	...	...	538		...	...	...	4
2818	Power-driven hand tools		...	...	...	4		...	...	...	28		...	...	...	...
2819	Other general-purpose machinery		...	...	159	224		...	...	3683	3278		...	...	35	32
282	Special-purpose machinery		...	...	214	273		...	...	14638	10265		...	...	137	99
2821	Agricultural and forestry machinery		...	...	29	36		...	...	2088	1536		...	...	16	13
2822	Metal-forming machinery and machine tools		...	...	38	41		...	...	3544	2477		...	...	34	24
2823	Machinery for metallurgy		...	...	...	...		...	...	...	...		...	...	...	...
2824	Mining, quarrying and construction machinery		...	...	19	29		...	...	3570	2282		...	...	33	22

ISIC Revision 4

Code	Description	(1)	(2)	(3)	(4)	(5)	(6)
2825	Food/beverage/tobacco processing machinery	11	28	753	740	9	8
2826	Textile/apparel/leather production machinery						
2829	Other special-purpose machinery	9	10	14260	12502	198	187
2910	Motor vehicles	26	29	2044	1620	21	17
2920	Automobile bodies, trailers and semi-trailers	97	117	41082	34338	338	300
2930	Parts and accessories for motor vehicles		45d/		3906d/		34d/
301	Building of ships and boats						
3011	Building of ships and floating structures						
3012	Building of pleasure and sporting boats	...d/	...d/	...d/	...d/	...d/	...d/
3020	Railway locomotives and rolling stock	3	...d/	325	...d/	3	...d/
3030	Air and spacecraft and related machinery	3	...d/	344	...d/	3	...d/
3040	Military fighting vehicles	8	...d/	241	...d/	2	...d/
309	Transport equipment n.e.c.		-		-		-
3091	Motorcycles		8		220		1
3092	Bicycles and invalid carriages	8					
3099	Other transport equipment n.e.c.	368	275	14077	12379	99	94
3100	Furniture	22	16	464	480	4	4
321	Jewellery, bijouterie and related articles	22	16	464	480	4	4
3211	Jewellery and related articles		-		5		-
3212	Imitation jewellery and related articles	4	4	6		2	2
3220	Musical instruments	14	21	306	384	4	2
3230	Sports goods	16	9	537	473	4	4
3240	Games and toys	67	98	3435	3084	26	24
3250	Medical and dental instruments and supplies						
3290	Other manufacturing n.e.c.	278	321	8890	8004	90	91
331	Repair of fabricated metal products/machinery	34	73	749	882	8	9
3311	Repair of fabricated metal products	156	147	3224	2563	30	32
3312	Repair of machinery	34	32	113	99	1	1
3313	Repair of electronic and optical equipment	30	26	896	579	9	5
3314	Repair of electrical equipment		21		3792		43
3315	Repair of transport equip., excl. motor vehicles		22		89		1
3319	Repair of other equipment	286	166	6063	4510	71	64
3320	Installation of industrial machinery/equipment						
C	Total manufacturing	8089	8044	441176	376783	3906	3502

a/ 1101 includes 1102, 1103 and 1104.
b/ 131 includes 139.
c/ 181 includes 1820.
d/ 301 includes 3020, 3030, 3040 and 309.

Slovakia

ISIC Revision 4		Output (millions of Euros)					Value added at factor values (millions of Euros)					Gross fixed capital formation (millions of Euros)		
ISIC	Industry	Note	2006	2007	2008	2009	Note	2006	2007	2008	2009	Note	2008	2009
1010	Processing/preserving of meat		...	...	599	501		...	...	73	74		30	34
1020	Processing/preserving of fish, etc.		...	...	37	36		...	...	8	11		5	4
1030	Processing/preserving of fruit,vegetables		...	...	85	...		...	...	15	...		6	...
1040	Vegetable and animal oils and fats		...	...	169	...		...	...	27	...		4	...
1050	Dairy products		...	...	535	430		...	...	53	68		40	58
106	Grain mill products,starches and starch products		...	...	238	...		...	...	32	...		13	9
1061	Grain mill products		...	...	...	67		...	...	...	13		...	...
1062	Starches and starch products		...	...	...	...		...	...	...	...		...	...
107	Other food products		...	...	912	855		...	...	249	257		100	70
1071	Bakery products		...	...	393	379		...	...	135	149		59	46
1072	Sugar		...	...	...	69		...	...	...	13		...	2
1073	Cocoa, chocolate and sugar confectionery		...	...	182	173		...	...	32	39		21	9
1074	Macaroni, noodles, couscous, etc.		...	...	29	24		...	...	2	1		1	2
1075	Prepared meals and dishes		...	...	...	...		...	...	...	...		...	...
1079	Other food products n.e.c.		...	...	...	...		...	...	...	...		...	...
1080	Prepared animal feeds		...	...	...	...		...	...	...	...		...	...
1101	Distilling, rectifying and blending of spirits		...	...	153	100		...	...	20	9		12	10
1102	Wines		...	...	685a/	656a/		...	...	160a/	161a/		81a/	57a/
1103	Malt liquors and malt		...	...	...a/	...a/		...	...	...a/	...a/		...a/	...a/
1104	Soft drinks,mineral waters,other bottled waters		...	...	...a/	...a/		...	...	...a/	...a/		...a/	...a/
1200	Tobacco products		...	...	3484	...		...	...	-12	...		...a/	...a/
131	Spinning, weaving and finishing of textiles		...	...	287b/	60		...	...	66b/	...		118	...
1311	Preparation and spinning of textile fibres		...	...	62	42		...	...	...	11		16b/	2
1312	Weaving of textiles		...	...	5	...		...	...	11	8		...	2
1313	Finishing of textiles		...	...	...b/	148		...	...	1	...		3	2
139	Other textiles		...	...	33	...		...	...	...b/	...		-	...
1391	Knitted and crocheted fabrics		...	...	86	52		...	...	8	45		...b/	9
1392	Made-up textile articles, except apparel		...	...	...	...		...	...	21	18		3	...
1393	Carpets and rugs		...	...	17	...		...	...	...	...		5	2
1394	Cordage, rope, twine and netting		...	...	54	15		...	...	3	4		...	...
1399	Other textiles n.e.c.		...	...	...	...		...	...	16	...		1	-
1410	Wearing apparel, except fur apparel		...	...	...	199		...	...	...	98		2	10
1420	Articles of fur		...	...	1	1		...	...	...	...		...	...
1430	Knitted and crocheted apparel		...	...	83	72		...	...	27	22		...	...
151	Leather;luggage,handbags,saddlery,harness;fur		...	...	38	32		...	...	15	15		2	1
1511	Tanning/dressing of leather; dressing of fur		...	...	18	13		...	...	4	5		6	3
1512	Luggage,handbags,etc.;saddlery/harness		...	...	21	19		...	...	11	11		-	-
1520	Footwear		...	...	350	365		...	...	97	97		7	2
1610	Sawmilling and planing of wood		...	...	324	215		...	...	77	61		20	24
162	Wood products, cork, straw, plaiting materials		...	...	453	361		...	...	74	70		66	45

Code	Industry						
1621	Veneer sheets and wood-based panels	209	155	14	14	47	23
1622	Builders' carpentry and joinery	150	125	36	39	12	11
1623	Wooden containers	52	40	10	7	5	2
1629	Other wood products;articles of cork,straw	42	40	14	10	1	9
1701	Pulp, paper and paperboard	686	595	154	132	48	25
1702	Corrugated paper and paperboard	174	139	47	43	19	10
1709	Other articles of paper and paperboard	392	402	69	87	45	33
181	Printing and service activities related to printing	377	365c/	115	115c/	34	58c/
1811	Printing	350	326	104	91	28	58
1812	Service activities related to printing	27	...	10	...	6	...c/
1820	Reproduction of recorded media	4	...c/	2	...c/	-	-
1910	Coke oven products	-	-	-	-	-	-
1920	Refined petroleum products	1515	1178	170	105	72	92
201	Basic chemicals,fertilizers, etc.	...	...	...	...	...	...
2011	Basic chemicals	...	...	...	...	...	...
2012	Fertilizers and nitrogen compounds	927	715	40	21	34	61
2013	Plastics and synthetic rubber in primary forms	213	229	36	40	24	28
202	Other chemical products	...	1	...	5	-	-
2021	Pesticides and other agrochemical products	47	39	8	5	2	1
2022	Paints,varnishes;printing ink and mastics	102	109	14	19	17	23
2023	Soap,cleaning and cosmetic preparations	64	80	14	16	5	4
2029	Other chemical products n.e.c.	143	104	-2	11	32	2
2030	Man-made fibres	257	...	61	...	24	...
2100	Pharmaceuticals,medicinal chemicals, etc.	...	...	179	173	134	86
221	Rubber products	828	646	133	128	120	74
2211	Rubber tyres and tubes	647	479	45	46	14	13
2219	Other rubber products	181	167	329	324	138	81
2220	Plastics products	1596	1432	...	89	...	30
2310	Glass and glass products	...	...	477	326	202	90
239	Non-metallic mineral products n.e.c.	1428	308	47	326	7	3
2391	Refractory products	167	1074	40	32	12	5
2392	Clay building materials	106	106	...	7	...	...
2393	Other porcelain and ceramic products	...	49	168	118	90	40
2394	Cement, lime and plaster	475	368	...	...	...	...
2395	Articles of concrete, cement and plaster	...	11	4	11	1	3
2396	Cutting, shaping and finishing of stone	11	25	...	...	...	...
2399	Other non-metallic mineral products n.e.c.	...	...	...	...	...	...
2410	Basic iron and steel	...	...	...	...	...	...
2420	Basic precious and other non-ferrous metals	289	208	39	53	29	13
243	Casting of metals	102	98	2	21	17	8
2431	Casting of iron and steel	186	110	37	32	12	6
2432	Casting of non-ferrous metals	...	...	...	...	...	...
251	Struct.metal products, tanks, reservoirs	805	556	185	147	53	48
2511	Structural metal products	467	398	68	55	35	18
2512	Tanks, reservoirs and containers of metal						

continued

Slovakia

ISIC	Industry	Output (millions of Euros) Note	2006	2007	2008	2009	Value added at factor values (millions of Euros) Note	2006	2007	2008	2009	Gross fixed capital formation (millions of Euros) Note	2008	2009
2513	Steam generators, excl. hot water boilers		...	...	...	...		...	...	...	...		...	...
2520	Weapons and ammunition		...	...	...	...		...	...	...	...		...	...
259	Other metal products;metal working services		...	...	1653	1221		...	...	465	293		164	116
2591	Forging,pressing,stamping,roll-forming of metal		...	...	159	84		...	...	36	18		35	8
2592	Treatment and coating of metals; machining		...	...	523	335		...	...	185	126		61	53
2593	Cutlery, hand tools and general hardware		...	...	100	66		...	...	32	21		7	2
2599	Other fabricated metal products n.e.c.		...	...	870	737		...	...	212	129		61	53
2610	Electronic components and boards		...	...	654	993		...	...	121	155		94	57
2620	Computers and peripheral equipment		...	...	90	83		...	...	32	18		2	3
2630	Communication equipment		...	...	69	106		...	...	20	18		3	4
2640	Consumer electronics		...	...	4792	4699		...	...	363	82		145	87
265	Measuring,testing equipment; watches, etc.		...	...	162	162		...	...	47	53		12	3
2651	Measuring/testing/navigating equipment,etc.		...	...	...	162		...	...	...	53		...	3
2652	Watches and clocks		...	...	...	9		...	...	...	-		...	...
2660	Irradiation/electromedical equipment,etc.		...	...	5	-		...	...	2	3		-	-
2670	Optical instruments and photographic equipment		...	...	...	7		...	...	...	1		-	-
2680	Magnetic and optical media		...	...	...	...		...	...	...	...		-	-
2710	Electric motors,generators,transformers,etc.		...	...	797	708		...	...	176	154		27	14
2720	Batteries and accumulators		...	...	1	3		...	...	...	1		-	-
273	Wiring and wiring devices		...	...	239	229		...	...	66	54		14	9
2731	Fibre optic cables		...	...	11	10		...	...	3	2		1	-
2732	Other electronic and electric wires and cables		...	...	222	194		...	...	61	48		13	8
2733	Wiring devices		...	...	7	24		...	...	2	4		1	-
2740	Electric lighting equipment		...	...	389	365		...	...	92	89		60	48
2750	Domestic appliances		...	...	407	342		...	...	-68	-32		23	8
2790	Other electrical equipment		...	...	398	254		...	...	98	41		15	6
281	General-purpose machinery		...	...	2114	1392		...	...	544	393		215	106
2811	Engines/turbines,excl.aircraft,vehicle engines		...	...	44	20		...	...	7	3		10	1
2812	Fluid power equipment		...	...	21	9		...	...	7	2		1	-
2813	Other pumps, compressors, taps and valves		...	...	486	350		...	...	101	69		42	24
2814	Bearings, gears, gearing and driving elements		...	...	986	646		...	...	292	201		96	59
2815	Ovens, furnaces and furnace burners		...	...	53	52		...	...	11	12		3	6
2816	Lifting and handling equipment		...	...	140	98		...	...	42	34		17	5
2817	Office machinery, excl.computers,etc.		...	...	...	23		...	...	...	6		...	...
2818	Power-driven hand tools		...	...	...	1		...	...	...	...		...	...
2819	Other general-purpose machinery		...	...	348	193		...	...	74	66		45	10
282	Special-purpose machinery		...	...	845	490		...	...	219	114		57	42
2821	Agricultural and forestry machinery		...	...	142	97		...	...	29	16		5	2
2822	Metal-forming machinery and machine tools		...	...	201	113		...	...	55	25		13	7
2823	Machinery for metallurgy		...	...	...	...		...	...	...	...		...	...
2824	Mining, quarrying and construction machinery		...	...	202	94		...	...	50	13		13	11

Code	Description	50	51	14	13	3	10
2825	Food/beverage/tobacco processing machinery	:..	:..	:..	:..	:..	:..
2826	Textile/apparel/leather production machinery	:..	:..	:..	:..	:..	:..
2829	Other special-purpose machinery	8373	6101	420	582	241	244
2910	Motor vehicles	196	111	38	20	11	8
2920	Automobile bodies, trailers and semi-trailers	4435	3409	555	513	253	176
2930	Parts and accessories for motor vehicles	:..	323d/	:..	84d/	:..	48d/
301	Building of ships and boats	:..	:..	:..	:..	:..	:..
3011	Building of ships and floating structures	:..	:..	:..	:..	:..	:..
3012	Building of pleasure and sporting boats	:..	:..	:..	..d/	:..	..d/
3020	Railway locomotives and rolling stock	15	..d/	:..	:..	1	..d/
3030	Air and spacecraft and related machinery	22	..d/	5	..d/	-	..d/
3040	Military fighting vehicles	11	..d/	6	..d/	1	..d/
309	Transport equipment n.e.c.	:..	-	3	-	:..	-
3091	Motorcycles	:..	9	:..	1	:..	-
3092	Bicycles and invalid carriages	:..	:..	:..	:..	:..	:..
3099	Other transport equipment n.e.c.	715	593	169	159	55	25
3100	Furniture	85	47	24	8	6	2
321	Jewellery, bijouterie and related articles	:..	47	8	8	:..	2
3211	Jewellery and related articles	:..	47	:..	:..	2	:..
3212	Imitation jewellery and related articles	:..	-	:..	:..	:..	-
3220	Musical instruments	37	11	14	3	4	-
3230	Sports goods	17	13	7	8	2	2
3240	Games and toys	141	123	55	48	12	15
3250	Medical and dental instruments and supplies	:..	:..	:..	:..	:..	:..
3290	Other manufacturing n.e.c.	622	474	106	100	38	30
331	Repair of fabricated metal products/machinery	57	51	17	12	4	5
3311	Repair of fabricated metal products	212	159	60	52	14	3
3312	Repair of machinery	7	6	4	1	-	-
3313	Repair of electronic and optical equipment	57	18	17	8	2	2
3314	Repair of electrical equipment	:..	232	:..	25	:..	22
3315	Repair of transport equip., excl. motor vehicles	:..	8	:..	2	-	-
3319	Repair of other equipment	493	359	141	120	18	17
3320	Installation of industrial machinery/equipment	:..	:..	:..	:..	:..	:..
C	Total manufacturing	54458	40328	7969	6279	3278	2233

a/ 1101 includes 1102, 1103 and 1104.
b/ 131 includes 139.
c/ 181 includes 1820.
d/ 301 includes 3020, 3030, 3040 and 309.

Slovakia

Index numbers of industrial production

ISIC Revision 4

(2005=100)

ISIC	Industry	Note	1999	2000	2001	2002	2003	2004	2005	2006	2007	2008	2009	2010
10	Food products		...	83	97	98	97	101	100	102	99	96	92	94
11	Beverages		...	127	127	122	102	107	100	100	101	104	94	89
12	Tobacco products		...	4228	3626	4251	2743	809	100	65	56	4	-	-
13	Textiles		...	156	164	113	95	101	100	98	90	64	36	47
14	Wearing apparel		...	112	122	121	116	105	100	211	213	233	225	236
15	Leather and related products		...	58	61	71	90	100	100	95	89	67	43	47
16	Wood/wood products/cork,excl. furniture		...	73	87	78	79	84	100	108	133	113	84	92
17	Paper and paper products		...	62	66	67	77	92	100	104	110	112	105	102
18	Printing and reproduction of recorded media		...	53	61	61	54	94	100	101	106	125	124	123
19	Coke and refined petroleum products		...	48	48	97	97	105	100	101	109	108	109	102
20	Chemicals and chemical products		...	87	91	87	86	91	100	125	145	142	147	160
21	Pharmaceuticals,medicinal chemicals, etc.		...	80	89	94	100	89	100	113	120	115	110	137
22	Rubber and plastics products		...	50	57	67	81	91	100	115	140	154	132	171
23	Other non-metallic mineral products		...	77	79	87	92	95	100	102	106	107	80	84
24	Basic metals		...	74	79	87	122	116	100	109	109	91	77	92
25	Fabricated metal products, except machinery		...	59	62	69	80	91	100	131	155	170	131	144
26	Computer, electronic and optical products		...	9	15	18	21	43	100	248	393	439	459	563
27	Electrical equipment		...	58	66	71	83	92	100	108	107	107	88	102
28	Machinery and equipment n.e.c.		...	82	70	74	94	111	100	125	152	165	126	185
29	Motor vehicles, trailers and semi-trailers		...	62	60	62	116	107	100	145	259	287	207	296
30	Other transport equipment		...	76	121	69	81	99	100	102	108	182	166	114
31	Furniture		...	111	120	121	136	145	100	108	129	103	96	102
32	Other manufacturing		...	53	55	80	116	94	100	92	76	86	58	64
33	Repair and installation of machinery/equipment		...	72	66	65	71	78	100	92	87	107	91	97
C	Total manufacturing		...	71	74	81	98	101	100	121	147	151	127	153

Slovenia

Supplier of information:
Statistical Office of the Republic of Slovenia, Ljubljana.

Basic source of data:
Annual census/exhaustive survey; administrative source.

Major deviations from ISIC (Revision 4):
None reported.

Reference period:
Calendar year.

Scope:
All registered enterprises.

Method of data collection:
Data for gross fixed capital formation are collected by questionnaires; all other data are mainly derived from administrative sources.

Type of enumeration:
Complete enumeration.

Adjusted for non-response:
Yes.

Concepts and definitions of variables:
Wages and salaries excludes payments in kind, housing and family allowances paid directly by the employer; it includes employers' contributions (in respect of their employees) paid to social security, pension and insurance schemes as well as the benefits received by employees under these schemes and severance and termination pay.
Output excludes net change between the beginning and end of the year in the value of work in process and stocks and goods to be shipped in the same condition as received; it includes revenue from non-industrial activities.

Related national publications:
Structural Business Statistics, published by the Statistical Office of the Republic of Slovenia, Ljubljana.

Slovenia

ISIC Revision 4

ISIC	Industry	Number of enterprises (number)					Number of employees (number)					Wages and salaries paid to employees (millions of Euros)				
		Note	2007	2008	2009	2010a/	Note	2007	2008	2009	2010a/	Note	2007	2008	2009	2010a/
1010	Processing/preserving of meat	...	...	163	171	173	...	...	4902	4676	4492	...	...	71	68	69
1020	Processing/preserving of fish, etc.	...	...	5	3	4	...	...	293	...	...	...	...	2	...	...
1030	Processing/preserving of fruit,vegetables	...	...	101	112	117	...	...	805	856	778	...	...	14	16	15
1040	Vegetable and animal oils and fats	...	...	31	32	36	...	...	160	160	...	...	...	3	3	...
1050	Dairy products	...	...	87	84	88	...	...	1450	1237	1190	...	...	24	21	23
106	Grain mill products,starches and starch products	...	...	41	37	39	...	...	1481	624	642	...	...	29	...	...
1061	Grain mill products	...	...	39	35	36	...	...	...	...	614	...	...	...	9	...
1062	Starches and starch products	...	...	2	2	3	...	...	...	...	28	...	...	...	...	...
107	Other food products	...	...	531	555	603	...	...	5970	6391	6332	...	...	85	100	101
1071	Bakery products	...	...	420	441	483	...	...	4859	4907	4980	...	...	70	70	73
1072	Sugar	...	...	1	2	2	...	...	...	...	...	...	...	...	...	...
1073	Cocoa, chocolate and sugar confectionery	...	...	16	17	17	...	...	447	347	317	...	...	5	5	5
1074	Macaroni, noodles, couscous, etc.	...	...	16	19	17	...	...	59	77	72	...	...	1	1	1
1075	Prepared meals and dishes	...	...	6	5	5	...	...	111	103	88	...	...	...	...	1
1079	Other food products n.e.c.	...	...	72	71	79	...	...	...	...	...	...	...	8	22	...
1080	Prepared animal feeds	...	...	16	14	12	...	...	416	...	...	...	...	8	8	9
1101	Distilling, rectifying and blending of spirits	...	...	28	30	29	...	...	...	...	...	...	...	...	...	...
1102	Wines	...	...	43	43	46	...	...	...	...	...	...	...	...	...	...
1103	Malt liquors and malt	...	...	14	12	12	...	...	710	692	705	...	...	19	20	20
1104	Soft drinks,mineral waters,other bottled waters	...	...	19	18	16	...	...	698	548	436	...	...	14	11	9
1200	Tobacco products	...	...	-	-	-	...	...	-	-	-	...	...	-	-	-
131	Spinning, weaving and finishing of textiles	...	...	58	54	58	...	...	1698	1073	1022	...	...	24	14	15
1311	Preparation and spinning of textile fibres	...	...	10	10	10	...	...	858	746	714	...	...	11	9	10
1312	Weaving of textiles	...	...	20	17	15	...	...	786	281	244	...	...	12	4	4
1313	Finishing of textiles	...	...	28	27	33	...	...	54	46	64	...	...	1	1	1
139	Other textiles	...	...	331	326	297	...	...	5266	4940	4103	...	...	70	68	66
1391	Knitted and crocheted fabrics	...	...	12	12	11	...	...	144	290	262	...	...	2	4	4
1392	Made-up textile articles, except apparel	...	...	176	176	156	...	...	4044	3237	2370	...	...	52	43	37
1393	Carpets and rugs	...	...	5	7	6	...	...	3	56	59	...	...	...	1	1
1394	Cordage, rope, twine and netting	...	...	12	10	12	...	...	132	122	126	...	...	2	2	2
1399	Other textiles n.e.c.	...	...	126	121	112	...	...	944	1233	1285	...	...	15	19	23
1410	Wearing apparel, except fur apparel	...	...	823	789	765	...	...	8732	6819	4110	...	...	90	61	50
1420	Articles of fur	...	...	5	6	5	...	...	6	6	5	...	...	...	...	...
1430	Knitted and crocheted apparel	...	...	99	95	90	...	...	878	1050	1024	...	...	11	12	13
151	Leather;luggage,handbags,saddlery,harness;fur	...	...	77	72	68	...	...	2157	1749	1732	...	...	24	22	24
1511	Tanning/dressing of leather; dressing of fur	...	...	13	14	13	...	...	670	271	279	...	...	8	6	6
1512	Luggage,handbags,etc.;saddlery/harness	...	...	64	58	55	...	...	1487	1478	1452	...	...	16	17	17
1520	Footwear	...	...	94	87	89	...	...	2156	1946	1635	...	...	27	24	22
1610	Sawmilling and planing of wood	...	...	519	514	515	...	...	1669	1396	1336	...	...	20	19	19
162	Wood products, cork, straw, plaiting materials	...	...	1182	1156	1148	...	...	8417	6815	6626	...	...	116	91	96

ISIC	Industry									
1621	Veneer sheets and wood-based panels	33	36	36	1904	1635	1759	29	22	27
1622	Builders' carpentry and joinery	570	562	572	4945	4053	3785	67	55	54
1623	Wooden containers	164	159	164	697	404	358	9	5	5
1629	Other wood products;articles of cork,straw	415	399	376	871	723	725	11	9	9
1701	Pulp, paper and paperboard	14	12	11	2226	2042	1958	43	44	42
1702	Corrugated paper and paperboard	89	80	78	1850	1405	1251	30	23	23
1709	Other articles of paper and paperboard	102	93	86	2463	1482	1337	40	23	24
181	Printing and service activities related to printing	1213	1219	1227	4978	4921	4446	81	82	74
1811	Printing	527	541	561	3912	3854	3502	65	65	59
1812	Service activities related to printing	686	678	666	1067	1067	945	16	17	15
1820	Reproduction of recorded media	21	20	21	24	10	17	…	…	…
1910	Coke oven products	-	-	-	-	-	-	-	-	-
1920	Refined petroleum products	5	4	3	92	-	-	2	-	-
201	Basic chemicals,fertilizers. etc.	52	52	51	2886	2362	2389	58	47	53
2011	Basic chemicals	27	29	29	1844	2078	2067	…	43	47
2012	Fertilizers and nitrogen compounds	5	7	5	…	…	…	…	…	…
2013	Plastics and synthetic rubber in primary forms	20	16	17	…	…	…	…	…	…
202	Other chemical products	109	110	116	…	…	…	…	…	…
2021	Pesticides and other agrochemical products	4	4	6	1460	1574	1505	31	30	33
2022	Paints,varnishes;printing ink and mastics	19	19	18	1535	1021	997	29	20	20
2023	Soap,cleaning and cosmetic preparations	43	42	46	851	1011	1071	21	23	24
2029	Other chemical products n.e.c.	43	45	46	…	…	…	…	…	…
2030	Man-made fibres	1	1	1	5778	5945	6233	247	251	243
2100	Pharmaceuticals,medicinal chemicals, etc.	16	16	17	3911	3259	3092	76	65	70
221	Rubber products	131	123	114	1627	1484	1451	35	31	35
2211	Rubber tyres and tubes	26	22	20	2283	1775	1640	41	34	35
2219	Other rubber products	105	101	94	9603	9112	9364	153	151	162
2220	Plastics products	986	951	937	2553	2194	2073	38	34	35
2310	Glass and glass products	70	69	74	6373	5854	6407	113	101	116
239	Non-metallic mineral products n.e.c.	500	515	507	38	54	57	1	1	1
2391	Refractory products	12	12	13	458	380	332	8	7	6
2392	Clay building materials	18	19	17	246	280	267	3	3	3
2393	Other porcelain and ceramic products	46	43	47	512	523	486	14	14	13
2394	Cement, lime and plaster	7	7	6	2223	1924	1908	38	33	34
2395	Articles of concrete, cement and plaster	158	155	147	840	834	816	13	12	12
2396	Cutting, shaping and finishing of stone	219	237	233	2056	1859	2541	36	31	47
2399	Other non-metallic mineral products n.e.c.	40	42	44	4370	…	3358	88	…	67
2410	Basic iron and steel	31	28	28	2306	…	979	46	…	19
2420	Basic precious and other non-ferrous metals	15	7	7	4085	4020	3928	68	64	68
243	Casting of metals	93	97	99	…	2166	2003	…	31	29
2431	Casting of iron and steel	24	24	26	…	1855	1925	…	33	38
2432	Casting of non-ferrous metals	69	73	73	…	…	…	…	…	…
251	Struct.metal products, tanks, reservoirs	675	696	703	7461	8375	7714	122	136	134
2511	Structural metal products	626	650	657	…	7365	6806	…	120	118
2512	Tanks, reservoirs and containers of metal	46	43	43	1110	1002	902	18	16	16

continued

Slovenia

ISIC	Industry	Number of enterprises (number)					Number of employees (number)					Wages and salaries paid to employees (millions of Euros)				
		Note	2007	2008	2009	2010a/	Note	2007	2008	2009	2010a/	Note	2007	2008	2009	2010a/
2513	Steam generators, excl. hot water boilers		...	3	3	3		...	...	8	6		...	...	...	...
2520	Weapons and ammunition		...	22	20	20		...	...	12	10		...	...	...	...
259	Other metal products;metal working services		...	3483	3453	3379		...	23305	21428	20640		...	371	331	339
2591	Forging,pressing,stamping,roll-forming of metal		...	120	117	115		...	2674	3295	3137		...	45	53	58
2592	Treatment and coating of metals; machining		...	2031	2032	2020		...	7331	7319	7163		...	104	99	102
2593	Cutlery, hand tools and general hardware		...	400	395	390		...	5048	4551	4350		...	89	80	78
2599	Other fabricated metal products n.e.c.		...	932	909	854		...	8252	6263	5990		...	133	99	101
2610	Electronic components and boards		...	93	110	109		...	687	2720	2172		...	11	42	36
2620	Computers and peripheral equipment		...	46	45	40		...	440	225	224		...	11	5	6
2630	Communication equipment		...	35	30	29		...	1467	1071	984		...	42	30	26
2640	Consumer electronics		...	18	19	29		...	...	324	331		...	1	5	6
265	Measuring,testing equipment; watches, etc.		...	85	82	82		...	2060	1903	1678		...	39	36	34
2651	Measuring/testing/navigating equipment,etc.		...	82	81	80		...	...	...	...		...	39	36	34
2652	Watches and clocks		...	3	1	2		...	...	...	...		...	...	...	...
2660	Irradiation/electromedical equipment,etc.		...	2	3	2		...	...	...	...		...	...	...	...
2670	Optical instruments and photographic equipment		...	27	16	16		...	...	375	...		...	...	7	...
2680	Magnetic and optical media		...	3	2	1		...	...	...	...		...	...	...	...
2710	Electric motors,generators,transformers,etc.		...	135	129	117		...	6433	6169	6196		...	103	97	116
2720	Batteries and accumulators		...	7	9	7		...	652	608	669		...	12	12	13
273	Wiring and wiring devices		...	57	50	45		...	1006	1557	1257		...	15	21	19
2731	Fibre optic cables		...	3	4	3		...	14	26	12		...	...	1	...
2732	Other electronic and electric wires and cables		...	28	23	20		...	499	275	15		...	7	4	7
2733	Wiring devices		...	26	23	22		...	494	1256	1231		...	7	17	18
2740	Electric lighting equipment		...	72	67	67		...	1196	1208	1244		...	23	24	26
2750	Domestic appliances		...	46	40	40		...	10055	9069	8920		...	167	153	159
2790	Other electrical equipment		...	130	126	130		...	2709	1139	1409		...	42	24	28
281	General-purpose machinery		...	436	425	411		...	10445	8899	8022		...	194	150	151
2811	Engines/turbines,excl.aircraft,vehicle engines		...	20	19	16		...	740	238	247		...	15	5	6
2812	Fluid power equipment		...	14	19	19		...	409	417	399		...	7	7	7
2813	Other pumps, compressors, taps and valves		...	49	43	40		...	2338	2548	2466		...	41	40	43
2814	Bearings, gears, gearing and driving elements		...	34	32	30		...	822	743	693		...	14	12	12
2815	Ovens, furnaces and furnace burners		...	29	30	30		...	225	...	...		...	5	...	...
2816	Lifting and handling equipment		...	96	93	92		...	2627	2580	2175		...	52	41	42
2817	Office machinery, excl.computers,etc.		...	4	2	2		...	92	...	...		...	2	...	...
2818	Power-driven hand tools		...	6	4	4		...	694	291	248		...	12	5	4
2819	Other general-purpose machinery		...	184	183	178		...	2499	1920	1625		...	45	36	33
282	Special-purpose machinery		...	402	392	369		...	6619	6500	5376		...	126	123	106
2821	Agricultural and forestry machinery		...	52	59	60		...	935	1196	1098		...	15	19	19
2822	Metal-forming machinery and machine tools		...	123	118	104		...	1270	2160	1319		...	27	47	27
2823	Machinery for metallurgy		...	16	11	9		...	841	549	519		...	17	10	10
2824	Mining, quarrying and construction machinery		...	35	25	23		...	1194	410	341		...	21	6	6

2825	Food/beverage/tobacco processing machinery	...	73	69	67	...	891	663	661	...	17	12	14
2826	Textile/apparel/leather production machinery	...	7	7	7	...	250	257	250	...	4	4	4
2829	Other special-purpose machinery	...	96	103	99	...	1239	...	...	...	25	...	...
2910	Motor vehicles	...	18	14	14	...	4168	3005	2908	...	76	57	59
2920	Automobile bodies, trailers and semi-trailers	...	32	35	35	...	727	1489	1420	...	13	26	27
2930	Parts and accessories for motor vehicles	...	100	92	95	...	9863	8487	8461	...	164	140	154
301	Building of ships and boats	...	54	54	48	...	791	483	292	...	14	9	6
3011	Building of ships and floating structures	...	14	16	14	...	51	40	29	...	1	1	...
3012	Building of pleasure and sporting boats	...	40	38	34	...	740	444	263	...	13	9	6
3020	Railway locomotives and rolling stock	...	-	2	2	...	-	...	...	...	-	...	...
3030	Air and spacecraft and related machinery	...	14	14	17	...	96	100	112	...	2	2	...
3040	Military fighting vehicles	...	-	-	-	...	-	-	-	...	-	-	-
309	Transport equipment n.e.c.	...	18	14	14	...	609	102	...	...	13	2	2
3091	Motorcycles	...	6	4	3	...	577	...	...	...	12	...	...
3092	Bicycles and invalid carriages	...	12	10	11	...	32	...	26	...	1	...	...
3099	Other transport equipment n.e.c.	...	-	-	-	...	-	-	-	...	-	-	-
3100	Furniture	...	1079	1065	1092	...	11936	9861	8598	...	160	130	120
321	Jewellery, bijouterie and related articles	...	184	179	180	...	440	382	365	...	6	5	6
3211	Jewellery and related articles	...	169	168	167	...	423	379	362	...	6	5	6
3212	Imitation jewellery and related articles	...	15	11	13	...	17	3	3	...	...	...	...
3220	Musical instruments	...	19	20	20	...	44	43	41	...	1	1	1
3230	Sports goods	...	45	44	43	...	558	490	150	...	9	8	3
3240	Games and toys	...	32	32	29	...	471	314	227	...	8	7	4
3250	Medical and dental instruments and supplies	...	241	299	309	...	2824	2516	2644	...	37	32	39
3290	Other manufacturing n.e.c.	...	257	249	240	...	462	529	575	...	6	8	9
331	Repair of fabricated metal products/machinery	...	1401	1397	1425	...	4333	3348	3494	...	81	62	69
3311	Repair of fabricated metal products	...	57	70	69	...	142	80	82	...	2	1	1
3312	Repair of machinery	...	887	892	922	...	2458	1952	1903	...	47	37	40
3313	Repair of electronic and optical equipment	...	101	99	94	...	72	56	56	...	1	1	1
3314	Repair of electrical equipment	...	224	207	201	...	181	160	161	...	3	3	3
3315	Repair of transport equip., excl. motor vehicles	...	118	113	124	...	1473	...	...	...	28	...	25
3319	Repair of other equipment	...	14	16	15	...	8	...	...	...	...	...	...
3320	Installation of industrial machinery/equipment	...	349	341	328	...	1416	1230	1392	...	25	24	27
C	Total manufacturing	...	17332	17172	17074	...	221409	197910	186393	...	3761	3347	3395

a/ Provisional data.

Slovenia

ISIC	Industry	Output — Note	Output 2007	Output 2008	Output 2009	Output 2010a/	VA — Note	VA 2007	VA 2008	VA 2009	VA 2010a/	GFCF — Note	GFCF 2009	GFCF 2010a/
			(millions of Euros)					(millions of Euros)					(millions of Euros)	
1010	Processing/preserving of meat		...	565	507	520		...	98	100	100		23	17
1020	Processing/preserving of fish, etc.		...	14	...	...		...	4	...	...		...	...
1030	Processing/preserving of fruit,vegetables		...	91	96	87		...	22	24	26		3	4
1040	Vegetable and animal oils and fats		...	42	32	...		...	6	7	...		...	...
1050	Dairy products		...	297	245	260		...	48	46	45		12	11
106	Grain mill products,starches and starch products		...	178	...	...		...	44	...	...		4	3
1061	Grain mill products		...	...	45	...		...	...	15	...		...	...
1062	Starches and starch products		...	...	...	...		...	...	...	...		...	...
107	Other food products		...	...	...	...		...	...	...	...		...	...
1071	Bakery products		...	369	447	446		...	143	146	162		39	25
1072	Sugar		...	269	269	270		...	109	99	104		20	16
1073	Cocoa, chocolate and sugar confectionery		...	36	33	30		...	15	8	7		6	2
1074	Macaroni, noodles, couscous, etc.		...	3	4	4		...	1	2	2		-	1
1075	Prepared meals and dishes		...	...	...	6		...	...	...	1		...	...
1079	Other food products n.e.c.		...	53	135	76		...	17	36	17		12	6
1080	Prepared animal feeds		...	81	74	...		...	10	10	...		1	11
1101	Distilling, rectifying and blending of spirits		...	...	2	...		...	...	1	...		-	...
1102	Wines		...	...	2	2		...	...	...	1		-	...
1103	Malt liquors and malt		...	185	176	161		...	62	68	53		...	...
1104	Soft drinks,mineral waters,other bottled waters		...	73	66	50		...	26	25	18		12	9
1200	Tobacco products		...	-	...	-		...	-	...	-		...	4
131	Spinning, weaving and finishing of textiles		...	...	...	...		...	...	...	...		-	-
1311	Preparation and spinning of textile fibres		...	102	67	91		...	26	18	22		6	...
1312	Weaving of textiles		...	54	46	69		...	15	12	17		5	...
1313	Finishing of textiles		...	40	15	14		...	10	5	3		1	...
139	Other textiles		...	8	6	8		...	1	1	2		-	...
1391	Knitted and crocheted fabrics		...	374	268	270		...	113	94	97		23	10
1392	Made-up textile articles, except apparel		...	5	12	12		...	2	4	4		6	4
1393	Carpets and rugs		...	267	140	111		...	79	51	43		...	1
1394	Cordage, rope, twine and netting		...	12	10	10		...	2	3	3		1	4
1399	Other textiles n.e.c.		...	92	11	12		...	29	2	3		15	...
1410	Wearing apparel, except fur apparel		...	210	148	119		...	106	70	61		5	4
1420	Articles of fur		...	...	...	29		...	...	...	...		...	2
1430	Knitted and crocheted apparel		...	37	28	...		...	16	14	16		1	...
151	Leather;luggage,handbags,saddlery,harness;fur		...	...	...	...		...	...	...	...		2	...
1511	Tanning/dressing of leather; dressing of fur		...	127	121	136		...	16	28	28		1	9
1512	Luggage,handbags,etc.;saddlery/harness		...	27	25	37		...	2	8	12		2	...
1520	Footwear		...	107	95	100		...	14	20	16		2	2
1610	Sawmilling and planing of wood		...	126	120	122		...	37	34	33		7	11
162	Wood products, cork, straw, plaiting materials		...	567	411	458		...	178	124	133		22	27

ISIC	Industry							
1621	Veneer sheets and wood-based panels	3	4	35	30	45	173	125	162
1622	Builders' carpentry and joinery	15	18	75	73	99	300	230	235
1623	Wooden containers	2	2	8	7	13	43	21	23
1629	Other wood products;articles of cork,straw	2	3	15	13	21	51	34	37
1701	Pulp, paper and paperboard	17	22	71	97	76	438	400	427
1702	Corrugated paper and paperboard	6	8	40	39	49	163	117	132
1709	Other articles of paper and paperboard	11	2	37	42	54	182	129	137
181	Printing and service activities related to printing	42	23	129	138	147	436	425	392
1811	Printing	37	17	98	102	111	347	331	307
1812	Service activities related to printing	5	5	32	35	35	89	94	86
1820	Reproduction of recorded media	-	...	...	...	1	3	1	1
1910	Coke oven products	-	-	-	-	-	-	-	-
1920	Refined petroleum products	...	...	...	...	3	11	...	...
201	Basic chemicals,fertilizers, etc.	27	21	110	85	103	466	328	405
2011	Basic chemicals	24	19	97	76	...	...	284	350
2012	Fertilizers and nitrogen compounds	-	...	...	...	...	...	...	...
2013	Plastics and synthetic rubber in primary forms	...	...	...	...	...	...	...	...
202	Other chemical products	...	...	...	...	...	...	...	...
2021	Pesticides and other agrochemical products	5	10	74	54	66	300	259	304
2022	Paints,varnishes;printing ink and mastics	5	5	57	49	57	203	176	188
2023	Soap,cleaning and cosmetic preparations	9	9	51	38	42	128	128	165
2029	Other chemical products n.e.c.	...	...	...	...	...	...	...	...
2030	Man-made fibres	132	138	640	621	734	1495	1330	1425
2100	Pharmaceuticals,medicinal chemicals, etc.	13	19	139	105	135	490	374	488
221	Rubber products	7	11	78	62	69	279	217	290
2211	Rubber tyres and tubes	7	8	61	44	66	211	156	198
2219	Other rubber products	65	58	287	270	286	938	845	920
2220	Plastics products	9	16	47	44	57	156	123	131
2310	Glass and glass products	60	38	220	189	252	776	590	704
239	Non-metallic mineral products n.e.c.	-	1	2	2	2	6	6	8
2391	Refractory products	1	1	10	10	21	52	33	32
2392	Clay building materials	-	-	3	3	1	6	7	6
2393	Other porcelain and ceramic products	26	4	28	34	51	141	107	84
2394	Cement, lime and plaster	18	14	61	60	82	266	204	214
2395	Articles of concrete, cement and plaster	4	7	21	21	24	61	51	50
2396	Cutting, shaping and finishing of stone	11	11	95	59	71	244	182	310
2399	Other non-metallic mineral products n.e.c.	...	26	126	...	216	1007	...	645
2410	Basic iron and steel	...	10	36	...	87	921	...	244
2420	Basic precious and other non-ferrous metals	13	26	115	101	94	357	285	346
243	Casting of metals	7	5	47	46	...	...	146	155
2431	Casting of iron and steel	5	21	68	55	...	...	139	191
2432	Casting of non-ferrous metals	...	36	200	196	200	...	632	639
251	Struct.metal products, tanks, reservoirs	30	35	184	176	200	639	632	639
2511	Structural metal products	...	1	16	20	25	78	570	587
2512	Tanks, reservoirs and containers of metal								

continued

Slovenia

ISIC	Industry	Output Note	Output 2007	Output 2008	Output 2009	Output 2010a/	VA Note	VA 2007	VA 2008	VA 2009	VA 2010a/	GFCF Note	GFCF 2009	GFCF 2010a/
				Output at factor values (millions of Euros)					**Value added at factor values (millions of Euros)**					**Gross fixed capital formation (millions of Euros)**
2513	Steam generators, excl. hot water boilers		...	...	1	1		...	...	...	...		-	-
2520	Weapons and ammunition		...	...	13	27		...	...	1	-1		-	-
259	Other metal products;metal working services		...	1874	1682	1966		...	642	486	589		95	104
2591	Forging,pressing,stamping,roll-forming of metal		...	294	521	636		...	70	60	102		14	26
2592	Treatment and coating of metals; machining		...	441	401	437		...	202	169	188		32	28
2593	Cutlery, hand tools and general hardware		...	356	268	293		...	141	105	117		19	22
2599	Other fabricated metal products n.e.c.		...	783	492	600		...	229	152	182		30	28
2610	Electronic components and boards		...	72	181	227		...	20	53	74		10	14
2620	Computers and peripheral equipment		...	51	28	27		...	15	7	8		2	1
2630	Communication equipment		...	151	56	57		...	53	16	24		8	5
2640	Consumer electronics		...	4	25	35		...	1	5	11		-	1
265	Measuring,testing equipment; watches, etc.		...	150	117	118		...	54	48	50		6	4
2651	Measuring/testing/navigating equipment,etc.		...	150	...	...		...	54	...	...		...	...
2652	Watches and clocks		...	...	...	...		...	...	...	...		...	...
2660	Irradiation/electromedical equipment,etc.		...	...	...	...		...	...	...	...		...	...
2670	Optical instruments and photographic equipment		...	...	...	...		...	...	...	...		...	...
2680	Magnetic and optical media		...	...	21	...		...	...	7	...		...	...
2710	Electric motors,generators,transformers,etc.		...	542	483	655		...	173	152	219		48	39
2720	Batteries and accumulators		...	119	95	140		...	31	22	28		7	5
273	Wiring and wiring devices		...	67	58	49		...	23	17	23		3	2
2731	Fibre optic cables		...	3	3	2		...	1	1	1		-	-
2732	Other electronic and electric wires and cables		...	39	20	2		...	12	5	1		-	-
2733	Wiring devices		...	25	36	46		...	11	11	21		3	2
2740	Electric lighting equipment		...	147	194	238		...	48	55	53		16	9
2750	Domestic appliances		...	1099	899	1046		...	286	222	295		28	38
2790	Other electrical equipment		...	191	116	128		...	68	38	50		2	3
281	General-purpose machinery		...	1187	747	815		...	348	200	252		35	37
2811	Engines/turbines,excl.aircraft,vehicle engines		...	92	25	33		...	31	12	19		2	6
2812	Fluid power equipment		...	33	23	30		...	13	10	13		3	1
2813	Other pumps, compressors, taps and valves		...	308	239	280		...	84	52	66		6	15
2814	Bearings, gears, gearing and driving elements		...	93	70	73		...	28	23	25		3	3
2815	Ovens, furnaces and furnace burners		...	28	...	...		...	9	...	...		1	-
2816	Lifting and handling equipment		...	372	218	221		...	97	42	65		13	7
2817	Office machinery, excl.computers,etc.		...	9	...	...		...	3	...	...		...	...
2818	Power-driven hand tools		...	52	14	16		...	16	3	5		...	...
2819	Other general-purpose machinery		...	200	143	144		...	68	50	52		7	5
282	Special-purpose machinery		...	648	517	436		...	214	185	155		29	18
2821	Agricultural and forestry machinery		...	82	85	96		...	27	25	30		3	5
2822	Metal-forming machinery and machine tools		...	149	215	93		...	45	73	34		14	4
2823	Machinery for metallurgy		...	94	43	37		...	33	18	16		2	3
2824	Mining, quarrying and construction machinery		...	104	22	27		...	32	12	8		2	3

ISIC Revision 4

2825	Food/beverage/tobacco processing machinery	...	77	52	66	27	20	22	2	3
2826	Textile/apparel/leather production machinery	...	15	12	14	6	5	6	...	1
2829	Other special-purpose machinery	...	126	...	...	45	...	...	...	...
2910	Motor vehicles	...	1528	1304	1337	198	148	143	1	...
2920	Automobile bodies, trailers and semi-trailers	...	89	235	302	21	46	49	...	45
2930	Parts and accessories for motor vehicles	...	1014	794	989	249	200	279	2	4
301	Building of ships and boats	...	74	43	44	15	5	7	-	-
3011	Building of ships and floating structures	...	3	1	1	1	1	1	2	4
3012	Building of pleasure and sporting boats	...	72	42	43	14	5	6	...	...
3020	Railway locomotives and rolling stock	...	-	...	...	-	4	...	2	...
3030	Air and spacecraft and related machinery	...	8	9	...	3	-	1	-	-
3040	Military fighting vehicles	...	-	-	-	17	1	1	...	-
309	Transport equipment n.e.c.	...	50	10	13	17	...	...	...	-
3091	Motorcycles	...	48	10	...	1	...	...	-	-
3092	Bicycles and invalid carriages	...	2	...	...	-	-	-	...	-
3099	Other transport equipment n.e.c.	...	-	-	-	...	...	...	29	23
3100	Furniture	...	687	451	425	226	158	148	1	...
321	Jewellery, bijouterie and related articles	...	24	21	25	12	9	12	1	...
3211	Jewellery and related articles	...	23	21	25	12	9	12	-	...
3212	Imitation jewellery and related articles	...	1	...	...	1	1	1	...	...
3220	Musical instruments	...	2	38	2	12	4	4	...	...
3230	Sports goods	...	46	42	10	24	12	6	4	2
3240	Games and toys	...	68	140	26	66	53	68	9	7
3250	Medical and dental instruments and supplies	...	41	43	53	12	15	17	2	2
3290	Other manufacturing n.e.c.	...	156	175	194	117	89	105	10	9
331	Repair of fabricated metal products/machinery	...	239	126	...	...	...	...	-	-
3311	Repair of fabricated metal products	...	8	5	6	4	2	3	8	5
3312	Repair of machinery	...	135	102	107	69	55	56	...	...
3313	Repair of electronic and optical equipment	...	9	6	14	3	6	7	1	2
3314	Repair of electrical equipment	...	15	13	61	7	...	38	...	-
3315	Repair of transport equip., excl. motor vehicles	...	71	...	1	33	...	...	...	-
3319	Repair of other equipment	...	1	...	...	...	...	...	4	5
3320	Installation of industrial machinery/equipment	...	126	128	132	46	45	55	...	...
C	Total manufacturing	...	23434	18550	20666	6743	5321	6020	1185	1073

a/ Provisional data.

Slovenia

Index numbers of industrial production

ISIC Revision 4

(2005=100)

ISIC	Industry	Note	1999	2000	2001	2002	2003	2004	2005	2006	2007	2008	2009	2010
10	Food products		105	112	114	112	114	102	100	100	99	91	85	86
11	Beverages		103	109	111	110	111	100	100	100	99	92	88	84
12	Tobacco products		…	…	…	…	…	…	…	…	…	…	…	…
13	Textiles		146	158	140	137	123	107	100	94	91	77	38	36
14	Wearing apparel		202	204	193	153	135	116	100	98	95	85	49	48
15	Leather and related products		133	138	136	115	100	94	100	105	83	86	64	72
16	Wood/wood products/cork,excl. furniture		98	99	91	94	90	94	100	103	115	107	81	85
17	Paper and paper products		94	98	96	103	97	98	100	99	97	88	79	80
18	Printing and reproduction of recorded media		96	98	91	94	98	96	100	99	99	109	95	91
19	Coke and refined petroleum products		…	…	…	…	…	…	100	94	99	30	23	11
20	Chemicals and chemical products		63	70	76	80	90	98	100	107	116	120	102	117
21	Pharmaceuticals,medicinal chemicals, etc.		…	…	…	…	…	…	…	…	…	…	…	…
22	Rubber and plastics products		75	82	83	82	85	95	100	106	115	127	106	122
23	Other non-metallic mineral products		132	127	127	128	129	107	100	106	112	115	83	82
24	Basic metals		82	92	96	98	105	97	100	120	128	88	62	67
25	Fabricated metal products, except machinery		75	84	88	92	93	91	100	107	117	148	114	121
26	Computer, electronic and optical products		73	78	81	84	106	96	100	109	116	163	130	125
27	Electrical equipment		57	63	71	76	74	99	100	112	117	124	105	129
28	Machinery and equipment n.e.c.		67	70	81	90	85	97	100	106	121	100	70	75
29	Motor vehicles, trailers and semi-trailers		48	53	56	59	61	86	100	97	100	105	100	117
30	Other transport equipment		56	64	58	59	63	92	100	112	112	133	107	61
31	Furniture		104	102	110	107	102	97	100	102	125	74	49	46
32	Other manufacturing		83	82	86	83	87	88	100	82	98	85	62	65
33	Repair and installation of machinery/equipment		64	70	73	77	82	94	100	113	79	130	103	101
C	Total manufacturing		81	86	89	91	92	96	100	106	115	118	96	102

South Africa

Concepts and definitions of variables:
Wages and salaries is compensation of employees.
Output is valued at basic prices.
Value added is valued at basic prices.

Related national publications:
Manufacturing production and sales, published by Statistics South Africa, Pretoria.

Supplier of information:
Statistics South Africa, Pretoria.

Basic source of data:
Quarterly employment statistics; periodic survey.

Major deviations from ISIC (Revision 3):
None reported.

Reference period:
Calendar year.

Scope:
All establishments.

Method of data collection:
Questionnaires.

Type of enumeration:
Sample survey.

Adjusted for non-response:
Yes.

South Africa

ISIC	Industry	Number of establishments (number)					Number of employees (thousands)					Wages and salaries paid to employees (millions of South African Rand)				
		Note	2007	2008	2009	2010	Note	2007	2008	2009	2010	Note	2007	2008	2009	2010
151	Processed meat,fish,fruit,vegetables,fats		1594	1691	1590	1443		57.7	57.0	57.2	...		2851	3216	3580	...
1511	Processing/preserving of meat		993	1056	996	900		...	...	...	...		...	...	...	...
1512	Processing/preserving of fish		192	203	185	158		...	...	...	...		...	...	...	...
1513	Processing/preserving of fruit & vegetables		307	324	303	284		...	...	...	...		...	...	...	...
1514	Vegetable and animal oils and fats		102	108	106	101		...	...	...	...		...	...	...	...
1520	Dairy products		277	306	268	273		...	...	...	...		...	...	...	...
153	Grain mill products; starches; animal feeds		605	663	643	616		17.7	17.7	17.9	...		1615	1802	1974	...
1531	Grain mill products		378	412	396	374		9.4	9.5	9.5	...		510	585	732	...
1532	Starches and starch products		3	3	4	4		...	...	...	...		...	...	...	...
1533	Prepared animal feeds		224	248	243	238		...	...	...	...		...	...	...	...
154	Other food products		3447	3669	3391	2987		...	...	...	...		...	...	...	...
1541	Bakery products		1431	1494	1374	1234		80.8	81.3	77.8	...		7367	8224	9333	...
1542	Sugar		40	41	40	38		...	...	...	...		...	...	...	...
1543	Cocoa, chocolate and sugar confectionery		211	217	195	171		...	...	...	...		...	...	...	...
1544	Macaroni, noodles & similar products		5	5	4	5		...	...	...	...		...	...	...	...
1549	Other food products n.e.c.		1760	1912	1778	1539		...	...	...	...		...	...	...	...
155	Beverages		1951	2050	1988	1927		...	...	...	...		...	...	...	...
1551	Distilling, rectifying & blending of spirits	b/	597	654	620	598		40.6	40.5	39.0	...		4717	5235	5525a/	...
1552	Wines	b/	...	...	...	...		...	...	...	...		...	...	...	...
1553	Malt liquors and malt		1028	1039	1026	1001		...	...	...	...		...	...	...	...
1554	Soft drinks; mineral waters		326	357	342	328		...	...	...	...		...	...	...	...
1600	Tobacco products		75	90	88	88		1.1	0.8	0.8	...		77	78	...a/	...
171	Spinning, weaving and finishing of textiles		150	151	155	161		...	...	...	...		...	...	...	...
1711	Textile fibre preparation; textile weaving		134	135	138	145		17.3	15.6	13.7	...		1049	1018	933	...
1712	Finishing of textiles		16	16	17	16		...	...	...	...		...	...	...	...
172	Other textiles		1908	1981	1846	1680		...	...	...	...		...	...	...	...
1721	Made-up textile articles, except apparel		480	507	466	439		31.3	31.5	27.2	...		1870	2018	1804	...
1722	Carpets and rugs		210	219	202	182		...	...	...	...		...	...	...	...
1723	Cordage, rope, twine and netting		72	72	70	64		...	...	...	...		...	...	...	...
1729	Other textiles n.e.c.		1146	1183	1108	995		...	...	...	...		...	...	...	...
1730	Knitted and crocheted fabrics and articles		304	309	306	287		7.0	7.0	5.5	...		324	313	296	...
1810	Wearing apparel, except fur apparel		2859	3002	2746	2407		63.7c/	55.9c/	49.7c/	...		2753c/	2640c/	2555c/	...
1820	Dressing & dyeing of fur; processing of fur		48	51	50	48		...c/	...c/	...c/	...		...c/	...c/	...c/	...
191	Tanning, dressing and processing of leather		548	597	555	497		...	...	...	...		...	...	...	...
1911	Tanning and dressing of leather		162	187	170	153		7.6	7.3	7.7	...		392	439	446	...
1912	Luggage, handbags, etc.; saddlery & harness		386	410	385	344		...	...	...	...		...	...	...	...
1920	Footwear		571	609	576	526		...	...	...	...		...	...	...	...
2010	Sawmilling and planing of wood		570	609	576	522		10.4	10.1	9.9	...		528	558	618	...
202	Products of wood, cork, straw, etc.		1432	1508	2439	1369		24.7	26.8	25.6	...		1217	1366	1254	...
2021	Veneer sheets, plywood, particle board, etc.		30	29	29	31		31.5	29.6	24.4	...		1671	1802	1639	...
2022	Builders' carpentry and joinery		266	266	266	282		...	...	...	...		...	...	...	...
2023	Wooden containers		102	115	115	116		...	...	...	...		...	...	...	...
2029	Other wood products; articles of cork/straw		1034	1098	2029	940		...	...	...	...		...	...	...	...
210	Paper and paper products		1318	1441	1365	1214		...	...	...	...		...	...	...	...
2101	Pulp, paper and paperboard		153	177	171	155		33.6	36.5	41.6	...		4491	5948	5946	...
2102	Corrugated paper and paperboard		539	582	560	488		...	...	...	...		...	...	...	...
2109	Other articles of paper and paperboard		626	682	634	571		...	...	...	...		...	...	...	...
221	Publishing		2468	2550	2473	2397		...	...	...	...		...	...	...	...
2211	Publishing of books and other publications		642	685	648	660		25.8	25.8	26.5	...		4091	4231	4291	...
2212	Publishing of newspapers, journals, etc.		895	945	909	825		...	...	...	...		...	...	...	...
2213	Publishing of recorded media		5	5	5	8		...	...	...	...		...	...	...	...
2219	Other publishing		926	915	911	904		...	...	...	...		...	...	...	...

Code	Description	(1)	(2)	(3)	(4)	(5)	(6)	(7)	(8)	(9)	(10)
222	Printing and related service activities	1696	1767	1648	1675	27.2	26.4	27.1	2644	2816	3241d/
2221	Printing	1571	1636	1522	1552	...	...	...	105	105	...d/
2222	Service activities related to printing	125	131	126	123	0.5	0.6	0.6	...	...	...
2230	Reproduction of recorded media	29	35	36	31	.../e/	.../e/	.../e/	.../e/	.../e/	.../e/
2310	Coke oven products	18	19	20	22	.../e/	.../e/	.../e/	.../e/	.../e/	.../e/
2320	Refined petroleum products	967	1116	1045	950	16.5e/	21.3e/	20.3e/	3406e/	4333e/	5613e/
2330	Processing of nuclear fuel	2	1	1	2	.../e/	.../e/	.../e/	.../e/	.../e/	.../e/
241	Basic chemicals	967	1040	997	960	21.1	20.7	19.9	3145	3515	3680
2411	Basic chemicals, except fertilizers	487	525	496	480	...	...	...	...	...	...
2412	Fertilizers and nitrogen compounds	210	233	220	222	...	...	...	...	...	...
2413	Plastics in primary forms; synthetic rubber	270	282	281	258	49.8	50.3	45.7	5568	6274	6912
242	Other chemicals	2194	2309	2259	2139	...	...	...	...	...	...
2421	Pesticides and other agro-chemical products	262	277	263	250	...	...	...	...	...	...
2422	Paints, varnishes, printing ink and mastics	578	601	576	533	...	...	...	...	...	...
2423	Pharmaceuticals, medicinal chemicals, etc.	288	309	309	307	...	...	...	...	...	...
2424	Soap, cleaning & cosmetic preparations	754	804	792	726	...	...	...	...	...	...
2429	Other chemical products n.e.c.	312	318	319	323	...	...	...	...	...	...
2430	Man-made fibres	1	1	1	1	14.6	14.7	13.8	1955	2108	2076
251	Rubber products	500	527	512	485	...	...	...	...	...	...
2511	Rubber tyres and tubes	189	200	193	187	38.1	37.0	32.5	3155	3237	3514
2519	Other rubber products	311	327	319	298	10.8	10.3	10.1	1160	1211	1318
2520	Plastic products	1733	1835	1790	1734	58.1	57.9	46.0	4179	4550	4151
2610	Glass and glass products	843	827	820	708	...	...	...	...	...	...
269	Non-metallic mineral products n.e.c.	1577	1682	1654	1549	...	...	...	...	...	...
2691	Pottery, china and earthenware	65	63	62	61	...	...	...	...	...	...
2692	Refractory ceramic products	418	470	467	408	...	...	...	...	...	...
2693	Struct.non-refractory clay; ceramic products	140	147	144	140	...	...	...	...	...	...
2694	Cement, lime and plaster	367	394	373	331	...	...	...	...	...	...
2695	Articles of concrete, cement and plaster	317	333	341	341	...	...	...	...	...	...
2696	Cutting, shaping & finishing of stone	74	75	69	67	...	...	...	...	...	...
2699	Other non-metallic mineral products n.e.c.	196	200	198	201	...	...	...	...	...	...
2710	Basic iron and steel	1792	1946	1823	1649	52.0	52.0	54.4	7083	8240	8483
2720	Basic precious and non-ferrous metals	1877	2083	1922	1712	25.9	24.3	21.7	2910	2981	3237
273	Casting of metals	115	130	124	122	41.3	40.2	37.8	3570	3911	4144
2731	Casting of iron and steel	96	108	102	101	...	...	...	...	...	...
2732	Casting of non-ferrous metals	19	22	22	21	83.7	80.9	73.8	7686	8300	8019
281	Struct.metal products;tanks;steam generators	1271	1346	1302	1269	...	...	...	...	...	...
2811	Structural metal products	1075	1149	1117	1092	...	...	...	...	...	...
2812	Tanks, reservoirs and containers of metal	91	90	86	83	...	...	...	...	...	...
2813	Steam generators	105	107	99	94	...	...	...	...	...	...
289	Other metal products; metal working services	7079	7341	6902	6383	...	...	...	...	...	...
2891	Metal forging/pressing/stamping/roll-forming	32	32	33	42	...	...	...	...	...	...
2892	Treatment & coating of metals	4032	4179	3907	3636	...	...	...	...	...	...
2893	Cutlery, hand tools and general hardware	355	370	356	342	...	...	...	...	...	...
2899	Other fabricated metal products n.e.c.	2660	2760	2606	2363	38.6	40.5	39.7	4313	4975	5844
291	General purpose machinery	3631	3808	3639	3365	...	...	...	...	...	...
2911	Engines & turbines (not for transport equipment)	108	125	126	117	...	...	...	...	...	...
2912	Pumps, compressors, taps and valves	759	797	764	703	...	...	...	...	...	...
2913	Bearings, gears, gearing & driving elements	70	69	69	65	...	...	...	...	...	...
2914	Ovens, furnaces and furnace burners	31	31	29	32	...	...	...	...	...	...
2915	Lifting and handling equipment	552	608	570	536	...	...	...	...	...	...
2919	Other general purpose machinery	2111	2178	2081	1912	61.4	61.2	57.5	7307	7902	8184
292	Special purpose machinery	3924	4175	3903	3664	...	...	...	...	...	...
2921	Agricultural and forestry machinery	824	864	794	736	...	...	...	...	...	...
2922	Machine tools	10	11	11	10	...	...	...	...	...	...
2923	Machinery for metallurgy	894	975	912	864	...	...	...	...	...	...
2924	Machinery for mining & construction	79	95	73	80	...	...	...	...	...	...
2925	Food/beverage/tobacco processing machinery	87	91	91	87	...	...	...	...	...	...
2926	Machinery for textile, apparel and leather	14	12	13	14	...	...	...	...	...	...
2927	Weapons and ammunition					...	...	...	...	...	...
2929	Other special purpose machinery	2016	2139	2009	1873	...	...	...	...	...	...

continued

South Africa

ISIC	Industry	Number of establishments (number)					Number of employees (thousands)					Wages and salaries paid to employees (millions of South African Rand)				
		Note	2007	2008	2009	2010	Note	2007	2008	2009	2010	Note	2007	2008	2009	2010
2930	Domestic appliances n.e.c.		524	563	524	493		4.3	4.4	4.3	...		403	421	483	...
3000	Office, accounting and computing machinery		2058	2242	2013	1755		10.0	11.2	8.8	...		1359	1503	1362	...
3110	Electric motors, generators and transformers		138	149	154	169		15.7f/	16.0f/	15.8f/	...		1558f/	1745f/	1905f/	...
3120	Electricity distribution & control apparatus		159	166	172	175		..f/	..f/	..f/	...		..f/	..f/	..f/	...
3130	Insulated wire and cable		141	147	142	146		5.8	6.4	5.3	...		846	910	786	...
3140	Accumulators, primary cells and batteries		116	124	112	108		4.5g/	4.8g/	5.0g/	...		490g/	607g/	569g/	...
3150	Lighting equipment and electric lamps		104	117	120	120		...g/	...g/	...g/	...		...g/	...g/	...g/	...
3190	Other electrical equipment n.e.c.		1129	1128	1107	1105		16.7	16.2	14.0	...		1683	1737	1438	...
3210	Electronic valves, tubes, etc.		75	82	82	90		8.2h/	7.4h/	7.5h/	...		782h/	823h/	967h/	...
3220	TV/radio transmitters; line comm. apparatus		138	149	144	141		..h/	..h/	..h/	...		..h/	..h/	..h/	...
3230	TV and radio receivers and associated goods		200	213	209	199		..h/	..h/	..h/	...		..h/	..h/	..h/	...
331	Medical, measuring, testing appliances, etc.		738	770	749	733		9.1i/	9.2i/	9.4i/	...		1281i/	1405i/	1646i/	...
3311	Medical, surgical and orthopaedic equipment		532	569	554	539		...	...	...	...		...	...	...	...
3312	Measuring/testing/navigating appliances,etc.		178	177	173	173		...	...	...	...		...	...	...	...
3313	Industrial process control equipment		28	24	22	21		...	...	...	...		...	...	...	...
3320	Optical instruments & photographic equipment		210	230	218	202		...i/	...i/	...i/	...		...i/	...i/	...i/	...
3330	Watches and clocks		32	33	33	32		...i/	...i/	...i/	...		...i/	...i/	...i/	...
3410	Motor vehicles		2071	2234	2071	1853		66.2j/	68.9j/	61.0j/	...		7628j/	8106j/	7226j/	...
3420	Automobile bodies, trailers & semi-trailers		457	497	494	463		...j/	...j/	...j/	...		...j/	...j/	...j/	...
3430	Parts/accessories for automobiles		4561	4731	4495	4185		65.0	64.6	59.0	...		6264	7011	6162	...
351	Building and repairing of ships and boats		127	127	129	122		13.1k/	13.2k/	12.4k/	...		1453k/	1822k/	2043k/	...
3511	Building and repairing of ships		80	78	79	75		...	...	...	...		...	...	...	...
3512	Building/repairing of pleasure/sport. boats		47	49	50	47		...	...	...	...		...	...	...	...
3520	Railway/tramway locomotives & rolling stock		81	97	99	91		...k/	...k/	...k/	...		...k/	...k/	...k/	...
3530	Aircraft and spacecraft		232	260	266	248		...k/	...k/	...k/	...		...k/	...k/	...k/	...
359	Transport equipment n.e.c.		386	388	378	357		...k/	...k/	...k/	...		...k/	...k/	...k/	...
3591	Motorcycles		187	191	182	164		...	...	...	...		...	...	...	...
3592	Bicycles and invalid carriages		17	17	17	16		...	...	...	...		...	...	...	...
3599	Other transport equipment n.e.c.		182	180	179	177		...	...	...	...		...	...	...	...
3610	Furniture		3255	3371	3159	2787		42.4	36.1	31.7	...		3060	2395	1967	...
369	Manufacturing n.e.c.		7734	8064	7624	7074		50.7	44.9	38.5	...		3428	3469	3283	...
3691	Jewellery and related articles		875	914	848	810		...	...	...	...		...	...	...	...
3692	Musical instruments		83	95	88	74		...	...	...	...		...	...	...	...
3693	Sports goods		190	201	202	184		...	...	...	...		...	...	...	...
3694	Games and toys		163	180	166	151		...	...	...	...		...	...	...	...
3699	Other manufacturing n.e.c.		6423	6674	6320	5855		...	...	...	...		...	...	...	...
3710	Recycling of metal waste and scrap		123	135	137	148		12.3	12.1	12.6	...		821	981	1730	...
3720	Recycling of non-metal waste and scrap		201	221	216	262		...	...	...	...		...	...	...	...
D	Total manufacturing	m/	75331	79503	76300	69920		1323.5	1306.6	1219.8	...		124762	136864	140640	...

a/ 155 includes 1600.
b/ 1551 includes 1552.
c/ 1810 includes 1820.
d/ 222 includes 2230.
e/ 2320 includes 2310 and 2330.
f/ 3110 includes 3120.
g/ 3140 includes 3150.
h/ 3210 includes 3220 and 3230.
i/ 331 includes 3320 and 3330.
j/ 3410 includes 3420.
k/ 351 includes 3520, 3530 and 359.
m/ Sum of available data.

South Africa

ISIC	Industry	Output (billions of South African Rand)					Value added (billions of South African Rand)					Gross fixed capital formation (billions of South African Rand)		
		Note	2007	2008	2009	2010	Note	2007	2008	2009	2010	Note	2009	2010
151	Processed meat,fish,fruit,vegetables,fats	a/	172.2	194.8	196.5	208.1	a/	34.5	40.9	44.8	48.6		…	…
1511	Processing/preserving of meat												…	…
1512	Processing/preserving of fish												…	…
1513	Processing/preserving of fruit & vegetables												…	…
1514	Vegetable and animal oils and fats												…	…
1520	Dairy products	a/					a/						…	…
153	Grain mill products; starches; animal feeds	a/					a/						…	…
1531	Grain mill products												…	…
1532	Starches and starch products												…	…
1533	Prepared animal feeds	a/					a/						…	…
154	Other food products												…	…
1541	Bakery products												…	…
1542	Sugar												…	…
1543	Cocoa, chocolate and sugar confectionery												…	…
1544	Macaroni, noodles & similar products												…	…
1549	Other food products n.e.c.	b/	57.8	69.4	66.4	70.8	b/	21.8	23.8	20.5	24.1		…	…
155	Beverages												…	…
1551	Distilling, rectifying & blending of spirits												…	…
1552	Wines												…	…
1553	Malt liquors and malt												…	…
1554	Soft drinks; mineral waters	b/					b/						…	…
1600	Tobacco products	c/	18.4	21.9	21.9	21.2	c/	3.8	3.6	3.6	3.4		…	…
171	Spinning, weaving and finishing of textiles												…	…
1711	Textile fibre preparation; textile weaving												…	…
1712	Finishing of textiles	c/					c/						…	…
172	Other textiles	c/					c/						…	…
1721	Made-up textile articles, except apparel												…	…
1722	Carpets and rugs												…	…
1723	Cordage, rope, twine and netting												…	…
1729	Other textiles n.e.c.	c/					c/						…	…
1730	Knitted and crocheted fabrics and articles												…	…
1810	Wearing apparel, except fur apparel	d/	14.9	18.1	17.9	18.4	d/	4.8	4.6	4.6	0.5		…	…
1820	Dressing & dyeing of fur; processing of fur	d/	4.3	5.5	5.2	5.3	d/	0.8	0.5	0.4	0.4		…	…
191	Tanning, dressing and processing of leather												…	…
1911	Tanning and dressing of leather												…	…
1912	Luggage, handbags, etc.; saddlery & harness												…	…
1920	Footwear	e/	5.7	7.0	7.0	6.9	e/	1.5	1.5	1.6	1.5		…	…
2010	Sawmilling and planing of wood	e/	25.6	31.3	29.7	29.0	e/	8.5	9.4	8.3	7.7		…	…
202	Products of wood, cork, straw, etc.												…	…
2021	Veneer sheets, plywood, particle board, etc.												…	…
2022	Builders' carpentry and joinery												…	…
2023	Wooden containers												…	…
2029	Other wood products; articles of cork/straw		48.0	60.1	58.1	57.6		10.7	11.4	10.7	9.9		…	…
210	Paper and paper products												…	…
2101	Pulp, paper and paperboard												…	…
2102	Corrugated paper and paperboard												…	…
2109	Other articles of paper and paperboard	f/	28.0	32.9	33.1	34.5	f/	8.8	9.8	10.6	11.3		…	…
221	Publishing												…	…
2211	Publishing of books and other publications												…	…
2212	Publishing of newspapers, journals, etc.												…	…
2213	Publishing of recorded media												…	…
2219	Other publishing												…	…

continued

South Africa

ISIC	Industry	Output Note	Output 2007	Output 2008	Output 2009	Output 2010	Value added Note	Value added 2007	Value added 2008	Value added 2009	Value added 2010	GFCF Note	GFCF 2009	GFCF 2010
			(billions of South African Rand)					(billions of South African Rand)					(billions of South African Rand)	
222	Printing and related service activities	f/					f/							
2221	Printing													
2222	Service activities related to printing													
2230	Reproduction of recorded media	f/					f/							
2310	Coke oven products													
2320	Refined petroleum products	g/	85.9	113.7	109.7	111.2	g/	20.5	25.9	24.3	24.5			
2330	Processing of nuclear fuel	g/	77.5	92.2	88.5	87.4	g/	15.7	20.2	18.5	18.2			
241	Basic chemicals	h/					h/							
2411	Basic chemicals, except fertilizers													
2412	Fertilizers and nitrogen compounds													
2413	Plastics in primary forms; synthetic rubber													
242	Other chemicals	h/	88.0	97.6	96.2	98.6	h/	20.0	21.8	22.2	22.9			
2421	Pesticides and other agro-chemical products													
2422	Paints, varnishes, printing ink and mastics													
2423	Pharmaceuticals, medicinal chemicals, etc.													
2424	Soap, cleaning & cosmetic preparations													
2429	Other chemical products n.e.c.													
2430	Man-made fibres													
251	Rubber products		11.5	14.7	14.8	14.3		3.3	3.6	4.0	3.7			
2511	Rubber tyres and tubes													
2519	Other rubber products													
2520	Plastic products		28.9	30.0	29.0	27.4		9.6	10.3	9.9	8.6			
2610	Glass and glass products		7.1	7.8	7.6	8.1		2.3	2.3	2.3	2.5			
269	Non-metallic mineral products n.e.c.		31.6	35.8	35.0	37.9		9.4	11.0	10.6	12.8			
2691	Pottery, china and earthenware													
2692	Refractory ceramic products													
2693	Struct.non-refractory clay; ceramic products													
2694	Cement, lime and plaster													
2695	Articles of concrete, cement and plaster													
2696	Cutting, shaping & finishing of stone													
2699	Other non-metallic mineral products n.e.c.													
2710	Basic iron and steel	i/	105.9	117.3	110.9	101.1	i/	23.6	22.6	19.1	14.8			
2720	Basic precious and non-ferrous metals		36.3	40.9	36.4	33.5	i/	11.8	14.3	11.8	9.5			
273	Casting of metals													
2731	Casting of iron and steel													
2732	Casting of non-ferrous metals	i/												
281	Struct.metal products;tanks;steam generators	j/	56.9	72.9	70.2	67.5	j/	16.5	21.0	19.7	17.7			
2811	Structural metal products													
2812	Tanks, reservoirs and containers of metal													
2813	Steam generators													
289	Other metal products; metal working services	j/					j/							
2891	Metal forging/pressing/stamping/roll-forming													
2892	Treatment & coating of metals													
2893	Cutlery, hand tools and general hardware													
2899	Other fabricated metal products n.e.c.													
291	General purpose machinery	k/	51.3	64.3	67.1	68.4	k/	14.0	17.0	20.6	20.9			
2911	Engines & turbines (not for transport equipment)													
2912	Pumps, compressors, taps and valves													
2913	Bearings, gears, gearing & driving elements													
2914	Ovens, furnaces and furnace burners													
2915	Lifting and handling equipment													
2919	Other general purpose machinery													

Code	Description	Note	(1)	(2)	(3)	(4)	Note	(5)	(6)	(7)	(8)
292	Special purpose machinery	k/	...	...	...	...	k/	...	...	...	...
2921	Agricultural and forestry machinery		...	...	...	...		...	...	...	...
2922	Machine tools		...	...	...	...		...	...	...	...
2923	Machinery for metallurgy		...	...	...	...		...	...	...	...
2924	Machinery for mining & construction		...	...	...	...		...	...	...	...
2925	Food/beverage/tobacco processing machinery		...	...	...	...		...	...	...	...
2926	Machinery for textile, apparel and leather		...	...	...	...		...	...	...	...
2927	Weapons and ammunition		...	...	...	...		...	...	...	...
2929	Other special purpose machinery		...	...	...	...		...	...	...	...
2930	Domestic appliances n.e.c.	k/	...	...	...	...	k/	...	...	...	...
3000	Office, accounting and computing machinery		33.6	40.6	39.4	40.0		8.1	8.2	7.9	7.6
3110	Electric motors, generators and transformers	m/	8.0	9.6	9.6	9.5	m/	2.4	2.4	2.5	2.4
3120	Electricity distribution & control apparatus	m/	...	...	...	...	m/	...	...	...	...
3130	Insulated wire and cable	m/	...	...	...	...	m/	...	...	...	...
3140	Accumulators, primary cells and batteries	m/	...	...	...	...	m/	...	...	...	...
3150	Lighting equipment and electric lamps	m/	...	...	...	...	m/	...	...	...	...
3190	Other electrical equipment n.e.c.	m/	...	...	...	...	m/	...	...	...	...
3210	Electronic valves, tubes, etc.	n/	5.5	6.6	6.5	6.6	n/	1.7	1.7	1.7	1.7
3220	TV/radio transmitters; line comm. apparatus	n/	...	...	...	...	n/	...	...	...	...
3230	TV and radio receivers and associated goods	n/	...	...	...	...	n/	...	...	...	...
331	Medical, measuring, testing appliances, etc.	p/	...	...	...	...	p/	...	...	...	...
3311	Medical, surgical and orthopaedic equipment		...	...	...	...		...	...	...	...
3312	Measuring/testing/navigating appliances,etc.		...	...	...	...		...	...	...	...
3313	Industrial process control equipment		...	...	...	...		...	...	...	...
3320	Optical instruments & photographic equipment	p/	...	...	...	...	p/	...	...	...	...
3330	Watches and clocks	p/	...	...	...	...	p/	...	...	...	...
3410	Motor vehicles	q/	160.5	156.8	152.4	163.0	q/	21.1	21.1	20.5	20.9
3420	Automobile bodies, trailers & semi-trailers	q/	...	...	...	...	q/	...	...	...	...
3430	Parts/accessories for automobiles	q/	...	...	...	...	q/	...	...	...	...
351	Building and repairing of ships and boats	r/	12.1	14.3	13.7	13.5	r/	3.7	4.0	3.7	3.6
3511	Building and repairing of ships		...	...	...	...		...	...	...	...
3512	Building/repairing of pleasure/sport. boats		...	...	...	...		...	...	...	...
3520	Railway/tramway locomotives & rolling stock	r/	...	...	...	...	r/	...	...	...	...
3530	Aircraft and spacecraft	r/	...	...	...	...	r/	...	...	...	...
359	Transport equipment n.e.c.		...	...	...	...		...	...	...	...
3591	Motorcycles		...	...	...	...		...	...	...	...
3592	Bicycles and invalid carriages		...	...	...	...		...	...	...	...
3599	Other transport equipment n.e.c.		...	...	...	...		...	...	...	...
3610	Furniture	s/	15.6	17.8	17.4	17.4	s/	3.6	3.1	3.4	2.9
369	Manufacturing n.e.c.		52.2	60.0	58.1	58.0		21.8	24.5	23.7	25.0
3691	Jewellery and related articles		...	...	...	...		...	...	...	...
3692	Musical instruments		...	...	...	...		...	...	...	...
3693	Sports goods		...	...	...	...		...	...	...	...
3694	Games and toys		...	...	...	...		...	...	...	...
3699	Other manufacturing n.e.c.		...	...	...	...		...	...	...	...
3710	Recycling of metal waste and scrap	s/	...	...	...	...	s/	...	...	...	...
3720	Recycling of non-metal waste and scrap	s/	...	...	...	...	s/	...	...	...	...
D	Total manufacturing	t/	1243.5	1434.1	1398.0	1415.3	t/	304.4	340.6	331.7	332.5

a/ 151 includes 1520, 153 and 154.
b/ 155 includes 1600.
c/ 171 includes 172 and 1730.
d/ 1810 includes 1820.
e/ 2010 includes 202.
f/ 221 includes 222 and 2230.
g/ 2310 includes 2320.
h/ 2330 includes 241.
i/ 2710 includes 273.
j/ 281 includes 289.

k/ 291 includes 292 and 2930.
m/ 3110 includes 3120, 3130, 3140, 3150 and 3190.
n/ 3210 includes 3220 and 3230.
p/ 331 includes 3320 and 3330.
q/ 3410 includes 3420 and 3430.
r/ 351 includes 3520 and 3530.
s/ 369 includes 3710 and 3720.
t/ Total manufacturing includes estimates of informal sectors.

South Africa

Index numbers of industrial production

ISIC Revision 3

(2005=100)

ISIC	Industry	Note	1999	2000	2001	2002	2003	2004	2005	2006	2007	2008	2009	2010
15	Food and beverages		88	86	89	86	88	94	100	101	105	110	112	117
16	Tobacco products		...	...	...	...	...	...	...	...	...	...	...	...
17	Textiles		103	105	108	117	101	104	100	101	100	95	76	70
18	Wearing apparel, fur		107	101	96	103	100	105	100	103	109	111	98	89
19	Leather, leather products and footwear		...	...	...	...	...	...	...	...	...	...	...	...
20	Wood products (excl. furniture)		80	84	84	92	92	94	100	105	106	100	82	86
21	Paper and paper products		90	96	94	99	96	98	100	108	109	122	104	113
22	Printing and publishing		95	91	87	85	89	93	100	106	107	101	86	85
23	Coke,refined petroleum products,nuclear fuel		99	97	97	99	100	102	100	94	97	96	95	93
24	Chemicals and chemical products		...	...	...	...	...	...	...	...	...	...	...	...
25	Rubber and plastics products		...	...	...	...	...	...	...	...	...	...	...	...
26	Non-metallic mineral products		...	...	...	...	...	...	...	...	...	...	...	...
27	Basic metals		...	...	...	...	...	...	...	...	...	...	...	...
28	Fabricated metal products		84	88	94	106	101	103	100	109	124	125	103	103
29	Machinery and equipment n.e.c.	a/	80	84	90	100	94	97	100	103	108	103	83	84
30	Office, accounting and computing machinery	a/	...	...	...	...	...	...	...	...	...	...	...	...
31	Electrical machinery and apparatus		104	109	110	110	107	102	100	106	111	125	121	128
32	Radio,television and communication equipment		111	108	82	83	83	89	100	104	108	118	102	93
33	Medical, precision and optical instruments		72	75	82	90	98	105	100	92	100	99	96	96
34	Motor vehicles, trailers, semi-trailers		64	75	82	82	82	89	100	113	112	105	75	93
35	Other transport equipment		104	109	113	129	108	103	100	105	113	117	125	115
36	Furniture; manufacturing n.e.c.		...	...	...	...	...	...	...	...	...	...	...	...
37	Recycling		...	...	...	...	...	...	...	...	...	...	...	...
D	Total manufacturing		86	90	92	95	93	97	100	105	110	110	96	101

a/ 29 includes 30.

Spain

Supplier of information:
Instituto Nacional de Estadística (I.N.E.), Ministerio de Economía y Hacienda, Madrid.
Industrial statistics for the OECD countries are compiled by the OECD secretariat, which supplies them to UNIDO.

Basic source of data:
Annual industrial survey; business register.

Major deviations from ISIC (Revision 4):
Data have been converted from the national NACE equivalent system to ISIC (Revision 4) by the OECD.

Reference period:
Calendar year.

Scope:
All units employing one or more persons.

Method of data collection:
Not reported.

Type of enumeration:
Not reported.

Adjusted for non-response:
Not reported.

Concepts and definitions of variables:
No deviations from the standard UN concepts and definitions are reported.

Related national publications:
None reported.

Spain

		Number of enterprises (number)					Number of employees (thousands)					Wages and salaries paid to employees (millions of Euros)				
ISIC	Industry (ISIC Revision 4)	Note	2006	2007	2008	2009	Note	2006	2007	2008	2009	Note	2006	2007	2008	2009
1010	Processing/preserving of meat		...	...	4152	4099		...	...	84.4	82.0		...	...	1777	1737
1020	Processing/preserving of fish, etc.		...	...	689	709		...	...	19.6	19.2		...	...	351	336
1030	Processing/preserving of fruit,vegetables		...	...	1264	1262		...	...	33.5	31.2		...	...	663	648
1040	Vegetable and animal oils and fats		...	...	1448	1512		...	...	13.0	12.6		...	...	294	333
1050	Dairy products		...	...	1463	1486		...	...	26.0	25.8		...	...	750	747
106	Grain mill products,starches and starch products		...	...	558	545		...	...	6.3	6.3		...	...	170	171
1061	Grain mill products		...	...	533	523		...	...	5.2	5.6		...	...	131	144
1062	Starches and starch products		...	...	25	22		...	...	1.0	0.7		...	...	39	27
107	Other food products		...	...	13687	12662		...	...	124.8	119.5		...	...	2603	2580
1071	Bakery products		...	...	10941	10010		...	...	76.9	73.0		...	...	1369	1338
1072	Sugar		...	...	41	45		...	...	1.7	1.6		...	...	55	48
1073	Cocoa, chocolate and sugar confectionery		...	...	752	709		...	...	14.6	17.5		...	...	340	515
1074	Macaroni, noodles, couscous, etc.		...	...	118	111		...	...	1.4	1.3		...	...	32	31
1075	Prepared meals and dishes		...	...	145	127		...	...	4.3	4.1		...	...	89	90
1079	Other food products n.e.c.		...	...	1692	1661		...	...	26.0	22.0		...	...	718	559
1080	Prepared animal feeds		...	...	837	840		...	...	13.9	13.4		...	...	368	361
1101	Distilling, rectifying and blending of spirits		...	...	4623a/	4335a/		...	...	49.5a/	46.2a/		...	...	1614a/	1541a/
1102	Wines		...	...	...a/	...a/		...	...	...a/	...a/		...	...	...a/	...a/
1103	Malt liquors and malt		...	...	...a/	...a/		...	...	...a/	...a/		...	...	...a/	...a/
1104	Soft drinks,mineral waters,other bottled waters		...	...	...a/	...a/		...	...	...a/	...a/		...	...	...a/	...a/
1200	Tobacco products		...	...	49	43		...	...	3.5	3.4		...	...	142	146
131	Spinning, weaving and finishing of textiles		...	...	2137	1854		...	...	23.5	18.1		...	...	536	419
1311	Preparation and spinning of textile fibres		...	...	702	577		...	...	7.7	5.6		...	...	171	133
1312	Weaving of textiles		...	...	490	421		...	...	7.6	6.3		...	...	178	147
1313	Finishing of textiles		...	...	945	856		...	...	8.2	6.2		...	...	188	138
139	Other textiles		...	...	5209	4701		...	...	31.3	25.9		...	...	632	548
1391	Knitted and crocheted fabrics		...	...	482	364		...	...	3.0	2.3		...	...	66	54
1392	Made-up textile articles, except apparel		...	...	3490	3138		...	...	18.1	14.0		...	...	331	262
1393	Carpets and rugs		...	...	136	115		...	...	1.2	1.2		...	...	30	26
1394	Cordage, rope, twine and netting		...	...	343	362		...	...	1.4	1.2		...	...	24	23
1399	Other textiles n.e.c.		...	...	758	722		...	...	7.6	7.2		...	...	182	184
1410	Wearing apparel, except fur apparel		...	...	10614	9394		...	...	66.8	54.4		...	...	1169	1057
1420	Articles of fur		...	...	294	290		...	...	0.8	0.7		...	...	13	11
1430	Knitted and crocheted apparel		...	...	842	799		...	...	8.4	7.1		...	...	154	134
151	Leather;luggage,handbags,saddlery,harness;fur		...	...	1472	1246		...	...	10.4	8.6		...	...	219	186
1511	Tanning/dressing of leather; dressing of fur		...	...	353	301		...	...	4.5	3.8		...	...	106	91
1512	Luggage,handbags,etc.;saddlery/harness		...	...	1118	945		...	...	5.9	4.8		...	...	113	95
1520	Footwear		...	...	3977	3347		...	...	29.3	22.2		...	...	451	344
1610	Sawmilling and planing of wood		...	...	1318	1229		...	...	9.1	7.6		...	...	172	137
162	Wood products, cork, straw, plaiting materials		...	...	13307	12472		...	...	70.8	57.4		...	...	1447	1194

1621	Veneer sheets and wood-based panels	:	481	411	:	12.4	9.8	:	299	236
1622	Builders' carpentry and joinery	:	9423	9041	:	41.3	32.9	:	799	651
1623	Wooden containers	:	929	893	:	7.5	7.2	:	149	150
1629	Other wood products;articles of cork,straw	:	2473	2127	:	9.7	7.5	:	200	157
1701	Pulp, paper and paperboard	:	273	233	:	13.4	11.6	:	474	437
1702	Corrugated paper and paperboard	:	747	808	:	22.8	21.5	:	634	581
1709	Other articles of paper and paperboard	:	1042	902	:	16.7	15.2	:	463	427
181	Printing and service activities related to printing	:	14866	14427	:	78.3	69.5	:	1943	1709
1811	Printing	:	11478	11370	:	61.0	55.3	:	1544	1371
1812	Service activities related to printing	:	3388	3058	:	17.2	14.2	:	399	338
1820	Reproduction of recorded media	:	1348	1242	:	2.4	2.2	:	56	55
1910	Coke oven products	:	13b/	14b/	:	8.8b/	8.9b/	:	456b/	454b/
1920	Refined petroleum products	:	...b/	...b/	:	...b/	...b/	:	...b/	...b/
201	Basic chemicals,fertilizers, etc.	:	1053	1018	:	32.5	28.9	:	1332	1275
2011	Basic chemicals	:	388	368	:	15.3	13.7	:	670	647
2012	Fertilizers and nitrogen compounds	:	260	274	:	3.7	3.8	:	117	113
2013	Plastics and synthetic rubber in primary forms	:	405	376	:	13.5	11.5	:	545	516
202	Other chemical products	:	2591	2595	:	57.0	52.8	:	1956	1820
2021	Pesticides and other agrochemical products	:	95	93	:	2.1	2.1	:	72	76
2022	Paints,varnishes;printing ink and mastics	:	549	534	:	16.6	14.7	:	544	500
2023	Soap,cleaning and cosmetic preparations	:	1125	1172	:	24.3	23.1	:	836	787
2029	Other chemical products n.e.c.	:	821	797	:	14.0	13.0	:	504	457
2030	Man-made fibres	:	49	42	:	3.4	2.8	:	115	99
2100	Pharmaceuticals,medicinal chemicals, etc.	:	368	347	:	40.0	39.0	:	1779	1729
221	Rubber products	:	873	800	:	28.4	24.1	:	884	716
2211	Rubber tyres and tubes	:	157	153	:	14.8	12.2	:	546	426
2219	Other rubber products	:	716	648	:	13.6	11.9	:	338	290
2220	Plastics products	:	4416	4305	:	85.3	75.0	:	2213	1951
2310	Glass and glass products	:	1267	1252	:	25.2	21.9	:	674	623
239	Non-metallic mineral products n.e.c.	:	10184	9344	:	152.5	121.8	:	4311	3509
2391	Refractory products	:	103	107	:	2.7	2.5	:	84	77
2392	Clay building materials	:	981	848	:	34.2	26.4	:	972	724
2393	Other porcelain and ceramic products	:	1060	996	:	8.5	6.7	:	260	211
2394	Cement, lime and plaster	:	205	201	:	10.9	9.7	:	531	498
2395	Articles of concrete, cement and plaster	:	3041	2891	:	54.3	43.6	:	1454	1161
2396	Cutting, shaping and finishing of stone	:	4489	3985	:	34.4	26.6	:	772	623
2399	Other non-metallic mineral products n.e.c.	:	307	314	:	7.4	6.5	:	237	216
2410	Basic iron and steel	:	581	549	:	38.5	35.1	:	1445	1240
2420	Basic precious and other non-ferrous metals	:	...	...	:	...	...	:	...	...
243	Casting of metals	:	667	637	:	21.3	18.1	:	627	503
2431	Casting of iron and steel	:	205	210	:	13.9	11.7	:	415	324
2432	Casting of non-ferrous metals	:	463	426	:	7.4	6.5	:	212	180
251	Struct.metal products, tanks, reservoirs	:	24572	22201	:	170.0	132.7	:	3810	3095
2511	Structural metal products	:	23594	21115	:	153.1	115.8	:	3357	2625
2512	Tanks, reservoirs and containers of metal	:	919	1028	:	14.9	15.1	:	392	415

continued

Spain

ISIC	Industry	Number of enterprises (number)					Number of employees (thousands)					Wages and salaries paid to employees (millions of Euros)				
		Note	2006	2007	2008	2009	Note	2006	2007	2008	2009	Note	2006	2007	2008	2009
2513	Steam generators, excl. hot water boilers		...	...	59	57		...	...	2.0	1.8		...	...	61	55
2520	Weapons and ammunition		...	...	67	58		...	...	1.6	1.3		...	...	49	40
259	Other metal products;metal working services		...	...	18311	17002		...	...	168.9	140.1		...	...	4572	3744
2591	Forging,pressing,stamping,roll-forming of metal		...	...	1772	1775		...	...	28.3	25.2		...	...	803	708
2592	Treatment and coating of metals; machining		...	...	8574	7908		...	...	71.1	56.1		...	...	1894	1450
2593	Cutlery, hand tools and general hardware		...	...	3954	3641		...	...	27.0	21.8		...	...	732	603
2599	Other fabricated metal products n.e.c.		...	...	4011	3678		...	...	42.5	37.0		...	...	1143	983
2610	Electronic components and boards		...	...	576	545		...	...	8.6	7.6		...	...	225	206
2620	Computers and peripheral equipment		...	...	851	...		...	...	3.5	...		...	...	89	...
2630	Communication equipment		...	...	256	240		...	...	6.5	5.9		...	...	207	187
2640	Consumer electronics		...	...	...	98		...	...	...	3.3		...	...	...	112
265	Measuring,testing equipment; watches, etc.		...	...	749	716		...	...	11.3	10.3		...	...	356	328
2651	Measuring/testing/navigating equipment,etc.		...	...	626	606		...	...	10.8	10.0		...	...	343	319
2652	Watches and clocks		...	...	124	110		...	...	0.5	0.3		...	...	13	9
2660	Irradiation/electromedical equipment,etc.		...	...	240	211		...	...	3.4	2.7		...	...	97	77
2670	Optical instruments and photographic equipment		...	...	...	...		...	...	...	...		...	...	...	...
2680	Magnetic and optical media		...	...	...	...		...	...	...	...		...	...	...	...
2710	Electric motors,generators,transformers,etc.		...	...	1137	1065		...	...	35.0	32.0		...	...	1174	1100
2720	Batteries and accumulators		...	...	17	17		...	...	2.9	2.7		...	...	86	90
273	Wiring and wiring devices		...	...	274	226		...	...	6.8	6.3		...	...	230	220
2731	Fibre optic cables		...	...	8	7		...	...	0.5	0.3		...	...	17	13
2732	Other electronic and electric wires and cables		...	...	183	160		...	...	4.6	4.0		...	...	152	124
2733	Wiring devices		...	...	83	59		...	...	1.6	2.0		...	...	61	83
2740	Electric lighting equipment		...	...	743	680		...	...	12.0	10.0		...	...	322	261
2750	Domestic appliances		...	...	351	330		...	...	16.6	13.6		...	...	456	400
2790	Other electrical equipment		...	...	301	348		...	...	9.7	8.1		...	...	316	244
281	General-purpose machinery		...	...	2842	2833		...	...	74.4	65.4		...	...	2278	1998
2811	Engines/turbines,excl.aircraft,vehicle engines		...	...	44	65		...	...	2.7	2.8		...	...	82	85
2812	Fluid power equipment		...	...	59	87		...	...	1.8	2.0		...	...	57	58
2813	Other pumps, compressors, taps and valves		...	...	323	307		...	...	9.7	8.4		...	...	281	248
2814	Bearings, gears, gearing and driving elements		...	...	182	169		...	...	4.6	4.3		...	...	148	136
2815	Ovens, furnaces and furnace burners		...	...	62	55		...	...	1.1	0.9		...	...	36	29
2816	Lifting and handling equipment		...	...	530	562		...	...	28.1	23.4		...	...	914	736
2817	Office machinery, excl.computers,etc.		...	...	92	75		...	...	0.5	0.5		...	...	12	16
2818	Power-driven hand tools		...	...	40	40		...	...	0.5	0.4		...	...	12	11
2819	Other general-purpose machinery		...	...	1511	1472		...	...	25.4	22.7		...	...	736	681
282	Special-purpose machinery		...	...	3929	3676		...	...	53.5	46.6		...	...	1592	1371
2821	Agricultural and forestry machinery		...	...	917	828		...	...	9.0	7.8		...	...	224	198
2822	Metal-forming machinery and machine tools		...	...	508	530		...	...	8.8	8.4		...	...	286	262
2823	Machinery for metallurgy		...	...	233	189		...	...	3.0	2.5		...	...	87	76
2824	Mining, quarrying and construction machinery		...	...	379	364		...	...	6.7	5.4		...	...	194	149

Code	Industry	(1)	(2)	(3)	(4)	(5)	(6)
2825	Food/beverage/tobacco processing machinery	685	673	9.5	8.5	288	243
2826	Textile/apparel/leather production machinery	304	253	2.6	2.1	74	60
2829	Other special-purpose machinery	904	840	14.0	11.9	440	382
2910	Motor vehicles	177	164	69.5	65.1	2278	2109
2920	Automobile bodies, trailers and semi-trailers	939	894	14.2	11.6	343	281
2930	Parts and accessories for motor vehicles	1063	1093	79.4	68.6	2351	2177
301	Building of ships and boats	527	521	15.5	13.7	513	488
3011	Building of ships and floating structures	478	469	13.9	12.5	470	450
3012	Building of pleasure and sporting boats	49	52	1.6	1.3	43	38
3020	Railway locomotives and rolling stock	48	72	11.1	10.8	413	413
3030	Air and spacecraft and related machinery	93	92	16.7	16.3	648	632
3040	Military fighting vehicles	...	...	...	...	...	...
309	Transport equipment n.e.c.	87	86	2.8	2.2	83	106
3091	Motorcycles	41	35	1.0	0.6	27	17
3092	Bicycles and invalid carriages	...	...	...	...	...	...
3099	Other transport equipment n.e.c.	17091	15155	103.9	81.6	2142	1685
3100	Furniture	2893	2684	7.9	6.9	169	147
321	Jewellery, bijouterie and related articles	2427	2224	6.7	5.5	147	121
3211	Jewellery and related articles	466	459	1.1	1.4	22	26
3212	Imitation jewellery and related articles	206	194	0.7	0.7	16	16
3220	Musical instruments	174	184	2.1	1.8	51	43
3230	Sports goods	371	293	3.9	3.2	106	92
3240	Games and toys	4278	4347	13.3	13.7	290	313
3250	Medical and dental instruments and supplies	1726	1613	9.7	8.6	223	199
3290	Other manufacturing n.e.c.	13472	11463	55.1	53.1	1429	1412
331	Repair of fabricated metal products/machinery	484	338	4.5	3.3	109	88
3311	Repair of fabricated metal products	10304	8523	28.5	27.0	728	694
3312	Repair of machinery	195	165	1.1	1.1	28	29
3313	Repair of electronic and optical equipment	378	425	5.5	5.7	145	171
3314	Repair of electrical equipment	1972	1864	14.7	15.4	403	418
3315	Repair of transport equip., excl. motor vehicles	141	148	0.8	0.5	18	12
3319	Repair of other equipment	287	307	9.4	11.5	285	367
3320	Installation of industrial machinery/equipment	...	...	...	...	...	...
C	Total manufacturing	207499	191973	2276.0	1988.3	60912	54391

a/ 1101 includes 1102, 1103 and 1104.
b/ 1910 includes 1920.

Spain

ISIC	Industry	Output Note	Output 2006	Output 2007	Output 2008	Output 2009	VA Note	VA 2006	VA 2007	VA 2008	VA 2009	GFCF Note	GFCF 2008	GFCF 2009
			(millions of Euros)					(millions of Euros)					(millions of Euros)	
1010	Processing/preserving of meat		...	...	19015	18087		...	...	3665	3541		912	668
1020	Processing/preserving of fish, etc.		...	...	3945	3838		...	...	734	722		212	133
1030	Processing/preserving of fruit,vegetables		...	...	7336	6943		...	...	1711	1563		357	336
1040	Vegetable and animal oils and fats		...	...	8809	7707		...	...	957	723		468	193
1050	Dairy products		...	...	9999	8855		...	...	1798	1880		354	273
106	Grain mill products,starches and starch products		...	...	3224	2758		...	...	609	364		140	113
1061	Grain mill products		...	...	2758	2483		...	...	481	339		120	95
1062	Starches and starch products		...	...	467	275		...	...	128	25		20	18
107	Other food products		...	...	16812	15560		...	...	5482	5132		1346	926
1071	Bakery products		...	...	6903	6203		...	...	2641	2456		724	364
1072	Sugar		...	...	706	580		...	...	201	167		44	94
1073	Cocoa, chocolate and sugar confectionery		...	...	2407	3273		...	...	731	958		102	148
1074	Macaroni, noodles, couscous, etc.		...	...	349	325		...	...	91	88		23	26
1075	Prepared meals and dishes		...	...	1047	1073		...	...	218	234		64	30
1079	Other food products n.e.c.		...	...	5400	4107		...	...	1600	1229		389	263
1080	Prepared animal feeds		...	...	9060	7568		...	...	903	895		223	203
1101	Distilling, rectifying and blending of spirits		...	...	16524a/	14960a/		...	...	4587a/	4634a/		1185a/	746a/
1102	Wines		...	...	...a/	...a/		...	...	...a/	...a/		...a/	...a/
1103	Malt liquors and malt		...	...	...a/	...a/		...	...	...a/	...a/		...a/	...a/
1104	Soft drinks,mineral waters,other bottled waters		...	...	...a/	...a/		...	...	...a/	...a/		...a/	...a/
1200	Tobacco products		...	...	941	891		...	...	458	467		10	9
131	Spinning, weaving and finishing of textiles		...	...	2727	2039		...	...	837	618		103	47
1311	Preparation and spinning of textile fibres		...	...	950	722		...	...	269	196		25	17
1312	Weaving of textiles		...	...	1055	812		...	...	285	218		38	15
1313	Finishing of textiles		...	...	723	505		...	...	284	205		40	15
139	Other textiles		...	...	3371	2768		...	...	1050	836		117	72
1391	Knitted and crocheted fabrics		...	...	349	241		...	...	104	70		10	6
1392	Made-up textile articles, except apparel		...	...	1671	1276		...	...	545	399		50	31
1393	Carpets and rugs		...	...	182	139		...	...	49	41		4	4
1394	Cordage, rope, twine and netting		...	...	164	166		...	...	49	47		19	8
1399	Other textiles n.e.c.		...	...	1005	947		...	...	302	279		35	24
1410	Wearing apparel, except fur apparel		...	...	6493	5557		...	...	2086	1743		199	105
1420	Articles of fur		...	...	51	41		...	...	20	13		1	-
1430	Knitted and crocheted apparel		...	...	872	762		...	...	253	231		15	10
151	Leather;luggage,handbags,saddlery,harness;fur		...	...	1300	1040		...	...	364	331		24	22
1511	Tanning/dressing of leather; dressing of fur		...	...	630	538		...	...	150	158		13	16
1512	Luggage,handbags,etc.;saddlery/harness		...	...	670	502		...	...	214	173		11	6
1520	Footwear		...	...	3081	2434		...	...	805	653		37	30
1610	Sawmilling and planing of wood		...	...	1063	786		...	...	296	237		45	24
162	Wood products, cork, straw, plaiting materials		...	...	8520	6148		...	...	2654	1962		431	186

1621	Veneer sheets and wood-based panels	2264	1634	518	397	209	57
1622	Builders' carpentry and joinery	4043	2777	1483	1022	156	78
1623	Wooden containers	1105	858	288	259	33	29
1629	Other wood products;articles of cork,straw	1108	878	365	284	33	22
1701	Pulp, paper and paperboard	4952	3765	1129	863	369	228
1702	Corrugated paper and paperboard	4558	3949	1268	1177	326	171
1709	Other articles of paper and paperboard	3304	2903	1046	997	135	102
181	Printing and service activities related to printing	8816	7787	3713	3104	544	358
1811	Printing	7256	6520	2956	2523	478	320
1812	Service activities related to printing	1560	1267	757	581	65	37
1820	Reproduction of recorded media	403	274	156	103	22	7
1910	Coke oven products	40268b/	24590b/	1736b/	1510b/	781b/	1999b/
1920	Refined petroleum products	...b/	...b/	...b/	...b/	...b/	...b/
201	Basic chemicals,fertilizers, etc.	19753	14281	3666	2259	1103	548
2011	Basic chemicals	9147	6288	2255	1246	700	282
2012	Fertilizers and nitrogen compounds	1573	909	372	133	84	47
2013	Plastics and synthetic rubber in primary forms	9032	7084	1039	880	319	219
202	Other chemical products	15691	12860	3990	3546	580	541
2021	Pesticides and other agrochemical products	660	597	160	158	9	12
2022	Paints,varnishes;printing ink and mastics	3758	2904	1038	858	138	90
2023	Soap,cleaning and cosmetic preparations	6699	5599	1671	1595	226	298
2029	Other chemical products n.e.c.	4574	3759	1122	934	208	141
2030	Man-made fibres	683	542	173	181	69	87
2100	Pharmaceuticals,medicinal chemicals, etc.	13169	12875	4358	3907	612	524
221	Rubber products	4743	3600	1614	1321	236	208
2211	Rubber tyres and tubes	2948	2272	1054	872	164	166
2219	Other rubber products	1795	1328	560	449	72	42
2220	Plastics products	15508	11700	4614	3600	912	478
2310	Glass and glass products	4039	3212	1447	1069	309	278
239	Non-metallic mineral products n.e.c.	28155	19161	9475	6446	1996	1058
2391	Refractory products	508	380	168	112	47	21
2392	Clay building materials	4868	3072	1676	1078	453	136
2393	Other porcelain and ceramic products	868	591	376	265	46	43
2394	Cement, lime and plaster	5012	3062	2398	1435	429	393
2395	Articles of concrete, cement and plaster	11578	8117	2948	2181	632	249
2396	Cutting, shaping and finishing of stone	3440	2376	1410	965	157	96
2399	Other non-metallic mineral products n.e.c.	1881	1563	499	411	232	119
2410	Basic iron and steel	22463	11926	3974	1477	1371	545
2420	Basic precious and other non-ferrous metals	...	...	...	...	...	...
243	Casting of metals	4674	2547	1227	779	251	101
2431	Casting of iron and steel	3398	1741	859	507	167	73
2432	Casting of non-ferrous metals	1276	806	368	272	83	28
251	Struct.metal products, tanks, reservoirs	20198	14116	7251	5142	751	518
2511	Structural metal products	17960	12233	6373	4338	683	446
2512	Tanks, reservoirs and containers of metal	1954	1642	770	702	57	58

continued

Spain

ISIC Revision 4		Output (millions of Euros)					Value added at factor values (millions of Euros)					Gross fixed capital formation (millions of Euros)		
ISIC	Industry	Note	2006	2007	2008	2009	Note	2006	2007	2008	2009	Note	2008	2009
2513	Steam generators, excl. hot water boilers		...	...	283	241		...	...	109	103		11	14
2520	Weapons and ammunition		...	...	341	283		...	...	115	83		17	6
259	Other metal products;metal working services		...	...	24949	17403		...	...	8758	6412		1276	586
2591	Forging,pressing,stamping,roll-forming of metal		...	...	6327	4552		...	...	1628	1170		321	141
2592	Treatment and coating of metals; machining		...	...	8311	5408		...	...	3550	2410		524	187
2593	Cutlery, hand tools and general hardware		...	...	3044	2041		...	...	1287	870		125	87
2599	Other fabricated metal products n.e.c.		...	...	7268	5403		...	...	2293	1961		306	171
2610	Electronic components and boards		...	...	1636	971		...	...	455	329		121	43
2620	Computers and peripheral equipment		...	...	708	...		...	...	139	...		11	...
2630	Communication equipment		...	...	1099	930		...	...	415	362		33	24
2640	Consumer electronics		...	...	...	969		...	...	...	208		...	8
265	Measuring,testing equipment; watches, etc.		...	...	2002	1511		...	...	817	664		91	94
2651	Measuring/testing/navigating equipment,etc.		...	...	1931	1466		...	...	790	647		89	93
2652	Watches and clocks		...	...	71	46		...	...	27	17		3	-
2660	Irradiation/electromedical equipment,etc.		...	...	416	312		...	...	187	125		13	4
2670	Optical instruments and photographic equipment		...	...	...	...		...	...	...	...		...	...
2680	Magnetic and optical media		...	...	...	...		...	...	...	...		...	...
2710	Electric motors,generators,transformers,etc.		...	...	11816	8843		...	...	2698	2275		341	197
2720	Batteries and accumulators		...	...	864	623		...	...	164	134		10	14
273	Wiring and wiring devices		...	...	2468	1534		...	...	431	348		72	42
2731	Fibre optic cables		...	...	140	71		...	...	25	17		6	1
2732	Other electronic and electric wires and cables		...	...	2101	1205		...	...	310	225		38	23
2733	Wiring devices		...	...	227	258		...	...	97	106		28	18
2740	Electric lighting equipment		...	...	1742	1312		...	...	531	408		69	40
2750	Domestic appliances		...	...	3229	2503		...	...	914	694		137	86
2790	Other electrical equipment		...	...	2277	1517		...	...	708	490		78	46
281	General-purpose machinery		...	...	14452	10186		...	...	4431	3654		440	427
2811	Engines/turbines,excl.aircraft,vehicle engines		...	...	1775	1015		...	...	253	365		53	42
2812	Fluid power equipment		...	...	331	312		...	...	111	112		15	9
2813	Other pumps, compressors, taps and valves		...	...	1667	1310		...	...	530	413		60	37
2814	Bearings, gears, gearing and driving elements		...	...	890	662		...	...	306	236		56	35
2815	Ovens, furnaces and furnace burners		...	...	147	97		...	...	60	41		2	-
2816	Lifting and handling equipment		...	...	5314	3494		...	...	1922	1484		133	226
2817	Office machinery, excl.computers,etc.		...	...	46	49		...	...	17	21		1	...
2818	Power-driven hand tools		...	...	46	31		...	...	22	14		2	1
2819	Other general-purpose machinery		...	...	4234	3217		...	...	1209	967		118	76
282	Special-purpose machinery		...	...	8605	6085		...	...	2990	2244		308	211
2821	Agricultural and forestry machinery		...	...	1280	996		...	...	419	351		50	36
2822	Metal-forming machinery and machine tools		...	...	1728	1184		...	...	482	402		48	35
2823	Machinery for metallurgy		...	...	625	475		...	...	193	157		27	25
2824	Mining, quarrying and construction machinery		...	...	1166	656		...	...	407	247		61	40

Code	Industry						
2825	Food/beverage/tobacco processing machinery	1385	1118	506	435	65	20
2826	Textile/apparel/leather production machinery	422	218	229	75	8	6
2829	Other special-purpose machinery	1999	1439	755	577	51	49
2910	Motor vehicles	33642	27420	4513	3612	1156	915
2920	Automobile bodies, trailers and semi-trailers	2316	1347	620	390	50	29
2930	Parts and accessories for motor vehicles	16997	13314	3852	3070	686	841
301	Building of ships and boats	4683	4233	973	672	126	92
3011	Building of ships and floating structures	4453	4057	914	600	123	88
3012	Building of pleasure and sporting boats	230	177	59	72	2	4
3020	Railway locomotives and rolling stock	3562	3426	1210	1137	65	72
3030	Air and spacecraft and related machinery	5922	4492	1135	1022	166	205
3040	Military fighting vehicles	781	520	166	106	21	30
309	Transport equipment n.e.c.	:	:	:	:	:	:
3091	Motorcycles	202	138	37	40	3	2
3092	Bicycles and invalid carriages	:	:	:	:	:	:
3099	Other transport equipment n.e.c.	9468	6962	3426	2507	416	191
3100	Furniture	833	675	295	236	11	8
321	Jewellery, bijouterie and related articles	742	518	262	184	9	6
3211	Jewellery and related articles	91	158	33	52	2	2
3212	Imitation jewellery and related articles	56	56	29	26	1	1
3220	Musical instruments	268	241	99	93	11	9
3230	Sports goods	762	617	237	161	58	24
3240	Games and toys	1359	1340	709	642	58	65
3250	Medical and dental instruments and supplies	1058	790	399	305	53	28
3290	Other manufacturing n.e.c.	:	:	:	:	:	:
331	Repair of fabricated metal products/machinery	5778	5034	2807	2426	180	106
3311	Repair of fabricated metal products	416	266	201	147	21	5
3312	Repair of machinery	2916	2457	1539	1231	74	39
3313	Repair of electronic and optical equipment	97	91	53	47	5	2
3314	Repair of electrical equipment	740	674	268	270	10	8
3315	Repair of transport equip., excl. motor vehicles	1524	1497	713	707	69	52
3319	Repair of other equipment	85	49	34	24	2	-
3320	Installation of industrial machinery/equipment	1146	1324	428	596	11	15
C	Total manufacturing	512471	394143	126704	100825	23070	16603

a/ 1101 includes 1102, 1103 and 1104.
b/ 1910 includes 1920.

Spain

Index numbers of industrial production

ISIC	Industry	Note	1999	2000	2001	2002	2003	2004	2005	2006	2007	2008	2009	2010
	ISIC Revision 4								(2005=100)					
10	Food products		89	88	90	94	96	98	100	100	102	101	101	103
11	Beverages		85	91	95	93	99	99	100	101	102	103	97	92
12	Tobacco products		143	147	123	130	123	103	100	85	87	85	74	71
13	Textiles		130	132	135	127	120	113	100	97	92	77	61	65
14	Wearing apparel		168	162	144	122	115	111	100	98	96	88	71	64
15	Leather and related products		163	160	157	151	134	116	100	94	86	79	63	65
16	Wood/wood products/cork,excl. furniture		115	116	99	100	100	102	100	102	99	78	58	54
17	Paper and paper products		88	91	89	94	98	101	100	101	103	101	92	97
18	Printing and reproduction of recorded media		74	74	73	86	85	92	100	101	106	94	83	83
19	Coke and refined petroleum products		89	89	86	88	92	97	100	102	100	104	93	94
20	Chemicals and chemical products		96	95	95	95	99	99	100	101	104	98	96	101
21	Pharmaceuticals,medicinal chemicals, etc.		88	91	95	101	107	101	100	110	118	127	127	139
22	Rubber and plastics products		85	91	91	96	97	99	100	102	104	93	77	84
23	Other non-metallic mineral products		91	96	97	96	97	98	100	104	103	81	58	55
24	Basic metals		80	93	91	95	96	102	100	106	107	100	76	84
25	Fabricated metal products, except machinery		94	96	89	93	95	95	100	105	109	99	76	71
26	Computer, electronic and optical products		163	177	156	119	110	109	100	104	111	114	84	87
27	Electrical equipment		92	89	89	92	97	101	100	111	114	107	78	76
28	Machinery and equipment n.e.c.		105	110	113	99	97	101	100	115	126	115	84	80
29	Motor vehicles, trailers and semi-trailers		96	106	103	100	104	106	100	105	109	93	67	75
30	Other transport equipment		107	107	112	101	102	100	100	100	108	114	100	88
31	Furniture		107	110	103	101	101	100	100	109	114	91	64	58
32	Other manufacturing		95	103	101	108	108	105	100	104	104	96	80	84
33	Repair and installation of machinery/equipment		...	...	...	85	87	121	100	153	145	158	131	106
C	Total manufacturing		96	99	98	97	99	100	100	104	107	98	81	82

Sri Lanka

Concepts and definitions of variables:

Output excludes value of goods shipped in the same condition as received less the amount paid for these goods; value of fixed assets produced by the unit for its own use; net change between the beginning and end of the year in the value of work in process and stocks of goods to be shipped in the same condition as received.
Gross fixed capital formation excludes intellectual property products such as products of R&D, computer software, databases, etc. It includes land, other construction and land improvements.

Related national publications:

Annual Survey of Industries, published by the Department of Census and Statistics, Colombo.

Supplier of information:

Department of Census and Statistics, Colombo

Basic source of data:

Annual survey of industries; sample survey.

Major deviations from ISIC (Revision 3):

None reported.

Reference period:

Calendar year.

Scope:

Establishments with 25 or more persons engaged.

Method of data collection:

Mail questionnaires; direct interview in the field.

Type of enumeration:

Complete enumeration; sample survey.

Adjusted for non-response:

Yes.

Sri Lanka

ISIC	Industry	Number of establishments (number)					Number of employees (number)					Wages and salaries paid to employees (millions of Sri Lankan Rupees)				
		Note	2007	2008	2009	2010	Note	2007	2008	2009	2010	Note	2007	2008	2009	2010
151	Processed meat,fish,fruit,vegetables,fats		57	124	116	104		8212	13420	12452	11258		1055	1850	1876	1880
1511	Processing/preserving of meat		…	…	…	…		…	…	…	…		…	…	…	…
1512	Processing/preserving of fish		…	…	…	…		…	…	…	…		…	…	…	…
1513	Processing/preserving of fruit & vegetables		…	…	…	…		…	…	…	…		…	…	…	…
1514	Vegetable and animal oils and fats		…	…	…	…		…	…	…	…		…	…	…	…
1520	Dairy products		14	33	29	34		4322	3996	4039	4001		1019	1086	1193	2133
153	Grain mill products; starches; animal feeds		29	63	26	26		4236	6486	2889	4032		715	1097	687	674
1531	Grain mill products		…	…	…	…		…	…	…	…		…	…	…	…
1532	Starches and starch products		…	…	…	…		…	…	…	…		…	…	…	…
1533	Prepared animal feeds		…	…	…	…		…	…	…	…		…	…	…	…
154	Other food products		936	858	744	707		82126	76825	71145	69195		9068	10075	10223	10969
1541	Bakery products		…	…	…	…		…	…	…	…		…	…	…	…
1542	Sugar		…	…	…	…		…	…	…	…		…	…	…	…
1543	Cocoa, chocolate and sugar confectionery		…	…	…	…		…	…	…	…		…	…	…	…
1544	Macaroni, noodles & similar products		…	…	…	…		…	…	…	…		…	…	…	…
1549	Other food products n.e.c.		…	…	…	…		…	…	…	…		…	…	…	…
155	Beverages		52	82	38	32		3803	6071	5350	4732		619	1842	1566	1455
1551	Distilling, rectifying & blending of spirits		…	…	…	…		…	…	…	…		…	…	…	…
1552	Wines		…	…	…	…		…	…	…	…		…	…	…	…
1553	Malt liquors and malt		…	…	…	…		…	…	…	…		…	…	…	…
1554	Soft drinks; mineral waters		…	…	…	…		…	…	…	…		…	…	…	…
1600	Tobacco products		21	32	23	22		3824	3782	3229	2677		1200	1089	1046	1050
171	Spinning, weaving and finishing of textiles		53	150	111	101		9901	16734	15335	14593		1219	2789	2899	2813
1711	Textile fibre preparation; textile weaving		…	…	…	…		…	…	…	…		…	…	…	…
1712	Finishing of textiles		…	…	…	…		…	…	…	…		…	…	…	…
172	Other textiles		117	79	57	54		21253	7575	6346	5338		2174	1080	1046	1052
1721	Made-up textile articles, except apparel		…	…	…	…		…	…	…	…		…	…	…	…
1722	Carpets and rugs		…	…	…	…		…	…	…	…		…	…	…	…
1723	Cordage, rope, twine and netting		…	…	…	…		…	…	…	…		…	…	…	…
1729	Other textiles n.e.c.		…	…	…	…		…	…	…	…		…	…	…	…
1730	Knitted and crocheted fabrics and articles		113	53	34	31		84943	19470	14751	15333		39330	3661	2776	2970
1810	Wearing apparel, except fur apparel		777	564	568	526		383254	340103	296540	260308		46703	41418	38173	36593
1820	Dressing & dyeing of fur; processing of fur		3	17	18	13		731	1515	1626	1512		98	226	213	233
191	Tanning, dressing and processing of leather		…	…	…	…		…	…	…	…		…	…	…	…
1911	Tanning and dressing of leather		…	…	…	…		…	…	…	…		…	…	…	…
1912	Luggage, handbags, etc.; saddlery & harness		…	…	…	…		…	…	…	…		…	…	…	…
1920	Footwear		26	20	22	27		8250	7663	7069	7635		1124	1284	1016	1198
2010	Sawmilling and planing of wood		2	12	14	11		179	1688	1326	892		34	255	227	181
202	Products of wood, cork, straw, etc.		71	53	28	23		3727	3208	1938	1790		315	350	263	239
2021	Veneer sheets, plywood, particle board, etc.		…	…	…	…		…	…	…	…		…	…	…	…
2022	Builders' carpentry and joinery		…	…	…	…		…	…	…	…		…	…	…	…
2023	Wooden containers		…	…	…	…		…	…	…	…		…	…	…	…
2029	Other wood products; articles of cork/straw		…	…	…	…		…	…	…	…		…	…	…	…
210	Paper and paper products		107	63	68	68		8528	5414	6012	5414		1849	906	973	1010
2101	Pulp, paper and paperboard		…	…	…	…		…	…	…	…		…	…	…	…
2102	Corrugated paper and paperboard		…	…	…	…		…	…	…	…		…	…	…	…
2109	Other articles of paper and paperboard		…	…	…	…		…	…	…	…		…	…	…	…
221	Publishing		1	5	3	3		42	421	222	176		4	117	70	22
2211	Publishing of books and other publications		…	…	…	…		…	…	…	…		…	…	…	…
2212	Publishing of newspapers, journals, etc.		…	…	…	…		…	…	…	…		…	…	…	…
2213	Publishing of recorded media		…	…	…	…		…	…	…	…		…	…	…	…
2219	Other publishing		…	…	…	…		…	…	…	…		…	…	…	…

Code	Product												
222	Printing and related service activities	3872	1875	4349	3171	13513	9905	15279	12896	81	85	83	95
2221	Printing												
2222	Service activities related to printing		146		13		261		55			1	4
2230	Reproduction of recorded media												
2310	Coke oven products	1784	725	1916		2771	2511	3047		2	2	2	
2320	Refined petroleum products												
2330	Processing of nuclear fuel	433	350	236	483	2291	1828	1531	2040	23	19	20	29
241	Basic chemicals												
2411	Basic chemicals, except fertilizers												
2412	Fertilizers and nitrogen compounds	1765	2030	2130	3761	8251	9432	10095	12891	80	90	94	67
2413	Plastics in primary forms; synthetic rubber												
242	Other chemicals												
2421	Pesticides and other agro-chemical products												
2422	Paints, varnishes, printing ink and mastics												
2423	Pharmaceuticals, medicinal chemicals, etc.												
2424	Soap, cleaning & cosmetic preparations												
2429	Other chemical products n.e.c.												
2430	Man-made fibres	5872	5533	5175	5009	29566	30777	35854	36514	160	155	181	246
251	Rubber products												
2511	Rubber tyres and tubes	2777	2821	2704	2156	15158	16711	17847	15121	121	120	107	73
2519	Other rubber products	267	263	19		589	568	195		5	4		
2520	Plastic products	3464	3300	3257	5785	12839	12393	13995	42262	76	85	98	219
2610	Glass and glass products												
269	Non-metallic mineral products n.e.c.												
2691	Pottery, china and earthenware												
2692	Refractory ceramic products												
2693	Struct.non-refractory clay; ceramic products												
2694	Cement, lime and plaster												
2695	Articles of concrete, cement and plaster												
2696	Cutting, shaping & finishing of stone												
2699	Other non-metallic mineral products n.e.c.	367	126			1274	670	1068	107	13	10	10	1
2710	Basic iron and steel	15	11	299	22	100	111	47		1	1	2	
2720	Basic precious and non-ferrous metals	660	878	762	908	2363	2640	2460	4446	21	24	24	35
273	Casting of metals												
2731	Casting of iron and steel												
2732	Casting of non-ferrous metals	345	385	603	141	2313	2659	3336	977	26	32	47	26
281	Struct.metal products;tanks;steam generators												
2811	Structural metal products												
2812	Tanks, reservoirs and containers of metal												
2813	Steam generators												
289	Other metal products; metal working services	366	389	378	811	2159	2654	2934	6443	29	37	41	86
2891	Metal forging/pressing/stamping/roll-forming												
2892	Treatment & coating of metals												
2893	Cutlery, hand tools and general hardware												
2899	Other fabricated metal products n.e.c.	126	164	2620	667	608	720	6824	4601	6	8	46	13
291	General purpose machinery												
2911	Engines & turbines (not for transport equipment)												
2912	Pumps, compressors, taps and valves												
2913	Bearings, gears, gearing & driving elements												
2914	Ovens, furnaces and furnace burners												
2915	Lifting and handling equipment												
2919	Other general purpose machinery	110	255	332	447	628	1049	1532	2238	10	15	25	18
292	Special purpose machinery												
2921	Agricultural and forestry machinery												
2922	Machine tools												
2923	Machinery for metallurgy												
2924	Machinery for mining & construction												
2925	Food/beverage/tobacco processing machinery												
2926	Machinery for textile, apparel and leather												
2927	Weapons and ammunition												
2929	Other special purpose machinery												

continued

Sri Lanka

ISIC Revision 3		Number of establishments (number)					Number of employees (number)					Wages and salaries paid to employees (millions of Sri Lankan Rupees)				
ISIC	Industry	Note	2007	2008	2009	2010	Note	2007	2008	2009	2010	Note	2007	2008	2009	2010
2930	Domestic appliances n.e.c.		3	8	6	7		791	1443	1199	1224		131	439	422	453
3000	Office, accounting and computing machinery		4	3	4	5		5200	2688	1546	2769		596	348	205	405
3110	Electric motors, generators and transformers		8	9	9	9		3125	2702	2341	2229		423	503	521	647
3120	Electricity distribution & control apparatus		23	12	14	15		2359	1432	1217	1976		334	220	238	434
3130	Insulated wire and cable		12	6	3	4		1697	1069	965	1035		261	227	162	176
3140	Accumulators, primary cells and batteries		5	4	4	4		963	411	416	374		385	148	157	160
3150	Lighting equipment and electric lamps		10	4	7	5		550	389	306	256		46	61	46	33
3190	Other electrical equipment n.e.c.															
3210	Electronic valves, tubes, etc.		6	7	6	6		1782	1465	1352	1326		302	335	327	254
3220	TV/radio transmitters; line comm. apparatus		2	1	1			134	74	62			13	10	7	
3230	TV and radio receivers and associated goods		4	3	3	4		490	283	272	349		60	49	37	53
331	Medical, measuring, testing appliances, etc.															
3311	Medical, surgical and orthopaedic equipment															
3312	Measuring/testing/navigating appliances,etc.															
3313	Industrial process control equipment															
3320	Optical instruments & photographic equipment		1	3	4			30	303	256			2	38	29	
3330	Watches and clocks															
3410	Motor vehicles		1	5	3	4		80	429	280	498		9	58	49	142
3420	Automobile bodies, trailers & semi-trailers		5	5	5	5		527	267	301	389		87	31	56	82
3430	Parts/accessories for automobiles		4	3	2			838	201	54			205	39	8	
351	Building and repairing of ships and boats															
3511	Building and repairing of ships		22	10	7	10		5473	3704	3512	3899		2025	1411	1334	1548
3512	Building/repairing of pleasure/sport. boats															
3520	Railway/tramway locomotives & rolling stock		1					196					18			
3530	Aircraft and spacecraft															
359	Transport equipment n.e.c.		9	7	5	5		3679	1672	1132	1199		475	279	157	197
3591	Motorcycles															
3592	Bicycles and invalid carriages															
3599	Other transport equipment n.e.c.															
3610	Furniture															
369	Manufacturing n.e.c.		93	96	61	62		9867	6589	5623	5953		1183	863	751	853
3691	Jewellery and related articles		208	110	113	102		23129	16277	13751	13423		2376	2179	2150	2640
3692	Musical instruments															
3693	Sports goods															
3694	Games and toys															
3699	Other manufacturing n.e.c.															
3710	Recycling of metal waste and scrap		3	2	1	3		430	136	68				21	10	
3720	Recycling of non-metal waste and scrap			5	3				638	441	421		59	73	20	31
D	Total manufacturing		3715	3295	2851	2730		832354	672170	580448	545397		140797	100081	91241	95900

Sri Lanka

ISIC	Industry	Output at producers' prices (millions of Sri Lankan Rupees)					Value added at producers' prices (millions of Sri Lankan Rupees)					Gross fixed capital formation (millions of Sri Lankan Rupees)		
	ISIC Revision 3	Note	2007	2008	2009	2010	Note	2007	2008	2009	2010	Note	2009	2010
151	Processed meat,fish,fruit,vegetables,fats		20675	35844	35290	33137		6885	18550	19330	16083		601	617
1511	Processing/preserving of meat		...	...	...	...		...	...	...	...		...	...
1512	Processing/preserving of fish		...	...	...	...		...	...	...	...		...	...
1513	Processing/preserving of fruit & vegetables		...	...	...	...		...	...	...	...		...	...
1514	Vegetable and animal oils and fats		47402	38798	40589	45213		10589	10703	11601	9627		1211	359
1520	Dairy products		68828	66511	55151	60010		19062	9824	11355	13211		242	677
153	Grain mill products; starches; animal feeds		...	...	...	...		...	...	...	...		...	...
1531	Grain mill products													
1532	Starches and starch products		...	...	...	...		...	...	...	...		...	...
1533	Prepared animal feeds		224835	164501	219873	209919		120734	72336	122859	88314		4719	6023
154	Other food products		...	...	...	...		...	...	...	...		...	...
1541	Bakery products		...	...	...	...		...	...	...	...		...	...
1542	Sugar													
1543	Cocoa, chocolate and sugar confectionery		...	...	...	...		...	...	...	...		...	...
1544	Macaroni, noodles & similar products		...	...	...	...		...	...	...	...		...	...
1549	Other food products n.e.c.		21419	25880	27438	27487		17038	14526	11115	12975		456	488
155	Beverages		...	...	...	...		...	...	...	...		...	...
1551	Distilling, rectifying & blending of spirits		...	...	...	...		...	...	...	...		...	...
1552	Wines													
1553	Malt liquors and malt		35988	40679	40285	64823		33270	38067	38044	62004		32	217
1554	Soft drinks; mineral waters		25371	40744	43556	42446		6186	13429	18325	17253		3340	831
1600	Tobacco products		...	...	...	...		...	...	...	...		...	...
171	Spinning, weaving and finishing of textiles		16356	8470	6935	6171		5804	3981	3135	2856		145	117
1711	Textile fibre preparation; textile weaving		...	...	...	...		...	...	...	...		...	...
1712	Finishing of textiles		...	...	...	...		...	...	...	...		...	...
172	Other textiles		...	...	...	...		...	...	...	...		...	...
1721	Made-up textile articles, except apparel		...	...	...	...		...	...	...	...		...	...
1722	Carpets and rugs													
1723	Cordage, rope, twine and netting		562375	29749	23168	25899		173244	15051	10860	11947		413	1035
1729	Other textiles n.e.c.		351965	328073	339305	313428		166690	132442	152094	147289		4561	3640
1730	Knitted and crocheted fabrics and articles		...	...	...	...		...	...	...	...		-	
1810	Wearing apparel, except fur apparel		692	1229	1268	1584		223	339	539	485		83	1
1820	Dressing & dyeing of fur; processing of fur		...	...	...	...		...	...	...	...		...	...
191	Tanning, dressing and processing of leather		...	...	...	...		...	...	...	...		...	...
1911	Tanning and dressing of leather		7458	7472	6744	8286		2955	3402	2596	3753		60	260
1912	Luggage, handbags, etc.; saddlery & harness		...	...	...	...		103	1695	1476	814		46	14
1920	Footwear		177	4398	2942	1927		547	1659	837	1635		59	84
2010	Sawmilling and planing of wood		1253	2801	1503	2708		...	...	...	...		...	...
202	Products of wood, cork, straw, etc.		...	...	...	...		...	...	...	...		...	...
2021	Veneer sheets, plywood, particle board, etc.		...	...	...	...		...	...	...	...		...	...
2022	Builders' carpentry and joinery													
2023	Wooden containers		...	...	...	...		...	...	...	...		...	...
2029	Other wood products; articles of cork/straw		31484	13621	14594	15603		7157	3995	4628	4789		367	370
210	Paper and paper products		...	...	...	...		...	...	...	...		...	...
2101	Pulp, paper and paperboard		...	...	...	...		...	...	...	...		...	...
2102	Corrugated paper and paperboard													
2109	Other articles of paper and paperboard		57	1624	1092	149		12	725	632	87		5	118
221	Publishing		...	...	...	...		...	...	...	...		...	...
2211	Publishing of books and other publications													
2212	Publishing of newspapers, journals, etc.		...	...	...	...		...	...	...	...		...	...
2213	Publishing of recorded media		...	...	...	...		...	...	...	...		...	...
2219	Other publishing		...	...	...	...		...	...	...	...		...	...

continued

Sri Lanka

			Output at producers' prices (millions of Sri Lankan Rupees)					Value added at producers' prices (millions of Sri Lankan Rupees)					Gross fixed capital formation (millions of Sri Lankan Rupees)	
ISIC	Industry (ISIC Revision 3)	Note	2007	2008	2009	2010	Note	2007	2008	2009	2010	Note	2009	2010
222	Printing and related service activities		21301	25998	18261	25620		8557	11464	6578	11166		658	4924
2221	Printing													
2222	Service activities related to printing								19	494				
2230	Reproduction of recorded media			40	561								3	
2310	Coke oven products													
2320	Refined petroleum products		125920	167660	108804			12298	9495	5968			172	
2330	Processing of nuclear fuel													
241	Basic chemicals		25504	11325	45388	47413		12619	4187	17293	20839		276	180
2411	Basic chemicals, except fertilizers													
2412	Fertilizers and nitrogen compounds													
2413	Plastics in primary forms; synthetic rubber													
242	Other chemicals		48981	48300	21707	32129		17076	17938	8461	16073		576	379
2421	Pesticides and other agro-chemical products													
2422	Paints, varnishes, printing ink and mastics													
2423	Pharmaceuticals, medicinal chemicals, etc.													
2424	Soap, cleaning & cosmetic preparations													
2429	Other chemical products n.e.c.													
2430	Man-made fibres													
251	Rubber products		80397	84937	62474	85332		39635	43640	30940	40257		877	1867
2511	Rubber tyres and tubes													
2519	Other rubber products		31613	36743	31072	32089		13448	11496	12997	10978		609	1036
2520	Plastic products			73	3612	3683			20	1913	1966		57	
2610	Glass and glass products		46975	78933	68599	73137		22377	24134	26107	27596		884	1679
269	Non-metallic mineral products n.e.c.													
2691	Pottery, china and earthenware													
2692	Refractory ceramic products													
2693	Struct.non-refractory clay; ceramic products													
2694	Cement, lime and plaster													
2695	Articles of concrete, cement and plaster													
2696	Cutting, shaping & finishing of stone													
2699	Other non-metallic mineral products n.e.c.													
2710	Basic iron and steel		2500	9832	3292	14554		73	1352	1113	1699		1	75
2720	Basic precious and non-ferrous metals		1354	478	677			404	154	202			-	
273	Casting of metals			17844	15196	12748			5143	5769	3756		354	329
2731	Casting of iron and steel													
2732	Casting of non-ferrous metals													
281	Struct.metal products;tanks;steam generators		1046	8278	5150	4928		692	5291	2534	2338		101	251
2811	Structural metal products													
2812	Tanks, reservoirs and containers of metal													
2813	Steam generators													
289	Other metal products; metal working services		7167	5633	4013	3445		2487	2215	1732	1485		46	35
2891	Metal forging/pressing/stamping/roll-forming													
2892	Treatment & coating of metals													
2893	Cutlery, hand tools and general hardware													
2899	Other fabricated metal products n.e.c.													
291	General purpose machinery		2197	49973	2449	1846		866	24969	1146	911		68	13
2911	Engines & turbines (not for transport equipment)													
2912	Pumps, compressors, taps and valves													
2913	Bearings, gears, gearing & driving elements													
2914	Ovens, furnaces and furnace burners													
2915	Lifting and handling equipment													
2919	Other general purpose machinery													

Code	Industry										
292	Special purpose machinery	6053	3065	1792	490	1648	1085	681	215	5	5
2921	Agricultural and forestry machinery	…	…	…	…	…	…	…	…	…	…
2922	Machine tools	…	…	…	…	…	…	…	…	…	…
2923	Machinery for metallurgy	…	…	…	…	…	…	…	…	…	…
2924	Machinery for mining & construction	…	…	…	…	…	…	…	…	…	…
2925	Food/beverage/tobacco processing machinery	…	…	…	…	…	…	…	…	…	…
2926	Machinery for textile, apparel and leather	…	…	…	…	…	…	…	…	…	…
2927	Weapons and ammunition	…	…	…	…	…	…	…	…	…	…
2929	Other special purpose machinery	4490	4869	4992	4999	664	1869	1669	1500	76	29
2930	Domestic appliances n.e.c.	6097	2665	1454	2332	2928	1124	691	1568	35	117
3000	Office, accounting and computing machinery	7227	13907	8821	11035	2544	5054	3507	5430	40	123
3110	Electric motors, generators and transformers	4585	3448	3322	5840	1597	1042	978	2235	44	283
3120	Electricity distribution & control apparatus	27179	4707	3425	3136	8437	2192	2190	1800	418	1
3130	Insulated wire and cable	4372	1908	2372	4564	1058	510	738	2551	17	14
3140	Accumulators, primary cells and batteries	349	435	438	218	21	194	229	72	1	…
3150	Lighting equipment and electric lamps	…	…	…	…	…	…	…	…	…	…
3190	Other electrical equipment n.e.c.	2427	4527	5134	4528	1018	2548	2856	1172	235	83
3210	Electronic valves, tubes, etc.	23	13	18	…	21	10	17	…	…	…
3220	TV/radio transmitters; line comm. apparatus	415	512	359	654	110	215	81	55	…	17
3230	TV and radio receivers and associated goods	…	…	…	…	…	…	…	…	…	…
331	Medical, measuring, testing appliances, etc.	…	…	…	…	…	…	…	…	…	…
3311	Medical, surgical and orthopaedic equipment	…	…	…	…	…	…	…	…	…	…
3312	Measuring/testing/navigating appliances,etc.	…	…	…	…	…	…	…	…	…	…
3313	Industrial process control equipment	6	116	66	…	3	67	39	…	…	…
3320	Optical instruments & photographic equipment	…	…	…	…	…	…	…	…	…	…
3330	Watches and clocks	…	…	…	…	…	…	117	409	…	37
3410	Motor vehicles	28	147	151	1719	26	111	117	122	…	…
3420	Automobile bodies, trailers & semi-trailers	67	38	115	144	27	23	88	…	…	…
3430	Parts/accessories for automobiles	1473	959	19	…	759	892	10	5843	28	56
351	Building and repairing of ships and boats	12434	11087	10914	12705	4634	4904	4801	…	…	…
3511	Building and repairing of ships	…	…	…	…	…	…	…	…	…	…
3512	Building/repairing of pleasure/sport. boats	…	…	…	…	…	…	…	…	…	…
3520	Railway/tramway locomotives & rolling stock	26	…	…	…	23	…	…	…	…	…
3530	Aircraft and spacecraft	9921	4042	3171	4441	5522	1200	591	1162	41	5
359	Transport equipment n.e.c.	…	…	…	…	…	…	…	…	…	…
3591	Motorcycles	…	…	…	…	…	…	…	…	…	…
3592	Bicycles and invalid carriages	…	…	…	…	…	…	…	…	…	…
3599	Other transport equipment n.e.c.	13640	13300	13046	17963	4442	4434	7710	9214	162	907
3610	Furniture	18208	18533	16819	22037	8413	8441	8613	9379	461	503
369	Manufacturing n.e.c.	…	…	…	…	…	…	…	…	…	…
3691	Jewellery and related articles	…	…	…	…	…	…	…	…	…	…
3692	Musical instruments	…	…	…	…	…	…	…	…	…	…
3693	Sports goods	…	…	…	…	…	…	…	…	…	…
3694	Games and toys	…	…	…	…	…	…	…	…	…	…
3699	Other manufacturing n.e.c.	…	…	…	…	…	…	…	…	…	…
3710	Recycling of metal waste and scrap	855	683	341	749	327	129	105	288	6	…
3720	Recycling of non-metal waste and scrap	…	1135	725	…	…	390	371	288	…	6
D	Total manufacturing	1932751	1446537	1328481	1417449	753382	538675	568757	605206	22591	28222

Sri Lanka

Index numbers of industrial production

ISIC Revision 3

(2005=100)

ISIC	Industry	Note	1999	2000	2001	2002	2003	2004	2005	2006	2007	2008	2009	2010
15	Food and beverages	a/	77	81	84	87	92	95	100	106	112	120	126	135
16	Tobacco products	a/	...	...	...	...	...	...	...	...	...	...	...	...
17	Textiles	b/	82	95	93	91	89	96	100	104	110	111	111	121
18	Wearing apparel, fur	b/	...	...	...	...	...	...	...	...	...	...	...	...
19	Leather, leather products and footwear	b/	...	...	...	...	...	...	...	...	...	...	...	...
20	Wood products (excl. furniture)		...	...	...	...	...	...	...	...	...	...	...	...
21	Paper and paper products		84	89	90	92	94	96	100	105	111	117	122	130
22	Printing and publishing		...	...	...	...	...	...	...	...	...	...	...	...
23	Coke,refined petroleum products,nuclear fuel	c/	70	77	79	80	84	88	100	108	115	133	136	153
24	Chemicals and chemical products	c/	...	...	...	...	...	...	...	...	...	...	...	...
25	Rubber and plastics products	c/	...	...	...	...	...	...	...	...	...	...	...	...
26	Non-metallic mineral products		79	84	92	90	88	94	100	111	121	125	120	135
27	Basic metals		77	79	80	84	87	94	100	106	113	117	118	124
28	Fabricated metal products	d/	82	88	90	92	95	97	100	104	109	114	118	129
29	Machinery and equipment n.e.c.	d/	...	...	...	...	...	...	...	...	...	...	...	...
30	Office, accounting and computing machinery	d/	...	...	...	...	...	...	...	...	...	...	...	...
31	Electrical machinery and apparatus	d/	...	...	...	...	...	...	...	...	...	...	...	...
32	Radio,television and communication equipment	d/	...	...	...	...	...	...	...	...	...	...	...	...
33	Medical, precision and optical instruments	d/	...	...	...	...	...	...	...	...	...	...	...	...
34	Motor vehicles, trailers, semi-trailers	d/	...	...	...	...	...	...	...	...	...	...	...	...
35	Other transport equipment	d/	...	...	...	...	...	...	...	...	...	...	...	...
36	Furniture; manufacturing n.e.c.		...	...	...	...	...	...	...	...	...	...	...	...
37	Recycling		...	...	...	...	...	...	...	...	...	...	...	...
D	Total manufacturing		85	86	89	93	94	97	100	104	109	114	118	127

a/ 15 includes 16.
b/ 17 includes 18 and 19.
c/ 23 includes 24 and 25.
d/ 28 includes 29, 30, 31, 32, 33, 34 and 35.

Sweden

Supplier of information:
Statistics Sweden, Stockholm.
Industrial statistics for the OECD countries are compiled by the OECD secretariat, which supplies them to UNIDO.

Basic source of data:
Various surveys; administrative data.

Major deviations from ISIC (Revision 4):
Data have been converted from the national NACE equivalent system to ISIC (Revision 4) by the OECD.

Reference period:
Calendar year.

Scope:
All enterprises.

Method of data collection:
Not reported.

Type of enumeration:
Not reported.

Adjusted for non-response:
Not reported.

Concepts and definitions of variables:
No deviations from the standard UN concepts and definitions are reported.

Related national publications:
None reported.

Sweden

ISIC	Industry	Number of enterprises (number)					Number of employees (number)					Wages and salaries paid to employees (millions of Swedish Kronor)				
		Note	2006	2007	2008	2009	Note	2006	2007	2008	2009	Note	2006	2007	2008	2009
1010	Processing/preserving of meat		…	…	494	488		…	…	11406	11506		…	…	3077	3239
1020	Processing/preserving of fish, etc.		…	…	214	217		…	…	…	1898		…	…	…	495
1030	Processing/preserving of fruit, vegetables		…	…	194	208		…	…	3656	3799		…	…	1139	1203
1040	Vegetable and animal oils and fats		…	…	56	57		…	…	…	…		…	…	…	…
1050	Dairy products		…	…	127	125		…	…	…	…		…	…	…	…
106	Grain mill products,starches and starch products		…	…	121	123		…	…	6976	6790		…	…	2083	2178
1061	Grain mill products		…	…	113	115		…	…	1728	1860		…	…	537	611
1062	Starches and starch products		…	…	8	8		…	…	1378	1595		…	…	428	529
107	Other food products		…	…	1942	1935		…	…	350	265		…	…	110	83
1071	Bakery products		…	…	1455	1427		…	…	24880	24044		…	…	6450	6392
1072	Sugar		…	…	6	7		…	…	16227	15664		…	…	3828	3733
1073	Cocoa, chocolate and sugar confectionery		…	…	214	217		…	…	…	…		…	…	…	…
1074	Macaroni, noodles, couscous, etc.		…	…	7	9		…	…	2765	2656		…	…	874	869
1075	Prepared meals and dishes		…	…	53	59		…	…	30	34		…	…	6	5
1079	Other food products n.e.c.		…	…	207	216		…	…	1690	1456		…	…	444	404
1080	Prepared animal feeds		…	…	100	97		…	…	…	…		…	…	…	…
1101	Distilling, rectifying and blending of spirits		…	…	…	…		…	…	…	…		…	…	…	…
1102	Wines		…	…	132a/	135a/		…	…	4965a/	4844a/		…	…	1778a/	1831a/
1103	Malt liquors and malt		…	…	…a/	…a/		…	…	…a/	…a/		…	…	…a/	…a/
1104	Soft drinks;mineral waters,other bottled waters		…	…	…a/	…a/		…	…	…a/	…a/		…	…	…a/	…a/
1200	Tobacco products		…	…	18	15		…	…	…	16883		…	…	…a/	…a/
131	Spinning, weaving and finishing of textiles		…	…	509	503		…	…	…	16883		…	…	8370	8060
1311	Preparation and spinning of textile fibres		…	…	30	29		…	…	1090	1025		…	…	274	255
1312	Weaving of textiles		…	…	141	130		…	…	46	39		…	…	10	7
1313	Finishing of textiles		…	…	338	344		…	…	476	471		…	…	131	124
139	Other textiles		…	…	1790	1774		…	…	568	515		…	…	134	123
1391	Knitted and crocheted fabrics		…	…	55	49		…	…	5016	4434		…	…	1367	1203
1392	Made-up textile articles, except apparel		…	…	828	822		…	…	475	438		…	…	134	119
1393	Carpets and rugs		…	…	41	39		…	…	1783	1553		…	…	442	387
1394	Cordage, rope, twine and netting		…	…	48	44		…	…	202	194		…	…	62	63
1399	Other textiles n.e.c.		…	…	818	820		…	…	…	…		…	…	…	…
1410	Wearing apparel, except fur apparel		…	…	1764	1791		…	…	1317	1202		…	…	359	341
1420	Articles of fur		…	…	60	58		…	…	47	41		…	…	10	8
1430	Knitted and crocheted apparel		…	…	59	59		…	…	259	210		…	…	62	51
151	Leather;luggage,handbags,saddlery,harness;fur		…	…	330	331		…	…	849	585		…	…	206	154
1511	Tanning/dressing of leather; dressing of fur		…	…	34	33		…	…	…	265		…	…	…	69
1512	Luggage,handbags,etc.;saddlery/harness		…	…	296	298		…	…	…	320		…	…	…	85
1520	Footwear		…	…	88	88		…	…	267	218		…	…	61	57
1610	Sawmilling and planing of wood		…	…	1414	1405		…	…	13694	12884		…	…	4059	3917
162	Wood products, cork, straw, plaiting materials		…	…	4704	4564		…	…	22901	19478		…	…	6360	5552

1621	Veneer sheets and wood-based panels	94	96	...	...	...	...
1622	Builders' carpentry and joinery	2852	2772	2465	2158	650	590
1623	Wooden containers	386	373	2110	1987	565	569
1629	Other wood products;articles of cork,straw	1372	1323	25931	23379	9862	9209
1701	Pulp, paper and paperboard	153	149	7924	4856	3189	1603
1702	Corrugated paper and paperboard	179	167	5181	4985	1778	1822
1709	Other articles of paper and paperboard	194	186	18321	16822	5699	5285
181	Printing and service activities related to printing	3321	3178	13851	12533	4305	3940
1811	Printing	2352	2224	4470	4289	1394	1345
1812	Service activities related to printing	969	954	395	162	62	40
1820	Reproduction of recorded media	219	208	...	2219b/	849b/	976b/
1910	Coke oven products	2	2	...	...	...b/	...b/
1920	Refined petroleum products	42	46	10598	9625	4421	4123
201	Basic chemicals,fertilizers, etc.	245	228	...	...	...	...
2011	Basic chemicals	166	148	...	517	...	178
2012	Fertilizers and nitrogen compounds	34	33	...	...	...	...
2013	Plastics and synthetic rubber in primary forms	45	47	66	39	15	12
202	Other chemical products	557	549	9546	9074	3399	3271
2021	Pesticides and other agrochemical products	13	13	4009	3628	1424	1301
2022	Paints,varnishes;printing ink and mastics	134	129	1995	1992	571	588
2023	Soap,cleaning and cosmetic preparations	235	242	3476	3415	1388	1370
2029	Other chemical products n.e.c.	175	165	10	9	3	2
2030	Man-made fibres	5	5	16883	...	8370	8060
2100	Pharmaceuticals,medicinal chemicals, etc.	146	146	5998	5166	1848	1667
221	Rubber products	245	238	483	419	135	116
2211	Rubber tyres and tubes	94	92	5514	4747	1713	1551
2219	Other rubber products	151	146	17445	15735	5328	4907
2220	Plastics products	1369	1354	...	...	...	...
2310	Glass and glass products	370	365	13594	12759	4527	4261
239	Non-metallic mineral products n.e.c.	1739	1703	680	580	228	188
2391	Refractory products	31	32	...	...	...	...
2392	Clay building materials	26	26	...	...	...	...
2393	Other porcelain and ceramic products	972	950	...	...	...	...
2394	Cement, lime and plaster	26	20	...	...	...	...
2395	Articles of concrete, cement and plaster	299	300	...	986	...	269
2396	Cutting, shaping and finishing of stone	325	324	1710	1548	551	481
2399	Other non-metallic mineral products n.e.c.	60	51	25792	22710	9099	7999
2410	Basic iron and steel	240	254	15522	13721	4734	4333
2420	Basic precious and other non-ferrous metals	103	99	3268	2509	924	710
243	Casting of metals	152	144	1693	1246	489	367
2431	Casting of iron and steel	60	59	1576	1263	436	343
2432	Casting of non-ferrous metals	92	85	...	...	...	...
251	Struct.metal products, tanks, reservoirs	1129	1122	13754	12281	4180	3866
2511	Structural metal products	971	966	...	...	...	...
2512	Tanks, reservoirs and containers of metal	152	150	...	...	...	...

continued

Sweden

ISIC	Industry	Number of enterprises (number) Note	2006	2007	2008	2009	Number of employees (number) Note	2006	2007	2008	2009	Wages and salaries paid to employees (millions of Swedish Kronor) Note	2006	2007	2008	2009
2513	Steam generators, excl. hot water boilers		...	...	6	6		...	...	...	...		...	...	...	...
2520	Weapons and ammunition		...	...	78	78		...	...	2599	2574		...	...	1038	1048
259	Other metal products;metal working services		...	...	10252	10116		...	...	65532	55976		...	...	19439	16789
2591	Forging,pressing,stamping,roll-forming of metal		...	...	767	742		...	...	2253	2040		...	...	644	585
2592	Treatment and coating of metals; machining		...	...	7273	7201		...	...	34856	29303		...	...	9747	8193
2593	Cutlery, hand tools and general hardware		...	...	875	830		...	...	13808	12421		...	...	4666	4271
2599	Other fabricated metal products n.e.c.		...	...	1337	1343		...	...	14615	12212		...	...	4382	3740
2610	Electronic components and boards		...	...	429	404		...	...	4083	4003		...	...	1261	1247
2620	Computers and peripheral equipment		...	...	224	205		...	...	1880	1585		...	...	691	579
2630	Communication equipment		...	...	295	281		...	...	...	...		...	...	...	...
2640	Consumer electronics		...	...	181	163		...	...	961	788		...	...	176	253
265	Measuring,testing equipment; watches, etc.		...	...	511	527		...	...	9805	9610		...	...	4153	3907
2651	Measuring/testing/navigating equipment,etc.		...	...	489	504		...	...	9632	9437		...	...	4105	3856
2652	Watches and clocks		...	...	22	23		...	...	173	173		...	...	48	52
2660	Irradiation/electromedical equipment,etc.		...	...	61	63		...	...	...	...		...	...	...	...
2670	Optical instruments and photographic equipment		...	...	101	103		...	...	609	523		...	...	211	182
2680	Magnetic and optical media		...	...	27	25		...	...	13	10		...	...	3	2
2710	Electric motors,generators,transformers,etc.		...	...	404	396		...	...	...	12589		...	...	4671	4910
2720	Batteries and accumulators		...	...	18	17		...	...	...	...		...	...	...	...
273	Wiring and wiring devices		...	...	74	78		...	...	4184	3038		...	...	1431	1026
2731	Fibre optic cables		...	...	9	9		...	...	41	...		...	...	10	...
2732	Other electronic and electric wires and cables		...	...	50	51		...	...	3335	2275		...	...	1171	789
2733	Wiring devices		...	...	15	18		...	...	807	...		...	...	250	...
2740	Electric lighting equipment		...	...	247	254		...	...	...	...		...	...	...	...
2750	Domestic appliances		...	...	99	99		...	...	4996	4398		...	...	1761	1473
2790	Other electrical equipment		...	...	165	170		...	...	3179	3009		...	...	1189	1156
281	General-purpose machinery		...	...	1541	1535		...	...	52118	47423		...	...	17529	16633
2811	Engines/turbines,excl.aircraft,vehicle engines		...	...	63	72		...	...	4706	5132		...	...	1831	2078
2812	Fluid power equipment		...	...	53	54		...	...	4518	3831		...	...	1288	1196
2813	Other pumps, compressors, taps and valves		...	...	142	140		...	...	6326	5891		...	...	2140	2056
2814	Bearings, gears, gearing and driving elements		...	...	91	92		...	...	5087	4485		...	...	1903	1706
2815	Ovens, furnaces and furnace burners		...	...	50	58		...	...	...	...		...	...	...	...
2816	Lifting and handling equipment		...	...	365	361		...	...	11378	10041		...	...	3601	3401
2817	Office machinery, excl.computers,etc.		...	...	34	38		...	...	1100	854		...	...	361	289
2818	Power-driven hand tools		...	...	23	23		...	...	...	...		...	...	...	...
2819	Other general-purpose machinery		...	...	720	697		...	...	15672	14133		...	...	5244	4835
282	Special-purpose machinery		...	...	1698	1691		...	...	32135	27820		...	...	10914	9942
2821	Agricultural and forestry machinery		...	...	202	196		...	...	4128	3983		...	...	1198	1525
2822	Metal-forming machinery and machine tools		...	...	435	426		...	...	3396	3073		...	...	1122	1034
2823	Machinery for metallurgy		...	...	17	17		...	...	688	627		...	...	280	244
2824	Mining, quarrying and construction machinery		...	...	151	156		...	...	10623	8345		...	...	3755	3019

2825	Food/beverage/tobacco processing machinery	…	100	101	…	…	744	1026	…	234	373
2826	Textile/apparel/leather production machinery	…	40	44	…	…	1482	1272	…	442	382
2829	Other special-purpose machinery	…	753	751	…	…	11074	9494	…	3885	3365
2910	Motor vehicles	…	170	180	…	…	77382 c/	38009	…	18590	15795
2920	Automobile bodies, trailers and semi-trailers	…	264	268	…	…	… c/	7206	…	2821	2180
2930	Parts and accessories for motor vehicles	…	625	623	…	…	… c/	18299	…	7675	5376
301	Building of ships and boats	…	717	712	…	…	2853	3317	…	822	1087
3011	Building of ships and floating structures	…	107	116	…	…	470	1524	…	137	564
3012	Building of pleasure and sporting boats	…	610	596	…	…	2384	1793	…	685	524
3020	Railway locomotives and rolling stock	…	27	30	…	…	902	1862	…	337	819
3030	Air and spacecraft and related machinery	…	36	38	…	…	…	…	…	…	…
3040	Military fighting vehicles	…	3	2	…	…	1705	1623	…	510	513
309	Transport equipment n.e.c.	…	149	146	…	…	…	…	…	…	…
3091	Motorcycles	…	40	40	…	…	1240	1227	…	361	381
3092	Bicycles and invalid carriages	…	64	61	…	…	…	…	…	…	…
3099	Other transport equipment n.e.c.	…	45	45	…	…	16759	15236	…	4832	4409
3100	Furniture	…	2273	2280	…	…	468	452	…	109	108
321	Jewellery, bijouterie and related articles	…	1219	1275	…	…	…	…	…	…	…
3211	Jewellery and related articles	…	1006	1055	…	…	151	143	…	36	36
3212	Imitation jewellery and related articles	…	213	220	…	…	730	754	…	211	225
3220	Musical instruments	…	232	223	…	…	168	173	…	48	44
3230	Sports goods	…	294	295	…	…	9884	9925	…	3447	3705
3240	Games and toys	…	218	212	…	…	2022	2005	…	574	569
3250	Medical and dental instruments and supplies	…	1180	1176	…	…	18482	16508	…	6283	5496
3290	Other manufacturing n.e.c.	…	1013	1038	…	…	456	600	…	131	191
331	Repair of fabricated metal products/machinery	…	4429	4580	…	…	8873	8838	…	2896	2887
3311	Repair of fabricated metal products	…	167	165	…	…	147	391	…	39	139
3312	Repair of machinery	…	2835	2956	…	…	914	634	…	305	208
3313	Repair of electronic and optical equipment	…	112	121	…	…	7692	5715	…	2802	1982
3314	Repair of electrical equipment	…	155	145	…	…	400	331	…	110	88
3315	Repair of transport equip., excl. motor vehicles	…	1102	1132	…	…	3228	2969	…	1131	1085
3319	Repair of other equipment	…	58	61	…	…	…	…	…	…	…
3320	Installation of industrial machinery/equipment	…	567	577	…	…	…	…	…	…	…
C	Total manufacturing	…	54347	53976	…	…	661850	613099	…	234212	216199

a/ 1101 includes 1102, 1103 and 1104.
b/ 1910 includes 1920.
c/ 2910 includes 2920 and 2930.

Sweden

ISIC	Industry	Note	Output (millions of Swedish Kronor) 2006	2007	2008	2009	Note	Value added at factor values (millions of Swedish Kronor) 2006	2007	2008	2009	Note	Gross fixed capital formation (millions of Swedish Kronor) 2008	2009
1010	Processing/preserving of meat		...	...	31657	32389		...	...	5355	5961		804	694
1020	Processing/preserving of fish, etc.		...	...	...	4500		...	...	...	1051		...	121
1030	Processing/preserving of fruit,vegetables		...	...	8768	9057		...	...	2289	2398		557	396
1040	Vegetable and animal oils and fats		...	...	...	...		...	...	...	...		...	...
1050	Dairy products		...	...	24052	21999		...	...	4103	4432		654	650
106	Grain mill products,starches and starch products		...	...	6024	5906		...	...	1495	1588		217	282
1061	Grain mill products		...	...	4802	5205		...	...	1289	1461		182	205
1062	Starches and starch products		...	...	1222	702		...	...	206	126		36	76
107	Other food products		...	...	38434	38242		...	...	12156	12214		1692	1732
1071	Bakery products		...	...	16075	15710		...	...	6405	6222		964	741
1072	Sugar		...	...	...	...		...	...	...	...		...	...
1073	Cocoa, chocolate and sugar confectionery		...	...	6640	6264		...	...	1681	1790		248	421
1074	Macaroni, noodles, couscous, etc.		...	...	28	18		...	...	11	6		-	2
1075	Prepared meals and dishes		...	...	2490	2425		...	...	804	828		92	67
1079	Other food products n.e.c.		...	...	...	...		...	...	...	...		...	...
1080	Prepared animal feeds		...	...	...	...		...	...	...	...		...	...
1101	Distilling, rectifying and blending of spirits		...	...	..a/	..a/		...	...	..a/	..a/		..a/	..a/
1102	Wines		...	...	16119a/	16154a/		...	...	4196a/	4636a/		689a/	424a/
1103	Malt liquors and malt		...	...	..a/	..a/		...	...	..a/	..a/		..a/	..a/
1104	Soft drinks,mineral waters,other bottled waters		...	...	..a/	..a/		...	...	..a/	..a/		..a/	..a/
1200	Tobacco products		...	...	74636	92519		...	...	36737	54464		2573	2108
131	Spinning, weaving and finishing of textiles		...	...	1324	1233		...	...	436	438		33	65
1311	Preparation and spinning of textile fibres		...	...	51	45		...	...	16	15		1	-
1312	Weaving of textiles		...	...	703	665		...	...	188	227		18	52
1313	Finishing of textiles		...	...	570	524		...	...	231	195		13	13
139	Other textiles		...	...	6556	5472		...	...	2482	2038		705	174
1391	Knitted and crocheted fabrics		...	...	712	547		...	...	252	159		12	2
1392	Made-up textile articles, except apparel		...	...	2056	1734		...	...	786	646		99	35
1393	Carpets and rugs		...	...	324	311		...	...	111	116		6	11
1394	Cordage, rope, twine and netting		...	...	...	...		...	...	...	...		...	...
1399	Other textiles n.e.c.		...	...	...	...		...	...	...	...		...	...
1410	Wearing apparel, except fur apparel		...	...	2511	2141		...	...	745	584		27	32
1420	Articles of fur		...	...	65	62		...	...	20	19		1	1
1430	Knitted and crocheted apparel		...	...	288	237		...	...	112	88		2	1
151	Leather;luggage,handbags,saddlery,harness;fur		...	...	1004	854		...	...	324	325		20	10
1511	Tanning/dressing of leather; dressing of fur		...	...	...	385		...	...	...	157		...	-
1512	Luggage,handbags,etc.;saddlery/harness		...	...	...	469		...	...	...	168		...	...
1520	Footwear		...	...	381	332		...	...	123	84		17	3
1610	Sawmilling and planing of wood		...	...	45020	41777		...	...	6726	7237		2922	2197
162	Wood products, cork, straw, plaiting materials		...	...	40497	34096		...	...	11816	10135		2622	1232

Code	Description											
1621	Veneer sheets and wood-based panels	⋮	⋮	⋮	⋮	⋮	⋮	⋮	⋮	⋮	⋮	⋮
1622	Builders' carpentry and joinery	⋮	⋮	4104	3406	⋮	⋮	1386	1071	⋮	⋮	212	138
1623	Wooden containers	⋮	⋮	4689	5027	⋮	⋮	1189	1208	⋮	⋮	992	373
1629	Other wood products;articles of cork,straw	⋮	⋮	⋮	⋮	⋮	⋮	⋮	⋮	⋮	⋮	⋮	⋮
1701	Pulp, paper and paperboard	⋮	⋮	105164	97238	⋮	⋮	23713	24389	⋮	⋮	6724	5221
1702	Corrugated paper and paperboard	⋮	⋮	15495	9463	⋮	⋮	5678	2898	⋮	⋮	587	445
1709	Other articles of paper and paperboard	⋮	⋮	12690	12816	⋮	⋮	3744	4069	⋮	⋮	525	517
181	Printing and service activities related to printing	⋮	⋮	27310	25080	⋮	⋮	9770	8639	⋮	⋮	1179	1066
1811	Printing	⋮	⋮	21779	20112	⋮	⋮	7328	6580	⋮	⋮	917	861
1812	Service activities related to printing	⋮	⋮	5530	4969	⋮	⋮	2433	2060	⋮	⋮	261	205
1820	Reproduction of recorded media	⋮	⋮	316	204	⋮	⋮	103	73	⋮	⋮	5	11
1910	Coke oven products	⋮	⋮	14359b/	15290b/	⋮	⋮	5090b/	4101b/	⋮	⋮	1312b/	1559b/
1920	Refined petroleum products	⋮	⋮	..b/	..b/	⋮	⋮	..b/	..b/	⋮	⋮	..b/	..b/
201	Basic chemicals,fertilizers, etc.	⋮	⋮	51559	46292	⋮	⋮	12840	12666	⋮	⋮	5210	3979
2011	Basic chemicals	⋮	⋮	⋮	⋮	⋮	⋮	⋮	⋮	⋮	⋮	⋮	⋮
2012	Fertilizers and nitrogen compounds	⋮	⋮	⋮	2227	⋮	⋮	⋮	629	⋮	⋮	⋮	116
2013	Plastics and synthetic rubber in primary forms	⋮	⋮	24635	24888	⋮	⋮	8035	7959	⋮	⋮	707	611
202	Other chemical products	⋮	⋮	⋮	⋮	⋮	⋮	⋮	⋮	⋮	⋮	⋮	⋮
2021	Pesticides and other agrochemical products	⋮	⋮	73	61	⋮	⋮	19	17	⋮	⋮	1	10
2022	Paints,varnishes;printing ink and mastics	⋮	⋮	11090	10333	⋮	⋮	3108	2913	⋮	⋮	216	139
2023	Soap,cleaning and cosmetic preparations	⋮	⋮	4558	4641	⋮	⋮	1404	1004	⋮	⋮	150	158
2029	Other chemical products n.e.c.	⋮	⋮	8914	9853	⋮	⋮	3505	4026	⋮	⋮	339	304
2030	Man-made fibres	⋮	⋮	10	13	⋮	⋮	6	6	⋮	⋮	-	⋮
2100	Pharmaceuticals,medicinal chemicals, etc.	⋮	⋮	74636	92519	⋮	⋮	36737	54464	⋮	⋮	2573	2108
221	Rubber products	⋮	⋮	10442	8749	⋮	⋮	3281	2663	⋮	⋮	396	536
2211	Rubber tyres and tubes	⋮	⋮	713	644	⋮	⋮	237	222	⋮	⋮	32	30
2219	Other rubber products	⋮	⋮	9729	8106	⋮	⋮	3044	2441	⋮	⋮	364	507
2220	Plastics products	⋮	⋮	30236	27219	⋮	⋮	9900	8874	⋮	⋮	1521	1114
2310	Glass and glass products	⋮	⋮	31711	26985	⋮	⋮	10423	8660	⋮	⋮	1717	1668
239	Non-metallic mineral products n.e.c.	⋮	⋮	⋮	⋮	⋮	⋮	⋮	⋮	⋮	⋮	⋮	⋮
2391	Refractory products	⋮	⋮	1129	874	⋮	⋮	418	339	⋮	⋮	26	7
2392	Clay building materials	⋮	⋮	⋮	⋮	⋮	⋮	⋮	⋮	⋮	⋮	⋮	⋮
2393	Other porcelain and ceramic products	⋮	⋮	⋮	⋮	⋮	⋮	⋮	⋮	⋮	⋮	⋮	⋮
2394	Cement, lime and plaster	⋮	⋮	⋮	⋮	⋮	⋮	⋮	⋮	⋮	⋮	⋮	⋮
2395	Articles of concrete, cement and plaster	⋮	⋮	4249	1287	⋮	⋮	1453	538	⋮	⋮	121	69
2396	Cutting, shaping and finishing of stone	⋮	⋮	⋮	3289	⋮	⋮	⋮	1049	⋮	⋮	⋮	92
2399	Other non-metallic mineral products n.e.c.	⋮	⋮	⋮	⋮	⋮	⋮	⋮	⋮	⋮	⋮	⋮	⋮
2410	Basic iron and steel	⋮	⋮	111995	68215	⋮	⋮	21089	9546	⋮	⋮	4963	4045
2420	Basic precious and other non-ferrous metals	⋮	⋮	4639	2772	⋮	⋮	1493	934	⋮	⋮	265	114
243	Casting of metals	⋮	⋮	⋮	⋮	⋮	⋮	⋮	⋮	⋮	⋮	⋮	⋮
2431	Casting of iron and steel	⋮	⋮	2513	1508	⋮	⋮	808	526	⋮	⋮	184	75
2432	Casting of non-ferrous metals	⋮	⋮	2127	1290	⋮	⋮	686	409	⋮	⋮	83	38
251	Struct.metal products, tanks, reservoirs	⋮	⋮	27078	22051	⋮	⋮	9161	7517	⋮	⋮	744	779
2511	Structural metal products	⋮	⋮	24006	19643	⋮	⋮	8136	6793	⋮	⋮	691	716
2512	Tanks, reservoirs and containers of metal	⋮	⋮	⋮	⋮	⋮	⋮	⋮	⋮	⋮	⋮	⋮	⋮

continued

Sweden

ISIC	Industry	Output Note	Output 2006	Output 2007	Output 2008	Output 2009	VA Note	VA 2006	VA 2007	VA 2008	VA 2009	GFCF Note	GFCF 2008	GFCF 2009
			(millions of Swedish Kronor)					(millions of Swedish Kronor)					(millions of Swedish Kronor)	
2513	Steam generators, excl. hot water boilers		:	:	5534	5723		:	:	2161	2177		68	87
2520	Weapons and ammunition		:	:				:	:					
259	Other metal products;metal working services		:	:	102255	77838		:	:	38488	28604		5537	3810
2591	Forging,pressing,stamping,roll-forming of metal		:	:	3965	2814		:	:	1261	868		144	211
2592	Treatment and coating of metals; machining		:	:	46997	35259		:	:	18878	13629		2610	1899
2593	Cutlery, hand tools and general hardware		:	:	23385	18039		:	:	9276	7530		1883	1029
2599	Other fabricated metal products n.e.c.		:	:	27907	21727		:	:	9074	6577		901	671
2610	Electronic components and boards		:	:	8855	8505		:	:	1913	1229		282	270
2620	Computers and peripheral equipment		:	:	3594	2591		:	:	990	920		63	19
2630	Communication equipment		:	:				:	:					
2640	Consumer electronics		:	:	1499	1205		:	:	541	459		51	5
265	Measuring,testing equipment; watches, etc.		:	:	22982	20357		:	:	8323	7728		361	304
2651	Measuring/testing/navigating equipment,etc.		:	:	22747	19996		:	:	8240	7638		360	302
2652	Watches and clocks		:	:	236	362		:	:	83	89		1	2
2660	Irradiation/electromedical equipment,etc.		:	:				:	:					
2670	Optical instruments and photographic equipment		:	:				:	:					
2680	Magnetic and optical media		:	:	1267	988		:	:	382	359		34	11
2710	Electric motors,generators,transformers,etc.		:	:	37	15		:	:	10	1		-	:
2720	Batteries and accumulators		:	:	30920	32644		:	:	9994	10418		466	370
273	Wiring and wiring devices		:	:				:	:					
2731	Fibre optic cables		:	:	13776	8866		:	:	3522	1731		311	261
2732	Other electronic and electric wires and cables		:	:	24	:		:	:	13	:		-	:
2733	Wiring devices		:	:	12384	7734		:	:	3065	1445		283	236
2740	Electric lighting equipment		:	:	1367	:		:	:	442	:		27	:
2750	Domestic appliances		:	:				:	:					
2790	Other electrical equipment		:	:	8052	5851		:	:	2782	1717		248	106
281	General-purpose machinery		:	:	7358	6871		:	:	2728	2175		86	68
2811	Engines/turbines,excl.aircraft,vehicle engines		:	:	119378	95471		:	:	39352	32274		3145	2462
2812	Fluid power equipment		:	:	17204	16580		:	:	4303	3940		370	476
2813	Other pumps, compressors, taps and valves		:	:	8036	5801		:	:	2899	2049		164	218
2814	Bearings, gears, gearing and driving elements		:	:	12354	11340		:	:	4933	4739		396	331
2815	Ovens, furnaces and furnace burners		:	:	9001	6641		:	:	3816	3429		445	174
2816	Lifting and handling equipment		:	:				:	:					
2817	Office machinery, excl.computers,etc.		:	:	27149	20221		:	:	7112	5756		562	416
2818	Power-driven hand tools		:	:	2568	1616		:	:	798	433		26	23
2819	Other general-purpose machinery		:	:	33142	27187		:	:	11084	9625		889	602
282	Special-purpose machinery		:	:	87093	56422		:	:	22566	10227		2961	1434
2821	Agricultural and forestry machinery		:	:	9865	7547		:	:	3194	2412		316	188
2822	Metal-forming machinery and machine tools		:	:	5931	4805		:	:	2100	1709		169	132
2823	Machinery for metallurgy		:	:	1706	1321		:	:	521	371		82	30
2824	Mining, quarrying and construction machinery		:	:	41685	19510		:	:	8637	29		1752	708

Code	Description						
2825	Food/beverage/tobacco processing machinery	1171	1943	426	342	18	45
2826	Textile/apparel/leather production machinery	2098	1579	779	468	65	44
2829	Other special-purpose machinery	24635	19715	6909	4899	558	288
2910	Motor vehicles	201721	123584	31834	11736	6989	6036
2920	Automobile bodies, trailers and semi-trailers	17944	11717	5279	4094	1367	870
2930	Parts and accessories for motor vehicles	56074	30786	13790	8228	1580	1534
301	Building of ships and boats	4535	4900	1224	1333	263	202
3011	Building of ships and floating structures	887	2245	187	595	62	52
3012	Building of pleasure and sporting boats	3648	2655	1036	738	202	150
3020	Railway locomotives and rolling stock	2260	5453	651	1650	37	47
3030	Air and spacecraft and related machinery	...	...	...	...	...	...
3040	Military fighting vehicles	...	...	...	...	...	...
309	Transport equipment n.e.c.	3573	3297	1096	1079	61	36
3091	Motorcycles	...	...	...	...	...	...
3092	Bicycles and invalid carriages	2743	2670	808	812	43	25
3099	Other transport equipment n.e.c.	...	...	...	...	...	...
3100	Furniture	27292	23372	9193	7471	888	924
321	Jewellery, bijouterie and related articles	787	645	272	272	25	16
3211	Jewellery and related articles	...	...	...	...	...	...
3212	Imitation jewellery and related articles	...	...	...	...	...	...
3220	Musical instruments	189	207	81	82	3	2
3230	Sports goods	1157	1224	470	441	34	23
3240	Games and toys	241	204	94	71	12	10
3250	Medical and dental instruments and supplies	20158	22237	8394	9157	687	552
3290	Other manufacturing n.e.c.	3251	3109	1222	1167	208	134
331	Repair of fabricated metal products/machinery	31132	27873	11144	9133	810	1046
3311	Repair of fabricated metal products	1249	1584	256	371	21	20
3312	Repair of machinery	12735	12535	5189	3921	398	448
3313	Repair of electronic and optical equipment	142	508	72	231	4	6
3314	Repair of electrical equipment	1325	1048	527	399	29	17
3315	Repair of transport equip., excl. motor vehicles	15282	11932	4910	4087	354	531
3319	Repair of other equipment	398	268	188	117	4	23
3320	Installation of industrial machinery/equipment	5232	4926	1967	1733	89	66
C	Total manufacturing	1844206	1561690	520007	469809	73735	57905

a/ 1101 includes 1102, 1103 and 1104.
b/ 1910 includes 1920.

Sweden

Index numbers of industrial production

ISIC Revision 4

ISIC	Industry	Note	1999	2000	2001	2002	2003	2004	2005	2006	2007	2008	2009	2010
									(2005=100)					
10	Food products		94	102	105	101	98	100	100	100	99	102	104	102
11	Beverages		...	104	104	101	98	98	100	105	111	109	102	101
12	Tobacco products		...	...	...	...	...	...	...	...	...	...	...	...
13	Textiles		...	...	...	...	...	...	...	...	...	...	...	...
14	Wearing apparel		...	...	...	...	...	...	...	...	...	...	...	...
15	Leather and related products		...	...	...	...	...	...	...	...	...	...	...	...
16	Wood/wood products/cork,excl. furniture		99	92	92	91	93	97	100	101	108	102	89	88
17	Paper and paper products		98	94	93	97	99	103	100	104	105	102	96	102
18	Printing and reproduction of recorded media		...	112	98	102	100	98	100	104	103	97	95	105
19	Coke and refined petroleum products		...	107	103	94	98	104	100	100	89	105	102	100
20	Chemicals and chemical products		100	97	93	91	90	97	100	106	106	104	90	99
21	Pharmaceuticals,medicinal chemicals, etc.		95	62	74	83	95	101	100	111	89	83	81	84
22	Rubber and plastics products		92	113	105	100	98	100	100	103	114	107	89	103
23	Other non-metallic mineral products		99	98	102	96	97	100	100	106	114	120	94	97
24	Basic metals		84	88	94	99	98	104	100	96	97	91	62	74
25	Fabricated metal products, except machinery		88	109	105	100	99	97	100	104	111	106	76	89
26	Computer, electronic and optical products		91	87	81	73	71	85	100	110	122	125	111	124
27	Electrical equipment		88	109	103	102	103	102	100	103	105	100	85	85
28	Machinery and equipment n.e.c.		99	87	85	87	92	96	100	110	122	121	78	86
29	Motor vehicles, trailers and semi-trailers		97	78	75	78	89	98	100	104	115	107	54	74
30	Other transport equipment		99	112	107	107	100	106	100	102	100	93	73	70
31	Furniture		95	108	102	99	100	98	100	102	109	87	72	77
32	Other manufacturing		94	92	91	101	91	99	100	102	110	110	109	117
33	Repair and installation of machinery/equipment		99	98	95	98	96	101	100	105	110	108	102	101
C	Total manufacturing		94	91	90	91	93	98	100	105	108	105	84	92

Syrian Arab Republic

Supplier of information:
Central Bureau of Statistics, Damascus.

Basic source of data:
Annual sample survey; administrative source.

Major deviations from ISIC (Revision 3):
None reported.

Reference period:
Fiscal year.

Scope:
All reported establishments.

Method of data collection:
Mail questionnaire for public sector; direct interview in the field for private sector.

Type of enumeration:
Complete enumeration; sample survey.

Adjusted for non-response:
No.

Concepts and definitions of variables:
Wages and salaries excludes housing and family allowance paid directly by the employer and payments in kind; it includes employers' contributions paid to social security, pension and insurance schemes as well as the benefits received by employees under these schemes and severance and termination pay.

Related national publications:
None reported.

Syrian Arab Republic

ISIC	Industry	Number of establishments (number)					Number of employees (number)						Wages and salaries paid to employees (millions of Syrian Pounds)				
		Note	2007	2008	2009	2010	Note	2007	2008	2009	2010a/	Note	2007	2008	2009	2010a/
15	Food and beverages		10700	10943	10964	...		86706	84889	79921	22058		8226	9049	9414	5431
16	Tobacco products		442	413	414	...		11698	11677	11767	10317		2067	2236	2305	2397
17	Textiles		7640	7689	7704	...		73774	72652	62385	24158		8428	9359	8757	5997
18	Wearing apparel, fur		15424	15480	15510	...		69911	70198	62402	1866		4445	5243	4824	478
19	Leather, leather products and footwear		3142	3109	3115	...		14869	15372	15115	879		1122	1385	1382	264
20	Wood products (excl. furniture)		10211	10257	10277	...		25692	26114	25129	94		803	983	948	33
21	Paper and paper products		385	374	375	...		3392	3319	3622	512		509	401	468	142
22	Printing and publishing		1441	1420	1423	...		6000	6011	7590	...		523	592	584	...
23	Coke,refined petroleum products,nuclear fuel		70	49	50	...		8310	8234	8149	7440		2764	3227	3270	3331
24	Chemicals and chemical products		974	984	986	...		16233	18212	19339	5648		2616	2932	3283	1918
25	Rubber and plastics products		2003	2034	2038	...		11697	12319	12710	1184		1254	1306	1442	412
26	Non-metallic mineral products		8500	8686	8703	...		55958	55954	51142	14823		6914	8061	8671	4966
27	Basic metals		1778	1772	1775	...		7720	8289	9869	1294		930	971	1084	422
28	Fabricated metal products		21068	21237	21278	...		56061	58090	56866	473		2350	2997	3755	124
29	Machinery and equipment n.e.c.		922	889	891	...		9474	9915	9302	1589		1265	1373	1413	543
30	Office, accounting and computing machinery		42	9	10	...		...	...	...	...		...	...	...	...
31	Electrical machinery and apparatus		254	224	225	...		2723	2733	2422	1284		453	532	510	432
32	Radio,television and communication equipment		123	90	93	...		1262	1156	977	707		212	221	216	200
33	Medical, precision and optical instruments		686	668	669	...		1099	1119	1355	...		39	49	44	...
34	Motor vehicles, trailers, semi-trailers		111	81	81	...		561	1381	640	...		39	214	98	...
35	Other transport equipment		69	39	43	...		192	290	300	...		15	24	23	...
36	Furniture; manufacturing n.e.c.		12789	12620	12809	...		32087	32577	35801	171		1218	1484	1831	43
37	Recycling		179	75	76	...		220	267	306	...		16	24	27	...
D	Total manufacturing		98953	99142	99509	...		495639	500768	477109	94497		46208	52663	54349	27133

a/ For public sector only.

Syrian Arab Republic

Index numbers of industrial production

ISIC Revision 3

(2005=100)

ISIC	Industry	Note	1999	2000	2001	2002	2003	2004	2005	2006	2007	2008	2009	2010
15	Food and beverages		91	89	92	102	95	105	100	106	107	119	113	118
16	Tobacco products		90	93	100	109	114	110	100	112	116	109	135	139
17	Textiles		67	72	79	84	87	100	100	102	93	89	93	95
18	Wearing apparel, fur		145	152	153	171	129	102	100	88	100	68	73	86
19	Leather, leather products and footwear		…	…	…	…	…	…	…	…	…	…	…	…
20	Wood products (excl. furniture)		221	125	155	115	135	114	100	129	114	130	54	39
21	Paper and paper products		191	185	165	119	94	94	100	80	65	63	33	13
22	Printing and publishing		…	…	…	…	…	…	…	…	…	…	…	…
23	Coke,refined petroleum products,nuclear fuel		99	97	102	103	84	101	100	104	105	95	91	87
24	Chemicals and chemical products		95	93	96	119	99	105	100	121	114	99	100	96
25	Rubber and plastics products		92	96	140	115	114	133	100	74	68	78	72	92
26	Non-metallic mineral products		98	90	100	98	97	94	100	92	93	94	83	92
27	Basic metals		113	106	116	101	98	89	100	96	84	70	65	60
28	Fabricated metal products		99	61	140	99	73	113	100	108	80	80	84	97
29	Machinery and equipment n.e.c.		234	108	100	122	104	78	100	97	97	120	84	71
30	Office, accounting and computing machinery		…	…	…	…	…	…	…	…	…	…	…	…
31	Electrical machinery and apparatus		67	67	98	101	101	103	100	84	82	77	82	109
32	Radio,television and communication equipment		344	417	333	396	279	142	100	146	88	83	67	133
33	Medical, precision and optical instruments		…	…	…	…	…	…	…	…	…	…	…	…
34	Motor vehicles, trailers, semi-trailers		…	…	…	…	…	…	…	…	…	…	…	…
35	Other transport equipment		…	…	…	…	…	…	…	…	…	…	…	…
36	Furniture; manufacturing n.e.c.		470	114	92	89	64	83	100	148	144	170	216	249
37	Recycling		…	…	…	…	…	…	…	…	…	…	…	…
D	Total manufacturing		94	93	99	103	92	102	100	104	104	99	98	97

The former Yugoslav Republic of Macedonia

Supplier of information:
State Statistical Office of the Republic of Macedonia, Skopje.

Basic source of data:
Administrative source.

Major deviations from ISIC (Revision 3):
None reported.

Reference period:
Calendar year.

Scope:
All establishments.

Method of data collection:
Not reported.

Type of enumeration:
Not reported.

Adjusted for non-response:
Not reported.

Concepts and definitions of variables:
Wages and salaries paid to employees includes employers' contributions (in respect of their employees) paid to social security, pension and insurance schemes as well as the benefits received by employees under these schemes and severance and termination pay. It excludes housing and family allowances paid directly by the employer.
Output excludes value of industrial work done or industrial services rendered to others, value of goods shipped in the same condition as received less the amount paid for these goods and value of fixed assets produced by the unit for its own use. It is valued at basic prices.
Value added is valued at basic prices.

Related national publications:
None reported.

The former Yugoslav Republic of Macedonia

		Number of establishments (number)					Number of employees (number)					Wages and salaries paid to employees (millions of Macedonia Denars)				
ISIC	**Industry**	**Note**	**2007**	**2008**	**2009**	**2010**	**Note**	**2007**	**2008**	**2009**	**2010**	**Note**	**2007**	**2008**	**2009**	**2010**
151	Processed meat,fish,fruit,vegetables,fats		190	179	223	242		2824	2991	3136	3380		853.7	897.7	957.6	1086.7
1511	Processing/preserving of meat		88	78	112	115		922	979	1237	1313		253.7	262.8	360.1	408.3
1512	Processing/preserving of fish		2	3	3	1		137	270	326	280		36.5	68.5	85.5	71.1
1513	Processing/preserving of fruit & vegetables		90	89	98	116		1207	1283	1261	1349		408.9	423.9	411.6	464.4
1514	Vegetable and animal oils and fats		10	9	10	10		558	459	311	438		154.5	142.4	100.4	142.9
1520	Dairy products		84	77	103	102		999	1093	1161	1292		288.7	387.3	416.8	552.0
153	Grain mill products; starches; animal feeds		98	96	100	98		1687	1432	1265	1080		426.3	399.3	399.8	361.8
1531	Grain mill products		75	76	77	73		1611	1347	920	761		404.1	378.5	285.0	258.0
1532	Starches and starch products		1	1	1	1		4	4	2	3		1.1	0.9	0.6	0.5
1533	Prepared animal feeds		22	19	22	24		72	81	343	315		21.1	19.9	114.2	103.2
154	Other food products		615	679	770	891		6459	7530	7796	8604		1405.0	1557.9	1984.2	2252.6
1541	Bakery products		483	542	638	753		4139	4995	4869	5766		719.4	848.5	1085.1	1372.4
1542	Sugar		1	1	2	2		225	204	201	160		69.1	38.7	43.4	44.0
1543	Cocoa, chocolate and sugar confectionery		39	38	42	41		1154	1253	1910	1852		368.9	400.9	639.4	615.1
1544	Macaroni, noodles & similar products		22	25	26	26		233	217	205	182		20.6	20.8	28.6	25.0
1549	Other food products n.e.c.		70	73	62	69		707	861	612	643		227.0	248.9	187.7	196.0
155	Beverages		90	106	100	110		1843	1928	2146	2493		755.6	833.2	1018.4	1692.1
1551	Distilling, rectifying & blending of spirits		5	5	5	4		81	82	90	67		18.5	13.1	32.2	5.2
1552	Wines		40	51	57	60		747	767	842	959		236.9	277.3	347.9	661.6
1553	Malt liquors and malt		4	2	2	2		697	605	206	225		408.9	388.8	103.0	105.3
1554	Soft drinks; mineral waters		41	48	36	44		318	474	1007	1242		91.4	154.0	535.3	920.0
1600	Tobacco products		22	22	18	15		3672	3301	2926	3529		920.3	1061.7	1410.9	2355.0
171	Spinning, weaving and finishing of textiles		63	70	66	72		1581	1275	1562	1306		271.5	241.3	283.6	230.1
1711	Textile fibre preparation; textile weaving		31	33	26	25		1410	1113	1225	937		250.3	214.9	240.9	164.7
1712	Finishing of textiles		32	37	40	47		171	163	337	369		21.2	26.4	42.6	65.4
172	Other textiles		213	224	155	154		3276	2979	1517	1412		567.8	446.4	234.2	234.4
1721	Made-up textile articles, except apparel		127	138	82	87		2346	2255	974	862		465.3	345.5	170.6	157.2
1722	Carpets and rugs		13	12	8	7		93	69	52	34		13.4	10.1	5.0	4.5
1723	Cordage, rope, twine and netting		5	6	6	6		35	19	18	13		1.8	1.2	1.2	1.2
1729	Other textiles n.e.c.		68	68	59	54		802	636	473	503		87.3	89.6	57.4	71.6
1730	Knitted and crocheted fabrics and articles		82	86	54	54		348	610	467	580		63.9	60.4	68.1	96.8
1810	Wearing apparel, except fur apparel		1578	1580	1141	1051		40025	41602	37658	34229		6072.1	6880.9	5909.5	6044.5
1820	Dressing & dyeing of fur; processing of fur		14	15	9	13		481	439	539	567		72.2	80.5	77.8	94.5
191	Tanning, dressing and processing of leather		266	241	62	59		862	852	434	259		106.2	112.1	42.6	33.5
1911	Tanning and dressing of leather		116	104	26	27		268	338	144	143		37.0	49.1	30.6	23.9
1912	Luggage, handbags, etc.; saddlery & harness		150	137	36	32		594	514	290	116		69.1	63.0	12.1	9.6
1920	Footwear		396	388	207	172		5100	5471	4522	4158		676.8	849.5	727.8	755.9
2010	Sawmilling and planing of wood		268	271	178	156		1034	1283	915	775		215.1	303.6	193.9	123.3
202	Products of wood, cork, straw, etc.		463	471	415	392		2282	2463	2672	2009		381.4	484.9	503.8	326.5
2021	Veneer sheets, plywood, particle board, etc.		10	11	20	21		51	64	272	235		19.8	26.5	73.9	51.0
2022	Builders' carpentry and joinery		204	214	216	191		1093	1230	1298	792		180.6	227.3	210.0	115.7
2023	Wooden containers		137	130	81	66		512	526	489	328		92.4	119.7	124.0	62.5
2029	Other wood products; articles of cork/straw		112	116	98	114		626	644	613	654		88.7	111.4	96.0	97.2
210	Paper and paper products		198	205	208	207		1829	1742	1848	1833		464.4	469.4	631.2	690.8
2101	Pulp, paper and paperboard		15	10	23	14		138	108	239	160		34.7	28.3	94.1	48.3
2102	Corrugated paper and paperboard		88	95	87	80		1190	1225	1105	1033		317.0	341.8	394.0	461.6
2109	Other articles of paper and paperboard		95	100	98	113		501	409	504	639		112.8	99.3	143.0	180.9
221	Publishing		260	252	248	239		1250	1239	974	1118		657.8	589.6	412.9	489.6
2211	Publishing of books and other publications		72	74	72	77		296	312	277	316		195.0	148.5	119.0	132.2
2212	Publishing of newspapers, journals, etc.		120	114	102	93		775	714	487	623		393.8	361.8	235.3	278.5
2213	Publishing of recorded media		26	24	25	21		50	67	46	26		18.8	22.5	13.1	4.7
2219	Other publishing		42	40	49	48		130	145	165	153		50.3	56.8	45.5	74.2

Code	Industry											
222	Printing and related service activities	384	397	429	449	2297	2476	2713	2772	812.6	900.2	970.2	992.2
2221	Printing	320	324	349	363	2004	2126	2279	2171	697.5	766.5	831.0	790.7
2222	Service activities related to printing	64	73	80	86	293	350	434	601	115.0	133.7	139.2	201.5
2230	Reproduction of recorded media	14	16	16	16	22	26	36	40	3.7	4.4	7.3	4.4
2310	Coke oven products	⋯	⋯	⋯	⋯	⋯	⋯	⋯	⋯	⋯	⋯	⋯	⋯
2320	Refined petroleum products	8	10	6	7	937	932	843	783	542.8	582.3	563.0	507.1
2330	Processing of nuclear fuel	⋯	⋯	⋯	⋯	⋯	⋯	⋯	⋯	⋯	⋯	⋯	⋯
241	Basic chemicals	31	28	35	34	358	326	293	325	321.0	324.2	170.4	161.8
2411	Basic chemicals, except fertilizers	23	21	18	20	278	254	202	222	230.7	212.5	130.4	128.3
2412	Fertilizers and nitrogen compounds	3	3	4	6	6	3	8	10	1.1	1.2	4.1	3.4
2413	Plastics in primary forms; synthetic rubber	5	4	13	8	74	69	83	93	89.1	110.4	35.9	30.2
242	Other chemicals	45	50	69	70	1819	1867	2243	2064	1398.6	1351.1	1459.3	1376.7
2421	Pesticides and other agro-chemical products	1	2	2	1	2	3	54	45	0.9	⋯	26.9	18.9
2422	Paints, varnishes, printing ink and mastics	9	12	17	15	105	109	178	149	113.6	96.2	78.3	59.4
2423	Pharmaceuticals, medicinal chemicals, etc.	6	6	5	5	1492	1517	1511	1366	1070.3	1058.5	1121.3	1099.1
2424	Soap, cleaning & cosmetic preparations	17	19	29	31	67	94	349	368	54.0	61.3	146.7	126.9
2429	Other chemical products n.e.c.	12	13	16	17	153	147	151	136	159.8	135.1	86.2	72.3
2430	Man-made fibres	⋯	⋯	⋯	⋯	⋯	⋯	⋯	⋯	⋯	⋯	⋯	⋯
251	Rubber products	73	80	67	75	285	298	217	215	40.1	47.0	38.0	41.9
2511	Rubber tyres and tubes	24	29	20	29	86	88	52	58	11.8	12.3	7.5	8.3
2519	Other rubber products	49	51	47	46	199	210	165	157	28.3	34.7	30.6	33.6
2520	Plastic products	361	375	357	384	3827	4331	3793	3444	717.0	842.3	762.2	735.5
2610	Glass and glass products	19	18	35	30	81	77	121	110	20.3	19.1	27.2	29.2
269	Non-metallic mineral products n.e.c.	144	176	224	229	3596	3656	4065	3159	1461.0	1626.6	1865.9	1401.1
2691	Pottery, china and earthenware	9	12	9	13	279	299	304	322	96.4	96.7	97.6	109.3
2692	Refractory ceramic products	9	9	10	11	387	416	291	304	143.5	177.5	132.7	118.4
2693	Struct.non-refractory clay; ceramic products	16	16	14	14	1574	1514	1242	571	451.0	535.2	448.9	233.5
2694	Cement, lime and plaster	7	8	11	12	701	688	444	369	589.8	599.2	538.6	345.6
2695	Articles of concrete, cement and plaster	36	44	88	93	226	242	1205	984	64.4	78.8	484.1	421.7
2696	Cutting, shaping & finishing of stone	55	72	81	73	257	308	388	392	61.6	77.7	102.1	104.4
2699	Other non-metallic mineral products n.e.c.	12	15	11	13	171	190	191	217	54.3	61.4	61.9	68.2
2710	Basic iron and steel	13	11	21	19	3660	3748	2800	2551	1405.3	1552.8	898.5	1044.8
2720	Basic precious and non-ferrous metals	21	21	20	15	975	988	876	875	560.3	554.1	384.9	401.2
273	Casting of metals	25	25	21	28	1640	1916	1874	1779	662.9	718.5	640.6	637.2
2731	Casting of iron and steel	9	9	8	11	1389	1572	1469	1359	565.7	604.0	528.3	496.5
2732	Casting of non-ferrous metals	16	16	13	17	251	344	405	420	97.2	114.5	112.3	140.7
281	Struct.metal products;tanks;steam generators	298	318	355	356	3405	3033	4125	3187	772.9	715.4	1113.4	963.1
2811	Structural metal products	269	287	326	317	3204	2784	3704	2721	727.0	649.2	1002.7	847.0
2812	Tanks, reservoirs and containers of metal	25	26	24	35	193	238	407	456	42.9	63.3	106.7	111.9
2813	Steam generators	4	5	5	4	8	11	14	10	2.9	2.9	4.0	4.2
289	Other metal products; metal working services	619	645	565	571	4178	4228	3560	4018	850.0	930.3	773.9	937.9
2891	Metal forging/pressing/stamping/roll-forming	61	63	56	48	453	431	386	367	97.0	108.0	70.5	80.0
2892	Treatment & coating of metals	234	255	250	240	1337	1403	1441	1537	244.8	278.1	306.7	340.8
2893	Cutlery, hand tools and general hardware	87	86	66	77	706	582	408	484	150.5	138.1	128.4	125.6
2899	Other fabricated metal products n.e.c.	237	241	193	206	1682	1812	1325	1630	357.7	406.1	268.3	391.5
291	General purpose machinery	90	94	85	94	917	1041	970	1123	258.7	313.7	300.5	352.5
2911	Engines & turbines (not for transport equipment)	6	7	7	8	253	246	239	252	87.1	87.6	102.4	157.3
2912	Pumps, compressors, taps and valves	21	21	21	21	200	231	199	187	51.7	63.8	56.5	43.0
2913	Bearings, gears, gearing & driving elements	9	10	10	8	27	47	49	39	6.6	12.3	11.1	10.0
2914	Ovens, furnaces and furnace burners	2	2	3	2	2	2	5	5	0.4	0.5	0.9	0.4
2915	Lifting and handling equipment	8	9	9	11	29	54	61	174	7.4	12.5	15.0	30.1
2919	Other general purpose machinery	44	45	34	44	406	461	417	469	105.5	136.9	114.6	111.8
292	Special purpose machinery	56	56	72	75	241	328	187	614	56.2	85.4	144.1	166.5
2921	Agricultural and forestry machinery	8	8	11	9	31	36	187	166	6.5	7.1	32.6	35.0
2922	Machine tools	26	26	28	32	98	122	107	143	24.5	42.6	45.3	60.2
2923	Machinery for metallurgy	1	1	4	2	1	⋯	5	7	0.2	3.7	1.2	1.4
2924	Machinery for mining & construction	1	2	1	1	33	33	92	65	9.3	10.5	9.1	9.4
2925	Food/beverage/tobacco processing machinery	6	6	12	11	43	43	128	134	⋯	⋯	32.7	34.0
2926	Machinery for textile, apparel and leather	⋯	⋯	1	1	⋯	⋯	⋯	1	15.8	21.5	⋯	⋯
2927	Weapons and ammunition	⋯	⋯	⋯	⋯	⋯	⋯	⋯	98	⋯	⋯	⋯	-
2929	Other special purpose machinery	14	13	15	18	70	93	98	98	⋯	⋯	23.3	26.4

continued

The former Yugoslav Republic of Macedonia

ISIC Revision 3

ISIC	Industry	Number of establishments (number)					Number of employees (number)					Wages and salaries paid to employees (millions of Macedonia Denars)				
		Note	2007	2008	2009	2010	Note	2007	2008	2009	2010	Note	2007	2008	2009	2010
2930	Domestic appliances n.e.c.		32	35	32	27		655	646	662	709		143.0	141.1	159.4	167.9
3000	Office, accounting and computing machinery		72	73	43	48		525	628	574	341		208.0	231.0	145.9	159.0
3110	Electric motors, generators and transformers		91	90	61	90		652	663	515	764		179.2	197.3	125.7	225.5
3120	Electricity distribution & control apparatus		28	26	26	20		582	653	884	606		157.9	187.7	253.6	161.3
3130	Insulated wire and cable		5	4	6	5		520	496	466	346		136.0	146.2	132.9	76.0
3140	Accumulators, primary cells and batteries		3	2	1	2		234	218	214	190		38.6	68.1	56.7	49.7
3150	Lighting equipment and electric lamps		17	18	13	14		105	115	116	82		26.0	27.8	18.6	18.4
3190	Other electrical equipment n.e.c.		81	78	60	71		771	816	678	670		162.2	228.1	233.4	250.1
3210	Electronic valves, tubes, etc.		27	27	11	11		112	115	60	51		24.1	30.0	23.7	10.9
3220	TV/radio transmitters; line comm. apparatus		28	28	18	16		206	223	84	84		44.3	49.6	20.7	19.9
3230	TV and radio receivers and associated goods		22	19	10	10		62	49	35	28		11.6	12.0	6.8	9.5
331	Medical, measuring, testing appliances, etc.		76	74	49	50		270	271	203	220		111.1	108.0	100.9	122.7
3311	Medical, surgical and orthopaedic equipment		45	44	26	24		158	160	122	139		62.8	63.3	60.1	61.9
3312	Measuring/testing/navigating appliances,etc.		26	25	15	17		91	86	47	49		36.7	31.0	16.0	16.2
3313	Industrial process control equipment		5	5	8	9		21	25	34	32		11.6	13.7	24.8	44.5
3320	Optical instruments & photographic equipment		6	7	5	6		41	45	43	43		15.7	14.4	14.7	17.6
3330	Watches and clocks		...	...	...	...		1	1	2	1		...	...	...	...
3410	Motor vehicles		4	3	10	3		70	169	288	64		14.8	33.9	54.8	21.4
3420	Automobile bodies, trailers & semi-trailers		10	8	7	4		95	12	12	9		9.8	4.0	2.1	3.1
3430	Parts/accessories for automobiles		34	38	25	22		1114	943	603	576		274.4	259.2	162.1	216.5
351	Building and repairing of ships and boats		1	1	1	2		11	1	1	1		0.2	2.5	5.4	0.1
3511	Building and repairing of ships		1	1	1	2		11	1	1	1		0.2	2.5	5.4	0.1
3512	Building/repairing of pleasure/sport. boats															
3520	Railway/tramway locomotives & rolling stock															
3530	Aircraft and spacecraft		2	2	2	2		694	697	562	475		212.9	208.0	192.3	202.8
359	Transport equipment n.e.c.		2	2	1	1		3	3	1	1		1.1	1.2	0.2	0.4
3591	Motorcycles		...	3	5	47		...	50	59	131		...	12.5	14.2	31.5
3592	Bicycles and invalid carriages		3	3	3	4		42	49	57	63		10.1	12.5	13.8	18.5
3599	Other transport equipment n.e.c.		...	...	2	43		...	1	2	68		...	...	0.4	13.0
3610	Furniture		529	567	588	615		3365	3611	3596	4136		606.6	683.0	702.5	692.4
369	Manufacturing n.e.c.		317	345	338	378		1175	1201	1171	1207		134.3	132.0	134.3	205.1
3691	Jewellery and related articles		217	243	239	247		723	773	787	711		80.9	73.5	81.7	119.9
3692	Musical instruments		1	1	5	15		4	3	10	32		0.1	0.1	0.5	10.0
3693	Sports goods		3	3	26	32		3	3	44	54		2.2	0.4	6.4	9.5
3694	Games and toys		6	7	6	5		37	36	31	15		6.1	6.1	4.7	2.7
3699	Other manufacturing n.e.c.		90	91	62	79		408	387	300	395		55.9	52.0	40.9	63.0
3710	Recycling of metal waste and scrap		122	118	90	74		411	415	368	284		81.9	95.8	78.8	69.2
3720	Recycling of non-metal waste and scrap		29	29	16	13		88	134	122	118		15.5	27.4	23.9	30.6
D	Total manufacturing		8642	8879	7852	8010		115595	119675	112000	106820		26712.3	29124.0	28056.2	29934.9

The former Yugoslav Republic of Macedonia

	ISIC Revision 3	Output (millions of Macedonia Denars)					Value added (millions of Macedonia Denars)					Gross fixed capital formation (millions of Macedonia Denars)		
ISIC	Industry	Note	2007	2008	2009	2010	Note	2007	2008	2009	2010	Note	2009	2010
151	Processed meat,fish,fruit,vegetables,fats		7605.7	9561.0	7553.0	9295.6		2333.6	3027.5	2812.6	2220.2		219.2	145.2
1511	Processing/preserving of meat		2233.8	2491.2	3098.7	3221.0		707.3	819.0	1156.6	727.0		43.9	55.9
1512	Processing/preserving of fish		386.5	463.8	431.4	454.2		117.9	163.5	185.3	95.0		...	5.6
1513	Processing/preserving of fruit & vegetables		3337.5	3892.7	3049.9	3295.0		999.4	1208.5	1122.2	960.0		142.2	66.8
1514	Vegetable and animal oils and fats		1647.9	2713.3	973.0	2325.4		509.0	836.6	348.5	438.2		33.1	16.9
1520	Dairy products		3557.6	5373.2	4356.0	5214.5		1072.5	1678.2	1596.7	1368.8		305.6	253.8
153	Grain mill products; starches; animal feeds		3130.5	3891.2	2659.7	2596.7		988.3	1242.3	989.9	645.8		224.8	88.4
1531	Grain mill products		2993.4	3685.5	1649.9	1587.9		943.5	1176.4	625.8	441.1		195.3	71.4
1532	Starches and starch products		2.8	4.2	1.4	1.1		1.6	1.3	0.7	0.9		29.5	17.0
1533	Prepared animal feeds		134.3	201.4	1008.4	1007.7		43.2	64.6	363.4	203.9		...	...
154	Other food products		7556.6	9449.0	10232.8	12272.3		2671.5	3404.3	3972.2	3647.7		274.7	423.2
1541	Bakery products		3397.7	4484.7	4232.3	5717.0		1375.4	1825.9	1823.9	2046.3		110.0	204.2
1542	Sugar		893.5	1075.2	669.5	1268.0		262.2	328.7	244.7	76.6		4.2	-0.6
1543	Cocoa, chocolate and sugar confectionery		1699.6	2141.0	3891.8	3993.4		519.5	670.0	1384.5	1118.3		102.6	167.0
1544	Macaroni, noodles & similar products		141.4	189.8	193.8	146.4		70.5	70.9	73.7	58.3		57.9	52.6
1549	Other food products n.e.c.		1424.4	1558.2	1245.3	1147.4		443.8	508.8	445.3	348.3		...	...
155	Beverages		8150.6	10117.9	10095.9	9959.3		2358.6	3057.5	3509.3	4249.1		1717.8	623.0
1551	Distilling, rectifying & blending of spirits		206.7	248.8	201.6	90.1		63.4	77.5	73.0	37.5		19.8	180.4
1552	Wines		2127.9	3477.0	2978.7	2949.8		631.4	1063.5	1046.6	1343.6		980.5	96.0
1553	Malt liquors and malt		5133.6	5187.8	974.7	1030.6		1450.7	1534.8	327.6	419.8		101.6	346.6
1554	Soft drinks; mineral waters		682.3	1204.2	5940.8	5888.9		213.1	381.7	2062.1	2448.2		615.8	...
1600	Tobacco products		6679.3	7815.1	6443.0	10083.2		2255.1	3015.7	2724.9	4752.4		231.7	278.0
171	Spinning, weaving and finishing of textiles		798.3	987.8	1196.7	1027.2		359.1	387.6	409.9	372.8		11.6	2.9
1711	Textile fibre preparation; textile weaving		680.9	847.7	1058.6	856.2		287.8	328.7	322.5	272.3		10.9	2.5
1712	Finishing of textiles		117.4	140.1	138.1	171.0		71.3	58.9	87.4	100.5		0.7	0.3
172	Other textiles		1780.1	1695.1	928.5	1455.4		660.5	660.4	338.4	452.3		14.1	12.1
1721	Made-up textile articles, except apparel		1459.3	1317.2	643.3	496.2		526.6	525.1	206.2	188.1		12.6	3.3
1722	Carpets and rugs		29.6	19.6	10.1	5.7		12.3	7.4	4.6	3.3		...	8.8
1723	Cordage, rope, twine and netting		16.2	16.6	7.5	10.4		6.1	6.2	3.9	5.6		1.6	...
1729	Other textiles n.e.c.		275.0	341.7	267.6	943.0		115.4	121.7	123.6	255.3		...	...
1730	Knitted and crocheted fabrics and articles		300.9	317.3	315.5	371.2		85.2	126.0	122.9	164.2		4.1	6.0
1810	Wearing apparel, except fur apparel		15672.8	15925.8	12966.7	13625.7		8661.7	9310.7	7964.3	7917.9		310.8	347.4
1820	Dressing & dyeing of fur; processing of fur		273.9	317.4	279.4	321.8		103.3	125.7	105.6	160.1		0.7	0.7
191	Tanning, dressing and processing of leather		355.7	384.5	221.9	177.6		192.2	211.5	107.7	91.4		0.1	35.3
1911	Tanning and dressing of leather		127.2	172.2	161.7	150.9		67.8	95.3	66.3	75.8		0.1	...
1912	Luggage, handbags, etc.; saddlery & harness		228.6	212.3	60.2	26.8		124.4	116.3	41.4	15.6		...	...
1920	Footwear		1945.6	2103.8	1482.2	1631.9		1040.9	1147.4	882.6	861.3		43.3	...
2010	Sawmilling and planing of wood		781.1	1039.6	574.5	512.8		289.3	483.5	267.7	175.1		1.9	9.6
202	Products of wood, cork, straw, etc.		1357.8	1573.6	1606.0	1329.9		507.6	735.5	667.3	485.6		27.8	12.6
2021	Veneer sheets, plywood, particle board, etc.		77.3	87.8	193.5	192.9		43.4	40.9	97.0	63.6		12.6	6.8
2022	Builders' carpentry and joinery		559.9	689.6	649.7	394.1		208.4	321.3	278.5	158.5		19.2	4.0
2023	Wooden containers		419.5	443.1	454.7	348.6		129.2	208.5	146.6	113.0		1.2	1.8
2029	Other wood products; articles of cork/straw		301.1	353.0	308.1	394.3		126.6	164.8	145.2	150.6		7.4	...
210	Paper and paper products		2402.4	2573.0	2643.9	2799.6		875.7	932.5	1024.3	1101.1		81.2	171.0
2101	Pulp, paper and paperboard		236.7	102.2	371.8	183.1		90.7	45.7	126.1	21.0		6.7	0.6
2102	Corrugated paper and paperboard		1609.6	1839.2	1711.2	1832.1		577.2	593.1	664.1	672.4		71.2	167.6
2109	Other articles of paper and paperboard		556.0	631.5	560.9	804.4		207.8	293.6	234.1	407.7		3.3	2.8
221	Publishing		2018.7	1975.3	1205.7	1683.0		844.1	917.9	574.9	783.8		12.8	114.1
2211	Publishing of books and other publications		519.5	471.0	389.1	715.9		203.4	213.2	225.3	374.7		9.4	103.5
2212	Publishing of newspapers, journals, etc.		1269.7	1257.3	599.9	760.2		540.5	584.5	248.0	292.3		...	8.7
2213	Publishing of recorded media		66.2	80.2	50.6	16.6		33.8	40.3	22.8	8.5		3.4	1.9
2219	Other publishing		163.4	166.8	166.0	190.3		66.3	80.0	78.8	108.2		...	...

continued

The former Yugoslav Republic of Macedonia

ISIC	Industry	Output Note	Output (millions of Macedonia Denars) 2007	2008	2009	2010	VA Note	Value added (millions of Macedonia Denars) 2007	2008	2009	2010	GFCF Note	Gross fixed capital formation (millions of Macedonia Denars) 2009	2010
222	Printing and related service activities		3277.7	4079.8	4167.7	4216.8		1318.6	1878.0	1698.1	1614.1		722.5	118.3
2221	Printing		2859.2	3547.4	3703.3	3496.9		1110.7	1617.6	1462.0	1279.4		694.8	75.3
2222	Service activities related to printing		418.5	532.3	464.4	719.9		208.0	260.3	236.1	334.7		27.8	43.0
2230	Reproduction of recorded media		11.7	23.4	23.5	14.9		2.0	11.8	10.6	2.2		…	…
2310	Coke oven products		…	…	…	…		…	…	…	…		…	…
2320	Refined petroleum products		27945.3	36556.1	21191.1	27509.6		3212.3	2060.4	2272.5	940.6		734.3	216.8
2330	Processing of nuclear fuel		…	…	…	…		…	…	…	…		…	…
241	Basic chemicals		1057.2	1173.6	961.6	1040.3		574.8	724.9	418.5	426.9		…	…
2411	Basic chemicals, except fertilizers		892.3	927.9	811.5	818.9		457.3	543.3	355.4	363.6		30.0	30.3
2412	Fertilizers and nitrogen compounds		1.5	2.0	5.6	7.5		0.6	1.6	3.6	5.3		30.0	29.7
2413	Plastics in primary forms; synthetic rubber		163.4	243.7	144.5	213.9		116.9	179.9	59.5	58.0		…	…
242	Other chemicals		5830.0	6135.7	6225.2	6498.2		3172.8	3407.6	3392.5	3614.2		…	…
2421	Pesticides and other agro-chemical products		1.1	…	245.3	131.6		0.9	0.9	69.9	47.8		…	0.6
2422	Paints, varnishes, printing ink and mastics		338.5	291.4	259.2	285.8		130.9	179.8	92.8	114.1		…	…
2423	Pharmaceuticals, medicinal chemicals, etc.		4858.3	5263.1	5017.5	5296.9		2754.8	2844.4	2936.8	3091.5		502.5	153.0
2424	Soap, cleaning & cosmetic preparations		89.7	103.9	332.1	390.8		60.8	82.8	155.1	206.6		4.5	3.4
2429	Other chemical products n.e.c.		542.3	477.4	371.0	393.1		225.2	300.6	138.0	154.1		2.2	…
2430	Man-made fibres		…	…	…	…		…	…	…	…		…	…
251	Rubber products		187.7	216.5	164.9	182.5		72.5	81.4	78.1	90.3		…	…
2511	Rubber tyres and tubes		65.8	76.0	33.6	46.6		24.5	28.7	12.5	19.5		486.3	144.2
2519	Other rubber products		121.9	140.5	131.4	135.9		48.0	52.7	65.6	70.8		1.9	0.8
2520	Plastic products		4651.6	6125.9	5597.1	5143.8		1693.0	2243.6	1888.0	1632.5		7.7	4.6
2610	Glass and glass products		69.4	75.9	104.9	98.3		37.6	38.1	43.1	31.1		218.8	480.7
269	Non-metallic mineral products n.e.c.		11140.8	11594.0	10703.4	9980.4		4967.8	5357.2	5083.4	4292.4		1295.5	488.4
2691	Pottery, china and earthenware		268.8	294.4	220.7	206.4		137.6	160.6	121.9	102.4		22.2	…
2692	Refractory ceramic products		1229.1	1215.1	849.8	1129.8		559.7	570.9	240.6	251.6		56.0	52.6
2693	Struct.non-refractory clay; ceramic products		1853.5	1862.1	1433.7	852.7		860.9	960.3	740.0	382.0		77.5	20.9
2694	Cement, lime and plaster		6340.3	6614.9	4155.9	3951.6		2743.6	2914.2	2511.6	2250.3		163.9	133.8
2695	Articles of concrete, cement and plaster		886.4	943.5	3150.5	2890.7		395.3	427.0	1129.9	932.5		900.2	194.4
2696	Cutting, shaping & finishing of stone		232.4	277.1	441.2	504.0		119.2	145.4	217.6	247.3		60.5	47.7
2699	Other non-metallic mineral products n.e.c.		330.4	386.9	451.6	444.9		151.5	178.8	121.7	126.4		15.2	39.0
2710	Basic iron and steel		32701.9	35696.3	10171.1	18024.4		2411.9	8799.7	2533.2	1711.3		534.1	692.4
2720	Basic precious and non-ferrous metals		24960.6	12292.7	7953.8	14036.3		12474.3	2992.8	1926.0	1282.7		224.1	765.2
273	Casting of metals		7232.2	7906.2	5713.4	7351.3		1311.1	1972.7	1429.3	719.6		737.9	146.6
2731	Casting of iron and steel		6415.9	7074.5	5065.4	6258.8		1139.3	1752.8	1253.7	613.9		735.7	92.4
2732	Casting of non-ferrous metals		816.3	831.5	648.0	1092.5		171.7	220.0	175.6	105.7		2.3	54.2
281	Struct.metal products;tanks;steam generators		4411.8	4396.1	5121.9	3623.1		1186.8	1207.8	1641.2	1211.6		…	…
2811	Structural metal products		4208.6	4158.2	4615.4	3284.4		1134.3	1125.4	1468.7	1102.3		563.0	223.3
2812	Tanks, reservoirs and containers of metal		196.6	231.6	498.0	331.9		49.2	80.4	168.6	106.0		563.0	198.0
2813	Steam generators		6.6	6.4	8.5	6.8		3.2	2.0	3.9	3.3		…	…
289	Other metal products; metal working services		4095.2	5091.9	3633.9	3753.1		1340.1	1767.9	1218.0	1362.1		…	25.3
2891	Metal forging/pressing/stamping/roll-forming		602.2	634.9	400.8	514.5		101.3	198.1	134.5	142.7		47.9	101.7
2892	Treatment & coating of metals		1019.3	1106.0	1059.0	987.8		439.7	505.3	491.0	549.6		5.5	1.5
2893	Cutlery, hand tools and general hardware		387.4	489.9	259.2	301.6		214.2	210.1	131.5	170.4		16.8	37.6
2899	Other fabricated metal products n.e.c.		2086.2	2861.0	1914.9	1949.1		584.8	854.3	460.9	499.5		0.2	…
291	General purpose machinery		1567.2	1683.2	1439.3	1798.0		621.0	684.6	547.3	922.7		25.3	62.6
2911	Engines & turbines (not for transport equipment)		476.1	440.3	388.7	489.2		180.7	173.0	200.5	273.7		28.7	21.0
2912	Pumps, compressors, taps and valves		470.7	548.9	334.0	263.8		186.8	219.3	128.7	112.1		2.8	9.7
2913	Bearings, gears, gearing & driving elements		43.2	59.9	33.3	33.4		17.3	25.2	17.9	13.8		10.5	9.5
2914	Ovens, furnaces and furnace burners		1.4	0.8	2.6	1.3		0.7	0.5	1.1	0.6		0.7	…
2915	Lifting and handling equipment		56.0	78.6	61.2	593.8		21.9	33.6	20.1	346.5		2.0	-1.1
2919	Other general purpose machinery		519.9	554.6	619.5	416.4		213.5	233.0	178.9	176.1		12.7	2.8

292	Special purpose machinery	407.4	496.4	548.8	682.8	160.7	200.4	230.3	298.6	48.3	47.1
2921	Agricultural and forestry machinery	35.5	41.6	81.9	83.6	13.9	17.0	47.0	40.4	15.9	8.1
2922	Machine tools	167.7	212.3	100.0	181.0	67.6	86.1	18.5	95.5	4.6	...
2923	Machinery for metallurgy	0.5	0.5	10.0	7.2	0.2	0.2	5.4	3.2	0.1	0.3
2924	Machinery for mining & construction	6.6	10.8	20.4	21.6	2.6	4.2	19.4	8.8	0.3	2.1
2925	Food/beverage/tobacco processing machinery	64.7	121.6	148.5	190.8	24.6	47.7	84.0	77.2	...	...
2926	Machinery for textile, apparel and leather	...	...	0.7	-	...	...	0.2	-	...	...
2927	Weapons and ammunition	132.5	109.6	187.3	198.6	51.8	45.2	55.8	73.4	27.4	36.7
2929	Other special purpose machinery	1291.8	1506.2	1283.6	1301.6	520.0	616.0	329.3	358.7	112.4	48.1
2930	Domestic appliances n.e.c.	933.9	1254.8	981.8	1104.4	337.8	456.7	366.1	353.2	11.7	30.4
3000	Office, accounting and computing machinery	819.6	958.7	553.3	685.5	334.3	398.1	231.1	339.1	14.3	52.7
3110	Electric motors, generators and transformers	844.9	918.4	732.4	480.0	341.5	385.5	318.9	182.1	34.3	15.3
3120	Electricity distribution & control apparatus	1117.4	1854.9	1117.6	291.7	441.4	753.1	460.5	13.6	56.5	20.2
3130	Insulated wire and cable	198.0	406.4	302.3	395.0	100.4	167.7	128.2	39.6	14.3	...
3140	Accumulators, primary cells and batteries	234.7	232.4	137.1	127.2	94.5	96.2	59.1	41.7	255.3	266.0
3150	Lighting equipment and electric lamps	732.7	934.3	1632.0	2756.1	310.2	393.6	662.1	344.7	...	...
3190	Other electrical equipment n.e.c.	96.2	112.7	74.8	64.8	46.5	38.5	28.2	22.1	7.3	2.4
3210	Electronic valves, tubes, etc.	224.8	347.1	72.8	109.8	82.6	147.3	33.1	36.4	...	...
3220	TV/radio transmitters; line comm. apparatus	45.4	39.7	20.8	24.5	20.0	14.8	10.8	11.2	4.0	0.8
3230	TV and radio receivers and associated goods	296.5	420.6	402.5	346.3	148.0	220.0	256.0	202.2	2.2	0.8
331	Medical, measuring, testing appliances, etc.	150.3	179.4	168.3	166.6	83.6	94.6	106.7	96.7	...	...
3311	Medical, surgical and orthopaedic equipment	109.1	151.8	43.2	54.8	44.5	79.2	22.6	19.0	1.8	1.8
3312	Measuring/testing/navigating appliances,etc.	37.0	89.4	190.9	124.9	19.9	46.2	126.7	86.5	0.9	0.9
3313	Industrial process control equipment	30.7	31.9	29.9	29.5	20.2	16.3	17.3	9.9	...	...
3320	Optical instruments & photographic equipment	1.0	0.9	2.5	0.8	0.6	0.5	1.4	0.6	...	...
3330	Watches and clocks	...	...	...	...	...	...	...	20.6	...	...
3410	Motor vehicles	128.9	186.0	640.6	57.8	107.6	72.2	270.2	6.7	3076.3	662.8
3420	Automobile bodies, trailers & semi-trailers	172.4	229.3	471.4	23.7	86.2	89.2	182.7	281.1	...	...
3430	Parts/accessories for automobiles	1126.1	1091.1	695.8	9029.3	369.8	437.7	281.1	3647.2	...	...
351	Building and repairing of ships and boats	...	2.7	5.4	0.1	...	1.3	5.2	...	...	...
3511	Building and repairing of ships	...	2.7	5.4	0.1	...	1.3	5.2	...	...	...
3512	Building/repairing of pleasure/sport. boats	684.4	559.1	419.6	524.5	366.3	273.6	206.7	199.1	...	64.7
3520	Railway/tramway locomotives & rolling stock	3.4	0.9	0.3	0.6	0.3	0.5	0.2	0.3	...	0.2
3530	Aircraft and spacecraft	142.8	142.8	150.0	158.8	73.1	73.1	41.5	73.0	0.4	0.2
359	Transport equipment n.e.c.	93.7	142.0	148.3	130.1	20.7	72.7	40.9	59.4	0.4	0.2
3591	Motorcycles	...	0.8	1.6	28.7	0.4	0.4	0.7	13.6	...	...
3592	Bicycles and invalid carriages	...	...	...	...	...	...	...	...	48.8	64.5
3599	Other transport equipment n.e.c.	2392.7	2773.6	2637.2	2849.5	784.3	1065.3	999.3	1127.4	2.3	8.3
3610	Furniture	286.4	609.8	600.9	744.0	225.3	356.1	363.3	482.8	2.3	8.3
369	Manufacturing n.e.c.	0.5	323.7	336.0	384.0	0.4	222.3	215.7	285.9	...	...
3691	Jewellery and related articles	11.9	0.4	2.2	28.8	0.9	0.4	1.7	17.1	...	...
3692	Musical instruments	...	1.3	29.8	31.3	6.6	-0.4	9.8	21.3	...	...
3693	Sports goods	9.7	11.1	12.7	7.1	6.6	6.2	6.8	3.8	...	...
3694	Games and toys	274.0	220.2	220.2	292.8	123.9	127.6	129.4	154.8	44.9	32.8
3699	Other manufacturing n.e.c.	...	273.3	...	...	...	...	...	...	15.2	7.5
3710	Recycling of metal waste and scrap	973.3	1057.7	714.6	720.1	572.1	607.4	273.7	119.8	...	...
3720	Recycling of non-metal waste and scrap	76.2	98.0	79.5	82.9	34.1	60.4	28.1	21.6	...	...
D	Total manufacturing	207016.4	224413.9	162241.7	200220.0	65353.2	70634.5	58035.2	57256.3	12868.8	7284.7

The former Yugoslav Republic of Macedonia

Index numbers of industrial production

(2005=100)

ISIC	Industry	Note	1999	2000	2001	2002	2003	2004	2005	2006	2007	2008	2009	2010
15	Food and beverages		86	88	86	79	100	96	100	101	108	117	114	115
16	Tobacco products		140	131	132	127	119	98	100	102	101	103	100	119
17	Textiles		177	161	140	153	112	99	100	89	82	84	56	55
18	Wearing apparel, fur		143	137	135	118	95	96	100	109	93	74	65	71
19	Leather, leather products and footwear		413	301	285	185	112	116	100	87	88	80	78	77
20	Wood products (excl. furniture)		68	65	61	77	126	126	100	93	93	71	42	44
21	Paper and paper products		100	114	112	116	93	92	100	123	124	118	111	114
22	Printing and publishing		280	192	190	205	100	103	100	108	95	152	204	154
23	Coke,refined petroleum products,nuclear fuel		70	86	85	58	83	86	100	112	110	111	101	91
24	Chemicals and chemical products		127	138	135	137	100	100	100	101	101	121	109	100
25	Rubber and plastics products		83	87	85	138	106	106	100	81	83	104	102	87
26	Non-metallic mineral products		56	73	69	96	80	82	100	111	115	112	98	83
27	Basic metals		59	72	68	55	66	75	100	109	146	137	79	97
28	Fabricated metal products		193	158	157	179	113	84	100	116	169	255	354	159
29	Machinery and equipment n.e.c.		116	120	107	116	99	92	100	103	143	154	126	135
30	Office, accounting and computing machinery	a/	209	210	209	166	111	92	100	101	76	96	68	52
31	Electrical machinery and apparatus	a/	...	...	...	...	...	...	...	...	...	...	...	...
32	Radio,television and communication equipment	a/	...	...	...	...	...	...	...	...	...	...	...	...
33	Medical, precision and optical instruments	a/	...	...	...	...	...	...	...	...	...	...	...	...
34	Motor vehicles, trailers, semi-trailers		109	103	103	198	140	136	100	70	51	47	29	25
35	Other transport equipment		...	...	...	...	...	...	100	...	...	...	...	...
36	Furniture; manufacturing n.e.c.		52	64	64	57	107	113	100	66	56	111	84	76
37	Recycling		49	56	55	47	61	74	100	129	83	180	159	242
D	Total manufacturing		...	98	94	90	95	93	100	104	109	116	105	98

a/ 30 includes 31, 32 and 33.

Turkey

Supplier of information:
State Institute of Statistics, Ankara.
Industrial statistics for the OECD countries are compiled by the OECD secretariat, which supplies them to UNIDO.

Basic source of data:
Survey.

Major deviations from ISIC (Revision 4):
None reported.

Reference period:
Calendar year.

Scope:
All enterprises.

Method of data collection:
Direct interview in the field.

Type of enumeration:
Full enumeration for enterprises with multiple local units or with more than 20 employees; sampling method is used for enterprises having single local unit.

Adjusted for non-response:
Yes.

Concepts and definitions of variables:
No deviations from the standard UN concepts and definitions are reported.

Related national publications:
None reported.

Turkey

ISIC Revision 4		Number of enterprises (number)					Number of employees (thousands)					Wages and salaries paid to employees (millions of Turkish Liras)				
ISIC	Industry	Note	2006	2007	2008	2009	Note	2006	2007	2008	2009	Note	2006	2007	2008	2009
1010	Processing/preserving of meat		...	...	...	454		...	...	...	27.9		...	...	...	437.7
1020	Processing/preserving of fish, etc.		...	...	...	52		...	...	...	3.8		...	...	...	46.4
1030	Processing/preserving of fruit,vegetables		...	...	...	1545		...	...	...	40.0		...	...	...	...
1040	Vegetable and animal oils and fats		...	...	...	819		...	...	...	10.8		...	...	...	212.7
1050	Dairy products		...	...	...	1570		...	...	...	24.5		...	...	...	...
106	Grain mill products,starches and starch products		...	...	...	4172		...	...	...	16.2		...	...	...	196.6
1061	Grain mill products		...	...	...	4161		...	...	...	15.5		...	...	...	177.5
1062	Starches and starch products		...	...	...	11		...	...	...	0.7		...	...	...	19.1
107	Other food products		...	...	...	30637		...	...	...	162.1		...	...	...	2571.6
1071	Bakery products		...	...	...	29087		...	...	...	99.0		...	...	...	962.2
1072	Sugar		...	...	...	66		...	...	...	20.0		...	...	...	...
1073	Cocoa, chocolate and sugar confectionery		...	...	...	1116		...	...	...	22.1		...	...	...	405.3
1074	Macaroni, noodles, couscous, etc.		...	...	...	29		...	...	...	2.1		...	...	...	37.5
1075	Prepared meals and dishes		...	...	...	...		...	...	...	...		...	...	...	...
1079	Other food products n.e.c.		...	...	...	339		...	...	...	18.8		...	...	...	...
1080	Prepared animal feeds		...	...	...	330		...	...	...	7.2		...	...	...	100.3
1101	Distilling, rectifying and blending of spirits		...	...	...	7		...	...	...	0.8		...	...	...	27.0
1102	Wines		...	...	...	86		...	...	...	...		...	...	...	...
1103	Malt liquors and malt		...	...	...	4		...	...	...	...		...	...	...	...
1104	Soft drinks;mineral waters,other bottled waters		...	...	...	401		...	...	...	8.7		...	...	...	176.1
1200	Tobacco products		...	...	...	24		...	...	...	17.3		...	...	...	511.5
131	Spinning, weaving and finishing of textiles		...	...	...	7484		...	...	...	162.1		...	...	...	1845.3
1311	Preparation and spinning of textile fibres		...	...	...	1164		...	...	...	60.2		...	...	...	633.0
1312	Weaving of textiles		...	...	...	4137		...	...	...	64.2		...	...	...	814.6
1313	Finishing of textiles		...	...	...	2183		...	...	...	37.7		...	...	...	397.7
139	Other textiles		...	...	...	10663		...	...	...	103.8		...	...	...	1189.4
1391	Knitted and crocheted fabrics		...	...	...	701		...	...	...	16.7		...	...	...	175.5
1392	Made-up textile articles, except apparel		...	...	...	5832		...	...	...	47.0		...	...	...	528.1
1393	Carpets and rugs		...	...	...	724		...	...	...	14.5		...	...	...	156.9
1394	Cordage, rope, twine and netting		...	...	...	136		...	...	...	0.9		...	...	...	9.2
1399	Other textiles n.e.c.		...	...	...	3270		...	...	...	24.8		...	...	...	319.7
1410	Wearing apparel, except fur apparel		...	...	...	46945		...	...	...	291.1		...	...	...	2835.7
1420	Articles of fur		...	...	...	51		...	...	...	0.9		...	...	...	8.4
1430	Knitted and crocheted apparel		...	...	...	4162		...	...	...	37.6		...	...	...	351.7
151	Leather;luggage,handbags,saddlery,harness;fur		...	...	...	2451		...	...	...	14.0		...	...	...	140.9
1511	Tanning/dressing of leather; dressing of fur		...	...	...	932		...	...	...	7.9		...	...	...	78.3
1512	Luggage,handbags,etc.;saddlery/harness		...	...	...	1519		...	...	...	6.1		...	...	...	62.6
1520	Footwear		...	...	...	4996		...	...	...	22.3		...	...	...	197.0
1610	Sawmilling and planing of wood		...	...	...	4793		...	...	...	8.6		...	...	...	70.8
162	Wood products, cork, straw, plaiting materials		...	...	...	22749		...	...	...	27.8		...	...	...	320.2

ISIC	Industry			
1621	Veneer sheets and wood-based panels	459	10.9	194.4
1622	Builders' carpentry and joinery	19833	11.6	81.6
1623	Wooden containers	1020	4.0	33.5
1629	Other wood products;articles of cork,straw	1437	1.2	10.7
1701	Pulp, paper and paperboard	279	5.2	98.3
1702	Corrugated paper and paperboard	1048	18.7	366.2
1709	Other articles of paper and paperboard	936	13.6	219.7
181	Printing and service activities related to printing	13050	43.0	530.1
1811	Printing	12241	41.2	506.5
1812	Service activities related to printing	809	1.8	23.5
1820	Reproduction of recorded media	61	0.1	1.7
1910	Coke oven products	10	5.9a/	353.7a/
1920	Refined petroleum products	129	...a/	...a/
201	Basic chemicals,fertilizers, etc.	855	15.2	472.4
2011	Basic chemicals	332	5.3	165.8
2012	Fertilizers and nitrogen compounds	121	2.9	83.3
2013	Plastics and synthetic rubber in primary forms	402	6.9	223.3
202	Other chemical products	2549	36.5	...
2021	Pesticides and other agrochemical products	40	1.3	304.4
2022	Paints,varnishes;printing ink and mastics	1084	14.0	381.3
2023	Soap,cleaning and cosmetic preparations	1145	14.9	186.3
2029	Other chemical products n.e.c.	280	6.3	...
2030	Man-made fibres	4	2.1	...
2100	Pharmaceuticals,medicinal chemicals, etc.	184	29.2	1461.4
221	Rubber products	1216	25.3	655.9
2211	Rubber tyres and tubes	248	7.9	361.9
2219	Other rubber products	968	17.4	294.0
2220	Plastics products	17028	100.7	1260.3
2310	Glass and glass products	1217	121.8	1798.3
239	Non-metallic mineral products n.e.c.	11731	1.8	37.6
2391	Refractory products	27	25.4	307.0
2392	Clay building materials	1723	10.2	153.1
2393	Other porcelain and ceramic products	675	15.1	496.6
2394	Cement, lime and plaster	148	33.3	444.8
2395	Articles of concrete, cement and plaster	1510	32.0	287.1
2396	Cutting, shaping and finishing of stone	7550	4.0	72.1
2399	Other non-metallic mineral products n.e.c.	98	...	...
2410	Basic iron and steel	367	...	...
2420	Basic precious and other non-ferrous metals	457	22.0	372.7
243	Casting of metals	1469	18.5	308.5
2431	Casting of iron and steel	1154	3.5	64.1
2432	Casting of non-ferrous metals	315	...	...
251	Struct.metal products, tanks, reservoirs	26959	74.1	639.3
2511	Structural metal products	26200	59.6	...
2512	Tanks, reservoirs and containers of metal	720	13.5	202.7

continued

Turkey

ISIC	Industry	Enterprises Note	(number) 2006	2007	2008	2009	Employees Note	(thousands) 2006	2007	2008	2009	Wages Note	(millions of Turkish Liras) 2006	2007	2008	2009
2513	Steam generators, excl. hot water boilers		…	…	…	39		…	…	…	1.0		…	…	…	…
2520	Weapons and ammunition		…	…	…	152		…	…	…	8.3		…	…	…	…
259	Other metal products;metal working services		…	…	…	23043		…	…	…	96.9		…	…	…	1251.2
2591	Forging,pressing,stamping,roll-forming of metal		…	…	…	441		…	…	…	11.1		…	…	…	187.4
2592	Treatment and coating of metals; machining		…	…	…	14605		…	…	…	29.3		…	…	…	276.1
2593	Cutlery, hand tools and general hardware		…	…	…	3088		…	…	…	16.7		…	…	…	229.9
2599	Other fabricated metal products n.e.c.		…	…	…	4909		…	…	…	39.9		…	…	…	557.8
2610	Electronic components and boards		…	…	…	142		…	…	…	3.7		…	…	…	54.6
2620	Computers and peripheral equipment		…	…	…	15		…	…	…	1.0		…	…	…	30.0
2630	Communication equipment		…	…	…	62		…	…	…	6.1		…	…	…	249.5
2640	Consumer electronics		…	…	…	19		…	…	…	…		…	…	…	…
265	Measuring,testing equipment; watches, etc.		…	…	…	317		…	…	…	7.0		…	…	…	117.8
2651	Measuring/testing/navigating equipment,etc.		…	…	…	309		…	…	…	6.8		…	…	…	116.4
2652	Watches and clocks		…	…	…	8		…	…	…	0.2		…	…	…	1.5
2660	Irradiation/electromedical equipment,etc.		…	…	…	23		…	…	…	0.3		…	…	…	4.2
2670	Optical instruments and photographic equipment		…	…	…	21		…	…	…	…		…	…	…	…
2680	Magnetic and optical media		…	…	…	14		…	…	…	0.5		…	…	…	7.1
2710	Electric motors,generators,transformers,etc.		…	…	…	1121		…	…	…	24.6		…	…	…	666.1
2720	Batteries and accumulators		…	…	…	45		…	…	…	1.9		…	…	…	47.4
273	Wiring and wiring devices		…	…	…	323		…	…	…	13.5		…	…	…	237.5
2731	Fibre optic cables		…	…	…	27		…	…	…	3.0		…	…	…	51.2
2732	Other electric and electric wires and cables		…	…	…	202		…	…	…	6.5		…	…	…	123.8
2733	Wiring devices		…	…	…	94		…	…	…	4.0		…	…	…	62.4
2740	Electric lighting equipment		…	…	…	3221		…	…	…	13.1		…	…	…	142.2
2750	Domestic appliances		…	…	…	2236		…	…	…	39.4		…	…	…	1027.7
2790	Other electrical equipment		…	…	…	229		…	…	…	2.8		…	…	…	38.9
281	General-purpose machinery		…	…	…	6075		…	…	…	70.7		…	…	…	1094.5
2811	Engines/turbines,excl.aircraft,vehicle engines		…	…	…	17		…	…	…	7.1		…	…	…	…
2812	Fluid power equipment		…	…	…	65		…	…	…	2.1		…	…	…	…
2813	Other pumps, compressors, taps and valves		…	…	…	889		…	…	…	12.7		…	…	…	180.6
2814	Bearings, gears, gearing and driving elements		…	…	…	111		…	…	…	5.4		…	…	…	94.7
2815	Ovens, furnaces and furnace burners		…	…	…	658		…	…	…	3.2		…	…	…	…
2816	Lifting and handling equipment		…	…	…	2128		…	…	…	13.8		…	…	…	50.6
2817	Office machinery, excl.computers,etc.		…	…	…	12		…	…	…	…		…	…	…	178.7
2818	Power-driven hand tools		…	…	…	2		…	…	…	…		…	…	…	…
2819	Other general-purpose machinery		…	…	…	2193		…	…	…	26.1		…	…	…	335.4
282	Special-purpose machinery		…	…	…	6705		…	…	…	50.1		…	…	…	688.5
2821	Agricultural and forestry machinery		…	…	…	1555		…	…	…	7.8		…	…	…	129.6
2822	Metal-forming machinery and machine tools		…	…	…	961		…	…	…	9.6		…	…	…	124.2
2823	Machinery for metallurgy		…	…	…	27		…	…	…	0.8		…	…	…	12.9
2824	Mining, quarrying and construction machinery		…	…	…	968		…	…	…	10.6		…	…	…	163.4

Code	Industry	(1)	(2)	(3)	(4)	(5)	(6)	(7)	(8)	(9)
2825	Food/beverage/tobacco processing machinery	720	...	...	...	7.9	...	...	...	101.6
2826	Textile/apparel/leather production machinery	1948	...	...	...	7.2	...	...	...	77.9
2829	Other special-purpose machinery	526	...	...	...	6.2	...	...	...	78.9
2910	Motor vehicles	28	...	...	...	40.2	...	...	...	1454.7
2920	Automobile bodies, trailers and semi-trailers	1486	...	...	...	9.1	...	...	...	94.8
2930	Parts and accessories for motor vehicles	3046	...	...	...	72.0	...	...	...	1324.4
301	Building of ships and boats	947	...	...	...	23.2	...	...	...	366.6
3011	Building of ships and floating structures	399	...	...	...	18.4	...	...	...	288.5
3012	Building of pleasure and sporting boats	548	...	...	...	4.8	...	...	...	78.1
3020	Railway locomotives and rolling stock	8	...	...	...	4.6	...	...	...	164.5
3030	Air and spacecraft and related machinery	8	...	...	...	4.4	...	...	...	...
3040	Military fighting vehicles	6	...	...	...	1.8	...	...	...	85.3
309	Transport equipment n.e.c.	98	...	...	...	1.8	...	...	...	...
3091	Motorcycles	8	...	...	...	0.5	...	...	...	6.8
3092	Bicycles and invalid carriages	70	...	...	...	1.1	...	...	...	17.6
3099	Other transport equipment n.e.c.	20	...	...	...	0.2	...	...	...	...
3100	Furniture	34427	...	...	...	97.1	...	...	...	942.6
321	Jewellery, bijouterie and related articles	3213	...	...	...	16.3	...	...	...	163.7
3211	Jewellery and related articles	3162	...	...	...	...	...	...	...	...
3212	Imitation jewellery and related articles	51	...	...	...	0.2	...	...	...	1.9
3220	Musical instruments	236	...	...	...	0.8	...	...	...	10.7
3230	Sports goods	98	...	...	...	2.0	...	...	...	17.2
3240	Games and toys	245	...	...	...	11.0	...	...	...	130.7
3250	Medical and dental instruments and supplies	1837	...	...	...	10.3	...	...	...	124.3
3290	Other manufacturing n.e.c.	1697	...	...	...	27.1	...	...	...	491.8
331	Repair of fabricated metal products/machinery	5624	...	...	...	0.3	...	...	...	4.2
3311	Repair of fabricated metal products	49	...	...	...	4.5	...	...	...	49.7
3312	Repair of machinery	2680	...	...	...	0.8	...	...	...	9.5
3313	Repair of electronic and optical equipment	273	...	...	...	2.7	...	...	...	36.7
3314	Repair of electrical equipment	1196	...	...	...	...	...	...	...	...
3315	Repair of transport equip., excl. motor vehicles	1426	...	...	...	...	...	...	...	14.1
3319	Repair of other equipment	...	...	...	...	...	...	...	...	...
3320	Installation of industrial machinery/equipment	104	...	...	...	0.9	...	...	...	...
C	Total manufacturing	320815	...	...	...	2264.2	...	...	...	35898.3

a/ 1910 includes 1920.

Turkey

ISIC	Industry	Output Note	2006	2007	2008	2009	Value added Note	2006	2007	2008	2009	GFCF Note	2008	2009
			(millions of Turkish Liras)					(millions of Turkish Liras)					(millions of Turkish Liras)	
1010	Processing/preserving of meat		...	...	...	7107		...	...	...	1133		...	667
1020	Processing/preserving of fish, etc.		...	...	...	784		...	...	...	199		...	42
1030	Processing/preserving of fruit,vegetables		...	...	...	11000		...	...	...	...		...	...
1040	Vegetable and animal oils and fats		...	...	...	6648		...	...	...	505		...	409
1050	Dairy products		...	...	...	...		...	...	...	...		...	...
106	Grain mill products,starches and starch products		...	...	...	6118		...	...	...	634		...	317
1061	Grain mill products		...	...	...	5641		...	...	...	522		...	277
1062	Starches and starch products		...	...	...	477		...	...	...	111		...	40
107	Other food products		...	...	...	21877		...	...	...	5068		...	1246
1071	Bakery products		...	...	...	7347		...	...	...	1813		...	336
1072	Sugar		...	...	...	4881		...	...	...	1260		...	184
1073	Cocoa, chocolate and sugar confectionery		...	...	...	5271		...	...	...	1017		...	474
1074	Macaroni, noodles, couscous, etc.		...	...	...	852		...	...	...	96		...	41
1075	Prepared meals and dishes		...	...	...	...		...	...	...	...		...	...
1079	Other food products n.e.c.		...	...	...	3526		...	...	...	881		...	212
1080	Prepared animal feeds		...	...	...	...		...	...	...	390		...	181
1101	Distilling, rectifying and blending of spirits		...	...	...	297		...	...	...	25		...	21
1102	Wines		...	...	...	...		...	...	...	...		...	...
1103	Malt liquors and malt		...	...	...	...		...	...	...	...		...	...
1104	Soft drinks,mineral waters,other bottled waters		...	...	...	3370		...	...	...	675		...	235
1200	Tobacco products		...	...	...	4347		...	...	...	1215		...	1100
131	Spinning, weaving and finishing of textiles		...	...	...	19006		...	...	...	4280		...	1554
1311	Preparation and spinning of textile fibres		...	...	...	7959		...	...	...	1576		...	385
1312	Weaving of textiles		...	...	...	7616		...	...	...	1934		...	932
1313	Finishing of textiles		...	...	...	3431		...	...	...	770		...	238
139	Other textiles		...	...	...	13206		...	...	...	2937		...	800
1391	Knitted and crocheted fabrics		...	...	...	3049		...	...	...	460		...	162
1392	Made-up textile articles, except apparel		...	...	...	5297		...	...	...	1280		...	201
1393	Carpets and rugs		...	...	...	2053		...	...	...	470		...	192
1394	Cordage, rope, twine and netting		...	...	...	79		...	...	...	22		...	...
1399	Other textiles n.e.c.		...	...	...	2728		...	...	...	704		...	...
1410	Wearing apparel, except fur apparel		...	...	...	25600		...	...	...	4945		...	1111
1420	Articles of fur		...	...	...	81		...	...	...	14		...	3
1430	Knitted and crocheted apparel		...	...	...	2802		...	...	...	698		...	163
151	Leather;luggage,handbags,saddlery,harness;fur		...	...	...	1514		...	...	...	307		...	60
1511	Tanning/dressing of leather; dressing of fur		...	...	...	1111		...	...	...	207		...	48
1512	Luggage,handbags,etc.;saddlery/harness		...	...	...	403		...	...	...	100		...	12
1520	Footwear		...	...	...	2055		...	...	...	419		...	109
1610	Sawmilling and planing of wood		...	...	...	1088		...	...	...	213		...	40
162	Wood products, cork, straw, plaiting materials		...	...	...	5076		...	...	...	1036		...	412

Code	Description			
1621	Veneer sheets and wood-based panels	3686	808	367
1622	Builders' carpentry and joinery	736	138	16
1623	Wooden containers	543	68	28
1629	Other wood products;articles of cork,straw	110	22	2
1701	Pulp, paper and paperboard	1390	307	339
1702	Corrugated paper and paperboard	4032	888	...
1709	Other articles of paper and paperboard	3133	549	254
181	Printing and service activities related to printing	4784	1219	241
1811	Printing	4606	1167	13
1812	Service activities related to printing	178	52	-
1820	Reproduction of recorded media	10	3	424a/
1910	Coke oven products	16858a/	1428a/	...a/
1920	Refined petroleum products	...a/	...a/	...a/
201	Basic chemicals,fertilizers, etc.	7582	1138	495
2011	Basic chemicals	1892	...	158
2012	Fertilizers and nitrogen compounds	2186	513	136
2013	Plastics and synthetic rubber in primary forms	3504	...	201
202	Other chemical products	...	...	...
2021	Pesticides and other agrochemical products	4525	769	208
2022	Paints,varnishes;printing ink and mastics	5401	1102	285
2023	Soap,cleaning and cosmetic preparations	2483	581	123
2029	Other chemical products n.e.c.	...	...	...
2030	Man-made fibres	...	...	...
2100	Pharmaceuticals,medicinal chemicals, etc.	8075	2639	362
221	Rubber products	4662	1415	310
2211	Rubber tyres and tubes	2347	717	155
2219	Other rubber products	2315	698	155
2220	Plastics products	16520	3629	1509
2310	Glass and glass products	20205	5161	2640
239	Non-metallic mineral products n.e.c.	...	...	...
2391	Refractory products	414	105	21
2392	Clay building materials	...	...	...
2393	Other porcelain and ceramic products	2439	689	208
2394	Cement, lime and plaster	6663	2168	1319
2395	Articles of concrete, cement and plaster	2663	712	281
2396	Cutting, shaping and finishing of stone	829	162	103
2399	Other non-metallic mineral products n.e.c.	...	...	...
2410	Basic iron and steel	...	...	...
2420	Basic precious and other non-ferrous metals	2553	801	171
243	Casting of metals	2114	674	140
2431	Casting of iron and steel	439	127	31
2432	Casting of non-ferrous metals	...	...	577
251	Struct.metal products, tanks, reservoirs	9103	1460	437
2511	Structural metal products	6879	522	129
2512	Tanks, reservoirs and containers of metal	2120	...	...

continued

Turkey

ISIC	Industry	Note	Output (millions of Turkish Liras) 2006	2007	2008	2009	Note	Value added (millions of Turkish Liras) 2006	2007	2008	2009	Note	Gross fixed capital formation (millions of Turkish Liras) 2008	2009
2513	Steam generators, excl. hot water boilers		…	…	…	104		…	…	…	…		…	10
2520	Weapons and ammunition		…	…	…	737		…	…	…	…		…	50
259	Other metal products;metal working services		…	…	…	12087		…	…	…	2753		…	911
2591	Forging,pressing,stamping,roll-forming of metal		…	…	…	1463		…	…	…	402		…	219
2592	Treatment and coating of metals; machining		…	…	…	3028		…	…	…	622		…	139
2593	Cutlery, hand tools and general hardware		…	…	…	1419		…	…	…	425		…	160
2599	Other fabricated metal products n.e.c.		…	…	…	6176		…	…	…	1304		…	392
2610	Electronic components and boards		…	…	…	368		…	…	…	116		…	34
2620	Computers and peripheral equipment		…	…	…	734		…	…	…	76		…	7
2630	Communication equipment		…	…	…	1276		…	…	…	…		…	66
2640	Consumer electronics		…	…	…	…		…	…	…	…		…	…
265	Measuring,testing equipment; watches, etc.		…	…	…	1055		…	…	…	327		…	44
2651	Measuring/testing/navigating equipment,etc.		…	…	…	1045		…	…	…	324		…	43
2652	Watches and clocks		…	…	…	9		…	…	…	3		…	1
2660	Irradiation/electromedical equipment,etc.		…	…	…	35		…	…	…	11		…	1
2670	Optical instruments and photographic equipment		…	…	…	…		…	…	…	3		…	…
2680	Magnetic and optical media		…	…	…	70		…	…	…	20			
2710	Electric motors,generators,transformers,etc.		…	…	…	6196		…	…	…	1986		…	438
2720	Batteries and accumulators		…	…	…	536		…	…	…	116		…	30
273	Wiring and wiring devices		…	…	…	4658		…	…	…	632		…	235
2731	Fibre optic cables		…	…	…	1074		…	…	…	162		…	71
2732	Other electronic and electric wires and cables		…	…	…	2959		…	…	…	319		…	142
2733	Wiring devices		…	…	…	624		…	…	…	151		…	22
2740	Electric lighting equipment		…	…	…	1410		…	…	…	292		…	60
2750	Domestic appliances		…	…	…	11724		…	…	…	2732		…	396
2790	Other electrical equipment		…	…	…	393		…	…	…	90		…	40
281	General-purpose machinery		…	…	…	9191		…	…	…	2604		…	910
2811	Engines/turbines,excl.aircraft,vehicle engines		…	…	…	…		…	…	…	…			
2812	Fluid power equipment		…	…	…	…		…	…	…	…			
2813	Other pumps, compressors, taps and valves		…	…	…	1569		…	…	…	415		…	208
2814	Bearings, gears, gearing and driving elements		…	…	…	560		…	…	…	178		…	96
2815	Ovens, furnaces and furnace burners		…	…	…	433		…	…	…	97		…	16
2816	Lifting and handling equipment		…	…	…	1748		…	…	…	422		…	146
2817	Office machinery, excl.computers,etc.		…	…	…	…		…	…	…	…		…	…
2818	Power-driven hand tools		…	…	…	…		…	…	…	…			
2819	Other general-purpose machinery		…	…	…	3255		…	…	…	795		…	233
282	Special-purpose machinery		…	…	…	5987		…	…	…	1605		…	497
2821	Agricultural and forestry machinery		…	…	…	1428		…	…	…	329		…	72
2822	Metal-forming machinery and machine tools		…	…	…	1042		…	…	…	290		…	133
2823	Machinery for metallurgy		…	…	…	104		…	…	…	34		…	13
2824	Mining, quarrying and construction machinery		…	…	…	1287		…	…	…	357		…	120

Code	Industry			
2825	Food/beverage/tobacco processing machinery	57	249	888
2826	Textile/apparel/leather production machinery	64	178	660
2829	Other special-purpose machinery	38	167	577
2910	Motor vehicles	1110	3881	22463
2920	Automobile bodies, trailers and semi-trailers	65	178	959
2930	Parts and accessories for motor vehicles	871	2512	10091
301	Building of ships and boats	553	842	3923
3011	Building of ships and floating structures	454	735	3394
3012	Building of pleasure and sporting boats	99	107	528
3020	Railway locomotives and rolling stock	...	245	446
3030	Air and spacecraft and related machinery	29	156	412
3040	Military fighting vehicles	12	...	...
309	Transport equipment n.e.c.	1	15	...
3091	Motorcycles	9	43	65
3092	Bicycles and invalid carriages	2	...	167
3099	Other transport equipment n.e.c.	428	1899	8435
3100	Furniture	34	617	7011
321	Jewellery, bijouterie and related articles	...	...	...
3211	Jewellery and related articles	...	...	...
3212	Imitation jewellery and related articles	-	3	12
3220	Musical instruments	7	17	85
3230	Sports goods	9	33	126
3240	Games and toys	100	294	868
3250	Medical and dental instruments and supplies	70	278	1056
3290	Other manufacturing n.e.c.	226	943	2280
331	Repair of fabricated metal products/machinery	1	5	26
3311	Repair of fabricated metal products	18	95	345
3312	Repair of machinery	2	25	54
3313	Repair of electronic and optical equipment	2	47	192
3314	Repair of electrical equipment	...	...	...
3315	Repair of transport equip., excl. motor vehicles	...	...	...
3319	Repair of other equipment	4	27	60
3320	Installation of industrial machinery/equipment	...	...	...
C	Total manufacturing	36597	84735	420381

a/ 1910 includes 1920.

Turkey

ISIC Revision 4 — Index numbers of industrial production

(2005=100)

ISIC	Industry	Note	1999	2000	2001	2002	2003	2004	2005	2006	2007	2008	2009	2010
10	Food products		...	...	...	...	...	...	100	106	109	113	112	120
11	Beverages		...	...	...	...	...	...	100	102	105	113	111	120
12	Tobacco products		...	...	...	...	...	...	100	110	110	118	116	101
13	Textiles		...	...	...	...	...	...	100	102	101	89	78	88
14	Wearing apparel		...	...	...	...	...	...	100	97	103	93	85	92
15	Leather and related products		...	...	...	...	...	...	100	116	107	102	93	110
16	Wood/wood products/cork,excl. furniture		...	...	...	...	...	...	100	131	150	161	161	208
17	Paper and paper products		...	...	...	...	...	...	100	108	114	115	112	123
18	Printing and reproduction of recorded media		...	...	...	...	...	...	100	107	119	123	127	127
19	Coke and refined petroleum products		...	...	...	...	...	...	100	105	106	107	85	90
20	Chemicals and chemical products		...	...	...	...	...	...	100	111	114	107	107	124
21	Pharmaceuticals,medicinal chemicals, etc.		...	...	...	...	...	...	100	111	132	144	147	146
22	Rubber and plastics products		...	...	...	...	...	...	100	105	114	111	101	121
23	Other non-metallic mineral products		...	...	...	...	...	...	100	110	113	110	97	111
24	Basic metals		...	...	...	...	...	...	100	114	126	123	105	116
25	Fabricated metal products, except machinery		...	...	...	...	...	...	100	110	121	113	96	115
26	Computer, electronic and optical products		...	...	...	...	...	...	100	81	72	62	52	70
27	Electrical equipment		...	...	...	...	...	...	100	116	124	123	122	155
28	Machinery and equipment n.e.c.		...	...	...	...	...	...	100	109	116	111	85	113
29	Motor vehicles, trailers and semi-trailers		...	...	...	...	...	...	100	109	119	126	85	118
30	Other transport equipment		...	...	...	...	...	...	100	114	200	230	88	117
31	Furniture		...	...	...	...	...	...	100	98	124	140	126	136
32	Other manufacturing		...	...	...	...	...	...	100	127	131	155	130	164
33	Repair and installation of machinery/equipment		...	...	...	...	...	...	100	110	169	132	147	100
C	Total manufacturing		...	...	...	...	...	...	100	107	114	113	100	114

Ukraine

Concepts and definitions of variables:

Wages and salaries was computed by UNIDO from reported monthly wages and salaries per employee. It excludes payment in kind and housing and family allowances paid directly by the employer.

Output corresponds to turnover. It excludes VAT for sales of goods and services and includes the value of all goods and services which were documented during the reporting period, regardless whether payment was made or delivery terms, according to the outstanding account balances, were met.

Related national publications:

Statistical Yearbook of Ukraine; Activity of Economic Entities; Activity of Small-Scaled Entities, all published by the State Statistics Service of Ukraine, Kiev.

Supplier of information:
State Statistics Service of Ukraine, Kiev.

Basic source of data:
Annual survey on registered enterprises.

Major deviations from ISIC (Revision 3):
None reported.

Reference period:
Calendar year.

Scope:
All registered enterprises.

Method of data collection:
Mail and e-mail questionnaires.

Type of enumeration:
Complete enumeration for medium and large enterprises; sample survey for small enterprises.

Adjusted for non-response:
Yes.

Ukraine

ISIC	Industry	Number of enterprises (number)				Number of employees (number)				Wages and salaries paid to employees (thousands of Ukrainian Hryvnias)			
		2007	2008	2009	2010	2007	2008	2009	2010	2007	2008	2009	2010
151	Processed meat,fish,fruit,vegetables,fats	2437	2277	1968	1933	123248	111104	103433	102241	1570673	1889212	1943924	2411118
1511	Processing/preserving of meat	1178	1071	941	897	71012	57824	53301	52801	854700	839604	787362	1087278
1512	Processing/preserving of fish	277	301	257	257	10895	9685	8611	7499	112306	124123	107775	113925
1513	Processing/preserving of fruit & vegetables	482	465	372	355	21586	23982	21091	20333	237532	430237	430003	503852
1514	Vegetable and animal oils and fats	500	440	398	424	19755	19613	20430	21608	366021	494954	618784	706063
1520	Dairy products	572	531	463	433	82879	77983	73999	68949	1008472	1264260	1257391	1436346
153	Grain mill products; starches; animal feeds	1208	1151	950	936	32200	32860	30414	29876	420017	598765	623000	704476
1531	Grain mill products	919	868	714	688	22741	23268	21081	20179	279169	392857	397672	426907
1532	Starches and starch products	19	21	13	17	2363	2429	2135	2136	42449	59783	56928	66464
1533	Prepared animal feeds	270	261	223	231	7096	7163	7198	7561	98436	146125	168347	210861
154	Other food products	2609	2424	2183	2076	195643	181409	163483	157164	2692830	3344394	3256581	3729773
1541	Bakery products	1701	1530	1386	1306	99770	93814	95126	89579	1150548	1468001	1592409	1727441
1542	Sugar	160	145	96	102	31294	22514	13581	15465	380410	374183	239732	339983
1543	Cocoa, chocolate and sugar confectionery	142	139	135	135	41787	41940	35651	33718	854962	1102183	1036588	1204542
1544	Macaroni, noodles & similar products	180	153	117	115	6706	8717	5989	4866	81840	132952	108852	125309
1549	Other food products n.e.c.	426	457	449	418	16086	14424	13136	13536	224110	267075	278851	332498
155	Beverages	997	970	834	774	73375	70378	60066	56678	1414964	1745945	1665030	1887377
1551	Distilling, rectifying & blending of spirits	189	187	158	145	25695	24251	22955	20283	416259	490937	466281	512349
1552	Wines	117	114	93	97	11161	11487	8615	9624	153352	192155	182259	241254
1553	Malt liquors and malt	86	95	83	78	16217	15945	13979	13173	517452	658592	667302	735844
1554	Soft drinks; mineral waters	605	574	500	454	20302	18695	14507	13598	327918	404261	349038	397497
1600	Tobacco products	21	14	13	17	5113	4613	4157	3768	279906	345089	431995	412279
171	Spinning, weaving and finishing of textiles	147	139	123	112	11922	10015	7737	7006	118314	131958	99436	106205
1711	Textile fibre preparation; textile weaving	121	111	90	87	11654	9776	7502	6772	115095	128222	95335	101336
1712	Finishing of textiles	26	28	33	25	268	239	235	234	3193	3731	4089	4869
172	Other textiles	602	596	512	466	17089	17051	14778	13976	180050	266609	247916	278269
1721	Made-up textile articles, except apparel	488	469	356	315	13757	13005	11036	10738	140817	169013	148854	185424
1722	Carpets and rugs	17	13	10	11	495	457	427	396	8114	9345	10228	10640
1723	Cordage, rope, twine and netting	29	29	26	26	916	1130	682	373	9475	16814	10345	4906
1729	Other textiles n.e.c.	68	85	120	114	1921	2459	2633	2469	21761	71321	78453	77299
1730	Knitted and crocheted fabrics and articles	220	191	148	137	6858	5908	4822	4732	57113	64728	60352	75125
1810	Wearing apparel, except fur apparel	2664	2343	2062	1900	85410	73217	63926	60993	726668	785472	711880	858537
1820	Dressing & dyeing of fur; processing of fur	56	53	46	47	1417	1064	844	757	12600	12564	10847	10438
191	Tanning, dressing and processing of leather	170	156	129	118	6440	5802	4922	4955	74962	82296	71763	92698
1911	Tanning and dressing of leather	72	67	53	46	3864	3304	2829	2539	54251	56300	48580	51400
1912	Luggage, handbags, etc.; saddlery & harness	98	89	76	72	2576	2498	2093	2416	20711	25959	23182	41285
1920	Footwear	437	386	317	301	17986	15695	14746	16289	154752	171766	176244	250590
2010	Sawmilling and planing of wood	1806	1649	1390	1283	19353	20172	17727	16006	157224	223667	219531	232983
202	Products of wood, cork, straw, etc.	2292	2016	1718	1591	34812	30547	26150	27085	385160	442817	353495	465429
2021	Veneer sheets, plywood, particle board, etc.	132	107	97	96	12608	10807	9360	10567	215899	248864	196448	264386
2022	Builders' carpentry and joinery	1697	1477	1229	1095	17334	15156	12834	12420	131253	144588	116276	148295
2023	Wooden containers	160	158	141	134	2401	2611	2202	2004	21234	30235	23491	27150
2029	Other wood products; articles of cork/straw	303	274	251	266	2469	1973	1754	2094	16799	19130	17280	25505
210	Paper and paper products	590	587	557	551	31189	30926	29052	28997	481309	591181	597904	733856
2101	Pulp, paper and paperboard	65	60	51	56	9606	9433	8405	8255	173369	215525	211201	243390
2102	Corrugated paper and paperboard	281	282	273	259	11787	11505	10911	10520	168743	209851	211455	253490
2109	Other articles of paper and paperboard	244	245	233	236	9796	9988	9736	10222	139182	165761	175248	236864
221	Publishing	2978	3001	3005	2975	32623	29974	28458	28903	536714	690961	655345	736680
2211	Publishing of books and other publications	680	739	760	755	5571	4475	4099	4370	72869	77006	69896	82960
2212	Publishing of newspapers, journals, etc.	1879	1879	1877	1831	23802	22814	21858	22379	427579	574365	544526	612558
2213	Publishing of recorded media	35	37	35	37	189	163	127	119	1742	1702	1268	1342
2219	Other publishing	384	346	333	352	3061	2522	2374	2035	34638	37769	39655	39634

Code	Description												
222	Printing and related service activities	3084	3010	2832	2808	47020	45867	40135	36904	653954	826156	733026	800763
2221	Printing	2726	2646	2496	2461	44603	43630	38436	34905	629973	798953	711681	769027
2222	Service activities related to printing	358	361	336	347	2417	2237	1699	1999	23725	27086	21305	31736
2230	Reproduction of recorded media	68	75	76	78	570	531	400	311	6710	9431	9278	8763
2310	Coke oven products	21	17	18	18	29813	28092	25035	23182	665068	811072	777487	901594
2320	Refined petroleum products	201	192	145	122	44210	16023	14582	14193	1394207	541834	535101	640218
2330	Processing of nuclear fuel	...	...	...	...	...	...	...	...	...	...	...	...
241	Basic chemicals	448	497	451	463	80109	78737	62622	60411	1614997	2011910	1432290	1841453
2411	Basic chemicals, except fertilizers	286	325	302	304	43003	42459	27883	26547	747220	935457	588889	704026
2412	Fertilizers and nitrogen compounds	61	67	55	70	32173	31609	30392	30451	791456	988097	760408	1055310
2413	Plastics in primary forms; synthetic rubber	101	105	94	89	4933	4669	4347	3413	76600	88356	82680	82117
242	Other chemicals	1190	1214	1135	1161	54304	50591	49134	49835	905791	1108550	1193635	1490864
2421	Pesticides and other agro-chemical products	40	44	34	41	220	301	324	312	1845	4056	6435	6623
2422	Paints, varnishes, printing ink and mastics	271	272	231	246	7992	7939	6281	6152	125155	154811	124213	135984
2423	Pharmaceuticals, medicinal chemicals, etc.	323	320	308	315	21099	20058	19295	20488	452194	562266	636040	809958
2424	Soap, cleaning & cosmetic preparations	252	256	252	260	7114	6999	7420	7894	106795	141604	188409	248756
2429	Other chemical products n.e.c.	304	322	310	299	17879	15294	15814	14989	219483	245560	238538	289947
2430	Man-made fibres	16	18	14	15	4414	3897	3256	2767	56464	61448	21568	16602
251	Rubber products	232	242	223	235	18929	17475	15144	13780	323232	384266	309378	345145
2511	Rubber tyres and tubes	33	32	29	27	11791	11035	9193	8153	229500	274374	205188	219348
2519	Other rubber products	199	210	194	208	7138	6440	5951	5627	93793	109892	104190	125797
2520	Plastic products	2096	2164	2003	1897	55995	53042	48432	46960	663877	789265	766582	971508
2610	Glass and glass products	324	354	311	294	25204	23260	18857	17971	389251	458594	333543	403269
269	Non-metallic mineral products n.e.c.	3475	3560	3035	2878	151641	149530	119252	104763	2456584	3124609	2230392	2330767
2691	Pottery, china and earthenware	121	143	124	121	10386	8626	6081	5296	109925	125871	108290	114076
2692	Refractory ceramic products	66	57	59	58	12676	11573	9132	9447	217976	244838	185745	257336
2693	Struct.non-refractory clay; ceramic products	763	734	622	552	33991	32496	25102	19954	446642	546323	362975	340974
2694	Cement, lime and plaster	105	109	89	91	17344	13609	12234	10841	363183	384264	369516	383511
2695	Articles of concrete, cement and plaster	1614	1748	1501	1424	59097	63402	49761	42639	1074383	1441761	886144	939934
2696	Cutting, shaping & finishing of stone	558	523	427	431	8171	7392	6238	6499	81677	71986	71487	84071
2699	Other non-metallic mineral products n.e.c.	248	245	213	201	9976	12432	10704	10087	162569	289566	246235	210617
2710	Basic iron and steel	312	309	273	272	311564	295438	257576	238729	8236506	9472924	8558735	9608365
2720	Basic precious and non-ferrous metals	96	123	104	103	24444	22523	16575	16123	512737	558120	422663	474403
273	Casting of metals	166	156	128	126	14767	10491	8213	7966	245959	202062	119234	196268
2731	Casting of iron and steel	119	112	86	80	13594	9399	6738	6610	233436	187228	101959	176725
2732	Casting of non-ferrous metals	47	44	42	46	1173	1092	1475	1356	12514	14834	17275	19543
281	Struct.metal products;tanks;steam generators	1823	1890	1682	1604	49955	52741	42607	36547	673194	915273	623341	651450
2811	Structural metal products	1595	1636	1430	1349	36456	40044	31561	25046	483407	678025	435163	411456
2812	Tanks, reservoirs and containers of metal	135	157	166	177	4058	3711	4194	4015	136177	170806	116511	155679
2813	Steam generators	93	97	86	78	9441	8986	6852	7486	53420	66442	71667	84315
289	Other metal products; metal working services	1871	1840	1723	1739	61445	58052	54793	53622	784530	962734	966599	1209753
2891	Metal forging/pressing/stamping/roll-forming	135	140	126	129	5949	4852	5236	4825	75899	78253	72257	104625
2892	Treatment & coating of metals	588	603	567	597	12086	12427	13218	13989	155764	207431	271709	339765
2893	Cutlery, hand tools and general hardware	221	205	189	199	10775	9257	7812	7539	133050	139522	116336	139049
2899	Other fabricated metal products n.e.c.	927	892	841	814	32635	31516	28527	27269	419817	537411	506297	626314
291	General purpose machinery	2294	2392	2293	2347	137372	133835	118012	110429	2190809	2797687	2509498	2876025
2911	Engines & turbines (not for transport equipment)	198	189	172	172	23986	22839	25474	25632	401238	497982	662426	777265
2912	Pumps, compressors, taps and valves	461	472	440	446	46021	43921	36694	33262	746092	916543	824734	892087
2913	Bearings, gears, gearing & driving elements	86	93	87	89	12584	12358	6836	6330	219415	289177	148806	188153
2914	Ovens, furnaces and furnace burners	61	49	46	45	2679	2082	2097	2222	34784	35652	26900	49835
2915	Lifting and handling equipment	490	530	541	589	26326	28289	25014	22451	437854	633108	491375	543673
2919	Other general purpose machinery	998	1059	1007	1006	25776	24346	21897	20532	352616	424789	355257	425012
292	Special purpose machinery	2669	2554	2221	2188	176657	177214	146471	136213	2815206	3691834	2816211	3445983
2921	Agricultural and forestry machinery	739	683	567	532	40508	30740	25908	26317	506026	515325	391107	541288
2922	Machine tools	450	425	329	319	36977	39824	29554	24449	555986	803808	623471	623156
2923	Machinery for metallurgy	163	157	125	147	26790	37611	31279	30007	695683	1056568	772466	983029
2924	Machinery for mining & construction	448	439	419	436	41876	42293	33459	31327	649246	844507	568535	743954
2925	Food/beverage/tobacco processing machinery	308	293	262	265	9175	8529	7889	7684	107568	133666	118524	136376
2926	Machinery for textile, apparel and leather	27	22	14	19	159	86	77	82	1366	723	537	939
2927	Weapons and ammunition	...	...	...	...	...	...	...	...	...	...	...	...
2929	Other special purpose machinery	534	528	505	470	21172	18131	18305	16347	299287	337237	341571	417241

continued

Ukraine

ISIC	Industry	Number of enterprises (number)					Number of employees (number)					Wages and salaries paid to employees (thousands of Ukrainian Hryvnias)				
		Note	2007	2008	2009	2010	Note	2007	2008	2009	2010	Note	2007	2008	2009	2010
2930	Domestic appliances n.e.c.		122	119	119	113		14622	14825	11606	10467		268109	310613	194145	271179
3000	Office, accounting and computing machinery		475	466	395	274		8384	8015	6669	3637		124653	173990	153734	145858
3110	Electric motors, generators and transformers		552	550	490	472		35882	36305	31195	29802		563634	772425	647234	756732
3120	Electricity distribution & control apparatus		716	725	673	650		27912	25567	22514	20438		348007	399766	332307	385788
3130	Insulated wire and cable		102	101	78	85		8220	7838	6580	6300		150031	192250	143865	182801
3140	Accumulators, primary cells and batteries		39	34	34	34		3138	3046	3324	3565		55844	77600	78739	117003
3150	Lighting equipment and electric lamps		96	110	93	96		6504	6184	5106	7282		84916	95728	78612	134834
3190	Other electrical equipment n.e.c.		692	685	631	635		27003	26046	25895	32235		412174	456013	506506	838626
3210	Electronic valves, tubes, etc.		164	145	107	100		6603	4532	3509	3861		120993	112466	82068	129730
3220	TV/radio transmitters; line comm. apparatus		323	296	274	257		13356	9359	5924	5051		186396	205748	122840	113708
3230	TV and radio receivers and associated goods		247	234	220	209		8739	6403	7589	7695		126261	131313	177218	180986
331	Medical, measuring, testing appliances, etc.		1381	1389	1327	1348		47403	48715	41709	37130		630270	825540	710700	830524
3311	Medical, surgical and orthopaedic equipment		471	457	434	446		9694	9677	9304	9977		144014	177321	165016	216940
3312	Measuring/testing/navigating appliances,etc.		794	794	758	751		36202	37792	30712	25910		462662	624475	513382	584349
3313	Industrial process control equipment		116	138	135	151		1507	1246	1693	1243		23527	23744	32302	29235
3320	Optical instruments & photographic equipment		53	54	50	42		3981	3801	4479	3403		35304	44791	64551	60723
3330	Watches and clocks		7	6	5	6		114	114	55	64		1234	1602	698	779
3410	Motor vehicles		77	74	68	55		37813	38415	23503	19718		792712	995717	410644	453356
3420	Automobile bodies, trailers & semi-trailers		63	79	71	57		3767	4118	3528	2758		49724	69726	53132	41138
3430	Parts/accessories for automobiles		175	178	161	131		15646	13838	9430	9250		224364	254730	144279	204573
351	Building and repairing of ships and boats		483	485	422	382		27294	27139	25272	21502		434630	563851	564805	489236
3511	Building and repairing of ships		436	435	381	336		26347	25809	24528	20540		422711	541060	554529	471516
3512	Building/repairing of pleasure/sport. boats		47	50	41	46		947	1330	744	962		11625	22791	10276	17720
3520	Railway/tramway locomotives & rolling stock		198	205	205	214		83031	79996	66218	67954		1584231	2025499	1292840	2153598
3530	Aircraft and spacecraft		96	105	111	104		68089	57309	59340	56868		1079347	1174605	1368618	1635069
359	Transport equipment n.e.c.		49	32	33	26		2151	876	943	491		33581	15326	17113	14583
3591	Motorcycles		8	2	5	4		585	37	301	...		8887	482	3027	23
3592	Bicycles and invalid carriages		20	17	20	20		1485	794	546	467		23718	14492	12226	14318
3599	Other transport equipment n.e.c.		21	13	8	2		81	45	96	21		979	350	1860	239
3610	Furniture		1824	1744	1549	1480		54067	51321	39761	38451		568352	671895	486198	587839
369	Manufacturing n.e.c.		780	813	769	750		21664	21436	17447	17407		263348	334789	266910	322935
3691	Jewellery and related articles		339	344	347	334		11524	11907	9890	9068		154606	199466	150130	163006
3692	Musical instruments		21	20	14	16		195	160	130	160		959	1133	864	1720
3693	Sports goods		56	65	59	59		2600	2459	2125	2478		40716	47951	50898	71842
3694	Games and toys		76	96	86	80		2213	2334	1512	1397		17580	27868	13717	18541
3699	Other manufacturing n.e.c.		288	288	263	261		5132	4576	3790	4304		49452	58371	51301	67762
3710	Recycling of metal waste and scrap		625	672	538	546		12588	11746	9184	9546		184893	221577	163328	206537
3720	Recycling of non-metal waste and scrap		355	403	354	351		3944	4956	3126	3464		39850	57509	36499	44436
D	Total manufacturing		49886	48810	43913	42415		2607885	2447957	2123716	2017420		43223662	51565982	44838842	52945170

Ukraine

ISIC	Industry	Note	Output at factor values (millions of Ukrainian Hryvnias) 2007	2008	2009	2010	Note	Value added (millions of Ukrainian Hryvnias) 2007	2008	2009	2010	Note	Gross fixed capital formation (millions of Ukrainian Hryvnias) 2009	2010
151	Processed meat,fish,fruit,vegetables,fats		34794	47379	55505	66935								
1511	Processing/preserving of meat		14232	20627	21204	23942								
1512	Processing/preserving of fish		1369	1899	2481	2502								
1513	Processing/preserving of fruit & vegetables		5168	6270	6925	7734								
1514	Vegetable and animal oils and fats		14025	18584	24895	32757								
1520	Dairy products		14435	17052	17169	23080								
153	Grain mill products; starches; animal feeds		7709	10625	11379	13607								
1531	Grain mill products		4130	5310	4902	5653								
1532	Starches and starch products		993	1269	1281	1805								
1533	Prepared animal feeds		2587	4045	5196	6149								
154	Other food products		25208	32082	37284	47446								
1541	Bakery products		8436	10976	12297	14146								
1542	Sugar		4560	4948	5253	8943								
1543	Cocoa, chocolate and sugar confectionery		7800	10319	12439	15923								
1544	Macaroni, noodles & similar products		854	1016	1074	1027								
1549	Other food products n.e.c.		3558	4824	6221	7406								
155	Beverages		21120	24771	28311	30789								
1551	Distilling, rectifying & blending of spirits		7010	8191	10002	10068								
1552	Wines		2656	3050	3896	4673								
1553	Malt liquors and malt		6868	8643	9500	10057								
1554	Soft drinks; mineral waters		4585	4888	4913	5991								
1600	Tobacco products		6694	7984	9902	10298								
171	Spinning, weaving and finishing of textiles		617	637	658	659								
1711	Textile fibre preparation; textile weaving		598	610	625	628								
1712	Finishing of textiles		20	28	33	31								
172	Other textiles		1695	2204	1955	2254								
1721	Made-up textile articles, except apparel		934	1075	1040	1343								
1722	Carpets and rugs		185	212	197	217								
1723	Cordage, rope, twine and netting		73	87	62	67								
1729	Other textiles n.e.c.		503	829	656	627								
1730	Knitted and crocheted fabrics and articles		293	338	399	531								
1810	Wearing apparel, except fur apparel		2230	2380	2203	2511								
1820	Dressing & dyeing of fur; processing of fur		105	97	82	85								
191	Tanning, dressing and processing of leather		1262	1562	1195	1186								
1911	Tanning and dressing of leather		1176	1470	1113	1058								
1912	Luggage, handbags, etc.; saddlery & harness		86	92	82	128								
1920	Footwear		831	984	1020	1305								
2010	Sawmilling and planing of wood		1678	2063	2102	2375								
202	Products of wood, cork, straw, etc.		4118	4724	4255	5010								
2021	Veneer sheets, plywood, particle board, etc.		2790	3121	2890	3555								
2022	Builders' carpentry and joinery		974	1167	1003	989								
2023	Wooden containers		215	292	210	250								
2029	Other wood products; articles of cork/straw		139	144	152	217								
210	Paper and paper products		7385	8914	10348	12789								
2101	Pulp, paper and paperboard		1421	1730	1757	2380								
2102	Corrugated paper and paperboard		3076	3643	4095	5154								
2109	Other articles of paper and paperboard		2888	3542	4496	5255								
221	Publishing		3369	4170	4010	4927								
2211	Publishing of books and other publications		543	663	733	1023								
2212	Publishing of newspapers, journals, etc.		2483	3131	2948	3548								
2213	Publishing of recorded media		39	33	19	25								
2219	Other publishing		304	343	311	331								

continued

Ukraine

ISIC	Industry	Output at factor values (millions of Ukrainian Hryvnias)					Value added (millions of Ukrainian Hryvnias)					Gross fixed capital formation (millions of Ukrainian Hryvnias)		
		Note	2007	2008	2009	2010	Note	2007	2008	2009	2010	Note	2009	2010
222	Printing and related service activities		5918	7306	7649	8174		…	…	…	…		…	…
2221	Printing		5516	6977	7250	7619		…	…	…	…		…	…
2222	Service activities related to printing		402	329	399	555		…	…	…	…		…	…
2230	Reproduction of recorded media		116	149	120	115		…	…	…	…		…	…
2310	Coke oven products		14110	23138	14916	27015		…	…	…	…		…	…
2320	Refined petroleum products		38418	42997	38831	45988		…	…	…	…		…	…
2330	Processing of nuclear fuel		…	…	…	…		…	…	…	…		…	…
241	Basic chemicals		21673	29289	19826	27975		…	…	…	…		…	…
2411	Basic chemicals, except fertilizers		8410	9042	7998	11868		…	…	…	…		…	…
2412	Fertilizers and nitrogen compounds		11152	18056	10515	14552		…	…	…	…		…	…
2413	Plastics in primary forms; synthetic rubber		2111	2192	1313	1555		…	…	…	…		…	…
242	Other chemicals		9082	10841	13423	16108		…	…	…	…		…	…
2421	Pesticides and other agro-chemical products		36	64	82	94		…	…	…	…		…	…
2422	Paints, varnishes, printing ink and mastics		1686	2085	1980	2203		…	…	…	…		…	…
2423	Pharmaceuticals, medicinal chemicals, etc.		3766	4318	6184	7839		…	…	…	…		…	…
2424	Soap, cleaning & cosmetic preparations		1770	2184	3185	3772		…	…	…	…		…	…
2429	Other chemical products n.e.c.		1825	2190	1992	2200		…	…	…	…		…	…
2430	Man-made fibres		265	193	70	50		…	…	…	…		…	…
251	Rubber products		2661	2862	2226	2695		…	…	…	…		…	…
2511	Rubber tyres and tubes		2000	2073	1463	1598		…	…	…	…		…	…
2519	Other rubber products		661	789	763	1097		…	…	…	…		…	…
2520	Plastic products		10231	12392	12930	15476		…	…	…	…		…	…
2610	Glass and glass products		3182	4079	3557	4744		…	…	…	…		…	…
269	Non-metallic mineral products n.e.c.		24282	30236	20431	23223		…	…	…	…		…	…
2691	Pottery, china and earthenware		441	458	624	765		…	…	…	…		…	…
2692	Refractory ceramic products		1458	1559	1341	1964		…	…	…	…		…	…
2693	Struct.non-refractory clay; ceramic products		2308	2827	2378	2711		…	…	…	…		…	…
2694	Cement, lime and plaster		6738	9315	5801	5645		…	…	…	…		…	…
2695	Articles of concrete, cement and plaster		11362	13969	8266	9305		…	…	…	…		…	…
2696	Cutting, shaping & finishing of stone		290	393	308	418		…	…	…	…		…	…
2699	Other non-metallic mineral products n.e.c.		1685	1715	1713	2416		…	…	…	…		…	…
2710	Basic iron and steel		132375	172643	117218	169052		…	…	…	…		…	…
2720	Basic precious and non-ferrous metals		8978	9678	8358	11177		…	…	…	…		…	…
273	Casting of metals		1781	1416	816	2022		…	…	…	…		…	…
2731	Casting of iron and steel		1520	1195	696	1818		…	…	…	…		…	…
2732	Casting of non-ferrous metals		261	221	120	204		…	…	…	…		…	…
281	Struct.metal products;tanks;steam generators		6427	8267	6125	6416		…	…	…	…		…	…
2811	Structural metal products		4959	6623	4705	4688		…	…	…	…		…	…
2812	Tanks, reservoirs and containers of metal		1111	1187	894	1195		…	…	…	…		…	…
2813	Steam generators		357	456	526	533		…	…	…	…		…	…
289	Other metal products; metal working services		7889	10032	8982	11234		…	…	…	…		…	…
2891	Metal forging/pressing/stamping/roll-forming		805	921	426	856		…	…	…	…		…	…
2892	Treatment & coating of metals		1635	1807	1532	2021		…	…	…	…		…	…
2893	Cutlery, hand tools and general hardware		604	645	545	619		…	…	…	…		…	…
2899	Other fabricated metal products n.e.c.		4846	6658	6478	7739		…	…	…	…		…	…
291	General purpose machinery		11589	15194	16142	17865		…	…	…	…		…	…
2911	Engines & turbines (not for transport equipment)		1680	2351	3624	3768		…	…	…	…		…	…
2912	Pumps, compressors, taps and valves		3367	4221	4586	4909		…	…	…	…		…	…
2913	Bearings, gears, gearing & driving elements		1109	1422	1306	1845		…	…	…	…		…	…
2914	Ovens, furnaces and furnace burners		242	295	214	313		…	…	…	…		…	…
2915	Lifting and handling equipment		2526	3495	2676	3116		…	…	…	…		…	…
2919	Other general purpose machinery		2665	3411	3737	3915		…	…	…	…		…	…

Code	Description				
292	Special purpose machinery	16342	19893	15959	19507
2921	Agricultural and forestry machinery	2860	3786	2316	3886
2922	Machine tools	3015	3196	3086	2948
2923	Machinery for metallurgy	2962	3733	3715	3821
2924	Machinery for mining & construction	4765	5927	3952	5307
2925	Food/beverage/tobacco processing machinery	707	943	817	950
2926	Machinery for textile, apparel and leather	16	23	9	11
2927	Weapons and ammunition	...	...	...	...
2929	Other special purpose machinery	2017	2285	2064	2583
2930	Domestic appliances n.e.c.	2170	2184	2145	2407
3000	Office, accounting and computing machinery	1312	1333	1095	1163
3110	Electric motors, generators and transformers	4658	6769	6603	5856
3120	Electricity distribution & control apparatus	2561	3127	2690	3244
3130	Insulated wire and cable	3082	3213	2016	3129
3140	Accumulators, primary cells and batteries	1241	1346	1229	2154
3150	Lighting equipment and electric lamps	591	637	614	845
3190	Other electrical equipment n.e.c.	2036	2688	3352	3731
3210	Electronic valves, tubes, etc.	700	696	538	631
3220	TV/radio transmitters; line comm. apparatus	1152	1094	716	705
3230	TV and radio receivers and associated goods	570	645	963	1160
331	Medical, measuring, testing appliances, etc.	3221	3745	4011	4856
3311	Medical, surgical and orthopaedic equipment	744	888	884	1150
3312	Measuring/testing/navigating appliances,etc.	2271	2436	2861	3329
3313	Industrial process control equipment	206	421	266	377
3320	Optical instruments & photographic equipment	80	270	668	223
3330	Watches and clocks	13	17	10	13
3410	Motor vehicles	23388	26422	5733	6872
3420	Automobile bodies, trailers & semi-trailers	422	555	492	358
3430	Parts/accessories for automobiles	1804	1896	1163	1624
351	Building and repairing of ships and boats	1894	2151	2960	2140
3511	Building and repairing of ships	1820	2044	2811	2014
3512	Building/repairing of pleasure/sport. boats	75	108	149	126
3520	Railway/tramway locomotives & rolling stock	16001	23997	9986	30077
3530	Aircraft and spacecraft	3295	3773	6613	7643
359	Transport equipment n.e.c.	219	134	135	148
3591	Motorcycles	17	6	7	5
3592	Bicycles and invalid carriages	150	116	111	126
3599	Other transport equipment n.e.c.	52	12	17	17
3610	Furniture	4412	5413	3900	4932
369	Manufacturing n.e.c.	1499	1842	1734	1899
3691	Jewellery and related articles	749	972	789	756
3692	Musical instruments	4	5	5	9
3693	Sports goods	182	234	322	391
3694	Games and toys	177	245	117	146
3699	Other manufacturing n.e.c.	388	385	502	596
3710	Recycling of metal waste and scrap	4597	5493	4051	9491
3720	Recycling of non-metal waste and scrap	383	458	497	626
D	Total manufacturing	530163	668466	559267	730544

Ukraine

ISIC Revision 3 — Index numbers of industrial production (2005=100)

ISIC	Industry	Note	1999	2000	2001	2002	2003	2004	2005	2006	2007	2008	2009	2010
15	Food and beverages		:	51	60	65	78	88	100	110	119	117	110	115
16	Tobacco products		:	:	:	:	:	:	:	:	:	:	:	:
17	Textiles	a/	:	:	:	:	:	:	:	:	:	:	:	:
18	Wearing apparel, fur	a/	:	70	82	82	85	97	100	95	92	82	59	65
19	Leather, leather products and footwear		:	:	:	:	:	:	:	:	:	:	:	:
20	Wood products (excl. furniture)		:	82	92	90	97	109	100	111	110	107	90	96
21	Paper and paper products	b/	:	34	43	54	66	83	100	114	128	126	97	107
22	Printing and publishing	b/	:	43	52	56	70	88	100	111	123	124	101	104
23	Coke,refined petroleum products,nuclear fuel		:	:	:	:	:	:	:	:	:	:	:	:
24	Chemicals and chemical products		:	51	79	102	111	115	100	88	90	78	77	77
25	Rubber and plastics products		:	62	66	72	83	93	100	101	108	97	77	97
26	Non-metallic mineral products		:	43	54	54	65	85	100	111	127	127	98	108
27	Basic metals	c/	:	53	59	62	72	88	100	112	127	125	78	84
28	Fabricated metal products	c/	:	72	76	79	90	101	100	109	117	103	82	92
29	Machinery and equipment n.e.c.		:	:	:	:	:	:	:	:	:	:	:	:
30	Office, accounting and computing machinery		:	51	61	62	75	89	100	103	106	105	68	82
31	Electrical machinery and apparatus		:	37	33	41	54	77	100	98	72	85	46	44
32	Radio,television and communication equipment		:	46	52	57	67	110	100	111	174	161	125	158
33	Medical, precision and optical instruments		:	40	56	56	71	78	100	99	104	83	64	77
34	Motor vehicles, trailers, semi-trailers	d/	:	61	70	75	86	109	100	117	122	121	80	100
35	Other transport equipment	d/	:	27	33	43	69	89	100	119	155	168	74	121
36	Furniture; manufacturing n.e.c.		:	:	:	:	:	:	:	:	:	:	:	:
37	Recycling		:	:	:	:	:	:	:	:	:	:	:	:
D	Total manufacturing		50	58	67	72	86	97	100	106	117	109	80	92

a/ 17 includes 18.
b/ 21 includes 22.
c/ 27 includes 28.
d/ 34 includes 35.

United Kingdom

Supplier of information:
Office for National Statistics, London.
Industrial statistics for the OECD countries are compiled by the OECD secretariat, which supplies them to UNIDO.

Basic source of data:
Annual employment survey; annual business inquiry.

Major deviations from ISIC (Revision 4):
Data have been converted from the national NACE equivalent system to ISIC (Revision 4) by the OECD.

Reference period:
Calendar year.

Scope:
All enterprises.

Method of data collection:
Mail questionnaires.

Type of enumeration:
Not reported.

Adjusted for non-response:
Not reported.

Concepts and definitions of variables:
No deviations from the standard UN concepts and definitions are reported.

Related national publications:
None reported.

United Kingdom

ISIC Revision 4		Number of enterprises (number)					Number of employees (thousands)					Wages and salaries paid to employees (millions of British Pounds)				
ISIC	Industry	Note	2006	2007	2008	2009	Note	2006	2007	2008	2009	Note	2006	2007	2008	2009
1010	Processing/preserving of meat		…	…	1035	1026		…	…	81	72		…	…	1589	1610
1020	Processing/preserving of fish, etc.		…	…	343	337		…	…	16	…		…	…	241	268
1030	Processing/preserving of fruit,vegetables		…	…	452	440		…	…	34	31		…	…	723	684
1040	Vegetable and animal oils and fats		…	…	47	34		…	…	1	…		…	…	28	39
1050	Dairy products		…	…	543	541		…	…	29	28		…	…	662	638
106	Grain mill products,starches and starch products		…	…	133	128		…	…	13	15		…	…	417	432
1061	Grain mill products		…	…	128	…		…	…	12	13		…	…	355	…
1062	Starches and starch products		…	…	5	…		…	…	1	2		…	…	63	…
107	Other food products		…	…	3515	3401		…	…	187	185		…	…	4317	4275
1071	Bakery products		…	…	2107	2079		…	…	102	88		…	…	1994	2047
1072	Sugar		…	…	3	…		…	…	2	…		…	…	…	…
1073	Cocoa, chocolate and sugar confectionery		…	…	283	292		…	…	23	…		…	…	650	547
1074	Macaroni, noodles, couscous, etc.		…	…	25	12		…	…	4	1		…	…	70	12
1075	Prepared meals and dishes		…	…	28	…		…	…	8	21		…	…	…	…
1079	Other food products n.e.c.		…	…	1069	957		…	…	47	50		…	…	1315	1217
1080	Prepared animal feeds		…	…	426	418		…	…	12	14		…	…	302	379
1101	Distilling, rectifying and blending of spirits		…	…	955 a/	938 a/		…	…	45 a/	…		…	…	1623 a/	1758 a/
1102	Wines		…	…	… a/	… a/		…	…	… a/	…		…	…	… a/	… a/
1103	Malt liquors and malt		…	…	… a/	… a/		…	…	… a/	…		…	…	… a/	… a/
1104	Soft drinks,mineral waters,other bottled waters		…	…	… a/	… a/		…	…	… a/	…		…	…	… a/	… a/
1200	Tobacco products		…	…	12	12		…	…	5	…		…	…	195	180
131	Spinning, weaving and finishing of textiles		…	…	1065	1037		…	…	21	17		…	…	358	327
1311	Preparation and spinning of textile fibres		…	…	149	136		…	…	5	…		…	…	59	55
1312	Weaving of textiles		…	…	251	231		…	…	8	…		…	…	160	148
1313	Finishing of textiles		…	…	665	670		…	…	8	6		…	…	139	124
139	Other textiles		…	…	3190	3031		…	…	41	38		…	…	766	681
1391	Knitted and crocheted fabrics		…	…	114	101		…	…	2	1		…	…	28	22
1392	Made-up textile articles, except apparel		…	…	2092	2039		…	…	22	21		…	…	383	319
1393	Carpets and rugs		…	…	201	171		…	…	7	6		…	…	161	151
1394	Cordage, rope, twine and netting		…	…	99	95		…	…	2	1		…	…	20	21
1399	Other textiles n.e.c.		…	…	684	625		…	…	8	8		…	…	173	167
1410	Wearing apparel, except fur apparel		…	…	3529	3301		…	…	28	…		…	…	420	322
1420	Articles of fur		…	…	12	9		…	…	…	…		…	…	2	1
1430	Knitted and crocheted apparel		…	…	285	262		…	…	6	-		…	…	82	75
151	Leather;luggage,handbags,saddlery,harness;fur		…	…	328	378		…	…	3	…		…	…	73	68
1511	Tanning/dressing of leather; dressing of fur		…	…	82	73		…	…	1	…		…	…	31	29
1512	Luggage,handbags,etc.;saddlery/harness		…	…	246	305		…	…	2	…		…	…	42	39
1520	Footwear		…	…	204	201		…	…	4	4		…	…	71	69
1610	Sawmilling and planing of wood		…	…	717	664		…	…	10	9		…	…	205	164
162	Wood products, cork, straw, plaiting materials		…	…	7175	7369		…	…	64	50		…	…	1225	1043

1621 Veneer sheets and wood-based panels	...	...	138	136	...	...	5	4	...	...	129	97
1622 Builders' carpentry and joinery	...	...	5214	5523	...	...	45	34	...	...	861	742
1623 Wooden containers	...	...	424	407	...	...	6	6	...	...	110	84
1629 Other wood products;articles of cork,straw	...	...	1399	1303	...	...	8	6	...	...	125	120
1701 Pulp, paper and paperboard	...	...	295	277	...	...	13	...	...	...	395	352
1702 Corrugated paper and paperboard	...	...	585	562	...	...	28	...	...	...	678	629
1709 Other articles of paper and paperboard	...	...	1749	1042	...	...	21	...	...	...	495	522
181 Printing and service activities related to printing	...	...	14943	14055	...	...	137	106	...	...	3207	2962
1811 Printing	...	...	11579	11111	...	...	116	89	...	...	2835	2599
1812 Service activities related to printing	...	...	3364	2944	...	...	21	17	...	...	372	363
1820 Reproduction of recorded media	...	...	1575	1378	...	...	4	3	...	...	84	99
1910 Coke oven products	...	...	-	-	...	...	-	...	...	...	-	-
1920 Refined petroleum products	...	...	245	208	...	...	10	...	...	...	467	483
201 Basic chemicals,fertilizers, etc.	...	...	925	845	...	...	46	118b/	...	...	1635	1491
2011 Basic chemicals	...	...	366	340	...	...	28	...	...	...	1043	1029
2012 Fertilizers and nitrogen compounds	...	...	71	66	...	...	2	...	...	...	94	81
2013 Plastics and synthetic rubber in primary forms	...	...	488	439	...	...	16	...	...	...	499	381
202 Other chemical products	...	...	1924	1850	...	...	76	...b/	...	...	2058	1985
2021 Pesticides and other agrochemical products	...	...	70	68	...	...	3	3	...	...	119	105
2022 Paints,varnishes;printing ink and mastics	...	...	463	444	...	...	18	...	...	...	537	482
2023 Soap,cleaning and cosmetic preparations	...	...	677	683	...	...	29	25	...	...	601	614
2029 Other chemical products n.e.c.	...	...	714	655	...	...	26	...	...	...	802	784
2030 Man-made fibres	...	...	17	17	...	...	2	...b/	...	...	60	107
2100 Pharmaceuticals,medicinal chemicals, etc.	...	...	375	463	...	...	44	40	...	...	2263	2202
221 Rubber products	...	...	684	650	...	...	26	24	...	...	664	580
2211 Rubber tyres and tubes	...	...	98	78	...	...	7	7	...	...	226	202
2219 Other rubber products	...	...	586	572	...	...	19	17	...	...	438	378
2220 Plastics products	...	...	5956	5615	...	...	160	128	...	...	3411	3163
2310 Glass and glass products	...	...	1076	968	...	...	...	22	...	...	625	570
239 Non-metallic mineral products n.e.c.	...	...	3332	3186	...	...	81	78	...	...	2122	1887
2391 Refractory products	...	...	124	114	...	...	4	...	...	...	102	92
2392 Clay building materials	...	...	315	283	...	...	10	8	...	...	263	186
2393 Other porcelain and ceramic products	...	...	380	355	...	...	10	...	...	...	200	173
2394 Cement, lime and plaster	...	...	21	24	...	...	6	...	...	...	143	108
2395 Articles of concrete, cement and plaster	...	...	1079	1014	...	...	35	...	...	...	1035	979
2396 Cutting, shaping and finishing of stone	...	...	1132	1130	...	...	8	9	...	...	159	138
2399 Other non-metallic mineral products n.e.c.	...	...	281	266	...	...	8	...	...	...	220	210
2410 Basic iron and steel	...	...	416	...	...	...	37	68c/	...	...	1179	...
2420 Basic precious and other non-ferrous metals	...	...	496	451	...	...	...	...c/	...	...	...	...
243 Casting of metals	...	...	672	617	...	...	20	...c/	...	...	359	300
2431 Casting of iron and steel	...	...	347	314	...	...	9	...	...	...	220	166
2432 Casting of non-ferrous metals	...	...	325	303	...	...	10	...	...	...	139	134
251 Struct.metal products, tanks, reservoirs	...	...	4994	4820	...	...	97	...	...	...	2309	2226
2511 Structural metal products	...	...	4522	4376	...	...	84	80	...	...	1973	1891
2512 Tanks, reservoirs and containers of metal	...	...	381	351	...	...	11	11	...	...	298	282

continued

United Kingdom

- 812 -

ISIC	Industry	Number of enterprises (number) Note	2006	2007	2008	2009	Number of employees (thousands) Note	2006	2007	2008	2009	Wages and salaries paid to employees (millions of British Pounds) Note	2006	2007	2008	2009
2513	Steam generators, excl. hot water boilers		...	...	91	93		...	...	2	...		...	...	39	53
2520	Weapons and ammunition		...	...	139	131		...	...	15	...		...	...	497	442
259	Other metal products;metal working services		...	...	21474	21866		...	...	218	216		...	...	4667	4011
2591	Forging,pressing,stamping,roll-forming of metal		...	...	918	895		...	...	24	19		...	...	578	406
2592	Treatment and coating of metals; machining		...	...	13514	14114		...	...	111	119		...	...	2266	2238
2593	Cutlery, hand tools and general hardware		...	...	2028	1936		...	...	25	23		...	...	530	379
2599	Other fabricated metal products n.e.c.		...	...	5014	4921		...	...	57	55		...	...	1293	988
2610	Electronic components and boards		...	...	1118	965		...	...	31	22		...	...	697	563
2620	Computers and peripheral equipment		...	...	801	949		...	...	11	...		...	...	374	315
2630	Communication equipment		...	...	1670	1683		...	...	26	...		...	...	666	519
2640	Consumer electronics		...	...	758	698		...	...	11	...		...	...	276	223
265	Measuring,testing equipment; watches, etc.		...	...	2468	2330		...	...	59	51		...	...	1814	1649
2651	Measuring/testing/navigating equipment,etc.		...	...	2387	2260		...	...	58	50		...	...	1800	1635
2652	Watches and clocks		...	...	81	70		...	...	2	1		...	...	14	13
2660	Irradiation/electromedical equipment,etc.		...	...	80	80		...	...	2	3		...	...	40	114
2670	Optical instruments and photographic equipment		...	...	166	...		...	...	3	...		...	...	97	...
2680	Magnetic and optical media		...	...	43	...		...	...	-	-		...	...	5	...
2710	Electric motors,generators,transformers,etc.		...	...	1066	1044		...	...	38	38		...	...	1022	1022
2720	Batteries and accumulators		...	...	97	80		...	...	3	...		...	...	110	71
273	Wiring and wiring devices		...	...	301	328		...	...	10	...		...	...	272	334
2731	Fibre optic cables		...	...	75	53		...	...	3	...		...	...	66	49
2732	Other electronic and electric wires and cables		...	...	181	216		...	...	7	...		...	...	177	192
2733	Wiring devices		...	...	45	59		...	...	1	...		...	...	30	93
2740	Electric lighting equipment		...	...	701	674		...	...	16	...		...	...	350	299
2750	Domestic appliances		...	...	385	348		...	...	20	16		...	...	430	432
2790	Other electrical equipment		...	...	741	484		...	...	7	8		...	...	211	235
281	General-purpose machinery		...	...	5208	5131		...	...	142	192d/		...	...	3763	4255
2811	Engines/turbines,excl.aircraft,vehicle engines		...	...	220	233		...	...	10	...		...	...	386	1168
2812	Fluid power equipment		...	...	145	139		...	...	6	...		...	...	141	150
2813	Other pumps, compressors, taps and valves		...	...	617	591		...	...	26	...		...	...	815	769
2814	Bearings, gears, gearing and driving elements		...	...	301	278		...	...	11	...		...	...	248	236
2815	Ovens, furnaces and furnace burners		...	...	169	165		...	...	3	2		...	...	75	70
2816	Lifting and handling equipment		...	...	916	974		...	...	20	19		...	...	469	488
2817	Office machinery, excl.computers,etc.		...	...	139	113		...	...	8	7		...	...	218	213
2818	Power-driven hand tools		...	...	24	19		...	...	2	1		...	...	43	27
2819	Other general-purpose machinery		...	...	2677	2619		...	...	57	42		...	...	1367	1134
282	Special-purpose machinery		...	...	4877	4078		...	...	66	...d/		...	...	1849	1485
2821	Agricultural and forestry machinery		...	...	461	337		...	...	5	6		...	...	133	162
2822	Metal-forming machinery and machine tools		...	...	1134	1080		...	...	9	...		...	...	247	229
2823	Machinery for metallurgy		...	...	19	16		...	...	1	1		...	...	35	16
2824	Mining, quarrying and construction machinery		...	...	341	297		...	...	17	16		...	...	508	383

ISIC	Industry	(1)	(2)	(3)	(4)	(5)	(6)
2825	Food/beverage/tobacco processing machinery	597	545	9	7	233	217
2826	Textile/apparel/leather production machinery	189	172	2	1	36	31
2829	Other special-purpose machinery	2136	1631	22	15	658	447
2910	Motor vehicles	751	712	76	…	2525	2379
2920	Automobile bodies, trailers and semi-trailers	895	860	24	22	577	458
2930	Parts and accessories for motor vehicles	1673	1429	76	…	1776	1322
301	Building of ships and boats	1093	1097	27	38	724	914
3011	Building of ships and floating structures	473	477	16	29	603	658
3012	Building of pleasure and sporting boats	620	620	10	9	121	256
3020	Railway locomotives and rolling stock	21	40	6	…	216	…
3030	Air and spacecraft and related machinery	379	440	87	…	3134	3173
3040	Military fighting vehicles	-	6	-	…	-	…
309	Transport equipment n.e.c.	280	286	3	…	66	73
3091	Motorcycles	89	86	1	…	26	24
3092	Bicycles and invalid carriages	80	84	1	…	18	37
3099	Other transport equipment n.e.c.	111	116	1	…	22	13
3100	Furniture	6397	6384	93	91	1956	1429
321	Jewellery, bijouterie and related articles	1491	1408	8	…	115	108
3211	Jewellery and related articles	…	…	…	…	…	…
3212	Imitation jewellery and related articles	…	…	…	…	…	…
3220	Musical instruments	275	279	1	1	20	15
3230	Sports goods	708	568	6	5	95	92
3240	Games and toys	591	567	6	…	104	112
3250	Medical and dental instruments and supplies	1809	1870	47	39	1147	931
3290	Other manufacturing n.e.c.	4512	5133	22	25	394	458
331	Repair of fabricated metal products/machinery	4061	4515	100	64	2846	2120
3311	Repair of fabricated metal products	366	316	7	10	360	358
3312	Repair of machinery	1870	1969	35	22	851	792
3313	Repair of electronic and optical equipment	151	133	2	3	88	59
3314	Repair of electrical equipment	562	660	11	5	216	100
3315	Repair of transport equip., excl. motor vehicles	883	951	43	23	1310	775
3319	Repair of other equipment	229	486	1	2	21	37
3320	Installation of industrial machinery/equipment	563	765	12	16	504	593
C	Total manufacturing	131817	128468	2726	2495	69616	65033

a/ 1101 includes 1102, 1103 and 1104.
b/ 201 includes 202 and 2030.
c/ 2410 includes 2420 and 243.
d/ 281 includes 282.

United Kingdom

ISIC	Industry	Output (millions of British Pounds) Note	2006	2007	2008	2009	Value added at factor values (millions of British Pounds) Note	2006	2007	2008	2009	Gross fixed capital formation (millions of British Pounds) Note	2008	2009
1010	Processing/preserving of meat		...	...	12926	14247		...	...	2600	2742		241	229
1020	Processing/preserving of fish, etc.		...	...	2066	2753		...	...	468	606		74	51
1030	Processing/preserving of fruit,vegetables		...	...	4109	3956		...	...	1437	1522		162	162
1040	Vegetable and animal oils and fats		...	...	867	1055		...	...	260	332		9	10
1050	Dairy products		...	...	6888	6513		...	...	1349	1338		218	252
106	Grain mill products,starches and starch products		...	...	5231	4764		...	...	1455	1208		101	123
1061	Grain mill products		...	...	3871	...		...	...	1362	...		...	...
1062	Starches and starch products		...	...	1360	...		...	...	94	...		...	...
107	Other food products		...	...	24168	24615		...	...	9733	9209		944	780
1071	Bakery products		...	...	9171	9030		...	...	3753	3958		407	304
1072	Sugar		...	...	...	...		...	...	184	...		...	...
1073	Cocoa, chocolate and sugar confectionery		...	...	4133	4344		...	...	2293	1835		117	119
1074	Macaroni, noodles, couscous, etc.		...	...	295	78		...	...	87	20		9	3
1075	Prepared meals and dishes		...	...	...	...		...	...	403	...		...	...
1079	Other food products n.e.c.		...	...	8342	8125		...	...	3012	2573		341	265
1080	Prepared animal feeds		...	...	4228	5084		...	...	846	1296		76	97
1101	Distilling, rectifying and blending of spirits		...	...	24237a/	27241a/		...	...	5492a/	6980a/		1057a/	887a/
1102	Wines		...	...	...a/	...a/		...	...	...a/	...a/		...a/	...a/
1103	Malt liquors and malt		...	...	...a/	...a/		...	...	...a/	...a/		...a/	...a/
1104	Soft drinks,mineral waters,other bottled waters		...	...	...a/	...a/		...	...	...a/	...a/		...a/	...a/
1200	Tobacco products		...	...	...a/	...a/		...	...	...a/	...a/		...a/	...a/
131	Spinning, weaving and finishing of textiles		...	...	1563	1431		...	...	552	470		35	26
1311	Preparation and spinning of textile fibres		...	...	248	214		...	...	83	58		6	3
1312	Weaving of textiles		...	...	707	602		...	...	245	205		17	12
1313	Finishing of textiles		...	...	608	616		...	...	225	207		12	11
139	Other textiles		...	...	3623	3149		...	...	1477	1341		104	81
1391	Knitted and crocheted fabrics		...	...	171	153		...	...	51	56		5	2
1392	Made-up textile articles, except apparel		...	...	1707	1581		...	...	797	768		29	30
1393	Carpets and rugs		...	...	821	584		...	...	286	183		20	16
1394	Cordage, rope, twine and netting		...	...	89	111		...	...	36	43		1	6
1399	Other textiles n.e.c.		...	...	836	720		...	...	307	291		50	27
1410	Wearing apparel, except fur apparel		...	...	2398	1879		...	...	913	556		24	19
1420	Articles of fur		...	...	5	3		...	...	2	...		-	-
1430	Knitted and crocheted apparel		...	...	315	305		...	...	146	94		2	2
151	Leather;luggage,handbags,saddlery,harness;fur		...	...	329	367		...	...	121	119		4	8
1511	Tanning/dressing of leather; dressing of fur		...	...	178	198		...	...	21	23		3	6
1512	Luggage,handbags,etc.;saddlery/harness		...	...	151	169		...	...	100	96		1	2
1520	Footwear		...	...	326	271		...	...	149	117		6	6
1610	Sawmilling and planing of wood		...	...	1246	829		...	...	437	288		56	56
162	Wood products, cork, straw, plaiting materials		...	...	6324	5020		...	...	2532	1700		132	154

1621	Veneer sheets and wood-based panels	995	774	248	157	27	15
1622	Builders' carpentry and joinery	4198	2794	1792	1148	86	124
1623	Wooden containers	532	455	270	186	10	7
1629	Other wood products;articles of cork,straw	599	997	222	208	8	7
1701	Pulp, paper and paperboard	2749	2320	716	640	102	69
1702	Corrugated paper and paperboard	3342	3454	1116	1029	97	72
1709	Other articles of paper and paperboard	3538	3598	893	944	86	92
181	Printing and service activities related to printing	12318	10269	5973	4766	679	569b/
1811	Printing	10972	9132	5222	4090	633	...
1812	Service activities related to printing	1346	1137	751	676	46	...b/
1820	Reproduction of recorded media	463	369	330	192	28	...
1910	Coke oven products	-	-	-	-	-	-
1920	Refined petroleum products	39790	31603	1518	1269	388	390
201	Basic chemicals,fertilizers, etc.	30664	18225	5502	4947	941	424
2011	Basic chemicals	23996	13483	4034	4123	768	...
2012	Fertilizers and nitrogen compounds	1837	1165	371	145	55	...
2013	Plastics and synthetic rubber in primary forms	4831	3577	1097	679	118	411
202	Other chemical products	13235	12249	4726	...	24	87
2021	Pesticides and other agrochemical products	658	682	251	205	84	40
2022	Paints,varnishes;printing ink and mastics	3222	3017	1032	1095	...	122
2023	Soap,cleaning and cosmetic preparations	3930	4036	1380	1174	...	162
2029	Other chemical products n.e.c.	5425	4514	2063	...	44	44
2030	Man-made fibres	520	1104	233	...	655	594
2100	Pharmaceuticals,medicinal chemicals, etc.	14224	14882	8612	7792	93	76
221	Rubber products	3574	2865	1410	986	26	22
2211	Rubber tyres and tubes	1829	1413	617	355	68	53
2219	Other rubber products	1746	1452	793	631	718	460
2220	Plastics products	16613	15588	6509	5646	715	376
2310	Glass and glass products	3276	2873	1144	903	11	37
239	Non-metallic mineral products n.e.c.	10462	9329	3683	2621	89	...
2391	Refractory products	396	304	142	99	...	...
2392	Clay building materials	878	629	340	193	...	...
2393	Other porcelain and ceramic products	664	548	319	247	...	30
2394	Cement, lime and plaster	717	705	287	256	30	...
2395	Articles of concrete, cement and plaster	6341	5533	2004	1196	15	20
2396	Cutting, shaping and finishing of stone	346	567	185	292	128	34
2399	Other non-metallic mineral products n.e.c.	1121	1043	406	337	...	...
2410	Basic iron and steel	11406	...	2950	...	...	...
2420	Basic precious and other non-ferrous metals	-	-	-	...	57	23
243	Casting of metals	1354	1085	596	473	36	15
2431	Casting of iron and steel	764	593	368	247	21	7
2432	Casting of non-ferrous metals	590	492	228	226	...	...
251	Struct.metal products, tanks, reservoirs	11249	9272	4405	3669	267	256
2511	Structural metal products	9840	7562	3805	2954	217	195
2512	Tanks, reservoirs and containers of metal	1230	1462	516	603	47	51

continued

United Kingdom

ISIC Revision 4

ISIC	Industry	Output Note	Output 2006	Output 2007	Output 2008	Output 2009	VA Note	VA 2006	VA 2007	VA 2008	VA 2009	GFCF Note	GFCF 2008	GFCF 2009
			\(millions of British Pounds\)					\(millions of British Pounds\)					\(millions of British Pounds\)	
2513	Steam generators, excl. hot water boilers		...	...	179	248		...	...	84	112		3	10
2520	Weapons and ammunition		...	...	2891	2492		...	...	1033	949		45	48
259	Other metal products;metal working services		...	...	18986	16044		...	...	8493	7154		646	370
2591	Forging,pressing,stamping,roll-forming of metal		...	...	2666	1690		...	...	923	505		63	45
2592	Treatment and coating of metals; machining		...	...	8575	7826		...	...	4435	3990		324	141
2593	Cutlery, hand tools and general hardware		...	...	1589	1454		...	...	907	725		79	38
2599	Other fabricated metal products n.e.c.		...	...	6155	5074		...	...	2228	1934		180	145
2610	Electronic components and boards		...	...	3685	2617		...	...	1646	955		104	57
2620	Computers and peripheral equipment		...	...	2013	2255		...	...	589	629		67	89
2630	Communication equipment		...	...	3711	2791		...	...	1405	1039		80	37
2640	Consumer electronics		...	...	1730	1305		...	...	697	974		...	...
265	Measuring,testing equipment; watches, etc.		...	...	8451	7223		...	...	3742	2981		177	137
2651	Measuring/testing/navigating equipment,etc.		...	...	8389	7168		...	...	3717	2954		176	137
2652	Watches and clocks		...	...	62	54		...	...	24	27		1	1
2660	Irradiation/electromedical equipment,etc.		...	...	178	726		...	...	81	212		4	7
2670	Optical instruments and photographic equipment		...	...	...	...		...	...	149	...		...	...
2680	Magnetic and optical media		...	...	...	...		...	...	15	...		...	...
2710	Electric motors,generators,transformers,etc.		...	...	4732	4622		...	...	2014	1749		104	110
2720	Batteries and accumulators		...	...	389	355		...	...	96	127		35	5
273	Wiring and wiring devices		...	...	1378	1573		...	...	403	528		32	34
2731	Fibre optic cables		...	...	421	340		...	...	68	101		...	3
2732	Other electronic and electric wires and cables		...	...	808	803		...	...	259	246		...	26
2733	Wiring devices		...	...	149	430		...	...	75	181		...	5
2740	Electric lighting equipment		...	...	1596	1501		...	...	652	459		1	...
2750	Domestic appliances		...	...	2321	2204		...	...	676	724		57	24
2790	Other electrical equipment		...	...	746	922		...	...	352	452		51	33
281	General-purpose machinery		...	...	19481	18663		...	...	6731	7763		11	11
2811	Engines/turbines,excl.aircraft,vehicle engines		...	...	2913	5037		...	...	645	2406		525	530
2812	Fluid power equipment		...	...	543	586		...	...	194	237		62	236
2813	Other pumps, compressors, taps and valves		...	...	3668	3153		...	...	1250	1396		19	10
2814	Bearings, gears, gearing and driving elements		...	...	1184	913		...	...	480	338		112	83
2815	Ovens, furnaces and furnace burners		...	...	341	293		...	...	143	111		40	18
2816	Lifting and handling equipment		...	...	2782	2389		...	...	918	681		...	2
2817	Office machinery, excl.computers,etc.		...	...	696	665		...	...	435	360		59	...
2818	Power-driven hand tools		...	...	182	98		...	...	65	38		30	26
2819	Other general-purpose machinery		...	...	7173	5529		...	...	2599	2194		195	90
282	Special-purpose machinery		...	...	10485	7809		...	...	4371	2797		229	191
2821	Agricultural and forestry machinery		...	...	1440	1476		...	...	272	284		21	41
2822	Metal-forming machinery and machine tools		...	...	1011	802		...	...	477	332		25	15
2823	Machinery for metallurgy		...	...	137	60		...	...	78	29		5	6
2824	Mining, quarrying and construction machinery		...	...	4013	2499		...	...	1166	686		106	87

Code						
2825	Food/beverage/tobacco processing machinery	825	915	439	370	15	10
2826	Textile/apparel/leather production machinery	109	94	56	44	4	2
2829	Other special-purpose machinery	2950	1964	1884	1052	54	31
2910	Motor vehicles	30860	23202	6301	3330	1114	1160
2920	Automobile bodies, trailers and semi-trailers	3026	2539	776	726	56	46
2930	Parts and accessories for motor vehicles	10122	6929	3145	1793	277	123
301	Building of ships and boats	2546	3695	905	1251	58	106
3011	Building of ships and floating structures	1971	2756	658	909	47	84
3012	Building of pleasure and sporting boats	574	939	247	342	10	22
3020	Railway locomotives and rolling stock	1373	1195	541	126	25	28
3030	Air and spacecraft and related machinery	18519	19288	6820	6410	493	538
3040	Military fighting vehicles	440	532	146	53	-	2
309	Transport equipment n.e.c.	283	507	89	53	14	12
3091	Motorcycles	68	292	35	20	10	9
3092	Bicycles and invalid carriages	88	154	22	60	2	2
3099	Other transport equipment n.e.c.	8548	6392	3525	2442	145	1
3100	Furniture	877	847	254	282	13	195
321	Jewellery, bijouterie and related articles	...	...	...	...	...	16
3211	Jewellery and related articles	...	...	...	...	...	...
3212	Imitation jewellery and related articles	69	56	34	23	9	6
3220	Musical instruments	471	334	252	146	16	11
3230	Sports goods	539	515	310	228	164	199
3240	Games and toys	4148	3753	2026	2177	38	85
3250	Medical and dental instruments and supplies	1924	1881	790	880	260	386
3290	Other manufacturing n.e.c.	13049	9013	5464	4186	20	14
331	Repair of fabricated metal products/machinery	1128	1043	545	577	88	112
3311	Repair of fabricated metal products	3515	2424	1603	1222	3	2
3312	Repair of machinery	523	313	220	92	18	6
3313	Repair of electronic and optical equipment	1498	420	529	190	128	249
3314	Repair of electrical equipment	6282	4692	2520	2029	3	3
3315	Repair of transport equip., excl. motor vehicles	102	121	47	78	22	31
3319	Repair of other equipment	1976	2045	813	1007	...	...
3320	Installation of industrial machinery/equipment	...	...	...	...	...	...
C	Total manufacturing	492664	439611	152983	134824	15201	12721

a/ 1101 includes 1102, 1103, 1104 and 1200.
b/ 181 includes 1820.

United Kingdom

Index numbers of industrial production

ISIC Revision 4 — (2005=100)

ISIC	Industry	Note	1999	2000	2001	2002	2003	2004	2005	2006	2007	2008	2009	2010
10	Food products		96	96	96	99	96	99	100	99	98	96	94	98
11	Beverages		96	96	99	102	100	100	100	102	103	100	99	101
12	Tobacco products		120	110	106	108	109	104	100	96	98	90	95	91
13	Textiles		136	132	114	110	112	103	100	98	96	95	88	92
14	Wearing apparel		145	142	124	114	112	100	100	103	100	103	90	93
15	Leather and related products		228	206	190	174	150	110	100	104	107	101	91	91
16	Wood/wood products/cork,excl. furniture		95	97	97	98	99	104	100	98	102	95	79	80
17	Paper and paper products		104	103	99	101	101	100	100	100	103	101	93	95
18	Printing and reproduction of recorded media		103	104	102	105	103	101	100	98	95	91	89	86
19	Coke and refined petroleum products		104	105	98	102	101	107	100	94	94	92	87	85
20	Chemicals and chemical products		96	100	100	98	97	101	100	102	104	104	88	85
21	Pharmaceuticals,medicinal chemicals, etc.		67	70	81	87	92	94	100	106	102	104	110	102
22	Rubber and plastics products		136	132	114	110	112	103	100	106	102	103	88	102
23	Other non-metallic mineral products		87	90	91	91	94	101	100	98	96	95	88	92
24	Basic metals		113	110	105	94	94	99	100	104	104	101	87	90
25	Fabricated metal products, except machinery		94	97	97	94	96	99	100	100	101	98	73	80
26	Computer, electronic and optical products		114	134	124	104	101	105	100	103	106	101	83	86
27	Electrical equipment		117	121	117	107	100	102	100	101	101	95	91	85
28	Machinery and equipment n.e.c.		98	99	100	95	95	98	100	105	107	105	82	90
29	Motor vehicles, trailers and semi-trailers		100	95	90	98	100	102	100	105	108	107	85	102
30	Other transport equipment		93	97	100	87	93	99	100	96	101	96	68	81
31	Furniture		102	101	100	105	101	101	100	109	110	113	119	151
32	Other manufacturing		93	94	95	96	100	101	100	99	101	97	85	87
33	Repair and installation of machinery/equipment		114	124	116	98	94	100	100	101	106	99	97	102
C	Total manufacturing		100	102	101	98	98	100	100	108	109	107	103	105

United Republic of Tanzania

Supplier of information:
National Bureau of Statistics, Dar es Salaam.

Basic source of data:
Annual survey of industrial production.

Major deviations from ISIC (Revision 4):
None reported.

Reference period:
Calendar year.

Scope:
All registered establishments.

Method of data collection:
Direct interview in the field and mail questionnaires.

Type of enumeration:
Complete enumeration of all establishments with 10 or more persons engaged.

Adjusted for non-response:
Yes.

Concepts and definitions of variables:
Wages and salaries includes employers' contributions (in respect of their employees) paid to social security, pension and insurance schemes as well as the benefits received by employees under these schemes and severance and termination pay. Gross fixed capital formation excludes intellectual property products of R&D, computer software, databases, etc.

Related national publications:
Annual Survey of Industrial Production Report, published by the National Bureau of Statistics, Dar es Salaam.

United Republic of Tanzania

ISIC	Industry (ISIC Revision 4)	Number of establishments (number)					Number of employees (number)					Wages and salaries paid to employees (millions of Tanzanian Shillings)				
		Note	2007	2008	2009	2010a/	Note	2007	2008	2009	2010a/	Note	2007	2008	2009	2010a/
1010	Processing/preserving of meat		…	1	1	1		…	38	38	43		…	78	78	88
1020	Processing/preserving of fish, etc.		…	15	13	13		…	3849	1805	2044		…	7068	3637	4115
1030	Processing/preserving of fruit,vegetables		…	3	3	3		…	162	136	154		…	259	276	313
1040	Vegetable and animal oils and fats		…	31	34	34		…	1014	1526	1728		…	1329	2850	3225
1050	Dairy products		…	…	…	…		…	…	…	…		…	…	…	…
106	Grain mill products,starches and starch products		…	…	…	…		…	…	…	…		…	…	…	…
1061	Grain mill products		…	61	58	58		…	2152	3123	3536		…	1446	6739	7626
1062	Starches and starch products		…	…	…	…		…	…	…	…		…	…	…	…
107	Other food products		…	…	…	…		…	…	…	…		…	…	…	…
1071	Bakery products		…	20	21	21		…	632	651	737		…	849	900	1019
1072	Sugar		…	10	9	9		…	14670	15075	17068		…	16471	23626	26733
1073	Cocoa, chocolate and sugar confectionery		…	2	3	3		…	3831	2688	3043		…	5458	8195	9273
1074	Macaroni, noodles, couscous, etc.		…	…	…	…		…	…	…	…		…	…	…	…
1075	Prepared meals and dishes		…	…	…	…		…	…	…	…		…	…	…	…
1079	Other food products n.e.c.		…	56	58	58		…	17093	11496	13016		…	19654	28736	32515
1080	Prepared animal feeds		…	4	6	6		…	50	130	147		…	75	94	106
1101	Distilling, rectifying and blending of spirits		…	7	8	8		…	761	785	889		…	6118	6905	7813
1102	Wines		…	2	4	4		…	200	221	250		…	1032	1687	1908
1103	Malt liquors and malt		…	2	1	1		…	1019	952	1078		…	15227	15123	17112
1104	Soft drinks,mineral waters,other bottled waters		…	22	22	22		…	3817	3429	3882		…	13897	27298	30888
1200	Tobacco products		…	4	3	3		…	6747	3815	4319		…	17375	8204	9283
131	Spinning, weaving and finishing of textiles		…	…	…	…		…	…	…	…		…	…	…	…
1311	Preparation and spinning of textile fibres		…	1	1	1		…	62	62	70		…	125	125	142
1312	Weaving of textiles		…	4	4	4		…	2120	2967	3359		…	3593	3986	4510
1313	Finishing of textiles		…	19	5	5		…	214	60	68		…	108	212	240
139	Other textiles		…	…	…	…		…	…	…	…		…	…	…	…
1391	Knitted and crocheted fabrics		…	…	…	…		…	…	…	…		…	…	…	…
1392	Made-up textile articles, except apparel		…	7	5	5		…	4000	3902	4418		…	5039	4468	5056
1393	Carpets and rugs		…	3	3	3		…	851	627	710		…	825	817	925
1394	Cordage, rope, twine and netting		…	…	…	…		…	…	…	…		…	…	…	…
1399	Other textiles n.e.c.		…	…	…	…		…	…	…	…		…	…	…	…
1410	Wearing apparel, except fur apparel		…	4	4	4		…	4438	4502	5097		…	495	428	485
1420	Articles of fur		…	2	1	1		…	67	16	18		…	77	11	12
1430	Knitted and crocheted apparel		…	…	…	…		…	…	…	…		…	…	…	…
151	Leather;luggage,handbags,saddlery,harness;fur		…	…	…	…		…	…	…	…		…	…	…	…
1511	Tanning/dressing of leather; dressing of fur		…	1	2	2		…	46	82	93		…	135	244	276
1512	Luggage,handbags,etc.;saddlery/harness		…	3	3	3		…	589	413	468		…	343	3233	3659
1520	Footwear		…	3	2	2		…	803	654	740		…	1032	239	271
1610	Sawmilling and planing of wood		…	11	10	10		…	305	237	268		…	224	321	363
162	Wood products, cork, straw, plaiting materials		…	…	…	…		…	…	…	…		…	…	…	…

Note: Column headings for this statistical table appear on a preceding page and are not printed here. The numeric columns below are grouped as they appear on the page (three data groups of three columns each); blank cells correspond to the dotted leaders ("…") shown in the source.

1621	Veneer sheets and wood-based panels	510	451	316	233	206	173		3	3
1622	Builders' carpentry and joinery				206	182	277	4	3	3
1623	Wooden containers	1109	981	220	524	463		2	5	5
1629	Other wood products;articles of cork,straw	4005	3540	3002	2315	2045	1602	2	2	2
1701	Pulp, paper and paperboard	974	861	380	370	327	257	2	3	3
1702	Corrugated paper and paperboard									
1709	Other articles of paper and paperboard									
181	Printing and service activities related to printing	12733	11253	14199	4324	3819	3451	51	49	49
1811	Printing	273	242	221	84	74	157	3	3	3
1812	Service activities related to printing									
1820	Reproduction of recorded media									
1910	Coke oven products									
1920	Refined petroleum products									
201	Basic chemicals,fertilizers, etc.									
2011	Basic chemicals	5610	4958	5684	1413	1248	1203	9	9	9
2012	Fertilizers and nitrogen compounds				11	10		9	9	9
2013	Plastics and synthetic rubber in primary forms							1	1	1
202	Other chemical products									
2021	Pesticides and other agrochemical products	1787	1580	2072	793	700	838	9	8	8
2022	Paints,varnishes;printing ink and mastics	2153	1903	1955	824	728	874	8	9	9
2023	Soap,cleaning and cosmetic preparations	129	114	101	58	51	39	3	4	4
2029	Other chemical products n.e.c.			1470				1	1	1
2030	Man-made fibres	4051	3580	3176	1119	988	557	7	6	6
2100	Pharmaceuticals,medicinal chemicals, etc.						1135			
221	Rubber products	344	304		60	53			1	1
2211	Rubber tyres and tubes								1	1
2219	Other rubber products	6812	6020	6272	4742	4188	4112	15	21	21
2220	Plastics products			21			69	1		
2310	Glass and glass products									
239	Non-metallic mineral products n.e.c.	2143	1894	1665	1420	1254	1216	19	21	21
2391	Refractory products	53	47		10	9				
2392	Clay building materials	18019	15925	73402	1016	897	1065	1	1	1
2393	Other porcelain and ceramic products	487	430	437	175	155		3	3	3
2394	Cement, lime and plaster	2	2		9	8	180	3	4	4
2395	Articles of concrete, cement and plaster							1	1	1
2396	Cutting, shaping and finishing of stone									
2399	Other non-metallic mineral products n.e.c.	1531	1353	1277	1044	922	539	6	8	8
2410	Basic iron and steel	150	133		102	90			1	1
2420	Basic precious and other non-ferrous metals									
243	Casting of metals	1167	1031	657	358	316	258	1	1	1
2431	Casting of iron and steel							1	1	1
2432	Casting of non-ferrous metals									
251	Struct.metal products, tanks, reservoirs	1331	1177	1183	453	400	525	2	2	2
2511	Structural metal products	176	155	137	27	24	22	1	1	1
2512	Tanks, reservoirs and containers of metal							1	1	1

continued

United Republic of Tanzania

ISIC	Industry	Est. Note	Est. 2007	Est. 2008	Est. 2009	Est. 2010a/	Emp. Note	Emp. 2007	Emp. 2008	Emp. 2009	Emp. 2010a/	Wage Note	Wage 2007	Wage 2008	Wage 2009	Wage 2010a/
			(number)					(number)					(millions of Tanzanian Shillings)			
2513	Steam generators, excl. hot water boilers		...	...	...	...		...	...	...	...		...	...	...	...
2520	Weapons and ammunition		...	...	...	...		...	...	...	...		...	...	...	...
259	Other metal products;metal working services		...	...	...	...		...	...	...	...		...	...	...	...
2591	Forging,pressing,stamping,roll-forming of metal		...	...	...	...		...	...	...	...		...	...	...	...
2592	Treatment and coating of metals; machining		...	...	...	...		...	...	...	...		...	...	...	...
2593	Cutlery, hand tools and general hardware		...	...	...	...		...	...	...	...		...	...	...	...
2599	Other fabricated metal products n.e.c.		...	...	...	...		...	...	...	...		...	...	...	...
2610	Electronic components and boards		...	28	20	20		...	1793	1565	1772		...	2840	2931	3317
2620	Computers and peripheral equipment		...	...	...	...		...	...	...	...		...	...	...	...
2630	Communication equipment		...	...	...	...		...	...	...	...		...	...	...	...
2640	Consumer electronics		...	...	...	...		...	...	...	...		...	...	...	...
265	Measuring,testing equipment; watches, etc.		...	...	...	...		...	...	...	...		...	...	...	...
2651	Measuring/testing/navigating equipment,etc.		...	...	...	...		...	...	...	...		...	...	...	...
2652	Watches and clocks		...	...	...	...		...	...	...	...		...	...	...	...
2660	Irradiation/electromedical equipment,etc.		...	...	...	...		...	...	...	...		...	...	...	...
2670	Optical instruments and photographic equipment		...	...	...	...		...	...	...	...		...	...	...	...
2680	Magnetic and optical media		...	...	...	...		...	...	...	...		...	...	...	...
2710	Electric motors,generators,transformers,etc.		...	...	...	...		...	...	...	...		...	...	...	...
2720	Batteries and accumulators		...	1	1	1		...	183	167	189		...	503	493	557
273	Wiring and wiring devices		...	...	...	...		...	...	...	...		...	...	...	...
2731	Fibre optic cables		...	...	...	...		...	...	...	...		...	...	...	...
2732	Other electronic and electric wires and cables		...	2	2	2		...	128	211	239		...	867	941	1065
2733	Wiring devices		...	...	...	...		...	...	...	...		...	...	...	...
2740	Electric lighting equipment		...	1	1	1		...	37	76	86		...	59	59	67
2750	Domestic appliances		...	...	...	...		...	...	...	...		...	...	...	...
2790	Other electrical equipment		...	...	...	...		...	...	...	...		...	...	...	...
281	General-purpose machinery		...	1	3	3		...	14	67	76		...	46	97	110
2811	Engines/turbines,excl.aircraft,vehicle engines		...	...	...	...		...	...	...	...		...	...	...	...
2812	Fluid power equipment		...	...	...	...		...	...	...	...		...	...	...	...
2813	Other pumps, compressors, taps and valves		...	...	...	...		...	...	...	...		...	...	...	...
2814	Bearings, gears, gearing and driving elements		...	2	2	2		...	30	30	34		...	172	176	199
2815	Ovens, furnaces and furnace burners		...	...	...	...		...	...	...	...		...	...	...	...
2816	Lifting and handling equipment		...	...	...	...		...	...	...	...		...	...	...	...
2817	Office machinery, excl.computers,etc.		...	1	...	...		...	219	...	...		...	450	...	...
2818	Power-driven hand tools		...	...	...	...		...	...	...	...		...	...	...	...
2819	Other general-purpose machinery		...	...	...	...		...	...	...	...		...	...	...	...
282	Special-purpose machinery		...	...	...	...		...	...	...	...		...	...	...	...
2821	Agricultural and forestry machinery		...	...	2	2		...	...	...	...		...	...	...	...
2822	Metal-forming machinery and machine tools		...	2	2	2		...	34	33	37		...	36	112	126
2823	Machinery for metallurgy		...	...	...	...		...	...	...	...		...	...	...	...
2824	Mining, quarrying and construction machinery		...	2	2	2		...	71	51	58		...	107	42	48

Code	Industry									
2825	Food/beverage/tobacco processing machinery	...	...	...	...	10	11	...	12	14
2826	Textile/apparel/leather production machinery	...	1	1	...	...	...	...	...	...
2829	Other special-purpose machinery	...	1	1	...	39	44	...	89	100
2910	Motor vehicles	3	4	4	58	87	99	115	223	253
2920	Automobile bodies, trailers and semi-trailers	1	3	3	36	85	96	47	115	131
2930	Parts and accessories for motor vehicles	...	...	...	...	...	...	...	...	...
301	Building of ships and boats	...	...	...	...	...	...	...	...	...
3011	Building of ships and floating structures	1	1	1	63	63	71	26	26	29
3012	Building of pleasure and sporting boats	...	...	...	...	...	...	...	...	...
3020	Railway locomotives and rolling stock	...	...	...	...	...	...	...	...	...
3030	Air and spacecraft and related machinery	...	...	...	...	...	...	...	...	...
3040	Military fighting vehicles	...	...	...	...	...	...	...	...	...
309	Transport equipment n.e.c.	...	...	...	...	...	...	...	...	...
3091	Motorcycles	1	1	1	8	8	9	43	43	49
3092	Bicycles and invalid carriages	1	1	1	17	17	19	7	7	8
3099	Other transport equipment n.e.c.	...	...	...	...	...	...	...	...	...
3100	Furniture	96	81	81	2425	2485	2813	2341	2782	3148
321	Jewellery, bijouterie and related articles	4	21	21	34	185	209	27	99	112
3211	Jewellery and related articles	...	...	...	...	...	...	...	...	...
3212	Imitation jewellery and related articles	...	...	...	...	...	...	...	...	...
3220	Musical instruments	...	...	...	...	...	...	...	...	...
3230	Sports goods	...	...	...	...	...	...	...	...	...
3240	Games and toys	1	1	1	46	46	52	19	19	21
3250	Medical and dental instruments and supplies	77	76	76	12852	11799	13359	31076	32903	37230
3290	Other manufacturing n.e.c.	...	...	...	...	...	...	...	...	...
331	Repair of fabricated metal products/machinery	...	1	1	...	9	10	...	15	17
3311	Repair of fabricated metal products	1	1	1	10	10	11	12	12	13
3312	Repair of machinery	...	...	...	...	...	...	...	...	...
3313	Repair of electronic and optical equipment	1	1	1	23	26	29	173	186	211
3314	Repair of electrical equipment	1	1	1	15	11	12	4	5	6
3315	Repair of transport equip., excl. motor vehicles	2	4	4	30	62	70	267	303	343
3319	Repair of other equipment	...	...	...	...	...	...	...	...	...
3320	Installation of industrial machinery/equipment	...	...	...	...	...	...	...	...	...
C	Total manufacturing	680b/	686b/	686b/	106205b/	95691b/	108340b/	275418b/	248297b/	280954b/

a/ Provisional data.
b/ Sum of available data.

United Republic of Tanzania

ISIC	Industry	Output at factor values (millions of Tanzanian Shillings)					Value added at factor values (millions of Tanzanian Shillings)					Gross fixed capital formation (millions of Tanzanian Shillings)		
		Note	2007	2008	2009	2010a/	Note	2007	2008	2009	2010a/	Note	2009	2010a/
1010	Processing/preserving of meat		...	3398	3398	3567		...	2405	2406	2329		1707	1793
1020	Processing/preserving of fish, etc.		...	274670	137527	144363		...	72209	30215	29254		2914	3060
1030	Processing/preserving of fruit,vegetables		...	5180	5179	5436		...	2290	2262	2190		180	189
1040	Vegetable and animal oils and fats		...	73828	295855	310559		...	32730	78025	75545		11023	11574
1050	Dairy products		...	...	...	...		...	...	...	...		...	...
106	Grain mill products,starches and starch products		...	...	...	...		...	...	...	...		...	...
1061	Grain mill products		...	...	...	...		...	...	...	...		...	...
1062	Starches and starch products		...	104473	150883	158383		...	34510	21181	20508		27379	28748
107	Other food products		...	...	...	...		...	...	...	...		...	...
1071	Bakery products		...	23125	26254	27559		...	11450	9704	9396		833	874
1072	Sugar		...	...	...	...		...	...	...	...		...	...
1073	Cocoa, chocolate and sugar confectionery		...	147504	191971	201512		...	81514	116277	112581		41053	43106
1074	Macaroni, noodles, couscous, etc.		...	46151	17770	18653		...	21236	4656	4508		79	83
1075	Prepared meals and dishes		...	...	...	...		...	...	...	...		...	...
1079	Other food products n.e.c.		...	...	...	...		...	...	...	...		...	...
1080	Prepared animal feeds		...	430288	679015	712764		...	220530	228481	221218		15422	16193
1101	Distilling, rectifying and blending of spirits		...	1083	1629	1710		...	369	502	486		16	17
1102	Wines		...	109310	122588	128681		...	54566	59488	57597		7413	7784
1103	Malt liquors and malt		...	39314	52579	55192		...	17224	49495	47922		936	983
1104	Soft drinks,mineral waters,other bottled waters		...	352967	350424	367841		...	123785	221507	214466		42266	44379
1200	Tobacco products		...	340801	336442	353164		...	109916	168864	163496		65218	68479
131	Spinning, weaving and finishing of textiles		...	262120	270390	283829		...	98945	138897	134482		19401	20371
1311	Preparation and spinning of textile fibres		...	...	...	...		...	...	...	...		...	...
1312	Weaving of textiles		...	39374	74059	77740		...	9694	47766	46248		376	395
1313	Finishing of textiles		...	34379	44575	46791		...	12333	25134	24335		2303	2419
139	Other textiles		...	717	718	754		...	541	302	292		...	...
1391	Knitted and crocheted fabrics		...	...	...	...		...	...	...	...		...	...
1392	Made-up textile articles, except apparel		...	...	...	...		...	...	...	...		...	...
1393	Carpets and rugs		...	55763	39583	41550		...	28758	22721	21998		2898	3042
1394	Cordage, rope, twine and netting		...	5727	26805	28138		...	2051	1717	1662		265	278
1399	Other textiles n.e.c.		...	...	...	...		...	...	...	...		...	...
1410	Wearing apparel, except fur apparel		...	52930	31282	32837		...	27098	14653	14187		1412	1483
1420	Articles of fur		...	798	142	149		...	492	98	95		...	...
1430	Knitted and crocheted apparel		...	...	...	...		...	...	...	...		...	...
151	Leather;luggage,handbags,saddlery,harness;fur		...	...	...	...		...	...	...	...		...	...
1511	Tanning/dressing of leather; dressing of fur		...	...	...	...		...	...	...	...		...	...
1512	Luggage,handbags,etc.;saddlery/harness		...	1766	1419	1490		...	800	109	106		2	2
1520	Footwear		...	7006	21153	22204		...	2023	3364	3257		496	521
1610	Sawmilling and planing of wood		...	8134	4907	5151		...	3182	1631	1579		12	12
162	Wood products, cork, straw, plaiting materials		...	5480	8720	9153		...	2888	4151	4019		200	210

Code	Description	(1)	(2)	(3)	(4)	(5)	(6)	(7)	(8)
1621	Veneer sheets and wood-based panels	...	12851	13490	1495	2459	2381	1403	1473
1622	Builders' carpentry and joinery	2826	7847	8237	...	6656	6445	5140	5397
1623	Wooden containers	3772	35855	37637	1520	5937	5748	460	483
1629	Other wood products;articles of cork,straw	9892	4424	4644	4951	795	769	329	346
1701	Pulp, paper and paperboard	11256	12949	13593	3584	1507	1460	1624	1705
1702	Corrugated paper and paperboard	...	...	...	...	...	...	...	...
1709	Other articles of paper and paperboard	...	...	...	...	...	...	...	...
181	Printing and service activities related to printing	156129	137646	144488	68234	45247	43808	4912	5157
1811	Printing	4679	2977	3125	2850	2295	2222	100	105
1812	Service activities related to printing	...	...	...	...	...	...	...	...
1820	Reproduction of recorded media	...	...	...	...	...	...	...	...
1910	Coke oven products	...	...	...	...	...	...	...	...
1920	Refined petroleum products	...	...	...	...	...	...	...	...
201	Basic chemicals,fertilizers, etc.	...	...	...	...	...	...	...	...
2011	Basic chemicals	149156	213860	224490	71540	75530	73130	6012	6312
2012	Fertilizers and nitrogen compounds	...	...	...	...	...	...	...	...
2013	Plastics and synthetic rubber in primary forms	...	...	...	...	...	...	...	...
202	Other chemical products	...	...	...	...	...	...	...	...
2021	Pesticides and other agrochemical products	82495	4654	4886	31589	240	232	1680	1764
2022	Paints,varnishes;printing ink and mastics	109390	92632	97236	52685	10503	10170	5088	5342
2023	Soap,cleaning and cosmetic preparations	1912	66860	70184	721	4372	4233	1067	1120
2029	Other chemical products n.e.c.	15247	1714	1799	2813	900	871	...	...
2030	Man-made fibres	...	...	...	...	...	...	...	...
2100	Pharmaceuticals,medicinal chemicals, etc.	68945	63952	67130	25268	55333	53574	1622	1703
221	Rubber products	...	12191	12797	...	899	871	3	3
2211	Rubber tyres and tubes	...	...	...	...	...	...	...	...
2219	Other rubber products	...	...	...	...	...	...	...	...
2220	Plastics products	427974	120297	126276	130866	72999	70679	19660	20643
2310	Glass and glass products	1022	...	...	524	...	...	...	...
239	Non-metallic mineral products n.e.c.	...	...	...	...	...	...	...	...
2391	Refractory products	13306	44034	46222	5660	35204	34085	3365	3533
2392	Clay building materials	...	586	615	...	115	112	3	3
2393	Other porcelain and ceramic products	325764	361848	379833	116240	161823	156679	79427	83399
2394	Cement, lime and plaster	5164	7198	7556	1356	734	711	20	21
2395	Articles of concrete, cement and plaster	...	36524	38339	...	19288	18675	...	...
2396	Cutting, shaping and finishing of stone	...	...	...	...	...	...	...	...
2399	Other non-metallic mineral products n.e.c.	26589	37594	39463	8227	11269	10911	1390	1459
2410	Basic iron and steel	...	3305	3469	...	540	523	76	80
2420	Basic precious and other non-ferrous metals	...	...	...	...	...	...	...	...
243	Casting of metals	12077	25227	26481	5342	23488	22741	904	949
2431	Casting of iron and steel	...	...	...	...	...	...	...	...
2432	Casting of non-ferrous metals	...	...	...	...	...	...	...	...
251	Struct.metal products, tanks, reservoirs	...	...	...	...	...	...	...	...
2511	Structural metal products	12962	11783	12368	3506	3674	3557	1816	1906
2512	Tanks, reservoirs and containers of metal	1156	952	999	139	19	19	4	4

continued

United Republic of Tanzania

ISIC	Industry	Output Note	Output 2007	Output 2008	Output 2009	Output 2010a/	VA Note	VA 2007	VA 2008	VA 2009	VA 2010a/	GFCF Note	GFCF 2009	GFCF 2010a/
				(millions of Tanzanian Shillings)					(millions of Tanzanian Shillings)				(millions of Tanzanian Shillings)	
2513	Steam generators, excl. hot water boilers		…	…	…	…		…	…	…	…		…	…
2520	Weapons and ammunition		…	…	…	…		…	…	…	…		…	…
259	Other metal products;metal working services		…	…	…	…		…	…	…	…		…	…
2591	Forging,pressing,stamping,roll-forming of metal		…	…	…	…		…	…	…	…		…	…
2592	Treatment and coating of metals; machining		…	…	…	…		…	…	…	…		…	…
2593	Cutlery, hand tools and general hardware		…	…	…	…		…	…	…	…		…	…
2599	Other fabricated metal products n.e.c.		…	169455	110172	115648		…	31629	18186	17608		3687	3871
2610	Electronic components and boards													
2620	Computers and peripheral equipment													
2630	Communication equipment													
2640	Consumer electronics													
265	Measuring,testing equipment; watches, etc.													
2651	Measuring/testing/navigating equipment,etc.													
2652	Watches and clocks													
2660	Irradiation/electromedical equipment,etc.													
2670	Optical instruments and photographic equipment													
2680	Magnetic and optical media		…	…	…	…		…	…	…	…		…	…
2710	Electric motors,generators,transformers,etc.		…	…	…	…		…	…	…	…		…	…
2720	Batteries and accumulators		…	15206	12620	13247		…	1459	9619	9313		374	392
273	Wiring and wiring devices													
2731	Fibre optic cables		…	…	…	…		…	…	…	…		…	…
2732	Other electronic and electric wires and cables			32125	21506	22575			8827	10144	9821		3032	3183
2733	Wiring devices			3231	3231	3392								
2740	Electric lighting equipment													
2750	Domestic appliances								452	452	438		25	26
2790	Other electrical equipment			78	272	285			44	131	127		6	7
281	General-purpose machinery		…	…	…	…		…	…	…	…		…	…
2811	Engines/turbines,excl.aircraft,vehicle engines													
2812	Fluid power equipment		…	…	…	…		…	…	…	…		…	…
2813	Other pumps, compressors, taps and valves													
2814	Bearings, gears, gearing and driving elements			1856	1894	1988			495	489	473		53	55
2815	Ovens, furnaces and furnace burners													
2816	Lifting and handling equipment			8678					1657					
2817	Office machinery, excl.computers,etc.		…	…	…	…		…	…	…	…		…	…
2818	Power-driven hand tools													
2819	Other general-purpose machinery		…	…	…	…		…	…	…	…		…	…
282	Special-purpose machinery		…	…	…	…		…	…	…	…		…	…
2821	Agricultural and forestry machinery			835	4094	4297			729	4074	3945			
2822	Metal-forming machinery and machine tools													
2823	Machinery for metallurgy		…	…	…	…		…	…	…	…		…	…
2824	Mining, quarrying and construction machinery		…	2432	1234	1296		…	344	711	688		522	549

		...	...	84	87	...	294	280	...
2825	Food/beverage/tobacco processing machinery	...	...	...	...	...	...	...	...
2826	Textile/apparel/leather production machinery	...	...	...	...	...	...	...	...
2829	Other special-purpose machinery	...	...	...	...	...	...	...	...
2910	Motor vehicles	2	3	200	206	...	539	514	...
2920	Automobile bodies, trailers and semi-trailers	60	63	221	228	378	2018	1923	1627
2930	Parts and accessories for motor vehicles	3	3	352	363	77	1109	1056	138
301	Building of ships and boats	...	...	...	...	...	...	...	...
3011	Building of ships and floating structures	...	...	...	...	...	...	...	...
3012	Building of pleasure and sporting boats	...	...	202	209	209	483	460	460
3020	Railway locomotives and rolling stock	...	...	...	...	...	...	...	...
3030	Air and spacecraft and related machinery	...	...	...	...	...	...	...	...
3040	Military fighting vehicles	...	...	...	...	...	...	...	...
309	Transport equipment n.e.c.	...	...	...	...	...	...	...	...
3091	Motorcycles	...	...	121	125	128	215	205	208
3092	Bicycles and invalid carriages	...	...	...	...	...	...	...	...
3099	Other transport equipment n.e.c.	5	5	18	18	-	287	273	256
3100	Furniture	539	566	20673	21352	8533	49208	46878	25722
321	Jewellery, bijouterie and related articles	...	...	...	...	...	...	...	...
3211	Jewellery and related articles	...	...	326	337	205	840	801	350
3212	Imitation jewellery and related articles	...	...	...	...	...	...	...	...
3220	Musical instruments	...	...	...	...	...	...	...	...
3230	Sports goods	...	...	...	...	...	...	...	...
3240	Games and toys	...	...	...	...	...	...	...	...
3250	Medical and dental instruments and supplies	16	17	1210	1249	313	1481	1411	474
3290	Other manufacturing	75402	79172	175988	181766	228022	547908	521965	578092
331	Repair of fabricated metal products/machinery	...	...	...	...	...	...	...	...
3311	Repair of fabricated metal products	...	...	26	27	...	57	54	...
3312	Repair of machinery	150	158	66	69	69	149	142	142
3313	Repair of electronic and optical equipment	...	...	...	...	...	...	...	...
3314	Repair of electrical equipment	21	22	452	467	305	961	916	834
3315	Repair of transport equip., excl. motor vehicles	...	...	8	9	7	18	17	17
3319	Repair of other equipment	1	1	896	925	855	1472	1402	1160
3320	Installation of industrial machinery/equipment	...	...	...	...	...	...	...	...
C	Total manufacturing	463803b/	486994b/	1981615b/	2046672b/	1797383b/	5194293b/	4948347b/	4711376b/

a/ Provisional data.
b/ Sum of available data.

United Republic of Tanzania

ISIC Revision 3

Index numbers of industrial production (2005=100)

ISIC	Industry	Note	1999	2000	2001	2002	2003	2004	2005	2006	2007	2008	2009	2010
15	Food and beverages	a/	42	60	73	80	88	95	100	100	108	188	214	…
16	Tobacco products		78	60	61	65	72	85	100	191	163	141	156	…
17	Textiles		44	61	101	119	161	161	100	159	159	244	169	…
18	Wearing apparel, fur		…	…	…	…	…	…	…	…	…	…	…	…
19	Leather, leather products and footwear		…	…	…	…	…	…	…	…	…	…	…	…
20	Wood products (excl. furniture)		57	75	37	67	60	55	100	91	103	639	464	…
21	Paper and paper products		11	12	139	143	105	125	100	43	157	275	265	…
22	Printing and publishing		…	…	…	…	…	…	…	…	…	…	…	…
23	Coke,refined petroleum products,nuclear fuel		…	…	…	…	…	…	…	…	…	…	…	…
24	Chemicals and chemical products		…	…	…	…	…	…	…	…	…	…	…	…
25	Rubber and plastics products		…	…	…	…	…	…	…	…	…	…	…	…
26	Non-metallic mineral products		61	63	67	76	86	88	100	101	129	150	188	…
27	Basic metals		…	…	…	…	…	…	…	…	…	…	…	…
28	Fabricated metal products		117	53	76	91	113	121	100	91	38	80	64	…
29	Machinery and equipment n.e.c.	b/	195	186	186	82	56	61	100	18	13	…	…	…
30	Office, accounting and computing machinery	b/	…	…	…	…	…	…	…	…	…	…	…	…
31	Electrical machinery and apparatus	c/	329	367	103	96	115	111	100	124	118	195	179	…
32	Radio,television and communication equipment	c/	…	…	…	…	…	…	…	…	…	…	…	…
33	Medical, precision and optical instruments		…	…	…	…	…	…	…	…	…	…	…	…
34	Motor vehicles, trailers, semi-trailers	d/	127	143	468	79	121	103	100	71	94	60	92	…
35	Other transport equipment	d/	…	…	…	…	…	…	…	…	…	…	…	…
36	Furniture; manufacturing n.e.c.		…	…	…	…	…	…	…	…	…	…	…	…
37	Recycling		…	…	…	…	…	…	…	…	…	…	…	…
D	Total manufacturing		49	56	69	78	91	97	100	120	124	203	188	…

a/ 15 excludes beverages.
b/ 29 includes 30.
c/ 31 includes 32.
d/ 34 includes 35.

United States of America

Supplier of information:
United States Census Bureau, U.S. Department of Commerce, Washington, D.C.
Industrial statistics for the OECD countries are compiled by the OECD secretariat, which
supplies them to UNIDO.

Basic source of data:
Census; annual survey of manufacturers and services; administrative data.

Major deviations from ISIC (Revision 4):
Data presented in accordance with ISIC (Revision 4) were originally classified in the
North American Industry Classification System (NAICS).

Reference period:
Calendar year.

Scope:
All manufacturing enterprises with at least one employee.

Method of data collection:
Data are collected by mail and other communication media.

Type of enumeration:
Not reported.

Adjusted for non-response:
Not reported.

Concepts and definitions of variables:
No deviations from the standard UN concepts and definitions are reported.

Related national publications:
None reported.

United States of America

		Establishments (number)					Number of employees (thousands)					Wages and salaries paid to employees (millions of US Dollars)				
ISIC	Industry (ISIC Revision 4)	Note	2005	2006	2007	2008	Note	2005	2006	2007	2008	Note	2005	2006	2007	2008
1010	Processing/preserving of meat		:	:	:	:		:	:	:	506		:	:	:	15217
1020	Processing/preserving of fish, etc.		:	:	:	:		:	:	:	37		:	:	:	1167
1030	Processing/preserving of fruit,vegetables		:	:	:	:		:	:	:	113		:	:	:	4255
1040	Vegetable and animal oils and fats		:	:	:	:		:	:	:	16		:	:	:	797
1050	Dairy products		:	:	:	:		:	:	:	132		:	:	:	5899
106	Grain mill products,starches and starch products		:	:	:	:		:	:	:	53		:	:	:	2635
1061	Grain mill products		:	:	:	:		:	:	:	45		:	:	:	2089
1062	Starches and starch products		:	:	:	:		:	:	:	8		:	:	:	546
107	Other food products		:	:	:	:		:	:	:	533		:	:	:	19795
1071	Bakery products		:	:	:	:		:	:	:	283		:	:	:	9743
1072	Sugar		:	:	:	:		:	:	:	13		:	:	:	589
1073	Cocoa, chocolate and sugar confectionery		:	:	:	:		:	:	:	49		:	:	:	2036
1074	Macaroni, noodles, couscous, etc.		:	:	:	:		:	:	:	3		:	:	:	131
1075	Prepared meals and dishes		:	:	:	:		:	:	:	67		:	:	:	2492
1079	Other food products n.e.c.		:	:	:	:		:	:	:	118		:	:	:	4803
1080	Prepared animal feeds		:	:	:	:		:	:	:	46		:	:	:	2007
1101	Distilling, rectifying and blending of spirits		:	:	:	:		:	:	:	8		:	:	:	421
1102	Wines		:	:	:	:		:	:	:	34		:	:	:	1485
1103	Malt liquors and malt		:	:	:	:		:	:	:	22		:	:	:	1278
1104	Soft drinks,mineral waters,other bottled waters		:	:	:	:		:	:	:	65		:	:	:	2909
1200	Tobacco products		:	:	:	:		:	:	:	18		:	:	:	1099
131	Spinning, weaving and finishing of textiles		:	:	:	:		:	:	:	99		:	:	:	3144
1311	Preparation and spinning of textile fibres		:	:	:	:		:	:	:	36		:	:	:	1033
1312	Weaving of textiles		:	:	:	:		:	:	:	25		:	:	:	777
1313	Finishing of textiles		:	:	:	:		:	:	:	38		:	:	:	1334
139	Other textiles		:	:	:	:		:	:	:	190		:	:	:	6218
1391	Knitted and crocheted fabrics		:	:	:	:		:	:	:	3		:	:	:	109
1392	Made-up textile articles, except apparel		:	:	:	:		:	:	:	72		:	:	:	2118
1393	Carpets and rugs		:	:	:	:		:	:	:	40		:	:	:	1281
1394	Cordage, rope, twine and netting		:	:	:	:		:	:	:	4		:	:	:	158
1399	Other textiles n.e.c.		:	:	:	:		:	:	:	72		:	:	:	2553
1410	Wearing apparel, except fur apparel		:	:	:	:		:	:	:	149a/		:	:	:	3382
1420	Articles of fur		:	:	:	:		:	:	:	...a/		:	:	:	-
1430	Knitted and crocheted apparel		:	:	:	:		:	:	:	...a/		:	:	:	505
151	Leather;luggage,handbags,saddlery,harness;fur		:	:	:	:		:	:	:	19		:	:	:	613
1511	Tanning/dressing of leather; dressing of fur		:	:	:	:		:	:	:	4		:	:	:	166
1512	Luggage,handbags,etc.;saddlery/harness		:	:	:	:		:	:	:	14		:	:	:	447
1520	Footwear		:	:	:	:		:	:	:	13		:	:	:	381
1610	Sawmilling and planing of wood		:	:	:	:		:	:	:	92		:	:	:	3394
162	Wood products, cork, straw, plaiting materials		:	:	:	:		:	:	:	370		:	:	:	12224

Code	Description			
1621	Veneer sheets and wood-based panels	...	50	...
1622	Builders' carpentry and joinery	...	230	...
1623	Wooden containers	...	56	...
1629	Other wood products;articles of cork,straw	...	34	...
1701	Pulp, paper and paperboard	...	123	...
1702	Corrugated paper and paperboard	...	177	...
1709	Other articles of paper and paperboard	...	107	...
181	Printing and service activities related to printing	...	570	...
1811	Printing	...	525	...
1812	Service activities related to printing	...	45	...
1820	Reproduction of recorded media	...	20	...
1910	Coke oven products	...	80b/	...
1920	Refined petroleum products	...	...b/	...
201	Basic chemicals,fertilizers, etc.	...	266	...
2011	Basic chemicals	...	152	...
2012	Fertilizers and nitrogen compounds	...	18	...
2013	Plastics and synthetic rubber in primary forms	...	96	...
202	Other chemical products	...	250	...
2021	Pesticides and other agrochemical products	...	10	...
2022	Paints,varnishes;printing ink and mastics	...	74	...
2023	Soap,cleaning and cosmetic preparations	...	104	...
2029	Other chemical products n.e.c.	...	62	...
2030	Man-made fibres	...	15	...
2100	Pharmaceuticals,medicinal chemicals, etc.	...	249	...
221	Rubber products	...	176	...
2211	Rubber tyres and tubes	...	57	...
2219	Other rubber products	...	119	...
2220	Plastics products	...	652	...
2310	Glass and glass products	...	94	...
239	Non-metallic mineral products n.e.c.	...	375	...
2391	Refractory products	...	9	...
2392	Clay building materials	...	21	...
2393	Other porcelain and ceramic products	...	12	...
2394	Cement, lime and plaster	...	23	...
2395	Articles of concrete, cement and plaster	...	206	...
2396	Cutting, shaping and finishing of stone	...	29	...
2399	Other non-metallic mineral products n.e.c.	...	74	...
2410	Basic iron and steel	...	184	...
2420	Basic precious and other non-ferrous metals	...	125	...
243	Casting of metals	...	163	...
2431	Casting of iron and steel	...	100	...
2432	Casting of non-ferrous metals	...	63	...
251	Struct.metal products, tanks, reservoirs	...	491	...
2511	Structural metal products	...	408	...
2512	Tanks, reservoirs and containers of metal	...	60	...

First data column values: 1970, 7743, 1480, 1032, 8052, 7921, 4699, 23840, 21947, 1893, 805, 7106b/, ...b/, 17800, 10880, 1033, 5887, 13529, 598, 3897, 5667, 3369, 666, 18771, 7667, 2977, 4691, 25300, 4227, 16454, 456, 776, 461, 1354, 8579, 1091, 3738, 11012, 6580, 7442, 4775, 2667, 21312, 17253, 2838

continued

United States of America

ISIC	Industry	Establishments (number)					Number of employees (thousands)					Wages and salaries paid to employees (millions of US Dollars)				
		Note	2005	2006	2007	2008	Note	2005	2006	2007	2008	Note	2005	2006	2007	2008
2513	Steam generators, excl. hot water boilers		...	...	...	...		...	...	...	22		...	...	...	1221
2520	Weapons and ammunition		...	...	...	...		...	...	...	32		...	...	...	1609
259	Other metal products;metal working services		...	...	...	...		...	...	...	1118		...	...	...	49972
2591	Forging,pressing,stamping,roll-forming of metal		...	...	...	...		...	...	...	207		...	...	...	9923
2592	Treatment and coating of metals; machining		...	...	...	...		...	...	...	393		...	...	...	16860
2593	Cutlery, hand tools and general hardware		...	...	...	...		...	...	...	207		...	...	...	9757
2599	Other fabricated metal products n.e.c.		...	...	...	...		...	...	...	311		...	...	...	13432
2610	Electronic components and boards		...	...	...	...		...	...	...	372		...	...	...	20486
2620	Computers and peripheral equipment		...	...	...	...		...	...	...	93		...	...	...	5908
2630	Communication equipment		...	...	...	...		...	...	...	133		...	...	...	8961
2640	Consumer electronics		...	...	...	...		...	...	...	14		...	...	...	663
265	Measuring,testing equipment; watches, etc.		...	...	...	...		...	...	...	313		...	...	...	22751
2651	Measuring/testing/navigating equipment,etc.		...	...	...	...		...	...	...	311		...	...	...	22651
2652	Watches and clocks		...	...	...	...		...	...	...	2		...	...	...	100
2660	Irradiation/electromedical equipment,etc.		...	...	...	...		...	...	...	82		...	...	...	6282
2670	Optical instruments and photographic equipment		...	...	...	...		...	...	...	23		...	...	...	1330
2680	Magnetic and optical media		...	...	...	...		...	...	...	7		...	...	...	489
2710	Electric motors,generators,transformers,etc.		...	...	...	...		...	...	...	144		...	...	...	6890
2720	Batteries and accumulators		...	...	...	...		...	...	...	26		...	...	...	1194
273	Wiring and wiring devices		...	...	...	...		...	...	...	82		...	...	...	3729
2731	Fibre optic cables		...	...	...	...		...	...	...	6		...	...	...	312
2732	Other electronic and electric wires and cables		...	...	...	...		...	...	...	28		...	...	...	1273
2733	Wiring devices		...	...	...	...		...	...	...	49		...	...	...	2144
2740	Electric lighting equipment		...	...	...	...		...	...	...	70		...	...	...	2930
2750	Domestic appliances		...	...	...	...		...	...	...	58		...	...	...	2296
2790	Other electrical equipment		...	...	...	...		...	...	...	128		...	...	...	6039
281	General-purpose machinery		...	...	...	...		...	...	...	716		...	...	...	35010
2811	Engines/turbines,excl.aircraft,vehicle engines		...	...	...	...		...	...	...	83		...	...	...	4355
2812	Fluid power equipment		...	...	...	...		...	...	...	71		...	...	...	3769
2813	Other pumps, compressors, taps and valves		...	...	...	...		...	...	...	108		...	...	...	5638
2814	Bearings, gears, gearing and driving elements		...	...	...	...		...	...	...	56		...	...	...	2672
2815	Ovens, furnaces and furnace burners		...	...	...	...		...	...	...	11		...	...	...	576
2816	Lifting and handling equipment		...	...	...	...		...	...	...	94		...	...	...	4309
2817	Office machinery, excl.computers,etc.		...	...	...	...		...	...	...	6		...	...	...	333
2818	Power-driven hand tools		...	...	...	...		...	...	...	8		...	...	...	346
2819	Other general-purpose machinery		...	...	...	...		...	...	...	280		...	...	...	13012
282	Special-purpose machinery		...	...	...	...		...	...	...	380		...	...	...	20446
2821	Agricultural and forestry machinery		...	...	...	...		...	...	...	76		...	...	...	3368
2822	Metal-forming machinery and machine tools		...	...	...	...		...	...	...	41		...	...	...	2402
2823	Machinery for metallurgy		...	...	...	...		...	...	...	3		...	...	...	186
2824	Mining, quarrying and construction machinery		...	...	...	...		...	...	...	133		...	...	...	6911

Code	Description		
2825	Food/beverage/tobacco processing machinery	935	19
2826	Textile/apparel/leather production machinery	449	11
2829	Other special-purpose machinery	6195	97
2910	Motor vehicles	12473	192
2920	Automobile bodies, trailers and semi-trailers	4269	110
2930	Parts and accessories for motor vehicles	18847	400
301	Building of ships and boats	6857	149
3011	Building of ships and floating structures	5252	105
3012	Building of pleasure and sporting boats	1605	44
3020	Railway locomotives and rolling stock	1652	30
3030	Air and spacecraft and related machinery	30892	440
3040	Military fighting vehicles	1021	17
309	Transport equipment n.e.c.	596	13
3091	Motorcycles	⋮	⋮
3092	Bicycles and invalid carriages	⋮	⋮
3099	Other transport equipment n.e.c.	⋮	⋮
3100	Furniture	15794	443
321	Jewellery, bijouterie and related articles	1241	32
3211	Jewellery and related articles	1058	27
3212	Imitation jewellery and related articles	183	5
3220	Musical instruments	499	12
3230	Sports goods	1936	46
3240	Games and toys	501	12
3250	Medical and dental instruments and supplies	16151	314
3290	Other manufacturing n.e.c.	4566	113
331	Repair of fabricated metal products/machinery	⋮	⋮
3311	Repair of fabricated metal products	⋮	⋮
3312	Repair of machinery	⋮	⋮
3313	Repair of electronic and optical equipment	⋮	⋮
3314	Repair of electrical equipment	⋮	⋮
3315	Repair of transport equip., excl. motor vehicles	⋮	⋮
3319	Repair of other equipment	⋮	⋮
3320	Installation of industrial machinery/equipment	⋮	⋮
C	Total manufacturing	606290	12748

a/ 1410 includes 1420 and 1430.
b/ 1910 includes 1920.

United States of America

ISIC	Industry	Output Note	Output 2005	Output 2006	Output 2007	Output 2008	Value added Note	Value added 2005	Value added 2006	Value added 2007	Value added 2008	GFCF Note	GFCF 2007	GFCF 2008
			(billions of US Dollars)					(billions of US Dollars)					(billions of US Dollars)	
1010	Processing/preserving of meat		...	...	...	169.9		...	...	...	50.8		...	4.3
1020	Processing/preserving of fish, etc.		...	...	...	10.2		...	...	...	4.1		...	0.4
1030	Processing/preserving of fruit, vegetables		...	...	...	46.9		...	...	...	19.6		...	1.4
1040	Vegetable and animal oils and fats		...	...	...	50.7		...	...	...	10.5		...	0.3
1050	Dairy products		...	...	...	98.1		...	...	...	27.1		...	2.2
106	Grain mill products,starches and starch products		...	...	...	49.1		...	...	...	21.3		...	1.1
1061	Grain mill products		...	...	...	33.8		...	...	...	14.1		...	0.6
1062	Starches and starch products		...	...	...	15.3		...	...	...	7.2		...	0.5
107	Other food products		...	...	...	175.3		...	...	...	96.1		...	4.9
1071	Bakery products		...	...	...	68.6		...	...	...	43.6		...	1.9
1072	Sugar		...	...	...	7.4		...	...	...	2.6		...	0.3
1073	Cocoa, chocolate and sugar confectionery		...	...	...	19.3		...	...	...	10.6		...	0.5
1074	Macaroni, noodles, couscous, etc.		...	...	...	2.0		...	...	...	0.9		...	-
1075	Prepared meals and dishes		...	...	...	23.6		...	...	...	11.0		...	0.7
1079	Other food products n.e.c.		...	...	...	54.5		...	...	...	27.4		...	1.4
1080	Prepared animal feeds		...	...	...	47.9		...	...	...	16.4		...	1.0
1101	Distilling, rectifying and blending of spirits		...	...	...	7.0		...	...	...	4.7		...	0.1
1102	Wines		...	...	...	13.4		...	...	...	8.2		...	0.8
1103	Malt liquors and malt		...	...	...	20.5		...	...	...	12.2		...	0.8
1104	Soft drinks,mineral waters,other bottled waters		...	...	...	47.3		...	...	...	19.4		...	1.6
1200	Tobacco products		...	...	...	37.4		...	...	...	31.0		...	0.4
131	Spinning, weaving and finishing of textiles		...	...	...	21.5		...	...	...	7.5		...	0.4
1311	Preparation and spinning of textile fibres		...	...	...	8.8		...	...	...	2.8		...	0.1
1312	Weaving of textiles		...	...	...	5.3		...	...	...	2.0		...	0.1
1313	Finishing of textiles		...	...	...	7.5		...	...	...	2.7		...	0.2
139	Other textiles		...	...	...	39.4		...	...	...	17.8		...	1.1
1391	Knitted and crocheted fabrics		...	...	...	0.7		...	...	...	0.3		...	-
1392	Made-up textile articles, except apparel		...	...	...	10.2		...	...	...	4.9		...	0.2
1393	Carpets and rugs		...	...	...	11.8		...	...	...	4.5		...	0.2
1394	Cordage, rope, twine and netting		...	...	...	0.8		...	...	...	0.4		...	-
1399	Other textiles n.e.c.		...	...	...	15.9		...	...	...	7.7		...	0.2
1410	Wearing apparel, except fur apparel		...	...	...	16.9		...	...	...	8.0		...	0.7
1420	Articles of fur		...	...	...	...		...	...	...	-		...	0.2
1430	Knitted and crocheted apparel		...	...	...	2.7		...	...	...	1.2		...	-
151	Leather;luggage,handbags,saddlery,harness;fur		...	...	...	3.5		...	...	...	1.6		...	-
1511	Tanning/dressing of leather; dressing of fur		...	...	...	1.4		...	...	...	0.4		...	0.1
1512	Luggage,handbags,etc.;saddlery/harness		...	...	...	2.1		...	...	...	1.2		...	-
1520	Footwear		...	...	...	1.9		...	...	...	1.1		...	-
1610	Sawmilling and planing of wood		...	...	...	24.3		...	...	...	7.3		...	0.6
162	Wood products, cork, straw, plaiting materials		...	...	...	63.7		...	...	...	27.3		...	1.9

Code	Product						
1621	Veneer sheets and wood-based panels	...	12.8	...	4.2	...	0.6
1622	Builders' carpentry and joinery	...	38.1	...	17.0	...	0.9
1623	Wooden containers	...	7.3	...	3.5	...	0.3
1629	Other wood products;articles of cork,straw	...	5.5	...	2.6	...	0.2
1701	Pulp, paper and paperboard	...	84.7	...	41.1	...	3.7
1702	Corrugated paper and paperboard	...	54.9	...	19.7	...	1.4
1709	Other articles of paper and paperboard	...	39.6	...	19.1	...	1.2
181	Printing and service activities related to printing	...	94.0	...	56.5	...	4.0
1811	Printing	...	88.8	...	52.5	...	3.8
1812	Service activities related to printing	...	5.2	...	4.0	...	0.2
1820	Reproduction of recorded media	...	4.1	...	2.7	...	0.2
1910	Coke oven products	...	747.6a/	...	84.4a/	...	18.4a/
1920	Refined petroleum products	...	...a/	...	...a/	...	...a/
201	Basic chemicals,fertilizers, etc.	...	369.7	...	121.2	...	12.1
2011	Basic chemicals	...	244.2	...	83.6	...	8.0
2012	Fertilizers and nitrogen compounds	...	24.4	...	11.4	...	1.0
2013	Plastics and synthetic rubber in primary forms	...	101.1	...	26.2	...	3.1
202	Other chemical products	...	179.7	...	88.9	...	4.1
2021	Pesticides and other agrochemical products	...	13.8	...	8.2	...	0.4
2022	Paints,varnishes;printing ink and mastics	...	37.3	...	17.7	...	0.7
2023	Soap,cleaning and cosmetic preparations	...	97.4	...	46.7	...	2.2
2029	Other chemical products n.e.c.	...	31.3	...	16.2	...	0.8
2030	Man-made fibres	...	7.1	...	2.6	...	0.3
2100	Pharmaceuticals,medicinal chemicals, etc.	...	194.5	...	142.8	...	5.1
221	Rubber products	...	43.4	...	18.6	...	1.7
2211	Rubber tyres and tubes	...	17.8	...	6.3	...	1.0
2219	Other rubber products	...	25.7	...	12.3	...	0.8
2220	Plastics products	...	167.4	...	76.5	...	6.5
2310	Glass and glass products	...	23.2	...	12.6	...	1.2
239	Non-metallic mineral products n.e.c.	...	115.0	...	56.6	...	5.3
2391	Refractory products	...	3.0	...	1.6	...	0.1
2392	Clay building materials	...	3.5	...	2.0	...	0.3
2393	Other porcelain and ceramic products	...	1.5	...	1.0	...	0.1
2394	Cement, lime and plaster	...	11.3	...	6.5	...	1.5
2395	Articles of concrete, cement and plaster	...	53.1	...	26.0	...	2.0
2396	Cutting, shaping and finishing of stone	...	3.8	...	2.4	...	0.1
2399	Other non-metallic mineral products n.e.c.	...	38.8	...	17.1	...	1.2
2410	Basic iron and steel	...	153.4	...	54.4	...	5.2
2420	Basic precious and other non-ferrous metals	...	100.2	...	27.0	...	2.9
243	Casting of metals	...	43.7	...	19.9	...	2.4
2431	Casting of iron and steel	...	30.7	...	13.5	...	1.8
2432	Casting of non-ferrous metals	...	13.0	...	6.5	...	0.6
251	Struct.metal products, tanks, reservoirs	...	116.0	...	55.8	...	3.2
2511	Structural metal products	...	95.0	...	44.9	...	2.3
2512	Tanks, reservoirs and containers of metal	...	14.7	...	7.5	...	0.5

continued

United States of America

ISIC	Industry	Output Note	Output 2005	Output 2006	Output 2007	Output 2008	VA Note	VA 2005	VA 2006	VA 2007	VA 2008	GFCF Note	GFCF 2007	GFCF 2008
			(billions of US Dollars)					(billions of US Dollars)					(billions of US Dollars)	
2513	Steam generators, excl. hot water boilers		…	…	…	6.3		…	…	…	3.4		…	0.4
2520	Weapons and ammunition		…	…	…	9.1		…	…	…	5.2		…	0.1
259	Other metal products;metal working services		…	…	…	234.9		…	…	…	125.5		…	9.0
2591	Forging,pressing,stamping,roll-forming of metal		…	…	…	57.9		…	…	…	25.0		…	2.5
2592	Treatment and coating of metals; machining		…	…	…	66.2		…	…	…	41.1		…	2.8
2593	Cutlery, hand tools and general hardware		…	…	…	36.9		…	…	…	22.6		…	1.3
2599	Other fabricated metal products n.e.c.		…	…	…	74.0		…	…	…	36.9		…	2.3
2610	Electronic components and boards		…	…	…	116.8		…	…	…	71.3		…	15.7
2620	Computers and peripheral equipment		…	…	…	68.1		…	…	…	38.7		…	1.2
2630	Communication equipment		…	…	…	53.9		…	…	…	30.5		…	2.4
2640	Consumer electronics		…	…	…	5.8		…	…	…	2.1		…	0.1
265	Measuring,testing equipment; watches, etc.		…	…	…	100.6		…	…	…	63.0		…	2.2
2651	Measuring/testing/navigating equipment,etc.		…	…	…	99.9		…	…	…	62.6		…	2.2
2652	Watches and clocks		…	…	…	0.7		…	…	…	0.4		…	-
2660	Irradiation/electromedical equipment,etc.		…	…	…	39.2		…	…	…	25.5		…	1.2
2670	Optical instruments and photographic equipment		…	…	…	7.1		…	…	…	4.0		…	0.2
2680	Magnetic and optical media		…	…	…	2.6		…	…	…	0.6		…	0.1
2710	Electric motors,generators,transformers,etc.		…	…	…	44.3		…	…	…	21.8		…	0.8
2720	Batteries and accumulators		…	…	…	9.7		…	…	…	3.9		…	0.4
273	Wiring and wiring devices		…	…	…	29.3		…	…	…	13.0		…	0.6
2731	Fibre optic cables		…	…	…	2.1		…	…	…	0.9		…	0.1
2732	Other electronic and electric wires and cables		…	…	…	13.6		…	…	…	4.2		…	0.3
2733	Wiring devices		…	…	…	13.6		…	…	…	7.9		…	0.2
2740	Electric lighting equipment		…	…	…	17.0		…	…	…	8.7		…	0.5
2750	Domestic appliances		…	…	…	21.9		…	…	…	9.1		…	0.4
2790	Other electrical equipment		…	…	…	25.3		…	…	…	14.3		…	0.8
281	General-purpose machinery		…	…	…	223.8		…	…	…	107.1		…	5.6
2811	Engines/turbines,excl.aircraft,vehicle engines		…	…	…	38.7		…	…	…	13.7		…	1.5
2812	Fluid power equipment		…	…	…	18.7		…	…	…	9.7		…	0.5
2813	Other pumps, compressors, taps and valves		…	…	…	39.2		…	…	…	21.6		…	0.8
2814	Bearings, gears, gearing and driving elements		…	…	…	15.7		…	…	…	9.4		…	0.5
2815	Ovens, furnaces and furnace burners		…	…	…	2.5		…	…	…	1.4		…	0.1
2816	Lifting and handling equipment		…	…	…	27.6		…	…	…	12.1		…	0.4
2817	Office machinery, excl.computers,etc.		…	…	…	2.0		…	…	…	1.2		…	-
2818	Power-driven hand tools		…	…	…	2.8		…	…	…	1.6		…	-
2819	Other general-purpose machinery		…	…	…	76.6		…	…	…	36.4		…	1.7
282	Special-purpose machinery		…	…	…	141.7		…	…	…	63.7		…	4.0
2821	Agricultural and forestry machinery		…	…	…	33.4		…	…	…	14.0		…	0.8
2822	Metal-forming machinery and machine tools		…	…	…	11.0		…	…	…	5.7		…	0.2
2823	Machinery for metallurgy		…	…	…	0.9		…	…	…	0.5		…	-
2824	Mining, quarrying and construction machinery		…	…	…	61.0		…	…	…	25.0		…	2.2

ISIC Revision 4

Code	Description						
2825	Food/beverage/tobacco processing machinery	0.1	⋮	2.5	⋮	4.5	⋮
2826	Textile/apparel/leather production machinery	0.1	⋮	1.1	⋮	2.0	⋮
2829	Other special-purpose machinery	0.5	⋮	15.0	⋮	29.0	⋮
2910	Motor vehicles	4.3	⋮	55.9	⋮	222.6	⋮
2920	Automobile bodies, trailers and semi-trailers	0.3	⋮	9.0	⋮	25.6	⋮
2930	Parts and accessories for motor vehicles	5.2	⋮	49.1	⋮	140.5	⋮
301	Building of ships and boats	1.0	⋮	16.7	⋮	30.4	⋮
3011	Building of ships and floating structures	0.6	⋮	12.8	⋮	21.3	⋮
3012	Building of pleasure and sporting boats	0.3	⋮	3.9	⋮	9.2	⋮
3020	Railway locomotives and rolling stock	0.3	⋮	5.3	⋮	15.8	⋮
3030	Air and spacecraft and related machinery	3.6	⋮	93.0	⋮	178.7	⋮
3040	Military fighting vehicles	0.1	⋮	6.4	⋮	12.6	⋮
309	Transport equipment n.e.c.	0.2	⋮	3.1	⋮	6.4	⋮
3091	Motorcycles	⋮	⋮	⋮	⋮	⋮	⋮
3092	Bicycles and invalid carriages	⋮	⋮	⋮	⋮	⋮	⋮
3099	Other transport equipment n.e.c.	⋮	⋮	⋮	⋮	⋮	⋮
3100	Furniture	1.2	⋮	42.8	⋮	78.0	⋮
321	Jewellery, bijouterie and related articles	0.1	⋮	4.2	⋮	8.8	⋮
3211	Jewellery and related articles	0.1	⋮	3.7	⋮	8.0	⋮
3212	Imitation jewellery and related articles	-	⋮	0.5	⋮	0.8	⋮
3220	Musical instruments	-	⋮	1.2	⋮	1.8	⋮
3230	Sports goods	0.2	⋮	7.2	⋮	12.4	⋮
3240	Games and toys	0.1	⋮	1.4	⋮	3.0	⋮
3250	Medical and dental instruments and supplies	2.8	⋮	60.4	⋮	84.0	⋮
3290	Other manufacturing n.e.c.	0.8	⋮	14.0	⋮	24.4	⋮
331	Repair of fabricated metal products/machinery	⋮	⋮	⋮	⋮	⋮	⋮
3311	Repair of fabricated metal products	⋮	⋮	⋮	⋮	⋮	⋮
3312	Repair of machinery	⋮	⋮	⋮	⋮	⋮	⋮
3313	Repair of electronic and optical equipment	⋮	⋮	⋮	⋮	⋮	⋮
3314	Repair of electrical equipment	⋮	⋮	⋮	⋮	⋮	⋮
3315	Repair of transport equip., excl. motor vehicles	⋮	⋮	⋮	⋮	⋮	⋮
3319	Repair of other equipment	⋮	⋮	⋮	⋮	⋮	⋮
3320	Installation of industrial machinery/equipment	⋮	⋮	⋮	⋮	⋮	⋮
C	Total manufacturing	168.3	⋮	⋮	⋮	5482.3	⋮

a/ 1910 includes 1920.

United States of America

ISIC Revision 4		Note	Index numbers of industrial production (2005=100)											
ISIC	Industry		1999	2000	2001	2002	2003	2004	2005	2006	2007	2008	2009	2010
10	Food products		92	94	94	96	97	97	100	101	101	100	100	99
11	Beverages		86	85	85	86	91	95	100	100	105	100	104	104
12	Tobacco products		111	112	110	92	96	96	100	96	87	77	71	72
13	Textiles		118	115	103	103	99	98	100	91	81	71	56	60
14	Wearing apparel		200	191	165	132	122	104	100	97	78	60	43	43
15	Leather and related products		167	162	131	93	91	92	100	100	88	82	66	75
16	Wood/wood products/cork, excl. furniture		95	94	88	91	91	94	100	101	94	81	62	64
17	Paper and paper products		110	107	101	102	100	100	100	99	99	95	85	87
18	Printing and reproduction of recorded media		107	108	104	103	99	100	100	99	101	95	79	79
19	Coke and refined petroleum products		92	91	91	95	92	98	100	102	106	103	104	102
20	Chemicals and chemical products		93	93	87	91	91	97	100	101	109	97	85	95
21	Pharmaceuticals, medicinal chemicals, etc.		77	80	86	93	96	96	100	104	105	103	97	90
22	Rubber and plastics products		99	100	94	98	98	99	100	101	98	89	74	81
23	Other non-metallic mineral products		94	93	90	91	92	95	100	101	99	87	68	71
24	Basic metals		109	105	96	96	94	103	100	103	105	105	78	95
25	Fabricated metal products, except machinery		102	106	97	96	95	96	100	104	109	104	79	87
26	Computer, electronic and optical products		53	70	71	69	78	88	100	114	131	139	122	135
27	Electrical equipment		112	117	106	99	97	98	100	101	105	101	80	84
28	Machinery and equipment n.e.c.		101	106	95	92	91	95	100	105	110	107	83	92
29	Motor vehicles, trailers and semi-trailers		96	95	87	95	99	99	100	99	97	78	57	75
30	Other transport equipment		108	95	101	95	91	90	100	106	125	127	116	116
31	Furniture		96	98	92	96	94	97	100	99	95	86	62	61
32	Other manufacturing		81	86	85	90	93	93	100	103	100	102	95	100
33	Repair and installation of machinery/equipment		…	…	…	…	…	…	…	…	…	…	…	…
C	Total manufacturing		91	95	91	92	93	96	100	103	106	101	87	92

Viet Nam

Supplier of information:
General Statistics Office of Viet Nam, Hanoi.

Basic source of data:
Survey.

Major deviations from ISIC (Revision 4):
None reported.

Reference period:
Calendar year.

Scope:
All registered enterprises.

Method of data collection:
Not reported.

Type of enumeration:
Complete enumeration.

Adjusted for non-response:
Not reported.

Concepts and definitions of variables:
No deviations from the standard UN concepts and definitions are reported.

Related national publications:
Statistical Yearbook of Viet Nam, published by the General Statistics Office of Viet Nam, Hanoi.

Viet Nam

ISIC	Industry	Number of enterprises (number)					Number of employees (thousands)					Wages and salaries paid to employees (billions of Vietnamese Dongs)				
		Note	2007	2008	2009	2010	Note	2007	2008	2009	2010	Note	2007	2008	2009	2010
1010	Processing/preserving of meat		132	160	203	225		8.2	9.0	9.1	10.7		283	389	429	520
1020	Processing/preserving of fish, etc.		845	1030	1071	1056		168.8	187.3	185.9	195.6		3089	4108	4744	6527
1030	Processing/preserving of fruit,vegetables		408	505	522	557		62.1	65.9	76.1	71.9		1026	1304	1717	1913
1040	Vegetable and animal oils and fats		50	51	60	67		4.4	4.9	4.9	4.7		231	293	272	324
1050	Dairy products		64	87	104	111		9.1	10.2	11.6	11.2		562	837	988	909
106	Grain mill products,starches and starch products		1214	1255	1297	1179		28.8	31.2	33.3	35.8		516	747	1205	1137
1061	Grain mill products		1101	1133	1160	1027		22.3	23.9	25.7	26.8		379	544	981	789
1062	Starches and starch products		113	122	137	152		6.5	7.4	7.6	9.0		137	203	224	348
107	Other food products		1031	1261	1380	1412		105.0	113.4	125.0	130.4		2383	3016	4069	5554
1071	Bakery products		186	234	261	284		14.6	21.3	23.2	21.8		368	638	767	873
1072	Sugar		38	40	44	48		18.4	18.6	18.7	19.6		518	616	670	881
1073	Cocoa, chocolate and sugar confectionery		100	136	154	170		10.5	8.8	16.0	17.2		184	209	493	700
1074	Macaroni, noodles, couscous, etc.		50	64	65	87		12.0	14.2	16.4	19.1		293	405	577	923
1075	Prepared meals and dishes		39	41	54	46		3.0	2.8	2.8	2.7		78	91	117	183
1079	Other food products n.e.c.		618	746	802	777		46.6	47.7	48.0	49.9		942	1057	1445	1994
1080	Prepared animal feeds		386	470	480	487		32.7	35.5	37.5	37.5		809	1277	1567	1799
1101	Distilling, rectifying and blending of spirits		59	92	130	127		1.9	2.4	2.7	3.1		111	127	154	176
1102	Wines		21	20	23	19		0.7	0.6	0.5	0.5		11	12	12	24
1103	Malt liquors and malt		162	153	156	143		16.0	14.1	17.4	18.7		759	677	901	1287
1104	Soft drinks,mineral waters,other bottled waters		939	1230	1400	1451		17.9	21.4	22.1	24.7		510	674	910	1058
1200	Tobacco products		25	26	27	26		13.7	13.9	13.6	13.6		668	781	1014	1220
131	Spinning, weaving and finishing of textiles		564	659	881	864		101.5	90.2	106.3	101.0		2155	3077	3067	3799
1311	Preparation and spinning of textile fibres		183	221	375	330		65.0	51.9	64.5	55.1		1453	2200	1927	2174
1312	Weaving of textiles		209	221	228	263		23.7	23.6	24.2	27.4		450	555	631	1006
1313	Finishing of textiles		172	217	278	271		12.9	14.8	17.6	18.5		252	322	508	620
139	Other textiles		-	-	-	-		-	-	-	-		-	-	-	-
1391	Knitted and crocheted fabrics		-	-	-	-		-	-	-	-		-	-	-	-
1392	Made-up textile articles, except apparel		-	-	-	-		-	-	-	-		-	-	-	-
1393	Carpets and rugs		-	-	-	-		-	-	-	-		-	-	-	-
1394	Cordage, rope, twine and netting		-	-	-	-		-	-	-	-		-	-	-	-
1399	Other textiles n.e.c.		-	-	-	-		-	-	-	-		-	-	-	-
1410	Wearing apparel, except fur apparel		2308	3115	3416	3831		697.6	749.9	760.6	841.4		12749	17201	20628	27590
1420	Articles of fur		9	10	17	13		1.4	1.0	1.1	0.4		23	27	23	19
1430	Knitted and crocheted apparel		177	190	197	183		26.8	21.8	17.1	16.7		478	452	422	569
151	Leather;luggage,handbags,saddlery,harness;fur		242	299	384	459		54.8	83.1	82.6	102.0		1135	1970	2432	3633
1511	Tanning/dressing of leather; dressing of fur		33	40	48	48		5.4	5.2	4.9	6.4		90	144	158	214
1512	Luggage,handbags,etc.;saddlery/harness		209	259	336	411		49.4	77.8	77.7	95.6		1045	1826	2275	3419
1520	Footwear		422	524	558	644		554.7	544.2	528.5	608.8		10825	10409	14177	17388
1610	Sawmilling and planing of wood		868	1097	1263	1414		24.6	26.7	28.4	37.2		404	532	671	1068
162	Wood products, cork, straw, plaiting materials		1508	2012	2300	2211		97.7	99.8	97.8	87.5		1399	1863	2059	2185

Code	Product												
1621	Veneer sheets and wood-based panels	233	340	417	392	18.8	21.3	21.5	21.9	338	505	556	683
1622	Builders' carpentry and joinery	245	313	426	510	5.6	7.7	8.7	11.7	82	158	201	308
1623	Wooden containers	36	49	56	95	1.0	1.2	1.6	2.1	18	33	38	56
1629	Other wood products;articles of cork,straw	994	1310	1401	1214	72.3	69.6	66.0	51.8	961	1167	1265	1137
1701	Pulp, paper and paperboard	319	368	400	352	23.7	21.9	23.7	20.2	606	705	773	792
1702	Corrugated paper and paperboard	564	759	789	844	36.1	38.5	40.3	43.8	759	1032	1320	1718
1709	Other articles of paper and paperboard	328	379	475	518	19.2	20.8	22.2	25.8	390	492	681	1576
181	Printing and service activities related to printing	1774	2171	2891	3332	42.8	48.6	54.7	57.0	1231	1633	2118	2573
1811	Printing	1488	1801	2428	2615	38.8	42.6	48.0	43.4	1154	1489	1899	2039
1812	Service activities related to printing	286	370	463	717	4.1	6.0	6.7	13.7	77	144	219	534
1820	Reproduction of recorded media	19	22	19	26	0.6	0.6	0.5	0.6	18	21	24	26
1910	Coke oven products	7	13	12	21	0.1	0.3	0.9	0.9	4	10	21	28
1920	Refined petroleum products	22	30	34	55	1.3	1.2	2.6	4.6	62	90	260	721
201	Basic chemicals,fertilizers, etc.	341	441	542	593	27.8	32.4	35.9	36.8	1102	1609	1767	2165
2011	Basic chemicals	90	116	158	170	5.9	6.7	7.0	8.2	223	317	312	481
2012	Fertilizers and nitrogen compounds	171	223	274	291	18.4	20.5	20.8	21.2	769	1111	1179	1348
2013	Plastics and synthetic rubber in primary forms	80	102	110	132	3.5	5.3	8.1	7.4	111	182	276	336
202	Other chemical products	793	947	1098	1139	40.7	42.2	49.7	48.4	1869	2302	2971	3341
2021	Pesticides and other agrochemical products	62	61	67	77	4.3	4.5	5.9	7.1	242	293	393	556
2022	Paints,varnishes;printing ink and mastics	290	352	387	427	13.0	13.7	14.4	17.8	494	635	823	1151
2023	Soap,cleaning and cosmetic preparations	198	268	311	337	10.9	11.8	13.5	14.1	644	737	933	1032
2029	Other chemical products n.e.c.	243	266	333	298	12.5	12.2	15.9	9.5	488	637	822	602
2030	Man-made fibres	21	26	18	16	2.3	2.2	1.8	1.2	29	31	42	36
2100	Pharmaceuticals,medicinal chemicals, etc.	224	263	276	290	29.1	32.4	34.9	35.6	1267	1535	1876	2179
221	Rubber products	54	56	64	67	12.4	13.6	13.5	14.7	393	445	631	731
2211	Rubber tyres and tubes	54	56	64	67	12.4	13.6	13.5	14.7	393	445	631	731
2219	Other rubber products	-	-	-	-	-	-	-	-	-	-	-	-
2220	Plastics products	1742	2059	2424	2576	118.6	131.9	145.7	161.3	2713	3574	4783	6167
2310	Glass and glass products	106	107	116	147	10.7	8.2	21.6	10.4	246	245	633	474
239	Non-metallic mineral products n.e.c.	1988	2436	2763	2960	230.5	245.0	262.5	281.8	5607	7328	9524	11434
2391	Refractory products	40	52	89	85	4.3	4.5	4.7	6.8	69	109	132	245
2392	Clay building materials	643	829	928	1005	76.9	83.6	94.7	101.6	1329	1928	2990	3154
2393	Other porcelain and ceramic products	372	381	403	395	40.6	40.5	34.4	37.8	837	969	1043	1241
2394	Cement, lime and plaster	132	140	170	188	54.6	53.4	57.5	64.1	2198	2523	3013	4069
2395	Articles of concrete, cement and plaster	386	498	598	642	33.2	39.8	45.9	42.1	799	1283	1628	1757
2396	Cutting, shaping and finishing of stone	260	360	374	471	14.5	16.5	17.0	21.8	248	384	476	673
2399	Other non-metallic mineral products n.e.c.	155	176	201	174	6.2	6.6	8.3	7.6	127	131	241	295
2410	Basic iron and steel	345	451	496	566	37.0	42.8	47.8	53.4	1243	1705	1912	2648
2420	Basic precious and other non-ferrous metals	39	55	92	126	6.8	6.1	7.1	10.8	236	168	231	436
243	Casting of metals	208	220	238	179	7.7	11.3	11.4	7.1	166	413	368	237
2431	Casting of iron and steel	146	158	169	145	5.7	6.6	6.8	5.1	127	252	233	185
2432	Casting of non-ferrous metals	62	62	69	34	1.9	4.7	4.7	2.0	39	160	136	52
251	Struct.metal products, tanks, reservoirs	1288	1664	2136	2976	52.2	56.4	68.2	83.1	1323	1758	2454	3835
2511	Structural metal products	1101	1422	1877	2738	42.2	46.6	57.7	73.5	1086	1453	2048	3349
2512	Tanks, reservoirs and containers of metal	144	191	199	165	8.6	8.0	8.6	7.5	191	240	324	367

continued

Viet Nam

ISIC	Industry	Note	Number of enterprises (number)				Note	Number of employees (thousands)				Note	Wages and salaries paid to employees (billions of Vietnamese Dongs)			
			2007	2008	2009	2010		2007	2008	2009	2010		2007	2008	2009	2010
2513	Steam generators, excl. hot water boilers		43	51	60	73		1.4	1.8	1.9	2.1		47	65	81	119
2520	Weapons and ammunition		1	3	7	1		-	-	5.4	-		-	1	178	-
259	Other metal products;metal working services		2449	3216	3886	3672		117.6	129.2	143.1	139.5		2780	3824	4685	5819
2591	Forging,pressing,stamping,roll-forming of metal		185	239	290	147		5.5	6.0	7.9	2.6		141	194	265	127
2592	Treatment and coating of metals; machining		592	848	1182	1121		13.5	16.5	23.0	19.0		289	451	724	897
2593	Cutlery, hand tools and general hardware		99	129	158	292		10.3	10.5	11.1	17.9		364	312	420	669
2599	Other fabricated metal products n.e.c.		1573	2000	2256	2112		88.2	96.2	101.0	99.9		1986	2867	3277	4127
2610	Electronic components and boards		109	173	253	261		35.6	44.1	54.9	67.3		705	1258	1625	2437
2620	Computers and peripheral equipment		30	43	69	44		16.0	17.6	27.4	24.4		357	1176	983	1743
2630	Communication equipment		44	42	64	73		10.8	9.7	22.2	26.4		252	297	687	987
2640	Consumer electronics		120	152	154	125		15.6	15.4	13.9	34.0		426	:::	649	1231
265	Measuring,testing equipment; watches, etc.		44	44	60	65		3.0	2.9	3.2	4.5		66	109	100	277
2651	Measuring/testing/navigating equipment,etc.		28	30	43	46		0.7	0.4	1.1	1.8		13	18	35	164
2652	Watches and clocks		16	14	17	19		2.4	2.4	2.1	2.7		53	91	65	114
2660	Irradiation/electromedical equipment,etc.		6	7	7	4		1.4	1.3	1.4	1.5		42	50	63	68
2670	Optical instruments and photographic equipment		4	4	5	18		2.7	2.0	1.9	7.7		68	56	53	245
2680	Magnetic and optical media		14	18	44	21		1.0	0.9	0.8	1.2		36	20	26	35
2710	Electric motors,generators,transformers,etc.		132	174	197	212		34.8	37.4	39.4	35.7		932	1200	1375	1715
2720	Batteries and accumulators		32	30	42	35		5.4	6.8	6.7	7.8		194	226	269	272
273	Wiring and wiring devices		151	180	200	210		51.8	49.5	50.0	56.7		1154	1628	1687	1919
2731	Fibre optic cables		14	12	17	20		2.4	1.9	2.3	1.2		87	81	83	67
2732	Other electronic and electric wires and cables		88	107	119	133		17.0	15.8	18.3	31.3		513	625	745	934
2733	Wiring devices		49	61	64	57		32.4	31.8	29.3	24.1		554	921	859	918
2740	Electric lighting equipment		49	66	92	104		7.6	5.9	7.5	10.0		192	222	258	376
2750	Domestic appliances		132	150	145	180		9.3	9.0	9.3	12.6		229	261	315	550
2790	Other electrical equipment		123	147	199	188		9.9	9.7	11.6	9.6		220	298	491	410
281	General-purpose machinery		276	294	370	421		24.6	25.0	25.2	31.6		551	755	900	1658
2811	Engines/turbines,excl.aircraft,vehicle engines		16	18	22	21		4.1	3.5	1.9	1.5		:::	111	52	64
2812	Fluid power equipment		4	4	7	8		0.1	0.5	1.0	1.0		2	21	45	49
2813	Other pumps, compressors, taps and valves		53	60	68	76		3.1	3.3	3.7	5.0		81	100	121	222
2814	Bearings, gears, gearing and driving elements		47	56	64	70		2.0	2.6	2.3	2.6		52	71	80	117
2815	Ovens, furnaces and furnace burners		15	8	15	18		0.3	0.1	0.2	0.5		7	4	9	15
2816	Lifting and handling equipment		42	37	49	91		4.6	3.7	3.9	7.4		137	99	125	413
2817	Office machinery, excl.computers,etc.		9	15	19	17		4.4	5.6	6.4	7.9		101	172	236	483
2818	Power-driven hand tools		8	6	10	5		0.8	0.1	0.5	0.3		12	3	14	6
2819	Other general-purpose machinery		82	90	116	115		5.3	5.5	5.4	5.4		126	173	219	289
282	Special-purpose machinery		408	510	570	595		22.4	25.2	27.4	23.2		632	906	1064	1044
2821	Agricultural and forestry machinery		69	81	100	102		4.0	4.3	4.3	3.4		88	117	141	119
2822	Metal-forming machinery and machine tools		49	53	60	82		1.6	1.9	1.8	3.1		27	48	57	107
2823	Machinery for metallurgy		1	1	1	6		-	-	-	0.4		-	-	-	15
2824	Mining, quarrying and construction machinery		26	43	49	66		4.2	4.1	4.8	1.9		142	145	207	78

Code	Category												
		a/				a/				a/			
2825	Food/beverage/tobacco processing machinery	44	48	53	64	2.8	3.1	2.9	3.3	119	151	127	180
2826	Textile/apparel/leather production machinery	21	33	35	28	1.0	2.1	1.9	1.7	22	59	56	62
2829	Other special-purpose machinery	198	251	272	247	8.9	9.7	11.7	9.5	234	385	477	483
2910	Motor vehicles	50	54	51	56	16.0	16.3	28.0	26.5	572	808	1240	1385
2920	Automobile bodies, trailers and semi-trailers	33	40	50	48	2.4	2.6	2.8	3.6	43	96	96	238
2930	Parts and accessories for motor vehicles	183	217	219	215	27.3	26.4	29.5	39.4	715	882	1114	1759
301	Building of ships and boats	244	311	400	349	56.3	61.2	66.9	49.1	1476	2166	2668	2376
3011	Building of ships and floating structures	224	271	338	306	55.8	59.4	65.9	48.3	1469	2049	2638	2346
3012	Building of pleasure and sporting boats	20	40	62	43	0.5	1.8	1.1	0.9	7	...	30	30
3020	Railway locomotives and rolling stock	4	4	6	3	1.2	1.1	0.8	0.6	43	37	20	24
3030	Air and spacecraft and related machinery	-	-	1	1	-	-	0.4	0.1	-	-	13	4
3040	Military fighting vehicles	-	-	-	-	-	-	-	-	-	-	-	-
309	Transport equipment n.e.c.	297	305	295	303	56.5	53.8	60.5	63.0	1573	1939	2243	2821
3091	Motorcycles	210	210	205	208	45.7	43.3	50.5	52.7	1295	1627	1895	2390
3092	Bicycles and invalid carriages	56	68	60	63	9.1	9.4	9.1	9.1	248	278	321	383
3099	Other transport equipment n.e.c.	31	27	30	32	1.7	1.1	0.9	1.2	30	34	26	48
3100	Furniture	1809	2388	2519	2718	280.0	272.2	265.8	278.2	5548	6760	7342	9400
321	Jewellery, bijouterie and related articles	58	85	95	89	7.9	8.7	7.8	9.3	200	238	268	343
3211	Jewellery and related articles	49	71	76	75	6.9	7.6	6.5	8.2	180	212	233	310
3212	Imitation jewellery and related articles	9	14	19	14	1.0	1.1	1.3	1.1	20	26	35	33
3220	Musical instruments	13	16	20	20	0.9	1.2	1.1	0.9	19	20	29	30
3230	Sports goods	42	53	52	58	11.9	13.6	12.8	15.8	226	312	390	520
3240	Games and toys	71	78	100	142	16.2	21.9	23.4	27.7	247	413	474	707
3250	Medical and dental instruments and supplies	78	96	104	121	5.0	5.6	8.0	11.1	105	152	238	411
3290	Other manufacturing n.e.c.	350	452	1089	825	39.6	35.6	45.3	43.1	791	926	1313	1565
331	Repair of fabricated metal products/machinery	289	367	522	638	7.0	8.3	13.5	10.8	178	304	476	546
3311	Repair of fabricated metal products	11	11	17	26	0.1	0.2	0.2	0.5	1	4	5	16
3312	Repair of machinery	87	123	159	191	1.1	1.4	2.2	2.2	24	43	66	84
3313	Repair of electronic and optical equipment	12	12	23	28	0.2	0.1	1.0	0.2	9	4	...	15
3314	Repair of electrical equipment	31	54	104	106	1.1	1.7	1.7	1.3	28	64	77	107
3315	Repair of transport equip., excl. motor vehicles	131	149	177	237	4.4	4.8	8.1	6.3	112	186	293	310
3319	Repair of other equipment	17	18	42	50	0.2	0.1	0.3	0.3	3	3	9	14
3320	Installation of industrial machinery/equipment	39	99	190	116	11.9	10.7	10.5	10.8	427	504	494	640
C	Total manufacturing	29300	36531	42829	45193	3637.9	3813.3	4035.4	4334.8	80389	105648	127675	163371

a/ Sum of available data.

Viet Nam

ISIC	Industry	Output (billions of Vietnamese Dongs)					Value added (billions of Vietnamese Dongs)					Gross fixed capital formation (billions of Vietnamese Dongs)		
		Note	2007	2008	2009	2010	Note	2007	2008	2009	2010	Note	2009	2010
1010	Processing/preserving of meat		:	:	:	:		1007	1220	1195	1285		1057	1470
1020	Processing/preserving of fish, etc.		:	:	:	:		9084	12455	12000	15644		23549	29673
1030	Processing/preserving of fruit,vegetables		:	:	:	:		1960	2914	2900	4028		3821	5397
1040	Vegetable and animal oils and fats		:	:	:	:		691	966	875	1122		1462	2123
1050	Dairy products		:	:	:	:		4169	5384	6329	8573		6938	7825
106	Grain mill products,starches and starch products		:	:	:	:		4093	5730	6430	9960		7580	10196
1061	Grain mill products		:	:	:	:		2458	3478	3691	5003		5447	6981
1062	Starches and starch products		:	:	:	:		1636	2252	2739	4958		2134	3215
107	Other food products		:	:	:	:		10693	14063	18116	22660		29932	33728
1071	Bakery products		:	:	:	:		645	1289	1285	1440		3605	4609
1072	Sugar		:	:	:	:		3483	3691	4434	6374		7198	8296
1073	Cocoa, chocolate and sugar confectionery		:	:	:	:		341	319	949	1030		2278	2492
1074	Macaroni, noodles, couscous, etc.		:	:	:	:		1950	2919	3707	4769		2563	3978
1075	Prepared meals and dishes		:	:	:	:		296	372	468	526		409	414
1079	Other food products n.e.c.		:	:	:	:		3978	5472	7272	8521		13879	13939
1080	Prepared animal feeds		:	:	:	:		14510	22861	29879	33209		14817	21044
1101	Distilling, rectifying and blending of spirits		:	:	:	:		431	597	814	881		1099	1696
1102	Wines		:	:	:	:		45	48	60	80		70	90
1103	Malt liquors and malt		:	:	:	:		9748	9832	13167	18663		28910	32116
1104	Soft drinks,mineral waters,other bottled waters		:	:	:	:		1475	2215	2481	3422		5771	7598
1200	Tobacco products		:	:	:	:		5952	6445	8110	9782		4486	4898
131	Spinning, weaving and finishing of textiles		:	:	:	:		8620	9356	12261	16462		38521	47766
1311	Preparation and spinning of textile fibres		:	:	:	:		6591	6975	9405	12638		30393	36451
1312	Weaving of textiles		:	:	:	:		1195	1298	1561	2530		5240	7526
1313	Finishing of textiles		:	:	:	:		834	1083	1294	1294		2889	3788
139	Other textiles		:	:	:	:		-	-	-	-		-	-
1391	Knitted and crocheted fabrics		:	:	:	:		-	-	-	-		-	-
1392	Made-up textile articles, except apparel		:	:	:	:		-	-	-	-		-	-
1393	Carpets and rugs		:	:	:	:		-	-	-	-		-	-
1394	Cordage, rope, twine and netting		:	:	:	:		-	-	-	-		-	-
1399	Other textiles n.e.c.		:	:	:	:		-	-	-	-		-	-
1410	Wearing apparel, except fur apparel		:	:	:	:		21217	26681	30061	40509		28605	35426
1420	Articles of fur		:	:	:	:		53	79	56	31		218	38
1430	Knitted and crocheted apparel		:	:	:	:		620	526	546	825		1221	1584
151	Leather;luggage,handbags,saddlery,harness;fur		:	:	:	:		1663	2819	3618	4437		4732	6247
1511	Tanning/dressing of leather; dressing of fur		:	:	:	:		406	423	382	674		1800	2246
1512	Luggage,handbags,etc.;saddlery/harness		:	:	:	:		1257	2397	3237	3764		2932	4000
1520	Footwear		:	:	:	:		15452	17530	18842	24262		25254	30275
1610	Sawmilling and planing of wood		:	:	:	:		1253	1615	1979	4143		3821	9223
162	Wood products, cork, straw, plaiting materials		:	:	:	:		3419	4236	4669	5630		7564	8209

1621	Veneer sheets and wood-based panels	1222	1612	1796	2345	3595	4192
1622	Builders' carpentry and joinery	211	354	533	773	709	1128
1623	Wooden containers	96	178	158	116	136	141
1629	Other wood products;articles of cork,straw	1891	2092	2183	2397	3124	2747
1701	Pulp, paper and paperboard	2387	2942	2886	3873	8403	7058
1702	Corrugated paper and paperboard	2429	3463	3751	5211	11696	12851
1709	Other articles of paper and paperboard	2208	3465	3874	5837	6295	6593
181	Printing and service activities related to printing	2221	3112	3437	5793	8482	10459
1811	Printing	2030	2673	2899	4404	7940	8989
1812	Service activities related to printing	191	439	538	1389	542	1470
1820	Reproduction of recorded media	52	54	55	55	241	113
1910	Coke oven products	10	49	51	506	1278	1487
1920	Refined petroleum products	2066	2486	11867	81624	44502	76019
201	Basic chemicals,fertilizers, etc.	6037	9210	20326	13676	12935	18807
2011	Basic chemicals	920	1199	11842	2420	3049	5632
2012	Fertilizers and nitrogen compounds	4658	7419	7870	10448	6665	9157
2013	Plastics and synthetic rubber in primary forms	458	592	614	808	3222	4018
202	Other chemical products	7046	9366	11699	14557	11913	17959
2021	Pesticides and other agrochemical products	759	968	1461	1906	1279	1809
2022	Paints,varnishes;printing ink and mastics	2487	3193	3583	5822	4030	7476
2023	Soap,cleaning and cosmetic preparations	2431	3262	4321	3807	3626	4419
2029	Other chemical products n.e.c.	1369	1944	2334	3022	2978	4256
2030	Man-made fibres	228	279	252	469	321	299
2100	Pharmaceuticals,medicinal chemicals, etc.	6043	7828	8970	11609	8458	10844
221	Rubber products	1257	1683	2058	2572	6639	7237
2211	Rubber tyres and tubes	1257	1683	2058	2572	6639	7237
2219	Other rubber products	-	-	-	-	-	-
2220	Plastics products	11299	15450	26143	23216	33530	38695
2310	Glass and glass products	1105	954	1537	2307	7059	8172
239	Non-metallic mineral products n.e.c.	18859	24935	37734	40690	146980	158559
2391	Refractory products	189	260	392	711	658	1350
2392	Clay building materials	4014	5537	6915	8366	14756	19312
2393	Other porcelain and ceramic products	2420	2757	2681	3318	5702	6321
2394	Cement, lime and plaster	8440	10511	14316	19069	87457	114678
2395	Articles of concrete, cement and plaster	2864	4614	7066	6974	15247	11038
2396	Cutting, shaping and finishing of stone	558	822	5740	1654	21871	3798
2399	Other non-metallic mineral products n.e.c.	373	435	625	598	1290	2062
2410	Basic iron and steel	6383	9904	10042	15675	42573	54911
2420	Basic precious and other non-ferrous metals	848	1430	2909	3021	3876	4779
243	Casting of metals	758	2161	2238	1208	3764	1446
2431	Casting of iron and steel	518	1839	1896	1067	2850	981
2432	Casting of non-ferrous metals	240	322	342	141	914	465
251	Struct.metal products, tanks, reservoirs	3890	5486	7070	11375	10613	14529
2511	Structural metal products	3055	4497	5990	10170	7739	12042
2512	Tanks, reservoirs and containers of metal	647	721	784	876	2640	2226

continued

Viet Nam

ISIC	Industry	Output (billions of Vietnamese Dongs)				Note	Value added (billions of Vietnamese Dongs)				Note	Gross fixed capital formation (billions of Vietnamese Dongs)		Note
		2007	2008	2009	2010		2007	2008	2009	2010		2009	2010	
2513	Steam generators, excl. hot water boilers	...	...	...	...		188	269	296	329		234	261	
2520	Weapons and ammunition	...	...	...	...		...	...	...	...		487	4	
259	Other metal products;metal working services	...	...	...	...		...	...	...	...				
2591	Forging,pressing,stamping,roll-forming of metal	...	...	...	...		6795	10374	11168	14488		31390	38027	
2592	Treatment and coating of metals; machining	...	...	...	...		335	466	479	250		3388	1721	
2593	Cutlery, hand tools and general hardware	...	...	...	...		307	480	626	1152		3498	5131	
2599	Other fabricated metal products n.e.c.	...	...	...	...		476	624	746	1419		1326	2820	
2610	Electronic components and boards	...	...	...	...		5676	8804	9318	11667		23178	28356	
2620	Computers and peripheral equipment	...	...	...	...		1994	3096	3443	4711		11267	15803	
2630	Communication equipment	...	...	...	...		2273	2778	3140	1682		4224	5824	
2640	Consumer electronics	...	...	...	...		605	561	1427	5128		5149	8723	
265	Measuring,testing equipment; watches, etc.	...	...	...	...		2492	2699	2724	3454		4463	4753	
2651	Measuring/testing/navigating equipment,etc.	...	...	...	...		159	234	184	402		370	1324	
2652	Watches and clocks	...	...	...	...		23	23	29	168		131	1047	
2660	Irradiation/electromedical equipment,etc.	...	...	...	...		136	211	155	235		239	277	
2670	Optical instruments and photographic equipment	...	...	...	...		151	185	247	265		289	271	
2680	Magnetic and optical media	...	...	...	...		154	146	156	3276		616	1925	
2710	Electric motors,generators,transformers,etc.	...	...	...	...		308	192	256	324		2193	2262	
2720	Batteries and accumulators	...	...	...	...		3043	3619	4503	5998		6417	7191	
273	Wiring and wiring devices	...	...	...	...		1010	1409	1489	2300		1370	1921	
2731	Fibre optic cables	...	...	...	...		4668	5345	5555	7440		12518	13185	
2732	Other electronic and electric wires and cables	...	...	...	...		164	127	116	167		2091	2509	
2733	Wiring devices	...	...	...	...		2918	3257	3528	4950		6572	7422	
2740	Electric lighting equipment	...	...	...	...		1586	1962	1910	2322		3855	3254	
2750	Domestic appliances	...	...	...	...		722	630	820	1211		1413	1644	
2790	Other electrical equipment	...	...	...	...		751	774	1106	2029		1797	2894	
281	General-purpose machinery	...	...	...	...		799	1133	1301	1519		1820	1464	
2811	Engines/turbines,excl.aircraft,vehicle engines	...	...	...	...		2192	2677	3191	5591		6768	12036	
2812	Fluid power equipment	...	...	...	...		309	349	63	93		473	844	
2813	Other pumps, compressors, taps and valves	...	...	...	...		1	45	74	85		130	157	
2814	Bearings, gears, gearing and driving elements	...	...	...	...		230	284	361	656		1050	1310	
2815	Ovens, furnaces and furnace burners	...	...	...	...		250	248	186	373		465	677	
2816	Lifting and handling equipment	...	...	...	...		14	8	7	19		10	20	
2817	Office machinery, excl.computers,etc.	...	...	...	...		227	146	160	611		1599	6582	
2818	Power-driven hand tools	...	...	...	...		848	1190	1774	3102		1914	1639	
2819	Other general-purpose machinery	...	...	...	...		21	3	12	14		9	9	
282	Special-purpose machinery	...	...	...	...		292	405	553	638		1118	797	
2821	Agricultural and forestry machinery	...	...	...	...		1931	2668	2890	3189		8395	4437	
2822	Metal-forming machinery and machine tools	...	...	...	...		122	177	204	208		409	442	
2823	Machinery for metallurgy	...	...	...	...		76	114	130	234		193	401	
2824	Mining, quarrying and construction machinery	...	...	...	...		232	266	314	136		685	376	

2825	Food/beverage/tobacco processing machinery	532	435	608	472	515	376
2826	Textile/apparel/leather production machinery	388	217	83	54	59	44
2829	Other special-purpose machinery	2186	6456	1894	1714	1536	1080
2910	Motor vehicles	9143	7846	9862	11014	8083	5976
2920	Automobile bodies, trailers and semi-trailers	1377	1010	764	452	444	233
2930	Parts and accessories for motor vehicles	10237	7685	6469	4011	3339	2690
301	Building of ships and boats	30891	27917	7766	18040	7554	5234
3011	Building of ships and floating structures	30842	27867	7644	17926	7453	5217
3012	Building of pleasure and sporting boats	48	49	122	114	101	17
3020	Railway locomotives and rolling stock	29	32	40	46	103	115
3030	Air and spacecraft and related machinery	121	41	23	12	-	-
3040	Military fighting vehicles	-	-	-	-	-	-
309	Transport equipment n.e.c.	22696	21204	19444	15164	12018	11555
3091	Motorcycles	21312	19896	18270	14152	11061	10775
3092	Bicycles and invalid carriages	1113	1096	1000	879	859	621
3099	Other transport equipment n.e.c.	271	212	175	133	98	158
3100	Furniture	28772	26954	22463	17180	16237	13700
321	Jewellery, bijouterie and related articles	587	647	529	1823	413	366
3211	Jewellery and related articles	490	511	509	1780	381	344
3212	Imitation jewellery and related articles	97	136	20	43	33	22
3220	Musical instruments	50	91	35	67	57	71
3230	Sports goods	1520	1545	695	536	418	308
3240	Games and toys	1152	797	923	677	559	309
3250	Medical and dental instruments and supplies	2363	1778	2680	1860	957	462
3290	Other manufacturing n.e.c.	4553	5091	3590	3187	1953	1846
331	Repair of fabricated metal products/machinery	1442	1565	1647	2197	760	393
3311	Repair of fabricated metal products	38	19	55	75	13	3
3312	Repair of machinery	510	314	845	1268	141	95
3313	Repair of electronic and optical equipment	20	62	25	41	11	9
3314	Repair of electrical equipment	57	102	259	216	198	103
3315	Repair of transport equip., excl. motor vehicles	765	1055	400	517	384	179
3319	Repair of other equipment	53	13	62	80	13	4
3320	Installation of industrial machinery/equipment	2925	456	11430	1600	1366	8652
C	Total manufacturing	988983	814590 a/	620252 a/	452756	344608	273236

a/ Sum of available data.

- 848 -

Viet Nam

Index numbers of industrial production

ISIC Revision 3

ISIC	Industry	Note	(2005=100)											
			1999	2000	2001	2002	2003	2004	2005	2006	2007	2008	2009	2010
15	Food and beverages		...	50	58	65	75	86	100	119	143	...	...	...
16	Tobacco products		...	51	60	68	82	90	100	100	105	99	109	112
17	Textiles		...	53	59	65	75	87	100	124	151	135	...	...
18	Wearing apparel, fur		...	39	46	53	68	84	100	125	156	161	...	...
19	Leather, leather products and footwear		...	47	53	59	72	85	100	119	144	130	...	...
20	Wood products (excl. furniture)		...	44	50	55	68	81	100	108	120	...	...	...
21	Paper and paper products		...	47	53	59	68	86	100	113	128	...	...	...
22	Printing and publishing		...	49	56	62	76	82	100	113	119	...	...	...
23	Coke,refined petroleum products,nuclear fuel		...	38	46	55	53	75	100	85	74	...	...	...
24	Chemicals and chemical products		...	47	54	62	68	80	100	120	143	...	...	...
25	Rubber and plastics products		...	35	44	53	62	83	100	117	137	124	...	...
26	Non-metallic mineral products		...	49	60	70	81	90	100	118	138	...	...	...
27	Basic metals		...	42	52	61	75	80	100	113	132	133	...	...
28	Fabricated metal products		...	33	41	48	61	74	100	130	155	...	...	...
29	Machinery and equipment n.e.c.		...	50	59	68	84	98	100	101	106	173	...	...
30	Office, accounting and computing machinery		...	40	36	31	48	58	100	163	238	...	...	...
31	Electrical machinery and apparatus		...	30	42	54	62	75	100	132	171	102	...	...
32	Radio,television and communication equipment		...	48	58	68	78	87	100	100	101	...	...	...
33	Medical, precision and optical instruments		...	56	61	65	76	89	100	94	81	...	...	...
34	Motor vehicles, trailers, semi-trailers		...	33	46	59	85	89	100	96	120	169	...	...
35	Other transport equipment		...	41	47	54	61	77	100	131	160	...	...	...
36	Furniture; manufacturing n.e.c.		...	29	37	45	59	76	100	135	168	110	...	...
37	Recycling		...	56	61	65	76	98	100	120	145	...	...	...
D	Total manufacturing		...	45	53	61	72	84	100	119	142	...	...	...